LE NORD AND PICARDY
Pages 192–205

CHAMPAGNE
Pages 206–217

ALSACE AND LORRAINE
Pages 218–233

BURGUNDY AND FRANCHE-COMTÉ
Pages 326–351

THE MASSIF CENTRAL
Pages 352–371

Reims

NORTHEAST FRANCE

Strasbourg

Troyes

Dijon

CENTRAL FRANCE AND THE ALPS

Lyon

ont-
and

Grenoble

THE RHÔNE VALLEY AND FRENCH ALPS
Pages 372–391

THE SOUTH OF FRANCE

LANGUEDOC-ROUSSILLON
Pages 476–497

PROVENCE AND THE CÔTE D'AZUR
Pages 498–531

Ajaccio

CORSICA
Pages 532–543

EYEWITNESS TRAVEL

FRANCE

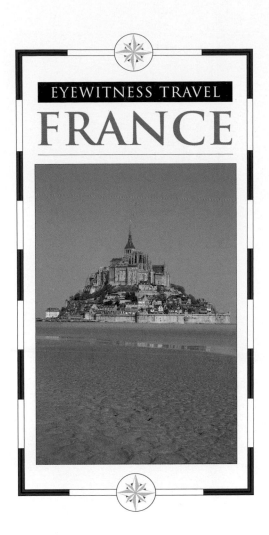

EYEWITNESS TRAVEL

FRANCE

LONDON, NEW YORK,
MELBOURNE, MUNICH AND DELHI
www.dk.com

PROJECT EDITOR Rosemary Bailey
ART EDITOR Janis Utton
EDITORS Tanya Colbourne, Fiona Morgan,
Anna Streiffert, Celia Woolfrey
DESIGNERS Joy FitzSimmons, Erika Lang, Clare Sullivan
MAP CO-ORDINATORS Simon Farbrother, David Pugh
RESEARCHER Philippa Richmond

MAIN CONTRIBUTORS
John Ardagh, Rosemary Bailey, Judith Fayard, Lisa Gerard-Sharp, Colin
Jones, Alister Kershaw, Alec Lobrano, Anthony Roberts, Alan Tillier,
Nigel Tisdall

PHOTOGRAPHERS
Max Alexander, Neil Lukas, John Parker, Kim Sayer

ILLUSTRATORS
Stephen Conlin, John Lawrence, Maltings Partnership,
John Woodcock

Reproduced by Colourscan (Singapore)
Printed and bound by South China Printing Co. Ltd., China

First American Edition, 1994

12 13 14 15 10 9 8 7 6 5 4 3 2 1

Published in the United States by DK Publishing, 375 Hudson Street,
New York, New York 10014

**Reprinted with revisions 1996, 1997, 1998, 1999, 2000,
2001, 2002, 2003, 2004, 2005, 2006, 2007, 2008, 2009, 2010, 2012**

Copyright © 1994, 2012 Dorling Kindersley Limited, London

Published in Great Britain by Dorling Kindersley Limited.

A catalog record for this book is available from the Library of Congress

ISSN 1542-1554
ISBN 978-0-75668-404-4

THROUGHOUT THIS BOOK, FLOORS ARE REFERRED TO IN ACCORDANCE WITH
EUROPEAN USAGE, I.E., THE "FIRST FLOOR" IS ONE FLIGHT UP.

Front cover main image: Mont-St-Michel, Normandy

MIX
Paper from
responsible sources
FSC www.fsc.org   FSC™ C018179

**The information in this DK Eyewitness Travel Guide
is checked regularly.**
Every effort has been made to ensure that this book is as up-to-date
as possible at the time of going to press. Some details, however,
such as telephone numbers, opening hours, prices, gallery hanging
arrangements, and travel information are liable to change. The
publishers cannot accept responsibility for any consequences arising
from the use of this book, nor for any material on third-party
websites, and cannot guarantee that any website address in this book
will be a suitable source of travel information. We value the views and
suggestions of our readers very highly. Please write to: Publisher,
DK Eyewitness Travel Guides, Dorling Kindersley, 80 Strand,
London WC2R 0RL, Great Britain, or email: travelguides@dk.com.

CONTENTS

The fishing village of St-Jean-de-Luz in the Pyrenees

Grape harvest in Alsace

Palais des Papes, Avignon

HOW TO USE THIS GUIDE

This guide helps you to get the most from your visit to France. It provides both expert recommendations and detailed practical information. *Introducing France* maps the country and sets it in its historical and cultural context. The 15 regional chapters, plus *Paris and Ile de France*, describe important sights, with maps, pictures, and illustrations. Throughout, features cover topics from food and wine to culture and beaches. Restaurant and hotel recommendations can be found in *Travelers' Needs*. The *Survival Guide* has tips on everything from the telephone system to transportation.

PARIS AND ILE DE FRANCE

The center of Paris has been divided into five sightseeing areas. Each has its own chapter, which opens with a list of the sights described. A further section covers Ile de France. All sights are numbered and plotted on an area map. The detailed information for each sight follows the map's numerical order, making sights easy to locate within the chapter.

Sights at a Glance lists the chapter's sights by category: Churches, Museums, and Galleries; Historic Buildings, Squares, and Gardens.

All pages relating to Paris and Ile de France have green thumb tabs.

A locator map shows where you are in relation to other areas of the city center.

1 Area Map
For easy reference, the sights are numbered and located on a map. Sights in the city center are also shown on the Paris Street Finder *on pages 156–69.*

2 Street-by-Street Map
This gives a bird's eye view of the key areas in each chapter.

A suggested route for a walk is shown in red.

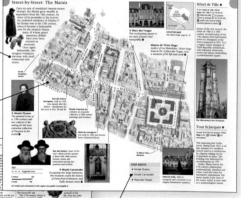

Stars indicate the sights that no visitor should miss.

3 Detailed information
The sights in Paris and Ile de France are described individually. Addresses, telephone numbers, opening hours, and information on admission charges and wheelchair access are also provided for each entry.

1 Introduction
The landscape, history, and character of each region is described here, showing how the area has developed over the centuries and what it offers to the visitor today.

FRANCE AREA BY AREA
Apart from Paris and Ile de France, France has been divided into 15 regions, each of which has a separate chapter. The most interesting towns and places to visit have been numbered on a *Regional Map*.

Each area of France can be quickly identified by its color coding, shown on the inside front cover.

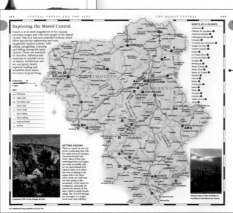

2 Regional Map
This shows the road network and gives an illustrated overview of the whole region. All interesting places to visit are numbered and there are also useful tips on getting around the region by car and train.

3 Detailed information
All the important towns and other places to visit are described individually. They are listed in order, following the numbering on the Regional Map. Within each town or city, there is detailed information on important buildings and other sights.

Story boxes highlight noteworthy features of the top sights.

For all the top sights, a Visitors' Checklist provides the practical information you will need to plan your visit.

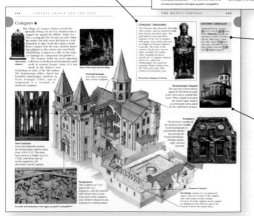

4 France's top sights
These are given two or more full pages. Historic buildings are dissected to reveal their interiors. The most interesting towns or city centers are shown in a bird's eye view, with sights picked out and described.

INTRODUCING
FRANCE

DISCOVERING FRANCE

T he chapters of this book have been divided into 16 color-coded regions that reflect the diversity of France. These are based on the country's historical regions that were often defined by their geography and landscape as much as by

Gothic detail from Le Nord region

their influence and power.

Each has developed its own special flavor: its own architecture, cuisine, customs, music, dress, dialect, and even language. The following pages give a taste of these areas and show you what there is to see and do.

Pyramide du Louvre in Paris, from across the fountain pools

PARIS AND THE ILE DE FRANCE

- Fantastic art at the Louvre
- Café life *par excellence*
- Captivating Versailles

The pleasures of Paris can be picked off at leisure any time of the year. The **Louvre** *(see pp100–3)*, **Picasso Museum** *(see pp90–1)*, and **Pompidou Center** *(see pp92–3)* may be on some people's ideal itinerary, while others may want to scale the **Eiffel Tower** *(see p113)* and shop

Les Deux Magots, one of Paris's most famous cafés

in the *grands boulevards*, or follow in the steps of the famous from **Montmartre** *(see pp132–3)* to the **Père Lachaise Cemetery** *(see p135)*. Whatever your interest, there are cafés and brasseries to soak up the atmosphere, particularly on the **Left Bank** *(see pp116–127)* and in the **Marais** *(see pp80–93)*. For a day excursion, there are plenty of châteaux to visit, none more exalted than Louis XIV's fabulous palace at **Versailles** *(see pp168–71)*.

LE NORD AND PICARDY

- Bustling Channel ports
- Lofty Gothic cathedrals
- Lille art collection

The countryside north of Paris undulates toward Flanders and to the cliffs and sandy beaches around the Channel ports of **Dunkerque** *(see p197)*, **Calais** *(see pp196–7)*, and **Boulogne-sur-**

Mer *(see p196)*. You can try your luck at the races, at **Chantilly** *(see pp204–5)* and **Le Touquet** *(see p196)*, or go to the lakes and woodland of the **Valley of the Somme** *(see p199)*, a name synonymous with the fatal trench warfare of World War I. High spots are the great Gothic cathedrals, such as **Amiens** *(see p200)*, the largest in France, and the city of **Lille** *(see p198)*, which has one of the best art galleries in the country.

CHAMPAGNE

- Sparkling Champagne houses
- Royal Reims
- Gothic churches in Troyes

Champagne means only one thing: sparkling white wine. Visit the producers' chalk caves in **Épernay** *(see p211)* and the premises of the *grandes marques* in **Reims** *(see pp210–1)*, where you will also

Heidsieck Champagne label

find a great slice of French history in **Reims Cathedral** *(see p212)*. Troyes *(see pp216–7)*, the region's former capital, is a delightful town of many Gothic churches, while the castle keep at **Chaumont** *(see p217)* has echoes of its former residents, the Counts of Champagne. On the wild side is the **Vallée de la Meuse** *(see p214)* in the rocky Ardennes, while the region around **Lac du Der-Chantecoq** *(see p215)* is known for its half-timbered churches.

◁ *The Pont du Gard, Nîmes*, by Hubert Robert

ALSACE AND LORRAINE

- **Alsace Wine Route**
- **Picturesque half-timbered towns**
- **Strasbourg, crossroads of Europe**

Abutting Germany and Switzerland, this is a delightful, gentle rural area of vineyards and orchards, and pretty, half-timbered villages and towns such as **Colmar** *(see p227)*, best seen along the 110-mile (180-km) **Route du Vin** *(see pp232–3)*. The **Vosges** mountains *(see p225)* attract skiers, and nearby is the **Gérardmer lake** *(see p225)* for summer water sports. The region is full of forts and castles, including the romantic **Château du Haut-Koenigsbourg** *(see pp228–9)*. The main town is **Strasbourg** *(see pp230–1)*.

Normandy's Mont-St-Michel, one of the most enchanting sights in France

The old town of Strasbourg, best explored on its pretty waterways

NORMANDY

- **D-Day beaches**
- **Cider and Calvados**
- **Magnificent Mont-St-Michel**

Visit Claude Monet's garden at **Giverny** *(see p266)* and see the lily pond and bridge just as he painted them. Normandy's blustery skies and billowing seas inspired the Impressionists who visited **Dieppe** *(see p263)*, **Le Havre** *(see p262)*, and pretty **Honfleur** *(see p262)*, while *tout* Paris used to decamp to the resorts of **Cabourg** *(see p255)*, **Deauville** *(see p255)* and **Trouville** *(see p255)*. Their beaches are known for the World War II D-Day landings. Normandy's farmlands are renowned for their cider, Calvados, butter, and cheese. Don't miss the **Abbaye de Mont-St-Michel** *(see pp256–61)* or **Rouen Cathedral** *(see pp264–5)*.

BRITTANY

- **Sandy beaches**
- **Mysterious Carnac**
- **Delightful fishing ports**

In the far northwest, this Celtic corner of France is a land with a language and culture of its own. Buffeted by the Atlantic, its rocky shores and sandy beaches, peppered with picturesque fishing ports, make it a prime spot for family beach vacations. Prehistory sighs in the wind here, and megalithic sites abound, especially in the mysterious rock formations at **Carnac** *(see p278)*.

To steep yourself in Breton culture, visit **Quimper** *(see p274)*, eat crêpes, drink cider, and try to attend a *pardon*, a feast of a local saint, when traditional costumes are worn. They take place between March and October. Find out about them at the **Musée de Bretagne** *(see p285)* in the region's capital, Rennes.

THE LOIRE VALLEY

- **Fairytale Renaissance châteaux**
- **Chartres Cathedral**
- **Le Mans, motor racing**

The fabulous châteaux of the Loire capture all the elegance and culture of France. Here the French nobles lived out the Renaissance in style. Wines have made towns such as **Saumur** *(see p292)* famous. Historic centers include **Tours** *(see pp296–7)* and **Chartres** *(see pp307–311)*, which has stunning stained glass in its magnificent cathedral windows, and **Orléans** *(see pp312–3)*, saved from the English by Joan of Arc, who is celebrated in a 10-day festival leading up to the anniversary of the city's liberation on 8 May. To the north is **Le Mans** *(see p291)*, another lovely old town, best known for its motor racing circuit. The 24-hour race is held in June.

Château de Chenonceau in the Loire Valley, across the River Cher

Côte de Nuits vineyard in Burgundy, part of the Côte d'Or region

BURGUNDY AND FRANCHE-COMTE

- Gastronomic paradise
- Impressive abbeys
- Fine trekking and skiing

Burgundy is corpulent France, conjuring up *boeuf bourguignon* and delicious wines that are among the most expensive in the world. The Dukes of Burgundy's legacy is splendid **Dijon** *(see pp340–2)*, but the true architectural gem is the **Hôtel-Dieu** in Beaune *(see pp346–7)*. The wealth of the Church is evident in harmonious Romanesque churches and abbeys, especially **Vézelay** *(see pp336–7)*. **The Franche-Comté's** *(see pp349–51)* lakes, mountains, woods, and waterfalls are perfect for trekking, canoeing and skiing.

MASSIF CENTRAL

- Wild, beautiful landscapes
- Dramatic Gorges du Tarn
- Treasures of Ste-Foy

This is the place to go to enjoy the great outdoors. A plateau of extinct volcanoes, spas, and lakes, the landscape reaches dramatic heights in the **Gorges du Tarn** *(see pp370–1)*. The **Cévennes** *(see p353)*, one of the least populated parts of the country, is known for its wild flowers and birds of prey. Remote villages and ancient churches top hills

and are tucked in valleys. The Abbaye de Ste-Foy in **Conques** *(see pp368–9)* has one of the most celebrated reliquaries in Christendom.

THE RHONE VALLEY AND FRENCH ALPS

- Lyon's enticing *bouchons*
- Grenoble and the ski slopes
- Elegant Evian-les-Bains

The south of France begins at **Lyon** *(see pp380–1)*, France's second largest city, where the River Saône joins the River Rhône and the Mediterranean starts to scent the air. The commercial and military capital of Roman Gaul is now a gastronomic capital known for its *bouchons* (bistros) and local wines from **Beaujolais** *(see p377)* as well as the Rhône. Natural attractions in the region include the dramatic, cave-pocked **Ardèche** *(see pp384–5)* and, to the east, **Grenoble** *(see pp388–9)* and the Alps where you'll find the elegant spa town of **Evian-les-Bains** *(see p391)* beside Lac Léman.

Wine from the Rhône Valley

POITOU AND AQUITAINE

- Marais Poitevin's canals
- Historic Poitiers
- Bordeaux wine châteaux

Set against a long coast of sandy beaches, this largely flat region runs from the port of **La Rochelle** *(see p416)* and

the popular holiday island of **Île d'Oléron** *(see p417)* to the Basque country. When La Rochelle is busy in summer, escape to the **Marais Poitevin** *(see pp408–9)*, a network of lily-blanketed canals teeming with wildlife. There are two historic centers – **Poitiers** *(see pp412–3)*, whose cathedral has the oldest carved choir stalls in France, and **Bordeaux** *(see pp420–3)*, beside the River Garonne. The latter has been long known as a wine port serving the magnificent surrounding châteaux estates.

PERIGORD, QUERCY AND GASCONY

- Sarlat Market
- Lascaux's famous caves
- Toulouse Space Park

Cut by the majestic Dordogne, Lot, and Tarn rivers, this is bucolic, green France where water activities help to beat the summer sun. Every town has a weekly market brimming with local produce, such as *foie gras* and **Agen** *(see p440)* prunes. Best known is the Wednesday market in **Sarlat-la-Caneda** *(see pp432–3)*, though stunning architecture makes it worth a visit any day of the week. **Rocamadour** *(see pp436–7)* and **Moissac** *(see pp442–3)* are other architectural high points, while prehistoric man has left his mark in the famous **Lascaux caves** *(see pp402–3)*. **Toulouse** *(see pp446–7)* is the major town. Try its sausages and visit the hi-tech Space Park.

Sarlat Market, famous for *foie gras* and walnuts

THE PYRENEES

- **Biarritz beaches**
- **Parc National des Pyrénées wildlife**
- **The shrine at Lourdes**

The Pyrenees mountain range stretches from the Atlantic to the Mediterranean, forming a natural border with Spain. On the Atlantic coast is the **Basque country** *(see p449)* where **Bayonne** *(see p452)* is known for its ham and **Biarritz** *(see p452)*, a surfers' town, is renowned for its bygone glories as the resort choice of kings. The **Parc National des Pyrénées** *(see pp460–1)* is at the heart of the mountains which are spectacular for walking and trekking. Skiers come in winter. **Lourdes** *(see pp458–9)* brings pilgrims all year round.

Flowers, butterflies, animals, and birds brighten the Pyrenees trails

LANGUEDOC-ROUSSILLON

- **Collioure, the artists' resort**
- **Carcassonne, fairytale walled town**
- **Pont du Gard, a Roman triumph**

These are sunny, rolling lands of olives, vines, cypress trees, and sunflowers, where old farm buildings have been baked by the sun. The Pyrenees reach the Mediterranean here, on the **Côte Vermeille** *(see p482)*, where the prettiest resort is **Collioure** *(see p483)*, long familiar to artists. To the

The fairytale sight of Carcassonne, restored in the 19th century

north is **Carcassonne** *(see pp488–9)*, a dreamy fortified town that has been perfectly restored. Romantics might also want to seek out **Montségur** *(see p463)* as the last stronghold of the persecuted Cathars. **Nîmes** *(see pp496–7)* was a major Roman city with a well-preserved amphitheater and an astonishing aqueduct, the **Pont du Gard** *(see p495)*. It was the highest bridge the Romans ever built.

PROVENCE AND THE CÔTE D'AZUR

- **The French Riviera**
- **Cannes' ritzy Film Festival**
- **Monte-Carlo Casino**

St-Tropez *(see p516)*, **Nice** *(see pp526–7)*, **Menton** *(see p529)* – the French Riviera is the most fabulous waterfront

in the world. Admire top yachts in **Antibes** *(see p521)*, catch the rising stars at **Cannes' film festival** *(see p520)*, and break the bank in **Monte-Carlo** *(see pp530–1)*. There is plenty to do all year round so it's best to avoid August when it can be incredibly busy. Away from the coast there are glorious ancient towns, from **Avignon** *(see p503)*, where popes built a palace, and **Aix** *(see p511)*, where good King Renée ruled, to Roman **Arles** *(see pp508–9)* and the cowboy country of the **Camargue** *(see pp510–1)*.

CORSICA

- **Myrtle-scented maquis**
- **Beautiful sandy beaches**
- **Fortified towns**

A mountainous island with coves and sandy beaches, Corsica is the place to hike, especially in spring, when the aromatic maquis puts on its best show. On the coast there are fortified towns such as **Bonifacio** *(see p543)* and **Porto** *(see p541)*, set in a magical bay. Napoleon Bonaparte was born in **Ajaccio** *(see p543)*. Find out about the island's history and customs in the Musée de la Corse in **Corte** *(see p540)*, which is a good base for exploring enchanting, remote Castagmiccia.

St-Tropez harbor, the most glamorous resort on the Provence coast

Putting France on the Map

France, one of the largest countries in Europe, has airline connections with most cities in the world. Paris is the major transport hub with two international airports; others include Bordeaux, Lille, Lyon, Nice, and Toulouse. There are good, high-speed rail links with the rest of Europe, and a network of efficient highways. A number of ferry routes cross the Mediterranean to Corsica and beyond. Cross-Channel ferries serve several ports, with the Channel Tunnel providing an alternative link by rail.

France, known as the "Hexagon" due to its six-sided shape, is bordered by six countries: Spain across the Pyrenees to the south; Italy and Switzerland beyond the Alps; Luxembourg and Belgium to the north; and Germany on the other side of the Rhine. The United Kingdom lies across the English Channel (La Manche).

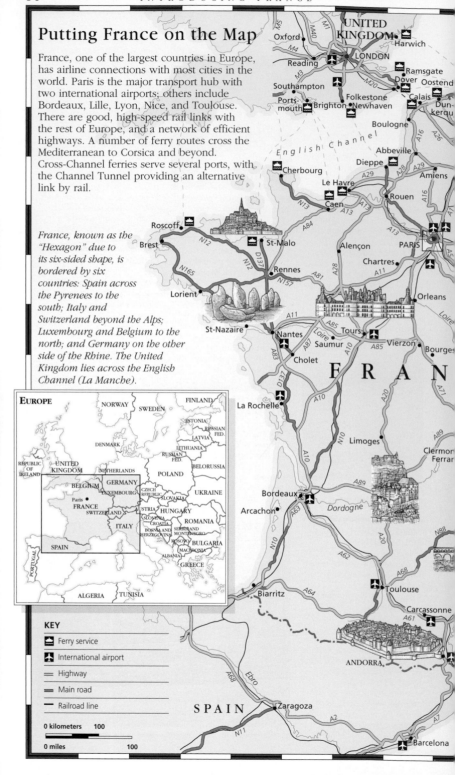

KEY

⛴	Ferry service
✈	International airport
━	Highway
━	Main road
─	Railroad line

0 kilometers	100
0 miles	100

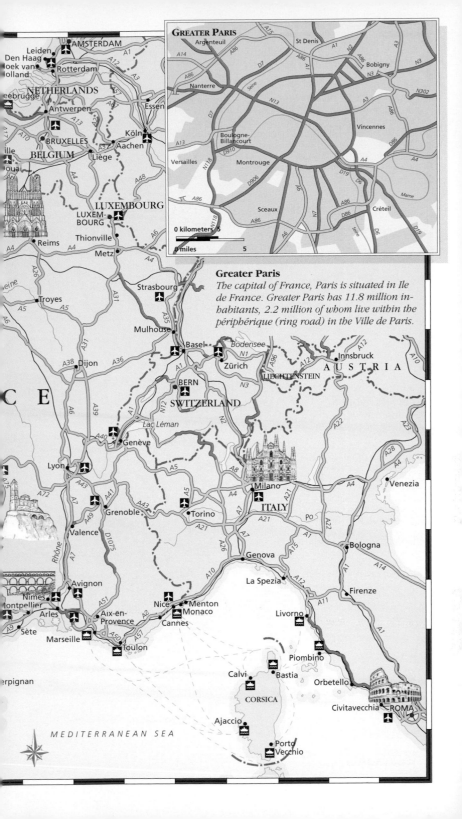

Greater Paris

The capital of France, Paris is situated in Ile de France. Greater Paris has 11.8 million inhabitants, 2.2 million of whom live within the périphérique (ring road) in the Ville de Paris.

GREATER PARIS

Argenteuil St Denis Bobigny Nanterre Boulogne-Billancourt Versailles Montrouge Vincennes Sceaux Créteil

Seine Marne

0 kilometers 5
0 miles 5

AMSTERDAM
Leiden
Den Haag
loek van
Iolland
Rotterdam

NETHERLANDS
Antwerpen Essen

BELGIUM
BRUXELLES
Köln
Aachen
Liège
ouai

Reims Thionville LUXEMBOURG LUXEM-BOURG

Metz
Troyes
Strasbourg
Mulhouse
Basel Bodensee Zürich Innsbruck
BERN LIECHTENSTEIN AUSTRIA
SWITZERLAND
Dijon
Lac Léman
Genève
Lyon
Milano
Venezia
Grenoble Torino ITALY
Valence
Bologna
Avignon Genova Firenze
Nîmes La Spezia
Montpellier Nice Menton Livorno
Arles Monaco Piombino
Sète Aix-en-Provence Cannes
Marseille Toulon Calvi Bastia
Orbetello
erpignan Civitavecchia ROMA
CORSICA
Ajaccio
MEDITERRANEAN SEA
Porto Vecchio

Regional France

France has a population of around 61 million, and
receives over 75 million visitors a year. It covers an
area of 210,025 sq miles (543,965 sq km). Paris is the
largest city, followed by Lyon, Marseille, and the
conurbation of Lille-Lens-Valenciennes. The Loire,
Seine, Garonne, and Rhône are the longest of France's
many rivers. This book divides the country into 15
regions, plus a separate
section for Paris and Ile de
France, although officially
France comprises 22 *régions*.

GETTING AROUND

In spite of its size, France is
relatively easy to travel around.
There is a well-organized rail
network, and traveling times
are considerably shortened
between towns with a high-
speed TGV link *(see p683)*.
Most highways have expensive
tolls but are fast and
efficient for longer distances.
City bypasses are usually free,
and some longer sections of
highway may also be free.
Smaller roads are usually
a more interesting way to
discover the country's varied
landscape *(pp686–8)*, and
they are almost invariably well-
maintained and signposted.

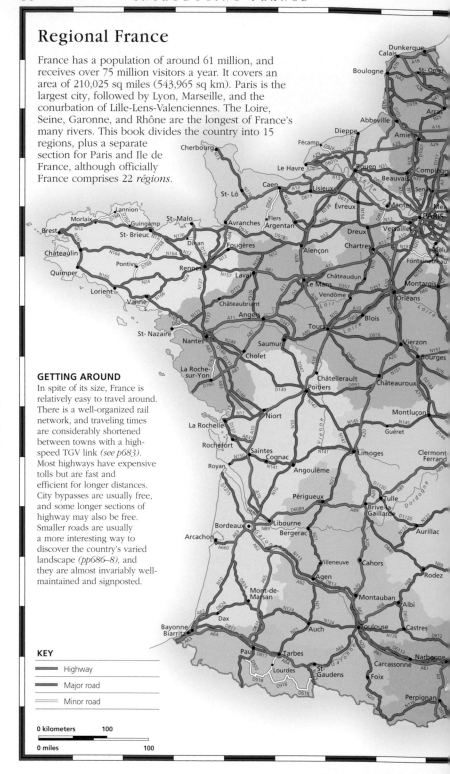

KEY

⎯⎯⎯	Highway
⎯⎯⎯	Major road
═══	Minor road

0 kilometers   100

0 miles   100

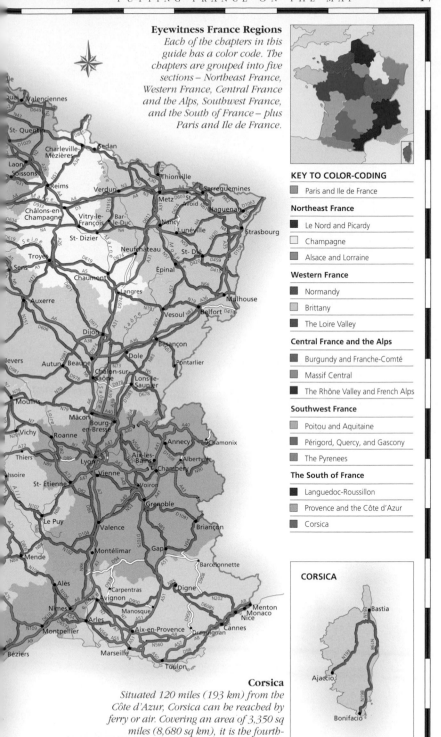

Eyewitness France Regions
Each of the chapters in this guide has a color code. The chapters are grouped into five sections – Northeast France, Western France, Central France and the Alps, Southwest France, and the South of France – plus Paris and Ile de France.

KEY TO COLOR-CODING

▢ Paris and Ile de France

Northeast France

▢ Le Nord and Picardy

▢ Champagne

▢ Alsace and Lorraine

Western France

▢ Normandy

▢ Brittany

▢ The Loire Valley

Central France and the Alps

▢ Burgundy and Franche-Comté

▢ Massif Central

▢ The Rhône Valley and French Alps

Southwest France

▢ Poitou and Aquitaine

▢ Périgord, Quercy, and Gascony

▢ The Pyrenees

The South of France

▢ Languedoc-Roussillon

▢ Provence and the Côte d'Azur

▢ Corsica

CORSICA

Corsica
Situated 120 miles (193 km) from the Côte d'Azur, Corsica can be reached by ferry or air. Covering an area of 3,350 sq miles (8,680 sq km), it is the fourth-largest island in the Mediterranean.

A PORTRAIT OF FRANCE

The French are convinced that their way of life is best, and that their country is the most civilized on earth. Many millions of visitors agree with them. The food and wine are justly celebrated. French culture, literature, art, cinema, and architecture can be both profound and provocative. Whether cerebral, sensual, or sportive, France is a country where anyone might feel at home.

France's landscape ranges from mountain plateaux to lush farmland, traditional villages to chic boulevards. Its regional identities are equally diverse. The country belongs to both northern and southern Europe, and encompasses Brittany with its Celtic maritime heritage, the Mediterranean sunbelt, Germanic Alsace-Lorraine, and the hardy mountain regions of the Auvergne and the Pyrenees. Paris remains the linchpin, with its famously brusque citizens and intense tempo. Other cities range from the industrial conglomeration of Lille in the north, to Marseille, the biggest port on the Mediterranean. The differences

Marianne, symbol of France

between north and south, country and city are well-entrenched, indeed cherished. Advances such as the TGV (high-speed train), Internet, and cell phone technology have helped reduce distance (both physical and emotional) yet have simultaneously provoked an opposite reaction: as life in France becomes more city-based and industrialized, so the desire grows to safeguard the old, traditional ways and to value rural life.

The idea of life in the country – *douceur de vivre* (the Good Life), tables set in the sun for the wine and anecdotes to flow – is as seductive as ever for residents and visitors

Château de Saumur, one of the Loire's most romantic and complete castles

◁ Café life in L'Isle sur la Sorgue, one of the country's many pleasures alike. Nevertheless, the rural way of life has been changing. Whereas in 1945 one person in three worked in farming, today it is only one in 25. France's main exports used to be luxury goods such as perfumes and Cognac; today, they have been overtaken by cars, aircraft, nuclear power stations, and telecommunications equipment.

The popular scooter

People remain firmly committed to their roots, and often retain a place in the country for holidays or retirement. On average, more French people have second homes than any other nationality. In many areas, such as Provence, dying villages have found a new life as chic summer residences for Parisians. Many artists and artisans now live and work in the country; and entrepreneurs have set up factory workshops there, more feasible in the age of the Internet.

Chanel chic

The decline in the influence of the Catholic Church has resulted in social changes. Today only 9 percent of people attend mass regularly. Many couples live together before marriage, and are allowed the same tax status as married couples. Abortion is now legal.

Feminism in France has quite a different look than in Anglo-Saxon countries. French feminists are unwilling to condemn frivolous sex-appeal. As EU citizens, women in France have legal equality with men, but French attitudes remain traditional. It may have seemed like a milestone in 1991, when Edith Cresson became France's first woman prime minister, but her unpopularity and the 1999 corruption case against her arguably held back women's equality in French politics. Ségolène Royal re-established a prominent political role for women when she won 47 percent of the vote in the 2007 presidential elections, as did Martine Aubry in 2008, when she became head of the French Socialist party.

SOCIAL CUSTOMS AND POLITICS

French social life, except between close friends, has always been marked by formality – handshaking, the use of titles, the preference for the formal *vous* rather than the intimate *tu*. However, this is changing among the younger generation, who now call you

The May 1968 disturbances, a catalyst for profound change in France

Farming in Alsace-Lorraine

by your first name. Standards of dress have become much more informal too, though the French still dress well.

Formality lingers on, however, and France remains very legalistic – whether you are buying a house or exporting an antique. But the French are insouciant about their famous red tape. Rules and laws are there to be ingeniously evaded, twisted, or made more human. This sport of avoiding cumbersome bureaucracy has a name of its own, *le système D*, to be accompanied with a shrug and a smile.

Charles de Gaulle

Since the end of the Cold War, the sharp Left/Right divisions in French society have been replaced by pragmatic centrism. Over a period of 14 years, President François Mitterrand – elected in 1981 as the head of a Socialist Communist coalition – steadily moved toward a more central-focused political agenda. In 1995, he was replaced by Jacques Chirac, who promised right-wing policies. He too moved to the center. By the 2002 presidential elections, immigration and security fears, broken electoral promises, and political corruption had caused widespread disenchantment and a swing to the Front National. The result was the elimination of Socialist Lionel Jospin in the first round and the election of Chirac by default in the second. Further electoral discontent was revealed by the rejection, in 2005, of the European Constitution.

In 2007, Chirac's Deputy Prime Minister, Nicolas Sarkozy, won the presidency by addressing public fears and promising an end to corruption. He has notably forged a closer relationship with the US, re-engaged France in the European Union, and opened up his government to ministers from the Left. But Sarkozy's popularity waned in 2010, after his plans to raise the retirement age provoked strikes, and the deportation of gypsies drew criticism from other European states.

CULTURE AND THE ARTS

Culture is taken seriously in France, and writers, intellectuals, artists, and fashion designers are held in high social esteem. As a result, the state finances

Designer Thierry Mugler at the Paris collections

a large network of provincial arts centers, and has traditionally given subsidies that allow experimentation in art and design. The French remain justly proud of their cinematic tradition and are determined to defend it against pressures from Hollywood. Other activities – from the music industry to the French language itself – are subject to the same protectionist attitudes.

Avant-garde art and literature and modern architecture all enjoy strong patronage in France. Some of the more exciting architectural projects range from the striking modern buildings in Paris – the Louvre

Traditional Breton costumes, worn for festivals and *pardons*

pyramid and La Grande Arche at La Défense – to the Post-Modern housing developments of Nîmes, Montpellier, and Marseille in the south.

MODERN LIFE

While one half of the French were heralding the new millennium in true Gallic style, the other half were plunged into darkness caused by some of the worst storms ever to hit Europe. This is an extreme illustration of French ambivalence toward modernism. France's agro-business is one of the most advanced in the world, but the peasant farmer is deeply revered. France hankers after a leading role in the world, yet the country effectively closes down for the whole of August, when the French take to the roads and coastal resorts of France! However, two factors have forced a change of pace: the Internet, which France has embraced keenly, and the Euro, which, in one fell swoop, has swept away Europe's oldest decimalized currency, the Franc.

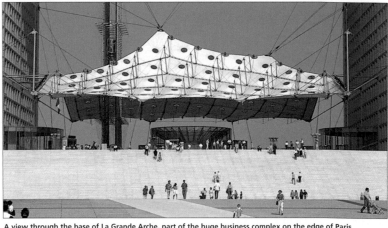

A view through the base of La Grande Arche, part of the huge business complex on the edge of Paris

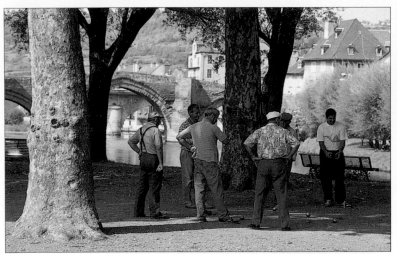

The traditional game of *boules or pétanque*, still extremely popular – especially in the south

The French are enthusiastic, discerning consumers. Even small towns have stylish clothes stores and street markets with the best local produce. France also has Europe's largest hypermarkets (superstores), which have been steadily ousting the local corner store or grocery. These are remarkably French in what they sell: a delicatessen counter may

Southern produce: melons, peaches, and apricots

display 100 or so French cheeses and charcuterie, while the range of fresh vegetables and fruit is a tribute to their role in French cuisine.

However, modern pressures have been changing eating habits in a curious way. The French used to eat well daily as a matter of course. Today many are in a hurry, and for most weekly meals will eat simply – either a quick steak or pasta dish at home, or a snack in town (hence the wave of fast-food places that have sprung up, in defiance of French tradition).

But meals still remain an important part of French culture – not just for the food and wines, but also for the pleasure of lengthy meals and good conversation around a table of family or friends. Gastronomy is now reserved for the once-or-twice-a-week special occasion, or the big family Sunday lunch, an important French ritual. It is at these times that the French zest for life really comes into its own.

Remote farm – a nostalgic reminder of rural life

The Classic French Menu

The traditional French meal consists of at least three courses. *Les entrées* or *hors d'oeuvre* (first courses or appetizers) include soups, egg dishes, salads, or *charcuterie*, such as sliced sausage or hams. There may be a separate fish course before the main course. Otherwise, *les plats* (main courses) will be a choice of meat and fish dishes, often served with a sauce and accompanied by potatoes, rice, or pasta and vegetables. The cheese course comes before the dessert. Desserts may include sorbets, fruit tarts, and creamy or chocolate concoctions. A fixed-price menu is the cheapest option. For more information on French restaurants, see pp596–9.

Fish soup

Endive salad with diced fried bacon

Goats cheese melted on toast with salad

Wild mushrooms sautéed with garlic and parsley

Sea bass grilled over fennel twigs, flamed in pastis

Scallops

Rabbit cooked "huntsman" style with mushrooms

Medallions of lamb

Steak with pepper sauce

Veal stew enriched with egg and cream

Breast of duck

Pork chops

Veal sweatbreads

HORS D'OEUVRE
Soupe de poissons
Escargots à la Bourguignonne
Salade frisée aux lardons
Crottin chaud en salade
Cèpes à la Bordelaise

POISSONS
Moules marinières
Loup au fenouil
Coquilles St-Jacques

VIANDES
Lapin chasseur
Noisettes d'agneau
Bifteck au poivre
Blanquette de veau
Magret de canard
Côte de porc
Ris de veau

Gratin Dauphinois
Carottes Vichy

Escargots à la Bourguignonne *In Bourgogne, snails are served in their shells with parsley and garlic butter.*

Moules marinières *In this classic dish, mussels are cooked in dry white wine with shallots and parsley.*

Gratin Dauphinois *Layers of potato are covered in cream, topped with Gruyère cheese and slowly baked.*

Carottes Vichy *Cooked in Vichy water with sugar, carrots take on a delicious, sweet glaze. They are served garnished with parsley.*

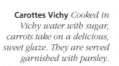

BREAKFAST

The French rarely eat cereal, eggs, or meat for breakfast; assorted breads, spread with butter and jams, are their morning choice. These include *croissants* (flaky, buttery crescent-shaped pastries); a piece of *baguette* (the classic long thin loaf); *pain au chocolat* (an oblong of croissant dough rolled round a tablet of chocolate, then baked); and *brioche* (an airy, egg-enriched yeast bread or roll). They are accompanied by coffee or tea, or hot chocolate for children. Hotels will usually offer fresh fruit juice, too. The most common form of coffee at breakfast is *café au lait*, espresso served with warm milk.

Typical French breakfast selection

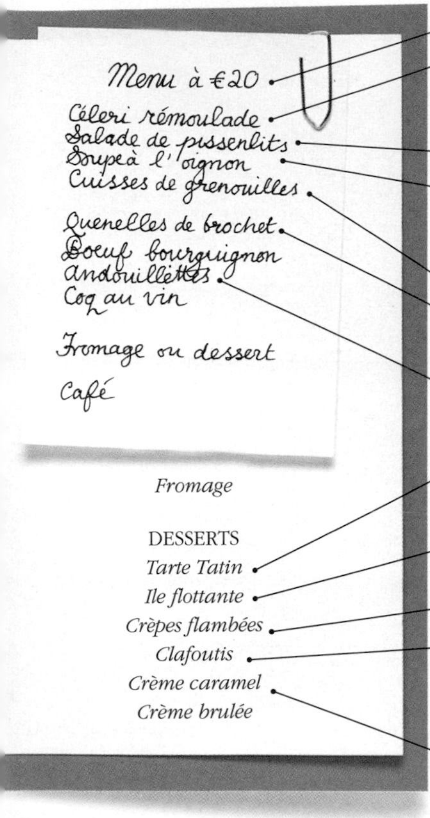

Menu à €20
Céleri rémoulade
Salade de pissenlits
Soupe à l'oignon
Cuisses de grenouilles

Quenelles de brochet
Boeuf bourguignon
Andouillettes
Coq au vin

Fromage ou dessert
Café

Fixed-price menu of the day

Grated celeriac in a piquant mayonnaise

Dandelion-leaf salad

Dark, rich onion soup topped with bread and grilled cheese

Frogs' legs

Light, fluffy poached pike dumplings

Small tripe sausages, usually grilled

Boeuf Bourguignon *Beef is cooked in red Burgundy wine with bacon, baby onions, and button mushrooms.*

Fromage

DESSERTS
Tarte Tatin
Ile flottante
Crèpes flambées
Clafoutis
Crème caramel
Crème brulée

Upside-down baked apple tart

Meringues floating in a creamy sauce

Sugared crêpes flamed in liqueur

Baked fruit and batter dessert, often made with cherries

Egg custard with a caramel sauce

Coq au vin *A male chicken is flamed in brandy, then stewed in wine with button mushrooms and onions.*

Fromage *Any good French restaurant will take pride in offering a good range of perfectly matured regional cheeses, including, as available, cows', ewes', and goats' milk, blue, soft, and hard varieties.*

Crème Brulée *This rich, creamy custard is covered with brown sugar, grilled to form a crisp topping.*

The Wine of France

Picker's hod

Winemaking in France dates back to pre-Roman times, although it was the Romans who disseminated the culture of the vine and the practice of winemaking throughout the country. The range, quality, and reputation of the fine wines of Bordeaux, Burgundy, the Rhône, and Champagne in particular have made them role models the world over. France's everyday wines can be highly enjoyable too, with plenty of good-value wines now emerging from the southern regions.

Traditional vineyard cultivation

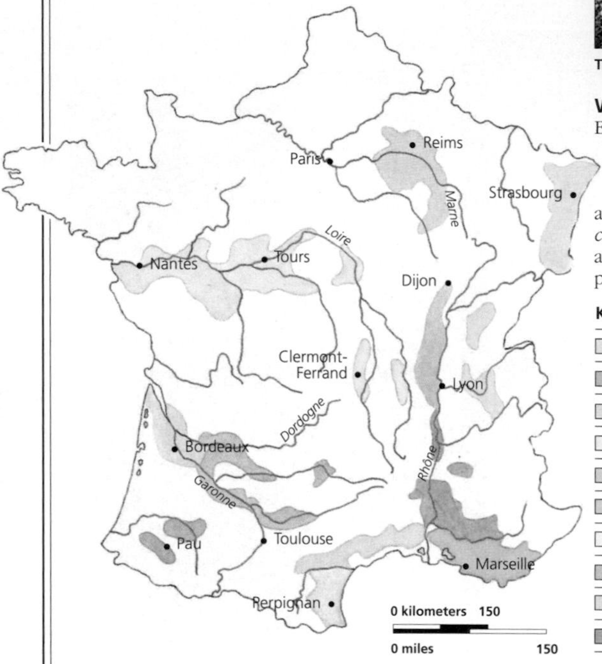

WINE REGIONS

Each of the 10 principal wine-producing regions has its own identity, based on grape varieties, climate, and *terroir* (soil). *Appellation contrôlée* laws guarantee a wine's origins and production methods.

KEY

- ☐ Bordeaux
- ☐ Burgundy
- ☐ Champagne
- ☐ Alsace
- ☐ Loire
- ☐ Provence
- ☐ Jura and Savoie
- ☐ The Southwest
- ☐ Languedoc-Roussillon
- ☐ Rhône

Map labels: Paris, Reims, Strasbourg, Nantes, Tours, Dijon, Marne, Loire, Clermont-Ferrand, Lyon, Bordeaux, Dordogne, Garonne, Rhône, Pau, Toulouse, Marseille, Perpignan

0 kilometers 150
0 miles 150

HOW TO READ A WINE LABEL

Even the simplest label will identify the wine and provide a key to its quality. It will bear the name of the wine and its producer, its vintage, if there is one, and whether it comes from a strictly defined area (*appellation contrôlée*) or is a more general *IGP* (*Indication Géographique Protégée*) wine or *vin de France*. It may additionally have a regional grading, as with the *crus classés* in Bordeaux. The shape and color of the bottle is also a guide to the kind of wine it contains. Green glass is often used, since this helps to protect the wine from light.

The property or producer

The vintage, from the French word *vendange*, or harvest

Pictures may be accurate or fanciful

Château-bottled, rather than from a merchant or growers' cooperative

The wine's *appellation contrôlée*

Capacity of the bottle

CHATEAU MARGAUX
2008
GRAND VIN
PREMIER GRAND CRU CLASSÉ

CHÂTEAU MARGAUX
PREMIER GRAND CRU CLASSÉ
MARGAUX
APPELLATION MARGAUX CONTROLEE
2008
MIS EN BOUTEILLE AU CHATEAU
S.C.A CHATEAU MARGAUX PROPRIETAIRE A MARGAUX · FRANCE

HOW WINE IS MADE

Wine is the product of the juice of freshly picked grapes, after natural or cultured yeasts have converted the grape sugars into alcohol during the fermentation process. The yeasts, or lees, are normally filtered out before bottling.

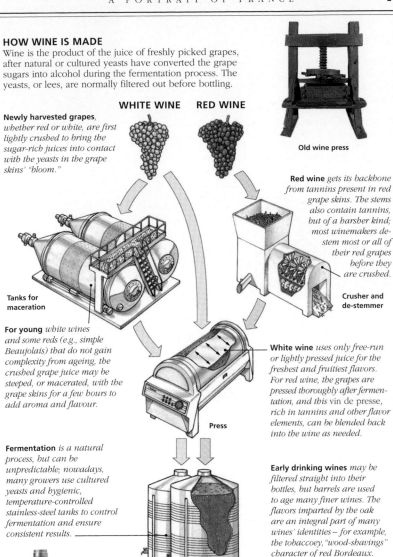

WHITE WINE   RED WINE

Newly harvested grapes, *whether red or white, are first lightly crushed to bring the sugar-rich juices into contact with the yeasts in the grape skins' "bloom."*

Old wine press

Red wine *gets its backbone from tannins present in red grape skins. The stems also contain tannins, but of a harsher kind; most winemakers de-stem most or all of their red grapes before they are crushed.*

Crusher and de-stemmer

Tanks for maceration

For young *white wines and some reds (e.g., simple Beaujolais) that do not gain complexity from ageing, the crushed grape juice may be steeped, or macerated, with the grape skins for a few hours to add aroma and flavour.*

White wine *uses only free-run or lightly pressed juice for the freshest and fruitiest flavors. For red wine, the grapes are pressed thoroughly after fermentation, and this vin de presse, rich in tannins and other flavor elements, can be blended back into the wine as needed.*

Press

Fermentation *is a natural process, but can be unpredictable; nowadays, many growers use cultured yeasts and hygienic, temperature-controlled stainless-steel tanks to control fermentation and ensure consistent results.*

Early drinking wines *may be filtered straight into their bottles, but barrels are used to age many finer wines. The flavors imparted by the oak are an integral part of many wines' identities – for example, the tobaccoey, "wood-shavings" character of red Bordeaux.*

Fermentation vat

Oak casks

Different shades of glass identify the wine regions

Bottle shapes typical of red Bordeaux (left) and Burgundy

Artists in France

Artists have always been inspired by France, especially since landscape became a legitimate subject for art in the 19th century. Art and tourism have been closely linked for over a century, when the establishment of artists' colonies in the forest of Fontainebleau, Brittany, and the south of France did much to make these areas attractive to visitors. Today, one of the pleasures of touring the countryside is the recognition of landscapes made famous in paintings.

Follower of *the French Classical tradition of landscape painting, Jean-Baptiste-Camille Corot recorded* The Belfry of Douai *(1871).*

Le Nord a
Picardy

Gustave Courbet*, socialist and leader of the Realist School of painting, captured this famous coastal town in* The Cliffs at Etretat after a Storm *(1869).*

Normandy

Paris
and Ile
Franc

Brittany

Loire Valley

Emile Bernard *was fascinated by the wild, almost primitive character of the Breton landscape and the individuality of its inhabitants. He was one of the community of artists based in Pont Aven. His* La Ronde Bretonne *(1892) portrays local Celtic customs.*

Poitou and
Aquitaine

Neo-Impressionist *artist and exponent of Pointillism, Paul Signac indulged his love of maritime subjects on the coasts of France.* Entrance to the Port at La Rochelle *(1921) shows his use of myriad dots of color to represent nature.*

Périgord,
Quercy and
Gascony

Pyrenees

Languedoc
Roussillon

Théodore Rousseau*, the leading light of the Barbizon School (see p181) of landscape painters, visited the Auvergne in 1830. It was here that he began to paint "en plein air" (in the open air). The results are seen in this sensitively observed scene,* Sunset, Auvergne *(c.1830).*

A few months *before his tragic death in July 1890, Vincent Van Gogh painted the* Church at Auvers. *He noted that the building "appears to have a violet-hued blue color; pure cobalt."*

In his Eiffel Tower *(1926) Robert Delaunay investigated the abstract qualities of color. His wife, artist Sonia Delaunay, said, "The Eiffel Tower and the Universe were one and the same to him."*

Alsace and Lorraine

Champagne

Scenes from *everyday life were realistically rendered by Gustave Courbet, as here in* Young Ladies of the Village Giving Alms to a Cow Girl in a Valley near Ornans *(1851–2).*

Burgundy and Franche-Comté

Maurice Utrillo *painted this village scene,* The Church of Saint Bernard in Summer *(1924), while staying at his mother's home. The somber tone and emptiness reflect his unhappy life.*

The Massif Central

The Rhône Valley and French Alps

Provence and the Côte d'Azur

Landscape at Collioure *(1905) depicts the vivid colors of this little Catalan fishing village. It was here that Henri Matisse founded the art movement of the Fauves, or "Wild Beasts," who used exceptionally bright, expressive colors.*

The French Riviera *attracted many artists (see pp472–3). Raoul Dufy particularly appreciated its pleasures, seen in this typical scene of blue skies and palm trees,* La Jetée Promenade à Nice *(1928).*

```
0 kilometers    100

0 miles            100
```

Writers in France

Writers and intellectuals traditionally enjoy high prestige in France. One of the most august of French institutions is the Academie Française, whose 40 members, most of them writers, have pronounced on national events and, on occasion, held public office.

Monument to Baudelaire

The work of many French novelists is deeply rooted in their native area, ranging from the Normandy of Gustave Flaubert to Jean Giono's Provence. In addition to their literary merit, these novels provide a unique guide to France's regional identities.

Colette's house in Burgundy

THE NOVEL

The farmland of the Beauce, where Zola based his novel, *La Terre*

The first great French writer was Rabelais in the 16th century, a boisterous, life-affirming satirist *(see p295)*. Many writers in the Age of Enlightenment that followed emphasized the tradition of reason, clarity, and objectivity in their work. The 19th century was the golden age of the French humanist novel, producing Balzac, with his vast fresco of contemporary society; Stendhal, a fierce critic of the frailties of ambition in *Scarlet and Black*; and Victor Hugo, known for epics such as *Les Misérables*. George Sand broke ground with her novels such as *The Devil's Pool* which depicted peasant life, albeit in an idealized way. In the same century, Flaubert produced his masterwork *Madame Bovary*, a study of provincialism and misplaced romanticism. In contrast, Zola wrote *Germinal*, *La Terre*, and other studies of lower-class life.

Marcel Proust combined a poetic evocation of his boyhood with a portrait of high society in his long novel, *Remembrance of Things Past*.

Marcel Proust, author of
Remembrance of Things Past

Others have also written poetically about their childhood, such as Alain-Fournier in *Le Grand Meaulnes* and Colette in *My Mother's House*.

A new kind of novel emerged after World War I. Jean Giono's *Joy of Man's Desiring* and François Mauriac's masterly *Thérèse Desqueyroux* explored the impact of landscape upon human character. Mauriac, and also George Bernanos in his *Diary of a Country Priest*, used lone spiritual struggle as a theme. The free-thinker André Gide was another leading writer of the inter-war years with his *Strait is the Gate* and the autobiographical *If it Die*.

In the 1960s Alain Robbe-Grillet and others experimented with the Nouveau Roman, which subordinated character and plot to detailed physical description. Critics held it in part responsible for the recent decline of the novel. Despite this, the 2008 Nobel Prize for literature was awarded to Franco-Mauritian Jean-Marie Gustave Le Clézio.

Hugo's novel *Les Misérables*, made into a musical in the 1980s

THEATER

The three classic playwrights of French literature, Racine, Molière, and Corneille, lived in the 17th century. Molière's comedies satirized the vanities and foibles of human nature. Corneille and Racine wrote noble verse tragedies. They were followed in the 18th century by Marivaux, writer of romantic comedies, and Beaumarchais whose *Barber of Seville* and *Marriage of Figaro* later became operas.

Molière, the 17th-century dramatist

Victor Hugo's dramas were the most vigorous product of the 19th century. The exceptional dramatists of the 20th century range from Jean Anouilh, author of urbane philosophical comedies, to Jean Genet, ex-convict critic of the establishment. In the 1960s, Eugene Ionesco from Romania and Samuel Beckett from Ireland were among the pioneers of a new genre, the "theater of the absurd." Since then, no major playwrights have emerged but experimental work flourishes in state-subsidized theater companies.

POETRY

The greatest of early French poets was Ronsard, who wrote sonnets about nature and love in the 16th century. Lamartine, a major poet of the early 19th century, also took nature as one of his themes (his poem *Le Lac* laments a lost love). Later the same century, Baudelaire *(Les Fleurs du mal)* and Rimbaud *(Le Bateau Ivre)* were judged to be provocative in their day. Nobel prizewinner in 1904, Frédéric Mistral wrote in his native Provençal tongue. The greatest poet of the 20th century is considered to be Paul Valéry, whose work is profoundly philosophical.

PHILOSOPHY

France has produced a large number of major philosophers in the European humanist tradition. One of the first was

Novels by Albert Camus, who won the Nobel Prize in 1957

Sartre and de Beauvoir in La Coupole restaurant in Paris, 1969

Montaigne, in the 16th century, an inspired moralist. Then came Descartes, the master of logic, and Pascal. The 18th century produced Voltaire, the supreme liberal, and Rousseau, who preached the harmonizing influence of living close to nature.

In the 20th century, Sartre, de Beauvoir, and Camus used the novel as a philosophical vehicle. Sartre led the existentialist movement in Paris in the early 1940s with his novel *Nausea* and his treatise *Being and Nothingness.* Camus' novel, *The Outsider,* was equally influential.

The 1970s and 1980s brought the structuralists, such as Foucault and Barthes, with their radical ideas. Poststructuralism took this rationalist approach into the 1990s, with Derrida, Kristeva, Deleuze, and Lyotard. In the 21st century, Badiou, known for his political ideas, is one of France's key philosophers.

FOREIGN WRITERS

Many foreign writers have visited and been inspired by France, from Petrarch in 14th-century Avignon to Goethe in Alsace in 1770–71. In the 20th century the Riviera attracted novelists Somerset Maugham, Katherine Mansfield, Ernest Hemingway, and Graham Greene. In 1919 the American Sylvia Beach opened the first Shakespeare and Company bookshop in Paris, which became a cultural center for expatriate writers. In 1922 she was the first to publish James Joyce's masterwork, *Ulysses.*

Hemingway with Sylvia Beach and friends, Paris 1923

Romanesque and Gothic Architecture in France

France is rich in medieval architecture, ranging from small Romanesque churches to great Gothic cathedrals. As the country emerged from the Dark Ages in the 11th century, there was a surge in Romanesque building, based on the Roman model of thick walls, round arches, and heavy vaults. French architects improved this basic structure, leading to the flowering of Gothic in the 13th century. Pointed arches and flying buttresses were the key inventions that allowed for much taller buildings with larger windows.

LOCATOR MAP

① Romanesque abbeys & churches

⑬ Gothic cathedrals

ROMANESQUE FEATURES

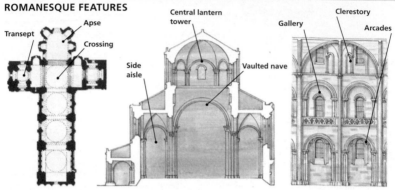

The plan of Angoulême *shows the cross-shape and the rounded eastern apse typical of Romanesque architecture.*

A section of Le Puy *reveals a high barrel-vaulted nave with round arches and low side aisles. Light could enter through windows in the side aisles and the central lantern tower.*

The massive walls *of the nave bays of St-Etienne support a three-storey structure of arcades, a gallery, and clerestory.*

GOTHIC FEATURES

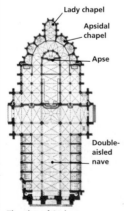

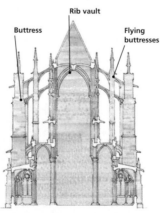

The plan of Amiens *shows the nave and apse flanked by a continuous row of chapels.*

A section of Beauvais *shows how the nave could be raised to staggering heights thanks to exterior support from flying buttresses.*

Pointed arches *withstood greater stress, permitting larger windows as in the nave at Reims.*

WHERE TO FIND ROMANESQUE ARCHITECTURE

① St-Etienne, Caen *p254*
② Mont-St-Michel, Normandy *p258*
③ St-Pierre, Angoulême *p419*
④ Notre-Dame, Le Puy *p365*
⑤ St-Pierre, Moissac *pp442–3*
⑥ St-Sernin, Toulouse *pp446–7*
⑦ Ste-Foy, Conques *pp358–9*
⑧ Sacré-Coeur, Paray-le-Monial *p345*
⑨ St-Philibert, Tournus *p344*
⑩ St-Etienne, Nevers *p338*
⑪ Ste-Madeleine, Vézelay *pp336–7*
⑫ Marmoutier, Saverne *p233*

WHERE TO FIND GOTHIC ARCHITECTURE

⑬ Notre-Dame, Strasbourg *p231*
⑭ Notre-Dame, Reims *pp212–3*
⑮ Notre-Dame, Laon *p205*
⑯ Notre-Dame, Amiens *pp202–3*
⑰ St-Pierre, Beauvais *p200*
⑱ St-Denis, Ile-de-France *p172*
⑲ Sainte-Chapelle, Paris *pp84–5*
⑳ Notre-Dame, Paris *pp86–7*
㉑ Notre-Dame, Chartres *pp308–11*
㉒ St-Etienne, Bourges *p313*

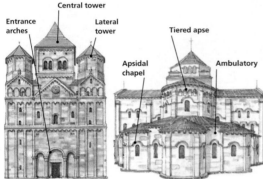

The west façade of Marmoutier Abbey *with its towers, narrow windows, and small portal give it a fortified appearance.*

The east end of Nevers *has a rounded apse surrounded by a semicircular ambulatory and radiating chapels. The chapels were added to provide space for altars.*

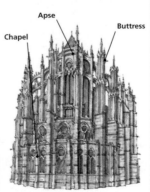

The west façade of Laon *has decorative, sculpted portals and a rose window characteristic of Gothic style.*

The east end of Beauvais, *with its delicate buttresses topped by pinnacles, is the culmination of High Gothic.*

TERMS USED IN THIS GUIDE

Basilica: Early church with two aisles and nave lit from above by clerestory windows.

Clerestory: A row of windows illuminating the nave from above the aisle roof.

 Rose: Circular window, often stained glass.

Buttress: Mass of masonry built to support a wall.

 Flying buttress: An arched support transmitting thrust of the weight downward.

Portal: Monumental entrance to a building, often decorated.

 Tympanum: Decorated space, often carved, over a door or window lintel.

Vault: Arched stone ceiling.

Transept: Two wings of a cruciform church at right angles to the nave.

Crossing: Center of cruciform where transept crosses nave.

Lantern: Turret with windows to illuminate interior, often with cupola (domed ceiling).

Triforium: Middle story between arcades and clerestory.

Apse: Termination of the church, often rounded.

Ambulatory: Aisle running round east end, passing behind the sanctuary.

Arcade: Set of arches and supporting columns.

Rib vault: Vault supported by projecting ribs of stone.

 Gargoyle: Carved grotesque figure, often a water spout.

Tracery: Ornamental carved stone pattern within Gothic window.

Flamboyant Gothic: Carved stone tracery resembling flames.

 Capital: Top of a column, usually carved.

Rural Architecture

French farmhouses are entirely products of the soil, built of stone, clay, or wood, depending on which materials are found locally. As the topography changes so does the architecture, from the steeply-sloped roofs covered in flat tiles in the north to the broad canal-tiled roofs of the south.

Despite this rich regional diversity, French farmhouses fall into three basic categories: the *maison bloc*, where house and outbuildings share the same roof; the high house, with living quarters upstairs and livestock or wine cellar below; and courtyard farmsteads, their buildings set around a central court.

Shuttered window in Alsace

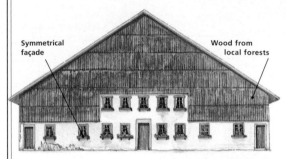

Symmetrical
façade

Wood from
local forests

The chalet *is typical of the Jura, Alps, and Vosges mountains. The* maison bloc *housed both family and livestock throughout the winter. Gaps between the gable planks allowed air to circulate around crops stored in the loft, and an earth ramp behind gave wagons access. Many lofts also had a threshing floor.*

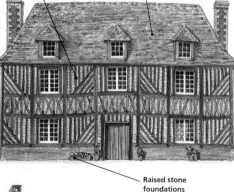

Normandy wood
structure

Flat-tiled roof

Half-timbered houses *are typical of Normandy, Alsace, Champagne, Picardy, the Landes, and Basque country. The filling between the timbers was wattle and daub or in some cases brick, but it is the arrangement of the smaller posts, different in each region, that best expresses the local style.*

Raised stone
foundations

Dovecote
with flat tiles

Steps to front
door

Animals or wine
housed here

The high house *is most prominent in the southeast, and is normally built of stone with an exterior stone staircase and upstairs porch. Wine growers' barrels could be stored on the ground floor without hoisting, or livestock stabled there. High houses in the Lot Valley often feature a dovecote.*

The long house *is the oldest form of* maison bloc, *with family and livestock at opposite ends of the building – originally one room. In this Breton version, separate doorways lead to house and stable. A dividing wall only became common in the 19th century.*

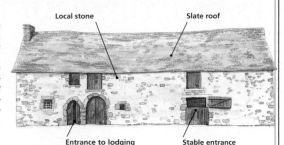

Local stone

Slate roof

Entrance to lodging

Stable entrance

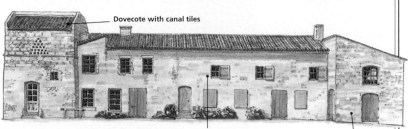

Dovecote with canal tiles

The word "mas" *generally refers to any Provençal farmhouse. In the Camargue and the Crau, it is a farmstead for large-scale sheep farming built in an "agglomerated" style: the outbuildings, although attached to one another, are of different heights. Often, a dovecote is included.*

Ochre and beige colors of the south

Rendered façade

Pebble and brick wall

Half-timber and brick

Compressed cob: *pisé*

Sun-dried adobe bricks

Pebbles in lime mortar

Brick, flint, and chalk

WALLS

Limestone, granite, sandstone and pebbles were all used for building walls. But if no stone was available, clay was dug for infilling half-timbered houses, as wattle and daub. The alternative was to use a cob mixture *(pisé)*, pressed into blocks in a process called *banchange*. Adobe (sundried brick) was also used but fired brick was fairly rare as it was expensive to bake. However, brick was sometimes used as trim or combined with chalk or pebbles in a "composite" walling. Walls were generally rendered with mortar.

Flat terra cotta tiles in colors of local sand

Pantiles, used in Flanders and Picardy

Canal clay tiles typical of the south

ROOFING

Two roof styles distinguish the north and south. Northern roofs are steeply pitched, so that any rainwater runs off easily. In the south, roofs are covered with canal clay tiles, and more gently sloped to prevent the tiles sliding off.

FRANCE THROUGH THE YEAR

The French, with their farming roots, are deeply aware of the changing seasons, and the mild climate means they can celebrate outdoors most of the year. History and tradition are honored with *fêtes*, such as Bastille Day (July 14). For culture lovers, thousands of arts festivals are held throughout France, ranging from the huge Avignon Theater Festival down to small village events. National sports events, such as the Tour de France bicycle race, are a key feature in the calendar. Throughout the year, festivals take place celebrating every kind of food and wine. In high summer, the cities empty and French and foreign visitors flock to the beaches and countryside.

SPRING

France's outdoor life resumes in spring, terrace-cafés filling up in the sunshine. Easter is a time of Catholic processions and concerts of sacred music. The Cannes Film Festival in May is the best known of the season's many conventions and trade fairs.

MARCH

International Half Marathon beginning and ending at Château de Vincennes.
Tinta' Mars *(two weeks)*, Langres. Cabaret and musical evenings at various venues.
Grenoble Jazz Festival *(two weeks Mar)*. Jazz concerts.
Banlieues Blues Jazz Festival *(Mar)*, Saint-Denis. Jazz music.

Rugby ball

Six Nations Rugby Tournament, Stade de France, Paris.

Formula One racing at the Monaco Grand Prix

Festival d'Amiens *(mid-Mar/early Apr)*. Celebrated jazz festival at various venues.
Europa Jazz Festival *(end Mar/early Apr)*, Le Mans. International jazz festival.

APRIL

Festival de Pâques *(Easter week)*, chamber music festival, Deauville *(see p255)*.
Feria Pascale *(Easter week)*. The whole town parties as the bull-fighting season begins, Arles *(see pp508–9)*.
Lourdes Pilgrimage *(Palm Sun to Oct, see p459)*.
Floréal Musical d'Epinal *(early Apr–mid-May)*. Multi-

genre music festival, Epinal.
Bourges Spring Festival *(end Apr/early May, see p313)*, modern music.
Joan of Arc Festival *(end Apr–early May)*, pageant and cathedral service, Orléans *(see p312)*.
Paris International Marathon from Place de la Concorde to Avenue Foch.

MAY

Spring asparagus

Asparagus harvest, notably in the Loire.
International Grand Prix de Monaco *(Ascension weekend, see p530)*.
La Bravade *(May 16–18)*, St-Tropez *(see p516)*.

La Bravade procession honoring Saint Torpes in St-Tropez

Cannes Film Festival *(second and third week)*.
Gypsy Pilgrimage *(late May)*, Stes-Maries-de-la-Mer *(see p510)*.
Fête de la Transhumance *(end May)*. Herds are taken up to summer pastures.
International Garden Festival *(May–mid-Oct)*, Chaumont sur Loire.
Nîmes Feria *(Pentecost)*, bullfights and street music festival *(see p496)*.
Grandes Eaux Musicales *(Apr –Oct: Sun; Jul –Sep: Sat –Sun)*, Versailles. Classical music in

Traditional transhumance of animals to summer pastures

the grounds of the château.
Puy-du-Fou Pageant *(May–Sep)*. Audio-guides and horse stunts evoke local life through the ages *(see p290)*.

Soccer Cup Final *(second week)*, Stade de France, Paris.
Le Printemps des Arts *(mid-May–Jun)*, Nantes area. Baroque dance and music.

SUMMER

The French vacation season begins in mid-July, with the return to work and school *(la rentrée)* in early September. Beaches, marinas, and camp sites are all full to bursting. Every village has its *fête* and there are festivals, sporting events, and flea markets.

JUNE

French Tennis Open *(last wk May –first wk Jun)*, Stade Roland Garros, Paris.
Strasbourg International Music Festival *(Jun– Jul)*.
International Sailing Week *(early Jun)*, La Rochelle.

Le Mans 24-Hour Automobile Race *(second or third w/e, see p291)*.
Fête de la Musique *(Jun 21)*, music events all over France.
Fête de St-Jean *(Jun 24)*, music, bonfires, and fireworks all over France.
Gay Pride March *(Jun 23)*, The march engulfs Paris.
Tarasque Festival *(last weekend)*, Tarascon *(see p507)*.

JULY

Festival d'Art Lyrique *(Jun–Jul)*, Aix-en-Provence *(see p511)*.
Avignon Theater Festival *(all month, see p503)*.
Paris-Plage *(mid-Jul–mid-Aug)*. Paris and other cities get an

Bullfighting in Mont-de-Marsan

annual temporary beach.
Tombées de la Nuit *(first week)*, Rennes. Arts festival.
Troménie *(2nd Sun Jul)*, Locronan. Procession of penitents *(see p273)*.
Comminges Music Festival *(Jul–end Aug, see p382)*.
Nice Jazz Festival *(late-Jul)*.
Mont-de-Marsan Feria *(third w/e)*. Bullfights and music *(see p425)*.
International Jazz Festival *(second half)*, Antibes and Juan-les-Pins *(see p521)*.
Jazz Vienne *(first two weeks)*, Vienne *(see p382)*.
Fête de St-Louis *(around Aug 25)*, Sète *(see p492)*.
Tour de France cycle race *(1st three weeks)*. The grand finale takes place on thè Champs-Elysées, Paris.
Francofolies *(mid-Jul)*, Music festival at La Rochelle.

The rose season in full bloom

Cyclists in the final stage of the Tour de France bicycle race

Vacationers on a crowded beach in Cannes on the Côte d'Azur

AUGUST

Pablo Casals Festival
(end Jul–mid-Aug),
Prades *(see p480)*.
**Les Rendezvous de
l'Erdre** *(last w/e)*,
Nantes. Jazz and
river-boats *(see p290)*.
Mimos *(1st week)*,
Périgueux. World-
famous international
mime festival.

Avignon Theater
Festival performer

Fête du Jasmin *(first w/e)*,
Grasse *(see p517)*. Floats,
music, dancing in town.
Foire aux Sorciers
(first Sun), Bué
(nr Bourges).
Costumed witch and
wizard festival and
folk groups.
**Parade of Lavender
Floats** *(first or
second weekends)*,
Digne *(see p517)*.

Fête de la Véraison
(first or second w/e), medieval
celebration of thanksgiving
for the bounty of the fruit
harvest, Châteauneuf-du-
Pape *(see p502)*.
Interceltic Festival *(second
week)*, Lorient, Celtic arts
and music.
Feria – Bullfight *(mid-Aug)*,
Dax *(see p425)*.
**St-Jean-Pied-de-Port-Basque
Fête** *(mid-Aug, see p454)*.

AUTUMN

In wine regions, the grape
harvest is the occasion for
much gregarious jollity, and
every wine village has its
wine festival. When the new
wine is ready in November
there are more festivities. The
hunting season begins –
everywhere there is game
shooting. In the southwest,
migrating birds are trapped.

SEPTEMBER

**Deauville American film
Festival** *(first two weeks)*.
Picardy Cathedral Festival
(mid-Sep), Classical concerts
in the region's cathedrals.
"Musicades" *(first fortnight)*,
Lyon. Classical concerts.
Le Puy "Roi de l'Oiseau,"
(second week). Renaissance-
style festival *(see p365)*.
Grape harvest, wine regions
throughout France.
Journées du Patrimoine,
(3rd w/e). Over 14,000 historical buildings can be visited,
many not normally open.

Ceremony for the Induction of new Chevaliers at the Hospice de Beaune

OCTOBER

Dinard British film festival
(first week, see p281).
Nuit Blanche *(first Sat)*,
Paris. Museums stay
open all night.
Prix de l'Arc de Triomphe
(first Sun). Horse racing
at Longchamp, Paris.
Espelette Pepper Festival
(last w/e, see p453).
**Festival de Lanvellec
and Trégor** *(mid-Oct)*.
Baroque music festival.

Classical cello

NOVEMBER

**Dijon International Food
and Wine Festival** *(first two
weeks)*. Traditional
gastronomic fair.
Apple Festival *(mid-
Nov)*, Le Havre.
**Wine Auctions and Les
Trois Glorieuses** *(third
weekend)*, Beaune
(see p346).
Truffle season *(until
Mar)*, Périgord, Quercy
and Provence.

WINTER

At Christmas, traditional nativity plays are held in churches and there are fairs and markets throughout France. In the Alps and the Pyrenees, and even the Vosges and Massif Central, the ski slopes are crowded. In Flanders and Nice, carnivals take place before Lent.

Christmas wreath

DECEMBER

Critérium International de la Première Neige *(early Dec)*, Val d'Isère. First competition of the season.

JANUARY

Monte-Carlo Rally *(usually mid-Jan, see p530)*.
Limoux Carnival *(until Mar)*. Street festival held since the Middle Ages.
Fashion shows. Summer

Downhill skier on the slopes in the French Alps

The Taj Mahal re-created at the Lemon Festival in Menton

collections, Paris.
Festival du Cirque *(end)*, Monaco. International event.
Festival de la Bande Dessinée *(last w/e)*. International strip cartoon festival, Angoulême.

FEBRUARY

Lemon Festival *(mid-Feb–Mar)*, Menton *(see p529)*.
Nice Carnival and the Battle of Flowers *(late Feb–early Mar, see p526)*.
Paris Carnaval, *(date varies, check)*, Quartier St-Fargeau.
Fête de Mimosa, *(3rd Sun)*, Bormes-les-Mimosas.

Celebrating the Nice Carnival and the Battle of Flowers

Bastille Day parade past the Arc de Triomphe

PUBLIC HOLIDAYS

New Year's Day (Jan 1)
Easter Sunday and Monday
Ascension Day (sixth Thursday after Easter)
Whit Monday (second Monday after Ascension)
Labor Day (May 1)
VE Day (May 8)
Bastille Day (Jul 14)
Assumption Day (Aug 15)
All Saints' Day (Nov 1)
Remembrance Day (Nov 11)
Christmas Day (Dec 25)

The Climate of France

Set on Europe's western edge, France has a varied, temperate climate. An Atlantic influence prevails in the northwest, with westerly sea winds bringing humidity and warm winters. The east experiences Continental temperature extremes with frosty, clear winters and often stormy summers. The south enjoys a Mediterranean climate with hot, dry summers and mild winters, punctuated by violent winds.

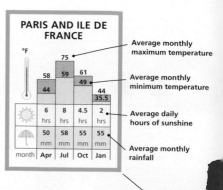

PARIS AND ILE DE FRANCE

°F			
		75	
58	59		61
44			49
			44
			35.5

- Average monthly maximum temperature
- Average monthly minimum temperature
- Average daily hours of sunshine
- Average monthly rainfall

☼	6 hrs	8 hrs	4.5 hrs	2 hrs
☂	50 mm	58 mm	55 mm	55 mm
month	Apr	Jul	Oct	Jan

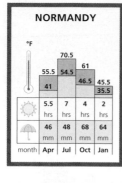

NORMANDY

°F			
	70.5		
55.5	54.5	61	
41		46.5	45.5
			35.5

☼	5.5 hrs	7 hrs	4 hrs	2 hrs
☂	46 mm	48 mm	68 mm	64 mm
month	Apr	Jul	Oct	Jan

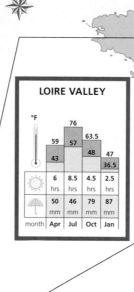

LOIRE VALLEY

°F			
	76		
59	57	63.5	
43		48	47
			36.5

☼	6 hrs	8.5 hrs	4.5 hrs	2.5 hrs
☂	50 mm	46 mm	79 mm	87 mm
month	Apr	Jul	Oct	Jan

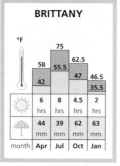

BRITTANY

°F			
	75		
58	55.5	62.5	
42		47	46.5
			35.5

☼	6 hrs	8 hrs	4.5 hrs	2 hrs
☂	44 mm	39 mm	62 mm	63 mm
month	Apr	Jul	Oct	Jan

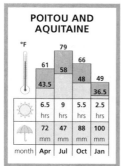

POITOU AND AQUITAINE

°F			
	79		
61	58	66	
43.5		48	49
			36.5

☼	6.5 hrs	9 hrs	5.5 hrs	2.5 hrs
☂	72 mm	47 mm	88 mm	100 mm
month	Apr	Jul	Oct	Jan

PYRENEES

°F			
	77		
59	56	66	
41		45.5	50
			33

☼	5 hrs	7.5 hrs	5.5 hrs	3.5 hrs
☂	98 mm	62 mm	78 mm	93 mm
month	Apr	Jul	Oct	Jan

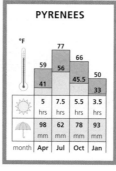

PÉRIGORD, QUERCY AND GASCONY

°F			
	80.5		
61.5	58	66	
43		48	47
			35.5

☼	6 hrs	9 hrs	4.5 hrs	2.5 hrs
☂	60 mm	50 mm	57 mm	66 mm
month	Apr	Jul	Oct	Jan

Le Havre

Rennes

Nantes

Tours

Bordeaux

Montauban

Biarritz

LE NORD AND PICARDY

°F			
	71.5		
55.5	54.5	59	
40		45.5	41
			33

5.5 hrs	6.5 hrs	3.5 hrs	1.5 hrs
48 mm	60 mm	64 mm	51 mm
month	**Apr**	**Jul**	**Oct**	**Jan**

CHAMPAGNE

°F			
	75		
57	53.5	60	
39		43.5	41
			31

5.5 hrs	7.5 hrs	4 hrs	1.5 hrs
43 mm	52 mm	52 mm	44 mm
month	**Apr**	**Jul**	**Oct**	**Jan**

ALSACE AND LORRAINE

°F			
	77		
57	56	59	
40		43.5	38
			29

5.5 hrs	7.5 hrs	3 hrs	1.5 hrs
48 mm	57 mm	43 mm	33 mm
month	**Apr**	**Jul**	**Oct**	**Jan**

BURGUNDY AND FRANCHE-COMTE

°F			
	80		
58	57	60	
41		48	39
			30

6 hrs	8.5 hrs	4 hrs	1.5 hrs
52 mm	51 mm	58 mm	59 mm
month	**Apr**	**Jul**	**Oct**	**Jan**

RHÔNE VALLEY AND FRENCH ALPS

°F			
	79.5		
59	59	62.5	
43		46.5	43
			31

6 hrs	9.5 hrs	4.5 hrs	2 hrs
68 mm	61 mm	80 mm	54 mm
month	**Apr**	**Jul**	**Oct**	**Jan**

PROVENCE AND CÔTE D'AZUR

°F			
	79.5		
62.5	67	70	
50		55.5	54.5
			41

7.5 hrs	11 hrs	6.5 hrs	5 hrs
62 mm	16 mm	108 mm	83 mm
month	**Apr**	**Jul**	**Oct**	**Jan**

MASSIF CENTRAL

°F			
	80		
59		63.5	
	55.5		44.5
39		44.5	31

5.5 hrs	8.5 hrs	4.5 hrs	2.5 hrs
45 mm	48 mm	51 mm	29 mm
month	**Apr**	**Jul**	**Oct**	**Jan**

LANGUEDOC-ROUSSILLON

°F			
	83		
63.5	62.5	68	
46.5		51	52
			35.5

7.5 hrs	11 hrs	6 hrs	4.5 hrs
55 mm	20 mm	110 mm	72 mm
month	**Apr**	**Jul**	**Oct**	**Jan**

CORSICA

°F			
	83		
63.5	64.5	70.5	
47		54.5	56
			41

7 hrs	11 hrs	6.5 hrs	4.5 hrs
66 mm	15 mm	107 mm	62 mm
month	**Apr**	**Jul**	**Oct**	**Jan**

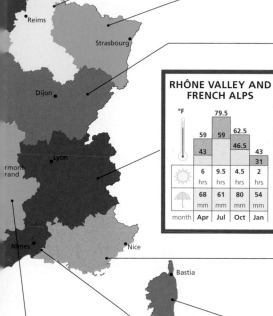

Reims
Strasbourg
Dijon
Lyon
rmont
rand
Nîmes
Nice
Bastia

THE HISTORY OF FRANCE

The only European country facing both the North Sea and the Mediterranean, France has been subject to a particularly rich variety of cultural influences. Though famous for the rootedness of its peasant population, it has also been a European melting pot, even before the arrival of the Celtic Gauls in the centuries before Christ, through to the Mediterranean immigrations of the 20th century.

Fleur-de-lys, the royal emblem

Roman conquest by Julius Caesar had an enduring impact, but from the 4th and 5th centuries AD, waves of Barbarian invaders destroyed much of the Roman legacy. The Germanic Franks provided political leadership in the following centuries, but when their line died out in the late 10th century, France was socially and politically fragmented.

THE FORMATION OF FRANCE

The Capetian dynasty gradually pieced France together over the Middle Ages, a period of great economic prosperity and cultural vitality. The Black Death and the Hundred Years' War brought setbacks, and the dynasty's power was seriously threatened by the rival Burgundian dukes. France recovered and, despite the wars of religion, flourished during the Renaissance, followed by the grandeur of Louis XIV's reign. During the Enlightenment, in the 18th century, French culture was the envy of Europe.

The Revolution of 1789 ended the absolute monarchy and introduced major social and institutional reforms, many of which were endorsed and consolidated by Napoleon. Yet the Revolution also inaugurated the instability that remained a hallmark of French politics until de Gaulle and the 5th Republic: since 1789, France has known five republics, two empires and three brands of royal power, plus the Vichy government in World War II.

Modernization in the 19th and 20th centuries proved a slow process. Railroads, the military service, and radical educational reforms were crucial in forming a sense of French identity among the citizens.

Rivalry with Germany dominated French politics for most of the late 19th and early 20th century. The population losses in World War I were traumatic for France, while during 1940–44 the country was occupied by Germany. Yet since 1945, the two countries have proved the backbone of the developing European Union.

Inlaid marble tabletop showing the map of France in 1684

◁ *La République*, painted by Charles Landelle in 1848

Prehistoric France

The earliest traces of human life in France date back to around 2 million BC. From around 40,000 BC, *Homo sapiens* lived an itinerant existence as hunters and gatherers. Around 6000 BC, following the end of the Ice Age, a major shift in lifestyle occurred, as people settled down to herd animals and cultivate crops. The advent of metal-working allowed more effective tools and weapons to be developed. The Iron Age is associated particularly with the Celts, who arrived from the east during the first millennium BC. A more complex social hierarchy developed, consisting of warriors, farmers, artisans, and druids (Celtic priests).

Bronze Age vase, Brittany

FRANCE IN 8000 BC

▢ *Former coastline*

▢ *Present-day land mass*

These carvings of horses' heads were found in the Pyrenees and date from around 9000 BC.

Carnac Stone Alignments *(4500–4000 BC)*
The purpose of the extensive networks of megaliths around Carnac (see p278) remains obscure. They possibly served in pagan rituals or as an astronomical calendar.

The mammoth, here carved from animal bone, was a thick-coated giant who died out after the end of the Ice Age.

Cro-Magnon Man
This skull, dating to c.25,000 BC, was discovered at Cro-Magnon in the Dordogne in 1868. In comparison with most of his predecessors, Cro-Magnon Man was tall, robust, and had a large head. He differed only marginally from us.

PREHISTORIC ART

The rich deposits of cave art in France have only been recognized as authentic for just over a century. They include wall paintings and daubings but also various engraved objects. Venus figurines, carved with flint tools, probably had ritual and religious rather than erotic purposes.

TIMELINE

		Painting of bulls in Lascaux
2,000,000 BC Early hominid societies	**30,000** Cro-Magnon Man	

2,000,000 BC	30,000	25,000	20,000

| | **400,000** Discovery of fire by *Homo erectus* | **28,000** The first Venus sculptures, possibly representing fertility goddesses | *Primitive stone tool* |

Doorway, Roquepertuse
Religion was an important part of Celtic life. The Celts made a cult of severed heads – presumably of their enemies – as seen in this sanctuary doorway dating from the 3rd century BC.

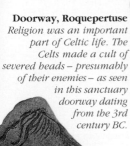

The prehistoric hunter's quarry is here represented by a flock of chamois carved on a piece of bone.

This carved bone, found in Laugerie Basse in the Dordogne, shows a bison chased by a man with a spear.

Copper Axe *(c.2000 BC)*
Copper tools preceded the arrival of the stronger and more malleable bronze alloy. Iron was to prove the toughest and most useful metal of all.

Bronze Armor
Bronze and Iron Age people were highly warlike. The Celtic Gauls were feared even by Romans. Their protective armor, such as this breastplate dating from 750–475 BC, was light but reasonably effective.

This highly stylized female figure, a Venus figurine found in southwest France, was carved from mammoth tusk in around 20,000 BC.

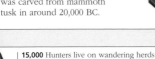

15,000 Hunters live on wandering herds of mammoth, rhinoceros, and reindeer. Art includes the Lascaux caves and Val Camonica/Mont Bego engravings

7000–4500 Neolithic revolution: farming, megaliths, and menhir stone sculptures

600 Greek colony at Marseille. Mediterranean luxury goods exchanged for tin, copper, iron, and slaves. Early urban development

15,000	10,000	5,000

10,000 End of Ice Age. More regions become inhabitable

10,000–6000 Mammoth herds disappear and hunters must rely on animals of the forest, including wild boar and aurochs

1200–700 Arrival of the Celts during the Bronze and Iron Ages

500 Celtic nobles bury their dead with riches such as the Vix treasure *(see p334)*

Celtic helmet

Roman Gaul

Roman mosaic
from Vienne

The Romans had annexed the southern
fringe of France by 125–121 BC. Julius
Caesar brought the rest of Gaul under
Roman control in the Gallic Wars (58–
51 BC). The province of Gaul prospered:
it developed good communications, a
network of cities crammed with public
buildings and leisure facilities such as baths
and amphitheaters, while in the countryside
large villas were established. By the 3rd
century AD, however, barbarian raids from
Germany were causing increasing havoc. From the 5th
century barbarians began to settle throughout Gaul.

FRANCE IN 58 BC

☐ Roman Gaul

Emperor Augustus, who was
considered a living God, was
worshipped at this altar.

Roman Dolce Vita
The Romans brought mate-
rial comfort and luxury,
and wine-growing became
widespread. This 19th-cen-
tury painting by Couture
conveys a contemporary
view of Roman decadence.

Vercingetorix
The Celtic chieftain Vercin-
getorix was Julius Caesar's
greatest military opponent.
This bronze statue is at Alise-
Sainte-Reine (see p334),the
Gauls' final stand in 51 BC.

LA TURBIE
This impressive monument
near Monaco was erected in 6 BC
by the Roman Senate. It celebrates Augustus's victory over
the Alpine tribes in 14–13 BC. Badly pillaged for
its stone, restoration only began in the 1920's.

TIMELINE

	125–121 BC Roman colonization of Southern Gaul	**31 BC** Frontiers of the Three Gauls (*Gallia Celtica, Gallia Aquitania* and *Gallia Belgica*) established by Augustus	*Augustus*
200 BC	100	0	AD 100
Julius Caesar	**58–51 BC** Julius Caesar's Gallic Wars result in establishment of Roman Gaul	**16 BC** Maison Carrée built in Nîmes (*see pp496–7*) **52–51 BC** Vercingetorix revolt	**AD 43** Lugdunum (Lyon) established as capital of the Three Gauls

Dancing Girl
Celtic art continued uninfluenced by Roman naturalistic ideals. This bronze statuette of a young woman dates from the 1st–2nd century AD.

A statue of Augustus was placed at the top of the original monument.

Enameled Brooch
This decorative Gallo-Roman brooch dates from the second half of the 1st century BC.

WHERE TO SEE GALLO-ROMAN FRANCE

Gallo-Roman remains are to be found all over France, many of them in Provence. In addition to La Turbie *(see p529)* there is the Roman amphitheater in Arles *(p485)* and the theater and triumphal arch in Orange *(p502)*. Elsewhere, there are ruins at Autun in Burgundy *(p339)*, the Temple d'Auguste et Livie in Vienne *(p382)*, Les Arènes at Nîmes *(pp496–7)*, and fragments of Vesunna in Périgueux *(p434)*.

Les Arènes in Nîmes, *built at the end of the 1st century AD, is still in use today.*

The Claudian Tables
In AD 48, Emperor Claudius persuaded the Senate to allow Gauls full Roman citizenship. The grateful Gauls recorded the event on stone tables found at Lyon.

The 44 tribes subjugated by Augustus are listed on an inscription, with a dedication to the emperor.

Emperor Augustus
Augustus, the first Roman Emperor (27 BC– AD 14), upheld the Pax Romana, an enforced peace which allowed the Gauls to concentrate on culture rather than war.

AD 177 First execution of Christian martyrs, Lyon. Sainte Blandine is thrown to the lions, who refuse to harm her

Sainte Blandine

360 Julian, prefect of Gaul, proclaimed Roman Emperor. Lutetia changes name to Paris

200	300	400

275 First Barbarian raids

313 Christianity officially recognized as religion under the rule of Constantine, the first Christian emperor

406 Barbarian invasion from the east. Settlement of the Franks and Germanic tribes

476 Overthrow of the last Roman emperor leads to end of the western Roman Empire

The Monastic Realm

The collapse of the Roman Empire led to a period of instability and invasions. Both the Frankish Merovingian dynasty (486–751) and the Carolingians (751–987) were unable to bring more than spasmodic periods of political calm. Throughout this turbulent period, the Church provided an element of continuity. As centers for Christian scholars and artists, the monasteries helped to restore the values of the ancient world. They also developed farming and viticulture and some became extremely powerful, dominating the country economically as well as spiritually.

9th-century gold chalice

FRANCE IN 751

☐ *Carolingian Empire*

Stable with lay brethren's quarters above

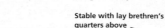

Charlemagne *(742–814)*
The greatest of Carolingian rulers, Charlemagne created an empire based on strictly autocratic rule. Powerful and charismatic, he could neither read nor write.

Bakery

The great infirmary hall could accommodate about 100 patients. It was flanked by the Lady Chapel.

Saint Benedict
Saint Benedict established the Benedictine rule: monks were to divide their time between work and prayer.

CLUNY MONASTERY

The Benedictine abbey of Cluny *(see p345)* was founded in 910 with the aim of major monastic reforms. This major religious cener, here shown as a reconstruction (after Conant), had great influence over hundreds of monasteries throughout Europe.

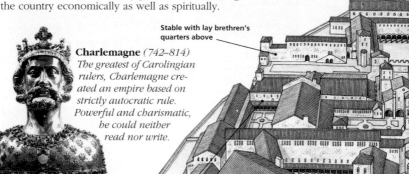

TIMELINE

481 Clovis the Frank becomes first Merovingian king

508 Paris made capital of the Frankish kingdom

c.590 Saint Colombanus introduces Irish monasticism to France

732 Battle of Poitiers: Charles Martel repulses Arab invasion

500   **600**   **700**

496 Conversion of Clovis, king of the Franks, to Christianity

629–37 Dagobert I, the last effective ruler of the Merovingian dynasty, brings temporary unity to the Frankish kingdom

Dagobert I

751 Pepin becomes first king of the Carolingian dynasty

Baptism of Clovis

The Frankish chieftain Clovis was the first barbarian ruler to convert to Christianity. He was baptized in Reims in 496.

The abbey church, begun in 1088, was the largest church in Europe before St Peter's was built in Rome in the 16th century.

Cemetery chapel

WHERE TO SEE MONASTIC FRANCE

The monastic realm has survived in austere Cistercian abbeys in Burgundy, such as Fontenay (*see pp332–3*). Little remains of Cluny, but some of the superb capitals can still be admired (*p345*). The best way to experience monastic France might be to retrace the steps of medieval pilgrims and visit the monastic centers on the route to Santiago de Compostela (*pp400–01*), such as Vézelay (*pp336–7*), Le Puy (*pp364–5*), Conques (*pp368–9*), Moissac (*pp442–3*), and St-Sernin in Toulouse (*pp446–7*).

Cluny capitals

Monastic Arts

In scriptoriums, talented artists dedicated their time to the meticulous art of illuminating and copying manuscripts for the libraries.

Monastic Labour

Monks of the Cistercian rule were renowned for their commitment to manual labor such as cultivating the land and producing wine and liqueurs.

1096 First Crusade

Carolingian soldiers

987 Hugh Capet, first Capetian ruler

1066 Conquest of England by the Normans

800	900	1000

843 Treaty of Verdun: division of the Carolingian Empire into three parts including West Francia

910 Foundation of the Benedictine monastery of Cluny

1077 Bayeux tapestry

800 Coronation of Charlemagne as Holy Roman Emperor

William the Conqueror steering his ship on the Bayeux tapestry

Gothic France

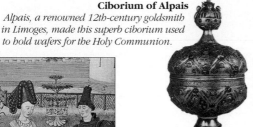

Medieval knights in combat

The Gothic style, epitomized by soaring cathedrals *(see pp32–3)*, emerged in the 12th century at a time of growing prosperity and scholarship, crusades, and an increasingly dominant monarchy. The rival French and Burgundian courts *(see p343)* became models of fashion and etiquette for all of Europe. *Chansons de gestes* (epic poems) performed by troubadours celebrated the code of chivalry.

FRANCE IN 1270

☐ *Royal territory*

▨ *Other fiefs*

Ciborium of Alpais
Alpais, a renowned 12th-century goldsmith in Limoges, made this superb ciborium used to hold wafers for the Holy Communion.

Courtly Love
According to the code of chivalry, knights dedicated their service to an ideal but unapproachable lady. Courtesy and romance were introduced in art and music.

Winch to lift up stone sections

The king supervised the building of the cathedral, accompanied by the architect.

Draper's Window
The textile trade benefited from the era of urban prosperity. This stained-glass window in a church in Semur-en-Auxois (see p335) shows wool washers at work.

TIMELINE

c.1100 First edition of the epic poem *Chanson de Roland*

1117 Secret marriage of the scholar Abelard and his student Héloise. Her uncle, canon Filibert, does not approve and forces him to become a monk while she retires as a nun

1154 Angevin Empire created by Anglo-Norman dynasty starting with Henry Plantagenet, count of Anjou and king of England (as Henry II)

1100	1125	1150	1175

1115 Saint Bernard founds the Cistercian abbey at Clairvaux

1120 Rebuilding of the abbey of St-Denis; birth of the Gothic style

King Philip Augustus, who adopted the fleur-de-lys emblem

1180–1223 Reign of Philip Augustus

The Crusades
In an attempt to win back the Holy Land from the Turks, Philip Augustus set out on the Third Crusade (1189) alongside England's Richard the Lion-Heart and Holy Roman Emperor Frederick Barbarossa.

Lacelike sculpture adorned the façades of the Gothic cathedrals.

Stone masons cut stones on site.

ELEANOR OF AQUITAINE
Strong-willed and vivacious Eleanor, duchess of independent Aquitaine, contributed to the conflict between France and England. In 1137 she married the pious Louis VII of France. Returning from a Crusade, Louis found that their marriage had broken down. After the annulment in 1152, Eleanor married Henry of Anjou, taking her duchy with her. Two years later Henry successfully claimed the throne of England. Aquitaine came under English rule and thus the Angevin Empire began.

Eleanor of Aquitaine *and Henry II are buried in Fontevraud (p294).*

Holy Relic
Throughout the Middle Ages most churches could boast at least one saint's relic. The cult of relics brought pilgrims and more riches.

St. Bernard *(1090–1153) Key figure of the Cistercian rule and counselor to the pope, St. Bernard preached rigorous simplicity of life.*

THE BUILDING OF A CATHEDRAL
In affluent, mercantile towns, skilled masons constructed towering Gothic cathedrals of revolutionary design, such as Chartres *(see pp308–11)* and Amiens *(pp202–3).* With their improbable height and lightness they were a testimony to both faith and prosperity.

Louis IX on his death bed

1226 Louis IX crowned king

1270 Death of Louis IX at Tunis in the Eighth Crusade

1305 Papacy established in Avignon

| 1200 | 1225 | 1250 | 1275 | 1300 |

1214 Battle of Bouvines. Philip Augustus begins to drive the English out of France

1259 Normandy, Maine, Anjou, and Poitou acquired from England

1285 Philip the Fair crowned

1297 Louis IX is canonized, becoming Saint Louis

The Hundred Years' War

The Hundred Years' War (1337–1453), pitting England against France for control of French land, had devastating effects. The damage of warfare was amplified by frequent famines and the ravages of bubonic plague in the wake of the Black Death in 1348. France came close to being permanently partitioned by the king of England and the duke of Burgundy. In 1429–30 the young Joan of Arc helped rally France's fortunes and within a generation the English had been driven out of France.

Public execution, in Froissart's 14th-century chronicle

FRANCE IN 1429
☐ France
■ Anglo-Burgundy

Angels with trumpets announce the Last Judgment.

Men of War
One of the reasons men enlisted as soldiers was hope for plunder. Both the French and English armies lived off the land, at the expense of the peasantry.

The elect, springing resurrected from their graves, are ushered into heaven.

The Black Death
The plague of 1348–52 caused 4–5 million deaths, about 25 percent of the French population. For want of medicines people had to put their faith in prayers and holy processions.

TIMELINE

1346 Battle of Crécy: French defeated by English

1328 Philip VI, first Valois monarch

1356 French defeat at Battle of Poitiers

14th-century flame-thrower

1325	1350	1375

1337 Start of the Hundred Years' War

Plague victims

1348–52 The Black Death

1358 Bourgeois uprising in Paris led by Etienne Marcel. The Jacquerie peasant uprising in Northern France

Medieval Medicine

The state of the heavens was widely held to influence earthly conditions, such as health, and a diagnosis based on the zodiac was considered reliable. The standby cure for all sorts of ailments was blood letting.

English Longbow

The king's troops fought against England, but the individual French duchies supported whichever side seemed more favorable. In the confused battles, English bowmen excelled. Their longbows caused chaos among the hordes of mounted French cavalry.

Christ as Supreme Judge is flanked by angels bearing the instruments of the Passion.

Archangel Michael, resplendent with peacock wings, holds the judgment scales. The weight of sinners outbalances the elect.

John the Baptist is accompanied by the 12 apostles and the Virgin Mary, dressed in blue.

The damned, with hideously twisted faces, fall into Hell.

THE LAST JUDGMENT

With war, plague, and famine as constant visitors, many people feared that the end of the world was nigh. Religious paintings, such as the great 15th-century altarscreen by Rogier van der Weyden in the Hôtel-Dieu in Beaune *(see pp346–7),* reflected the moral fervor of the time.

Attack on Heresy

The general anxiety spilled over into anti-Semitic pogroms and attacks on alleged heretics, who were burned at the stake.

1415 Battle of Agincourt. French defeat by Henry V of England

1429 Intervention of Joan of Arc: Charles VII crowned king

1453 End of the Hundred Years' War. Only Calais remains in English hands

| 1400 | 1425 | 1450 |

1411 *Les Très Riches Heures du Duc du Berry* prayer book, by Paul and Jean de Limbourg *(see p204)*

1431 Joan of Arc burned at stake as witch by the English

1419 Charles VI of France makes Henry V of England his heir

Joan of Arc

Renaissance France

As a result of the French invasion of Italy in 1494, the ideals and aesthetic of the Italian Renaissance spread to France, reaching their height during the reign of François I. Known as a true Renaissance prince, he was skilled in letters and art as well as sports and war. He invited Italian artists, such as Leonardo and Cellini, to his court and enjoyed Rabelais' bawdy stories. Another highly influential Italian was Catherine de' Medici (1519–89). Widow of Henri II, she virtually ruled France through her sons, François II, Charles IX, and Henri III. She was also one of the major players in the Wars of Religion (1562–93) between Catholics and Protestants, which divided the nobility and tore the country to pieces.

Masked lute player

FRANCE IN 1527

☐ *Royal territory*

☐ *Other fiefs*

The corner towers are a Gothic feature transformed by Italian lightness of touch into pure decoration.

Galerie François I, Fontainebleau
The artists of the School of Fontainebleau blended late Italian Renaissance style with French elements.

Power Behind the Throne
Catherine de' Medici dominated French politics from 1559–89.

AZAY-LE-RIDEAU
One of the loveliest of the Loire châteaux, Azay was begun in 1518 *(see p296)*. Italian influences are visible and it is clear that this is a dwelling meant for pleasure rather than defense.

TIMELINE

1470 First printing presses established in France

Prototype tank by Leonardo da Vinci

1519 Leonardo da Vinci dies in the arms of François I at the French court in Amboise

1536 Calvin's *Institutes of the Christian Religion* leads to a new form of Protestantism

1470	1480	1490	1500	1510	1520	1530

1477 Final defeat of the Dukes of Burgundy, who sought to establish a middle kingdom between France and Germany

1494–1559 France and Austria fight over Italian territories in the Italian Wars

1515 Reign of François I begins

Golden coin showing the fleur-de-lys and the salamander of François I

Gold Pomander
Pomanders containing sweet-smelling herbs such as amber and cinnamon were carried in time of plague to ward off the bad air held responsible for contagion.

Ballroom with Flemish tapestries

The staircase was in the new Italian fashion with double flights of steps rather than a spiral.

The Red Room

WHERE TO SEE RENAISSANCE FRANCE

In Paris, many churches and the impressive place des Vosges (*see p91*) date from the Renaissance. There are countless 16th-century châteaux in the Loire and Burgundy. Among the finest are Chenonceau (*pp298–9*) and Tanlay (*p331*). Salers (*p363*) is a virtually intact Renaissance town. The historic center of Toulouse (*p446*) has many elegant Renaissance palaces.

This fireplace *stands in François I's room at Château de Chenonceau.*

François I and the Italian Influence
François I, here receiving Raphael's painting The Holy Family *in 1518, collected Italian art at Fontainebleau. Among the favored painters were Michelangelo, Leonardo, and Titian.*

New France
French expansion and quest for colonies started with Cartier's expedition to Canada in 1534 (see p282).

1539 Edict of Villers Cotterets makes French the official language of state

1559 Treaty of Cateau–Cambrésis ends the Italian Wars

1562 Wars of Religion between Catholics and Protestants start

1572 Massacre of Protestants on St. Bartholomew's Eve in Paris

St. Bartholomew's Eve Massacre

1589 Henry III murdered. The Huguenot Henry IV becomes first Bourbon king of France

1593 Henry IV converts to Catholicism and ends the Wars of Religion

1598 Edict of Nantes: tolerance for Protestantism

1608 Foundation of Quebec

1540	1550	1560	1570	1580	1590	1600

The Grand Siècle

Emblem of the Sun King

The end of the Religious Wars heralded a period of exceptional French influence and power. The cardinal ministers Richelieu and Mazarin paved the way for Louis XIV's absolute monarchy. Political development was matched by artistic styles of unprecedented brilliance: enormous Baroque edifices, the drama of Molière and Racine, and the music of Lully. Versailles (*see pp174–7*), built under the supervision of Louis' capable finance minister Colbert, was the glory of Europe, but its cost and Louis XIV's endless wars proved expensive for the French state and led to widespread misery by the end of his reign.

FRANCE IN 1661

☐ *Royal territory*
▨ *Avignon (papal enclave)*

Molière *(1622–73)*
Actor-playwright Molière performed many plays for Louis XIV and his court, though some of his satires were banned. After his death, his company became the basis of the French state theater, the Comédie Française.

Madame (married to Monsieur) as Flora

Monsieur, the king's brother

Madame de Maintenon
In 1684, following the death of his first wife Marie-Thérèse, Louis secretly married his mistress Mme. de Maintenon, then aged 49.

THE SUN KING AND HIS FAMILY
Claiming to be monarch by divine right, Louis XIV commanded court painter Jean Nocret to devise this allegorical scene in 1665. Surrounded by his family, the king appears as the sun god Apollo.

TIMELINE

Cardinal Richelieu

1610–17 Marie de' Medici acts as Regent for Louis XIII	**1624** Cardinal Richelieu becomes principal minister	**1634** Foundation of the literary society Académie Française	**1642–3** Death of Louis XIII and Cardinal Richelieu. Accession of Louis XIV with Mazarin as principal minister	
1610	**1620**	**1630**	**1640**	**1650**
1617 Louis XIII accedes at the age of 17	**1631** Foundation of *La Gazette*, France's first newspaper	**1635** Richelieu actively involves France in the Thirty Years' War **1637** Descartes' *Discourse on Method*	**1648–52** The Fronde: French civil wars	

Louis XIV's Book of Hours
After a lively and libertine youth, Louis became increasingly religious. His Book of Hours *(1688–93) is in Musée Condé (see p205).*

Royal Wedding
Louis XIII and Anne of Austria were married in 1615. After his death, Anne became regent for the young Louis XIV with Cardinal Mazarin as minister.

Louis XIV as Apollo

Anne of Austria as Cybele

Baroque Figurine
The royal glory was reflected in the arts. This objet d'art features a Christ in jasper on a pedestal decorated with gilded cherubs and rich enameling.

The dauphin (the king's son)

Grande Mademoiselle, the king's cousin, as Diana

Queen Marie-Thérèse as Juno

WHERE TO SEE ARCHITECTURE OF THE GRAND SIÈCLE

Paris boasts many imposing Grand Siècle buildings, such as the Hôtel des Invalides *(see p114)*, the Dôme church *(p115)*, and the Palais du Luxembourg *(pp126–7)*, but the Château de Versailles *(pp174–7)* is the ultimate example of the flamboyance of the period. Reminders of this glory include the sumptuous Palais Lascaris in Nice *(p528)* and the Corderie Royale in Rochefort *(p417)*. At the same time, military architect Vauban constructed mighty citadels, such as Neuf-Brisach *(see p226)*.

Versailles' *interior is a typical example of the gilded Baroque style.*

Playwright Jean Racine (1639–99)

1661 Death of Mazarin: Louis XIV becomes his own principal minister

1662 Colbert, finance minister, reforms finances and the economy

1680 Creation of the theater Comédie Française

1685 Revocation of the Edict of Nantes of 1598: Protestantism banned

1682 Royal court moves to Versailles

1686 Opening of the Café Procope (first coffee house in Paris)

1689 Major wars of Louis XIV begin

1709 Last great famine in French history

1660	1670	1680	1690	1700

17th-century cannon

Enlightenment and Revolution

In the 18th century, Enlightenment philosophers such as Voltaire and Rousseau redefined man's place within a framework of natural principles, thus challenging the old aristocratic order. Their essays were read across Europe and even in the American colonies. But although France exported worldly items as well as ideas, the state's increasing debts brought social turmoil, triggering the 1789 Revolution. Under the motto "Liberty, Equality, Fraternity," the new Republic and its reforms had a far-reaching impact on the rest of Europe.

Plate of Louis XVI's execution

FRANCE IN 1789

☐ *Royal France*
■ *Avignon (papal enclave)*

Voltaire *(1694–1778)*
Voltaire, master of satire, wrote numerous essays and the novel Candide. *His fierce critiques sometimes forced him into exile abroad.*

National Assembly

Jacobin Club

The Guillotine
This infamous invention was introduced in 1792 as a humane alternative to other forms of capital punishment, which had usually involved torture.

Place de la Révolution
(see p98) is where Louis XVI's execution took place in 1793.

The Tuileries

Café Le Procope was the haunt of Voltaire and Rousseau.

Palais Royal
The private residence of the Duke of Orléans, the Palais Royal (see p99) became a center of revolutionary agitation from 1789. It was also the site of several printing presses.

TIMELINE

1715 Death of Louis XIV, accession of Louis XV

1743–64 Mme. de Pompadour, Louis XV's favorite, uses her influence to support artists and philosophers during her time at court

| 1715 | 1725 | 1735 | 1745 | 1755 |

Physician's protective costume worn during the plague

1720 Last outbreak of plague in France: population of Marseille decimated

1751 Publication of the first volume of Diderot's *Encyclopaedia*

1756–63 Seven Years' War: France loses Canada and other colonial possessions

Revolutionary Symbols
The motifs of the Revolution such as the blue, white, and red of the tricolor even appeared on wallpaper in the 1790s.

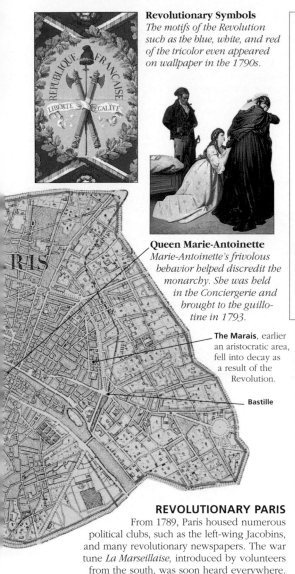

WHERE TO SEE 18TH-CENTURY FRANCE

The Palais de l'Elysée, built in 1718 *(see p108)*, is an outstanding example of 18th-century Parisian architecture. Examples across France include the curious Saline Royale in Arc-et-Senans *(p350)*, the Grand Théâtre in Bordeaux *(p422)*, the elegant mansions in Condom *(p440)*, and the merchants' houses in Ciboure *(p453)*. The Château de Laàs in Sauveterre de Béarn is a feast of 18th-century art and furniture *(p454)*.

The Grand Théâtre *in Bordeaux is an excellent example of elegant 18th-century architecture.*

Queen Marie-Antoinette
Marie-Antoinette's frivolous behavior helped discredit the monarchy. She was held in the Conciergerie and brought to the guillotine in 1793.

The Marais, earlier an aristocratic area, fell into decay as a result of the Revolution.

Bastille

REVOLUTIONARY PARIS
From 1789, Paris housed numerous political clubs, such as the left-wing Jacobins, and many revolutionary newspapers. The war tune *La Marseillaise,* introduced by volunteers from the south, was soon heard everywhere.

Revolutionary Calendar
A new calendar was introduced, the months named after seasonal events. This engraving shows Messidor, the month of harvest.

1768 Annexation of Corsica

1789 Storming of the Bastille, and establishment of constitutional monarchy: abolition of feudal laws

1783 First balloon ascent by the Montgolfier brothers

Model of the Bastille

1765	1775	1785	1795

1774 Accession of Louis XVI

Electors' card for the Convention of 1792

1794 Overthrow of Robespierre and end of the Terror

1762 Rousseau's *Emile* and the *Social Contract*

1778–83 France aids the 13 colonies in the War of American Independence

1792 Overthrow of Louis XVI: establishment of First Republic

Napoleonic France

Two generations of Napoleons dominated France
from 1800 to 1870. Napoleon Bonaparte took the
title of Emperor Napoleon I. He extended his
empire throughout most of western Europe,
placing his brothers and sisters on the thrones of
conquered countries. Defeated in 1814 and
replaced by the restored Bourbon dynasty,
followed by the 1830 Revolution and the so-
called July Monarchy, the Napoleonic clan made
a comeback after 1848. Napoleon I's nephew,
Louis Napoleon, became President of the Second
Republic, then made himself emperor as Napoleon III.
During his reign Paris was modernized and the
industrial transformation of France began.

**Légion
d'Honneur**

EUROPE IN 1812
- ☐ Napoleonic rule
- ■ Dependent states

The Laurel, crown of
the Roman emperors

Napoleon, as First Consul, is crowned
by Chronos, the God of Time.

Musée du Louvre
*The museum had opened in 1792, but
it flourished during Napoleon's reign.
He took a personal interest in both
acquisitions and organization.*

The revolutionary
tricolor flag was
kept throughout
the empire.

Imperial Insignia
*Napoleon I
created a new
titled aristocracy,
who were allowed
coats of arms. Only his,
however, was permitted a
crown. The eagle symbol
was adopted in 1800, an
evocation of Imperial Rome.*

Légion d'Honneur medal

TIMELINE

1804 Napoleon crowned
as Emperor. Napoleonic
Civil Code established

Josephine's bed at Malmaison

1800 Establishment of
the Bank of France

1809 Josephine and
Napoleon divorce.
She retains Château
Malmaison (see p173)

1814 Defeat of Napoleon by the
Allies (England, Russia, Austria, and
Prussia). Napoleon exiled to Elba

1800   **1810**   **1820**

1802 Treaty of Amiens
brings temporary
peace to Europe

1806 Arc de
Triomphe
commissioned

1803 Resumption of wars
to create the Napoleonic
Empire

1815 The "Hundred
Days": Napoleon returns
from Elba, is defeated
at Waterloo and exiled
to St. Helena

1802 Establishment of
the Légion d'Honneur

July Revolution
Three days of street-fighting in July 1830 ended unpopular Bourbon rule.

The Napoleons
This imaginary group portrait depicts Napoleon I (seated), his son "Napoleon II" – who never ruled (right), Napoleon's nephew Louis Napoleon (Napoleon III), and the latter's infant son.

The Civil Code, created by Napoleon, is here shown as a tablet.

Napoleon on Campaign
A dashing general in the late 1790s, Napoleon remained a remarkable military commander throughout his reign.

EMPIRE FASHION

Greek and Roman ideals were evident in architecture, furniture, design, and fashion. Women wore light, Classical tunics, the most daring with one shoulder or more bare. David and Gérard were the fashionable portraitists, while Delacroix and Géricault created many Romantic masterpieces.

Madame Récamier *held a popular salon and was renowned for her beauty and wit. David painted her in 1800.*

NAPOLEONIC GLORY

Though professing himself a true revolutionary, Napoleon developed a taste for imperial pomp. However, he also achieved some long-lasting reforms such as the Civil Code, the new school system, and the Bank of France.

Train on the Paris – St-Germain line

The Belle Epoque

Art Nouveau vase by Lalique

The decades before World War I became the *Belle Epoque* for the French, remembered as a golden era forever past. Nevertheless this was a politically turbulent time, with working-class militancy, organized socialist movements, and the Dreyfus Affair polarizing the country between Left and anti-semitic Right. New inventions such as electricity and vaccination against disease made life easier at all social levels. The cultural scene thrived and took new forms with Impressionism and Art Nouveau, the realist novels of Gustave Flaubert and Emile Zola, cabaret and cancan, and, in 1895, the birth of the cinema.

FRANCE IN 1871

☐ *Under Third Republic*

■ *Alsace and Lorraine*

Statue of Apollo by Aimé Millet

Universal Exhibition

The 1889 Paris exhibition was attended by 3.2 million people. Engineer Eiffel's breathtaking iron structure dominated the exhibition and caused great controversy at the time.

Stage

Copper-green roofed cupola

Backstage area

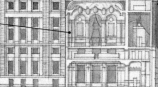

Peugeot Car *(1899)*
The car and bicycle brought new freedom, becoming a part of people's leisure time. Peugeot, Renault, and Citroën were all founded before World War I.

The auditorium in gold and purple seated over 2,000 guests.

TIMELINE

1869 Opening of the Suez Canal, built by Ferdinand de Lesseps

1871 The Paris Commune leads to the Third Republic

Woman on the barricades in 1871

1880s Scramble for colonies in Africa and Asia begins

1889 Universal Exhibition in Paris; Eiffel Tower built

1865	1870	1875	1880	1885	1890

1870–71 Franco-Prussian War: defeat and overthrow of Napoleon III; France cedes Alsace and Lorraine to Germany

1874 Impressionist movement begins

1881–6 Reforms in education by Jules Ferry

1885 Pasteur produces vaccine for rabies, the first tested on a human

1890 Peugeot constructs one of the earliest automobiles

Poster Art

The poster was revolutionized by Art Nouveau, with designs by Alphonse Mucha particularly popular. This one from 1897 is for beer, the beverage of the lost Alsace and Lorraine, which became a "patriotic" drink.

WHERE TO SEE THE BELLE EPOQUE

Belle Epoque buildings include the Negresco Hotel, Nice *(see p526)*, the Grand Casino in Monte-Carlo *(p530)*, and the Palais Hotel in Biarritz *(p452)*. The Musée d'Orsay in Paris *(pp120–21)* exhibits Art Nouveau objects and furniture.

Staircase at the Opera

The grand staircase had colored marble columns and a frescoed ceiling. As this painting by Beroud from 1887 shows, it soon became a showcase for high society.

Guimard's *Metro entrance is a typical example of the elegant, swirling lines of Art Nouveau.*

Emperor's pavilion

Grand Foyer with balconies and lavishly decorated ceiling

Grand staircase

OPERA NATIONAL GARNIER

Founded by Napoleon III in 1862, the new opera was opened to great public acclaim in 1875 and became a focus of Belle Epoque social life. Designed by Charles Garnier, its extravagant exterior was matched by its sumptuous interior decor.

The Divine Sarah

Actress Sarah Bernhardt (1844–1923) worked in all theatrical genres, dominating the Paris stage.

1895 First public cinema by the Lumière brothers

Caricature of Zola

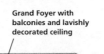

1894–1906 The alleged treason of Dreyfus sparks the Dreyfus Affair, involving the author Zola among others

1918 Germany asks for armistice to end war

1909 Blériot flies the Channel

1917 Mutinies in the army suppressed by Pétain

1916 Battle of Verdun

| 1895 | 1900 | 1905 | 1910 | 1915 |

1905 Official separation of church and state

1913 Publication of Proust's first volume of *Remembrance of Things Past*

1898 Marie and Pierre Curie discover radium

1914 World War I breaks out

French recruit, 1916

1919 Treaty of Versailles

Avant-Garde France

Despite the devastation wrought by two world wars, France retained its international renown as a center for the avant garde. Paris in particular was a magnet for experimental writers, artists, and musicians. The cafés were full of American authors and jazz musicians, French surrealists, and film makers. The French Riviera also attracted colonies of artists and writers, from Matisse and Picasso to Hemingway and F. Scott Fitzgerald, along with the wealthy industrialists and aristocrats arriving in automobiles or the famous Train Bleu. And from 1936 paid vacations meant that the working classes could also enjoy the new fashion for sunbathing.

FRANCE IN 1919

☐ *French territory*

African Gods of Creation

Art Deco 1925
The International Exhibition in Paris in 1925 launched the Art Deco style: geometrical shapes and utilitarian designs, adapted for mass production.

EXPOSITION INTERNATIONALE ■ ARTS DÉCORATIFS ET INDUSTRIELS MODERNES ■ AVRIL-OCTOBRE

Dancers in heavy cardboard costumes

The Jazz Age
Paris welcomed American jazz musicians, such as Sidney Bechet in 1925 and Dizzy Gillespie (left), co-founder of Bebop in the 1940s.

Citroën Goddess (1956)
This elegant model became an icon of the new French consumerism evident in the 1950s and '60s.

The costumes and scenery by the Cubist Léger were striking and made to look partly mechanical.

TIMELINE

Air France aircraft, 1937

1920 French Communist Party founded. Publication of Tristan Tzara's Dadaist Manifesto

1928 Premiere of *Un Chien Andalou* by Luis Buñuel and Salvador Dalí

1933 Air France begins operation

1937 Premiere of *La Grande Illusion* by Jean Renoir

1920

1930

1924 Olympic Games in Paris. André Breton publishes the *Surrealist Manifesto*

Detail of poster for the 1924 Olympics

1929–39 The Depression

1936–38 The "Popular Front": radical social program introduced, including paid vacations

1938 Munich Conference: height of appeasement

Coco Chanel *(1883–1971)*

Chanel, here photographed by Man Ray, revolutionized fashion in the 1920s with her elegant but comfortable clothes.

Par Avion

France pioneered the use of airmail, starting in 1927.

First Man and Woman

WORLD WAR II

Following the collapse of the Third Republic in 1940, Paris and the north and west parts of France were occupied by the Germans until the Liberation in 1944. Southeast France formed the collaborationist Vichy state, led by Marshal Pétain and Pierre Laval. Meanwhile, the Free French movement was led by Charles de Gaulle, with Jean Moulin coordinating the operations of the many different Resistance factions.

German soldiers *liked to pose in front of the Eiffel Tower during the occupation of Paris.*

LA CREATION DU MONDE *(1923)*

Artistic experimentation thrived in the early 20th century. *La Création du Monde* by Les Ballets Suédois had costumes by Léger and music by Milhaud. Diaghilev's Ballets Russes also competed for avant-garde artists like Picabia, Cocteau, Satie, and Sonia Delaunay.

The African theme was based on text by Blaise Cendrars.

Josephine Baker *(1906–75)*
The music hall flourished in the 1920s with Mistinguett and Josephine Baker as its undisputed queens.

1940 The Fall of France. Vichy government led by Pétain. De Gaulle fights on from London

1942 The whole of France controlled by Germany

1949 Establishment of NATO. Founding of the Council of Europe

1958 5th Republic begins under President de Gaulle

1956 Late in her career, Edith Piaf crowns her success at Carnegie Hall, New York

1940

1950

1944 D-Day: Allied landings in Normandy (June). Liberation of Paris (August)

1939 Declaration of World War II

1946 Sartre establishes *Les Temps Modernes*. First Cannes Film Festival

1945 End of the war. 4th Republic begins. Votes for women

1954 France withdraws from Indo-China after Battle of Dien Bien Phu. Start of Algerian insurrection

Modern France

After the 1950s, the traditional foundations of French society changed: the number of peasant farmers plummeted, old industries decayed, jobs in the service sector and high-technology industries grew dramatically, and the French came to enjoy the benefits of mass culture and widespread consumerism. High prestige projects, such as Concorde, TGV, La Défense, and the Pompidou Center, brought international acclaim. Efforts for European integration and the inauguration of the Channel Tunnel aim toward closer relations with France's neighbors.

Lemon squeezer by Philippe Starck

FRANCE TODAY
☐ France
■ European Union

Pompidou Center *(1977)*
The Pompidou Center's controversial building changed the aspect of the historic quarter of Beaubourg. A major arts center, it has revital-ized the formerly rundown area (see pp92–3).

La Grande Arche was opened in 1989 to commemorate the bicentenary of the Revolution.

Shopping centre

New Wave Film
Directors like Godard and Truffaut launched a refreshing, personal style of films, such as Jules et Jim *(1961).*

LA DÉFENSE

The huge modernist business center at La Défense *(see p130)*, on the edge of Paris, was developed in the 1960s and has become a prime site for the headquarters of major multinational companies.

TIMELINE

1960 First French atomic bomb. Decolonization of black Africa

1967 Common Agricultural Policy, subsidizing Europe's farmers

1973 Extension of the Common Market (EU) from six to nine states

1974 Giscard d'Estaing elected president

1980 Giverny, Monet's garden, opens to the public *(see p266)*

1981 Socialist Mitterrand becomes president for 14 years

1989 Bicentennial celebration of the French Revolution

1960 **1970** **1980**

1962 Evian agreements lead to Algerian independence

1963 First French nuclear power station

1968 May demonstrations

1969 Pompidou replaces de Gaulle as president

1976 Concorde's first commercial flight

1977 Jacques Chirac first mayor of Paris since 1871. Opening of the Pompidou Center

1987 Mitterrand and Thatcher sign agreement for Channel Tunnel. Trial in Lyon of ex-SS Officer Klaus Barbie

François Mitterran

THE HISTORY OF FRANCE

EU Flag
*France has been one
of the leading forces
in the European
Union ever since the
move toward closer
European collaboration
began in the 1950s.*

TGV
*The TGV (Train à Grande
Vitesse) is one of the
world's fastest trains (see
pp682–3). It typifies the
French government's
commitment to high
technology and improved
communications.*

**The Areva (Fiat)
Tower** is one of
Europe's tallest
towers, at 584 ft
(178 m).

Fashion by Lacroix
*Despite less demand
for haute couture,
Paris is still a major
fashion center.
The designs shown
on the catwalk,
here by Christian
Lacroix, remain
proof of the world-
renowned skills of
French designers.*

MAY 1968

The events of May 1968 began as a
political revolt by left-wing students
against the Establishment and had
a profound influence on French
society. Around 9 million workers,
and leading intellectuals like Jean-
Paul Sartre, joined the rebellion,
demanding better pay, better study
conditions, and the overhaul of
traditional values and institutions.

Student riots *starting in Nanterre, just
outside Paris, sparked widespread riot-
ing and industrial unrest in France.*

Palais de la Défense was
built first and houses the
center for industry.

1994
Channel
Tunnel
opens

2002 National Front
defeat Socialists in 1st
round of presidential
campaign. France re-
elects Jacques Chirac

Prince Albert II

2008 Jean-Marie Gustave Le Clézio
wins the Nobel Prize for literature

2010 The head of France's King Henry IV
is found after it was lost in 1793

990	2000	2010	2020

1991 Edith Cresson
is first woman
prime minister

2002 Euro replaces
franc as legal tender

1996 Mitterrand dies
after a long illness

2007 Center-right Nicolas
Sarkozy is elected president

2005 Prince Rainier III
of Monaco dies and is
succeeded by his only
son, Prince Albert II

Kings and Emperors of France

Following the break-up of the Roman Empire, the Frankish king Clovis consolidated the Merovingian dynasty. It was followed by the Carolingians, and from the 10th century by Capetian rulers. The Capetians established royal power, which passed to the Valois branch in the 14th century, and then to the Bourbons in the late 16th century, following the Wars of Religion. The Revolution of 1789 seemed to end the Bourbon dynasty, but it made a brief come-back in 1814–30. The 19th century was dominated by the Bonapartes, Napoleon I and Napoleon III. Since the overthrow of Napoleon III in 1870, France has been a republic.

768–814 Charlemagne

954–986 Lothaire

898–929 Charles III, the Simple

743–751 Childéric III

716–721 Chilpéric II

695–711 Childebert II

1137–80 Louis VII

566–584 Chilpéric I

674–691 Thierri III

884–888 Charles II, the Fat

987–996 Hugh Capet

558–562 Clothaire I

879–882 Louis III

447–458 Merovich

655–668 Clothaire III

1031–60 Henri I

840–877 Charles I, the Bald

458–482 Childéric I

628–637 Dagobert I

1060–1108 Philippe I

400	500	600	700	800	900	1000	1100
MEROVINGIAN DYNASTY				CAROLINGIAN DYNASTY		CAPETIAN DYNASTY	
400	500	600	700	800	900	1000	1100

751–768 Pépin the Short

996–1031 Robert II, the Pious

721–737 Thierri IV

986–987 Louis V

711–716 Dagobert III

936–954 Louis IV, the Foreigner

691–695 Clovis III

888–898 Odo, Count of Paris

668–674 Childéric II

882–884 Carloman

637–655 Clovis II

584–628 Clothaire II

877–879 Louis II, the Stammerer

562–566 Caribert

511–558 Childebert I

814–840 Louis I, the Pious

1108–37 Louis VI, the Fat

482–511 Clovis I

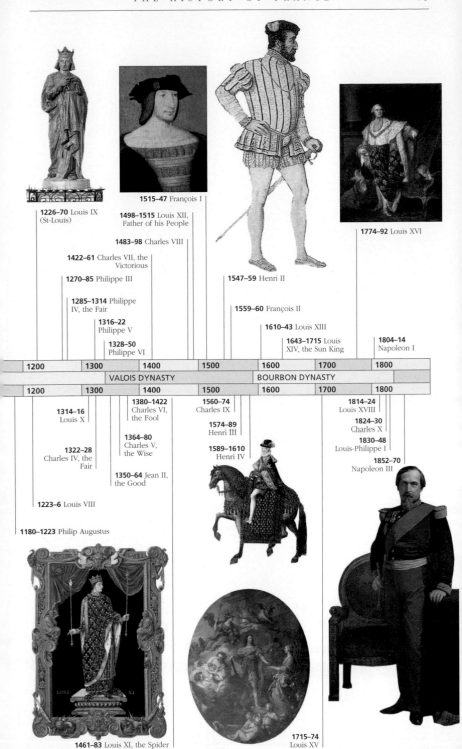

1226–70 Louis IX (St-Louis)

1515–47 François I

1498–1515 Louis XII, Father of his People

1483–98 Charles VIII

1422–61 Charles VII, the Victorious

1270–85 Philippe III

1285–1314 Philippe IV, the Fair

1316–22 Philippe V

1328–50 Philippe VI

1774–92 Louis XVI

1547–59 Henri II

1559–60 François II

1610–43 Louis XIII

1643–1715 Louis XIV, the Sun King

1804–14 Napoleon I

1200	1300	1400	1500	1600	1700	1800
	VALOIS DYNASTY			BOURBON DYNASTY		
1200	1300	1400	1500	1600	1700	1800

1314–16 Louis X

1380–1422 Charles VI, the Fool

1560–74 Charles IX

1574–89 Henri III

1589–1610 Henri IV

1364–80 Charles V, the Wise

1322–28 Charles IV, the Fair

1350–64 Jean II, the Good

1814–24 Louis XVIII

1824–30 Charles X

1830–48 Louis-Philippe I

1852–70 Napoleon III

1223–6 Louis VIII

1180–1223 Philip Augustus

1461–83 Louis XI, the Spider

1715–74 Louis XV

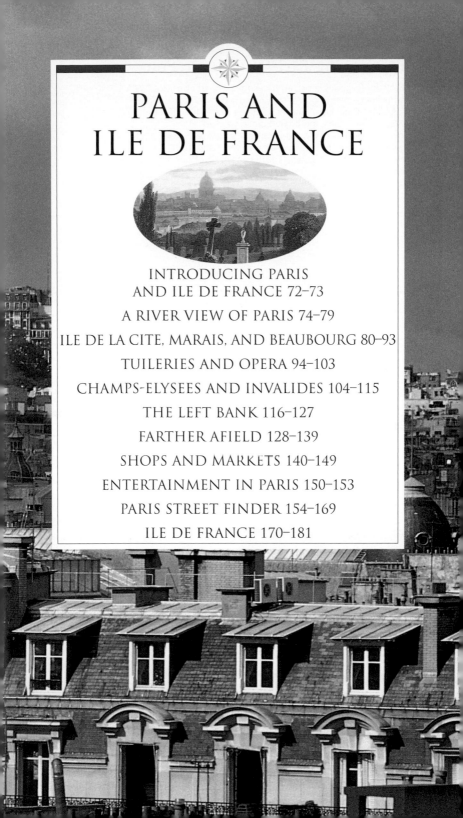

PARIS AND ILE DE FRANCE

Introducing Paris and Ile de France

The French capital is rich in museums, art galleries, and monuments. The Louvre, Eiffel Tower, and Pompidou Center are among the most popular sights.

Surrounding Paris, the Ile de France takes in 4,600 sq miles (12,000 sq km) of busy suburbs and commuter towns punctuated by châteaux, the most celebrated being Versailles. Farther out, suburbia gives way to farmland, forests, and the magnificent palace of Fontainebleau.

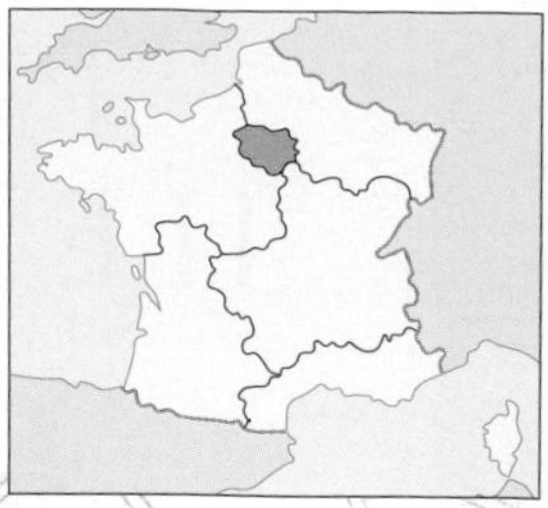

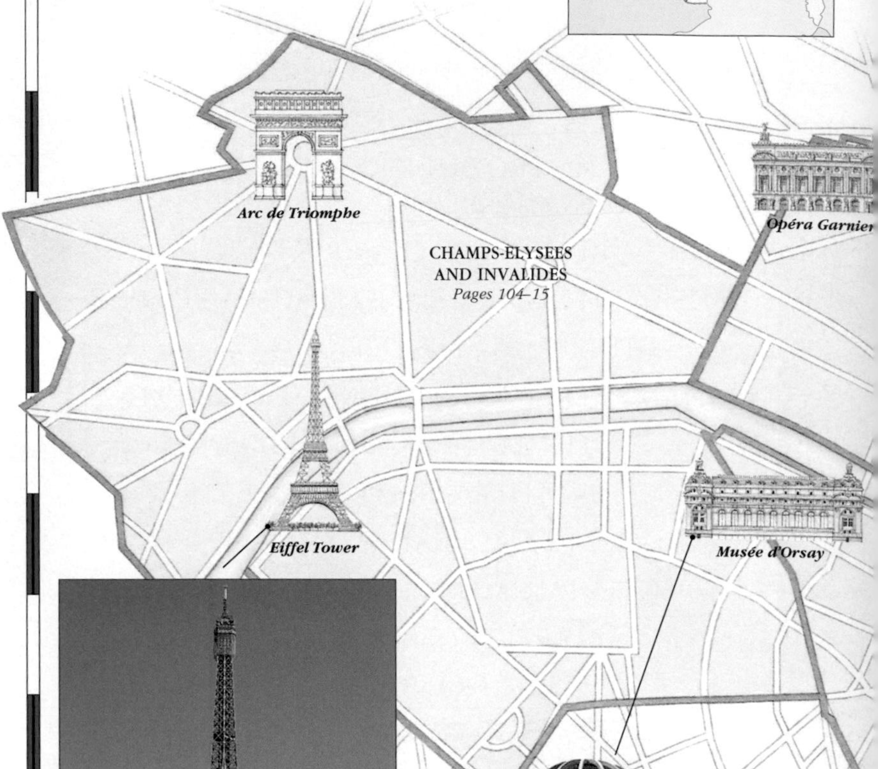

Arc de Triomphe

Opéra Garnier

CHAMPS-ELYSEES
AND INVALIDES
Pages 104–15

Eiffel Tower

Musée d'Orsay

The Eiffel Tower, *designed for the Universal Exhibition of 1889, scandalized contemporary critics but is now the capital's most famous landmark (see p113).*

The Musée d'Orsay, *opened in 1986, was created from a late 19th-century railroad terminus (see pp120–1). Its magnificent collection of 19th- and early 20th-century art (notably Impressionist art) ncludes Jean-Baptiste Carpeaux's* Four Quarters of the World *(1872).*

◁ **Rooftop view of Sacré-Coeur and the Butte Montmartre**

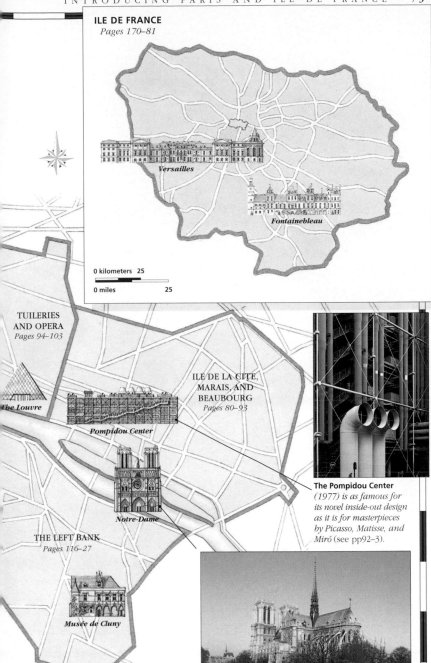

ILE DE FRANCE
Pages 170–81

Versailles

Fontainebleau

0 kilometers   25

0 miles   25

TUILERIES
AND OPERA
Pages 94–103

The Louvre

ILE DE LA CITÉ,
MARAIS, AND
BEAUBOURG
Pages 80–93

Pompidou Center

Notre-Dame

THE LEFT BANK
Pages 116–27

Musée de Cluny

0 kilometers   1

0 miles   0.5

The Pompidou Center
*(1977) is as famous for
its novel inside-out design
as it is for masterpieces
by Picasso, Matisse, and
Miró* (see pp92–3).

Notre-Dame, *a stunning example of Gothic architecture begun in 1163, took two centuries and armies
of medieval workers to complete* (see pp86–7). *Architect
Viollet-le-Duc designed the spire in the 19th century.*

A RIVER VIEW OF PARIS

Sculpture on the Pont Alexandre III

The remarkable French music-hall star Mistinguett described the Seine as a "pretty blonde with laughing eyes." The river most certainly has a beguiling quality, but the relationship that exists between it and the city of Paris is far more than one of flirtation.

No other European city defines itself by its river in the same way as Paris. The Seine is the essential point of reference to the city: distances are measured from it, street numbers determined by it, and it divides the capital into two distinct areas, the Right Bank on the north side of the river and the Left Bank on the south side. These are as well-defined as any of the official boundaries. The city is also divided historically: the east is linked to the city's ancient roots and the west to the 19th–20th centuries.

Practically every building of note in Paris is either along the river bank or within a stone's throw of it. The quays are lined by fine bourgeois apartments, magnificent townhouses, world-renowned museums, and striking monuments.

Above all, the river is very much alive. For centuries fleets of small boats used it, but motorized land traffic stifled this once-bustling scene. Today, the river is busy with commercial barges and massive *bâteaux mouches* pleasure boats carrying sightseers up and down the river.

The Latin Quarter Quayside is on the Left Bank of the Seine. Associated with institutes of learning since the Middle Ages, it acquired its name from the early Latin-speaking students.

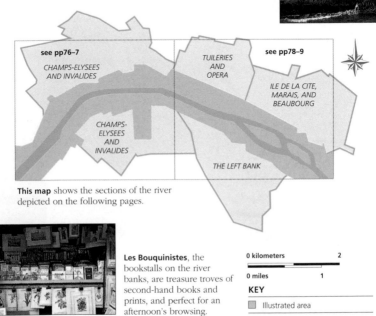

see pp76–7

CHAMPS-ELYSEES AND INVALIDES

TUILERIES AND OPERA

see pp78–9

ILE DE LA CITE, MARAIS, AND BEAUBOURG

CHAMPS-ELYSEES AND INVALIDES

THE LEFT BANK

This map shows the sections of the river depicted on the following pages.

Les Bouquinistes, the bookstalls on the river banks, are treasure troves of second-hand books and prints, and perfect for an afternoon's browsing.

0 kilometers 2

0 miles 1

KEY

Illustrated area

◁ Point Alexandre III, encrusted with exuberant statuary

From Pont de Grenelle to Pont de la Concorde

The grand monuments along this stretch of the river are remnants of the Napoleonic era and the Industrial Revolution. The elegance of the Eiffel Tower, the Petit Palais and the Grand Palais is matched by more recent buildings, such as the Palais de Chaillot and the Musée du Quai Branly.

Palais de Chaillot
Built for the 1937 Exhibition, the spectacular colonnaded wings house several museums and a theater (p110).

The Palais de Tokyo
Bourdelle's statues adorn the façades (p110).

Trocadéro Ⓜ

Bateaux Parisiens
Tour Eiffel
Vedettes de Paris
Ile de France

The Pont Bir-Hakeim has a dynamic statue by Wederkinch rising at its north end.

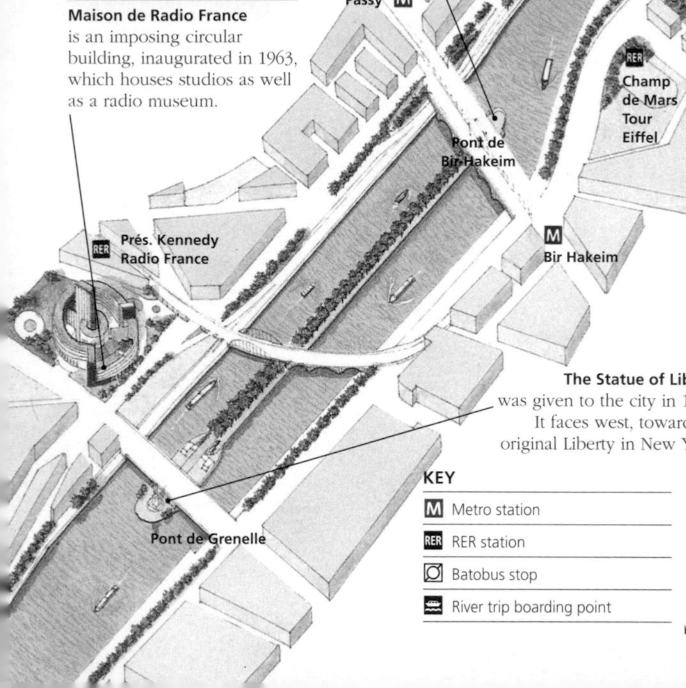

Passerelle Debilly

Pont d'Iéna

Musée du Quai Branly

Maison de Radio France
is an imposing circular building, inaugurated in 1963, which houses studios as well as a radio museum.

Passy Ⓜ

Eiffel Tower
This is Paris's most identifiable landmark (p113).

Champ de Mars Tour Eiffel Ⓡ

Pont de Bir-Hakeim

Ⓡ Prés. Kennedy Radio France

Ⓜ
Bir Hakeim

The Statue of Liberty
was given to the city in 1885. It faces west, toward the original Liberty in New York.

Pont de Grenelle

KEY

Ⓜ	Metro station
Ⓡ	RER station
ⓞ	Batobus stop
⛴	River trip boarding point

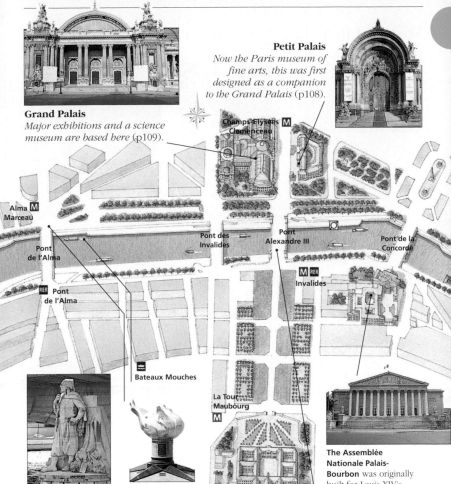

Grand Palais
Major exhibitions and a science museum are based here (p109).

Petit Palais
Now the Paris museum of fine arts, this was first designed as a companion to the Grand Palais (p108).

Champs-Élysées Clemenceau Ⓜ

Alma Ⓜ Marceau

Pont de l'Alma

Pont des Invalides

Pont Alexandre III

Pont de la Concorde

ⓇⒺ Pont de l'Alma

Ⓜ ⓇⒺⓇ Invalides

Bateaux Mouches

La Tour Maubourg Ⓜ

The Zouave, a statue on the central pier, is a useful gauge for checking flood levels.

The Liberty Flame is a memorial to the fighters of the French Resistance during World War II.

The Assemblée Nationale Palais-Bourbon was originally built for Louis XIV's daughter. It has accommodated the lower house of the French Parliament since 1830.

Dôme Church
The majestic gilded dome (p115) is here seen from Pont Alexandre III. Napoleon's tomb is installed in the crypt.

Pont Alexandre III
Flamboyant statuary decorates Paris's most ornate bridge (p109).

From Pont de la Concorde to Pont de Sully

The historic heart of Paris lies on the banks and islands of the east river. At its center is the Ile de la Cité, a natural stepping-stone across the Seine and the cultural core of medieval Paris. Today it is still vital to Parisian life.

Jardin des Tuileries
These are laid out in the formal style (pp98–9).

Musée du Louvre
Before becoming the world's greatest museum and home to the Mona Lisa, this was Europe's largest royal palace (pp100–3).

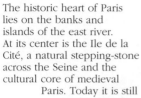
Concorde M

Pont de la Concorde

Assemblée Nationale M

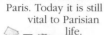
Passerelle Solférino

RER
Musée d'Orsay

Pont Royal

Pont du Carrousel

Passerelle des Arts

Musée de l'Orangerie
An important collection of 19th-century paintings is on display here (p98).

Musée d'Orsay
This converted train station houses Paris's outstanding collection of Impressionist art (pp120–21).

Bateaux Vedettes du Pont Neuf

BATOBUS CRUISES

The boarding points are: **Eiffel Tower. Map** 6 D3. **M** Bir Hakeim. **Champs-Elysées. Map** 7 A1. **M** Champs-Elysées-Clemenceau. **Musée d'Orsay. Map** 8 D2. **M** Assemblée Nationale. **Louvre. Map** 8 D2. **M** Palais Royal-Musée du Louvre. **Hôtel de Ville. Map** 9 B4. **M** Hôtel de Ville. **Notre-Dame. Map** 9 B4. **M** St-Michel. **St-Germain-des-Prés. Map** 8 E3. **M** St-Germain des Prés. **Jardin des Plantes. Map** 13 C1. **M** Jussieu. *Departures mid-Feb–mid-Mar, mid-Nov–mid-Dec: 10:30am–4:30pm (to 5:30pm mid-Dec–early Jan); mid-Mar–May, Sep–11 Nov: 10am–7pm (to 9:30pm Jun–Aug); every 15–30 min daily.* **www.batobus.com**

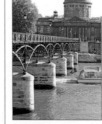

Passerelle des Arts This steel reconstruction of Paris's first cast-iron bridge (1804) was inaugurated in 1984.

Monnaie de Paris, the Mint, was built in 1778, and has an extensive coin and medallion collection in its old milling halls.

HOW TO TAKE A SEINE CRUISE

Bateaux Vedettes du Pont-Neuf Seine Cruise
Boarding point is: **Square du Vert-Galant** (Pont Neuf). **Map** 8 F3. **Tel** 01 46 33 98 38. **M** Pont Neuf. **RER** Châtelet/St-Michel. **27**, 58, 67, 70, 72, 74, 75. **Departures** 15 Mar–31 Oct: 10:30am, 11:15am, noon, 1:30–10:30pm (every 30 mins) daily; Nov–14 Mar: 10:30am, 11:15am, noon, 2–6:30pm (every 45 mins), 8pm, 9pm, 10pm Mon–Thu; 10:30am, 11:15am, noon, 2–6:30pm, 8pm, 9–10pm (every 30 min) Fri–Sun. **Duration** 1 hr. Snacks available. **www.** vedettesdupontneuf.fr

Bateaux Mouches Seine Cruise
Boarding point is: Pont de l'Alma. **Map** 6 F1. **Tel** 01 42 25 96 10. **M** Alma-Marceau. **RER** Pont de l'Alma. **28**, 42, 63, 72, 80, 81, 92. **Departures** Apr–Sep: 10:15am–11pm daily (every 20–45 min); Oct–Mar: 10:15am–9pm daily (every 30–60 min). **Duration** 1hr 15 min. **Lunch cruise** 1pm Sat, Sun, public hols (boarding 12:15pm). **Dinner cruise** boarding 7:30–8:30pm daily. **Duration** 2 hr 15 min. Jacket and tie. **www.** bateaux-mouches.fr.

Vedettes de Paris Ile de France Seine Cruise
Main boarding point is: **Port du Suffren. Map** 6 D3. **Tel** 01 44 18 19 50. **M** Trocadéro, Bir Hakeim. **RER** Champ-de-Mars–Tour Eiffel. **22**, 30, 32, 42, 44, 63, 69, 72, 82, 87. **Departures** 10:30am–10pm daily (11am–7:15pm Oct–Apr, until 9pm Sat–Sun) (every 20–45 min). **Duration** 1hr. **Champagne cruise** 6pm Thu–Sat. Taste 3 champagnes on a 1-hr trip. **Dinner cruise** 8pm Sat. **Duration** 2 hr 30 min. www.vedettes deparis.com

Bateaux Parisiens Tour Eiffel Seine Cruise
Boarding point is: **Pont d'Iéna** & **Quai de Montbello** (Apr–Nov). **Map** 6 D2. **Tel** 08 25 01 01 01. **M** Trocadéro, Bir Hakeim. **RER** Champ-de-Mars–Tour Eiffel. **42**, 82. **Departures** Apr–Sep: 10am–10:30pm; Oct–Mar: 10:30am–10pm (every 30 min). **Lunch cruise** daily 12:15pm. **Duration** 2 hr 15 min. **Dinner cruise** daily, boarding 7:15–8:15pm. **Duration** 3 hr. Jacket and tie. **www.** bateauxparisiens.com

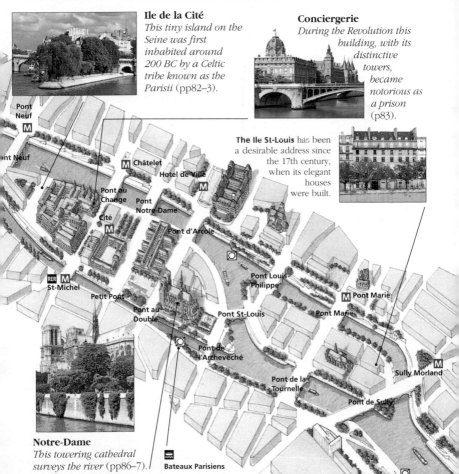

Ile de la Cité
This tiny island on the Seine was first inhabited around 200 BC by a Celtic tribe known as the Parisii (pp82–3).

Conciergerie
During the Revolution this building, with its distinctive towers, became notorious as a prison (p83).

The Ile St-Louis has been a desirable address since the 17th century, when its elegant houses were built.

Pont Neuf **M**

nt Neuf

M Châtelet

Hôtel de Ville **M**

Pont au Change

Pont Notre-Dame

Cité **M**

Pont d'Arcole

RER M St-Michel

Petit Pont

Pont au Double

Pont de l'Archevêché

Pont St-Louis

Pont Louis Philippe

Pont Marie **M**

Pont Marie

Pont de la Tournelle

Pont de Sully

Sully Morland **M**

Notre-Dame
This towering cathedral surveys the river (pp86–7).

Bateaux Parisiens

ILE DE LA CITE, MARAIS, AND BEAUBOURG

The Right Bank is dominated by the modernistic Forum des Halles and Pompidou Center in the Beaubourg. These are Paris's most thriving public areas, with millions of tourists, shoppers, and students flowing between them. Young people flock to Les Halles, shopping for the latest street fashions, but you should avoid the area at night. Renovations to improve Les Halles should be completed by 2017. All roads from here appear to lead to the Pompidou Center, an avant-garde assembly of pipes, ducts, and cables housing the Musée National d'Art Moderne. The smaller streets around the center are full of art galleries housed in

The crest of the city of Paris

crooked, gabled buildings. The neighboring Marais, abandoned by its royal residents during the 1789 Revolution, descended into architectural wasteland before being rescued in the 1960s. It has since become a very fashionable address, though small cafés, bakeries, and artisans still survive in its streets.

Notre-Dame cathedral, the Palais de Justice, and Sainte-Chapelle continue to draw tourists to the Ile de la Cité, despite its extensive redevelopment in the last century. At the eastern end a bridge connects with the Ile St-Louis, a former swampy pastureland transformed into a residential area with pretty, tree-lined quays and mansions.

SIGHTS AT A GLANCE

Islands & Squares
Ile St-Louis ❼
Forum des Halles ⓭
Place des Vosges ⓲
Place de la Bastille ㉑

Churches
Sainte-Chapelle ❹
Notre-Dame pp86–7 ❻
St-Gervais–St-Protais ❾
St-Eustache ⓬

Historic Buildings
Conciergerie ❷
Palais de Justice ❸
Hôtel de Ville ❿
Tour St-Jacques ⓫

GETTING THERE
Metro stations include Châtelet, Hôtel-de-Ville, and Cité. Buses 47 and 29 serve Beaubourg and the Marais respectively. Several bus routes cross Ile de la Cité and Ile St-Louis.

Museums and Galleries
Crypte Archéologique ❺
Hôtel de Sens ❽
Pompidou Center pp92–3 ⓮
Musée d'Art et d'Histoire du Judaisme ⓯
Hôtel de Soubise ⓰
Musée Picasso ⓱
Musée Carnavalet ⓲
Maison de Victor Hugo ⓴

Bridges
Pont Neuf ❶

KEY

- Street by Street map *pp82–3*
- Street by Street map *pp88–9*
- Ⓜ Metro station
- Batobus boarding point
- **RER** RER station

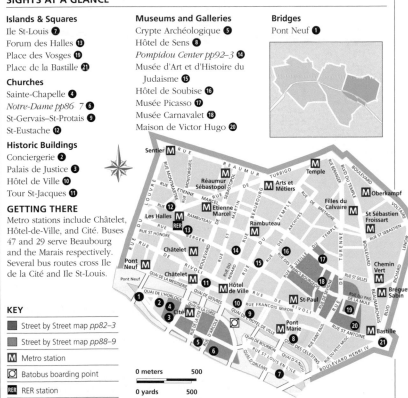

◁ **View of the Conciergerie and the Pont au Change**

Street-by-Street: Ile de la Cité

The origins of Paris are on the Ile de la Cité, the boat-shaped island on the Seine first inhabited by Celtic tribes in the 3rd century BC. One tribe, the Parisii, eventually gave its name to the city. The island offered a convenient river crossing on the route between northern and southern Gaul and was easily defended. In later centuries the settlement was expanded by the Romans, the Franks, and the Capetian kings to form the nucleus of today's city.

Remains of the first buildings can still be seen today in the archaeological crypt of the great medieval cathedral of Notre-Dame. At the other end of the island is Sainte-Chapelle, another Gothic masterpiece.

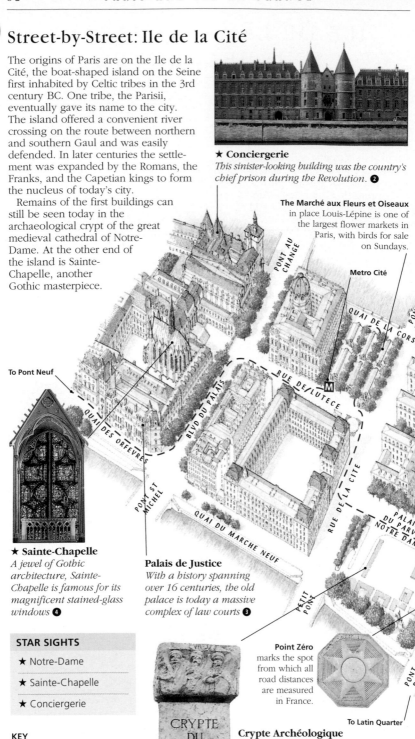

★ **Conciergerie**
This sinister-looking building was the country's chief prison during the Revolution. ❷

The Marché aux Fleurs et Oiseaux in place Louis-Lépine is one of the largest flower markets in Paris, with birds for sale on Sundays.

Metro Cité

To Pont Neuf

★ **Sainte-Chapelle**
A jewel of Gothic architecture, Sainte-Chapelle is famous for its magnificent stained-glass windows ❹

Palais de Justice
With a history spanning over 16 centuries, the old palace is today a massive complex of law courts ❸

Point Zéro marks the spot from which all road distances are measured in France.

To Latin Quarter

STAR SIGHTS

- ★ Notre-Dame
- ★ Sainte-Chapelle
- ★ Conciergerie

KEY

– – – Suggested route

Crypte Archéologique
Deep under the square lie remnants of houses dating back 2,000 years ❺

Hôtel Dieu, the oldest hospital in Paris, was founded in AD 651 by St. Landry, Bishop of Paris.

LOCATOR MAP
See Street Finder maps 8, 9

Pont Neuf, the city's oldest bridge

Pont Neuf ❶

75001. **Map** 8 F3. Ⓜ *Pont Neuf, Cité.*

Despite its name (New Bridge), this bridge is the oldest in Paris and has been immortalized by major literary and artistic figures. The first stone was laid by Henri III in 1578, but it was Henri IV (whose statue stands at the center) who inaugurated it and gave it its name in 1607.

Conciergerie ❷

2 bd du Palais 75001. **Map** 9 A3. **Tel** 01 53 40 60 80. Ⓜ *Cité.* ⬤ 9:30am 6pm daily (9am–5pm Nov–Feb; last adm 30 min before closing). ⬤ Jan 1, May 1, Dec 25. 🎫 Combined ticket with Sainte-Chapelle (see p84) available. 📷 ✆ call to check. 🚻

Forming part of the huge Palais de Justice, the historic Conciergerie served as a prison from 1391–1914. Henri IV's assassin, François Ravaillac, was imprisoned and tortured here in 1610.

During the Revolution the building was packed with over 4,000 prisoners. Its most celebrated inmate was Marie-Antoinette, who was held in a tiny cell until her execution in 1793. Others included Charlotte Corday, who stabbed Revolutionary leader Marat.

The Conciergerie has a superb four-aisled Gothic hall, where guards of the royal household once lived. Renovated during the 19th century, the building retains its 11th-century torture chamber and 14th-century clock tower.

★ **Notre-Dame**
This cathedral, with its magnificent south-facing rose window and impressive array of gargoyles, is one of the finest examples of French Gothic architecture ❻

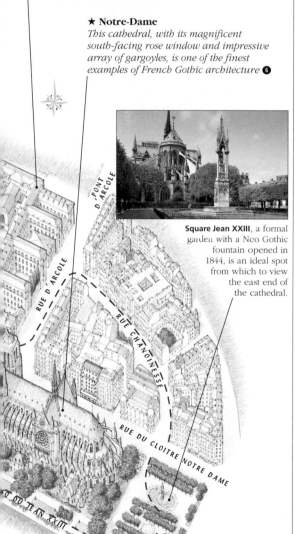

Square Jean XXIII, a formal garden with a Neo Gothic fountain opened in 1844, is an ideal spot from which to view the east end of the cathedral.

0 meters 100
0 yards 100

A sculptured relief on the Palais de Justice

Palais de Justice ❸

4 bd du Palais (entrance at 8 bd du Palais) 75001. **Map** 9 A3.
Tel 01 44 32 52 52. **M** Cité.
◯ 9am–6pm Mon–Fri.
⬤ public hols & Aug recess.

This huge block of buildings making up the law courts of Paris stretches the entire width of the Ile de la Cité. It is a splendid sight with its Gothic towers lining the quays. The site has been occupied since Roman times when it was the governors' residence. It was the seat of royal power until Charles V moved the court to the Marais following a bloody revolt in 1358. In April 1793 the notorious Revolutionary Tribunal began dispensing justice from the Première Chambre Civile, or first civil chamber. Today the site embodies Napoleon's great legacy – the French judicial system.

Sainte-Chapelle ❹

6 bd du Palais 75001.
Map 9 A3. **📱** 01 53 40 60 80.
M Cité. ◯ Mar–Oct: 9:30am–6pm daily; Nov–Feb: 9am–5pm daily.
⬤ Jan 1, May 1, Dec 25.
🎫 Combined ticket with Conciergerie (see p83) available. No sharp objects permitted. 📷 ✉ 📱

Ethereal and magical, Sainte-Chapelle has been hailed as one of the greatest architectural masterpieces of the Western world. In the Middle Ages the devout likened this church to "a gateway to heaven." Today no visitor can fail to be transported by the blaze of light created by the 15 magnificent stained-glass windows, separated by pencil-like columns soaring 50 ft (15 m) to the star-studded roof. The windows portray more than 1,000 biblical scenes in a kaleidoscope of red, gold, green, and blue. Starting from the left near the entrance and proceeding clockwise, you can trace the scriptures from Genesis through to the Crucifixion and the Apocalypse.

The chapel was completed in 1248 by Louis IX to house what was believed to be Christ's Crown of Thorns and fragments of the True Cross (now in the treasury at Notre-Dame). The king, who was canonized for his good works, purchased the relics from the Emperor of Constantinople, paying three times more for them than for the entire construction of Sainte-Chapelle.

The building actually consists of two separate chapels. The somber lower chapel was used by servants and lower court officials, while the exquisite upper chapel, reached by means of a narrow spiral staircase, was reserved for the royal family and its courtiers. A discreetly placed window enabled the king to take part in the celebrations unobserved.

During the Revolution the building was badly damaged and became a warehouse. It was renovated a century later by architect Viollet-le-Duc.

Today, evening concerts of classical music are held regularly in the chapel, taking advantage of its superb acoustics.

Crypte Archéologique ❺

Parvis Notre-Dame–pl Jean-Paul II 75004. **Map** 9 A4. **Tel** 01 55 42 50 10. **M** Cité. ◯ 10am–6pm Tue–Sun (last adm 30 mins before closing).
⬤ Jan 1, May 1 & 8, Nov 1 & 11, Dec 25. 🎫 📷 📱

Situated beneath the *parvis* (main square) of Notre-Dame and stretching 393 ft (120 m) underground, the crypt was opened in 1980.

There are Gallo-Roman streets and houses with an underground heating system, sections of Lutetia's 3rd-century BC wall, and remains of the cathedral. Models explain the development of Paris from a settlement of the Parisii, the Celtic tribe who inhabited the island 2000 years ago.

Notre-Dame ❻

See pp86–7.

The magnificent interior of Sainte-Chapelle

Ile St-Louis ❼

75004. **Map** 9 B-C4-5. Ⓜ *Pont Marie, Sully Morland.* **St-Louis-en-l'Ile** *19 bis rue Saint-Louis en l'Ile.* **Tel** *01 46 34 11 60.* ◯ *9:30am–1pm, 2–7:30pm (7pm Sun, public hols).* **Concerts** *www.stlouisenlile.com*

Across Pont St-Louis from Ile de la Cité, smaller Ile St-Louis is a little haven of quiet streets, riverside quays, and luxurious restaurants and stores, including the famous ice-cream maker Berthillon. Almost everything on the Ile was built in classical style in the 17th century. The church of **St-Louis-en-l'Ile**, with its marble and gilt Baroque interior, was completed in 1726 from plans by royal architect Louis de Vau. Note the 1741 iron clock at the church entrance, the pierced iron spire, and a plaque given in 1926 by St. Louis, Missouri. The church is twinned with Carthage cathedral in Tunisia, where St. Louis is buried.

The interior of St-Louis-en-l'Ile

Hôtel de Sens ❽

1 rue du Figuier 75004. **Map** 9 C4. **Tel** *01 42 78 14 60.* Ⓜ *Pont-Marie.* ◯ *10am–7:30pm Wed & Thu (from 1pm Tue, Fri, Sat).* ⬤ *public hols.* 🎫

One of only a handful of medieval buildings still standing in Paris, the Hôtel de Sens is home to the Forney arts library. During the period of the Catholic League in the 16th century, it was turned into a fortified mansion and occupied by the Bourbons, the Guises, and Cardinal de Pellevé.

St-Gervais–St-Protais ❾

Pl St-Gervais 75004. **Map** 9 B3. **Tel** *01 48 87 32 02.* Ⓜ *Hôtel de Ville.* ◯ *5:30am–9pm daily.* **Organ concerts**

Named after Gervase and Protase, two Roman soldiers martyred by the Emperor Nero, the origins of this magnificent church go back to the 6th century. It boasts the earliest Classical façade in Paris, dating from 1621, with a triple-tiered arrangement of Doric, Ionic and Corinthian columns.

Behind the façade lies a late Gothic church renowned for its association with religious music. François Couperin (1668–1733) composed his two masses for this church's organ.

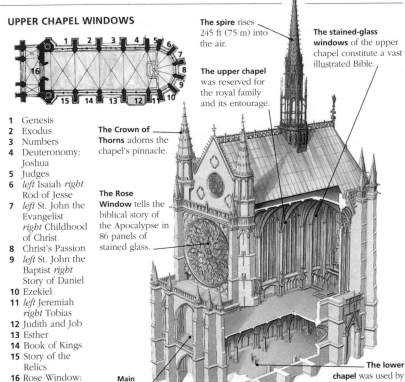

UPPER CHAPEL WINDOWS

1 Genesis
2 Exodus
3 Numbers
4 Deuteronomy: Joshua
5 Judges
6 *left* Isaiah *right* Rod of Jesse
7 *left* St. John the Evangelist *right* Childhood of Christ
8 Christ's Passion
9 *left* St. John the Baptist *right* Story of Daniel
10 Ezekiel
11 *left* Jeremiah *right* Tobias
12 Judith and Job
13 Esther
14 Book of Kings
15 Story of the Relics
16 Rose Window: The Apocalypse

The spire rises 245 ft (75 m) into the air.

The stained-glass windows of the upper chapel constitute a vast illustrated Bible.

The upper chapel was reserved for the royal family and its entourage.

The Crown of Thorns adorns the chapel's pinnacle.

The Rose Window tells the biblical story of the Apocalypse in 86 panels of stained glass.

Main portals

The lower chapel was used by servants and commoners.

Notre-Dame ❻

No other building epitomizes the history of Paris more than Notre-Dame. Built on the site of a Roman temple, the cathedral was commissioned by Bishop de Sully in 1159. The first stone was laid in 1163, marking the start of two centuries of toil by armies of Gothic architects and medieval craftsmen. It has been witness to great events of French history ever since, including the coronations of Henry VI in 1422 and Napoleon Bonaparte in 1804. During the Revolution the building was desecrated and rechristened the Temple of Reason. Extensive renovations (including the addition of the spire and gargoyles) were carried out in the 19th century by architect Viollet-le-Duc.

★ **West Façade**
The beautifully proportioned west façade is a masterpiece of French Gothic architecture.

387 steps lead to the top of the south tower, where the famous Emmanuel bell is housed.

★ **Galerie des Chimères**
The cathedral's legendary gargoyles (chimères) gaze menacingly from the cathedral's ledge.

★ **West Rose Window**
This window depicts the Virgin in a medallion of rich reds and blues.

STAR FEATURES

- ★ West Façade and Portals
- ★ Flying Buttress
- ★ Rose Windows
- ★ Galerie des Chimères

The Kings' Gallery features 28 stone images of the kings of Judah.

Portal of the Virgin
The Virgin surrounded by saints and kings is a fine composition of 13th-century statues.

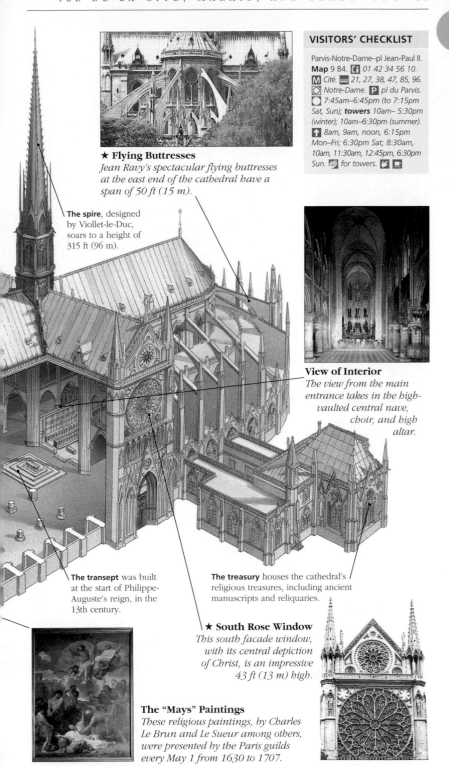

★ **Flying Buttresses**
Jean Ravy's spectacular flying buttresses at the east end of the cathedral have a span of 50 ft (15 m).

The spire, designed by Viollet-le-Duc, soars to a height of 315 ft (96 m).

VISITORS' CHECKLIST

Parvis-Notre-Dame–pl Jean-Paul II.
Map 9 B4. 01 42 34 56 10.
Cité. 21, 27, 38, 47, 85, 96.
Notre-Dame. *pl du Parvis.*
7:45am–6:45pm (to 7:15pm
Sat, Sun); **towers** 10am–5:30pm
(winter); 10am–6:30pm (summer).
8am, 9am, noon, 6:15pm
Mon–Fri; 6:30pm Sat; 8:30am,
10am, 11:30am, 12:45pm, 6:30pm
Sun. for towers.

View of Interior
The view from the main entrance takes in the high-vaulted central nave, choir, and high altar.

The transept was built at the start of Philippe-Auguste's reign, in the 13th century.

The treasury houses the cathedral's religious treasures, including ancient manuscripts and reliquaries.

★ **South Rose Window**
This south façade window, with its central depiction of Christ, is an impressive 43 ft (13 m) high.

The "Mays" Paintings
These religious paintings, by Charles Le Brun and Le Sueur among others, were presented by the Paris guilds every May 1 from 1630 to 1707.

Street by Street: The Marais

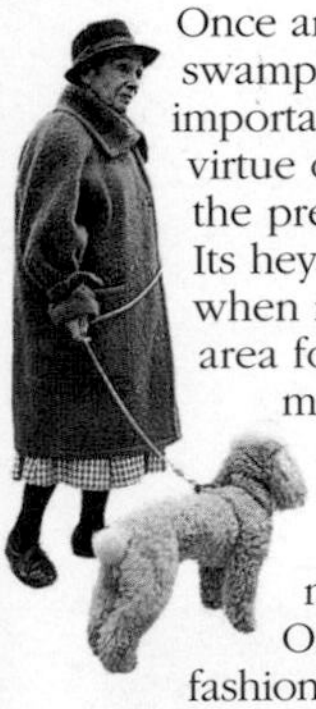

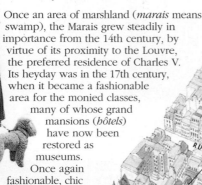

Once an area of marshland (*marais* means swamp), the Marais grew steadily in importance from the 14th century, by virtue of its proximity to the Louvre, the preferred residence of Charles V. Its heyday was in the 17th century, when it became a fashionable area for the monied classes, many of whose grand mansions (*hôtels*) have now been restored as museums. Once again fashionable, chic designer boutiques alternate with small restaurants and stores.

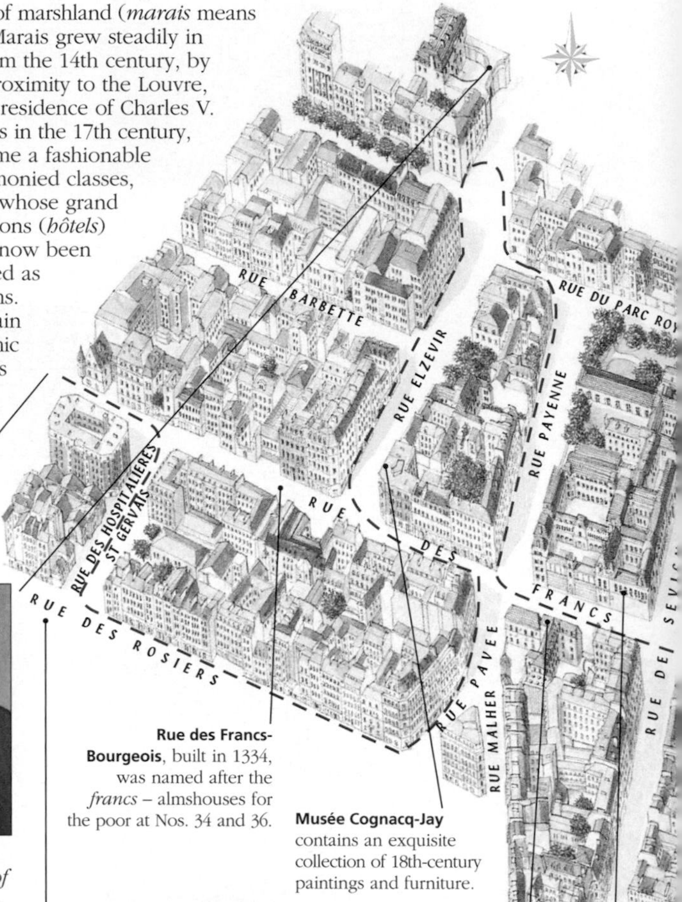

To the Pompidou Centre

★ **Musée Picasso**
The palatial home of a 17th-century salt-tax collector houses the most extensive collection of Picassos in the world ⑰

Rue des Francs-Bourgeois, built in 1334, was named after the *francs* – almshouses for the poor at Nos. 34 and 36.

Musée Cognacq-Jay contains an exquisite collection of 18th-century paintings and furniture.

Hôtel de Lamoignon was built in 1584 and houses Paris's historical library.

Rue des Rosiers, heart of the city's oldest Jewish quarter, is lined with 18th-century houses, stores, and cafés serving dishes such as hot pastrami and borscht.

★ **Musée Carnavalet**
Occupying two large mansions, this museum covers the history of Paris from Prehistoric and Gallo-Roman times ⑱

KEY

– – – Suggested route

0 meters 100
0 yards 100

For hotels and restaurants in this region see pp550–5 and pp600–6

★ Place des Vosges
This enchanting square is an oasis of peace and tranquility ⑲

LOCATOR MAP
See Street Finder maps 9, 10

Maison de Victor Hugo
Author of Les Misérables, *Victor Hugo lived at No. 6 place des Vosges, now a museum of his life and work* ⑳

RUE DE BEARN

RUE DE TURENNE

URGEOIS

RUE DE BIRAGUE

To Metro Sully Morland

STAR SIGHTS

★ Musée Picasso

★ Musée Carnavalet

★ Place des Vosges

Hôtel de Sully, with its orangerie and courtyard, is an elegant Renaissance mansion.

Hôtel de Ville ⑩

Pl de l'Hôtel de Ville 75004.
Map 9 B3. **Tel** *01 42 76 40 40*.
Ⓜ *Hôtel-de-Ville.* ⬜ to groups: phone to arrange (01 42 76 54 04). ⬤ public hols, and for official functions (phone to check). ♿

Home of the city council, the Hôtel de Ville is a 19th-century reconstruction of the 17th-century town hall burned down by insurgents of the Paris Commune in 1871. It is a highly ornate example of Third Republic architecture, with elaborate stonework, turrets, and statues overlooking a pedestrianized square.

The 16th-century Tour St-Jacques

Tour St-Jacques ⑪

Square de la Tour St-Jacques 75004.
Map 9 A3. Ⓜ *Châtelet.*
⬜ *gardens only.*

This imposing late Gothic tower, dating from 1523, is all that remains of a medieval church used as a rendezvous by pilgrims setting out for Compostela in Spain. The building was destroyed by revolutionaries in 1797.
Earlier, Blaise Pascal, the 17th-century philosopher, mathematician, physicist, and writer, used the tower for barometric experiments. His statue stands at the base of the tower, which is now used as a meteorological station.

St-Eustache ⑫

2 impasse St-Eustache 75001.
Map 9 A1. **Tel** 01 42 36 31 05.
Ⓜ Les Halles. RER Châtelet-Les-Halles.
◯ 9:30am–7pm Mon–Fri, 10am–
7pm Sat & Sun. ✝ 12:30pm Mon–
Fri, 6pm Sat, 11am, 6pm Sun.
Concerts www.saint-eustache.org

With its Gothic plan and
Renaissance decoration, St-
Eustache is one of Paris's
most beautiful churches. Its
massive interior is modeled on
Notre-Dame, with five naves
and side and radial chapels.
The 105 years (1532–1637) it
took to complete the church
saw the flowering of the
Renaissance style, which is
evident in the magnificent
arches, pillars, and columns.
   St-Eustache has hosted many
ceremonial events, including
the baptisms of Cardinal
Richelieu and Madame de
Pompadour, and the funerals
of fabulist La Fontaine, Colbert
(prime minister of Louis XIV),
17th-century dramatist Molière,
and the revolutionary orator
Mirabeau. It was here that
Berlioz first performed his *Te
Deum* in 1855. Today talented
choir groups perform regularly
and organ recitals are often
held here.

Forum des Halles ⑬

75001. **Map** 13 A2. Ⓜ Les Halles.
RER Châtelet-Les-Halles. **Le Forum des
Images**: 2 rue du Cinéma. ◯ 12:30–
11:30pm Tue–Fri, 2–11:30pm Sat, Sun.

Known simply as Les Halles
and built amid much controversy on the site of the famous
old fruit and vegetable market,
the complex occupies 750,000
sq ft (7 ha), partly above and
partly below ground, and has
a reputation for being unsafe,
particularly at night. The
underground levels 2 and 3
are occupied by a varied
array of stores, from clothes
boutiques to megastores, as
well as two multiscreen movie
theaters and a cinema resource
center, **Le Forum des Images**.
Above ground there are well-
tended gardens, pergolas and
mini-pavillions. Extensive renovations to improve the area
were due to start in 2006 but
work is slow to commence.

**St-Eustache and sculptured head,
l'Ecoute, by Henri de Miller**

Pompidou Center ⑭

See pp92–3.

Musée d'Art et d'Histoire du Judaïsme ⑮

Hôtel de St-Aignan, 71 rue du Temple
75003. **Map** 13 B2. **Tel** 01 53 01 86
60. Ⓜ Rambuteau. ◯ 11am–6pm
Mon–Fri, 10am–6pm Sun. ◯ Jewish
hols. 🈳 ♿ ▤ 🏠 www.mahj.org

This museum in a Marais
mansion, the elegant Hôtel de
St-Aignan, brings together
collections formerly scattered
around the city, and commemorates the culture of French
Jewry from medieval times to
the present. Visitors learn that
there has been a sizeable
Jewish community in
France since Roman
times, and some of the
world's greatest Jewish
scholars – Rashi, Rabenu
Tam, the Tosafists – were
French. Much exquisite
craftsmanship is dis-
played, with elaborate
silverware, Torah covers,
fabrics, and items of fine
Judaica and religious
objects for use both in
the synagogue and in the
home. There are also
photographs, paintings,
and cartoons and
historical documents,
including some on the
antisemitic Dreyfus Affair
more than a century ago.

Hôtel de Soubise ⑯

60 rue des Francs-Bourgeois 75003.
Map 9 C2. Ⓜ Rambuteau.
◯ 10am–12:30pm, 2–5:30pm Mon,
Wed–Fri, 2–5:30pm Sat & Sun.
◯ public hols.

This imposing mansion, built
from 1705 to 1709 for the
Princesse de Rohan, is one of
two main buildings housing the
national archives (the other
one being the Hôtel de Rohan).
It boasts a majestic courtyard
and 18th-century interior decoration by some of the best-
known artists of the time.
   Notable items held here
include Natoire's *rocaille* work
in the Princess's bedchamber
and Napoleon's will. Unfortunately the interior is only
accessible by appointment to
historical researchers.

Musée Picasso ⑰

Hôtel Salé, 5 rue de Thorigny,
75003. **Map** 10 D2. 🛈 01 42 71 25
21. Ⓜ St-Sébastien Froissart.
◯ Closed for renovation work until
2012. 🈳 ◯ 🛗 📷 groups by
appointment only. 🏠 ▤
www.musee-picasso.fr

On the death of the Spanish-
born artist Pablo Picasso
(1881–1973), who lived most
of his life in France, the
French State inherited one
quarter of his works in lieu of
death duties. In 1986, it used
them to create the Musée
Picasso in the beautifully

**Woman Reading (1932) by
Pablo Picasso**

restored Hôtel Salé, one of the loveliest buildings in the Marais. It was built in 1656 for Aubert de Fontenay, collector of the dreaded salt tax (*salé* means "salty").

Comprising over 200 paintings, 158 sculptures, 88 ceramic works, and some 3,000 sketches and engravings, this unique collection shows the enormous range and variety of Picasso's work, including examples from his Blue, Pink, and Cubist periods.

Highlights to look out for are his Blue period *Self-portrait*, painted at age 20; *Still Life with Caned Chair*, which introduced collage to Cubism; the Neoclassical *Pipes of Pan*; and *The Crucifixion*.

The museum frequently loans canvases for special exhibitions elsewhere, so some pieces will be on show in other galleries. The museum closed in August 2009 for major renovation work, which should be finished by late 2012.

A magnificent 17th-century ceiling painting by Charles Le Brun

Musée Carnavalet ⑱

23 rue de Sevigné 75003. **Map** 10 D3.
Tel 01 44 59 58 58. Ⓜ St-Paul.
◯ 10am–6pm Tue–Sun (rooms open in rotas: phone to check). ⬤ public hols. ⬤ ⬤ ring for times. ⬛
www.carnavalet.paris.fr

Devoted to the history of Paris since Prehistoric times, this vast museum is in two adjoining mansions. They include entire decorated rooms with gilded paneling, furniture, and *objets d'art*; many works of art, such as paintings and sculptures of prominent personalities; and engravings showing Paris being built.

The main building is the Hôtel Carnavalet, built as a town house in 1548 by Nicolas Dupuis. The literary hostess Madame de Sévigné lived here between 1677 and 1696, entertaining the intelligentsia of the day and writing her celebrated *Lettres*. Many of her possessions are in the first-floor exhibit covering the Louis XIV era.

The 17th-century Hôtel le Peletier, opened in 1989, features reconstructions of early 20th-century interiors and artifacts from the Revolution and Napoleonic era. The Orangery houses a department devoted to Prehistory and Gallo-Roman Paris. The collection includes pirogues discovered in 1992, during an archaeological dig in the Parc de Bercy, which unearthed a neolithic village.

Place des Vosges ⑲

75003, 75004. **Map** 10 D3.
Ⓜ Bastille, St-Paul.

This perfectly symmetrical square, laid out in 1605 by Henri IV, is considered among the most beautiful in the world. Thirty-six houses, nine on each side, are built over arcades which today accommodate antiques stores and fashionable cafés. The square has been the scene of many historical events over the centuries, including a three-day tournament in a celebration of the marriage of Louis XIII to Anne of Austria in 1615.

Maison de Victor Hugo ⑳

6 pl des Vosges 75004. **Map** 10 D4.
Tel 01 42 72 10 16. Ⓜ Bastille.
◯ 10am–6pm Tue–Sun.
⬤ public hols. ⬤ **Library**
www.musee-hugo.paris.fr

The French poet, dramatist, and novelist lived on the second floor of the former Hôtel de Rohan-Guéménée, the largest house on the square, from 1832 to 1848. It was here that he wrote most of *Les Misérables*. On display are reconstructions of some of the rooms in which he lived, complete with his desk, furniture he made, his drawings, and mementos from key periods of his life, from his childhood to his exile between 1852 and 1870. There are also regular temporary exhibitions.

Marble bust of Victor Hugo by Auguste Rodin

Place de la Bastille ㉑

75004. **Map** 10 E4. Ⓜ Bastille.

Nothing remains of the infamous prison stormed by the revolutionary mob on July 14, 1789, the event that sparked the French Revolution.

The 164-ft (50-m) Colonne de Juillet stands in the middle of the traffic-clogged square to honor the victims of the July Revolution of 1830. On the south side of the square (at 120 rue de Lyon) is the 2,700-seat **Opéra National Bastille**, completed in 1989, the bicentennial of the French Revolution.

The "genius of liberty" statue on top of the Colonne de Juillet

Pompidou Center ⑭

The Pompidou is like a building turned inside out: escalators, elevators, air and water ducts, and even the massive steel struts that make up the building's skeleton are all on the outside. This allowed the architects, Richard Rogers, Renzo Piano, and Gianfranco Franchini, to create a flexible exhibition space. Among the artists featured in the museum are Matisse, Picasso, Miró, and Pollock, representing such schools as Fauvism, Cubism, and Surrealism. The Pompidou also keeps abreast of the Paris art scene with frequently changing temporary exhibitions. Outside in the Piazza, crowds gather to watch street performers.

KEY

☐ Exhibition space

☐ Nonexhibition space

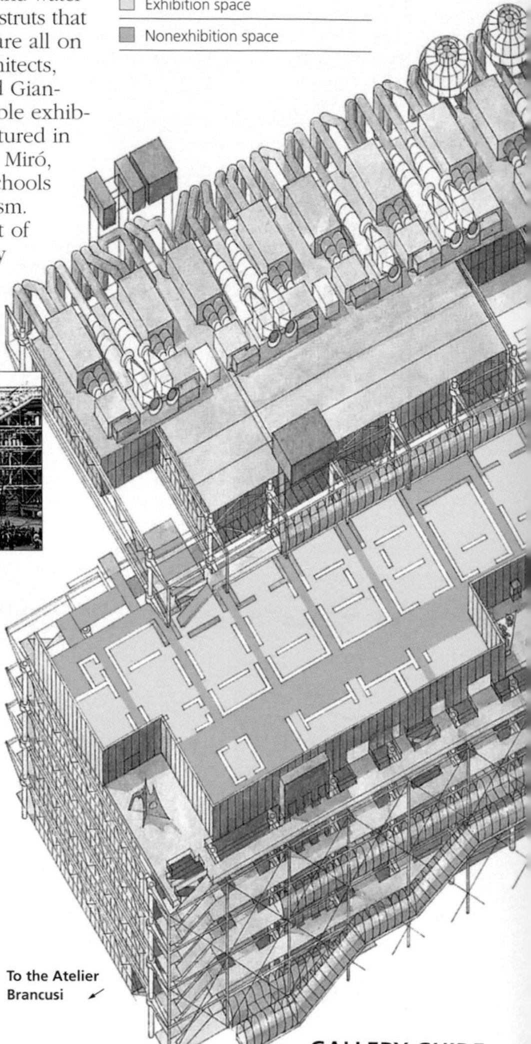

This riotous jumble of glass and steel, known as Beaubourg, is Paris's top tourist attraction, built in 1977 and drawing over seven million visitors a year.

Mobile on Two Planes *(1955)*
20th-century American artist Alexander Calder introduced the mobile as an art form.

To the Atelier Brancusi ⤢

GALLERY GUIDE

The permanent collections are on the fifth and fourth levels: works from 1905–60 are on the former, contemporary art on the latter. The first and sixth levels are for temporary exhibitions; the second and third house a library. The lower levels make up "The Forum," the focal public area, with a performance center, movie theater, shops, and children's workshop.

Sorrow of the King *(1952)*
This collage was created by Matisse using gouache-painted paper cutouts.

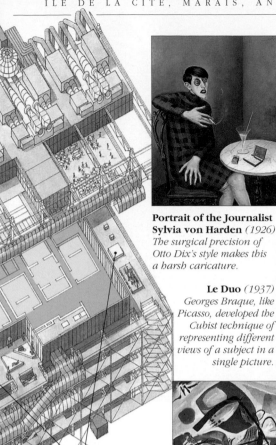

Portrait of the Journalist
Sylvia von Harden *(1926)*
The surgical precision of
Otto Dix's style makes this
a harsh caricature.

Le Duo *(1937)*
Georges Braque, like
Picasso, developed the
Cubist technique of
representing different
views of a subject in a
single picture.

Basin and
Sculpture Terrace

With the Black Arc
(1912) The transition
to Abstraction, one of
the major art forms of
the 20th century, can
be seen in the works of
Wassily Kandinsky.

Stravinsky Fountain
This fountain, which was
inaugurated in 1983, is in
the place Igor Stravinsky
near the Pompidou Center.
It was designed by sculptors
Jean Tinguely and Niki de
Saint Phalle, both of whom
are represented in the
Pompidou Center.

BRANCUSI WORKSHOP

The Atelier Brancusi, on the
rue Rambuteau side of the
piazza, is a reconstruction of the
workshop of the Romanian-
born artist Constantin Brancusi
(1876–1957), who lived and
worked in Paris. He bequeathed
his entire collection of works to
the French state on condition
that his workshop be rebuilt as
it was. The collection includes
over 200 sculptures and plinths,
1600 photographs exhibited in
rotation, and tools Brancusi
used to create his works.
Also featured are some of his
more personal items such as
documents, pieces of furniture,
and his book collection.

Interior of the Brancusi work-
shop, designed by Renzo Piano

TUILERIES AND OPERA

The 19th-century grandeur of Baron Haussmann's *grands boulevards* offsets the bustle of bankers, theater-goers, sightseers, and shoppers who frequent the area around the Opéra. A profusion of shops and department stores, ranging from the exclusively expensive to the popular, draws the crowds. Much of the area's older character is found in the early 19th-century shopping arcades, with elaborate steel and glass roofs. They are known as *galeries* or *passages*, and were restored to their former glory in the 1970s. Galerie Vivienne, which is the fanciest, has an elaborate, patterned mosaic floor. The passage des Panoramas, passage Verdeau, and tiny passage des Princes are more old-style Parisian. These streets abound with curious stores

Lamppost of vestal virgin outside the Opéra

of all kinds, from mouthwatering food shops to antiquarian bookstores and stamp collectors.

The Tuileries area lies between the Opéra and the river, bounded by the vast place de la Concorde in the west and the Louvre to the east. The Louvre palace combines one of the world's greatest art collections with I.M. Pei's avant-garde glass pyramid. Elegant squares and formal gardens give the area its special character. Monuments to monarchy and the arts coexist with modern luxury at its most ostentatious. Place Vendôme, home to exquisite jewelry stores and the luxurious Ritz Hotel, is a heady mix of the wealthy and the chic. Parallel to the Jardin des Tuileries are two of Paris's foremost shopping streets, the rue de Rivoli and rue St-Honoré, full of expensive boutiques, bookstores, and deluxe hotels.

SIGHTS AT A GLANCE

Museums and Galleries
Grévin ❸
Galerie Nationale du Jeu
   de Paume ❻
Musée de l'Orangerie ❽
Musée des Arts Décoratifs ⓫
Musée du Louvre pp100–3 ⓮

Squares, Parks, and Gardens
Place Vendôme ❺
Place de la Concorde ❼
Jardin des Tuileries ❾

Monuments
Arc de Triomphe du
   Carrousel ⓬

Historic Buildings
Opéra de Paris Garnier ❷
Palais Royal ⓭

Churches
La Madeleine ❶
St-Roch ❿

Stores
Les Passages ❹

GETTING THERE
This area is well served by the metro system, with stations at Tuileries, Pyramides, Palais Royal, Madeleine, and Opéra, among others. Bus route 72 passes along rue de Rivoli and quai du Louvre, while routes 21, 27, 29, and 81 serve avenue de l'Opéra.

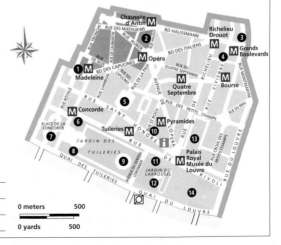

KEY

▓	Street-by-Street map *pp96–7*
Ⓜ	Metro station
ℹ	Tourist information

0 meters   500

0 yards   500

◁ **View of the place de la Concorde and the Obelisk**

Street-by-Street: Opéra Quarter

It has been said that the whole world will pass you by if you sit for long enough at the Café de la Paix (opposite the Opéra National Garnier). During the day, the area is a center of commerce, tourism, and shopping, with mammoth department stores lining the *grands boulevards*. In the evening, the clubs and theaters attract a totally different crowd, and the cafés along boulevard des Capucines throng with life.

Statue by Gumery on the Opéra

★ **Opéra National de Paris Garnier**
Dating from 1875, the grandiose opera house has come to symbolize the opulence of the Second Empire ❷

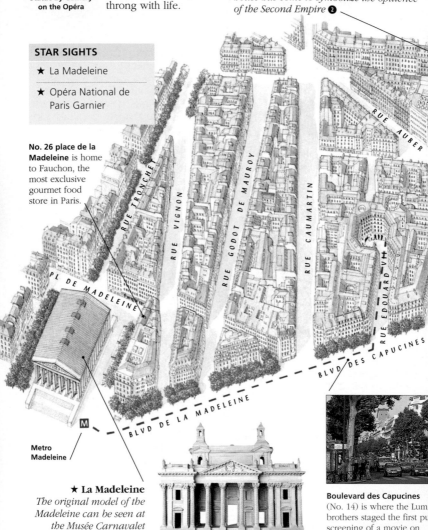

STAR SIGHTS

★ La Madeleine

★ Opéra National de Paris Garnier

No. 26 place de la Madeleine is home to Fauchon, the most exclusive gourmet food store in Paris.

RUE TRONCHET

RUE VIGNON

RUE GODOT DE MAUROY

RUE CAUMARTIN

RUE EDOUARD VII

RUE AUBER

PL DE MADELEINE

BLVD DES CAPUCINES

BLVD DE LA MADELEINE

Ⓜ

Metro Madeleine

★ **La Madeleine**
The original model of the Madeleine can be seen at the Musée Carnavalet (see p91) ❶

Boulevard des Capucines
(No. 14) is where the Lumière brothers staged the first public screening of a movie on December 28, 1895.

For hotels and restaurants in this region see pp550–5 and pp600–6

LOCATOR MAP
*See Street Finder
maps 4, 7, 8*

KEY

— — — Suggested route

0 meters	100
0 yards	100

Musée de l'Opéra contains the scores of every ballet and opera performed at the Opéra, and memorabilia ranging from Nijinsky's dancing shoes to Pavlova's tiara.

Metro Opéra

Place de l'Opéra was designed by Baron Haussmann and is one of Paris's busiest intersections.

Marochetti's *Mary Magdalene Ascending to Heaven* in La Madeleine

La Madeleine ❶

Pl de la Madeleine 75008. **Map** 3 C5.
Tel 01 44 51 69 00. Ⓜ *Madeleine.*
🕙 *9:30am–7pm daily.* ✝ *12:30pm Mon–Fri, 6:30pm Thu–Fri, 6pm Sat, 9:30am, 11am, 7pm Sun.* 📷
🎵 ***Concerts***

Modeled after a Greek temple, La Madeleine was begun in 1764 but not consecrated until 1845. Before that, there were proposals to turn it into a stock exchange, bank, or theater. Corinthian columns encircle the building, supporting a sculptured frieze. Three ceiling domes crown the inside, which is richly decorated with sculptures, rose marble, and gilt.

Opéra National de Paris Garnier ❷

Pl de l'Opéra 75009. **Map** 4 DF.
🎫 0892 89 90 90. Ⓜ *Opéra.*
🕙 *10am–4:30pm daily (until 5:30pm Jun–Sep and 12:30pm on matinée days).* ● *public hols.* ♿
💻 *www.operadeparis.fr*

Sometimes compared to a giant wedding cake, this lavish building was designed by Charles Garnier for Napoleon III in 1862. The Prussian War and the 1871 uprising delayed the opening until 1875.
The interior is famous for its Grand Staircase made of white Carrara marble, topped by a huge chandelier, as well as for its auditorium bedecked in red velvet and gold, with a false ceiling painted by Chagall in 1964. Restored to its full

glory, it is primarily used for dance, but shares operatic productions with the Opéra Bastille (see p153).

Grévin ❸

10 bd Montmartre 75009. **Map** 4 F4. ***Tel*** 01 47 70 85 05. Ⓜ *Grands Boulevards.* 🕙 *10am–6:30pm Mon–Fri (7pm Sat, Sun & school hols).* 📷 💻 *www.grevin.com*

Founded in 1882, this is a Paris landmark, on a par with Madame Tussauds. The historical scenes include Louis XIV at Versailles and the arrest of Louis XVI. Notable figures from the worlds of art, politics, film, and sports are also on display. On the first floor is a holography museum devoted to optical tricks. The museum also houses a 320-seat theater.

Sign outside the Grévin

Les Passages ❹

75002. **Map** 4 F5. Ⓜ *Bourse.*

The early 19th-century glass-roofed shopping arcades (known as *galeries* or *passages*) are concentrated between boulevard Montmartre and rue St-Marc. They house an eclectic mixture of small stores selling anything from designer jewelry to rare books and art supplies. One of the most charming is the Galerie Vivienne (off the rue Vivienne or the rue des Petits Champs) with its mosaic floor and excellent tearoom.

Place Vendôme **❺**

75001. **Map** 8 D1. **Ⓜ** *Tuileries.*

Perhaps the best example of 18th-century elegance in the city, the architect Jules Hardouin-Mansart's royal square was begun in 1698. The original plan was to house academies and embassies behind its arcaded façades, but instead bankers moved in and created sumptuous mansions for themselves. The square's most famous residents include Frédéric Chopin, who died here in 1849 at No. 12, and César Ritz, who established his famous hotel at No. 15 in 1898.

Monet's *Waterlilies (Nymphéas)* on display in the Musée de l'Orangerie

Galerie Nationale du Jeu de Paume **❻**

Jardin des Tuileries, place de la Concorde 75008. **Map** 7 C1. **Tel** 01 47 03 12 50. **Ⓜ** *Concorde.* ◯ *noon–9pm Tue, noon–7pm Wed–Fri, 10am–7pm Sat.* ● *Jan 1, May 1, Dec 25.* 🎦 ⓑ 📷 🖥 🖳 **www**.jeudepaume.org

The Jeu de Paume – literally "game of the palm" – was built as two royal tennis courts by Napoleon III in 1851 on the north side of the Tuileries gardens. The courts were later converted into an art gallery and exhibition space. The Jeu de Paume has rotating exhibitions of contemporary art and houses the Centre National de la Photographie. Its sister site is the Hôtel de Sully *(see p89).*

Place de la Concorde **❼**

75008. **Map** 7 C1. **Ⓜ** *Concorde.*

One of Europe's most magnificent and historic squares, covering over 20 acres (8 ha), the place de la Concorde was a swamp

The 3,200-year-old obelisk from Luxor

until the mid-18th century. It became the place Louis XV in 1775 when royal architect Jacques-Ange Gabriel was asked by the king to design a suitable setting for an equestrian statue of himself.

The monument, which lasted here less than 20 years, was replaced by the guillotine (the Black Widow, as it came to be known), and the square was renamed place de la Révolution. On January 21, 1793 Louis XVI was beheaded, followed by over 1,300 other victims including Marie Antoinette, Madame du Barry, Charlotte Corday (Marat's assassin), and revolutionary leaders Danton and Robespierre.

The blood-soaked square was optimistically renamed place de la Concorde after the Reign of Terror finally came to an end in 1794. A few decades later the 3,200-year-old Luxor obelisk was presented to King Louis-Philippe as a gift from the viceroy of Egypt (who also donated Cleopatra's Needle in London).

Flanking the rue Royale on the north side of the square are two of Gabriel's Neoclassical mansions, the Hôtel de la Marine and the exclusive Hôtel Crillon.

Musée de l'Orangerie **❽**

Jardin des Tuileries, place de la Concorde 75001. **Map** 7 C1. **Tel** 01 44 77 80 07. **Ⓜ** *Concorde.* ◯ *9am–6pm Wed–Mon.* ● *May 1, Dec 25.* 🎦 📷 ⓑ 🖥 *by appt.* 🖳 **www**.musee-orangerie.fr

Paintings from Claude Monet's crowning work, representing part of his waterlily series, fill the two oval upper floor rooms. Known as the *Nymphéas*, most of the canvases were painted between 1899 and 1921.

This superb work is complemented by the Walter-Guillaume collection, including 27 Renoirs, notably *Young Girls at the Piano*, works by Soutine and 14 Cézannes, including *The Red Rock.* Picasso is represented by works including *The Female Bathers*, and Rousseau by 9 paintings, notably *The Wedding.* Other works are by Matisse, Derain, Utrillo, and Modigliani.

Jardin des Tuileries **❾**

75001. **Map** 8 D1. **Ⓜ** *Tuileries, Concorde.* ◯ *Apr–May: 7am–9pm, Jun–Aug: 7am–11pm, Sep: 7am–9pm, Oct–Mar: 7:30am–7:30pm.*

These Neo-Classical gardens once belonged to the Palais des Tuileries, which the Communards razed to the ground in 1871. They were laid out in the 17th century by André Le Nôtre, who created the broad central avenue and geometric topiary. Ongoing restoration has created a new garden with lime and chestnut trees, and modern sculptures.

St-Roch 🔟

284 rue St-Honoré 75001. **Map** 8 E1. **Tel** *01 42 44 13 20.* 🅜 *Tuileries.* 🔵 *8:30am–7pm daily.* 🔵 *non-religious public hols.* 📷 **Concerts**

This huge church was designed by Jacques Lemercier, architect of the Louvre, and its foundation stone was laid by Louis XIV in 1653. It is a treasure house of religious art, much of it from now-vanished churches and monasteries, and contains the tombs of the playwright Pierre Corneille, the royal gardener André Le Nôtre, and the philosopher Denis Diderot.

Vien's *St. Denis Preaching to the Gauls* (1767) in St-Roch

Musée des Arts Décoratifs 1️⃣1️⃣

Palais du Louvre, 107 rue de Rivoli 75001. **Map** 8 E2. **Tel** *01 44 55 57 50.* 🅜 *Palais Royal, Tuileries.* 🔵 *11am–6pm Tue–Sun (until 9pm Thu).* **Library** 🔵 *public hols.* 📷 www.lesartsdecoratifs.fr

Occupying the northwest wing of the Palais du Louvre (along with the Musée de la Publicité and the Musée de la Mode et du Textile), this

The Buren Columns in the main courtyard of the Palais Royal

museum offers an eclectic mix of decorative art and domestic design from the Middle Ages to the present day. The Art Nouveau and Art Deco rooms include a reconstruction of the home of couturier Jeanne Lanvin. Other floors show Louis XIV, XV, and XVI styles of decoration and furniture. Contemporary designers are also represented. The restaurant has breathtaking views over the Tuileries gardens.

Arc de Triomphe du Carrousel 1️⃣2️⃣

Pl du Carrousel 75001. **Map** 8 E2. 🅜 *Palais Royal.*

This rose-marble arch was built by Napoleon to celebrate various military triumphs, notably the Battle of Austerlitz in 1805. The crowning statues, added in 1828, are copies of the famous Horses of St Mark's which Napoleon stole from Venice, which he was subsequently forced to return after his defeat at Waterloo in 1815.

Palais Royal 1️⃣3️⃣

Pl du Palais Royal 75001. **Map** 8 E1. 🅜 *Palais Royal.* **Buildings** 🔵 *to the public.*

This former royal palace has had a turbulent history. It was built by Cardinal Richelieu in the early 17th century, passing to the Crown on his death and becoming the childhood home of Louis XIV. Under the 18th-century royal dukes of Orléans, it became the epicenter of brilliant gatherings, interspersed with periods of gambling and debauchery. It was from here that the clarion call to revolution roused the mobs to storm the Bastille on July 14, 1789.

Today the southern section of the building houses the Councils of State and the Ministry of Culture. Just west of the palace at 2 rue de Richelieu is the Comédie Française, established by Louis XIV in 1680. Luxury stores occupy the rear section of the palace, where artists such as Colette and Cocteau once lived.

The Arc de Triomphe du Carrousel crowned by Victory riding a chariot

Musée du Louvre ⑭

The Musée du Louvre, containing one of the most important art collections in the world, has a history dating back to medieval times. First built as a fortress in 1190 by King Philippe-Auguste to protect Paris against Viking raids, it lost its keep in the reign of François I, who replaced it with a Renaissance-style building. Thereafter, four centuries of kings and emperors improved and enlarged it. Visitors should request a schedule of room closures from the information point since not all rooms are open on any given day.

The Louvre's east façade, facing St-Germain l'Auxerrois

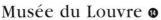

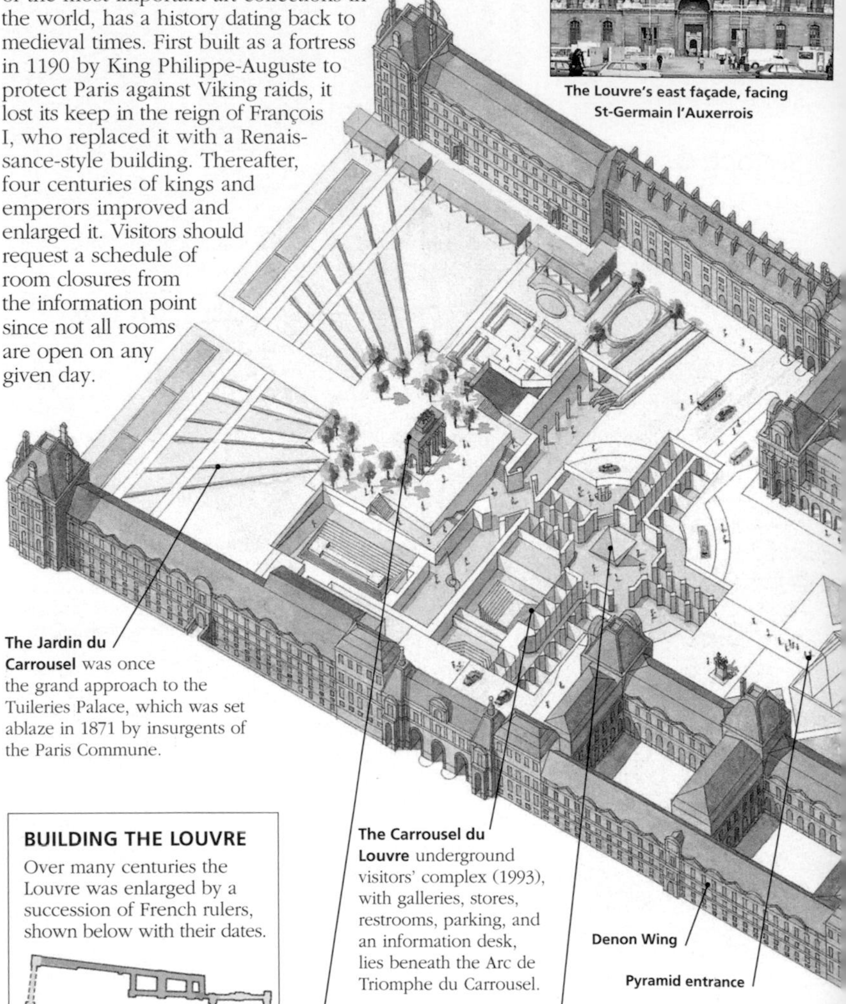

The Jardin du Carrousel was once the grand approach to the Tuileries Palace, which was set ablaze in 1871 by insurgents of the Paris Commune.

The Carrousel du Louvre underground visitors' complex (1993), with galleries, stores, restrooms, parking, and an information desk, lies beneath the Arc de Triomphe du Carrousel.

Denon Wing

Pyramid entrance

The inverted glass pyramid brings light to the subterranean complex, echoing the museum's main entrance in the Cour Napoléon.

BUILDING THE LOUVRE

Over many centuries the Louvre was enlarged by a succession of French rulers, shown below with their dates.

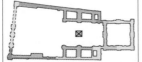

MAJOR ALTERATIONS

▨	Reign of François I (1515–47)
▨	Catherine de' Medici (about 1560)
▨	Reign of Henri IV (1589–1610)
▨	Reign of Louis XIII (1610–43)
▨	Reign of Louis XIV (1643–1715)
▨	Reign of Napoleon I (1804–15)
▨	Reign of Napoleon III (1852–70)
▨	IM Pei (1989) (architect)

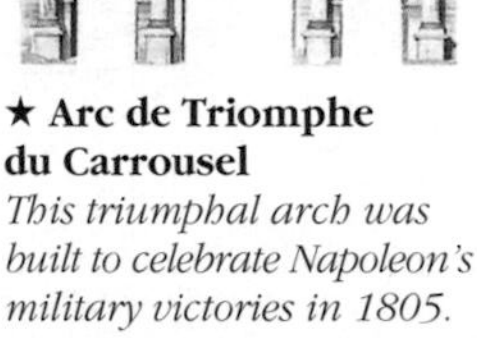

★ **Arc de Triomphe du Carrousel**
This triumphal arch was built to celebrate Napoleon's military victories in 1805.

STAR FEATURES

★ Perrault Colonnade

★ Medieval Moats

★ Arc de Triomphe du Carrousel

For hotels and restaurants in this region see pp550–5 and pp600–6

THE GLASS PYRAMID

Plans for the modernization and expansion of the Louvre were first conceived in 1981. They included the transfer of the Ministry of Finance from the Richelieu wing of the Louvre to new offices elsewhere, as well as a

new main entrance designed by architect I.M. Pei in 1989. Made of metal and glass, the pyramid enables the visitor to see the buildings around the palace, while allowing light down into the underground visitors' reception area.

VISITORS' CHECKLIST

Map 12 E2. *Automatic ticket booths at Carrousel du Louvre, 99 rue de Rivoli, 75001.* Ⓜ *Palais Royal, Musée du Louvre.* 🚌 *21, 24, 27, 39, 48, 68, 69, 72, 81, 95.* Ⓡ *Châtelet-Les-Halles.* Ⓟ *Louvre.* Ⓟ *Carrousel du Louvre (entrance via av du Général Lemonnier); pl du Louvre, rue St-Honoré.* 🕐 *9am–6pm Mon, Thu, Sat, & Sun, 9am–10pm Wed & Fri. History of the Louvre rooms open Sat, Sun only.* 🕐 *1 Jan, 1 May, 25 Dec.* 🎟 *(free 1st Sun of each month and for under 18; reduced price for Nocturnals after 6pm).* 🔧 *partial 01 40 20 59 90.* 📷 *phone 01 40 20 52 09.* 🎭 ***Lectures, films, concerts** 01 40 20 55 55.* 🔴🔵🟢 www.louvre.fr ***Advance bookings:*** www.ticketweb.com

Cour Marly is the glass-roofed courtyard that now houses the *Marly Horses (see p103)*.

Richelieu Wing

Cour Puget

Hall Napoléon is situated under the pyramid.

Cour Khorsabad

Sully Wing

Cour Carrée

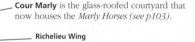

★ **Perrault's Colonnade**
The east façade, with its majestic rows of columns, was built by Claude Perrault, who worked on the Louvre with Louis Le Vau in the mid-17th century.

The Salle des Caryatides is named after the four monumental statues created by Jean Goujon in 1550 to support the upper gallery. Built for Henri II, it is the oldest room in the palace.

Cour Napoléon

The Louvre of Charles V
In about 1360, Charles V transformed Philippe-Auguste's old fortress, with its distinctive tower and keep, into a royal residence.

★ **Medieval Moats**
The base of the twin towers and the drawbridge support of Philippe-Auguste's fortress can be seen in the excavated area.

Exploring the Louvre's Collection

Owing to the vast size of the Louvre's collection, it is useful to set a few viewing priorities before starting. The collection of European paintings (1400–1848) is comprehensive, with over half the works by French artists. The extensively renovated departments of Oriental, Egyptian, Greek, Etruscan, and Roman antiquities feature numerous new acquisitions and rare treasures. The varied display of *objets d'art* includes furniture and jewelry.

The Raft of the Medusa (1819)
by Théodore Géricault

EUROPEAN PAINTING: 1200 TO 1848

Painting from northern Europe (Flemish, Dutch, German, and English) is well covered. One of the earliest Flemish works is Jan van Eyck's *Madonna of the Chancellor Rolin* (about 1435), showing the Chancellor of Burgundy kneeling in prayer before the Virgin and Child. Hieronymus Bosch's *Ship of Fools* (1500) is a satirical account of the futility of human existence.

Mona Lisa (about 1504) by
Leonardo da Vinci

In the fine Dutch collection, Rembrandt's *Self-portrait*, his *Disciples at Emmaus* (1648), and *Bathsheba* (1654) are examples of the artist's genius.

The three major German painters of the 15th and 16th centuries are represented by important works. There is a youthful *Self-portrait* (1493) by Albrecht Dürer, a *Venus* (1529) by Lucas Cranach, and a portrait of the humanist scholar Erasmus by Hans Holbein.

The impressive collection of Italian paintings is arranged in chronological order from 1200 to 1800. The father figures of the early Renaissance, Cimabue and Giotto, are here, as is Fra Angelico, with his *Coronation of the Virgin* (1430–32), and Raphaël, with his stately portrait of Count Baldassare Castiglione (1514–15). Several paintings by Leonardo da Vinci are on display, for instance the *Virgin with the Infant Jesus and St. Anne*, which is as enchanting as his *Mona Lisa*.

The Louvre's fine collection of French painting ranges from the 14th century to 1848.

Paintings after this date are housed in the Musée d'Orsay *(see pp120–21)*. Outstanding is Jean Fouquet's portrait of Charles VII (1450–55). The great 18th-century painter of melancholy, J.A. Watteau, is represented, as is J.H. Fragonard, master of the Rococo, whose delightfully frivolous subjects are evident in *The Bathers* from 1770.

EUROPEAN SCULPTURE: 1100 TO 1848

Early Flemish and German sculpture in the collection has many masterpieces such as Tilman Riemenschneider's *Virgin of the Annunciation* from the end of the 15th century and a life-sized nude figure of the penitent Mary Magdalen by Gregor Erhart (early 16th century). An important work of Flemish sculpture is Adrian de Vries's long-limbed *Mercury and Psyche* from 1593, which was originally made for the court of Rudolph II in Prague.

The French section opens with early Romanesque works, such as the figure of Christ by a 12th-century Burgundian sculptor, and a head of St. Peter. With its eight black-hooded mourners, the late 15th-century tomb of Philippe Pot (a high-ranking official in Burgundy) is one of the more unusual pieces. Diane de Poitiers, Henri II's mistress, had a large figure of her namesake Diana, goddess of the hunt, installed in the courtyard of her castle west of Paris. It is now in the Louvre.

The tomb of Philippe Pot (late 15th century) by
Antoine le Moiturier

The celebrated *Marly Horses* (1745) by Guillaume Coustou

The works of French sculptor Pierre Puget (1620–94) have been assembled in the Cour Puget. They include a figure of Milo of Crotona, the Greek athlete who got his hands caught in the cleft of a tree stump and was eaten by a lion. The wild horses of Marly now stand in the Cour Marly, surrounded by other masterpieces of French sculpture, including Jean-Antoine Houdon's early 19th-century busts of famous men such as Diderot and Voltaire.

The collection of Italian sculpture includes such splendid exhibits as Michelangelo's *Slaves* and Benvenuto Cellini's Fontainebleau *Nymph*.

ORIENTAL, EGYPTIAN, GREEK, ETRUSCAN, AND ROMAN ANTIQUITIES

A substantial overhaul of the Louvre has boosted its collection of antiquities, which range from the Neolithic period to the fall of the Roman Empire. Among the exhibits are Greek and Roman glassware dating from the 6th century BC. Important works of Mesopotamian art include one of the world's oldest legal documents, a basalt block bearing the code of the Babylonian King Hammurabi, dating from about 1700 BC.

The warlike Assyrians are represented by delicate carvings and a spectacular reconstruction of part of Sargon II's (722–705 BC) palace with its winged bulls. A fine example of Persian art is the enameled brickwork depicting the king of Persia's personal guard of archers (5th century BC).

Most Egyptian art was made for the dead, who were provided with the things they needed for the afterlife. Examples include the lifelike funeral portraits such as the *Squatting Scribe*, and several sculptures of married couples.

The departments of Greek, Roman and Etruscan antiquities contain a vast array of fragments, among them some exceptional pieces. There is a geometric head from the Cyclades (2700 BC) and an elegant swan-necked bowl hammered out of a gold sheet (2500 BC). The two most famous Greek marble statues, the *Winged Victory of Samothrace* and the *Venus de Milo*, both belong to the Hellenistic period (late 3rd to 2nd century BC), when more natural-looking human forms were produced.

The undisputed star of the Etruscan collection is the terra cotta sarcophagus of a married couple who look as though they are attending an eternal banquet, while the highlight of the Roman section is a 2nd-century bronze head of the Emperor Hadrian.

***Squatting Scribe* (about 2500 BC), a lifelike Egyptian funeral sculpture**

Venus de Milo (Greece, late 3rd–early 2nd century BC)

OBJETS D'ART

The catchall term *objets d'art* (art objects) covers a vast range of items: jewelry, furniture, clocks, watches, sundials, tapestries, miniatures, silver and glassware, cutlery, Byzantine and Parisian carved ivory, Limoges enamels, porcelain, French and Italian stoneware, rugs, snuffboxes, scientific instruments, and armor. The Louvre has well over 8,000 pieces, from many ages and regions.

Many of these precious objects came from the Abbey of St-Denis, where the kings of France were crowned. The treasures include a serpentine stone plate from the 1st century AD with a 9th-century border of gold and precious stones, a porphyry vase which Super Abbot of St-Denis, had mounted in gold in the shape of an eagle, and the golden scepter made for King Charles V in around 1380.

The French crown jewels include the coronation crowns of Louis XV and Napoleon, scepters, swords, and other accessories of the coronation ceremonies. On view also is the Regent, one of the purest diamonds in the world, which Louis XV wore at his coronation in 1722.

One whole room is taken up with a series of tapestries called the *Hunts of Maximilian*, originally executed for Emperor Charles V in 1530. The large collection of French furniture ranges from the 16th to the 19th centuries and is assembled by period, or in rooms devoted to donations by distinguished collectors. On display are pieces by exceptionally prominent furniture-makers such as André-Charles Boulle, cabinet-maker to Louis XIV, who worked at the Louvre in the late 17th to mid-18th centuries.

Gilded bronze statues by a number of sculptors, decorating the central square of the Palais de Chaillot

CHAMPS-ELYSEES AND INVALIDES

The River Seine bisects this area, much of which is built on a monumental scale, from the imposing 18th-century buildings of Les Invalides to the Art Nouveau avenues surrounding the Eiffel Tower. Two of Paris's grandest avenues dominate the neighborhood to the north of the Seine: the Champs-Elysées has many fine hotels and stores but today is more downmarket;

Ornate lamppost on Pont Alexandre III

while the more chic rue du Faubourg St-Honoré has the heavily guarded Palais de l'Elysée. The village of Chaillot was absorbed into the city in the 19th century, and many of its opulent Second Empire mansions are now embassies or company headquarters. Streets around the place du Trocadéro and Palais de Chaillot are packed full of museums and elegant cafés.

SIGHTS AT A GLANCE

Historic Buildings and Streets
Avenue des Champs-Elysées ❷
Palais de l'Elysée ❸
Les Egouts ⓮
No 29 Avenue Rapp ⓱
Champ-de-Mars ⓲
Ecole Militaire ⓳
Hôtel des Invalides ㉑

Museums and Galleries
Petit Palais ❹
Grand Palais ❺
Musée d'Art Moderne de la Ville de Paris ❼
Musée Galliera ❽

Musée National des Arts Asiatiques Guimet ❾
Cité de l'Architecture et du Patrimoine ⓾
Musée Dapper ⓫
Palais de Chaillot ⓭
Musée du Quai Branly ⓯
Musée de l'Armée ㉒
Musée Rodin ㉕
Musée Maillol ㉗

Churches
St-Louis-des-Invalides ㉓
Dôme Church ㉔
Sainte-Clotilde ㉖

Monuments and Fountains
Arc de Triomphe ❶
Eiffel Tower p113 ⓰

Modern Architecture
UNESCO ⓴

Gardens
Jardins du Trocadéro ⓬

Bridges
Pont Alexandre III ❻

GETTING THERE
Metro stations in this area include Etoile, Trocadéro, and Champs-Elysées. Bus routes 42 and 73 serve the Champs-Elysées; routes 82 and 69 serve avenue de Suffren and rue St-Dominique respectively.

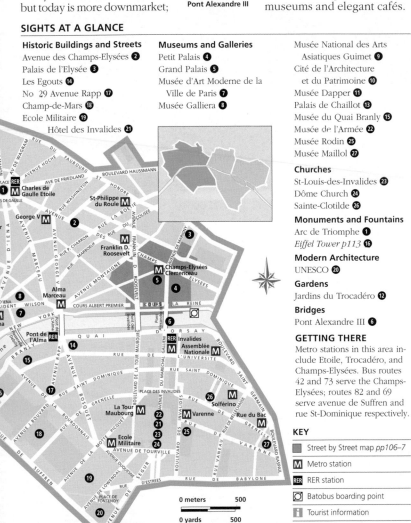

KEY
▨	Street by Street map *pp106–7*
Ⓜ	Metro station
RER	RER station
⧠	Batobus boarding point
ⓘ	Tourist information

0 meters   500
0 yards   500

Street by Street: Champs-Elysées

The formal gardens that line the Champs-Elysées from the place de la Concorde to the Rond-Point have changed little since they were laid out by the architect Jacques Hittorff in 1838. The gardens were used as the setting for the World Fair of 1855, which included the Palais de l'Industrie, Paris's response to London's Crystal Palace. The Palais was later replaced by the Grand Palais and the Petit Palais, which was created as a showpiece of the Third Republic for the Universal Exhibition of 1900. They sit on either side of an impressive vista that stretches from the place Clémenceau across the elegant curve of the Pont Alexandre III, with its four strong anchoring columns, to the Invalides.

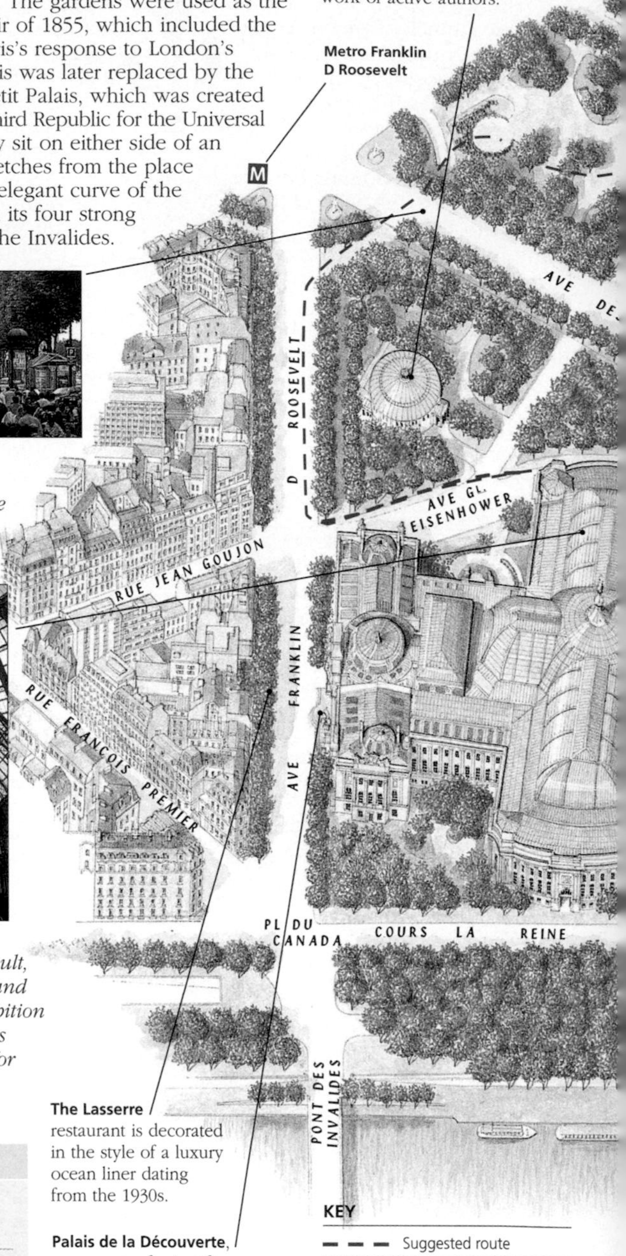

Théâtre du Rond Point, an original Champs-Elysées building, presents the work of active authors.

Metro Franklin D Roosevelt

★ **Avenue des Champs-Elysées**
This was the setting for the victory parades following the two World Wars ❷

★ **Grand Palais**
Designed by Charles Girault, and built between 1897 and 1900, this elaborate exhibition hall with its splendid glass dome is frequently used for major exhibitions ❺

The Lasserre
restaurant is decorated in the style of a luxury ocean liner dating from the 1930s.

Palais de la Découverte,
a museum of scientific discovery, was originally opened in the Grand Palais for the World Fair of 1937.

STAR SIGHTS

★ Avenue des Champs-Elysées

★ Grand Palais

★ Petit Palais

KEY

- - - Suggested route

| 0 meters | 100 |
| 0 yards | 100 |

The Jardins des Champs-Elysées, with their fountains, flowerbeds, and pleasure pavilions, have been a popular spot since the 19th century.

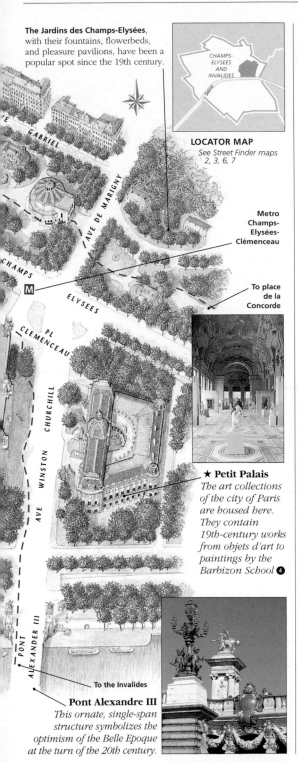

LOCATOR MAP
See Street Finder maps 2, 3, 6, 7

Metro
Champs-
Elysées-
Clémenceau

To place de la Concorde

★ **Petit Palais**
The art collections of the city of Paris are housed here. They contain 19th-century works from objets d'art to paintings by the Barbizon School ❹

To the Invalides

Pont Alexandre III
This ornate, single-span structure symbolizes the optimism of the Belle Epoque at the turn of the 20th century.

The east façade of the Arc de Triomphe

Arc de Triomphe ❶

Place Charles de Gaulle, 75008. **Map** 2 D4. Ⓜ *Charles de Gaulle-Etoile.* **Tel** *01 55 37 73 77.* **Museum** ◯ *Apr–Sep: 10am–11pm daily; Oct–Mar: 10am–10:30pm daily (last adm 30 mins earlier).* ● *Jan 1, May 1, May 8, Jul 14, Nov 11, Dec 25.*
◯ ♨ ▯

After his greatest victory, the Battle of Austerlitz in 1805, Napoleon promised his men they would "go home beneath triumphal arches." The first stone of what was to become the world's most famous triumphal arch was laid the following year. But disruptions to architect Jean Chalgrin's plans and the demise of Napoleonic power delayed completion. Standing 164 ft (50 m) high, the Arc is encrusted with reliefs, shields, and sculptures. The viewing platform offers spendid views.

On November 11, 1920 the body of the Unknown Soldier was placed beneath the arch to commemorate the dead of World War I. The tomb's eternal flame is lit every evening.

High relief by J.P. Corot, celebrating the Triumph of Napoleon

BARON HAUSSMANN

A lawyer by training and civil servant by profession, Georges-Eugène Haussmann (1809–91) was appointed Prefect of the Seine in 1852 by Napoleon III. For 17 years Haussmann was responsible for the urban modernization of Paris. With a team of the best architects and engineers of the day, he demolished the crowded, insanitary streets of the medieval city and created a well-ventilated and ordered capital within a geometrical grid. The new scheme involved redesigning the area at one end of the Champs-Elysées and creating a star of 12 avenues, which were centered on the new Arc de Triomphe.

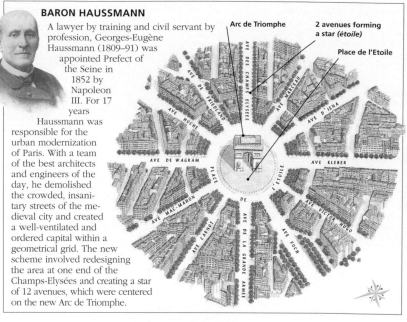

Avenue des Champs-Elysées ❷

75008. **Map** 3 A5. **M** *Charles de Gaulle-Etoile, George V, Franklin D Roosevelt, Champs-Elysées - Clemenceau, Concorde.*

The majestic avenue "of the Elysian Fields" (the name refers to a mythical Greek heaven for heroes), first laid out in the 1660s by the landscape designer André Le Nôtre, forms a 2 mile (3 km) straight line from the huge place de la Concorde to the Arc de Triomphe. The 19th century saw it transformed from horseride into elegant boulevard. Today it's a crowded tourist trap with notorious traffic, but the Champs-Elysées keeps its style, its memories, and a special place in the French heart. National parades are held here, the finish of the annual Tour de France bicycle race is always in the Champs-Elysées, and, above all, it is where Parisians instinctively go at times of great national celebration.

Palais de l'Elysée ❸

55 rue du Faubourg-St-Honoré 75008. **Map** 3 B5. **M** *St-Philippe-du-Roule.* ● *to the public.*

Elysée guard

Amid splendid gardens, the Elysée Palace was built in 1718 and has been the official residence of the President of the Republic since 1848. Several occupants left their mark. Louis XV's mistress, Madame de Pompadour, had the whole site enlarged. After the Revolution, it became a dance hall. In the 19th century, it was home to Napoleon's sister (Caroline Murat) and his wife, Empress Josephine. The President's Apartments are today on the first floor.

Petit Palais ❹

Av Winston Churchill 75008. **Map** 7 B1. **Tel** *01 53 43 40 00.* **M** *Champs-Elysées-Clemenceau.* ◐ *10am–6pm Tue–Sun.* ● *public hols.* ✎ ✚ *for exhibitions.* ◙ ♿ 🖥 *www.petitpalais.paris.fr*

Built for the Universal Exhibition in 1900 to stage a major display of French art, this jewel of a building was renovated in 2005 and houses the Musée des Beaux-Arts de la Ville de Paris. The architect, Charles Girault, arranged the

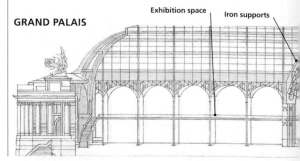

GRAND PALAIS

Pont Alexandre III, built 1896–1900 for the Universal Exhibition

palace around a semicircular courtyard and garden. Permanent exhibits, housed on the Champs-Elysées side, include the Dutuit Collection of medieval and Renaissance *objets d'art*, paintings, and drawings; the Tuck Collection of 18th-century furniture and *objets d'art*; and the City of Paris collection, with work by Ingres, Delacroix, and Courbet,

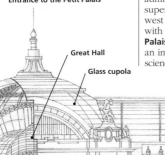

Entrance to the Petit Palais

and the landscape painters of the Barbizon School. Temporary exhibitions are housed in the Cours de la Reine wing.

Grand Palais ❺

Porte A, av Général Eisenhower 75008. **Map** 7 A1. **Tel** *01 44 13 17 17.* Ⓜ *Champs-Elysées-Clemenceau.* ◯ *for temporary exhibitions only; 10am–8pm Wed–Mon.* ● *May 1, Dec 25.* 🎫 🗑 🕭 🗂 🏠 ☐ 🛈
Palais de la Decouverte: *av Franklin D. Roosevelt 75008.* **Tel** *01 56 43 20 21.* Ⓜ *Franklin D. Roosevelt.* ◯ *9:30am–6pm Tue–Sat, 10am–7pm Sun & public hols.* 🎫 ☐ 🛈 www.grandpalais.fr

Built at the same time as the Petit Palais opposite, this huge, glass-roofed palace has a fine Classical façade adorned with statuary and Art Nouveau ironwork. Bronze flying horses and chariots stand at the four corners. The Great Hall and the glass cupola can be admired during the palace's superb exhibitions. On the west side of the building, with a separate entrance, the **Palais de la Découverte** is an imaginative child-oriented science museum.

Pont Alexandre III ❻

75008. **Map** 7 A1. Ⓜ *Champs-Elysées-Clemenceau.*

This is Paris's prettiest bridge, with exuberant Art Nouveau decoration of gilt and bronze lamps, cupids and cherubs, nymphs, and winged horses at either end. It was built between 1896 and 1900 to commemorate the 1892 French-Russian alliance, and in time for the Universal Exhibition in 1900. Pont Alexandre III was named after Tsar Alexander III (father of Nicholas II), who laid the foundation stone in October 1896.

The style of the bridge reflects that of the Grand Palais, to which it leads on the Right Bank. The construction of the bridge is a marvel of 19th-century engineering. It consists of an 18-ft (6-m) high single-span steel arch across the Seine. The design was subject to strict controls that prevented the bridge from obscuring the view of the Champs-Elysées or the Invalides, so today you can still enjoy the magnificent views from here.

Great Hall

Glass cupola

Quadriga **(chariot and four horses) by Récipon**

Musée d'Art Moderne de la Ville de Paris ❼

Palais du Tokyo, 11 av du Président-Wilson 75016. **Map** 6 E1. **Tel** 01 53 67 40 00. Ⓜ *Iéna, Alma-Marceau.* ◯ *10am-6pm Tue-Sun (until 10pm Thu for temporary exhibitions).* ⬤ *Dec 25, Jan 1.* 🎫 *for temporary exhibitions.* ♿ 🎥 📷 🛈 **www.**mam.paris.fr

This museum in the east wing of the Palais de Tokyo covers trends in 20th-century art. The Fauves and Cubists are well represented here. Highlights include Raoul Dufy's gigantic mural, *The Spirit of Electricity* (created for the 1937 World Fair), and Matisse's *The Dance* (1932). There is also a collection of Art Deco furniture.

Musée Galliera ❽

10 ave Pierre 1er de Serbie 75116. **Map** 6 D1. **Tel** 01 56 52 86 00. Ⓜ *Iéna, Alma-Marceau.* ◯ *10am-6pm daily & 2–6pm some public hols (check website).* ⬤ *for renovation until spring 2012.* 🎫 **Children's room. www.**galliera.paris.fr

Devoted to the evolution of fashion, this museum, also known as the Musée de la Mode et du Costume, is housed in the Renaissance-style palace built for the Duchesse Maria de Ferrari Galliera in 1892. The collection includes more than 100,000 outfits and fashion accessories from the 18th century to the present day. Donations have been made by such fashionable women as Baronne Hélène de Rothschild and Princess Grace of Monaco. Eminent couturiers such as Balmain and Balenciaga have donated their designs to the museum.

Often extremely fragile, the fashion exhibits are displayed in rotation, usually in two major exhibitions each year. These shows can highlight a particular couturier's career or explore a single theme.

Trocadéro fountains in front of the Palais de Chaillot

Musée Dapper ⓫

35bis rue Paul-Valéry, 75016. **Map** 2 D5. **Tel** 01 45 00 91 75. Ⓜ *Victor-Hugo.* ◯ *11am– 7pm Wed–Mon.* 🎫 **www.**dapper.com.fr

A world-class ethnographic research center, this is one of France's premier showcases of African art and culture. Located in an attractive building with an "African" garden, it is a treasure house of color and powerful, evocative work from the black nations. The focus is on pre-colonial folk arts, with sculpture, carvings, and tribal work, but there is later art, too. The highlight is tribal masks, with a dazzling, extra-ordinary array of richly carved religious, ritual, and funerary masks, as well as theatrical ones used for comic, magical, or symbolic performances.

Jardins du Trocadéro ⓬

75016. **Map** 6 D2. Ⓜ *Trocadéro.* *Cinéaqua Tel 01 40 69 23 23.* ◯ *10am–8pm daily.* ⬤ *Jul 14.* 🎫

These beautiful gardens cover 25 acres (10 ha). Their centerpiece is a long rectangular ornamental pool, bordered by stone and bronze-gilt statues, which looks spectacular at night when the fountains are illuminated. The statues include *Woman* by Georges Braque and *Horse* by Georges Lucien Guyot. On either side of the pool, the slopes of the Chaillot hill lead gently down to the Seine and the Pont d'Iéna. Cinéaqua, the hi-tech aquarium here, has over 25 sharks and a petting pool for children.

Palais de Chaillot ⓭

Pl du Trocadéro 75016. **Map** 5 C2. Ⓜ *Trocadéro.* **Théâtre National de Chaillot Tel** 01 53 65 30 00. **Musée de l'Homme Tel** 01 44 05 72 72. ◯ *Wed–Mon.* **Musée de la Marine Tel** 01 53 65 69 69. ◯ *Wed–Mon.* ⬤ *Jan 1, May 1, Dec 25.*

The Palais, with its huge, curved colonnaded wings each culminating in a vast pavilion, has three museums and a theater. Designed in Neoclassical style for the 1937 Paris Exhibition by Azéma, Louis-Auguste Boileau, and Jacques Carlu, it is adorned with sculptures and low reliefs. On the walls of the pavilions are gold inscriptions that were written by the poet and essayist, Paul Valéry. The square *(parvis)* between the two pavilions has bronze

Musée National des Arts Asiatiques Guimet ⑨

6 pl d'Iéna 75016. **Map** 6 D1.
Tel 01 56 52 53 00. Ⓜ *Iéna.*
⬜ *10am–6pm Wed–Mon.* 📷 📱 ♿
🔲 *Panthéon Bouddhique, 19 av d'Iéna. Tel 01 40 73 88 00.*
www.guimet.fr

One of the world's leading museums of Asian art, the Guimet has a fine collection of Cambodian (Khmer) art. It was set up in Lyon in 1889 by Emile Guimet, and later moved to Paris. It includes a comprehensive Asian research center.

Buddha head from Musée Guimet

Cité de l'Architecture et du Patrimoine ⑩

Palais de Chaillot, pl du Trocadéro 75016. **Map** 5 C2. *Tel 01 58 51 52 00.* Ⓜ *Trocadéro.* ⬜ *11am–7pm Wed–Mon (until 9pm Thu).* ⚫ *Jan 1, May 1, Dec 25.* 📷 🍴 🏠
www.citechaillot.fr

This museum charts French architecture through the ages and includes models of great French cathedrals, such as Chartres (*see pp308–11*). In addition, there is a reconstruction of an apartment designed by Le Corbusier.

PALAIS DE CHAILLOT

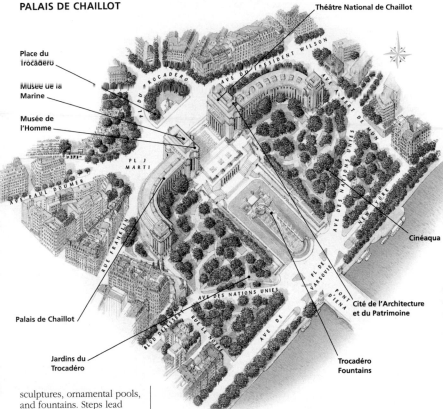

Théâtre National de Chaillot

Place du Trocadéro

Musée de la Marine

Musée de l'Homme

Cinéaqua

Cité de l'Architecture et du Patrimoine

Palais de Chaillot

Jardins du Trocadéro

Trocadéro Fountains

sculptures, ornamental pools, and fountains. Steps lead down from the terrace to the **Théatre National de Chaillot**, which has an experimental approach to productions covering all genres.

The **Musée de l'Homme**, in the west wing, stages tempor-ary exhibitions tracing human evolution through a series of anthropological exhibits. The museum is undergoing extensive renovation. Next door is the **Musée de la Marine**, devoted to French naval history and aspects of the modern-day navy. The east wing contains the **Cité de l'Architecture et du Patrimoine** (*see above*).

Les Egouts ⑭

Opposite 93 quai d'Orsay 75007.
Map 6 F2. ⓕ *01 53 68 27 81 (in
English).* Ⓜ *Alma-Marceau.*
ⓇⒺⓇ *Pont-de-l'Alma.* ◯ *11am–4pm
(5pm in summer) Sat–Wed.*
◯ *last 3 wks Jan.* 🎞 ✇ ▯

One of Baron Haussmann's
finest achievements, the majority of Paris's sewers (*égouts*)
date from the Second Empire. If
laid end to end the 1,490 miles
(2,400 km) of sewers would
stretch from Paris to Istanbul.
Tours of this popular attraction
have been limited to an area
around the quai d'Orsay
entrance and are on foot. Visitors
can discover the mysteries of
underground Paris in the
sewer museum. There are also
displays showing how the
machinery used in the sewers
has changed over the years.

Musée du Quai Branly ⑮

37 quai Branly 75007. **Map** 6 E2.
Tel *01 56 61 70 00.* Ⓜ *Alma-
Marceau.* ⓇⒺⓇ *Pont-de-l'Alma.*
◯ *11am–7pm Tue, Wed, Sun, 11am–
9pm Thu, Fri, Sat.* ◯ *May 1, Dec 25.*
🎞 *free 1st Sun of month & for
18–25s after 6pm Sat.*
🈸 ▯ *Exhibitions,
theater, film, library.*
www.quaibranly.fr

Built to give the
arts of Africa,
Asia, Oceania,
and the Americas
a platform as shin-
ing as that for
Western art in the
city, this museum
has a massive collec-
tion of more than
300,000 objects. It is particularly
strong on Africa, with stone,
wooden, and ivory masks, as
well as ceremonial tools. The
Jean Nouvel-designed building, which is raised on stilts, is
a worthwhile sight in itself,
while the ingenious use of
glass in its construction allows
the surrounding greenery to
act as a natural backdrop.

**Aztec mask, Musée
du Quai Branly**

Eiffel Tower ⑯

See p113.

**Original Art Nouveau doorway at
No. 29 avenue Rapp**

No. 29 Avenue Rapp ⑰

75007. **Map** 6 E2. Ⓜ *Alma-
Marceau.* ⓇⒺⓇ *Pont-de-l'Alma.*

A prime example of Art
Nouveau architecture,
No. 29 avenue Rapp won its
designer, Jules Lavirotte, first
prize at the Concours des
Façades de la Ville de Paris
in 1901. Its ceramics and
brickwork are decorated with
animal and flower motifs
intermingling with female
figures. These are super-
imposed on a multi-
colored sandstone
base to produce a
façade that is
deliberately erotic,
and was certainly
subversive in its
day. Also worth
visiting nearby is
Lavirotte's building,
complete with watch-
tower, which can be
found in the square Rapp.

Champ-de-Mars ⑱

75007. **Map** 6 E3. Ⓜ *Ecole-Militaire.*
ⓇⒺⓇ *Champ-de-Mars–Tour-Eiffel.*

The vast gardens stretching
from the Eiffel Tower to the
Ecole Militaire (Military
School) were originally a
parade ground for young
officer cadets. The area has
since been used for horse-
racing, balloon ascents, and
mass ceremonies to celebrate

the anniversary of the
Revolution on July 14th. The
first ceremony was held in
1790 in the presence of a
glum captive, Louis XVI.
Mammoth exhibitions were
held here in the late 19th
century, among them the
1889 World Fair for which the
Eiffel Tower was erected.

Ecole Militaire ⑲

1 pl Joffre 75007. **Map** 6 F4.
Ⓜ *Ecole-Militaire.* **Visits** *by special
permission only – contact the
Commandant in writing.*

The Royal Military Academy
of Louis XV was founded in
1751 to educate 500 sons of
impoverished officers. Louis
XV and Madame de
Pompadour commissioned
architect Jacques-Ange
Gabriel to design a building
that would rival Louis XIV's
Hôtel des Invalides. Financing
the building became a
problem so a lottery was
authorized and a tax was
raised on playing-cards. One
of the main features is the
central pavilion – a magnificent example of the French
Classical style, with ten
Corinthian columns and a
quadrangular dome. Four
figures adorn the entablature
frieze, symbolizing France,
Victory, Force, and Peace.
An early cadet at the
academy was Napoleon,
whose final report stated that
"he could go far if the cir-
cumstances are right."

**A 1751 engraving showing the
planning of the Ecole Militaire**

Eiffel Tower ⑯

Eiffel Tower seen from the Trocadéro

Built for the Universal Exhibition of 1889, and to commemorate the centennial of the Revolution, the 1,063 ft (324 m) Eiffel Tower (Tour Eiffel) was meant to be a temporary addition to Paris's skyline. Designed by Gustave Eiffel, it was fiercely decried by 19th-century aesthetes. It stood as the world's tallest building until 1931, when New York's Empire State Building was completed.

VISITORS' CHECKLIST

Champ-de-Mars, 75007. **Map** 6 D3. **Tel** 08 92 70 12 39. Ⓜ Bir Hakeim. 🚌 42, 69, 72, 82, 87 to Champ-de-Mars. 🆁 Champ-de-Mars. Ⓞ Tour Eiffel. ◯ mid-Jun–Aug: 9am–12:45am; Sep–mid-Jun: 9:30am–11:45pm daily. 🅿 ⭕ 🍴 📷 ♿ www.tour-eiffel.fr

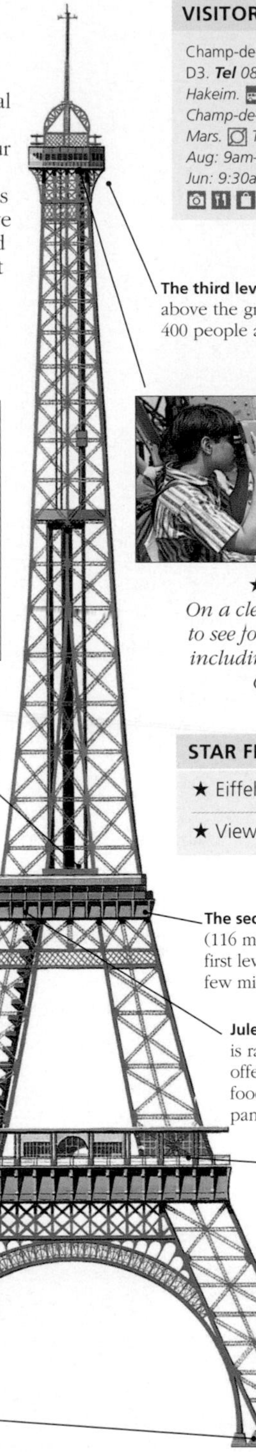

The third level, 905 ft (276 m) above the ground, can hold 400 people at a time.

DARING FEATS

The tower has always inspired crazy stunts. In 1912, Reichelt, a Parisian tailor, attempted to fly from the parapet with only a cape for wings. He plunged to his death in front of a large crowd.

Stuntman Reichelt

★ **Viewing Gallery**
On a clear day it is possible to see for 45 miles (72 km), including a distant view of Chartres Cathedral.

STAR FEATURES

★ Eiffel Bust

★ Viewing Gallery

The double-decker elevators have a limited capacity, and during the tourist season there can be long waits. Waiting in line for the elevators requires patience and a good head for heights.

Cineiffel
This small audio-visual museum shows historical film footage of the tower.

The second level is at 380 ft (116 m), separated from the first level by 359 steps or a few minutes in the elevator.

Jules Verne restaurant is rated highly in Paris, offering not only superb food but a breathtaking panoramic view.

★ **Eiffel Bust**
The achievement of Eiffel (1832–1923) was honored by Antoine Bourdelle, who placed this bust under the tower in 1929.

The first level, 187 ft (57 m) high, can be reached by elevator or by 345 steps.

LES INVALIDES

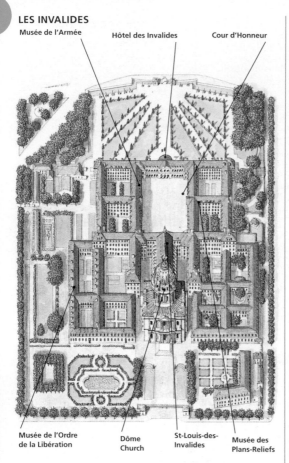

Musée de l'Armée   Hôtel des Invalides   Cour d'Honneur

Musée de l'Ordre de la Libération   Dôme Church   St-Louis-des-Invalides   Musée des Plans-Reliefs

Designed by Libéral Bruand, it was completed in 1676 by Jules Hardouin-Mansart. He later incorporated the Dôme Church, with its golden roof, which was built as Louis XIV's private chapel. Nearly 6,000 soldiers once lived here. Today there are fewer than 100.

The harmonious Classical façade is one of the most impressive sights in Paris. The building houses the Musée de l'Armée and the Musée de l'Ordre de la Libération. This was set up to honor feats of heroism during World War II under the leadership of Charles de Gaulle. The story is told using film, photographs, and mementos. The Musée des Plans-Reliefs also houses a large collection of military models of French forts.

Musée de l'Armée 22

129 rue Grenelle 75007. **Map** 7 A3. **Tel** *08 10 11 33 99.* M *Varenne, Latour-Maubourg, Invalides.* RER *Invalides.* ◯ *10am–6pm (7pm Tue, 5pm Oct–Mar) daily.* ● *1st Mon of month, Jan 1, May 1, Nov 1, Dec 25.* 🎟 ◯ 🔲 📷 🛒 🔲
🖥 www.invalides.org

This is one of the most comprehensive museums of military history in the world. It is housed in two galleries, situated on either side of the magnificent courtyard of the Hôtel des Invalides and in the newly opened "Priests' Wing" with the World War II galleries.

A major exhibit recalls the victories and defeats of France through history, dedicated mainly to the Napoleonic era. The emperor's death mask and stuffed horse, Vizier, are on display. Other exhibits include François I's ivory hunting horns, Oriental arms from Japan, and a model of the 1944 Normandy landing.

UNESCO 20

7 pl de Fontenoy 75007. **Map** 6 F5. 🎟 *01 45 68 10 60 (in English).* M *Ségur, Cambronne.* ◯ *for guided tours only (reservations essential): 3pm Mon (French), 3pm Wed (English).* ● *public hols.* ♿ 🛒 🍴
🖥 www.unesco.org

This is the headquarters of the United Nations Educational, Scientific and Cultural Organization (UNESCO). Its aim is to contribute to international peace through education, science, and culture.

UNESCO is a treasure-trove of modern art, including an enormous mural by Picasso, beautiful ceramics by Joan Miró and sculptures by Henry Moore. Outside, there is a peaceful Japanese garden by Nogushi. Exhibitions and movies are also held here.

Hôtel des Invalides 21

75007. **Map** 7 A3. **Tel** *01 44 42 38 77.* M *Latour-Maubourg, Invalides, Varenne.* ◯ *10am–6pm (5pm winter) daily.* ● *Jan 1, May 1, Nov 1, Dec 25.* 🎟 *(call to reserve on 01 44 42 37 72).*
www.invalides.org

This imposing building, from which the area takes its name, was commissioned by Louis XIV in 1670 for his wounded and homeless veterans.

The façade of the Musée de l'Armée

Altar of St-Louis-des-Invalides with banners seized in battle

St-Louis-des-Invalides ㉓

Hôtel des Invalides 75007. **Map** 7 A3.
M Invalides, Latour-Maubourg, Varenne. **Tel** 01 44 42 37 65.
◯ 10am–5:30pm (4:30pm winter) daily. **www**.invalides.org

Also known as the "soldiers' church," this is the chapel of the Hôtel des Invalides. It was built from 1679 to 1708 by Jules Hardouin-Mansart, according to Bruand's design. The stark, Classical interior is well-proportioned, designed in the shape of a Greek cross.

There is a fine 17th-century organ on which the first performance of Berlioz's *Requiem* was given on December 5, 1837, with more than 200 musicians and choristers participating.

Dôme Church ㉔

Hôtel des Invalides, 129 rue de Grenelle, 75007. **Map** 7 A3.
Tel 01 44 42 38 77. **M** Latour-Maubourg, Varenne, Invalides.
▦ 82, 92 to Les Invalides.
RER Invalides. ◯ Tour Eiffel.
◯ Apr–Sep: 10am–6pm daily (Jul & Aug: to 7pm); Oct–Mar: 10am–5pm.
● 1st Mon of month, Jan 1, May 1, Jun 17, Nov 1, Dec 25. ▦ ◯ ⓵ restr. ◢ ▢ ⓵ **www**.invalides.org

Jules Hardouin-Mansart was asked in 1676 by the Sun King, Louis XIV, to build the Dôme Church to complement the existing buildings of the Invalides military refuge, designed by Libéral Bruand. The Dôme was to be reserved for the exclusive use of the Sun King and as the location of royal tombs.

The resulting masterpiece is one of the greatest examples of 17th-century French architecture, the period known as the *grand siècle*. After Louis XIV's death, plans to bury the royal family in the church were abandoned.

The main attraction is the tomb of Napoleon; 20 years after his death on the island of St. Helena, his body was returned to France and installed in this magnificent crypt, encased in six coffins in a vast red porphyry sarcophagus.

Dôme Church with cupola, first gilded in 1715

Musée Rodin ㉕

79 rue de Varenne 75007. **Map** 7 B3.
Tel 01 44 18 61 10. **M** Varenne.
◯ 10am–5:45pm Tue–Sun. ● Jan 1, May 1, Dec 25. ▨ Free 1st Sun of month & for 18–25s after 6pm Sat.
⓵ restricted. ▢ ⓵ **www**.musee-rodin.fr

Auguste Rodin (1840–1917), regarded as one of the greatest French sculptors, lived and worked in the Hôtel Biron, an elegant 18th-century mansion, from 1908 until his death. In return for a state-owned apartment and studio, Rodin left his work to the nation, and it is now exhibited here.

Some of his most celebrated sculptures are on display in the garden: *The Burghers of Calais*, *The Thinker*, *The Gates of Hell (see p120)*, and *Balzac*.

The indoor exhibits are arranged in chronological order, spanning the whole of Rodin's career. Highlights include *The Kiss* and *Eve*.

Sainte-Clotilde ㉖

23 bis rue Las Cases 75007.
Map 7 B3. ⓵ 01 44 18 62 60.
M Solférino, Varenne, Invalides.
◯ 9am–7:30pm Mon–Fri, 10am–8pm Sat, Sun. ● non-religious public hols. **Concerts**

Designed by the German-born architect Franz Christian Gau and built in 1846–56, this Neo-Gothic church was inspired by the 19th-century enthusiasm for the Middle Ages, popularized by such writers as Victor Hugo.

Inside are wall paintings by James Pradier and stained-glass windows with scenes relating to the patron saint of the church. The composer César Franck was organist here from 1858 to 1890.

Musée Maillol ㉗

61 rue de Grenelle 75007.
Map 7 C4. **Tel** 01 42 22 59 58.
M Rue du Bac, Sèvres-Babylone.
◯ 10:30am–7pm (9:30am Fri).
● publ hols. ⓵ ▢ ⓵
www.museemaillol.com

This museum was created by Dina Vierny, muse to Aristide Maillol. His work is exhibited here in all its diverse forms: drawings, engravings, paintings, sculpture, and decorative objects. The museum also plays host to two major temporary exhibitions each year. Allegorical figures of the city of Paris and the four seasons adorn Bouchardon's fountain outside.

Rodin's *The Thinker* in museum garden

THE LEFT BANK

The Left Bank has long been associated with poets, philosophers, artists, and radical thinkers of all kinds. It still has its share of bohemian street life and sidewalk cafés, but the stylish set has moved in, patronizing Yves St-Laurent and the exclusive interior design shops in rue Jacob.

The Latin Quarter is the ancient area lying between the Seine and Luxembourg Gardens, and is today filled with bookstores, art galleries, and cafés. The boulevard St-Michel, bordering the Latin quarter and St-Germain-des-Prés, has slowly given way to commerce, and is full of

Clock in the Musée d'Orsay

fast-food outlets and cheap stores. The surrounding maze of narrow, cobbled streets has retained its character, with ethnic stores and avant-garde theaters dominated by the façade of the Sorbonne, France's first university, built in 1253. Many Parisians dream of living near the Luxembourg Gardens, a quiet area with charming old streets, gateways, and elaborate gardens full of paths, lawns, and tree-lined avenues. Students come here to chat, and on warm days, old men still meet underneath the chestnut trees to play chess or the traditional French game of *boules*.

SIGHTS AT A GLANCE

Churches
St-Germain-des-Prés ⑤
St-Séverin ⑨
St-Julien-le-Pauvre ⑩
St-Etienne-du-Mont ⑫
Panthéon ⑬

St-Sulpice ⑮
Val-de-Grâce ⑰

Museums and Galleries
Musée d'Orsay pp120–1 ①
Musée Eugène Delacroix ⑥
Musée de Cluny ⑧

Fountains
Fontaine de l'Observatoire ⑯

Historic Buildings and Streets
Boulevard St-Germain ②
Quai Voltaire ③
Ecole Nationale Supérieure
   des Beaux Arts ④
Rue de l'Odéon ⑦
La Sorbonne ⑪
Palais du Luxembourg ⑭

GETTING THERE
This area is served by metro stations at St-Germain-des-Prés, St-Michel, and St-Sulpice, among others, with RER stations at Musée d'Orsay and Luxembourg. Bus routes 63 and 87 serve boulevard St-Germain; route 38 serves boulevard St-Michel.

KEY

▨	Street-by-Street map pp118–19
▨	Street-by-Street map pp124–5
▨	Street-by-Street map pp126–7
M	Metro station
RER	RER station
◙	Batobus boarding point

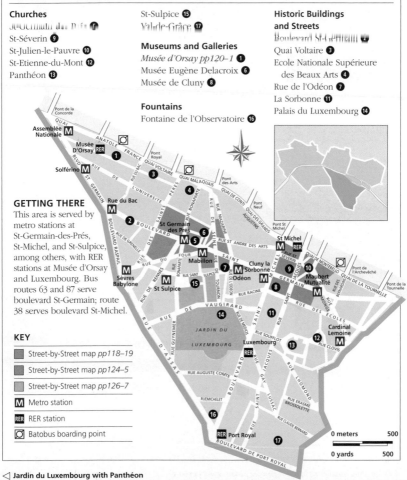

◁ **Jardin du Luxembourg with Panthéon**

Street by Street: St-Germain-des-Prés

After World War II, St-Germain des-Prés became synonymous with intellectual life centered on bars and cafés. Philosophers, writers, actors, and musicians mingled in the cellar nightspots and brasseries, where existentialist philosophy co-existed with American jazz. The area is now more stylish than in the heyday of Jean-Paul Sartre and Simone de Beauvoir, the enigmatic singer Juliette Greco, and the New Wave film-makers.

Organ grinder in St-Germain

Les Deux Magots became a focus of bohemian and literary activity in the 1920s.

However, the writers are still around, enjoying the pleasures of sitting in Les Deux Magots, Café de Flore, and other haunts. The 17th-century buildings have survived, but signs of change are evident in the affluent shops dealing in antiques, books, and fashion.

Café de Flore, the former favorite haunt of Jean-Paul Sartre, Simone de Beauvoir, and other French intellectuals, still has a classic Art Deco interior.

RUE DU DRAGON

RUE DU SABOT

RUE DE RENNES

RUE BONAPARTE

BLVD ST

M

RUE DU FOUR

Brasserie Lipp, decorated with colorful ceramics, is a renowned brasserie frequented by politicians.

Metro St-Germain-des-Prés

★ **St-Germain-des-Prés**
The philosopher René Descartes is among the notables buried here in Paris's oldest church **5**

★ **Boulevard St-Germain**
Café terraces, boutiques, movie theaters, restaurants, and bookstores characterize the central section of the Left Bank's main street **2**

For hotels and restaurants in this region see pp550–5 and pp600–6

STAR SIGHTS

★ St-Germain-des-Prés

★ Boulevard St-Germain

★ Musée Delacroix

KEY

- - - Suggested route

LOCATOR MAP
See Street Finder maps 7, 8

★ Musée Delacroix
The home of the Romantic painter Eugène Delacroix (1798–1863) is now a museum devoted to his art ⑥

Palais Abbatial was the residence of abbots from 1586 until the 1789 Revolution.

Rue de Buci was for centuries an important street and the site of some Real Tennis courts. It now holds a lively market.

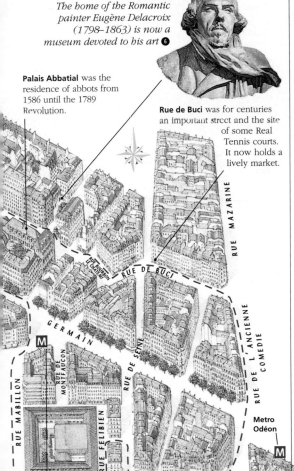

RUE MAZARINE

RUE DE BUCI

GERMAIN

M

RUE DE MONTFAUCON

RUE DE SEINE

RUE DE L'ANCIENNE COMÉDIE

RUE MABILLON

RUE FÉLIBIEN

Metro Odéon

M

CARREFOUR DE L'ODÉON

Metro Mabillon

0 meters 100
0 yards 100

Musée d'Orsay ❶

See pp120–21.

Boulevard St-Germain ❷

75006, 75007. **Map** 8 D4. Ⓜ
Solférino, Rue du Bac, St-Germain-des-Prés, Mabillon, Odéon, Cluny-La Sorbonne, Maubert-Mutualité.

The Left Bank's most celebrated thoroughfare curves across three districts from the Ile St-Louis to the Pont de la Concorde. The architecture is homogeneous because the boulevard was another of Baron Haussmann's bold strokes of urban planning, but it encompasses a wide range of different lifestyles from bohemian to bourgeois.

Starting from the east, it passes Musée de Cluny and the Sorbonne. It is most lively from boulevard St-Michel to St-Germain-des-Prés, with its café culture.

Quai Voltaire ❸

75006, 75007. **Map** 8 D3.
Ⓜ *Rue du Bac.* ⓇⒺⓇ *Musée d'Orsay.*

The quai Voltaire is now home to some of the most important antiques dealers in Paris. Many famous people have lived in the attractive 18th-century houses, among others Voltaire at No. 27 and Richard Wagner, Jean Sibelius, and Oscar Wilde at No. 19.

Plaque marking the house in quai Voltaire where Voltaire died in 1778

Musée d'Orsay ①

In 1986, 47 years after it had closed as a major train
station, Victor Laloux's turn-of-the-century building
reopened as the Musée d'Orsay. Built as the Orléans
railroad terminus in the heart of Paris, it narrowly
avoided demolition in the 1970s. In the conversion
to a museum, much of the original architecture was
retained. The museum presents the rich diversity
of visual arts from 1848 to 1914 and explains
the social and technological context in
which they were created. Exhibits include
paintings, sculptures, furniture, and
decorative objects. The museum also
has a program of classical music concerts.
Exhibits and access are subject
to change due to major
ongoing renovations.

**Young Dancer of
Fourteen (1881)
by Edgar Degas**

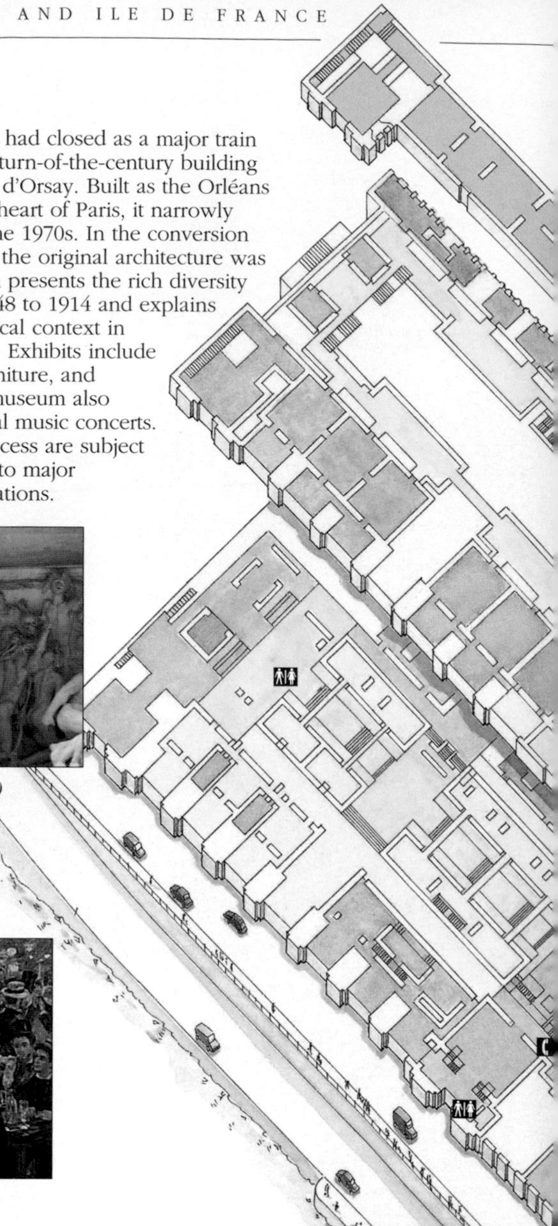

The Gates of Hell *(1880–1917)*
*Rodin included figures that he
had already created, such as*
The Thinker *and* The Kiss, *in
this famous gateway.*

**Dancing at the Moulin
de la Galette** *(1876)*
*Renoir painted this picture
outside to capture the light
as it filtered through the trees.*

The Dance *(1867–8)*
*Carpeaux's dynamic
sculpture caused a
scandal when it was
first unveiled in 1869.*

KEY TO FLOOR PLAN

- Architecture & Decorative Arts
- Sculpture
- Painting before 1870
- Impressionism
- Neo-Impressionism
- Naturalism and Symbolism
- Art Nouveau
- Temporary exhibitions
- Nonexhibition space

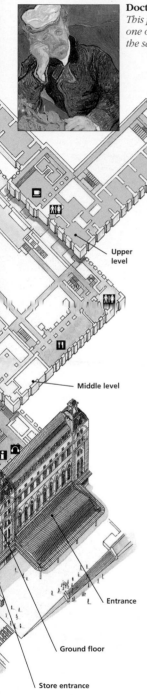

Doctor Paul Gachet *(1890)*
This portrait by Van Gogh is one of three and was painted the same year the artist died.

GALLERY GUIDE

The ground floor has works from the mid- to late 19th century. The middle level features Art Nouveau decorative art and late 19th- to early 20th-century paintings and sculptures. The upper level is currently not open to the public.

Upper level

Middle level

Entrance

Ground floor

Store entrance

VISITORS' CHECKLIST

Quai Anatole France 75007.
Map 8 D2. **Tel** 01 40 49 48 14.
M Solférino. 24, 68, 69, 84 to quai A. France; 73 to rue de la Légion d'Honneur; 63, 83, 84, 94 to bd St-Germain. **RER**
Musée d'Orsay. **P** Quai A. France. 9:30am–6pm Tue–Sun (9:45pm Thu; last entry 1 hr before closing). Jan 1, May 1, Dec 25. **Concerts** phone 01 40 49 47 50.
www.musee-orsay.fr

EXPLORING THE MUSÉE D'ORSAY

Many of the paintings in the Musée d'Orsay came from the Louvre and the Impressionist collection once in the Jeu de Paume. Paintings from before 1870 are on the ground floor, presided over by Thomas Couture's massive *Romans of the Decadence*. Neo-Classical masterpieces, like Ingres's *La Source*, hang near Romantic works like Delacroix's turbulent *Tiger Hunt*. These exotic visions contrast with Realist works by artists like Courbet and early canvases by Degas and Manet, including the latter's famous *Olympia*.

The museum's central aisle overflows with sculpture, from Daumier's satirical busts of members of parliament to Carpeaux's exuberant *The Dance* and Rodin's *The Gates of Hell*. Decorative arts and architecture are on the middle level, where there is also a display of Art Nouveau – sinuous lines

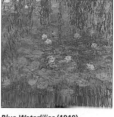

Blue Waterlilies (1919)
by Claude Monet

characterize Lalique's jewelry and glassware and the designs of Hector Guimard, who produced the characteristic curvy entrances of the Paris metro.

Among the many highlights of the Impressionist rooms are Monet's *Rouen Cathedral* series *(see p267)* and Renoir's joyful *Moulin de la Galette*. The Post-Impressionist collection on the middle level includes the *Eglise d'Auvers* by Van Gogh, Seurat's pointillist composi-tions such as *Le Cirque*, Gauguin's highly coloured Symbolist works, and Toulouse-Lautrec's depictions of Parisian nightlife. Among the highlights of the post-1900 display is Matisse's *Luxe, Calme et Volupté*. Some exhibits may be moved due to renova-tion work.

Le Déjeuner sur l'Herbe (1863) by Edouard Manet

The façade of the Ecole Nationale Supérieure des Beaux Arts

Ecole Nationale Supérieure des Beaux Arts ❹

14 rue Bonaparte 75006. **Map** 8 E3.
Tel 01 47 03 50 00. Ⓜ *St-Germain-des-Prés.* ⬤ *groups by appt only*
(01 47 03 50 00 to reserve). 📷 📷
Library www.ensba.fr

The main French school of fine arts has an enviable position at the corner of the rue Bonaparte and the river-side quai Malaquais. It is housed in several buildings, the most imposing being the 19th-century Palais des Etudes. A host of budding French and foreign painters and architects have crossed the courtyard, which contains a 17th-century chapel, to learn in the ateliers of the school. Many American architects have studied here over the past century.

St-Germain-des-Prés ❺

3 pl St-Germain-des-Prés 75006.
Map 8 E4. **Tel** 01 55 42 81 33.
Ⓜ *St-Germain-des-Prés.* ⬤ *8am–7pm daily.* **Concerts** 8pm Tue, Thu.
www.eglise-sgp.org

This is the oldest church in Paris, originating in 542 as a basilica to house holy relics. It became an immensely power-ful Benedictine abbey, rebuilt in the 11th century, but most of it was destroyed by fire in 1794. Major restoration took place in the 19th century. One of the three original towers survives, housing one of the oldest belfries in France. The interior is an interesting mix of architectural styles, with 6th-century marble columns, Gothic vaulting, and Roman-esque arches. Famous tombs include that of 17th-century philosopher René Descartes.

Musée Eugène Delacroix ❻

6 rue de Fürstenberg 75006. **Map** 8 E4.
Tel 01 44 41 86 50. Ⓜ *St-Germain-des-Prés.* ⬤ *9.30am–5pm Wed–Mon.* ⬤
Jan 1, May 1, Dec 25. 📷 *Free 1st Sun of month & for 18–25s (EU residents).*
📷 📷 www.musee-delacroix.fr

The leading Romantic painter Eugène Delacroix lived and worked here from 1857 until his death in 1863. Here he painted *The Entombment of Christ* and *The Way to Calvary* (which hang in the museum). He also created superb murals for the Chapel of the Holy Angels in the nearby St-Sulpice church.
The apartment and studio has a portrait of George Sand and Delacroix self-portraits.

Jacob Wrestling with the Angel by
Delacroix, in St-Sulpice *(see p127)*

Rue de l'Odéon ❼

75006. **Map** 8 F5. Ⓜ *Odéon.*

Opened in 1779 to improve access to the Odéon theater, this was the first street in Paris to have sidewalks with gutters and it still has many 18th-century houses.
Sylvia Beach's bookstore, the original Shakespeare & Company, stood at No. 12 from 1921 to 1940. It was a magnet for writers like James Joyce, Ezra Pound, and Hemingway.

Musée de Cluny ❽

6 pl Paul-Painlevé. **Map** 9 A5.
Tel 01 53 73 78 16. Ⓜ *St-Michel, Odéon, Cluny.* Ⓡ *St-Michel.*
⬤ *9:15am– 5:45pm Wed–Mon.*
⬤ *Jan 1, May 1, Dec 25.*
📷 📷 📷 *Concerts.*
www.musee-moyenage.fr

The museum (officially the Musée National du Moyen Age) is a unique combination

Stone heads of the Kings of Judah carved around 1220

St-Séverin ❾

1 rue-des-Prêtres-St-Séverin 75005.
Map 9 A4. **Tel** 01 42 34 93 50.
Ⓜ *St-Michel.* ⬤ *11am–7:30pm Mon–Sat, 9am–8:30pm Sun.* 📷

St-Séverin, one of the most beautiful churches in Paris, is named after a 6th-century hermit who lived in the area. It is a perfect example of the Flamboyant Gothic style. Finished in the early 16th cen-tury, it includes a remarkable double aisle encircling the chancel. In the garden stands the church's medieval gable-roofed charnel house.

Gargoyles adorning the gables of the Flamboyant Gothic St-Séverin

For hotels and restaurants in this region see pp550–5 and pp600–6

The School woodcarving (English, early 16th century)

The poetic elegance of a unicorn on the sixth tapestry

of Gallo-Roman ruins, incorporated into a medieval mansion (in newly created medieval gardens), and one of the world's finest collections of medieval art and crafts. Its name comes from Pierre de Chalus, Abbot of Cluny, who bought the ruins in 1330. The present building dates from 1485–98. Among the star exhibits are the tapestries, remarkable for their quality, age and state of preservation. The highlight of the sculpture section is the Gallery of the Kings, while one of Cluny's most precious items, the Golden Rose of Basel from 1330, is found in the collection of jewelry and metalwork. Other treasures include stained glass, woodcarvings, and books of hours.

St-Julien-le-Pauvre ❿

1 rue St-Julien-le-Pauvre 75005. **Map** 9 A4. **Tel** 01 43 54 52 16. M St-Michel. ◯ 9:30am–1pm, 3–6:30pm daily. ✚ 10am, 11am, 6pm Sun. **Concerts**

The church is one of the oldest in Paris, dating from between 1165 and 1220. The university held its official meetings in the church until 1524, when a student protest created so much damage that university meetings were barred from the church by parliament. It has belonged to the Greek Orthodox Melchite sect since 1889, and is now the setting for classical and religious concerts.

La Sorbonne ⓫

47 rue des Ecoles 75005. **Map** 9 A5. **Tel** 01 40 46 22 11. M Cluny-La Sorbonne, Maubert-Mutualité. 📷 only by appt. Write to Service des Visites. **www**.paris-sorbonne.fr

The Sorbonne, seat of the University of Paris until 1969, was established in 1253 by Robert de Sorbon, confessor to Louis IX, for 16 poor scholars to study theology. It went on to become the center of scholastic theology. In 1469, three printing machines were brought from Mainz, and the first printing house in France was founded. The college's opposition to liberal 18th-century philosophical ideas led to its suppression during the Revolution. It was re-established by Napoleon in 1806, and the 17th-century buildings replaced. In 1969 the Sorbonne split into 13 separate universities, but the building still holds some lectures.

St-Etienne-du-Mont ⓬

Pl Ste-Geneviève 75005. **Map** 13 A1. **Tel** 01 43 54 11 79. M Cardinal Lemoine. ◯ 8:45am–7:30pm Tue–Sun. ◯ lunchtime Sat & Sun. 📷 🚻

This remarkable church houses the shrine of Saint Geneviève, the legendary patron saint of Paris, and the remains of the great literary figures Racine and Pascal. Some parts of the building are Gothic, others Renaissance, including the eye-catching rood screen.

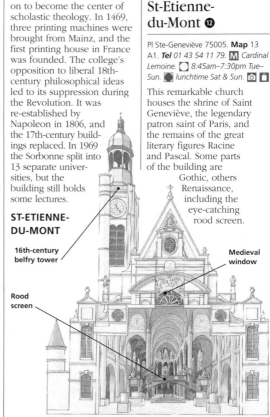

ST-ETIENNE-DU-MONT

16th-century belfry tower

Rood screen

Medieval window

Street by Street: Latin Quarter

Since the Middle Ages this riverside quarter has been dominated by the Sorbonne, and acquired its name from the early Latin-speaking students. It dates back to the Roman town across from the Ile de la Cité; at that time the rue St-Jacques was one of the main roads out of Paris. The area is generally associated with artists, intellectuals, and a bohemian way of life; it also has a history of political unrest. In 1871, the place St-Michel became the center of the Paris Commune, and in May 1968 it was a site of student uprisings. Today the eastern half has become sufficiently chic, however, to house members of the Establishment.

Latin jazz

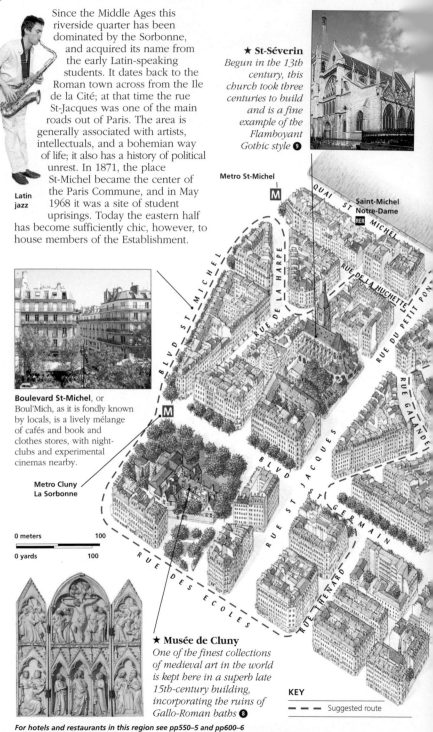

★ **St-Séverin**
Begun in the 13th century, this church took three centuries to build and is a fine example of the Flamboyant Gothic style ❾

Metro St-Michel

Saint-Michel Notre-Dame

Boulevard St-Michel, or Boul'Mich, as it is fondly known by locals, is a lively mélange of cafés and book and clothes stores, with night-clubs and experimental cinemas nearby.

Metro Cluny La Sorbonne

0 meters	100
0 yards	100

★ **Musée de Cluny**
One of the finest collections of medieval art in the world is kept here in a superb late 15th-century building, incorporating the ruins of Gallo-Roman baths ❽

KEY

– – – Suggested route

LOCATOR MAP
See Street Finder maps 8, 9, 12, 13

★ **St-Julien-le-Pauvre**
*Rebuilt in the 17th century,
this church was used to
store animal feed in
the Revolution* ⑩

Metro
Maubert
Mutualité

STAR SIGHTS

- ★ Musée de Cluny
- ★ St-Séverin
- ★ St-Julien-le-Pauvre

Panthéon ⑬

Pl du Panthéon 75005. **Map** 13 A1.
Tel *01 44 32 18 00.* **M** *Maubert-
Mutualité, Cardinal-Lemoine.*
RER *Luxembourg.* ☐ *Apr–Sep:
10am–6:30pm daily; Oct–Mar:
10am–6pm daily.* ● *Jan 1, May 1,
Dec 25.* **http**://pantheon.
monuments-nationaux.fr

When Louis XV recovered
from illness in 1744, he was so
grateful that he conceived
a magnificent church to
honor Saint Geneviève, the
patron saint of Paris. The
French architect Jacques-
Germain Soufflot planned the
church in Neo-Classical
style. Work began in 1764
and was completed in 1790

The Panthéon Interior
*The interior has four
aisles arranged in the
shape of a Greek cross,
from the center of which
the great dome rises.*

Entrance

under the control of
Guillaume Rondelet. But with
the Revolution underway, the
church was soon turned into
a pantheon – a monument
housing the tombs of France's
great heroes. Napoleon
returned it to the Church in
1806, but it was secularized
and then desecularized once
more before finally being
made a civic building in 1885.

The façade, inspired by the
Rome Pantheon, has a pediment relief depicting the
mother country granting lau-
rels to her great men. Those
resting here include Voltaire,
Rousseau, and Zola, and the
ashes of Pierre and Marie
Curie and André
Malraux.

**Iron-
Framed
Dome**
The fresco
in the dome's
stone cupola *represents
the* Glorification of Sainte
Geneviève, *commissioned
by Napoleon in 1811.*

The dome lantern

The dome
galleries

Crypt
*Under the building, the vast crypt
divides into galleries flanked by
Doric columns. Many French
notables rest here, including
Voltaire and Emile Zola.*

Street by Street: Luxembourg Quarter

Situated only a few steps from the bustle of St-Germain-des-Prés, this graceful and historic area offers a peaceful haven in the heart of a modern city. The Jardin du Luxembourg and Palais du Luxembourg dominate the surroundings. The gardens became fully open to the public in the 19th century under the ownership of the Comte de Provence (later to become Louis XVIII), when for a small fee visitors could come in and feast on fruit from the orchard. Today the gardens, palace, and old houses on the streets to the north remain unspoiled and attract many visitors.

STAR SIGHTS

- ★ St-Sulpice
- ★ Palais du Luxembourg

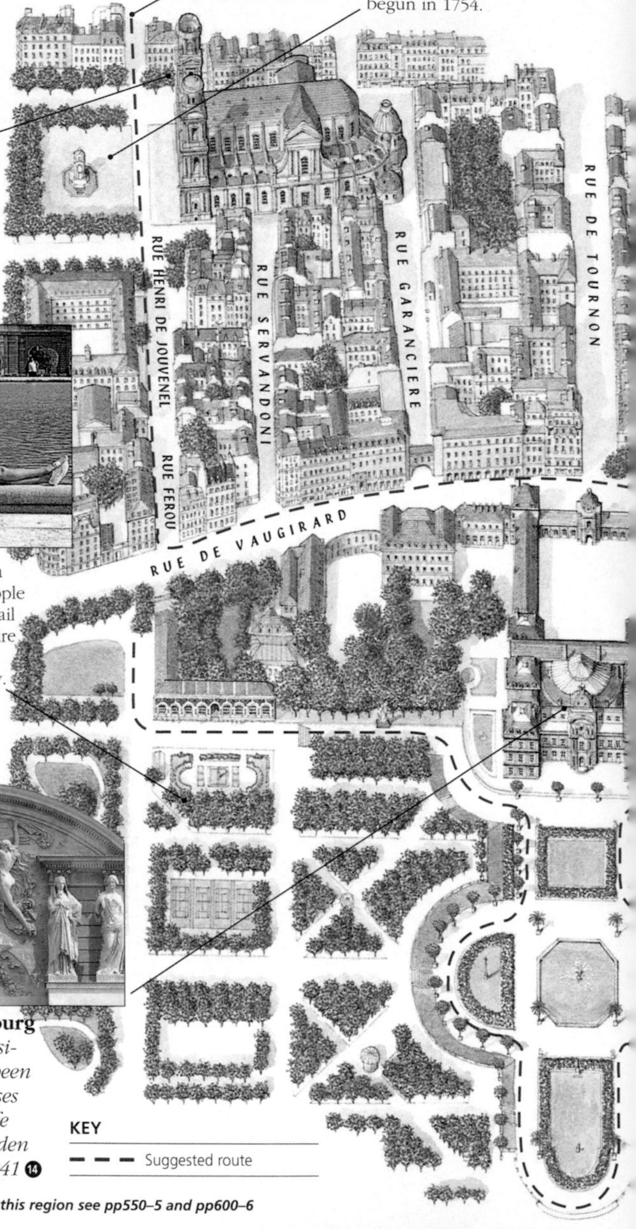
To St-Germain-des-Prés
RUE HENRI DE JOUVENEL
RUE SERVANDONI
RUE GARANCIERE
RUE DE TOURNON
RUE FEROU
RUE DE VAUGIRARD

Place St-Sulpice, ringed by flowering chestnut trees, was begun in 1754.

★ St-Sulpice
This huge Classical church, by six different architects, took more than a century to build ⓯

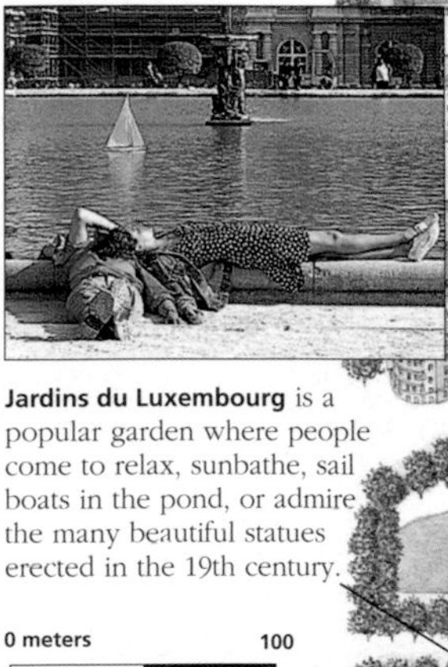

Jardins du Luxembourg is a popular garden where people come to relax, sunbathe, sail boats in the pond, or admire the many beautiful statues erected in the 19th century.

0 meters 100
0 yards 100

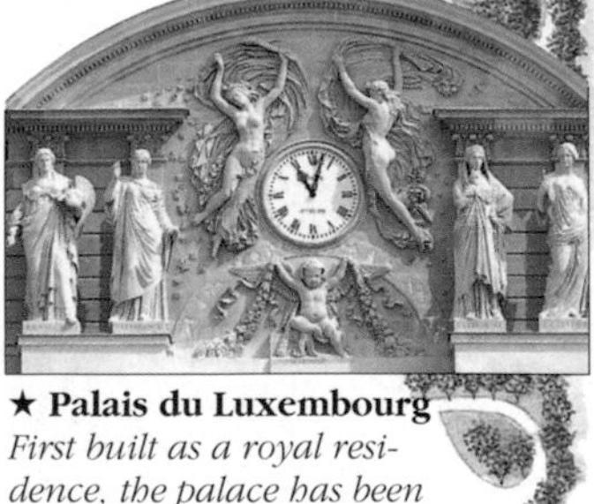

★ Palais du Luxembourg
First built as a royal residence, the palace has been used for various purposes from prison to Luftwaffe headquarters. This garden façade was added in 1841 ⓮

KEY

– – – Suggested route

For hotels and restaurants in this region see pp550–5 and pp600–6

LOCATOR MAP
See Street Finder maps 8, 12, 13

Fontaine de Médicis is a 17th century fountain in the style of an Italian grotto. It is thought to have been designed by Salomon de Brosse.

Saint Geneviève, patron saint of Paris, whose prayers saved Paris from the Huns in AD 451, is honored by this statue by Michel-Louis Victor in 1845.

Palais du Luxembourg ⑭

15 rue de Vaugirard 75006. **Map** 8 E5. *Tel* 01 44 54 19 49. Ⓜ *Odéon*. ⓇⒺⓇ *Luxembourg*. 🎫 *groups: Mon, Fri, Sat (apply 3 months in advance); individuals: one Sat per month. Tel* 01 44 54 19 49. 🖥 www.senat.fr **Museum** ⬭ *daily during exhibitions*. 🏷 www.museeduluxembourg.fr

Now the home of the French Senate, this palace was built to remind Marie de' Médici, widow of Henri IV, of her native Florence. It was designed by Salomon de Brosse in the style of Florence's Pitti Palace. By the time it was finished (1631) she had been banished from Paris, but it remained a royal palace until the Revolution. In World War II it became the Luftwaffe headquarters. The Musée du Luxembourg in the east gallery hosts world-class art exhibitions.

St-Sulpice ⑮

Pl St-Sulpice 75006. **Map** 8 F5. *Tel* 01 42 34 59 98. Ⓜ *St-Sulpice*. ⬭ 7:30am–7:30pm daily. 📷 **Concerts**

This huge and imposing church was started in 1646 and took more than a century to finish. The result is a simple façade with two tiers of elegant columns and two mismatched towers at the ends. Large arched windows fill the vast interior with light.
 In the side chapel to the right are murals by Eugène Delacroix, including *Jacob Wrestling with the Angel (see p122)* and *Heliodorus Driven from the Temple*.

The Classical two-story west front of St-Sulpice with its two towers

Carpeaux's fountain sculpture

Fontaine de l'Observatoire ⑯

Pl Ernest Denis, av de l'Observatoire 7500. **Map** 12 E2. ⓇⒺⓇ *Port Royal*.

Situated at the southern tip of the Jardin du Luxembourg, this is one of the finest fountains in Paris. The central sculpture, by Jean-Baptiste Carpeaux, was erected in 1873. Made of bronze, it has four women holding aloft a globe representing six continents – the seventh, Australia, was left out for reasons of symmetry. There are some subsidiary figures, including dolphins, horses, and a turtle.

Val-de-Grâce ⑰

1 pl Alphonse-Laveran 75005. **Map** 12 F2. *Tel* 01 40 51 51 92. Ⓜ *Gobelins*. ⓇⒺⓇ *Port Royal*. ⬭ *noon– 6pm Tue–Sun*. ⬛ *Aug*. 🎫 🏷 *except for nave*. ♿

This is one of the most beautiful churches in France, and forms part of a military hospital complex. Built for Anne of Austria (wife of Louis XIII) in gratitude for the birth of her son, young Louis XIV himself laid the first stone in 1645.
 The church is noted for its dome. In the cupola is Pierre Mignard's enormous fresco, with over 200 triple-life-sized figures. The six huge marble columns framing the altar are similar to St. Peter's in Rome.

FARTHER AFIELD

Many of Paris's famous sights are slightly out of the city center. Montmartre, long a mecca for artists and writers, still retains much of its bohemian atmosphere, and Montparnasse is full of bustling cafés and theater crowds. The famous Cimetière du Père Lachaise numbers Chopin, Oscar Wilde, and Jim Morrison among its dead, and, along with the parks and gardens, provides a tranquil escape from sightseeing. Modern architecture can be seen at Fondation Le Corbusier and La Défense, and there is a huge selection of museums to visit. To the northeast, the science museum at La Villette provides an educational family day out.

SIGHTS AT A GLANCE

Museums and Galleries
Musée Marmottan
   Claude Monet ⑤
Musée du Cristal de
   Baccarat ⑥
Musée Gustave Moreau ⑨
*Cité des Sciences et
   de l'Industrie pp136–7* ⑮
Cité Nationale de l'Histoire de
   l'Immigration ⑳
Musée National d'Histoire
   Naturelle ㉔

Churches and Mosques
St-Alexandre-Nevsky ⑦
Sacré-Coeur ⑪
Mosquée de Paris ㉗

Parks and Gardens
Bois de Boulogne ②
Parc Monceau ⑧

Parc des Buttes-Chaumont ⑰
Parc Montsouris ㉓
Jardin des Plantes ㉕
Parc André Citroën ㉘

Cemeteries
Cimetière de Montmartre ⑬
Cimetière du Père Lachaise ⑱
Cimetière du Montparnasse ㉚

Historic Districts
Montmartre pp132–3 ⑩
Canal St-Martin ⑯
Montparnasse ㉙

Historic Buildings and Streets
Rue La Fontaine ④

Moulin Rouge ⑫
Château de Vincennes ㉑
Catacombes ㉛

Modern Architecture
La Défense ①
Fondation Le Corbusier ③
Bercy ⑲
Bibliothèque Nationale
   de France ㉒
Institut du Monde Arabe ㉖

Markets
Marché aux Puces
   de St-Ouen ⑭

KEY

	Main sightseeing area
═══	Major roads

0 kilometers   4

0 miles   2

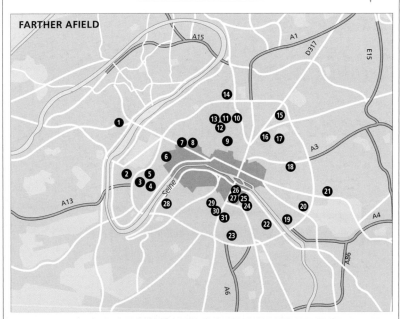

FARTHER AFIELD

West of the City

La Défense ❶

La Grande Arche. **Tel** 01 49 07 27 55. **RER** La Défense. ⬤ for renovation; call for information. 🖼 🚻 📷 See **The History of France** pp66–7. **www**.grandearche.com

This skyscraper business city on the western edge of Paris is the largest office development in Europe. La Grande Arche is an enormous hollow cube large enough to contain Notre-Dame cathedral. Designed by Danish architect Otto von Spreckelsen in the late 1980s, the arch houses a gallery and a conference center, and has superb views.

La Grande Arche in La Défense

Bois de Boulogne ❷

75016. Ⓜ Porte Maillot, Porte Dauphine, Porte d'Auteuil, Sablons. ◯ 24 hrs daily. 🔲 to specialist gardens and museum. ♿.

Located between the western edges of Paris and the River Seine, this 2,137-acre (865-ha) park offers a vast belt of greenery for strolling, biking, riding, boating, picnicking, or spending a day at the races. The Bois de Boulogne was once part of the immense Forêt du Rouvre. In the mid-19th century Napoleon III had the Bois designed and landscaped by Baron Haussmann along the lines of Hyde Park in London. Several self-contained parks within the forest include the

Jardin d'Acclimatation, a fun park for children, Pré Catalan and the Bagatelle gardens, with architectural follies and an 18th-century villa famous for its rose garden. The villa was built in just 64 days after a bet between the Comte d'Artois and Marie-Antoinette.

By day the Bois is busy with families, joggers, and walkers, but after dark it is notoriously seedy – and best avoided.

Fondation Le Corbusier ❸

8–10 square du Docteur-Blanche 75016. **Tel** 01 42 88 41 53. Ⓜ Jasmin. ◯ 1:30–6pm Mon, 10am–6pm Tue–Thu, 10am–5pm Fri & Sat. ⬤ pub hols, Aug, Dec 24–Jan 2. 🎞 **Films, videos. www**.fondationlecorbusier.fr

In a quiet corner of Auteuil stand the villas La Roche and Jeanneret, the first two Parisian houses built by the influential 20th-century architect Charles-Edouard Jeanneret, better known as Le Corbusier. Built at the start of the 1920s, they demonstrate his revolutionary use of white concrete in Cubist forms. Rooms flow into each other allowing maximum light and volume, and the houses stand on stilts with windows along their entire length.

Villa La Roche was owned by the art patron Raoul La Roche. Today, the villas hold lectures on Le Corbusier and his work.

An Art Nouveau window in the rue la Fontaine

Rue la Fontaine ❹

75016. **Map** 5 A4. Ⓜ Michel-Ange-Auteuil, Jasmin. **RER** Radio-France.

The rue la Fontaine and surrounding streets act as a showcase for some of the most exciting early 20th-century, low-cost architecture, featuring sinuous decorative detail. At No. 14 stands the Castel Béranger, which firmly established the reputation of architect Hector Guimard. He went on to design the city's Art Nouveau metro entrances.

Musée Marmottan-Claude Monet ❺

2 rue Louis Boilly 75016. **Tel** 01 44 96 50 33. Ⓜ Muette. ◯ 11am–6pm Wed–Sun (9pm Tue). ⬤ Jan 1, May 1, Dec 25. 🖼 ♿ 📷 **www**.marmottan.com

The museum was created in the 19th-century mansion of the famous art historian, Paul Marmottan, in 1932. He bequeathed his house, plus his Renaissance, Consular, and First Empire paintings and furniture, to the Institut de France.

In 1966 the museum acquired a fabulous collection of work by Impressionist painter Claude Monet, the bequest of his son, Michel. Some of Monet's most famous paintings are here, including

A landscaped island in the Bois de Boulogne

Impression – Sunrise (hence the term "Impressionist"), a painting of Rouen Cathedral *(see p267)*, and the *Waterlilies* series *(see p98)*. Also here is the work painted at Giverny during the last years of Monet's life. This includes *The Japanese Bridge* and *The Weeping Willow*. The iridescent colors and daring brush-strokes make these some of the museum's most powerful works.

Part of Monet's personal art collection was passed on to the museum, including work by fellow Impressionists Camille Pissarro, Pierre-Auguste Renoir, and Alfred Sisley. The museum also displays medieval illuminated manuscripts and 16th-century Burgundian tapestries Piano and chamber music concerts are held on the third Tuesday of each month.

Musée du Cristal de Baccarat ❻

11 pl des Etats Unis 75016. **Tel** 01 40 22 11 00. Ⓜ *Boissière.*
◯ *10am–6:30pm Mon, Wed–Sat (last adm 6pm).* ◑ *public hols.* ▓
✇ *by appt.* **www**.baccarat.fr

The Musée du Cristal, also known as the Galerie-Musée Baccarat, displays over 400 items made by the Baccarat company, which was founded in 1764 in Lorraine in eastern France. These include dinner services created for the royal and imperial courts of Europe and many of the best contemporary pieces produced in the workshops, such as fine vases, candelabras, decanters, and perfume bottles, as well as watches and jewelry.

In the glassworks itself you can see some of the technical skills used to shape and decorate the crystal ware, such as fine cutting, wheel-engraving, gilding and enameling.

Le Vase d'Abyssinie, made of Baccarat crystal and bronze

Colonnade beside the *naumachia* basin in Parc Monceau

North of the City

St-Alexandre-Nevsky Cathedral

St-Alexandre-Nevsky ❼

12 rue Daru 75008. **Map** 2 F3.
Tel 01 42 27 37 34. Ⓜ *Courcelles, Ternes.* ◯ *3–5pm Tue & Fri; 10am–12:30pm, 3–6pm Sun.* ✇
🕆 *6pm Sat, 10:30am Sun.*

This imposing Russian Orthodox cathedral with its five golden-copper domes signals the presence of a large Russian community in Paris. Designed by members of the St. Petersburg Fine Arts Academy and financed jointly by Tsar Alexander II and the local Russian community, it was completed in 1861.

Inside, a wall of icons divides the church in two. The Greek-cross plan and the rich mosaics and frescoes decorating the interior are Neo-Byzantine, while the exterior and gilt domes are traditional Russian Orthodox.

Parc Monceau ❽

Bd de Courcelles 75017. **Map** 3 A3.
Tel 01 42 27 08 64. Ⓜ *Monceau.*
◯ *7am–8pm daily (10pm summer).*
✇ *by appt.*

This green haven dates back to 1778 when the Duc de Chartres commissioned the painter-writer and amateur landscape designer Louis Carmontelle to create a magnificent garden. The result was an exotic landscape full of architectural follies in the English and German style.

In 1852 the garden became a chic public park. A few of the original features remain, among them the *naumachia* basin – an ornamental version of a Roman pool used for simulating naval battles.

Musée Gustave Moreau ❾

14 rue de la Rochefoucauld 75009.
Map 4 E3. **Tel** 01 48 74 38 50.
Ⓜ *Trinité.* ◯ *10am–12:45pm, 2–5:15pm Wed–Mon.* ◑ *some public hols.* ▓ 📷 🚹
www.musee-moreau.fr

The Symbolist painter Gustave Moreau (1826–98), known for his symbolic works depicting biblical and mythological fantasies, lived and worked in this handsome town house. *Jupiter and Semele,* one of the artist's outstanding works, is displayed here, along with other major paintings, and some of the collection's 7,000 drawings and 1,000 oils and watercolors.

Montmartre ⑩

The steep *butte* (hill) of Montmartre has been associated with artists for 200 years.

Streetside painter

Théodore Géricault and Camille Corot came here at the start of the 19th century, and in the 20th century Maurice Utrillo immortalized the streets in his works. Today, street artists thrive predominantly on the tourist trade, but much of the area still preserves its rather louche, villagey prewar atmosphere. The name of the area is ascribed to martyrs who were tortured and killed in the area around AD 250, hence *mons martyrium.*

Montmartre Vineyard
This is the last Parisian vineyard. The harvest is celebrated on the first Saturday in October.

Metro
Lamarck
Caulaincourt

RUE ST-VINCENT
RUE DE L' ABREUVOIR
RUE DES SAULES
RUE CORTO
RUE
RUE ST-RUST
NORVINS
RUE LEPIC
R. DE LA CLEMENT
RUE POULBOT
RUE DE LA MIRE
RAVIGNAN
PL E GOUDEAU
RUE
RUE DREVET
RUE
RUE
DES TROIS FRERES

Au Lapin Agile
"The Agile Rabbit," once a literary haunt, is now a nightclub.

A la Mère Catherine
This was a favorite restaurant of Russian cossacks. They would shout "Bistro!" (meaning "quick") – which gave the bistro its name.

MAISON CATHERINE
A LA MERE CATHERINE

Espace Montmartre Salvador Dalí
Some 330 works by the Surrealist painter and sculptor are on display here.

Place du Tertre
The tourist center of Montmartre is full of portraitists. Artists first exhibited in the square in the 19th century.

KEY

— — — Suggested route

0 meters	100
0 yards	100

Musée de Montmartre
Changing, Montmarte-related exhibitions usually include works by artists who lived here, such as this Portrait of a Woman (1918) by Amedeo Modigliani.

LOCATOR MAP
See Street Finder maps 3, 4

Sacré-Coeur
This Neo-Romanesque church, started in the 1870s and completed in 1914, contains many treasures, such as this figure of the Virgin Mary and Child (1896) by P. Brunet ⑪

St-Pierre de Montmartre
This is an early Parisian church with origins dating back to the 6th century.

The funiculaire, or cable railroad, at the end of the rue Foyatier takes you to the foot of the basilica of the Sacré-Coeur. Metro tickets are valid for it.

Square Willette lies below the forecourt of the Sacré-Coeur. It is laid out on the side of the hill in a series of descending terraces with lawns, shrubs, trees, and flowerbeds.

Musée de la Halle Saint Pierre
Exhibitions here showcase Outsider Art and Art Brut, such as this piece by S. Feleggakis.

To metro Anvers

Sacré-Coeur ⓫

Parvis de Notre Dame 75018. **Map** 4
F1. **Tel** 01 53 41 89 00. Ⓜ Abbesses
(then funiculaire to steps of Sacré-
Coeur), Anvers. 🚌 30, 31, 80, 85.
Basilica ◯ 6am–10:30pm daily.
Dome & crypt ◯ 9am–6pm daily.
🎵 ✝ 7am, 11:15am, 6:30pm,
10pm Mon–Thu, Sat; 3pm Fri; 11am,
6pm, 10pm Sun (Vespers 4pm).
www.sacre-coeur-montmartre.com

The Sacré-Coeur basilica,
dedicated to the Sacred Heart
of Christ and consecrated in
1919, was built as a result of a
private religious vow made at
the outbreak of the Franco-
Prussian war. Two Catholic
businessmen, Alexandre
Legentil and Hubert Rohault
de Fleury, promised to finance
the basilica should France be
spared from assault. Despite
the war and the Siege of
Paris, invasion was averted
and work began in 1875 to
Paul Abadie's designs. Never
considered very graceful, the
basilica is vast and impressive, and one of France's
most important Roman
Catholic buildings.

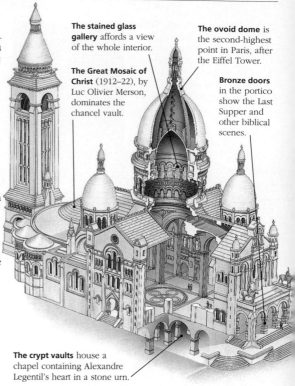

**The stained glass
gallery** affords a view
of the whole interior.

The ovoid dome is
the second-highest
point in Paris, after
the Eiffel Tower.

**The Great Mosaic of
Christ** (1912–22), by
Luc Olivier Merson,
dominates the
chancel vault.

Bronze doors
in the portico
show the Last
Supper and
other biblical
scenes.

The crypt vaults house a
chapel containing Alexandre
Legentil's heart in a stone urn.

Moulin Rouge ⓬

82 bd de Clichy 75018. **Map** 4 E1.
Tel 01 53 09 82 82. Ⓜ Blanche.
Shows at 9pm & 11pm daily; two
matinées per month at 1pm Sun. 🎵
www.moulinrouge.com

Built in 1885, the Moulin Rouge
was turned into a dance hall
as early as 1900. Henri de
Toulouse-Lautrec immortalized
the wild and colorful cancan
shows here in his posters and
drawings of famous dancers
such as Jane Avril. The high-
kicking routines continue today
in glitzy, Las Vegas-style revues.

Cimetière de
Montmartre ⓭

20 av Rachel 75018. **Map** 4 D1.
Tel 01 53 42 36 30. Ⓜ Place de
Clichy. ◯ 8:30am–5:30pm Mon–Sat,
9am–5:30pm Sun (6pm summer). ♿

This has been the resting
place for many luminaries of
the creative arts since the
beginning of the 19th century.

The composers Hector Berlioz
and Jacques Offenbach (who
wrote the famous cancan
tune), Russian dancer Vaslav
Nijinsky, and film director
François Truffaut are just a
few of the famous people
who have been buried here
over the years.

There is also a Montmartre
cemetery near square Roland-
Dorgelès, known as the St-
Vincent cemetery. This is
where the French painter
Maurice Utrillo is buried.

**African stall in the Marché aux
Puces de St-Ouen**

Marché aux Puces
de St-Ouen ⓮

Rue des Rosiers, St-Ouen 93406
Ⓜ Porte-de-Clignancourt. ◯ 9am–
6pm Sat–Mon. See **Shops and
Markets** p142. **www**.les-puces.com

This is the oldest and largest
of the Paris flea markets,
covering 15 acres (6 ha)
near the Porte de Clignancourt.
In the 19th century, rag merchants and tramps would
gather outside the fortifications that marked the city
limits and offer their wares
for sale. Today the area is
divided into separate markets,
and is well-known for its
heavy Second Empire furniture and ornaments. Although
there are few bargains to be
had, this does not deter the
huge weekend crowds.

Cité des Sciences et
de l'Industrie ⓯

See pp136–7.

Canal St-Martin

M *Jaurès, J Bonsergent, Goncourt.*

A walk along the quays on either side of the Canal St-Martin gives a glimpse of how this thriving, industrial, working-class area of the city looked at the end of the 19th century. The 3-mile (5-km) canal, opened in 1825, provided a shortcut for river traffic between loops of the Seine. A smattering of brick-and-iron factories and warehouses survive from this time along the quai de Jemmapes. Here, too, is the legendary Hôtel du Nord, from Marcel Carné's 1930s film of the same name. The canal itself is quietly busy with barges and anglers; around it are tree-lined quays with quirky stores and cafés, iron footbridges and public gardens. At Jaurès, it meets the Canal de l'Ourcq, which offers a pleasant stroll to Parc de la Villette *(see p136).*

Parc des Buttes-Chaumont

Place Armand Carrel 75019. *No phone.* M *Botzaris, Buttes-Chaumont.* ◯ *May–Sep: 7am–10pm daily; Oct–Apr: 7am–9pm daily.*

For many this is the most pleasant park in Paris. Urban planner Baron Haussmann converted the hilly site from a garbage dump and quarry, with gallows at the foot, to English-style gardens in the 1860s. His colleague was landscape architect Adolphe Alphand, who was also responsible for a vast 1860s program to provide Haussmann's new sidewalk-lined Parisian avenues with benches, streetlights, kiosks, and urinals *(see p108).*

Others involved in the creation of this highly praised park were the engineer Darcel and the landscape gardener Barillet-Deschamps. They created a lake, made an island with real and artificial rocks, gave it a Roman-style temple, and added a waterfall, streams, and footbridges

Boats moored at Port de l'Arsenal

leading to the island. Today, in summer, visitors will also find boating facilities, donkey rides, and beautiful lawns.

East of the City

Cimetière du Père Lachaise

16 rue du Repos, 75020. *Tel 01 55 25 82 10.* M *Père Lachaise, A Dumas.* ▭ *60, 69, 102 to pl Gambetta.* P *Pl Gambetta.* ◯ *8am–5:30pm (6pm Apr–Nov; from 9am Sun & hols) daily.* 🖥 www.pere-lachaise.com

Paris's most prestigious cemetery is set on a wooded hill overlooking the city. The land was once owned by Père de la Chaise, Louis XIV's confessor, but it was bought by order of Napoleon in 1803. The cemetery became so popular that the boundaries were extended six times during the 19th century. Here are buried celebrities such as writer Honoré de Balzac and composer Frédéric Chopin, and actors Yves Montand and Simone Signoret.

Bercy

75012. M *Bercy, Cour St-Emilion.* ▭ *24, 64, 87.* **Cinémathèque Française**: *51 rue de Bercy.* *Tel 01 71 19 32 00.* ◯ *noon–7pm Mon–Sat, 10am–8pm Sun.* ♿ *(call 01 71 19 33 33).*

This former wine-trading quarter just east of the city center, with its once-grim riverside warehouses and pavilions and slum housing, has been transformed into an ultramodern district beside the Seine. A new automatic metro line (Line 14) links it to the heart of the city.

The centerpiece of this district is the Palais d'Omnisports de Paris-Bercy (POPB), which is the city center's principal concert venue, as well as its premier sports stadium. The vast pyramidal structure, its sides clad with real lawns, has become a landmark for the eastern part of central Paris.

Other architecturally adventurous buildings dominate the skyline, notably Chemetov's Ministry of Finance building and Frank Gehry's American Center, which houses the **Cinémathèque Française**, a cinema museum with film screenings, a library, and retrospectives on directors.

At the foot of these structures, the 173-acre (70-ha) Parc de Bercy provides a welcome green space. Former wine stores and cellars along Cours St. Emilion have been restored as restaurants, bars, and stores. Some of the warehouses have been restructured as the Pavillons de Bercy, one of which contains the Musée des Arts Forains (Fairground Museum).

Bercy's striking American Center, designed by Frank Gehry

Cité des Sciences et de l'Industrie ⑮

This hugely popular science and technology museum occupies the largest of the old Villette slaughterhouses, which now form part of a massive urban park. Architect Adrien Fainsilber has created an imaginative interplay of light, vegetation, and water in the high-tech, five-story building, which soars 133 ft (40 m) high, stretching over 7 acres (3 ha). At the museum's heart is the Explora exhibit, a fascinating guide to the worlds of science and technology. Visitors can take part in computerized games on space, the earth and ocean, computers, and sound. On other levels there are a children's science city, cinemas, a science newsroom, a library, and shops.

Modern folly in the Parc de la Villette

Planetarium
In this 260-seat auditorium you can watch eclipses and fly over Martian landscapes, thanks to the 3-D video system.

Le Nautile
This full-scale model of the Nautile, France's technologically advanced exploration submarine, represents one of the most sophisticated machines in the world.

★ **The Story of the Universe**
An exploration of the birth of the universe, this exhibit takes you back 13.7 billion years to the creation of the first atom.

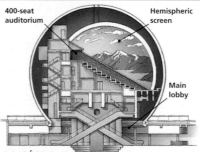

400-seat auditorium

Hemispheric screen

Main lobby

LA GÉODE
This giant entertainment sphere houses a huge hemispherical movie screen, 11,000 sq ft (1,000 sq m), showing IMAX films on nature, travel, history, and space.

The moat was designed by Fainsilber so that natural light could penetrate into the lower levels of the building.

The main hall is vast, with a soaring network of shafts, bridges, escalators, and balconies, and has a cathedral-like atmosphere.

For hotels and restaurants in this region see pp550–5 and pp600–6

STAR EXHIBITS

★ Children's City

★ Story of the Universe

★ La Géode

Cupolas
*The two glazed domes,
56 ft (17 m) in diameter,
filter the flow of natural
light into the main hall.*

VISITORS' CHECKLIST

30 av Corentin-Cariou 75019.
☎ 01 40 05 80 00. M Porte
de la Villette. 🚌 139, 150, 152,
249, 375, PC2. ⬜ 10am–6pm
Tue–Sat (7pm Sun). 🅿 ♿ ⭐
⬜ ⬜ ⬜ Shows, films,
videos, library, conference
center. www.cite-sciences.fr

The greenhouse is a
square hothouse, 105 ft
(32 m) high and wide,
linking the park to
the building.

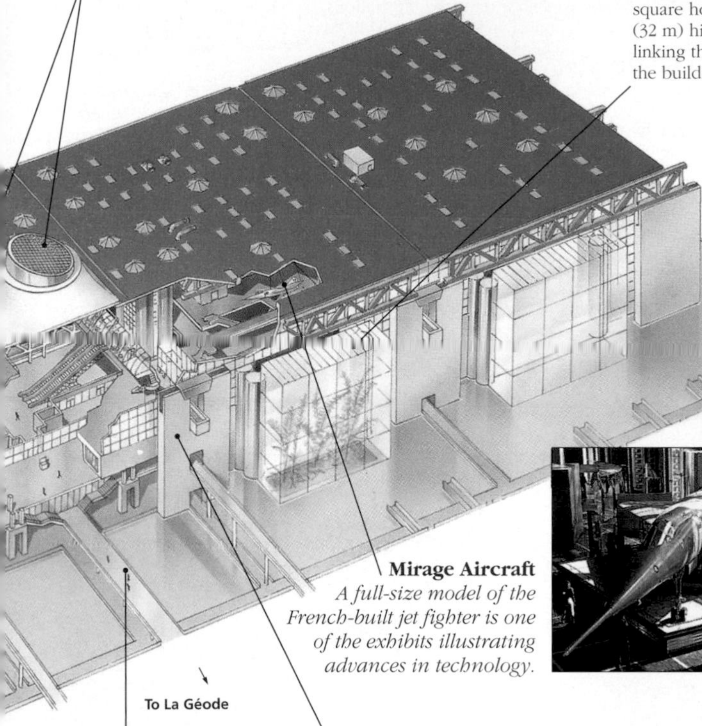

Mirage Aircraft
*A full-size model of the
French-built jet fighter is one
of the exhibits illustrating
advances in technology.*

To La Géode

Walkways
*The walkways cross the
encircling moat to link the
various floors of the museum
to the Géode and the park.*

★ Children's City
*In this lively, extensive
area children can
experiment and play
with machines that
show how scientific
principles work.*

Bibliothèque Nationale de France

Cité Nationale de l'Histoire de l'Immigration ⑳

293 av Daumesnil 75012.
Tel 01 53 59 58 60. Ⓜ *Porte Dorée.*
◯ *10am–5:30pm Tue–Fri (7pm Sat & Sun).* ● *May 1, Jul 14, Dec 25.*
🖾 ♿ *restricted.* ⬛

Housed in the Palais de la Porte Dorée, this museum is devoted to immigration in France. The palace itself is an Art Deco building designed by architects Albert Laprade and Léon Jaussely for the city's grand colonial exhibition in 1931.

The cellar also contains tropical fish collections, along with tortoises and crocodiles.

Château de Vincennes ㉑

Av de Paris 94300 Vincennes.
Tel 01 48 08 31 20. Ⓜ *Château de Vincennes.* 🚆 *Vincennes.*
◯ *10am–5pm daily (6pm May–Aug).* ● *Jan 1, May 1, Nov 1 & 11, Dec 25.* 🖾 🖾 ⬛ www.chateau-vincennes.fr

The Château de Vincennes was the permanent royal residence until the 17th century, before the court moved to Versailles. The donjon, the tallest fortified medieval building in Europe, the Gothic chapel, 17th-century pavilions, and moat are all worth seeing.

Beyond lies the Bois de Vincennes. Once a royal hunting ground, it is now a landscaped forest with ornamental lakes and a racecourse.

Bibliothèque Nationale de France ㉒

Quai François-Mauriac 75013. *Tel* 01 53 79 59 59. Ⓜ *Bibliothèque François-Mitterrand.* ◯ *10am–7pm Tue–Sat, 1–7pm Sun.* ● *public hols, 2 wks mid-Sep.* 🖾 ♿ ⬛ www.bnf.fr

These four great book-shaped towers house 10 million volumes. The libraries offer over 400,000 titles. Other resources include digitized illustrations, sound archives, and CD-ROMs. There are also frequent temporary exhibitions.

South of the City

Parc Montsouris ㉓

Bd Jourdan 75014. *Tel* 01 41 71 75 60.
Ⓜ *Pte d'Orléans.* 🚆 *Cité Universitaire.*
◯ *8am–8:30pm (5:30pm winter) daily.* 🖾 ♿

This English-style park, the second largest in Paris, was laid out by Adolphe Alphand from 1865–1878. Its restaurant, lawns, and lake – home to a variety of birds – are popular with students and children.

Skull of the reptile dimetrodon

Musée National d'Histoire Naturelle ㉔

36 rue Geoffroy Saint-Hilaire 75006.
Map 14 D1. *Tel* 01 40 79 54 79.
Ⓜ *Jussieu, Austerlitz.* ◯ *10am–6pm Wed–Mon.* ● *May 1.* 🖾 🖾 ♿ ⬛ ⬛ 🖾 *Library* www.mnhn.fr

The highlight of the museum is the Grande Galerie de l'Evolution. There are also four other departments: palaeontology, featuring skeletons, casts of various animals, and an exhibition showing the evolution of the vertebrate skeleton; palaeo-botany, devoted to plant fossils; mineralogy, including gemstones; and entomology, with some of the oldest fossilized insects on earth. The bookstore is in the house that was occupied by the naturalist Buffon from 1772 until his death in 1788.

Jardin des Plantes ㉕

57 rue Cuvier 75005. **Map** 13 C1. *Tel* 01 40 79 56 01. Ⓜ *Jussieu, Austerlitz.*
◯ *8am–5:30pm (5pm winter) daily.*

The botanical gardens were established in 1626 when Jean Hérouard and Guy de la Brosse, Louis XIII's physicians, obtained permission to found a royal medicinal herb garden. A school of botany, natural history, and pharmacy followed and the garden opened to the public in 1640. One of the city's great parks, it contains a natural history museum, botanical school, and zoo.

As well as beautiful vistas and walkways flanked by ancient statues, the park has an alpine garden with plants from Corsica, Morocco, the Alps, and the Himalayas, and an unrivaled display of herbaceous and wild plants. The Cedar of Lebanon here, originally from Britain's Kew Gardens, was the first to be planted in France.

Rue Mouffetard, one of several markets near Jardin des Plantes

For hotels and restaurants in this region see pp550–5 and pp600–6

Institut du Monde Arabe 26

1 rue des Fossés St-Bernard,
Pl Mohammed V 75005. **Map** 9 C5.
Tel 01 40 51 38 38. **M** Jussieu,
Cardinal-Lemoine. **Museum & temp**
exhibs ◯ 10am–6pm Tue–Sun.
Library ◯ 1–8pm Tue–Sat. 🎫 📷
♿ 📧 🍴 www.imarabe.org

This magnificent modern
building was designed by
French architect Jean Nouvel,
and cleverly combines high-
tech details with the spirit of
traditional Arab architecture.
From the fourth to seventh
floors there is a comprehensive
display of Islamic art from the
9th to 19th centuries, including
glassware, ceramics, and sculpture. The museum's highlight
is its collection of *astrolabes*,
the much prized tool used by
ancient Arabic astronomers.

Institut du Monde Arabe, covered with photosensitive lightscreens

Mosquée de Paris 27

2 pl du Puits de l'Ermite 75005.
Tel 01 45 35 97 33. **M** Place Monge.
◯ 9am–noon, 2–6pm Sat–Thu.
⬤ Muslim hols. 🎫 📷 📧 🍴
Library www.mosquee-de-paris.org

Built in the 1920s in the
Hispano-Moorish style, these
buildings are the center for
Paris's Muslim community.
Once solely by scholars,
the mosque has expanded
over the years and now
houses some salubrious
but fun Turkish baths, a fine
restaurant, and a beautiful
salon de thé.

Parc André Citroën 28

Quai Andre Citroën 75015. **Tel** 01 40
71 75 60. **M** Balard. ◯ Mar–Oct:
9am–dusk (Nov–Feb: to 5pm) daily. ♿

Designed by both landscapers
and architects, this park is a
fascinating blend of styles,
ranging from wildflower
meadow in the north to sophisticated monochrome mineral and sculpture gardens in
the southern section. Modern
water sculptures dot the park.

Tour Montparnasse

Montparnasse 29

75014 & 75015. **Map** 11 & 12.
M Montparnasse, Vavin, Raspail, Edgar
Quinet. **Tour Montparnasse** ◯ Apr–
Sep: 9:30am–11:30pm; Oct–Mar:
9:30am–10:30pm (11pm Fri & Sat).

The name Montparnasse was
first used ironically in the 17th
century, when arts students
performed their work on a
"mount" of rubble left over
from quarrying. In ancient
Greece, Mount Parnassus was
dedicated to poetry, music, and
beauty. By the 19th century,
crowds were drawn to the
local cabarets and bars by
duty-free prices. The mixture
of art and high living was particularly potent in the 1920s
and 1930s when Hemingway,
Picasso, Cocteau, Giacometti,
Matisse, and Modigliani were
"Montparnos," as the residents
were called. The modern
quartier is dominated by the
much-hated **Tour Montparnasse**,
although the view from the top
(the 56th floor) is spectacular.

Cimetière du Montparnasse 30

3 bd Edgar Quinet 75014. **Map** 12 D3.
Tel 01 44 10 86 50. **M** Edgar Quinet.
◯ mid-Mar–Nov: 8am–6pm Mon– Fri,
8:30am–6pm Sat, 9am–6pm Sun;
Dec–mid-Mar: closes 5:30pm.

Montparnasse cemetery
opened in 1824. Among
those buried here are Serge
Gainsbourg, Charles
Baudelaire, Jean Paul Sartre
and Simone de Beauvoir,
and Guy de Maupassant.

Catacombes 31

1 av du Colonel Henri Rol-Tanguy
75014. **Map** 12 E3. **Tel** 01 43 22 47
63. **M** Denfert-Rochereau. ◯ 10am–
5pm Tue–Sun. ⬤ public hols. 🎫 📷
www.catacombes-de-paris.fr

A long series of quarry
tunnels built in Roman times,
the catacombs are now lined
with ancient bones and
skulls. Thousands of rotting
corpses were transported
here in the 1780s to absorb
the excess from the insanitary
Les Halles cemetery.

Skulls and bones stored in the catacombes

SHOPS AND MARKETS

For many people, Paris epitomizes luxury and good living. Exquisitely dressed men and women sip wine by the banks of the Seine against the backdrop of splendid French architecture, or shop at small specialty stores. The least expensive way of joining the chic set is to create French style with accessories or costume jewelry. Alternatively, try shopping in the January or July sales. If your budget allows, take the opportunity to buy world-famous Paris fashions, or feast on the wonderful gourmet delicacies displayed with consummate artistry. Parisian shopping streets and markets are the ideal place to indulge in the French custom of strolling for the express purpose of seeing and being seen. For up-to-the-minute high fashion, the rue du Faubourg-St-Honoré is hard to beat, with its exquisite couture window displays. Browsing around the bookstalls along the Seine is another favorite French pastime. A survey of some of the best and most famous places to shop follows.

Shopping in avenue Montaigne

OPENING HOURS

Stores are usually open from 10am–7pm, Monday to Saturday, but hours can vary. Many department stores stay open late on Thursday, while boutiques may shut for an hour or two at midday. Markets and local neighborhood stores usually close on Mondays. Some places shut for the summer, usually in August, but they may leave a note on the door suggesting an open equivalent nearby.

PAYMENT AND TAX

Cash is readily available from the ATMs in most banks, which accept both credit and bank debit cards. Visa and MasterCard are the most widely accepted credit cards.

A sales tax (TVA) from 5.5–19.6 per cent is imposed on most goods and services in EU countries. Non-EU residents shopping in France are entitled to a refund of this if they spend a minimum of 175€ in one store in one day. You must have been resident in France for less than six months and either carry the goods with you out of the country within three months of purchase, or get the store to forward them to you. Larger stores will generally supply a form (*bordereau de détaxe* or *bordereau de vente*) and help you to fill it in. When you leave France or the EU you present the form to Customs, who either permit you to be reimbursed straightaway, or forward

The Chanel logo, recognized worldwide

your claim to the place where you bought the merchandise; the shop eventually sends you a refund.

SALES

The best sales (*soldes*) are held in January and July, although you can sometimes find sale items before Christmas. If you see goods labelled *Stock*, it means that they are stock items, reduced for clearance. *Dégriffé* means designer labels, (with the label cut out) marked down, frequently from the previous year's collections. *Fripes* indicates that clothes are second-hand.

THE CENTER OF PARIS COUTURE

The couture houses are concentrated on the Right Bank, around rue du Faubourg-St-Honoré and avenue Montaigne.

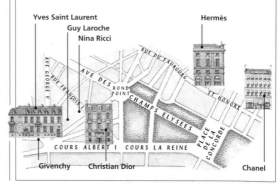

Yves Saint Laurent · Guy Laroche · Nina Ricci · Hermès · Givenchy · Christian Dior · Chanel

DEPARTMENT STORES

Much of the pleasure of shopping in Paris is derived from going to the small specialty stores. But if time is short, try the *grands magasins* (department stores). Some still operate a ticket system for selling goods. The store assistant writes up a ticket for goods from their own boutique which you take to one of the cashiers. You then return with your validated ticket to pick up your purchase. This can be time-consuming, so go early in the morning and don't shop on

The 1865 façade of Au Printemps department store

Kenzo designerwear in the place des Victoires

Saturdays, unless you enjoy a crowd. The French do not pay much attention to lines so be assertive! One peculiarity of a visit is that the security guards may ask to inspect your bags as you leave. These are random checks and should not be taken as an implication of theft.

All department stores have places to eat, although the stores themselves tend to have different emphases. **Au Printemps** is noted for its exciting and innovative household goods section, vast cosmetic range, and large menswear store. The clothes departments for women and children are well stocked. Fashion shows are held at 10am on Tuesdays (and each Friday from April to October: by invitation only). The lovely domed restaurant in the cupola often hosts chic after-hours parties, which are

private, but a visit to the restaurant during shopping hours is worthwhile.

BHV (Le Bazar de l'Hôtel de Ville) is a home improver's paradise, and sells a host of other items, such as fashion decor. The Left Bank's **Le Bon Marché** was Paris's first department store and today is its chicest. The designer clothing sections are well-sourced, the high-end accessories are excellent, and the own-brand linen has a good quality to price ratio. The prepared food sections serve restaurant-quality fare to take out.

Galeries Lafayette is perhaps the best-known department store and has a wide range of clothes available at all price levels. Its first-floor trends section plays host to lots of innovative designers. Galeries Lafayette Gourmet, the food court, sells a range of French and international delicacies. Across the road is the store's housewares

Cartier, one of the world's most exclusive stores

building, which stocks a good range of kitchenware.

Virgin Megastore is open until late and has an excellent record selection and an impressive book section. **FNAC** specializes in records, books (foreign editions can be found at Les Halles), and electronic equipment, while **FNAC Odeón** sells a wide range of the latest technological equipment.

ADDRESSES

Au Printemps
64 bd Haussmann 75009.
Map 4 D4. **Tel** 01 42 82 50 00.
www.printemps.com

BHV
55 rue de la Verrerie 75004.
Map 9 B3. **Tel** 01 42 74 90 00.
www.bhv.com

Le Bon Marché
24 rue de Sèvres 75007.
Map 7 C5. **Tel** 01 44 39 80 00.
www.lebonmarche.com

FNAC
Forum des Halles, 1 rue Pierre Lescot 75001. **Map** 9 A2.
Tel 0825 020 020.
www.fnac.com

FNAC Odeón
77–81 bd St-Germain 75006.
Map 9 A5. **Tel** 0825 020 020.

Galeries Lafayette
40 bd Haussmann 75009. **Map** 4 E4.
Tel 01 42 82 34 56.
www.galerieslafayette.com

Virgin Megastore
52–60 av des Champs-Elysées 75008. **Map** 2 F5. **Tel** 01 49 53 50 00. **www**.virginmegastore.fr

Clothes and Accessories

For many people Paris is synonymous with fashion, and Parisian style is the ultimate in chic. More than anywhere else in the world, women in Paris seem to be in tune with current trends and when a new season arrives appear, as one, to don the look. Though less trend-conscious generally, Parisian men are aware of style, and mix and match patterns and colors with *élan*. Finding the right clothes at the right price means knowing where to shop. For every luxury boutique on the avenue Montaigne, there are ten young designers' stores waiting to become the next Jean-Paul Gaultier – and hundreds more selling imitations.

HAUTE COUTURE

Paris is the home of *haute couture*. The original *couture* garments, as opposed to the imitations and adaptations, are one-time creations, designed by one of the nine *haute couture* houses listed with the Fédération Française de la Couture. The rules for being classified are fairly strict, and many of the top designers are not included. Astronomical prices put *haute couture* beyond the reach of all but a few immensely deep pockets, but it is still the lifeblood of the fashion industry, providing inspiration for the mass market.

WOMEN'S CLOTHES

Most *couture* houses are found on or near the rue du Faubourg-St-Honoré and avenue Montaigne: **Christian Dior**, **Pierre Cardin**, **Chanel**, **Christian Lacroix**, **Versace**, **Givenchy**, **Nina Ricci**, **Giorgio Armani**, and **Yves Saint Laurent**.

Hermès has classic country chic. **MaxMara's** Italian elegance is popular in France and no one can resist a **Giorgio Armani** suit. The legendary **Prada** store has stuck to the Right Bank but many fashion houses prefer the Left Bank.

Many designers have a Left Bank branch in addition to their Right Bank bastions, and they all have ready-to-wear shops here. For sheer quality there's **Georges Rech**, and **Jil Sander** for exquisite tailoring. Try **Sonia Rykiel** for knitwear and **Barbara Bui** for soft, feminine clothes. **Comptoir des Cotonniers** has branches

throughout Paris and stocks excellent basics, and **Vanessa Bruno** is extremely popular for feminine flair.

For ready-to-wear head to place des Victoires. **Kenzo** is here (although its flagship store is located near the Pont Neuf), along with fellow Japanese designers **Comme des Garçons**, with its quirky fashion for both sexes. In nearby rue du Jour find the timeless elegance of **Agnès B**.

The Marais is a haven for up-and-coming designers. One of the best streets is the rue des Rosiers, which includes the wonderful **L'Eclaireur**. **Anne Fontaine** is on the neighboring rue des Francs-Bourgeois, and daring designer **Azzedine Alaïa's** is just around the corner.

The Bastille area has trendy boutiques, as well as established stores, including **Jean-Paul Gaultier** and mainstream names like **Petit Bateau**. **Isabel Marant's** boutique is renowned for its originality.

Young designers' clothes are found at **Colette**, **Stella Cadente**, and **Zadig and Voltaire**.

CHILDREN'S CLOTHES

Lots of options for children exist in various styles and many price ranges. Many top designers of adult clothes also have boutiques for children. These include **Kenzo**, **Baby Dior**, **Agnès B**. Ready-to-wear such as **Jacadi** and **Du Pareil au Même** are serviceable and wide-ranging; and **Tartine et Chocolat's** best-selling garments are overalls.

Bonpoint stocks adorably chic clothing for mini-Parisians. **Petit Bateau** is coveted as much by grown-ups as it is by children. The inevitable has finally happened – children now have their own concept store in **Bonton**.

For little feet, **Froment-Leroyer** probably offers the best all-round classics.

MEN'S CLOTHES

Men don't have the luxury of *haute couture* dressing and their choice is limited to ready-to-wear. On the Right Bank, there's **Giorgio Armani**, **Pierre Cardin**, **Lanvin** (also good for accessories), and **Yves Saint Laurent**. On the Left Bank, **Michel Axel** and **Jean-Charles de Castelbajac** are known for their ties and **Francesco Smalto's** elegant creations are worn by some of the world's leading movie stars. Yohji Yamamoto's clothes in **Y3** are for those who are intent on making a serious fashion statement, while **Gianni Versace** is classic, suave, and Italian in style.

The ultimate in Parisian elegance for men, however, is a suit, custom-made shirt, or silk tie from **Charvet**.

VINTAGE AND SECOND-HAND STORES

The vintage craze hit Paris some time back and there are some wonderful stores to plunder for a retro look. The best of the bunch is **Didier Ludot**, where an Aladdin's Cave of chic *haute couture* is elegantly displayed. The **Depôt-Vente de Buci-Bourbon** is another good place to bargain hunt. A cheaper option is to head for one of the second-hand consignment stores. Chic Parisians discard their outfits with the seasons so it is very easy to pick up some quality items, often in top condition, from places such as **Réciproque** in Passy or **Alternatives** in the Marais.

A cheaper option for sample pieces and sale stock can be found at **Le Mouton à Cinq Pattes**.

JEWELRY

The *couture* houses probably stock some of the best jewelry and scarves. **Chanel's** jewels are classics and **Christian Lacroix**'s are fun. **Boutique YSL** is a great place for accessories.

Among the main expensive Paris jewelry outlets are **Boucheron**, **Mauboussin**, and **Poiray**. They are for the serious jewelry buyer. Other top retailers include **Harry Winston** and **Cartier**. **Dinh Van** has some quirky pieces, whilst **Mikimoto** is a must for pearls, and **H Stern** has some innovative designs using semiprecious and precious stones. For a range of more unusual jewelry

and accessories, try the **Swarovski Boutique**, which is owned by the Swarovksi crystal family.

SHOES AND BAGS

For both classic and wild footwear designs, you can't beat **Miu Miu**. **Rodolphe Ménudier** and **Christian Louboutin** are mainstays for sexy stilettos. **Carel** stocks stylish basics and **Jonak** is a must for good imitations of designer footwear.

For ladies handbags, nothing beats **Chanel** or **Dior** at the top end of the scale, although **Goyard** comes close. Mid-range bags from **Furla** are a great compromise. Fabric bags from **Jamin Puech**

or **Vanessa Bruno** are a feature in every chic Parisian closet. For those with tighter purse strings, cheap, cheerful, and stylish bags can be found at **Lollipops**.

LINGERIE

For modern lingerie go to **Fifi Chachnil**, whose store is filled with coloufu underwear. **La Boîte à Bas** sells fine French stockings, whereas **Princesse Tam Tam** offers quality items at reasonable prices, while divine designer underwear can be found at cult store **Sabbia Rosa**. The ultimate in Parisian lingerie can be bought off the peg or made to order at **Cadolle**, the store which invented the bra.

DIRECTORY

DIRECTORY

CHILDREN'S CLOTHES

Bonpoint
320 rue St-Honoré 75001.
Map 9 A2.
Tel 01 49 27 94 82.
www.bonpoint.com

Bonton
82 rue de Grenelle 75007.
Map 6F3.
Tel 01 44 39 09 20.
www.bonton.fr

Du Pareil au Même
1 rue St-Denis 75001.
Map 9 B3.
Tel 01 42 36 07 57.
www.dpam.com

Froment-Leroyer
7 rue Vavin 75006.
Map 12 E1.
Tel 01 43 54 33 15.
www.froment-leroyer.fr

Jacadi
17 rue Tronchet 75008.
Map 3 C5.
Tel 01 42 65 84 98.
www.jacadi.fr

Petit Bateau
116 av des Champs
Elysées 75008. **Map** 2 E4.
Tel 01 40 74 02 03.
www.petit-bateau.fr

Tartine et Chocolat
84 rue du Faubourg-St-
Honoré 75008. **Map** 3 B5.
Tel 01 45 62 44 04.
www.tartine-et-chocolat.fr

MEN'S CLOTHES

Charvet
28 pl Vendôme
75001. **Map** 4 D5.
Tel 01 42 60 30 70.

Francesco Smalto
44 rue François 1er
75008. **Map** 2 F5.
Tel 01 47 20 96 04.
www.smalto.com

Gianni Versace
45 av Montaigne 75008.
Map 2 F5.
Tel 01 47 42 88 02.
www.versace.com

Giorgio Armani
(see p143).

Jean-Charles de Castelbajac
61 rue des Saints Pères
75006. **Map** 8 D4. *Tel* 09
64 48 48 54. www.jc-de-
castelbajac.com

Kenzo
(see p143).

Lanvin
15 rue du Faubourg
St-Honoré 75008.
Map 10 F4.
Tel 01 44 71 31 25.
www.lanvin.com

Michel Axel
44 rue du Dragon 75006.
Map 8 E4.
Tel 01 42 84 13 86.

Pierre Cardin
(see p143).

Y3
47 rue Etienne
Marcel 75001. **Map** 9 A1.
Tel 01 45 08 82 45.

Yves Saint Laurent
12 pl St-Sulpice 75006.
Map 8 D4.
Tel 01 43 26 84 40.

VINTAGE AND SECOND-HAND STORES

Alternatives
18 rue du Roi-de-Sicile
75004. **Map** 9 C3.
Tel 01 42 78 31 50.

Depôt-Vente de Buci-Bourbon
6 rue de Bourbon-le-
Château 75006.
Map 8 E4.
Tel 01 46 34 45 05.

Didier Ludot
24 Galerie Mont-pensier
75001. **Map** 8 E1.
Tel 01 42 96 06 56.
www.didierludot.fr

Le Mouton à Cinq Pattes
8 rue St-Placide 75006.
Map 8 D5.
Tel 01 45 48 86 26.
www.moutonacinq
pattes.com

Réciproque
95 rue de la Pompe
75016. **Map** 5 A1.
Tel 01 47 04 30 28.
www.reciproque.fr

JEWELRY

Boucheron
26 pl Vendôme 75001.
Map 4 D5.
Tel 01 42 61 58 16.
www.boucheron.com

Cartier
13 rue de la Paix 75002.
Map 4 D5.
Tel 01 58 18 23 00.
www.cartier.fr

Dinh Van
16 rue de la Paix 75002.
Map 4 D5.
Tel 01 42 61 74 49.
www.dinhvan.com

H Stern
3 rue Castiglione 75001.
Map 8 D1.
Tel 01 42 60 22 27.
www.hstern.net

Harry Winston
29 av Montaigne 75008.
Map 6 F1.
Tel 01 47 20 03 09.
www.harrywinston.com

Mauboussin
20 pl Vendôme 75001.
Map 4 D5.
Tel 01 44 55 10 00.
www.mauboussin.com

Mikimoto
8 pl Vendôme 75001.
Map 4 D5.
Tel 01 42 60 33 55.
www.mikimoto.fr

Poiray
1 rue de la Paix 75002.
Map 4 D5.
Tel 01 42 61 70 58.
www.poiray.com

Swarovski Boutique
146 av des Champs-
Elysées 75008. **Map** 2 E4.
Tel 01 45 61 13 80.
www.swarovski.com

SHOES AND BAGS

Carel
4 rue Tronchet 75008.
Map 4 D4.
Tel 01 42 66 21 58.
www.carel.fr

Christian Louboutin
38-40 rue de Grenelle
75007. **Map** 6 F3.
Tel 01 42 22 33 07.
www.christian
louboutin.com

Furla
8 rue de Sèvres 75006.
Map 7 C5.
Tel 01 40 49 06 44.
www.furla.com

Goyard
233 rue St-Honoré 75001.
Map 3 C5.
Tel 01 42 60 57 04.

Jamin Puech
26 rue Gambon 75001.
Map 4 D5.
Tel 01 40 20 40 28.

Jonak
70 rue de Rennes 75006.
Map 12 D1.
Tel 01 45 48 27 11.

Lollipops
60 rue Tiquetonne 75002.
Map 9 A1.
Tel 01 42 33 15 72.
www.lollipops.fr

Miu Miu
219 rue St-Honoré
75001. **Map** 8 D1.
Tel 01 58 62 53 20.
www.miumiu.com

Rodolphe Ménudier
14 rue de Castiglione
75001. **Map** 8 D1.
Tel 01 42 60 86 27.

Vanessa Bruno
25 rue St-Sulpice 75006.
Map 8 E5.
Tel 01 43 54 41 04.
www.vanessabruno.com

LINGERIE

La Boîte à Bas
27 rue Boissy-d'Anglas
75008. **Map** 3 C5.
Tel 01 42 66 26 85.

Cadolle
4 rue Cambon 75001.
Map 4 D5.
Tel 01 42 60 94 22.

Fifi Chachnil
231 rue St-Honoré
75001. **Map** 8 D1.
Tel 01 42 61 21 83.
www.fifichachnil.com

Princesse Tam Tam
52 bd St-Michel 75006.
Map 8 F5.
Tel 01 42 34 99 31.

Sabbia Rosa
73 rue des Sts-Pères
75006. **Map** 8 D4.
Tel 01 45 48 88 37.

Gifts and Souvenirs

Paris has a wealth of stylish gift options, from designer accessories to Eiffel Tower paperweights. Stores on the rue de Rivoli and around major tourist attractions offer a range of cheap vacation paraphernalia, or go to one of the souvenir stores such as **Les Drapeaux de France.**

PERFUME

Many shops advertise discounted perfume. They include **Eiffel Shopping** near the Eiffel Tower. The **Sephora** chain has a big selection, or try the department stores for a range of beauty brands which are hard to find elsewhere.

Parfums Caron has many scents created at the turn-of-the-19th century, which are unavailable elsewhere. Beautifully packaged perfumes made from natural essences are available from **Annick Goutal. Guerlain** has the ultimate in beauty care, while the elegant stores of **L'Artisan Parfumeur** specialize in exquisitely packaged scents evoking specific memories.

HOUSEHOLD GOODS

It is difficult to ignore some of the world's most elegant tableware. Luxury homeware stores line the rue Royale. **Lalique's** Art Nouveau and Art Deco glass sculptures are collected all over the world. Impeccable silverware comes from **Christofle.**

For significant savings on porcelain and crystal, try **Lumicristal,** which stocks Baccarat, Daum, and Limoges crystal, or why not go to **Baccarat** itself.

La Chaise Longue has a selection of fun gift ideas to suit most tastes and **BoConcept** has a wide range of contemporary goods to add a new lease of life to any home.

BOOKS

Some department stores have a books section, and there are several English-language bookstores such as **W H Smith** and **Brentano's.** The cozy **Shakespeare & Company** and **Red Wheelbarrow Bookstore** are good for convivial browsing among expats. French-language bookstores include **La Hune,** specializing in art, film, fashion, and photography, and **Gilbert Joseph** for educational books.

SPECIALTY STORES

A La Civette is perhaps Paris's most beautiful tobacconists, stocking a vast range of cigars behind specially humidified store windows.

One of the world's most famous and delightful toystores is **Au Nain Bleu** while the name **Cassegrain** is synonymous with high-quality stationery and paper products.

DIRECTORY

SOUVENIR STORES

Les Drapeaux de France
1 pl Colette 75001.
Map 8 E1.
Tel *01 40 20 00 11.*

PERFUME

Annick Goutal
16 rue de Bellechasse 75007. **Map** 7 C3.
Tel *01 45 51 36 13.*
www.annickgoutal.com

L'Artisan Parfumeur
24 bd Raspail 75007.
Map 12 D1.
Tel *01 42 22 23 32.*
One of several branches.

Eiffel Shopping
9 av de Suffren 75007.
Map 6 D3.
Tel *01 45 66 55 30.*

Guerlain
68 av des Champs-Elysées 75008. **Map** 2 F5.
Tel *01 45 62 52 57.*
www.guerlain.com

Parfums Caron
34 av Montaigne 75008.
Map 6 F1.
Tel *01 47 23 40 82.*
www.parfumscaron.com

Sephora
70 av des Champs-Elysées 75008. **Map** 7 B1.
Tel *01 53 93 22 50.*
www.sephora.fr

HOUSEHOLD GOODS

Baccarat
11 pl de la Madeleine 75008. **Map** 3 C5.
Tel *01 42 65 36 26.*

BoConcept
8 bd Sebastopol 75004.
Map 9 A3.
Tel *01 42 78 66 66.*

La Chaise Longue
30 rue Croix-des-Petits-Champs 75001. **Map** 8 F1.
Tel *01 42 96 32 14.*

Christofle
24 rue de la Paix 75002.
Map 4 D5. **Tel** *01 42 65 62 43.* www.christofle.com

Lalique
11 rue Royale 75008.
Map 3 C5.
Tel *01 53 05 12 12.*

Lumicristal
29 rue de Paradis 75010.
Tel *01 42 46 60 29.*

BOOKS

Brentano's
37 av de l'Opéra 75002.
Map 4 E5.
Tel *01 42 60 87 37.*
www.brentanos.fr

Gibert Joseph
26 bd St-Michel 75006.
Map 8 F5.
Tel *01 44 41 88 88.*

La Hune
170 bd St-Germain 75006. **Map** 8 D4.
Tel *01 45 48 35 85.*

Red Wheelbarrow Bookstore
22 rue St-Paul 75004.
Map 10 D4.
Tel *01 48 04 75 08.*
www.theredwheel barrow.com

Shakespeare & Company
37 rue de la Bûcherie 75005. **Map** 9 A4.
Tel *01 43 25 40 93.*
www.shakespeare andcompany.com

W H Smith
248 rue de Rivoli 75001.
Map 7 C1.
Tel *01 44 77 88 99.*
www.whsmith.fr

SPECIALTY STORES

A La Civette
157 rue St-Honoré 75001. **Map** 8 F2.
Tel *01 42 96 04 99.*

Au Nain Bleu
5 bd Malesherbes 75008.
Map 3 C5.
Tel *01 42 65 20 00.*
www.aunainbleu.com

Cassegrain
422 rue St-Honoré 75008. **Map** 3 C5.
Tel *01 42 60 20 08.*
www.cassegrain.fr.

Food and Drink

Paris is as famous for food as it is for fashion. Gastronomic treats include *foie gras*, cold meats from the *charcuterie*, cheese, and wine. Certain streets are so overflowing with food stores that you can put together a picnic for 20 in no time: try the rue Montorgueil *(see Map 9 A1)*. The rue Rambuteau, running on either side of the Pompidou Center, has a marvelous row of fish stores and delicatessens.

BREAD AND CAKES

There is a vast range of breads and pastries in France's capital. The *baguette* is often translated as "French bread;" a *bâtard* is similar but thicker, while a *ficelle* is thinner. A *fougasse* is a crusty, flat loaf often filled with onions, cheese, herbs, or spices.

Croissants can be bought *ordinaire* or *au beurre* – the latter is flakier and more buttery. *Pain au chocolat* is a chocolate-filled pastry eaten for breakfast, and *chausson aux pommes* is filled with apples. There are also pear, plum, and rhubarb variations. A *pain aux raisins* is a bread-like wheel filled with custard and raisins.

Poilâne sells perhaps the only bread in Paris known by the name of its baker (the late Lionel, brother of Max) and his hearty wholewheat loaves are tremendously popular.

Many think **Ganachaud** bakes the best bread in Paris. Thirty different kinds, including ingredients such as walnuts and fruit, are made in the old-fashioned ovens.

Les Panetons is a good chain bakery. Favorites here include five-grain bread, sesame rolls, and *mouchoir aux pommes*, a variation on the traditional *chausson*.

Many of the Jewish delicatessens have the best ryes and the only pumpernickels in town. One of the best is **Sacha Finkelsztajn**.

Le Moulin de la Vierge uses a wood fire to bake organic breads and rich pound cakes. **J L Poujauran** is known for his black-olive bread and nut-and-raisin wholegrain breads.

Pierre Hermé is to cakes what Chanel is to fashion, while **Ladurée**'s macaroons are legendary.

CHOCOLATE

Like all food in France, chocolate is to be savored. **Christian Constant's** low-sugar creations are made with pure cocoa and are known to connoisseurs. **Dalloyau** makes all types of chocolate and is not too expensive (it is also known for its pâtisserie and cold meats). **Fauchon** is world famous for its luxury food products. Its chocolates are excellent, as is the pâtisserie. Robert Linxe at **La Maison du Chocolat** is constantly inventing fresh, rich chocolates with mouthwatering exotic ingredients. **Richart** boasts beautifully presented and hugely expensive chocolates, which are usually coated with dark chocolate or liqueur-filled.

CHARCUTERIE AND FOIE GRAS

Charcuteries often sell cheese, snails, truffles, smoked salmon, caviar, and wine as well as cold meats. **Fauchon** has a good grocery, as does the department store **Le Bon Marché**. **Hédiard** is a luxury store similar to Fauchon, and **Maison de la Truffe** sells *foie gras* and sausages as well as truffles. For Beluga caviar, Georgian tea, and Russian vodka, go to **Petrossian**.

The Lyon and Auvergne regions of France are the best known for their *charcuterie*, and **Jean-Jacques Chrétienne** sells excellent examples. **Maison Pou** is a sparklingly clean and popular store selling *pâté en croute* (pâté baked in pastry), *boudins* (black and white puddings), Lyonnais sausages, ham, and *foie gras*. Just off the Champs-Elysées, **Vignon** has superb *foie gras* and Lyonnais

sausages as well as popular prepared food.

Together with truffles and caviar, *foie gras* is the ultimate in gourmet food. Though most specialty food stores sell *foie gras*, you can be sure of quality at **Comtesse du Barry**, which has six outlets in Paris. **Divay** is relatively inexpensive and will ship overseas. **Labeyrie** has a range of beautifully packaged *foie gras* suitable for giving as presents.

CHEESE

Although camembert is undoubtedly a favorite, there is an overwhelming range of cheeses available and a friendly *fromager* will always help you choose. **Marie-Anne Cantin** is one of the leading figures in the fight to protect traditional production methods, and her fine cheeses are available from the store that she inherited from her father. Some say that **Alléosse** is the best cheese delicatessen in Paris – all the cheeses are made according to traditional methods. **Crèmerie Quatrehomme** sells farm-made cheeses, many of which are in danger of becoming extinct; these include a rare and delicious truffle Brie (when in season). **Le Jardin Fromager** is one of the best stores in Paris for all types of cheese – the *chèvre* (goat's cheese) is particularly good, as are the *camemberts au lait cru* (cheese made with unpasteurized milk), which ooze over the plate. **Barthélémy** in the rue de Grenelle has a truly exceptional Roquefort. **Androuët** is a Parisian institution with several branches across the city. Try a pungent Munster or a really ripe Brie. A charming cheese store, **La Fermette**, offers a dazzling array of dairy products, which the staff will encase in plastic for the journey home, imperative when bringing cheese through customs.

Well-heeled locals line up in the street to buy oozing *livarot* and sharp *chèvre* from **La Fromagerie d'Auteuil**.

WINE

The chain store which has practically cornered the everyday tippling market is **Nicolas** – there is a branch in every neighborhood with a range of wines to suit all pockets. As a rule, the salespeople are knowledgeable and helpful. Try the charming **Legrand Filles et Fils** for a carefully chosen selection of high-end champagnes. **Caves Taillevent** on the rue du Faubourg-St-Honoré is worth a sightseeing tour. It is an enormous, overwhelming cellar with some of the most expensive wine.

Cave Péret on the rue Daguerre has a vast selection of wines and can offer personal advice to help you with your purchase. The beautiful **Ryst-Dupeyron**, in the St-Germain quarter, displays whiskies, wines, ports, and Monsieur Ryst's own Armagnac. He will even personalize a bottle for that special occasion.

Other great wine stores include **Lavinia**, which is the largest in Europe, and, by contrast, **Renaud Michel** at Place de la Nation, whose small boutique is very well stocked and well connected. The staff in **Les Caves Augé** are also very knowledgeable and friendly.

DIRECTORY

BREAD AND CAKES

Ganachaud
226 rue des Pyrénées 75020.
Tel 01 43 58 42 62.

J L Poujauran
18 rue Jean-Nicot 75007.
Map 6 F2.
Tel 01 43 17 35 20.

Ladurée
75 av des Champs-Elysées 75008. **Map** 2 F5.
Tel 01 40 75 08 75.

Le Moulin de la Vierge
105 rue Vercingétorix 75014. **Map** 11 A4.
Tel 01 45 43 09 84.

Les Panetons
113 rue Mouffetard 75005. **Map** 13 B2.
Tel 01 47 07 12 08.

Pierre Hermé
72 rue Bonaparte 75006.
Map 8 E4.
Tel 01 43 54 47 77.

Poilâne
8 rue du Cherche-Midi 75006. **Map** 8 D4.
Tel 01 45 48 42 59.

Sacha Finkelsztajn
27 rue des Rosiers 75004.
Map 9 C3.
Tel 01 42 72 78 91.

CHOCOLATE

Christian Constant
37 rue d'Assas 75006.
Map 12 E1.
Tel 01 53 63 15 15.

Dalloyau
101 rue du Faubourg-St-Honoré 75008. **Map** 3 B5.
Tel 01 42 99 90 00.

Fauchon
26 pl de la Madeleine 75008. **Map** 3 C5.
Tel 01 70 39 38 00.

La Maison du Chocolat
225 rue du Faubourg-St-Honoré 75008. **Map** 2 E3.
Tel 01 42 27 39 44.

Richart
258 bd St-Germain 75007. **Map** 7 C2.
Tel 01 45 55 66 00.

CHARCUTERIE AND FOIE GRAS

Comtesse du Barry
1 rue de Sèvres 75006.
Map 8 D4.
Tel 01 45 48 32 04.

Divay
4 rue Bayen 75017. **Map** 2 D2. *Tel 01 43 80 16 97.*

Hédiard
21 pl de la Madeleine 75008. **Map** C5.
Tel 01 43 12 88 88.

Jean-Jacques Chrétienne
58 rue des Martyrs 75009. **Map** 4 F2.
Tel 01 48 78 96 45.

Labeyrie
11 rue d'Auteuil 75016.
Map 5 A5.
Tel 01 42 24 17 62.

Le Bon Marché
24 rue de Sèvres 75007.
Map 7 C5.
Tel 01 44 39 80 00.

Maison de la Truffe
19 pl de la Madeleine 75008. **Map** 3 C5.
Tel 01 42 65 53 22.

Maison Pou
16 av des Ternes 75017.
Map 2 D3.
Tel 01 43 80 19 24.

Petrossian
18 bd Latour-Maubourg 75007. **Map** 7 A2.
Tel 01 44 11 32 25.

Vignon
13 rue Clément-Marot 75008. **Map** 2 E5.
Tel 01 47 20 10 01.

CHEESE

Alléosse
13 rue Poncelet 75017.
Map 2 E3.
Tel 01 46 22 50 45.

Androuët
134 rue Mouffetard 75005. **Map** 13 B1.
Tel 01 45 87 85 05.

Barthélémy
51 rue de Grenelle 75007. **Map** 8 D4.
Tel 01 45 48 56 75.

Crèmerie Quatrehomme
62 rue de Sèvres 75007.
Map 7 C5.
Tel 01 47 34 33 45.

La Fermette
86 rue Montorgueil 75002. **Map** 9 A1.
Tel 01 42 36 70 96.

La Fromagerie d'Auteuil
58 rue d'Auteuil 75016.
Map 5 A5.
Tel 01 45 25 07 10.

Le Jardin Fromager
53 rue Oberkampf 75011.
Map 10 E1.
Tel 01 48 05 19 96.

Marie-Anne Cantin
12 rue du Champ-de-Mars 75007.
Map 6 F3.
Tel 01 45 50 43 94.

WINE

Cave Péret
6 rue Daguerre 75014.
Map 12 F4.
Tel 01 43 22 08 64.

Les Caves Augé
116 bd Haussman 75008.
Map 3 C4.
Tel 01 45 22 16 97.

Caves Taillevent
199 rue du Faubourg-St-Honoré 75008.
Map 2 F3.
Tel 01 45 61 14 09.

Lavinia
3–5 bd de la Madeleine 75008.
Map 4 D5.
Tel 01 42 97 20 20.

Legrand Filles et Fils
1 rue de la Banque 75002.
Map 8 F1.
Tel 01 42 60 07 12.

Nicolas
35 bd Malesherbes 75008.
Map 3 C5.
Tel 01 42 65 00 85.

Renaud Michel
12 pl de la Nation 75012.
Tel 01 43 07 98 93.

Ryst-Dupeyron
79 rue du Bac 75007.
Map 8 D3.
Tel 01 45 48 80 93.

Arts and Antiques

In Paris you can either buy art and antiques from stores and galleries with established reputations, or from flea markets and avant-garde galleries. Many of the prestigious antiques stores and galleries are located around the rue du Faubourg-St-Honoré and are worth a visit even if you can't afford to buy. On the Left Bank is Le Carré Rive Gauche, an organization of 30 antiques dealers.

EXPORTING

Objets d'art over 50 years old, worth more than a given amount, will require a *Certificat pour un bien culturel* to be exported (provided by the vendor), plus a *licence d'exportation* for non-EU countries. Seek professional advice from the large antique stores. The **Centre des Renseignements des Douanes** has a booklet, *Bulletin Officiel des Douanes*, with all the details.

ANTIQUES

If you wish to buy antiques, you might like to stroll around the areas that boast the most galleries – in Le Carré Rive Gauche around quai Malaquais, try **L'Arc en Seine** and **Anne-Sophie Duval** for Art Nouveau and Art Deco. Rue Jacob is still one of the best places to seek beautiful objects, antique or modern. Close to the Louvre, the

Louvre des Antiquaires comprises 250 stores selling mainly expensive, quality furniture. Many of the prestigious antiques stores are near rue du Faubourg-St-Honoré including **Didier Aaron**, expert on furniture from the 17th and 18th centuries. **Village St-Paul** is the most charming group of antiques shops and is also open on Sundays. In the south of the city, **Le Village Suisse** also groups many art and antiques dealers.

ART GALLERIES

Established art galleries are located on or around the avenue Montaigne. The **Louise Leiris** gallery was founded by D.H. Kahnweiler, the dealer who "discovered" both Georges Braque and Pablo Picasso. The gallery still shows Cubist masterpieces.

On the Left Bank **Galerie Maeght** has a tremendous stock of paintings at prices to

suit most budgets; he also publishes fine art books.

Rue Louise-Weiss, known as Scène Est, has become the area for cutting-edge creativity and innovation. The **Air de Paris** gallery is popular.

In the Marais try **Yvon Lambert** and **Galerie du Jour Agnès B.**, in the Bastille, **Lavignes-Bastille** and **L et M Durand-Dessert**, also a fashionable place to buy catalogs on new artists, if not their works.

AUCTION HOUSES

The great Paris auction center, in operation since 1858, is **Drouot-Richelieu**. Bidding can be intimidating since most of it is done by dealers. Beware of the auctioneer's high-speed patter. *La Gazette de L'Hôtel Drouot* tells you which auctions are coming up when. Drouot-Richelieu also has its own auction catalog. The house only accepts cash and French checks, but there is an exchange desk in-house. A 10–15 percent commission to the house is charged, so remember to add it onto any price you hear. You may view from 11am–6pm on the day before the sale, and from 11am to noon on the morning of the sale.

DIRECTORY

Markets

For eye-catching displays of wonderful food, or a lively shopping atmosphere, there is no better place than a Paris market. There are large covered food markets, markets where stalls change regularly, and permanent street markets. Some of the more famous markets, with approximate opening times, follow. While you are enjoying browsing round the stalls, remember to keep an eye on your money and be prepared to bargain.

FOOD MARKETS

The French still shop daily, hence food markets are always packed. Most fruit and vegetable markets are open from around 8am–1pm and from 4–7pm Tuesday to Saturday, and from 9am–1pm Sunday. Watch out for rotten produce – buy produce loose, not in boxes. A little language is useful for specifying *pas trop mûr* (not too ripe), or *pour manger ce soir* (to be eaten tonight).

FLEA MARKETS

It is often said that you can no longer find bargains at the Paris flea markets. Though this may be true, it is still worth going to one for the sheer fun of browsing. Whether you pick up any real bargains has as much to do with luck as with judgement. Often the sellers themselves have little or no idea of the true value of their goods – which can work either for or against you. The biggest and most famous market, incorporating several smaller ones, is the Marché aux Puces de St-Ouen. Keep an eye on your wallet, as pickpockets frequent these markets.

Marché d'Aligre

Pl d'Aligre 75012. **Map** 10 F5. M *Ledru-Rollin.* ◯ *9am–1pm & 4–7:30pm Tue–Sat, 9am–1:30pm Sun.*

Reminiscent of a Moroccan bazaar, this must be the cheapest and liveliest market in the city. Here traders hawk ingredients such as North African olives, groundnuts, and hot peppers, and there are even a few halal butchers. Stalls on the square sell mostly second-hand clothes and bric-a-brac. This is a less affluent area of town with few tourists and many Parisians.

Marché Enfant Rouges

39 rue de Bretagne 75003. **Map** 10 D2. M *Temple, Filles-du-Calvaire.* ◯ *8:30am–1pm, 4–7pm Tue–Sat (8pm Fri, Sat), 8:30am–2pm Sun.*

This part-covered fruit and vegetable market dates from 1620. Famous for the freshness of its produce, on Sunday mornings street singers and accordionists help enliven the proceedings. There are also plenty of cheap eateries here.

Marché Raspail

75006. **Map** 8 D4. M *Rennes.* ◯ *7am–2:30pm Tue & Fri, 9am–3pm Sun.*

Conveniently situated between Montparnasse and St-Germain, Raspail market sells fresh produce during the week and organic only produce on Sundays.

Marché St-Germain

4–8 rue Lobineau 75006. **Map** 8 E4. M *Mabillon.* ◯ *10am–7:30pm Mon–Sat.*

St-Germain is one of the few covered markets left in Paris. Here you can buy Italian, Mexican, Greek, Asian, and organic produce.

Rue Montorgueil

75001 & 75002. **Map** 9 A1. M *Les Halles.* ◯ *9am–7pm daily (subject to change).*

The paved rue Montorgueil is what remains of the old Les Halles market. Here you can buy exotic fruit and vegetables like green bananas and yams, or sample offerings from the delicatessens. Expect high prices.

Rue Mouffetard

75005. **Map** 13 B2. M *Pl Monge.* ◯ *8am–1pm Tue–Sun.*

This is one of the oldest market streets in Paris, and although it has become touristy it is still a charming winding street full of quality food. There is also a lively African market down the nearby side street of rue Daubenton.

Rue Poncelet

75017. **Map** 2 E3. M *Ternes.* ◯ *8am–noon, 4–7:30pm Tue–Sat, 8am–12:30pm Sun.*

Situated away from the main tourist areas, this market street is worth visiting for its authentic French atmosphere. Choose from many bakeries, pâtisseries, and *charcuteries*.

Marché de la Porte de Vanves

Av Georges-Lafenestre & av Marc-Sangnier 75014. M *Porte-de-Vanves.* ◯ *7am–3 or 5pm Sat & Sun.*

Porte de Vanves is a small market selling good-quality bric-a-brac and junk as well as some second-hand furniture. It's best to get to the market early on Saturday morning for the best choice of wares. Artists exhibit nearby.

Marché aux Puces de Montreuil

Porte de Montreuil, 93 Montreuil 75020. M *Porte-de-Montreuil.* ◯ *7am–7:30pm Sat–Mon.*

Go early to the Porte de Montreuil flea market, where you'll have a better chance of picking up a bargain. The substantial second-hand clothes section attracts many young people. Stalls sell everything from used bicycles to bric-à-brac and exotic spices.

Marché aux Puces de St-Ouen

(see p134.)

This is the most well known, the most crowded, and the most expensive of all the flea markets. Here you'll find a range of markets, locals dealing from their car trunks, and a number of large buildings packed with stalls. Some of them are very upmarket; others sell junk. A *Guide des Puces* (guide to the flea markets) can be obtained from the information kiosk in the Marché Biron on the rue des Rosiers.

Rue de Seine and Rue de Buci

75006. **Map** 8 E4. M *Odéon.* ◯ *8am–1pm, 4–7pm Tue–Sat, 9am–1pm Sun.*

The stalls here are expensive and crowded but sell quality fruit and vegetables. There is also a large flower shop and two excellent pâtisseries.

ENTERTAINMENT IN PARIS

Whether your preference is for classical drama, avant-garde theater, ballet, opera or jazz, cinema, or dancing the night away, Paris has it all. There is plenty of free entertainment, too, from the street performers outside the Pompidou Center to musicians busking all over town and in the metros.

Parisians themselves like nothing better than strolling along the boulevards or sitting at a sidewalk café

nursing a drink as they watch the world go by. If, however, you're looking for the ultimate "Oh la-la!" experience, you can visit any of the celebrated nightclubs.

Spectator sports fans have tennis, the Tour de France, or horse racing. Recreation centers and gyms cater to the more active. And for those disposed to more leisurely pursuits, there is always a quiet game of boules to be played in the park.

The glass façade of the Bastille Opéra

BUYING TICKETS

Depending on the event, tickets can often be bought at the door, but for popular events it is wiser to purchase tickets in advance at the **FNAC** chains or **Virgin Megastore**. Theater box offices open daily from about 11am–7pm. Most accept credit card reservations by telephone.

THEATER

From the grandeur of the **Comédie Française** to slapstick farce and avant-garde drama, theater is flourishing, both in Paris and in its suburbs. Founded in 1680 by royal decree, the Comédie Française is the bastion of French theater, aiming to keep classical drama in the public eye and to perform works by the best modern playwrights. Formerly the second theater of the Comédie Française, the **Odéon Théâtre de l'Europe** now specializes in plays from other countries, performed in their original language. In an

underground auditorium in the Art Deco Palais de Chaillot, the **Théâtre National de Chaillot** is famed for staging some very lively productions of European classics. The **Théâtre National de la Colline** specializes in contemporary drama.

Among the most important of the serious independents is the **Comédie des Champs-Elysées**, while for over 100 years the **Palais Royal** has been known as the temple of risqué farce. The café theaters such as **Théâtre d'Edgar** and **Le Point Virgule** are always good venues for seeing the best of the emerging new talent.

In the summer, street theater thrives in tourist areas such as the Pompidou Center, Les Halles, and St-Germain-des-Prés. Open-air performances of Shakespeare and classic French plays are given at the Shakespeare Garden in the Bois de Boulogne.

CLASSICAL MUSIC

Paris has many first-class venues with an excellent range of opera, classical, and contemporary music productions. Opened in 1989, the stylish, 2,700-seat **Opéra National de Paris Bastille** stages classic and modern operas. The beautifully renovated **Opéra National Garnier** puts on mostly ballets.

The **Salle Pleyel** is Paris's principal concert hall, housing the Orchestre de Paris and Radio France's Philharmonic Orchestra. Both the **Théâtre des Champs-Elysées** and the **Théâtre du Châtelet** are recommended for their varied high-quality programs. Venues for chamber music include the **Salle Gaveau** and the **Théâtre de la Ville**. The **Cité**

LISTINGS MAGAZINES

Pariscope, Zurban, and *L'Officiel des Spectacles* are the best listings magazines in Paris. Published every Wednesday, you can pick them up at any newsstand. *Le Figaro* also has a good listings section on Wednesdays. *The City* is published quarterly in English, and is available at news-stands or W H Smith *(see p145)*.

The famous silhouette of the Moulin Rouge nightclub

de la **Musique** in the Parc de la Villette is one of Paris' most vibrant concert halls. The venue is renowned for its eclectic music programs and workshops, while the museum charts the history of music, and exhibits over 4,000 instruments.

DANCE

The French are very vocal in their appreciation or dislike of dance, and those who fail to please are subjected to boos, hisses, and mass walkouts in mid-performance.

The opulent **Opéra National Garnier** has space for 450 artists and is home to the Ballet de l'Opéra de Paris, which has earned a reputation as one of the best classical ballet companies in the world. Government support has helped the **Théâtre de la Ville** to become Paris's most important venue for modern dance, with subsidies keeping ticket costs relatively low.

The **Maison des Arts de Créteil** stages famous overseas companies, as well as its own much praised productions.

CLUBS AND CABARET

Music in Paris clubs tends to follow the trends set in the U.S. and Britain. Only a few clubs such as **Balajo**, once frequented by Edith Piaf, and the ultrahip **Showcase**, under the Alexandre III bridge, are genuinely up-to-the-minute with their music.

Showcase attracts a young crowd to its big-name DJ nights. **Le Baron** is a trendy nightspot, attracting people from the fashion world and from show business.

For comedy in English, try **La Java**. The stage of this club, where Edith Piaf once performed, now showcases British and American comedians.

When it comes to picking a cabaret, the rule of thumb is simple: the better known places are best. The **Folies-Bergère** is the oldest music hall in Paris and probably the most famous in the world. It is closely rivaled by the **Lido** and the **Moulin Rouge**, birthplace of the cancan. **Paradis Latin** is the most "French" cabaret in the city. It shows variety acts whose sketches are enlivened by remarkable special effects and scenery.

ROCK, JAZZ AND WORLD MUSIC

The top international acts are usually to be found at the enormous arenas such as **Palais Omnisports Paris-Bercy** or the **Zenith**. For a more intimate atmosphere, the legendary **Olympia** has assigned seating and good acoustics. To hear indigenous rock groups like Les Negresses Vertes and Mano Negra go to **La Cigale** or **Elysée-Montmartre** in the Pigalle area.

Jazz-crazy Paris has innumerable packed clubs where the best talent in the world can be heard on any evening. All the great jazz musicians have performed at **New Morning**, which also hosts African, Brazilian, and other sounds. For Dixieland go to **Le Petit Journal St-Michel**.

World music and jazz lovers alike can see top acts and dance until dawn at the excellent **Chapelle des Lombards**.

The spectacular façade of the Opéra National Garnier

MOVIES

Paris is the world's capital of film appreciation. It was the cradle of the cinematograph nearly 100 years ago. Then in the late 1950s and early 1960s the city nurtured that very Parisian vanguard movement, the New Wave, when movie directors such as François Truffaut and Jean-Luc Godard revolutionized the way movies were made and perceived.

There are now more than 370 screens within the city limits, distributed among over 100 movie theaters. Most are concentrated in cinema belts, which enjoy the added appeal of nearby restaurants and stores. The Champs-Elysées has the densest movie theater strip in town, where you can see the latest Hollywood smash or French *auteur* triumph, as well as some classic re-issues.

In the vicinity of the Opéra de Paris Garnier, the theaters in the Grands Boulevards include two notable landmarks: the 2,800-seat **Le Grand Rex**, with its Baroque decor, and the **Max Linder Panorama**, which was completely refurbished in the 1980s. The place de Clichy is the last Parisian stronghold of Pathé, while the hub of Right Bank cinema is in the Forum des Halles mall. France's largest screen is at **La Géode**.

On the Left Bank, Odéon St-Germain-des-Prés has taken over from the Latin Quarter as the city's heartland for art and repertory movie theaters. The huge **MK2 Bibliothèque** points to the future with its collection of 14 screens, a bar, stores, and exhibition space.

The dome of the 2,800-seat Le Grand Rex movie theater

SPORTS

Paris is host to some of the foremost sporting events in the world. City-wide frenzy sweeps Paris when the Tour de France bicycle race finishes there in July. From late May to mid-June Parisians live and breathe tennis during the **Roland Garros** national tennis championship. The Prix de l'Arc de Triomphe, held at the **Hippodrome de Longchamp** on the first Sunday in October, provides the opportunity to see the rich in all their finery as well as first-class flat racing.

The **Palais Omnisports Paris-Bercy** is the venue for a vast range of events, including the Paris tennis open, and rock concerts, as is the new **Stade de France** at St-Denis. **Parc des Princes** is home to Paris's top football team, Paris St-Germain.

THE CELEBRATED CAFES OF PARIS

One of the most enduring images of Paris is the Left Bank café scene where great artists, writers, and eminent intellectuals consorted. Before World War I, hordes of Russian revolutionaries, including Lenin and Trotsky, whiled away their days in the Rotonde and the Dôme in Montparnasse. In the 1920s, Surrealists dominated café life. Later came the American writers led by Ernest Hemingway and F. Scott Fitzgerald, whose haunts included La Coupole. After World War II, Jean-Paul Sartre and other Existentialists shifted the cultural scene northward to St-Germain.

Newspaper reading remains a typical café pastime

DIRECTORY

BUYING TICKETS

FNAC
26–30 av des Ternes
75017. **Map** 2 D3.
Tel 08 25 02 00 20.
Forum Les Halles, 1 rue
Pierre Lescot 75001.
Map 9 A2. *Tel* 08 25 02
00 20. www.fnac.com

Virgin Megastore
52–60 av des Champs-
Elysées 75008. **Map** 2 F5.
Tel 01 49 53 50 00.
www.virginmegastore.fr

THEATER

Comédie des
Champs-Elysées
15 av Montaigne 75008.
Map 6 F1.
Tel 01 53 23 99 19.

Comédie Française
1 pl Colette 75001. **Map**
8 E1. *Tel* 0825 10 16 80.
www.comedie-francaise.fr

Odéon Théâtre
de l'Europe
Pl de l'Odéon 75006. **Map**
12 F5. *Tel* 01 44 85 40 40.
www.theatre-odeon.fr

Palais Royal
38 rue Montpensier
75001. **Map** 8 E1.
Tel 01 42 97 40 00.

Le Point Virgule
7 rue Ste-Croix de la
Bretonnerie 75004. **Map**
9 C3. *Tel* 01 42 78 67 03.

Théâtre d'Edgar
58 bd Edgar-Quinet
75014. **Map** 12 D2.
Tel 01 42 79 97 97.

Théâtre National
de Chaillot
Pl du Trocadéro 75016.
Map 5 C2.
Tel 01 53 65 30 00.
www.theatre-chaillot.fr

Théâtre National
de la Colline
15 rue Malte-Brun 75020.
Tel 01 44 62 52 52.
www.colline.fr

CLASSICAL MUSIC

Cité de la Musique
221 av Jean-Jaurès 75019.
Tel 01 44 84 44 84.
www.cite-musique.fr

Opéra National de
Paris Bastille
120 rue de Lyon 75012.
Map 10 E4.
Tel 08 92 89 90 90.
www.operadeparis.fr

Opéra National
de Paris Garnier
Pl de l'Opera 75009. **Map**
4 E5. *Tel* 08 92 89 90 90.

Salle Gaveau
45 rue la Boétie 75008.
Map 3 B4.
Tel 01 49 53 05 07.
www.sallegaveau.com

Salle Pleyel
252 rue du Faubourg St-
Honoré 75008. **Map** 2 E3.
Tel 01 42 56 13 13.
www.sallepleyel.fr

Théâtre des
Champs-Elysées
15 av Montaigne 75008.
Map 6 F1. *Tel* 01 49 52
50 00. www.theatre
deschampselysees.fr

Théâtre du Châtelet
Pl du Châtelet 75001.
Map 9 A3. *Tel* 01 40 28
28 40. www.chatelet-
theatre.com

Théâtre de la Ville
2 pl du Châtelet 75004.
Map 9 A3. *Tel* 01 42 74
22 77. www.theatre
delaville-paris.com

DANCE

Maison des Arts
de Créteil
Pl Salvador Allende 94000
Créteil. *Tel* 01 45 13 19 19.
www.maccreteil.com

Opéra Garnier
(See Classical Music.)

Théâtre de la Ville
(See Classical Music.)

CLUBS AND
CABARET

Balajo
9 rue de Lappe 75011.
Map 10 E4. *Tel* 09 54 94
54 09. www.balajo.fr

Le Baron
6 av Marceau 75008.
Map 6 E1.
Tel 01 47 20 04 01.

Folies-Bergère
32 rue Richer 75009.
Tel 08 92 68 16 50.
www.foliesbergere.com

La Java
105 rue du Faubourg-du-
Temple 75010.
Tel 01 42 02 20 52.

Lido
116 bis av des Champs-
Elysées 75008. **Map** 2 E4.
Tel 01 40 76 56 10.
www.lido.fr

La Machine du
Moulin Rouge
90 bd de Clichy 75018.
Map 4 D1.
Tel 01 56 55 52 04.

Moulin Rouge
82 bd de Clichy 75018.
Map 4 E1. *Tel* 01 53 09 82
82. www.moulinrouge.fr

Paradis Latin
28 rue du Cardinal-
Lemoine 75005. **Map** 9
B5. *Tel* 01 43 25 28 28.

Showcase
Porte des Champs-Elysées
75008. **Map** 7 A1.
Tel 01 45 61 25 43.
www.showcase.fr

ROCK, JAZZ, AND
WORLD MUSIC

Chapelle des
Lombards
19 rue de Lappe 75011.
Map 10 F4.
Tel 01 43 57 24 24.

La Cigale
120 bd Rochechouart
75018. **Map** 4 F2.
Tel 01 49 25 89 99.

Elysée-Montmartre
72 bd Rochechouart
75018. **Map** 4 F2.
Tel 01 44 92 45 36.

New Morning
7–9 rue des Petites-
Ecuries 75010.
Tel 01 45 23 51 41.

Olympia
28 bd des Capucines
75009. **Map** 4 D5.
Tel 08 92 68 33 68.
www.olympiahall

Palais Omnisports
Paris-Bercy
8 bd de Bercy 75012.
Map 14 F2. *Tel* 08 92 39
04 90. www.bercy.fr

Le Petit Journal
St-Michel
71 bd St-Michel 75005.
Map 12 F1.
Tel 01 43 26 28 59.

Zénith
211 av de Jean-Jaurès
75019. *Tel* 08 90 71 02 07.
www.zenith-paris.com

MOVIES

La Géode
26 av Corentin-Cariou
75019.
📞 08 92 68 45 40.
www.lageode.fr

Le Grand Rex
1 bd Poissonnière 75002.
📞 08 92 68 05 96.
www.legrandrex.com

Max Linder
Panorama
24 bd Poissonnière
75009.
📞 08 92 68 00 31.

MK2 Bibliothèque
128–162 av de France
75013. 📞 08 92 69 84
84. www.mk2.com

SPORTS

Hippodrome de
Longchamp
Route des Tribunes
75016. *Tel* 01 44 30
75 00.

Palais Omnisports
Paris-Bercy
(see Rock section.)

Parc des Princes
24 rue du Commandant-
Guilbaud 75016.
Tel 3275.

Stade de France
La Plaine St-Denis 93210.
Tel 08 92 70 09 00.
www.stadedefrance.fr

Stade Roland
Garros
2 av Gordon-Bennett
75016. *Tel* 01 47 43
48 00. www.fft.fr/
rolandgarros/

PARIS STREET FINDER

The map references given with sights, stores, and entertainment venues described in the Paris section of the guide refer to the maps on the following pages. Map references are also given for Paris hotels *(see pp550–5)* and restaurants *(pp600–6),* and for useful addresses in the *Travelers' Needs* and *Survival Guide* sections at the back of the book. The maps include not only the main sightseeing areas but also the most important districts for hotels, restaurants, shopping, and entertainment venues. The key map below shows the area of Paris covered by the *Street Finder,* with the *arrondissement* numbers for the various districts. The symbols used for sights and other features on the *Street Finder* maps are listed opposite.

Paris is divided into 20 *arrondissements,* outlined in orange and numbered on this map.

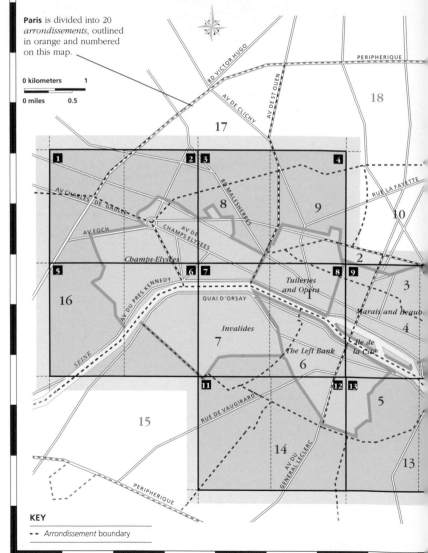

0 kilometers   1

0 miles   0.5

KEY

- - - *Arrondissement* boundary

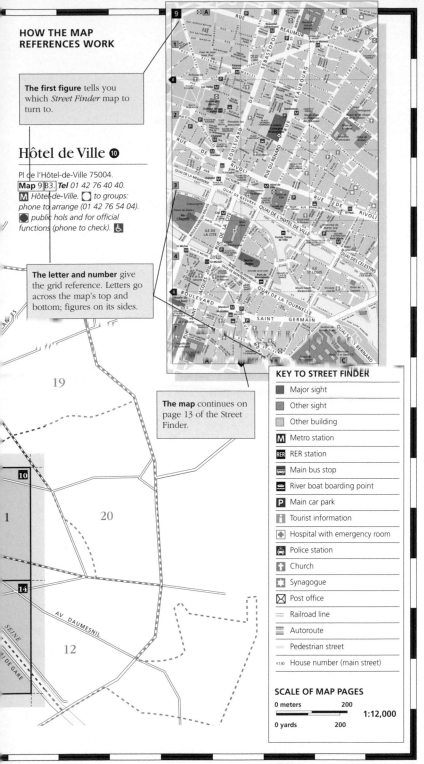

HOW THE MAP REFERENCES WORK

The first figure tells you which *Street Finder* map to turn to.

Hôtel de Ville ⓾

Pl de l'Hôtel-de-Ville 75004.
Map 9 B3. **Tel** 01 42 76 40 40.
Ⓜ *Hôtel-de-Ville.* ⬜ to groups: phone to arrange (01 42 76 54 04).
⬤ public hols and for official functions (phone to check). ♿

The letter and number give the grid reference. Letters go across the map's top and bottom; figures on its sides.

The map continues on page 13 of the Street Finder.

KEY TO STREET FINDER

- 🟥 Major sight
- 🟫 Other sight
- ⬜ Other building
- Ⓜ Metro station
- RER RER station
- 🚌 Main bus stop
- 🚤 River boat boarding point
- 🅿 Main car park
- ℹ Tourist information
- 🏥 Hospital with emergency room
- 🚓 Police station
- ✝ Church
- ✡ Synagogue
- ⊠ Post office
- ═ Railroad line
- ▬ Autoroute
- ▬ Pedestrian street
- ‹130 House number (main street)

SCALE OF MAP PAGES

| 0 meters | 200 |
| 0 yards | 200 |

1:12,000

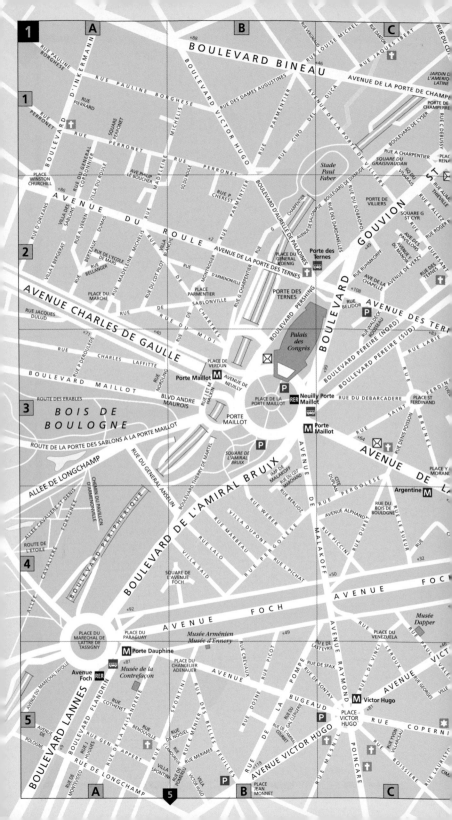

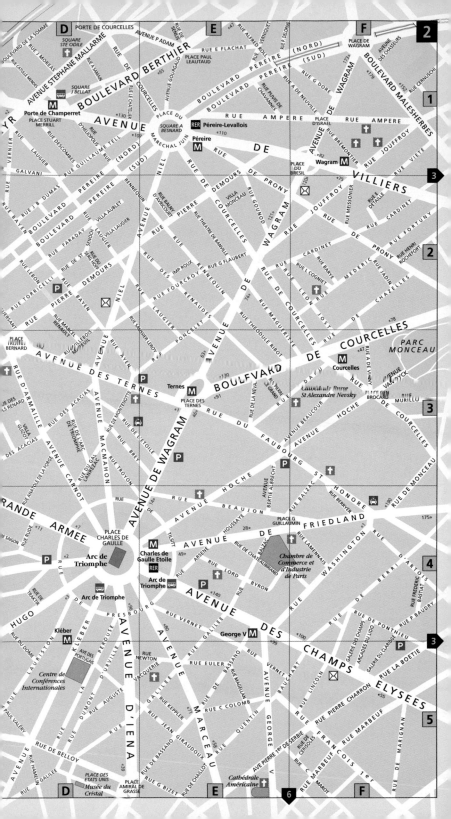

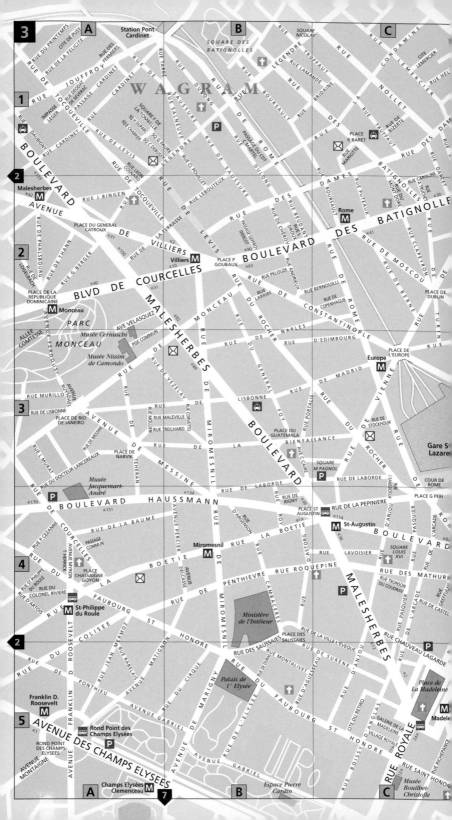

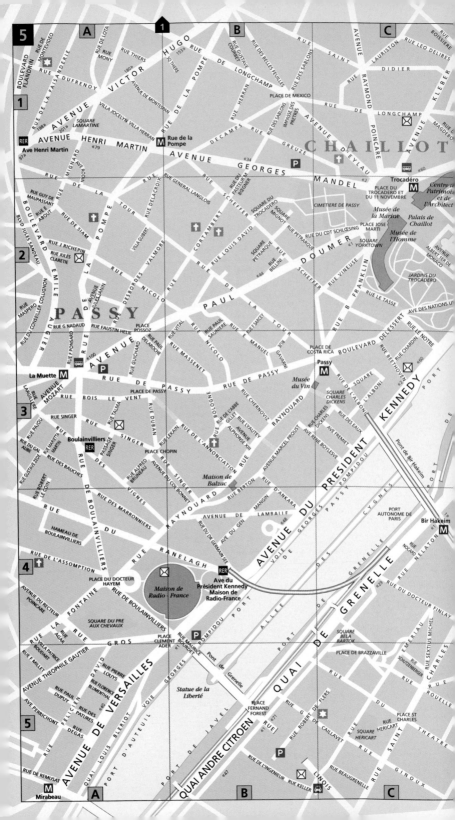

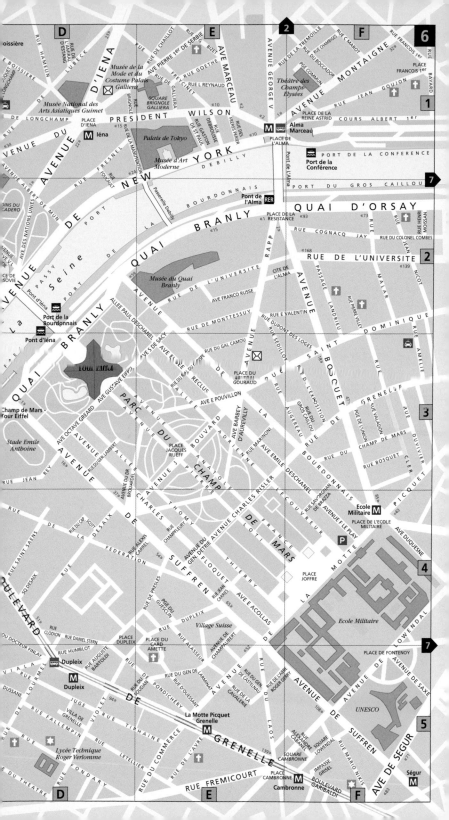

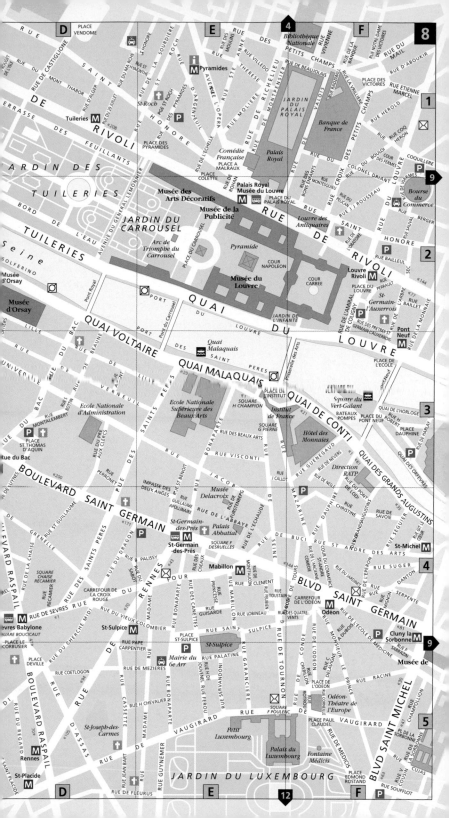

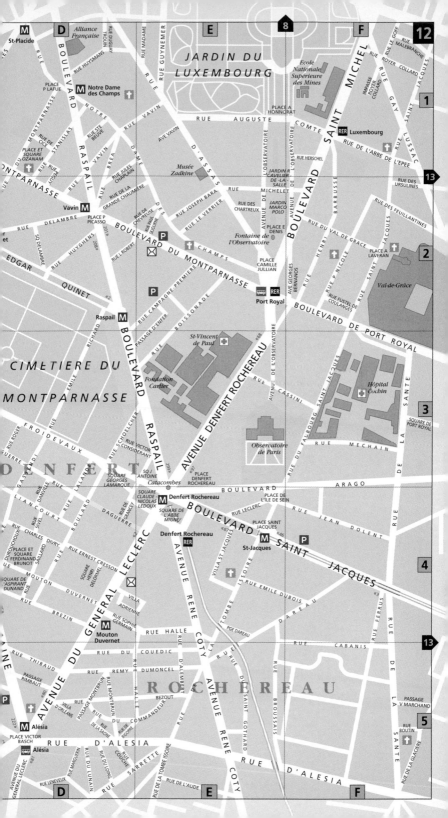

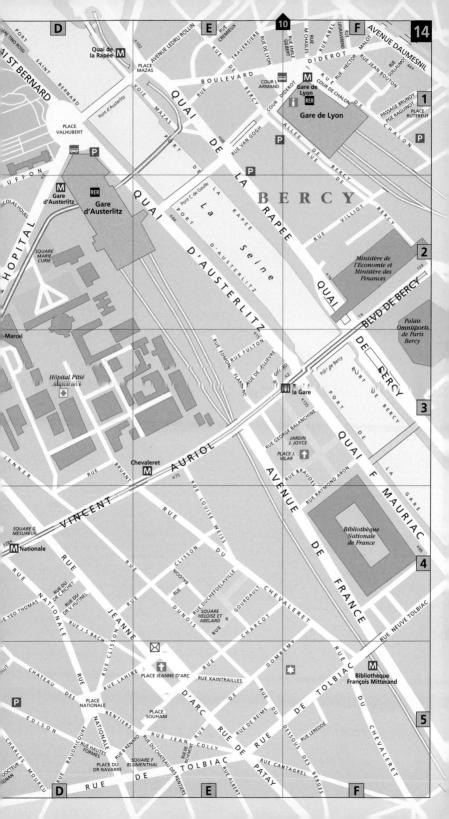

ILE DE FRANCE

Set at the heart of France, with Paris as its hub, Ile de France extends well beyond the densely populated suburbs of the city. Its rich countryside incorporates a historic royal region of monumental splendour central to *"la gloire de la France."*

The region became a favorite with French royalty after François I transformed Fontainebleau into a Renaissance palace in 1528. Louis XIV kept the Ile de France as the political axis of the country when he started building Versailles in 1661. This Classical château created by the combined genius of Le Nôtre, Le Vau, Le Brun, and Jules Hardouin-Mansart is France's most visited sight. It stands as a monument to the power of the Sun King and is still used for state occasions. Rambouillet, closely linked with Louis XVI, is now the summer residence of the French president, while Malmaison was the favorite home of Empress Josephine. To the north, the Château d'Ecouen offers a showcase of Renaissance life and to the south Vaux-le-Vicomte boasts some of the loveliest formal gardens in France.

Nourished by the Seine and Marne rivers, the Ile de France is a patchwork of chalky plains, wheatfields and forests. The serene, poplar-lined avenues and rustic charm of the region have been an inspiration to painters such as Corot, Rousseau, Pissarro, and Cézanne.

SIGHTS AT A GLANCE

Châteaux and Museums
Château de Dampierre **8**
Château de Fontainebleau **13**
Château de Malmaison **5**
Château de Rambouillet **9**
Château de Sceaux **7**
Château de Vaux-le-Vicomte **11**
Château de Versailles **6**
Musée National de la
  Renaissance **2**

Towns
Provins **12**
St-Germain-en-Laye **4**

Abbeys and Churches
Abbaye de Royaumont **1**
Basilique St-Denis **3**

Theme Parks
Disneyland Resort Paris **10**

KEY

▢	Greater Paris
▣	Central Paris
✈	International airport
═	Highway
═	Major road
═	Minor road

0 kilometers 20
0 miles 10

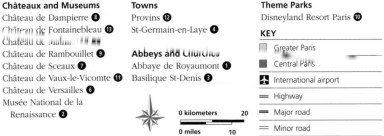

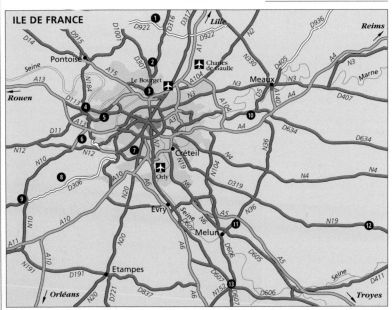

ILE DE FRANCE

◁ **Magnificent formal gardens at the Château Vaux-le-Vicomte**

The vaulted Gothic refectory of Abbaye de Royaumont

Abbaye de Royaumont ❶

Fondation Royaumont, Asnières-sur-Oise, Val-d'Oise. **Tel** 01 30 35 59 70. ◯ daily. 📷 ♿ 🎧 phone 01 30 35 59 00. 🎵 **Concerts.**
www.royaumont.com

Set among woods "near water and far from mankind," 22 miles (35 km) north of Paris, Royaumont is the finest Cistercian abbey in the Ile de France. Chosen for its remoteness, the abbey's stark stonework and simplicity of line reflect the austere teachings of St-Bernard. However, unlike his Burgundian abbeys, Royaumont was founded in 1228 by Louis IX and his mother, Blanche de Castille. "St-Louis" showered the abbey with riches and chose it as a royal burial site.

The abbey retained its royal links until the Revolution, when much of it was destroyed. It was then a textiles mill and orphanage until its revival as a cultural center. The original pillars still remain, along with a gravity-defying corner tower and the largest Cistercian cloisters in France, which enclose a charming Classical garden. The monastic quarters border one side of the cloisters.

The Château de Royaumont, erected as the abbot's palace on the eve of the Revolution, is set apart and resembles an Italianate villa. In the grounds are monks' workshops, woods, ponds, and Cistercian canals.

In summer, concerts are held in the abbey on weekends (call 01 34 68 05 50 for details).

Musée National de la Renaissance ❷

Château d'Ecouen, Val-d'Oise. **Tel** 01 34 38 38 50. ◯ Wed–Mon. 🔴 Jan 1, May 1, Dec 25. **Park** ◯ Apr–Sep: 8am–7pm (Oct–Mar: 6pm); no animals. 🎨 museum only. ♿ 📷 🚻 **www**.musee-renaissance.fr

This imposing moated château is curiously adrift, halfway between St-Denis and Royaumont. Now a Renaissance museum, Ecouen's magnificent quadrilateral exterior provides an authentic setting for an impressive collection of paintings, tapestries, coffers, carved doors and staircases salvaged from other 16th-century châteaux.

Ecouen was built in 1538 for Anne de Montmorency, adviser to François I and Commander-in-Chief of his armies. As the second most powerful person in the kingdom, he employed Ecole de Fontainebleau artists and craftsmen to adorn his palace. Their influence is apparent in the ravishing painted fireplaces depicting biblical and Classical themes in mysterious landscapes. The most striking room is the chapel, containing a gallery and vaulted ceilings painted with the Montmorency coat of arms.

Upstairs is one of the finest series of 16th-century tapestries in France. Equally compelling are the princely apartments, the library of illuminated manuscripts, vivid ceramics from Lyon, Nevers, Venice, Faenza, and Iznik, and a display of early mathematical instruments. Recent acquisitions include 16th- and 17th-century engravings from France, Italy, and Germany.

Basilique St-Denis ❸

1 rue de la Légion d'Honneur, St-Denis, Seine-St-Denis. **Tel** 01 48 09 83 54. Ⓜ Line 13 Basilique de St-Denis. ◯ daily. 🔴 Jan 1, May 1, Dec 25. 🎨 ♿ ✝ 8:30am, 10am Sun.

According to legend, the decapitated St-Denis struggled here, clutching his head, and an abbey was erected to commemorate the martyred bishop. Following the burial of Dagobert I in the basilica in 638, a royal link with St-Denis began, which was to span 12 centuries. Most French kings were entombed in St-Denis, and all the queens of France were crowned here. The elegant, early Gothic basilica rests on Carolingian and Romanesque crypts. Of the medieval effigies, the most impressive are of Charles V (1364) and a 12th-century likeness in enameled copper of Blanche de France with her dog. The mask-like

Statue of Louis XVI at St-Denis

The west wing of Musée National de la Renaissance

The Renaissance tomb of Louis XII and Anne de Bretagne in St-Denis

serenity of these effigies is in sharp contrast with the graphically realistic Renaissance portrayal of agony present in the grotesque mausoleum of Louis XII and Anne de Bretagne. Both are represented as naked figures, their faces eerily captured at the moment of death. Above the mausoleum, effigies of the finely dressed royal couple contemplate their own nakedness. As a reflection of humanity in the face of death, the tombs have few rivals.

St-Germain-en-Laye ❹

Yvelines. 🏙 42,200. 🚊 🚌 ❚
Maison Claude Debussy, 38 rue au Pain.
Tel *01 34 51 05 12.* 🗓 *Tue–Wed, Fri–Sun.*

Dominating the Place Général de Gaulle in this chic suburb is the legendary Château de St-Germain, birthplace of Louis XIV. Louis VI built the original

stronghold in 1122 but only the keep and St-Louis chapel remain. Under François I and Henri II, the medieval upper tiers were demolished, leaving a moated pentagon. Henri IV built the pavilion and terraces that run down to the Seine, and Louis XIV had Le Nôtre landscape the gardens before leaving for Versailles in 1682.

Today the château houses the **Musée des Antiquités Nationales**, which exhibits archeological finds from pre-history to the Middle Ages. Created by Napoleon III, the collection includes a 22,000-year-old carved female, a megalithic tomb, a bronze helmet from the 3rd century BC, and Celtic jewelry. The finest treasure is the Gallo-Roman mosaic pavement.

🏛 Musée des Antiquités Nationales
Château de St-Germain-en-Laye.
Tel *01 39 10 13 00.* 🗓 *10am–5:15pm Wed–Mon.* 🗓🗓🗓🗓🗓
www.musee-antiquitesnationales.fr

Château de Malmaison ❺

Rueil-Malmaison, Hauts-de-Seine.
Tel *01 41 29 05 55.* 🗓 *Apr–Sep: 10am–5:45pm Wed–Mon (6:15pm Sat & Sun); Oct–Mar: 10am–5:15pm Wed–Mon (5:45pm Sat & Sun).* 🗓 *Jan 1, Dec 25.* 🗓🗓
www.chateau-malmaison.fr

Situated 9 miles (15 km) west of Paris, this 17th-century estate is now best known for its Napoleonic associations. Bought by Josephine as a retreat from the formality of the Emperor's residences at the Tuileries and Fontainebleau, it has charming rural grounds. While Josephine loved this country manor, Napoleon scorned its entrance as fit only for servants, and so he had a curious drawbridge built at the back of the château.

The finest rooms are the frescoed and vaulted library, the canopied campaign room, and the sunny Salon de Musique. Napoleon's restrained yellow canopied bedroom contrasts with the bedchamber Josephine died in, a magnificent indulgence bedecked in red. Many of the rooms overlook the romantic "English" gardens and the famous rose garden Josephine cultivated after her divorce.

Memorabilia abound, from imperial eagles to David's moody portrait of Napoleon, or Gérard's painting of the languid Josephine reclining on a chaise-longue.

Château Bois Préau, set in the wooded grounds, houses a museum dedicated to Napoleon's exile and death.

Empress Josephine's bed at Château de Malmaison

Château de Versailles ❻

Garden statue of a flautist

The present palace, started by Louis XIV in 1668, grew around Louis XIII's original hunting lodge. Architect Louis Le Vau built the first section, which expanded into an enlarged courtyard. From 1678, Jules Hardouin-Mansart added north and south wings and the Hall of Mirrors. He also designed the chapel, completed in 1710. The Opera House (L'Opéra) was added by Louis XV in 1770. André Le Nôtre enlarged the gardens and broke the monotony of the symmetrical layout with expanses of water and creative use of uneven ground. Opposite the château is the Academie du Spectacle Equestre, where you can watch dressage shows.

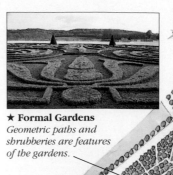

★ Formal Gardens
Geometric paths and shrubberies are features of the gardens.

The Orangery was built beneath the Parterre du Midi to house exotic plants in winter.

Fountain of Latona
Four marble basins rise to Balthazar Marsy's statue of the goddess Latona.

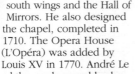

Water Parterre

★ Château
Under Louis XIV, Versailles became the center of political power in France.

Dragon Fountain
The fountain's centerpiece is a winged monster.

The King's garden features a mirror pool in the 19th-century garden created by Louis XVIII.

Colonnade
Mansart designed this circle of marble arches in 1685.

VISITORS' CHECKLIST

Versailles, Yvelines. *Tel 01 30 83 78 00.* 171 from Paris. Versailles Rive Gauche. Versailles Chantiers, Versailles Rive Droite. **Château** 9am–6:30pm (5:30pm Nov–Mar) Tue–Sun. some public hols; phone to check. **Grand Trianon & Petit Trianon** noon–7pm (5:30pm winter) daily (last adm: 30 mins before closing). Jan 1, May 1, Dec 25. **Academie du Spectacle Equestre** Thu, Sat, Sun. with Château ticket. Les Fêtes de Nuit (Aug–Sep); Les Grandes Eaux Nocturnes (Apr–Sep: Sat). **www**.chateauversailles.fr

The Grand Canal was the setting for Louis XIV's boating parties.

Petit Trianon
Built in 1762 as a retreat for Louis XV, this small château became a favorite with Marie-Antoinette.

Fountain of Neptune
Groups of sculptures spray spectacular jets of water in Le Nôtre's 17th-century garden.

STAR FEATURES

★ Château

★ Formal Gardens

★ Grand Trianon

★ Grand Trianon
Louis XIV built this small palace of stone and pink marble in 1687 to escape the rigors of court life and to enjoy the company of Madame de Maintenon.

Inside the Château de Versailles

The sumptuous main apartments are on the first floor of this vast château complex. Around the Marble Courtyard are the private apartments of the king and queen. On the garden side are the state apartments where official court life took place. These were richly decorated by Charles Le Brun with marble, stone and wood carvings, murals, velvet, silver, and gilded furniture. Beginning with the Salon d'Hercule, each state room is dedicated to an Olympian deity. The climax is the Hall of Mirrors, where 17 great mirrors face tall arched windows. Not all rooms are open at the same time so check on arrival.

★ Queen's Bedroom
In this room the queens of France gave birth to the royal children in public view.

KEY TO FLOOR PLAN

- ☐ South wing
- ☐ Coronation room
- ☐ Madame de Maintenon's apartments
- ☐ Queen's apartments and private suite
- ☐ State apartments
- ☐ King's apartments and private suite
- ☐ North wing
- ☐ Nonexhibition space

The Marble Courtyard is overlooked by a gilded balcony.

Entrance

Entrance

The Salon du Sacre is adorned with huge paintings of Napoleon by Jacques-Louis David.

★ Salon de Vénus
A statue of Louis XIV stands amid the rich marble decor of this room.

Stairs to ground floor reception area

★ Chapelle Royale
The chapel's first floor was reserved for the royal family and the ground floor for the court. The beautiful interior is decorated with Corinthian columns and white marble, gilding, and Baroque murals.

STAR FEATURES

- ★ Chapelle
- ★ Salon de Vénus
- ★ Hall of Mirrors
- ★ Queen's Bedroom

★ Hall of Mirrors
Great state occasions were held in this room stretching 233 ft (70 m) along the west façade. Here in 1919 the Treaty of Versailles was ratified, ending World War I.

Oeil-de-Boeuf

The King's Bedroom is where Louis XIV died in 1715.

The Cabinet du Conseil was used by the king to receive his ministers and family.

Salon de la Guerre
The room's theme of war is reinforced by Antoine Coysevox's stuccoed relief of Louis XIV riding to victory.

Louis XVI's library features Neoclassical paneling and the king's terrestrial globe.

Salon d'Hercule

Salon d'Apollon
Designed by Le Brun and dedicated to the god Apollo, this was Louis XIV's throne room. A copy of Hyacinthe Rigaud's famous portrait of the king (1701) hangs here.

TIMELINE

1667 Grand Canal begun	*Louis XV*		**1793** Louis XVI and Marie-Antoinette executed	**1833** Louis-Philippe turns the château into a museum
1668 Construction of new château by Le Vau	**1722** 12-year-old Louis XV occupies Versailles			
1650	**1700**	**1750**	**1800**	**1850**
1671 Interior decoration by Le Brun begun	**1715** Death of Louis XIV. Versailles abandoned by court		**1789** King and Queen forced to leave Versailles for Paris	
				1919 Treaty of Versailles signed on June 28
1661 Louis XIV enlarges château	**1682** Louis XIV and Marie-Thérèse move to Versailles		**1774** Louis XVI and Marie-Antoinette live at Versailles	

Château de Sceaux ❼

Sceaux, Hauts-de-Seine. **Tel** 01 41 87 29 50. ◯ Apr–Oct: 10am–6pm Wed–Mon (6:30pm Sun); Nov–Mar: 10am–5pm Wed–Mon. ● public hols & lunchtimes. & ✓ **www**.domaine-des-sceaux.fr

The Parc de Sceaux, bounded by elegant villas, is an appealing mixture of formal gardens, woods, and water containing Classical gardens designed by Le Nôtre. The gardens use water to great effect, with tiered waterfalls and fountains presenting a moving staircase that cascades into an octagonal basin. This feeds into the Grand Canal and offers a poplar-lined view to the Pavillon de Hanovre, one of several pavilions that adorn the park, which also contains Mansart's Classical Orangerie. Today this is the setting for exhibitions and music concerts.

Built for Colbert in 1670, the original château was demolished and rebuilt in Louis XIII style in 1856. The stylish fake contains the Musée de l'Ile de France, which celebrates the landscapes and châteaux of the region with paintings, furniture, and sculpture.

Château de Dampierre ❽

Dampierre-en-Yvelines, Yvelines. **Tel** 01 30 52 53 24. ◯ Apr–mid-Oct: daily. ● Sun lunch. 📷 & restricted. ✓ 🍴 **www**.chateau-de-dampierre.fr

After Versailles and Rambouillet, Dampierre is the most celebrated château southwest of Paris. Built in 1675 for the Duc de Chevreuse, the exterior of the château is a harmonious composition of rose-colored brick and cool stone, designed by Hardouin-Mansart.

By contrast, the interior sumptuously evokes Versailles, particularly in the royal apartments and the Louis XIV dining room. The grandest room is the frescoed Salle des Fêtes, remodeled in the 19th century in triumphal Roman style. The rooms overlook gardens landscaped by Le Nôtre.

Château de Rambouillet

Château de Rambouillet ❾

Rambouillet, Yvelines. **Tel** 01 34 83 00 25. ◯ Wed–Mon. ● Jan 1, May 1, Nov 1 & 11, Dec 25, when the president in residence & lunchtimes. 📷 ✓ **http**://chateau-rambouillet. monuments-nationaux.fr

The château borders the deep Forêt de Rambouillet, once the favorite royal hunting ground. This ivy-covered red-brick château, flanked by five stone towers, is curious rather than beautiful. Adopted as a feudal castle, country estate, royal palace, and Imperial residence, it reflects a composite of French royal history. Since 1897, it has been the president's official summer residence.

Inside, oak-paneled rooms are adorned with Empire-style furnishings and Aubusson tapestries. The main façade overlooks Classical parterres. Nearby is the Queen's Dairy, given by Louis XVI to Marie-Antoinette so that she could play milkmaid.

Environs About 17 miles (28 km) north on the D11 is the **Château de Thoiry**, which has a safari park and an innovative play area for children.

Disneyland Resort Paris ❿

Marne-la-Vallée, Seine-et-Marne. **Tel** 08 25 30 02 22. ◯ daily. 🚇 RER Marne-la-Vallée-Chessy. 🚄 TGV from Lille or Lyon. 🚌 from both airports. 📷 & **www**.disneylandparis.com

Disneyland Resort Paris covers 500 acres (200 ha), with two theme parks, seven hotels, facilities for shopping and dining, and convention centers. Most interesting are the Parks – the first with its five themed Lands, offering magic dominated by Sleeping Beauty Castle, and Walt Disney Studios.

Minnie Mouse

Château de Vaux-le-Vicomte ⓫

Maincy, Seine-et-Marne. **Tel** 01 64 14 41 90. 🚌 shuttle from Melun train station. ◯ mid-Mar–early Nov. ● Wed (except Jul & Aug). 📷 🍴 **www**.vaux-le-vicomte.com

Set north of Melun, not far from Fontainebleau, the château enjoys a peaceful rural

---

SÈVRES PORCELAIN

In 1756 Madame de Pompadour and Louis XV opened a porcelain factory near Versailles at Sèvres to supply the royal residences with tableware and *objets d'art*. Thus began the production of exquisite dinner services, statuettes, Etruscan-style vases, romantic cameos, and porcelain paintings, depicting grand châteaux or mythological scenes. Sèvres porcelain is typified by its translucence, durability, and narrow palette of colors.

Le Pugilat (1832), one of a pair of vases from Sèvres

ANDRE LE NÔTRE

As the greatest French landscape gardener, Le Nôtre (1613–1700) created masterpieces in château gardens all over France. His Classical vision shaped many in the Ile de France, such as those at Dampierre, Sceaux, and Vaux-le-Vicomte. At Vaux he perfected the concept of the *jardin à la française*: avenues framed by statues and box hedges; water gardens with fountains and ornate pools; graceful terraces and geometrical parterres "embroidered" with motifs. His genius lay in architectural orchestration and a sense of symmetry, typified by the sweeping vistas of Versailles, his greatest triumph.

location. Nicolas Fouquet, a powerful court financier to Louis XIV, challenged the architect Le Vau and the decorator Le Brun to create the most sumptuous palace of the day. The result is one of the greatest 17th-century French château. However, it also led to his downfall. Louis and his ministers were so enraged – because its luxury cast the royal palaces into the shade – that they arrested Fouquet.

The interior is a gilded banquet of frescoes, stucco, caryatids, and giant busts. The Salon des Muses boasts Le Brun's magnificent frescoed ceiling of dancing nymphs and poetic sphinxes. La Grande Chambre Carrée is decorated in Louis XIII style with paneled walls and an impressive triumphal frieze, evoking Rome. However, its many rooms feel intimate and the scale is not overwhelming.

Yet Vaux-le-Vicomte's continuing fame is due to André Le Nôtre's stunning gardens. The landscape designer's early training as a painter is evident in the magnificent succession of terraces, ornamental lakes, and fountains, which descend to a formal canal. On Saturday evenings from May to October, the castle is lit with over 2,000 candles and classical music is played in the gardens.

Provins **12**

Seine-et-Marne. 🏠 *12,000.* 🚉 🚌
ℹ️ *Chemin de Villecran (01 64 60 26 26).* 🕒 *Sat.* **www**.provins.net

As a Roman outpost, Provins commanded the border of Ile de France and Champagne. Today, it offers a coherent vision of the medieval world. Ville Haute, the upper town, is clustered within high 12th-century ramparts, complete with crenelations and defensive ditches. The ramparts to the west are the best preserved. Here, between the fortified gateways of Porte de Jouy and Porte St-Jean, the fortifications are dotted with square, round, and rectangular towers.

The town is dominated by Tour César, a keep with four corner turrets and a pyramid shaped roof. The moat and fortifications were added by the English during the Hundred Years' War. A guard-room leads to a gallery and views over the place du Châtel, a busy square of medieval gabled houses, and over the wheatfields beyond.

Provins is proud of its crimson roses. Every June, a floral celebration is held in the riverside rose garden, marked by a medieval festival with falconry and jousting.

Château de Vaux-le-Vicomte seen across the gardens designed by Le Nôtre

Château de Fontainebleau ⓭

Ceiling detail from the Salle de Bal

Fontainebleau is not the product of a single vision but is a bewildering cluster of styles from different periods. Louis VII built an abbey here which was consecrated by Thomas Becket in 1169. A medieval tower survives but the present château harks back to François I. Originally drawn by the local hunting, the Renaissance king created a decorative château modeled on Florentine and Roman styles.

Fontainebleau's abiding charm comes from its relative informality and spectacular forest setting. While impossible to cover in a day, the *grands appartements* provide a sumptuous introduction to this royal palace.

Ground floor

Jardin de Diane
Now more romantic than Classical, the garden features a bronze fountain of Diana as huntress.

★ Escalier du Fer-à-Cheval
This imposing horseshoe-shaped staircase by Jean Androuet du Cerceau, built in 1634, lies at the end of Cour du Cheval Blanc. Its ingenious design allowed carriages to pass beneath the two arches.

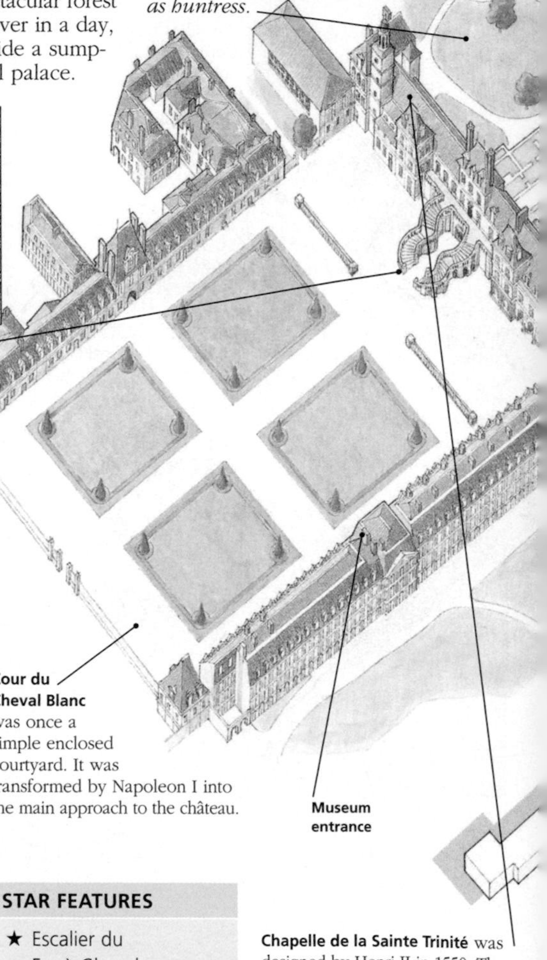

KEY TO FLOOR PLAN

- Petits Appartements
- Galerie des Cerfs
- Musée Chinois
- Musée Napoléon
- Grands Appartements
- Salle Renaissance
- Appartements de Madame de Maintenon
- Grands Appartements des Souverains
- Escalier de la Reine/ Appartements des Chasses
- Chapelle de la Trinité
- Appartement Intérieur de l'Empereur

Cour du Cheval Blanc was once a simple enclosed courtyard. It was transformed by Napoleon I into the main approach to the château.

Museum entrance

Chapelle de la Sainte Trinité was designed by Henri II in 1550. The chapel acquired its vaulted and frescoed ceiling under Henri IV and was completed by Louis XIII.

STAR FEATURES

- ★ Escalier du Fer-à-Cheval
- ★ Salle de Bal
- ★ Galerie François I

For hotels and restaurants in this region see pp555–6 and pp606–7

Porte Dorée
Originally a feudal gate-house, this was transformed into the entrance pavilion to the forest by Gilles Le Breton for François I.

Cour Oval

First floor

VISITORS' CHECKLIST

Seine-et-Marne. *Tel 01 60 71 50 70.* ☐ 9:30am–5pm (6pm Apr–Sep) Wed–Mon. 🖼 ♿ 🅿 ▯
Gardens ☐ 9am–5pm (6pm Mar–Apr & Oct, 7pm May–Sep).
▮ Jan 1, May 1, Dec 25. **www**.chateaudefontainebleau.fr

★ **Salle de Bal**
The Renaissance ballroom, designed by Primaticcio (1552), was finished under Henri II. His emblems adorn the walnut coffered ceiling, forming a pattern reflected in the parquet floor.

The Appartements de Napoléon I
house his grandiose throne in the Emperor's Salle du Trône, formerly the Chambre du Roi.

Cour de la Fontaine

★ **Galerie François I**
This gilded gallery is a tribute to the Italian artists in the Ecole de Fontainebleau. *Rosso Fiorentino's allegorical frescoes pay homage to the king's wish to create "a second Rome."*

The Jardin Anglais
is a romantic "English" garden, planted with cypress and plantain trees. It was re-designed in the 19th century by Maximilien-Joseph Hurtault.

THE BARBIZON SCHOOL

Artists have been drawn to the glades of Fontainebleau since the 1840s, when a group of landscape painters, determined to paint only from nature, formed around Théodore Rousseau and Millet. They settled in the nearby hamlet of Barbizon where the Auberge Ganne, a museum dedicated to the *Ecole de Barbizon*, is located.

Spring at Barbizon, painted by Jean-François Millet (1814–75)

NORTHEAST FRANCE

Introducing Northeast France

The rolling plains of Northern France run from the
English Channel to the wooded Ardennes hills and
the Vosges mountains of Alsace. Apart from somber
battle memorials, the area has France's finest Gothic
cathedrals – and a long tradition of brewing good
quality beers. There is fine wine, too, in Champagne
and Alsace. The old heavy industry has gone,
while Lille's growth as a transportation hub has brought new
prosperity. This map
shows some of the most
interesting sights.

LE NORD AND PICARDY
(See pp192–205)

Amiens Cathedral

Amiens cathedral *is renowned
for its fine wood carvings and
its nave, the highest in France*
(see pp202–3).

*Beauvais
Cathedral*

Château de Compiègne

*Rein...
Cathea...*

The pride of Beauvais *is its Gothic
cathedral and astronomical clock
(see p200) which escaped heavy
bombing during World War II.*

*Troyes
Cathedral*

Half-timbered houses *and
Renaissance mansions line the
streets and alleys of Troyes' Old
Town (see p216), rebuilt after the
great fire in 1524. Its cathedral has
remarkable stained-glass windows.*

The legacy of World War I *is strong in this area of former battlefields. The Douaumont Memorial outside Verdun* (see pp190–91), *with its 15,000 graves, is only one of many memorials and cemeteries here.*

Haut-Koenigsbourg, *a castle painstakingly rebuilt by Kaiser Wilhelm II when Alsace-Lorraine was under German rule, is one of Alsace's most popular attractions* (see p228).

Strasbourg, *seat of the Council of Europe, has a fine Gothic cathedral* (see pp230–31) *surrounded by delightful historic buildings.*

Douaumont Memorial

Porte Chaussée Verdun

Place Stanislas, Nancy

Strasbourg Cathedral

CHAMPAGNE
(See pp206–217)

ALSACE AND LORRAINE
(See pp218–33)

Haut-Koenigsbourg

| 0 kilometers | 50 |
| 0 miles | 50 |

The Flavors of Northeast France

The cuisine of northeast France is robust and warming, with rich beef stews, suckling pig, sausages and hams, dumplings, and sauerkraut dishes, many of them closely related to German or Flemish staples. There is good fish from the Atlantic and from freshwater lakes and rivers. Vegetables and fruit are produced in abundance, and often served in a variety of savory and sweet tarts, of which *quiche lorraine*, with bacon, eggs, and cream, is the best known. Rich cakes are popular, especially *Kougelhopf*, a ring-shaped cake of raisins and almonds soaked in kirsch, and madeleine sponge cakes.

Leeks from a local market

Golden mirabelle plums alongside the more usual variety

LE NORD AND PICARDY

The northern coast offers a wide variety of fish dishes, the most popular being steamed mussels served with chips (fries). Herrings are pickled, soused, grilled, or smoked and North Sea shrimps fried and eaten whole. Chicken may be cooked in beer, duck is made into pies and terrines, and eel served smoked as a starter. The market gardens (*hortillons*) of Picardy are famous for their vegetables, often made into delicious soups. Leeks or chicory, braised or in gratins, accompany many dishes. Strong, washed-rind cheeses, such as Maroilles, are typical of the region.

Beer is often drunk with meals in the northeast, where traditional methods and small breweries thrive.

CHAMPAGNE

Champagne encompasses arable plains and wooded uplands as well as vineyards, and produces game, *charcuterie*, and delicious freshwater fish. Nothing, however, can compete with its main claim to fame, Champagne itself, which is often used as a luxury cooking ingredient as well as, of course, being enjoyed in its own right.

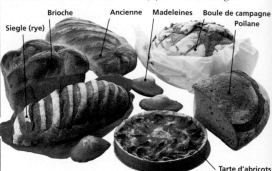

Brioche Ancienne Madeleines Boule de campagne Poilane
Siegle (rye)

Tarte d'abricots

Selection of typical regional breads and patisserie

REGIONAL DISHES AND SPECIALTIES

The classic dish of the region is *choucroute garni*, a platter of pickled cabbage flavored with juniper berries and cooked with white wine, ham hock, and smoked pork belly. Smoked Montbeliard and Strasbourg sausages are added toward the end of cooking. Sausages come in many variations, from *saucisses de Strasbourg* to *bratwurst*, made from veal and pork, *lewerzurscht* (liver sausage), *andouillettes* (spicy chitterling sausages), *boudin noir* (black pudding of pork and pig's blood), and *boudin blanc* (white meat without blood). There are also smoked hams, cooked hams and many different terrines, such as *presskopf* (pig's brawn in jelly) and the jellied white meat terrine, *potjevleesch*. *Langue lucullus* is smoked ox tongue studded with *foie gras*, a specialty of Valenciennes.

Beetroot

Ficelle picardie *Pancakes are filled with mushrooms and ham in creme fraîche sauce, and baked with grated cheese.*

Display of traditional northern French charcuterie

Wild boar, deer, rabbit, hare, quail, partridge, and wood-cock are all found in the Ardennes, made into game pâtés and terrines as well as roasts and stews. The Ardennes is also noted for its fine quality smoked ham, while *jambon de Reims* is cooked ham with mustard, champagne, and Reims vinegar. Troyes is famous for its *andouillettes*, usually served with onions or baked in a creamy mustard sauce. Fish come from the small lakes east of Troyes and trout are abundant in the clear streams of the Ardennes. The two best cheeses of Champagne are Chaource and Langres.

ALSACE AND LORRAINE

Rolling pastures, orchards, pine forests, and rivers produce the ingredients of Alsatian cooking. Meat is important, particularly pork, roasted or made into hams and sausages. In winter, game stews abound. There is a strong tradition of raising geese; after all, *foie gras* production originated in

Shopping at the fish market in the port of Boulogne

Strasbourg. The rivers are a good source of pike, trout, crayfish, and carp, often cooked in beer and served on festive occasions. Locally grown vegetables include cabbage, potatoes, and turnips, and fruit includes bilberries, quince, redcurrants, and the golden mirabelle plums of Lorraine, the latter prized for both jam and *eau de vie* (fruit brandy). The best-known cheese is Munster, a soft cow's milk cheese.

The white wines of Alsace range from steely, bone-dry Riesling (the region's finest variety) to aromatic Muscat and Gewurztraminer. For more on the wines of Alsace, see pp232–3.

ON THE MENU

Anguille au vert Eel baked with green herbs and potatoes.

Cassolette de petits gris Snails in champagne sauce.

Flamiche aux poireaux Leek tart.

Flammekueche Pizza-style tart topped with bacon, creme fraîche, and onions.

Marcassin à l'Ardennaise Wild boar with celeriac.

Potée champenoise Pork, ham, sausage, beans, and vegetable stew.

Potée Lorraine Casserole of salt pork with vegetables.

Zewelwai A rich onion tart.

Truite à l'Ardennaise *Trout is stuffed with breadcrumbs and finely chopped Ardennes ham, then baked.*

Carbonnade de boeuf *Steak and caramelized onions are covered with beer and cooked for three hours.*

Babas au rhum *These are dry yeast cakes of raisins, eggs, and butter, doused in rum and served with cream.*

France's Wine Regions: Champagne

Since its fabled "invention" by the monk Dom Pérignon in the 17th century, no other wine has rivaled champagne as the symbol of luxury and celebration. Only wines made in this region by the *Méthode Champenoise* can be called champagne *(see p210)*. Most champagne is non-vintage: the skill of the blenders, using reserves of older wines, creates consistency and excellence year on year. The "big names" *(grandes marques)* command the prestige and prices, but many small growers and cooperatives also produce excellent-value wines well worth seeking out.

Giant carved barrel, Épernay

LOCATOR MAP
■ *Champagne wine region*

Grapes going for pressing, Montagne de Reims

WINE REGIONS

Champagne is a compact wine region, largely in the French *département* of the Marne. Certain areas within it are particularly identified with certain styles of wine. The Aube produces 25 per cent of all champagne as well the exclusive Rosé des Riceys.

Soissons

Château Thierry

La Ferté-sous-Jouarre

Petit Morin

Grand Morin

KEY FACTS ABOUT CHAMPAGNE

Location and Climate
The cool, marginal climate creates the finesse that other sparkling wines strive for, but seldom achieve. Chalky soils and east- and north-facing aspects help produce the relatively high acidity champagne needs.

Grape Varieties
Three varieties are grown: red ***Pinot Noir*** and ***Pinot Meunier***, and white ***Chardonnay***. Most champagne is a blend of all three, though Blanc de Blancs is 100 percent Chardonnay and Blanc de Noirs, although white, is made only from red grapes.

Good Producers
Grandes Marques: Bollinger, Gosset, Krug, Möet et Chandon, Joseph Perrier, Louis Roederer, Pol Roger, Billecart-Salmon, Veuve Clicquot, Taittinger, Ruinart, Laurent Perrier, Salon.
Négociants, cooperatives & growers: Boizel, M. Arnould, Cattier, Bricout, Drappier, Ployez-Jacquemart, H. Blin, Gimmonet, Andre Jacquart, Chartogne-Taillet, Vilmart, Alfred Gratien, Emile Hamm, B. Paillard, P. Gerbais.

Good Vintages
2005, 2003, 2000, 1998, 1996, 1990.

BOLLINGER
Spécial Cuvée
BRUT
Champagne — *Ay France*

From a name *famous even to non-wine lovers, this is in the classic* brut *(dry) style; only* brut non dosage *or* brut sauvage *is drier.*

Nogent-sur-Seine

KEY

■	Champagne *appellation* area
□	Vallée de la Marne district
■	Montagne de Reims district
■	Côte de Sézanne district
□	Côte des Blancs district
□	Aube district

0 kilometers 15

0 miles 15

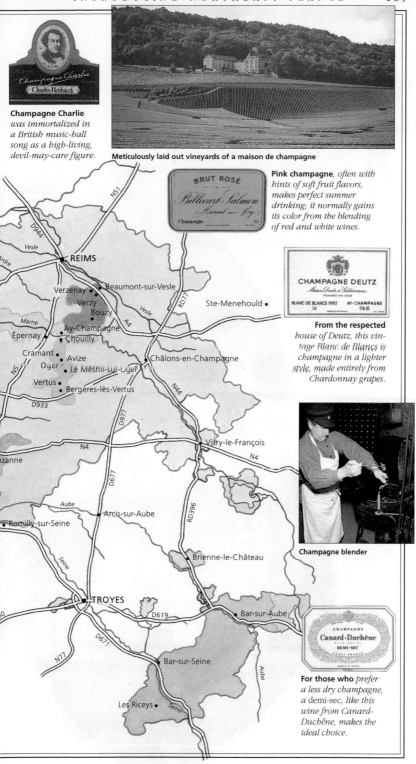

Champagne Charlie *was immortalized in a British music-hall song as a high-living, devil-may-care figure.*

Meticulously laid out vineyards of a maison de champagne

Pink champagne, *often with hints of soft fruit flavors, makes perfect summer drinking; it normally gains its color from the blending of red and white wines.*

BRUT ROSÉ
Billecart-Salmon
Mareuil-sur-Ay
Champagne

CHAMPAGNE DEUTZ
Maison Deutz et Geldermann
FONDÉE EN 1838
BLANC DE BLANCS 1982   AY-CHAMPAGNE

From the respected *house of Deutz, this vintage Blanc de Blancs is champagne in a lighter style, made entirely from Chardonnay grapes.*

Champagne blender

CHAMPAGNE
Canard-Duchêne
DEMI-SEC

For those who *prefer a less dry champagne, a* demi-sec, *like this wine from Canard-Duchêne, makes the ideal choice.*

Map labels:

N51
D944
Vesle
'Ardre
Vesle
REIMS
Verzenay • Beaumont-sur-Vesle
Verzy
Marne   Bouzy   Vesle   RD77   Ste-Menehould •
Épernay • Ay-Champagne   A4
Chouilly
Cramant • Avize   Châlons-en-Champagne
N5   Oger • Le Mesnil-sur-Oger
Vertus •   N44
Bergères-lès-Vertus
D933
D977
N4   Vitry-le-François
D677   N4
ézanne
Aube   RD396
• Romilly-sur-Seine   Arcis-sur-Aube
Seine   • Brienne-le-Château
TROYES
60   D619   • Bar-sur-Aube
D671
N77   • Bar-sur-Seine   Aube
Les Riceys •   Seine

The Battle of the Somme

The many cemeteries that cover the Somme region serve as a poignant reminder of the mass slaughter that took place on the Western Front in World War I (which ended with the Armistice on November 11, 1918). Between July 1 and November 21, 1916 the Allied forces lost more than 600,000 men and the Germans at least 465,000. The Battle of the Somme, a series of campaigns conducted by British and French armies against fortified positions held by the Germans, relieved the hard-pressed French at Verdun, but hopes of a breakthrough never materialized, and the Allies only managed to advance 10 miles (16 km).

British World War I soldier

Beaumont Hamel Memorial Park, a tribute to the Royal Newfoundland Regiment, has a huge bronze caribou.

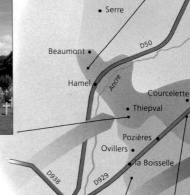

Thiepval Memorial was designed by Sir Edwin Lutyens. It dominates the landscape of Thiepval, one of the most hard-fought areas of the battle, appropriately chosen as a memorial to the 73,367 British soldiers with no known grave.

Albert *was the site of heavy bombardment by German artillery in 1916. Today, the town is a convenient center for visiting the battlefields. The Albert Basilique, with its leaning Virgin statue, was damaged but is now restored. It was a landmark for thousands of troops.*

Lochnager Mine Crater, formed by the largest of the British mines exploded on July 1, 1916, lies on the ridge by La Boiselle.

The British Tank Memorial, *on the main road from Albert to Bapaume, commemorates the first use of tanks in warfare on September 15, 1916. The attack was a limited success; the tanks of World War I were too few before 1918 to transform warfare dominated by artillery, machine guns, and barbed wire.*

Propaganda in World War I *was employed by both sides to maintain support at home. This French postcard has a popular image for civilian consumption. It shows a dying soldier kissing the flag, under the tender gaze of a ministering nurse, affirming his faith in the cause with his last breath.*

Delville Wood South African Memorial and Museum show the importance of Commonwealth forces in the Somme.

VISITORS' CHECKLIST

D929, D938 from Albert. 🚹 *30 pl de la République, 80800 Corbie.* **Tel** *03 22 96 95 76.* **www**.tourisme-albert.net. **Albert Basilique, Beaumont Hamel Memorial Park, Delville Wood, La Boiselle, Thiepval, & Pozières memorials** ⬜ *daily.* **Ulster Tower** ⬜ *Feb–Mar: Tue–Sun; Apr–Nov: daily.* **South African Memorial,** Delville Wood, Longueval. **Tel** *03 22 85 02 17.* ⬜ *Feb–Nov: Tue–Sun.* ⬤ *hols.* **Historial de Péronne** **Tel** *03 22 83 14 18.* ⬜ *May–Sep: daily; Oct– Apr: Tue–Sun.* ⬤ *mid-Dec–mid-Jan.* 🎫 ♿ ✉ 🖥 📷 **www**.historial.org

Bapaume

N17

D1017

A1

A2

• Flers

Morval •

Ginchy •

ricourt   • Maurepas

D1017

Canal du Nord

D917

Poppies *were one of the few plants to grow on the battlefield. Ghengis Khan brought the first white poppy from China and, according to legend, it turned red after battle. Today poppies are a symbol of remembrance.*

al de la Somme

A1   D1

Péronne

KEY

🟥	Allied forces
⬜	German forces
⬜	Front Line before July 1, 1916
🟦	Front Line progress July–September 1916
🟦	Front Line progress September–November 1916

0 kilometers   5

0 miles   5

The Front Line trenches *stretched from the North Sea to the Swiss frontier; only by keeping underground could men survive the terrible conditions. Trenches remain in a few areas, including the Beaumont Hamel Park.*

LE NORD AND PICARDY

PAS DE CALAIS · NORD · SOMME · OISE · AISNE

*B*eneath the modern skin of France's northernmost region, the sights and monuments bear witness to the triumphs and turbulence of its past: soaring Gothic cathedrals, stately châteaux along the river Oise, and the battlefields and memorials of World War I.

The Channel ports of Dunkerque, Calais, and Boulogne, and the refined resort of Le Touquet, are the focal points along a busy coastline that stretches from the Somme estuary to the Belgian frontier. Boulogne has a genuine maritime flavor, and the White Cliffs running from here to Calais provide the most dramatic scenery along the Côte d'Opale.

Flemish culture holds sway along the border with Belgium: an unfamiliar France of windmills and canals where the local taste is for beer, stews, and festivals with gallivanting giants. Lille is the dominant city here, a sprawling modern metropolis with a lively historic heart and an excellent art museum. To the southwest, the grace of Flemish architecture is handsomely displayed in the central squares of Arras, the capital of Artois.

From here to the Somme valley the legacy of World War I, with its memorial cemeteries and poppy-strewn battlefields, makes compelling viewing.

Cathedrals are the main appeal of Picardy. In Amiens, its capital, Cathédrale Notre-Dame is a pinnacle of the Gothic style – its magnificence echoed by the dizzying achievements at Beauvais further south. Splendid cathedrals at Noyon, Senlis, and the delightful hilltop town of Laon chart the evolution of the Gothic. Closer to Paris, two châteaux command attention. Chantilly, the epicenter of French equestrianism, boasts gardens by Le Nôtre and a 19th-century château housing copious art treasures. Compiègne, bordered by a large and inviting forest, plays host to a lavish royal palace favored by French rulers from Louis XV to Napoleon III.

Memorial cemetery in Vallée de la Somme, an area still haunted by the memory of World War I

◁ Catamarans on the busy beach of Le Touquet Paris-Plage

Exploring Le Nord and Picardy

As the gateway to England and Belgium, this northern corner of France is buzzing with business and industries, with the large, Euro-oriented city of Lille offering great culture as well as a new high-tech district. Yet peace and quiet is never far away. The coast between the historic port of Boulogne-sur-Mer and the Vallée de la Somme has a rich birdlife and is perfect for a relaxing seaside visit. Inland, the many Gothic cathedrals such as Amiens and Beauvais make an impressive tour, and the World War I battlefields and memorials provide an important insight into 20th-century history. Further south, the grand châteaux at Compiègne and Chantilly – which has the fascinating Musée Condé – are easily visited en route to or from Paris.

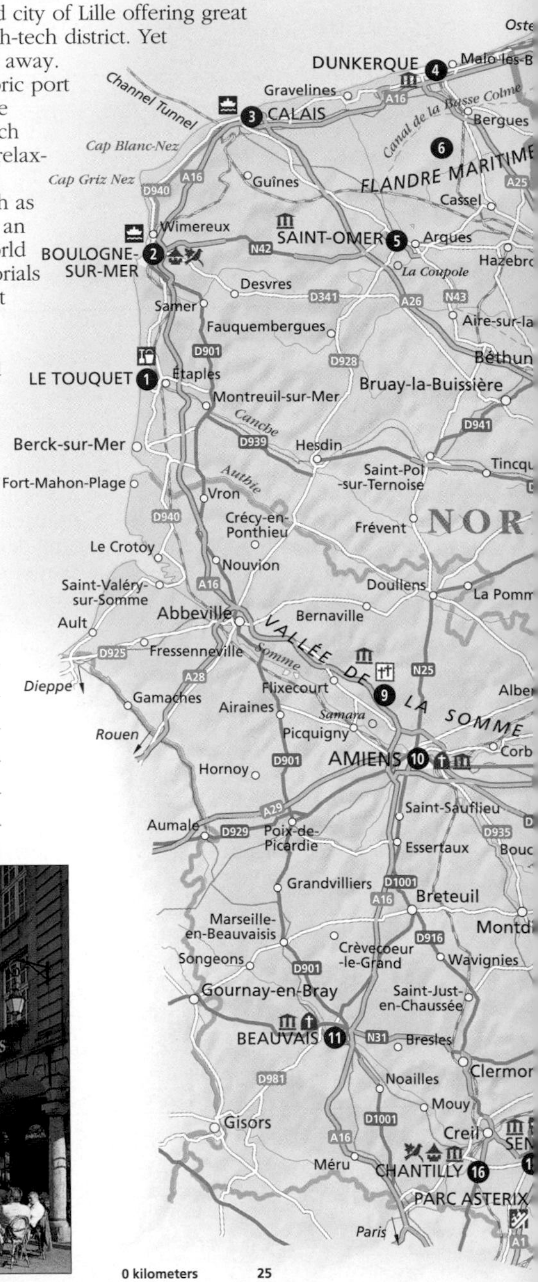

KEY

▬	Highway
▬	Major road
▬	Secondary road
═	Minor road
─	Scenic route
┄	Main railroad
─	Minor railroad
▬	International border
▬	Regional border

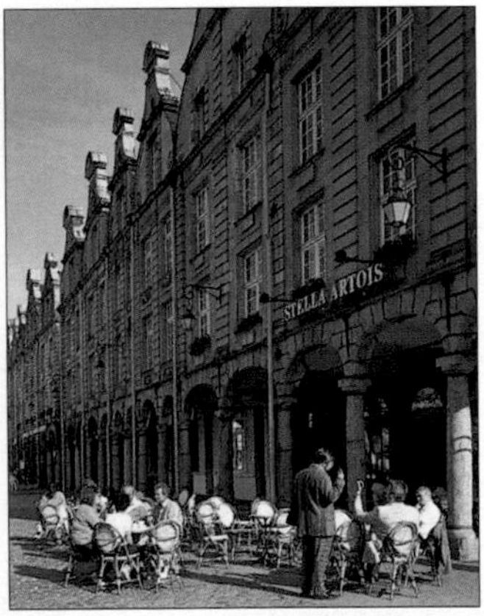

Lively outdoor café in the historic Grand' place in the heart of Arras

0 kilometers 25

0 miles 25

Oste

DUNKERQUE 4 Malo-les-B

Channel Tunnel

Gravelines

CALAIS 3

Bergues

Canal de la Basse Colme

6

Cap Blanc-Nez

Cap Griz Nez

Guînes

FLANDRE MARITIME

Cassel

Wimereux

SAINT-OMER 5 Arques

BOULOGNE-SUR-MER 2

La Coupole

Hazebro

Desvres

Samer

Fauquembergues

Aire-sur-la

LE TOUQUET 1 Étaples

Montreuil-sur-Mer

Canche

Béthun

Bruay-la-Buissière

Berck-sur-Mer

Hesdin

Saint-Pol-sur-Ternoise

Tincqu

Fort-Mahon-Plage

Vron

Crécy-en-Ponthieu

Frévent

NOR

Le Crotoy

Nouvion

Doullens

La Pomm

Saint-Valéry-sur-Somme

Abbeville

Bernaville

Ault

Fressenneville

VALLÉE DE

9

N25

Dieppe

Gamaches

Flixecourt

Alber

Airaines

Samara

LA SOMME

Rouen

Picquigny

AMIENS 10 Corb

Hornoy

Saint-Sauflieu

Aumale

Poix-de-Picardie

Essertaux

Bouc

Grandvilliers

Breteuil

Marseille-en-Beauvais

Crèvecœur-le-Grand

Montd

Songeons

Wavignies

Gournay-en-Bray

Saint-Just-en-Chaussée

BEAUVAIS 11 Bresles

Clermor

Noailles

Mouy

Gisors

Creil

SEN

Méru

CHANTILLY 16

PARC ASTERIX

Paris

SIGHTS AT A GLANCE

The meandering waters in the Vallée de la Somme

GETTING AROUND

The main entry point into the region is Calais (and the Channel Tunnel terminal 2 miles/3 km south). From here, autoroutes A16 and A26/A1, several major N and D roads, and mainline rail services run directly to Paris. In addition, TGVs serve Calais-Frethun, Lille, and Paris. There is a dense road network throughout the region. With their many local bus and train connections, Lille and Amiens make good bases. The A26 (or *Autoroute des Anglais*) crosses the whole region from Calais to Troyes, via Arras and Laon, giving easy access to eastern Picardy. It's also a useful route if you're heading south and want to avoid Paris.

Poppies, the symbol of World War I battlefields, in the Vallée de la Somme

Le Touquet beach at low tide

Le Touquet ❶

Pas de Calais. 🏠 5,500. 🚋 🚌
ℹ️ Palais de l'Europe (03 21 06 72 00).
🔄 Thu & Sat (Jun–mid-Sep: also Mon).
www.letouquet.com

Properly known as Le
Touquet Paris-Plage, this
resort was created in the 19th
century and became fashionable with the rich and famous
between the two World Wars.

A vast pine forest, planted in
1855, spreads around the
town sheltering stately villas.
To the west, a grid of chic
hotels, vacation residences,
and sophisticated stores and
restaurants borders a long,
sandy beach. A racecourse
and casino are complemented
by seaside amusements and
sports facilities, including two
excellent golf courses, horse-
riding, and land yachting.

Farther inland, the hilltop
town of **Montreuil** has lime-
washed 17th-century houses,
abundant restaurants, and a
tree-shaded rampart walk.

Boulogne-sur-Mer ❷

Pas de Calais. 🏠 45,000. 🚋 🚌
ℹ️ Parvis de Nausicaa (03 21 10 88
10). 🔄 Wed & Sat (pl Dalton), Sun
(pl Vignon). www.tourisme-
boulognesurmer.com

An important fishing port
and busy marina, Boulogne
rewards its visitors well. Its
attractions come neatly boxed
in a walled Haute Ville, with
the Porte des Dunes opening
onto a 17th–19th-century

ensemble of Palais de Justice,
Bibliothèque, and Hôtel de
Ville in **place de la Résistance**.

The 19th-century **Basilique
Notre-Dame** is capped by a
dome visible for miles. Inside,
a bejeweled wooden statue
represents Boulogne's
patroness, Notre-Dame de
Boulogne. She is wearing a
soleil, a head-dress also worn
by women during the *Grande
Procession* held annually in
her honor. Nearby, the powerful moated 13th-century
Château, built for the Counts
of Boulogne, is now a well-
organized historical museum.

In the center of town, stores,
hotels, and fish restaurants
line the quai Gambetta on the
east bank of the river Liane.
To the north lie Boulogne's
beach and **Nausicaa**, a vast,
spectacular and innovative
aquarium and Sea Center.

North of the town, the
Colonne de la Grande Armée
was erected in 1841 as a monument to Napoleon I's planned
invasion of England in 1803–5.
From the top there is a panoramic view along the coast
toward Calais. This is the
most scenic stretch of the Côte
d'Opale (Opal Coast), with the

windblown headlands of **Cap
Gris-Nez** and **Cap Blanc-Nez**
offering breathtakingly extensive views across the Channel.

⛪ **Château**
Rue de Bernet. **Tel** 03 21 10 02 20.
🔄 Tue–Sun. 🔄 Jan 1, May 1,
Dec 24–Jan 2. 🔄

🐟 **Nausicaa**
Bd Sainte-Beuve. **Tel** 03 21 30 99 99.
🔄 daily. 🔄 3 weeks in Jan, Dec 25.
🔄 ♿ www.nausicaa.fr

Calais ❸

Pas de Calais. 🏠 76,000. 🚋 🚌
🚢 ℹ️ 12 bd Clémenceau (03 21 96
62 40). 🔄 Wed, Thu, & Sat.
www.calais-cotedopale.com

Calais is a busy cross-Channel
port with a sandy beach to the
west. Clumsily rebuilt after
World War II, it seems to have
little to offer at first sight. Many
visitors never get closer than
the huge Cité Europe shopping
mall by the Eurotunnel exit.

The **Musée des Beaux Arts**,
however, has works by the
Dutch and Flemish Schools.
Also on show are studies for
Auguste Rodin's famous statue
The Burghers of Calais (1895).

The windswept Cap Blanc-Nez on the Côte d'Opale

The Burghers of Calais by Auguste Rodin (1895)

The statue stands outside the Hôtel de Ville and celebrates an event during Edward III's siege of Calais in 1347, when six burghers offered their lives to save the rest of the town.

The **Cité de la Dentelle et de la Mode** recalls the town's lace-making industry.

Musée de la Guerre, housed in a battle-scarred German blockhouse, offers a detailed account of local events during World War II.

Musée des Beaux Arts
25 rue Richelieu. **Tel** 03 21 46 48 40. ☐ Tue–Sat, Sun pm. ✍ ✦

Cité de la Dentelle
Quai du Commerce. **Tel** 03 21 46 43 14. ☐ Wed–Sun. ✍

Musée de la Guerre
Parc Saint Pierre. **Tel** 03 21 34 21 57. ☐ call for opening times. ✍ ✦

Dunkerque ❹

Nord. � 376,000. ☐ ☐ ☐ ☐ *Rue Amiral Ronarc'h (03 28 66 79 21).* ☐ Wed, Sat. **www**.ot-dunkerque.fr

Though a major industrial port, Dunkerque has much Flemish character. Start a tour from place du Minck, with its fresh fish stalls. Nearby **Musée Portuaire** celebrates the town's maritime history. In the old center, a statue commemorates local hero Jean Bart, a 17th-century corsair, who lies in **Eglise St-Eloi**. Its belfry (1440) offers fine views.

La Mémorial du Souvenir has an exhibition of the dramatic evacuation of 350,000

British and French troops in 1940. The **Lieu d'Art et d'Action Contemporaine (LLAC)** features ceramics and glassware.

Musée Portuaire
9 quai de la Citadelle. **Tel** 03 28 63 33 39. ☐ Wed–Mon. ☐ Jan 1, May 1, Dec 25. ✍ ✦

The port at Dunkerque

La Mémorial du Souvenir
32 Courtines du Bastion. **Tel** 03 28 66 79 21. ☐ Wed–Mon. ☐ Jan 1, Nov 1, Dec 25. ✍ ✦ ground floor only.

Lieu d'Art et d'Action Contemporaine
Av des Bains. **Tel** 03 28 29 56 00. ☐ Tue–Sun. ☐ public hols. ✍ ✦

St-Omer ❺

Pas de Calais. � 15,000. ☐ ☐ ☐ *4 rue Lion d'Or (03 21 98 08 51).* ☐ Sat. **www**.tourisme-saintomer.com

Refined St-Omer seems untouched. Pilasters adorn the 17th- and 18th-century houses lining the cobbled streets, one of which, **Hôtel Sandelin**, is now a museum of fine and decorative arts. The cathedral has original 13th-century tiles and a huge organ. The **Bibliothèque Municipale** contains rare manuscripts from the Abbayé St-Bertin, a ruined 15th-century abbey east of town.

Three miles (5 km) from St-Omer, **La Coupole** is an informative WWII museum inside a converted bunker.

Hôtel Sandelin
14 rue Carnot. **Tel** 03 21 38 00 94. ☐ Wed–Sun. ✍ ✦ ground floor.

Bibliothèque Municipale
40 rue Gambetta. **Tel** 03 21 38 35 08. ☐ Tue–Sat. ☐ public hols.

La Coupole
Tel 03 21 12 27 27. ☐ daily. ☐ last week Dec–1st week Jan.

CHANNEL CROSSINGS

Calais is only 22 miles (36 km) southeast of the English coast, and crossing the waters of the Channel – which the French know as La Manche (the Sleeve) – has inspired many intrepid exploits. The first crossing by balloon was in 1785 by Jean Pierre Blanchard; Captain M. Webb made the first swim in 1875; and Louis Blériot's pioneering flight followed in 1909. Plans for an undersea tunnel, first laid as early as 1751, were finally achieved in 1994 with the opening of a railroad link between Fréthun and Folkestone.

Children watching Louis Blériot taking off, 1909

Flandre Maritime ⑥

Nord. 🕅 5,000. 🚈 Lille. 🚉 Bergues.
🚌 Dunkerque. 🚹 Bergues, Le Beffroi,
pl Henri Billiaert (03 28 68 71 06).

South of Dunkerque lies a flat, agricultural plain with narrow waterways and expansive skies – an archetypal Flemish landscape with canals, bicyclists, and ancient windmills. The **Noordmeulen**, built just north of Hondschoote in 1127, is thought to be the oldest windmill in Europe.

From Hondschoote the D3 follows the Canal de la Basse Colme west to Bergues, a fortified wool town with fine 16th–17th-century Flemish works in its **Musée Municipal**. Farther south, the hilltop town of **Cassel** has a cobbled Grande place with 16th–18th-century buildings, and views across Flanders and Belgium from its Jardin Public.

🏛 Musée Municipal
1 rue du Mont de Piété, Bergues.
Tel 03 28 68 13 30. ☐ Thu–Mon.
⬤ Oct–Apr. ⬛

Lille ⑦

Nord. 🕅 282,000. 🛬 🚉 🚍 🚹
Palais Rihour (03 59 57 94 00). 🚌
daily. **www**.lilletourism.com

Transformed in recent years, not least by the advent of Eurostar and the city's election as European City of Culture

Musicians in place du Général de Gaulle, in the heart of Vieux Lille

Flower stalls in the arcades of the Vieille Bourse in Lille

2004, Lille has excellent stores and markets and a powerful sense of its historic Flemish identity – the Flemish name (Rijssel) is still used and some of the area's million residents speak a Franco-Flemish patois. With heavy industry declining, the city has turned to hi-tech. A modern commercial quarter, including the Euralille shopping complex, adjoins Lille Europe station, the TGV/ Eurostar/ Thalys rail interchange. The city's metro, VAL, is a driverless automatic train.

The city's charm lies in its historic center, Vieux Lille – a mass of cobbled squares and narrow streets that are packed with stylish stores, cafés, and restaurants. Place du Général de Gaulle forms its hub, with façades including the 17th-century **Vieille Bourse** (Old Exchange). Adjacent stand the **Nouvelle Bourse** and the **Opéra**, both built in the early 20th century. The moated

five-point brick Citadel by Vauban is also worth a look.

⛪ Musée de l'Hospice Comtesse
32 rue de la Monnaie. **Tel** 03 28 36 84 00. ☐ Wed–Sun, Mon pm. ⬛
A hospital was founded here in 1237. Now its 15th- and 17th- century buildings house exhibitions. The Sick Room has a barrel-vaulted ceiling, the Community Wing a Delft kitchen. There is a collection of ancient instruments.

🏛 Palais des Beaux-Arts
Pl de la République. **Tel** 03 20 06 78 00.
☐ Wed–Sun, Mon pm. ⬛ ⬛ ⬛ ⬛
One of the best art collections outside Paris, the museum is strong on Flemish works, including Rubens and Van Dyck. Other highlights are *Paradise and Hell* by Dirk Bouts, Van Goyen's *The Skaters*, Goya's *The Letter*, Delacroix's *Médée*, works by Courbet, and Impressionist paintings.

Arras ❽

Pas de Calais. 🏠 45,000. 🚇 🚌 ℹ️
Hôtel de Ville, pl des Héros
(03 21 51 26 95). 🛒 Wed, Sat.
www.ot-arras.fr

The center of Arras, capital of the Artois region, is graced by two picturesque cobbled squares enclosed by 155 houses with 17th-century Flemish-style façades. A triumph of postwar reconstruction, each residence in the **Grand' place** and the smaller place des Héros has a slightly varying design, with some original store signs still visible.

A monumental **Hôtel de Ville**, rebuilt in the Flamboyant Gothic style, stands at the west end of place des Héros – in the foyer are two giants, Colas Dédé and Jacqueline, who swagger round the town during local festivals. From the basement you can take an elevator up to the belfry for superb views, or take a guided tour into the labyrinth of underground passages below Arras. These were cut in the limestone in the 10th century. They have often served as shelter and during World War I as a subterranean army camp.

The huge Abbaye St-Vaast includes an 18th–19th-century Neoclassical cathedral and the **Musée des Beaux-Arts**. The museum contains some fine examples of medieval sculp-

Roadside shrine, Somme Valley

ture including a pair of beautiful 13th-century angels. Among other exhibits are a local *arras* (hanging tapestry) and 19th-century works by the School of Arras, a group of realist landscape painters.

🏛 **Hôtel de Ville**
Pl des Héros. *Tel* 03 21 51 26 95. ◯ Jul–Aug daily. ✔️ oblig. for tunnels. ♿

🏛 **Musée des Beaux-Arts**
22 rue Paul Doumer. *Tel* 03 21 71 26 43. ◯ Wed–Mon. ● public hols. ♿

Vallée de la Somme ❾

Somme. 🚆 🚌 🚗 Amiens. ℹ️ 16 pl André Audinot, Péronne (03 22 84 42 38). www.somme-tourisme.com

The name of the Somme is synonymous with the slaughter and horror of trench warfare during World War I *(see pp190–91)*. Yet the Somme valley also means pretty countryside, a vast estuary wetland, and abundant wildlife. Lakes and woods alongside provide enjoyable camping, walking, and fishing.

Battlefields lie along the river and its tributaries north and northeast of Amiens, and extend north to Arras. Tidy World War I Commonwealth cemeteries cover the area. The **Historial de la Grande Guerre** at Péronne gives a thoughtful introduction. Parc Mémorial Beaumont-Hamel,

Boating on the river Somme

near Albert, is a real battlefield being allowed to disappear in its own time. Travel to Vimy Ridge Canadian Memorial, near Arras, to see a bloodbath battle site preserved as it was, and to Notre-Dame de Lorette, the landmark French National Cemetery.

West of Amiens, **Samara** – Amiens' Gallo-Roman name – is France's largest archeological park, with reconstructions of prehistoric dwellings and exhibitions explaining early crafts like flint-cutting and corn-grinding. Farther downstream, Eglise St-Vulfran at Abbeville is noted for its Flamboyant Gothic west front with beautifully carved 16th-century door panels.

St-Valéry-sur-Somme is a charming harbor resort with a historic upper town and a tree-lined promenade looking across the estuary. William departed for England from here in 1066. Birdwatchers should visit the Maison de l'Oiseau on the D3 nearby, or the Parc Ornithologique de Marquenterre on the far shore near delightful Le Crotoy. In summer, a little train links the two sides, passing through dunes and marshes.

🏛 **Historial de la Grande Guerre**
Château de Péronne. *Tel* 03 22 83 14 18. ◯ Apr–Sep: daily; Oct–Mar: Tue–Sun. ● mid-Dec–mid-Jan. ✔️ ♿ ✔️ www.historial.org

🏛 **Samara**
La Chaussée-Tirancourt. *Tel* 03 22 51 82 83. ◯ mid-Mar–mid-Nov: daily. ✔️ ♿ ✔️ www.samara.fr

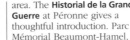

16th-century carvings on Eglise St-Vulfran in Abbeville, Somme Valley

Amiens ⑩

Somme. 🏠 130,000. 🚉 🚌
ℹ️ *6 bis rue Dusevel (03 22 71 60 50).*
🛒 *Wed & Sat.*
www.amiens-tourisme.com

There is more to Amiens, the
capital of Picardy, than its
Cathédrale Notre-Dame *(see
pp202–3)*. The picturesque
quarter of St-Leu is a pedestrianized area of low houses and
flower-lined canals with waterside restaurants, bars, and
artisans' stores. Farther east are
Les Hortillonnages, a colorful
patchwork of marshland
market gardens, once tended
by farmers using punts which
now ferry visitors around the
protected natural site.

The **Musée de Picardie** has
many fine medieval and
19th-century sculptures and
16th–20th-century paintings,
including a remarkable set of
16th-century group portraits,
commissioned as offerings to
the cathedral. To the south is
the Cirque d'Hiver which Jules
Verne (1828–1905) inaugurated in 1889. **Maison de Jules
Verne**, his renovated home,
has over 700 objects spread
over four floors relating to the
famous author, who lived here
from 1882 until 1900.

🏛 **Musée de Picardie**
48 rue de la République.
Tel *03 22 97 14 00.* ⬜ *Tue–Sun.*
⬛ *Jan 1, May 1, Nov 1 & 11,
Dec 25.* 🎟 ♿

🏛 **Maison de Jules Verne**
2 rue Charles Dubois. ***Tel*** *03 22 45
45 75.* ⬜ *Easter–mid-Oct: daily;
mid-Oct– Easter: Wed–Mon.* 🎟

The clock depicts
Christ surrounded by
the 12 apostles.

Mechanical figures
perform scenes from
the Last Judgment.

**Clock
showing
age of the
world**

**Solstice
indicator**

Astronomical clock in Beauvais cathedral

Beauvais ⑪

Oise. 🏠 61,000. ✈ 🚉 🚌 ℹ️ *1 rue
Beauregard (03 44 15 30 30).* 🛒
Wed, Sat. **www**.beauvaistourisme.fr

Heavily bombed in World
War II, Beauvais is now a
modern town with one
outstanding jewel. Though
never completed, **Cathédrale
St-Pierre** is a poignant,
neck-cricking finale to the
vaulting ambition that created

the great Gothic cathedrals. In
1227 work began on a building
designed to soar above all
predecessors, but the roof of
the chancel caved in twice
from lack of support before its
completion in the early 14th
century. Delayed by wars and
inadequate funds, the transept
was not completed until 1550.
In 1573 its crossing collapsed
after a tower and spire were
added. What remains today is
nevertheless a masterpiece,
rising 157 ft (48 m) high.
In the transept much of the
original 16th-century stained
glass survives, while near the
north door is a 90,000-part
astronomical clock assembled
in the 1860s. What would
have been the nave is still
occupied by the remnants of
a 10th-century church known
as the Basse-Oeuvre.

The former Bishop's Palace
is now home to the **Musée
Départemental de l'Oise**. The
collection includes archeological finds, medieval
sculpture, tapestries, and local
ceramics. Beauvais has a long
tradition of tapestry manufacture, and examples from

VIOLLET-LE-DUC

The renowned architectural theorist Viollet-le-Duc (1814–79)
was the first to fully appreciate Gothic architecture. His
1854 dictionary of architecture celebrated medieval building
techniques, showing that the
arches and tracery of Gothic
cathedrals were solutions
to architectural problems,
not mere decoration. His
restoration work included
Château de Pierrefonds,
Notre-Dame in Paris
(see pp86–7), and Car-
cassonne *(see pp488–9)*.

**Medieval architects, as
drawn by Viollet-le-Duc**

the French national collection are shown in the **Galerie Nationale de la Tapisserie.**

🏛 **Musée Départemental de l'Oise**
Ancien Palais Episcopal, 1 rue du Musée. *Tel 03 44 10 40 50.* ⬜ *Wed–Mon.* ⬤ *Jan 1, Easter, May 1, Jun 9, Nov 1, Dec 25.* 🖼

🏛 **Galerie Nationale de la Tapisserie**
22 rue St-Pierre. *Tel 03 44 15 39 10.* ⬜ *Tue–Sun.* 🖼 ⬤ *Jan 1, May 1, Dec 25.*

Noyon ⓬

Oise. 🏘 *15,200.* 🚆 ❓ *pl de l'Hôtel de Ville (03 44 44 21 88).* ⬛ *Wed & Sat, first Tue of each month.* **www**.noyon-tourisme.com

Noyon has long been a religious center. The **Cathédrale de Notre-Dame**, dating from 1150, is the fifth to be built on this site and was completed by 1290. It provides a harmonious example of the transition from Romanesque to Gothic style.

A local history museum, the **Musée du Noyonnais** occupies part of the former Bishop's Palace, and at the cathedral's east end is a rare half-timbered chapter library built in 1506.

Jean Calvin, the Protestant theologian and one of the leaders of the Reformation, was born here in 1509 and is commemorated in the small **Musée Jean Calvin.**

🏛 **Musée du Noyonnais**
Ancien Palais Episcopal, 7 rue de l'Evêché. *Tel 03 44 09 43 41.* ⬜ *Wed-Mon.* ⬤ *Jan 1, Nov 11, Dec 25.* 🖼

The rib-vaulted nave of Cathédrale de Notre-Dame, Noyon

Path through Forêt de Compiègne

Compiègne ⓭

Oise. 🏘 *70,000.* 🚆 🚌 ❓ *pl de l'Hôtel de Ville (03 44 40 01 00).* ⬛ *Wed & Sat.* **www**.compiegne-tourisme.fr

Compiegne is where Joan of Arc was captured by the Burgundians in 1430. A 16th-century Hôtel de Ville with a towering belfry rules over the center, but the town is most famous for its royal **Château**.

Designed as a summer residence for Louis XV, the château was completed by Louis XVI, restored by Napoleon, and later became a residence of Napoleon III and Empress Eugénie. Tours of the Imperial Apartments take in private chambers, such as the sumptuous bedrooms of Napoleon I and Marie-Louise.

Within the château, the Musée du Second Empire and Musée de l'Impératrice display furniture, memorabilia, and portraits, while the Musée de la Voiture is an entertaining assembly of historic carriages, bicycles, and early motor cars.

South and east of the town the old hunting grounds of **Forêt de Compiègne** spread as far as Pierrefonds, with ample space for walks and picnics beneath its oaks and beeches. East of the D130 Les Beaux Monts provide majestic views back to the château.

The Clairière de l'Armistice, north of the N31, marks the spot where the armistice of World War I was signed on November 11, 1918. The small **Musée Wagon de l'Armistice** has a replica of the railroad

carriage where the ceremony took place, which was used again in World War II by Hitler as a humiliating venue for the signing of the French surrender on June 22, 1940.

♣ **Château de Compiègne**
Pl du Général de Gaulle. *Tel 03 44 38 47 02.* ⬜ *Wed–Mon.* ⬤ *Jan 1, May 1, Dec 25.* 🖼 **www**.musee-chateau-compiegne.fr

🏛 **Musée Wagon de l'Armistice**
Clairière de l'Armistice (direc. Soissons). *Tel 03 44 85 14 18.* ⬜ *Wed–Mon.* ⬤ *Jan & Feb am, Jan 1, Dec 25.* 🖼

Château de Pierrefonds

Château de Pierrefonds ⓮

Oise. *Tel 03 44 42 72 72.* ⬜ *daily.* ⬤ *Mon (Sep 5–Apr), Jan 1, May 1, Nov 1 & 11, Dec 25.* 🖼 🎫 **Concerts**

The immense Château de Pierrefonds dominates the small village below. A mighty castle was constructed here by Louis d'Orléans in the 14th century, but by 1813 it had become a picturesque ruin which Napoleon I purchased for less than 3,000 francs.

In 1857, Napoleon III commissioned the architect Viollet-le-Duc to restore it, and in 1884 Pierrefonds was reborn as a museum of fortification. The exterior, with its moat, drawbridge, towers, and double sentry walks, is a diligent reconstruction of medieval military architecture. The interior, by contrast, is enlivened by the romantic fancies of Viollet-le-Duc and his patron. There are guided tours and a historical exhibition.

Amiens Cathedral

Work on France's largest cathedral started around 1220. It was built to house the head of St. John the Baptist, brought back from the Crusades in 1206, which is still displayed here. Within 50 years, Notre-Dame was complete, a masterpiece of engineering – Gothic architecture carried to a bold extreme. Restored in the 1850s by Viollet-le-Duc *(see p200)*, and having miraculously survived two World Wars, the cathedral is famous for its statues and reliefs, which inspired John Ruskin's *The Bible of Amiens* in 1884. The annual *La Cathédrale en Couleurs* sound and light show re-creates the original colors of the statuary around the west door.

★ West Front
The King's Gallery, a row of 22 colossal statues repre-senting the kings of France, spans the west front. The statues are also thought to symbolize the Kings of Judah.

Weeping Angel
Sculpted by Nicolas Blasset in 1628, this sentimental statue in the ambulatory became a popular image during World War I.

St-Firmin Portal is decorated with figures and scenes from the life of St. Firmin, the martyr who brought Christianity to Picardy and became the first bishop of Amiens.

The Calendar shows signs from the Zodiac, with the corresponding monthly labors below. It depicts everyday life in the 13th century.

Central Portal
Scenes from the Last Judg-ment adorn the tympanum, with the Beau Dieu, a statue of Christ, between the doors.

STAR FEATURES

- ★ West Front
- ★ Nave
- ★ Choir Stalls
- ★ Choir Screens

Towers
Two towers of unequal height frame the west front. The south tower was completed in 1366; the north in 1402. The spire was replaced twice, in 1627 and 1887.

The Flamboyant tracery of the rose window was created in the 16th century.

A double row comprising 22 elegant flying buttresses supports the construction.

★ **Nave**
Soaring 138 ft (42 m) high, with support from 126 slander pillars, the brightly illuminated interior of Notre-Dame is a hymn to the vertical.

★ **Choir Stalls**
The 110 oak choir stalls (1508–19) are delicately carved with over 4,000 biblical, mythical, and real life figures.

The flooring was laid down in 1288 and reassembled in the late 19th century. The faithful followed its labyrinthine shape on their knees.

★ **Choir Screens**
Vivid scenes from the lives of St. Firmin and St. John, carved in the 15th–16th centuries, adorn the ambulatory.

Senlis ❶

Oise. ⛪ *17,000*. 🚌 🛈 *pl du Parvis Notre-Dame (03 44 53 06 40)*. 🏛 *Tue & Fri*. www.senlis-tourisme.fr

Senlis, 6 miles (10 km) east of Chantilly, is worth visiting for its Gothic cathedral and the well-preserved historic streets in the old town that surround it. **Cathédrale Notre-Dame** was constructed during the 12th century, and the sculpted central doorway of its west front, depicting the Assumption of the Virgin, influenced later cathedrals such as Amiens (*see pp202–3*). The south tower's spire dates from the 13th century, while the Flamboyant south transept, built in the mid-16th century, makes an ornate contrast with the austerity of earlier years. Opposite the west front, a gateway leads to the ruins of the Château Royal and its gardens. Here the **Musée de la Vénerie**, housed in a former priory, celebrates hunting through paintings, old weapons, and trophies.

The **Musée d'Art** recalls the town's Gallo-Roman past, and also has an excellent collection of early Gothic sculpture.

🏛 **Musée de la Vénerie**
Château Royal, pl du Parvis Notre-Dame. *Tel 03 44 32 00 81.* ⭕ *Mon, Wed pm, Thu, Sun.* ⬤ *Jan 1, May 1, Dec 25.* 📷 🎫 *oblig.*

🏛 **Musée d'Art et d'Archéologie**
Ancien Evêché, 2 pl Notre-Dame. *Tel 03 44 32 00 81.* ⭕ *Mon, Wed pm, Thu, Sun.* ⬤ *Jan 1, May 1, Dec 25.* 📷

Les Très Riches Heures du Duc de Berry, on show in Chantilly

Chantilly ❷

Oise. ⛪ *11,200*. 🚌 🚉 🛈 *60 av du Maréchal Joffre (03 44 67 37 37)*. 🏛 *Wed & Sat*. www.chantilly-tourisme.com

The horse-racing capital of France, Chantilly offers a classy combination of château, park, and forest that has long made it a popular excursion. With origins in Gallo-Roman times, the château of today started to take shape in 1528 when the famous Anne de Montmorency, Constable of France, had the old fortress replaced and added the Petit Château. During the time of the Great Prince of Condé (1621–86), renovation work continued and Le Nôtre created a park and fountains which made even Louis XIV jealous. Destroyed in the Revolution,

---

CHANTILLY HORSE RACING

Chantilly is the capital of thoroughbred racing in France, a shrine to the long-standing love affair between the French upper classes and the world of horses. It was the firm belief of Prince Louis-Henri de Bourbon, creator of Chantilly's monumental Grandes Ecuries, that he would one day be reincarnated as a horse. Horse racing was introduced from England around 1830 and soon became very popular. The first official race meeting was held here in 1834 and today around 3,000 horses are trained in the surrounding forests and countryside. Every June, Chantilly becomes the focus of the social and flat racing season when top riders and their thoroughbreds compete for its two historic trophies, the Prix du Jockey-Club and Prix de Diane-Hermès.

Prix Equipage de Hermès, one of many prestigious races at Chantilly

the Grand Château was again rebuilt and its receptions and hunting parties became crowded by the fashionable high society of the 1820s–30s. It was finally replaced by a Renaissance-style château in the late 19th century.

Today the Grand Château and the Petit Château form the **Musée Condé**, displaying art treasures collected by its last private owner, the Duke of Aumale. These include work by Raphael, Botticelli, Poussin, and Ingres, and an entertaining gallery of 16th-century portraits by the Clouet brothers. Among the most precious items is the famous 15th-century illuminated manuscript *Les Très Riches Heures du Duc de Berry*, reproductions of which are on view. You can also tour the stately apartments, with decorative conceits ranging from frolicking monkeys to triumphant battles.

Asterix with friends, Parc Astérix

Both châteaux are somewhat upstaged by the magnificent stables (Grandes Ecuries), an equestrian palace designed by Jean Aubert in 1719 which could accommodate 240 horses and 500 dogs. It is occupied by the **Musée Vivant du Cheval**, presenting various breeds of horses and ponies, and riding displays.

🏛 **Musée Condé**
Château de Chantilly. **Tel** 03 44 62 62 62. ◻ Wed–Mon. ✒🖪

🏇 **Musée Vivant du Cheval**
Grandes Ecuries du Prince de Condé, Chantilly. **Tel** 03 44 27 31 80. ◻ call for information. ✒⌧

Parc Astérix ⑰

Plailly. 🆔 08 26 30 10 40. ◻ Jun–Aug daily & French school hols (check). ✒🖪 www.parcasterix.fr

Near Charles de Gaulle Airport a small fortified Gaulish village has its own customs controls, currency, and radio station (Menhir FM). One of the most popular

theme parks in France, it is dedicated to Asterix the Gaul and all the other characters in Goscinny and Uderzo's famous cartoon strip: Getafix, Obelix, Cacofonix *et al*. The Romans are driven crazy as they try to subdue these larger-than-life Gauls, who dodge patrolling Roman centurions. Hilarious battles take place.

The Parc is as much about French history as about the cartoons. Via Antiqua and the Roman City are lighthearted but genuinely educational. Rue de Paris shows Paris through the centuries, including the construction of Notre-Dame cathedral. There are nonhistorical attractions too, like a dolphinarium and Zeus' Thunder high-speed roller-coaster. Grab on the latest rides – there's usually something new every year.

Laon ⑱

Aisne. 🏠 27,000. 🚉 🛈 *Hôtel-Dieu, pl du Parvis Gauthier de Montagne (03 23 20 28 62).* 🔄 *Wed–Thu & Sat.* www.tourisme-paysdelaon.com

The capital of the Aisne *département*, Laon occupies a dramatic site on top of a

The pedestrianized rue Châtelaine, a main shopping street in Laon

Rose window in the 13th-century Cathédrale de Notre-Dame, Laon

long, narrow ridge surrounded by wide plains. The old town, on top of the mount, is best approached by Poma, an automated cable car that swings up from the train station to the place du Général Leclerc.

The pedestrianized rue Châtelaine leads to Laon's splendid **Cathédrale do Notre-Dame**. Completed in 1235, the cathedral lost two of its original seven towers in the Revolution but remains an impressive monument to the early Gothic style.

Details include the deep porches of the west façade, the four-story nave, and the carved Renaissance screens enclosing its side chapels. The immense 13th-century rose window in the apse represents the Glorification of the Church. Protruding from the cathedral's western towers are statues paying tribute to the oxen used to haul up stone for its construction.

The rest of medieval Laon rewards casual strolling: a promenade rings the 16th-century **Citadelle** farther east, while to the south you can follow the ramparts past the Porte d'Ardon and Porte des Chenizelles to **Eglise St-Martin**, with views of the cathedral from rue Thibesard.

South of Laon is Chemin des Dames, named after Louis XV's daughters who used to take this route, but more often remembered as a World War I battlefield and lined with cemeteries and memorials.

CHAMPAGNE

MARNE · ARDENNES · AUBE · HAUTE-MARNE

Champagne is a name of great resonance, conjuring up images of celebration and the world-famous cathedral at Reims. Yet beyond the glamor lies an unspoiled rural idyll of two strikingly contrasting landscapes: the rolling plains of Champagne, giving way to lakes and water meadows to the south, and the dense forests and hills of the Ardennes in the north.

The so-called "sacred triangle of Champagne," linking Épernay, Reims, and Châlons-en-Champagne, is like a magnet for wine lovers. Here, the experience of drinking fine champagne is enhanced by gourmet meals of stuffed trout, Ardennes ham, and the famous sausages called *andouillettes*.

The sign posted *route touristique du Champagne* winds its way through vineyards towards endless cereal plains stretching southward to the "lake district," an area of oak forests, water meadows, and streams.

On the border between France and Belgium lies the Ardennes, named after the Celtic word for deep forest. This wild border land of dramatic valleys, deciduous forests, and hills is cut by the meanderings of the river Meuse. Border fortifications include the vast citadel of Sedan and the star-shaped town and fortress of Rocroi, as well as the Maginot Line outposts built before World War II. The Ardennes may offer appealing countryside but Champagne is culturally superior, with impressive towns that have painstakingly restored historic centers. It has some striking churches, from the Gothic majesty of Reims cathedral to the rustic charm of its typical half-timbered *champenoises* churches. These feature vivid stained-glass windows by the famous School of Troyes, whose subtle craftsmanship seems to typify the appeal of this quiet region.

Timber-framed *champenoise* church at Lac du Der-Chantecoq

◁ Cathédrale St-Etienne at Châlons-en-Champagne

Exploring Champagne

Champagne's fizz draws wine lovers to the sacred triangle between Reims, Épernay, and Châlons-en-Champagne, but the region also attracts culture lovers to its great churches, notably Reims Cathedral. Reims abounds in gastronomic restaurants but Troyes, the former capital of Champagne, makes the most delightful base. Much of Champagne is flat or gently undulating, and the wild and wooded Ardennes to the north attracts walkers and nature-lovers. North of Reims, the Ardennes canal can be explored by barge or pleasure boat from Rethel; to the south, watersports are popular on the lakes to the east of Troyes.

Fishing by a canal in Montier-en-Der near Lac du Der-Chantecoq

GETTING AROUND

The region's main autoroute is the A26, which reaches Reims in under 3 hours from Calais, and also provides easy access to most of the region all the way down to Troyes and Langres (via the A5). The A4 motorway also links Reims to Paris and Alsace. Paris-Reims by the TGV high-speed train takes 45 minutes. Rail transport within the region is reasonably good, and so are the roads. To explore the wine-growing region, follow the signposted roads marked "Route de Champagne."

Windmill at Verzenay, Parc Naturel de la Montagne de Reims

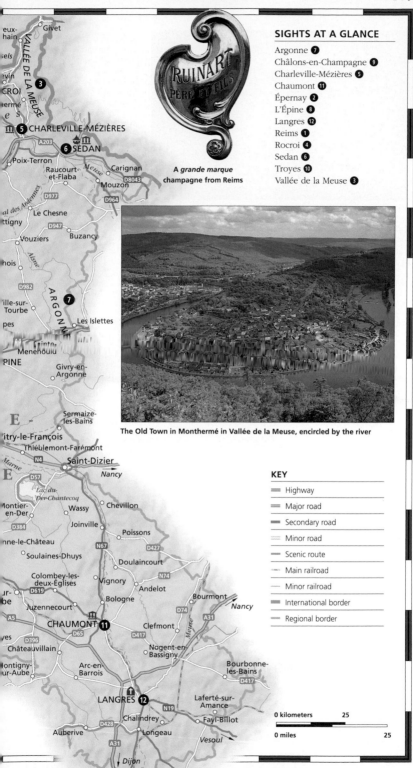

A *grande marque*
champagne from Reims

The Old Town in Monthermé in Vallée de la Meuse, encircled by the river

KEY

▬	Highway
▬	Major road
▬	Secondary road
═	Minor road
▬	Scenic route
➤	Main railroad
—	Minor railroad
▬	International border
▬	Regional border

0 kilometers   25

0 miles   25

Gilded reliquary (1896), with body of St Remi, in Basilique St-Remi, Reims

Reims ❶

Marne. 🏛 185,000. ✈ 🚊 🚌
ℹ 2 rue Guillaume de Machault
(08 92 70 13 51). 🛥 daily.
www.reims-tourisme.com

Pronounced like the French word "prince" without the "p," Reims is home to some of the best known *grandes marques* in Champagne, and several are grouped around the Basilique St-Remi. But the city has another, much earlier, claim to fame: since the 11th century all the kings of France have come to this "city of coronations" to be crowned in its remarkable Gothic **Cathédrale Notre-Dame** *(see pp212–13)*.

Although World War II bombing destroyed much of Reims' architectural coherence, there are some remarkable monuments here. The **Crypto-portique**, part of the forum, and Porte Mars, a triumphal Augustan arch, recall the Roman past. In 1945, the German surrender was taken in the **Musée de la Reddition** in Eisenhower's French HQ during World War II.

Musée des Beaux-Arts houses a fine collection of 15th- and 16th-century canvases depicting biblical scenes, portraits by the Cranachs, *The Death of Marat* by David, and more than 20 land-scapes by Corot. Also here are the Barbizons, Impressionists, and modern masters.

In 1996 Reims celebrated the 1,500-year anniversary of the baptism of Clovis, first King of the Franks, in its cathedral.

🏛 Ancien Collège des Jésuites & Planetarium

1 pl Museux. **Tel** 03 26 35 34 70.
Collège 🏛 *(Planetarium).*
Founded in 1606, this college was a hospice until 1976. Nowadays its 300-year-old vines, Romanesque wine cellars, and Baroque interior play their part as atmospheric film sets, notably for the film of Zola's *Germinal* (1992) and *Queen Margot* (1993). High-lights include the refectory's ceiling and the kitchen, the only room where fireplaces were permitted in an austere Jesuit establishment. A double spiral staircase leads to a Baroque library with yet another magnificent ceiling. Housed in the same building since 1979 is the **Planetarium**, with views of the sky from everywhere in the world.

⚓ Basilique St-Remi

Pl St-Rémi. 🕐 *daily.* ♿
This Benedictine abbey church, the oldest church in Reims, began as a Carolingian basilica dedicated to Saint Rémi (440–533). Inside, an Early Gothic choir and radiating

Porte Mars, a reminder of Reims in Roman times

METHODE CHAMPENOISE

To produce its characteristic bubbles, champagne has to undergo a process of double fermentation.

First fermentation: The base wine, made from rather acidic grapes, is fermented at 68°–71.6°F in either stainless steel tanks or, occasionally, in oak barrels. It is then siphoned off from the sediment and kept at colder temperatures to clear completely, before being drawn off and blended with wines from other areas and years (except in the case of vintage champagne). The wine is bottled and the *liqueur de tirage* (sugar, wine, and yeast) is added. **Second fermentation:** The bot-tles are stored for a year or more in cool, chalky cellars. The yeast converts the sugar to alcohol and carbon diox-ide, which produces the sparkle, and the yeast cells die leaving a deposit. To remove this, the inverted bottles are turned and tapped daily *(remuage)* to shift the deposits into the neck of the bottle. Finally, the deposits are expelled by the process known as *dégorgement*, and a bit of sugar syrup *(liqueur d'expédition)* is added to adjust the sweetness before the final cork is inserted.

Champagne Mumm of Reims

chapels can be seen, as well as sculpted Romanesque capitals in the north transept.

🏛 Musée St-Remi
53 rue Simon. *Tel 03 26 85 00 01.* ◯ *daily pm only.* ● *Jan 1, May 1, Jul 14, Nov 1 & 11, Dec 25.* 🖥

Set in the former abbey, the adjoining museum encloses the original Gothic chapterhouse within its cloistered 17th-century shell. On display are archeological artifacts, 15th-century tapestries depicting the life of Saint Remi, and a collection of weapons dating from the 16th–19th centuries.

🏰 Fort de la Pompelle
5 miles (8km) southeast of Reims. *Tel 03 26 49 11 85.* ◯ *Wed–Mon.* 🖥 ♿

Built to protect Reims after the Franco-Prussian War, this fort houses a museum of German Imperial military headgear.

Épernay ❷
Marne. 👥 *25,000.* 🚂 🚌 *7 av de Champagne (03 26 53 33 00).* 🛍 *Wed, Sat & Sun.* **www**.ot-epernay.fr

The sole reason for visiting Épernay is to burrow into the chalky *caves* and taste the champagne. This rather undistinguished town lives off the

Statue of Dom Perignon at Moët

fruits of its profitable champagne industry. As proof, the avenue de Champagne quarter abounds in mock-Renaissance mansions. **Moët & Chandon**, dating back to 1743, is the largest and slickest *maison*, the star of the Moët-Hennessy stable. Its cellars stretch some 18 miles (28 km) underground.

The group also owns other champagne houses, such as Mercier, Krug, Pommery, Veuve Clicquot, and Canard Duchêne.

There is little to choose between a visit to the cellars of Moët & Chandon or **Mercier** – both are in Avenue de Champagne. Mercier has the distinction of displaying a giant tun (cask) created for the 1889 Paris Exhibition, and takes you through the *caves* in an electric train.

De Castellane offers a more personalized tour, accompanied by a heady *dégustation*.

🏰 Moët & Chandon
20 av de Champagne. *Tel 03 26 51 20 20.* ◯ *end Mar–mid-Nov: daily; mid-Nov–Dec, Feb–end Mar: Mon–Fri.* 🖥 🎫 *only.* **www**.moet.com

🏰 Mercier
70 av de Champagne. *Tel 03 26 51 22 22.* ◯ *mid-Mar–Nov: daily; Dec–mid-Mar: Thu–Mon.* 🖥 ♿ 🎫 *oblig.* **www**.champagnemercier.com

🏰 De Castellane
57 rue de Verdun. *Tel 03 26 51 19 19.* ◯ *daily (Jan–Mar: Sat & Sun only).* 🖥 ♿ *restr.* 🎫 *obligatory.* **www**.castellane.com

Dégorgement *is the final removal of the yeast deposits from the bottle. The neck of the bottle is plunged in freezing brine and the frozen block of sediment is then removed.*

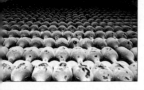

Seductive marketing *of champagne since the 19th century has ensured its continuing success.*

The bubbles in champagne *are produced during the second fermentation. Champagnes, especially vintage ones, improve with ageing.*

Reims Cathedral

The magnificent Gothic Cathédrale Notre-Dame at
Reims is noted for its harmony and monumentality.
A cathedral has stood on this site since 401, but the
present building was begun in 1211. Reims has been
the backdrop for coronations from medieval times until
1825, when Charles X was crowned. The coronation of
Charles VII here in 1429 was attended by Joan of Arc.

During the Revolution, the rood screen and windows
were destroyed but the stonework survived. World War I
damage was finally fully restored in 1996, to coincide
with the 1,500th anniversary of the baptism of Clovis,
King of the Franks, at Reims, which was considered the
first coronation of a French king.

The Nave
*Compared with the nave at
Chartres (see pp308–11),
Reims is taller. Its elegant
capitals are decorated with
naturalistic floral motifs
such as ivy and berries.*

★ Great Rose Window
*Best seen at sunset, the
13th-century window
shows the Virgin sur-
rounded by the apostles
and angel musicians. It is
set within a larger window,
a feature common in
13th-century architecture.*

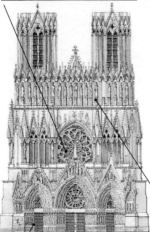

WEST FAÇADE

SOUTH FAÇADE

★ Smiling Angel
*Rich in statuary,
Reims is often called
"the cathedral of
angels." Situated
above the left (north)
portal, this enigmatic
angel with unfurled
wings is the most cele-
brated of the many
that grace the building.*

★ Gallery of the Kings
*The harmonious west façade, decorated
with over 2,300 statues, is the most notable
feature at Reims. Fifty-six stone effigies of
French kings form the Gallery of the Kings.*

PALAIS DU TAU

The archbishop's palace adjoining the cathedral is named after its T-shaped design, based on early episcopal crosses. (Tau is Greek for T.) The palace, built in 1690 by Mansart and Robert de Cotte, encloses a Gothic Chapel and the 15th-century Salle du Tau, rooms associated with French coronations. On the eve of a coronation, the future king would spend the night in the palace. After being crowned in the cathedral, he held a magnificent banquet in the palace. The Salle du Tau, or banqueting hall, is the finest room in the palace, with a magnificent barrel-vaulted ceiling and walls hung with 15th-century

Arras tapestries. The palace now houses a museum of statuary and tapestries from the cathedral, including a 15th-century tapestry of the baptism of Clovis, the first Christian king.

Salle du Tau – the banqueting hall

VISITORS' CHECKLIST

Cathédrale Notre-Dame, pl du Cardinal Luçon. **Tel** 03 26 47 55 34. ◯ 7:30am–7:30pm daily. ⬛ 8am & 7pm Mon, Wed, Fri; 8am Tue, Thu, Sat; 9:30am & 11am Sun. ◻ ◻ ◻ by appt only. **www**.cathedrale-reims. com **Palais du Tau Tel** 03 26 47 81 79. ◯ Tue–Sun. ⬛ Jan 1, May 1, Nov 1 & 11, Dec 25. ◻

Apse Gallery
The restored claire-voie (open work) gallery on the apse is crowned by statues of mythological beasts.

The radiating chapels of the apse are supported by flying buttresses and adorned with octagonal pinnacles.

south transept

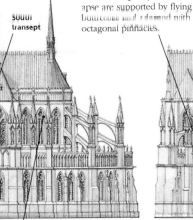

APSE

SIDE SECTION

The clerestory windows pioneered Gothic tracery by dividing the lights with slender bars of stone, creating a decorative, intersecting pattern.

Pinnacles on the flying buttresses shelter guardian angels, symbolic protectors of the cathedral.

STAR FEATURES

★ Gallery of the Kings

★ Smiling Angel

★ Great Rose Window

Chagall Window
The windows in the axial chapel were designed by the 20th-century artist Marc Chagall and made by local craftsmen. This one depicts the Crucifixion and the Sacrifice of Isaac.

The *sentier touristique*, a walk along the ramparts of Rocroi

Vallée de la Meuse ❸

Ardennes. 🏠 *8,900.* 🚉 *Revin.*
ℹ️ *65 quai Edgar Quinet, Revin (03 24 40 19 59).* **www**.*meuselavallee.org*

The Meuse meanders through the Ardennes among spectacular scenery of wild gorges, woods, and warped rock formations of granite or schist.

Dramatically situated on a double meander of the Meuse, **Revin** is an unremarkable town in an exceptional site, with the Vieille Ville enfolded in the north bend. From the quay, you can see wooded **Mont Malgré Tout** and a route dotted with observation points and steep trails. Just south is **Dames de la Meuse**, a rocky outcrop over the river gorge.

Monthermé lies on two banks, with the Vieille Ville clustered on the charming left bank. The rocky gorges around **Roche à Sept Heures** on the far bank entice climbers and ramblers. The jagged crest of **Rocher des Quatre Fils d'Aymon** suggests the silhouette of four legendary local horsemen.

Rocroi ❹

Ardennes. 🏠 *2,430.* 🚉 🚉 *Revin.*
ℹ️ *14 pl d'Armes (03 24 54 20 06).*
🍴 *Tue & 1st Mon of month.*
www.*otrocroi.com*

Set on the Ardennes plateau, the star-shaped citadel of Rocroi was originally built under Henri II in 1555, and later made impregnable by Vauban in 1675 *(see p226).*

The main attraction is the walk along the ramparts from the southern gateway. The nature preserve at Rièzes is home to orchids and carnivorous plants.

Charleville-Mézières ❺

Ardennes. 🏠 *58,000.* 🚉 🚉
ℹ️ *4 pl Ducale (03 24 55 69 90).*
🍴 *Tue, Thu, & Sat.*
www.*charleville-tourisme.com*

This riverside ford was originally two towns. The somber medieval citadel of Mézières only merged with the neat Classical town of Charleville in 1966. Mézières has irregular slate-covered houses curving around a bend in the Meuse. Battered fortifications and gateways are visible from avenue de St-Julien. Tucked into the ramparts is the much remodeled Gothic **Notre-Dame de l'Espérance**.

The centrepiece of Charleville is **place Ducale**, a model of Louis XIII urban planning,

echoing place des Vosges in Paris *(see p91).* The poet Arthur Rimbaud was born nearby in 1854. His modest birthplace at No. 12 rue Bérégovoy is still there, along with his childhood home on the Meuse at 7 quai Arthur Rimbaud.

Just along the quayside is the Vieux Moulin, the town house whose view inspired *Le Bateau Ivre*, Rimbaud's greatest poem. Inside is the small **Musée Rimbaud**, with manuscripts and photographs by the poet.

🏛 **Musée Rimbaud**
Quai Arthur Rimbaud. **Tel** *03 24 32 44 65.* 🕐 *Tue–Sun.* 🔴 *Jan 1, May 1, Dec 25.* 📷 *(free first Sun of month).*

Sedan ❻

Ardennes. 🏠 *20,000.* 🚉 🚉
ℹ️ *32 rue du Menil (03 24 27 73 73).* 🍴 *Wed & Sat.*
www.*tourisme-sedan.fr*

Just to the east of Charleville is the **Château de Sedan**, the largest fortified castle in Europe. There has been a bastion on these slopes since the 11th century, but each Ardennes conflict has spelled a new tier of defenses for Sedan.

In 1870, during the Franco-Prussian War, with 700 Prussian cannons turned on Sedan, Napoleon III surrendered and 83,000 French prisoners were deported to Prussia. In May 1940 after capturing Sedan, German forces reached the French coast a week later.

The seven-storied bastion contains sections dating from

The 19th-century poet Rimbaud, whose birthplace was Charleville

medieval times to the 16th
century. Highlights of any
visit are the ramparts, the 16th-
century fortifications, and the
magnificent 15th-century eaves
in one tower. The **Musée du
Château**, in the south wing, is
rather jumbled, with a section
on military campaigns.

The bastion is surrounded by
17th-century slate-roofed
houses which hug the banks
of the Meuse. These reflect
the city's earlier prosperity as
a Huguenot stronghold.

🏛 **Musée du Château**
1 pl du Château. *Tel 03 24 27 73 73.*
◯ *July & Aug: daily; Sep–mid-Mar:
Tue–Sun.* 📷 *Tue–Fri pms.*

Environs
Farther south is **Fort de Villy-
la-Ferté**, one of the few forts
on the Maginot line to have
been captured in combat with
the enemy in 1940.

**Courtyard inside the heavily
fortified Château de Sedan**

Gargoyle on Basilique de Notre-Dame de l'Epine

Argonne ❼

Ardennes & Meuse. 🚍 *Châlons.*
🚆 *Ste-Menehould.* 🛈 *5 pl du
Général Leclerc, Ste-Menehould (03
26 60 85 83).* **www.argonne.fr**

East of Reims, the Argonne
is a compact region of picturesque valleys and forests,
dotted with priories, trenches,
and war cemeteries.

As a wooded border
between the rival bishoprics
of Champagne and Lorraine,
the Argonne was home to
abbeys and priories. Now
ruined, the Benedictine abbey
of **Beaulieu-en-Argonne**
boasts a 13th-century wine
press and has forest views.

Just north is **Les Islettes**,
known for its faïence pottery
and tiles. The hilly terrain
here was a battleground
during the Franco-Prussian
War and World War I. The
disputed territory of **Butte de
Vauquois**, north of Les Islettes,
bears a war memorial.

L'Épine ❽

Marne. 🏠 *670.* 🚍 *Châlons.*
🛈 *Mairie (03 26 66 96 99).*

L'Épine is worth visiting if
only for a glimpse of the
**Basilique de Notre-Dame de
l'Épine** surrounded by wheatfields. Designed on the scale of
a cathedral, this 15th-century
Flamboyant Gothic church
has been a pilgrimage site
since medieval times. Even
French kings have come here
to venerate a "miraculous"
statue of the Virgin.

On the façade, three gabled
portals are offset by floating
tracery, a gauzy effect reminiscent of Reims cathedral. All
around are gruesome gar-
goyles, symbolizing evil spirits
and deadly sins, chased out by
the holy presence within.
Unfortunately, the most risqué
sculptures were destroyed,
judged obscene by 19th-
century puritans. The subdued
Gothic interior contains a 15th-
century rood-screen and the
venerated statue of the Virgin.

CHAMPAGNE TIMBER CHURCHES

Skirting Lac du Der-Chantecoq lies a region of woodland
and water meadows, containing twelve Romanesque and
Renaissance half-timbered churches with curious pointed
gables and *caquetoirs*, rickety wooden porches.
They have intimate and often beautifully
carved interiors with stained-glass windows
designed in the vivid colors
of the School of Troyes.
Rural roads link
churches at Bailly-le-
Franc, Chatillon-sur-
Broué, Lentilles,
Vignory, Outines,
Chavanges, and
Montier-en-Der.

**16th-century timber
church in Lentilles**

Châlons-en-Champagne ❾

Marne. 🏛 *48,000*. 🚊 🚌 ⓘ
3 quai des Arts (03 26 65 17 89).
🗓 *Wed, Fri am, Sat, Sun am.*
www.chalons-tourisme.com

Encircled by the river Marne and minor canals, Châlons' sleepy bourgeois charm is made up of half-timbered houses and gardens mirrored in canals. Nearby are vineyards producing Blanc de Blancs.

From quai de Notre-Dame there are views of old bridges and the Romanesque towers of **Notre-Dame-en-Vaux**, a masterpiece of Romanesque-Gothic. Behind the church is a well-restored medieval quarter and the **Musée du Cloître**, containing the original Romanesque cloisters.

Cathédrale St-Etienne, by the canal, is a cool Gothic affair with a Baroque portal, Romanesque crypt and vivid medieval windows. Beyond is **Le Petit Jard**, riverside gardens overlooking the Château du Marché, and a turreted toll gate built by Henri IV. Excellent river tours of the city are available from the tourist office.

🏛 **Musée du Cloître de Notre-Dame-en-Vaux**
Rue Nicolas Durand. *Tel 03 26 69 38 53.* ◯ *Wed–Mon.* ⬤ *Jan 1, May 1, Nov 1 & 11, Dec 25.* 🎟 🅿

Troyes ❿

Aube. 🏛 *63,000*. 🚊 🚌 ⓘ *16 bd Carnot (03 25 82 62 70).* 🗓 *daily.*
www.tourisme-troyes.com

Troyes is a delight, a city of magnificent Gothic churches and charming 16th-century courtyards, in a historical center shaped like a champagne cork. The city is famous for its heritage of stained glass and sausages *(andouillettes)*, its knitwear industry, and factory stores.

The battered Flamboyant Gothic west front of the **Cathédrale St-Pierre-et-St-Paul** opens onto a splendid vaulted interior. The nave is bathed in mauvish-red rays

Statuary in Troyes' Cathédrale St-Pierre-et-St-Paul

from the 16th-century rose window, complemented by the discreet turquoise of the Tree of Jesse window and the intense blue of the medieval windows of the apse.

Nearby, **Eglise St-Nizier** glitters in the faded quarter behind the cathedral with its shimmering tiled Burgundian roof. Inside, it is lit by windows in a range of warm mauves and soothing blues.

The Gothic **Basilique St-Urbain** boasts grand flying buttresses and particularly fine 13th-century windows. **Eglise Ste-Madeleine** is noted for its elaborate 16th-century rood screen resembling lacy

Rue Larivey, a typical street with half-timbered houses, in Troyes

foliage, grapes, and figs. Beyond is a wall of windows in browns, reds, and blues. The ruelle des Chats, which is a quaint covered passageway, connects rue Charbonnet and rue Champeaux.

Set in one of the best-preserved quarters, **Eglise St-Pantaléon** faces a Renaissance mansion. A Gothic and Renaissance interior houses an imposing collection of 16th-century statuary and severe *grisaille* windows.

🏛 **Musée d'Art Moderne**
14 pl St-Pierre. *Tel 03 25 76 26 80.* ◯ *Tue–Sun.* ⬤ *public hols.* 🎟 🅿
Beside the cathedral, the former episcopal palace is now a museum of modern art, with a sculpture by Rodin, and an especially fine collection of Fauvist paintings, as well as other modern art.

🏛 **Hôtel du Petit Louvre**
Rue de la Montée St-Pierre.
Courtyard only ◯ *daily.*
Set off quai Dampierre, this well-restored *hôtel particulier* boasts a fish-scale roof, medieval tower, Renaissance courtyard, staircase, and well. The highlight is a façade adorned with quizzical multicolored faces.

For hotels and restaurants in this region see pp558–61 and pp610–12

Environs

The city's green playground, **Lac et Forêt d'Orient**, is 15 miles (25 km) east of Troyes. The forest is dotted with marshes, nature preserves, and smaller lakes. Lac d'Orient, the largest artificial lake in Europe, is popular for sailing, with water-skiing on Lac Amance, and fishing at Lac du Temple.

Chaumont ⓫

Haute-Marne. 🏠 26,000. 🚂
🛈 37 rue de Verdun (03 25 03 80 80). 🛒 Wed & Sat. **www**.tourisme-chaumont-champagne.com

As the former residence of the Counts of Champagne, this feudal town enjoyed great prestige in the 13th century. On the far side of a ravine, the old town is on a rocky spur, with the Palais de Justice and the medieval castle keep dominating.

The keep is a reminder that this quiet administrative center had a formidable past. This impression is confirmed by the Renaissance town houses which are bulging with *tourelles d'escaliers*, turreted staircases.

Basilique St-Jean-Baptiste, a gray-stone Champenois church, is the most remarkable monument in Chaumont. The interior is enlivened by a spider's web of vaulting, a striking turreted staircase and Renaissance galleries. Near the entrance is a tiny chapel containing an unsettling *Mise au Tombeau* (1471), an intense multicolored stone group of 10 mourners gathered around Christ laid out on a shroud in his tomb. In the left transept is a bizarre but beguiling *Tree of Jesse*. On this ill-lit Renaissance stone relief, a family tree sprouts from the sleeping Jesus.

Environs

Fourteen miles (23 km) northwest of Chaumont, **Colombey-les-Deux-Eglises** will forever be associated with General Charles de Gaulle (1890–1970). The de Gaulles bought their home, **La Boisserie**, in 1933, but had to abandon it during the war,

Cathédrale St-Mammès in Langres

when it was badly damaged. After its restoration, de Gaulle would return to La Boisserie from Paris at weekends to write his memoirs. He died here on November 9, 1970. The house is now a museum.

In the village churchyard, the General lies in a simple tomb, but a giant granite cross of Lorraine, erected in 1972, dominates the skyline. At its foot is the **Mémorial**, a museum dedicated to de Gaulle's life.

🏛 **La Boisserie**
Colombey-les-Deux-Eglises.
Tel 03 25 01 52 52. 🕐 mid-Apr–mid-Oct: daily; mid-Oct–mid-Apr: Wed–Mon. 🚫 🚻

🏛 **Mémorial Charles de Gaulle**
Tel 03 25 30 90 80. 🕐 May–Sep: daily; Oct–Apr: Wed–Mon. 🚫
www.memorial-charlesdegaulle.fr

Langres ⓬

Haute-Marne. 🏠 9,000. 🚂
🚌 🛈 square Olivier Lahalle (03 25 87 67 67). 🛒 Fri.
www.tourisme-langres.com

Set on a rocky spur, Langres lies beyond Chaumont, in the backwaters of southern Champagne. This ancient bishopric was one of the gateways to Burgundy and the birthplace of the encyclopedist, Denis Diderot (1713–84). Langres promotes itself as a land of springs, claiming that its proximity to the sources of the Seine and Marne grant it mystical powers.

Virtually the whole town is enclosed by medieval ramparts, Langres' undoubted attraction. A succession of towers and parapets provide glimpses of romantic town gates and sculpted Renaissance mansions, with panoramic views of the Marne valley, the Langres plateau, the Vosges, and, on a clear day, even Mont Blanc.

Near Porte Henri IV is the much-remodeled **Cathédrale St-Mammès**. The gloomy vaulted interior, in Burgundian Romanesque style, is redeemed by the sculpted capitals in the apse, reputedly taken from a temple of Jupiter. The town's Musée d'Art et d'Histoire has some interesting collections.

Langres' lively summer season includes historical re-enactments, theater, and fireworks.

Memorial to General de Gaulle at Colombey-les-Deux-Eglises

ALSACE AND LORRAINE

MEURTHE-ET-MOSELLE · MEUSE · MOSELLE · BAS-RHIN
HAUT-RHIN · VOSGES

*A*s border regions, Alsace and Lorraine have been fought over for centuries by France, Austria, and Germany, their beleaguered past recalled by many a military stronghold and cemetery. Today, the region presents only a peaceful aspect with pastel-painted villages, fortified towns, and sleepy vineyards.

At the northeast frontier of France, bordered by the Rhine, Alsace forms a fertile watershed between the mountains of the Vosges and the Black Forest in Germany. Lorraine, with its rolling landscape on the other side of the mountains, is the poorer cousin but is more overtly French in character.

EMBATTLED TERRITORY

Caught in the wars between France and Germany, Alsace and part of Lorraine have changed nationality four times since 1871. Centuries of strife have made border citadels of Metz, Toul, and Verdun in Lorraine, while Alsace abounds with castles, from the faithfully reconstructed Haut-Koenigsbourg to Saverne's ruined fortress, built to guard a strategic pass in the Vosges. However, the area has a strong identity of its own, taking pride in local costumes, traditions, and dialects. In Alsace, Route des Vins vineyards nudge pretty villages in the Vosges foothills. Strasbourg, the capital, is a cosmopolitan city with a 16th-century center, while Nancy, Lorraine's historical capital, represents elegant 18th-century architecture.

Much of the attraction of this region lies in its cuisine. Lorraine offers beer and quiche lorraine. In Alsace, cozy *winstubs*, or wine cellars, serve sauerkraut and flowery white wines, such as Riesling and Gewürztraminer. There are also fine restaurants here.

Villagers enjoying the view from their window in Hunspach, north of Strasbourg in the northern Vosges

◁ Half-timbered houses with flower-clad balconies along the Route du Vin in Alsace

Exploring Alsace and Lorraine

Visitors seeking art and architecture will be amply rewarded
by the charming medieval towns and excellent city
museums of the region. Undiscovered Lorraine is the place
to clamber over military citadels, walk in unspoiled
countryside, and unwind at relaxing
spas. By contrast, Alsace offers
magnificent forests and rugged
mountain drives in the Vosges,
quaint villages and rich wines.
The Route des Vins *(see pp232–
3)* is one of the region's many
scenic routes. It is particularly
popular during the wine harvest festivities but is worth
visiting in any season.

SIGHTS AT A GLANCE

Betschdorf **18**
Château du Haut-
    Koenigsbourg **13**
Colmar **10**
Eguisheim **9**
Gérardmer **5**
Guebwiller **7**
Metz **3**
Mulhouse **6**
Nancy **4**
Neuf-Brisach **8**
Obernai **15**
Ribeauvillé **12**
Riquewihr **11**
Saverne **17**
Sélestat **14**
Strasbourg **16**
Toul **2**
Verdun **1**

Field of sunflowers just outside the village of Turckheim

0 kilometers   20

0 miles   10

For additional map symbols see back flap

The picturesque village of Riquewihr on the Route du Vin

GETTING AROUND

There are good road and rail links between Strasbourg, Colmar, Metz, and Nancy, and on to Switzerland and Germany. The main roads to and through the regions are the N4, A31, and A35, the A4 to Paris, and the N59 and the tunnel under the Vosges. The spectacular journey over the Vosges and along the Route des Vins is best made by car or on organized trips from Colmar or Strasbourg. The TGV link to the region from Paris takes 2 hours 20 minutes.

KEY

▬	Highway
▬	Major road
▬	Secondary road
▭	Minor road
—	Scenic route
▬	Main railroad
—	Minor railroad
▬	International border
—	Regional border
△	Summit

The Ossuaire de Douaumont, a sentinel for the regiments of crosses on the battlefields of Verdun

Verdun ●

Meuse. 🏠 *21,000.* 🚊 🚌 **i** *pl de la Nation (03 29 86 14 18).* 🎪 *Fri.* **www**.verdun-tourisme.com

Verdun will be forever remembered for the horrors of the 1916–1917 Battle of Verdun, when about a million men died in almost a whole year of continuous bloodshed that is considered the worst single battle of the Great War. The Germans intended to strike a blow at French morale by destroying the forts of Douaumont and Vaux (which had been built to prevent a repeat of the humiliating French defeat of the Franco-Prussian war of 1870) and capture Verdun, France's northeastern stronghold. The French fought simply to prevent the town being taken. The stalemate and the killing continued here right up to the end of the war, and not until 1918 did the Germans draw back from their positions just 3 miles (5 km) from the town.

Several poignant museums, memorials, battle sites, and cemeteries can be visited in the hills just outside Verdun on the north side. In this devastated region, nine villages were obliterated without trace. The **Musée-Memorial de Fleury** tells their story. Nearby, the **Ossuaire de Douaumont** contains the unidentified bones of over 130,000 French and German dead. One of the most striking monuments to the Battle of Verdun is Rodin's memorial in Verdun itself. It depicts the winged figure of Victory unable to soar

triumphant because she has become caught in the remains of a dead soldier.

The town of Verdun was heavily fortified over the centuries. The crenelated **Porte Chaussée**, a medieval river gateway, still guards the eastern entrance to the town and is the most impressive of the remaining fortifications.

Although battered by war damage, the **Citadelle de Verdun** retains its 12th-century tower, the only relic from the original abbey that Vauban incorporated into his new military design. Now a war museum, the **Citadelle Souterraine** recreates Verdun's role in WWI. The citadel casemates come to life as grim trenches, and the presentation ends by showing how the "Unknown Soldier" was chosen for the symbolic tomb under the Arc de Triomphe in Paris *(see p107).*

The town center is dominated by the cathedral, where Romanesque elements were rediscovered after the 1916 bombardments.

The 16th-century cloisters of Eglise St-Gengoult in Toul

🏛 Citadelle Souterraine
Ave du 5ième R.A.P. **Tel** 03 29 86 14 18. ⭘ daily. ⬤ Jan & Dec 25. 🎞 &

Toul ●

Meurthe-et-Moselle. 🏠 *16,500.* 🚊 🚌 **i** *1 pl Charles de Gaulle (03 83 64 90 60).* 🎪 *Wed & Fri.* **www**.lepredenancy.fr

Lying within dark forests west of Nancy, the octagonal fortress city of Toul is encircled by the Moselle and the Canal de la Marne. Along with Verdun and Metz, Toul was one of the 4th-century bishoprics. In the early 18th century, Vauban built the cita-del, from which the ring of defensive waterways, the octagonal city ramparts, and the **Porte de Metz** remain.

The **Cathédrale St-Etienne**, begun in the 13th century, took over 300 years to build. It suffered damage in World War II but the purity of the Champenois style has survived, notably in the arched, high-galleried interior. The imposing Flamboyant Gothic façade is flanked by octagonal towers. Rue du Général-Gengoult, behind the Gothic **Eglise St-Gengoult**, contains a clutch of sculpted Renaissance houses. North of the city the local "gray" Côtes de Toul wines are produced.

Environs
South of Toul, near the town of Neufchâteau, is the birth-place of Joan of Arc at **Domrémy-La-Pucelle**. Next door to the house where she

was born is an exhibition about her remarkable life.

The vast **Parc Régional de Lorraine** takes in red-tiled cottages, vineyards, forests, cropland, *chaumes* (high pastureland), marshes, and lakes. Inns in the area are especially noted for their quiche lorraine and *potée lorraine*, a bacon casserole.

Column of Merten in La Cour d'Or

Metz ❸

125 Moselle. 🏛 125,000. ✈ 🚉 🚌
🛈 pl d'Armes (03 87 55 53 76).
🚩 Sat. www.tourisme.metz.fr

An austere yet appealing city, Metz sits at the confluence of the Moselle and the Seille. Twenty bridges criss-cross the rivers and canals, and there are pleasant walks along the banks. This Gallo-Roman city, now the capital of Lorraine, has always been a pawn in the game of border chess – annexed by Germany in 1871, regained by France in 1918.

Set on a hill above the Moselle, the **Cathédrale St-Etienne** overlooks the historic center. Inside there are stained-glass windows, including some by Chagall.

To the northwest of the cathedral, a narrow wooden bridge leads across to the island of Petit Saulcy, site of the oldest French theater still in use. Located on the other side of the cathedral, the **Porte des Allemands**, spanning a river, more resembles a medieval castle because of its bridge, defensive towers, and 13th-century gate with pepper-pot towers.

In the Vieille Ville, place St-Louis is a delightful square bordered by lofty, arcaded 14th-century mansions. **Eglise St-Pierre-aux-Nonnains** claims to be one of France's oldest churches. The external walls and the façade date from Roman times, while much of the rest belongs to the 7th century. Nearby is the 13th-century **Chapelle des Templiers**, built by the Knights Templar.

🏛 Centre Pompidou Metz
1 parvis des Droits de l'Homme.
Tel 03 87 15 39 39. ☐ Mon–Wed.
⬤ May 1. 🖼
This museum is an annex to the Pompidou Center in Paris (*see pp92–3*). Modern European art is displayed inside an unusual hexagonal building.

🏛 Musée de la Cour d'Or
2 rue du Haut-Poirier. *Tel* 03 87 20 13 20. ☐ Wed–Mon. ⬤ publ hols. 🖼
Also known as the Musée d'Art et d'Histoire, this is set in the Pulau Camtral, an incorporated 17th-century monastery incorporating Gallo-Roman thermal baths and a medieval barn. On display are Merovingian stone carvings; Gothic painted ceilings; and a variety of German, Flemish, and French paintings.

WHITE STORKS
Until recently, the white stork, traditionally a symbol of good fortune in Alsace, was a frequent sight in northeast France. White storks spend the winter in Africa, but migrate north to breed. However, the gradual draining of marshy ground, pesticides, and electric cables have threatened their survival here. A program to reintroduce them to the area has set up breeding centers, as at Molsheim and Turckheim, which means these striking birds can once again be seen in Alsace-Lorraine.

The 13th-century Chapelle des Templiers with restored frescoes in Metz

Place Stanislas in Nancy with the statue of Stanislas Leczinski, Duke of Lorraine and father-in-law of Louis XV

Nancy ❶

Meurthe-et-Moselle. 🏙 108,000.
🚉 🏢 🚌 🚏 14 pl Stanislas
(03 83 35 22 41). 🛍 Tue–Sat.
www.ot-nancy.fr

Lorraine's historic capital backs onto the Canal du Marne and the river Meurthe. In the 18th century, Stanislas Leczinski, Duke of Lorraine (see p302), transformed the city, making it a model of 18th-century urban planning.

Nancy's second golden age was the turn of this century, when glassmaker Emile Gallé founded the Ecole de Nancy, a forerunner of the Art Nouveau movement in France.

Nancy's principal and most renowned landmark is **place Stanislas**. Laid out in the 1750s, this elegantly proportioned square is enclosed by highly ornate gilded wrought-iron gates and railings, which have been beautifully restored. Lining the square are fine *hôtels particuliers* (town houses) and chic restaurants.

An Arc de Triomphe leads to Place de la Carrière, a gracious, tree-lined square. At the far end, flanked by semicircular arcades, is the Gothic **Palais du Gouvernement**. Next door in the Parc de la Pépinière is Rodin's statue of Claude Lorrain, the landscape painter, born near Nancy.

The Grande Rue provides a glimpse of medieval Nancy. Of the original fortifications only the Porte de la Craffe remains, which was used as a prison after the Revolution.

🏛 Eglise et Couvent des Cordeliers et Musée Régional des Arts et Traditions Populaires
64 & 66 grande rue. **Tel** 03 83 32 18 74. ⭘ Tue–Sun. ⬤ Jan 1, May 1, Jul 14, Nov 1, Dec 25. 📷
The Dukes of Lorraine are buried in the crypt and the adjoining converted monastery contains the Musée Régional des Arts et Traditions Populaires, covering folklore, furniture, costumes, and crafts.

🏛 Musée des Beaux-Arts
3 pl Stanislas. **Tel** 03 83 85 30 72. ⭘ Wed–Mon. ⬤ some public hols. 📷 ♿ 📷
Recent renovation and a modern extension have enabled 40 percent more of the museum's remarkable collection of 14th- to 20th-century European art to be seen, including works by Delacroix, Manet, Monet, Utrillo and Modigliani. The Daum glassware is stunning.

🏛 Musée Historique Lorraine
Palais Ducal, 64 grande rue.
Tel 03 83 32 18 74. ⭘ Tue–Sun. ⬤ Jan 1, May 1, Jul 14, Nov 1, Dec 25. 📷
The Museum of the History of Lorraine has a rich collection of archeological finds, sculptures, and paintings, including two by Georges de la Tour.

🏛 Musée de l'Ecole de Nancy
36–38 rue de Sergent Blandan.
Tel 03 83 40 14 86. ⭘ Wed–Sun. ⬤ Jan 1, May 1, July 14, Nov 1, Dec 25. 📷 📷
Exhibits in reconstructed Art Nouveau settings include furniture, fabrics, and jewelry, as well as the fanciful glassware of Emile Gallé, founder of the Ecole de Nancy.

Arc de Triomphe in place Stanislas, leading to place de la Carrière

Vosges landscape seen from the Route des Crêtes

THE ROUTE DES CRÊTES

This strategic mountain road, 50 miles (83 km) long, connects the Vosges valleys from Col du Bonhomme to Cernay, east of Thann, often through woodland. Hugging the western side of the Vosges, the Route des Crêtes was created during World War I to prevent the Germans from observing French troop movements. When not shrouded in mist, there are breathtaking views over Lorraine from its many "ridges" *(crêtes)*.

Gérardmer ❺

Vosges. 🏠 10,000. 🚉
🚌 ℹ️ 4 pl des Déportés
(03 29 27 27 27). 🛒 Thu & Sat.
www.gerardmer.net

Nestling on the Lorraine side of the Vosges, on the shore of a magnificent lake stretching out before it, Gérardmer is a setting rather than a city. In November 1944, just before its liberation, Gérardmer was razed by the Nazi scorched-earth policy, but has since been reconstructed. Saw mills and wood-carving remain local trades, though tourism is fast replacing the textile industry.

Gérardmer is now a popular vacation resort. In winter, the steep slopes of the Vosges Cristallines around the town turn it into a ski resort, while the lake is used for watersports in summer. The town's attractions also include lakeside walks and boat trips, as well as Géromée cheese, similar to the more famous Munster from just over the Alsatian border. Gérardmer also boasts the oldest tourist information office in the country, dating from 1875.

The scenic drives and mountain hikes in the Vosges attract adventurous visitors. Most leave the lakeside bowl to head for the Alsatian border and the magnificent **Route des Crêtes**, which can be joined at the mountain pass of Col de la Schlucht.

Recreating village crafts in Ecomusée d'Alsace in Ungersheim

Mulhouse ❻

Haut Rhin. 🏠 115,000. ✈️ 🚉
🚌 ℹ️ 9 av du Maréchal Foch
(03 89 35 48 48). 🛒 Tue, Thu & Sat.
www.tourisme-mulhouse.com

Close to the Swiss border, Mulhouse is an industrial city that was badly damaged in World War II. However, there are technical museums and shopping galleries, as well as Alsatian taverns and Swiss wine bars. Most visitors use the city as a base for exploring the rolling hills of the Sundgau on the Swiss border.

Of the museums, **Musée de l'Impression sur Etoffes**, at 14 rue Jean-Jaques Henner, is devoted to textiles and fabric painting, while **Musée Français du Chemin de Fer**, at 2 rue Alfred Glehn, has a collection of steam and electric locomotives. A revamped **Musée National de l'Automobile**, at 192 avenue de Colmar, boasts over 100 Bugattis, a clutch of Mercedes and Ferraris, and Charlie Chaplin's Rolls Royce. In Place de la République is the **Musée Historique**, in the Renaissance former town hall

Alsatian black pig in Ecomusée d'Alsace in Ungersheim

Environs

At Ungersheim, north of Mulhouse, the **Ecomusée d'Alsace** displays and preserves the region's rural heritage. The 12th-century fortified house from Mulhouse is a dramatic building, complete with Gothic garden. Farms are run along traditional lines, with livestock such as the Alsatian black pig. Rural crafts can be seen in their original settings.

🏛 **Ecomusée d'Alsace**
Chemin du Grosswald. **Tel** 03 89 74 44 65. ◯ Apr–Oct & Dec: daily.
🅿️ ♿ 📷

The lake at Gérardmer, offering sporting and leisure activities

Guebwiller ⑦

Haut Rhin. 🏘 *12,000.* 🚍
ℹ️ *73 rue de la République (03
89 76 10 63).* 🚍 *Tue & Fri.*
www.tourisme-guebwiller.fr

Surrounded by vineyards
and flower-filled valleys,
Guebwiller is known as
"the gateway to the valley of
flowers." However, as an
industrial town producing
textiles and machine tools,
it feels cut off from this
rural setting. The *caves* and
churches make it worth a visit.

Set on a pretty square,
Eglise Notre-Dame combines
Baroque theatricality with
Neoclassical elegance, while
Eglise des Dominicains boasts
Gothic frescoes and a fine
rood screen. **Eglise St-Léger**,
the richly decorated
Romanesque church, is the
most rewarding, especially the
façade, triple porch, and portal.

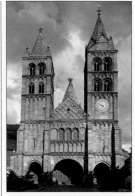

Eglise St-Léger in Guebwiller

Environs
The scenic Lauch valley, northwest of Guebwiller, is known
as "Le Florival" because of its
floral aspect. **Lautenbach** is
used as a starting point for
hikes through this recognized
zone de tranquillité. The

village has a pink Roman-
esque church, whose portal
depicts human passion and
the battle between Good and
Evil. The square leads to the
river, a small weir, *lavoir*
(public washing place), and
houses overhanging the water.

Neuf-Brisach ⑧

Haut Rhin. 🏘 *2,100.* 🚍 ℹ️ *Palais
du Gouverneur, 6 pl d'Armes (03 89
72 56 66).* 🚍 *Sat.* **www**.tourisme-
rhin.com

Situated near the German
border, this octagonal citadel
is the military strategist
Vauban's masterpiece. Built
between 1698 and 1707, the
citadel forms a typical star-
shaped pattern, with
symmetrical towers enclosing
48 equal squares. In the center,
from where straight streets
radiate for ease of defense,

THE CITADEL OF NEUF-BRISACH

The outer ring of defenses
was built around two moats.

Porte de Bâle

Place d'Armes,
once the parade
ground, provided the
innermost refuge.

**Porte de
Strasbourg**
was originally
protected
by a draw-
bridge.

Bastion

The fortress
is divided
into 48 ilôts
or squares.

The fortress walls
are 30 ft (9 m) high
and 14.5 ft (4.5 m)
wide at their base.

The Porte de Belfort
houses the Musée
Vauban. A walk links
Porte de Belfort with
Porte de Colmar.

Porte de Colmar

The celebrated Issenheim altarpiece by Matthias Grünewald in Colmar

is the place d'Armes and the Eglise St-Louis, which was added in 1731–6. This was the usual homage to Louis XV, implying that the church was dedicated to the King, rather than the saint.

The Porte de Belfort houses the **Musée Vauban**, which includes a model of the town, showing the original fort, now concealed by woodland. They represent Vauban's barrier to the fortress and it is to his credit that the citadel was never taken.

🏛 **Musée Vauban**
Pl Porte de Belfort.
Tel *03 89 72 03 93.*
⏰ *May–Oct: Wed–Mon; Nov–Apr: groups only, by appt.* 📷 ♿

Eguisheim ❾

Haut Rhin. 🏘 *1,600.* 🚇 🚌 ℹ *22a grand'rue (03 89 23 40 33).*
www.ot-eguisheim.fr

Eguisheim is an exquisite small town, laid out within three concentric rings of 13th-century ramparts. The en-semble of austere fortifications and domestic elegance within makes for a surprisingly harmonious whole.

In the center of town is the octagonal feudal **castle** of the Counts of Eguisheim. A Renaissance fountain in front has the statue of Bruno Eguisheim, born here in 1002. He became Pope Léon IX and was later canonized.

The grand'rue is lined with half-timbered houses, many showing their construction

date. Close to the castle is the **Marbacherhof**, a monastic tithe barn and cornhall. On a neighboring square, the modern parish church retains the original Romanesque sculpted tympanum.

The rest of the town has its share of Hansel-and-Gretel atmosphere, while inviting courtyards offer tastings of *grands crus*. From within the Hautvilliers, outside the faint parts, a marked path leads through scenic vineyards.

Colmar ❿

Haut Rhin. 🏘 *68,000.* 🚇 🚌 ℹ *4 rue d'Unterlinden (03 89 20 68 92).* 🛒 *Mon, Wed, Thu & Sat.* **www**.ot-colmar.fr

Colmar is the best preserved city in Alsace. As a trading post and river port, Colmar had its heyday in the 16th century, when wine merchants shipped their wine along the waterways running through

the picturesque canal quarter, now known as **Petite Venise**. "Little Venice" is best seen on a leisurely boat trip that takes you from the tanners' quarter to the Rue des Tanneurs. The adjoining Place de l'Alsacienne Douane is dominated by the **Koïfhüs**, a galleried customs house with a Burgundian tiled roof overlooking half-timbered pastel houses which sport sculpted pillars.

Nearby, the place de la Cathédrale quarter is full of 16th-century houses. **Eglise St-Martin**, essentially Gothic, has a noted south portal. To the west, the place des Dominicains, with cafés, is dwarfed by the Gothic **Eglise Dominicaine**. Inside is *La Vierge au Buisson de Roses* (1473), the red and gold "Virgin of the Rosebush" by Martin Schongauer, a renowned painter and native son of Colmar.

Place d'Unterlinden, the adjoining square, has the **Musée d'Unterlinden**. Set in a 13th-century convent, it dis-plays early Rhenish paintings. The highlight is the Issenheim altarpiece. A masterpiece of emotional intensity, it is part of an early 16th-century Alsatian panel painting by Matthias Grünewald.

In the historic center, the quaint rue des Têtes has the former wine exchange, a Renaissance town house known as the Maison des Têtes because of the grimacing heads on the gabled façade. And in rue Mercière, **Maison Pfister**, with its slender stair turret and galleried flower-decked façade, has come to typify the city.

Along the Quai de la Poissonerie in the Petite Venise area of Colmar

Riquewihr ⓫

Haut Rhin. 🏘 *1,300.* 🖼
ℹ *2 rue de 1ère Armée
(03 89 73 23 23).* 🚌 *Fri.*
www.ribeauville-riquewihr.com

Vineyards run right up to the
ramparts of Riquewihr, the
prettiest village on the Route
du Vin *(see pp232–3)*. Deeply
pragmatic, Riquewihr
winemakers plant roses at the
end of each row of vines –
both for their pretty effect
and as early detectors of
parasites. The village belonged
to the Counts of Wurtemberg
until the Revolution and has
grown rich on wine, from
Tokay and Pinot Gris to
Gewürztraminer and Riesling.
Virtually an open-air museum,
Riquewihr abounds in
cobbled alleys, geranium-clad
balconies, galleried courtyards,
romantic double ramparts,
and watchtowers.

From the Hôtel de Ville, the
rue du Général de Gaulle
climbs gently past medieval
and Renaissance houses, half-
timbered, stone-clad, or
corbeled. Oriel windows vie
with sculpted portals and
medieval sign boards. On the

right lies the idyllic **place des
Trois Eglises**. A passageway
leads through the ramparts
to the vineyards on the hill.
Further up lies the **Dolder**, a
13th-century belfry, followed
by the **Tour des Voleurs** (both
are museums, the latter with a
medieval torture chamber),
marking the second tier of
ramparts. Beyond the gateway
is the **Cour des Bergers**,
gardens laid out around the
16th-century ramparts.
Visitors outnumber the locals,
in summer or during the
superb Christmas market.

**The pretty – and popular – village
of Riquewihr, set among vineyards**

Ribeauvillé ⓬

Haut Rhin. 🏘 *5,000.* 🚆 🖼
ℹ *1 grand'rue (03 89 73 23 23).*
🚌 *Sat.* www.ribeauville-
riquewihr.com

Overlooked by three ruined
castles, Ribeauvillé is stiflingly
prettified, as may be expected
from a favored town on the
Route du Vin. This status is
partly due to healthy sales
of the celebrated *grands
crus* of Alsace, especially
Riesling. There are ample
opportunities for tastings,
particularly near the park, in
the lower part of town *(see
pp232–3)*.

On the grand'rue (No. 14)
is the **Pfifferhüs**, the minstrels'
house. As locals declare,
Ribeauvillé is the capital of the
kougelhopf, the almond-
flavored Alsatian cake.

Tortuous alleys wind past
steep-roofed artisans' and
vignerons' houses in the upper
part of the town. Beyond are
Renaissance fountains, painted
façades, and **St Grégoire-le-
Grand**, the Gothic parish
church. A marked path, which
begins in this part of town,
leads into the vineyards.

Château du Haut-Koenigsbourg ⓭

Orschwiller. *Tel 03 88 82 50 60.*
⭕ *daily.* ⬤ *Jan 1, May 1, Dec 25.*
🔳🔳🔳🔳🔳
www.haut-koenigsbourg.fr

Looming above the pretty
village of St-Hippolyte, this
castle is the most popular
attraction in Alsace. In 1114,
the Swabian Emperor,
Frederick of Hohenstaufen,
built the first Teutonic castle
here, which was destroyed in
1462. Rebuilt and added to
under the Habsburgs, it
burned down in 1633. At the
end of the 19th century, Kaiser
Wilhelm II commissioned
Berlin architect Bodo Ebhardt
to restore the castle. The
result of his painstaking work
was a precise reconstruction
of the original building.

With a drawbridge, fierce
keep, and rings of fortifications,
this warm sandstone hybrid is

a sophisticated feudal
château. The Cour d'Honneur
is a breathtaking re-creation,
with a pointed corner turret
and creaky arcaded galleries.
Inside are gloomy "Gothic"
chambers and "Renaissance"
rooms. La Grande Salle is the
most far-fetched, with a Neo-
Gothic gallery and ornate
paneling. From the

Upper garden

West bastion

battlements, almost 2,500 ft
(750 m) above the Alsace
plain, stretches a Rhineland
panorama bordered by the
Black Forest and the Alps. On
the other side are views
from the high Vosges to
villages and vineyards
below.

West wing

Outer walls

Chapelle St-Sébastien outside Dambach-la-Ville, along the Route du Vin

Sélestat ⑭

Bas Rhin. 🏠 17,000. 🚆 🚌 🛈 Commanderie Saint Jean, bd du Général Leclerc (03 88 58 87 20). 🗓 Tue, Sat. www.selestat-tourisme.com

During the Renaissance, Sélestat was the intellectual center of Alsace, with a tradition of humanism fostered by Beatus Rhenanus, a friend of Erasmus. The **Bibliothèque Humaniste** has a collection of editions of some of the earliest printed books, including the first book to name America, in 1507. Nearby are the Cour des Prélats, a turreted ivy-covered mansion, and the Tour de l'Horloge, a clocktower. **Eglise Ste-Foy** is 12th-century, with an octagonal belltower. Opposite is **Eglise St-Georges**, glittering with green and red "Burgundian tiles."

🏛 **Bibliothèque Humaniste**
1 rue de la Bibliothèque.
Tel 03 88 58 07 20. ☐ Mon, Wed–Sat am; (Jul–Aug: Wed–Mon exc. Sun am). ● public hols. 🗗 www. bibliotheque-humaniste.eu

Environs
Medieval **Dambach-la-Ville**, another pretty town, is linked to Andlau and red-tiled Itterswiller by a delightful rural road through vineyards.
Ebersmunster, a picturesque hamlet, has an onion-domed abbey church, whose Baroque interior is a sumptuous display of gilded stucco.

Obernai ⑮

Bas Rhin. 🏠 11,000. 🚆 🚌 🛈 pl du Beffroi (03 88 95 64 13). 🗓 Thu. www.obernai.fr

At the north end of the Route du Vin, Obernai retains a flavor of authentic Alsace: residents speak Alsatian, at festivities women wear traditional costume, and church services are well-attended

Young Alsaciens in traditional costume

Neo-Gothic **Eglise St-Pierre-et-St-Paul**. The place du Marché is well-preserved and features the gabled **Halle aux Blés**, a 16th-century corn hall (now a restaurant) above a former butcher's store, with a façade adorned with cows' and dragons' heads. Place de la Chapelle, the adjoining square, has a Renaissance fountain and the 16th-century **Hôtel de Ville** and the **Kapellturm**, the galleried Gothic belfry. Side streets have Renaissance and medieval timber-framed houses. A stroll past the cafés on rue du Marché ends in a pleasant park by the ramparts.

Environs
Odile, Alsace's seventh-century patron saint, was born in Obernai but is venerated on **Mont Sainte-Odile**, to the west.
Molsheim, a former bishopric and fortified market town 6 miles (10 km) north, is noted for its Metzig, a Renaissance-style butchers' guildhall.
Le Mémorial de l'Alsace-Moselle at Schirmeck commemorates the 10,000 who died at the Struthof concentration camp across the valley.

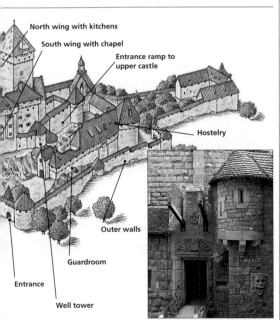

North wing with kitchens
South wing with chapel
Entrance ramp to upper castle
Hostelry
Outer walls
Guardroom
Entrance
Well tower

Drawbridge within the walls of Château du Haut-Koenigsbourg

For hotels and restaurants in this region see pp561–2 and pp612–14

Strasbourg ⑯

Halfway between Paris and Prague, Strasbourg is not surprisingly often known as "the crossroads of Europe." The city wears its European cosmopolitanism with ease – after all, its famous cathedral has catered to both Catholic and Protestant congregations – and as one of the capitals of the European Union has sensibly located the futuristic European Parliament building some way from the historic center. One of the ways to see this, along with the more traditional city sights, is to take a boat trip along the waterways encircling the Old Town. On the way you will take in the Ponts-Couverts, covered bridges linked by medieval watchtowers that provide an observation point for the four Ill canals, and the scenic Petite France, once the tanners' district, dotted with mills and criss-crossed by bridges.

Cathedral statue

Barge on the canal

The central portal of the west façade of the cathedral

⛪ Cathédrale Notre-Dame

A masterpiece of stone lace-work, the sandstone cathedral "rises like a most sublime, wide-arching tree of God," as Goethe marveled. Though construction began in the late 11th century (the choir is Romanesque, the nave is Gothic), it ended only in 1439, with the completion of the west façade, begun in 1277. The three portals are ornamented with statues. But the crowning glory is the rose window. The south portal leads to the Gothic Pillar of Angels (c. 1230), set beside the Astronomical Clock: mechanical figures appear accompanied by chimes at 12:31pm. There are wonderful views over the city from the viewing platform, and on some summer evenings there are organ concerts.

In place de la Cathédrale, Maison Kammerzell, now a popular restaurant, was once a rich merchant's mansion, its highly elaborate, carved façade dating from mid-15th–late-16th centuries.

🏛 Palais Rohan

2 pl du Château. **Tel** 03 88 80 50 50. ☐ Wed–Mon. ⬤ Jan 1, Good Fri, May 1, Nov 1 & 11, Dec 25. 🈺 🔗 www.musee-strasbourg.org
Designed by the king's architect, Robert de Cotte, in 1730, this grand Classical palace was intended for the Prince-Bishops of Strasbourg. It houses three museums: the Musée des Beaux Arts; the Musée Archéologique; and the Musée des Arts Décoratifs, which contains the sumptuous State Apartments and one of the finest collections of ceramics in France.

The Musée d'Art Moderne et Contemporain on Strasbourg's waterfront

VISITORS' CHECKLIST

Bas Rhin. 🏘 500,000.
✈ 7.5 miles (12 km) SW
Strasbourg. 🚉 pl de la Gare
(08 92 35 35 35). 🚌 pl des
Halles (03 88 23 43 23).
🛈 17 pl de la Cathédrale (03
88 52 28 28). 🛒 Wed, Fri, & Sat.
🎵 International Music Festival
(Jun–Jul). www.ot-strasbourg.fr

STRASBOURG CITY CENTER

Cathédrale Notre-Dame ④
Maison Kammerzell ③
Musée Alsacien ⑦
Musée de l'Oeuvre
Notre-Dame ⑤
Palais Rohan ⑥
Petite France ②
Ponts-Couverts ①

0 meters	250
0 yards	250

Key to Symbols see back flap

has fascinating exhibits on
local traditions and popular
arts and crafts.

🏛 Musée de l'Oeuvre Notre-Dame

3 pl du Château. **Tel** 03 88 52 50
00. ◯ Tue–Sun. ● Jan 1, Good
Fri, May 1, Nov 1, Dec 25. 🎟 ♿
ground floor.

The cathedral's impressive
museum contains much
of its original sculpture,
as well as magnificent
11th-century stained
glass. This somber
gabled house also
displays a collection
of Medieval and Renais-
sance Alsatian art.

🏛 Musée d'Art Moderne et Contemporain

1 pl Hans-Jean Arp. **Tel** 03 88 23 31
31. ◯ Tue–Sun. ● Jan 1, Good Fri,
May 1, Nov 1 & 11, Dec 25. 🎟 ♿
🍴 🎬 Concerts, movie theater.

Adrien Fainsilber's cultural
flagship for the 21st century is
a marvel of glass and light
(particularly at night when it
appears to float on the river).
Its superb collections run from
1860–1950 and from 1950
on-ward. The Art Café is welcome respite for art-weary feet.

🏛 Musée Historique

3 pl de la Grande Boucherie. **Tel** 03
88 52 50 00. ◯ Tue–Sun. ● Jan 1,
Good Fri, May 1, Nov 1 & 11, Dec 25.
🎟 ♿

The museum occupies the
16th-century city abattoir and
focuses on Strasbourg's political and military history.

🏛 Musée Alsacien

23 quai St-Nicolas. **Tel** 03 88
52 50 00. ◯ Wed–Mon. ●
Jan 1, Good Fri, May 1, Nov 1,
Dec 25. 🎟

Housed in a series of
interconnecting Renaissance
buildings, the museum

Ponts-Couverts with medieval
watchtowers over the canals

The Alsace Route des Vins

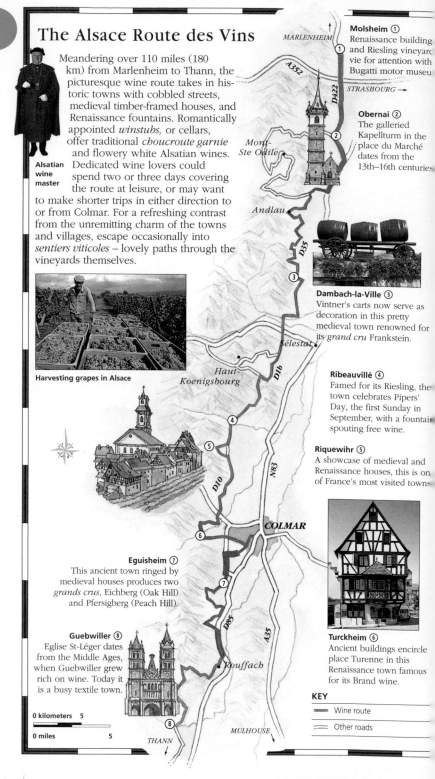

Meandering over 110 miles (180 km) from Marlenheim to Thann, the picturesque wine route takes in historic towns with cobbled streets, medieval timber-framed houses, and Renaissance fountains. Romantically appointed *winstubs*, or cellars, offer traditional *choucroute garnie* and flowery white Alsatian wines. Dedicated wine lovers could spend two or three days covering the route at leisure, or may want to make shorter trips in either direction to or from Colmar. For a refreshing contrast from the unremitting charm of the towns and villages, escape occasionally into *sentiers viticoles* – lovely paths through the vineyards themselves.

Alsatian wine master

Harvesting grapes in Alsace

MARLENHEIM

STRASBOURG →

Mont-Ste Odile

Andlau

Haut Koenigsbourg

Sélestat

COLMAR

Rouffach

MULHOUSE

THANN

Molsheim ①
Renaissance building and Riesling vineyard vie for attention with Bugatti motor museum

Obernai ②
The galleried Kapellturm in the place du Marché dates from the 13th–16th centuries

Dambach-la-Ville ③
Vintner's carts now serve as decoration in this pretty medieval town renowned for its *grand cru* Frankstein.

Ribeauvillé ④
Famed for its Riesling, the town celebrates Pipers' Day, the first Sunday in September, with a fountain spouting free wine.

Riquewihr ⑤
A showcase of medieval and Renaissance houses, this is one of France's most visited towns.

Eguisheim ⑦
This ancient town ringed by medieval houses produces two *grands crus*, Eichberg (Oak Hill) and Pfersigberg (Peach Hill).

Guebwiller ⑧
Eglise St-Léger dates from the Middle Ages, when Guebwiller grew rich on wine. Today it is a busy textile town.

Turckheim ⑥
Ancient buildings encircle place Turenne in this Renaissance town famous for its Brand wine.

KEY

— Wine route
═ Other roads

0 kilometers 5

0 miles 5

The 12th-century chapel of the Château du Haut-Barr, near Saverne

Saverne ⓱

Bas Rhin. 🏘 12,300. 🚉 🚌
🅸 37 grand rue (03 88 91 80 47).
📅 Tue & Thu. **www**.ot-saverne.fr

Named by hills, and situated on the river Zorn and the Marne-Rhine canal, Saverne is a pretty sight. The town was a fief of the prince-bishops of Strasbourg and its sandstone Château des Rohan was a favorite summer residence. Today, it houses the **Musée du Château des Rohan**, whose collection traces Saverne's past. On the far side of the château, the grand'rue is studded with restaurants and timber-framed Renaissance houses.

🏛 Musée du Château des Rohan
Château des Rohan. **Tel** 03 88 91 06 28. ☐ Jan–mid-Jun & mid-Sep–Dec: Mon–Fri pm, 10am–6pm Sat & Sun; mid-Jun–mid-Sep: 10am–6pm daily. ● Tue. 🎦 ♿ restricted.

Environs
To the southwest, perched on a rocky spur, the ruined **Château du Haut-Barr** – the "Eye of Alsace" – once commanded the pass of Col de Saverne. In **Marmoutier**, 3.5 miles (6 km) south, is an abbey church with a Romanesque-Lombard façade and octagonal towers.

Betschdorf ⓲

Bas Rhin. 🏘 4,000. 🅸 La Mairie (03 88 54 44 92). **www**.betschdorf.com

The vibrant village of Betschdorf borders the forest of Haguenau, 27 miles (45 km) north of Strasbourg. Many residents occupy timber-framed houses dating from the 18th century, when pottery made the village prosperous. Generations of potters have passed down the knowledge of the characteristic blue-gray glaze to their sons, while the women have been entrusted with decorating it in cobalt blue. A pottery museum, with a work-shop attached, dis-plays rural ceramics.

Betschdorf pottery

Betschdorf is a good place to try *tartes flambées* – hot, crispy bases topped with cheese or fruit.

Environs
Another pottery village, **Soufflenheim**, lies 6 miles (10 km) southeast. Its earth-colored pottery is usually painted with bold flowers. To the north, close to the German border, the picturesque town of **Wissembourg** has many half-timbered houses and the sec-ond-largest church in Alsace after Strasbourg Cathedral, Eglise St-Pierre et St-Paul.

WESTERN FRANCE

Introducing Western France

The western regions of France have played very different historical roles, from the royal heartland of the Loire Valley to separatist Celtic Brittany. These are mainly rich farming regions, with fishing important along the coasts. Heavy industry and oil refineries are concentrated around Rouen and Le Havre. Visitors come for the wonderful beaches, quiet rural byways, and the sumptuous Loire châteaux. This map shows some of the region's most celebrated sights.

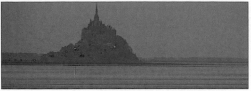

The evocative silhouette of Mont-St-Michel *has welcomed pilgrims since the 11th century. Today nearly one million visitors a year walk across the causeway to the island abbey* (see pp256–61).

Guimiliau Parish Close

Mont-St-Michel

BRITTANY
(See pp268–85)

Carnac Megaliths

The megaliths of Carnac *are evidence of early settlers in Brittany. These ancient granite blocks, arranged in intriguing patterns, date back to 4000 BC and are thought to have had a religious or astronomical purpose* (see p279).

The Bayeux Tapestry (see pp252–3) *shows William the Conqueror's invasion of England from the French point of view. Among its 58 scenes, key events such as the Battle of Hastings in 1066 are depicted with great vigor and finesse. Here, two of William's messengers are shown hurrying to meet him.*

Bayeux Tapestry

Rouen Cathedral

Château de Chambord *is the largest and most extravagant of the Loire châteaux (see pp302–3). François I transformed the original hunting lodge into a luxurious moated castle in 1519. Its splendor was completed by Louis XIV in 1685. Inside the 440 rooms are François' salamander emblem and 365 fireplaces, one for every day of the year.*

NORMANDY
(See pp246–67)

Chartres Cathedral

Le Mans Cathedral

Château de Chambord

Château de Villandry

Château de Chenonceau

THE LOIRE VALLEY
(See pp286–313)

0 kilometers 50

0 miles 50

The Flavors of Western France

The Atlantic coast, the rich agricultural hinterland of dairy farms, orchards, and vegetable fields, and the rivers of the Loire Valley combine to produce some of France's best loved food. Vegetables are grown in abundance in Brittany and the alluvial soils of the Loire, and the orchards of Normandy are bountiful. Fish from the windswept coast of Brittany or the channel ports of Normandy play a key role in the cuisine. Hearty meat dishes range from the celebrated duck of Rouen to the rabbit and game of the Sologne in the Loire. Fine cheeses are made here, and butter is the favored cooking medium.

Normandy apples

Norman cheese-producer displaying his wares

NORMANDY

Normandy's lush green pastures, dotted with brown and white cows, and orchards heavy with apples, make it a great source of veal, milk, cheese, cream, butter, apples, and pears. Duck is a specialty, as is *pre-salé* lamb from the salt-rich marshes around Mont-St-Michel. Many vegetables are grown

and wild mushrooms thrive in the damp meadows and woodlands in the fall. Fish is important, with catches of sole, plaice, and mackerel, skate and herrings, and 80 percent of France's scallops, plus a great variety of shellfish.

Camembert is Normandy's most famous cheese; others include Pont l'Evêque, the pungent-smelling Livarot, rich Brillat-Savarin, and Petit-Suisse, a small, fresh white cheese eaten with sugar.

Apples symbolize Normandy above all, and cider is traditionally drunk with food while Calvados, the powerful apple brandy, is served with meals as *le trou normand*.

BRITTANY

The extensive coastline yields an abundance of fish and seafood. Oysters are highly prized, as are mussels, harvested both wild and cultivated. Other fish caught

Some of the favorite vegetables of western France

Artichokes — Asparagus — Shallots — Watercress — Broccoli — Radishes

REGIONAL DISHES AND SPECIALTIES

Fish dominates the menus here, most spectacularly in the *plateau de fruits de mer*, featuring oysters, crabs, langoustines, prawns, shrimp, cockles, and clams, piled on a bed of ice. Oysters are served simply with lemon or shallot vinegar, but can also come stuffed, gratinéed, or wrapped in pastry. Fresh fish may be grilled, baked in sea salt (*sel de Guérande* is the best), braised in cider, or served with *beurre blanc* ("white butter" sauce with shallots, wine vinegar, and cream). Lobster is often served *à l'Armoricaine. Cotriade,* the Breton fish stew, combines a selection of the catch of the day with onions and potatoes. *Moules marinières* (mussels steamed in white wine with shallots and butter) is the popular classic. As a change from fish, look for *gigot de sept heures* – lamb slowly pot-roasted for seven hours.

Pears

Homard à l'armoricaine
Lobster, served in a herby tomato and onion sauce, enriched with brandy.

Superb Breton oysters for sale at a regional fish market

include monkfish, tuna, sardines, scallops, and lobster. Pig-rearing is important, so expect roast pork, smoked sausages, hams, and *boudin noir* (black/blood pudding), delicious served with apples. A great delicacy is the *pre-salé* lamb from the Gouesnou, served with haricot beans. Artichokes are the symbol of Brittany, an indication of the importance of vegetables, especially winter produce like cauliflower, onions, and potatoes.

Crêpes (pancakes), both sweet and savory, are a key element of the Breton diet. They come as buckwheat *galettes* with savory fillings such as ham, cheese, spinach, or mushrooms, or as lacy light dessert versions with sweet fillings and known as *crêpes dentelles* (*dentelle* meaning "lace").

THE LOIRE VALLEY

This huge region takes pride in a truly diverse range of specialties. Grass-fed cattle are raised in Anjou, and sheep in the Berry region. Excellent free-range chick-

Cheese and charcuterie at Loches market in the Loire Valley

ens, *poulet fermier Loué*, are raised in Touraine and the Orléanais. The forests and lakes of the Sologne yield deer, wild boar, pheasant, partridge, hare, and duck. Charcuterie includes *rillettes* (shredded and potted pork) and ham from the Vendée. The Atlantic coast produces a variety of fish and the Loire itself is a source of pike, shad, tench, salmon, eels, and lampreys. Mushrooms are cultivated in the limestone caves around Saumur, but of the many vegetables grown, best of all is Sologne asparagus. Superb goats' cheeses include St-Maure de Touraine, ash-coated Valençay, and the little Crottins de Chavignol.

ON THE MENU

Alose à l'oseille Shad in a sorrel sauce.

Côte de veau vallée d'Auge Veal in mushrooms, cream, and cider or Calvados.

Far aux pruneaux Egg batter pudding baked with prunes.

Kig ha farz Meat and vegetable stew with buckwheat dumpling.

Marmite Dieppoise Assorted fish stewed in cider or white wine with cream.

Tergeule Creamy baked rice pudding with cinnamon.

Tripes à la Mode de Caen Tripe with calves' feet, onions or leeks, herbs, and cider.

Sole Normande *Baked sole in sauce of egg and cream, garnished with mussels, oysters, mushrooms, and shrimp.*

Canard Rouennais *Duclair duck, part-roasted then finished in a rich sauce of duck liver and shallots.*

Tarte tatin *Caramelized upside-down apple tart, originally made at the Hotel Tatin in the Loire Valley.*

France's Wine Regions: the Loire

With a few exceptions, the Loire is a region of good rather than great wines. The fertile agricultural soils of the meandering flatlands of the "Garden of France" are fine for fruit and vegetables, less so for the production of great wines. The cool, northern, Atlantic-influenced climate nonetheless produces refreshing reds and summer rosés, both dry and lusciously sweet white wines and attractively bracing sparkling wines. Dry white wines are very much in the majority here, and are usually intended for early consumption, so vintages in the Loire tend to matter less than in the classic red wine regions.

Cabernet Franc, red grape of the Loire

LOCATOR MAP
☐ *Loire wine region*

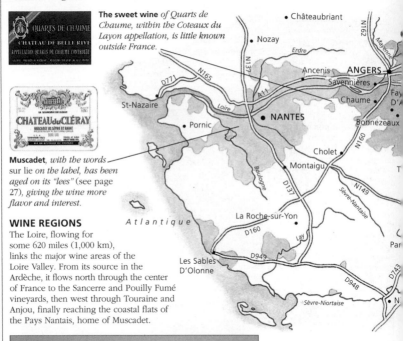

The sweet wine *of Quarts de Chaume, within the Coteaux du Layon appellation, is little known outside France.*

Muscadet, *with the words sur lie on the label, has been aged on its "lees" (see page 27), giving the wine more flavor and interest.*

WINE REGIONS

The Loire, flowing for some 620 miles (1,000 km), links the major wine areas of the Loire Valley. From its source in the Ardèche, it flows north through the center of France to the Sancerre and Pouilly Fumé vineyards, then west through Touraine and Anjou, finally reaching the coastal flats of the Pays Nantais, home of Muscadet.

Map labels: Châteaubriant • Nozay • Erdre • Ancenis • ANGERS • Savennières • Chaume • St-Nazaire • Loire • NANTES • Bonnezeaux • Pornic • Cholet • Montaigu • La Roche-sur-Yon • *Atlantique* • Boulogne • Sèvre-Nantaise • Les Sables D'Olonne • Lay • Sèvre-Niortaise
N162, N137, N165, D771, A11, N160, N149, D137, D160, D949, D948, D743

Clos de l'Echo, Chinon, producer of fine, herbaceous red wine

KEY
☐ Pays Nantais
☐ Anjou-Saumur
☐ Haut-Poitou
☐ Touraine
☐ Central Vineyards

0 kilometers   15

0 miles   15

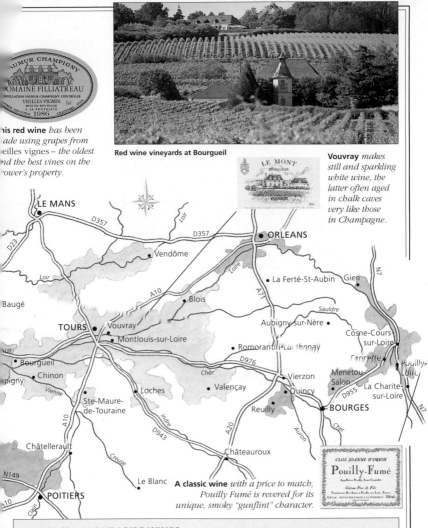

Red wine vineyards at Bourgueil

his red wine has been ade using grapes from eilles vignes – the oldest nd the best vines on the ower's property.

Vouvray *makes still and sparkling white wine, the latter often aged in chalk caves very like those in Champagne.*

A classic wine *with a price to match, Pouilly Fumé is revered for its unique, smoky "gunflint" character.*

KEY FACTS ABOUT LOIRE WINES

Location and Climate
Fertile agricultural soils support fruit, vegetables, and cereals; the poorer soils support grapes. The climate is cool, influenced by the Atlantic, giving the wines a refreshing acidity.

Grape Varieties
The **Melon de Bourgogne** makes simple, dry white wines. The **Sauvignon** makes gooseberryish, flinty dry whites, finest in Sancerre and Pouilly Fumé but also good in Touraine. The **Chenin Blanc** makes dry and medium Anjou, Savennières, Vouvray, Montlouis, and Saumur, sparkling Vouvray and Saumur, and the famous sweet whites, Bonnezeaux,

Vouvray, and Quarts de Chaume. Summery reds are made from the **Gamay** and the fruity, herbaceous **Cabernet Franc**.

Good Producers
Muscadet: Sauvion, Guy Bossard, Michel Bregeon. *Anjou, Savennières, Vouvray*: Richou, Ogereau, Nicolas Joly, Huet, Domaine des Aubuissières, Bourillon-Dorléans, Jacky Blot, Domaine Gessey. *Touraine* (white): Pibaleau. *Saumur-Champigny* (red): Filliatreau, Chateâu du Hureau. *Chinon, Bourgueil*: Couly-Dutheil, Yves Loiseau. *Sancerre, Pouilly Fumé, Ménétou-Salon*: Francis Cotat, Vacheron, Mellot, Vincent Pinard.

From Defense to Decoration

The great châteaus of the Loire Valley gradually evolved from purely defensive structures to decorative palaces. With the introduction of firearms, castles lost their defensive function and comfort and taste predominated. Defensive elements like towers, battlements, moats, and gatehouses were retained largely as symbols of rank and ancestry. Renaissance additions, such as galleries and dormer windows, added elegance.

Salamander emblem of François 1

Slate and stone walls

Angers (see p291), *a fortress built from 1230–40 by Louis IX, stands on a rocky hill in the town center. In 1585, Henri III removed the pepper-pot shaped towers from 17 fortifications which were formerly 30 m (98 ft) high.*

Chaumont (see p306) *was rebuilt in 1445–1510 in Renaissance style by the Amboise family. Although it has a defensive appearance, with circular towers, corbeled walkways, and a gatehouse, these features are mainly decorative. It was restored after c.1833.*

Fortifications with pepper-pot towers removed

Circular tower, formerly defensive

Corbelled walkways, once useful in battle

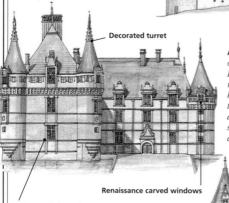

Decorated turret

Azay-le-Rideau (see p296), *regarded as one of the most elegant and well-designed Renaissance châteaux, was built by finance minister Gilles Berthelot (1518–1527) and his wife Philippa Lesbahy. It is a mixture of traditional turrets with Renaissance pilasters and pinnacles. Most dramatic is the interior staircase with its three storys of twin bays and an intricately decorated pediment.*

Renaissance carved windows

Pilasters (columns)

Cylindrical tower

Dormer windows

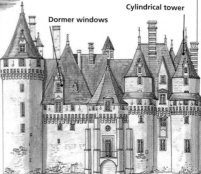

Ussé (see p295) *was built in 1462 by Jean de Bueil as a fortress with parapets containing openings for missiles, battlements, and gunloops. The Espinay family, chamberlains to both Louis XI and Charles VIII, bought the château and changed the walls overlooking the main court-yard to Renaissance style with dormer windows and pilasters. In the 17th century the north wing was demolished to create palatial terraces.*

Breton Traditions

Brittany was christened Breiz Izel (Little Britain) by the Welsh and Cornish migrants who fled here in the 5th and 6th centuries AD and imposed their customs, language, and religion on the local Gauls. Brittany resisted Charlemagne, the Vikings, the Normans, English alliances, and even French rule until 1532. Today, Breton is taught in some schools, and a busy calendar keeps Brittany in touch with its past and with other Celtic regions.

Bigouden lace headdresses

Breton music *has strong Celtic links. Instruments like the* biniou, *similar to the bagpipes, and the oboe-like* bombarde *are often heard at local festivals.*

A pardon *is an annual religious honour to a local saint. The name derives from the granting of indulgences to pardon the sins of the past year. Some* padons, *like those at Ste- Anne d'Auray and Ste- Anne-la-Palud, still attract thousands of pilgrims who carry banners and holy relics through the streets. Most* pardons *take place between April and September.*

Lace *coiffe* — **Felt hat** — **Linen** *coiffe* — **Small headdress**

Wooden clogs

Embroidered apron

Baggy Breton trousers

Breton costumes, *still seen at pardons and weddings, varied since each area had distinctive headdresses or* coiffes. *Artists like Gauguin often painted the costumes. There are good museum collections in Quimper (see p274) and Pont l'Abbé in Pays Bigouden (see p273).*

Brittany's Coastal Wildlife

With its granite cliffs, sweeping bays, rias, and deep estuaries, the Brittany coastline contains a wealth of varied wildlife habitats. Parts of the coast have a tidal range of more than 150 ft (50 m), the highest in France, and this great variation in sea level divides marine life into several distinct zones. Most of the

Starfish region's famous shellfish, including mussels, clams, and oysters, live on the lower shore, either on rocks or in muddy sand where they are submerged for most of the day. Higher zones are the preserve of limpets and barnacles and several kinds of seaweed which can survive out of the water for long periods. Above the sea, towering cliffs offer a nursery for seabirds and a foothold for many kinds of wild flowers.

Cliffs at the Pointe du Raz, Brittany

The Ile de Bréhat at low tide

FEATURES OF THE COAST

This scene shows some of the wildlife habitats found on the Brittany coastline. When exploring the shore, make a note of the tide times, particularly if you plan to walk along the foot of the cliffs.

Salt-marsh flowers are a their best in late summer

Dunes, where marram grass grows, stabilize the sand.

Mud and sand is inhabited by clams and cockles which filter food from the water.

Rock stacks provide secure nurseries for nesting seabirds.

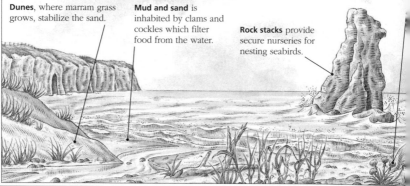

OYSTER BEDS

Like most marine molluscs, oysters begin their lives as tiny floating larvae. The first step in *ostréiculture*, or oyster cultivation, consists of providing the larvae with somewhere to settle, which is usually a stack of submerged tiles. The developing oysters are later transferred to beds and left to mature before being collected for the market.

Oyster beds at Cancale

Clifftop turf often contains a narrow band of wild flowers sandwiched between fields and the sea.

Rockpools are flooded twice daily by the tide. They are inhabited by fish, molluscs, sea anemones, and sponges.

COASTAL WILDLIFE

The structure of this shore determines the wildlife that lives on it. In a world beset by wind and waves, rocks provide solid anchorage for plants and a secure habitat for many small animals. Muddy sand is rich in nutrients, and has a greater abundance of life – although most of this is concealed beneath the surface.

Cliffs

The rock dove *is a cliff-dwelling ancestor of the well-known city pigeon.*

Thrift *is a common spring flower, found on exposed ledges near the sea.*

Rocks and Rockpools

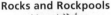

Seaweed *of many different varieties is exposed each day by the falling tide.*

The limpet, *a slow-moving creature, scrapes tiny plants from the rock surface.*

The goby, *with its sharp eyesight, dashes for cover at the first sign of movement above.*

Mud and Sand

Crabs *live at many different water depths. Some species are extremely good swimmers.*

Cockles *live in large numbers just beneath the surface of muddy sand.*

The curlew *has a forceps-like curved beak for extracting shell-fish from mud and sand.*

NORMANDY

EURE · SEINE-MARITIME · MANCHE · CALVADOS · ORNE

The quintessential image of Normandy is of a lush, pastoral region of apple orchards and contented cows, cider, and pungent cheeses – but the region also spans the windswept beaches of the Cotentin and the wooded banks of the Seine valley. Highlights include the great abbey churches of Caen, the mighty island of Mont-St-Michel, and Monet's garden at Giverny.

Normandy gets its name from the Viking Norsemen who sailed up the river Seine in the 9th century. Pillagers turned settlers, they made their capital at Rouen – today a cultured cathedral city that commands the east of the region. Here the Seine meanders seaward past the ancient abbeys at Jumièges and St-Wandrille to a coast that became an open-air studio for Impressionist painters during the mid- and late 19th century.

North of Rouen are the chalky cliffs of the Côte d'Albâtre. The mood softens at the port of Honfleur and the elegant resorts of the Côte Fleurie to the west. Inland lies the Pays d'Auge, with its half-timbered manor houses and patch-eyed cows. The western half of Normandy is predominantly rural, a *bocage* countryside of small, high-hedged fields with windbreaks composed of beech trees.

The modern city of Caen is worth visiting for its two great 11th-century abbey churches built by William the Conqueror and his queen, Matilda. Close by in Bayeux, the story of William's invasion of England is told in detail by the town's famous tapestry. Memories of another invasion, the D-Day Landings of 1944, still linger along the Côte de Nacre and the Cotentin Peninsula. Thousands of Allied troops poured ashore onto these magnificent beaches in the closing stages of World War II. The Cotentin Peninsula is capped by the port of Cherbourg, still a strategic naval base. At its western foot stands one of France's greatest attractions: the monastery island of Mont-St-Michel.

Half-timbered manor house in the village of Beuvron-en-Auge, near Lisieux

◁ **Rich pastures and brown and white Norman cattle, the traditional wealth of the province**

Exploring Normandy

Normandy's rich historical sights and diverse land-scape make it ideal for touring by car or bicycle. Rewarding coastal drives and good beaches can be found along the windswept Côte d'Albâtre and the Cotentin Peninsula. Further south is one of France's most celebrated sights, Mont-St-Michel. Inland, follow the meanders of the Seine valley, passing cider orchards and half-timbered houses along the way, to visit historic Rouen and Monet's garden at Giverny.

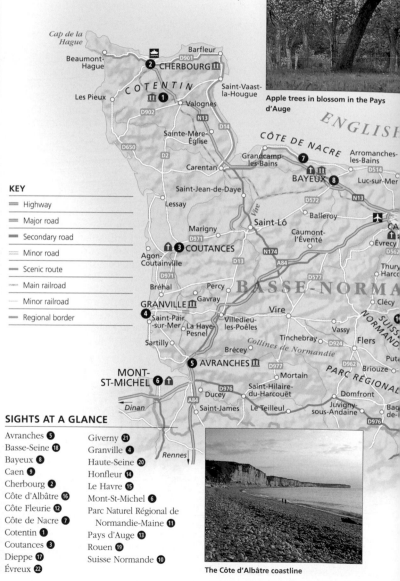

Apple trees in blossom in the Pays d'Auge

KEY

- Highway
- Major road
- Secondary road
- Minor road
- Scenic route
- Main railroad
- Minor railroad
- Regional border

SIGHTS AT A GLANCE

The Côte d'Albâtre coastline

GETTING AROUND

Access to and through the region from Calais
is quick and direct on the A16, which links up
with the A28–A29 and A13 highways to Paris,
and runs west to Caen, and beyond on the
A84. There are also main road and rail links
to the cross-Channel ports of Dieppe, Le
Havre, Caen (Ouistreham), and Cherbourg.
Travel by public transportation beyond these
arteries is limited. The region is threaded
with minor roads, particularly delightful
in the Pays d'Auge and Cotentin
Peninsula. The main airports
are at Rouen, Le Havre,
and Caen.

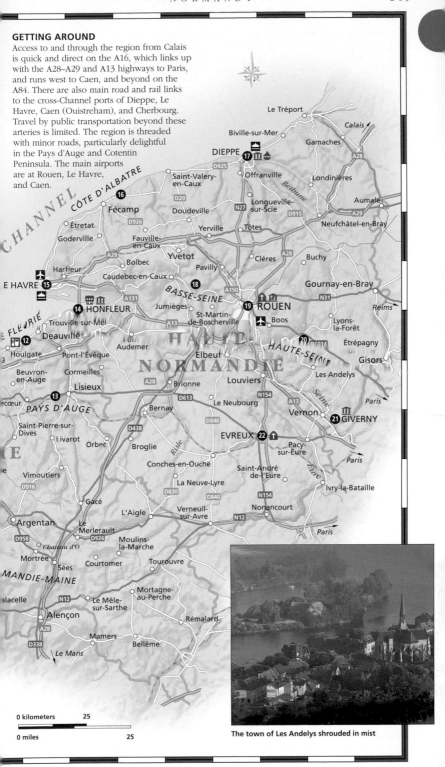

Le Tréport
Calais
Biville-sur-Mer
Gamaches
DIEPPE 17
Londinières
Saint-Valery-
en-Caux
Offranville
Aumale
CÔTE D'ALBATRE 16
Longueville-
sur-Scie
Neufchâtel-en-Bray
Fécamp
Doudeville
Étretat
Yerville
Tôtes
Goderville
Fauville-
en-Caux
Clères
Buchy
Harfleur
Bolbec
Yvetot
Pavilly
Gournay-en-Bray
E HAVRE 15
Caudebec-en-Caux
BASSE-SEINE 18
Jumièges
St-Martin-
de-Boscherville
ROUEN 19
Reims
HONFLEUR 14
Boos
Lyons-
la-Forêt
Trouville-sur-Mer
HAUTE-SEINE
Étrépagny
Deauville 12
Audemer
HAUTE
20
Gisors
Houlgate
Pont-l'Évêque
Elbeuf
NORMANDIE
Les Andelys
Beuvron-
en-Auge
Cormeilles
Louviers
Brionne
Paris
ecœur
Lisieux
Le Neubourg
Vernon
PAYS D'AUGE 13
Bernay
GIVERNY 21
Saint-Pierre-sur-
Dives
Livarot
Orbec
Broglie
EVREUX 22
Pacy-
sur-Eure
Vimoutiers
Conches-en-Ouche
Saint-André-
de-l'Eure
Paris
Gacé
La Neuve-Lyre
Ivry-la-Bataille
Argentan
L'Aigle
Verneuil-
sur-Avre
Nonancourt
Le
Merlerault
Paris
Mortrée
Château d'O
Moulins-
la-Marche
Sées
Courtomer
Tourouvre
MANDIE-MAINE
Mortagne-
au-Perche
alacelle
Le Mêle-
sur-Sarthe
Alençon
Rémalard
Mamers
Bellême
Le Mans

0 kilometers 25

0 miles 25

The town of Les Andelys shrouded in mist

Rugged cliffs on the Cotentin Peninsula

Cotentin **●**

Manche. 🕊 🚌 🚋 🚢 *Cherbourg*.
🛈 *2 quai Alexandre III, Cherbourg
(02 33 93 52 02).*
www.manchetourisme.com

Thrusting into the English
Channel, the Cotentin
Peninsula has a landscape
similar to Brittany's. Its long
sandy beaches have wild and
windblown headlands around
Cap de la Hague and Nez de
Jobourg. The latter is popular
among bird-watchers –
gannets and shearwaters fly
by in large numbers. Along
the east coast stretches Utah
Beach, where American troops
landed as part of the Allied
invasion on June 6, 1944.
Inland, Ste-Mère-Eglise commemorates these events with
its **Musée Airborne** (Airborne
Troops Museum). Just outside
Ste-Mère-Eglise, the **Ferme
Musée du Cotentin** has farm
animals and activities which
give an insight into rural life in
the early 1900s, while farther
north in the market town of
Valognes, the **Musée Régional
du Cidre et du Calvados** celebrates the thriving local talent
for making cider and Calvados.
Two fishing ports command
the Peninsula's northeast
corner: Barfleur and St-Vaast-la-
Hougue, the latter famous for
oysters and a base for boat
trips to the Ile de Tatihou. The
Val de Saire is ideal for a scenic
drive, with a view point at La
Pernelle the best place to
survey the coast. On the west
side of the Peninsula, warmed
by the Gulf Stream, the resort

of Barneville-Carteret offers
sandy beaches and summer
boat trips to the Channel
Islands. The low-lying, marshy
landscape east of Carentan
forms the heart of the Parc
Régional des Marais du
Cotentin et du Bessin.

🏛 **Musée Airborne**
14 rue Eisenhower, Ste-Mère-Eglise.
Tel *02 33 41 41 35.* ⏰ *Feb–Nov:
daily & Christmas hols.* ● *Dec–Jan.*
🈚 🚻 **www**.musee-airborne.com

🏛 **Ferme Musée du Cotentin**
Rte de Beauvais, Ste-Mère-Eglise.
Tel *02 33 95 40 20.* ⏰ *Jun–Sep:
daily; Feb school vacations–May &
Nov school vacations: daily pms.* 🈚

🏛 **Musée Régional du Cidre
et du Calvados**
Rue du Petit-Versailles, Valognes. **Tel**
02 33 40 22 73. ⏰ *Apr–Sep: Wed–
Mon (Jul & Aug: daily).* ● *Sun am.* 🈚

Cherbourg **❷**

Manche. 🏘 *44,100.* 🕊 🚌 🚋
🚢 🛈 *2 quai Alexandre III (02 33 93
52 02).* 🔁 *Tue, Thu, & Sat.*
www.otcherbourgcotentin.fr

Cherbourg has been a strategic
port and naval base since the
mid-19th century. The French
Navy still uses its harbors, as do
transatlantic ships and cross-
Channel ferries from England
and Ireland. For a good view
of the port, drive to the hilltop
Fort du Roule, which houses
the **Musée de la Libération**,
recalling the D-Day invasion
and the subsequent liberation
of Cherbourg. Most activity is
centered on the flower-filled
market square, place Général

de Gaulle, and along shopping
streets such as rue Tour-Carrée
and rue de la Paix. The fine art
in the **Musée Thomas-Henry**
includes 17th-century Flemish
works, and portraits by Jean
François Millet, born in
Gréville-Hague. **Parc Emmanuel
Liais** has small botanical gardens and a densely packed
Musée d'Histoire Naturelle.
The **Cité de la Mer**, a completely bilingual center, has a
cylindrical deep-sea aquarium,
the world's largest visitable
submarine, and other wonders.

🏛 **Musée de la Libération**
Fort du Roule. **Tel** *02 33 20 14 12.*
⏰ *May–Sep: Mon pm–Sat & Sun
pm; Oct– Apr: Wed–Sun pms.*
● *public hols.* 🈚 *Free Sun.*

🏛 **Musée Thomas-Henry**
Rue Vastel. **Tel** *02 33 23 39 30.*
⏰ *May–Sep: Tue–Sat & Sun pm;
Oct–Apr: Tue–Sun pms.*
● *public hols.* 🚻

🏛 **La Cité de la Mer**
Gare Maritime Transatlantique. **Tel**
02 33 20 26 69. ⏰ *Feb–Oct: daily;
Nov–Dec: Tue–Sun.* ● *Jan, Dec 25.*
🈚 🚻 🚻 🚻 **www**.citedelamer.com

Cherbourg town center

Coutances **❸**

Manche. 🏘 *11,500.* 🚌 🚋 🛈
pl Georges Leclerc (02 33 19 08 10).
🔁 *Thu.* **www**.coutances.fr

From Roman times until the
Revolution, the hilltop town
of Coutances was the capital
of the Cotentin. The slender
Cathédrale Notre-Dame, a
fine example of Norman
Gothic architecture, has a
soaring 217 ft (66 m) lantern
tower. Founded in the 1040s
by Bishop Geoffroi de
Montbray, it was financed by
the local de Hauteville family
using monies gained in Sicily
where they had founded a
kingdom a few years earlier.
The town was badly damaged
during World War II but the

cathedral, the churches of St. Nicholas and St. Peter, and the beautiful public gardens with their rare plants all survived.

The back of Coutances cathedral with its squat lantern tower

Granville ❹

Manche. 🏠 13,500. 🚊 🚍 🛳
ℹ️ 4 cours Jonville (02 33 91 30 03).
📅 Sat. www.ville-granville.fr

Ramparts enclose the upper town of Granville, which sits on a spur overlooking the Baie du Mont-St-Michel. The walled town was developed from fortifications built by the English in 1439.

The **Musée de Vieux Granville**, in the town gate-house, recounts Granville's long-seafaring tradition. The chapel walls of the **Eglise de Notre-Dame** are lined with tributes from local fishermen to their patroness, Notre-Dame du Cap Lihou.

The lower town is an old-fashioned seaside resort with a casino, promenades, and public gardens. From the port there are boat trips to the Iles Chausey, a scattering of low-lying granite islands.

Le Musée Christian Dior is housed in Les Rhumbs, the fashion designer's childhood home, surrounded by a beautiful cliff garden.

🏛 **Musée de Vieux Granville**
2 rue Le Carpentier.
Tel 02 33 50 44 10. ⬤ Apr–Sep; Wed–Mon; Oct– Mar: Wed, Sat & Sun pms. ⬤ Nov 1, Dec 22–Jan. 🎫

🏛 **Musée Christian Dior**
Villa les Rhumbs. *Tel 02 33 61 48 21.* ⬤ mid-May–Sep: daily; gardens open all year. 🎫

D-DAY LANDINGS

In the early hours of June 6, 1944, Allied forces began landing on the shores of Normandy. The first step in a long-planned invasion of German-occupied France, known as Operation Overlord. Parachutists were dropped near Ste-Mère-Eglise and Pegasus Bridge, and seaborne assaults were made along a string of code-named beaches. U.S. troops landed on Utah and Omaha in the west, while British and Canadian troops, which included a contingent of Free French commandos, landed at Gold, Juno, and Sword. Over 60 years on, the beaches are still referred to by their code names.

American troops coming ashore during the Allied invasion of France

Pegasus Bridge, where the first French house was liberated, is a natural starting point for a tour around the sights and memorials. Farther west, evocative ruins of the artificial harbor towed across from England survive at Arromanches-les-Bains. There are British, German, and American war cemeteries at La Cambe, Ranville, and St-Laurent-sur-Mer. War museums at Bayeux, Caen, St-Mère-Eglise, and Cherbourg provide background on D-Day and the ensuing Battle for Normandy.

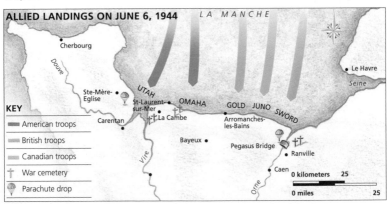

ALLIED LANDINGS ON JUNE 6, 1944 — LA MANCHE

KEY
▬ American troops
▬ British troops
▬ Canadian troops
† War cemetery
⬤ Parachute drop

By the end of D-Day, over 135,000 men had been brought ashore, with losses totaling around 10,000.

Avranches ❺

Manche. 🏃 9,500. 🚉 🚌 ℹ 2 rue
Général-de-Gaulle (02 33 58 00 22).
🗓 Sat. **www**.ot-avranches.com

Avranches has been a religious
center since the 6th century
and is the final staging-post for
visitors to the abbey on Mont-
St-Michel. The origins of the
famous abbey lie in a vision
experienced by Aubert, the
Bishop of Avranches. One night
in 708 the Archangel Michael
instructed him to build a church
on the nearby island. Aubert's
skull, with the finger-hole made
in it by the angel, can be seen
in the treasury of **St-Gervais**
in Avranches. The best views
of Mont-St-Michel are from the
Jardin des Plantes, where
spectacular light shows are
held on summer evenings.
After the Revolution, 203
illuminated manuscripts were
rescued from Mont-St-Michel's
abbey. These and many others
are held in the **Musée des
Manuscrits du Mont-St-Michel**.
The **Musée d'Art et d'Histoire**
details life in the Cotentin over
the centuries, with a collection
devoted to representations of
Mont-St-Michel.

🏛 **Musée des Manuscrits du
Mont-St-Michel**
Pl d'Estouteville. **Tel** 02 33 79 57 00.
◯ Tue–Sun (Jul–Aug: daily). ● Jan,
May 1, Nov 1, Dec 25. 🖼
🏛 **Musée d'Art et d'Histoire**
Place Jean de Saint-Avit. ◯ Jun–
Sep: daily. 🖼

Remains of Mulberry Harbor from World War II off the Côte de Nacre

Mont-St-Michel ❻

See pp256–9.

Côte de Nacre ❼

Calvados. ✈ Caen. 🚉 🚌 Caen,
Bayeux. ⛴ Caen-Ouistreham.
ℹ pl St-Pierre, Caen (02 31 27 14 14).
🗓 Fri, Sun. **www**.tourisme.caen.fr

The stretch of coast between
the mouths of the rivers Orne
and Vire was dubbed the
Côte de Nacre (Mother of
Pearl Coast) in the 19th
century. More recently it has
become known as the site of
the D-Day Landings when
Allied troops poured ashore
at the start of Operation
Overlord (see p251). The
associated cemeteries,
memorials, and museums, and
the remnants of the Mulberry
Harbor at Arromanches-les-
Bains, provide focal points
for a visit. However, the
coastline is equally popular as
a summer vacation destination,
offering long, sandy beaches
backed by seaside resorts
such as Courseulles-sur-Mer
and Luc-sur-Mer, which are
more relaxed than the resorts
of the Côte Fleurie farther east.

Bayeux ❽

Calvados. 🏃 15,500. 🚉 🚌 ℹ
Pont-St-Jean (02 31 51 28 28). 🗓 Sat,
Wed. **www**.bessin-normandie.com

Bayeux was the first town to
be liberated by the Allies in
1944 and fortunate to escape
war damage. Today, an
attractive nucleus of 15th–
19th-century buildings remains
around its central main

BAYEUX TAPESTRY

A lively comic strip justifying William the Conqueror's
invasion of England, this 230-ft (70-m) long
embroidered hanging was commissioned by Bishop
Odo of Bayeux. Offering insights into 11th-century
life and an action-packed account of Harold, King of
England's defeat at the Battle of Hastings, the tapestry
is valued as a work of art, a historical document, an
early example of spin, and an entertaining read.

Harold's retinue sets off for France
to inform William that he will
succeed to the English throne.

Trees with interlacing branches
are sometimes used to divide
the tapestry's 58 scenes.

streets, rue St-Martin and rue St-Jean. The latter is lined with stores and cafés.

Above the town rise the spires and domed lantern tower of the Gothic **Cathédrale Notre-Dame**. Beneath its interior is an 11th-century crypt decorated with restored 15th-century frescoes of angels playing musical instruments. The original Romanesque church that stood here was consecrated in 1077, and it is likely that Bayeux's famous tapestry was commissioned for this occasion by one of its key characters, Bishop Odo.

The tapestry is displayed in a renovated seminary, **Centre Guillaume-le-Conquérant-Tapisserie de Bayeux**, which gives a detailed audiovisual explanation of events leading up to the Norman conquest. On the southwest side of the town, the restored **Musée Mémorial de la Bataille de Normandie** tells the full story of the Battle of Normandy in World War II, with an excellent film compilation made from contemporary newsreels.

🏛 **Centre Guillaume-le-Conquérant-Tapisserie**
Rue de Nesmond. *Tel* 02 31 51 25 50. ◯ daily. ● 1st wk Jan, Dec 25–26. 🏷 ⬥ www.tapisserie-bayeux.fr

🏛 **Musée Mémorial de la Bataille de Normandie**
Bd Fabian-Ware. *Tel* 02 31 51 46 90. ◯ Mar–Dec: daily. ● Jan 1, Dec 25–26. 🏷 ⬥

The Abbaye aux Hommes in Caen

Caen ❾

Calvados. 🏠 117,200. ✈ 🚉 🚌 ⛴
ℹ pl St-Pierre (02 31 27 14 14).
🛒 Fri & Sun www.tourisme.caen.fr

In the mid-11th century Caen became the favored residence of William the Conqueror and Queen Matilda, and despite the destruction of three-quarters of the city during World War II, much remains of their creation. The monarchs built two great abbeys and a castle on the north bank of the river Orne, bequeathing Caen a core of historic interest that justifies penetrating its industrial estates and postwar housing.

Much-loved by the citizens of Caen, the **Eglise St-Pierre** was built on the south side of the castle in the 13th–14th centuries, with an impressively ornate Renaissance east end added in the early 16th century. The frequently copied 14th-century belltower was destroyed in 1944 but has now been restored. To the east, rue du Vaugeux is the central street in Caen's small Vieux Quartier (Old Quarter). Now pedestrianized, the street still has some lovely half-timbered buildings. A walk west, along rue St-Pierre or boulevard du Maréchal Leclerc, leads to the city's main shopping district.

The English have a last meal on land before boarding with hunting dogs and falcons.

Wide moustaches distinguish the English characters from the clean-shaven Normans.

The colored wool used to embroider the linen has faded little since the 11th century.

Latin inscriptions caption each main scene in the work and embody the heroic ideals shared by all the participants.

Borders provide wry comment through fables and asides.

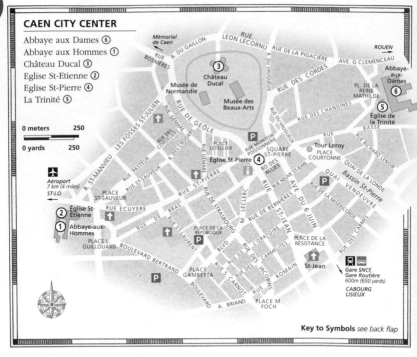

CAEN CITY CENTER

Abbaye aux Dames ⑥
Abbaye aux Hommes ①
Château Ducal ③
Eglise St-Etienne ②
Eglise St-Pierre ④
La Trinité ⑤

0 meters   250
0 yards   250

Key to Symbols *see back flap*

🔒 Abbaye-aux-Hommes

Esplanade Jean-Marie Louvel. *Tel 02 31 30 42 81.* ☐ *daily.* ● *Jan 1, May 1, Dec 25.* 📷 ♿ 🎫 *oblig.*
Work began on William's Abbey for Men in 1063 and was almost complete by his death 20 years later. The abbey church, **Eglise St-Etienne**, is a masterpiece of Norman Romanesque, with a severe, unadorned west front crowned with 13th-century spires. The sparingly decorated nave was roofed in the early 12th century with stone vaulting that anticipates the Gothic style.

🔒 Abbaye-aux-Dames

Pl de la Reine Mathilde. *Tel 02 31 06 98 98.* ☐ *daily pms.* ● *Jan 1, May 1, Dec 25.* 🎫 *oblig.* ♿
Like William's Abbaye-aux-Hommes, Matilda's Abbey for Women also has a Norman Romanesque church, **La Trinité**, flanked by 18th-century buildings. Begun in 1060, it was consecrated 6 years later. Queen Matilda lies buried in the choir under a slab of black marble, and her beautifully restored abbey, with its creamy Caen stone, makes a serene, dignified mausoleum.

🏛 Château Ducal

Esplanade du Château. **Musée des Beaux Arts** *Tel 02 31 30 47 70.* ☐ *Wed–Mon.* **Musée de Normandie** *Tel 02 31 30 47 60.* ☐ *Jun–Oct: daily; Nov–May: Wed–Mon.* ● *Jan 1, Easter, May 1, Ascension, Nov 1, Dec 25 (both museums).* 📷 ♿
The ruins of Caen's castle, one of the largest fortified enclosures in Europe, offer spacious lawns, museums, and rampart views. A fine art collection, strong on 17th-century French and Italian painting, is exhibited in the **Musée des Beaux Arts**. The **Musée de Normandie** recalls traditional life in the region with utensils and displays on farming and lace.

🏛 Mémorial de Caen

Esplanade Dwight-Eisenhower. *Tel 02 31 06 06 45.* ☐ *mid-Feb–Oct: daily; Nov–mid-Feb: Tue–Sun.* ● *3 weeks in Jan, Dec 25.* 📷 ♿ www.memorial-caen.fr
Northwest of Caen, close to the N13 ring-road (exit 7), this museum is dedicated to peace, placing D-Day into the context of World War II using a host of interactive and audiovisual techniques, including stunning compilations of archive and fictional film.

A modern extension gives a wider perspective on cultural, religious, border, and ecological conflicts in the second half of the 20th century.

Lush Orne valley in the Suisse Normande

For hotels and restaurants in this region see pp563–6 and pp614–18

Suisse Normande ⑩

Calvados & Orne. 🚉 *Caen.* 🚌 🚍
Caen, Argentan. 🛈 *2 pl St-Sauveur,
Thury-Harcourt (02 31 79 70 45).*
www.ot-suisse-normande.com

Though hardly like the
mountains of Switzerland, the
cliffs and valleys carved out
by the river Orne as it winds
north to Caen have become
popular for walking,
climbing, camping, and river
sports. The area is also ideal
for a rural drive. Its highest
and most impressive point is
the Oëtre Rock, off the D329,
where you can look down
over the dramatic gorges
created by the river Rouvre.

Parc Naturel Régional de Normandie-Maine ⑪

Orne & Manche. 🚉 *Alençon.* 🚌
🚍 *Argentan.* 🛈 *Carrouges (02 33
26 78 43).* **www**.parc-naturel-
normandie-maine.fr

The southern fringes of
central Normandy have
been incorporated into
France's largest regional park.
Among the farmland and
forests of oak and beech are
several small towns. **Domfront** rests on a spur overlooking the river Varenne.
The spa town **Bagnoles-de-
l'Orne** offers a casino and
sports facilities, while **Sées**
has a Gothic cathedral. The
Maison du Parc at Carrouges

Poster of Deauville, about 1930

has information on walks,
bicycling, and canoeing.

🏛 Maison du Parc
Carrouges. **Tel** *02 33 81 13 33.*
⬭*Jun–Sep: daily; Oct–May: Mon–
Fri, Sat & Sun pms.* ⬤ *public hols.*

Environs
Just north of the park is the
Château d'O, a Renaissance
château with fine 17th-century
frescoes. The **Haras du Pin** is
France's national stud,
called "a horses' Versailles"
for its 17th-century
architecture. Horse shows,
dressage events, and various
tours take place throughout
the year.

Côte Fleurie ⑫

Calvados. 🚉 🚌 🚍 *Deauville.*
🛈 *pl de la Mairie, Deauville (02 31
14 40 00).* **www**.deauville.org

The Côte Fleurie (Flowery
Coast) between Villerville and
Cabourg has been planted
with chic resorts which burst

into bloom every summer.
Trouville was once a humble
fishing village, but in the mid-
19th century caught the
attention of writers Gustave
Flaubert and Alexandre
Dumas. By the 1870s Trouville
had acquired grand hotels,
a train station, and pseudo-
Swiss villas along the
beachfront. It has, however,
long been outclassed by its
neighbor, **Deauville**, created
by the Duc de Morny in the
1860s. This resort boasts a
casino, racecourses, marinas,
and the famous beachside
catwalk, Les Planches.
  For something quieter,
head west to smaller resorts
such as Villers-sur-Mer or
Houlgate. **Cabourg** farther
west is dominated by the
turn-of-the-century Grand
Hôtel *(see p551)* where
novelist Marcel Proust spent
many summers. Proust used
the resort as a model for the
fictional Balbec in his novel
Remembrance of Things Past.

Pays d'Auge ⑬

Calvados. 🚉 *Deauville.* 🚌
🚍 *Lisieux.* 🛈 *11 rue d'Alençon,
Lisieux (02 31 48 18 10).*
www.lisieux-tourisme.com

Inland from the Côte Fleurie,
the Pays d'Auge is classic
Normandy countryside, lushly
woven with fields, wooded
valleys, cider orchards, dairy
farms and manor houses. Its
capital is **Lisieux**, a cathedral
town devoted to Ste-Thérèse
of Lisieux, canonized in 1925,
who attracts hundreds of
thousands of pilgrims each
year. Lisieux is an obvious base
for exploring the region, but
nearby market towns, such as
St-Pierre-sur-Dives and Orbec,
are smaller and more attractive.
  The best way to enjoy the
Pays d'Auge is to mosey
around its minor roads. Two
tourist routes are devoted
to cider and cheese, while
picturesque manor houses,
farmhouses, and châteaus
testify to the wealth of this
fertile land. **St-Germain-de-
Livet** can be visited, as can
Crèvecoeur-en-Auge, and
the half-timbered village of
Beuvron-en-Auge is charming.

APPLES AND CIDER

Apple orchards are a familiar feature of the Normandy
countryside, and their fruit a fundamental ingredient in the
region's gastronomic repertoire. No self-respecting
pâtisserie would be without its *tarte normande* (apple
tart), and every country lane seems to sport an *Ici Vente
Cidre* (cider sold here) sign. Much of the harvest forms the
raw material for cider and Calvados, an apple brandy aged
in oak barrels for at least two years. A local brew is also
made from pears, and known as *poiré* (perry).

A crop ranging from sour cider apples to sweet eating varieties

Mont-St-Michel ➏

The 10th-century abbey

Shrouded by mist, encircled by sea, soaring proudly above glistening sands – the silhouette of Mont-St-Michel is one of the most enchanting sights in France. Now linked to the mainland by a causeway, the island of Mont-Tombe (Tomb on the Hill) stands at the mouth of the river Couesnon, crowned by a fortified abbey that almost doubles its height. Lying strategically on the frontier between Normandy and Brittany, Mont-St-Michel grew from a humble 8th-century oratory to become

St Michael

The 11th-century abbey

a Benedictine monastery that had its greatest influence in the 12th and 13th centuries. Pilgrims known as *miquelots* journeyed from afar to honor the cult of St. Michael, and the monastery was a renowned center of medieval learning. Major engineering works to reverse the silting up of the sea around the island will be in place until 2015.

The mid-18th-century abbey

St. Aubert's Chapel
A small 15th-century chapel built on an outcrop of rock is dedicated to Aubert, the founder of Mont-St-Michel.

★ Gabriel Tower
Three floors of cannons pointed in all directions from this imposing 16th-century tower.

Entrance

TIMELINE

		1434 Last assault by English forces. Ramparts surround the town	1789 French Revolution: abbey becomes a political prison	1874 Abbey declared a national monument
966 Benedictine abbey founded by Duke Richard I	**1211–28** Construction of La Merveille			
				1922 Services again held in abbey church

700	1000	1300	1600	1900

1017 Work on abbey church starts		**1516** Abbey falls into decline	**1877–9** Causeway built	**1895–7** Belfry, spire, and statue of St. Michael added
708 St. Aubert builds an oratory on Mont-Tombe		**1067–70** Mont-St-Michel depicted in Bayeux Tapestry *Bayeux Tapestry detail*		**2007** Benedictine monks leave abbey; they are replaced by the Fraternité de Jérusalem

VISITORS' CHECKLIST

to Pontorson, then bus.
bd de l'Avancée (02 33 60 14 30). www.ot-montsaintmichel. com **Abbey Tel** 02 33 89 80 00. May–Aug: 9am–7pm; Sep– Apr: 9:30am–6pm. Nocturnal visits in summer (recommended). Jan 1, May 1, Dec 25. 12:15pm Tue–Sat, 11:30am Sun. www.mont-saint- michel.monuments-nationaux.fr

Tides of Mont-St-Michel
Extremely strong tides in the Baie du Mont-St-Michel act as a natural defense. They rise and fall with the lunar calendar and can reach speeds of 6 mph (10 km/h).

★ Abbey
Protected by high walls, the abbey and its church occupy an impregnable position on the island.

Gautier's Leap
At the top of the Inner Staircase, this terrace is named after a prisoner who leaped to his death.

Eglise St-Pierre

Liberty Tower

The Arcade Tower provided lodgings for the abbot's soldiers.

King's Tower

STAR FEATURES

★ Abbey

★ Ramparts

★ Grande Rue

★ Grande Rue
Now crowded with restaurants, the pilgrims' route, followed since the 12th century, climbs up past Eglise St-Pierre to the abbey gates.

The Abbey of Mont-St-Michel

The present buildings bear witness to the time when the abbey served both as a Benedictine monastery and, for 73 years after the Revolution, as a political prison. In 1017 work began on a Romanesque church at the island's highest point, building over its 10th-century predecessor, now the Chapel of Our Lady Underground. A monastery built on three levels, La Merveille (The Miracle) was added to the church's north side in the early 13th century.

Cross in the choir

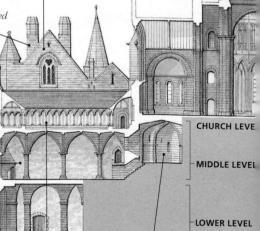

★ Church
Four bays of the Romanesque nave survive. Three were pulled down in 1776, creating the West Terrace.

★ La Merveille
The Miracle is a Gothic masterpiece – a three-story monastic complex built in only 16 years.

Refectory
The monks ate their meals in this long, narrow room, which is flooded with light through tall windows.

Knights' Room
The rib vaults and finely decorated capitals are typically Gothic.

CHURCH LEVEL

MIDDLE LEVEL

LOWER LEVEL

Crypt of the Thirty Candles is one of two 11th-century crypts built to support the transepts of the main church.

★ Cloisters
The cloisters with their elegant columns in staggered rows are a beautiful example of early 13th-century Anglo-Norman style.

VISITING THE ABBEY

The three levels of the abbey reflect the monastic hierarchy. The monks lived at the highest level, in an enclosed world of church, cloister, and refectory. The abbot entertained his noble guests on the middle level. Soldiers and pilgrims farther down on the social scale were received at the lowest level. Guided tours begin at the West Terrace at the church level and end in the almonry, where alms were dispensed to the poor. The almonry is now a bookstore and souvenir hall.

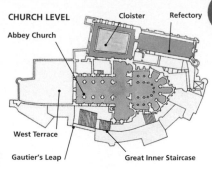

CHURCH LEVEL

Cloister · Refectory · Abbey Church · West Terrace · Gautier's Leap · Great Inner Staircase

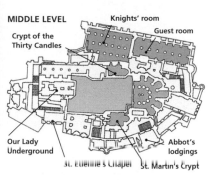

MIDDLE LEVEL

Knights' room · Guest room · Crypt of the Thirty Candles · Our Lady Underground · St. Etienne's Chapel · St. Martin's Crypt · Abbot's lodgings

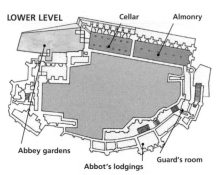

LOWER LEVEL

Cellar · Almonry · Abbey gardens · Abbot's lodgings · Guard's room

Church interior
A Flamboyant Gothic choir was built in 1446–1521, held up by crypts with massive supporting pillars.

St-Martin's Crypt is an 11th-century barrel-vaulted chapel that preserves the austere forms of the original Romanesque abbey.

The abbot's lodgings were close to the abbey entrance, and he received prestigious visitors in the guest room. Poorer pilgrims were received in the almonry.

West Terrace
Guided tours start here, at the West Terrace. The Fraternité de Jérusalem, a small monastic community, lives in the abbey and welcomes visitors.

STAR FEATURES

★ Church

★ La Merveille

★ Cloisters

Mont-St-Michel by night ▷

Honfleur ⓮

Calvados. ⫣ 8,500. ☐ Deauville.
🛈 quai Lepaulmier (02 31 89 23 30).
☐ Wed, Sat; Thu, Sun: fish market
at harbor. www.ot-honfleur.fr

A major defensive port in the 15th century, Honfleur has become one of Normandy's most appealing harbors. At its heart is the 17th-century **Vieux Bassin** (Old Dock), with its pretty tall houses (6-7 storys).

Honfleur became a center of artistic activity in the 19th century. Eugène Boudin, the painter, was born here in 1824, as was the composer Erik Satie in 1866. Courbet, Sisley, Renoir, Pissarro, and Cézanne all visited Honfleur, often meeting at the Ferme St-Siméon, now a luxury hotel. Painters still work from Honfleur's quayside, and exhibit in the **Greniers à Sel**, two salt warehouses built in 1670. These lie to the east of the Vieux Bassin in an area known as l'Enclos, which made up the fortified heart of the town in the 13th-century.

The **Musée d'Ethnographie et d'Art Populaire Normand** displays mementos of Honfleur's nautical past, with a warren of Norman interiors next door in the former prison. Place Ste-Catherine has an unusual 15th-century church built by ship's carpenters. The **Musée Eugène-Boudin** documents the artistic appeal of Honfleur and the Seine estuary, with works from Boudin to Raoul Dufy. **Les Maisons Satie** use extracts from Satie's music to guide you round reconstructions of the rooms.

🏛 Greniers à Sel
Rue de la Ville. 🛈 02 31 89 23 30.
☐ for guided tours & exhibitions.
🗹 obligatory, except during summer exhibs. 📷 ⚿

🏛 Musée d'Ethnographie et d'Art Populaire Normand
Quai St Etienne. **Tel** 02 31 89 14 12.
☐ mid-Feb–Mar, Oct–mid-Nov:
Tue–Fri (pms only), Sat, Sun; Apr–Sep: Tue–Sun. ● May 1. 📷 ⚿

🏛 Musée Eugène-Boudin
Pl Erik Satie, rue de l'Homme de Bois. **Tel** 02 31 89 54 00. ☐ mid-Mar–Sep: Wed–Mon; Oct–Dec & mid-Feb–mid-Mar: Wed–Mon pms, Sat, Sun. ● May 1, Jul 14, Dec 25. 📷 ⚿

🏛 Les Maisons Satie
67 bd Charles V. **Tel** 02 31 89 11 11.
☐ mid-Feb–Dec: Wed–Mon.
● public hols. 📷

Quai St-Etienne in Honfleur

Le Havre ⓯

Seine-Maritime. ⫣ 194,000. ✈ ☐
☐ ⛴ 🛈 186 bd Clemenceau
(02 32 74 04 04). ☐ daily.
www.lehavretourisme.com

Strategically positioned on the Seine estuary, Le Havre (The Harbor) was created in 1517 by François I after the nearby port of Harfleur silted up.

During World War II it was virtually obliterated by bombing, but despite a industrial zone which sta beside the port, it still ha appeal. It is an important yachting center, and its bea has two blue flags (very clea

Much of the city center wa rebuilt in the 1950s–1960s by August Perret, whose towering **Eglise St-Joseph** (a UNESCO World Heritage site) pierces the skyline. On the seafront, the **Musée Malraux** has works by, among others, local artist Raoul Dufy. France's biggest skateboard park is also on the seafront.

🏛 Musée Malraux
2 bd Clemenceau. **Tel** 02 35 19 62 62. ☐ Wed–Mon. ● public hols. 📷

Côte d'Albâtre ⓰

Seine-Maritime. ☐ 🚌 ⛴ 🛈 quai du Carénage, Dieppe (02 32 14 40 60). www.dieppetourisme.com

The Alabaster Coast gets its name from the chalky cliffs and milky waters that characterize the Normandy coastline between Le Havre and Le Tréport. It is best known for the **Falaise d'Aval** west of Etretat, eroded into an arch. The author Guy de Maupassant, born near Dieppe in 1850, compared these cliffs to an elephant dipping its trunk into the sea. From Etretat, a chain of coastal roads runs east across a switchback of breezy headlands and wooded valleys to Dieppe.

Fécamp is the only major town along this route. Its Benedictine abbey was once an important pilgrimage center after a tree trunk said to contain drops of Christ's Blood washed ashore here in the 7th century. This is enshrined in a reliquary at the entrance to the Lady Chapel of the abbey church, La Trinité.

The vast **Palais Bénédictine** is a Neo-Gothic-and-Renaissance homage to the ego of Alexander Le Grand, a local wine and spirits merchant who rediscovered the monks' recipe for Bénédictine, the famous herbal liqueur. Built

Woman with Parasol (1880) by Boudin in the Musée Eugène-Boudin

For hotels and restaurants in this region see pp563–6 and pp614–18

The cliffs at Falaise d'Aval, famously likened to an elephant dipping its trunk into the sea

in 1882, it incorporates a distillery and an eccentric museum packed with curios. The adjacent halls provide an aromatic account and tastings of the 27 herbs and spices that make up the elixir.

🏛 Palais Bénédictine
110 rue Alexandre Le Grand, Fécamp.
Tel *02 35 10 26 10.* ◯ *daily.*
🌑 *Jan, May 1, Dec 25.* 📷 🔲

View of Dieppe from the château and museum above the town

Dieppe ⓱

Seine-Maritime. 🏠 *36,000.* 🚋 🚌
🚤 🛈 *Pont Jean Ango (02 32 14 40 60).* 🛒 *Tue, Thu, & especially Sat.*
www.dieppetourisme.com

Dieppe exploits a break in the chalky cliffs bordering the Pays de Caux, and has won historical prestige as a Channel fort, port, and resort. Prosperity came during the 16th and 17th centuries, when local privateer Jehan Ango raided the Portuguese and English fleets, and a trading post called Petit Dieppe was founded on the West African coast. At that time, Dieppe's population was already 30,000, and included a 300-strong

community of craftsmen carving imported ivory. This maritime past is celebrated in **Le Château-Musée**, the 15th-century castle crowning the headland to the west of the seafront. Here you can see historical maps and model ships, a collection of Dieppe ivories, and paintings that evoke the town's development as a fashionable seaside resort during the 19th century. Dieppe had the nearest beach to Paris and it quickly responded to the developing passion for promenading, seawater cures, and bathing.

Today Dieppe's broad seafront is given over to lawns, seaside amusements, and parking lots, and its liveliest streets surround the battle-scarred **Eglise St-Jacques** to the south. If the weather is poor, visit **L'Estran-La Cité de la Mer**, an exhibition center with maritime models.

🏛 Le Château-Musée
Tel *02 35 06 61 99.* ◯ *Jun–Sep: daily; Oct–May: Wed–Mon.*
🌑 *Jan 1, May 1, Nov 1, Dec 25.* 📷
🔲 **www**.mairie-dieppe.fr

🏛 L'Estran-La Cité de la Mer
37 rue de l'Asile Thomas.
Tel *02 35 06 93 20.* ◯ *daily.*
🌑 *Jan 1, Dec 25.* 📷 ♿

Basse-Seine ⓲

Seine-Maritime & Eure. ✈ *Le Havre, Rouen.* 🚋 🚌 *Yvetot.* 🚤 *Le Havre.*
🛈 *Yvetot (02 35 95 08 40).*

Meandering seaward from Rouen to Le Havre, the river Seine is crossed by three spectacular road bridges: the Pont de Brotonne, the Pont de Tancarville, and the Pont de

Normandie (completed in 1995, it links Le Havre and Honfleur). The grace and daring of these modern bridges echo the soaring aspirations of the abbeys founded on the river's banks in the 7th and 8th centuries. The abbeys now provide good stepping stones for a tour of the Lower Seine valley.

West of Rouen is the harmonious Eglise de St-Georges at **St-Martin-de-Boscherville** which, until the Revolution, was the church of a small walled abbey. Its 12th-century chapter house has remarkable biblical statues and carved capitals. From here the D67 runs south to the riverside village of La Bouille.

As you head northwest, an hourly car ferry at Mesnil-sous-Jumièges takes you over to the colossal ruins of the **Abbaye de Jumièges**. The abbey was founded in 654 and once housed 900 monks and 1,500 servants. The main abbey church dates from the 11th century; its consecration in 1067 was a major event, with William the Conqueror in attendance.

The D913 strikes through oak and beech woods in the Parc Régional de Brotonne to the 7th-century **Abbaye de St-Wandrille**. The Musée de la Marine de Seine at **Caudebec-en-Caux** gives an engrossing account of many aspects of life on this great river since the late 19th century.

Monk from Abbaye de St-Wandrille

Rouen ⑲

Founded at the lowest point where the Seine could be bridged, Rouen has prospered through maritime trade and industrialization to become a rich and cultured city. Despite the severe damage of World War II, the city boasts a wealth of historic sights on its right bank, all within walking distance of the central Cathédrale Notre-Dame, frequently painted by Monet. In turn a Celtic trading post, Roman garrison, and Viking colony, Rouen became the capital of the Norman Duchy in 911. It was captured by Henry V in 1419 after a siege during the Hundred Years' War. In 1431 Joan of Arc was burned at the stake here in place du Vieux-Marché.

Rouen, a thriving port on the river Seine

Exploring Rouen

From the cathedral, the rue du Gros Horloge runs west under the city's Great Clock, to the place du Vieux Marché and its post-war Eglise Ste-Jeanne-d'Arc. Rue aux Juifs leads past the 15th-century Gothic **Palais de Justice**, once Normandy's parliament, to the fancy stores and cafés around rue des Carmes. Farther east, between the St-Maclou and St-Ouen churches, are half-timbered houses in the rue Damiette and rue Eau de Robec. North, in place Général de Gaulle, is the 18th-century **Hôtel de Ville**.

🏛 Cathédrale Notre-Dame

This Gothic masterpiece is dominated by the famous west façade (*see p267*), painted

Cathédrale Notre-Dame, Rouen

by Monet, which is framed by two unequal towers – the northern Tour St-Romain, and the later Tour du Beurre, supposedly paid for by a tax on butter consumption in Lent. Above the central lantern tower rises a Neo-Gothic spire, made from cast iron and erected in 1876. Recently restored, both the 14th-century northern Portail des Libraires and the 14th-century southern Portail de la Calende are worth seeing for their precise sculpting and delicate tracery. Many of the cathedral's riches are accessible by guided tour only, including the tomb of Richard the Lionheart, whose heart was buried here, and the rare 11th-century semicircular hall crypt, rediscovered in 1934. The choir/chancel was badly hit by the 1999 storm.

🏛 Eglise St-Maclou

This Flamboyant Gothic church has an intensively

For hotels and restaurants in this region see pp563–6 and pp614–18

SIGHTS AT A GLANCE

Aître St-Maclou ⑨
Cathédrale Notre-Dame ⑦
Eglise St-Maclou ⑧
Eglise St-Ouen ⑩
Gros-Horloge ②
Hôtel de Ville ⑪
Musée des Beaux Arts ⑤
Musée de la Céramique ④
Musée d'Histoire Naturelle ⑫
Musée le Secq des Tournelles ⑥
Palais de Justice ③
Place du Vieux-Marché ①

timbers of its buildings, set around the quadrangle, are carved with a macabre array of grinning skulls, crossed bones, coffins, and grave-diggers' implements.

🏛 Musée d'Histoire Naturelle

198 rue Beauvoisine. **Tel** 02 35 71 41 50. ☐ Tue–Sun pms. 🌀

The Musée d'Histoire Naturelle is the second largest museum of its kind in France, holding more than 800,000 objects.

🔒 Eglise St-Ouen

Once part of a formi-dable Benedictine abbey, St-Ouen is a solid Gothic church with a lofty, unadorned interi-or made all the more beautiful by its restored 14th-century stained glass. Behind the church there is a pleasant park which is ideal for picnics.

🏛 Musée des Beaux Arts

Square Verdrel. **Tel** 02 35 71 28 40. ☐ Wed–Mon. ☐ public hols except Easter & Whitsun. 🌀 ♿

The city's collection includes major art works: masterpieces by Caravaggio and Velázquez, and paintings by Normandy-born artists Théodore Géricault, Eugène Boudin, and Raoul Dufy. Also on display is Monet's *Rouen Cathedral, The Portal, Gray Weather*.

🏛 Musée de la Céramique

Hôtel d'Hocqueville, 1 rue Faucon. **Tel** 02 35 07 31 74. ☐ Wed–Mon. ☐ public hols. 🌀

Exhibits of 1,000 pieces of Rouen faïence – colorful glazed earthenware – together with other pieces of French and foreign china are displayed in a 17th-century town house. The works trace the history of Rouen faïence to its zenith in the 18th century.

Jug from Musée de la Céramique

🏛 Musée Le Secq des Tournelles

Rue Jacques-Villon. **Tel** 02 35 88 42 11. ☐ Wed–Mon. ☐ public hols. 🌀 ♿ ground floor only.

Located in a 16th-century church, this wrought ironwork museum exhibits antique iron work ranging from keys to corkscrews and Gallo-Roman spoons to mighty tavern signs.

🏛 Musée Flaubert

51 rue de Lecat. **Tel** 02 35 15 59 95. ☐ Tue–Sat. ☐ public hols. 🌀

Flaubert's father was a sur-geon at Rouen Hospital, and his family home combines memorabilia with an awesome – and occasionally gruesome – display of 17th–19th-century medical equipment.

GUSTAVE FLAUBERT

The novelist Gustave Flaubert (1821–80) was born and raised in Rouen, and the city provides the backdrop for some memorable scenes in his masterpiece, *Madame Bovary*.

Published in 1857, this realistic study of a country doctor's wife driven to despair by her love affairs provoked a scandal that made Flaubert's name. His famous stuffed green parrot, which can be seen in the Musée Flaubert, was always perched on his writing desk.

Flaubert's stuffed parrot

decorated west façade with a five-bay porch and carved wooden doors depicting biblical scenes. Behind the church, its *aître*, or ossuary, is a rare surviving example of a medieval cemetery for the burial of plague victims. The

Château Gaillard and the village of Les Andelys, in a loop of the river Seine

Haute-Seine ⑳

Eure. ✈ Rouen. 🚉 Vernon, Val de
Reuil. 🚌 Gisors, Les Andelys.
🛈 Les Andelys (02 32 54 41 93).
http://office-tourisme.ville-andelys.fr

Southeast of Rouen, the river
Seine follows a convoluted
course, with most points of
interest on its north bank.
At the center of the Forêt de
Lyons, once the hunting
ground for the Dukes of
Normandy, is the country
town of **Lyons-la-Forêt**, with
half-timbered houses and an
18th-century covered market.
    To the south the D313
follows the gracefully curving
Seine to the town of **Les
Andelys**. Above it tower the
ruins of Château Gaillard
which Richard the Lionheart,
as King of England and Duke
of Normandy, built in 1197 to
defend Rouen from the
French. They eventually took
the castle in 1204.

Giverny ㉑

Eure. 🏠 600. 🛈 36 rue Carnot,
Vernon (02 32 51 39 60).
www.cape-tourisme.fr

In 1883 the Impressionist
painter Claude Monet rented
a house in the small village of

Giverny, and worked here
until his death. The house,
known as the **Fondation
Claude Monet**, and its garden
are open to the public. The
house is decorated in the
color schemes that Monet
admired; the gardens are
famous as the subject of
some of the artist's studies.
Only copies are on show, but
there are outstanding original
19th- and 20th-century art
works in the **Musée des
Impressionnismes** nearby.

🏛 **Fondation Claude Monet**
Giverny, Gasny. **Tel** 02 32 51 28 21.
⬚ Apr–Oct: daily. 🖼
www.fondation-monet.fr

🏛 **Musée des
Impressionnismes**
99 rue Claude Monet, Giverny.
Tel 02 32 51 94 65. ⬚ Apr–Oct.
🖼 ♿

Évreux ㉒

1 Eure. 🏠 55,000. 🚉 🚌
🛈 1ter pl du Général de Gaulle
(02 32 24 04 43). 🛒 Wed & Sat.
www.grandevreuxtourisme.fr

Though considerably dam-
aged in the war, Évreux is a
pleasant cathedral town set in
wide, agricultural plains. At
its heart, the **Cathédrale Notre-
Dame** is renowned for its
14th–15th century stained
glass. The building is predominantly Gothic, though
Romanesque arches survive
in the nave and Renaissance
screens adorn its chapels.
Next door, the former Bishop's
Palace houses the **Musée de
l'Ancien Evêché**, with Roman
bronze statues of Jupiter and
Apollo and fine 18th-century
furniture and decorative art.

Monet's garden at Giverny, restored to its original profuse glory

For hotels and restaurants in this region see pp563–6 and pp614–18

Monet's Cathedral Series

n the 1890s Claude Monet made almost 30 paintings of Rouen's cathedral, several of which are now in the Musée d'Orsay in Paris *(see pp120–21)*. He studied the effects of changing light on its façades, and described both the surface detail and huge bulk, putting color before contour. The archetypal Impressionist, Monet said he conceived this series when he watched the effects of light on a country church, "as the sun's rays slowly dissolved the mists … that wrapped the golden stone in an ideally vaporous envelope."

HARMONY IN BLUE AND GOLD *(1894)*
Monet selected a close vantage point for the series and was partial to this southwest view. The sun would cast afternoon shadows across the carved west front, accentuating the cavernous portals and the large rose window.

Monet's sketch, *one of many of Rouen, parallels the shimmering effect of the paintings.*

Harmony in Brown *(1894) is the only finished version of a frontal view of the west façade. Analysis has shown that it was begun as a southwest view like the others.*

Harmony in Blue *(1894), compared with Harmony in Blue and Gold, shows the stone of the west façade further softened by the diffuse light of a misty morning.*

The Portal, Gray Weather *(1894) was one of several canvases in the gray color group which showed the cathedral façade in the soft light of an overcast day.*

BRITTANY

FINISTÈRE · CÔTES D'ARMOR · MORBIHAN · ILLE-ET-VILAINE

J*utting defiantly into the Atlantic, France's northwest corner has long been culturally and geographically distinct from the main bulk of the country. Known to the Celts as Armorica, the land of the sea, Brittany's past swirls with the legends of drowned cities and Arthurian forests. Prehistoric megaliths arise mysteriously from land and sea, and the medieval is never far from the modern.*

A long, jagged coastline is the region's great attraction. Magnificent beaches line its northern shore, swept clean by huge tides and interspersed with well-established seaside resorts, seasoned fishing ports, and abundant oysterbeds. The south coast is gentler, with wooded river valleys and a milder climate, while the west, being exposed to the Atlantic winds, has a drama that justifies the name Finistère – the End of the Earth.

Inland lies the Argoat – once the Land of the Forest, now a patchwork of undulating fields, woods, and rolling moorland. Parc Régional d'Armorique occupies much of central Finistère, and it is in western Brittany that Breton culture remains most evident. In Quimper, and in the Pays Bigouden, crêpes and cider, traditional costumes, and Celtic music are still a genuine part of the Breton lifestyle. Eastern Brittany has a more conventional appeal. Vannes, Dinan, and Rennes, the Breton capital, have well-preserved medieval quarters where half-timbered buildings shelter inviting markets, stores, crêperies, and restaurants. The walled port of St-Malo on the Côte d'Emeraude recalls the region's maritime prowess, while the remarkably intact castles at Fougères and Vitré are reminders of the mighty border-fortresses that protected Brittany's eastern frontier before its final union with France in 1532.

Women dressed in traditional costume and *coiffe*, the typical Breton lace head-dress

◁ Characteristic pink granite cliffs on the Côte de Granit Rose, northern Brittany

Exploring Brittany

Ideal for a seaside vacation, Brittany offers enjoyable drives along the headlands and beaches of the northern Côte d'Emeraude and Côte de Granit Rose, while the south coast has wooded valleys and the prehistoric sites of Carnac and the Golfe du Morbihan. The parish closes *(see pp276–7)* provide an intriguing insight into Breton culture, as does the cathedral town of Quimper. Be sure to visit the regional capital, Rennes, and the great castle at Fougères, and in summer take a boat trip to one of Brittany's islands.

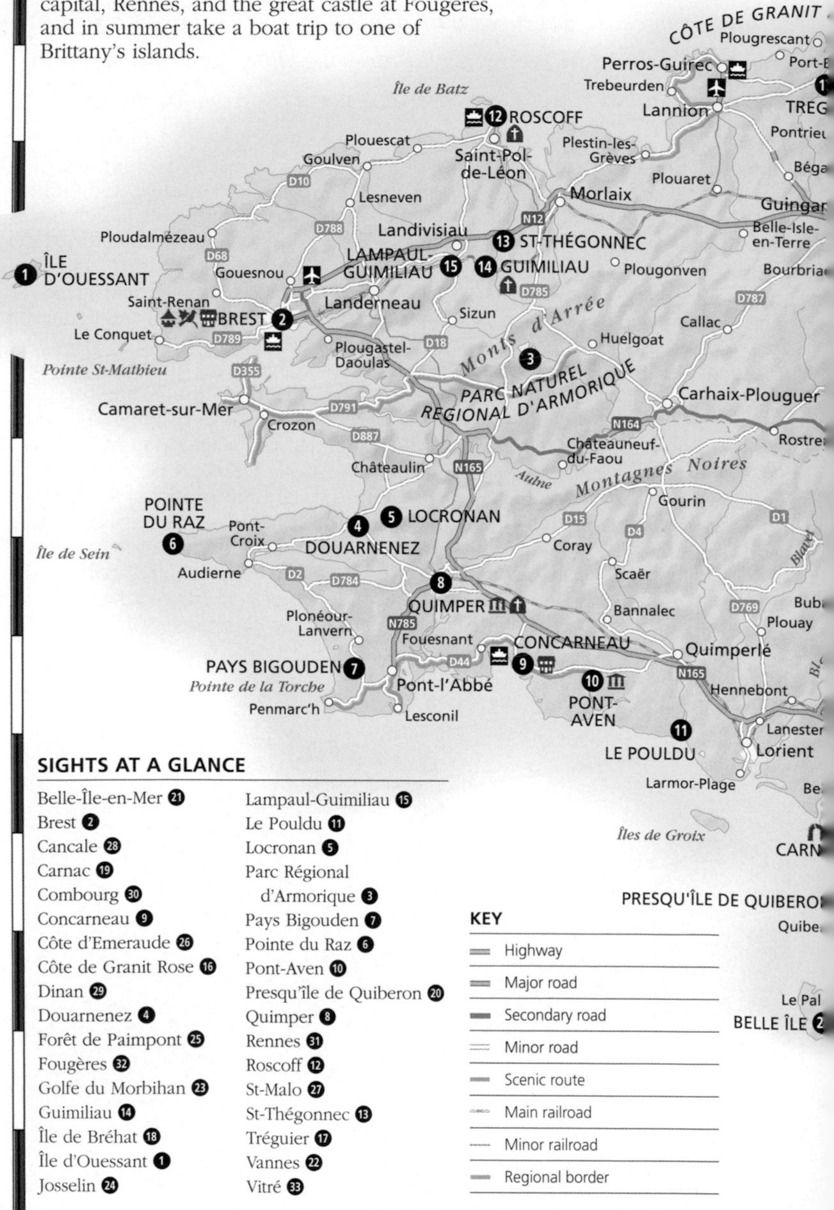

SIGHTS AT A GLANCE

KEY

▬▬	Highway
▬▬	Major road
▬▬	Secondary road
▭▭	Minor road
▭▭	Scenic route
▬▬	Main railroad
----	Minor railroad
▬▬	Regional border

For additional map symbols *see back flap*

GETTING AROUND
Expressways N12/N165 encircle Brittany, giving easy access to coastal areas, while the N12 and N24 give direct access to Rennes, Brittany's capital. Brittany can be reached by air to Brest, Nantes, and Rennes airports, by Channel ferries to St. Malo and Roscoff, by autoroutes from Normandy, the Loire, and A11 from Paris, or by TGV direct from Paris and Lille.

Lighthouse on the Île de Bréhat, Côte de Granit Rose

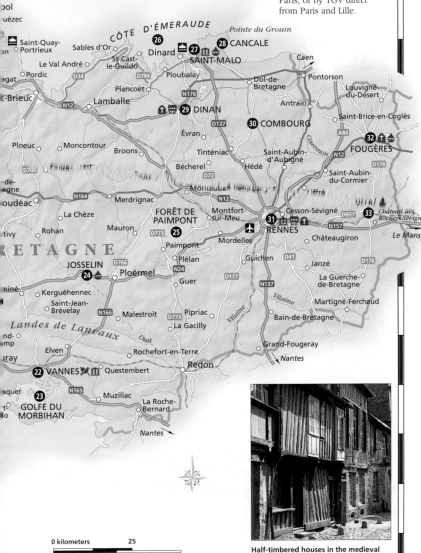

Half-timbered houses in the medieval part of Rennes

0 kilometers 25

0 miles 25

Île d'Ouessant ➊

Finistère. 🏘 930. ✈ Ouessant
(via Brest). 🚂 Brest, then boat.
🚢 Le Conquet, then boat. ℹ️ pl de
l'Eglise, Lampaul (02 98 48 85 83).
www.ot-ouessant.fr

A well-known Breton proverb
declares "He who sees
Ouessant sees his own blood."
Also known as Ushant, the
island is notorious among
sailors for its fierce storms and
strong currents. However, this
westerly point of France has a
pleasant climate in summer
and, though often bleak and
stormy, can be surprisingly
mild in winter. Part of the Parc
Naturel Régional d'Armorique,
the windswept island supports
migrating birds and a small
seal population, which may
be observed from the Pern
and Pen-ar-Roc'h headlands.

Two museums shed light on
the island's defiant history,
dogged by shipwreck and
tragedy. At Niou Uhella, the
Ecomusée d'Ouessant has
furniture made from driftwood
and wrecks, often painted blue
and white in honor of the
Virgin Mary. Nearby at Phare
du Créac'h, the **Musée des
Phares et Balises** explains the
history of Brittany's many
lighthouses and their keepers.

🏛 **Ecomusée d'Ouessant**
Maison du Niou. **Tel** 02 98 48 86
37. ⏷ Apr–Sep: daily; Oct–Mar:
Tue–Sun pms. ▨ ♿

🏛 **Musée des Phares et Balises**
Pointe de Créac'h. **Tel** 02 98 48 80
70. ⏷ Apr–Sep: daily; Oct–Mar:
Tue–Sun pms. ▨

Brest ➋

Finistère. 🏘 153,000. ✈ 🚂 🚢
🛥 to islands only. ℹ️ place de
la Liberté (02 98 44 24 96).
🛒 daily. **www**.brest-metropole-
tourisme.fr

A natural harbor protected by
the Presqu'île de Crozon,
Brest is France's premier
Atlantic naval port with a rich
maritime history. Heavily
bombed during World War II,
it is now a modern commercial city where cargo vessels,
yachts, and fishing boats ply
the waters. The Cours Dajot

Windswept moorlands near Ménez-Meur, Parc Régional d'Armorique

promenade has good views
of the Rade de Brest. The
Château houses a naval museum with historic maps, maritime paintings, model ships,
carved wooden figureheads,
and nautical instruments.

Across the Penfeld river –
reached by Europe's largest
lifting bridge, the Pont de
Recouvrance – is the 14th-
century **Tour de la Motte
Tanguy**. By the Port de
Plaisance, **Océanopolis** "sea
center" has three vast pavilions simulating temperate,
tropical, and polar ecosystems.

⚓ **Château de Brest**
Tel 02 98 22 12 39. ⏷ Apr–Sep:
daily; Oct–Dec & Feb–Mar: pms only
daily. ⏺ May 1, Dec 25. ▨

🏯 **Tour de la Motte Tanguy**
Sq Pierre Peron. **Tel** 02 98 00 88 60.
⏷ Jun–Sep: daily; Oct–May: Wed–
Thu, Sat–Sun pms. ⏺ Jan 1, May 1,
Dec 25.

🐋 **Océanopolis**
Port de Plaisance du Moulin Blanc.
Tel 02 98 34 40 40. ⏷ mid-Apr–
Sep: daily; Oct–mid-Apr: Tue–Sun.
⏺ 2 wks Jan, Dec 25. ▨ ♿ ℹ️
🖥 **www**.oceanopolis.com

Traditional boatbuilding at Le Port
Musée, Douarnenez

Parc Naturel
Régional
d'Armorique ➌

Finistère. ✈ Brest. 🚂 Chateaulin,
Landernau. 🚢 Le Faou, Huelgoat,
Carhaix. ℹ️ Le Faou (02 98 81 90 08).

The Armorican Regional
Nature Park stretches west
from the moorlands of the
Monts d'Arrée to the Presqu'île
de Crozon and Ile d'Ouessant.
Within this protected area lies
a mixture of farmland, heaths,
remains of ancient oak forest
and wild, open spaces. The
park and its scenic coastline
is ideal for walking, riding,
and touring by bicycle or car.

Huelgoat is a good starting
point for inland walks, while
Ménez-Hom (1,082 ft/330 m)
at the beginning of the Crozon
Peninsula, has excellent views.

The main information centrer
for the park is at **Le Faou**.
Nearby at **Ménez-Meur** is a
wooded estate with wild and
farm animals, and a Breton
horse museum. Scattered
around the park are 16 small,
specialist museums, some
paying tribute to country
traditions like hunting, fishing, and tanning. The **Musée
de l'Ecole Rurale** at Trégarvan
recreates an early 20th-century
rural school, while other
museums cover subjects as
diverse as medieval monastic
life, junk dealers, and the lifestyle of a Breton country
priest. Contemporary crafts and
art can be seen at the **Maison
des Artisans** in Brasparts.

Douarnenez ❹

Finistère. 🏠 16,700. 🖼
🛈 2 rue du Docteur Mével (02 98
92 13 35). 🖼 Mon–Sat.
www.douarnenez-tourisme.com

At the start of this century
Douarnenez used to be
France's leading sardine port;
today it is still devoted to
fishing, but is also a tourist
resort with beaches on both
sides of the Pouldavid estuary.

Nearby lies the tiny **Île
Tristan**, linked with the tragic
love story of Tristan and Iseult.
In the 16th century it was the
stronghold of a notorious
brigand, La Fontenelle.

The picturesque **Port du
Rosmeur** offers cafés, fish
restaurants, and boat trips
around the bay, with a lively
early morning *criée* (fish
auction) held in the nearby
Nouveau Port. The Port-Rhu
has been turned into a floating
museum, **Le Port Musée**, with
over 100 boats and several
shipyards. Some of the larger
vessels can be visited.

🏛 **Le Port Musée**
Pl de l'Enfer. **Tel** 02 98 92 65 20.
☐ Jul–Aug: daily; Sep–Jun: Wed–
Mon. 🗐 🛦 www.port-musee.org

**Locronan's 15th-century Eglise
St-Ronan, seen from the churchyard**

Locronan ❺

Finistère. 🏠 1,000. 🛈 pl de la
Mairie (02 98 91 70 14).
www.locronan.org

During the 15th–17th
centuries Locronan grew
wealthy from the manufacture
of sail-cloth. After Louis XIV
ended the Breton monopoly
on this trade, the town
declined – leaving an elegant

The awe-inspiring cliffs at Pointe du Raz

ensemble of Renaissance
buildings that attract many
visitors. In the town's central
cobbled square stands a late
15th-century church dedicated
to the Irish missionary
St. Ronan. Down Rue Moal is
the delightful **Chapelle Notre-
Dame-de-Bonne-Nouvelle**
with a calvary and a fountain.
Every July Locronan is the
scene of a *Troménie,* a
hilltop pilgrimage held in
honor of St. Ronan. The more
elaborate *Grande Troménie*
takes place every six years.

Pointe du Raz ❻

Finistère. 🚄 Quimper. 🚍 Quimper,
then bus. 🛈 Audierne (02 98 70 12
20); Maison du Site (02 98 70 67 18).
www.pointeduraz.com

The dramatic Pointe du Raz,
almost 262 ft (80 m) high, is a
headland jutting into the
Atlantic at the tip of Cap
Sizun. The views of jagged
rocks and pounding seas are
breathtaking. Further west is
the flat Ile de Sein and
beyond that the lighthouse of
Ar Men. Despite being only
5 ft (1.5 m) above sea level,

Ile de Sein is nevertheless
home to 260 inhabitants, and
can be reached by boat from
Audierne in an hour.

Pays Bigouden ❼

Finistère. 🚍 Pont l'Abbé. 🛈 Pont
l'Abbé (02 98 82 37 99).
www.ot-pontlabbe29.fr

Brittany's southwest tip
is known as the Pays
Bigouden, a windy peninsula
with proud and ancient traditions. The region is famous
for the women's tall *coiffes* still
worn at festivals and *pardons*
(see p243), which can also be
seen at the **Musée Bigouden**.

Along the Baie d'Audierne
is a brooding landscape of
hamlets and isolated chapels –
the 15th-century calvary at
Notre-Dame-de-Tronoën is the
oldest in Brittany. There are
invigorating sea views from
Pointe de la Torche (a good
surfing spot) and from the
Eckmühl lighthouse.

🏛 **Musée Bigouden**
Le Château, Pont l'Abbé. **Tel** 02 98
66 00 40. ☐ Apr–May: Tue–Sun
pms; Jun–Sep: daily. 🔴 May 1. 🗐

Quimper ⑧

Finistère. 🏠 *67,250.* ✈ 🚌 🚇
ℹ *pl de la Résistance (02 98 53 04 05).* 🚋 *Wed, Sat.* www.quimper-tourisme.com

The ancient capital of Cornouaille, Quimper has a distinctly Breton character. Here you can find Breton language books and music on sale, buy a traditional costume, and enjoy some of the best crêpes and cider in Brittany. Quimper gets its name from *kemper*, a Breton word meaning the confluence of two rivers, and the Steir and Odet still flow through this relaxed cathedral city.

West of the cathedral lies a pedestrianized area known as **Vieux Quimper**, full of stores, crêperies, and half-timbered houses. Rue Kéréon is the main thoroughfare, with the place au Beurre and the picturesque *hôtels particuliers* (mansions) of rue des Gentilshommes to the north.

Quimper has been producing faïence, elegant hand-painted pottery since 1690. The design often features decorative flowers and animals framed by blue and yellow borders. Now mainly decorative, faïence is today exported to collectors all over the world. In the southwest of the city lies the oldest factory, **Faïenceries HB-Henriot**, which is open to visitors all year round.

🔓 **Cathédrale St-Corentin**

Quimper's cathedral is dedicated to the city's founder-bishop St-Corentin. Begun in 1240 – its colorfully painted interior now restored – it is the earliest Gothic building in Lower Brittany, and was bizarrely constructed with its choir at a slight angle to the nave, perhaps to fit in with some since-disappeared buildings. The two spires of the west façade were added in 1856. Between them rides a statue of King Gradlon, the

The Martyrdom of St Triphine (1910) by Sérusier, Pont-Aven School

Typical faïence plate from Quimper

mythical founder of the drowned city of Ys. After this deluge he chose Quimper as his new capital and St-Corentin as his spiritual guide.

🏛 **Musée des Beaux-Arts**
40 pl St-Corentin. **Tel** *02 98 95 45 20.* ◯ *Jul–Aug: daily; Sep–Jun: Wed–Mon.* ⬤ *most public hols; Nov–Mar: Sun am.* 📷 ♿ www.musee-beauxarts.quimper.fr
Quimper's art museum is one of the best in the region. The collection is strong on late 19th- and early 20th-century artists, and their work – such as Jean-Eugène Buland's *Visite à Ste-Marie de Bénodet* – offers a valuable insight into the way visiting painters perpetuated a romantic view of Brittany. Also on show are works by members of the Pont-Aven School and local artists like J-J Lemordant and Max Jacob.

🏛 **Musée Départemental Breton**
1 rue de Roi-Gradlon. **Tel** *02 98 95 21 60.* ◯ *Jun–Sep: daily; Oct–May: Tue– Sat; Sun pm.* 📷 ♿
The 16th-century Bishop's Palace has collections of Breton costumes, furniture, and faïence, including Cornouaille *coiffes*, ornately carved box-beds and wardrobes, and turn-of-the-century tourist posters for Brittany.

Concarneau ⑨

Finistère. 🏠 *20,000.* 🚇 ⛴ *only for islands.* ℹ *quai d'Aiguillon (02 98 97 01 44).* 🚋 *Mon & Fri.* www.tourismeconcarneau.fr

An important fishing port, Concarneau's principal attraction is its 14th-century **Ville Close** (walled town), built on an island in the harbor and encircled by massive lichen-covered granite ramparts. Access is by bridge from place Jean Jaurès. Parts of the ramparts can be toured, and the narrow streets are full of shops and restaurants. The **Musée de la Pêche**, housed in the port's ancient barracks, explains the local techniques and history of sea-fishing.

🏛 **Musée de la Pêche**
3 rue Vauban. **Tel** *02 98 97 10 20.* ◯ *Feb–Sep: daily.* ⬤ *public hols.* 📷 ♿

Fishing boats in Concarneau's busy harbor

Pont-Aven ❿

Finistère. 🏠 3,000. 🚇 🚌 5 pl de
l'Hôtel de Ville (02 98 06 04 70).
🚢 Tue, Sat. www.pontaven.com

Once a market town of
"14 mills and 15 houses,"
Pont-Aven's picturesque
location in the wooded Aven
estuary made it attractive to
many late 19th-century artists.
In 1888 Paul Gauguin,
along with like-minded painters Emile Bernard and Paul
Sérusier, developed a crude,
colorful style of painting
known as Synthetism.
Drawing inspiration from the
Breton landscape and its
people, the Ecole de Pont-
Aven (Pont-Aven School)
worked here and in nearby
Le Pouldu until 1896.
The town is devoted to art
and has 50 private galleries,
along with the informative
Musée de Pont-Aven which
documents the artistic activities
of the Pont-Aven School. The
surrounding woods proved
inspirational to many artists,
and offer pleasant walks –
one leads through the Bois
d'Amour to the Chapelle de
Trémalo, where the wooden
Christ in Gauguin's Le Christ
Jaune still hangs.

🏛 Musée de Pont-Aven
Pl de l'Hôtel de Ville. Tel 02 98 06
14 43. ◯ daily. ⬤ early Jan–mid-
Feb; between exhibitions. 🈶 ♿
🎫 📷

Notre-Dame-de-Kroaz-Baz, Roscoff

Le Pouldu ⓫

Finistère. 🏠 4,000. 🚇 🚌 Pouldu
Plage, rue C. Filiger (02 98 39 93 42).

A quiet port at the mouth of
the river Laïta, Le Pouldu has
a small beach and good
walks. Its main attraction is
Maison Musée du Pouldu, a
reconstruction of the inn
where Paul Gauguin and other
artists stayed between 1889
and 1893. They covered every
inch of the dining room,
including the windowpanes,
with self-portraits, caricatures,
and still-lifes. These were
discovered in 1924 beneath
layers of wallpaper.

🏛 Maison Musée du Pouldu
10 rue des Grands Sables. Tel 02 98
39 98 51. ◯ Apr–Oct (call for hours).
🈶 www.museedupouldu.clohars-
carnoet.fr

Roscoff ⓬

Finistère. 🏠 3,690. 🚇 🚌 ⛴ 🚌
quai d'Auxerre (02 98 61 12 13). 🚢
Wed. www.roscoff-tourisme.com

Once a Corsairs' haunt,
Roscoff is a thriving Channel
port and seaside resort. Signs
of its wealthy seafaring past
can be found in the old port,
along rue Amiral Réveillère
and in place Lacaze-Duthiers.
Here the granite façades of the
16th- and 17th-century ship-
owners' mansions, and the
weather-beaten caravels and
cannon decorating the 16th-
century **Eglise Notre-Dame-
de-Kroaz-Baz**, testify to the
days when the privateers of
Roscoff were as notorious as
those of St-Malo (see p282).
The famous French onion
sellers (Johnnies) first crossed
the Channel in 1828, selling
their braided onions door to
door. The **Maison des Johnnies**
tells their colorful history. The
Thalado is an informative seaweed exhibition center. From
the harbor you can take a
boat trip to the peaceful **Ile de
Batz**. Near Pointe de Bloscon
are tropical gardens.

🏛 Maison des Johnnies
48 rue Brizeux. Tel 02 98 61 25 48.
◯ mid-Jun–mid-Sep: Mon, Tue,
Thu, & Fri pms. ⬤ Jan. 🈶

🏛 Thalado
5 rue Victor Hugo. Tel 02 98 69
77 05. ◯ daily. ⬤ Sep–mid-Jul:
Sun. 🈶

PAUL GAUGUIN IN BRITTANY

**Carving,
Chapelle
de Trémalo**

Paul Gauguin's (1848–1903)
story reads like a romantic
novel. At the age of 35 he left
his career as a stockbroker to
become a full-time painter.
From 1886 to 1894 he lived and
worked in Brittany, at Pont-Aven and Le
Pouldu, where he painted the landscape
and its people. He chose to concentrate
on the intense, almost "primitive" quality
of the Breton Catholic faith, attempting to
convey it in his work. This is evident in
Le Christ Jaune (Yellow Christ), inspired
by a woodcarving in the Trémalo chapel. In
Gauguin's painting, the Crucifixion is a reality
in the midst of the contemporary Breton
landscape, rather than a remote or symbolic
event. This theme recurs in many of his
paintings from the period, including Jacob
Wrestling with the Angel (1888).

Le Christ Jaune (1889) by Paul Gauguin

St-Thégonnec ⑬

Finistère. 🚉 🅿 *daily.* ♿

This is one of the most complete parish closes in Brittany. Passing through its triumphal archway, the ossuary is to the left. The calvary, directly ahead, was built in 1610 and perfectly illustrates the extraordinary skills Breton sculptors developed as they worked with the local granite. Among the many animated figures surrounding the central cross, a small niche contains a statue of St-Thégonnec with a cart pulled by wolves.

Guimiliau ⑭

Finistère. 🅿 *daily.* ♿

Almost 200 figures adorn Guimiliau's intensely decorated calvary (1581–88), many wearing 16th-century dress. Among them you can contemplate the legendary torment of Katell Gollet, a servant girl tortured by demons for stealing a consecrated wafer to please her lover.

The church is dedicated to St-Miliau and has a richly decorated south porch. The baptistry's elaborate carved oak canopy dates from 1675.

Font canopy from 1675, Guimiliau

Lampaul-Guimiliau ⑮

Finistère. 🅿 *daily.* ♿

Entering through the monumental gate, the chapel and ossuary lie to the left, while the calvary is to the right. Here, however, it is the church that demands most attention. The interior is zealously painted and carved, including some naive scenes from the Passion depicted along the 16th-century rood-beam dividing the nave and choir.

Parish Closes

Reflecting the religious fervor of the Bretons, the Enclos Paroissiaux (parish closes) were built during the 15th–18th centuries. At that time Brittany had few urban centers but many wealthy rural settlements that profited from maritime trading and the manufacture of cloth. Grand religious monuments, some taking over 200 years to complete, were built by small villages inspired by spiritual zeal and the more earthly desire to rival their neighbors. Some of the finest parish closes lie in the Elorn valley, linked by a well-signposted Circuit des Enclos Paroissiaux.

The enclosure, *surrounded by a stone wall, is the hallowed area. By following the wall, visitors are drawn towards the triumphal arch, shown here in Pleyben.*

The small cemetery reflects the size of the community that built these great churches.

GUIMILIAU PARISH CLOSE

The three essential features of a parish close are a triumphal gateway marking the entry into the hallowed enclosure, a calvary depicting scenes from the Passion and Crucifixion, and an ossuary beside the church porch.

The calvary *is unique to Brittany, and may have been inspired by the crosses set on top of menhirs (see p279) by the early Christians. They provide a walk-around Bible lesson, often with the characters in 17th-century costumes as in this example from St-Thégonnec.*

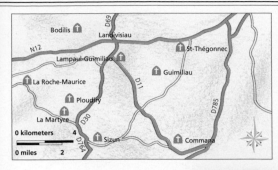

Brittany's parish closes *are mostly in the Elorn Valley. As well as St-Thégonnec, Lampaul-Guimiliau, and Guimiliau, other parish closes to visit include Bodilis, La Martyre, La Roche-Maurice, Ploudiry, Sizun, and Commana. Farther afield lie Plougastel-Daoulas and Pleyben, while Guéhenno is in the Morbihan region.*
🛈 *rue de Kerven, Landivisiau (02 98 68 33 33).*

Church interiors *are usually adorned with depictions of local saints and scenes from their lives, along with ornately carved beams and furniture. This is the altarpiece in Guimiliau.*

In the ossuary bones exhumed from the cemetery would be stored. Built close to the church entrance, the ossuary was considered a bridge between the living and the dead.

Church

South Porch

Calvary

Funeral Chapel

Field of the Dead

Triumphal Arch

The triumphal arch *at St-Thégonnec, a monumental entrance, heralds the worshipper's arrival on sacred ground, like the righteous entering heaven.*

Carvings in stone *were created as biblical cartoons to instruct and inspire visitors. Their clear message is now often obscured by weather and lichen, but this one in St-Thégonnec is well preserved.*

The chapel of Notre-Dame, perched on the cliffs above the beach of Port-Blanc, Côte de Granit Rose

Côte de Granit Rose ⓰

Côtes d'Armor. ✈ 🚊 🚌 *Lannion.*
🅸 *Lannion (02 96 46 41 00).* 🄳
Thu. **www**.ot-lannion.fr

The coast between Paimpol and Trébeurden is known as the Côte de Granit Rose due to its pink cliffs. These are best between Trégastel and Trébeurden; their granite is also used in neighboring towns. The coast between Trébeurden and Perros-Guirec is one of Brittany's most popular family vacation areas.

Farther east there are quieter beaches and coves, as at **Trévou-Tréguignec** and **Port-Blanc**. Beyond Tréguier, **Paimpol** is a working fishing port that once sent huge cod and whaling fleets to fish off Iceland and Newfoundland.

Tréguier ⓱

Côtes d'Armor. 🏠 *2,950.*
🅸 *13 pl de l'Eglise, Penvenan (02 96 92 81 09).* 🄳 *Wed.*

Overlooking the estuary of the Jaundy and Guindy rivers, Tréguier stands apart from the resorts of the Côte de Granit Rose. It is a typically Breton market town, with one main attraction, the 14th–15th-century **Cathédrale St-Tugdual**. It has three towers: one Gothic, one Romanesque, and one 18th-century. The last, financed by Louis XVI with winnings from the Paris Lottery, has holes in the shapes of playing card suits.

Environs
Chapelle St-Gonery in Plougrescant has a leaning lead spire and a 15th-century painted wooden ceiling.

Ile de Bréhat ⓲

Côtes d'Armor. 🏠 *420.* 🚊 🚌
Paimpol, then bus to Pointe de l'Arcouest (Mon–Sat winter; daily summer), then boat. 🅸 *Paimpol (02 96 20 83 16).* **www**.paimpol-goelo.com

A 15-minute crossing from the Pointe de l'Arcouest, the Ile de Bréhat is actually two islands, joined by a bridge, which together are only 2.2 miles (3.5 km) long. With motorized traffic banned, and a climate mild enough for mimosa and a variety of fruit trees to flourish, it has a relaxing atmosphere. Bicycle rental and boat tours are available in the main town, **Port-Clos**, and you can walk to the island's highest point, the **Chapelle St-Michel**.

Chapelle St-Michel, a landmark on Ile de Bréhat

Carnac ⓳

Morbihan. 🏠 *4,600.* 🚌 🅸 *74 avenue des Druides (02 97 52 13 52).* **www**.ot-carnac.fr

Carnac, a popular seaside resort, is also one of the world's great prehistoric sites, with almost 3,000 menhirs in parallel rows, and an excellent **Musée de Préhistoire**.

The 17th-century **Eglise St-Cornély** is dedicated to St. Cornelius, patron saint of horned animals. His life is depicted on its ceiling.

♉ Maison des Megaliths
Tel *02 97 52 29 81.* 🄳 *daily.*
🄲 *Jan 1, May 1, Dec 25.* 🅿
summer only. 🅿 *oblig. Apr–Sep.*

🏛 Musée de Préhistoire
10 pl de la Chapelle. **Tel** *02 97 52 22 04.* 🄳 *Feb–Jun & Sep–Dec: Wed–Mon; Jul–Aug: daily.*
🄲 *Jan, May 1, Dec 25.* 🄳 ♿

Presqu'île de Quiberon ⓴

Morbihan. 🏠 *5,200.* ✈ *Quiberon (via Lorient).* 🚊 *Jul–Aug.* 🚌 🚌
Quiberon. 🅸 *Quiberon (08 25 13 56 00).* 🄳 *Sat, Wed (summer).*
www.quiberon.com

Once an Island, the slender Quiberon peninsula has a bleak west coast with sea-punished cliffs, known as the Côte Sauvage. The east is more benign. At the peninsula's southern tip is the fishing port and resort of **Quiberon**, with a car ferry to Belle-Ile. In 1795 10,000 Royalist troops were massacred here in an ill-fated attempt to reverse the French Revolution.

Brittany's Prehistoric Monuments

At Carnac, thousands of ancient granite rocks were arranged in mysterious lines and patterns by Megalithic tribes as early as 4,000 BC. Their original purpose remains obscure: the significance was probably religious, but the precise patterns also suggest an early astronomical calendar. Celts, Romans and Christians have since adapted them to their own beliefs.

The Gavrinis Tumulus, Golfe du Morbihan

MEGALITHS

There are many different formations of megaliths, all with a particular purpose. Words from the Breton language, such as *men* (stone), *dole* (table), and *hir* (long), are still used to describe them.

Menhirs, the most common of megaliths, are upright stones standing alone or arranged in lines. Those in circles are known as cromlechs.

Dolmen, *two upright stones roofed by a third, were used as a burial chamber, such as the Merchant's Table at Locmariaquer.*

Allée couverte, *upright stones placed in a row and roofed to form a covered alley, can be seen at Carnac.*

A tumulus *is a dolmen covered with stones and soil to form a burial mound.*

KEY

- Megalithic sites
- Alignments

0 kilometers   5

0 miles   5

Brittany's major megalithic sites

BAIE DE QUIBERON

Carnac

Gavrinis

Quiberon

Alignment at Carnac

Menhirs of all shapes in a field near Carnac

Belle-Île-en-Mer  ㉑

Morbihan. 🚩 5,200. ✈ Quiberon (via Lorient). 🚢 from Quiberon. 🛈 quai Bonnelle, Le Palais (02 97 31 81 93). 🏪 daily. **www.**belle-ile.com

Brittany's largest island lies 9 miles (14 km) south of Quiberon and can be reached in 45 minutes by car ferry from Quiberon. The coast has cliffs and good beaches; inland lie exposed highlands intersected by sheltered valleys. In the main town, Le Palais, stands the **Citadelle Vauban**, a 16th-century star-shaped fortress, and there are fine walks and views along the southern Côte Sauvage.

Cloisters of St-Pierre in Vannes

Vannes ㉒

Morbihan. 🚩 58,000. 🚌 🚆 🛈 1 quai Tabarly (08 25 13 56 10). 🏪 Wed & Sat. **www.**tourisme-vannes.com

Standing at the head of the Golfe du Morbihan, Vannes was the capital of the Veneti, a seafaring Armorican tribe defeated by Caesar in 56 BC. In the 9th century Nominoë, the first Duke of Brittany, made it his power base. The city remained influential up until the signing of the union with France in 1532, when Rennes became the Breton capital. Today it is a busy commercial city with a well-preserved medieval quarter, and a good base for exploring the Golfe du Morbihan.

The impressive eastern walls of old Vannes can be viewed from the promenade de la Garenne. Two of the city's old gates survive at either end: Porte-Prison in the

Breton seafarer, off Belle-Ile's coast

north, and the southern Porte-Poterne with a row of 17th-century wash houses close by.

Walking up from Porte St-Vincent, you find the city's old market squares, still in use today. The **place des Lices** was once the scene of medieval tournaments and the streets around the rue de la Monnaie are full of well-preserved 16th-century houses.

Begun in the 13th century, **Cathédrale St-Pierre** has since been drastically remodeled and restored. The Chapel of the Holy Sacrament houses the revered tomb of Vincent Ferrier, a Spanish saint who died in Vannes in 1419.

Opposite the west front of the cathedral, the old covered market **La Cohue** (meaning throng or hubbub) was once the city's central meeting place. Parts of the building date from the 13th century, and a small museum inside displays art and artifacts relevant to the history of the area.

Housed in the 15th-century Château Gaillard, the **Musée**

d'Histoire is a rich assembly of finds from Morbihan's many prehistoric sites, including jewelry, pottery, and weapons. There is also a gallery of medieval and Renaissance *objets d'art*.

🏛 **Musée d'Histoire**
Château Gaillard, 2 rue Noé. **Tel** 02 97 01 63 00. 🕐 Jun–Sep: daily. ⬤ public hols. 📷

Environs
To the south of the city the **Parc du Golfe** is a beautiful leisure park with many amusements, a butterfly greenhouse, an automaton museum, and an aquarium that boasts over 400 species of fish. Northeast of Vannes, off the N166, lie the romantic ruins of the 15th-century **Tours d'Elven**.

Golfe du Morbihan ㉓

Morbihan. ✈ Lorient. 🚆 🚌 🚢 Vannes. 🛈 Vannes (08 25 13 56 10). **www.**tourisme-vannes.com

Morbihan means "little sea" in Breton, an apt description for this landlocked expanse of tidal water. Only connected to the Atlantic by a small channel between the Locmariaquer and Rhuys peninsulas, the gulf is dotted with islands. Around 40 are inhabited, with the **Ile d'Arz** and the **Ile aux Moines** the largest. These are served by regular ferries from Conleau and Port-Blanc respectively.

Around the gulf several small harbors earn a living from fishing, oyster cultivation, and

The picturesque fishing port of Le Bono in Golfe du Morbihan

Young vacationers on the beach at Dinard, a classic seaside resort on the Emerald Coast

tourism. There is a wealth of megalithic sites, notably the island of **Gavrinis** where stone carvings have been excavated *(see p279)*. There are boat trips to Gavrinis from Larmor-Baden and around the gulf from Locmariaquer, Auray, Vannes, and Port Navalo.

The medieval Château de Josselin on the banks of the river Oust

Josselin ㉔

Morbihan. 🏠 2,500. 🚌 🏨 26 rue de Trente (02 97 22 36 43). 🅰 Sat. www.josselin-communaute.fr

Overlooking the river Oust, Josselin is dominated by a medieval **Château** owned by the de Rohan family since the end of the 15th century. Only four of its nine towers survive. The elaborate inner granite façade incorporates the letter "A" – a tribute to the much-loved Duchess Anne of Brittany (1477–1514), who presided over Brittany's "Golden Age." Tours are given of the 19th-century interior, and in the former stables there is a Musée des Poupées with 600 dolls. In the town, **Basilique Notre-Dame-du-Roncier**

contains the mausoleum of the castle's most famous owner and constable of France, Olivier de Clisson (1336–1407). West of Josselin at Kerguéhennec, the grounds of an 18th-century château have become a modern sculpture park.

🏯 **Château de Josselin**
Tel 01 97 22 36 45. ☐ Apr–Sep: daily (Apr–mid-Jul: pms); Oct: Sat & Sun pms. 🎦 🅯 www.chateau josselin.com

Forêt de Paimpont ㉕

Ille-et-Vilaine. 🚂 Rennes. 🚌 Monfort-sur-Meu. 🚍 Rennes. ℹ️ Montauban de Bretagne (02 99 06 86 07).

Also known as the Forêt de Brocéliande, this is a remnant of the dense primeval woods that once covered much of Armorica. It has long been associated with the legends of King Arthur, and visitors still

Legendary sorcerer Merlin and Viviane, the Lady of the Lake

search for the magical spring where the sorcerer Merlin first met the Lady of the Lake. The small village of **Paimpont** is a good base for exploring both the forest and its myths.

Côte d'Emeraude ㉖

Ille et Vilaine & Côtes d'Armor. 🚂 ✈ Dinard–St-Malo. 🚌 🚍 ℹ️ Dinard (02 99 46 94 12). www.ot-dinard.com

Between Le Val-André and the Pointe du Grouin, near Cancale, sandy beaches, rocky headlands, and classic seaside resorts stretch along Brittany's northern shore. Known as the Emerald Coast, its self-proclaimed Queen is the aristocratic resort of **Dinard**, "discovered" in the 1850s and still playing host to the international rich.

To its west are resorts like St-Jacut-de-la-Mer, St-Cast-le-Guildo, Sables d'Or-les-Pins, and Erquy, all with tempting beaches. In the Baie de la Frênaye, the medieval **Fort La Latte** provides good views from high in its ancient watchtower, while the light-house that dominates **Cap Fréhel** nearby offers even more extensive panoramas.

East of Dinard, the D186 runs across the **Barrage de la Rance** to St-Malo. Built in 1966 it was the world's first dam to generate electricity by using tidal power. Beyond St-Malo, coves and beaches surround La Guimorais, while around the Pointe du Grouin the seas are often truly emerald.

SEAFARERS OF ST-MALO

St-Malo owes its wealth and reputation to the exploits of its mariners. In 1534 Jacques Cartier, born in nearby Rothéneuf, discovered the mouth of the St. Lawrence river in Canada and claimed the territory for France. It was Breton sailors who voyaged to South America in 1698 to colonize the Iles Malouines, known today as Las Malvinas or the Falklands. By the 17th century St-Malo was the largest port in France and famous for its corsairs – privateers licensed by the king to prey on foreign ships. The most illustrious were the swashbuckling René Duguay-Trouin (1673–1736), who captured Rio de Janeiro from the Portuguese in 1711, and the intrepid Robert Surcouf (1773–1827), whose ships hounded vessels of the British East India Company. The riches won by trade and piracy enabled St-Malo's ship-owners to build great mansions known as *malouinières*.

Explorer Jacques Cartier (1491–1557)

St-Malo ㉗

Ille-et-Vilaine. 🏛 53,000. ✈ 🚉
🚌 ⛴ 🛈 esplanade St-Vincent
(08 25 13 52 00). 🛒 Tue & Fri.
www.saint-malo-tourisme.com

Once a fortified island, St-Malo stands in a commanding position at the mouth of the river Rance.

The city is named after Maclou, a Welsh monk who came here in the 6th century to spread the Christian message. During the 16th–19th centuries the port won prosperity and power through the exploits of its seafarers. St-Malo was heavily bombed in 1944 but has since been scrupulously restored and is now a major port and ferry terminal as well as a resort.

The old city is encircled by ramparts that provide fine views of St-Malo and its islands. Take the steps up by the **Porte St-Vincent** and walk clockwise, passing the 15th-century **Grande Porte**.

Within the city is a web of cobbled streets with tall 18th-century buildings housing stores, fish restaurants, and crêperies. Rue Porcon-de-la-Barbinais leads to **Cathédrale St-Vincent**, with its somber 12th-century nave contrasting with the stained glass of the chancel. On cour La Houssaye, the 15th-century Maison de la Duchesse Anne has been carefully restored.

St-Malo seen at low tide through the gate of Fort National

♜ Château de St-Malo

Pl Châteaubriand, near the Marina.
Tel 02 99 40 71 57. 🕙 Apr–Sep: daily; Oct–Mar: Tue–Sun. 🔴 Jan 1, May 1, Nov 1 & 11, Dec 25. 🎟
St-Malo's castle dates from the 14th–15th centuries. The great keep contains a museum of the city's history, including the adventures of its state-sponsored corsairs. From its watch towers there is an impressive view. Nearby, in the place Vauban, a tropical aquarium has been built into the ramparts, while on the edge of town, the Grand Aquarium has a shark tank and simulated submarine rides.

🏰 Fort National

🕙 Jun–Sep: daily at low tide. 🎟
Constructed in 1689 by Louis XIV's famous military architect, Vauban, this fort can be reached on foot at low tide

and offers good views of St-Malo and its ramparts. At low tide you can also walk out to **Petit Bé Fort** (open Easter–mid-Nov) and **Grand Bé**, where St-Malo-born writer François-René de Chateaubriand lies buried. From the top there are great views along the whole of Côte d'Emeraude (see p281).

🏰 Tour Solidor

St-Servan. **Tel** 02 99 40 71 58. 🕙 Apr–Oct: daily; Nov–Mar: Tue–Sun. 🔴 Jan 1, May 1, Nov 1 & 11, Dec 25. 🎟
To the west of St-Malo in St-Servan, the three-towered Tour Solidor was built in 1382. Formerly a toll house, it was also a prison under the Revolution, and now houses an intriguing museum devoted to the ships and sailors that rounded Cape Horn, with ship models, logs, and various nautical instruments.

Environs

When the tide is out, good beaches are revealed around St-Malo and in the nearby suburbs of St-Servan and Paramé. A passenger ferry runs to Dinard in summer (see p281) and the Channel Islands and there are boat trips up the Rance to Dinan, and out to the Iles Chausey, Ile de Cézembre, and Cap Fréhel.

At Rothéneuf you can visit the **Manoir Limoëlou**, home of the navigator Jacques Cartier. Nearby, on the coast, Les Rochers Sculptés is a

Cancale oysters, prized for their taste since Roman times

beguiling array of granite faces and figures carved into the cliffs by a local priest, Abbé Fouré, at the end of the 19th century.

☗ Manoir Limoëlou
Rue D. Macdonald-Stuart, Limoëlou-Rothéneuf. **Tel** 02 99 40 97 73. ◯ Jul–Aug: daily. ● public hols. 🖼 🎫 oblig. ♿

Cancale 28

Ille-et-Vilaine. 🏘 5,350. 🚆
🛈 44 rue du Port (02 99 89 63 72).
🚍 Sun. **www**.cancale-tourisme.fr

A small port with views across the Baie du Mont-St-Michel, Cancale is entirely devoted to the cultivation and consumption of oysters. Prized by the Romans, the acclaimed flavor of Cancale's oysters is said to derive from the strong tides that wash over them daily. You can survey the beds from a *sentier des douaniers* (coastguards' footpath, the GR34) running along the cliffs.

There are plenty of opportunities for sampling the local specialty provided by a multitude of bars and restaurants along the busy quays of the Port de la Houle, where the fishing boats arrive at high tide. Devotees should pay a visit to the **Musée de l'Huître, du Coquillage et de la Mer.**

🏛 Musée de l'Huître, du Coquillage et de la Mer – La Ferme Marine
Aurore. **Tel** 02 99 89 69 99.
◯ mid-Feb–Jun & mid-Sep–Oct: Mon–Fri pms. 🎫 🖼

Dinan 29

Côtes d'Armor. 🏘 10,000. 🚆 🚍
🛈 9 rue du Château (02 96 87 69 76).
🚍 Thu. **www**.dinan-tourisme.com

Set on a hill overlooking the wooded Rance valley, Dinan is a modern market town with a medieval heart. Surrounded by ramparts, the well-kept, half-timbered houses and cobbled streets of its Vieille Ville have an impressive, unforced unity best appreciated by climbing to the top of its 15th-century **Tour d'Horloge**, in rue de l'Horloge. Nearby, **Basilique St-Sauveur** contains the heart of Dinan's most famous son, the 14th-century warrior Bertrand du Guesclin.

Behind the church, Les Jardins Anglais offer good views of the river Rance and the viaduct spanning it. A couple of streets farther north, the steep, geranium-decorated rue du Jerzual winds down through the 14th-century town gate to the port. Once a busy harbor from which cloth was shipped, it is now a quiet backwater where you can take a pleasure cruise, or walk along a towpath to the restored 17th-century **Abbaye St-Magloire** at Léhon.

The **Musée du Château** houses a small museum of local history. Next to it is the 15th-century **Tour de Coëtquen**. From here are walks beside the ramparts along the promenade des Petits Fossés and the promenade des Grands Fossés.

♠ Musée du Château
Château de la Duchesse Anne, rue du Château. **Tel** 02 96 39 45 20. ◯ daily (Oct–May: pms only). ● Jan, 1 week Feb, public hols. 🖼

Author and diplomat François-René de Chateaubriand (1768–1848)

Combourg 30

Ille-et-Vilaine. 🏘 5,000. 🚆 🚍
🛈 23 pl Albert Parent (02 99 73 13 93). 🚍 Mon. **www**.combourg.org

A small, sleepy town beside a lake, Combourg is completely overshadowed by the great, haunting **Château de Combourg**. The buildings seen today date from the 14th and 15th centuries. In 1761 the château was bought by the Comte de Chateaubriand, and the melancholic childhood spent there by his son, the author and diplomat François-René de Chateaubriand (1768–1848), is candidly described in his entertaining chronicle, *Mémoires d'Outre-Tombe*.

Empty after the Revolution, the château was restored in the 19th century and is open for tours. One room has the belongings of François-René de Chateaubriand.

♠ Château de Combourg
23 rue des Princes. **Tel** 02 99 73 22 95. ◯ Apr–Jun & Sep–Oct: Mon–Fri & Sun pm; Jul–Aug: daily. 🎫 🖼
www.combourg.net

View over Dinan and the Gothic bridge crossing the river Rance

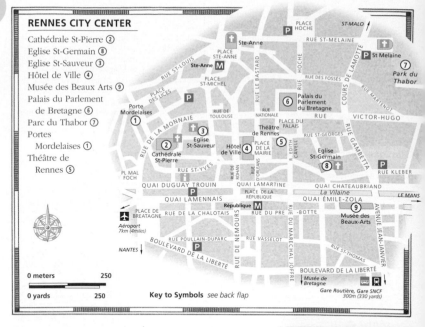

RENNES CITY CENTER

Cathédrale St-Pierre ②
Eglise St-Germain ⑧
Eglise St-Sauveur ③
Hôtel de Ville ④
Musée des Beaux Arts ⑨
Palais du Parlement
    de Bretagne ⑥
Parc du Thabor ⑦
Portes
    Mordelaises ①
Théâtre de
    Rennes ⑤

0 meters   250
0 yards   250

Key to Symbols *see back flap*

Rennes ③

Ille-et-Vilaine. 👥 214,800. ✈ 🚌 🚊 🛈
11 rue St-Yves (02 99 67 11 11). 🛒
Tue–Sat. www.tourisme-rennes.com

Founded by the Gauls and
colonized by the Romans,
Rennes is strategically located
where the Vilaine and Ille
rivers meet. After Brittany's
union with France in 1532, the
town became regional capital.
In 1720 a fire lasting for six
days devastated the city. Today
a small part of the medieval
city survives, together with
the neat grid of 18th-century

**The lively market at place des Lices
in the heart of Rennes**

buildings that arose from the
ashes. Around this historic
core are the tower blocks and
high-tech factories of modern
Rennes – a confident provincial
capital with two universities
and a thriving cultural life.
    Wandering through the
streets that radiate from the
place des Lices and the place
Ste-Anne, it is easy to imagine
what Rennes was like before
the Great Fire. Now mostly
pedestrianized, this area has
become the city's youthful
heart with plenty of bars,
crêperies and designer shops.
At the western end of rue de
la Monnaie stands the 15th-
century **Portes Mordelaises**,
once part of the city's ramparts.
    Close by, **Cathédrale St-Pierre**
was completed in 1844, the
third on this site. Note the
carved 16th-century Flemish
altarpiece. Nearby is the
18th-century **Eglise St-Sauveur**.
Just south of the attractive rue
St-George, **Eglise St-Germain**
has a typically Breton belfry
and wooden vaulting. In the
place de la Mairie stands the
early 18th-century **Hôtel de
Ville** and the Neo-Classical
Théâtre de Rennes. The **Parc
du Thabor**, once part of a
Benedictine monastery,
is ideal for walks and picnics.

**Half-timbered houses lining the
narrow streets of old Rennes**

🏛 Palais du Parlement
de Bretagne

Pl du Parlement. ☐ *Tourist Office
for guided tours (02 99 67 11 66).*
www.tourisme-rennes.com
Rennes' Law Courts, built in
1618–55, were the seat of
the region's governing body
until the Revolution. Severely
damaged by fire during riots
over fish prices in 1994, the
major restoration work is
all but complete, including the
unique coffered ceiling and
gilded woodwork of the
Grande Chambre. Today,
the Salle des Pas Perdus, with
its vaulted ceilings, can again
be admired by the public.

For hotels and restaurants in this region see pp566–8 and pp618–20

🏛 **Musée des Beaux Arts**
20 quai Zola. *Tel 02 23 62 17 45.*
⭕ *Tue–Sun.* ⚫ *public hols.* 📷
www.mbar.org. **Musée Bretagne** 10
cours des Alliés. *Tel 02 23 40 66 70.*
⭕ *Tue–Sun pms only.* ⚫ *public hols.*
📷 ♿ www.musee-bretagne.fr

The **Musée des Beaux Arts**
has a wide-ranging collection
of art from the 14th century to
the present, including a room
of art on Breton themes. There
are paintings by Gauguin,
Bernard, and other members of
the Pont-Aven School *(see p275)*,
and three works by Picasso,
including the lively *Baigneuse*
painted at Dinard in 1928.

Housed in the Rennes
cultural center along with the
Science Museum and Plane-
tarium, the **Musée de Bretagne**
includes examples of traditional
Breton furniture and costume,
and displays on Brittany's prehistoric megaliths, the growth
of Rennes, rural crafts, and
the fishing industry.

Environs

Just south of Rennes, the
Eco-musée du Pays de Rennes
traces the history of a local
farm since the 17th century.

Some 10 miles (16 km) to
the southeast of Rennes is
Châteaugiron, a charming
medieval village, with an
imposing castle and houses
preserving their wooden eaves.

🏛 **Ecomusée du Pays de
Rennes**
Ferme de la Bintinais, rte de
Châtillon-sur-Seiche. *Tel 02 99 51
38 15.* ⭕ *Apr–Sep: Tue–Sun; Oct–
Mar: Tue–Fri (Sat, Sun pm only).*
⚫ *public hols.* 📷 ♿ www.
ecomusee-rennes-metropole.fr

♣ **Château de Châteaugiron**
⭕ *mid-Jun–mid-Sep: daily;
call 02 99 37 89 02.* 📷

Fougères ❸❷

Ille-et-Vilaine. 🏠 *23,000.* 🚌
ℹ️ *2 rue Nationale (02 99 94 12 20).*
🚃 *Sat.* www.ot-fougeres.fr

A fortress town close to the
Breton border, Fougères rests
on a hill overlooking the
Nançon river. In the valley
below, and still linked to the
Haute Ville by a curtain of
ancient ramparts, stands the
mighty 11th–15th century

The mighty fortifications of Château de Fougères

Château de Fougères. To
get a good overview of the
château, go to the gardens of
place aux Arbres behind the
16th-century **Eglise St-Léonard**.
From here you can descend
to the river and the medieval
houses around place du
Marchix. The Flamboyant
Gothic **Eglise St-Sulpice**, with
its 18th-century wood-panelled
interior and granite retables,
is well worth visiting.

A walk around the castle's
massive outer fortifications
reveals the ambitious scale
of its construction, with
13 towers and walls over 10 ft
(3 m) thick. You can still climb
the castle's ramparts to get a
feel of what it was like to live
within its staggered defences.
Much of the action in Balzac's
novel *Les Chouans* (1829)
takes place in and around
Fougères and its castle.

♣ **Château de Fougères**
Pl Pierre-Simon. *Tel 02 99 99 79
59.* ⭕ *Feb–Dec: daily.* 📷
www.chateau-fougeres.com

Overhanging timber-frame houses
on rue Beaudrairie, Vitré

Vitré ❸❸

Ille-et-Vilaine. 🏠 *16,000.* 🚌 🚃
ℹ️ *pl Général de Gaulle
(02 99 75 04 46).* 🚃 *Mon & Sat.*
www.ot-vitre.fr

The fortified town of Vitré is
set high on a hill overlooking
the Vilaine valley. Its medieval
Château is complete with
pencil-point turrets and
picturesque 15th–16th century
buildings in attendance. The
castle was rebuilt in the
14th–15th centuries and
follows a triangular plan,
with some of its ramparts
walkable. There is a museum
in the Tour St-Laurent.

To the east, rue Beaudrairie
and rue d'Embas have overhanging timber-frame houses
with remarkable patterning.

The 15th–16th century
Cathédrale Notre-Dame, built
in Flamboyant Gothic style,
has a south façade with an
exterior stone pulpit. Further
along rue Notre-Dame, the
promenade du Val skirts
around the town's ramparts.

To the southeast of Vitré on
the D88, the **Château des
Rochers-Sévigné** was once the
home of Mme de Sévigné
(1626–96), famous letter-writer
and chronicler of life at the
court of Louis XIV. The park,
chapel and some of her
rooms are open to the public.

♣ **Château de Vitré**
Tel 02 99 75 04 54. ⭕ *Apr–Sep:
daily; Oct–Mar: Wed–Mon (closed
Sun am).* ⚫ *Jan 1, Easter,
Nov 1, Dec 25.* 📷

♣ **Château des Rochers-
Sévigné**
Tel 02 99 96 76 51. ⭕ *Apr–Sep:
daily; Oct–Mar: Fri–Sun pms.*
📷 ♿ *restricted.*

THE LOIRE VALLEY

E · INDRE-ET-LOIRE · LOIR-ET-CHER · LOIRET · EURE-ET-LOIR
R · VENDEE · MAINE-ET-LOIRE · LOIRE-ATLANTIQUE · SARTHE

enowned for its sumptuous châteaux, the glorious valley of the Loire, now classified a UNESCO World Heritage Site, is rich both in history and architecture. Like the river Loire, this vast region runs through the heart of French life. Its sophisticated cities, luxuriant landscape, and magnificent food and wine create a bourgeois paradise.

The lush Loire Valley is supremely regal. Orléans was France's intellectual capital in the 13th century, attracting artists, poets, and troubadours to the royal court. But the medieval court never stayed in one place for long, which led to the building of magnificent châteaux all along the Loire. Chambord and Chenonceau, the two greatest Renaissance châteaux, remain prestigious symbols of royal rule, resplendent amid vast hunting forests and waterways.

Due to its central location, culture, and fine cuisine, Tours is the natural visitors' capital. Angers is a close second but more authentic are the historic towns of Saumur, Amboise, Blois, and Beaugency, strung out like jewels along the river. This is the classic Loire Valley, a château trail which embraces the Renaissance gardens of Villandry and the fairytale turrets of Ussé. Venture northward and the cathedral cities of Le Mans and Chartres reign supreme, their medieval centers bordered by Gallo-Roman walls. Nantes in the west is a breezy, forward-looking port and gateway to the Atlantic.

Southward, the windswept Vendée is edged by a wild, sandy coastline that is perfect for windsurfers and nature lovers alike. Inland, the Loire's more peaceful tributaries and the watery Sologne beg to be explored. Also ripe for discovery are troglodyte caves, sleepy hamlets, and small Romanesque churches decorated with frescoes. Inviting inns offer game, fish, and abundant fresh vegetables to be lingered over with a light white Vouvray wine or a fruity Bourgeuil. Overindulgence is no sin in this rich region.

The river Loire at Montsoreau, southeast of Saumur

◁ The fairytale Château de Saumur towering above the town and the river Loire

Exploring the Loire Valley

The lush valley landscape, studded with France's greatest châteaux, is the main attraction. Numerous river cruises are available, while the sandy Atlantic coast offers beach holidays. Peaceful country holidays can be had in the Vendée, and in the Loir and Indre valleys. Wine tours focus on Bourgueil, Chinon, Muscadet, Saumur, and Vouvray vintages. The most charming bases are Amboise, Blois, Beaugency, and Saumur, but culture-lovers are well provided for throughout the region.

Countryside around Vouvray

The 16th-century Château de Villandry and its famous gardens

KEY

▬ Highway	
▬ Major road	▬ Main railroad
▬ Secondary road	--- Minor railroad
▬ Minor road	▬ Regional border
▬ Scenic route	△ Summit

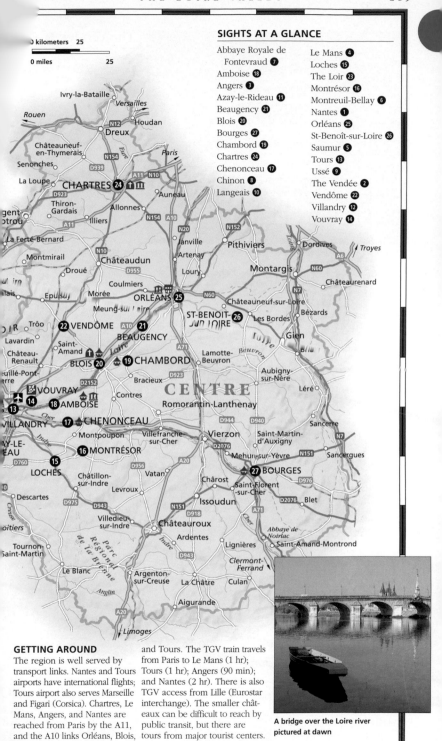

SIGHTS AT A GLANCE

Abbaye Royale de
  Fontevraud **7**
Amboise **18**
Angers **3**
Azay-le-Rideau **11**
Beaugency **21**
Blois **20**
Bourges **27**
Chambord **19**
Chartres **24**
Chenonceau **17**
Chinon **8**
Langeais **10**

Le Mans **4**
Loches **15**
The Loir **23**
Montrésor **16**
Montreuil-Bellay **6**
Nantes **1**
Orléans **25**
St-Benoît-sur-Loire **26**
Saumur **5**
Tours **13**
Ussé **9**
The Vendée **2**
Vendôme **22**
Villandry **12**
Vouvray **14**

0 kilometers 25
0 miles 25

A bridge over the Loire river
pictured at dawn

GETTING AROUND

The region is well served by
transport links. Nantes and Tours
airports have international flights;
Tours airport also serves Marseille
and Figari (Corsica). Chartres, Le
Mans, Angers, and Nantes are
reached from Paris by the A11,
and the A10 links Orléans, Blois,
and Tours. The TGV train travels
from Paris to Le Mans (1 hr);
Tours (1 hr); Angers (90 min);
and Nantes (2 hr). There is also
TGV access from Lille (Eurostar
interchange). The smaller châteaux can be difficult to reach by
public transit, but there are
tours from major tourist centers.

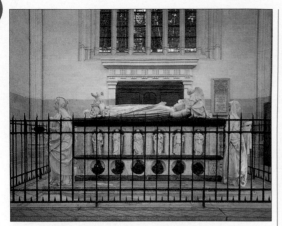

Tomb of François II and his wife, Marguerite de Foix, in Cathédrale St-Pierre

Nantes ❶

Loire-Atlantique. 🏛 270,000. ✈
🚉 🚌 🛈 3 cours Olivier-de-Clisson
(08 92 46 40 44). 🛒 Tue–Sun.
www.nantes-tourisme.com

For centuries, Nantes disputed with Rennes the title of capital of Brittany. Yet links with the Plantagenets and Henri IV also bound it to the "royal" river Loire. Since the 1790s it has officially ceased to be part of Brittany and, though still Breton at heart, it is today capital of the Pays de la Loire.

Visually, Nantes is a city of variety, with hi-tech towers overlooking the port, canals, and Art Nouveau squares. Chic bars and restaurants cram the medieval nucleus, bounded by place St-Croix and the château.

The **Cathédrale St-Pierre et St-Paul**, completed in 1893, is notable both for its sculpted Gothic portals and Renaissance tomb of François II, the last duke of Brittany.

More impressive is the **Château des Ducs de Bretagne**, where Anne of Brittany was born in 1477 and where the Edict of Nantes was signed by Henri IV in 1598, granting Protestants religious freedom. Following major restoration work, the château now houses the lively, interactive **Musée d'Histoire**. It charts the history of Nantes through 32 rooms of exhibits, including Turner's painting of the Loire embanments in Nantes and a virtual visit of the city in 1757.

♦ Château des Ducs de Bretagne
Pl Marc Elder. *Tel* 08 11 46 46 44.
🕐 Jul–Aug: daily; Sep–Jun: Wed–Mon. 🔴 Jan 1, May 1, Nov 1, Dec 25.
🎫 ♿

Environs
From Nantes, boats cruise the Erdre and Sèvre Nantaise rivers, passing châteaux and vineyards. Some 20 miles (30 km) southeast of Nantes is **Clisson**, a town razed to the ground during the Vendée Uprising of 1793, and later rebuilt by sculptor François-Frédéric Lemot along Italian lines, with Neo-Classical villas, and red-tiled roofs. On a spur overlooking the Sèvre Nantaise river is the ruined 13th-century **Château de Clisson**.

♦ Château de Clisson
Tel 02 40 54 02 22. 🕐 Wed–Mon (Oct–Apr: Wed–Mon pms only).
🔴 May 1, Christmas hols. 🎫 🎫

The Vendée ❷

Vendée and Maine-et-Loire.
✈ Nantes. 🚉 🚌 La Roche-sur-
🛈 La Roche-sur-Yon (02 51 36 00 ᴥ
www.vendee-tourisme.com

The counter-revolutionary movement which swept western France between 1793 and 1799 began as a series of uprisings in the Vendée, still an evocative name to the French. As a bastion of the *Ancien Régime*, the region rebelled against urban Republican values. But a violent massacre in 1793 left 80,000 royalists dead in one day as they tried to cross the Loire at St-Florent-le-Vieil. The Vendée farmers were staunch royalists, and, although they ultimately lost, the region remains colored by conservatism and religious fervor to this day.

This local history is dramatically retraced at **Le Puy du Fou** in Les Epesses, south of Cholet, with its spectacular summer evening live show, "Cinéscenie." More sober accounts are given at Logis de La Chabotterie near St-Sulpice-de-Verdon, and the Musée du Textile in Cholet, whose flax and hemp textiles provided the royalist heroes with their kerchiefs: originally white, then blood-red.

The tranquil Vendée offers green tourism inland, in the *bocage vendéen*, a wooded backwater with paths and nature trails. The Atlantic coast between the Loire and La Rochelle has beaches, yet the only sizeable resort here is **Les Sables d'Olonne**, with boat trips to the salt-marshes, out to sea, or to the nearby **Ile**

The harbor at Ile de Noirmoutier in the Vendée

d'Yeu. To the north, the marshy **Ile de Noirmoutier** is connected to the mainland at low tide via the Gois causeway.

Inland lies the remote **Marais Poitevin** *(see p408)*, its marshes home to bird sanctuaries and fine churches (Maillezais, Vix, Maillé) in hamlets bordered by canals. It is France's largest complex of manmade waterways, largely reclaimed for farming in the west, while farther east is a nature lover's paradise. Coulon is the main center for renting punts.

The Apocalypse Tapestry in Angers

Angers ❸

Maine-et-Loire. 🏠 156,300.
✕ 🚊 🚌 📘 7 pl Kennedy (02 41 23 50 00). 🚏 Tue–Sun.
www.angersloiretourisme.com

Angers is the historic capital of Anjou, home of the Plantagenets and gateway to the Loire Valley. The town has a formidable 13th-century **Château** *(see p242)*. Inside is the longest (338 ft) and one of the finest medieval tapestries in the world. It tells the story of the Apocalypse, with battles between hydras and angels.

A short walk from the castle is the **Cathédrale St-Maurice**, noted for its façade and 13th-century stained-glass windows. Close by is Maison d'Adam, with carvings showing the tree of life. The nearby **Galerie David d'Angers**, housed in the glass-covered ruins of a 13th-century church, celebrates the sculptor born in Angers. Across the river Maine, the Hôpital St-Jean, a hospital for the poor from 1174 to 1854, houses the **Musée Jean Lurçat**. Its prize exhibit is the exquisite *Chant du Monde* tapestry, which was created by Lurçat in 1957. In the same building is **Le Musée de la Tapisserie Contemporaine**, with displays of ceramics and paintings.

⛪ **Château d'Angers**
Tel 02 41 86 48 77. ⏲ daily. ⬤ Jan 1, May 1, Nov 1 & 11, Dec 25. 🎫 🎦

🏛 **Galerie David d'Angers**
33 bis rue Toussaint. **Tel** 02 41 05 38 90. ⏲ Jun–Sep: daily; Oct–May: Tue–Sun. ⬤ most public hols. 🎫

🏛 **Musée Jean Lurçat / Le Musée de la Tapisserie Contemporaine**
4 bd Arago. **Tel** 02 41 24 18 45. ⏲ Jun–Sep: daily; Oct–May: Tue–Sun. ⬤ most public hols. 🎫 ♿

Environs
Within a 13-mile (20-km) radius of Angers lie the Classical **Château de Serrant** and the moated **Château du Plessis-Bourré**, a decorative pleasure dome encased in a feudal shell. Follow the Loire east along the sandbanks and dykes, enjoying the fish restaurants en route.

⛪ **Château de Serrant**
St-Georges-sur-Loire. **Tel** 02 41 39 13 01. ⏲ call or check website for opening schedules. 🎫 🎦 oblig. 📷
www.chateau-serrant.net

⛪ **Château du Plessis-Bourré**
Ecuillé. **Tel** 02 41 32 06 72. ⏲ Jul–Aug: daily; Apr–Jun & Sep: Thu pm–Tue (Feb, Mar, Oct, Nov: Thu–Tue pms only). 🎫 🎦 oblig.
www.plessis-bourre.com

Le Mans ❹

Sarthe. 🏠 150,000. ✕ 🚊 🚌 📘 rue de l'Etoile (02 43 28 17 22). 🚏 Tue–Sun. **www**.lemanstourisme.com

Ever since Monsieur Bollée became the first designer to place an engine under a car hood, Le Mans has been synonymous with the motor trade. Bollée's son created an embryonic Grand Prix, since when the event *(see p37)* and associated **Musée Automobile**

Stained-glass Ascension window in the Cathédrale St-Julien, Le Mans

de la Sarthe have remained star attractions. Cité Plantagenét, the ancient fortified center, is surrounded by the greatest Roman walls in France, best seen from the quai Louis Blanc. Once insalubrious and abandoned, the area has been restored, and is now used for filming epics such as *Cyrano de Bergerac*, set among its Renaissance mansions, half-timbered houses, arcaded alleys, and tiny courtyards. The crowning point is the Gothic **Cathédrale St-Julien,** borne aloft by flying buttresses, with its Romanesque portal rivaling that of Chartres. Inside, the Angevin nave opens into a Gothic choir, complemented by sculpted capitals and a 12th-century Ascension window.

🏛 **Musée Automobile de la Sarthe**
9 pl Luigi Chinetti. **Tel** 02 43 72 72 24. ⏲ daily (call for hours). 🎫 ♿

Le Mans racetrack: a 1933 print from the French magazine *Illustration*

Saumur ⑤

Maine-et-Loire. 🏠 32,000. 🚉 ✈ ℹ
pl de la Bilange (02 41 40 20 60). 🛒 *Thu,
Sat.* www.saumur-tourisme.com

Saumur is celebrated for its
fairytale château, cavalry
school, mushrooms, and
sparkling wines. Its stone
mansions recall the city's
17th-century heyday, when it
was a bastion of Protestantism
and vied with Angers as the
intellectual capital of Anjou.

High above both town and
river is the turreted **Château
de Saumur**. The present
structure was
started in the 14th-
century by Louis I
of Anjou and
remodeled later by
his grandson, King
René. Collections
include medieval
sculpture and
equestrian exhibits.

The Military
Cavalry School,
established in
Saumur in 1814, led
to the creation of the **Musée
des Blindés**, which exhibits
150 different armored vehicles,
and the prestigious Cadre
Noir horse-riding formation.

The Château de Saumur and spire of St-Pierre seen from the Loire

**King René's
coat of arms**

Morning training sessions and
stable visits, along with
occasional evening performances, can be seen at the
Ecole Nationale d'Equitation.
The nearby subterranean
**Parc Pierre et
Lumière** (sculptures
in the tufa cave walls
of prominent local
tourist sites), is well
worth a visit; as is
Europe's largest
dolmen, with its
collection of pre-
historic implements,
in Bagneux.

Before you leave
the area, be sure to
sample the local
méthode champenoise sparkling
wine – the best in France outside Champagne – in one of
the many wine cellars or at
the Maison des Vins in town.

⛪ **Château de Saumur**
Tel 02 41 40 24 40. ⬤ *for
renovation (call for details).*

Ecole Nationale d'Equitation
St-Hilaire-St-Florent. *Tel 02 41 53 50
60.* ⬤ *call for details of performance
times.* ⬤ *public hols.* 🎦 ♿ ✔
oblig. 🖥 www.cadrenoir.fr

Environs
The lovely **Eglise Notre-Dame**
at Cunault, an 11th-century
Romanesque priory church,
has a fine west door and
carved capitals, while an
amazing subterranean fort and
myriad caves and tunnels can
be seen at **Château de Brézé**.

Montreuil-Bellay ⑥

Maine-et-Loire. 🏠 4,500. 🚉 ✈
ℹ *pl du Concorde (02 41 52 32 39).*
🛒 *Tue (& Sun, mid-Jun–mid-Sep).*
www.ville-montreuil-bellay.fr

Set on the river Thouet 11
miles (17 km) south of Saumur,
Montreuil-Bellay is one of the
region's most gracious small
towns and is an ideal base for
touring Anjou. The towering
roofline of the Gothic collegiate
church overlooks walled mansions and surrounding vineyards
(wine-tasting recommended).
The **Chapelle St-Jean** was an
ancient hospice and pilgrimage center.

The imposing **Château de
Montreuil-Bellay**, established
in 1025, is a veritable fortress
with its 13 interlocking towers,
barbican, and ramparts.

A 15th-century house lies
beyond the fortified gateway,
complete with vaulted medieval
kitchen and an oratory decorated with 15th-century frescoes.

⛪ **Château de
Montreuil-Bellay**
Tel 02 41 52 33 06. ⬤ *Apr–Oct:
Wed–Mon (Jul–Aug: daily).* 🎦 ✔

TROGLODYTE DWELLINGS

Some of the best troglodyte settlements in France have been
carved out of the soft limestone (tufa) of the Loire Valley, especially around Saumur, Vouvray, and along the river Loir. The
caves, cut out of cliff-faces or dug underground, have been a
source of cheap, secure accommodations for centuries. Today
they are popular as *résidences secondaires*, or used for wine
storage and mushroom growing. Some are now restaurants or
hotels, and old quarries at Doué-la-Fontaine accommodate a
zoo and a 15th-century amphitheater. At Rochemenier, near
Saumur, is a well-preserved troglodyte village museum. A
central pit is surrounded by a warren of caves, barns, wine
cellars, dwellings, and even a simple underground chapel.

Heralded by chimney pots, the underground hamlet of
La Fosse was inhabited until the late 20th century by three
families, and is now a museum of family life underground.

A typical troglodyte dwelling

Court Life in the Renaissance

François I's reign, from 1515 to 1547, witnessed the apogee of the French Renaissance, characterized by an intense period of château-building and an interest in humanism and the arts. The itinerant court traveled between the pleasure palaces of Amboise, Blois, and Chambord in the Loire. Days were devoted to hunting, falconry, *fêtes champêtres* (country festivals), or *jeu de paume*, a forerunner of tennis. Nights were given over to feasting, balls, poetry, and romantic assignations.

Lute and mandolin *music were much in vogue, as were Italian recitals and masquerades. Musicians played at the twice-weekly balls, where the pavane and galliard were danced.*

The antics *of François I's fools, Triboulet and Caillette, amused the court. Yet they were often mistreated: courtiers regularly nailed Caillette's ears to a post for fun, daring him to remain silent.*

RENAISSANCE FEASTS

Dinner usually took place before 7pm to the accompaniment of Italian music. Humanist texts were read aloud and the king's fools amused the courtiers.

Courtiers used their own knives at dinner. Forks were still rare, although their use was spreading from Italy.

A typical royal dinner comprised smoked eel, salted ham, veal pâté, egg and saffron soups, roast game and boiled meats, as well as fish dishes in lemon or gooseberry sauce.

The cost of lavish damask, satin, and silk costumes often sent courtiers into debt.

Diane de Poitiers *(1499–1566) became the mistress of the future Henri II when he was 12 years old. Two years later he married Catherine de' Medici, but Diane remained his favorite until his death.*

Artists symbolized love *in different ways during the Renaissance. Winged hearts charmingly perform the function here.*

The Grand Moûtier cloisters

Abbaye Royale de Fontevraud ⑦

Maine-et-Loire. 🚌 *from Saumur.* ***Tel*** *02 41 51 73 52.* ⬜ *Feb–mid-Apr: Tue–Sun; mid-Apr–Dec: daily.* ⬛ *Jan, Dec 25.* 🎦 **www**.abbaye-fontevraud.com

The Abbaye Royale de Fontevraud is the largest and most remarkably intact medieval abbey in Europe. It was founded in the early 12th century by Robert d'Arbrissel, a visionary itinerant preacher who set up a Benedictine community of

THE PLANTAGENETS

The legendary counts of Anjou were named after the *genêt*, the sprig of broom Geoffrey Plantagenet wore in his cap. He married Matilda, daughter of England's Henry I. In 1154, when their son Henry – who had married Eleanor of Aquitaine *(see p51)* – acceded to the English throne, the Plantagenet dynasty of English kings was founded, fusing French and English destinies for 300 years.

Effigies of Henry II, Plantagenet king of England, and Eleanor of Aquitaine

monks, nuns, nobles, lepers, and vagabonds. The radical founder entrusted the running of the abbey to an abbess, usually from a noble family, and the abbey became a favorite sanctuary for the female aristocracy, including Eleanor of Aquitaine.

From 1804 to 1963 the abbey was used as a prison, since when the buildings have been undergoing painstaking restoration by the French State. Wandering around the abbey buildings and gardens gives a fascinating insight into monastic life.

The focal point was the Romanesque abbey church, consecrated in 1119. It features beautifully carved capitals and an immense nave with four domes, one of the finest examples of a cupola nave in France. Inside are the painted effigies of the Plantagenets dating from the early 13th century: Henry II of England, his redoubtable wife Queen Eleanor of Aquitaine, their crusading son Richard the Lion-Heart, and Isabelle d'Angoulême, widow of his infamous brother, King John of England.

The abbey's nuns lived around the Renaissance **Grand Moûtier cloisters**, forming one of the largest nunneries in France, and the leper colony was housed in the **St-Lazare priory**, now the atmospheric abbey hotel *(see p555)*. The monastic quarters of **St. Jean de l'Habit** no longer exist. Most impressive is the octagonal kitchen with its fireplaces and chimneys in the **Tour Evraud**, a rare example of secular Romanesque architecture.

The abbey, now an important arts center, regularly hosts concerts and exhibitions.

TOUR EVRAUD

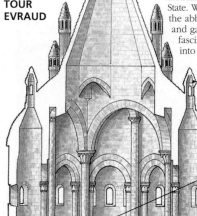

Pepperpot chimneys top the towers of the kitchen, restored in the 20th century.

Fireplace alcoves that look like side chapels housed the ovens.

Chinon ⑧

Indre-et-Loire. 🏯 *9,000.* 🚉 🚌 🛈 *pl Hofheim (02 47 93 17 85).* 🛒 *Thu.* **www**.chinon-valdeloire.com

The Château de Chinon is an important shrine in Joan of Arc country and, as such, wheedles money from all passing pilgrims. It was here in 1429 that the saint first recognized the disguised dauphin (later Charles VII),

and persuaded him to give her an army to drive the English out of France. Before that, Chinon was the Plantagenet kings' favorite castle. Although the **château** is now mostly in ruins, the ramparts are an impressive sight from the opposite bank of the Vienne river. The town's bijou center is like a

Stallholder at Chinon's market

medieval film set. **Rue Voltaire,** lined with 15th- and 16th-century houses and once enclosed by the castle walls, represents a cross-section of Chinonais history. At No. 12 is the **Musée Animé du Vin**, where animated figures tell the story of wine-making. **No. 44** which houses the Musée d'Art et d'Histoire, is a

Vineyard in the Chinon wine region

stone mansion where, in 1199, Richard the Lion-Heart is said to have died. The grandest mansion is the **Palais du Gouverneur,** with its double staircase and loggia. More charming is the **Maison Rouge** in the Grand Carroi, studded with a red-brick herringbone pattern.

The 15th-century **Hostellerie Gargantua**, where Rabelais' lawyer father once practised, is now an agreeable inn *(see p569)*. The great Renaissance writer lived nearby in the Rue de la Lamproie.

The 1900s market, with stallholders in period costume, folk dancing and music is a must (3rd Sat Aug).

🏛 **Musée Animé du Vin**
12 rue Voltaire. **Tel** 02 47 93 25 63.
◯ Easter–Sep: daily. 🖼 🗺

Environs
Three miles (5 km) southwest of Chinon is **La Devinière**, birthplace of François Rabelais, the 16th-century writer, priest, doctor and humanist scholar.

🏛 **La Devinière**
Seuilly. **Tel** 02 47 95 91 18. ◯ Wed–Mon. ● Jan 1, Dec 25. 🖼 🗺

Château d'Ussé ❾

Indre-et-Loire. 🚊 *Chinon,* then taxi. **Tel** 02 47 95 54 05.
◯ mid-Feb–mid-Nov: daily. 🖼 🗺
www.chateaudusse.fr

The fairytale Château d'Ussé enjoys a bucolic setting by the river Indre. Its romantic turrets, pointed towers, and chimneys inspired Charles Perrault's *Sleeping Beauty*.

Constructed in the 15th century, the castle was gradually

transformed into an aristocratic château, which is still privately owned *(see p242)*. However, the sunless and musty interior is rather disappointing and the *Sleeping Beauty* tableaux are clumsily presented.

The château's delightful Renaissance chapel, framed by the oak forest of Chinon, has lost its Aubusson tapestries, but retains a lovely della Robbia terra cotta *Virgin*.

Château de Langeais ❿

Indre-et-Loire. 🚊 *Langeais.*
Tel 02 47 96 72 60. ◯ daily.
● Jan 1, Dec 25. 🖼 🗺
www.chateau-de-langeais.com

Compared with neighboring towns, Langeais is distinctly untouristy and has a welcoming, unpretentious feel. Its château is fiercely feudal, built strictly for defense with a drawbridge, portcullis, and no concessions to the Renaissance. It was constructed by Louis XI in just four years, from 1465–9, with hardly an alteration since then. The ruins of an impressive keep, built by Foulques Nerra in AD 994, stand in the small château courtyard.

A *son et lumière* in the Salle de la Chapelle represents the marriage of Charles VIII and Anne of Brittany in 1491. Many of the rooms have intricate designs on the tiled floors, and all are hung with fine 15th- and 16th-century Flemish and Aubusson tapestries.

FRANÇOIS RABELAIS

Rabelais, born in 1494, was a priest, doctor, diplomat, and humanist scholar noted for his wisdom and tolerance. He is best remembered for his many ribald satires (written as "medicine" for his patients), such as *Pantagruel* and *Gargantua*, set around his native Chinon.

Infant Pantagruel, depicted by Doré in 1854, was fed on the milk of 17,913 cows

Château d'Azay-le-Rideau ⓫

Indre-et-Loire. 🚉 🚌 Azay-le-Rideau. **Tel** 02 47 45 42 04.
◯ daily. ◯ Jan 1, May 1, Dec 25.
📷 🎬 **Son et Lumière:** Jul–Aug.

Balzac called Azay-le-Rideau "A multifaceted diamond set in the Indre." It is the most beguiling and feminine of Loire châteaux, created in the early 16th century by Philippa Lesbahy, wife of François I's corrupt finance minister. Although Azay is superficially Gothic (see pp54–55, 242), it clearly shows the transition to the Renaissance: the turrets are purely decorative and the moats are picturesque pools. Azay was a pleasure palace, lived in during fine weather and deserted in winter.

The interior is equally delightful, an airy, creaking mansion smelling faintly of cedarwood and full of lovingly re-created domestic detail. The first floor is furnished in the Renaissance style, with a fine example of a portable Spanish cabinet and exquisite tapestries. The ground floor has 19th-century furniture, dating from the period of the château's restoration. The four-story grand staircase is unusual for its time, being straight as opposed to spiral.

Wine-tasting opportunities in the village are a welcome reminder that vineyards are all around. Unlike most Loire villages, Azay is lively at night, thanks to the château's poetic son et lumière.

The Château de Villandry's *jardin d'ornement*

Château de Villandry ⓬

Indre-et-Loire. 🚌 Tours, then taxi.
Tel 02 47 50 02 09. ◯ **Château:** mid-Feb–mid-Nov & mid-Dec–early Jan: daily. **Gardens:** daily. 📷 🎬 🚻 Mar–Oct. www.chateauvillandry.com

Villandry was the last great Renaissance château built in the Loire Valley, a perfect example of 16th-century architecture. Its gardens were restored to their original splendor early in the last century by Dr. Joachim Carvallo, whose grandson continues his work.

The result is a patchwork of sculpted shrubs and flowers on three levels: the kitchen garden (*jardin potager*), the ornamental garden (*jardin d'ornement*), and, on the highest level, the water garden (*jardin d'eau*). There are signs to explain the history and meaning behind each plant: the marrow, for instance, symbolized fertility; the cabbage, sexual and spiritual corruption. Plants were also prized for their medicinal properties: cabbage was thought to help cure hangovers, while pimento aided digestion.

The delicate roots of the 32 miles (52 km) of box hedge that outline and highlight each section mean that the whole 10 acres of gardens must be hand-weeded.

A *chocolatier* in Tours

Tours ⓭

Indre-et-Loire. 🏛 140,000. ✈ 🚉
🚌 🛈 78 rue Bernard Palissy (02 47 70 37 37). 🛒 Tue–Sun. www.ligeris.com

Tours is the most appealing of the major Loire cities, thanks to bourgeois prosperity, an intelligent restoration program and its university population. It is built on the site of a Roman town, and was a center of Christianity in the 4th century under St. Martin, bishop of Tours. In 1461 Louis XI made the city the French capital. However, during Henri IV's reign the city lost favour with the monarchy and the capital left Tours for Paris.

Bombarded by the Prussians in 1870, and bombed in World War II, Tours suffered extensive damage. By 1960, the middle classes had abandoned the historic center and it became a slum, full of

Château d'Azay-le-Rideau reflected in the river Indre

...mbling medieval masonry. ...generation of the city has ...cceeded due to the popular ...olicies of Jean Royer, mayor ...f Tours from 1958 to 1996.

The pedestrianized **place Plumereau** is Tours' most atmospheric quarter, set in the medieval heart of the city and full of cafés, boutiques, and galleries. Streets such as rue Briçonnet reveal half-timbered façades, hidden courtyards, and crooked towers. A gateway leads to place St-Pierre-le-Puellier, a square with sunken Gallo-Roman remains and a Romanesque church converted into a café. Nearby in place de Châteauneuf lies the Romanesque **Tour Charlemagne**, all that remains of St. Martin's first church. West of here is the highly yuppified artisans' quarter, centered on the rue du Petit St-Martin.

The **Cathédrale St-Gatien**, in the eastern sector of the city, was begun in the early 13th century and completed in the 16th. Its Flamboyant Gothic façade is blackened and crumbling but still truly impressive, as are the medieval stained-glass windows.

The **Musée des Beaux Arts**, set in the former archbishop's palace nearby, overlooks

Cathédrale St-Gatien in Tours

Classical gardens and a giant cedar of Lebanon. Its star exhibits are *Christ in the Garden of Olives* and *The Resurrection* by Mantegna, and a room devoted to the modern artist Olivier Debré.

Further west is the **Eglise St-Julien**, whose Gothic monastic cells and chapterhouse contain a small wine museum. Next door, the **Musée du Compagnonnage** displays hundreds of finely created works by master craftsmen of the guilds. Across the rue Nationale lies the town's

finest Renaissance building, the **Hôtel Goüin**, which houses regular art exhibitions.

🏛 Musée des Beaux Arts
18 pl François Sicard. **Tel** 02 47 05 68 73. ◯ Wed–Mon. ● Jan 1, May 1, Jul 14, Nov 1 & 11, Dec 25. 🖼

🏛 Musée du Compagnonnage
8 rue Nationale. **Tel** 02 47 21 62 20. ◯ mid-Jun–mid-Sep: daily; mid-Sep–mid-Jun: Wed–Mon. ● Jan 1, May 1, Jul 14, Nov 1 & 11, Dec 25. 🖼 ♿

Environs
Just outside Céré la Ronde, on the D764 from Montrichard to Loches, lies the 15th-century **Château de Montpoupon** and its excellent Musée du Veneur, which looks at the important role of horses in hunting.

Backgammon players in Tours' place Plumereau

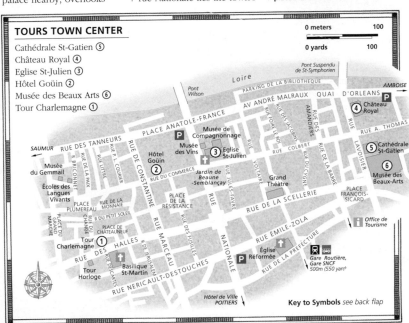

TOURS TOWN CENTER

Cathédrale St-Gatien ⑤
Château Royal ④
Eglise St-Julien ③
Hôtel Goüin ②
Musée des Beaux Arts ⑥
Tour Charlemagne ①

0 meters 100
0 yards 100

Pont Suspendu de St-Symphorien

Loire

AMBOISE

Pont Wilson

PARKING DE LA BIBLIOTHÈQUE
AV ANDRÉ MALRAUX QUAI D'ORLEANS
④ Château Royal

PLACE ANATOLE-FRANCE
RUE A. THOMAS

SAUMUR RUE DES TANNEURS
Musée de Compagnonnage

Hôtel Goüin ②
Musée des Vins ③ Eglise St-Julien
RUE COLBERT
⑤ Cathédrale St-Gatien
⑥ Musée des Beaux Arts

Musée du Gemmail
Écoles des Langues Vivants

Jardin de Beaune -Semblançay

Grand Théâtre

PLACE FRANÇOIS-SICARD

PLACE PLUMEREAU
Tour Charlemagne ①
RUE DE LA SCELLERIE

RUE ÉMILE-ZOLA
Office de Tourisme

Eglise Réformée
Gare Routière, Gare SNCF 500m (550 yards)

Basilique St-Martin
Tour Horloge

NATIONALE

Hôtel de Ville POITIERS

Key to Symbols see back flap

Château de Chenonceau ⑰

A romantic pleasure palace, Chenonceau was created from the Renaissance onwards by a series of aristocratic women. A magnificent avenue bordered by plane trees leads to symmetrical gardens and the serene vision that Flaubert praised as "floating on air and water." The château stretches across the river Cher with a 197-ft (60-m) gallery built over a series of arches, its elegant beauty reflected in the languid waters. The grandeur continues inside with splendidly furnished rooms, airy bedchambers, and fine paintings and tapestries.

Turreted Pavilion
This was built between 1513 and 1521 by Catherine Briçonnet and her husband, Thomas Bohier, over the foundations of an old water mill.

Chapelle
The chapel has a vaulted ceiling and pilasters sculpted with acanthus leaves and cockleshells. The stained glass, destroyed by a bomb in 1944, was replaced in 1953.

Catherine de' Medici's Garden
Lavish court receptions and transvestite balls were held under Catherine's auspices.

TIMELINE

Catherine de' Medici

1533 Marriage of Catherine de' Medici (1519–89) to Henri II (1519–59). Chenonceau becomes a Loire royal palace

1559 On Henri's death, Catherine forces the disgraced Diane to accept the Château de Chaumont in exchange for Chenonceau

1789 Chenonceau is spared in the French Revolution, thanks to Madame Dupin

1500	1600	1700	1800

1575 Louise de Lorraine (1554–1601) marries Henri III, Catherine's third and favorite son

1547 Henri II offers Chenonceau to Diane de Poitiers, his lifelong mistress

1513 Thomas Bohier acquires medieval Chenonceau. His wife, Catherine Briçonnet, rebuilds it in Renaissance style

1863 Madame Pelouz[e] restores the château [to] its original sta[te]

1730–99 Madame Dupin, a "farmer-general's" wife, makes Chenonceau a salon for writers and philosophers

VISITORS' CHECKLIST

🅿 Chenonceaux. 🚌 from Tours.
Tel 02 47 23 90 07. ◯ daily. 📷
📷 ♿ gr. fl. only. 🍴 🛒 🎁 🛍
Classical music: Jun–Aug.
www.chenonceau.com

The Creation of Chenonceau

The women responsible for Chenonceau each left their mark. Catherine Briçonnet, wife of the first owner, built the turreted pavilion and one of the first straight staircases in France; Henri II's mistress, Diane de Poitiers, added the formal gardens and arched bridge over the river; Catherine de' Medici transformed the bridge into an Italian-style gallery (having evicted Diane following her husband's death in 1559); Louise de Lorraine, bereaved wife of Henri III, inherited the château in 1590 and painted the ceiling of her bedchamber black and white (the colors of royal mourning); Madame Dupin, a cultured 18th-century châtelaine, saved the château from destruction in the Revolution; and Madame Pelouze undertook a complete restoration in 1863.

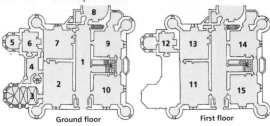

Ground floor — First floor

Grande Galerie
The elegant gallery crowning the bridge is Florentine in style, created by Catherine de' Medici from 1570 – 76.

CHÂTEAU GUIDE

The main living area was in the square-shaped turreted pavilion in the middle of the river Cher. Four principal rooms open off the Vestibule on the ground floor: the Salle des Gardes and the Chambre de Diane de Poitiers, both hung with 16th-century Flemish tapestries; the Chambre de François I, with a Van Loo painting; and the Salon Louis XIV. On the first floor, reached via the Italianate staircase, are other sumptuous apartments including the Chambre de Catherine de' Médicis and the Chambre de Vendôme.

1 Vestibule
2 Salle des Gardes
3 Chapelle
4 Terrasse
5 Librairie de Catherine de' Médicis
6 Cabinet Vert
7 Chambre de Diane de Poitiers
8 Grande Galerie
9 Chambre de François I
10 Salon Louis XIV
11 Chambre des Cinq Reines
12 Cabinet des Estampes
13 Chambre de Catherine de' Médicis
14 Chambre de Vendôme
15 Chambre de Gabrielle d'Estrées

1913 The château is bought by the Menier family, the *chocolatiers* who still own it today

1941 Chenonceau chapel is damaged in a bombing raid

Diane de Poitiers

Chambre de Catherine de' Médicis

Vouvray ❿

Indre-et-Loire. 🏠 3,500.
ℹ️ 12 rue Rabelais (02 47 52 68 73).
🚌 Tue & Fri. **www**.tourisme
vouvray-valdeloire.com

Just east of Tours is the village of Vouvray, home of the delicious white wine that Renaissance author Rabelais likened to taffeta.

The quality of Vouvray's wines has not changed. The star vineyard is **Huet** where, since 1990, grapes have been grown according to biodynamic methods: manual weeding and natural fertilizers. In the preface to his novel *Quentin Durward*, Sir Walter Scott sang the praises of its dry white wines which are still matured in chestnut barrels. Gaston Huet also hit the headlines in 1990 with his protests against the building of tracks for the TGV train over Vouvray vineyards. A compromise was eventually reached and tunnels were built under the hilly vineyards.

The **Chateau de Montcontour**, where monks first planted vines in the 4th century, has its own wine-making museum in the impressive 10th-century cellars hewn out of the tufa rock.

The medieval town of Loches

Huet
11–13 rue de la Croix-Buisée.
Tel 02 47 52 78 87. ⏰ Jul–Aug:
Mon–Sat for wine tastings; cellar visits by reservation only.
⬤ public hols.

⛪ Château de Moncontour
Route de Rochecorbon. **Tel** 02 47 52 60 77. ⏰ Easter–Sep: daily; Oct–before Easter: Mon–Fri. 🎫 📷 Visits can be followed by wine tastings.
www.moncontour.com

Loches ⓯

Indre-et-Loire. 🏠 7,000. 🚉 🚌
ℹ️ pl de la Marne (02 47 91 82 82).
🚌 Wed & Sat. **www**.loches-tourainecotesud.com

This unspoiled medieval town is removed from the château trail in the Indre valley. It is a backwater of late Gothic gateways and sculpted façades. Its keep has the deepest dungeons in the Loire. The Logis Royal is associated with Charles VII and his mistress Agnès Sorel. It is also where Joan of Arc pleaded with Charles to go to Reims and be crowned. Anne of Brittany's chapel is decorated with ermines, and contains an effigy of Agnès Sorel.

⛪ Logis Royal de Loches
Tel 02 47 59 01 32. ⏰ daily.
⬤ Jan 1, Dec 25. 🎫 📷

THE HEROINE OF FRANCE

Joan of Arc is the quintessential French national heroine, a virginal warrior, a woman martyr, a French figurehead. Her divinely led campaign to "drive the English out of France" during the Hundred Years' War has inspired plays, poetry, and movies from Voltaire to Cecil B. de Mille. Responding to heavenly voices, she appeared on the scene as champion of the dauphin, the uncrowned Charles VII. He faced an Anglo-Burgundian alliance which held most of northern France, and had escaped to the royal châteaux on the Loire. Joan con-

Earliest known drawing of Joan of Arc (1429)

vinced him of her mission, mustered the French troops, and in May 1429 led them to victory over the English at Orléans. She then urged the dithering Charles to go to Reims to be crowned. However, in 1430 she was captured and handed over to the English. Accused of witchcraft, she was burned at the stake in Rouen in 1431 at the age of 19. Her legendary bravery and tragic martyrdom led to her canonization in 1920.

Portrait of Joan of Arc *in the Maison Jeanne d'Arc in Orléans* (see p312). *She saved the city from the English on May 8, 1429, a date the Orléannais still celebrate annually.*

Montrésor ⑯

Indre-et-Loire. 🏠 *400.* 🛈 *43 grande rue (02 47 92 70 71).* **www.**tourisme-valdindrois-montresor.com

Classed as one of "the most beautiful villages in France," Montrésor does not disappoint. Set on the river Indrois, it became a Polish enclave in the 1840s. In 1849 a Polish nobleman, Count Branicki, bought the 15th-century **Château**, built on the site of one of Foulques Nerra's 11th-century fortifications. It

Farm building and poppy fields near the village of Montrésor

has remained in the family ever since, its interior unchanged.

♠ **Château de Montrésor**
Tel 02 47 92 60 04. ◯ *Apr–Nov 11: daily; mid-Nov–Mar: Sat & Sun pms.*
📷 🎧 ♿

Château de Chenonceau ⑰

See pp288–9.

Amboise ⑱

Indre-et-Loire. 🏠 *12,000.* 🚌 🚉
🛈 *quai du Général de Gaulle (02 47 57 09 28).* 🏪 *Fri & Sun am.*
www.amboise-valdeloire.com

Few buildings are more historically important than the **Château d'Amboise**. Louis XI lived here; Charles VIII was born and died here; François I was brought up here, as were Catherine de Medici's 10 children. The château was also the setting for the 1560 Amboise Conspiracy, an ill-fated Huguenot plot against François II. Visitors are shown the metal lacework balcony which served as a gibbet for 12 of the 1,200 conspirators who were put to death. The **Tour des Minimes**, the château's original entrance, is

Amboise seen from the Loire

famous for its huge spiral ramp up which horsemen could ride to deliver provisions.

On the ramparts is the beautifully restored Gothic **Chapelle St-Hubert**, Leonardo da Vinci's burial place. Under the patronage of François I, the artist lived in the nearby manor house of **Clos-Lucé,** whose gardens exhibit models of Leonardo's inventions constructed from his sketches.

♠ **Château d'Amboise**
Tel 02 47 57 00 98. ◯ *daily.*
● *Jan 1, Dec 25.* 📷 🎧
www.chateau-amboise.com

🏛 **Clos-Lucé**
2 rue de Clos-Lucé. *Tel 02 47 57 00 73.*
◯ *daily.* ● *Jan 1, Dec 25.* 📷 ♿
restricted. **www.**vinci-closluce.com

A romantic heroine, *Joan of Arc was a popular subject for artists. This painting of her is by François Léon Benouville (1821–59).*

Burned at the stake – *a scene from* St. Joan, *Otto Preminger's 1957 epic movie, which starred Jean Seberg.*

Château de Chambord ⑲

Henry James once said, "Chambord is truly royal – royal in its great scale, its grand air, and its indifference to common considerations." The Loire's largest residence, brainchild of the extravagant François I, began as a hunting lodge in the Forêt de Boulogne. In 1519 this was razed and the creation of present-day Chambord began, to a design probably initiated by Leonardo da Vinci. By 1537 the towers, keep, and terraces had been completed by 1,800 men and three master masons. At one point, François suggested diverting the Loire to flow in front of his château, but he settled for redirecting the nearby Cosson instead. His son Henry II continued his work, and Louis XIV completed the 440-roomed edifice in 1685.

The Château de Chambord with the river Cosson, a tributary of the Loire, in the foreground

The Salamander
François I chose the salamander as his enigmatic emblem. It appears over 800 times throughout the château.

★ Roof Terraces
This skyline of delicate cupolas has been likened to a miniature Oriental town. The roof terraces include a forest of elongated chimney pots, miniature spires, shell-shaped domes, and richly sculpted gables.

The chapel was begun by François I shortly before his death in 1547. Henri II added the second story and Louis XIV the roof.

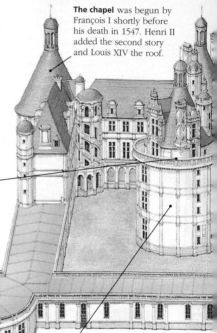

The central keep (donjon), with its four circular towers, forms the nucleus of the château.

STAR FEATURES

- ★ Roof Terraces
- ★ Vaulted Guardrooms
- ★ Grand Staircase

TIMELINE

1519–47 The Count of Blois' hunting lodge demolished by François I and the château created

1547–59 Henri II adds the west wing and second story of the chapel

1547 Death of François I

1669–85 Louis XIV completes the building, then abandons it

1670 Molière's *Le Bourgeois Gentilhomme* staged at Chambord

Molière

1725–33 Inhabited by Stanislas Leczinski, exiled king of Poland who was made duke of Lorraine

1748 The Maréchal de Saxe acquires Chambord. On his death two years later, the château yet again falls into decline

1840 Chambord declared a *Monument Historique*

1970s Chambord is restored and refurnished and the moats re-dug.

1500	1600	1700	1800	1900

★ Vaulted Guardrooms

Arranged in the form of a Greek cross around the Grand Staircase, the vaulted guardrooms were once the setting for royal balls and plays. Their ceilings are decorated with François I's initials and salamander motif.

The lantern tower is 105 ft (32 m) high. Surmounting the terrace, it is supported by arched buttresses and crowned by a fleur-de-lys.

François I's Bedchamber is where the king, hurt by a failed romance, scratched a message on a pane of glass: " *Souvent femme varie, bien fol est qui s'y fie.*" (Every woman is fickle, he who trusts one is a fool.)

Cabinet de François I
The king's barrel-vaulted study (cabinet) in the outer north tower was turned into an oratory in the 18th century by Queen Catherine Opalinska, wife of Stanislas Leczinski (Louis XV's father-in-law).

★ Grand Staircase

This innovative double-helix staircase was supposedly designed by Leonardo da Vinci. It ensures that the person going up and the person going down cannot meet.

Louis XIV's Bedchamber
Louis XIV's bedchamber lies within the Sun King's state apartments, the grandest quarters in the château.

For hotels and restaurants in this region see pp568–72 and pp620–5

Blois's Cathédrale St-Louis and Hôtel de Ville seen from across the Loire

Blois ⑳

Loir-et-Cher. 🏠 60,000. 🚉 🚌
i 23 pl du château (02 54 90 41
41). 🛒 Fri (organic market), Sat.
www.bloispaysdechambord.com

Once a fief of the counts of
Blois, the town rose to
prominence as a royal domain
in the 15th century, retaining
its historic façades and refined
atmosphere to this day. Architectural interest abounds in
Vieux Blois, the hilly, partially
pedestrianized quarter enclosed
by the château, cathedral, and
river. Four well-signposted
walking tours act as a gentle
introduction to the noble
mansions and romantic courtyards that grace the Loire's
most beguiling town.

Set back from the north
bank of the river, the **Château
Royal de Blois** was the principal
royal residence until Henri IV
moved the court to Paris in
1598 – Louis XIV's creation
of Versailles (see pp174–7)
was to mark the final eclipse
of Blois. The château's four
contrasting wings make a

harmonious whole. The Salle
des Etats Généraux, the only
part of the building surviving
from the 13th century, housed
the council and court; it is the
largest and best-preserved
Gothic hall in France. The
adjoining late-15th-century
Louis XII wing, which houses
the **Musée des Beaux Arts**,
infuses Gothic design with
Renaissance spirit, sealed with
the king's porcupine symbol.

The 16th-century François I
wing is a masterpiece of the
French Renaissance containing
a monumental spiral staircase
in an octagonal tower. By
contrast, the 17th-century
Gaston d'Orléans wing is a
model of Classical sobriety.

Blois is authentically furnished and hung with
paintings portraying its
troubled past. These
include a graphic
portrayal of the
murder of the Duc
de Guise in 1588.
Suspected of
heading a Catholic
plot against Henri
III, he was stabbed

King Louis XII's porcupine symbol

to death by guards in the
king's chamber. The most
intriguing room is Catherine
de' Medici's study where, of
the 237 carved wooden wall
panels, four are secret cabinets

François I Staircase

*Built between 1515 and
1524, this octagonal
staircase is a master-
piece of the
early French
Renaissance.*

The gallery
provided an
ideal setting
for viewing
jousts and re-
ceptions held
in the inner
courtyard.

**François I's
salamander
motif** adorns
the openwork
balustrades.

The staircase
within the
tower slopes
appreciably
more steeply
than the bal-
ustrades.

Louis XII wing of the Château Royal de Blois

For hotels and restaurants in this region see pp568–72 and pp620–5

said to have stored her poisons.
Dominating the eastern sector
of the city, the **Cathédrale
St-Louis** is a 17th-century
reconstruction of a Gothic
church that was almost
completely destroyed by a
hurricane in 1678. Behind the
cathedral the former bishop's
palace, built in 1700, is the
Hôtel de Ville (town hall). The
surrounding terraced gardens
have lovely views over the
city and river. Opposite the
cathedral is the **Maison des
Acrobates**, carved with characters from medieval farces
including acrobats and jugglers.

Place Louis-XII, the marketplace, is overlooked by
splendid 17th-century façades.
Rue Pierre de Blois, a quaint
alley straddled by a Gothic
passageway, winds downhill
to the medieval Jewish ghetto.
The rue des Juifs boasts
several distinguished *hôtels
particuliers* (mansions),
including the galleried **Hôtel
de Condé** with its Renaissance
archway and courtyard, and the
Hôtel Jassaud, with magnificent 16th-century low reliefs
above the main doorway. On
the rue du Puits-Châtel, also
rich in Renaissance mansions,
is the galleried **Hôtel Sardini**.

Place Vauvert is the most
charming square in Vieux
Blois, with a fine example of
a half-timbered house.

🏰 **Château Royal de Blois**
Tel 02 54 90 33 33. ⬜ Jan–Mar &
Nov–Dec: 9am–12:30pm & 1:30–
5:30pm daily; Apr–Jun & Sep:
9am–6:30pm daily; Jul–Aug:
9am–7pm daily; Oct: 9am–6pm
daily. ⬤ Jan 1, Dec 25. 🎫 📷

Covered Gothic passageway in Rue
Pierre de Blois

The nave of the abbey church of Notre-Dame in Beaugency

Beaugency ㉑

Loiret. 🏠 7,500. 🚉 🚌 🛈 3 pl
de Docteur-Hyvernaud (02 38 44 54
42). 🛒 Sat. **www**.beaugency.fr

Beaugency has long been the
eastern gateway to the Loire.
This compact medieval town
makes a peaceful base for
exploring the Orléanais
region. Exceptionally for the
Loire, it is possible to walk
along the river banks and stone
levées. At quai de l'Abbaye
there is a good view of the
11th-century bridge which,
until modern times, was the
only crossing point between
Blois and Orléans. An obvious
target for enemy attack, it was
captured four times by the
English during the Hundred
Years' War before being retaken by Joan of Arc in 1429.

The town center is domin-
ated by a ruined 11th-century
watchtower. It stands on
place St-Firmin, along with a
16th-century belltower (the
church was destroyed in the
Revolution) and a statue of

Joan of Arc. Period houses line
the square. Farther down is
the **Château Dunois**, built on
the site of the feudal castle by
one of Joan of Arc's *compag-
non d'armes*. Its regional
museum features an array of
costumes, furniture, and
antique toys. Facing the
Château Dunois is **Notre-
Dame**, a Romanesque abbey
church that witnessed the
annulment of the marriage
between Eleanor of Aquitaine
and Louis VII in 1152, leaving
Eleanor free to marry the
future Henry II of England.

Nearby is the medieval
clocktower in rue du Change
and the Renaissance **Hôtel de
Ville**, with its façade adorned
with the town's arms. Equally
charming is the nearby
ancient mill district, around
the rue du Pont and the rue
du Rü, with its streams and
riot of flowers.

🏰 **Château Dunois (Musée
Daniel Vannier)**
3 pl Dunois. **Tel** 02 38 44 54 42.
⬤ call for details. 🎫 📷 oblig.

Châteaux Tour of the Sologne

The mysterious Sologne is a secretive landscape of woods and marshes edged by vineyards. Wine-lovers can indulge in tastings of Loire Valley wines accompanied, in season, by a dinner of succulent wild game from the region's forests, popular hunting grounds for centuries. The Sologne is a hunter's paradise and devotees of the sport can see today's hounds, as well as hunting trophies of the past.

This ambling rural route takes in some of the Loire's most varied châteaux. The five on this tour – for which a couple of days is required – represent a delightful encapsulation of regional architecture. All styles are here, from feudal might to Renaissance grace and Classical elegance. Several are inhabited but can still be visited.

Château de Beauregard ②
Beauregard was built around 1520 as a hunting lodge for François I. It contains a gallery with 327 portraits of royalty.

N152

① D751

← AMBOISE

D764

Château de Chaumont ①
Chaumont is a feudal castle with Renaissance embellishments and lofty views over the river Loire *(see p242)*.

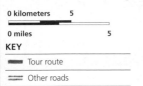

| 0 kilometers | 5 |
| 0 miles | 5 |

KEY

━━ Tour route

═══ Other roads

Pontlevóy

Vendôme ㉒

Loir-et-Cher. 🏠 18,500. 🚉 🚌
🚩 47 rue Poterie (02 54 77 05 07).
🗓 Fri & Sun. www.vendome.eu

Once an important stop for pilgrims en route to Compostela in Spain, Vendôme is still popular with modern pilgrims, thanks to the TGV rail service. Though a desirable address with Parisian commuters, the town still manages to retain its provincial charm. Vendôme's old stone buildings are encircled by the river Loir, its lush gardens and chic restaurants reflected in the water.

The town's greatest monument is the abbey church of **La Trinité**, founded in 1034. Its Romanesque belltower (all that remains of the original structure) is overshadowed by the church portal, a masterpiece of Flamboyant Gothic tracery. The interior is embellished with Romanesque capitals and 15th-century choir stalls.

Commanding a rocky spur high above the Loir is the ruined **château**, built by the counts of Vendôme in the 13th –14th centuries. Down below, rowing boats may be rented for gently exploring the meandering backwaters of the Loir, past a medieval *lavoir*, elegant buildings, and a plane tree planted in 1759.

Vendôme's native son Rochambeau, hero of the American Revolution

The Loir ㉓

Loir-et-Cher. 🚌 Tours. 🚉 Vendôme.
🚌 Montoire-sur-le-Loir. 🚩 16 pl Clémenceau, Montoire-sur-le-Loir (02 54 85 23 30).

Compared with the royal river Loire, the tranquil Loir to the north has a rural charm. The stretch between Vendôme and Trôo is the most rewarding, offering troglodyte caves *(see p292)*, walking trails, wine-tasting, fishing, and boat trips.

Les Roches-l'Evêque is a fortified village with cave dwellings visible in the cliff-face. Just downstream is **Lavardin**, with its Romanesque church, half-timbered houses, Gothic bridge, and ruined château ringed by ramparts. In **Montoire-sur-le-Loir**, the Chapelle St-Gilles, a former leper colony, has Romanesque frescoes. **Trôo**, the next major village, is known for its Romanesque Eglise de St-Martin and a labyrinth

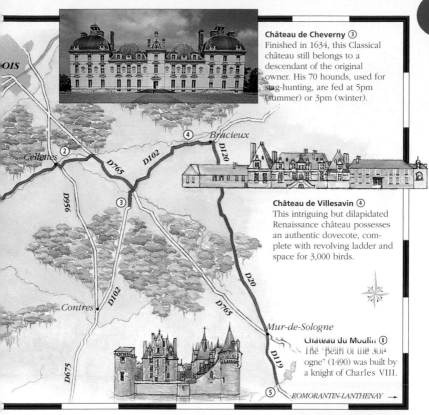

Château de Cheverny ③
Finished in 1634, this Classical château still belongs to a descendant of the original owner. His 70 hounds, used for stag-hunting, are fed at 5pm (summer) or 3pm (winter).

Château de Villesavin ④
This intriguing but dilapidated Renaissance château possesses an authentic dovecote, complete with revolving ladder and space for 3,000 birds.

Mur-de-Sologne

Château du Moulin ⑤
"The pearl of the Sologne" (1490) was built by a knight of Charles VIII.

ROMORANTIN-LANTHENAY →

---

of troglodyte dwellings. **St-Jacques-des-Guérets**, facing the village of Trôo, has a frescoed Romanesque chapel, as does **Poncé-sur-le-Loir**, farther downstream. On the slopes are vineyards producing Jasnières and Côteaux du Vendômois. Wine-tastings enliven sleepy **Poncé** and **La Chartre-sur-le-Loir**. The cliffs on the opposite bank are studded with caves, commonly used as wine cellars.

Northward, the **Forêt de Bercé** abounds with paths and streams, while to the west the small town of **Le Lude** sits on the south bank of the Loir, dominated by its romantic 15th-century château.

Some 12 miles (20 km) west of Le Lude lies **La Flèche**, whose main attraction is the Prytanée Nationale Militaire, originally a Jesuit college founded by Henri IV in 1603. Philosopher René Descartes was one of the college's earliest and most illustrious pupils.

Chartres ㉔

Eure-et-Loir. 42,400. 🚉 🚌
🛈 pl de la Cathédrale (02 37 18 26 26). 🛒 Tue, Thu, Sat.
www.chartres-tourisme.com

Chartres has the greatest Gothic cathedral in Europe (*see pp308–11*), and its churches should not be ignored. The Benedictine abbey church of **St-Pierre** has lovely medieval stained-glass windows, while **St-Aignan** abuts 9th-century ramparts. By the river is the Romanesque **Eglise de St-André**, a deconsecrated church used for art exhibitions and concerts. The **Musée des Beaux Arts**, in the former episcopal palace, offers a fine collection of 17th and 18th-century furniture, Renaissance enamels, and paintings by Vlaminck.

As one of the first urban conservation sites in France, Chartres is a success story. Quirky half-timbered houses

One of the many washhouses along the Eure river

abound along such cobbled streets as the rue des Ecuyers. Steep staircases known as *tertres* lead down to the river Eure providing views of mills, humpback stone bridges, washhouses, and the cathedral.

In the Grenier de Loens, next to the cathedral, is the Centre International du Vitrail. The building's 13th-century vaulted storerooms are also used for temporary exhibitions.

🏛 **Musée des Beaux Arts**
29 cloître Notre-Dame. **Tel** 02 37 90 45 80. ☐ Wed–Mon. ● Sun am, and Jan 1, May 1 & 8, Nov 1 & 11, Dec 25. 🗓 🎫

Chartres Cathedral

According to art historian Emile Male, "Chartres is the mind of the Middle Ages manifest." Begun in 1020, the Romanesque cathedral was destroyed by fire in 1194. Only the north and south towers, south steeple, west portal, and crypt remained; the sacred *Veil of the Virgin* relic was the sole treasure to survive. Peasant and lord alike helped to rebuild the church in just 25 years. Few alterations were made after 1250 and, fortunately, Chartres was unscathed by the Wars of Religion and the French Revolution. The result is a Gothic cathedral with a true "Bible in stone" reputation.

Part of the Vendôme Window

Elongated Statues
These statues on the Royal Portal represent Old Testament figures.

The taller of the two spires dates from the start of the 16th century. Flamboyant Gothic in style, it contrasts sharply with the solemnity of its Romanesque counterpart.

STAR FEATURES

★ Stained-Glass Windows

★ South Porch

★ Royal Portal

Gothic Nave
As wide as the Romanesque crypt below it, the nave reaches a lofty height of 121 ft (37 m).

★ Royal Portal
The central tympanum of the Royal Portal (1145–55) shows Christ in Majesty.

The lower half of the west front is a survivor of the original Romanesque church, the portal and the three windows dating from the mid-12th century.

Labyrinth

THE LABYRINTH

The 13th-century labyrinth, inlaid in the nave floor, was a feature of most medieval cathedrals. Pilgrims followed the tortuous route on their knees, echoing the way to Jerusalem and the complexity of life, in order to reach Christ. The journey – 851 ft (262 m) of broken concentric circles – took at least 1 hour.

VISITORS' CHECKLIST

Pl de la Cathédrale. *Tel* 02 37 21 75 02. ◯ 8:30am–6:45pm daily. ⏹ 9am Tue & Fri; 11:45am & 6:15pm Mon–Sat (6pm Sat); 9:15am (in Latin), 9:15am, & 11am Sun. ⬛ ♿ 📷 🚻
http://cathedrale.chartres.free.fr

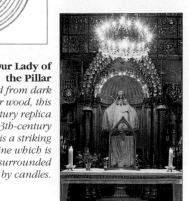

Our Lady of the Pillar
Carved from dark pear wood, this 16th-century replica of a 13th-century statue is a striking shrine which is often surrounded by candles.

Vaulted Ceiling
A network of ribs supports the vaulted ceiling.

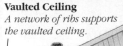

★ **Stained-Glass Windows**
The windows cover a surface area of over 28,000 sq ft (2,600 sq m).

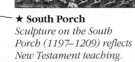

★ **South Porch**
Sculpture on the South Porch (1197–1209) reflects New Testament teaching.

The Crypt
This is the largest crypt in France, most of it dating from the early 11th century. It houses the Veil of the Virgin relic and comprises two galleries, a series of chapels, and the 9th-century St-Lubin's vault.

The Stained Glass of Chartres

Donated by royalty, aristocracy, priests, and the merchant brotherhoods between 1210 and 1240, this glorious collection of stained glass is world-renowned. Around 176 windows illustrate biblical stories and daily life in the 13th century. During both World Wars the windows were dismantled piece by piece and removed for safety. There is an ongoing program, begun in the 1970s, to restore the windows in the cathedral.

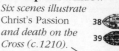

Stained glass above the apse

Redemption Window
Six scenes illustrate Christ's Passion *and death on the Cross (c.1210).*

★ Tree of Jesse
This 12th-century stained glass shows Christ's genealogy. The tree rises up from Jesse, father of David, at the bottom, to Christ enthroned at the top.

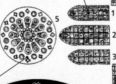

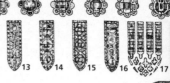

★ West Rose Window
This window (1215), with Christ seated in the center, shows the Last Judgment.

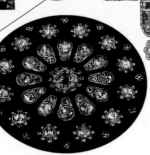

KEY

1 Tree of Jesse	**12** Noah	**22** St. Anthony and St. Paul	**33** St. Theodore and St. Vincent
2 Incarnation	**13** St. John the Evangelist	**23** Blue Virgin	**34** St. Stephen
3 Passion and Resurrection	**14** Mary Magdalene	**24** Life of the Virgin	**35** St. Cheron
4 North Rose Window	**15** Good Samaritan and Adam and Eve	**25** Zodiac Window	**36** St. Thomas
5 West Rose Window	**16** Assumption	**26** St. Martin	**37** Peace Window
6 South Rose Window	**17** Vendôme Chapel Windows	**27** St. Thomas Becket	**38** Modern Window
7 Redemption Window	**18** Miracles of Mary	**28** St. Margaret and St. Catherine	**39** Prodigal Son
8 St. Nicholas	**19** St. Apollinaris	**29** St. Nicholas	**40** Ezekiel and David
9 Joseph	**20** Modern Window	**30** St. Remy	**41** Aaron
10 St. Eustache	**21** St. Fulbert	**31** St. James the Greater	**42** Annunciation-Visitation
11 St. Lubin		**32** Charlemagne	**43** Isaiah and Moses
			44 Daniel and Jeremiah

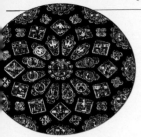

North Rose Window
This depicts the Glorification of the Virgin, *surrounded by the kings of Judah and the prophets (c.1230).*

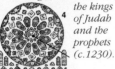

4

GUIDE TO READING THE WINDOWS

Each window is divided into panels, usually read from left to right, bottom to top (earth to heaven). The number of figures or abstract shapes used is thought to be symbolic: three stands for divinity, while the number four symbolizes the material world or the four elements.

Mary and Child in the sacred mandorla (c.1150)

Two angels doing homage before the celestial throne

Christ's triumphal entry into Jerusalem on Palm Sunday

Upper panels of the Incarnation Window

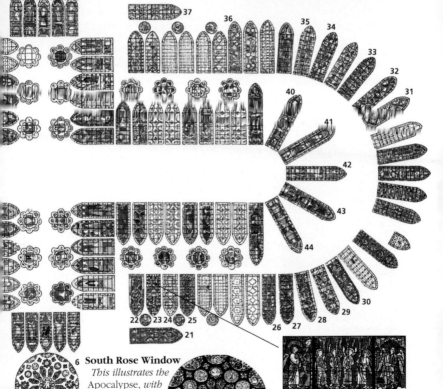

37 36 35 34 33 32 31 40 41 42 43 44 30 29 28 27 26 22 23 24 25 21

6 **South Rose Window**
This illustrates the Apocalypse, *with* Christ in Majesty *(c.1225).*

STAR WINDOWS

★ West Rose Window

★ Tree of Jesse

★ Blue Virgin Window

★ **Blue Virgin Window**
The window's bottom panel depicts the conversion of water into wine by Christ at The Marriage at Cana.

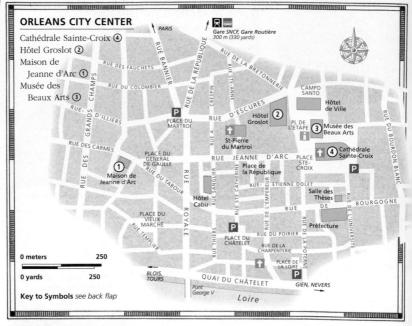

ORLEANS CITY CENTER

Cathédrale Sainte-Croix ④
Hôtel Groslot ②
Maison de
  Jeanne d'Arc ①
Musée des
  Beaux Arts ③

0 meters   250
0 yards   250

Key to Symbols *see back flap*

Orléans' Cathédrale Sainte-Croix

Orléans ㉕

Loiret. 🏙 *112,500.* ✈ 🚉 🚌
ℹ *2 pl Etape (02 38 24 05 05).*
🗓 *Tue–Sun.* www.tourisme-
orleans.com

Orléans' dazzling contemporary bridge symbolizes the
city's increasing importance
at the geographic heart of
both France and Europe. As
a tourist, however, one is
struck by the city's continued
attachment to its past, most
particularly to Joan of Arc. It

was from here that the Maid
of Orléans saved France from
the English in 1429 *(see p300).*
Since her martyrdom at
Rouen in 1431, Joan remains
a presence in Orléans. Every
April 29 and May 1, 7, and 8
her liberation of the city is re-
enacted in a pageant and a
blessing in the cathedral.

Orléans' historic center was
badly damaged in World War
II, but much has been reconstructed, and a faded grandeur
lingers in Vieil Orléans, the
quarter bounded by the cathedral, the river Loire, and the
place du Martroi. The latter, a
Classical but rather windswept square, has an equestrian statue of the city's heroine.
Nearby, the half-timbered
Maison de Jeanne d'Arc was
rebuilt from period dwellings
in 1961 on the site where
Joan had lodgings in 1429.

From place du Martroi, the
rue d'Escures leads past
Renaissance mansions to the
cathedral. **Hôtel Groslot** is the
grandest, a 16th-century red-
brick mansion where kings
Charles IX, Henri III, and
Henri IV all stayed. The 17-
year-old François II died here
in 1560 after attending a
meeting of the Etats Généraux

with his child-bride, Mary,
later Queen of Scots. The
building served as Orléans'
town hall from 1790 to
1982, and the sumptuously
decorated interior, with its
Joan memorabilia, is still
used for marriages and
official ceremonies.

Virtually opposite the Hôtel
Groslot and alongside the
new town hall is the **Musée
des Beaux Arts**, displaying
European works of art from
the 16th to the 20th centuries.

The **Cathédrale Sainte-Croix**
nearby is an imposing edifice
begun in the late 13th century,
destroyed by the Huguenots
(Protestants) in 1568, and
then rebuilt in supposedly
Gothic style between the
17th and 19th centuries.

🏛 **Hôtel Groslot**
Pl de l'Etape. *Tel 02 38 79 22 30.*
🗓 *daily.* ⬤ *sporadically.*

🏛 **Musée des Beaux Arts**
Pl Ste-Croix. *Tel 02 38 79 21
55.* 🗓 *Tue–Sun.* ⬤ *Jan 1,
May 1, May 8, Nov 1 & 11,
Dec 25.* 🎟 *free 1st Sun of
month.* ♿

🏛 **Maison de Jeanne d'Arc**
3 pl du Général de Gaulle.
Tel 02 38 52 99 89. ⬤ *call for
further information.*

Joan of Arc stained-glass window in Orléans' Cathédrale Sainte-Croix

St-Benoît-sur-Loire ㉖

Loiret. 🏠 *2,000.* 🚄 🛈 *44 rue Orléanaise (02 38 35 79 00).*
www.saint-benoit-sur-loire.fr

Situated along the river Loire between Orléans and Gien, St-Benoît-sur-Loire boasts one of the finest Romanesque abbey churches in France (1067–1108). It is all that survives of an important monastery founded in AD 650 and named after St. Benedict, patron saint of Europe. His relics were brought from Italy at the end of the 7th century.

The church's belfry porch is graced with carved capitals depicting biblical scenes. The nave is tall and light, and the choir floor is an amazing patchwork of Italian marble. Daily services with Gregorian chant are open to the public.

Bourges ㉗

Cher. 🏠 *80,000.* 🚄 🛈
🛈 *21 rue Victor Hugo (02 48 23 02 60).* 🗓 *Tue–Sun.*
www.bourgestourism.com

This Gallo-Roman city retains its original walls but is best known as the city of Jacques Coeur, financier and foreign minister to Charles VII. The greatest merchant of the Middle Ages and a self-made man *par excellence*, it was in his capacity as an arms dealer that he established a tradition maintained for four centuries, as Napoléon III had cannons manufactured here in 1862.

Built over part of the walls, the **Palais Jacques Coeur** is a Gothic gem and a lasting memorial to its first master. It was finished in 1453, and incorporates Coeur's two emblems, scallop shells and hearts, as well as his motto: *"A vaillan coeur, rien impossible"* – to the valiant heart, nothing is impossible. The obligatory tour reveals a barrel-vaulted gallery, a painted chapel, and a chamber that had Turkish baths.

Bourges also flourishes as a university town and cultural mecca, renowned for its spring festival of music.

Rue Bourbonnoux leads to **St-Etienne**, the widest Gothic cathedral in France and the one most similar to Paris's Notre-Dame. The west façade has five sculpted portals, the

Stained-glass window in the Cathédrale St-Etienne

central one depicting an enthralling *Last Judgment*. In the choir are vivid 13th-century stained-glass windows presented by the guilds. The crypt holds the marble tomb of the 14th-century Duc de Berry, best known for commissioning the illuminated manuscript the *Très Riches Heures (see pp204–5).* From the top of the north tower stretch views of the beautifully restored medieval quarter and the marshes beyond. Beside the cathedral is a tithe barn and the remains of the Gallo-Roman ramparts.

Statue of Jacques Coeur

The **Jardin des Prés Fichaux**, set along the river Yèvre, contains pools and an open-air theater. To the north lie the **Marais de Bourges**, where gardeners transport their produce by boat.

🏛 **Palais Jacques Coeur**
Rue Jacques Coeur. **Tel** *02 48 24 79 42.* 🗓 *daily.* ⬤ *Jan 1, May 1, Nov 1 & 11, Dec 25.* 🅰 🖼

Environs
About 22 miles (35 km) south of Bourges in the Berry region is the **Abbaye de Noirlac**. Founded in 1136, it is one of the best-preserved Cistercian abbeys in France.

Statue in the Jardin des Prés Fichaux

CENTRAL FRANCE AND THE ALPS

Introducing Central France and the Alps

The geological contrasts of this region reflect
its enormous variety, from the industrial and
gastronomic metropolis of Lyon to the largely
agricultural landscape of Burgundy. The mountains
of the Massif Central and the Alps attract visitors for
winter sports, superb walking, and other outdoor
activities. The major sights of this richly rewarding
area, both natural and architectural, are shown here.

Basilique Ste-Madeleine,
*the famous pilgrimage church
crowning the hilltop village of
Vézelay, is a masterpiece of
Burgundian Romanesque.
It is renowned for its vividly
decorated tympanum and
capitals (see pp336–7).*

The Abbaye de Ste-Foy *in the village
of Conques (see pp366–7) is one of the
great pilgrimage churches of France,
with a fabulous treasury of medieval
and Renaissance gold reliquaries.*

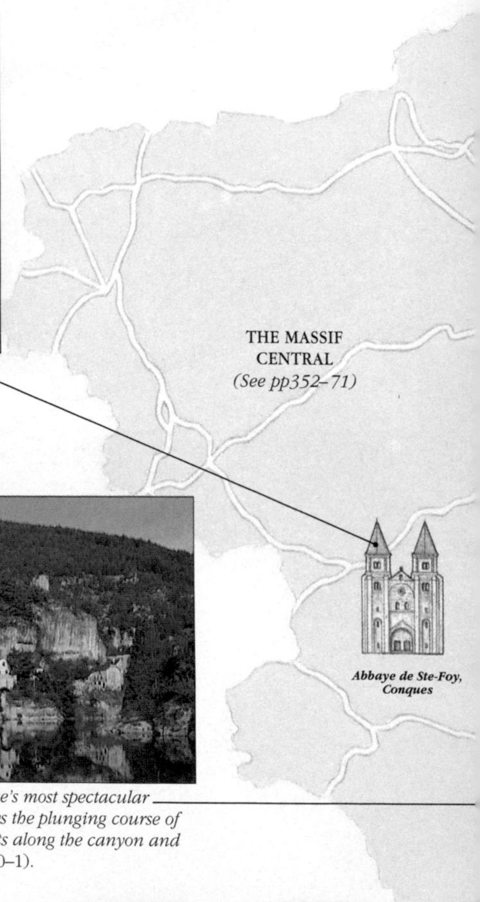

**THE MASSIF
CENTRAL**
(See pp352–71)

*Abbaye de Ste-Foy,
Conques*

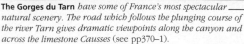

The Gorges du Tarn *have some of France's most spectacular
natural scenery. The road which follows the plunging course of
the river Tarn gives dramatic viewpoints along the canyon and
across the limestone Causses (see pp370–1).*

The Abbaye de Fontenay, *founded by Saint Bernard in the early 12th century, is the oldest Cistercian monastery in France (see pp332–3). This well-preserved Romanesque abbey is a perfect testimony to the severe ideal of the Cistercian life.*

Abbaye de Fontenay

adeleine,
zelay

Palais des Ducs, Dijon

BURGUNDY AND FRANCHE-COMTE
(See pp326–51)

Théâtre Romain, Autun

Brou Abbey Church, Bourg-en-Bresse

Mont Blanc

Temple d'Auguste et Livie, Vienne

THE RHONE VALLEY AND FRENCH ALPS
(See pp372–91)

Palais Idéal du Facteur Cheval, Hauterives

Le Puy

Gorges du Tarn

0 kilometers   50

0 miles   50

The Flavors of Central France

The renowned gastronomic tradition of Lyon and the rich wine and food of Burgundy combine to make central France a gourmet paradise. The great chefs of the region have a wide choice of excellent local produce: fine Bresse chicken, Charolais beef, and Morvan ham; wildfowl and frogs from the marshes of the Dombe; fish from the Saône and the Rhône; and fat snails called "oysters of Burgundy." Franche-Comté and the Jura contribute smoked sausages, farmhouse cheeses, walnut oil, and fish from glacier-fed lakes. In the Massif Central, sturdy regional fare features salted hams, pork, Cantal cheese, the celebrated green lentils of Le Puy, and wild mushrooms.

Chanterelle mushrooms

A mountain farmer shows off his fine salt-cured ham

BURGUNDY AND FRANCHE-COMTE

Burgundy is one of France's top wine regions so, not surprisingly, wine plays a major role in the cuisine, such as in the signature dish, *boeuf bourguignon*, made from Charolais beef marinated and then stewed in good red wine, with baby onions, bacon, and mush-

rooms added. Other specialties include *coq au vin* and *oeufs en meurette*. Dijon's famous mustard appears most classically with steak and in *moutarde au lapin*, rabbit in a creamy mustard sauce. Burgundy and Franche-Comté produce some of the most celebrated French cheeses: Epoisses, a cow's milk cheese washed with *marc de Bourgogne*, Cîteaux, made by monks, and the magnificent Vacherin-Mont d'Or, a winter

treat to be scooped straight from its wooden box. Blackcurrants are widely grown and contribute to many desserts as well as the famous Kir: white wine with cassis (blackcurrant liqueur).

THE MASSIF CENTRAL

The peasant cuisine of the Auvergne is well known in France due to the many cafés run by Auvergnats in Paris, where they serve local

Tomme de Savoie | **Fourme d'Ambert** | **Raclette** | **Roquefort**
St-Nectaire | **Emmenthal** | **Reblochon**

Mouthwatering array of classic French cheeses

REGIONAL DISHES AND SPECIALTIES

The cuisine of central France is rich with sauces using wine, butter, and cream, which enhance almost every dish: snails in butter and garlic; potatoes cooked with cheese and cream; and beef, lamb, and chicken stewed slowly in reduced wine sauces, often with cream or butter added at the end of cooking. Mushrooms are cooked in cream sauces, and fish is often baked in a creamy gratin. Most indulgent of all is the Alpine fondue, where cheeses are melted, together with Kirsch and wine, in a special earthenware fondue pot. This is placed on a burner on the table, and cubes of bread are speared onto special long forks and dipped into the cheese. Traditionally, anyone who loses their bread in the pot must kiss everyone else at the table.

String of onions

Oeufs en meurette *This Burgundian dish is eggs poached in red wine with onions, mushrooms, and bacon.*

Traditional charcuterie on sale in a Lyon market

dishes like pork stuffed with cabbage, or *aligot*. Le Puy lentils, grown in the fertile volcanic soils of the Puy-en-Velay basin, combine well with sausages or *petit salé*, or are served cold as a salad. Good beef comes from the Salers cattle of the Auvergne or from the Limousin, where there is also plentiful game. Wild mushrooms are eagerly sought in season. Cheeses include Cantal, one of the country's oldest and similar in flavor to Cheddar, and the famous blue Roquefort, ripened in the limestone caves of the Lozère.

THE RHONE VALLEY AND THE FRENCH ALPS

Lyon is famous for its traditional bistros, *bouchons*, where the cooks are often women, known as *mères*, who dish up substantial fare like onion soup, lyonnais sausages, and *charcuterie*. The markets of Lyon are equally famous, stocked with the region's wide range of fruit, particularly apricots, peach, and juicy berries.

Redcurrants and blackberries for sale by the punnet

Vegetables include onions, chard, and cardoons, and the most northerly outpost of the olive is at Nyons. The Bresse region is famous for its high-quality chickens.

The Dombes lakes and the Alps are good sources of fish, such as perch, trout, and lake salmon. Bony perch is most delicious eaten as *quenelles de brochet*, filleted fish blended, made into dumplings, and baked in a creamy sauce. From the Alps comes a wide range of cheeses. As well as being delicious to eat fresh, they will often be found melted as *raclettes* or fondues, or layered with sliced potato to make an unctuous *gratin dauphinois*.

ON THE MENU

Chou farci Cabbage stuffed with pork and herbs.

Gigot Brayaude Leg of lamb baked over sliced potatoes and lardons of bacon.

Gougère Cheesy choux pastry baked in a ring shape.

Jambon persillé Ham and parsley in aspic jelly.

Pochouse Freshwater fish (carp, pike, eel, and trout) stewed in white wine.

Potée savoyarde Stew made with vegetables, chicken, ham, and sausage.

Salade auvergnate Cubes of Auvergne ham, Cantal cheese, and walnuts.

Petit salé *A specialty of the Auvergne region, salt pork is cooked in wine with tiny green Puy lentils.*

Aligot *Slivers of Cantal cheese are beaten into buttery, garlicky mashed potato until the mixture forms long strands.*

Clafoutis *This is usually made with black cherries, baked in batter and laced with Kirsch, a cherry liqueur.*

France's Wine Regions: Burgundy

Grape-picker's basket

Burgundy and its fine wines have inspired awe for centuries. The fame of the region's wines spread throughout Europe in the 14th century, under the Valois Dukes of Burgundy. The system of dividing wine areas into designated *appellations*, of which there are a bewildering number, came into effect in 1935. Even today, the classification system remains dauntingly complex. But despite its impenetrable image, this is unmissable territory for the "serious" wine lover, with its rich vinous history and tradition and dazzling *grands crus*.

LOCATOR MAP

Burgundy wine region

Clos de Vougeot on the Côte de Nuits

WINE REGIONS

Between Chablis in the north and the Côte Chalonnaise and Mâconnais in the south is the Côte d'Or, incorporating Côte de Nuits and Côte de Beaune. The Beaujolais region (*see pp376–7*) lies below Mâcon.

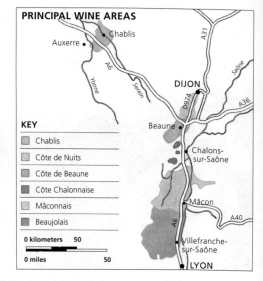

PRINCIPAL WINE AREAS

Chablis
Auxerre
DIJON
Beaune
Chalons-sur-Saône
Mâcon
Villefranche-sur-Saône
LYON

Yonne · Serein · A6 · A31 · Saône · A36 · D974 · A40 · A6

KEY

- Chablis
- Côte de Nuits
- Côte de Beaune
- Côte Chalonnaise
- Mâconnais
- Beaujolais

0 kilometers 50

0 miles 50

KEY FACTS ABOUT BURGUNDY

Location and Climate
The continental climate (bleak winters and hot summers) can be very variable, making vintages a crucial quality factor. The best vineyards have chalky soil and face south or east.

Grape Varieties
Burgundy is at least relatively simple in its grape varieties. Red Burgundy is made from **Pinot Noir**, with its sweet flavors of raspberries, cherries, and strawberries, while the **Gamay** makes red Mâcon and Beaujolais. **Chardonnay** is the principal white variety for Chablis and white Burgundy, though small amounts of **Aligoté** and **Pinot Blanc** are grown and the **Sauvignon** is a specialty of St-Bris.

Good Producers
White Burgundy: Jean-Marie Raveneau, René Dauvissat, La Chablisienne, Comtes Lafon, Guy Roulot, Etienne Sauzet, Pierre Morey, Louis Carillon, Jean-Marc Boillot, André Ramonet, Hubert Lamy, Jean-Marie Guffens-Heynen, Olivier Merlin, Louis Latour, Louis Jadot, Olivier Leflaive.
Red Burgundy: Denis Bachelet, Daniel Rion, Domaine Dujac, Armand Rousseau, Joseph Roty, De Montille, Domaine de la Pousse d'Or, Domaine de l'Arlot, Jean-Jacques Confuron, Robert Chevillon, Georges Roumier, Leroy, Drouhin.

Good Vintages
(*Reds*) 2009, 2005, 2002, 1999.
(*Whites*) 2008, 2005, 2001, 1996.

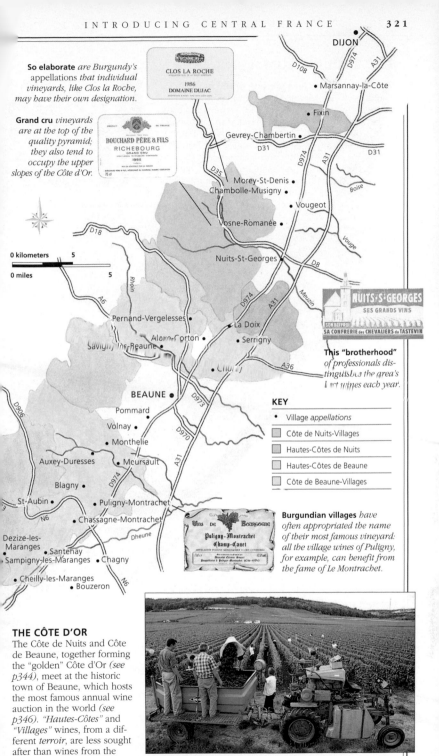

So elaborate *are Burgundy's appellations that individual vineyards, like Clos la Roche, may have their own designation.*

CLOS LA ROCHE
1986
DOMAINE DUJAC

Grand cru *vineyards are at the top of the quality pyramid; they also tend to occupy the upper slopes of the Côte d'Or.*

BOUCHARD PÈRE & FILS
RICHEBOURG
GRAND CRU
1986

DIJON

Marsannay-la-Côte

Fixin

Gevrey-Chambertin

Morey-St-Denis
Chambolle-Musigny

Vougeot

Vosne-Romanée

Nuits-St-Georges

0 kilometers   5
0 miles   5

Pernand-Vergelesses
Aloxe-Corton
La Doix
Savigny-lès-Beaune
Serrigny
Chorey

NUITS·S·GEORGES
SES GRANDS VINS
SON BEFFROI
SA CONFRERIE des CHEVALIERS du TASTEVIN

This "brotherhood" *of professionals distinguishes the area's best wines each year.*

BEAUNE
Pommard
Volnay
Monthelie
Auxey-Duresses
Meursault
Blagny
St-Aubin
Puligny-Montrachet
Chassagne-Montrachet
Dezize-les-Maranges
Santenay
Sampigny-les-Maranges
Chagny
Cheilly-les-Maranges
Bouzeron

KEY

•	Village *appellations*
▢	Côte de Nuits-Villages
▢	Hautes-Côtes de Nuits
▢	Hautes-Côtes de Beaune
▢	Côte de Beaune-Villages

Vins de Bourgogne
Puligny-Montrachet
Champ-Canet

Burgundian villages *have often appropriated the name of their most famous vineyard: all the village wines of Puligny, for example, can benefit from the fame of Le Montrachet.*

THE CÔTE D'OR

The Côte de Nuits and Côte de Beaune, together forming the "golden" Côte d'Or *(see p344)*, meet at the historic town of Beaune, which hosts the most famous annual wine auction in the world *(see p346)*. "Hautes-Côtes" and "Villages" wines, from a different *terroir*, are less sought after than wines from the starry individual *appellations*.

Teams of grape-pickers at the vineyards of Nuits-St-Georges

The French Alps

In any season, the Alps are one of the most spectacular regions of France – a majestic mountain range stretching south from Lake Geneva almost to the Mediterranean, and climaxing in Europe's loftiest peak, the 15,770-ft (4,800-m) Mont Blanc. The area encompasses the old regions of Dauphiné and Savoie, once remote and independent (Savoie only became part of France in 1860). They have prospered since alpine holidays and skiing became popular over the last century, but are still very conscious of their distinct identity.

Children in traditional Savoie costumes

The Alpine landscape in winter: chalets and skiers on the slopes at Courchevel

WINTER

The ski season usually starts just before Christmas, and finishes at the end of April. Most resorts offer both cross-country and downhill skiing,

A cable car at Courchevel, part of Les Trois Vallées complex

with many pistes linking two or more ski stations. The less energetic can still enjoy the landscape from some of the highest cable cars (*téléphériques*) in the world.

Of the 100 or more French Alpine resorts, the most popular include **Chamonix-Mont Blanc**, the historic capital of Alpine skiing and site of the first Winter Olympics in 1924; **Megève**, which boasts one of the best ski schools in Europe; **Morzine**, a year-round resort on the Swiss border, overlooked by the modern, car-free resort of **Avoriaz**; modern **Albertville**, site of the 1992 Winter Olympics; **Les Trois Vallées**, which include glamorous

A downhill skier at Val d'Isère

Courchevel and **Méribel**, and the lesser-known **Val Thorens/Les Ménuires**; **Tignes**, a year-round resort; **Les Arcs** and **La Plagne**, both purpose-built; and **Val d'Isère**, a favorite among the rich and famous.

ALPINE FLOWERS

In spring and early summer the pastures of the French Alps are ablaze with flowers. These include blue and yellow gentians, bellflowers, lilies, saxifrages and a variety of orchids. Steep mountain meadows cannot be farmed intensively, and the absence of fertilizers and weed killers enables wild flowers to flourish.

Spring gentian (Gentiana verna)

Martagon lily (Lilium martagon)

The French Alps in spring: flower-filled meadows overlooked by brilliant white peaks

SPRING AND SUMMER

The Alpine summer season starts in late June, extending to early September – most resorts close in October and November

Bell-ringing dairy cows in an Alpine pasture

between the hiking and skiing seasons. After the spring thaw, flower-filled pastures, snow-fed mountain lakes, and a huge number of marked trails make this area a hiker's paradise. In the Chamonix area alone there are over 195 miles (310 km) of hiking trails. The best known long-distance route is the **Tour du Mont Blanc**, a 10-day hike via France, Italy, and Switzerland. The **GR5** traverses the entire Alps, passing through the **Parc National de la Vanoise** and **Parc Régional du Queyras** *(see p387)* to the south. *Téléphériques* give access to the higher trails, where the views are even more awesome. Be sure to bring plenty of warm,

waterproof clothing: the weather can change very quickly.

Many resorts are now concentrating on broadening their summer appeal – golf, tennis, mountain biking, horseback-riding, paragliding, canoeing, white water rafting, glacier skiing, and mountain climbing are all widely available.

Mountain climbers scaling the heights around Mont Blanc

Geology of the Massif Central

The Massif Central covers almost one-fifth of France and is over 250 million years old. Most of its peaks have been eroded to form a vast plateau split into deep valleys. The heart of the Massif consists of hard, igneous rocks like granite, with softer rocks such as limestone at its margins. Different rock types are reflected in the landscape and buildings; in the eroded Gorges du Tarn, the houses are built of russet-colored limestone. Massive granite farmhouses are a feature of Limousin, and Le Puy-en-Velay is distinguished by its giant basalt pillars.

LOCATOR MAP

   Extent of the Massif Central

Basalt *is a dark, fine-grained rock formed by volcanic lava. A common building stone in the Auvergne, it is often cut into blocks and bonded with lighter-colored mortar. In the medieval town of Salers (see p363), basalt was used for most of the buildings, including this one in the Grande Place.*

This granite portal *is found in the Romanesque church at Moutier d'Ahun (see p356). Granite underlies much of the Massif Central.*

Montluçon

Moutier d'Ahun

Limoges

Clermont-Ferrand

Dordogne

Salers

Schist tiling *is featured on these roofs at Argentat. Schist is a crystalline rock which splits readily into layers. It is particularly common on the edge of the Massif, and provides an effective roofing material.*

Argentat

Cère

Lot

Limestone walls *can be seen on houses in Espalion (see p366). Of all the rocks in the Massif Central, it is among the most easily worked. It splits readily and is soft enough to be cut into blocks with a hand saw. As with granite, its color and consistency vary from area to area.*

Milla

Tarn

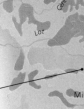

0 kilometers   50

0 miles   50

Crystallized lava, *like this dramatic curtain of columns at Prades, formed when liquid basalt seeped through the surrounding rock and solidified to form giant crystals.*

KEY

◼	Sedimentary rock
◼	Surface volcanic rock
◼	Granite
◻	Metamorphic rock

Nevers

Loire

Saône

Lyon

St-Étienne

Le-Puy-en-Velay

Rhône

Limestone plateaux (causses) *are typical of this region. Gorges, where rivers have cut through layers of this slightly soluble rock, run deep into the Massif Central.*

This mature landscape *at Mont Aigoual is the highest point in the Cévennes (see p367), dividing rivers flowing into the Atlantic and the Mediterranean. Its granite and schist rocks show erosion.*

RECOGNIZING ROCKS

Geologists divide rocks into three groups. Igneous rocks, like granite, are formed by volcanic activity and either extruded on to the surface or intrude into other rocks below ground. Sedimentary rocks are produced by sediment build-up. Metamorphic rocks have been transformed by heat or pressure.

SEDIMENTARY ROCK

Oolitic limestone *often contains fossils and small amounts of quartz.*

SURFACE VOLCANIC ROCK

Basalt, *which can form very thick sheets, is the most common lava rock.*

GRANITE

Pink granite, *a coarse-grained rock, is formed deep in the earth's crust.*

METAMORPHIC ROCK

Muscovite schist *is a medium-grained mud or clay-based rock.*

BURGUNDY AND FRANCHE-COMTE

YONNE · NIEVRE · COTE D'OR · SAONE-ET-LOIRE HAUTE-SAONE · DOUBS · JURA

B*urgundy considers itself the heart of France, a prosperous region with world-renowned wine, earthy but excellent cuisine, and magnificent architecture. Franche-Comté to the east combines gentle farmland with lofty Alpine forests.*

Under the dukes of Valois, Burgundy was France's most powerful rival, with territory extending well beyond its present boundaries. By the 16th century, however, the duchy was ruled by governors appointed by the French king, but it still managed to keep its privileges and traditions. Once a part of Burgundy, Franche-Comté – the Free County – struggled to remain independent of the French crown, and was a province of the Holy Roman Empire until annexed by Louis XIV in 1674.

Burgundy, now as in the past, is a wealthy region, a center of medieval religious faith which produced Romanesque masterpieces at Vézelay, Fontenay, and Cluny. Dijon is a splendid city, filled with the great palaces of the old Burgundian nobility and a collection of great paintings and sculptures in the Musée des Beaux Arts. The vineyards of the Côte d'Or, the Côte de Beaune, and Chablis yield some of the world's most venerated wines. Other richly varied landscapes – from the wild forests of the Morvan to the lush farmland of the Brionnais – produce snails, Bresse chickens, and Charolais beef.

Franche-Comté has none of this opulence, though its capital, Besançon, is an elegant 17th-century city with a tradition of clockmaking. Topographically the Franche-Comté is divided into two, with gently rolling farmland in the Saône valley and high Alpine scenery to the east. This forest country of Alpine torrents filled with trout is also the home of great cheeses, notably Vacherin and Comté, and of the characteristic yellow wine of Arbois.

The prehistoric site of the Roche de Solutré near Mâcon

◁ Vineyards at Santenay in the world-renowned Côte de Beaune district

Exploring Burgundy and Franche-Comté

Burgundy is arguably France's richest province – historically, culturally, gastronomically, and economically. This lush kernel of a once great power possesses a concentration of unique Romanesque architecture in Fontenay and Vézelay, along with some of the world's most venerated wines. Dijon is a must for lovers of art, architecture, and food. Franche-Comté is better suited for outdoor holidays, such as trekking and canoeing in wild scenery and crystal-clear rivers.

Burgundian riverscape near Fontenay

Distinctive Burgundian glazed roof tiles, Hôtel Aubriot in Dijon

KEY

━━━	Highway
━━━	Major road
━━━	Secondary road
═══	Minor road
━━━	Scenic route
∙━∙━	Main railroad
────	Minor railroad
▬▬▬	International border
━━━	Regional border
△	Summit

0 kilometers   25

0 miles   25

For additional map symbols *see back flap*

Champigny · SENS ① · Villeneuve-l'Archevêque · Paris · Villeneuve-sur-Yonne · Joigny · Charmoy · Brienon · Saint-Florentin · Les Riceys · Charny · Aillant-sur-Tholon · Pontigny · CHABLIS ④⑤ ⑥ TANLAY · CHÂTIL SUR-S · AUXERRE ③ · TONNERRE ⑦ · ANCY-LE-FRANC · Toucy · Bléneau · St-Fargeau · Vermenton · Noyers · ABBAYE DE FONTENAY ⑨ · St-Sauveur-en-Puisaye · Courson-les-Carrières · Montbard ⑨ · Château de Bussy-Rabutin · LA PUISAYE ② · St-Amand · Château d'Epoisses · ⑩ AL STE · Cosne-Cours-sur-Loire · Clamecy · VÉZELAY ⑫ · ⑬ AVALLON · SEMUR-EN-AUXOIS · Varzy · Château de Bazoches · Quarré-les-Tombes · BOURGOGNE · Donzy · Somb · ⑮ SAULIEU · La Charité · Corbigny · Montsauche · Pouilly-en-Auxois · Prémery · MORVAN · Lucenay-l'Évêque · Arn le-D · Guérigny · Châtillon-en-Bazois · Château-Chinon ⑭ · Haut Folin 901m · NEVERS ⑯ · Saint-Benin-d'Azy · Saint-Léger-sous-Beuvray · ⑰ AUTUN · St-Parize-le-Châtel · Imphy · La Machine · Saint-Honoré · Bourges · Decize · Fours · Luzy · Le Creusot · Mont · Issy-l'Évêque · Blanzy · Montceau-les-Mines · Bourbon-Lancy · Gueugnon · Cor · Digoin ㉓ · Saint-Bonnet-de-Joux · PARAY-LE-MONIAL · Charolles · CLUN · Marcigny · BRIONNAIS · La Clayette · St-Christophe ㉔ · Loire

SIGHTS AT A GLANCE

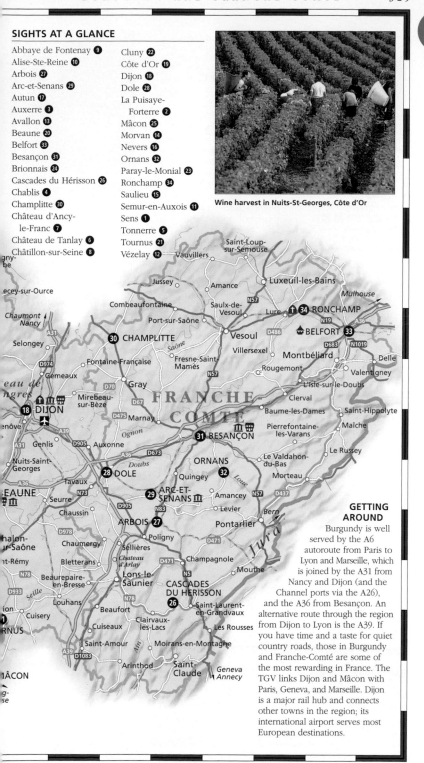

Wine harvest in Nuits-St-Georges, Côte d'Or

GETTING AROUND

Burgundy is well served by the A6 autoroute from Paris to Lyon and Marseille, which is joined by the A31 from Nancy and Dijon (and the Channel ports via the A26), and the A36 from Besançon. An alternative route through the region from Dijon to Lyon is the A39. If you have time and a taste for quiet country roads, those in Burgundy and Franche-Comté are some of the most rewarding in France. The TGV links Dijon and Mâcon with Paris, Geneva, and Marseille. Dijon is a major rail hub and connects other towns in the region; its international airport serves most European destinations.

La Sainte Châsse, 11th-century reliquary in the Treasury in Sens

Sens ❶

Yonne. 🏠 30,000. 🚉 🚌
🛈 pl Jean-Jaurès (03 86 65 19 49).
🗓 Mon, Wed, Fri, & Sat.
www.office-de-tourisme-sens.com

The little town of Sens, at the confluence of the rivers Yonne and Vanne, was important before Caesar came to Gaul. It was the Senones whose attempt to sack the Roman Capitol in 390 BC was thwarted by a flock of geese.

The **Cathédrale St-Etienne** is Sens' outstanding glory. Begun before 1140, it is the oldest of the great Gothic cathedrals and its noble simplicity influenced many other churches. Louis IX (see p51) did the town the honor of getting married here in 1234.

The exquisite stained-glass windows from the 12th–16th centuries show biblical scenes, including the Tree of Jesse, and a tribute to Thomas Becket who was exiled here. His liturgical robes are in the Treasury (part of the **Musées de Sens**), which has one of the finest collections in France, including a beautiful Byzantine reliquary.

🏛 **Les Musées de Sens**
Pl de la Cathédrale. **Tel** 03 86 64 46 22. ◻ Jun–Sep: Wed–Mon; Oct–May: Wed, Sat, Sun (Mon, Thu, Fri pms only). 🖼 🚻 🗲

La Puisaye-Forterre ❷

Yonne, Nièvre. 🚉 Auxerre, Clamecy, Bonny-sur-Loire, Cosne-Cours-sur-Loire. 🚌 St-Fargeau, St-Sauveur-en-Puisaye. 🛈 Charny (03 86 63 65 51).

The strange, secret forest country of La Puisaye-Forterre was immortalized by Colette (1873–1954), who was born at **St-Sauveur** in "a house that smiled only on its garden side…." This 17th-century château now houses the **Musée Colette**.

The best way to explore the region is on foot or by bike around its watery woodlands, orchards, and meadows. Alternatively, take a ride on the *Transpoyaudin*, a 17-mile (27-km) train ride from St-Sauveur to Villiers St-Benoît.

A hands-on visit can be made to **Château de Guédelon**, a 25-year project recreating a medieval castle, using only original building methods and materials found locally. Nearby is the genuine 13th-century **Château de Ratilly**, with pottery, art exhibitions, concerts, and music workshops. More of this can be seen in **St-Amand**, the center of Puisaye stoneware production, much of which was traditionally fired in the 18th-century horizontal kiln at Moutiers. Both the pottery

Colette in the 1880s at St-Sauveur

and local frescoes (see the churches at **Moutiers** and **La Ferté-Loupière**) made use of locally mined ocher, a major export in the 19th century. The pink brick **Château de St-Fargeau** housed the exiled Grande Mademoiselle (p57).

🏛 **Musée Colette**
Château St-Sauveur-en-Puisaye. **Tel** 03 86 45 61 95. ◻ Apr–mid–Nov: Wed–Mon. 🖼

Auxerre ❸

Yonne. 🏠 40,000. 🚉 🛈 1–2 quai de la République (03 86 52 06 19).
🗓 Tue & Fri. www.ot-auxerre.fr

Beautifully sited overlooking the Yonne river, Auxerre justly prides itself on a fine collection of churches along with a charming pedestrianized main square, the place Charles-Surugue.

The Gothic **Cathédrale St-Etienne** took more than three centuries to build and was completed around 1560. It is famous for its intricate 13th-century stained glass. The choir with its slender columns and colonettes is the epitome of Gothic elegance, while the western portals are decorated with beautiful flamboyant sculpture which, unfortunately, has been mutilated by war and weather. The Romanesque crypt is adorned by unique 11th–13th-century frescoes, including one depicting Christ on a white horse. The badly pillaged treasury has an interesting collection of illuminated manuscripts.

Château de St-Fargeau in the Puisaye-Forterre region

For hotels and restaurants in this region see pp572–5 and pp625–9

St. Germanus, mentor of St. Patrick and bishop of Auxerre in the 5th century, was buried at the former abbey church of **St-Germain**. The abbey was founded by Queen Clothilde, wife of Clovis (see pp48–9), the first Christian king of France, and is an important shrine. The crypt is partly Carolingian, with tombs and 11th–13th century frescoes. The former abbey houses the **Musée St-Germain** with local Gallo-Roman finds.

🏛 **Musée St-Germain**
2 pl St-Germain. **Tel** 03 86 18 05 50. ☐ Apr–Sep: Wed–Sun; Oct–May: Wed–Fri ams, Sat & Sun. ● some public hols. 🗺 🖪

Medieval fresco in Cathédrale St-Etienne at Auxerre

Chablis ❹

Yonne. 🏠 2,700. 🚉 🛈 1 rue du Maréchal de Lattre de Tassigny (03 86 42 80 80). ☺ Sun. www.chablis.net

There can be no question that Chablis tastes best in Chablis. Although this is one of the

The intriguing spring of Fosse Dionne in Tonnerre

most famous wine villages on earth, its narrow stone streets still have an air of sleepy prosperity. February processions in nearby Fyé, attended by the wine brotherhood of Piliers Chablisiens, honor St-Vincent, patron saint of wine-growers.

Tonnerre ❺

Yonne. 🏠 6,200. 🚉 🖪 🛈 pl Marguerite de Bourgogne (03 86 55 14 48). ☺ Sat & Wed. www.tonnerre.fr

The mystical cloudy-green spring of **Fosse Dionne** is a good reason to visit the small town of Tonnerre. An astonishing volume of water bursts up from the ground into an 18th-century washing place. Due to its depth and strong currents it has never been thoroughly explored, and local legend has it that a serpent lives on undisturbed.

The **Hôtel-Dieu** is 150 years older than the Hôtel-Dieu in Beaune (see p346–7).

It was founded by Margaret of Burgundy in 1293 to care for the poor. In the Revolution it lost its tiling, but the barrel-vaulted oak ceiling survived.

🏥 **Hôtel-Dieu & Musée**
Rue du Prieuré. **Tel** 03 86 55 14 48. ☐ daily. ● Oct–Mar: Wed, Sun, & some public hols. 🗺 🖪 🖪

Château de Tanlay ❻

Tanlay. **Tel** 03 86 75 70 61. ☐ Apr–mid-Nov: Wed–Mon. 🗺 🖪 oblig.

The moated Château de Tanlay is a beautiful example of French Renaissance, built in the mid-16th century. There is a trompe l'oeil in the Grande Galerie and, in the corner tower, an intriguing School of Fontainebleau painted ceiling. Its antique divinities represent famous Protestants and Catholics in the 16th century, such as Diane de Poitiers as Venus.

The Renaissance façade and cour d'honneur of Château de Tanlay

Abbaye de Fontenay ❾

The tranquil Abbey of Fontenay is the oldest surviving Cistercian foundation in France and offers a rare insight into the Cistercian way of life. It represents the spirit of the order in the sublime gravity of its Romanesque church and its plain but elegant chapterhouse, in early Gothic style. The abbey was founded in 1118 by St-Bernard. Situated deep in the forest, it offered the peace and seclusion the Cistercians sought. Supported by the local aristocracy, the abbey began to thrive and remained in use until the Revolution when it was sold and converted into a paper mill. In 1906 the abbey came under new ownership and was restored to its original appearance.

Dovecote
A magnificent circular dovecote, built in the 13th century, is situated next to the kennel where the precious hunting dogs of the dukes of Burgundy were guarded by servants.

The 17th-century abbot's lodgings were built when the abbots were appointed by royal favor.

The bakehouse is no longer intact but the 13th-century oven and chimney have survived.

The visitors' hostel is where weary wanderers and pilgrims were offered board and lodging by the monks.

★ Cloisters
For a 12th-century monk a walk through the cloisters was an opportunity for meditation and provided shelter from the weather.

Warming Room

In the forge monks produced their own tools and hardware.

Fontenay "Prison"
It may be that this 15th-century building was actually used to lock up not local miscreants but important abbey archives, in order to protect them from damage by rats.

Scriptorium
Manuscripts were copied here. The adjacent Warming Room was used to warm chilled hands

★ **Abbey Church**
Rich decoration has no place in this church from the 1140s. But the severe architectural forms, the warm color of the stone, and the diffused light convey a grandeur of their own.

VISITORS' CHECKLIST

Marmagne. *Tel 03 80 92 15 00.*
🚉 Montbard. ⬜ 10am–6pm
daily (mid-Nov–mid-Apr: 10am–noon & 2–5pm). 🖼 ♿ 📷 📷
www.abbayedefontenay.com

Dormitory
Monks slept in long rows on straw mattresses in this large, unheated room. The timberwork roof is from the late 15th century.

The herb garden was skilfully cultivated by the monks in order to grow healing herbs for medicines and potions.

STAR FEATURES

★ Abbey Church

★ Cloisters

Chapterhouse
Once a day, monks and abbot assembled in this room to discuss matters concerning the community. It derives much of its charm from the elegant 12th-century piers and the rib-vaults.

Infirmary

ST-BERNARD AND THE CISTERCIANS

In 1112 Bernard, a young Burgundian nobleman, joined the Cistercians. At the time the order was still obscure, founded 14 years earlier by a group of monks who wanted to turn their back on the elaborate lifestyle of Cluny *(see pp48–9)*, renounce the world, and espouse poverty and simplicity of life. During Bernard's lifetime the Cistercians became one of the largest and most famous orders of its time. Part of this success was clearly due to Bernard's powerful personality and his skills as a writer, theologian, and statesman. He reinforced the poverty rule, rejecting all forms of embellishment. In 1174, only 21 years after his death, he was canonized.

The Virgin Protecting the Cistercian Order, by Jean Bellegambe

Château d'Ancy-le-Franc 7

Ancy-le-Franc. **Tel** *03 86 75 14 63.* ⬤ *mid-Mar–mid-Nov: Tue–Sun.* 📷 ✔ *oblig.* **www**.chateau-ancy.com

The classical Renaissance façade of Château d'Ancy-le-Franc gives an austere impression. Its inner courtyard, however, has rich ornamentation. The château was built in the 1540s by the Italian Sebastiano Serlio for the Duke of Clermont-Tonnerre. Most of the interior decoration was carried out by Primaticcio and other members of the Fontainebleau School *(see pp180–81).* Diane de Poitiers, the duke's sister-in-law and mistress of Henry II, is portrayed in the *Chambre de Judith et Holophernes.*

The château holds monthly classical music concerts and cooking workshops.

The vase of Vix in the Musée du Châtillonnais, Châtillon-sur-Seine

Châtillon-sur-Seine 8

Côte d'Or. 🚌 *5,837.* 🚆 🚌 🛈 *rue du Bourg (03 80 91 13 19).* 🚍 *Sat.* **www**.tourisme-chatillonnais.fr

World War II left Châtillon a ruin, hence the town's largely modern aspect. But the past is still present in the **Musée du Pays du Châtillonnais**, where the Vix treasure is displayed. In 1953, the tomb of a Gaulish princess, from the 6th century BC, was discovered near Vix at Mont Lassois. The trove of jewelry and artifacts of Greek origin includes a stunning bronze vase, 66 in (164 cm) high and weighing 459 lb (208 kg). Also of interest is the

The staid façade of Château d'Ancy-le-Franc

Romanesque **Eglise St-Vorles** containing an *Entombment* with Christ and mourners splendidly sculpted (1527).

At the nearby source of the river Douix, which runs into the Seine, is a beautiful grotto.

🏛 **Musée du Pays du Châtillonnais**
Rue de la Libération. **Tel** *03 80 91 24 67.* ⬤ *daily.* ⬤ *Jan 1, May 1, Dec 25.* 📷 ✔ **www**.musee-vix.fr

Abbaye de Fontenay 9

See pp332–3.

Alise-Ste-Reine 10

Côte d'Or. 🚌 *3,275.* 🛈 *pl Bingerbrück (03 80 96 89 13).* **www**.alesia-tourisme.net

Mont Auxois, above the village of Alise-Ste-Reine, was the site of Caesar's final victory over the heroic Gaulish chief-

tain Vercingétorix in 52 BC after a six-week siege *(see p46).* The first excavations here were undertaken in the mid-19th century, and they uncovered the vestiges of a thriving Gallo-Roman town, with theater, forum, and well-laid-out street plan. The **Musée Alésia** houses artifacts, jewelry, and bronze figures from the site.

Alise is dominated by Aimé Millet's gigantic moustachioed statue of Vercingétorix, which was placed here in 1865 to commemorate the first excavations. Cynics feel that it bears a more than passing resemblance to Napoleon III, who sponsored the dig.

🏛 **Musée Alésia**
Rue de l'Hôpital. **Tel** *03 80 96 96 22.* ⬤ *daily.* 📷 **www**.alesia.com

Environs
In the vicinity lies **Château de Bussy-Rabutin**. The spiteful 17th-century soldier and wit Roger de Bussy-Rabutin created its highly individualistic

Excavations at the Roman site near Alise-Ste-Reine

decor while exiled from Louis XIV's court. One room is dedicated to portraits of his many mistresses, as well as a couple of imaginary ones.

⚜ **Château de Bussy-Rabutin**
Bussy-le-Grand. *Tel 03 80 96 00 03.*
◻ *Tue–Sun.* ● *Jan 1, Nov 1 & 11, Dec 25.* 🖼

Semur-en-Auxois ⓫

Côte d'Or. 🏠 *5,000.* 🚉 🛈 *2 place Gaveau (03 80 97 05 96).* 🚌 *Sun.* **www**.ville-semur-en-auxois.fr

Approached from the west, Semur-en-Auxois comes as a surprise on an otherwise uneventful road. Its massive round bastions built in the 14th century (one of them with an unnerving gash in it) suddenly appear, towering over the Pont Joly and the peaceful river Armançon.

The **Eglise Notre-Dame** dates from the 13th and 14th centuries, and was modeled on the cathedral of Auxerre. The fragile high walls had to be restored in the 15th and 19th centuries. The church houses significant artworks, from the tympanum showing the legend of Doubting Thomas on the north doorway, to the 15th-century *Entombment* by Antoine le Moiturier. The stained glass presents the legend of Saint Barbara, and the work of different guilds such as butchers and drapers.

Environs
The village of Epoisses is the site of the moated **Château d'Epoisses**, its 11th–18th-century construction blending medieval towers with fine Renaissance details, and a huge 15th-century dovecote. Epoisses is also the home of one of Burgundy's most re-

Stained-glass window in Eglise Notre-Dame at Semur-en-Auxois

Semur-en-Auxois by the river Armançon

nowned cheeses, to be sampled at the local café or *fromagerie*.

⚜ **Château d'Epoisses**
Epoisses. *Tel 03 80 96 40 56.*
◻ *Jul–Aug: Wed–Mon (grounds: all year).* 🖼 📷 ♿ *ground floor only.*

Vézelay ⓬

See pp336–7.

Avallon ⓭

Yonne. 🏠 *9,000.* 🚉 🚌 🛈 *6 rue Bocquillot (03 86 34 14 19).* 🚌 *Sat & Thu.* **www**.avallonnais-tourisme.com

A fine old fortified town, Avallon is situated on a granite spur between two ravines by the river Cousin.

Avallon suffered in the wars of Saracens, Normans, English, and French, which accounts for its defensive aspect. The town is quiet and rather beautiful, full of charming details. The main monument is the 12th-century Romanesque **Eglise St-Lazare**, with two carved doorways. The larger illustrates the signs of the zodiac, the labors of the month, and the horsemen of

the Apocalypse. The nave is decorated with sophisticated acanthus capitals and polychrome statuary.

The **Musée de l'Avallonnais** features an intricate Venus mosaic from the 2nd century AD, and Georges Rouault's (1871–1958) series of Expressionist etchings, the *Miserere*.

🏛 **Musée de l'Avallonnais**
5 rue du College. *Tel 03 86 34 03 19.*
◻ *call for information.* 🖼 🛈

Environs
To the southwest of Avallon is the 12th-century Château de Bazoches, given to Maréchal de Vauban by Louis XIV in 1675, and transformed by him into a military garrison.

***Miserere** by Georges Rouault in the Musée d'Avallonnais, Avallon*

Vézelay ⑫

Decorated capital

The golden glow of the Basilique Ste-Madeleine crowning Vézelay's hill is visible from afar. Tourists follow in the footsteps of medieval pilgrims, ascending the narrow street up to the former abbey church. In the 12th century, at the height of its glory, the abbey claimed to house relics of Mary Magdalene and was also an important meeting point for pilgrims en route to Santiago de Compostela in Spain *(see pp400–1)*. Today its attraction lies in the Romanesque church with its magnificent sculpture and Gothic choir.

View of Vézelay
The abbey dominates Vézelay's surroundings as it once dominated the religious and worldly affairs of the area.

Tour St-Michel was built in 1150–1250. It derives its name from the statue of the archangel in the tower's southwest corner.

Nave of Ste-Madeleine

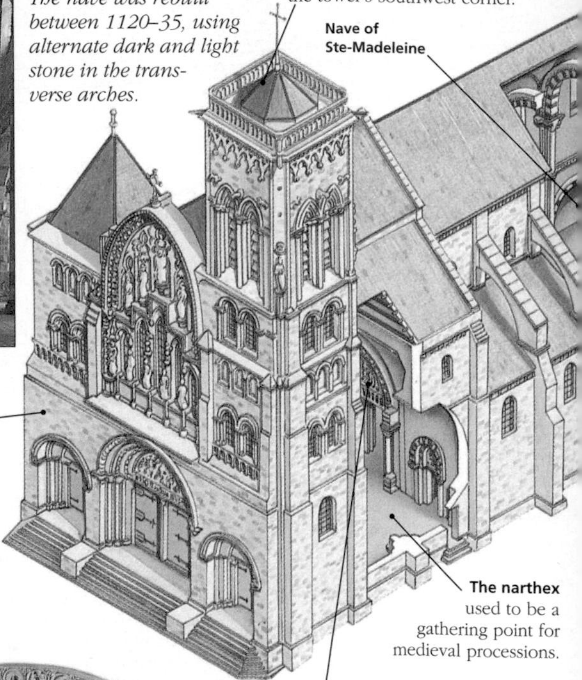

Nave of Ste-Madeleine
The nave was rebuilt between 1120–35, using alternate dark and light stone in the transverse arches.

The façade dates from 1150 and has a large 13th-century window. It was about to collapse when Viollet-le-Duc was commissioned to restore it according to old plans in 1840.

The narthex used to be a gathering point for medieval processions.

★ Tympanum
This masterpiece of sculpture (1120–35) shows Christ on His throne, stretching out His hands from which rays of light descend on to the apostles.

STAR FEATURES

★ Tympanum

★ Capitals

Tour St-Antoine was built at the same time as the choir, in the late 12th century. Its counterpart on the north side was never finished.

VISITORS' CHECKLIST

Basilique Ste-Madeleine, Vézelay.
Tel 03 86 33 39 50. 🚉 Sermizelles.
⬤ 6am–8pm daily (7am–dusk winter). ✝ 6:30pm Mon–Fri; 12:30pm, 6pm (winter), 7pm (summer) Sat; 11am Sun. 📷
www.vezelay.cef.fr

The chapterhouse and cloister are the only parts remaining from the 12th-century monastic buildings. Viollet-le-Duc rebuilt part of the cloister and restored the rib-vaulted chapterhouse, once a graceful background for the monks' daily assemblies.

Crypt of Ste-Madeleine
The Romanesque crypt houses relics once thought to be Mary Magdalene's. The vault was rebuilt in 1165.

★ Capitals
The capitals in the nave and narthex are exquisitely carved and give a vivid rendering of the stories of Classical antiquity and the Bible. The master who created them remains unknown.

Choir of Ste-Madeleine
The choir was rebuilt in the last quarter of the 12th century in the then modern Gothic style of the Ile de France.

Morvan, a region of rivers and forests well-suited to fishing and other outdoor pursuits

Morvan ⑭

Yonne, Côte d'Or, Nièvre, Saône et
Loire. 🚊 Dijon. 🚌 Autun, Mombard.
🏠 Château-Chinon, Saulieu, Avallon.
🏨 6 bd République, Château-Chinon
(03 86 85 06 58); Maison du Parc,
St-Brisson (03 86 78 79 57).
www.parcdumorvan.org

Morvan is a Celtic word
meaning Black Mountain,
which is a good description
of this area seen from afar.
The immense, sparsely
inhabited plateau of granite
and woodland appears sud-
denly in the center of the rich
Burgundy hills and farmland.
Stretching roughly north to
south, it gains altitude as it
proceeds southward, reaching
a culminating point of 2,928 ft
(901 m) at **Haut-Folin**.
   The Morvan's two sources
of natural wealth are abundant water and dense forests
of oak, beech, and conifer. In
the old days lumber used to
be floated out of the area to
Paris via a network of lakes
and rivers. Today it travels by
truck, and the Yonne, Cousin,
and Cure rivers are instead
used for recreation and the
production of electricity.
   The Morvan has always
been a poor, remote area.
Each of its largest towns,
Château-Chinon in the center
and Saulieu on the outskirts,
has barely 3,000 inhabitants.
   During World War II the
Morvan was a bastion of the
French Resistance. Today a
Regional Nature Park, its attraction is its wildness. Information
on a wide variety of outdoor
activities, including bicycling,

canoeing, skiing, and horse
trekking, is available at the
Maison du Parc at St-Brisson
where there is also the very
moving **Musée de la
Resistance**. There are plenty
of short walking trails, and
two well-signed long-distance
paths: the GR13 (Vézelay to
Autun) and the Tour du
Morvan par les Grands Lacs.

🏛 **Musée de la Résistance**
Maison du Parc, St-Brisson. **Tel** 03
86 78 72 99. ⬜ Easter–mid-Nov:
Wed–Mon (Jul & Aug: daily). 🎫 🎦
🔲 ♿

Saulieu ⑮

Côte d'Or. 🏃 3,000. 🚌 🚉
🏨 24 rue d'Argentine (03 80 64
00 21). 🛒 Sat. **www**.saulieu.fr

On the edge of the Morvan,
Saulieu has been a shrine of
Burgundian cooking ever
since the 17th century. The
town was then a
staging post on the
Paris to Lyon
coach road. To-
day the tradition
is maintained
by the famous
chef Bernard
Loiseau at the
Côte d'Or
restaurant (see
p598). Yet there is
more to Saulieu than
ris de veau de lait
braisé or poularde
truffée à la vapeur.
The Romanesque **Basilique St-
Andoche**, built in the early
12th century, has decorated
capitals with representations
of the Flight into Egypt and a

comical version of the story
of Balaam and his donkey
waylaid by the Angel.

Nevers ⑯

Nièvre. 🏃 41,000. 🚌 🚉 🏨 Palais
Ducal, rue Sabatier. (03 86 68 46 00).
🛒 Sat. **www**.nevers-tourisme.com

Like all Burgundian towns
fronting the Loire, Nevers
should be approached from
the west side of the river for
a full appreciation of its noble
site. Though lacking historical
importance, the town has
much to show. Considered to
be the earliest of the Loire
châteaux, the **Palais Ducal**
has a long Renaissance
façade framed by polygonal
towers and a broad esplanade.
The Romanesque 11th-century
Eglise St-Etienne has graceful
monolithic columns and a
wreath of radiating chapels.
In the crypt of the
Gothic **Cathédrale
St-Cyr** is a 16th-
century sculpted
Entombment,
and the found-
ations of a
6th-century bap-
tistry, discovered
in 1944, after
heavy bombing.
The contemporary
stained-glass windows
are also noteworthy.
Nevers faïence The overlordship of
vase Nevers passed to the
Gonzaga family in the
16th century. They brought
with them an Italian school
of artists skilled in faïence
making and glass-blowing.

The industry has remained and the modern pottery is still traditionally decorated in blue, white, yellow, and green, with its curious trademark, the little green arabesque knot, or *noeud vert*. The best place to view it is at the **Musée Municipal** and the best place to buy it is the 17th-century **Faïencerie Montagnon**.

🏛 **Musée Municipal Frédéric Blandin**
16 rue Saint-Geneste. *Tel 03 86 68 44 60.* ⬤ *for renovation until mid-2012; call for details.*

Environs
Just south of Nevers, the 19th-century **Pont du Guetin** carries the Loire Canal majestically across the Allier river. The church at **St-Parize-le-Châtel** has a jolly Burgundian menagerie sculpted on the capitals of the crypt.

The *Temptation of Eve* in Autun

Autun ⑰

Saône-et-Loire. 🏠 *18,000.* 🚉
🚌 ℹ *13 rue Général Demetz (03 85 86 80 38).* 🛒 *Wed & Fri.*
www.autun-tourisme.com

Augustodunum, the town of Augustus, was founded in the late 1st century BC. It was a

The imposing Porte St-André in Autun, once part of the Roman wall

great center of learning, with a population four times what it is today. Its theater, built in the 1st century AD, could seat 20,000 people.

Today Autun is still a delight, deserving gastronomic as well as cultural investigation. The magical **Cathédrale St-Lazare** was built in the 1100 century. It is special because of its sculptures, most of them by the mysterious 12th-century artist Gislebertus. He sculpted both the capitals inside and the glorious Last Judgment tympanum over the main portal. This masterpiece, called a "Romanesque Cézanne" by André Malraux, escaped notice and was saved from destruction during the Revolution because it had been plastered over in the 18th century. Inside, some of the capitals can be seen close-up in a room in the tower. Look also for the

sculpture of Pierre Jeannin and his wife. Jeannin was the president of the Dijon parliament who prevented the Massacre of St. Bartholomew *(see pp54–5)* spreading with the perceptive remark, "the commands of very angry monarchs should be obeyed very slowly."

The brilliant collection of medieval art at the **Musée Rolin** includes the famous *Temptation of Eve*, by Gislebertus. There is also the 15th-century painted stone Virgin of Autun, and the *Nativity of Cardinal Rolin* by the Master of Moulins, from about 1480.

The monumental **Porte St-André** and **Porte d'Arroux**, and the ruins of the **Théâtre Romain** and the **Temple de Janus**, are reminders of Autun's glorious Roman past.

🏛 **Musée Rolin**
3 rue des Bancs. *Tel 03 85 52 09 76.* ⬤ *Wed–Sat, Sun am.* ⬤ *mid-Dec–mid-Feb, public hols.* 📷 ✔

Remains of the Roman theatre at Autun, dating from the 1st century AD

Street by Street: Dijon

The center of Dijon is noted for its
architectural splendor – a legacy from
the Dukes of Burgundy *(see p343)*.
Wealthy parliament members also had
elegant *hôtels particuliers* built in the
17th–18th centuries. The capital of
Burgundy, Dijon today has a rich cultural
life and a renowned university. The
city's great art treasures are housed in
the Palais des Ducs. Dijon is also famous
for its mustard *(see p318)* and *pain
d'épices* (gingerbread), a reminder of the
town's position on the spice route. It
became a major rail hub during the 19th
century and now has a TGV link to Paris.

Hôtel de Vogüé
*This elegant 17th-century mansion is
decorated with Burgundian cabbages
and fruit garlands by Hugues Sambin.*

★ **Notre-Dame**
*This magnificent 13th-century
Gothic church has a
façade with
gargoyles,
columns, and
the popular
Jacquemart
clock. The
chouette (owl)
is reputed to
bring good luck
when touched.*

Musée des Beaux Arts
*The collection of Flemish masters
here includes this 14th-century
triptych by Jacques de Baerze
and Melchior Broederlam.*

Place de la Libération was
created by Mansart in the 17th century.

★ **Palais des Ducs**
*The dukes of Burgundy held court here, but
the building seen today was mainly built
in the 17th century for the parliament.
It now houses the Musée des Beaux Arts.*

Rue Verrerie
This cobbled street in the old merchants' quarter is lined with medieval half-timbered houses. Some have fine wood carvings, such as Nos. 8, 10, and 12.

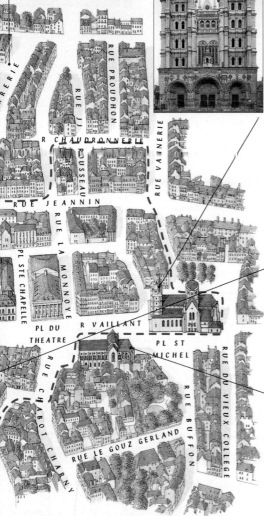

★ St-Michel
Begun in the 15th century and completed in the 17th century, St-Michel's façade combines Flamboyant Gothic with Renaissance details. On the richly carved porch, angels and biblical motifs mingle with mythological themes.

Musée Magnin
A collection of French and foreign 16th–19th-century paintings are displayed among period furniture in this 17th-century mansion.

Eglise St-Etienne dates back to the 11th century but has been rebuilt many times. Its characteristic lantern was added in 1686.

STAR SIGHTS

★ Palais des Ducs

★ Notre-Dame

★ St-Michel

KEY

- - - Suggested route

0 meters 100
0 yards 100

Well of Moses by Claus Sluter, in the Chartreuse de Champmol

Exploring Dijon

The center of Dijon is a warren of little streets that reward exploration. The rue des Forges, behind the Palais de Ducs, was the main street until the 18th century and is named after the jewelers and goldsmiths who had workshops there. Hôtel Chambellan at No. 34 is Flamboyant Gothic with a stone spiral staircase and wooden galleries. At No. 38 the Maison Maillard, built in 1560, has a stone façade decorated by Hugues Sambin.

Rue Chaudronnerie has a number of houses of note, especially the Maison des Cariatides at No. 28, with ten fine stone carved caryatids framing the windows. Place Darcy is lined with hotels and restaurants; the Jardin Darcy is delightful.

🏛 Musée des Beaux Arts

Palais des Etats de Bourgogne, Cour de Bar. *Tel* 03 80 74 52 70. ◯ Wed–Mon. ● Jan 1, May 1 & 8, Jul 14, Nov 1 & 11, Dec 25. ⑤ limited. 🖼

Dijon's prestigious art collection is housed in the former Palais des Ducs *(see p340)*. The Salle des Gardes on the first floor is dominated by the giant mausoleums of the dukes, with tombs sculpted by Claus Sluter (c.1345–1405). Other exhibits include two gilded Flemish retables and a portrait of Philip the Good by Rogier van der Weyden.

The art collection has Dutch and Flemish masters and sculpture by Sluter and Rude. There are also Swiss and German primitives, 16th–18th century French paintings, and the Donation Granville of 19th- and 20th-century French art. Also note the ducal kitchens with six fireplaces, and the Tour Philippe le Bon, 150 ft (46 m) tall with a fine view of Burgundian tiled roof tops.

🏰 Cathédrale St-Bénigne

Pl Ste-Bénigne. *Tel* 03 80 30 39 33. ◯ daily. 🖼 ⑤

Little remains of the 11th-century Benedictine abbey first founded in honor of St-Bénigne. Beneath the church is a Romanesque crypt with a fine rotunda ringed by three circles of columns.

🏛 Musée Archéologique

5 rue du Docteur Maret. *Tel* 03 80 30 88 54. ◯ Wed–Mon. ● most public hols.

The museum is housed in the old dormitory of the Benedictine abbey of St-Bénigne. The 11th-century chapterhouse, its stocky columns supporting a barrel-vaulted roof, houses a fine collection of Gallo-Roman sculpture. The ground floor, with its lovely fan vaulting, houses the famous head of Christ by Claus Sluter, originally from the *Well of Moses*.

🏯 Chartreuse de Champmol

1 bd Chanoine Kir. ◯ daily by appt (0892 70 05 58).

This was originally the site of a family necropolis built by Philip the Bold, destroyed during the Revolution. All that remains is a chapel doorway and the famous *Well of Moses* by Claus Sluter. It is now in the grounds of a psychiatric hospital east of Dijon train station, not very easy to find but definitely worth the effort. Despite its name, it is not a well but a monument, its lower part probably originally surrounded by water. Sluter is renowned for his deeply cut carving and here his work, depicting six prophets, is exquisitely lifelike.

The tomb of Philip the Bold by Claus Sluter, now in the Salle des Gardes of the Musée des Beaux Arts

For hotels and restaurants in this region see pp572–5 and pp625–9

The Golden Age of Burgundy

the French Capetian dynasty
at in the Hundred Years' War *(see
2–3)*, the dukes of Burgundy built
one of the most powerful states in
urope, which included Flanders and
arts of Holland. From the time of
Philip the Bold (1342–1404), the ducal
court became a cultural force, supporting many of Europe's finest artists, such as painters Rogier Van der Weyden and the Van Eyck brothers and sculptor Claus Sluter. The duchy's dominions were, however, broken up after the death of Duke Charles the Bold in 1477.

The tomb of Philip the Bold *in Dijon was made by the Flemish sculptor Claus Sluter, who was among the most brilliant artists of the Burgundian golden age. The dramatic realism of the mourners is one of the most striking features of this spectacular tomb, begun while the duke was still alive.*

BURGUNDY IN 1477

■ *Extent of the duchy at its peak*

THE MARRIAGE OF PHILIP THE GOOD

Philip the Good, duke from 1419–67, married Isabella of Portugal in 1430. This 17th-century copy of a painting by Van Eyck shows the sumptuous wedding feast, when Philip also inaugurated the chivalric Order of the Golden Fleece.

The dukes surrounded themselves with luxury, including fine gold and silverware.

Isabella of Portugal

The Duchess of Bedford, Philip's sister

Greyhounds were popular hunting animals at the Burgundian court.

Philip the Good is dressed in white ceremonial finery.

Burgundian art, *such as this Franco-Flemish Book of Hours, reflected the Flemish origins of many of the dukes' favorite artists.*

Dijon's Palais des Ducs *was rebuilt in 1450 by Philip the Good to reflect the glory of the Burgundian court, a center of art, chivalry, and glorious feasts. Empty after Charles the Bold's death, it was reconstructed in the 17th century.*

Wine harvest in the vineyards of Nuits-St-Georges, part of the Côte d'Or district

Côte d'Or ⑲

Côte d'Or. ✈ Dijon. 🚍 🚌 Dijon, Nuits-St-Georges, Beaune, Santenay. 🛈 Dijon (08 92 70 05 58). www.cotedor-tourisme.com

In winemaking terms, the Côte d'Or includes the Côte de Beaune and the Côte de Nuits in a nearly unbroken line of vines from Dijon to Santenay. Squeezed in between the flat plain of the Saône to the southeast and a plateau of woodland to the northwest, this narrow escarpment is about 30 miles (50 km) long. The grapes of the great Burgundy vineyards grow in the golden reddish soil of the slope (hence the area's name).

The classification of the characteristics of the land is fabulously technical and elaborate, but for the layman a rough rule of thumb might be that 95 percent of the best

A narrow street in the historic center of Beaune

vines are on the uphill side of the N74 thoroughfare (see pp320–21). The names on the signposts haunt the dreams of wine lovers the world over: Gevrey-Chambertin, Vougeot, Chambolle-Musigny, Vosne-Romanée, Nuits-St-Georges, Aloxe-Corton, Meursault, and Chassagne Montrachet.

Typical grape basket in the Musée du Vin de Bourgogne at Beaune

Beaune ⑳

Côte d'Or. 🏠 23,000. 🚍 🚌 🛈 6 bd Perpeuil (03 80 26 21 30). 🗓 Sat, Wed. 🎵 Baroque Music (Jul). www.ot-beaune.fr

The old center of Beaune, snug within its ramparts and encircling boulevards, is easy to explore on foot. Its indisputable treasure is the **Hôtel-Dieu** (see pp346–7). The Hôtel des Ducs de Bourgogne, built in the 14th–16th centuries, houses the **Musée du Vin de Bourgogne**. The building, with its flamboyant façade, is as interesting as its display of traditional winemaking equipment.

Farther to the north lies the **Collégiale Notre-Dame**, begun in the early 12th century. Inside this mainly Romanesque church hang five very fine 15th-century woolen and silk tapestries. With hints

of early Renaissance style, they delicately illustrate the life of the Virgin Mary in 19 scenes.

🏛 **Musée du Vin de Bourgogne**
Rue d'Enfer. **Tel** 03 80 22 08 19. ◯ Apr–Nov: daily; Dec–Mar: Wed–Mon. ● Jan 1, Dec 25. 🖼

Tournus ㉑

Saône-et-Loire. 🏠 6,500. 🚍 🚌 🛈 pl de l'Abbaye (03 85 27 00 20). 🗓 Sat. www.tournugeois.fr

The Abbaye de St-Philibert is one of Burgundy's oldest and greatest Romanesque buildings. It was founded by a group of monks from Noirmoutier who had been driven from their island by invading Normans in the 9th century, who brought with them relics of their patron saint, Philibert (still in the choir). Rebuilt in the 10th–12th centuries, the well-fortified abbey church is

Dovecote in Cormatin château gardens, Mâconnais

Nave of St-Philibert in Tournus

made from lovely pale pink stone, with black and white vaulting inside.

The 17th-century Hôtel-Dieu has its original rooms intact with the furniture, equipment, and pharmacy on display. It also houses the **Musée Greuze** dedicated to Tournus' most famous son, the artist Jean-Baptiste Greuze (1725–1805).

Environs
Southwest of Tournus lies the Mâconnais landscape of hills, vineyards, orchards, red-tiled farmhouses, and Romanesque churches. **Brancion** is a pretty hill village, **Chapaize** has an 11th-century church and there is a sumptuous Renaissance château at **Cormatin**. The village of **Taizé** is the center of a world-famous ecumenical community. To the north, **Chalon-sur-Saône** features the Musée Niepce, dedicated to the inventor of photography.

Cluny ㉒

Saône-et-Loire. 🚶 4,800. 🚌 🚶 6 rue Mercière (03 85 59 05 34). 🚌 Sat. **www**.cluny-tourisme.com

The little town of Cluny is overshadowed by the ruins of its great abbey. The **Ancienne Abbaye de Cluny** was once the most powerful monastic foundation in Europe (see pp48–9). The abbey was founded by William the Pious, Duke of Aquitaine in 910. Within 200 years, Cluny had become the head of a major reforming order with monasteries all over Europe. Its

abbots were considered as powerful as monarchs or popes, and four of them are venerated as saints. By the 14th century, however, the system was in decline. The abbey was closed in 1790 and the church was later dismantled.

The guided tour presents the abbey remains, notably the Clocher de l'Eau Bénite (Holy Water Belltower); **Musée d'Art**, housed in the former abbot's palace; and its figured capitals displayed in the 13th-century flour store. In town, don't miss 12th-century **Eglise St-Marcel**.

Southwest of the town, the chapel in **Berzé-la-Ville** is decorated with superb 12th-century frescoes, similar to those once seen at Cluny.

🏛 Ancienne Abbaye de Cluny
Tel 03 85 59 15 93. ⬜ daily. ● Jan 1, Dec 25. 🎫 ☑

🏛 Musée d'Art
Palais Jean de Bourbon. Tel 03 85 59 15 93. ⬜ daily. ● Jan 1, May 1, Nov 1 & 11, Dec 25. 🎫 ☑

Paray-le-Monial ㉓

Saône-et-Loire. 🚶 10,000. 🚌 🚌 🚶 25 av Jean-Paul II (03 85 81 10 92). 🚌 Fri. **www**.paraylemonial.fr

Dedicated to the cult of the Sacred Heart of Jesus, the **Basilique du Sacré-Coeur** has made Paray-le-Monial one of the most important sites of pilgrimage in modern France. Marguerite-Marie Alacoque, who was born here in 1647, had rather gory visions from which the cult later developed, sweeping across France in the 19th century. The church is a small version of the now lost abbey church of Cluny, with particularly harmonious and pure Romanesque architecture.

A visit to the **Musée de Paul Charnoz** provides an insight into industrial artistic tile production in the 19th and 20th centuries.

Situated on place Guignaud is the ornate **Maison Jayet**, dating from the 16th century, which houses the town hall,

Basilique du Sacré-Coeur at Paray-le-Monial

Hôtel-Dieu

Christian-de-Pitié

After the Hundred Years' War, many of Beaune's inhabitants suffered the effects of poverty and famine. To remedy this, the chancellor, Nicolas Rolin, and his wife founded a hospice here in 1443, which was inspired by the architecture of Northern French hospitals. The Rolins provided an annual grant and salt-works for income. Today the hospice is considered a medieval jewel, with its superb geometric multicolored Burgundian roof tiles. It houses two religious masterpieces: the *Christ-de-Pitié* statue, carved from oak, and Rogier van der Weyden's *Last Judgment* polyptych.

★ **Great Hall of the Poor**
The hall, with its carved, painted roof, has 28 four-poster beds, each often used by two patients at a time. Meals were served at central tables.

Tribute to Rolin's Wife
A recurring motif features the entwined letters N and G, birds and stars, and the word "Seulle" referring to Rolin's wife Guigone, his "one and only."

Saint Hugues' Room contains a painting of the saint curing two children. Frescoes by Isaac Moillon show the miracles of Christ.

Entrance

Saint Anne's Room has a tableau of nuns working in what was once the linen room, and a colorful feast day tapestry.

ANNUAL CHARITY WINE AUCTION

On the third Sunday in November, an annual charity auction in Beaune is the centerpiece of three days of festivities known as *Les Trois Glorieuses*. Saturday sees the banquet of the Confrérie des Chevaliers du Tastevin at the Château Clos de Vougeot. On Sunday the auction of wine from the 151 acres (61 ha) of vineyards, owned by nearby hospitals, takes place. Its prices are the benchmark for the entire vintage. On Monday at La Paulée de Meursault there is a party where growers bring along bottles of their best vintages to enjoy.

Hospices de Beaune
1986
BEAUNE
Appellation Beaune Contrôlée
Cuvée Nicolas-Rolin

Wine sold at the famous auction

STAR FEATURES

★ Great Hall

★ Last Judgment Polyptych by Rogier van der Weyden

Kitchen
The centerpiece of the kitchen is a Gothic fireplace with a dual hearth and a mechanical spit, made in 1698, which is turned by a wooden "robot."

VISITORS' CHECKLIST

Rue de L'Hôtel-Dieu, Beaune. *Tel* 03 80 24 45 00. ☐ Apr–mid Nov: 9–6:30pm daily; mid-Nov–Mar: 9–11:30am, 2–5:30pm daily. 🖼 📷 📹 **Wine Auction** 3rd Sun Nov: Les Halles de Beaune (03 80 24 45 00). **www**.hospices-de-beaune.com

Cour d'Honneur
The buildings of Hôtel-Dieu are arranged around a splendid central courtyard. This is flanked by a wooden gallery, above which rise high dormer windows topped by weathervanes. The courtyard well is a fine example of Gothic wrought-iron work.

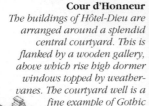

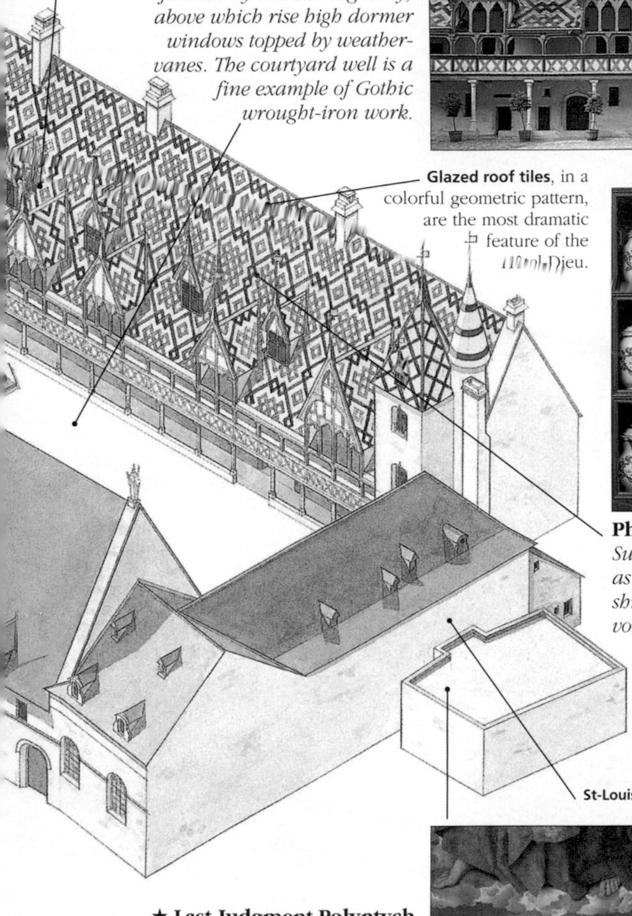

Glazed roof tiles, in a colorful geometric pattern, are the most dramatic feature of the Hôtel-Dieu.

Pharmacy
Such unusual potions as woodlouse powder, shrimps' eyes, and vomit nut powder are stored in these earthenware pots. Nearby is a bronze mortar used to prepare the remedies.

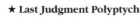

St-Louis' Room

★ Last Judgment Polyptych
The naked figures shown in Rogier van der Weyden's 15th-century polyptych were briefly given clothing in the 19th century. At the same time, the altarpiece was cut in half so that the outer and inner panels could be seen together.

Château de Pierreclos in the Mâconnais region

Brionnais ㉔

Saône-et-Loire. ✕ *Mâcon.*
🚊 *Paray-le-Monial, Roanne.*
🚌 *Paray-le-Monial.*
ℹ️ *Marcigny (03 85 25 39 06).*

The Brionnais is a small and peaceful rural district, squeezed between the river Loire and the Beaujolais foot-hills in the far south of Burgundy.

Its agricultural staple is the white Charolais cow, which can be seen grazing everywhere. For a closer look at this regional symbol, visit the lively cattle-market in **St-Christophe** on Wednesday afternoons.

The area has an abundance of Romanesque churches, most of which are built of the local ocher-colored stone. The 11th-century church of **Anzy-le-Duc** has a majestic

Capital in St-Julien-de-Jonzy

three-tiered polygonal tower and exquisitely carved capitals. **Semur-en-Brionnais** was the birthplace of Cluny's famous abbot St-Hugues. Its church is inspired by his great monastery. The church at **St-Julien-de-Jonzy** has a very finely carved tympanum.

A small town by the river Genette, **La Clayette** is graced by a château set in a lake. It is not open to the public, but has a vintage car museum and in summer is the setting for a *son et lumière* show.

Southeast of La Clayette the lonely **Montagne de Dun** rises just over 2,300 ft (700 m) and offers a pano-rama over the gentle, green Brionnais hills. This is some of the best picnic country in Burgundy, full of sleepy corners and quiet byways.

Mâcon ㉕

Saône-et-Loire. 👥 *36,000.* ✕
🚊 🚌 ℹ️ *1 pl Saint Pierre (03 85 21 07 07).* 🛒 *Sat.*
www.macon-tourism.com

At the frontier between Burgundy and the south, Mâcon is an industrial town and wine center on the Saône.

The lack of churches is due to fervent anticlericalism during the Revolution, when 14 were destroyed. A 17th-century convent has been turned into the **Musée des Ursulines**. Its collections include French and Flemish painting and an exhibition on the prehistoric site of Solutré. On the charming place aux Herbes, where the market is held, the **Maison de Bois** is a 15th-century wooden house covered with bizarre carvings.

🏛 **Musée des Ursulines**
Allée de Matisco. **Tel** *03 85 39 90 38.* ⬜ *Tue–Sat & Sun pm.* ⬤ *Jan 1, May 1, Jul 14, Nov 1, Dec 25.* 📷

Environs

The great **Roche de Solutré** rises dramatically above the Pouilly-Fuissé vineyards in the Mâconnais district *(see p.345).* Below the rock, finds from the Stone Ages have established it as a major archeological site.

Mâconnais is also the land of the Romantic poet Lamartine (1790–1869). Born in Mâcon, he spent his childhood at Milly Lamartine and later lived at Château de St-Point. **Château de Pierreclos** is associated with his epic poem *Jocelyn.*

Charolais cattle grazing on the gentle hills of the Brionnais

nche-Comté

egion of woods and
ter, the Franche-Comté
ers exceptional natural
eauty combined with
opportunities for canoe-
ng, trekking, and skiing.
Apart from towns well
worth visiting, this is a
region to explore in the
wild. Glorious scenery with
grottoes and cascading
waterfalls can be found all
along the Vallée du Doubs.
Farther south are the spectacular sources of the rivers
Lison and Loue. The
Reculées is an area of
extraordinary formations of
ridges and waterfalls such
as Baume-les-Messieurs.
In Région des Lacs, the
silent, peaceful lakes are
surrounded by mountain
peaks and virgin forests.

Nature at its purest at Source du Lison in the Franche-Comté

Cascades du Hérisson ㉖

Pays-des-Lacs. 🚐 *Clairvaux-les-Lacs
(03 84 25 27 47).* 🛒 *Wed.*

The village of Doucier, at the
foot of the Pic de l'Aigle, is
the starting point for the valley
of the river Hérisson, one of
the finest natural settings in the
Jura. Leave the car at the park
by the Moulin Jacquand and
walk up the trail through the
woods to a spectacular waterfall, the 213-ft (65-m) Cascade
de L'Eventail, and beyond
to the equally impressive
Cascade du Grand Saut. The
walk, which takes about two
hours there and back, is steep
at times and can be slippery,
so sturdy shoes are essential.

Arbois ㉗

Jura. 👥 *3,600.* 🚊 🚐 *17 rue de
l'Hôtel de Ville (03 84 66 55 50).* 🛒 *Fri.*
www.arbois.com

The jolly wine town of Arbois
lies on the vine-covered
banks of the river Cuisance. It
is famous for the sherry-like
vin jaune (yellow wine) of the
district. On the north side of

the town is **Maison de Pasteur**,
the preserved house and lab-
oratory of the great scientist
Louis Pasteur (1822–95), the
first to test vaccines on
human beings.

Environs
Southeast of Dole is the 18th-
century **Château d'Arlay** with
immaculately kept gardens.

Dole ㉘

Jura. 👥 *28,000.* 🚊 🚐 🚌 *6 pl Grévy
(03 84 72 11 22).* 🛒 *Tue, Thu, & Sat.*
www.tourisme-paysdedole.fr

The busy town of Dole lies
where the Doubs meets the
Rhine-Rhône canal. The former
capital of the Comté was always a symbol of the region's
resistance to the French. The
region had become used to
relative independence, first
under the Counts of Burgundy
and then as part of the Holy
Roman Empire. Though
always French-speaking, its
people did not appreciate the

idea of the French absolute
monarchy and, in 1636, en-
dured a long siege. The town
finally submitted to Louis XIV,
first in 1668, and again in 1674.

There is a charming historic
quarter in the center of town,
full of winding alleys, houses
dating back to the 15th century, and quiet inner courtyards. Place aux Fleurs offers
an excellent view of this part
of town and the mossy-roofed,
16th-century **Eglise Notre-Dame**.

**Virgin and Child on the north portal
of Eglise Notre-Dame, Dole**

The Saline Royale at Arc-et-Senans

Arc-et-Senans ㉙

Doubs. 🏛 1,400. 🚇 ℹ️ *Ancienne Saline Royale (03 81 57 43 21).* **www**.ot-arcetsenans.fr

Designated a World Heritage Site since 1982, the Saline Royale (royal salt works) at Arc-et-Senans were designed by the great French architect Claude-Nicolas Ledoux (1736–1806). He envisaged a development built in concentric circles around the main buildings. However, the only ones to be completed (in 1775) were the buildings used for salt production. Nevertheless, these show the staggering scale of Ledoux's idea: salt water was to be piped from Salins-les-Bains nearby, and fuel to reduce it was to come from the Chaux forest. The enterprise, which was never a success, was closed down in 1895, but the buildings remain.

The **Musée Ledoux Lieu du Sel** displays intriguing models of the grand projects imagined by the visionary architect.

🏛 Musée Ledoux Lieu du Sel
Saline Royale. **Tel** 03 81 54 45 45. ◯ daily. ⬤ Jan 1, Dec 25. 📷 ✅ 🔊 ⬇️ gr. floor.

Champlitte ㉚

Haute Saône. 🏛 1,900. 🚇 ℹ️ 33B rue de la République (03 84 67 67 19).

In the small town of Champlitte, the **Musée des Arts et Traditions Populaires** was created by a local shepherd who collected artifacts connected with disappearing local customs. One of the poignant displays housed in this Renais-sance château recalls the emigration of 400 citizens to Mexico in the mid-19th century.

🏛 Musée des Arts et Traditions Populaires
Pl de l'Eglise. **Tel** 03 84 67 82 00. ◯ Apr–Jun & Sep: Wed–Fri (Sat–Sun pms only); Jul–Aug: Mon–Fri (Sat–Sun pms only); Oct–Mar: Wed–Mon pms. ⬤ Jan 1, Nov 1, Dec 25. 📷 ✅ 🔊

Besançon ㉛

Doubs. 🏛 120,000. 🚇 🚄 ℹ️ 2 pl de la Première Armée Française (03 81 80 92 55). 🚌 Tue–Sat & Sun am. **www**.besancon-tourisme.com

Besançon supplanted Dole as the capital of the Franche-Comté in the 17th century. It began as an ecclesiastical center and is now an industrial one, specializing in precision engineering. The stately architecture of the old town, with its elegant wrought-iron work, is a 17th-century legacy.

Behind the fine Renaissance façade of the Palais Granvelle, in the grande rue, is the **Musée du Temps**, a fine collection of 'time-pieces' of all ages – a timely tribute to Besançon's renown as a clock and watch-making center. An interactive exhibition on the third floor invites reflection on the relativity of the notion of time.

Farther along the same street are the birthplaces of novelist Victor Hugo (1802–85) at No. 140 and the Lumière brothers (*see p63*) at place Victor Hugo. Behind **Porte Noire**, a Roman arch, is the 12th-century Cathédrale St-Jean. In its belltower is the **Horloge Astronomique** with its automatons that pop out on the hour.

The stunning **Musée des Beaux Arts et d'Archéolog** occupies the old corn mar Its collection includes wor by Bellini, Cranach, Ruben Fragonard, Boucher, Ingres, Goya, Matisse, and Picasso.

Vauban's citadel overlookin the river Doubs has magnificent views and the intriguing **Musée Comtois**, with a collection of local artifacts, an insectarium, and an aquarium.

🏛 Musée du Temps
Palais Granvelle, 96 grande rue. **Tel** 03 81 87 81 50. ◯ Tue–Sun. ⬤ Jan 1, May 1, Nov 1, Dec 25. 📷 ✅ ⬇️

⏰ Horloge Astronomique
Rue de la Convention. **Tel** 03 81 81 12 76. ◯ Apr–Sep: Wed–Mon; (Thu–Mon winter). ⬤ Jan, May 1, Nov 1 & 11, Dec 25. 📷 ✅

🏛 Musée des Beaux Arts et d'Archéologie
1 pl de la Révolution. **Tel** 03 81 87 80 49. ◯ Wed–Mon. 📷 free Sun. 📷 ⬇️

🏛 Musée Comtois
La Citadelle, rue des Fusillés de la Résistance. **Tel** 03 81 87 83 33. ◯ Apr–Oct: daily; Nov–Mar: Wed–Mon. ⬤ Jan 1, Dec 25. 📷 ✅ 🔊 📷

The fantastic astronomical clock in Besançon, made in 1857–60

Ornans ㉜

Doubs. 🏛 4,300. 🚇 ℹ️ 7 rue Pierre Vernier (03 81 62 21 50). 🚌 3rd Tue of month. **www**.valleedelaloue.com

The great Realist painter Gustave Courbet was born at Ornans in 1819. He painted the town in every possible light. His *Enterrement à*

The striking **Chapelle Notre-Dame du Haut** by Le Corbusier at Ronchamp

Ornans proved to be one of the most influential paintings of the 19th century. Courbet's work is displayed in three historic buildings, including his childhood home, which make up the **Musée Courbet**.

🏛 **Musée Courbet**
Pl Robert Fernier. **Tel** 03 81 86 22 88. ◯ Wed–Mon. ◯ Jan 1, May 1, Nov 1, Dec 25. 🎟 🏠 ◻ ◻
http://musee-courbet.doubs.fr

Environs
A canoeist's paradise, the **Vallée de la Loue** is the loveliest in the Jura. The D67 follows the river from Ornans eastward to Ouhans, from where it is only a 15-minute walk to its magnificent source. Various belvederes offer splendid views over the area.
Southwest of Ornans, the spectacular **Source du Lison** (*see p349*) is a 20-minute walk from Nans-sous-Ste-Anne.

Belfort ⓧ

Territoire de Belfort. 🏘 52,000. 🚉
🚌 🛈 2 bis rue Clemenceau (03 84 55 90 90). ◻ Wed–Sun.
www.ot-belfort.fr

The symbol of Belfort is an enormous pink sandstone lion. It was built (rather than

carved) by Frédéric Bartholdi (1834–1904), whose other major undertaking was the Statue of Liberty.
Belfort's immensely strong **citadel**, designed by Vauban under Louis XIV, withstood three sieges, in 1814, 1815, and 1870. Today this remarkable array of fortifications provides an interesting walk and extensive views of the surroundings. The **Musée d'Art et d'Histoire**, housed in some of the billets, displays models of the original fortifications as well as regional art and artifacts (closed Tuesday in winter).

Ronchamp ⓧ

Haute-Saône. 🏘 3,000. 🚉
🛈 14 pl du 14 juillet (03 84 63 50 82). ◻ Sat.
www.ot-ronchamp.fr

Le Corbusier's **Chapelle Notre-Dame-du-Haut** dominates this former miners' town. A sculpture rather than a building, its swelling concrete form was finalized in 1955. Inside, light, shape, and space form a unity.
There is also a **Musée de la Mine** evoking the industry and the life of local miners.

Le Miroir d'Ornans in the Musée Courbet, Ornans

THE MASSIF CENTRAL

ALLIER · AVEYRON · CANTAL · CORRÈZE · CREUSE · HÂUTE-LOIRE
HAUTE-VIENNE · LOZÈRE · PUY DE DOME

The Massif Central is a region of strange, wild beauty – one of France's best-kept secrets. It is surprisingly little known beyond its sprinkling of spas and the major cities of Clermont-Ferrand, Vichy, and Limoges. However, the new autoroutes through the heart of its uplands have started to open up this previously remote region.

The huge central plateau of ancient granite and crystalline rock that makes up the Massif Central embraces the dramatic landscapes of the Auvergne, Limousin, Aveyron, and more. Once a testing crossroads for pilgrims, and strung with giant volcanoes, it is a region of unsuspected richness, from the spectacular town of Le Puy-en-Velay to the unique treasures at Conques.

With its crater lakes and hot springs, the Auvergne is the Massif Central's lush volcanic core, an outdoor paradise offering activities from hiking in summer to skiing in winter. It also has some of France's most beautiful Romanesque churches, medieval castles, and Renaissance palaces. To the east are the mountain ranges of Forez, Livardois, and Velay; to the west are the giant chains of extinct volcanoes, the Monts Dômes, Monts Dore, and the Monts du Cantal. The Limousin, on the northwestern edge of the Massif Central, is gentler country with green pastures and blissfully empty roads.

The Aveyron spreads into the southwest from the Aubrac mountains, carrying with it the rivers Lot, Aveyron, and Tarn through gorges and valleys with their cliff-hanging villages. To the east in the Lozère are the Grands Causses, the vast, isolated uplands of the Cévennes. These barren plateaus give farmers a poor living, but have been a favorite route with adventurous travelers across the centuries.

La Bourboule, a spa town in the Monts Dore

◁ The summit of Puy Mary, 5,863 ft (1,787 m), offering a superb view to walkers who attempt the ascent

Exploring the Massif Central

Nature is at its most magnificent in the volcanic mountain ranges and wild river gorges of the Massif Central. This is a vast and unspoiled territory which offers spectacular sightseeing and every imaginable outdoor activity, with rafting, paragliding, canoeing, and hiking among the many choices. There are hundreds of churches, châteaus, and museums to nourish lovers of history, architecture, and art; and good, hearty regional cooking and wonderful local wines for lovers of good living.

KEY

━━━	Highway
━━━	Major road
━━━	Secondary road
┈┈┈	Minor road
───	Scenic route
╼╼╼	Main railroad
───	Minor railroad
━━━	Regional border
△	Summit

Limestone cliffs of the Gorges du Tarn

GETTING AROUND

There is a good air and rail service connecting Paris with the major towns of Limoges, Clermont-Ferrand, and Vichy. Many of the most interesting towns and sights are easily accessible only by car, and motorail from Calais to Brive is an effortless way of getting to the region with a car. Most minor roads are well kept, but slow going in the mountains. A few roads are vertiginous, especially the road to the summit of Puy Mary, which is utterly breathtaking. The A71/A75 (toll-free) through the Auvergne is a magnificent road.

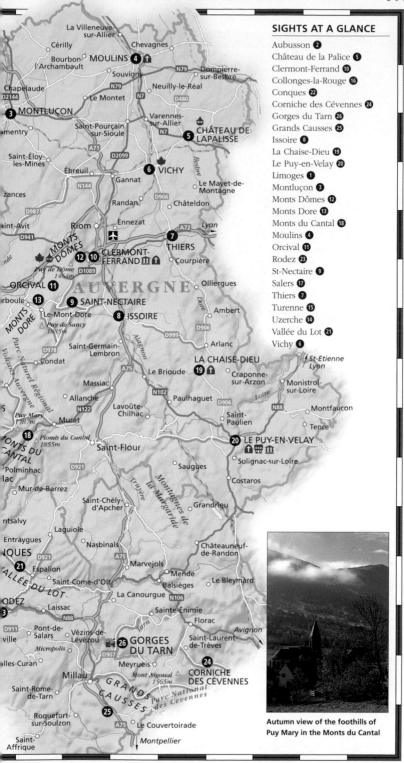

La Villeneuve-sur-Allier
Cérilly
Bourbon-l'Archambault
Chapelaude
D2144
MONTLUÇON
mentry
Saint-Éloy-les-Mines
zances
D987
int-Avit
D941
rboule
S
 route
Chevagnes
MOULINS
Souvigny
N79
Le Montet
N7
Saint-Pourçain-sur-Sioule
A71
D2099
Ébreuil
Gannat
N144
Randan
Riom
Ennezat
MONTS DÔMES
Puy de Dôme 146 1m
D1089
CLERMONT-FERRAND
ORCIVAL
Le-Mont-Dore
MONTS DORE
Puy de Sancy 1885m
D978
Condat
Saint-Germain-Lembron
D999
Massiac
A75
Le Brioude
Allanche
N122
Lavoûte-Chilhac
Puy Mary 1787m
Murat
Plomb du Cantal 1855m
Saint-Flour
Polminhac
lac
D921
Mur-de-Barrez
ntsalvy
Laguiole
Entraygues
IQUES
D921
Espalion
Saint-Come-d'Olt
ODEZ
Laissac
ville
N88
D911
Pont-de-Salars
Micropolis
lles-Curan
Millau
Saint-Rome-de-Tarn
Roquefort-sur-Soulzon
Saint-Affrique
Vézins-Lévézou
D907
Dompierre-sur-Besbre
N79
Neuilly-le-Réal
D480
Varennes-sur-Allier
N7
CHÂTEAU DE LAPALISSE
VICHY
Le Mayet-de-Montagne
D906
Châteldon
Lyon
A72
THIERS
Courpière
AUVERGNE
SAINT-NECTAIRE
ISSOIRE
Dore
Ollierges
Ambert
D906
Arlanc
LA CHAISE-DIEU
Craponne-sur-Arzon
Paulhaguet
D906
Saint-Paulien
LE PUY-EN-VELAY
Solignac-sur-Loire
Saugues
Costaros
Montagnes de la Margeride
Grandrieu
Saint-Chély-d'Apcher
A75
Nasbinals
Châteauneuf-de-Randon
Marvejols
Mende
Le Bleymard
Balsièges
La Canourgue
N106
Sainte-Énimie
Florac
Tarn
GORGES DU TARN
Saint-Laurent-de-Trèves
Meyrueis
Mont Aigoual 1565m
CORNICHE DES CÉVENNES
GRANDS CAUSSES
Parc National des Cévennes
A75
Le Couvertoirade
Montpellier
St-Etienne Lyon
Monistrol-sur-Loire
N88
Montfaucon
Tence
Avignon

Autumn view of the foothills of Puy Mary in the Monts du Cantal

A Limoges enamel plaque, *The Bad Shepherd*

Limoges **❶**

Haute-Vienne. 🏠 200,000. ✈ 🚉
🚌 🚻 *12 bd de Fleurus (05 55 34
46 87).* 🍴 *daily.*
www.limoges-tourisme.com

The capital of the Limousin
has two hearts: the old Cité
and the rival château, now
the commercial center of the
modern city. The Cité was
ravaged by the Black Prince
during the Hundred Years'
War and today it is a quiet
place of half-timbered houses
and narrow streets.

It was not until the 1770s
that Limoges became
synonymous with porcelain.
The legendary local ware is on
display at the superb **Musée
National Adrien-Dubouché**.
More than 10,000 exhibits
trace the history of ceramics.
The **Musée des Beaux-Arts de
Limoges** houses an Egyptian
collection, archaeological
artifacts tracing the history of
Limoges, over 600 Limousin
enamels, and Impressionist
paintings. This area was a
center of Resistance operations in World War II; the
Musée de la Résistance et

de la Déportation has a
collection of exhibits relating
to Resistance activities.

🏛 **Musée National
Adrien-Dubouché**
Pl Winston Churchill. **Tel** 05 55 33
08 50. ◯ *Wed–Mon.* ● *Jan 1,
May 1, Dec 25.* 🎫 🔲
www.musee-adriendubouche.fr

🏛 **Musée des Beaux-Arts
de Limoges**
1 pl de l'Evêché. **Tel** 05 55 45 98 10.
◯ *Wed–Mon.* ● *Jan 1, May 1, Nov
1 & 11, Dec 25.* www.museebal.fr

🏛 **Musée de la Résistance et
de la Déportation**
Rue de la Règle, Jardin de L'Evêché.
Tel 05 55 45 98 23.
◯ *Wed–Mon pms.*

Environs
Resistance activity in the
Limousin led to severe reprisals.
On June 10, 1944 at the village
of **Oradour-sur-Glane**, 16 miles
(25 km) northwest of Limoges,
SS troops burned alive the
entire population. The ruins
have been kept as a shrine,
and a new village built nearby.
The town of St-Junien close by
has been a glove-making town
since the Middle Ages, and it
still supplies today's designers
with luxury leather items.

Aubusson **❷**

Creuse. 🏠 5,000. 🚌 🚻 *rue
Vieille (05 55 66 32 12).* 🍴 *Sat.*
www.ot-aubusson.fr

Aubusson owes its renown to
the exceptionally pure waters
of the Creuse, perfect for
making the delicately colored
dyes used for tapestries and
rugs. Tapestry production was
at its zenith in the 16th and
17th centuries, but by the end
of the 18th century the
Revolution and patterned
wallpaper had swept away
the clientele.

In the 1940s, Aubusson was
revived, largely due to the
artist Jean Lurçat, who persuaded other modern artists
to design for tapestry. The
**Musée Départemental de la
Tapisserie** displays a
permanent collection of these
modern works. All 30 workshops welcome visitors – at
the **Manufacture St Jean** you
can watch tapestries and
custom-made carpets being
made by hand and restored.

🏛 **Musée Départemental de
la Tapisserie**
Av des Lissiers. **Tel** 05 55 83 08 30.
◯ *Wed–Mon (Tue pm Jul–Aug).*
● *1 week Apr, 1 week Nov.* 🎫 ♿

🏛 **Manufacture St Jean**
3 rue St Jean. **Tel** 05 55 66 10 08.
◯ *Mon–Fri.* 🎫 🎫

Environs
A single street of 15th-century
houses and a Roman bridge
comprise **Moûtier-d'Ahun**,

Tapestry restoration at the
Manufacture St Jean in Aubusson

Romanesque church at Moûtier-d'Ahun near Aubusson

early Renaissance. Moulins' most celebrated sight is the Flamboyant Gothic **Cathédrale Notre-Dame**, where members of the Bourbon court appear amid the saints in the 15th- and 16th-century stained-glass windows. The treasury contains a luminous 15th-century Virgin and Child triptych by the "Master of Moulins." Benefactors Pierre II, Duke of Bourbon, and his wife Anne de Beaujeu, bedecked in embroidery and jewels, are shown being introduced to a less richly dressed Madonna.

The tower keep and the single remaining wing of the Bourbon **Vieux Château** house a superb collection of sculpture, painting, and decorative art from the 12th to the 16th centuries. Housed in the former cavalry barracks is a magnificent collection of 10,000 theatrical costumes.

🏛 **Cathédrale Notre-Dame**
Pl de la Déportation. **Tel** 04 70 20 89 65 **Treasury** 🕙 Tue–Sat. Dec 25.

tucked into the lush Creuse valley. Vestiges of a Benedictine abbey can still be detected in the half-Romanesque, half-Gothic church with its elaborate stone portal. The choir has wooden stalls, for visit to the church. They are masterpieces of late 17th-century carving with fantastical and intricately worked motifs of flora and fauna representing the many different facets of Good and Evil in figurative form. Today there is a garden where the nave once was.

Montluçon ❸

Allier. 👥 45,000. 🚊 🚌 🛈 67 ter bd de Courtais (04 70 05 11 44). 🛒 Tue, Thu, Sun. **www**.montlucontourisme.com

Montluçon is the economic center of the region, a small town with a medieval core. At its heart there is a Bourbon château which now houses temporary exhibitions. **Jardin Wilson**, a pleasant *jardin à la française* in the medieval quarter, sits on the original ramparts of the town. Mostly destroyed in the 18th century, little remains of the ramparts now. The restored rose garden and spectacular flower beds are worth a visit. The 12th-century **Eglise de St-Pierre** is a surprise, with giant stone columns and a huge barrel-vaulted ceiling.

Moulins ❹

Allier. 👥 23,000. 🚊 🚌 🛈 rue François Péron (04 70 44 14 14). 🛒 Fri, Sun. **www**.moulins-tourisme.com

Capital of the Bourbonnais and seat of the Bourbon Dukes since the 16th century, Moulins flourished during the

Stained-glass windows at the Cathédrale Notre-Dame in Moulins

Château de la Palice ❺

Allier. *Tel 04 70 99 37 58.*
⏺ *Easter–Oct: daily.* 🏛 ▮

In the early 16th century, the Marshal of France, Jacques II de Chabannes, hired Florentine architects to reconstruct the feudal château-fort at Lapalisse, creating a refined Renaissance castle, which has been inhabited ever since by his descendants. The *salon doré* (gilded room) has a beamed ceiling paneled in gold and two huge 15th-century Flemish tapestries showing the Crusader Knight Godefroy de Bouillon and Greek hero Hector, two of the nine classic braves of chivalric legend.

Environs

From Lapalisse, the D480 leads up through the beautiful Besbre valley past a handful of other small, well-preserved châteaus, including **Château de Thoury**.

🔺 **Château de Thoury**
Dompierre. *Tel 04 70 42 00 41.*
Courtyard and exterior ⏺ *Apr–May: Sat, Sun & public hols (pms only); Jun–Nov: Wed–Mon.*

Gilded ceiling, Château de La Palisse

Vichy ❻

Allier. 🏘 *27,000.* 🚉 ✈ 🚌 ❶ *19 rue du Parc (04 70 98 71 94).* 🛒 *Wed.*
www.vichytourisme.com

This small city on the river Allier has long been known for its hot and cold springs, and reputed cures for rheumatism, arthritis, and digestive complaints. The letter-writer Madame de Sévigné and the daughters of Louis XV visited in the late 17th and 18th centuries – the former compared the showers to "a rehearsal for Purgatory." The

Interior of the original Thermal Establishment building in Vichy

visits of Napoleon III in the 1860s put Vichy on the map and made taking the waters fashionable. The small town was spruced up and became a favorite among the French nobility and the world's wealthy middle classes. These days, the grand old Thermal Establishment, built in 1900, has been turned into shopping galleries. The modern baths are state-of-the-art and strictly

Vichy poster (about 1930–50) by Badia-Vilato

for medical purposes. A doctor's prescription and a reservation 30 days in advance are required for all treatments.

Vichy's fortunes changed for the better once again in the 1960s with the damming of the Allier, creating a huge lake in the middle of town, which rapidly became a thriving center for watersports and international events. For a small fee, you can have a taste of sports from aikido to waterskiing or learn canoeing on the 2-mile (3-km) long artificial river.

The focal point of life in Vichy is the **Parc des Sources** in the center of town, with its turn-of-the-century bandstand (afternoon concerts in season), Belle Epoque glass-roofed shopping galleries, and the Grand Casino and Opera House. Here there is gambling every afternoon and musical performances in the evenings, and an atmosphere of gaiety pervades. Also open to the public are the beautiful bronze taps of the **Source**

Célestin, in a riverside park containing vestiges of a convent bearing the same name. Only by making an effort to imagine the city in grainy black-and-white newsreel style is there the slightest reminder of the wartime Vichy government which was based in the town from 1940–44 (see p65).

🍀 **Source Célestin**
Bd du Président Kennedy. ⬜ daily. 🟢 Dec–Jan. ♿

Thiers ❼

Puy de Dôme. 🏘 13,500. 🚉 🚌
🛈 pl de Pirou (04 73 80 65 65).
📅 Thu & Sat. **www**.ville-thiers.fr

According to the writer La Bruyère, Thiers "seems painted on the slope of the hill," hanging dramatically as it does on a ravine over a sharp bend in the river Durolle. The city has been renowned for silverware since the Middle Ages, when legend has it that Crusaders brought back techniques of metalwork from the Middle East. With grindstones powered by dozens of waterfalls on the opposite bank of the river, Thiers produced everything from table knives to guillotine blades, and silverware remains its major industry today, much of it on display in the Silverware Museum, the **Musée de la Coutellerie**.

The Old Town is filled with mysterious quarters like "the Corner of Chance" and "Hell's Hollow," honeycombed with tortuous streets and well-restored 14th–17th-century houses. Many have elaborately carved wooden façades, like the Maison du Pirou in place

Pirou. The view to the west from the rampart terrace, toward Monts Dômes and Monts Dore, is particularly splendid at sunset.

🏛 **Musée de la Coutellerie**
58 rue de la Coutellerie. **Tel** 04 73 80 58 86. ⬜ Jun–Sep: daily; Oct–May: Tue–Sun. 🟢 Jan 25, May 1, Dec 25. 📷🎥
www.musee-coutellerie-thiers.com

Issoire ❽

Puy de Dôme. 🏘 15,000. 🚉 🚌
🛈 9 pl St-Paul (04 73 89 15 90).
📅 Sat. **www**.sejours-issoire.com

Most of old Issoire was destroyed in the 16th-century Wars of Religion. The present-day town has been an important industrial center since the end of World War II.

Not only does Issoire have a thriving aeronautical tradition it is also a mecca for glider pilots who come from miles around to take advantage of the strong local air currents.

Issoire's colorful 12th-century abbey church of **St-Austremoine** is one of the great Romanesque churches of the region. The capitals depict scenes from the *Life of Christ* (one of the Apostles at the Last Supper has fallen asleep at table), and imaginary demons and beasts. The 15th-century fresco of the *Last Judgment* shows Bosch-like figures of sinners being cast into the mouth of a dragon or carted off to hell. The nearby Tour de l'Horloge has scenes of Renaissance history.

Thiers from the south, spreading over the slopes above the river Durolle

St-Nectaire 🄰

Puy de Dôme. 🏠 *750.* 🚉.
ℹ️ *Les Grands Thermes (04 73 88 50 86).* 🄰 *Jul–Aug: Sun am.*
www.sancy.com

The Auvergne is noted for Romanesque churches. The **Eglise St-Nectaire** in the upper village of St-Nectaire-le Haut, with its soaring, elegant proportions, is one of the most beautiful. The 103 stone capitals, 22 of them polychrome, are vividly carved, and the treasury includes a gold bust of St-Baudime and a wooden Notre-Dame-du-Mont-Cornadore, both marvels of 12th-century workmanship. The lower village, St-Nectaire-le-Bas, has more than 40 hot and cold springs.

Environs
The 12th-century citadel of **Château de Murol**, partially in ruins, offers costumed guides demonstrating medieval life and knightly pursuits. It is wonderful for children.

🏰 Château de Murol
Murol. **Tel** *04 73 26 02 00.*
🄰 *Apr–Sep: daily; Oct–Mar: Sat & Sun.* 🄰 📷
www.chateaudemurol.fr

Fontaine d'Amboise (1515) in Clermont-Ferrand

Clermont-Ferrand 🄰

Puy de Dôme. 🏠 *141,000.* ✈
🚉 🚌 ℹ️ *pl de la Victoire (04 73 98 65 00).* 🄰 *Mon–Sat.*
www.clermont-fd.com

Clermont-Ferrand began as two distinct – and rival – cities, united only in 1630. Clermont is a lively commercial center and student town, with thriving cafés and restaurants. It was a Celtic settlement before the Roman era, had a cathedral as early as the 5th century, and by 1095 was significant enough for the pope to announce the First Crusade there. The Counts of Auvergne, challenging the episcopal power of Clermont, made their base in what is now old Montferrand, a short drive from Clermont city center. Built on a bastide pattern, it is a time warp of quiet streets and Renaissance houses.

Clermont's more ancient origins are well illustrated at the **Musée Bargoin** with its remarkable collections of locally found Roman domestic artifacts (closed Mondays).

Place St-Pierre is Clermont's principal marketplace, with a daily food market – especially good on Saturdays. Nearby, the pedestrianized rue du Port leads steeply downhill from the **Fontaine d'Amboise** (1515) to the **Basilique Notre-Dame-du-Port**. This is one of the most important Romanesque churches in the region and has benefited from extensive renovation. The stone interior is beautifully proportioned, with a magnificent raised choir and vivid carved capitals – Charity battles Avarice, in the form of two knights.

The contrast with the black lava **Cathédrale Notre-Dame-de-l'Assomption** is startling, from austere 12th-century Romanesque to high-flying 13th-century Gothic. The

Raised choir in the Basilique Notre-Dame-du-Port

For hotels and restaurants in this region see pp575–7 and pp629–31

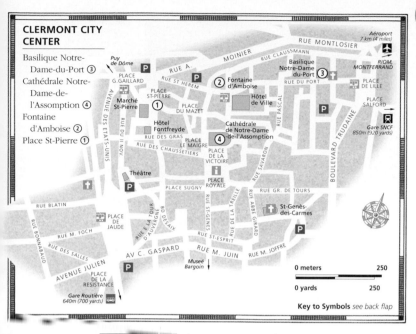

CLERMONT CITY CENTER

Basilique Notre-
Dame-du-Port ③
Cathédrale Notre-
Dame-de-
l'Assomption ④
Fontaine
d'Amboise ②
Place St-Pierre ①

0 meters 250

0 yards 250

Key to Symbols *see back flap*

---

graceful lines of the
interior are due to
the strong local
stone used for con-
struction, allowing
pillars to be thinner
and the whole
structure lighter.
The dark volcanic
rock provides a foil
for the jewel-like
12th–15th-century
stained-glass win-
dows, which are
believed to be from
the same workshop
as Sainte-Chapelle's
in Paris (*see p84*).

The old section of Mont-
ferrand thrived from the 13th
to the 17th centuries, and
many fine houses – known as
hôtels particuliers – built by
prosperous merchants have
survived. Some of the best of

Michelin man, c.1910

**Choir inside the Cathédrale
Notre-Dame-de-l'Assomption**

these, with italian
loggias, mullioned
windows, and in-
triguing courtyards,
line ancient **rue
Kléber**. Between
Clermont and old
Montferrand lies a
third mini-city, the
headquarters and
factories of the
Michelin rubber-
and-tire company,
founded here in
1830, which domin-
ates the town.

Environs

Once the rival of Clermont-
Ferrand for supremacy in
Auvergne, **Riom** is a somber
provincial town of black stone
houses and lava fountains.
The 14th-century château of
Duke Jean de Berry was razed
in the 19th century to build
the Palais de Justice; all that
remains is the delicate Sainte-
Chapelle with its lovely 15th-
century stained-glass windows.

Riom's greatest treasure is a
graceful Madonna holding an
infant with a small bird in his
hand. The statue is housed in
the Eglise de Notre-Dame-du-
Marthuret, originally built in
the 14th century, but much
rearranged since then.

Orcival ⚓

Puy de Dôme. 🚶 300.
🚉 Le Bourg (04 73 65 89 77).
www.terresdomes-sancy.com

Crowded in summer, Orcival
is nevertheless well worth
visiting for its Romanesque
church, the **Basilique
d'Orcival**, which many would
say is the best in the region.
Completed at the beginning
of the 12th century and
typically Auvergne Roman-
esque in style, the apse is
multitiered and the side walls
are supported by powerful
buttresses and strong arches.
Inside, the ornate silver and
vermilion *Virgin and Child* (in
the forward-facing position
known as "in majesty") is
enigmatic in its rigid,
square chair. With
an interior lit by 14
windows and a
spacious crypt,
the propor-
tions of the
building itself
are the most
graceful aspect.

*Virgin and
Child* in the
**Basilique
d'Orcival**

Aerial view of Puy de Dôme in the Monts Dômes range

Monts Dômes ⑫

Puy de Dôme. 🎿 🚌 🚠 *Clermont-Ferrand*. 🛈 *Montlosier (04 73 65 64 00).* **www**.parc-volcans-auvergne.com

The youngest range of the Auvergne volcanoes, at 4,000 years old, the Monts Dômes (or Chaîne des Puys), encompasses 112 extinct volcanoes aligned over a 19-mile (30-km) stretch just west of Clermont-Ferrand. At the center, the **Puy de Dôme** towers above a high plateau. A road off the N922 spirals up the peak at a steady 12 percent gradient, while the steeper Roman path is still used by hikers. For a less strenuous route, there is the mountain railroad (call 04 73 42 21 32 for details).

At the summit, half an hour farther, are the vestiges of the Roman temple of Mercury and a meteorological/telecommunications tower. On a rare clear day, the view across the volcano will take away whatever breath you have left.

The volcanic Roche Tuilière below Col de Guéry in the Monts Dore

The controversial **Parc Européen du Volcanisme, Vulcania** uses the latest technology to simulate volcanic activity in its 5 acre (2 ha) underground circuit.

In the southwest corner of the Monts Dômes region is the **Château de Cordès**, a small, privately owned 15th-century manor house with formal gardens designed by Le Nôtre *(see p179).*

🌋 **Vulcania**
D941B, Saint-Ours-les-Roches. *Tel* 08 20 82 78 28. ⭕ *mid-Mar–Aug: daily; Sep–mid-Nov: Wed–Sun.* 📷 ♿ 🍴 🎦 🏠 *Documentation center* **www**.vulcania.com

🏰 **Château de Cordès**
Orcival. *Tel* 04 73 65 81 34. ⭕ *gardens only (call 04 73 21 15 89 for hours).* 📷 🅿

Monts Dore ⑬

Puy de Dôme. 🎿 *Clermont-Ferrand.* 🚌 🚠 *Le Mont-Dore.* 🛈 *Montlosier, Aydat (04 73 65 64 00).*

Three giant volcanoes – the Puy de Sancy, the Banne d'Ordanche, and the Puy de l'Aiguiller – and their secondary cones make up the Monts Dore: dark green, heavily wooded mountains laced with rivers and lakes and dotted with summer and winter resorts for skiing, hiking, paragliding, canoeing and sailing.

The 6,185-ft (1,886-m) **Puy de Sancy** is the highest point in Central France. It can be reached by taking a shuttle from the town of Le Mont-Dore to the cable car which goes up to the peak, followed by a long

hike across open terrain. From Le Mont-Dore, there is a scenic drive on the D36 which leads to the **Couze-Chambon valley**, a beautiful stretch of high moorland threaded with waterfalls.

The area has two popular spa towns, **La Bourboule**, for children's ailments, with its casino, and Le Mont-Dore, with its grandiose turn-of-the-century **Etablissement Thermal**.

Below the Col de Guéry on the D983, the eroded volcanic **Roche Sanadoire** and **Roche Tuilière** stand up like two huge gateposts. From their peaks are far-reaching views over the wooded Cirque de Chausse and beyond.

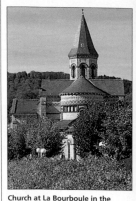

Church at La Bourboule in the Monts Dore

Uzerche ⑭

Corrèze. 🏘 *3,000.* 🚌 🚠 🛈 *pl de la Libération (05 55 73 15 71).* 🛒 *20th of the month.* **www**.pays-uzerche.fr

Uzerche is an impressive sight: gray slate roofs, turrets, and belltowers rising from a hill above the Vézère river. This prosperous town never capitulated during the conflicts of the Middle Ages, and earlier withstood a seven-year siege by Moorish forces in 732: the townspeople sent a feast out to their enemy – in fact, the last of their supplies. The Moors, thinking such lavish offerings meant the city had stores to spare, gave up.

The Romanesque **Église St-Pierre** crests the hill above the town. Beyond Uzerche, the Vézère cuts through the green gorges of the Saillant.

CANTAL CHEESE

Transhumance is still practised in the Auvergne, with the local Salers cattle kept in barns in the valleys during winter and led up to mountain pastures for the summer. The robust grasses and flowers – gentian, myrtle, anemone – on which the cows graze produce a flavorful milk that is the basis for the region's great cheese, Cantal. Curds were once turned and pressed through cheesecloth by hand, but now modern methods prevail. Cantal is the key ingredient in *aligot* – the potato-and-cheese purée flavored with garlic that is one of the region's most famous dishes.

Salers cattle enjoying rich pastures

Turenne ⓯

Corrèze. 🏠 750. 🚊 🚌
🛈 *le Bourg (05 55 24 08 00).*

Turenne is one of the most appealing medieval towns in the Corrèze. Crescent-shaped and about ... of the town, the town was the last independent feudal fiefdom in France, under the absolute rule of the La Tour d'Auvergne family until 1738. Henri de la Tour d'Auvergne, their most illustrious member, was a marshal of France under Louis XIV, and one of the greatest soldiers of modern times.

Now the sole remains of the **Château de Turenne** are the 13th-century Clock Tower and 11th-century Tower of Caesar, from which there is a quite stunning 360-degree view of the Cantal mountains across to the Dordogne

valley. Not far away is the 16th-century collegiate church and the **Chapelle des Capucins** dating from the 18th century.

⛪ Château de Turenne
Tel *05 55 85 90 66.* 🕙 *Apr–Oct: daily, Nov–Mar: Sun pm.* 🎫
www.chateau-turenne.com

Collonges-la-Rouge ⓰

Corrèze. 🏠 400. 🚊 *Brive, then bus to Collonges.* 🛈 *av de l'Auvitrie (05 55 25 47 57).*

There's something a little unsettling about Collonges' unique carmine sandstone architecture, quite beautiful in individual houses, though the overall effect is both austere and fairytale-like.

Founded in the 8th century, Collonges came under the rule

of Turenne, whose burghers built the sturdy turreted houses in the surrounding vineyards. Look out for the communal bread oven in the marketplace, and the 11th-century church, later fortified with a tower keep. The church's unusual carved white limestone tympanum shows a man driving a bear and other lively figures.

Salers ⓱

Cantal. 🏠 400. 🚊 *summer only.* 🛈 *pl Tyssandier d'Escous (04 71 40 58 08).* 🛒 *Wed.*
www.salers-tourisme.fr

A handsome town of gray lava houses and 15th-century ramparts, Salers sits atop a steep escarpment at the edge of the Cantal mountains. It is one of few virtually intact Renaissance villages in the region. The church has an admirable polychrome *mise au tombeau* (entombment), dated 1495, and five 17th-century Aubusson tapestries.

From the fountain, streets lead up to the cliff edge and allow views of the surrounding valleys, with the ever-present sound of cowbells in the distance. The town is very crowded in summer, but it makes a good starting point for excursions to the Puy Mary (*see p364*), the huge barrage at Bort-les-Orgues, the nearby Château de Val, and the Cère valley to the south.

Medieval Château de Val at Bort-les-Orgues near Salers

Puy Mary peak in the volcanic Monts du Cantal

Monts du Cantal ⑱

Cantal. ✈ *Aurillac.* 🚌 🚃 *Lioron.*
ℹ *Aurillac (04 71 48 46 58).*
www.iaurillac.com

The Cantal mountains were originally one enormous volcano – the oldest and the largest in Europe, dating from the Tertiary period. The highest peaks, the **Plomb du Cantal** at 6,086 ft (1,855 m) and the **Puy Mary** at 5,863 ft (1,787 m), are surrounded by crests and deep river valleys. Driving the narrow roads is a thrill, compounded by the views at every hairpin turn. Between peaks and gorges, rich mountain pastures provide summer grazing for red-gold Salers cows *(see p363)*. From the **Pas de Peyrol**, the highest road pass in the country at 5,191 ft (1,589 m), it's about a 25-minute journey on foot to the summit of the Puy Mary.

Environs
One of the finest of the Auvergne châteaux, **Château d'Anjony** was built by Louis II d'Anjony, a supporter of Joan of Arc *(see pp300–1)*. Highlights are the 16th-century frescoes: in the chapel, scenes from the Life and Passion of Christ, and upstairs in the *Salle des Preux* (Knights' Room), a dazzling series of the nine heroes of chivalry. To the south lies the small town of **Aurillac**, a good base for exploring the Cantal region.

♣ **Château d'Anjony**
Tournemire. **Tel** *04 71 47 61 67.*
◐ *Jul–Aug: daily; mid-Feb–mid-Nov: daily pms.* 🎫 🎥 *obligatory.*

La Chaise-Dieu ⑲

Haute-Loire. 🏠 *700.* 🚌 ℹ *pl de la Mairie (04 71 00 01 16).* 🅰 *Thu.*
www.la-chaise-dieu.info

Somber and massive, midway between Romanesque and Gothic, the 14th-century abbey church of **St-Robert** is the prime reason to visit the small village of La Chaise-Dieu. The building is an amalgam of styles; the choir, however, is sensational: 144 oak stalls carved with figures of Vice and Virtue. Above them, entirely covering the walls, are some of the loveliest tapestries in France. Made in Brussels and Arras in the early 16th century and depicting scenes from the Old and New Testaments, they are rich in color and detail.

Statue of Notre-Dame-de-France at Le Puy

On the outer walls of the choir the 15th-century wall painting of the *Danse Macabre* shows Death in the form of skeletons leading rich and poor alike to their inevitable end. Beyond the cloister is the Echo room, in which two people whispering in opposite corners can hear one another perfectly. A Baroque Music Festival from mid-August to September makes the abbey crowded.

Le Puy-en-Velay ⑳

Haute-Loire. 🏠 *20,500.* ✈ 🚌 🚃
ℹ *2 pl de Clauzel (04 71 09 38 41).*
🅰 *Sat.* 🎪 *Sep.*
www.ot-lepuyenvelay.fr

Located in the bowl of a volcanic cone, the town of Le Puy teeters on a series of rock outcrops and giant basalt pillars. The town has three peaks, each topped with a landmark church or statue. Seen from afar, this is one of the most impressive sights in France.

Now a commercial and tourist-oriented town, Le Puy's star attraction is its medieval **Holy City**. This became a pilgrimage center after the Bishop of Le Puy, Gotescalk, made one of the first pilgrimages to Santiago de Compostela in 962, and built the **Chapelle St-Michel d'Aiguilhe** on his return.

Detail of *Danse Macabre* at St-Robert, in La Chaise-Dieu

THE AUVERGNE'S BLACK MADONNAS

The cult of the Virgin Mary has always been strong in the Auvergne and this is reflected in the concentration of her statues in the region. Carved in dark walnut or cedar, now blackened with age, the Madonnas are believed to originate from the Byzantine influence of the Crusaders. Perhaps the most famous Madonna is the one in Le-Puy-en-Velay, a 17th-century copy of one which belonged to Louis IX in the Middle Ages.

Louis IX's Black Virgin

Pilgrims from eastern France and Germany assembled at the **Cathédrale de Notre-Dame** with its famous Black Madonna and "fever stone" – a small crescent stone with healing powers in one of its walls – before setting off for Compostela.

Built on an early pagan site, the Cathédrale de Notre-Dame is a huge Romanesque structure. Multiform arches, carved palm and leaf designs, and a checkerboard façade show the influences of Moorish Spain, and indicate the considerable cultural exchange that took place with southern France in the 11th and 12th centuries. In the transept are Romanesque frescoes, notably an 11th–12th-century St. Michael; in the sacristy, the treasury includes the Bible of Theodolphus, a handwritten document from the era of Charlemagne. The cathedral is the center of the Holy City complex that dominates the upper town, encompassing a baptistry, cloister, Prior's house, and Penitents' chapel.

The colossal red statue of **Notre-Dame-de-France**, on the pinnacle of the Rocher Corneille, was erected in 1860, cast from 213 cannons captured at Sebastopol during the Crimean War. The statue is reached by a steep pathway and can be climbed by an iron ladder on the inside.

The Chapelle St-Michel, like the cathedral, shows Moorish influences in the trefoil decoration and colored mosaics on the rounded arch over the main entrance. It seems to grow out of a giant finger of lava rock and is reached by a steep climb. The chapel is thought to be located on the site of an earlier temple to Mercury, and its center dates from the 10th century, although most of the building was constructed a century later. The floor has been constructed to follow the contours of the rock in places,

and the interior is ornamented with faded 10th-century murals and 20th-century stained-glass.

In the lower city, narrow streets of 15th- and 16th-century houses lead to the Vinay Garden and the **Musée Crozatier**, which has a collection of handmade lace from the 16th century to the present. The museum also has a good collection of medieval *objets d'art* and 15th-century paintings. Once begun, renovation work will close the museum for several years so call ahead.

In mid-September, Le Puy transforms itself into masked and costumed Renaissance carnival for the Bird King Festival, an ancient tradition celebrating the skill of the city's best archers (see p38).

Chapelle St-Michel d'Aiguilhe
Aiguilhe. *Tel* 04 71 09 50 03. mid-Feb–mid-Dec: daily; mid-Dec–mid-Feb: pms only. Jan 1, Dec 25.

Notre-Dame-de-France
Rocher Corneille. *Tel* 04 71 05 45 52. daily (except Christmas hols).

Musée Crozatier
Jardin Henri Vinay. *Tel* 04 71 06 62 40. for renovations until 2014.

Chapelle St-Michel d'Aiguilhe, standing on a finger of lava rock

Ruins of the Castle of Calmont d'Olt at Espalion in the Lot Valley

Vallée du Lot ㉑

Aveyron. ✈ Aurillac, Rodez.
🚉 Rodez, Séverac-le-Château.
🚌 Espalion, Rodez. ℹ️ Espalion (05
65 44 10 63). www.valleedulot.com

From Mende and the old river port of La Canourgue all the way to Conques, the river Lot (or Olt in old usage) courses through its fertile valley past orchards, vineyards, and pine forests. **St Côme d'Olt**, near the Aubrac mountains, is an unspoiled, fortified village whose 15th-century church is surrounded by Medieval and Renaissance houses. At **Espalion**, the pastel stone houses and a turreted 16th-century castle are reflected in the river, which runs beneath a 13th-century arched stone bridge. The town has one of the best markets in the region on Friday mornings. Just outside town is the 11th-century Perse Church, whose carved capitals portray battling knights and imaginary birds sipping from a chalice.
  Estaing was once the fiefdom of one of the greatest families of the Rouergue, dating back to the 13th-century. The village nestles beneath its massive château (open May–Sep) on the river bank. The road passes through the Lot Gorge on the way to **Entraygues** ("between waters") where the old quarter and 13th-century Gothic bridge are worth a visit. Beyond Entraygues the river widens to join the Garonne.

Conques ㉒

See pp368–9.

Rodez ㉓

Aveyron. 🏠 26,000. 🚆 🚉 🚌
ℹ️ pl Foch (05 65 75 76 77).
🕑 Wed, Sat. www.ot-rodez.fr

Like many medieval French cities, Rodez was politically divided: the store-lined **place du Bourg** on one side of town and **place de la Cité** near the cathedral on the other, reflect

Entombment in Rodez Cathedral

conflicting secular and ecclesiastical interests. Rodez's commercial center, the largest in the region, is probably the main attraction now, though the 13th-century huge pink stone **Cathédrale Notre-Dame** is worth a look, with its fortress-like west façade, and its magnificent, ornate belltower. The 15th-century choir stalls show a superb panoply of creatures, including a winged lion and one naughty fellow exposing his derrière.

Environs

Southeast (28 miles/45 kms) lies Saint Léons, birthplace of Jean-Henri Fabre, the famous entymologist. Here is **Micropolis**, part interactive museum, part theme park, dedicated to the glory of insects (closed Nov–mid-Feb). Watch the breathtaking movie of the same name, if nothing else.

ROBERT LOUIS STEVENSON

Robert Louis Stevenson (1850–94), best known for his novels *Treasure Island, Kidnapped,* and *Dr. Jekyll and Mr. Hyde,* was also an accomplished travel writer. In 1878, he set off across the remote Cévennes mountain range with only a small donkey, Modestine, for company. His classic account of this eventful journey, *Travels with a Donkey in the Cévennes,* was published in the following year.

Robert Louis Stevenson

Dramatic scenery in Corniche des Cévennes national park

Corniche des Cévennes ㉔

Lozère, Gard. 🚉 *Nîmes.* 🚌 *Alès.*
🚌 *St-Jean-du-Gard.*
ℹ️ *St-Jean-du-Gard (04 66 85 32 11).*
www.cevennes-parcnational.fr

The dramatic Corniche road from Florac on the Tarn to St-Jean-du-Gard was cut in the early 18th century by the troops of Louis XIV in pursuit of the Camisards, Protestant rebels who had no uniforms but fought in their ordinary shirts (*camiso* in the *langue d'oc*). The route of the D983 makes a spectacular drive. Fascination with the history of the Camisards was one of the reasons that Robert Louis Stevenson undertook his fabled trek in the Cévennes with Modestine, recounted in his *Travels with a Donkey*.

At St-Laurent-de-Trèves, where fossil remains suggest dinosaurs once roamed, there is a view of the Grands Causses and the peaks of Lozère and Aigoual. The Corniche ends in St-Jean-du-Gard, where the **Musée des Vallées Cévenoles**, depicting peasant life, is located in a former 17th-century inn.

🏛 **Musée des Vallées Cévenoles**
95 grand' rue, St-Jean-du-Gard.
Tel *04 66 85 10 48.* ⭕ *Jul–Aug: 10am–7pm daily; Apr–Jun, Sep–Oct: 10am–noon, 2–7pm daily; Nov–Mar: by appt only.* 🔲 ⭕ *public hols.* 📶
🖥 www.museedescevennes.com

Grands Causses ㉕

Aveyron. ✈️ *Rodez-Marcillac.* 🚌
🚌 *Millau.* ℹ️ *Millau (05 65 60 02 42).*
📅 *Wed & Fri.* **www**.ot-millau.fr

The Causses are vast, arid limestone plateaus, alternating with surprisingly green, fertile canyon valleys. The only sign of life at times is a bird of prey wheeling in the sky, or an isolated stone farm or shepherd's hut. The whole area makes for some desolate hiking for those who like solitude.

The four Grands Causses – Sauveterre, Méjean, Noir, and Larzac – stretch out east of the city of Millau, which boasts the tallest vehicular bridge in the world. They extend from Mende in the north to the valley of the Vis river in the south.

Among the sights in the Causses are the *chaos* – bizarre rock formations reputed to resemble ruined cities, and named accordingly: there's the chaos of **Montpellier-le-Vieux**, **Nîmes-le-Vieux**, and **Roquesaltes**. **Aven Armand** and the **Dargilan Grotto** are vast and deep natural underground grottoes.

A good place to head for in the Larzac Causse is the strange, rough-hewn stone village of **La Couvertoirade**, a fully-enclosed citadel of the Knights Templar in the 12th century. The unpaved streets and medieval houses are an austere reminder of the dark side of the church. Entry into the village is free, with a fee for the tour of the ramparts.

The Causse du Larzac's best-known village is probably **Roquefort-sur-Soulzon**, a small gray town terraced on the side of a crumbled limestone outcrop. It has one main street and one major product, Roquefort cheese. This is made from unpasteurized sheep's milk, seeded with a distinctive blue mould grown on loaves of bread, and aged in the warren of damp caves above the town.

View over Méjean, one of the four plateaux of the Grands Causses

Conques ㉒

The village of Conques clusters around the splendid Abbaye de Ste-Foy, hemmed into a rugged site against the hillside. Sainte-Foy was a young girl who became an early Christian martyr; her relics were first kept at a rival monastery in Agen. In the 9th century a monk from Conques stole the relics, thereby attracting pilgrims to this remote spot and firmly establishing Conques as a halt on the route to Santiago de Compostela *(see pp400–1)*.

The treasury holds the most important collection of medieval and Renaissance gold

12th-century reliquary

work in western Europe. Some of it was made in the abbey's own workshops as early as the 9th century. The Romanesque abbey church has beautiful stained-glass windows by Pierre Soulages (1994), and its tympanum is a triumph of medieval sculpture.

View of the church from the village

The broad transepts were able to accommodate crowds of pilgrims.

Nave Interior
Pure and elegantly austere, the Romanesque interior dates from 1050–1135. The short nave soars to a height of 72 ft (22 m), with three tiers of arches topped by 250 decorative carved capitals.

Tympanum
This sculpture from the early 12th century depicts the Last Judgment, with the Devil in Hell (shown) in the lower part of the sculpture and Christ in Heaven in the tympanum's central position.

CONQUES' TREASURES

The treasures date from the 9th to the 19th century, and are prized for both their beauty and their rarity. The gold-plated wood and silver reliquary of Ste-Foy is studded with gems, rock crystal, and even an *intaglio* of Roman Emperor Caracalla. The body is 9th century, but the face may be older, possibly 5th century. Other magnificent pieces include an "A"-shaped reliquary said to be a gift from Charlemagne, the small but exquisite Pépin's shrine from AD 1000, and a late 16th-century processional cross.

The precious reliquary of Ste-Foy

Romanesque Chapels

The east end is three-tiered, topped by the blind arcades of the choir and a central bell-tower. Three chapels surround the eastern apse, built to accommodate extra altars for the celebration of mass.

Treasury

The precious contents of the treasury were hidden by the townspeople to prevent their destruction during the French Revolution. Perhaps surprisingly, all were returned.

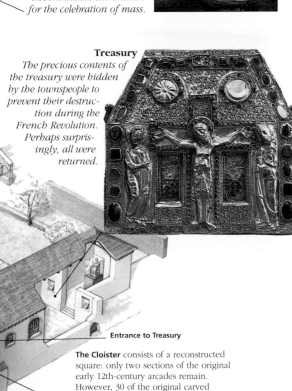

Entrance to Treasury

The Cloister consists of a reconstructed square: only two sections of the original early 12th-century arcades remain. However, 30 of the original carved capitals are displayed in the refectory and in the Musée Fau.

Gorges du Tarn ❷⑥

Near the beginning of its journey to meet the river Garonne, the Tarn flows through some of Europe's most spectacular gorges. For millions of years, the Tarn and its tributary the Jonte have eaten their way down through the limestone plateaus of the Cévennes, creating a sinuous forked canyon some 15 miles (25 km) long and nearly 1,300 ft (400 m) deep. The gorges are flanked by rocky bluffs and scaled by roads with dizzying bends and panoramic views, which are incredibly popular in the high season. The surrounding plateaus, or *causses*, are eerily different, forming an open, austere landscape, dry in summer and snow-clad in winter, where wandering sheep and isolated farms are sometimes the only signs of life.

Point Sublime
From 2,600 ft (800 m) up, there are stunning views of a major bend in the Tarn gorge, with the Causse Méjean visible in the distance.

Outdoor Activities
The Tarn and Jonte gorges are popular for canoeing and river-rafting. Although relatively placid in summer, melting snow can make the rivers hazardous in spring.

Pas de Souci
Just upriver from Les Vignes, Pas de Souci flanks a narrow point in the gorge as the Tarn makes its way northwards.

Chaos de Montpellier-le-Vieux
Situated on the flank of the Causse Noir off the D110 is a remarkable geological site – bizarre rock formations created by limestone erosion.

La Malène
*An old crossing-point between the Causse de Sauveterre
and the Causse Méjean, this village, with its 16th-century
fortified manor, is a good starting point for boat trips.*

VISITORS' CHECKLIST

Lozère. 🚉 Rodez-Marcillac.
🚌 Mende, Banassac,
Séverac-le-Château. 🚌 Milau.
ℹ️ Le Rozier (05 65 62 60 89).
St-Enimie (04 66 48 53 44).
www.ot-gorgesdutarn.com

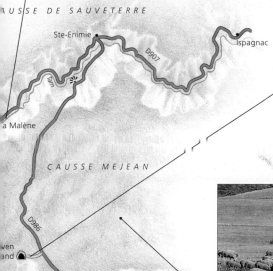

CAUSSE DE SAUVETERRE

Ste-Enimie

Ispagnac

D907

Tarn

La Malène

CAUSSE MEJEAN

D986

ven
and 🔺

D996

Jonte

te de
gilan 🔺

D39

Meyrueis

Aven Armand Caves
*On the Causse Méjean,
many stalactites in the caves
are linned by minerals that
are deposited by the
slowly trickling water.*

Causse Méjean
The high plateaus or causses *are a botanist's
paradise in spring and summer, with over
900 species of wild flowers, including orchids.*

THE WILD CEVENNES

One of the least populated
parts of France, this area is well
known for its wild flowers and
birds of prey, and griffon
vultures were once common here. These
giant but harmless
scavengers nearly
died out in the 20th century
through being hunted, but
now a reintroduction
program has led to growing
numbers breeding in the
Gorges de la Jonte.

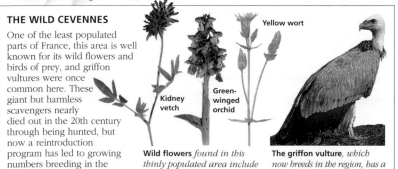

Yellow wort

Kidney
vetch

Green-
winged
orchid

Wild flowers *found in this
thinly populated area include
unusual alpine plants.*

The griffon vulture, *which
now breeds in the region, has a
wingspan of over 8 ft (2.5 m).*

THE RHONE VALLEY
AND FRENCH ALPS

LOIRE · RHONE · AIN · ISEZERE · DROME
ARDECHE · HAUTE-SAVOIE · SAVOIE · HAUTES-ALPES

*I*ts two most important geographical features, the Alps and the river
*Rhône, give this region both its name and its dramatic character.
The east is dominated by majestic snowcapped peaks, while the
Rhône provides a vital conduit between north and south.*

The Romans recognized
this strategic route when
they founded Lyon over
2,000 years ago. Today Lyon,
with its great museums and
fine Renaissance buildings,
is the second city of France.
It is one of the country's most
vital commercial and cultural centers
as well as the undisputed capital of
French gastronomy. To the north lie
the flat marshlands of the Dombes and
the rich agricultural Bresse plain.
Here, too, are the famous Beaujolais
vineyards which, along with the
Rhône vineyards, make the region
such an important wine producer.

The French Alps are among the most
popular year-round resort areas in the
world, with internationally renowned
ski stations such as Chamonix, Mégève,
and Courchevel, and his-
toric cities like Chambéry,
capital of Savoy before it
joined France. Elegant spa
towns line the shores of
Lac Léman (Lake Geneva).
Grenoble, a bustling
university city and hi-tech
center, is flanked by two of the most
spectacular nature reserves in France,
the Chartreuse and the Vercors.

To the south, orchards and fields of
sunflowers give way to brilliant rows
of lavender interspersed with vineyards and olive groves. Châteaus and
ancient towns dot the landscape.
Mountains and pretty, old-fashioned
spa towns characterize the rugged
Ardèche, and the deeply scoured
gorges along the river Ardèche offer
some of the wildest scenery in France.

The restored Ferme de la Forêt at St-Trivier-de-Courtes, north of Bourg-en-Bresse

◁ **Annecy's medieval quarter**

Exploring the Rhône Valley and French Alps

Lyon is the region's largest city, famed for its historic buildings and gastronomic tradition. Wine lovers can choose between the vineyards of the Beaujolais, Rhône Valley, and Drôme region to the south. To the west, the Ardèche offers rugged wilderness, canoeing, and climbing. Spa devotees from around the world flock to Évian-les-Bains and Aix-les-Bains, while the Alps are a favorite destination for sports enthusiasts *(see pp322–3)*.

SIGHTS AT A GLANCE

- Aix-les-Bains 22
- Annecy 23
- The Ardèche 11
- Bourg-en-Bresse 1
- Briançon 16
- Chambéry 21
- The Chartreuse 20
- The Dombes 2
- Grenoble 18
- Grignan 14
- Lac Léman 24
- Le Bourg d'Oisans 17
- Lyon 4
- Montélimar 13
- Nyons 15
- Palais Idéal du Facteur Cheval 8
- Pérouges 3
- St-Étienne 7
- St-Romain-en-Gal 6
- Tournon-sur-Rhône 9
- Valence 10
- Vals-les-Bains 12
- The Vercors 19
- Vienne 5

KEY

- Highway
- Major road
- Secondary road
- Minor road
- Scenic route
- Main railroad
- Minor railroad
- International border
- Regional border
- Summit

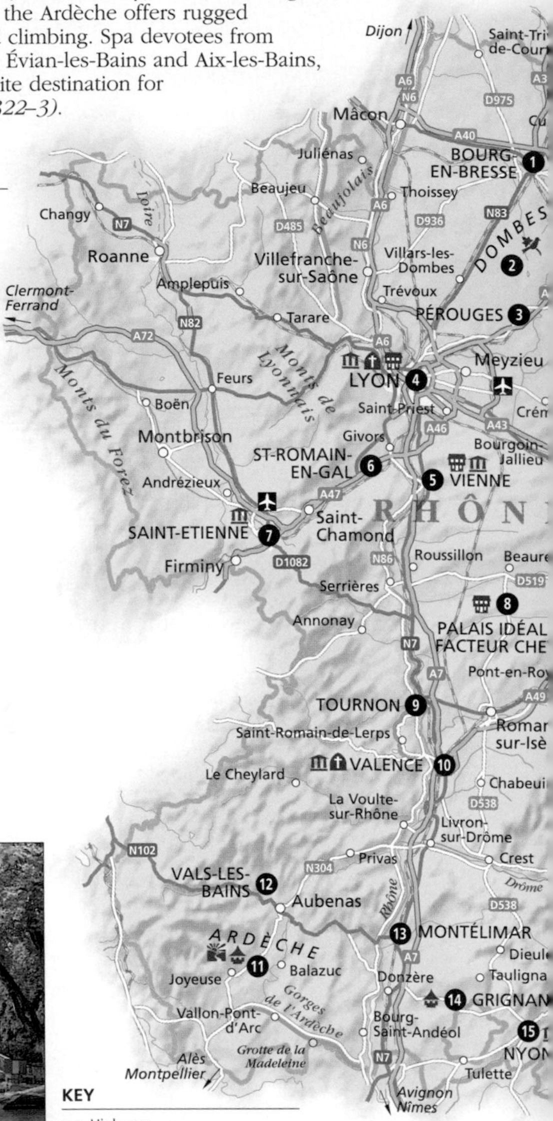

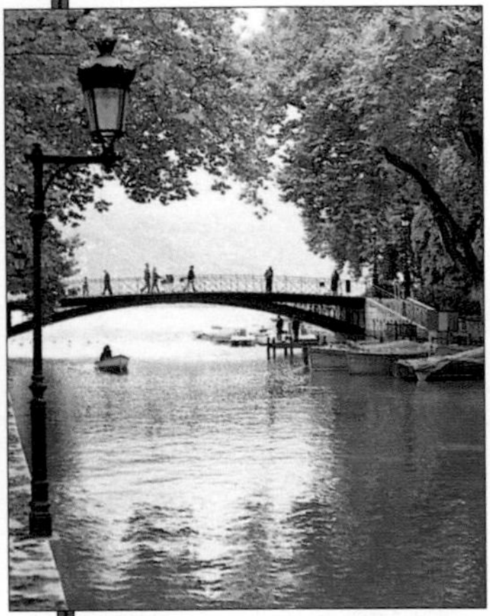

The Pont des Amours in Annecy

For additional map symbols *see back flap*

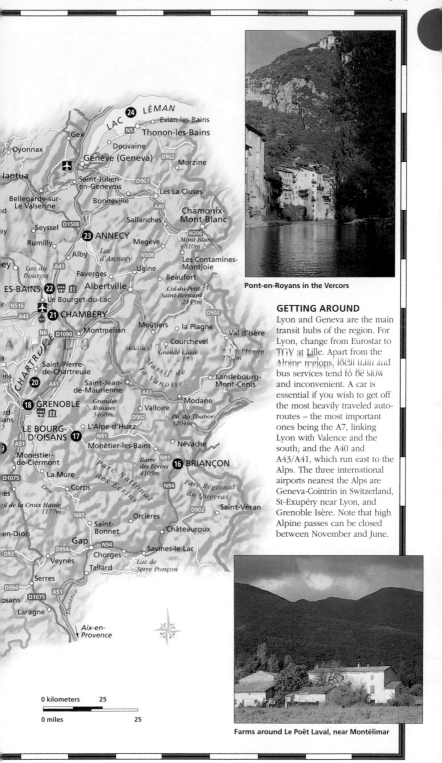

Pont-en-Royans in the Vercors

GETTING AROUND

Lyon and Geneva are the main transit hubs of the region. For Lyon, change from Eurostar to TGV at Lille. Apart from the Alpine regions, local train and bus services tend to be slow and inconvenient. A car is essential if you wish to get off the most heavily traveled auto-routes – the most important ones being the A7, linking Lyon with Valence and the south; and the A40 and A43/A41, which run east to the Alps. The three international airports nearest the Alps are Geneva-Cointrin in Switzerland, St-Exupéry near Lyon, and Grenoble Isère. Note that high Alpine passes can be closed between November and June.

Farms around Le Poët Laval, near Montélimar

0 kilometers 25

0 miles 25

Bourg-en-Bresse ❶

Ain. ⌘ *43,000*. 🚆 🚌 ℹ️ *Centre Culturel Albert Camus, 6 av Alsace-Lorraine (04 74 22 49 40)*. 🛍️ *Wed & Sat*. www.bourgenbressetourisme.fr

Bourg-en-Bresse is a busy market town, with some beautifully restored half-timbered buildings. It is best known for its tasty *poulet de Bresse* (chickens raised in the flat agricultural region of Bresse and designated *appellation contrôlée, see p319*); and its abbey church of **Brou** on the southeast edge of town.

The latter, no longer a place of worship, has become one of the most visited sites in France. Flamboyant Gothic in style, it was built between 1505 and 1536 by Margaret of Austria after the death of her husband Philibert, Duke of Savoy, in 1504.

The couple's finely sculpted Carrara marble tombs can be seen in the choir, along with the tomb of Margaret of Bourbon, Philibert's mother, who died in 1483. Notice also the beautifully carved choir stalls, stained-glass windows, and rood screen with its elegant basket-handle arching.

The adjacent cloisters house a small museum with a good collection of 16th- and 17th-century Dutch and Flemish masters, as well as contemporary works by local artists.

Environs

About 15 miles (24 km) north of Bourg-en-Bresse at St-Trivier-de-Courtes, the restored **Ferme-Musée de la Forêt** offers a look at farm life in the region during the 17th century. The ancient house has what is known locally as a Saracen chimney, with a brick hood in the center of the room, similar to constructions in Sicily and Portugal, and a collection of antique farm implements.

Tomb of Margaret of Austria in the abbey church of Brou at Bourg-en-Bresse

Bresse chickens

🏛 **Ferme-Musée de la Forêt**
Tel *04 74 30 71 89*. ⬜ *Jul–Sep: daily; Apr–Jun & Oct: w/e & public hols*. ● *Mon am*. 📷 ♿

The Dombes ❷

Ain. ✈️ *Lyon*. 🚆 *Lyon, Villars les Dombes, Bourg-en-Bresse*. 🚌 *Villars-les-Dombes (from Bourg-en-Bresse)*. ℹ️ *3 pl de Hôtel de Ville, Villars-les-Dombes (04 74 98 06 29)*.

This flat, glacier-gouged plateau south of Bourg-en-Bresse is dotted with small hills, ponds and marshes, making it popular with anglers and bird-watchers.

In the middle of the area at **Villars-les-Dombes** is an ornithological park, the **Parc des Oiseaux**. Over 400 species of native and exotic birds live here, including tufted herons, vultures, pink flamingoes, emus, and ostriches.

🦅 **Parc des Oiseaux**
Route Nationale 83, Villars-les-Dombes. **Tel** *04 74 98 05 54*.
⬜ *daily*. ● *Dec–Feb*. 📷 ♿

Pérouges ❸

Ain. ⌘ *900*. 🚆 *Meximieux-Pérouges*. 🚌 ℹ️ *04 74 46 70 84*. www.perouges.org

Originally the home of immigrants from Perugia, Pérouges is a fortified hilltop village of medieval houses and cobblestoned streets. In the 13th century it was a center of linen-weaving, but with the mechanization of the industry in the 19th century, the local population fell from 1,500 to 90.

Restoration of its historic buildings and a new influx of craftsmen have breathed new life into Pérouges. Not surprisingly, the village has often been used as the setting for historical dramas such as *The Three Musketeers and Monsieur Vincent*. The village's main square, place de la Halle, is shaded by a huge lime tree planted in 1792 to honor the Revolution.

A Tour of Beaujolais

Beaujolais is an ideal area for wine tasting, offering delicious, affordable wine and glorious countryside. The south of the region produces most of the Beaujolais Nouveau, released fresh from the cellars on the third Thursday of November each year. In the north are the ten superior quality *cru* wines – St-Amour, Juliénas, Moulin-à-Vent, Chénas, Fleurie, Chiroubles, Morgon, Brouilly, Côte de Brouilly, and Regnié – most of which can be visited in a day's drive. The distinctive *maisons du pays* have living quarters built over the wine cellar. Almost every village has its *cave* (wine cellar), offering tastings and a glimpse of the wine culture that dominates local life.

Côte de Brouilly

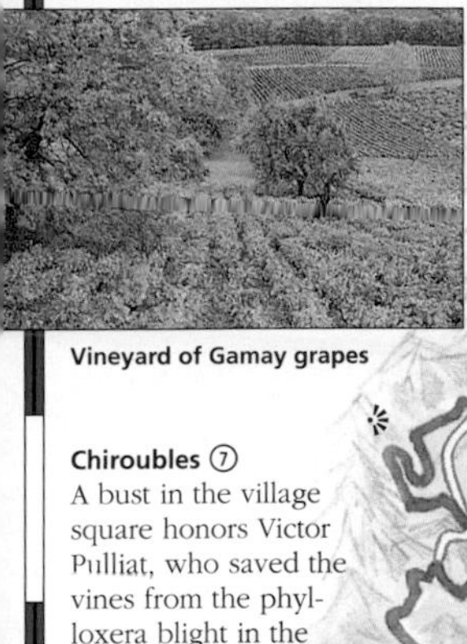

Juliénas ①
Famous for *coq au vin*, this village stores and sells wine in its church, at the Château du Bois de la Salle, and at several private cellars.

Moulin-à-Vent ②
This 17th-century windmill has lovely views of the Saône valley. Tastings of the oldest *cru* in the region are held in the *caves* next door.

MACON →

Chénas

Romanèche-Thorins

Vineyard of Gamay grapes

Chiroubles ⑦
A bust in the village square honors Victor Pulliat, who saved the vines from the phylloxera blight in the 1880s by using American vine stocks.

Fleurie ③
The chapel of the Madonna (1875) stands guard over the vineyards, and village restaurants serve local *andouillettes au Fleurie*.

Villié-Morgon ④
Wine-tasting takes place in the cellars of the 18th-century Château Fontcrenne in the village center.

Régnié-Durette

Cercié

KEY

▬▬▬	Tour route
═══	Other roads
☀	Viewpoint

0 kilometers 2

0 miles 1

Beaujeu ⑥
Once the ancient capital of the region, Beaujeu offers tastings in its 17th-century hospices. This Renaissance wooden building houses a store, information center, and museum.

VILLEFRANCHE-SUR-SAONE ↓

Brouilly ⑤
The hill, with its tiny 19th-century chapel of Notre-Dame du Raisin, offers fine views and an annual Beaujolais wine festival.

Street-by-Street: Lyon ❹

On the west bank of the river Saône, the restored old
quarter of Vieux Lyon is an atmospheric warren of
cobbled streets, *traboules* (covered passageways),
Renaissance palaces, first-class restaurants, lively
bouchons (bistros), and bohemian stores. It is also
the site of the Roman city of Lugdunum, the
commercial and military capital of Gaul
founded by Julius Caesar in 44 BC.
Vestiges of this prosperous city can be
seen in the superb Gallo-Roman
museum at the top of Fourvière hill.
Two excavated Roman theaters still stage
performances from opera to rock concerts.
At the foot of the hill is the finest collection
of Renaissance mansions in France. The
spectacular Musée des Confluences makes an
exciting new addition to the city in 2013.

★ Théâtres Romains
*There are two Roman
amphitheaters here: the
Grand Théâtre, the oldest
theater in France, built in
15 BC to seat 30,000
spectators and still used for
modern performances; and
the smaller Odéon, with its
geometric tiled flooring.*

**★ Musée de la Civilisation
Gallo-Romaine**
*This underground museum
contains a rich collection of
statues, mosaics, coins, and
inscriptions evoking Lyon's
Roman past.*

Entrance
to funicular

STAR SIGHTS

★ Théâtres Romains

★ Musée de la
   Civilisation
   Gallo-Romaine

★ Basilique Notre-Dame
   de Fourvière

Cathédrale St-Jean
*Begun in the late 12th century,
cathedral has a 14th-century astr
nomical clock that shows religi
feast days until the year 2019.*

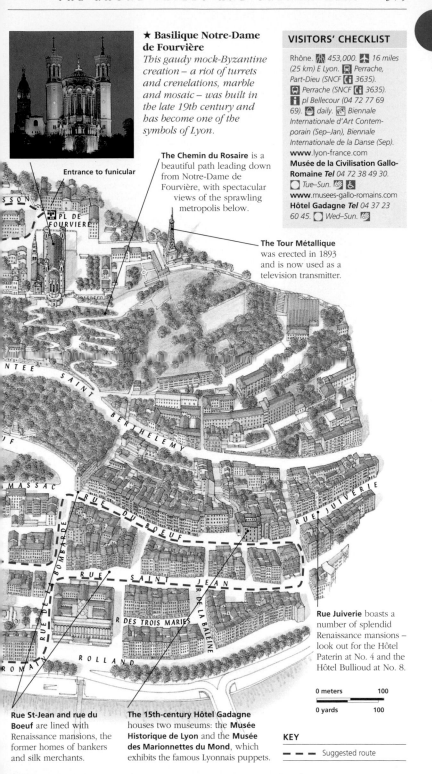

★ **Basilique Notre-Dame de Fourvière**
This gaudy mock-Byzantine creation – a riot of turrets and crenelations, marble and mosaic – was built in the late 19th century and has become one of the symbols of Lyon.

Entrance to funicular

The Chemin du Rosaire is a beautiful path leading down from Notre-Dame de Fourvière, with spectacular views of the sprawling metropolis below.

The Tour Métallique was erected in 1893 and is now used as a television transmitter.

VISITORS' CHECKLIST

Rhône. 453,000. 16 miles (25 km) E Lyon. Perrache, Part-Dieu (SNCF 3635). Perrache (SNCF 3635). pl Bellecour (04 72 77 69 69). daily. Biennale Internationale d'Art Contemporain (Sep–Jan), Biennale Internationale de la Danse (Sep). www.lyon-france.com
Musée de la Civilisation Gallo-Romaine *Tel* 04 72 38 49 30. Tue–Sun. www.musees-gallo-romains.com
Hôtel Gadagne *Tel* 04 37 23 60 45. Wed–Sun.

Rue Juiverie boasts a number of splendid Renaissance mansions – look out for the Hôtel Paterin at No. 4 and the Hôtel Bullioud at No. 8.

| 0 meters | 100 |
| 0 yards | 100 |

Rue St-Jean and rue du Boeuf are lined with Renaissance mansions, the former homes of bankers and silk merchants.

The 15th-century Hôtel Gadagne houses two museums: the **Musée Historique de Lyon** and the **Musée des Marionnettes du Mond**, which exhibits the famous Lyonnais puppets.

KEY

– – – Suggested route

Exploring Lyon

France's second city, dramatically sited on the banks of the Rhône and Saône rivers, has been a vital gateway between the north and south since ancient times. On arriving you immediately feel a *brin du sud*, or touch of the south. The crowds are not as quick-stepping as they are in Paris, and the sun is often shining here when it's rainy and cold in the north. Despite its importance as a banking, textile, and pharmaceutical center, most of the French immediately associate Lyon with their palates. The city is packed with restaurants, ranging from simple *bouchons* (bistros) to some of the most opulent tables in France.

The rue St-Jean in Vieux Lyon

The Presqu'île

The heart of Lyon is the Presqu'île, the narrow peninsula of land between the Saône and Rhône rivers, just north of their confluence. A pedestrianized shopping street, the rue de la République, links the twin poles of civic life: the vast **place Bellecour**, with its equestrian statue of Louis XIV in the middle, and the **place des Terreaux**. The latter is overlooked by Lyon's ornate 17th-century Hôtel de Ville (town hall) and the Palais St-Pierre, a former Benedictine convent and now the home of the **Musée des Beaux Arts**. In the middle of the square is a monumental 19th-century fountain by Bartholdi, sculptor of the Statue of Liberty.

Behind the town hall, architect Jean Nouvel's futuristic **Opéra de Lyon** – a black barrel vault of steel and glass encased in a Neoclassical shell – was remodeled in a controversial design in 1993.

A few blocks to the south, the **Musée de l'Imprimerie** illustrates Lyon's contribution to the early days of printing in the late 15th century.

Two other museums worth visiting in the Presqu'île are the **Musée des Tissus**, which houses an extraordinary collection of silks and tapestries dating from early Christian times to the present day, and the **Musée des Arts Décoratifs**, which displays a range of tapestries, furniture, porcelain, and *objets d'art*.

Nearby, the **Abbaye St-Martin d'Ainay** is an impressively restored Carolingian church dating from 1107.

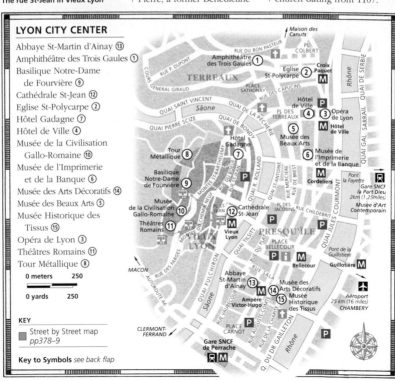

LYON CITY CENTER

Abbaye St-Martin d'Ainay ⑬
Amphithéâtre des Trois Gaules ①
Basilique Notre-Dame
de Fourvière ⑨
Cathédrale St-Jean ⑫
Eglise St-Polycarpe ②
Hôtel Gadagne ⑦
Hôtel de Ville ④
Musée de la Civilisation
Gallo-Romaine ⑩
Musée de l'Imprimerie
et de la Banque ⑥
Musée des Arts Décoratifs ⑭
Musée des Beaux Arts ⑤
Musée Historique des
Tissus ⑮
Opéra de Lyon ③
Théâtres Romains ⑪
Tour Métallique ⑧

0 meters 250
0 yards 250

KEY

▢ Street by Street map
pp378–9

Key to Symbols *see back flap*

Food market on quai St-Antoine

La Croix-Rousse

This area north of Presqu'île became the center of the city's silk-weaving industry in the 15th century. It is traced with covered passages known as *traboules*, used by weavers to transport their finished fabrics. To get a sense of them, enter at No. 6 place des Terreaux and continue along until you reach the **Eglise St-Polycarpe**. From here, it is a short walk to the ruins of the **Amphithéâtre des Trois Gaules**, built in AD 19, and the **Maison des Canuts**, with its traditional silk loom.

La Part-Dieu

This modern business area on the east bank of the Rhône has a TGV station, a huge shopping complex, and the **Auditorium Maurice-Ravel** for important cultural events.

🏛 Musée de l'Imprimerie
13 rue de la Poulaillerie.
Tel 04 78 37 65 98. ⬤ Wed–Sun.
⬤ public hols. 📷 📷 📷

🏛 Musée des Tissus
34 rue de la Charité. ***Tel*** 04 78 38 42 00. ⬤ Tue–Sun. ⬤ public hols. 📷

🏛 Musée Arts Décoratifs
30 rue de la Charité. ***Tel*** 04 78 38 42 00. ⬤ Tue–Sun. ⬤ public hols. 📷

🏛 Maison des Canuts
10–12 rue d'Ivry. ***Tel*** 04 78 28 62 04. ⬤ Mon–Sat. ⬤ public hols.
📷 📷 📷

Environs

Bourgoin-Jallieu, southeast of Lyon, still prints silk for fashion houses, and has a fine textile collection in its museum.

Musée des Beaux Arts

Lyon's Musée des Beaux Arts showcases the country's largest and probably most important collection of art after the Louvre. The museum is housed in the 17th-century Palais St-Pierre, a former Benedictine convent for the daughters of the nobility. The Musée d'Art Contemporain, formerly located in the Palais St-Pierre, is now at 81 quai Charles de Gaulle, north of the Parc Tête d'Or. Housed in a building designed by Renzo Piano, it specializes in works from the mid-20th century.

ANTIQUITIES

Included in this wide-ranging collection on the first floor are Egyptian archeological finds, Etruscan statuettes, and 4,000-year-old Cypriot ceramics. Temporary exhibits, with a separate entrance on 16 rue Edouard Herriott, are also on the ground and first floors.

SCULPTURE AND OBJETS D'ART

Occupying the old chapel on the ground floor, the sculpture department includes works from the French Romanesque period and Italian Renaissance, as well as late 19th- and early 20th-century pieces. Represented are Rodin and Bourdelle (whose statues also appear in the courtyard), Maillol, Despiau, and Pompon among others. The huge *objets d'art* collection, on the first floor, comprises medieval ivories, bronzes, and ceramics, coins, medals, weapons, jewelry, furniture, and tapestries.

Odalisque (1841) by James Pradier

PAINTINGS AND DRAWINGS

The museum's superb collection of paintings occupies the first and second floors. It covers all periods and includes works by Spanish and Dutch masters, the French schools of the 17th, 18th, and 19th centuries, Impressionist

Fleurs des Champs (1845) by Louis Janmot of the Lyon School

and modern paintings, as well as works by the Lyon School, whose exquisite flower paintings were used as sources of inspiration by the designers of silk fabrics through the ages. On the first floor, the Cabinet d'Arts Graphiques has over 4,000 drawings and etchings by such artists as Delacroix, Poussin, Géricault, Degas, and Rodin (by appointment only).

🏛 Musée des Beaux Arts
Palais St-Pierre, 20 pl des Terreaux.
Tel 04 72 10 17 40. ⬤ Wed–Mon.
⬤ public hols. 📷 📷 📷

La Méduse (1923) by Alexeï von Jawlensky

Châtiment de Lycurgue in the Musée Archéologique, St-Romain-en-Gal

Vienne ❺

Isère. 🏠 30,000. 🚉 🚌 ℹ cours Brillier (04 74 53 80 30). 🛒 Sat. 🎷 International Jazz Festival (end Jun–mid-Jul). **www**.vienne-tourisme.com

No other city in the Rhône Valley offers such a concentration of architectural history as Vienne. Located in a natural basin of land between the river and the hills, this site was recognized for both its strategic and aesthetic advantages by the Romans, who vastly expanded an existing village when they invaded the area in the 1st century BC.

The center of the Roman town was the **Temple d'Auguste et Livie** (10 BC) on place du Palais, a handsome structure supported by

Vienne's Temple d'Auguste et Livie (1st century BC)

Corinthian columns. Not far away off place de Miremont are the remains of the **Jardin Archéologique de Cybèle**, a temple dedicated to the goddess Cybèle.

The **Théâtre Romain**, at the foot of Mont Pipet off rue du Cirque, was one of the largest amphitheaters in Roman France, capable of seating over 13,000 spectators. It was restored in 1938, and is now used for a variety of events, including an international jazz festival. From the very top seats the view of the town and river is spectacular.

Other interesting Roman vestiges include a fragment of Roman road in the public gardens and, on the southern edge of town, the **Pyramide du Cirque**, a curious structure about 65 feet (20 m) high that was once the centerpiece of the chariot racetrack. The **Musée des Beaux Arts et d'Archéologie** also has a good collection of Gallo-Roman artifacts, as well as 18th-century French faïence. This museum may close when the city's museums are re-grouped so check before visiting.

The **Cathédrale de St-Maurice** is the city's most important medieval monument. It was built between the 12th and 16th century and represents an unusual hybrid of Romanesque and Gothic styles. The cathedral is being restored, so some areas may

be closed. Two of Vienne's earliest Christian churches are the 12th-century **Eglise St-André-le-Bas**, with richly carved capitals in its nave and cloister, and the **Eglise St-Pierre**, parts of which date from the 5th and 6th centuries. The latter houses the **Musée Lapidaire**, a museum of stone-carving, with low reliefs and statues from Gallo-Roman buildings.

🏛 **Musée des Beaux Arts et d'Archéologie**
Pl de Miremont. **Tel** 04 74 85 50 42. 🕐 Apr–Oct: Tue–Sun; Nov–Mar: Tue–Fri & Sat–Sun pms. 🌑 Jan 1, May 1, Nov 1 & 11, Dec 25. 🖼

🏛 **Musée Lapidaire**
Pl St-Pierre. **Tel** 04 74 85 20 35. 🕐 Apr–Oct: Tue–Sun; Nov–Mar: Tue–Fri & Sat–Sun pms. 🌑 Jan 1, May 1, Nov 1 & 11, Dec 25. 🖼 ♿ 📷 🏠

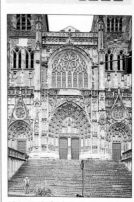

Vienne's Cathédrale de St-Maurice

St-Romain-en-Gal ❻

Rhône. 🏠 1,300. 🚉 Vienne. ℹ Vienne (04 74 53 80 30).

In 1967, building work in this commercial town directly across the Rhône from Vienne revealed extensive remains of a significant Roman community dating from 100 BC to AD 300. It comprises the remnants of villas, public baths, stores, and warehouses. Of particular interest is the House of the Ocean Gods, with a magnificent mosaic floor depicting the bearded Neptune and other ocean images.

Much of what has been unearthed during the ongoing excavations is housed in the **Musée Archéologique** adjoining the ruins. The impressive collection includes household objects, murals, and mosaics. The star exhibit is the *Châtiment de Lycurgue*, a mosaic discovered in 1907.

🏛 **Musée Archéologique**
Tel 04 74 53 74 01. ⬤ *Tue–Sun.* ⬤ *some publ hols.* 🈳 🔲 🔥 *restr.* 🔲
🔢 **www**.musees-gallo-romains.com

St-Étienne ❼

Loire. 🚶 *180,000.* 🚉 🚌 🚃
ℹ️ *16 av de la Libération (04 77 49 39 00).* 🛒 *daily.* **www**.tourisme-st-etienne.com

The dour industrial renown brought to this city by coal-mining and armaments is slowly being shaken off, with urban redevelopment well under way and an efficient tramway network. The downtown area around place des Peuple is lively. Nearby, Jean-Michel Wilmotte has overhauled the **Musée d'Art et d'Industrie**, which covers St-Étienne's industrial history, including the development of the revolutionary Jacquard loom, and world-class collections of bicycles and ribbon-making machines.

To the north of the city, the **Musée d'Art Moderne** has a collection of 20th-century art, including works by Andy Warhol and Frank Stella.

Detail of the bizarre Palais Idéal du Facteur Cheval at Hauterives

🏛 **Musée d'Art et d'Industrie**
2 pl Louis Comte. *Tel* 04 77 49 73 00. ⬤ *Wed–Mon.* ⬤ *some public hols.* 🈳 🔥 🔲

🏛 **Musée d'Art Moderne**
La Terrasse. *Tel* 04 77 79 52 52. ⬤ *Wed–Mon.* ⬤ *some public hols & when exhibitions change.* 🈳 🔥 🔲 **www**.mam-st-etienne.fr

Palais Idéal du Facteur Cheval ❽

Hauterives, Drôme. 🚌 🚉 *Romans-sur-Isère. Tel* 04 75 68 81 19.
⬤ *daily.* ⬤ *Jan 1 & 15–31, Dec 25.* 🈳 🎫 🔲 🔥 *restricted.* **www**.facteurcheval.com

At Hauterives, 15 miles (25 km) north of Roman-sur-Isère on the D538, is one of the greatest follies of France, an eccentric "palace" made of stones and evoking Egyptian, Roman, Aztec, and Siamese styles of architecture. It was built by a local mailman, Ferdinand Cheval, who collected the stones during his daily rounds. His neighbors thought him crazy, but the project attracted the admiring attention of Picasso, the surrealist André Breton, and others.

The interior of the palace is inscribed with numerous mottos and exhortations by Cheval, the most poignant of which refers to his assiduous efforts to realize his lifelong fantasy: "1879–1912: 10,000 days, 93,000 hours, 33 years of toil."

THE RHÔNE'S BRIDGES

The Rhône has played a crucial role in French history, transporting armies and commercial traffic between the north and south. It has always been dangerous, a challenge to boatmen and builders for centuries. In 1825 the brilliant engineer, Marc Seguin, built the first suspension bridge using steel wire cables. This was followed by another 20 along the length of the Rhône, forever transforming communications between east and west.

Suspension bridge over the Rhône at Tournon-sur-Rhône

The town of Tournon-sur-Rhône

Tournon-sur-Rhône ⑨

Ardèche. 🏠 10,000. 🚆
🛈 Hôtel de la Tourette
(04 75 08 10 23). 🔁 Wed & Sat
www.ville-tournon.com

Situated at the foot of impressive granite hills, Tournon is a lovely town with gracious tree-lined promenades and an imposing 11th–16th-century **château**. The latter houses a museum of local history, and has fine views of the town and river from its terraces.

The adjacent **Collégiale St-Julien**, with its square bell-tower and elaborate façade, is an interesting example of the Italian influence on architecture in the region during the 14th century. Inside is a powerful *Résurrection*, painted in 1576 by Capassin, a pupil of Raphael.

On quai Charles de Gaulle, the **Lycée Gabriel-Fauré** is the oldest high school in France,

dating from 1536. Directly across the Rhône from Tournon, the village of **Tain l'Hermitage** is famous for its steep-climbing vineyards which produce both red and white Hermitage, the finest of all Rhône wines.

Environs
From Tournon's main square, the place Jean Jaurès, a narrow, twisting road signposted the **Route Panoramique** leads via the villages of Plats and St-Romain-de-Lerps to St-Péray. This route offers breathtaking views at every turn, and, at St-Romain, you are rewarded with a superb panorama extending over 13 *départements*.

Valence ⑩

Drôme. 🏠 67,000. 🚆 🚆 🛈 11 bd Bancel (08 92 70 70 99). 🔁 Thu & Sat. 🎵 Summer Music (Jul).
www.valencetourisme.com

Valence is a large, thriving market town set on the east bank of the Rhône and looking across to the cliffs of the Ardèche. Its principal sight is the Romanesque **Cathédrale St-Apollinaire** on place des Clercs, founded in 1095 and rebuilt in the 17th century.

Alongside the cathedral in the former bishop's palace, the small **Musée des Beaux Arts** contains a collection of late 18th-century chalk drawings of Rome by Hubert Robert.

A short walk from here are two Renaissance mansions. The **Maison des Têtes** at No. 57 Grande Rue was built

in 1532 and is embellished with the sculpted heads of ancient Greeks including Aristotle, Homer, and Hippocrates. On rue Pérollerie, the **Maison Dupré-Latour** has a finely sculptured porch and staircase.

The **Parc Jouvet**, south of avenue Gambetta, offers 14 acres (6 ha) of pools and gardens, with fine views across the river to the ruined **Château de Crussol**.

🏛 **Musée des Beaux Arts**
4 pl des Ormeaux. **Tel** 04 75 79 20 80. ● until 2013. 🎫

The limestone Pont d'Arc

The Ardèche ⑪

Ardèche. ✈ Avignon. 🚆 Montélimar. 🚌 Montélimar, Vallon Pont d'Arc. 🛈 Vallon Pont d'Arc (04 75 88 04 01). www.vallon-pont-darc.com

Over the course of thousands of years, wind and water have endowed this south-central region of France

---

CÔTES DU RHÔNE

Rising in the Swiss Alps and traveling south to the Mediterranean, the mighty Rhône is the common thread that links the many vineyards of the Rhône Valley. A hierarchy of *appellations* divides into three levels of quality: at the base, the regional Côtes du Rhône provides the bulk of the Rhône's wines; next, Côtes du Rhône-Villages comprises a plethora of picturesque villages; and, at the top, there are 13 individual *appellations*. The most famous are the steep slopes of Hermitage and Côte Rôtie in the northern Rhône, and historic Châteauneuf-du-Pape (*see p503*) in the south. The lion's share of production is of red wine, which, based on the syrah grape, is often spicy, full-bodied, and robust.

Harvest in a Côtes du Rhône vineyard

with such a wild and rugged landscape that it is often more reminiscent of the American southwest than the verdure commonly associated with the French countryside. This visible drama is repeated underground as well, since the Ardèche is honeycombed with enormous stalagmite- and stalactite-ornamented caves. The most impressive are the **Aven d'Orgnac** (*aven* meaning pothole) to the south of Vallon-Pont-d'Arc, and the **Grotte de la Madeleine**, reached via a signposted path from the D290.

For those who prefer to stay above ground, the most arresting natural scenery in the region is the **Gorges de l'Ardèche**, best seen from the D290, a two-lane road with frequent viewpoints that parallels the recessed river for 20 miles (32 km). Nearly at the head of the gorge, heading west, is the **Pont d'Arc**, a natural limestone "bridge" spanning the river, created by erosion and the elements.

Canoeing and white-water rafting are the two most popular sports here. All the equipment necessary can be rented locally; operators at Vallon-Pont-d'Arc (among many other places) rent out two-person canoes and organize return transportation from St-Martin d'Ardèche, 20 miles (32 km) downstream. Note that the river Ardèche is one of France's fastest flowing rivers – it is safest in May and June; by autumn its waters can be

The Gorges de l'Ardèche, between Vallon-Pont-d'Arc and Pont St-Esprit

The village of Vogüé on the banks of the river Ardèche

unpredictable and dangerous, especially for beginners.

The softer side of the region is found in its ancient and picturesque villages, gracious spa towns, vineyards and plantations of Spanish chestnuts (from which the delectable *marron glacé* is produced).

Some 8 miles (13 km) south of Aubenas, the 12th-century village of **Balazuc** is typical of the region, its stone houses built on a clifftop overlooking a secluded gorge of the river Ardèche. There are fine views as you approach on the D294.

Neighboring **Vogüé** is nestled between the river Ardèche and a limestone cliff. A tiny but atmospheric village, its most commanding sight is the 12th-century **Château de Vogüé**, once the seat of the barons of Languedoc. Rebuilt in the 17th century, the building houses a museum featuring exhibitions about the region.

♣ **Château de Vogüé**
Tel 04 75 37 01 95. ☐ *Easter–Jun: Wed–Sun; Jul–mid-Sep: daily; mid-Sep–mid-Nov: Wed–Sun.* 🏛 📷
www.chateaudevogue.net

Vals-les-Bains ⑫

Ardèche. 🏘 3,700. ☐ *Montélimar.*
🛈 *rue Jean Jaurès (04 75 89 14 97).*
🗓 *Thu & Sun (& Tue in summer).*

This small spa town retains a hint of its past elegance. It is situated in the valley of the Volane, where there are at least 150 springs, of which all but two are cold. The water, which contains bicarbonate of soda and other minerals, is said to aid digestive problems, rheumatism, and diabetes.

Discovered around 1600, Vals-les-Bains is one of the few spas in southern France to have been overlooked by the Romans. The town reached the height of its popularity in the late 19th century, and most of its parks and architecture retain something of the Belle Epoque. Vals is a convenient first stop for an exploration of the Ardèche, with plenty of hotels and restaurants.

Environs
About 5 miles (8 km) east of Vals is the superb Romanesque church of **St-Julien du Serre**.

A farm near Le Poët Laval, east of Montélimar

Montélimar ⓭

Drôme. 👥 33,000. 🚌 🚆
🈯 allées Provençales
(04 75 01 00 20). 🛒 Wed–Sat.
www.montelimar-tourisme.com

Whether you choose to make a detour to Montélimar will largely depend on how sweet a tooth you might have. The main curiosity of this market town is its medieval center, chock-full of shops selling almond-studded nougat. This splendid confection has been made here since the start of the 17th century, when the almond tree was first introduced into France from Asia.

The **Château des Adhémar**, a mélange of 12th-, 14th-, and 16th-century architecture, surveys the town from a tall hill to the east.

⛪ **Château des Adhémar**
Tel 04 75 00 62 30. ◯ Apr–Oct: daily; Nov–Mar: Wed–Mon (for exhibitions only). ⬤ Jan 1, Dec 25. 🈯 ♿

Environs
The countryside east of Montélimar is full of picturesque medieval villages and scenic routes. **La Bégude-de-Mazenc** is a thriving little vacation center, with its fortified Old Town perched on a hilltop. Farther east is **Le Poët Laval**, a tiny medieval village of honey-colored stone buildings set in the Alpine foothills. **Dieulefit**, the capital of this beautiful region, has several small hotels and restaurants, as well as facilities for tennis, swimming, and fishing. To the south, the fortified village of **Taulignan** is known for its truffles.

Grignan ⓮

Drôme. 👥 1,360. 🚌 🚆 🈯 pl du Jeu de Ballon (04 75 46 56 75). 🛒 Tue.
www.tourisme-paysdegrignan.com

Attractively situated on a rocky hill surrounded by fields of lavender, this charming little village owes its fame to Madame de Sévigné (see p91), who wrote many of her celebrated letters while staying at the **Château de Grignan**.

Built during the 15th and 16th centuries, the château is one of the finest Renaissance structures in this part of France. Its interior contains a good collection of Louis XII furniture and Aubusson tapestries.

From the château's terrace, a panoramic view extends as far as the Vivarais mountains in the Ardèche. Directly below the terrace, the **Eglise de St-Saveur** was built in the 1530s, and contains the tomb of Madame de Sévigné, who died here in 1696 at the age of 69.

⛪ **Château de Grignan**
Tel 04 75 91 83 55. ◯ Apr–Oct: daily; Nov–Mar: Wed–Mon.
⬤ Jan 1, Dec 25. 🈯 🈯

Nyons ⓯

Drôme. 👥 7,000. 🚌 🈯 pl de la Libération (04 75 26 10 35). 🛒 Thu.
www.paysdenyons.com

As a major center of olive production, Nyons is synonymous with olives in France. All manner of olive products are on sale at the Thursday morning market, from soap to *tapenade*, the olive paste so popular in the south.

The **Quartier des Forts** is Nyons' oldest quarter, a warren of narrow streets and stepped alleyways, the most rewarding of which is the covered rue des Grands Forts. Spanning the river Aygues is a graceful 13th-century bridge; on its town side are several old mills turned into stores where you can see the enormous presses once used to extract olive oil. The **Musée de l'Olivier** further explains the cultivation of the olive tree and the myriad local uses found for its fruit.

There is a fine view of the area from the belvedere overlooking the town. Sheltered by mountains, Nyons enjoys an almost exotic climate, with all the trees and plants of the Riviera to be found here.

🏛 **Musée de l'Olivier**
Pl Olivier des Serre.
Tel 04 75 26 12 12. ◯ daily.
🈯 for guide. 🈯 📷 ♿

Environs
From Nyons, the D94 leads west to **Suze-la-Rousse**, a pleasant wine-producing village which, during the Middle Ages, was the most important town in the area. Today, it is best known for its "university of wine," one of the most respected centers of oenology in

The hilltop town of Grignan and its Renaissance château

Olive groves just outside Nyons

the world. It is housed in the 14th-century **Château de Suze-la-Rousse**, the hunting lodge of the princes of Orange. The interior courtyard is a masterpiece of Renaissance architecture and some rooms preserve original paint and stuccowork.

⌂ Château de Suze-la-Rousse
Tel 04 75 04 81 44. ☐ *Apr–Oct: daily; Nov–Mar: Wed–Mon.* ● *Jan 1, Dec 25.* 🖼 🎦 📷

Playing *boules* in Nyons

Briançon ⓰

Hautes Alpes. 🏛 *12,000.* ☐ ☐
ℹ *1 pl du Temple (04 92 21 08 50).* ☐ *Wed.* 🎷 *Altitude Jazz Festival (early Feb).* **www**.ot-briancon.fr

Briançon – the highest town in Europe at 4,330 ft (1,320 m) – has been an important stronghold since pre-Roman times, guarding as it does the road to the Col de Montgenèvre,

one of the oldest and most important passes into Italy. At the beginning of the 18th century, the town was fortified with ramparts and gates – still splendidly intact – by Louis XIV's military architect, Vauban. If driving, park at the Champs de Mars, and enter the pedestrianized Old Town via the **Porte de Pignerol**.

This leads to the **grande rue**, a steep, narrow street with a stream running down the middle, bordered by lovely period houses. The nearby **Eglise de Notre-Dame** dates from 1718, and was also built by Vauban with an eye to defense. To visit Vauban's **citadel**, stop by the tourist office, which organizes guided tours.

Briançon is a major sports center, with skiing in winter; rafting, biking, and parapente in summer *(see pp660–61).*

Environs
Just west of Briançon, the **Parc National des Ecrins** is the largest of the French national parks, offering lofty peaks and glaciers, and a magnificent variety of Alpine flowers.

The **Parc Régional du Queyras** is reached from Briançon over the rugged Col de l'Izoard. A wall of 9,850-ft (3,000-m) peaks separates this wild and beautiful national park from neighboring Italy.

Le Bourg d'Oisans ⓱

Isère. 🏛 *3,000.* ☐ *to Grenoble.* ☐ *to Le Bourg d'Oisans.* **ℹ** *quai Girard (04 76 80 03 25).* ☐ *Sat.* **www**.bourgdoisans.com

Le Bourg d'Oisans is an ideal base from which to explore the Romanche valley, providing numerous opportunities for sports such as bicycling, rock-climbing, and skiing, in the nearby resort of **L'Alpe d'Huez**.

Silver and other minerals have been mined here since the Middle Ages, and today the town has a scientific reputation as a center for geology and mineralogy. Its **Musée des Minéraux et de la Faune des Alpes** is renowned for its collection of crystals and precious stones.

🏛 Musée des Minéraux et de la Faune des Alpes
Pl de l'Eglise. *Tel 04 76 80 27 54.* ☐ *2–6pm Wed–Mon (Jul–Aug: 11am–6pm).* ● *Jan 1, Nov, Dec 25.* 🖼

LIFE ON HIGH

The Alpine ibex is one of the rarest inhabitants of the French Alps, living high above the tree line for all but the coldest part of the year. Until the creation of the Parc National de la Vanoise *(see p323)*, this sure-footed climber had become almost extinct in France, but after rigorous conservation there are now over 500. Both males and females have horns; in the oldest males these can be almost 3 ft (1 m) long.

An ibex in the Parc National de la Vanoise

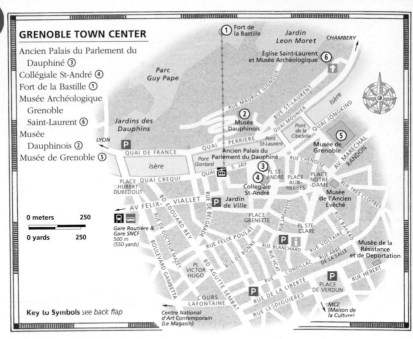

GRENOBLE TOWN CENTER

Ancien Palais du Parlement du
   Dauphiné ③
Collégiale St-André ④
Fort de la Bastille ①
Musée Archéologique
   Grenoble
   Saint-Laurent ⑥
Musée
   Dauphinois ②
Musée de Grenoble ⑤

Key to Symbols *see back flap*

**Hôtel Lesdiguières, Grenoble's
imposing former town hall**

Grenoble ⑱

Isère. 🏔 165,000. ✈ 🚍 🚌
🛈 *14 rue de la République
(04 76 42 41 41).* 🗓 *Tue–Sun.*
www.grenoble-tourisme.com

Ancient capital of the
Dauphiné region and site of
the 1968 Winter Olympics,
Grenoble is a thriving city,
home to the science-oriented
University of Grenoble, and a
center of chemical and electronics industries and nuclear
research. It is attractively situated at the confluence of the
Drac and Isère rivers, with the
Vercors and Chartreuse
massifs to the west and north.

A cable car starting at quai
Stéphane-Jay whisks you up
to the 19th-century **Fort de**

la Bastille, which has superb
views of the city and surrounding mountains. Paths
lead down through the Parc
Guy Pape and Jardin des
Dauphins to the **Musée
Dauphinois**, a regional
museum in a 17th-century
convent devoted to local
history, arts, and crafts.
Nearby, **Musée Archéologique
Grenoble Saint-Laurent**, located
in a medieval former church
with a 6th-century crypt,
exhibits medieval artifacts and
decorative and religious art.

On the left bank of the Isère,
the focus of life is the pedestrian area around the place
Grenette. Nearby, the place
St-André is the heart of the
medieval city, overlooked by
Grenoble's oldest buildings
including the 13th-century
Collégiale St-André and the
16th-century **Ancien Palais du
Parlement du Dauphiné**.
The **Musée de Grenoble**
exhibits works by Chagall,
Picasso, and Matisse. The
Musée de l'Ancien Evêché
recounts the history of Isère,
and includes a visit to the
4th-century baptistry. On rue
Hébert, the **Musée de la Résistance et de la Déportation**
has documents relating to the
French Resistance. Displays

of contemporary art can be
seen at **Le Magasin** (Centre
National d'Art Contemporain),
a renovated warehouse on
the cours Berriat. In the
Quartier Malherbe, **MC2**
(Maison de la Culture) hosts
concerts, dance, and theater.

🏛 **Musée Dauphinois**
30 rue Maurice Gignoux. *Tel 04 57
58 89 01.* 🗓 *Wed–Mon.* ● *Jan 1,
May 1, Dec 25.*

🏛 **Musée Archéologique
Grenoble Saint-Laurent**
Pl St-Laurent. *Tel 04 76 44 78 68.*
🗓 *call for details.* www.musee-
archeologique-grenoble.fr

Grenoble's gondola cable car

🏛 **Musée de Grenoble**
5 pl de Lavalette. **Tel** 04 76 63 44
44. ⬭ Wed–Mon. ⬤ Jan 1, May 1,
Dec 25. 🖼 ⬭ 🖼 🖥 🖥

🏛 **Musée de l'Ancien Evêché**
2 rue Très Cloîtres. **Tel** 04 76 03 15
25. ⬭ daily. ⬤ Tue am. ⬭

🏛 **Musée de la Résistance et
de la Déportation**
14 rue Hébert. **Tel** 04 76 42 38 53.
⬭ daily. ⬤ Tue am, Jan 1, May 1,
Dec 25. 🖼 ⬭

🏛 **Le Magasin (CNAC)**
155 cours Berriat. **Tel** 04 76 21 95
84. ⬭ Tue–Sun pms only (during
exhibitions). 🖼 ⬭

🏛 **MC2**
4 rue Paul Claudel. **Tel** 04 76 00 79
00. ⬭ varies – call to check. 🖼 ⬭
www.mc2grenoble.fr

The Vercors ⑲

Isère & Drôme. ✈ Grenoble. 🚋
Romans-sur-Isère, St-Marcellin, Grenoble. 🚌 Pont-en-Royans, Romans-
sur-Isère. 🛈 Pont-en-Royans (04 76
36 09 10). **www**.parc-du-vercors.fr

To the south and west of
Grenoble, the Vercors is one
of the most magnificent
regional parks in France – a
wilderness of pine forests,
mountains, waterfalls, caves,
and deep, narrow gorges.

The D531 out of Grenoble
passes through **Villard-de-
Lans** – a good base for
excursions – and continues to
the dark **Gorges de la
Bournes**. About 5 miles (8 km)
farther west, the hamlet of
Pont-en-Royans is sited on a
limestone gorge, its stone
houses built into rocks
overlooking the river Bourne.

South of Pont-en-Royans
along the D76, the **Route de
Combe-Laval** snakes along a
sheer cliff above the roaring
river. The **Grands Goulets**,
4 miles (6.5 km) to the east,
is a spectacularly deep,
narrow gorge overlooked by
sheer cliffs that virtually shut
out the sky above. The best-
known mountain in the park
is the **Mont Aiguille**, a soaring
outcrop of 6,844 ft (2,086 m).

The Vercors was a key base
for the French Resistance
during World War II. In July
1944 the Germans launched
an aerial attack on the region,
flattening several of its villages.
There are Resistance museums
at Vassieux and Grenoble.

Cows grazing in the Chartreuse

The Chartreuse ⑳

Isère & Savoie. ✈ Grenoble,
Chambéry. 🚋 Grenoble, Voiron.
🚌 St-Pierre-de-Chartreuse. 🛈 St-
Pierre-de-Chartreuse (04 76 88 64 00).

From Grenoble, the D512
leads north toward Chambéry
into the Chartreuse, a majestic
region of mountains and
forests where hydroelectricity
was invented in the late 19th
century. The **Monastère de la
Grande Chartreuse** is the main
local landmark, situated just
west of St-Pierre-de-Chartreuse
off the D520-B.

Founded by St-Bruno in
1084, the monastery owes its
fame to the sticky green and
yellow Chartreuse liqueurs first
produced by the monks in
1605. The recipe, based on
a secret herbal elixir of 130
ingredients, is now produced
in the nearby town of Voiron.

The monastery itself is
inhabited by about 40 monks
who live in silence and seclusion. It is not open to visitors,
but there is a museum at the
entrance, the **Musée de la
Correrie**, which faithfully
depicts the daily routine of
the Carthusian monks.

🏛 **Musée de la Correrie**
St-Pierre-de-Chartreuse. **Tel** 04 76 88
60 45. ⬭ Apr–Nov: daily. 🖼

A farm in the pine-clad mountains of the Chartreuse

Chambéry ㉑

Savoie. 🚶 61,000. 🛬 🚌 🚊
ℹ 5 bis pl Palais de Justice
(04 79 33 42 47). 🛒 Tue, Sat.
www.chambery-tourisme.com

Once the capital of Savoy,
this dignified city has aristocratic airs and a distinctly
Italianate feel. Its best-loved
monument is the splendidly
extravagant **Fontaine des
Eléphants** on rue de Boigne.
It was erected in 1838 to
honor the Comte de Boigne,
a native son who left to his
home town some of the
fortune he amassed in India.

The **Château des Ducs de
Savoie**, at the opposite end of
rue de Boigne, was built in the
14th century and is now mostly
occupied by the Préfecture.
Only parts of the building can
be visited, such as the late
Gothic Ste-Chapelle.

On the southeast edge of
town is the 17th-century
country house, **Les
Charmettes**, where
the philosopher
Rousseau lived with
his mistress Madame
de Warens. It is
worth a visit for its
gardens and museum
of memorabilia.

🏛 **Les Charmettes**
892 chemin des
Charmettes. **Tel** 04 79 33
39 44. ◻ Wed–Mon.
⬤ public hols. 📷 📷

The Lac du Bourget at Aix-les-Bains

Aix-les-Bains ㉒

Savoie. 🚶 26,000. 🛬 🚌
ℹ pl Maurice Mollard (04 79 88 68
00). 🛒 Wed & Sat am. 🎦 Festival
Musilac (Jul). **www**.aixlesbains.com

The great Romantic poet
Lamartine rhapsodized over
the beauty of Lac du Bourget,
site of the gracious spa
town of Aix-les-Bains.
The heart of the town
is the 19th-century
Thermes Nationaux,
thermal baths which
were first enjoyed by
the Romans over 2,000
years ago – in the base-
ment are the remains
of the original Roman
baths. The ruins
are closed to visitors
due to safety reasons,
but the Thermes

Roman statue in
the Temple of Diana

Nationaux spa is open all
year. Opposite the baths, the
2nd-century AD **Temple of
Diana** contains a collection of
Gallo-Roman artifacts. The
nearby **Musée Faure** has some
stunning Impressionist
paintings by Degas and Sisley,
Rodin sculptures, and
Lamartine memorabilia.

🏛 **Thermes Nationaux**
Pl Maurice Mollard. **Tel** 04 79 35 38
50. ◻ Mon–Sat. 📷 for treatment.
◻ **www**.thermaix.com

🏛 **Musée Faure**
Villa des Chimères, 10 bd des Côtes.
Tel 04 79 61 06 57. ◻ Wed–Mon
(mid-Nov–Feb: Wed–Sun). ⬤ Dec
18–Jan 2, public hols. 📷 📷

Environs
Boats leave from Aix's Grand
Port and sail across Lac du
Bourget to the **Abbaye
d'Hautecombe**, a Benedictine
abbey containing the mausoleum of the Savoyard dynasty.

The small town of **Le
Revard**, just east of Aix on the
D913, has spectacular views
of the lake and Mont Blanc.

Annecy ㉓

Haute Savoie. 🚶 51,000. 🛬 🚌
🚊 ℹ 1 rue Jean Jaurès (04 50 45
00 33). 🛒 Tue, Fri–Sun. **www**.lac-
annecy.com 🎦 Fête du Lac (firework
display; 1st Sat Aug).

Annecy is one of the most
charming towns in the Alps,
set at the northern tip of Lac

Annecy's 12th-century Palais de l'Isle, with the Thiou canal in the foreground

Cycling along the shores of Lac Léman (Lake Geneva)

d'Annecy and surrounded by snow-capped mountains. Its small medieval quarter is laced with canals, flower-covered bridges, and arcaded streets. Strolling around is the main attraction here, though there are a couple of specific sights worth having a look at more closely: the formidable **Palais de l'Isle**, a 12th-century prison in the middle of the Thiou canal; and the **Château d'Annecy**, set high on a hill above the town with impressive views of Vieil Annecy and the crystal-clear lake beyond.

The best spot for swimming and watersports is at the eastern end of the avenue d'Albigny near the Imperial Palace hotel, while boat trips leave from quai Napoléon III.

Environs
One of the best ways to enjoy the area's spectacular scenery is to take a boat from Annecy to **Talloires**, a tiny lakeside village celebrated for its hotels and restaurants. Facing Talloires across the lake is the 15th-century **Château de Duingt** (not open to visitors).

On the west bank of the lake, the Semnoz mountain and its summit, the **Crêt de Châtillon**, offer superb views of Mont Blanc and the Alps (see pp322–3).

Lac Léman ②

Haute-Savoie & Switzerland.
✈ Geneva. ⊟ ⊟ Geneva,
Thonon-les-Bains, Évian-les-Bains.
ℹ Thonon-les-Bains (04 50 71 55
55). www.thononlesbains.com

The stirring scenery and gentle climate of the French shore of Lake Geneva (Lac Léman to the French) has made it a popular and fashionable resort area since the first spa buildings were erected at Évian-les-Bains in 1839.

Yvoire is a fine place to begin a visit to the area. This medieval port is guarded by a massive 14th-century castle, and its houses are bedecked with colorful flower boxes.

Farther east along Lac Léman is **Thonon-les-Bains**, a prosperous, well-manicured little spa town perched on a cliff overlooking the lake. A funicular takes you down to Rives, the small harbor at the foot of the cliffs, where sailboats can be rented and excursion boats to the Swiss cities of Geneva and Lausanne stop. Just outside the town is the 15th-century **Château de Ripaille**, made famous by its one-time resident, Duke Amadeus VIII, who later became antipope (Felix V).

Though it has been modernized and acquired an international reputation for its eponymous spring water, **Évian-les-Bains** still exudes a polite fin de rose charm. The tree-lined lakefront promenade teems with leisurely strollers, while more energetic types can avail themselves of all kinds of sports facilities including tennis, golf, riding, sailing, and skiing in the winter. State-of-the-art spa treatments are available, and the exotic domed casino is busy at night, with blackjack, roulette, and baccarat, among other games.

From Évian there are daily ferries across Lake Geneva to Lausanne in Switzerland, as well as bus excursions into the surrounding mountains.

The elegant Hôtel Royal in Évian-les-Bains (see p578)

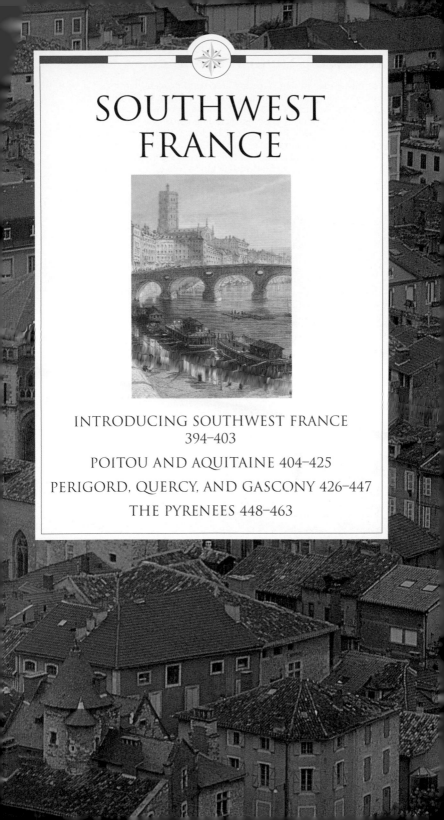

SOUTHWEST FRANCE

Introducing Southwest France

The southwest is farming France, a green and peaceful land nurturing crops from sunflowers to *foie gras*. Other key country products include Landes forest timber, Bordeaux wines, and Cognac. Major modern industries, including aerospace, are focused on the two chief cities, Bordeaux and Toulouse. Visitors are mainly drawn to the wide Atlantic beaches, the ski slopes of the Pyrenees, and the rural calm of the Dordogne. The major sights of this favored region are shown here and include some of France's most celebrated Romanesque buildings.

La Rochelle

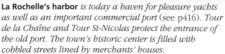

Roman Ruins, Saintes

La Rochelle's harbor *is today a haven for pleasure yachts as well as an important commercial port (see p416). Tour de la Chaîne and Tour St-Nicolas protect the entrance of the old port. The town's historic center is filled with cobbled streets lined by merchants' houses.*

Grand Théâtre, Bord

Bordeaux *is a town of grand buildings and monuments, including its theater. The Monument aux Girondins, with its magnificent bronze statues and fountains, stands at the 18th-century Esplanade des Quinconces (see pp420–22).*

POITOU AND AQUITAINE
(See pp404–25)

THE PYRENEES
(See pp448–63)

| 0 kilometers | 50 |
| 0 miles | 50 |

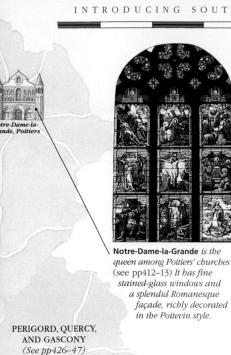

Notre-Dame-la-Grande *is the queen among Poitiers' churches (see pp412–13) It has fine stained-glass windows and a splendid Romanesque façade, richly decorated in the Poitevin style.*

PERIGORD, QUERCY, AND GASCONY
(See pp426–47)

Rocamadour *is both a place of pilgrimage and a tourist sight, its chapels and shrines clinging to the edge of the rocky hillside (see pp436–7). Among its many venerated features is the shrine of the Black Virgin and Child.*

Lascaux

Rocamadour

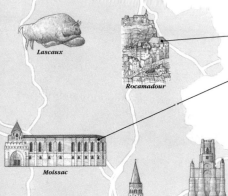

Moissac

Albi Cathedral

St-Sernin, Toulouse

Cirque de Gavarnie

Moissac Abbey *is the pre-eminent medieval monastery in southwest France (see pp442–3). Its tympanum, representing the Apocalypse, and the cloister capitals are outstanding examples of Romanesque sculpture.*

tre-Dame-la-nde, Poitiers

The Flavors of Southwest France

"Great cooking and great wines make a paradise on earth," said Henri IV of his own region, Gascony. The southwest does indeed fulfill the requirements of the most demanding gourmet. The Atlantic coast supplies fine seafood; Bordeaux produces some of France's best wines to complement its rich cooking; geese and ducks provide the fat that is key to local cuisine; and regional produce includes delicacies such as *foie gras*, truffles, and wild mushrooms. The Pyrenees offer beef and lamb grazed on mountain pastures, cheese and *charcuterie*, and the Basque country adds the spicy notes of red peppers and fine chocolate.

Espelette peppers

Walnuts, one of the southwest's most famous products

POITOU AND AQUITAINE

The coast is famous for its seafood, and is the most important oyster-producing region of France – the oysters of Marennes-Oleron are of especially high quality. The species of blue algae on which they feed give them a distinctive green coloring. Oysters are usually served simply with lemon or shallot vinegar, but in Bordeaux they like to eat them with little sausages. Mussels are also raised here, and the sea yields a variety of fish. Eels, lamprey and sturgeon are caught in the Gironde estuary.

Poitou-Charentes is one of France's main goat-rearing areas, producing cheeses such as *chabichou de Poitou*, a small, soft, cylindrical cheese of distinct flavor.

PERIGORD, QUERCY, AND GASCONY

High-quality ducks, geese, and poultry form the basis of the cuisine of this region, and their fat is a key ingredient of many dishes from simple *pommes sarladaises* (potatoes cooked in goose fat) to *confit*, where entire duck legs are preserved in their own fat. The ultimate

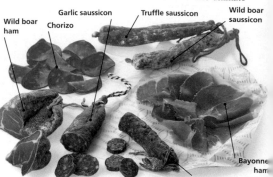

Wild boar ham   Garlic saussicon   Chorizo   Truffle saussicon   Wild boar saussicon   Bayonne ham   Bilberry saussicon

Selection of traditional southwestern *charcuterie*

REGIONAL DISHES AND SPECIALTIES

Duck is one of the essential ingredients of southwestern cooking, and is served in a variety of ways. The *magret* is the breast – the best of all coming from a duck that has been bred for *foie gras*. Usually served pink *(rose)*, it may be served with a variety of sauces but is most perfectly complemented by the smoky flavor of local cèpe mushrooms in season. Duck *confit* is usually made with the legs, but gizzards are also preserved in this way. *Foie gras* is the most expensive (and controversial) product, resulting from the process of *gavage*, when the duck or goose is force-fed maize to enlarge and enrich its liver. *Foie gras* can be eaten freshly cooked, served with sauce or fruit, or preserved and served with toast or brioche, ideally accompanied by a sweet white wine such as Sauternes.

Pink garlic

Omelette aux truffes *For this luxurious omelet the filling is local black truffles, with more sliced over the top.*

Fattened Toulouse geese, the source of *foie gras*

southwestern dish has to be *cassoulet*, a stew of duck or goose, sausages, pork, and white beans topped with a crust of breadcrumbs; it arouses fierce competition among the dedicated chefs of the region.

Luxury ingredients enhance these basics: walnut oil is added to salads and slivers of expensive truffles perfume sauces or omelets. Wild mushrooms are eagerly sought in season, and are most delicious cooked simply with garlic, shallots, and parsley. The region is one of the main producers of garlic, which appears studded into meat or served as whole baked heads. The finest fruits include *reines-claudes* (green-gages) and the celebrated plums of Agen, which are dried as prunes or added to dishes of rabbit or hare.

THE PYRENEES

From the mountains pastures come beef and lamb of high quality, including Barèges mutton, as well as river trout, and an array of excellent *charcuterie*. Strong cheeses

Fishermen opening oysters at a local maritime festival

of goat's or ewe's milk are sometimes served with jam made from the black cherries of Itxassou. One of the most popular dishes is *garbure*, a hearty stew of cabbage, bacon, and confit of duck or goose.

Basque cuisine has its own distinct identity, with the red Espelette pepper adding a touch of spice to chorizo, *piperade*, or chipirones (baby squid cooked in their own ink). Succulent Bayonne ham is made from pigs that forage for acorns and chestnuts. Bayonne was also home to the first chocolatiers in France, 17th-century Jewish refugees from the Inquisition, and the town still makes top-quality dark, bitter chocolate.

ON THE MENU

Cagouilles à la charentaise Snails with sausage meat, herbs, and wine.

Entrecôte à la bordelaise Steak in sauce of red wine, shallots, and bone marrow.

Farçi poitevin Cabbage stuffed with bacon, pork, and sorrel.

Gasconnade Leg of lamb with garlic and anchovy.

Mouclade Mussels in curry sauce, from the spice port of La Rochelle.

Salade landaise Salad of *foie gras*, gizzards, and *confit*.

Ttoro Basque mixed fish and shellfish stew with potatoes, tomatoes, and onions.

Cassoulet *This is a stew of white beans cooked with a variety of sausages and cuts of meat, such as pork or duck.*

Piperade *Eggs are added to a stew of peppers, onions, tomatoes, and garlic, with Bayonne ham laid on top.*

Croustade *Thin pastry is layered with melted butter and apples, perfumed with Armagnac and vanilla.*

France's Wine Regions: Bordeaux

Bordeaux is the world's largest fine wine region, and, for red wines, certainly the most familiar outside France. Following Henry II's marriage to Eleanor of Aquitaine, three centuries of courtly commerce with England ensured that claret was served at the finest foreign tables. In the 19th century, canny merchants capitalized on this fame and brought fantastic financial prosperity to the region, and with it, the famous 1855 Classification of the Médoc, a league table of châteaux that is still very much in force today.

Barrel-making

LOCATOR MAP

☐ Bordeaux wine region

Picking red Merlot grapes at Château Palmer

Cos d'Estournel, *like all the châteaux included in the 1855 league of crus classés ("classed growths"), proudly proclaims the fact on its label.*

Lac d'

WINE REGIONS

The great wine-producing areas of Bordeaux straddle two great rivers; the land between the rivers ("Entre-Deux-Mers") produces lesser, mainly white wines. The rivers, and the river port of Bordeaux itself, have been crucial to the trade in Bordeaux wines; some of the prettiest châteaux line the river banks, enabling easy transportation.

KEY FACTS ABOUT BORDEAUX WINES

Location and Climate
Climatic conditions may vary not only from one year to another, but also within the region itself. The soils tend to be gravelly in the Médoc and Graves, and clayey on the right bank.

Grape Varieties
The five main red grape varieties are **Cabernet Franc**, **Cabernet Sauvignon**, **Merlot, Petit Verdot**, and **Malbec**. Cabernet Sauvignon is the dominant grape on the west side of the Gironde, Merlot to the east. Most Bordeaux reds are, however, a blend of grapes. **Sauvignon Blanc** and **Sémillon** are grown and often blended for both dry and sweet whites.

Good Producers
(reds) Latour, Margaux, Haut-Brion, Cos d'Estournel, Léoville Las Cases, Léoville Barton, Lascombes, Pichon Longueville, Pichon Lalande, Lynch-Bages, Palmer, Rausan-Ségla, Duhart Milon, d'Angludet, Léoville Poyferré, Branaire Ducru, Ducru Beaucaillou, Malescot St-Exupéry, Cantemerle, Phélan-Ségur, Chasse-Spleen, Poujeaux, Domaine de Chevalier, Pape Clément, Cheval Blanc, Canon, Pavie, l'Angelus, Troplong Mondot, La Conseillante, Lafleur, Trotanoy.

Good Vintages
(reds) 2009, 2006, 2005, 2003, 2000, 1998, 1996.

Haut-Brion, *in the top division of Bordeaux's Classification, was and still is the single Graves château in this league of Médoc properties.*

Arcacho

Cap Ferret

Lac de C et de Sang

The famous legend *that guarantees château-bottling originated in Bordeaux, as a check to unscrupulous merchants.*

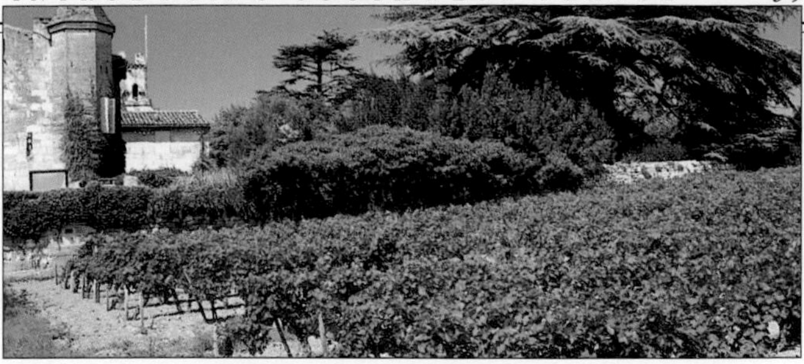

One of many wine-producing properties in the St-Emilion district

Entre-Deux-Mers, *largely undistinguished, has some good producers.*

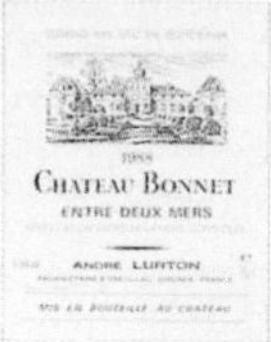

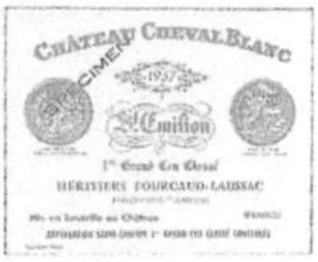

CHÂTEAU BONNET
ENTRE DEUX MERS

St-Emilion *has its own crus classés league: Cheval Blanc shares top ranking.*

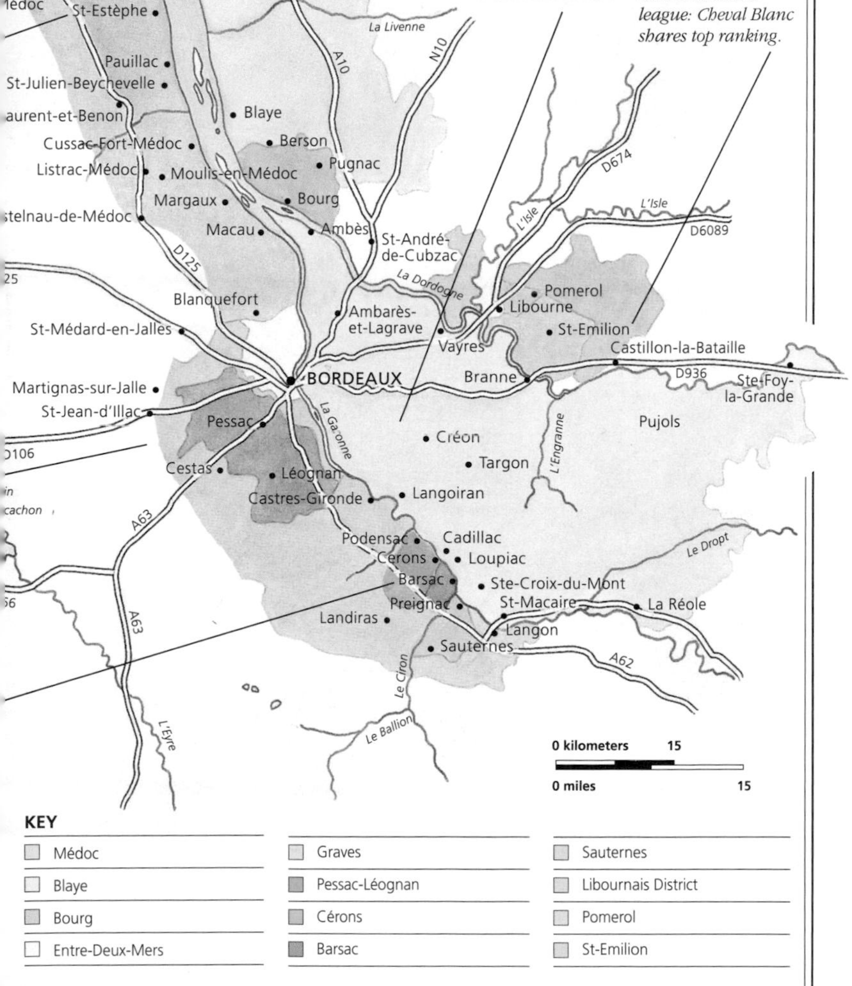

Verdon-Mer

Gironde

St-Christoly-Médoc

arre-Médoc   St-Estèphe

St-Seurin-de-Cadourne   Montendre

La Livenne

A10   N10

Pauillac

St-Julien-Beychevelle

aurent-et-Benon   Blaye

Cussac-Fort-Médoc   Berson

Listrac-Médoc   Moulis-en-Médoc   Pugnac

Margaux   Bourg

stelnau-de-Médoc   Macau   Ambès

St-André-de-Cubzac

La Dordogne

D674

L'Isle

L'Isle

D6089

25

Blanquefort   Ambarès-et-Lagrave

Pomerol
Libourne

St-Médard-en-Jalles   Vayres   St-Emilion

Castillon-la-Bataille

Martignas-sur-Jalle   **BORDEAUX**   Branne

D936   Ste-Foy-la-Grande

St-Jean-d'Illac

La Garonne

Pujols

0106   Pessac

Créon

Cestas   Léognan   Targon

L'Engranne

in   Castres-Gironde   Langoiran

cachon

Podensac   Cadillac

Cérons   Loupiac

Barsac   Ste-Croix-du-Mont

Le Dropt

Preignac   St-Macaire   La Réole

66   Landiras   Langon

Sauternes   A62

Le Ciron

L'Eyre

Le Ballion

| 0 kilometers | 15 |
| 0 miles | 15 |

KEY

▢ Médoc	▢ Graves	▢ Sauternes
▢ Blaye	▢ Pessac-Léognan	▢ Libournais District
▢ Bourg	▢ Cérons	▢ Pomerol
▢ Entre-Deux-Mers	▢ Barsac	▢ St-Emilion

The Road to Compostela

Scallop symbol

Throughout the Middle Ages millions of Christians visited Santiago de Compostela in Spain to pay homage at the shrine of St. James (Santiago). They traveled across France staying in monasteries or simple shelters and would return with a scallop shell, the symbol of St. James, as a souvenir. Most pilgrims went in hope of redemption and were often on the road for years. In 1140, a monk called Picaud wrote one of the world's first travel guides about the pilgrimage. Today, travelers can follow the same routes, passing through ancient towns and villages with their magnificent shrines and churches.

Foreign pilgrims joined at ports such as St-Malo.

The original cathedral *of Santiago de Compostela was built in 813 by Alfonso II over the tomb of St. James. In 1075 construction started on the grandiose Romanesque church seen today which has, among other later additions, a resplendent 17th–18th-century Baroque façade.*

The routes converged on Santiago de Compostela.

Most pilgrims crossed the Pyrenees at Roncesvalles.

James the Greater, *an apostle, came to Spain to spread the Gospel, according to legend. On his return to Judaea, he was martyred by Herod. His remains were taken to Spain by boat and lay hidden for 800 years.*

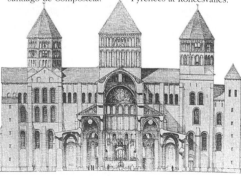

The powerful Cluny monastery *in Burgundy (see pp48–9), and its affiliated monasteries, played an important role in promoting the pilgrimage. They built shelters and set up churches and shrines housing precious relics, to encourage the pilgrims on their way.*

THE PILGRIMS' WAY

Paris, Vézelay *(see pp336–7)*, Le Puy *(see p364)*, and Arles are the rallying points for the four "official" routes across France. They cross the Pyrenees at Roncesvalles and Somport, and merge at Puente la Reina to form one route, culminating at the shrine on the Galician coast.

WHAT TO SEE TODAY

Huge Romanesque churches, including Ste-Madeleine at Vézelay *(see p336)*, Ste-Foy at Conques *(pp368–9)*, and St-Sernin at Toulouse *(p447)*, along with many small chapels, were built to accommodate large numbers of pilgrims.

Basilique Ste-Madeleine, Vézelay

Conques purloined relics to boost its prestige.

Le Puy was a main rallying point for pilgrims.

The first recorded pilgrim *was the bishop of Le Puy in 951. But pilgrims have probably been coming to Santiago since 814, soon after the saint's tomb was found.*

The reliquary *of Ste-Foy, at Conques, is in one of many elaborate shrines on the way which drew crowds of pilgrims. A saint's relics were thought to have miraculous powers.*

The name *Santiago de Compostela is believed to originate from the Latin* Campus stellae *(field of stars). Legend has it that strange stars were seen hovering over a field in 814 and on July 25, now the feast of Santiago, the saint's remains were found. Subsequent evidence showed that St. James's remains were never in Compostela after all.*

Caves of the Southwest

Southwest France is well-known for its spectacular rock formations, created by the slow accumulation of dissolved mineral deposits. Caves and rock shelters exist throughout limestone country in France. But in the foothills of the Pyrenees and the Dordogne they also have something else to offer the visitor: a collection of extraordinary rock paintings, some dating back to the last Ice Age. These art forms were created when prehistoric peoples evolved and began engraving, painting, and carving. This unique artistic tradition lasted for more than 25,000 years, reaching its zenith around 17,000 years ago. Some very fine examples of cave painting are still visible today.

Ancient cave paintings at Lascaux

CAVES OF THE DORDOGNE

There are many different cave systems to visit in or near the Dordogne valley. The entire Périgord region contains one of the densest concentrations of prehistoric sites anywhere in the world. In an uncertain climate, its rivers flanked by caves and rock shelters proved very attractive to prehistoric man.

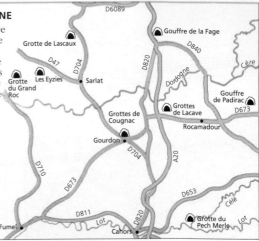

CAVE FORMATION

Limestone is laid down in layers containing fissures that allow water to penetrate beneath the surface. Over thousands of years, the water slowly dissolves the rock, first forming potholes and then larger caverns. Stalactites develop where water drips from the cave roof; stalagmites grow upward from the floor.

Grotte du Grand Roc in the Vézère valley, Périgord

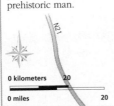

Fissure / Limestone layers

Impermeable rock

1 Water percolates through fissures, slowly dissolving the surrounding rock.

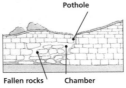

Pothole

Fallen rocks / Chamber

2 The water produces potholes and loosens surrounding rocks, which gradually fall away.

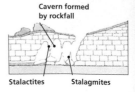

Cavern formed by rockfall

Stalactites / Stalagmites

3 Dripping water containing dissolved limestone forms stalactites and stalagmites.

GOUFFRE DE PADIRAC

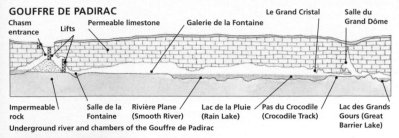

Chasm entrance · **Lifts** · **Permeable limestone** · **Galerie de la Fontaine** · **Le Grand Cristal** · **Salle du Grand Dôme**

Impermeable rock · **Salle de la Fontaine** · **Rivière Plane (Smooth River)** · **Lac de la Pluie (Rain Lake)** · **Pas du Crocodile (Crocodile Track)** · **Lac des Grands Gours (Great Barrier Lake)**

Underground river and chambers of the Gouffre de Padirac

Prehistoric caves at Les Eyzies

VISITING THE CAVES

Cougnac contains chasms ("gouffres") and galleries and its prehistoric paintings include human figures. Around **Les Eyzies** *(see pp434–5)* are the caves of **Les Combarelles**, and **Font de Gaume**, which have beautiful prehistoric paintings, drawings, and engravings, as does **Rouffignac** in its network of caves. **Grand Roc** has chambers containing a profusion of stalactites and stalagmites. Northeast of Les Eyzies is the rock shelter of **L'Abri du Cap Blanc**, with its rare frieze of horses and bison dating from around 14,000 years ago.

On the south bank of the Dordogne, an underground river and lake with extraordinary rock formations can be seen at **Lacave**. The gigantic chasm and caverns at **Padirac** *(p438)* are even more spectacular. The caves at **Lascaux** with the finest prehistoric paintings have been closed, but the exceptional replica at **Lascaux II** *(p434)* is well worth seeing. Further south, **Pech-Merle's** caverns *(p438)* have impressive rock formations. **Niaux**, in the foothills of the Pyrenees, can also be visited.

THE STORY OF CAVE ART

The first prehistoric cave paintings in Europe were discovered in northwest Spain in 1879. Since then, over 200 decorated caves and rock shelters have been found in Spain and France, mainly in the Dordogne region. A wide range of clues, from stone lamps to miraculously preserved footprints, has helped prehistorians to work out the techniques the cave artists used. But their motives are still not clear. Nearly all the paintings are of animals, with few humans, and many of them are in inaccessible underground chambers. The paintings undoubtedly had a symbolic or magical significance; a new theory suggests they were the work of shamans.

The techniques used by Ice Age artists, who worked by lamplight, included cutting outlines into soft rock, using natural contours as part of the design. Black lines and shading were produced by charcoal, while color washes were applied with mineral pigments such as kaolin and hematite. Hand silhouettes were made by sucking up diluted pigment and blowing it through a plant stem to form a fine spray. When the hand was removed from the rock, its eerie shape was left behind.

Decorated stone lamp discovered in Lascaux cave

Kaolin

Charcoal

Hematite

The Great Bull from the Hall of Bulls frieze at Lascaux

POITOU AND AQUITAINE

DEUX-SEVRES · VIENNE · CHARENTE-MARITIME
CHARENTE · GIRONDE · LANDES

This vast area of southwest France spans a quarter of the country's windswept Atlantic coastline, a great expanse of fine sandy beaches. The region stretches from the marshes of the Marais Poitevin to the great pine forests of the Landes. Central to it is the celebrated wine region of Bordeaux and its great châteaux.

The turbulent history of Poitou and Aquitaine, fought over for centuries, has left a rich architectural and cultural heritage. The great arch and amphitheater at Saintes bear witness to Roman influence in the area. In the Middle Ages, the pilgrimage route to Santiago de Compostela *(see pp400–1)* created an impressive legacy of Romanesque churches, such as those at Poitiers and Parthenay, as well as tiny chapels and glowing frescoes. The Hundred Years' War *(see pp52–3)* caused great upheaval but also resulted in the construction of mighty defense keeps by the English Plantagenet kings. As a result of the Wars of Religion *(see pp54–5)*, many towns, churches, and châteaus were destroyed and had to be rebuilt.

Present-day Poitiers is a big, thriving commercial centre. To the west are the historic ports of La Rochelle and Rochefort. Farther south, the wine-producing district of Bordeaux combines with Cognac, famous for its brandy, to supply an important part of the region's income. The city of Bordeaux is as prosperous today as in Roman times, combining a lively cultural scene with elegant 18th-century architecture. Its wines complement the region's cuisine: lampreys, mussels, and oysters from the coast; and salty lamb and goat's cheeses from the inland pastures.

Shuttered houses in St-Martin-de-Ré, on Ile de Ré, off the coast of La Rochelle

◁ The seaside resort of Arcachon by the sandy dunes of the Bassin d'Arcachon

Exploring Poitou and Aquitaine

Blessed with a seemingly endless Atlantic coastline, abundant navigable waterways, excellent ports, and the finest wine and brandy in the world, the region is ideal for a relaxing holiday. Today most summer visitors head straight for the beaches with their thundering waves, but there is also a lush countryside inland with a lot to offer. Fine medieval architecture can be seen along the pilgrim's route to Santiago de Compostela (see pp400–1), and châteaux of all shapes and sizes characterize the wine districts around Bordeaux. The only modern city of major importance in the region, Bordeaux is worth a visit for its elegant 18th-century architecture as well as for its rich cultural life. The vast man-made forest of Les Landes also adds to this greatly undervalued corner of France.

Beachlife in Bassin d'Arcachon on the Côte d'Argent

GETTING AROUND

The region's main highway is the A10 connecting Paris and Poitiers with Bordeaux and points east, such as Toulouse, west to Rochefort, and south to Bayonne and Spain. This road carries most of the area's heavy traffic, relieving the excellent smaller roads. Bordeaux can be reached by TGV direct from Lille (Eurostar interchange), and the Paris–Poitiers–Angoulême–Bordeaux TGV line has halved rail travel times (Paris–Bordeaux 3¼ hr). Bordeaux, Poitiers, and La Rochelle have international airports (direct flights to UK), and Bordeaux also has bus services to most European capitals. Poitiers has buses to nearby towns.

For additional map symbols see back flap

One of the Ile de Ré's picturesque harbors

SIGHTS AT A GLANCE

0 kilometers   25

0 miles   25

KEY

— Highway

— Major road

— Secondary road

— Minor road

— Scenic route

— Main railroad

— Minor railroad

— Regional border

Boats moored at Coulon in the Marais Poitevin

Rose window of St-Médard, Thouars

Thouars ❶

Deux-Sèvres. 🏘 *10,500.*
🚉 🚌 🛈 *3 bis bd Pierre Curie
(05 49 66 17 65).* 🛒 *Tue & Fri.*
www.tourisme-paysthouarsais.fr

Thouars, on a rocky outcrop surrounded by the river Thouet, is on the border between Anjou and Poitou. There are as many roofs of northern slate as of southern red tiles.

In the center stands **Eglise St-Médard**. Its Romanesque façade is a perfect example of the Poitevin style that is typical of the region *(see p412)*, although a splendid Gothic rose window has been added. Lined with half-timbered medieval houses, the rue du Château leads up to the 17th-century château which dominates the town. It now houses a school, and is open to the public during the summer.

East of Thouars lies the moated **Château d'Oiron**, which now hosts contemporary art exhibitions. A masterpiece of Renaissance architecture, it was largely built from 1518–49.

⚜ **Château d'Oiron**
79100 Oiron. *Tel 05 49 96 51 25.*
◯ *daily.* ◯ *some public hols.* 🖼

Parthenay ❷

Deux-Sèvres. 🏘 *11,000.* 🚉 🚌 🛈 *8 rue de la Vau-St-Jacques (05 49 94 90 05).* 🛒 *Wed.* **www**.cc-parthenay.fr

Parthenay is a classic, sleepy provincial town, except on Wednesday mornings, when France's second biggest livestock market is held here. In the Middle Ages, the town was an important halt on the route to Santiago de Compostela *(see pp400–1)* and it is easy to imagine the processions of pilgrims in the medieval quarter. Steep and cobbled, rue de la Vau-St-Jacques winds up to the 13th-century ramparts, leading on from the fortified Porte St-Jacques which guards a 13th-century bridge over the river Thouet.

West of Parthenay, the 12th-century church of **St-Pierre de Parthenay-le-Vieux** has a splendid Poitevin façade, featuring Samson and the Lion and a cavalier with a falcon.

Marais Poitevin ❸

Charente-Maritime, Deux-Sèvres, Vendée. ✈ *La Rochelle.*
🚉 *Niort, La Rochelle.* 🚌 *Coulon, Arçais, Marans.* 🛈 *place de la Couture, Coulon (05 49 35 81 04).*
www.parc-marais-poitevin.fr

The Poitevin marshes, which have been slowly drained with canals, dikes, and sluices for a thousand years, cover about 197,000 acres (80,000 ha) between Niort and the sea. The area is now a regional park, divided into two parts. To the north and south of the Sèvre estuary is the Marais Désséché (dry marsh), where cereal and other crops are grown. The huge swathe of the Marais Mouillé (wet marsh) is upstream toward Niort.

The wet marshes, known as the Venise Verte (Green Venice), are the most interesting. They are crisscrossed by a labyrinth of weed-choked canals, adorned by waterlilies and irises, shaded by poplars and beeches, and support a rich variety of birds and other wildlife. The *maraîchins* who live here stoutly maintain that much of the huge, water-logged forest is unexplored. The picturesque whitewashed villages hereabouts are all built on higher ground, and the customary means of transportation is a flat-bottomed boat, known as a *platte*.

Coulon, St-Hilaire-la-Palud, La Garette and Arçais, as well as Damvix and Maillezais in the Vendée, are all convenient starting points for boat trips

Medieval houses lining the cobbled rue de la Vau-St-Jacques in Parthenay

Flat-bottomed boats moored at Coulon in the Marais Poitevin

around the marshes. Boats can be rented with or without a guide. Make sure you bring plenty of insect repellent.

Coulon is the largest and best equipped village, and a popular base for visiting the area. **La Maison du Marais Poitevin** presents an account of life in the marshes in times gone by, along with details of the wetlands' flora and fauna.

The Plantagenet donjon in Niort, now housing a local museum

Niort ❹

Deux-Sèvres. 🏠 60,000. 🚊 🚌 ℹ *place de la Brèche (05 49 24 18 79).* 🗓 *Thu & Sat.* **www**.niortmaraispoitevin.com

Once a medieval port by the green waters of the Sèvre, Niort is now a prosperous industrial town specializing in machine tools, electronics, chemicals, and insurance.

Its closeness to the marshes is evident in local specialties – eels, snails, and angelica. This herb has been cultivated in the wetlands for centuries and is used for anything from liqueur to ice cream.

The town's immediate attraction is the huge 12th-century donjon overlooking the Vieux Pont. Built by Henry II and Richard the Lion-Heart, it played an important role during the Hundred Years' War and was later used as a prison. One prisoner was the father of Madame de Maintenon *(see p56),* who

spent her childhood in Niort. The donjon is now a museum of local arts and crafts and archeology. The **Musée d'Agesci** in avenue de Limoges exhibits ceramics, sculpture, and paintings from the 16th to 20th centuries.

Environs

Halfway to Poitiers is the small town of **St-Maixent-L'Ecole**. A marvel of light and space, its abbey church is a Flamboyant Gothic reconstruction by François Le Duc (1670) of a building destroyed during the Wars of Religion. Farther west, the **Tumulus de Bougon** consists of five tumuli (burial mounds), the oldest dating from 4500 BC.

Melle ❺

Deux-Sèvres. 🏠 4,000. 🚌 ℹ *rue E Traver (05 49 29 15 10).* 🗓 *Fri.* **www**.ville-melle.fr

A Roman silver mine was the origin of Melle, which in the 9th century had the only mint in Aquitaine. Later its fame derived from the *baudet du Poitou,* an especially sturdy mule bred in the area. Now Melle is better known for its churches, of which the finest is **St-Hilaire**. It has a 12th-century Poitevin façade with an equestrian statue of the Emperor Constantine above the north door.

Environs

To the northwest, the abbey in **Celles-sur-Belle** has a great Moorish doorway which contrasts strongly with the rest of the church, a 17th-century restoration in Gothic style.

Equestrian statue of Constantine on the façade of St-Hilaire, Melle

Canal in the Venise Verte region of the Marais Poitevin ▷

Poitiers ❻

Three of the greatest battles in French history were fought around Poitiers, the most famous in 732 when Charles Martel halted the Arab invasion. After two periods of English rule *(see p51)* the town thrived during the reign of Jean de Berry (1369–1416), the great sponsor of the arts. Its university, founded in 1431, made Poitiers a major intellectual center and saw Rabelais among its students. The Wars of Religion left Poitiers in chaos and not until the late 19th century did any major development take place. Today, however, the town is a modern and dynamic regional capital with a rich architectural heritage in its historic center.

Fresco in Eglise St-Hilaire-le-Grand

🔒 Notre-Dame-la-Grande
Despite its name, Notre-Dame-la-Grande is not a large church. One of Poitiers' great pilgrim churches, it is most celebrated as a masterpiece of lively 12th-century Poitevin sculpture, notably its richly detailed façade. In the choir is a Romanesque fresco of Christ and the Virgin. Most of the chapels were added in the Renaissance.

🏛 Palais de Justice
Pl Alphonse Lepetit. *Tel 05 49 50 22 00.* ☐ *Mon–Fri.*
Behind the bland Renaissance façade is the 12th-century great hall of the palace of the Angevin kings, Henry II and Richard the Lion-Heart. This is thought to be the scene of Joan of Arc's examination by a council of theologians in 1429.

🔒 Cathédrale St-Pierre
The 13th-century carved choir stalls in St-Pierre are by far the oldest in France. Note the huge 12th-century east window showing the Crucifixion. The

Pillars with colorful geometrical patterns in Notre-Dame-la-Grande

NOTRE-DAME-LA-GRANDE

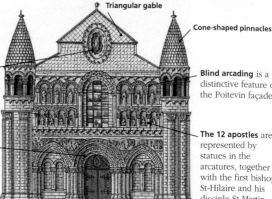

Triangular gable

Cone-shaped pinnacles

Christ in Majesty is shown in the center of the gable, surrounded by symbols of the evangelists.

Blind arcading is a distinctive feature of the Poitevin façade.

The portals on the Poitevin façade are deep and richly sculpted, often showing a pronounced Moorish influence.

The 12 apostles are represented by statues in the arcatures, together with the first bishop St-Hilaire and his disciple St-Martin.

tiny figures of the cathedral's patrons (Henry II and Eleanor of Aquitaine) are crouched at the foot of the window. Its organ (1787–91), made by François-Henri Cliquot, is one of the most prestigious and beautiful in Europe.

🏛 Espace Mendès France

1 pl de la Cathédrale. *Tel 05 49 50 33 08.* ◯ *daily.* ● *Jun–Aug: Sun; some public hols.* 🖼
This museum contains a state-of-the-art planetarium, with laser shows to help explain the mysteries of the universe, plus events and exhibitions.

🔒 Eglise St-Hilaire-le-Grand

Fires and reconstructions have made St-Hilaire a mosaic of different styles. With its origins in the 6th century, the church still displays an 11th-century belltower and a 12th-century nave.

🔒 Baptistère St-Jean

Rue Jean Jaurès.
◯ *Wed–Mon.* 🖼
The polygonal 4th-century Baptistère St-Jean is one of the oldest Christian buildings in France. Many of the earliest converts were baptized here. Now a museum, it contains Romanesque frescoes of

Christ and Emperor Constantine, and some Merovingian sarcophagi.

🏛 Musée Sainte-Croix

3 bis rue Jean Jaurès. *Tel 05 49 41 07 53.* ◯ *Tue–Sun pms.* ● *some public hols.* 🖼
Musée Sainte-Croix exhibits prehistoric, Gallo-Roman, and medieval archeology, and a wide range of paintings and 19th-century sculpture. Five bronzes by Camille Claudel are on show, including *La Valse.* There is also a large collection of contemporary art.

🏛 Médiathèque François Mitterrand

4 rue de l'Université. *Tel 05 49 52 31 51.* ◯ *Tue–Sat.* ● *public hols.*
This modern building, in the historic quarter, is home to the **Maison du Moyen Age**, which displays a collection of medieval manuscripts, maps, and engravings.

VISITORS' CHECKLIST

Vienne. 🏠 92,000. ✈ 3 miles (5 km) W Poitiers. 🚉 🚌 🛈 45 pl Charles de Gaulle (05 49 41 21 24). 🔄 Sat, Tue & Thu. 🎭 Les Expressifs (Oct).
www.ot-poitiers.fr

One of Futuroscope's most popular attractions: the large-screen cinema

Futuroscope ❼

Jaunay-Clan. 🚉 *Tel 05 49 49 11 22.* ◯ *daily.* ● *Jan–early Feb.* 🖼 🍴 🛅
www.futuroscope.com

Futuroscope is a fantastic theme park 4.5 miles (7 km) north of Poitiers, exploring visual technology in a futuristic environment. Attractions evolve yearly and include simulators, 3D and 360° screens and the "magic carpet" cinema, with one of its screens on the floor, creating the sensation of "flying." The cinema has the biggest screen in Europe.

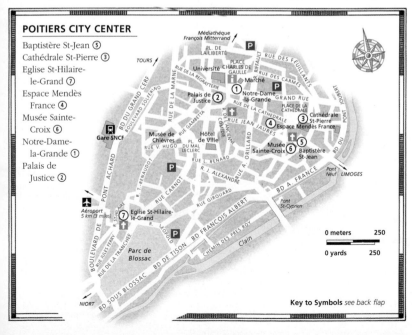

POITIERS CITY CENTER

Baptistère St-Jean ⑤
Cathédrale St-Pierre ③
Eglise St-Hilaire-le-Grand ⑦
Espace Mendès France ④
Musée Sainte-Croix ⑥
Notre-Dame-la-Grande ①
Palais de Justice ②

0 meters 250
0 yards 250

Key to Symbols see back flap

The castle ruins of Angles-sur-l'Anglin with the old watermill in the foreground

Abbaye de Nouaillé-Maupertuis ❽

Nouaillé-Maupertuis. **Tel** 05 49 55 35 69. **Church** ⬭ 9am–6pm (7pm in summer). ♿ limited. 🎦 summer only.

On the banks of the river Miosson lies the Abbaye de Nouaillé-Maupertuis. First mentioned in 780, the abbey became independent in 808 and followed the Benedictine rule. Apart from the beauty of the site, it is also worth visiting the church, built in the 11th–12th centuries and reconstructed several times. Behind the altar is the 10th-century sarcophagus of St-Junien, with three great heraldic eagles carved on the front.

More interesting is the nearby battlefield, scene of the great English victory at Poitiers by the Black Prince in 1356. The view has altered little since the 14th century. Drive down the small road to La Cardinerie (to the right off the D142), which leads to the river crossing at Gué de l'Omme, the epicenter of the battle. There is a monument halfway up the hill where the heaviest fighting took place and where the French king Jean le Bon was captured. He had put up a heroic resistance with nothing but his battle-axe and his small son Philippe to tell him where the next English knight was coming from.

Chauvigny ❾

Vienne. 🏠 7,000. 🚍 ℹ 5 rue St-Pierre (05 49 46 39 01). 🚌 Tue, Thu, Sat. **www**.chauvigny.fr

Chauvigny, on its steep promontory overlooking the broad river Vienne, displays the ruins of no fewer than four fortified medieval castles. Stone from the local quarry was so plentiful that nobody ever bothered to demolish earlier castles for building material.

Nevertheless, the best thing in this town is the 11th–12th-century **Eglise St-Pierre**, whose decorated capitals are a real treasure – particularly those in the choir stalls. The carvings represent biblical scenes along with monsters, sphinxes, and

Monster capitals in Eglise St-Pierre in Chauvigny

sirens. Look for the one that says *Gofridus me fecit* (Gofridus made me), with wonderfully natural scenes of the Epiphany.

Environs
Nearby is the lovely **Château de Touffou**, a Renaissance dream on the banks of the Vienne, with terraces and hanging gardens. Just north of it is the sleepy village of **Bonneuil-Matours**, with fine choir stalls in its Romanesque church.

🏰 **Château de Touffou**
Bonnes. **Tel** 05 49 56 08 48.
⬭ May–mid-Jun: Sat, Sun, & public hols; mid-Jun–mid-Sep: Wed–Mon. 🅿️

Angles-sur-l'Anglin ❿

Vienne. 🏠 400. ℹ 2 rue du Four Banal (05 49 48 86 87). 🚌 Sat & Sun. **www**.anglessuranglin.com

The village of Angles lies in an extremely beautiful riverside setting, dominated by its castle ruins. Adding to the charm is an old watermill by the slow-running river Anglin, graced by waterlilies and swaying reeds. Try to avoid visiting in summer, since the narrow streets become too crowded for comfort.

Angles is also famous for its tradition of fine needlework, the *jours d'Angles*, which is determinedly maintained by the local women today (their workshops can be visited).

t-Savin ⓫

lienne. 🏠 1,000. 🚌 🚹 20 pl de la
libération (05 49 84 30 00). 🚲 Fri.
www.abbaye-saint-savin.fr

The glory of St-Savin is its
11th-century abbey church
with its slender Gothic spire
and huge nave.

The abbey had enormous
influence until the Hundred
Years' War, when it was
burned down. It was later
pillaged several times during
the Wars of Religion. Despite
restoration work by monks in
the 17th century and again in
the 19th century, the church
appears quite untouched.

Its interior contains the most
magnificent series of 12th-
century Romanesque frescoes
in Europe. These wall paintings were among the very first
in France to be classified as a
Monument Historique in 1836.
Some of the frescoes were
restored in 1967–74 and since
1983 they have been protected by UNESCO. A full-scale
replica of the St-Savin murals
can be seen at the Palais de
Chaillot in Paris _(see pp110–
11)._ The abbey-museum
explains the historical context
and techniques of the murals.

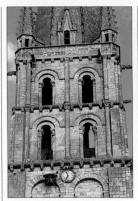

Belltower of St-Savin

Montmorillon ⓬

Vienne. 🏠 7,000. 🚌 🚹 2 pl du
Maréchal Leclerc (05 49 91 11 96).
🚲 Wed. **www**.tourisme-
montmorillon.fr

Montmorillon, built on the
river Gartempe, has its origins
in the 11th century. Like
most towns in the region, it
had a difficult time during the
Hundred Years' War and the
Wars of Religion. Some
buildings survived, such as
Eglise Notre-Dame, which
has beautiful frescoes in its

12th-century crypt (contact
tourist office for key). They
include scenes from the life
of St. Catherine of Alexandria.

Environs
Half an hour's walk from the
Pont de Chez Ragon, south of
Montmorillon, is the **Portes
d'Enfer**, a dramatically shaped
rock above the sudden rapids
of the Gartempe.

Confolens ⓭

Charente. 🏠 3,000. 🚌 🚹 rue
Fontaine des Jardins (05 45 84 14
08). 🚲 Wed & Sat.

On the border with Limousin,
Confolens was once an
important frontier town,
but now suffers from rural
exodus. Efforts to prevent
the town's isolation include
the annual international
folklore festival. Every
August the town is
transformed by a mix of
music, costumes, and crafts
from all over the world.

Of historical interest is the
medieval bridge across the
Vienne, heavily restored in
the early 18th century.

Charroux ⓮

Vienne. 🏠 1,200. 🚹 2 route de
Chatain (05 49 87 60 12). 🚲 Thu.
www.charroux-en-poitou.com

The 8th-century **Abbaye
St-Sauveur** in Charroux was
once one of the richest abbeys
in the region. Today it is a
ruin open to the sky (call the
tourist office to arrange a visit).

Its chief contribution to
history was made in the 10th
century, when the Council of
Charroux declared the "Truce
of God," the earliest-known
attempt to regulate war in the
manner of the Geneva
Convention. Rules included:
"Christian soldiers may not
plunder churches, strike
priests, or steal peasants' livestock while campaigning."

The huge tower marking
the center of the church, and
some superb sculpture from
the original abbey portal in
the small museum here, give
an idea of its original splendor.

ST-SAVIN WALL PAINTINGS

The frescoes of St-Savin represent Old Testament history
from the Creation to the Ten Commandments. The sequence
starts to the left of the entrance with the Creation of the
stars and of Eve. It continues with scenes from Noah's Ark
to the Tower of Babel, the story of Joseph, and the parting
of the Red Sea. It is believed that all the frescoes were
created by the same group of artists, due to the similarity
in style. Their harmonious colors – red and yellow ocher,
green, black, and white – have been softened by time.

Noah's Ark, from a 12th-century wall painting in St-Savin

Aulnay 🅕

Charente-Maritime. 🏠 *1,500.*
🛈 *290 av de l'Eglise (05 46 33
14 44).* 🄰 *Thu & Sun.*
www.aulnaytourisme.com

Perhaps the most unusual fact
about the lovely 12th-century
Eglise St-Pierre at Aulnay is
that it was all built at once;
there is no ill-fitting apse or
transept added to an original
nave. Surrounded by nothing
but cypresses, it has remained
the same since the time of the
great pilgrimages.

The church is covered in
glorious sculpture, particularly
the outside of the south transept. It is a rare example of a
complete Romanesque façade,
with myriad raucous monsters
and graceful human figures.
Look for the donkey with a
harp. Inside the church a pillar
decorated with elephants is
inscribed "Here be Elephants."

Façade of Eglise St-Pierre at Aulnay

La Rochelle 🅖

Charente-Maritime. 🏠 *80,000.* ✈
🚌 🚍 🛈 *2 quai Georges Simenon,
Le Gabut (05 46 41 14 68).* 🄰 *daily.*
www.larochelle-tourisme.com

La Rochelle, a commercial
center and busy port since
the 11th century, has suffered
much from a distressing ten-
dency to back the wrong side
– the English and the Calvin-
ists, for example. This led to
the ruthless siege of the city
by Cardinal Richelieu in 1628,
during which 23,000 people
starved to death. The walls

Tour St-Nicolas in La Rochelle

were destroyed and the city's
privileges withdrawn. The
glory of La Rochelle is the old
harbor surrounded by stately
buildings. The harbor is now
the biggest yachting center on
France's Atlantic coast. On
either side of its entrance are
Tour de la Chaîne and **Tour
St-Nicolas**. A huge chain used
to be strung between them to
ward off attack from the sea.

La Rochelle is easy to
explore on foot, though its
cobbled streets and arcades
can be congested in high
summer. To get an overview,
climb the 15th-century **Tour
de la Lanterne**. Its inner walls
were covered in graffiti by
prisoners, mostly mariners, in
the 17th–19th centuries. Ships
are the most common motif.

The study of the 18th-century
scientist Clément Lafaille is
preserved in the renovated
Muséum d'Histoire Naturelle,
complete with shell collection
and display cabinets. There are
also stuffed animals and
African masks. The town's
relation to the New World is
treated in the **Musée du Nouveau Monde**. Emigration,
commerce, and the slave trade
are explained through old
maps, paintings, and artifacts.

The richly decorated 16th-
century courtyard façade of
the **Hôtel de Ville** is worth a
visit, as is the delightful
collection of perfume bottles
in the **Musée du Flacon à
Parfum** in the parfumerie at
No. 33 rue du Temple.

Next to the Vieux Port is the
huge **Aquarium**. Transparent
tunnels lead through tanks
with different marine biotopes,
including sharks and turtles.

🏯 Tour de la Lanterne
Rue des Murs, Le Port. **Tel** *05 46
41 56 04.* ☐ *daily.* ⬤ *Jan 1, May
1, Nov 1 & 11, Dec 25.* 🈺

**🏛 Muséum d'Histoire
Naturelle**
28 rue Albert Premier. **Tel** *05 46 41
18 25.* ☐ *Tue–Sun.* 🈺 ♿

**🏛 Musée du Nouveau
Monde**
10 rue Fleuriau. **Tel** *05 46 41 46
50.* ☐ *Wed–Mon.* ⬤ *Sat am (Oct–
Mar), Sun am, Jan 1, May 1, Jul 14,
Nov 1 & 11, Dec 25.* 🈺

🐠 Aquarium
Bassin des Grands Yachts, quai
Louis Prunier. **Tel** *05 46 34 00 00.*
☐ *daily.* 🈺 ♿ 🛒 🍴 🎁 📷
www.aquarium-larochelle.com

Environs
Ile de Ré, also known as the
white island, is a long stretch
of chalky cliffs and dunes
with a rich birdlife. Since 1988
it has been connected to
the mainland by a 2-mile
(3-km) long bridge. Head
for **Ars-en-Ré** or the island's
main town, **St-Martin-de-Ré**.
There are plenty of seafood
restaurants serving locally
grown oysters.

Arcade in rue du Palais, La Rochelle

Rochefort 🅗

Charente-Maritime. 🏠 *27,000.* 🚍
🚍 🛈 *av Sadi-Carnot (05 46 99 08
60).* 🄰 *Tue, Thu, & Sat.*
www.rochefort-ocean.com

The historic rival of La Rochelle,
Rochefort was purpose-built
by Colbert *(see pp56–7)* in the

Phare des Baleines on the eastern point of the Ile de Ré, opposite La Rochelle

17th century to be the greatest shipyard in France, producing over 300 sailing vessels per year.

This maritime heritage can be traced in the beautifully restored **Corderie Royale** from 1670. The building houses an exhibition on ropemaking. The **Musée de la Marine** displays models of the ships built in the arsenal.

Rochefort is also famous as the birthplace of the writer Pierre Loti (1850– 1923). The author's extravagant **Maison de Pierre Loti** is filled with lush souvenirs in an oriental decor.

Outside the town is **Pont Transbordeur**, France's last ferry bridge, built in 1897 to connect Rochefort with southern points.

🏯 **La Corderie Royale**
Centre International de la Mer, rue Audebert. **Tel** 05 46 87 01 90. ◯ daily. ● Jan 1, 7–25, Dec 25. 🖼️ & 🅿️ www.corderie-royale.com

🏛 **Musée de la Marine**
Pl de la Galissonnière. **Tel** 05 46 99 86 57. ◯ daily. ● Jan, May 1, Dec 25. 🖼️🅿️ www.musee-marine.fr

🏛 **Maison de Pierre Loti**
141 rue Pierre Loti. **Tel** 05 46 99 16 88. ◯ Wed–Mon. ● Jan, Nov 1 & 11, Dec 25. 🖼️🅿️ only.

🏛 **Pont Transbordeur**
3 av Maurice Chupin, Parc des Fourriers. **Tel** 05 46 83 30 86. ◯ Apr–Sep: daily; Oct, Feb–Mar: Wed–Sun. www.pont-transbordeur.fr

Environs
Ile d'Aix is served by a ferry from Fouras on the mainland. Napoleon was briefly kept here before being exiled to St-Helena. There are Napoleonic

mementos in the **Musée Napoléonien**. The camel he rode in the Egyptian campaign is in the **Musée Africain**.

🏛 **Musée Napoléonien**
30 rue Napoléon. **Tel** 05 46 84 66 40. ◯ Wed–Mon. ● May 1. 🖼️

🏛 **Musée Africain**
Rue Napoléon. **Tel** 05 46 84 66 40. ◯ Wed–Mon. ● May 1. 🖼️ &

Napoleon, who was detained at Ile d'Aix in 1814

Île d'Oléron ⓲

Charente-Maritime. ✈️ La Rochelle. 🚆 Rochefort, La Rochelle, Saintes then bus. ⛴️ from La Rochelle (in summer). 🅸 Bourcefranc (05 46 85 65 23). www.ile-oleron-marennes.com

Accessible from the mainland by bridge, Oleron is the second largest French island after Corsica, and a very popular vacation resort. Its south coast, the **Côte Sauvage**, is all dunes and pine forest, with excellent

beaches at Vert Bois and Grande Plage, near the fishing port of La Cotinière. The north is used for farming and fishing.

The train from **St-Trojan** makes an interesting excursion through dunes and woodlands to the Pointe de Maumusson (Easter–Oct).

Brouage ⓳

Charente-Maritime. 🏠 580. 🅸 2 rue de Québec (05 46 85 19 16).

Cardinal Richelieu's fortress at Brouage, his base during the Siege of La Rochelle (1627–8), once overlooked a thriving harbor, but its wealth and population declined in the 18th century as the ocean receded. In 1659, Marie Mancini was sent into exile here by her uncle, Cardinal Mazarin, who did not approve of her liaison with Louis XIV. The king never forgot the beautiful Marie. Even on his way back from his wedding, he stayed alone at Brouage in the room once occupied by his first great love. Today the **ramparts** make a peaceful place to stroll and admire the view.

Environs
There are two reasons to go to **Marennes**, southwest of Brouage: the famous green-tinged oysters and the view from the steeple of Eglise St-Pierre-de-Sales. Nearby is the 18th-century **Château de la Gataudière** with an exhibition of horsedrawn vehicles.

One of Royan's five popular beaches

Royan ⑳

Charente-Maritime. 🏠 *20,000.*
🚉 🚌 🛥️ *to Verdon only.* ℹ️ *1 bd
de la Grandière (05 46 23 00 00).*
🛒 *Tue–Sun, daily in summer.*
www.royan-tourisme.com

Badly damaged by Allied
bombing in World War II,
Royan is now thoroughly
modern and different in tone
from the rest of the towns
on this weather-beaten coast.
With five beaches of fine
sand, here called *conches*, it
becomes a heavily populated
resort in the summer months.
    Built between 1955 and
1958, **Eglise Notre-Dame** is a
remarkable early example of
reinforced concrete architecture. Its interior is flooded
with color and light by the
stained-glass windows.
    The outstanding Renaissance
Phare de Cordouan, visible in
the distance from the coast,
offers a change from all the
modern architecture. Various
lighthouses have been erected
on the site since the 11th
century. The present one was

finished in 1611, with a chapel
inside. The construction was
later reinforced and heightened. Since 1789, nothing
has changed but the lighting
method. Boat trips in summer
ferry visitors to Phare de
Cordouan from Royan harbor.

Talmont-sur-Gironde ㉑

Charente-Maritime. 🏠 *79.*
ℹ️ *rue de l'Église (05 46 90 16 25).*

The tiny Romanesque **Eglise
Ste-Radegonde** is perched on
a spit of land overlooking the
Gironde. Built in 1094, the
church's apse was designed to
resemble the prow of a ship –
which is apt, since the nave
has already fallen into the
estuary. A 15th-century façade
closes off what's left. Inside
are richly decorated capitals,
including a tableau of St.
George and the Dragon.
    Talmont is a jewel of a
village, packed full of little
white houses and colorful
hollyhocks in summer.

Saintes ㉒

Charente-Maritime. 🏠 *28,000.*
🚉 🚌 ℹ️ *place Bassompierre
(05 46 74 23 82).* 🛒 *Tue–Sun.*
www.ot-saintes.fr

Capital of the Saintonge
region, Saintes has an extra-
ordinarily rich architectural
heritage. For centuries it
boasted the only bridge over
the lower Charente, well used
by pilgrims on their way to
Santiago de Compostela.
The Roman bridge no longer
exists but you can still admire
the magnificent **Arch of
Germanicus** (AD 19), which
used to mark its entrance.
    On the same side of the
river is the beautiful **Abbaye
aux Dames**. Consecrated in
1047, it was modernized in
the 12th century. During the
17th–18th centuries noble
ladies were educated here.
Look for the decorated portal
and the vigorous 12th-century
head of Christ in the apse.
    On the left bank is the 1st-
century Roman **amphitheater**.
Farther away lies the rather
unknown gem, **Eglise St-
Eutrope**. In the 15th century,
this church had the misfortune
to effect a miraculous cure of
the dropsy on Louis XI. In a
paroxysm of gratitude, he did
his best to wreck it with ill-
considered Gothic additions.
Luckily, its rare Romanesque
capitals have survived.

Arch of Germanicus in Saintes

Cognac ㉓

Charente. 🏠 *20,000.* 🚉 🚌 ℹ️ *16
rue du 14 Juillet (05 45 82 10 71).* 🛒
Tue–Sun. **www**.tourism-cognac.com

Wherever you spot the black
lichen stains from alcohol
evaporation on the exterior
of the buildings in this river

Necropolis in the monolithic Eglise St-Jean in Aubeterre-sur-Dronne

port, you may be sure that you are looking at a storehouse of cognac.

All the great cognac houses offer tours – a good one is chez **Cognac Otard**, situated in the 15th–16th-century château where François I was born. The distillery was established in 1795 by a Scot named Otard, who demolished an old chapel in the process. Luckily much of the Renaissance architecture was saved and can be seen during the tour, which includes a cognac-tasting.

Cognac in traditional snifter

The basic material for cognac is local white wine low in alcohol, which is then distilled. The resultant pale spirit is aged in oak barrels for 4–40 years before being bottled. The skill lies in the blending – therefore the only guide to quality is the name and the duration of ageing.

🏭 Cognac Otard
Château de Cognac, 127 bd Denfert-Rochereau. *Tel 05 45 36 88 86.*
⭕ Apr–Oct: daily; Nov–Dec: by appt.
● May 1 & public hols in winter.
🎦 🔲 obligatory. **www**.otard.com

Angoulême ㉔

Charente. 🏠 46,000. 🚉 🚌
🛈 7 bis rue du Chat (05 45 95 16 84). 🍴 daily.
www.angouleme-tourisme.com

The celebrated 12th-century **Cathédrale St-Pierre**, which dominates this industrial center, is the fourth to be built on the

site. One of its most interesting features is the Romanesque frieze on the façade. Some restoration work was done by the 19th-century architect Abadie. In his eagerness to wipe out all details added after the 12th century, he destroyed a 6th-century crypt. Unfortunately he was also let loose on the old château, transforming it into a Neo-Gothic **Hôtel de Ville** (town hall). However, the 15th-century tower where Marguerite d'Angoulême was born in 1492 still stands. A statue of her can be seen in the garden. Sister of François I, she spoke six languages, had an important role in foreign policy, and wrote a popular work, *Heptaméron*.

The ramparts offer a long, bracing walk, with views over the Charente Valley. A vintage car race takes place there in mid-September. Angoulême

has become the capital of comic book art *(band dessinée)*, hosting the prestigious Festival de la Band Dessinée (Jan/Feb). The **Cité Internationale de la Bande-Dessinée et de l'Image** has a reference collection of French print and movie cartoons dating back to 1946. From here, a footbrige leads to the Musée de la Band Dessinée, where the history, techniques, and aesthetics of the art form are explained.

🏛 Cité Internationale de la Bande-Dessinée et de l'Image
121 rue de Bordeaux. *Tel 05 45 38 65 65.* ⭕ Tue–Sun (w/e pms only).
● Jan, public hols. 🎦 🔲 📷 🔲
Cinema **www**.cnbdi.fr

Aubeterre-sur-Dronne ㉕

Charente. 🏠 430. 🚌 🛈 8 pl du Champ de Foine (05 45 98 57 18). 🍴 Sun. **http://**aubeterresurdronne.com

The chief ornament of this pretty white village is the staggering monolithic **Eglise St-Jean**. Dug out of the white chalky cliff that gave the village its name (Alba Terra – White Earth), some parts of it date back to the 6th century. Between the Revolution and 1860, it served as the village's cemetery. It contains an early Christian baptismal font and an octagonal reliquary.

The Romanesque Eglise St-Jacques is also of note for its fine sculpted façade.

Detail from the Romanesque façade of Cathédrale St-Pierre in Angoulême

Street-by-Street: Bordeaux ㉖

Built on a curve of the river Garonne,
Bordeaux has been a major port since pre-
Roman times and for centuries a crossroads
of European trade. Today Bordeaux shows
little visible evidence of the Romans,
Franks, English, or the Wars of Religion
that have marked its past. This forward-
looking town, the seventh largest in France,
is an industrial and maritime sprawl
surrounding a noble 18th-century center.

Along the waterfront of this wealthy wine
metropolis is a long sweep of elegant
Classical façades, first built to mask the
medieval slums behind. Adding to the
magnificence are the Esplanade des
Quinconces, the Grand Théâtre,
and the place de la Bourse.

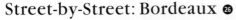

**Eglise Notre-
Dame, built
1684–1707**

★ Grand Théâtre
*Built in 1773–80, the theater
is a masterpiece of the
Classical style, crowned by
9 statues of the muses.*

STAR SIGHTS

* ★ Grand Théâtre
---
* ★ Esplanade des
  Quinconces
---
* ★ Place de la Bourse

KEY

— — — Suggested route

0 meters	100
0 yards	100

The quais, lined with graceful
façades, make a beautiful
walk along the Garonne.

★ Place de la Bourse
*This elegant and harmonious
square is flanked by two
majestic 18th-century
buildings, Palais de la Bourse
and Hôtel des Douanes.*

For hotels and restaurants in this region see pp580–2 and pp635–7

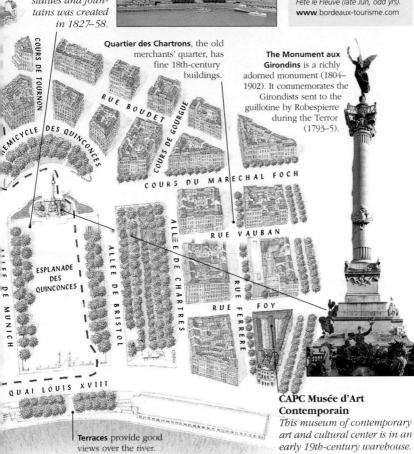

★ **Esplanade des Quinconces**
Replacing the 15th-century Château de Trompette, this vast space of tree-lined esplanades with statues and fountains was created in 1827–58.

Quartier des Chartrons, the old merchants' quarter, has fine 18th-century buildings.

The Monument aux Girondins is a richly adorned monument (1804–1902). It commemorates the Girondists sent to the guillotine by Robespierre during the Terror (1793–5).

COURS DE TOURNON

RUE BOUDET

HEMICYCLE DES QUINCONCES

COURS DE GOURGUE

COURS DU MARECHAL FOCH

ALLEE DE MUNICH

ESPLANADE DES QUINCONCES

ALLEE DE BRISTOL

ALLEE DE CHARTRES

RUE VAUBAN

RUE FERRERE

RUE FOY

QUAI LOUIS XVIII

Terraces provide good views over the river.

CAPC Musée d'Art Contemporain
This museum of contemporary art and cultural center is in an early 19th-century warehouse.

Loading wine barrels in 19th-century Bordeaux

THE BORDEAUX WINE TRADE

After Marseille, Bordeaux is the oldest trading port in France. From Roman times the export of wine was the basis for a modest prosperity, but under English rule (1154–1453, *see pp50–53*), the merchants began making immense fortunes from their monopoly of wine sales to England. After the discovery of the New World, Bordeaux took advantage of its Atlantic position to diversify and extend its wine market. Today the Bordeaux region produces over 60 million cases of wine per year.

GRAND THÉÂTRE DE BORDEAUX

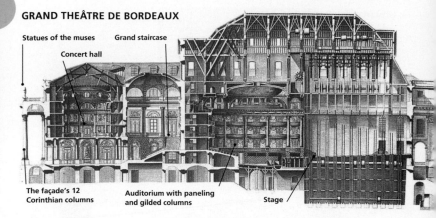

Statues of the muses   Grand staircase

Concert hall

The façade's 12
Corinthian columns

Auditorium with paneling
and gilded columns

Stage

Exploring Bordeaux

Much of central Bordeaux is grand streets and 18th-century mansions. A triangle made by cours Clemenceau, cours de l'Intendance, and allées de Tourny has chic boutiques and cafés. Cathédrale St-André is another focal point, with good museums nearby. Both the *quais* and the Chartrons district around the Jardin Public are worth exploring.

♨ Grand Théâtre
Place de la Comédie. *Tel* 05 56 00 85 95. ☐ *by appointment only.* ⚙
Built by the architect Victor Louis, the 18th-century Grand Théâtre is one of the finest Classical constructions of its type in France. The auditorium is renowned for its extraordinary acoustics. The spectacular main staircase was later imitated by Garnier for the Paris Opéra *(see p97)*.

⛪ Eglise St-Seurin
This church is somewhat chaotic with a patchwork of styles ranging from the 11th to the 18th century. Most interesting are the 6th-century Gallo-Roman sarcophagi in the crypt and a fine 14th-century bishop's throne.

⛪ Basilique St-Michel
It took 200 years to build the massive Basilique St-Michel, begun in 1350. This triple-naved edifice has a remarkable statue of St. Ursula with her flock of penitents. Its freestanding belfry, built in 1472–92, is the tallest in southern France (374 ft).

⛫ Musée des Beaux-Arts
20 cours d'Albret. *Tel* 05 56 10 20 56. ☐ *Wed–Mon.* ⬤ *public hols.* 🎫 ♿
Housed in two wings of the Hôtel de Ville, the excellent collection of paintings here ranges from the Renaissance to our time. Masterpieces include works by Titian, Veronese, Rubens, Delacroix, Corot, Renoir, Matisse, and Boudin.

⛫ Musée des Arts Décoratifs
39 rue Bouffard. *Tel* 05 56 10 14 00. ☐ *Wed–Mon.* ⬤ *public hols.* 🎫 🖵
If you're interested in elegant furnishings and fine porcelain, stop off at this exceptional collection, housed in the suitably refined 18th-century Hôtel de Lalande.

⛫ Musée d'Aquitaine
20 cours Pasteur. *Tel* 05 56 01 51 00. ☐ *Tue–Sun.* ⬤ *public hols.* ♿
This important museum traces life in the region from pre-historic times to the present, through artifacts, furniture, and viticulture tools. Among

Calm street in Bordeaux by the Porte de la Grosse Cloche

its more spectacular exhibits are the Tayac treasure from the 2nd century BC and the Garonne treasure, a hoard of over 4,000 Roman coins.

⛪ Cathédrale St-André
The nave of this gigantic church was begun in the 11th century and modified 200 years later. The Gothic choir and transepts were added in the 14th and 15th centuries. The excellent medieval sculptures on the Porte Royale include scenes from the Last Judgement.

⛫ CAPC Musée d'Art Contemporain
Entrepôt Lainé, 7 rue Ferrère. *Tel* 05 56 00 81 50. ☐ *Tue–Sun.* ⬤ *public hols.* 🎫 ♿ 🖵 🖵
This superbly converted 19th-century warehouse merits a visit, whatever you make of its high-profile temporary exhibitions and permanent collection of contemporary art.

St-Émilion ㉗

Gironde. 🚶 2,100. 🚉 🚌 🛈 *pl des Créneaux (05 57 55 28 28).* 🛍 *Sun.* **www**.saint-emilion-tourisme.com

This charming village, in the middle of the red wine district to which it gives its name, dates back to an 8th-century hermit, Émilion, who dug out a cave for himself in the rock. A monastery followed, and by the Middle Ages St-Émilion had become a small town. Today medieval houses still line the narrow streets, and parts of the

12th-century ramparts remain. The interior of the church dug out of the chalky cliff by followers of Saint Émilion after his death is somewhat ruined by concrete columns put up to prevent its collapse.

Famous châteaus in the district include the elegant **Figeac, Cheval Blanc,** and **Ausone,** all of them St-Émilion Premiers Grands Crus Classés.

Vineyard close to Margaux in the Médoc region west of Bordeaux

Pauillac ㉘

Gironde. 🚶 *5,400.* 🚉 🚌 🛈 *La Verrerie (05 56 59 03 08).* 🛒 *Sat.*
www.pauillac-medoc.com

One of the most famous areas in the Médoc wine region *(see pp398–9)* is the commune of Pauillac. Three of its châteaux are Médoc Premiers Grands Crus Classés.

The **Château Mouton-Rothschild** uses leading artists to create its wine labels and has a small museum of paintings on wine themes from all over the world. The **Château Lafite-Rothschild** is of medieval origin and the **Château Latour** is recognizable by its distinctive stone turret. They can be visited by appointment

(contact the tourist office). The town of Pauillac is situated on the west bank of the Gironde. In the 19th century it was the bustling arrival point for transatlantic steamships, but now the sleepy port is mostly used by pleasure boats. There are picturesque river views from the quais and plenty of cafés serving the local wine.

BORDEAUX WINE CHÂTEAUS

The château is at the heart of the quality system in Bordeaux, the world's largest fine wine region. A château includes a vineyard and a building which can range from the most basic to the grandest, historic as well as modern. But the château is also the symbol of a tradition and the philosophy that a wine's quality and character spring from the soil. Some châteaus welcome visitors for wine tasting as well as buying. Every major wine town has a Maison du Vin, which can provide information on visits to a château.

Latour *in Pauillac is famous for its powerful wines and the medieval stone turret that appears on its label.*

Cheval Blanc, *a great château in the St-Émilion area, boasts a rich, spicy Premier Grand Cru.*

Margaux, *built in 1802, produces a classic Margaux Premier Cru of the same elegant proportions as its Palladian façade.*

Palmer, *dating from 1856, is Neo-Renaissance in style and produces a very fine Margaux Troisième Cru.*

Gruaud-Larose *is a cream-colored château with a Classical façade, distinguished by its full-bodied St-Julien Deuxième Cru Classé.*

Vieux Château Certan *is Belgian-owned and one of the great historic properties of Pomerol. Its wines are consistently in the first rank in the district, challenged only by Pétrus.*

The immense Dune du Pilat, stretching almost 2 miles (3 km) south of the inlet to Bassin d'Arcachon

La Côte d'Argent ㉙

Gironde, Landes. ✈ Bordeaux, Biarritz.
🚆 Soulac-sur-Mer, Arcachon, Labenne,
Dax. 🚌 Lacanau, Arcachon, Mimizan.
ℹ️ Lacanau (05 56 03 21 01),
Mimizan-Plage (05 58 09 11 20),
Capbreton (05 58 72 12 11).

The long stretch of coast between Pointe de Grave on the Gironde estuary and Bayonne (see p452) is called La Côte d'Argent – the Silver Coast. It is virtually one vast beach of shifting sand dunes. Treeplanting has now slowed down their progress.

The coast is dotted with sea-side resorts like **Soulac-sur-Mer** in the north, followed by the big **Lacanau-Océan** and **Mimizan-Plage**. Down in the south is **Hossegor** with its salty lake, and **Capbreton**. Modern vacation resorts have been integrated with the old.

Inland are lakes popular for fishing and boating. They are connected to each other and the ocean by lively water currents, such as the **Courant d'Huchet** from Etang de Léon. Boat trips are available.

Bassin d'Arcachon ㉚

Gironde. 🏛 12,000. 🚢 to Cap Ferret.
🚆 ℹ️ espl Georges Pompidou
(05 57 52 97 97). 🛒 daily.
www.arcachon.com

In the middle of the Côte d'Argent the straight coastline suddenly forms a lagoon. Famous for its natural beauty,

fine beaches, and oysters, the Bassin d'Arcachon is a protected area, perfect for vacationers, sailing enthusiasts, and oyster-eaters.

The basin is dotted with smaller amorphous resorts, beaches, and fishing/oyster villages, all worth exploring.

Cap Ferret, the northern headland that protects the basin from stiff Atlantic winds, is a preserve of the wealthy, whose luxurious villas stand among the pines. Look for the small road under the trees from Lège, which leads to the wild, magnificent beach of Grand-Crohot.

Between Cap Ferret and Arcachon, near Gujan-Mestras, the **Parc Ornithologique du Teich** provides care and shelter for damaged birds and endangered species. For the bird watcher, there are two fascinating walks, each carefully marked: an introductory one, and another of greater length. Both

provide concealed observation points from which people can watch the wild fowl without disturbing them.

Arcachon was created as a seaside resort in 1845. Its popularity grew and in the late 19th and early 20th centuries the elegant villas in Ville d'Hiver were built. The livelier Ville d'Eté, facing the lagoon, has a casino and sports facilities.

The immense **Dune du Pilat** is the largest sand dune in Europe. It is nearly 2 miles (3 km) long, 340 ft (104 m) high, and 1,625 ft (500 m) wide. Aside from the view, the dune is a great vantage point in the fall for viewing flocks of migratory birds as they pass overhead on their way to the sanctuary at Le Teich.

✈ Parc Ornithologique du Teich
Le Teich. **Tel** 05 56 22 80 93.
🕐 daily. 🖼 ♿ 🏪 🛍 **www**.
parc-ornithologique-du-teich.com

Parc Ornithologique du Teich, a bird sanctuary in Bassin d'Arcachon

LANDES FOREST

The vast, totally artificial 19th-century forest of Les Landes was an ambitious project to make use of an area of sand and marshes. Pines and grasses were planted to anchor the coastal dunes, and inland dunes were stabilized with a mixture of pines, reeds and broom. In 1855 the land was drained, and is now covered with pine groves and undergrowth, preserving a delicate ecological balance.

Pine trees in the Landes forest

Les Landes ③

Gironde, Landes. 🚉 Bordeaux, Biarritz. 🚉 Morcenx, Dax, Mont-de-Marsan. 🚌 Mont-de-Marsan. 🛈 Mont-de-Marsan (05 58 05 87 37).

Almost entirely covered by an immense pine forest, the Landes area extends over the two *départements* of Gironde and Landes. The soil here is uniformly sandy. Until a century ago the whole region became a swamp in winter, because of a layer of tufa (porous rock) just under the surface that retained water from the brackish lakes. Any settlement or agriculture close to the sea was impossible, due to the constantly shifting dunes. Furthermore, the mouth of the Adour river kept moving from Capbreton to Vieux-Boucau and back, a distance of 20 miles (32 km).

The Adour was fixed near Bayonne by a canal in the 16th century. This was the start of the slow conquest of the Landes. The planting of pine trees ultimately wiped out the migrant shepherds and their flocks. Today the inner Landes is still very under-populated,

but wealthy from its pinewood and pine derivatives. The coastal strip has a large influx of vacationers.

In 1970, part of the forest was made into a nature park. At **Marqueze**, in the **Écomusée de la Grande Lande**, a typical 19th-century *airial* (clearing) has been restored. It commemorates the vanished world of Les Landes before the draining of the marshes, when shepherds still used stilts to get around. There are traditional *auberges landaises*, wooden houses with sloping roofs, as well as henhouses built on stilts because of the foxes. In **Luxey** a museum recalls old techniques of tapping and distillation of resin.

Levignacq, near the coast, is a perfect Landais village with a remarkable 14th-century fortified church full of charming naive frescoes.

Mont-de-Marsan ③

Landes. 🚶 32,000. 🚉 🚌 🛈 6 pl du Général Leclerc (05 58 05 87 37). 🚌 Tue & Sat. **www**.tourisme-montdemarsan.fr

A bullfighting mecca, Mont-de-Marsan attracts all the great bullfighters of France and Spain in the summer season. A less bloodthirsty local variant of the sport is the *course landaise*, in which the object is to vault over the horns and back of a charging cow.

The administrative capital of the Landes is also known for its hippodrome and the production of poultry and *foie gras*.

Sculpture from the first half of the 20th century can be seen at **Musée Despiau-Wlérick**.

Dax ③

Landes. 🚶 21,500. 🚉 🚌 🛈 cours Foch (05 58 56 86 86). 🚌 Sat, Sun am. **www**.dax-tourisme.com

The thermal spa of Dax is second only to Aix-les-Bains *(see p390)* in importance. Its hot springs, with a constant temperature of 147° F (64° C) and tonic mud from the Adour, have been soothing aches and pains since the time of Emperor Augustus.

Apart from the 13th-century doorway of the otherwise 17th-century **Cathédrale Notre-Dame**, there isn't much of architectural interest in this warm, peaceful town. But the promenade along the river Adour is charming and the bullring is world-renowned.

La Force (1937) by Raoul Lamourdieu, in the bullfighting capital of Mont-de-Marsan

PERIGORD, QUERCY, AND GASCONY

DORDOGNE · LOT · TARN · HAUTE GARONNE
LOT-ET-GARONNE · TARN-ET-GARONNE · GERS

*S*outhwest France is an archeologist's heaven, for the region has been continuously inhabited by mankind for tens of thousands of years, longer than any other area in Europe. The landscape of these historic regions seems to have an ancient familiarity, derived from centuries of people living in harmony with the land.

The great cave sites around Les Eyzies and Lascaux harbor the earliest evidence we possess of primitive art. The castles, bastides *(see p445)*, and churches that grace the countryside from Périgueux to the Pyrenees, from the Bay of Biscay to Toulouse, and beyond to the Mediterranean, belong to a far more recent past. From the coming of Christianity until the late 18th century, this lovely region was the battlefield for a string of conflicts. The English fought and lost the Hundred Years' War for Aquitaine (1345–1453); this was followed by intermittent Wars of Religion, in which Catholics fought Huguenots (French Protestants) in a series of massacres and guerilla wars *(see pp52–3)*.

Today nothing is left of these old struggles but crumbling ramparts, keeps, and bastides, which are part of the region's cultural and artistic heritage, attracting thousands of visitors every year. Yet it is as well to remember that all the great sights here, from the abbey church at Moissac, whose 12th-century portal is a masterpiece of Romanesque art, to the awesome clifftop site of Rocamadour, have suffered at one time or another from the attacks of marauding soldiers.

Over the last 50 years, the rural southwest has gone through a radical demographic shift. There has been a steady decline in the old peasant way of life, with fewer and fewer people cultivating the land. A steady migration by the young to the cities has been matched by an influx of downsizers and commuters looking for a more relaxed way of life.

Périgord geese, reared for the area's celebrated *foie gras*

◁ La Roque-Gageac in the Dordogne Valley

Exploring Périgord, Quercy, and Gascony

The market towns of Périgueux, Cahors, and Albi make good bases for exploring the region, and are quieter alternatives to Toulouse – the only major urban center. Elsewhere, the green hills and sleepy villages of Gascony and Périgord (also known as the Dordogne) are mainly for those who appreciate the slow pace of life in the countryside. But if you want more than peace and good food, this region offers some of France's finest medieval architecture, and Europe's most important prehistoric caves, notably Lascaux.

The medieval hilltop town of Cordes

GETTING AROUND

The west–east Autoroute des Deux Mers (A62-A61) is the main road through the region, linking Bordeaux, the Atlantic coast, and the Mediterranean. The A20 from Montauban to Limoges provides access to the Dordogne and Quercy. Buses and mainline railroads, including a Bordeaux–Marseille TGV, pass along the same two axes. They meet at Toulouse, where an international airport has daily flights to and from most European destinations.

KEY

═══	Highway
═══	Major road
──	Secondary road
═══	Minor road
──	Scenic route
┄┄	Main railroad
┄┄	Minor railroad
──	Regional border

SIGHTS AT A GLANCE

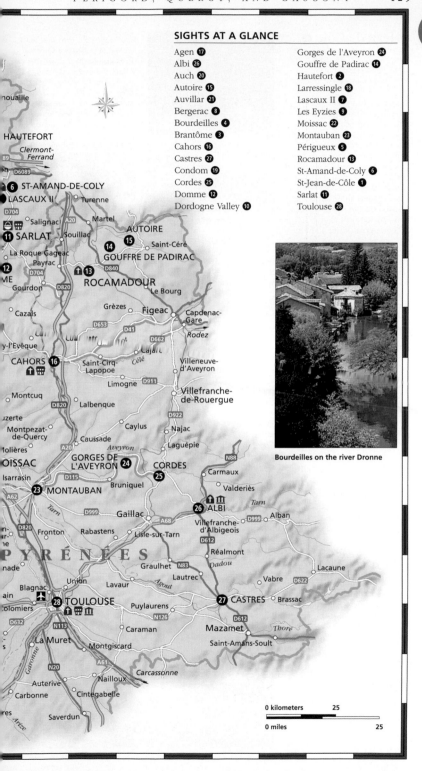

Bourdeilles on the river Dronne

St-Jean-de-Côle ●

Dordogne. 350. *pl du Château (05 53 62 14 15).* Floralies (Apr–May). www.ville-saint-jean-de-cole.fr

St-Jean-de-Côle's medieval, humpbacked bridge gives the best view of this lovely Dordogne village set in hilly countryside. Stone and half-timbered houses, roofed with the distinctive red-brown tiles of the region, cram the narrow streets around the main square. Here stand a covered market place, château, and 12th-century church.

The cupola of the church used to be the largest in the region – too large, it seems, for it fell down twice in the 18th and 19th centuries. The second time it happened the builders gave up, and there has been a plank ceiling ever since.

Main square in the lovely village of St-Jean-de-Côle

Hautefort ●

Tel 05 53 50 40 27. **Château** Feb, Mar & early Nov: Sat, Sun & hols pms only; Apr– Sep: daily (Oct: daily, pms only). mid-Nov–Feb. oblig. limited. www.chateau-hautefort.com

Hautefort clings to the sides of a steep hill topped by a massive 17th-century château, one of the finest in southwest France. Partially fortified, and built as a pleasure palace in honor of King Louis XIII's secret love, the Marquis de Hautefort's sister Marie, the castle sits among French gardens on terraces with superb views of the rolling countryside of northeast Périgord. In the village, the hospice, of a similar date, has a museum of early medical implements.

Brantôme Abbey, with belfry

Brantôme ●

Dordogne. 2,200. inside the abbey (05 53 05 80 52). Fri. www.ville-brantome.fr

Surrounded by the river Dronne, Brantôme is often called the Venice of the Périgord Vert. Its medieval abbey and 11th-century belfry (reputedly the oldest in France), together with the verdant rockface behind, provide a dramatic backdrop for this picturesque town.

Pierre de Bourdeille, the poet (1540–1614), was appointed abbot here in his youth. His lovers allegedly included Mary, Queen of Scots. After a crippling fall, Bourdeille retired here in 1569 to write his racy memoirs. It is possible to wander the stone staircases and cloisters, and through the main courtyard to the intriguing troglodyte dwellings in the cliff behind. In one is a huge crucifixion scene cut into the stone during the 16th century.

Just 7 miles (12 km) northeast lies the Renaissance **Château de Puyguilhem** and **Grotte de Villars**. Discovered in 1953, these caves lead to several different levels. Apart from spectacular rock formations, there are some marvelous 1,700-year-old cave paintings.

Château de Puyguilhem
Villars. *Tel 05 53 54 82 18.* Apr–Sep: daily; Oct–Mar: Wed–Sun. Jan 1, May 1, Nov 1 & 11, Dec 25. http://puyguilhem. monuments-nationaux.fr

Grotte de Villars
Villars. *Tel 05 53 54 82 36.* Apr–Oct: daily. oblig. www.grotte-villars.com

Bourdeilles ●

Dordogne. 800. *63 place Tilleuls (05 53 03 42 96).*

This small town has everything – a Gothic bridge with cutwater piers spanning the Dronne, a mill, and a medieval **château**. The 16th-century additions to the castle were designed in a hurry by the châtelaine Jacquette de Montbron, when expecting Queen Catherine de' Medici to visit. When the royal visit was called off, so were the building works. The highlight is the gilded salon, decorated in the 1560s by Ambroise le Noble, of the Fontainebleau School.

Château de Bourdeilles
Tel 05 53 03 73 36. Feb–Mar & Nov–mid-Dec: Mon, Wed, Thu, & Sun; Jul–Aug: daily; Sep–Oct & late Dec: Wed–Mon. Jan. www.bourdeilles.com

The impressive Château de Bourdeilles towering above the town

Cathédrale St-Front in Périgueux, restored in the 19th century

Périgueux **5**

Dordogne. 🏛 *31,000.* ✈ 🚆
🚌 ℹ *26 pl Francheville*
(05 53 53 10 63). 🛒 *daily.*
www.tourisme-perigueux.fr

The ancient and truly gastronomic city of Périgueux, like
its neighbors Bergerac and
Riberac, should be visited on
market day, when stalls in the
lively squares in the medieval
part of town offer the pick
of local specialties, including truffles (Nov–Mar),
charcuterie, and the succulent pies called *pâtés
de Périgueux.*

Périgueux, now
the busy regional
capital, has long
been the crossroads
of Périgord. The
earliest part re-
maining today is the
quarter known as **La
Cité**, once the import-
ant Gallo-Roman settle-
ment of Vesunna. La
Domus de Vesonne, a
Gallo-Roman museum,
has just opened on site.
From Roman times to
the Middle Ages, this

was the focus of Périgueux.
Most of the fabric of Vesunna
was pulled down in the 3rd
century, but some vestiges of
a temple, a huge arena, and a
sumptuous villa remain. The
Eglise St-Etienne nearby dates
back to the 12th century.

Walking up the hill from La
Cité to the city's dazzling white
cathedral you pass through
bustling streets and squares,
each with its market activity.
This is the medieval quarter
of **Le Puy St-Front**,
which began to flou-
rish as pilgrims on
their way to Santiago de
Compostela *(see p400)*
visited the cathedral.
As they brought
prestige and wealth
to the quarter, it grad-
ually eclipsed La Cité.
At the top stands the
imposing **Cathédrale
St-Front**, the largest in
southwestern France.
The Romanesque con-
struction was heavily
restored in the 19th
century, when architect

**19th-century stained glass
in Cathédrale St-Front**

Paul Abadie added the
fanciful domes and cones.
He later used St-Front as
inspiration for the Sacré-
Coeur in Paris *(see p134).*

Other gems of medieval
and Renaissance architecture
include **Maison Estignard**,
at No. 3 rue Limogeanne,
with its unusual corkscrew
staircase, and houses along
rue Aubergerie and rue de
la Constitution.

Also in the cathedral quarter
is the **Musée d'Art et d'Archéologie du Périgord**, one of the
most comprehensive prehistory
museums in France, with
remnants of burials dating
back 70,000 years. Beautiful
Roman glass, mosaics,
earthenware, and other
artifacts from Vesunna are in
the Gallo-Roman museum.

🏛 **Musée d'Art et
d'Archéologie du Périgord**
22 cours Tourny. **Tel** *05 53 06 40 70.*
⬜ *Wed–Mon.* ⬤ *public hols.* 🈁

St-Amand-de-
Coly **6**

Dordogne. **Tel** *Maison du Patrimoine
(05 53 51 04 56, summer only);
La Mairie.* ⬜ *daily.*
www.saint-amand-de-coly.org

This abbey church is an outstanding example of fortress
architecture, built in the
12th–13th centuries by
Augustinian monks to protect
their monastery. There are
two lines of defense: a high
stone rampart and, behind it,
the arched tower of the church
itself. The tower looks more
like a castle keep, and was
once pierced by arrow slits.

Inside, the church is beautifully simple, with pure lines, a
flat ribbed vault, a 12th-century
cupola, a soaring nave, and a
stone floor sloping up to the
altar. Yet even this interior
was arranged for defense,
with a gallery from which
enemies within the building
could be attacked.

St-Amand was damaged
during the Hundred Years'
War. Later, in 1575, it survived
a siege by Huguenot cavalry
and a six-day bombardment
by cannon. Religious life here
ended after the Revolution.

Sarlat

Sculptures of geese in Sarlat

Sarlat-la-Canéda possesses the highest concentration of medieval, Renaissance, and 17th-century façades of any town in France. Its prosperity was a reflection of the privileged status it was granted in return for loyalty to the French crown during the Hundred Years' War. Behind the nondescript rue de la République are narrow lanes and archways, and ancient, ocher-colored stone town houses rich in ornamental detail. Protected by law since 1962, Sarlat's buildings now form an open-air museum. The town is also famous for one of the best markets in France.

Place de la Liberté
The Renaissance heart of Sarlat is no[w] lined with luxury stores and cafés.

Rue des Consuls contains 15th-, 16th-, and 17th-century mansions, built for the town's middle-class merchants, magistrates and church officials.

Rue Jean-Jacques Rousseau was the main street until rue de la République (known as "La Traverse") was built in the 19th century.

Walnuts, a key Périgord crop

SARLAT MARKET

Every Wednesday, the great Sarlat food market is held in place de la Liberté, and every Saturday there is a full-scale fair which attracts locals from all around. Sarlat lies at the heart of the nation's *foie gras* and walnut trades. These typical Périgord products absorb much of the town's attention and supply a good proportion of its revenue, as they did during Sarlat's heyday in the 14th and 15th centuries. Other local specialties are black truffles dug up in the woods in January, and wild mushrooms. Seek out, too, the cheeses of every shape, age, and hue, and the huge range of pork delicacies available, which may be potted, fresh, smoked, dried, salted, fried, baked, or boiled.

Bulbs of pink garlic

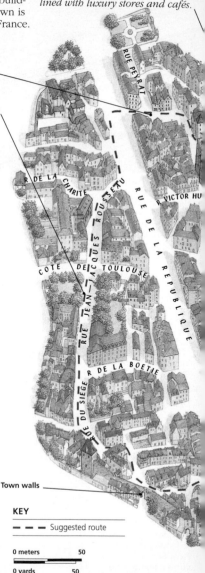

Town walls

KEY

– – – Suggested route

| 0 meters | 50 |
| 0 yards | 50 |

Rue de la Salamandre
This lane was named after the salamander emblem of King François I, seen on many of the town's 16th-century houses.

VISITORS' CHECKLIST

Dordogne. 10,500.
av de la Gare.
3 rue Tourny (05 53 31 45 45). Wed & Sat.
Theater (Jul–Aug); Film (Nov).
www.sarlat-tourisme.com

Lanterne des Morts (Lantern of the Dead)
The conical tower in the cemetery was built to commemorate St-Bernard's sermons in Sarlat in August 1147.

Cathédrale St-Sacerdos
Built largely in the 16th and 17th centuries, the cathedral is remarkable for its magnificent 18th-century organ.

The Chapelle des Pénitents Bleus, built in pure Romanesque style, is the last vestige of the 12th-century abbey.

The former Bishop's Palace, with remains of a 16th-century loggia and a Renaissance interior, is now a tourist office which puts on excellent summer exhibitions.

Cour des Fontaines
A pure spring here attracted the monks who founded Sarlat's first abbey in the 9th century.

Painting of a bull from the original cave at Lascaux

Lascaux II ❼

Montignac. **Tel** 05 53 05 65 65.
◯ Feb–mid-Nov daily; mid-Nov–Feb:
Tue–Sun; times vary – phone to
check. ◉ Jan, Dec 25. 📷 ✓
www.lascaux.culture.fr

Lascaux is the most famous
of the prehistoric sites
clustered around the junction
of the rivers Vézère and Beune
(see pp402–3). Four boys
came across the caves and
their astonishing paleolithic
paintings in 1940, and the
importance of their discovery
was swiftly recognized.
Lascaux has been closed to
the public since 1963 because
of deterioration, but an exact
copy has been created a few
minutes' walk down the hillside, using the same materials.
The replica is beautiful and
should not be spurned: high-
antlered elk, bison, bulls, and
plump horses cover the walls,
surrounded by arrows and
geometric symbols thought to
have had ritual significance.

Bergerac ❽

Dordogne. 👥 26,000. ✈ 🚃 🚌
ℹ 97 rue Neuve d'Argenson
(05 53 57 03 11). 🗓 Wed & Sat.
www.bergerac-tourisme.com

This small port, a tobacco
farming and commercial
center, spreads itself over
both sides of the Dordogne.
Chief attractions are its extraordinary **Musée du Tabac**
(tobacco museum), and its
food and wine which are
invariably excellent. Bergerac's

most celebrated wine is Monbazillac, a sweet white wine,
often drunk on ceremonial
occasions. On show in the
small, lively museum are
some Native American pipes.

🏛 **Musée du Tabac**
Maison Peyrarède, pl du Feu.
Tel 05 53 63 04 13. ◯ Tue–Sun.
◉ Sun ams (Oct–Mar: Sun all day),
public hols. 📷 ♿

Les Eyzies ❾

Dordogne. 👥 900. 🚃 ℹ 19 av
de la Préhistoire (05 53 06 97 05).
🗓 Mon (Apr–Oct).
www.tourisme-vezere.com

Four major prehistoric sites
and a group of smaller caves
cluster around the unassuming village of Les Eyzies.
Head first for the **Musée
National de Préhistoire**, in a
new building at the foot of a
16th-century castle over-
looking the village. The
timelines and other exhibits
are useful for putting the vast
warren of prehistoric painting
and sculpture into context.
The **Grotte de Font de
Gaume** is the logical first stop
after the museum at Les
Eyzies. This cave, discovered
in 1901, contains probably
the finest prehistoric paintings
still on public view in France.
Close by is the **Grotte des
Combarelles**, with engravings
of bison, reindeer, magic
symbols, and human figures.

Les Eyzies, a center for the area's concentration of prehistoric caves

Farther on, you reach the rock shelter of **Abri du Cap Blanc**, discovered in 1909, with a rare, lifesize frieze of horses and bison sculpted in the rock.

On the other side of Les Eyzies is the cave system at **Rouffignac**, a favorite place for excursions since the 15th century. There are 5 miles (8 km) of caves here, 1.5 miles (2.5 km) of which are served by electric train. The paintings include drawings of mammoths and a frieze of two bison challenging each other to combat.

Tickets for all the caves sell out fast, especially in summer, so arrive early. Some must be reserved two weeks ahead.

Musée National de Préhistoire

🏛 **Musée National de Préhistoire**
Tel 05 53 06 45 45. ⭕ *Jul & Aug: daily; Sep–Jun: Wed–Mon.* ⭕ *Jan 1, Dec 25.* 🈂 🔥 📷 🎧
🎟 **Grotte de Font de Gaume**
Tel 05 53 06 86 00. ⭕ *Sun–Fri by appt; reserve 2 months in advance.* ⭕ *some public hols.*
🎟 **Grotte des Combarelles**
Tel 05 53 06 86 00. ⭕ *Sun–Fri; reserve fortnight in advance.* ⭕ *some public hols.* 🈂
🎟 **Abri du Cap Blanc**
Marquay, Les Eyzies. *Tel 05 53 06 86 00.* ⭕ *Apr–Oct: daily.* ⭕ *some public hols.* 🈂 🔥
🎟 **Grotte de Rouffignac**
Tel 05 53 05 41 71. ⭕ *Apr–Oct: daily.* 🈂 🔥

Dordogne Valley ⑩

Dordogne. ✈ *Bergerac.* 🚉 *Bergerac, Le Buisson de Cadouin.* 🚌 *Beynac.* ⓘ *Le Buisson de Cadouin (05 53 22 06 09)*

Probably no river in France crosses so varied a landscape and such different geological formations as the Dordogne. Starting in deep granite gorges in the Massif Central, it continues through fertile lowlands, then enters the limestone Causse country around Souillac. By the time the Dordogne has wound down to the Garonne, it is almost 2 miles (3 km) wide.

Don't be put off by the valley's touristy image. It is a beautiful area for wandering. Several villages make good stopping-off points, such as Limeuil, Beynac, and La Roque-Gageac from where *gabarres* (river boats) ferry visitors (Easter–Oct).

Perched high above the river, southwest of Sarlat, is the 17th-century **Château de Marqueyssac**. Its topiary park offers panoramic views from Domme to Beynac, and of the Château de Castelnaud on the opposite river bank.

Sarlat ⑪

See pp432–3.

View of Domme from the medieval gateway of Porte de la Combe

Domme ⑫

Dordogne. 🏠 *1,030.* ⓘ *pl de la Halle (05 53 31 71 00).* 🛒 *Thu.* **www**.ot-domme.com

Henry Miller wrote, "Just to glimpse the black, mysterious river at Domme from the beautiful bluff…is something to be grateful for all one's life." Domme itself is a neat bastide *(see p445)* of golden stone, with medieval gateways still standing. People come here to admire the view, which takes in the Dordogne valley from Beynac in the west to Montfort in the east, and wander the maze of old streets inside the walls. There is also a large cavern under the 17th-century covered market where the inhabitants hid at perilous moments during the Hundred Years' War and the 16th-century Wars of Religion. Despite a seemingly impregnable position, 30 intrepid Huguenots managed to capture Domme by scaling the cliffs under cover of night and opening the gates.

A *cingle* (loop) of the river Dordogne, seen from the town of Domme

Rocamadour ⓑ

Rocamadour became one of the most famous centers of pilgrimage following a spate of miracles heralded, it is claimed, by the bell above the Black Virgin and Child in the Chapel of Notre-Dame. This was followed by the discovery in 1166 of an ancient grave and sepulchre containing an undecayed body, said to be that of the early Christian hermit St. Amadour. Although the town suffered with the decline of pilgrimages in the 17th and 18th centuries, it was heavily restored in the 19th century. Still a holy shrine, as well as a popular tourist destination, Rocamadour's site on a rocky plateau above the Alzou valley is phenomenal. The best views are to be had from the ramparts of the château, reached from the hamlet of L'Hospitalet.

Black Virgin and Child

The Château stands on the site of a fort which protected the sanctuary from the west.

St. Michael's Chapel contains well-preserved 12th-century frescoes.

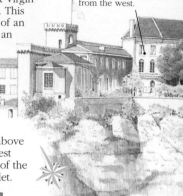

General View
Rocamadour is at its most breathtaking in the sunlight of early morning: the cluster of medieval houses, towers, and battlements seems to sprout from the base of the cliff.

The Tomb of St-Amadour once held the body of the hermit called *roc amator* (lover of rock), from whom the town took its name.

Grand Stairway
Pilgrims would climb this broad flight of steps on their knees as they said their rosaries. The stairway leads to a square on the next level, around which the main pilgrim chapels are grouped.

For hotels and restaurants in this region see pp582–5 and pp637–40

The Chapel of St. John the Baptist faces the fine Gothic portal of the Basilica of St-Sauveur.

The Basilica of St-Sauveur, a late 12th-century sanctuary, backs onto the bare rock face.

St. Anne's Chapel dates from the 13th century, and contains a 17th-century gilded altar screen.

Ramparts

Cross of Jerusalem

VISITORS' CHECKLIST

Lot. 🚶 670. 🚉 3 miles (5 km) SW Rocamadour. 🛈 Maison du Tourisme (05 65 33 22 00). **Chapel of Notre-Dame** ⬤ 9am–6:30pm daily (to 9pm Jun–Sep). 📷 www.rocamadour.com

Stations of the Cross
Pilgrims encounter the Cross of Jerusalem and 14 stations marking Jesus's journey to the Cross on their way up the hillside to the château.

Chapel of St-Blaise (13th century)

Rocamadour Town
Now a pedestrian precinct, its main street is lined with souvenir stores to tempt the throngs of pilgrims.

Chapel of Notre-Dame (Miracles)
St. Amadour's body was found in the cliff, near the Black Virgin Chapel. A statue of the Black Virgin, the supreme object of veneration, stands on the altar.

Gouffre de Padirac ⑭

Lot. **Tel** 05 65 33 64 56.
☐ Apr–Oct: daily. 🏛 🔲
www.gouffre-de-padirac.com

Formed by the collapse of a cave, this huge crater measures 115 ft (35 m) wide and 337 ft (103 m) deep. The underground river and stunning succession of galleries (see p403) were discovered in 1889. The immense Salle du Grand Dôme dwarfs the tallest of cathedrals. Bring a jacket, since the cave is 55° F (13° C).

Autoire ⑮

Lot. 🏛 370. 🚹 Saint Céré
(05 65 38 11 85).
www.tourisme.saint.cere.com

This is one of the loveliest places in Quercy, the fertile area east of Périgord. There are no grand monuments or dramatic history, just an unspoiled site at the mouth of the Autoire gorge. The **Château de Limarque** on the main square, and the **Château de Busqueille** overlooking it, are both built in characteristic Quercy style, with turrets and towers. Elsewhere, elaborate dovecotes stand in fields or are attached to houses.

Outside Autoire, past a 100-ft (30-m) waterfall, a path climbs to a rock amphitheater, giving panoramic views of the region.

The picturesque village of Autoire, seen from across the gorge

Cahors ⑯

Lot. 🏛 21,200. 🚇 🚌
🚹 pl François Mitterrand (05 65 53 20 65). 🛒 Wed & Sat am.
www.tourisme-cahors.com

The capital of the Lot *département*, Cahors is renowned for its dark, heady wine, which was produced as far back as Roman times. It is also famous for being the birthplace of the statesman Léon Gambetta (1838–82), who led France to recovery after the war with Prussia in 1870. The main street of Cahors – like many towns in France – is named after him.

Cathédrale de St-Etienne, entrenched behind the narrow streets of Cahors' Old Town, dates back to 1119. It has some fine medieval details; don't miss the lively figures of the Romanesque north door and tympanum, which depict the Ascension, or the huge cupola above the nave (said

---

A Tour of Two Rivers

Flanked by spectacular limestone cliffs, the beautiful Lot and Célé valleys feature ancient medieval villages and castles, narrow gorges, and rushing waterfalls along lazy stretches of river. An unhurried tour of both valleys, around 100 miles (160 km), is best spread over 2 days to savor the gastronomic delights and the superb views.

From Cahors, the route follows the Lot, then meanders slowly up the peaceful and picturesque Célé valley to reach Figeac, a handsome town full of charming stores, cafés, and restaurants. The return route is via the busier Lot Valley, which has more sights, including the spectacular village of St-Cirq-Lapopie (allow time to park above or below the village and to enter on foot).

Grotte de Pech-Merle ①
This 25,000-year-old prehistoric site outside Cabrerets has huge chambers painted with mammoths, horses, bison, and human figures.

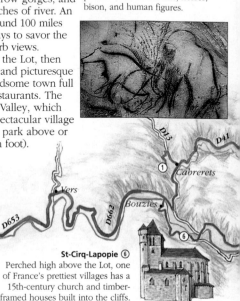

CAHORS

St-Cirq-Lapopie ⑥
Perched high above the Lot, one of France's prettiest villages has a 15th-century church and timber-framed houses built into the cliffs.

to be the largest in France). They are covered in 14th-century frescoes depicting the stoning of St. Stephen (St-Étienne). The Renaissance cloisters are decorated with some intricate, though damaged, carvings.

Also worth seeking out in the cathedral quarter is the ornate 16th-century **Maison de Roaldès**, its north façade decorated with tree, sun, and rose of Quercy motifs. It was here that Henri of Navarre (who later became King Henri IV) stayed for one night in 1580 after besieging and capturing Cahors.

The town's landmark monument is the **Pont Valentré**, a fortified bridge with seven pointed arches and three towers that spans the river. It was built between 1308 and 1360, and has withstood many attacks since then. It is claimed that the bridge is one of the most photographed monuments in the whole of

The fortified Pont Valentré spanning the river Lot at Cahors

France. An alternative way to enjoy the scenery is to take a leisurely 90-minute boat trip through the lock from a wharf near the bridge (Apr–Oct).

Environs

Cahors makes a good base from which to explore the sights of the Lot. Visit the historic towns of Figeac,

birthplace of Jean-François Champollion who first deciphered Egyptian hieroglyphs, and the **Grotte de Pech-Merle** with its extraordinary painted walls.

🏠 **Grotte de Pech-Merle**
Cabrerets. *Tel* 05 65 31 27 05.
◯ Apr–Oct daily. 🚫
www.pechmerle.com

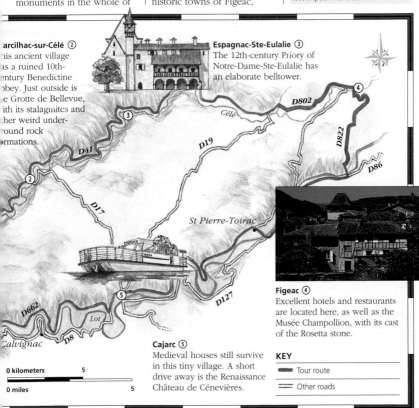

arcilhac-sur-Célé ②
his ancient village as a ruined 10th-entury Benedictine obbey. Just outside is e Grotte de Bellevue, ith its stalagmites and her weird underground rock rmations.

Espagnac-Ste-Eulalie ③
The 12th-century Priory of Notre-Dame-Ste-Eulalie has an elaborate belltower.

Célé

D802

D822

D41

D19

D86

②

③

D17

St Pierre-Toirac

D662

D127

Lot

alvignac

D8

⑤

Figeac ④
Excellent hotels and restaurants are located here, as well as the Musée Champollion, with its cast of the Rosetta stone.

Cajarc ⑤
Medieval houses still survive in this tiny village. A short drive away is the Renaissance Château de Cénevières.

| 0 kilometers | 5 |
| 0 miles | 5 |

KEY

▬▬ Tour route

═══ Other roads

Orchards and vineyards outside Agen

Agen ⑰

Lot-et-Garonne. 🏠 35,000. ✈ 🚉
🚌 ℹ 38 rue Garonne (05 53 47 36
09). 🏛 Tue–Sun. www.ot-agen.org

Vast orchards of regimented
plum trees – producing the
celebrated *pruneaux d'Agen* –
characterize the landscape
around this small provincial
city. Crusaders returning from
the Middle East brought the
fruit to France in the 11th
century, and monks in the Lot
valley nearby were the first to
dry plums for prunes in
commercial quantities.

Agen's **Musée Municipal des
Beaux-Arts** contains paintings
by Goya, including his *Ascent
in a Hot-Air Balloon*, Sisley's
September Morning, Corot's
landscape *L'étang de Ville
d'Avray*, and works by
Picabia. Undisputed jewel
of the collection is the
Vénus du Mas, a beautifully
proportioned marble statue

dating from the 1st century BC,
discovered nearby in 1876.

🏛 Musée Municipal des Beaux-Arts
Pl du Docteur Esquirol. **Tel** 05 53 69
47 23. 🏛 Wed–Mon. 🔴 Jan 1,
May 1, Nov 1, Dec 25. 🖼

Environs
The fortified village of Moirax,
5 miles (8 km) south of Agen,
has a 12th-century Roman-
esque church of great beauty
and symmetry. Two of the
appealingly sculpted capitals
depict biblical accounts of
Daniel in the lions' den, and
Original Sin.

The bastide town *(see p445)*
of Villeneuve-sur-Lot, 21 miles
(34 km) south of Agen, stands
astride the River Lot. It has a
tall, 14th-century tower that
once formed a defensive gateway. The red-brick Romano-
Byzantine church of Ste-
Catherine was built in 1909 but
contains restored 15th-century

stained-glass windows. Just to
the east of Villeneuve is the
pretty medieval hilltop village
of Penne D'Agenais.

Larressingle ⑱

Gers. 🏠 200. 🚌 to Condom.
ℹ Condom (05 62 28 00 80).

With its ramparts, ruined
donjon (defense tower), and
fortress gate, Larressingle is a
tiny fortified village in the
middle of the Gascon countryside. It dates from the 13th
century, and is one of the last
remaining Gascon villages
with its walls still intact. The
state of preservation is unique,
and gives an idea of what life
must have been like for the
small, embattled local communities who had to live for
decades under conditions of
perpetual warfare.

Condom ⑲

Gers. 🏠 7,500. 🚌 ℹ 50 bd de la
Libération (05 62 28 00 80). 🏛 Wed,
Sat am. www.tourisme-tenareze.com

Long a center for the
Armagnac trade, Condom is a
market town built around the
late-Gothic **Cathédrale St-
Pierre**. In 1569 during
the Wars of Religion, the
Huguenot (French Protestant)
army threatened to demolish
the cathedral, but Condom's
citizens averted this by paying
a huge ransom.

The river Baïse skirts the
town center. Notable among
Condom's fine 17th–18th-
century mansions is the **Hôtel
de Cugnac** on rue Jean-Jaurès,
with its ancient *chai* (wine
and spirit storehouse) and
distillery. On the other side of
the town center, the **Musée
de l'Armagnac** is the place to
find out, finally, what the
difference between the
brandy of Armagnac and
Cognac really is.

🏛 Musée de l'Armagnac
2 rue Jules Ferry. **Tel** 05 62
28 47 17. 🏛 Apr–Oct:
Wed–Mon; Nov–Mar:
Wed–Sun pms. 🔴 Jan, public
hols. 🖼 ♿

ARMAGNAC

Armagnac is one of the world's most expensive brandies. It is also one of the leading
products of southwest France: approximately
6 million bottles are produced annually, 45
percent of which are exported to 132
countries. The vineyards of Armagnac
roughly straddle the border between the
Gers and the Lot-et-Garonne regions
and the Landes. Similar in style to
Cognac, its more famous neighbor,
Armagnac's single distillation leaves
more individual flavors in the spirit.
The majority of small, independent
producers offer direct sale to the
public: look out for the battered,
often half-hidden farm signs
advertising *Vente Directe*.

A Tenarèze Armagnac

D'ARTAGNAN

Gascons call their domain the "Pays d'Artagnan" after Alexandre Dumas' rollicking hero from *The Three Musketeers* (1844). The character of d'Artagnan was based on Charles de Batz, a typical Gascon whose chivalry, passion, and impetuousness made him ideal as a musketeer, or royal bodyguard. De Batz's life was as fast and furious as that of the fictional hero, and he performed a feat of courtliness by arresting Louis XIV's most formidable minister without causing the slightest offense. The French have other opinions on the Gascon nature, too: a *promesse de Gascon,* for example, means an empty promise.

Statue of Dumas' musketeer d'Artagnan in Auch

windows show a mix of prophets, patriarchs, and apostles, with 360 individually characterized figures and exceptional colors. Three depict the key biblical events of Creation, the Crucifixion, and the Resurrection.

Auch went through an urbanization program in the 18th century, when the allées d'Etigny, flanked by the grand Hôtel de Ville and Palais de Justice, were built. Some fine houses from this period line the pedestrianized rue Dessoles. Auch's restaurants are known for their hearty dishes, including *foie gras de canard* (fattened duck liver).

Auch ⓴

Gers. 🏠 23,500. 🚉 🚌 ℹ️ 1 rue Dessoles (05 62 05 22 89). 🗓 Thu & Sat. www.auch-tourisme.com

The ancient capital of the Gers department, Auch (pronounced "Ohsh") has long been a sleepy place which comes alive on market days. The new town by the station is not a place which encourages you to linger. Head instead for the Old Town on the outcrop

Medallion from Cathédrale Ste-Marie

overlooking the river Gers. If you climb the 234 stone steps from the river, you arrive directly in front of the restored late-Gothic **Cathédrale Ste-Marie**, begun in 1489. The furnishings of the cathedral are remarkable: highlights are the carved wooden choir stalls depicting more than 1,500 biblical, historical, and mythological characters, and the equally magnificent 15th-century stained glass, attributed to Arnaud de Moles. The

Auvillar ⓶

Tarn-et-Garonne. 🏠 1,000. ℹ️ pl de la Halle (05 63 39 89 82).

A perfect complement to the high emotion of Moissac *(see pp442–3)*, Auvillar is one of the loveliest hilltop villages in France. It has a triangular marketplace lined with half-timbered arcades at its center, and extensive views from the promenade overlooking the river Garonne. There are picnic spots along this panoramic path plus an orientation map. This includes all but the chimneys visible in the distance, belonging to the nuclear plant at Golfech.

Sunflowers, a popular crop in southwest France grown for their seeds and oil

Moissac ㉒

Abbot Durand

At the core of this otherwise unremarkable riverside town is the abbey of St-Pierre, one of the undisputed masterpieces of French Romanesque art. Founded in the 7th century by a Benedictine monk, the abbey was subsequently ransacked by Arabs, Normans, and Hungarians. In 1047, Moissac abbey was united with the rich foundation at Cluny and prospered under the direction of Abbot Durand de Bredon. By the 12th century it had become the pre-eminent monastery in southwest France. The superb south portal was created during this period.

Abbey of St-Pierre
The church's exterior belongs to two periods: one part (in stone) is Romanesque, the other (in brick) is Gothic.

Tympanum
The lower register of the balanced, compact tympanum shows the expressive "24 Elders with crowns of gold" from St. John's vision.

Christ in Majesty
The figure of Christ sits in judgment at the center of the scene. He holds the Book of Life in His left hand and raises His right in benediction.

★ **South Portal**
The carved south portal (1100–1130) is a masterful translation into stone of St. John's dramatic vision of the Apocalypse (Book of Revelation, Chapters 4 and 5). The Evangelists Matthew, Mark, Luke, and John appear as "four beasts full of eyes." Moorish details on the door jambs reflect the contemporary cultural exchange between France and Spain.

VISITORS' CHECKLIST

Tarn-et-Garonne. 🏘 *13,000.* 🚊
🚌 **i** *6 pl Durand de Bredon
(05 63 04 01 85).* 🛒 *Sat & Sun
ams.* **Abbey** ◯ *daily.* **Cloisters**
◯ *daily (call for details).*
✝ *6:30pm Mon–Fri, 7:30pm Sat,
10:30am Sun.* 📷 📹
http://tourisme.moissac.fr

★ Cloister
*The late 11th-century
cloister is lined with
alternate double and single
columns in white, pink,
green, and gray marble.
In all, there are 76 richly
decorated arches.*

FLOOR PLAN: CHURCH AND CLOISTER

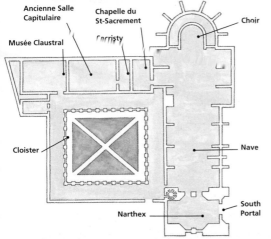

Ancienne Salle
Capitulaire

Chapelle du
St-Sacrement

Choir

Musée Claustral

Sacristy

Cloister

Nave

Narthex

South
Portal

Cloister Capitals
*Flowers, beasts, and
scenes from both the Old
and New Testaments are
featured in these superbly
sculptured 11th-century
Romanesque capitals.*

STAR FEATURES

★ South Portal

★ Cloister

Montauban ㉓

Tarn-et-Garonne. 🏘 *58,000.* 🚊 🚌
i *4 rue du Collège (05 63 63 60 60).*
🛒 *Sat, Wed.* **www**.montauban-
tourisme.com

Montauban deserves more
attention than it usually gets,
as Toulouse's little pink-brick
sister and the capital of the
17th-century "Protestant
Republic" of southern France.
The painter Ingres was born
here in 1780, and the town's
great treasure is the **Musée
Ingres**, a 17th-century palace
with an exceptional bequest
of paintings and 4,000 drawings, plus works by Van Dyck,
Tintoretto, Courbet, and sculptor Emile Bourdelle, an associate of Rodin, also from here.

Above all, Montauban is a
civilized shopping center, with
a double-arcaded main square
(place Nationale) built in the
17th and 18th centuries. A few
streets away lies the stark white
Cathédrale Notre-Dame, built
on the orders of Louis XIV in
1692, in the backlash against
Protestant heresy.

🏛 Musée Ingres
Palais Episcopal, 13 rue de l'Hôtel
de Ville. **Tel** *05 63 22 12 91.*
◯ *Tue–Sun (Jul–Aug: daily).* ● *Jan
1, Jul 14, Nov 1 & 11, Dec 25.* 📷

Gorges de l'Aveyron ㉔

Tarn-et-Garonne. ✈ *Toulouse.* 🚊
Montauban, Lexos. 🚌 *Montauban.*
i *Mairie, St-Antonin-Noble-Val
(05 63 30 63 47).* **www**.tourisme-
saint-antonin-noble-val.com

At the Gorges de l'Aveyron, the
sweltering plains of Montauban
change to cool, wooded hills.
Here the villages are of a
different stamp from those of
Périgord and Quercy, displaying an obsession with defense.

The château at Bruniquel,
founded in the 6th century, is
built over the lip of a preci-
pice. Farther along the D115,
the village of Penne's position
on the tip of a giant rock fang
is even more extreme. The
gorge narrows and darkens;
from St-Antonin-Noble-Val,
beside the river, the valley
turns toward Cordes.

Cordes ㉕

Tarn. 🏠 1,050. 🚗 🚆 ℹ️ pl Jeanne
Ramel-Cals (05 63 56 00 52). 🏛️ Sat.
www.cordessurciel.fr

Sometimes known as
Cordes-sur-Ciel, this is a
fitting description since the
town seems suspended
against the sky-line. During
the 13th-century Cathar
wars the entire town was
excommunicated. Devastating
epidemics of plague later
sent it into decline, and the
town was in an advanced
state of decay at the beginning of the 20th century.

Restoration work began in
the 1940s and the ramparts
and many of the gates built in
1222 have been well preserved.
Also intact are Gothic houses
like the 14th-century **Maison
du Grand Fauconnier**.

Today, Cordes still exudes
a sense of loss. The town of
which Albert Camus wrote
"Everything is beautiful there,
even regret," is now dependent
on tourism. "Medieval" crafts
aimed at visitors abound and
a collection at the **Musée
d'Art Moderne et
Contemporain** evokes Cordes'
former embroidery industry.
It also houses works of
modern art by such artists as
Picasso and Miro. The **Jardin
des Paradis** offers a corner
of beauty and hope.

🏛️ **Musée d'Art Moderne et
Contemporain**
Maison du Grand Fauconnier.
Tel 05 63 56 14 79.
⬜ mid-Mar–mid-Nov: daily.
⬛ Jan. 🈳 🚻

Cathédrale Ste-Cécile perched above the town of Albi

Albi ㉖

Tarn. 🏠 51,275. 🚗 🚆
ℹ️ pl Ste-Cécile (05 63 36 36 00).
🏛️ Tue–Sun. www.albi-tourisme.fr

Like many another large town
in this region, Albi is not only
red, but also red hot, and not
ideal for afternoon visits in
summer. You need to get up in
the cool early morning to
walk the streets around the
market and the cathedral.

Then make for the **Musée
Henri de Toulouse-Lautrec** in
the Palais de la Berbie ahead
of the crowds. The museum
contains the most complete
permanent collection of the
artist's work in existence,
including paintings, drawings,
and his famous posters for
the Moulin-Rouge. There are
also canvases by Matisse,
Dufy and Yves Brayer. After
a stroll around the beautiful
terraced gardens, step next
door to the vast red-brick
Cathédrale Ste-Cécile, built
in the aftermath of the
Albigensian crusade in 1265.
It was intended as a reminder
to potential heretics that the
Church meant business. From
a distance, its semicircular
towers and narrow windows
give it the appearance more
of a fortress than a place of
worship. Every feature, from
the huge belltower to the
apocalyptic fresco of the *Last
Judgement*, is on a giant scale,
built deliberately to dwarf the
average person. The effect is
breathtaking.

🏛️ **Musée Toulouse-Lautrec**
Palais de la Berbie.
Tel 05 63 49 58 97.
⬜ Apr–Sep: daily; Oct–Mar:
Wed–Mon.
⬛ Jan 1, May 1, Nov 1, Dec 25.
🈳 ♿ 🚻 🎧
www.musee-toulouse-lautrec.com

Castres ㉗

Tarn. 🏠 45,000. ✈️ 🚗 🚆
ℹ️ 2 pl de la République (05 63 62
63 62). 🏛️ Tue–Sun.
www.tourisme-castres.fr

Castres has been a center for
the cloth industry since the
14th century. Today it is also
the headquarters of one of
France's biggest pharma-
ceutical companies. In the
large collection of Spanish art
in the **Musée Goya**, the artist
himself is well represented by
a large, misty council scene
and by a series of powerful
prints, *Los Caprichos*. Outside,
the formal gardens between
the town hall and the river
Agout were designed in the
17th century by Le Nôtre
(*see p179*), the landscape
architect of Vaux-le-Vicomte
and Versailles.

🏛️ **Musée Goya**
Hôtel de Ville. **Tel** 05 63 71 59 30 or
05 63 71 59 27. ⬜ Jul–Aug: daily;
Sep–Jun: Tue–Sun. ⬛ Jan 1, May 1,
Nov 1, Dec 25. 🈳

TOULOUSE-LAUTREC

Comte Henri de Toulouse–
Lautrec was born in Albi
in 1864. Crippled at 15 as
a result of two falls, he
moved to Paris in 1882,
recording the life of the
city's cabarets, brothels,
racecourses, and circuses.
A dedicated craftsman, his
bold, vivid posters did
much to establish litho-
graphy as a major art form.
Alcoholism and syphilis
led to his early death at
the age of 36.

Lautrec's *La Modiste* (1900)

Bastide Towns

Bastide towns were hurriedly built in the 13th century by both the English and the French, to encourage settlement of empty areas before the Hundred Years' War. They are the medieval equivalent of "new towns," with their planned grid of streets and fortified perimeters. Over 300 bastide towns and villages still survive between Périgord and the Pyrenees.

A broad arcaded marketplace *is the central feature of most bastides. Montauban's arcades still shelter a variety of stores.*

The central square is surrounded by a grid of interconnecting streets and alleys. This differs markedly from the usual jumble of medieval houses and lanes.

Lauzerte, *founded in 1241 by the Count of Toulouse, is a typical bastide town of gray stone houses. The town, long an English outpost, is perched for security on the brow of a hill.*

The church could be used as a keep when the bastide's outer fortifications had been breached.

Stone houses protected the perimeter.

MONFLANQUIN
This military bastide town was built by the French in 1256 on a strategic north–south route. It changed hands several times during the Hundred Years' War.

Today, the bastides *form a convenient network of market towns, known as the* route des bastides. *The best time to visit them is on market day, when the central squares are crammed with stalls.*

Porte de la Jane *in Cordes is a typical bastide feature. These narrow gateways were easily barred by portcullises.*

Toulouse ㉘

Toulouse, the most important town in southwest France, is the country's fourth largest metropolis, and a major industrial and university city. The area is also famous for its aerospace industry (Concorde, Airbus, and the Ariane space rocket all originated here), as shown by the Cité de l'Espace just outside the city.

Best seen on foot, Toulouse has fine cuisine, one of France's most striking churches, lively street life, and a rose-brick Old Town, which is described as "pink at dawn, red at noon, and mauve at dusk."

The river Garonne, crossed by the Pont Neuf

Houseboats at their moorings on the Canal du Midi

Exploring Toulouse

This warm southern city has steadily expanded, crescent-like, from its original Roman site on the Garonne. First it was a flourishing Visigoth city, then a Renaissance town of towered brick palaces built with the wealth generated by the *pastel* (blue pigment) and grain trades. The grandest of these palaces still survive in the Old Town, centered around place du Capitole and the huge 18th-century **Hôtel de Ville**. Here, and in place St-Georges and rue Alsace-Lorraine, is the main concentration of shops, bars, and cafés. The city's large student population keeps prices down in the numerous cafés, oyster bars, and bookstores, and in the fleamarket, held on Sundays in place St-Sernin.

A ring of 18th- and 19th-century boulevards encircles the city, surrounded in turn by a tangle of autoroutes. The left bank of the Garonne is under development (St-Cyprien) and

is linked to Toulouse's driverless metro. The former abattoir has been superbly converted into a center for modern and contemporary art, **Les Abattoirs** (Wed–Sun), the highlight of which is Picasso's theater backdrop *Minotaur disguised as Harlequin*.

🏠 Les Jacobins

This church was begun in 1229 and completed over the next two centuries. It was the first Dominican convent, founded to combat dissent. The Jacobins' convent became the founding institution of Toulouse University. Its church, a Gothic masterpiece, features a soaring, 22-branched palm tree vault in the apse. The delicate Gothic Chapelle St-Antonin (1337) contains frescoes of the Apocalypse dating from 1341.

🏛 Musée des Augustins

21 rue de Metz. **Tel** 05 61 22 21 82.
🔲 daily. 🔲 Jan 1, May 1, Dec 25.
🖼 ♿ 🌐 www.augustins.org

Palm vaulting in the apse of Les Jacobins

Toulouse became a center of Romanesque art owing to its position on the route to Santiago de Compostela *(see p400)*. The museum has sculpture from the period and 12th-century Romanesque capitals, as well as cloisters from a 14th-century Augustinian priory. There are also 16th–19th-century French, Italian, and Flemish paintings here, including work by Ingres, Delacroix, Constant, and Laurens.

Façade of Musée des Augustins

♣ Fondation Bemberg

Hôtel d'Assézat, 7 pl d'Assézat. **Tel** *05 61 12 06 89.* ◯ *Tue–Sun.* ◯ *Jan 1, Dec 25.* 🎦 🚻 🖼
This 16th-century palace houses the collection of local art lover Georges Bemberg, and covers Renaissance paintings, 19th–20th-century French paintings, *objets d'art*, and bronzes.

♙ Basilique St-Sernin

Pl St-Sernin. **Tel** *05 61 21 80 45.* ◯ *daily.*
This is the largest Romanesque basilica in Europe, built in the 11th–12th centuries to accommodate pilgrims. Highlights are the octagonal brick belfry, with rows of decorative brick arches topped by an enormously tall spire. Beautiful 11th-century marble bas-reliefs of Christ and the symbols of the Evangelists by Bernard Gilduin are in the ambulatory.

🏛 Cité de l'Espace

Av Jean Gonord. **Tel** *08 20 37 72 23.* ◯ *daily in summer.* ◯ *Jan.* 🎦 🚻 🅿 🍴 🎁 **www**.cite-espace.com
Southeast of the city center, this vast "space park" includes two planetariums, interactive exhibits related to space exploration, the Terradome "film-experience" on the history of the earth, an IMAX theater, and a lifesize replica of the Ariane 5 rocket, where visitors can learn how, in theory at least, to launch rockets and satellites.

The tiered, 12th-century tower of Basilique St-Sernin

SIGHTS AT A GLANCE

Basilique St-Sernin ①
Fondation Bemberg ④
Le Capitole ②
Les Jacobins ③
Musée des Augustins ⑤

0 meters   250
0 yards   250

Key to Symbols *see back flap*

THE PYRENEES

PYRENEES-ATLANTIQUES · HAUTES-PYRENEES
ARIEGE · HAUTE-GARONNE

The mountains of the Pyrenees form a conspicuous frontier across southwestern France. Over centuries this remote terrain has fostered tenacious people, many descended from Spanish emigrants and refugees. Today it is the last remaining wilderness in southern Europe and a habitat for rare animal species.

Heading east from the Atlantic coast, the hills are wonderfully lush after the plains of Aquitaine. The deeper the Pyrenees are penetrated, the steeper the valley sides and the more gigantic the snow-clad peaks become. This is magnificent, empty, dangerous country, to be approached with caution and respect. In summer the region offers over 1,000 miles (1,600 km) of walking trails, as well as camping, fishing, and climbing. In winter there is both cross-country and downhill skiing at the busy resorts along the border, much livelier than their Spanish counterparts.

Historically, the Pyrenees are known as the birthplace of Henri IV, who put an end to the Wars of Religion in 1593 and united France, though the region has been characterized more often by independent fiefdoms. The region's oldest inhabitants, the Basque people *(see p455)* have maintained their own language and culture, and their resorts of Bayonne, Biarritz, and St-Jean-de-Luz reflect this, looking to the sea and to summer visitors for their livelihood.

Inland, Pau, Tarbes, and Foix rely on tourism and medium-scale industry, while Lourdes receives four million pilgrims every year. For the rest, life has been regulated by agriculture, though economic constraints today are causing an exodus from the land.

Countryside around St-Lizier, in the heart of the Pyrenean countryside

◁ Barèges, a ski resort and spa town in the Hautes-Pyrénées

Exploring the Pyrenees

The towering Pyrenees cut across southwest France from the Mediterranean to the Atlantic coast, encompassing the craggy citadel of Montségur, the pilgrimage center of Lourdes, Pau, capital of the hilly Béarn country, and the Basque port of Bayonne. This formidable range, an un-spoiled paradise for walkers, fishermen, and skiers, is as lush on its French side as it is arid in Spain, and contains the wild and beautiful Parc National des Pyrénées. Throughout the region, visitors can expect cool temperatures and grandiose scenery. Lovers of history and architecture will be richly rewarded by St-Bertrand-de-Comminges and St-Jean-de-Luz, among the region's important sights.

Marzipan sweets, a specialty of southwest France

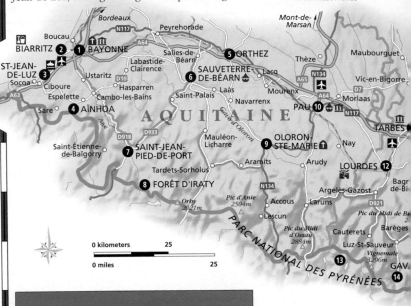

The galleried church in the Basque village of Espelette

GETTING AROUND

Access to the Basque coast in the western Pyrenees is via the A63/N10 from Bordeaux. The length of the Pyrenees, including the mountain valleys, is served by the A64, which runs from Bayonne to Toulouse, via Orthez, Pau, Tarbes and St-Gaudens. Once you are high up, expect narrow, twisting roads and slow driving. The scenic but demanding D918/D618 road crosses 18 high passes between the Atlantic and the Mediterranean.

There are airports at Biarritz, Pau and Lourdes. Both Pau and Lourdes, together with Orthez and Tarbes, are on the rail route which loops south between Bordeaux and Toulouse.

SIGHTS AT A GLANCE

Wild pottock ponies on moorland in the Forêt d'Iraty

St-Jean-de-Luz seen from Ciboure, across the Nivelle estuary

KEY

▬	Highway
▬	Major road
▬	Secondary road
▭	Minor road
▬	Scenic route
▬	Main railroad
---	Minor railroad
▬	International border
▬	Regional border
△	Summit

Bayonne ❶

Pyrénées-Atlantiques. 🗠 46,000.
🚉 🚌 ℹ pl des Basques (820 42
64 64). 🌐 daily. www.bayonne-
tourisme.com

Bayonne, capital of the
French Basque country, lies
between two rivers – the
turbulent Nive which arrives
straight from the mountains,
and the wide, languid Adour.
An important town since
Roman times because of its
command of one of the few
easily passable roads to
Spain, Bayonne prospered as
a free port under English rule
from 1154 to 1451. Since then
it has successfully withstood
14 sieges, including a particularly bloody one directed by
Wellington in 1813.

Grand Bayonne, the district
around the cathedral, can be
easily explored on foot. The
13th-century **Cathédrale
Ste-Marie** was begun under
English rule and is northern
Gothic in style. Look for the
handsome cloister and the
15th-century knocker on the
north door – if a fugitive could
put a hand to this, he was
entitled to sanctuary. The pedestrianized streets around form
a lively shopping area, especially the arcaded rue du Port
Neuf, with cafés serving hot
chocolate, a Bayonne specialty.
(Fine-quality chocolate-making
was introduced by the Jews
who fled Spain at the end of
the 15th century, and it has
remained a specialty of the

Lighthouse at Biarritz

town.) Bayonne is also
famous for its ham.

Petit Bayonne lies on the
opposite side of the quay-
lined river Nive. The **Musée
Basque** gives an excellent
introduction to the customs
and traditions of the Basque
nation, with reconstructed
house interiors and exhibits
on seafaring. Nearby, the
Musée Bonnat has a superb
art gallery. The first floor here
is a must for art lovers, with
sketches by Leonardo, Van
Dyck, Rubens, and Rembrandt
and paintings by Goya, Corot,
Ingres, and Constable.

🏛 **Musée Basque**
37 quai des Corsaires. **Tel** 05 59
59 08 98. ⬜ Tue–Sun (Jul–Aug:
daily). ⬤ public hols. 🎟 ♿ 🖬
www.musee-basque.com

🏛 **Musée Bonnat**
5 rue Jacques Lafitte. **Tel** 05 59 59
52. ⬜ Wed–Mon. ⬤ public hols.
🎟 ♿ www.musee-bonnat.com

Biarritz ❷

Pyrénées-Atlantiques. 🗠 27,000.
✈ 🚉 🚌 ℹ Javalquinto, square
d'Ixelles (05 59 22 37 00). 🌐 daily.
www.biarritz.fr

Biarritz, west of Bayonne, has
a grandiose center, but has
been developed along the
coast by residential suburbs.
The resort began as a whaling
port but was transformed into
a playground for the European
rich in the 19th century. Its
popularity was assured when
Empress Eugénie discovered
its mild winter climate during
the reign of her husband,
Napoleon III. The town has

three good beaches, with the
best surfing in Europe, two
casinos, and one of the last
great luxury hotels in Europe,
the Palais (see p586), formerly
the residence of Eugénie.

In the port des Pêcheurs, the
Musée de la Mer aquarium is
home to specimens of some
of the marine life found in the
Bay of Biscay. Below it, a narrow causeway leads across to
the Rocher de la Vierge, offering far-reaching views along
the whole of the Basque coast.
The Musée du Chocolat is fine
compensation for a rainy day.

🏛 **Musée de la Mer**
Esplanade du Rocher-de-la-Vierge,
14 plateau de l'Atalaye. **Tel** 05 59
22 75 40. ⬜ Apr–Oct: daily; Nov–
Mar: Tue–Sun. ⬤ Jan 1, 2nd–3rd
week Jan, Dec 25. 🎟 ♿ 🖬 🖬
www.museedelamer.com

Altar in Eglise St-Jean-Baptiste

St-Jean-de-Luz ❸

Pyrénées-Atlantiques. 🗠 14,500.
✈ Biarritz. 🚉 🚌 ℹ 20 bd Victor
Hugo (05 59 26 03 16). 🌐 Tue & Fri.
www.saint-jean-de-luz.com

St-Jean is a quiet fishing town
out of season and a scorching
tourist resort in August, with
stores to rival the chic rue du
Faubourg St-Honoré in Paris.
In the 11th century whale
carcasses were towed here
to feed the whole village.
The natural harbor protects
the shoreline, making it
one of the few beaches safe
for swimming along this
stretch of coast.

An important historical
event took place in St-Jean:
the wedding of Louis XIV
and the Infanta Maria Teresa

**Grand Bayonne, clustered around
the twin-spired cathedral**

St-Jean-de-Luz, a fishing village that explodes into life in summer

of Spain in 1660, a union that had the effect of sealing the long-awaited alliance between France and Spain, only to embroil the two countries ultimately in the War of the Spanish Succession. This wedding took place at the **Eglise St-Jean-Baptiste**, still the biggest and best of the great Basque churches, a triple-galleried marvel with a glittering 17th-century altarpiece and an atmosphere of gaiety and fervor. The gate through which the Sun King led his bride was immediately walled up by masons: a plaque now marks the place. The **Maison Louis XIV**, with its contemporary furnishings, is where the king stayed in 1660, and is worth a look.

The port is busy in summer, while the restaurants behind the covered markets serve sizzling bowls full of *chipirons* – squid cooked in their own ink – a local specialty. Place Louis XIV is a lovely place to sit and watch the world go by.

🏛 **Maison Louis XIV**
Place Louis XIV. **Tel** 05 59 26 27 58.
⬜ Apr–Oct: daily. 📷 🎥
www.maison-louis-xiv.fr

Environs
On the other side of the river Nivelle, Ciboure was the birthplace of composer Maurice Ravel. It is characterized by 18th-century merchants' houses, steep narrow streets,

and seafood restaurants. A two-hour coastal walk leads to the neighboring village of **Socoa**, where the lighthouse on the clifftop offers a fine view of the coast all the way to Biarritz.

Basque men in traditional berets

Aïnhoa ❹

Pyrénées-Atlantiques. 👥 680. 🚌
ℹ️ La Mairie (05 59 29 92 60).
www.ainhoa.fr

A tiny township on the road to the Spanish border, Aïnhoa was founded in the 12th century as a waystation on

the road to Santiago de Compostela *(see pp400–1)*. The main street of 17th-century whitewashed Basque houses and a galleried church from the same period survive.

Environs
There is a similar church in the village of Espelette nearby. Typically Basque in style, the galleries boosted the seating capacity and separated the men from the women and children. Espelette is the trading center for *pottocks*, an ancient local breed of pony, auctioned here at the end of January. It is also the shrine of the local crop, the red pimento pepper, especially in October when a pepper festival is held here.

At the foot of the St-Ignace pass lies the pretty mountain village of **Sare**. From the pass you can reach the summit of la Rhune by cog railroad. This provides the best vantage point in the entire Pays Basque. The descent on foot is worthwhile.

11th-century château, Espelette

Sauveterre-de-Béarn and the remains of the fortified bridge over the Gave d'Oloron, the Pont de la Légende

Orthez **5**

Pyrénées-Atlantiques. *11,000.*
*Maison Jeanne d'Albret, rue
Bourg Vieux (05 59 38 32 84).*
Tue; Nov–Mar: foie gras market Sat.
www.tourisme-bearn-gaves.com

Orthez is an important Béarn
market town, its 13th–14th-
century fortified bridge a vital
crossing point over the Gave
de Pau river in the Middle
Ages. It has a spectacular
Saturday morning market held
from November to February,
selling *foie gras*, smoked and
air-cured Bayonne hams, and
all kinds of fresh produce.
Fine buildings line the rue
Bourg Vieux, especially the
house of Jeanne d'Albret,
mother of Henry IV, on the
corner of rue Roarie. Jeanne's
enthusiasm for the Protestant
faith alienated both her own
subjects and Charles X, and
ultimately caused the Béarn
region to be drawn into the
Wars of Religion (1562–93).

Sauveterre-de-
Béarn **6**

Pyrénées-Atlantiques. *1,400.*
pl Royale (05 59 38 50 17).
Sat. **www**.tourisme-bearn-
gaves.com

An attractive market town,
Sauveterre is well worth a
night's stay. It has stunning
views over the Gave d'Oloron,
the graceful single arch of the
river's fortified bridge, and the
16th-century **Château de Nays**.
Fishermen gather here for the
annual world salmon-fishing
championships, in the fast-
flowing Oloron (April to July).

Be sure, also, to visit the
Château de Laàs, 5.5 miles
(9 km) along the D27 from
Sauveterre, which has an excellent collection of 18th-century
decorative art and furniture –
notably the bed Napoleon
slept in on the night after his
defeat at Waterloo. There is
also a pretty park with a maze.

🏛 **Château de Laàs**
Tel *05 59 38 91 53.* ☐ *Apr–Oct:
Wed– Mon (Apr: pm only; Jul–Aug:
daily).*

The Château de Nays at Sauveterre
in the Béarn region

St-Jean-Pied-
de-Port **7**

Pyrénées-Atlantiques. *1,700.*
*14 pl du Général de
Gaulle (0810 75 36 71).* ☐ *Mon.*
www.pyrenees-basques.com

The old capital of Basse-
Navarre lies at the foot of the
Roncesvalles Pass. Here the
Basques crushed the rear-
guard of Charlemagne's army
in 778 and killed its commander, Roland, later glorified
in the *Chanson de Roland*.

Throughout the Middle Ages
this red sandstone fortress-
town was famous as the last
rallying point before entering
Spain on the pilgrim road to
Santiago de Compostela *(see
pp400–1)*. As soon as a group
of pilgrims was spotted, the
townsfolk would ring the
church bells to show them the
way, and the pilgrims would
sing in response.

Visitors and pilgrims in all
seasons still provide St-Jean
with its income. They enter
the narrow streets of the upper
town on foot from the Porte
d'Espagne, and pass cafés,
hotels, and restaurants on the
way up. The ramparts are
worth the steep climb, as is the
citadel with panoramic views.

On Mondays the town hosts
a craft market, Basque *pelote*
games and, in summer,
shows with bulls.

...t d'Iraty ❽

...es-Aquitaine. 🚌 St-Jean-Pied-
...t 🚉 🛈 St-Jean-Pied-de-Port
...75 36 71), Larrau (05 59
...2 80).

...plateau of beech woods
...nd moorland, the Forêt
...'Iraty is famous for its cross-
country skiing and walking.
Here the ancient breed of
Basque ponies, the *pottocks*,
run half-wild. These creatures
have not changed since the
prehistoric inhabitants of the
region traced their silhouettes
on the walls of local caves.

The tourist office at St-Jean-
Pied-de-Port publishes maps
of local walks. The best begins
at the Chalet Pedro parking lot,
south of the lake on the Iraty
plateau, and takes you along
the GR10 to 3,000-year-old
standing stones on the western
side of the Sommet d'Occabé.

Oloron-Ste-Marie ❾

Pyrénées-Atlantiques. 👥 12,000. 🚉
🚌 🛈 allées du Compte de Tréville
(05 59 39 98 00). 🏪 Fri.
www.tourisme-oloron.com

Oloron, a small town at the
junction of the Aspe and the
Ossau valleys, has grown
from a Celtiberian settlement.
There are huge agricultural
fairs here in May and
September, and the town is
famed for producing the

Cathédrale Ste-Marie

famous classic French berets.
The town's great glory is the
doorway of the Romanesque
Cathédrale Ste-Marie, with its
biblical and Pyrenean scenes.
Spain lies just on the other
side of the Somport pass at

the head of the mountainous
Aspe valley, and the influence
of Spanish stonemasons is
evident in Oloron's **Eglise
Sainte-Croix** with its Moorish-
style vaulting.

Environs
Head up the Aspe valley to
try one of the area's famous
ewe's cheeses, or mixed cow
and goat's cheeses. A side
road leads to Lescun, huddled
around its church, beyond
which is a spectacular range
of saw-toothed peaks topped
by the **Pic d'Anie** at 8,215 ft
(2,504 m), one of the most
beautiful sights in the Pyrenees.
This is also one of the last
refuges of the Pyrenean
brown bear, whose numbers
have been drastically
diminished by human activity,
particularly hunting and the
building of roads and houses.

High moorland above the Forêt d'Iraty, long denuded of timber for use by the French and Spanish navies

Gobelin tapestry in the Château de Pau

Pau ⑩

Pyrénées-Atlantiques. 🏠 86,000.
❌ 🚉 🚌 ℹ️ pl Royale (05 59 27
27 08). 🗓️ Mon–Sat.
www.pau-pyrenees.com

A lively university town, with
elegant Belle Epoque
architecture and shady parks,
Pau is the capital of the Béarn
region, and the most interesting big town in the central
Pyrenees. The weather in the
fall and winter is mild, so this
has been a favorite resort of
affluent foreigners, especially
the English, since the early
19th century.

Pau is chiefly famous as the
birthplace of King Henry IV.
His mother, Jeanne d'Albret,
traveled for 19 days from
Picardy, in the eighth month
of her pregnancy, just to have
her baby here. She sang
during her labor, convinced
that if she did so, Henry
would grow up as tough as
she was. As soon as the infant
was born, his lips were
smeared with garlic and local
Jurançon wine, in keeping
with the traditional custom.

The town's principal sight
is the **Château de Pau**, first
remodeled in the 14th
century for the ruler of Béarn,
Gaston Phoebus (see p463).
It was heavily restored
400 years later. Marguerite
d'Angoulême, sister of the
King of France, resided here
in the late 16th century, and
transformed the town into a
center for the arts and free

thinking. The château's 16th-
century Gobelin tapestries,
made by Flemish weavers
working in Paris, are
fabulous. (The Maison Carrée
in Nay – 11 miles toward
Lourdes – exhibits the former
Musée Béarnais' important
collection of artifacts retracing
the history, traditions, and
culture of the Béarn.)

Outside, the boulevard des
Pyrénées affords glorious
views of some of the highest
Pyrenean peaks, which are
often snowcapped year
round. Continue from here to
the eclectic **Musée des Beaux-
Arts**, where there is a
splendid Degas, the *Cotton
Exchange, New Orleans*;
Rubens' *Last Judgment,* and
a work by El Greco.

♠ Château de Pau
Rue du Château. **Tel** 05 59 82 38 02.
🗓️ daily. ⬤ Jan 1, May 1,
Dec 25. 🎫 🧥 🚻
www.musee-chateau-pau.fr

🏛 Musée des Beaux-Arts
Rue Mathieu Lalanne **Tel** 05 59 27
33 02. 🗓️ Wed–Mon. ⬤ some
public hols. 🧥 🚻 restricted.

Tarbes ⑪

Hautes-Pyrénées. 🏠 46,500. ✈
🚉 🚌 ℹ️ 3 cours Gambetta
(05 62 51 30 31). 🗓️ Thu.
www.tarbes.com

Tarbes is the capital of the
Bigorre region and hosts a
major agricultural fair.
The **Jardin Massey** in the
middle of town was designed
at the turn of the 19th
century and is one of the
loveliest parks in the
southwest, with many rare
plants, including the North
American sassafras, and a
14th-century cloister with
finely carved capitals.

The **Maison du Cheval** and
the Haras National (National
Stud), with its thoroughbred
stallions, should not be missed.

🏛 La Maison du Cheval
Chemin du Mauhourat. **Tel** 05 62 56
30 80. 🗓️ daily pms. ⬤ public hols.
🧥 🎫 Jul–Aug & French school hols.

Lourdes ⑫

Hautes-Pyrénées. 🏠 16,000. ✈
🚉 🚌 ℹ️ pl Peyramale (05 62
42 77 40). 🗓️ Mon–Sat.
www.lourdes-infotourisme.com

Lourdes, one of the great
shrines of Europe, owes its
celebrity to visions of the
Virgin experienced by
14-year-old Bernadette
Soubirous in 1858. Five

Château de Pau, birthplace of Henry IV in 1553

◁ St-Lizier in the foothills of the Pyrenees

million people annually visit **Grotte Massabielle**, where the visions occurred, and rue des Petits-Fossés, where Bernadette lived, in search of a miracle cure. The **Musée de Lourdes** gives information about Bernadette and the shrine.

Visit the **Grottes de Bétharram** for underground rides by boat and train, or the **Musée Pyrénéen**, about the pioneers who opened up these ranges.

🏛 **Musée de Lourdes**
Parking de l'Egalité. *Tel* 05 62 94 28 00. ◯ Apr–Oct: daily; Nov–Mar: Mon–Sat. 🔲 ♿

🎿 **Grottes de Bétharram**
St-Pé-de-Bigorre. *Tel* 05 62 41 80 04. ◯ Feb–late Mar: Mon–Fri pms; late Mar–Oct: daily. 🔲 ♿ www.betharram.com

Spectacular limestone formations at the Grottes de Bétharram

Pilgrims participating in open-air mass at Lourdes

🏛 **Musée Pyrénéen**
Château Fort, rue du Fort. *Tel* 05 62 42 37 37. ◯ daily. ● Jan 1, Nov 1 & 11, Dec 25. 🔲

Parc National des Pyrénées ⑬

See pp460–61.

Luz-St-Sauveur ⑭

Hautes-Pyrénées. 🔲 1,200. 🔲 to Lourdes. 🔲 🔲 pl du 8 mai (05 62 92 30 30). ● Mon am. www.luz.org

Luz-St-Sauveur is an attractive spa town, with an unusual church built in the 14th century by the Hospitaliers de Saint Jean de Jérusalem (later the Knights of Malta), an order established to protect pilgrims. The church is fortified with gun slits that look out over the town and valley, and provided protection for pilgrims on the way to Santiago de Compostela.

Environs
The elegant spa town of **Cauterets** makes a good base for climbing, skiing, and walking in the rugged mountains of the Bigorre region.

Gavarnie is a former waystation on the Santiago de Compostela pilgrim route. A good track, accessible on foot or by donkey, leads from the village to the spectacular natural rock amphitheater known as the **Cirque de Gavarnie**. Here the longest waterfall in Europe, at 787 ft (240 m), cascades off the mountain into space, encircled by eleven 9,800-ft (3,000-m) peaks.

Tourists can now share much of the **Observatoire Pic du Midi de Bigorre** with scientists. Access is by cablecar from La Mongie to Le Taoulet and then up to the summit. Alternatively there are a number of walks up to the Pic (4 hours minimum).

The French are justly proud of the Observatory, which has supplied the clearest images of Venus and other planets so far obtained from Earth. The 3.2-ft (1-m) telescope mapped out the moon for NASA's Apollo missions.

🏛 **Observatoire Pic du Midi de Bigorre**
Tel 08 25 00 28 77. ◯ Jan, Apr, May, Dec: Wed–Mon; Feb, Mar, Jun–Sep: daily. ● Oct–Nov. 🔲 🔲 🔲 www.picdumidi.com

THE MIRACLE OF LOURDES

In 1858 a young girl named Bernadette Soubirous experienced 18 visions of the Virgin at the Grotte Massabielle near the town. Despite being told to keep away from the cave by her mother – and the local magistrate – she was guided to a spring with miraculous healing powers. The church endorsed the miracles in the 1860s, and since then, many people claim to have been cured by the holy water. A religious city of shrines, churches, and hospices has since grown up around the spring, with a dynamic tourist industry to match.

Bernadette's vision

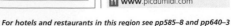

Parc National des Pyrénées ⓭

Pyrenean ibex

The Pyrenees National Park, designated in 1967, extends 62 miles (100 km) along the French and Spanish frontier. It boasts some of the most spectacular scenery in Europe, ranging from meadows glimmering with butterflies to high peaks, snow-capped even in summer. Variations in altitude and climate make the park rich in flora and fauna. One of the most enjoyable ways to see it is on foot: within the park are 217 miles (350 km) of well-marked footpaths.

Vallée d'Aspe
Jagged peaks tower above the Vallée d'Aspe and the Cirque de Lescun. A access road to Somport Tunnel has be built here (see p455).

OLORON-STE-MARIE

PAU

Laruns

PIC D'ANIE
2,504 m
(8,215 ft)

N134

D934

PIC DE LA SAGETTE
2,301 m
(7,550 ft)

PIC DU MIDI D'OSSAU
2,884 m
(9,462 ft)

Col du Somport, the Somport pass (5,354 ft/1,632 m), is a rugged route into Spain that is now by-passed by a tunnel.

Pic d'Anie
The limestone-flanked 8,215-ft (2,504-m) Pic d'Anie overlooks rich upland pastures watered by melting snow. In spring, the ground is ablaze with Pyrenean varieties of gentian and columbine, found nowhere else.

Pic du Midi d'Ossau
A tough trail leads from the Bious-Artigues lake a the base of the Pic du Midi d'Ossau and encircles the formidable tooth-shaped summit (9,462 ft/ 2,884 m).

PYRENEAN WILDLIFE

The Pyrenees are home to a rich variety of wild creatures, many of them unique to the range. The ibex, a member of the antelope family, is still numerous in the valleys of Ossau and Cauterets. Birds of prey include the Egyptian, griffon, and bearded vultures. Ground predators range from the rare Pyrenean lynx, to civet, pine marten, and stoat. The desman, a tiny aquatic mammal related to the mole, is found in many of the mountain streams.

Pyrenean fritillary *flowers through late spring and early summer in mountain pastures.*

The Turk's Cap Lily *flowers June–August on rocky slopes at up to 7,218 ft (2,200 m).*

rèche de Roland
*he famous breach in the sheer
rest of the Cirque de Gavarnie
rms a gateway for climbers
etween France and Spain.*

The GR10 long-distance trail
is one of the great walks of
France, linking the Atlantic
with the Mediterranean.

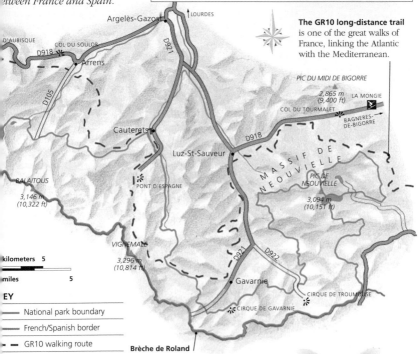

Argelès-Gazost
LOURDES
D'AUBISQUE
COL DU SOULOR
D918
Arrens
D105
Cauterets
PIC DU MIDI DE BIGORRE
2,865 m (9,400 ft)
LA MONGIE
COL DU TOURMALET
BAGNERES-DE-BIGORRE
D918
Luz-St-Sauveur
MASSIF DE NEOUVIELLE
PONT D'ESPAGNE
BALAITOUS
3,146 m (10,322 ft)
PIC DE NEOUVIELLE
3,094 m (10,151 ft)

kilometers 5
miles 5

EY
— National park boundary
— French/Spanish border
– – GR10 walking route

VIGNEMALE
3,296 m (10,814 ft)
D921
D922
Gavarnie
CIRQUE DE TROUMOUSE
CIRQUE DE GAVARNIE
Brèche de Roland

he Egyptian vulture *is seen
ll over the Pyrenees, especially
n rocky cliff faces.*

Pyrenean bears *are close to
extinction but a few still live in
the Ossau and Aspe valleys.*

Cleopatra

Scarce Swallowtail

These butterflies *are among
several colorful species found
at high altitudes.*

Arreau ⑮

Hautes-Pyrénées. 🚶 865. 🚌
ℹ️ *Château des Nestes (05 62 98 63 15).* 🛒 *Thu.* **www**.vallee-aure.com

Arreau stands at the junction of the rivers Aure and Louron. A small, bustling half-timbered town with good stores and restaurants, this is the place to buy the basics for hiking or fishing in the mountains. The town surrounds a handsome town hall with a covered marketplace beneath it. Next door is a 16th-century house, the Maison de Lys, which has a façade ornamented with the fleur-de-lis motif.

Environs
St-Lary Soulan is a nearby ski resort and a good base for exploring the entire Massif du Néouvielle. Head for the village of Fabian and the smattering of lakes above it, where the GR10 (*see p461*) and other well-marked trails criss-cross the peaks. Here you may see golden eagles or an enormous lammergeier.

St-Bertrand-de-Comminges ⑯

Haute-Garonne. 🚶 260.
🚉 *Montrejeau, then taxi.*
🚌 ℹ️ *Les Olivetains, parvis de la Cathédrale (05 61 95 44 44).*
🎵 *music festival (mid-Jul–end Aug).*

The pretty hilltop town of St-Bertrand is the most remarkable artistic and historic site in the Central Pyrenees and the venue for an acclaimed music festival

Cloisters in the Cathédrale Ste-Marie, St-Bertrand-de-Comminges

in summer (*see p37*). Some of the best sculpture in the region adorns the portal of the **Cathédrale Ste-Marie**. The adjoining Romanesque and Gothic cloisters contain sarcophagi, carved capitals, and statues of the four Evangelists.

St-Bertrand's origins lie on the plain below, in the city founded by the great Roman statesman Pompey in 72 BC. At that time it consisted of two thermal baths, a theater, a temple, a market, and a Christian basilica. All were destroyed by Gontran, the grandson of Clovis (*see p212*) in 585, and six centuries were to pass before the Bishop of Comminges, Bertrand de l'Isle, saw the site as a potential location for a new cathedral and monastery. The town, which was relatively unimportant in political terms, became a major religious center.

Inside the cathedral, look out for the 66 magnificent carved choirstalls and the 16th-century organ case. The tomb of Bertrand de l'Isle is situated at the far end of the choir, with

an altar beside it; the beautiful marble tomb in the Virgin's chapel just off the nave is that of Hugues de Châtillon, a bishop who provided funds for the completion of the cathedral in the 14th century.

🏛 **Cathédrale Ste-Marie**
Tel *05 61 89 04 91.* ⭕ *daily.*
⭕ *Sun am.* 📷 🎫 *cloisters.*

Fresco in the Cathédrale St-Lizier

St-Lizier ⑰

Ariège. 🚶 *1,500.* 🚌 ℹ️ *pl de l'Eglise (05 61 96 77 77).*
www.ariege.com/st-lizier

St-Lizier is located in the Ariège, a region famous for its steep-sided valleys and wild mountain scenery. The village dates back to Roman times, and by the Middle Ages was an important religious center. St-Lizier has two cathedrals; the finer is the 12th–14th-century **Cathédrale St-Lizier** in the lower town. It boasts Romanesque frescoes and a cloister with carved columns, but the **Cathédrale de la Sède** in the upper town has the better view.

The imposing 12th-century Cathédrale Ste-Marie in St-Bertrand

St-Lizier, with snow-capped mountains in the distance

Foix ⑱

Ariège. 🏠 10,000. 🚆 🚌 🚺 29 rue Delcassé (05 61 65 12 12). 🛒 Fri & 1st, 3rd & 5th Mon of each month. www.tourisme-foix-varilhes.fr

With its battlements and towers, Foix stands four-square at the junction of the rivers Arget and Ariège. In the Middle Ages, Foix's dynasty of counts ruled the whole of the Béarn area. Count Gaston Phoebus (1331–91) was the most flamboyant, a poet who wrote a famous treatise on hunting. He was a ruthless politician, who had his brother and his son put to death.

Some of the pleasures of the medieval court are re-created in the local summer fair, the largest in the southwest. At any time, the 15th-century keep of the **Château de Foix** is worth climbing just for the view. The restored 14th-century **Eglise de St-Volusien** is delightful in its simplicity and grace.

🏰 Château de Foix
Tel 05 34 09 83 83. ⭘ Wed–Mon & daily in sch hols. ⭘ Jan 1, Dec 25. 🎟 www.sesta.fr/chateau-de-foix.html

Environs
The **Grotte de Niaux**, 9 miles (15 km) south of Foix, has prehistoric cave paintings.

⛰ Grotte de Niaux
Tel 05 61 05 10 10. ⭘ by appt only. 🎟 🅿 oblig.

Montségur ⑲

Ariège. 🏠 100. 🚺 05 61 03 03 03. 🎟 🅿 for the château (summer only). www.montsegur.fr

Montségur is famous as the last stronghold of the Cathars *(see p491)*. From the parking lot at the foot of the mount, a path leads up to the small castle above, occupied in the 13th century by *faidits* (dispossessed aristocrats) and a Cathar community. The Cathars themselves lived outside the fortress, in houses clinging to the rock. Opposed to Catholic authority, Cathar troops marched on Avignonnet in 1243 and massacred members of the Inquisitional tribunal. In retaliation, an army of 10,000 laid siege to Montségur for 10 months. When captured, 205 Cathars refused to convert and were burned alive.

Mirepoix ⑳

Ariège. 🏠 3,300. 🚌 🚺 pl du Maréchal Leclerc (05 61 68 83 76). 🛒 Mon & Thu. www.tourisme-mirepoix.com

Mirepoix is a solid country bastide town *(see p445)* with a huge main square – one of the loveliest in the southwest – surrounded by beamed 13th–15th-century arcades and half-timbered houses.

The **cathedral**, begun in 1317 with the last additions made in 1867, has the widest Gothic nave (72 ft/22 m) in France.

The best times to visit the town are on market days, when stalls in the square sell a mass of local produce.

The arcaded main square at Mirepoix

THE SOUTH
OF FRANCE

Introducing the South of France

The South is France's most popular vacation region, drawing millions of visitors each year to the Riviera resorts and modern beach cities to the west. Agriculture is a mainstay of the economy, producing early fruits and an abundance of affordable wine. The new hi-tech industries of Nice and Montpellier reflect the region's key role in the developing south coast sunbelt, while Corsica still preserves much of its natural beauty. The map shows the major sights of this sun-blessed region.

Pont du Gard, *a 2,000-year-old bridge (see p495), is a major feat of Roman engineering. It was a key link in the 10.5-mile (17-km) aqueduct, parts of which were underground, carrying fresh water from a spring at Uzes to Nîmes.*

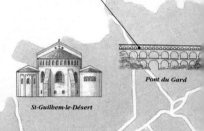

St-Guilhem-le-Désert

Pont du Gard

LANGUEDOC-ROUSSILLON
(See pp476–97)

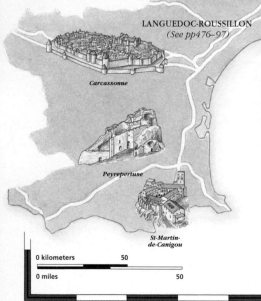

Carcassonne

Peyrepertuse

St-Martin-de-Canigou

The Camargue *lies at the mouth of the Rhône delta, where marshland and inland seas support a rich selection of wildlife. Three visitors' centers give a good introduction to this fragile area and its population of pink flamingoes and white horses (see pp510–11).*

| 0 kilometers | 50 |
| 0 miles | 50 |

Avignon, enclosed by massive ramparts, became papal territory when popes decamped from Rome (see p503) in the 14th century, taking up residence in the Palais des Papes which towers over the town. In the summer the town is the scene of the popular Avignon Festival.

alais des Papes, Avignon

Camargue

PROVENCE AND THE COTE D'AZUR
(See pp498–531)

Giacometti statue,
St-Paul-de-Vence

Musée Matisse, Nice

The Côte d'Azur *has attracted sunworshippers and celebrities since the 1920s (see pp474–5). The coast also offers some prize collections of 20th-century art (pp472–3) and yearly events such as the Cannes Film Festival and Antibes Jazz Festival.*

CORSICA
(see pp532–43)

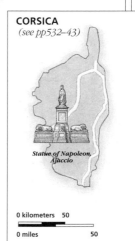

Statue of Napoleon,
Ajaccio

0 kilometers   50

0 miles   50

The Flavors of the South of France

Mediterranean France has a fresh, sunny cuisine, with ripe and flavorful fruit and vegetables, fresh fish and seafood, and lean meat from mountain pastures. Good dishes are enhanced by key ingredients: olive oil, garlic, and aromatic herbs. Markets are a colorful feast of seasonal produce all year round. Whether you opt for a picnic choice of local hams, sausage, bread, and cheese to eat on the beach, share a simple lunch of tomato salad and grilled fish or lamb in a village bistro, or indulge in the sophisticated cuisine of one of France's top chefs, you can be sure of food that is not only authentic and delicious, but healthy, too.

Local olives and olive oil

Preserving anchovies in seasoned olive oil in Languedoc-Roussillon

LANGUEDOC-ROUSSILLON

There is a robust Catalan flavor to the food of this region bordering Spain. Spices and almonds add an exotic touch to the fruit and vegetables produced in abundance on the Roussillon plain, and the grass-fed beef and lamb of the Mediterranean Pyrenees. Fish is plentiful: Sète is the largest fishing port on the French Mediterranean, huge oyster and mussel beds thrive in the saltwater lagoons of the coast, and the little fishing port of Collioure is famous for its anchovies. Local dishes include *brandade de morue*, a specialty of Nîmes, squid stuffed with anchovies, and snails with garlic and ham. Roussillon is famous for its peaches and apricots, and the cherries of Ceret are always the first to be harvested in France. Goat's milk is the main source of cheese, with round, orange-rinded Pélardon the most common.

PROVENCE

This is the land of the olive and of rich green olive oil. These are evident in a wide range of dishes, such as *aioli*, a rich mayonnaise of olive oil and garlic, served with vegetables or fish;

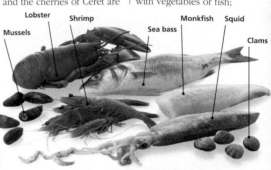

Lobster   Shrimp   Monkfish   Squid
Mussels   Sea bass   Clams

Selection of Mediterranean seafood available in the south of France

REGIONAL DISHES AND SPECIALTIES

The *cuisine du soleil*, "cuisine of the sun," has produced several classic dishes. *Bouillabaisse* is the most famous. The ingredients of this fish stew vary from place to place, though Marseille claims the original recipe. A variety of local seafood (always including *rascasse*, or scorpion fish) is cooked in stock with tomatoes and saffron. The fish liquor is traditionally served first, with croûtons spread with *rouille*, a spicy mayonnaise, and the fish served afterward. Once a fishermen's meal, it is now a luxury item you may need to order 24 hours in advance. A simpler version is *bourride*, a garlicky fish soup. Rich red wine stews, known as *daubes*, are another specialty, usually made with beef, but sometimes tuna or calamari. Other classics include *ratatouille* and *salade niçoise*.

Fresh figs

Artichauts à la barigoule
Small violet artichokes are stuffed with bacon and vegetables, cooked in wine.

Dried spices and herbs on sale at the market in Nice

tapenade, a purée of olives, anchovies, and capers; and *pissaladière*, a type of pizza made with onions, olives, and anchovies, with a distinct Italian accent. Vegetables play a leading role: courgettes (zucchini) or tomatoes stuffed in the Niçois style with meat, rice, and herbs; baby artichokes sautéed with bacon; or aromatic *pistou*, a bean and vegetable soup laced with a sauce of basil and garlic. Mediterranean fish is highly prized, and is often best appreciated simply grilled. Meat includes game and rabbit, Sisteron lamb, grazed on high mountain pastures, and the bull's meat stew of the Camargue, served with nutty local red rice. There is also ripe fruit aplenty, from juicy figs to fragrant Cavaillon melons to the vivid lemons of Menton.

CORSICA

The cuisine of Corsica is a robust version of the Mediterranean diet. Chestnuts were once the staple food of the island, and the flour is still widely used. There is a

Ripe chestnuts on the tree in a Corsican forest

huge variety of *charcuterie*, including flavorful hams and sausages, smoked, cured, or air-dried in the traditional way. Wild boar is a delicacy, stewed with chestnuts in red wine. Roast goat *(cabri roti)* is served as a festive meal, spiked with garlic and rosemary. Game, from rabbit to pigeon and partridge, is also very popular. On the coast there is locally caught fish and seafood, including monkfish, squid, sea urchins, and sardines, the latter most delicious stuffed with herbs and Brocciu, a ricotta-style soft cheese. Local honey is redolent of mountain herbs, and jams are made from a huge variety of ingredients.

ON THE MENU

Beignets des fleurs de courgette Courgette (zucchini) flower fritters.

Estoficada Salt cod stewed with tomatoes, potatoes, garlic, and olives.

Fougasse Flat olive oil bread often studded with olives.

Ratatouille Stew of aubergine (eggplant), tomatoes, courgettes (zucchini), and peppers.

Salade Niçoise Lettuce with hard-boiled egg, olives, green beans, tomatoes, and anchovies.

Socca Chickpea (garbanzo) pancakes, a specialty of Nice.

Tourte des blettes Pie of chard, raisins, and pine nuts.

Brandade de morue *Dried salted cod is cooked in water, then beaten with olive oil and milk to make a purée.*

Bœuf en daube *Beef is marinated in red wine, onions, and garlic, then stewed with orange peel and tomato.*

Crème catalane *Originating in Spain, this dessert is an egg custard topped with a flambéed sugar crust.*

France's Wine Regions: the South

A massive arc stretching from Banyuls, in the extreme southern corner of France, to Nice, close to the Italian border, encompasses the Mediterranean vineyards of Languedoc-Roussillon and Provence. This was for a century an area of mass-produced wine, and much is still of *vin de France* quality. Today, however, the more dynamic producers are applying new technology to traditional and classic grape varieties to revive southern France's nobler heritage of generous, warm, aromatic wines, redolent of sunbaked stone, the scent of wild herbs, and the shimmering waters of the Mediterranean.

Cellar sign, Banyuls

LOCATOR MAP

■ *Languedoc-Roussillon & Provence*

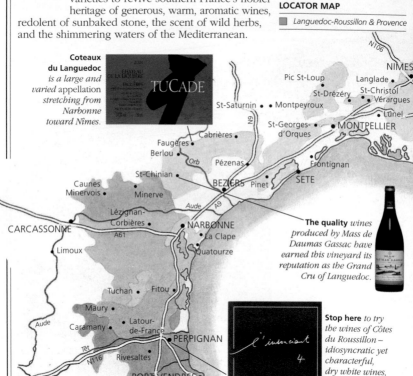

Coteaux du Languedoc *is a large and varied* appellation *stretching from Narbonne toward Nîmes.*

The quality *wines produced by Mass de Daumas Gassac have earned this vineyard its reputation as the Grand Cru of Languedoc.*

Stop here *to try the wines of Côtes du Roussillon – idiosyncratic yet characterful, dry white wines, dry rosés, and medium reds.*

0 kilometers   25

0 miles   25

KEY

■ Collioure & Banyuls	☐ Costières du Gard
■ Côtes de Roussillon	☐ Coteaux d'Aix en Provence
■ Côtes de Roussillon Villages	☐ Côtes de Provence
☐ Fitou	■ Cassis
☐ Corbières	☐ Bandol & Côtes de Provence
■ Minervois	☐ Coteaux Varois
☐ Coteaux du Languedoc	☐ Bellet

Rugged valley slopes in Corbières

Hand-picking grapes for Côtes de Provence red wine

WINE REGIONS

Both in the Provence wine region, east of Aix and
Marseille, and in the larger Languedoc-Roussillon
area to the west, new quality wine *appellations* such
as Cabardès (north of Carcassonne), are
joining the more familiar names.

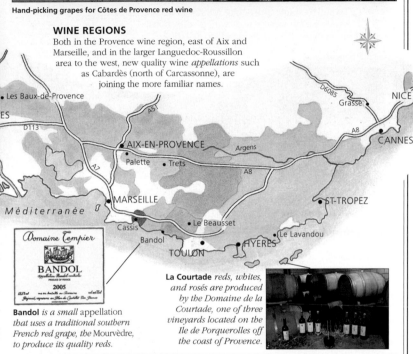

Bandol *is a small* appellation
*that uses a traditional southern
French red grape, the* Mourvèdre,
to produce its quality reds.

La Courtade *reds, whites,
and rosés are produced
by the Domaine de la
Courtade, one of three
vineyards located on the
Ile de Porquerolles off
the coast of Provence.*

KEY FACTS ABOUT WINES OF THE SOUTH

Location and Climate
A warm and sunny climate helps
to create generously alcoholic
wines. The flat coastal plains
support acres of vines, but generally the best
sites are on the schist and limestone hillsides.

Grape Varieties
Mass-production grapes such as
Aramon are giving way to quality
varieties such as **Syrah**,
Mourvèdre, and **Grenache**. **Cabernet
Sauvignon**, **Merlot**, and **Syrah**, and the
whites **Chardonnay**, **Sauvignon Blanc**, and
Viognier, are increasingly used for IGPs.
Rich, sweet whites are made from the
aromatic, honeyed **Muscat** grape.

Good Producers
Corbières & Minervois: La Voulte
Gasparets, Saint Auriol, Lastours,
Villerambert-Julien.
Faugères: Château des Estanilles,
Château de la Liquiere.
St Chinian: Château Cazal-Viel, Domaine
Navarre, Cave de Roquebrun.
Coteaux du Languedoc and IGPs:
Mas Jullien, Château de Capitoul, Domaine
de la Garance, Mas de Daumas Gassac,
Pech-Celeyran. *Roussillon*: Domaine Gauby,
Domaine Sarda Malet. *Provence*: Domaine
Tempier, Château Pibarnon, Domaine de
Trévallon, Mas de la Dame, Domaine
Richeaume, La Courtade, Château Simone,
Château Pradeaux, Château de Bellet.

Artists and Writers in the South of France

Monet's palette

Artists and writers have helped create our image of the South of France – the poet Stephen Liégeard even gave the Côte d'Azur its name in 1887. Many writers, French and foreign, found a haven in the warmth of the south. From Cézanne to Van Gogh, Monet to Picasso, artists have been inspired by the special light and brilliant colors of this seductive region. Today it is rich in art museums, some devoted to single artists like Matisse, Picasso, and Chagall, others with varied collections such as those in Céret, Nîmes, Montpellier, St-Tropez, St-Paul-de-Vence, and Nice *(see pp482–527)*.

Picasso and Françoise Gilot on the Golfe Juan, 1948

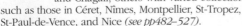

Paul Cézanne's studio in Aix-en-Provence *(see p511)*

THE WILD BEASTS

The Fauves, dubbed "Wild Beasts" for their unnaturally bright and wild colors, led one of the first 20th-century avant-garde movements, founded by Matisse in Collioure in 1905 *(see p29)*. Other Fauves included Derain, Vlaminck, Marquet, Van Dongen, and Dufy. Matisse visited Corsica in 1898, and then St-Tropez, and was inspired by the sensuality of Provence to paint the celebrated *Luxe, Calme, et Volupté*. Eventually he settled in Nice, where he painted his great series of Odalisques. He wrote, "What made me stay are the great colored reflections of January, the luminosity of daylight." The exquisite blue-and-white chapel he designed in Vence is one of the most moving of his later works *(see p523)*.

FESTIVE LIGHT

The Impressionists were fascinated by the effects of light, and Monet was entranced by "the glaring festive light" of the south which made colors so intense he said no one would believe they were real if painted accurately. In 1883 Renoir came with him to the south, returning often to paint his voluptuous nudes in the filtered golden light. Bonnard, too, settled here, painting endless views of the red tiled roofs and palm trees.

Post-Impressionists Van Gogh and Gauguin arrived in 1888, attracted by the region's rich colors. Cézanne, who was born in Aix in 1839, analyzed and painted the structure of nature, above all the landscape of Provence and his beloved Mont-Ste-Victoire. Pointillist Paul Signac came to St-Tropez to paint sea and sky in a rainbow palette of dots.

Vincent Van Gogh's *Sunflowers* (1888)

PICASSO COUNTRY

The South of France is, without question, Picasso country. His nymphs and sea urchins, his monumental women running on the beach, his shapes and colors, ceramics and sculpture are all derived from the hard shadows and bright colors of the south.

Pablo Picasso was born in Malaga in Spain in 1881, but he spent much of his life on the French Mediterranean, developing Cubism with Braque in Céret in 1911, and arriving in Juan-les-Pins in 1920. He was in Antibes when war broke out in 1939, where he painted *Night Fishing at Antibes*, a luminous nocturnal seascape. He returned in 1946 and was given the Grimaldi Palace to use as a studio. It is now a Picasso Museum *(see p521)*. He also worked in Vallauris, producing ceramics and sculptures *(see p522)*.

Deux Femmes Courant sur la Plage (1933) by Pablo Picasso

LOST CAVIAR DAYS

Just as F. Scott Fitzgerald wrote the Jazz Age into existence, he created the glittering image of life on the Riviera with *Tender is the Night*. He and Zelda arrived in 1924 attracted, like many expatriate writers, by the warm climate and the cheap, easy living. "One could get away with more on the summer Riviera, and whatever happened seemed to have something to do with art," he wrote. They passed their villa on to another American, Ernest Hemingway. Many other writers flocked there including Katherine Mansfield, D.H. Lawrence, Aldous Huxley, Friedrich Nietzsche, Lawrence Durrell, and Graham Greene. Some, like Somerset Maugham, led a glamorous lifestyle surrounded by exotic guests. Colette was an early visitor to St-Tropez, and in 1954, Françoise Sagan captured the youthful hedonism of the time in her novel, *Bonjour Tristesse*.

F. Scott and Zelda Fitzgerald with daughter

NEW REALISM

In the 1950s Nice produced its own school of artists, the *Nouveaux Réalistes*, including Yves Klein, Arman, Martial Raysse, Tinguely, César, Niki de Saint Phalle, and Daniel Spoerri *(see pp526–7)*. They explored the possibilities of everyday objects – Arman sliced violins, packaged and displayed trash; Tinguely exploded TV sets and cars. They had a light-hearted approach, "We live in a land of vacations, which gives us the spirit of nonsense," said Klein. He painted solid blue canvases of his personal color, International Klein Blue, taking the inspiration of the Mediterranean to its limit.

PROVENÇAL WRITERS

The regions of Provence and Languedoc have always had a distinct literary identity, ever since the troubadours in the 12th–13th centuries composed their love poetry in the *langue d'oc* Provençal, a Latin-based language. In the last century, many regional writers have been inspired by the landscape and local traditions. They were influenced by the 19th-century Felibrige movement to revive the language, led by Nobel prize-winning poet Frédéric Mistral. Some, like Daudet and film-maker turned writer Marcel Pagnol, celebrate the Provençal character; others, such as Jean Giono, explore the connection between nature and humanity.

Frédéric Mistral in the *Petit Journal*

L'HOMMAGE DE LA PROVENCE A MISTRAL

Beaches in the South of France

The glamorous Mediterranean coast is France's foremost vacation playground. To the east lie the Riviera's big, traditional resorts such as Menton, Nice, Cannes, and Monte-Carlo. To the west are smaller resorts in coves and bays like St-Tropez and Cassis. Farther on is the Camargue reserve at the mouth of the Rhône. West of the Rhône, making a majestic curve reaching almost to the Spanish border, is the long, sandy shore of Languedoc-Roussillon, where a string of purpose-built resorts range from modernistic beach cities to replicas of fishing villages.

The beaches are sandy west of Antibes; eastward, they are naturally shingly, so any sand is imported. Anti-pollution drives mean that most beaches are now clean, except in a few spots west of Marseille and around Nice. Beaches around towns often charge fees but are usually well equipped.

The Carlton Hotel logo

A rail poster by Domergue advertising the Côte d'Azur

0 kilometers   25

0 miles   25

Sète *(p492)* is a seaport with a network of canals. Stretching southward are 9.5 miles (15 km) of unspoiled, sandy beaches with lots of room, even in high season.

Stes-Maries-de-la-Mer *(p510)*, set among the sand dunes of the Camargue, offers white sandy beaches and a naturist beach 4 miles (6 km) to the east. Horse-riding is available.

Cap d'Agde (p487) *is a vast modern resort with long, golden sandy beaches and sports facilities of all kinds. It has Europe's largest naturist resort, accommodating 20,000 visitors.*

La Grande-Motte (p495) *is a huge purpose-built beach resort with excellent sports facilities, famous for its bizarre ziggurat architecture.*

In Victorian times *the Côte d'Azur, or Riviera, was the fashionable vacation venue of Europe's royalty and rich. They came to gamble and escape northern winters. Summer bathing did not come into vogue until the 1920s. Today the Riviera is busy all year round with the glamorous beaches and nightlife still a major attraction.*

Menton *(p529)* has a warm climate in winter, giving beach weather all year. Its sheltered, shingly beaches are backed by beautiful villas.

Cannes *(p520) takes great pride in its golden beaches, keeping them scrupulously clean: most are private with entrance fees.*

Cassis *(p513) is a charming fishing village with a popular casino, white cliffs, and some lovely hidden creeks nearby.*

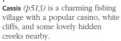

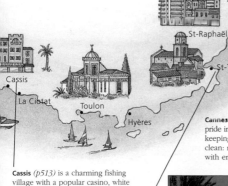

Cap Ferrat (p528) *is a wooded peninsula which has a 6-mile (10-km) craggy cliff walk offering glimpses of grand villas and private beaches.*

St-Tropez (p516) *is flanked by golden beaches mostly occupied by stylish "clubs" offering amenities at a price.*

Nice (p526), *has a visually dramatic waterfront with a wide, handsome promenade, but the beach itself is stony and has a busy highway alongside.*

LANGUEDOC-ROUSSILLON

AUDE · GARD · HERAULT · PYRENEES-ORIENTALES

*T**he two distinct provinces of Languedoc and Roussillon stretch from the foothills of the Pyrenees on the Spanish border to the mouth of the Rhône. The flat beaches and lagoons of the coast form a purpose-built sunbelt accommodating millions of vacationers every year. In between is a dry, sunburned land producing half of France's table wine and the season's first peaches and cherries.*

Beyond such sensuous pleasures are many layers of history, not least the unification of the two provinces. The formerly independent Languedoc once spoke Occitan, the tongue of the troubadours, and still cherishes its separate identity. Roussillon was a Spanish possession until the treaty of the Pyrenees in 1659. Its Catalan heritage is displayed everywhere from the road signs to the Sardana dance, and the flavor of Spain is evident in the popularity of bullfights, paella, and gaudily painted façades.

This stretch of coastline was the first place in Gaul to be settled by the Romans, their enduring legacy evident in the great amphitheater at Nîmes and the magnificent engineering of the Pont du Gard. The abbeys of St-Martin-du-Canigou, St-Michel-de-Cuxa, and St-Guilhem-le-Désert are superb examples of early Romanesque architecture, unaffected by Northern Gothic. The great craggy Cathar castles and the perfectly restored medieval Cité of Carcassonne bear witness to the bloody battles of the Middle Ages.

In parts, the region remains wild and untamed: from the high plateaus of the Cerdagne, to the wild hills of the Corbières or the remote uplands of Haut Languedoc. But it also has the most youthful and progressive cities in France: Montpellier, the ancient university city and capital of the region, and Nîmes with its exuberant *feria* and bullfights. The whole area is typified by an insouciant mixture of ancient and modern, from Roman temples and postmodern architecture in its cities to solar power and ancient abbeys in the mountains.

A sunny stretch of coastline at Cap d'Agde

◁ **The abbey of Saint-Martin-du-Canigou perched on Mount Canigou**

Exploring Languedoc-Roussillon

Languedoc-Roussillon combines miles of gentle
coastline with a rugged hinterland. Its clean, sandy
beaches are perfect for family holidays, with resorts
ranging from traditional fishing villages to new
purpose-built resorts. Inland is quieter, with acres of
vineyards in the Corbières and Minervois and
mountain walks in the Haut Languedoc and
Cerdagne. A rich architectural heritage ranges from
Roman to Romanesque, contrasting with the
modern, vibrant atmosphere of the main cities.

**Jousting on the canal, a regular
summer event in Sète**

SIGHTS AT A GLANCE

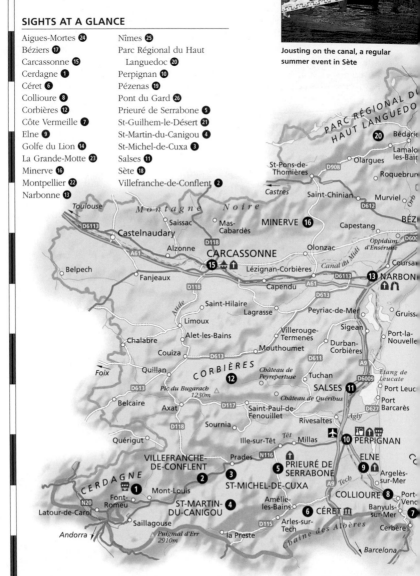

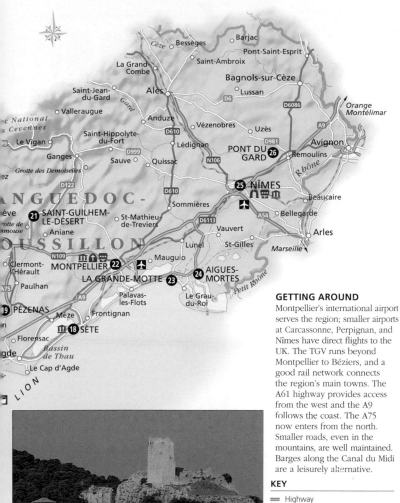

Barjac
Bessèges
Pont-Saint-Esprit
Cèze
La Grand-
Combe
Saint-Ambroix
Saint-Jean-
du-Gard
Alès
Bagnols-sur-Cèze
Lussan
Vallerauge
D6
D6086
Orange
Montélimar
Parc National
des Cévennes
Anduze
Vézenobres
Uzès
A9
Le Vigan
Saint-Hippolyte-
du-Fort
D610
Lédignan
PONT DU
GARD 26
D981
Avignon
Ganges
Sauve
Quissac
D999
N106
Remoulins
Rhône
Grotte des Demoiselles
D122
D610
NÎMES
Beaucaire
ANGUEDOC-
Sommières
25
SAINT-GUILHEM-
LE-DÉSERT 21
St-Mathieu-
de-Treviers
Bellegarde
rotte de
mouse
Aniane
D6113
Vauvert
A54
Arles
OUSSILLON
Lunel
St-Gilles
Marseille
Clermont-
l'Hérault
N109
MONTPELLIER 22
Mauguio
AIGUES-
MORTES 24
Paulhan
LA GRANDE-MOTTE 23
Petit Rhône
A9
PÉZENAS 19
Palavas-
les-Flots
Mèze
Frontignan
Le Grau-
du-Roi
Florensac
SÈTE 18
Bassin
de Thau
Le Cap d'Agde
LION

GETTING AROUND

Montpellier's international airport
serves the region; smaller airports
at Carcassonne, Perpignan, and
Nîmes have direct flights to the
UK. The TGV runs beyond
Montpellier to Béziers, and a
good rail network connects
the region's main towns. The
A61 highway provides access
from the west and the A9
follows the coast. The A75
now enters from the north.
Smaller roads, even in the
mountains, are well maintained.
Barges along the Canal du Midi
are a leisurely alternative.

KEY

▬▬	Highway
▬▬	Major road
▬▬	Secondary road
══	Minor road
▬	Scenic route
▬▪▬	Main railroad
---	Minor railroad
▬▬	International border
▬▬	Regional border
△	Summit

0 kilometers   25

0 miles   25

The ruined Barbarossa tower at Gruissan on the Golfe du Lion

Cerdagne ❶

Pyrénées-Orientales. ✈ Perpignan.
🚆 🚌 Mont Louis, Bourg Madame.
ℹ Mont Louis (04 68 04 21 97).
www.mont-louis.net

The remote Cerdagne, an independent state in the Middle Ages, is today divided between Spain and France. Its high plateaus offer skiing and walking among clear mountain lakes and pine and chestnut forests. The Little Yellow Train is an excellent way to sample it in a day. Stops include **Mont Louis**, a town fortified by Vauban, Louis XIV's military architect, which still accommodates French troops; the huge ski resort of **Font-Romeu**, **Latour-de-Carol**, and the tiny village of **Yravals** below it. Nearby **Odeillo** is the site of a huge solar furnace, 150 ft (45 m) tall and 165 ft (50 m) wide. Established in 1969, its giant curved mirrors create a remarkable sight in the valley.

Villefranche-de-Conflent ❷

Pyrénées-Orientales. 🚶 240. 🚆 🚌
ℹ pl de l'Eglise (04 68 96 22 96).

In medieval times Villefranche's position at the narrowest point of the Têt valley made it an eminently defensible fortress against Moorish invasion. Today, fragments of 11th-century walls remain, along with massive ramparts, gates, and Fort Liberia high above the gorge, all built by Vauban

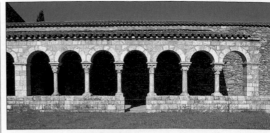
Abbey cloisters of St-Michel-de-Cuxa

in the 17th century. The 12th-century **Eglise de St-Jacques** has fine carved capitals from the workshops of St-Michel-de-Cuxa, and Catalan painted wooden statues, including a 14th-century *Virgin and Child*. The 13th-century oak door is embellished with intricate local wrought ironwork, a craft which still features on many of the shop signs in town. From the streets

Statue in St-Jacques, Villefranche

of locally quarried pink marble you can make the climb up to the **Grottes des Canalettes**, a superb underground setting for concerts. The Little Yellow Train will take you to the magnificent mountain plain of the Cerdagne (call 08 06 88 60 91 to reserve your seat).

St-Michel-de-Cuxa ❸

Prades, Pyrénées-Orientales. **Tel** 04 68 96 15 35. ◯ daily. ⬤ Sun am, religious hols. 📷

Prades, a small, pink marble town in the Têt valley, is typical of the local style. The **Eglise St-Pierre** has a southern Gothic wrought iron belfry and a Baroque Catalan interior. But the town is distinguished by the beautiful pre-Romanesque abbey of St-Michel-de-Cuxa which lies 2 miles (3 km) farther up the valley, and by the legacy of the Spanish cellist Pablo Casals. Casals spent many years here in exile from Franco's Spain; every August the abbey provides the setting for the Prades music festival held in his memory.

An early example of monastic architecture, St-Michel-de-Cuxa abbey was founded by Benedictine monks in 878 and rapidly became renowned throughout France and Spain. Distinctive keyhole arches showing Moorish influence pierce the massive walls of the abbey church, which was consecrated in 974. The mottled pink marble cloisters, with their superbly carved capitals, were added later, in the 12th century.

After the Revolution the building was abandoned, and

THE LITTLE YELLOW TRAIN

Arrive early for the best seats in the railroad cars of *Le Petit Train Jaune* which winds its way on narrow-gauge tracks through gorges and across towering viaducts up into the Cerdagne, stopping at small mountain stations along the way. Built in 1910 to improve access to the mountains, it now operates mainly for tourists, beginning at Villefranche-de-Conflent and terminating at Latour-de-Carol.

The Little Yellow Train, with open cars for summer visitors

For hotels and restaurants in this region see pp588–90 and pp643–6

its famous carvings looted. From 1913, George Grey Bernard, a visiting American artist, began to discover some of the capitals incorporated in local buildings. He sold the carvings to the Metropolitan Museum of Art in New York in 1925, where they formed the basis of the Cloisters Museum – a faithful re-creation of a Romanesque abbey in the unlikely setting of Manhattan.

St-Martin-du-Canigou ❹

Casteil. *Tel 04 68 05 50 03.*
☐ *(guided tours only: tour lasts 1 hour; times vary with seasons) Jun–Sep: daily; Oct–May: Tue–Sun.* ● *Jan.* 🦽

Saint-Martin-du-Canigou is situated in a spectacularly remote site a third of the way up Pic du Canigou, on a jagged spur of rock approached only by jeep or a 40-minute climb on foot from Casteil or by renting a jeep from Vernet-les-Bains. The abbey was built between 1001 and 1026, and financed by Guifred, Count of Cerdagne, who abandoned his family and entered the monastery in 1035. He was buried there 14 years later in a tomb he carved from the rock himself, which can still be seen. The church is early

Nun at St-Martin

Serrabone priory's chapel tribune, with columns of local marble

Romanesque, based on a simple basilican plan. Two churches are built, quite literally one on top of the other, making the lower church the crypt for the upper building.

The abbey complex is best viewed from above by continuing up the path. From there, its irregular design clinging to the rock is framed by the dramatic mountain setting – the ensemble a tribute to the ingenuity and vitality of its early builders.

Prieuré de Serrabone ❺

Boule d'Amont. *Tel 04 68 84 09 30 (tourist office).* ☐ *daily.* ● *Jan 1, May 1, Nov 1, Dec 25.* 🦽

Perched high up on the northern flanks of Pic du Canigou, the sacred mountain of the Catalans, is the priory of Serrabone. A final lap of hairpin bends on the approach road (the D618) reveals the simple square tower and round apse of this remote Romanesque abbey, surrounded by a botanical garden of local herbs and woodland plants clinging to the mountainside.

Inside the cool, austere 12th-century building is a surprisingly elaborate chapel tribune, its columns and arches glowing from the local red-veined marble, carved by the anonymous Master of Cuxa, whose work appears throughout the region. Note the strange beasts and verdant flora featured in the capital carvings, especially the rose of Roussillon.

The 11th-century cloister of St-Martin-du-Canigou

Céret ❻

Pyrénées-Orientales. 🏠 *8,000.* 🚃
ℹ️ *av Clémenceau (04 68 87 00 53).*
🏪 *Sat, Tue eve Jul–Aug.* 🎉 *Fête des Cerises (May/Jun).* **www**.ot-ceret.fr

Céret is a cherry town, surrounded by a cloud of pink blossom in the early spring, and producing the very first fruits of the year. The tiled and painted façades and loggias of the buildings have a Spanish feel and the town was popular with Picasso, Braque, and Matisse. Today Céret is distinguished by the **Musée d'Art Moderne**, its sophisticated modern architecture housing a remarkable collection which includes Catalan artists Tapiès and Capdeville, 50 works donated by Picasso, including a series of bowls painted with bullfighting scenes, and works by Matisse, Chagall, Juan Gris, and Salvador Dalí.

The town's Catalan heritage is evident in regular bullfights held in the arena, and in its Sardana dance festivals in July.

🏛 Musée d'Art Moderne
8 bd Maréchal Joffre. **Tel** *04 68 87 27 76.* 🕐 *Apr–Sep: daily; Oct–Mar: Wed–Mon.* 🔴 *some public hols.*
📷 ♿ **www**.musee-ceret.com

Environs
From Céret the D115 follows the Tech valley to the spa

Statue by Aristide Maillol, Banyuls

town of **Amélie-les-Bains**, where fragments of Roman baths have been discovered. Beyond, in **Arles-sur-Tech**, the Eglise de Ste-Marie contains 12th-century frescoes, and a sarcophagus beside the church door which, according to local legend, produces drops of unaccountably pure water every year.

Catalan flag

Côte Vermeille ❼

Pyrénées-Orientales. ✈️ *Perpignan.*
🚉 *Collioure, Cerbère.* 🚌 *Collioure, Banyuls-sur-Mer.* ℹ️ *Collioure (04 68 82 15 47), Cerbère (04 68 88 42 36).* **www**.collioure.com

Here the Pyrenees meet the Mediterranean, the coast road twisting and turning around secluded pebbly coves and rocky outcrops. The *vermeille* (vermilion-tinted) rock of the headlands gives this stretch of coast, the loveliest in the region, its name.

The Côte Vermeille extends all the way to the Costa Brava in northern Spain. With its Catalan character, it is as redolent of Spain as of France. **Argelès-Plage** has three sandy beaches and a palm-fringed promenade, and is the largest camping center in Europe. The small resort of **Cerbère** is the last French town before the border, flying the red and gold Catalan flag to signal its true allegiance. All along the coast, terraced vineyards cling to the rocky hillsides, producing strong, sweet wines like Banyuls and Muscat. The difficult terrain makes harvesting a laborious process. Vines were first cultivated here by Greek settlers in the 7th century BC, and Banyuls itself has wine cellars dating back to the Middle Ages.

Banyuls is also famous as the birthplace of Aristide Maillol, the 19th-century sculptor, whose work can be seen all over the region. **Port Vendres**, with fortifications built by the indefatigable Vauban (architect to Louis XIV) is a fishing port, renowned for its anchovies and sardines.

The spectacular Côte Vermeille, seen from the coast road south of Banyuls

For hotels and restaurants in this region see pp588–90 and pp643–6

Collioure harbor, with one of its beaches and the Eglise Notre-Dame-des-Anges

Collioure ⑧

Pyrénées-Orientales. 🚶 3,000.
🚆 🚌 ℹ pl du 18 juin
(04 68 82 15 47). 🛒 Wed & Sun.
www.collioure.com

The colors of Collioure first attracted Matisse here in 1905: brightly stuccoed houses sheltered by cypresses and gaily painted fishing boats, all bathed in the famous luminous light and washed by a gentle sea. Other artists including André Derain worked here under Matisse's influence and were dubbed *fauves* (wild beasts) for their wild experiments with color. Art galleries and souvenir stores now fill the cobbled streets, but this small fishing port has changed little since then, with anchovies still its main business. Two salting houses, which can be visited, are evidence of this tradition.

Three sheltered beaches, both pebble and sand, nestle around the harbor, dominated by the bulk of the **Château Royal**, which forms part of the harbor wall. It was first built by the Knights Templar in the 13th century, and Collioure became the main port of entry for Perpignan, remaining under the rule of Spanish Aragon until France took over in 1659. The outer fortifications were reinforced ten years later by Vauban, who demolished much of the

original town in the process. Today the château can be toured, or visited for its exhibitions of modern art.

The **Eglise Notre-Dame-des-Anges** on Collioure's quayside was rebuilt in the 17th century to replace the church which was destroyed by Vauban. A former lighthouse was incorporated as a belltower. Inside the church are no fewer than five Baroque altarpieces by Joseph Sunyer and other Catalan masters of the genre.

Be warned that Collioure is extremely popular in July and August, with visitors cramming the tiny streets. Long lines of traffic are possible, too, though the building of another route, the D86, has helped to ease congestion.

⚓ Château Royal
Tel 04 68 82 06 43. ☐ daily.
🔴 Jan 1, May 1 & Dec 25. 🈂

Elne ⑨

Pyrénées-Orientales. 🚶 8,000. 🚆 🚌
ℹ pl Sant-Jordi (04 68 22 05 07).
🛒 Mon, Wed, Fri. www.ot-elne.fr

The ancient town of Elne accommodated Hannibal and his elephants in 218 BC on his epic journey to Rome, and was one of the most important towns in Roussillon until the 16th century. Today it is famed for the 11th-century **Cathédrale de Ste-Eulalie et Ste-Julie**, with its superb cloister. Milky blue-veined marble has been carved into exquisite capitals, embellished with a riot of flowers, figures, and arabesques. The side nearest the cathedral dates from the 1100s; the remaining three are 13th–14th-century. From the front of the cathedral are views of the vines and orchards of the surrounding plain.

Carved capital at Elne, showing "The Dream of the Magi"

Entrance to the Palais des Rois de Majorque, Perpignan

Perpignan ⑩

Pyrénées-Orientales. 🏛 *120,000.*
✈ 🚃 🚌 ℹ *Palais des Congrès
(04 68 66 30 30).* 🕭 *daily.*
www.perpignantourisme.com

Catalan Perpignan has a
distinctly southern feel, with
palm trees lining the Têt river
promenade, house and store
façades painted vibrant
turquoise and pink, and the
streets of the Arab quarter
selling aromatic spices, couscous, and paella.

Today Perpignan is the
vibrant capital of Roussillon,
and has an important position
on the developing Mediterranean sunbelt. But it reached
its zenith in the 13th and 14th
centuries under the kings of
Majorca and the kings of
Aragón, who controlled great
swathes of northern Spain
and southern France. Their
vast **Palais des Rois de
Majorque** still straddles a
substantial area in the
southern part of the city.

Perpignan's strong Catalan
identity is evident during the
twice-weekly summer cel-
ebrations when the Sardana
is danced in the
place de la
Loge. It is a
key Catalan
symbol. Arms raised,
concentric circles of
dancers keep step to the
accompaniment of a
Catalan woodwind band.

One of Perpignan's finest
buildings, the **Loge de Mer**
lies at the head of the
square. Built in 1397 to
house the Maritime
Exchange, only the eastern
section retains the original
Gothic design. The rest of
the building was rebuilt
in Renaissance style in
1540 with sumptuous
carved wooden ceilings
and sculpted window frames.
While visitors are sometimes

**Devout Christ
in St-Jean**

offended by the sight of a
fast-food restaurant inside, the
result is that the Loge de Mer
has avoided becoming a
hushed museum piece.
Instead, it remains the
center of
Perpignan life
– elegant cafés
cluster around it,
producing a constant
buzz of activity.

Next door is the **Hôtel
de Ville** with its pebble
stone façade and wrought
iron gates. Inside, parts
of the arcaded courtyard
date back to 1315; at the
center is Aristide Maillol's
allegorical sculpture, *The
Mediterranean* (1950).

To the east is the laby-
rinthine cathedral
quarter of St-Jean, made
up of small streets and
squares containing
some fine 14th- and
15th-century buildings.

🏛 **Cathédrale St-Jean**
Pl de Gambetta. 🕭 *daily.*
Topped by a wrought iron
belfry, this cathedral was
begun in 1324 and was finally
ready for use in 1509. It is
constructed almost entirely
from river pebbles layered
with red brick, a style
common throughout the
region due to the scarcity of
other building materials.

Inside the gloomy interior
the nave is flanked by gilded
altarpieces and painted wood-
en statues, with a massive pre-
Romanesque marble font. A
cloistered cemetery adjoins
the church and the Chapel of
the Devout Christ with its

THE ANNUAL PROCESSION DE LA SANCH

There is a very Catalan
atmosphere in Perpignan
during the annual Good
Friday procession of the
Confraternity of La Sanch
(Brotherhood of the Holy
Blood). Originally dedi-
cated to the comfort of
condemned prisoners in
the 15th century, members
of the brotherhood still
wear macabre red or black
robes as they carry sacred
relics and the crucifix from
the Chapel of the Devout
Christ to the cathedral.

For hotels and restaurants in this region see pp588–90 and pp643–6

...cious, poignantly realistic ...edieval wooden Crucifixion. ...he cathedral replaced the 11th-century church of St-Jean-le-Vieux, whose superb Romanesque doorway can be glimpsed to the left of the main entrance. Some areas may be restricted due to ongoing restoration work.

🏛 Palais des Rois de Majorque

2 rue des Archers. **Tel** 04 68 34 48 29. ⬜ daily. ⚫ Jan 1, May 1, Nov 1, Dec 25. 📷

Access to the vast 13th-century fortified palace of the Kings of Majorca is as circuitous today as it was intended to be for invading soldiers. Flights of steps zigzag within the sheer red-brick ramparts, begun in the 15th century and added to successively over the next two centuries. Eventually, the elegant gardens and substantial castle within are revealed, entered by way of the Tour de l'Hommage, from the top of which is a panoramic view of city, mountains, and sea.

The palace itself is built around a central arcaded courtyard, flanked on one side by the Salle de Majorque, a great hall with a triple fireplace and giant Gothic arched windows. Adjacent, two royal chapels built one above the other show southern Gothic style at its best: pointed arches, patterned frescoes, and elaborate tilework demonstrating a distinct Moorish influence. The fine rose marble doorway of the upper King's Chapel is typical of the Roussillon Romanesque style, although the sculpted

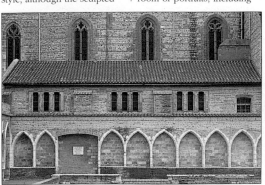

The pebble and red-brick Cathédrale de St-Jean in Perpignan

Courtyard in the Hôtel de Ville

capitals are Gothic. Today the great courtyard is sometimes used for concerts.

🏛 Musée Josep Deloncle de l'Histoire de la Catalogue Nord

Le Castillet. **Tel** 04 68 35 42 05. ⬜ Tue–Sun. ⚫ Jan 1, May 1, Nov 1. 📷

The red-brick tower and pink belfry of the Castillet, built as the town gate in 1368, was at one time a prison and is all that remains of the town walls. It now houses a collection of Catalan craft objects, agricultural implements, kitchen furniture, looms, and terra cotta pots for storing water and oil. It also holds art exhibitions.

🏛 Musée Rigaud

16 rue de l'Ange. **Tel** 04 68 35 43 40. ⬜ Tue–Sun. ⚫ public hols. 📷 ♿

This magnificent 18th-century mansion has an eclectic art collection dominated by the work of Hyacinthe Rigaud (1659–1743), who was born in Perpignan and was court painter to Louis XIV and Louis XV. The first floor has a room of portraits, including

works by David, Greuze, and Ingres; the Dufy, Picasso, and Maillol room; and the Primitifs Catalan, 14th–16th-century Catalan and Spanish paintings, among them the *Retable de la Trinité* (1489) by the Master of Canapost.

The museum also represents the 20th century: Alechinsky, Appel, and others from the late 1940s European Cobra movement; the Catalan artist Pierre Daura; and modern Roussillon painters like Brune, Terrus, and Violet.

Fortress tower and ramparts, Salses

Salses ⓫

Pyrénées-Orientales. 🏘 3,000. 🚉 🏢 ℹ pl de la République (04 68 38 66 13). 🗓 Wed. **www**.salses. monuments-nationaux.fr

Looking like a giant sand-castle against the ocher earth of the Corbières vineyards, the **Forteresse de Salses** stands at the old frontier of Spain and France. It guards the narrow defile between the Mediterranean lagoons and the mountains, and was built by King Ferdinand of Aragon between 1497 and 1506 to defend Spain's possession of Roussillon. Its massive walls and rounded towers are a classic example of Spanish military architecture, designed to deflect the new threat posed by gunpowder.

Inside were underground stables for 300 horses and a subterranean passageway.

There is a wonderful view from the keep over the lagoons and surrounding coastline.

Vineyards covering the hilly terrain of the Corbières

Corbières 🕛

Aude. ✈ Perpignan. 🚆 Narbonne,
Carcassonne, Lézignan-Corbières.
🚌 Narbonne, Carcassonne,
Lézignan-Corbières. 🛈 Lézignan-
Corbières (04 68 27 05 42).
www.lezignan-corbieres.fr/tourisme

Still one of the wildest parts
of France with few roads, let
alone villages, the Corbières
is best known for its wine
and the great craggy hulks of
the Cathar castles (see p491).
Much of the land is untamed
garrigue (scrubland), fragrant
with honeysuckle and broom;
south-facing slopes have been
cleared and planted with vines.
    To the south are the spec-
tacular medieval castles of
Peyrepertuse and Quéribus,
the latter one of the last Cathar
strongholds. The guided visits
around the remarkable Cathar
château at Villerouge-Termenes
reveal some of its turbulent
past. To the west is the barren,
uninhabited Razès area in the
upper Aude valley. Its best-
kept secret is the village of
Alet-les-Bains, with beautifully
preserved half-timbered houses
and the remains of a Benedictine abbey, battle-scarred
from the Wars of Religion.

Narbonne 🕚

Aude. 👥 52,000. 🚆 🚌 🛈 pl
Roger Salengro (04 68 65 15 60).
🗓 Thu & Sun.
www.mairie-narbonne.fr

Narbonne is a medium-
sized, cheerful town profiting
from the booming wine
region that surrounds it. The
town is bisected by the tree-
shaded Canal de la Robine; to
the north is the restored
medieval quarter with many
elegant stores and good restaurants. Located here is one
of Narbonne's most intriguing
tourist attractions, the
Horreum. This underground
warren of granaries and grain
chutes dates from the 1st
century BC, when Narbonne
was a major port and capital
of the largest Roman province
in Gaul.
    The town prospered through
the Middle Ages until the 15th
century when the harbor
silted up and the course of
the river Aude altered, taking
Narbonne's fortunes with it.
By then, an important bishopric had been established and
an ambitious cathedral project,
modeled on the great Gothic
cathedrals of the North, was

underway. However, the f
grandiose design was abar.
doned and just the chancel,
begun in 1272, became the
Cathédrale St-Just et St-
Pasteur we see today.
    It is still enormous, en-
hanced by 14th-century
sculptures, fine stained-glass
windows, and an 18th-century
carved organ. Aubusson and
Gobelin tapestries adorn the
walls, and the Chapel of the
Anonciade houses a treasury
of manuscripts, jeweled
reliquaries and tapestries.
    The unfinished transept
now forms a courtyard, and
between the cathedral and
the Palais des Archevêques
(Archbishops' Palace), lie
cloisters with four galleries of
14th-century vaulting.
    This huge palace and cath-
edral complex dominates the
center of Narbonne. Between
the Palais des Archevêques'
massive 14th-century towers
is the town hall, with a 19th-
century Neo-Gothic façade by
Viollet-le-Duc (see p200), the
architect who so determinedly

The vaulted chancel of Cathédrale
St-Just et St-Pasteur in Narbonne

CANAL DU MIDI

From Sète to Toulouse the 149-mile (240-km)
Canal du Midi flows between plane trees,
vineyards, and villages. The complex system
of locks, aqueducts, and bridges is a remarkable
feat of engineering, built by the Béziers salt-
tax baron Paul Riquet. Completed in 1681, it
encouraged Languedoc trade and established
a vital link, via the Garonne river, between the
Atlantic and the Mediterranean. Today it is plied
by vacation barges (www.canal-du-midi.org).

Tranquil waterway of the Canal du Midi

The Cistercian Abbaye de Fontfroide (1093), southwest of Narbonne

restored medieval France. The palace itself is divided into the Palais Vieux (Old Palace) and the Palais Neuf (New Palace). Narbonne's most important museums are in the Palais Neuf, on the left as you enter through the low medieval arches of the passage de l'Ancre. The **Musée d'Archéologie et de Préhistoire** collection includes fragments of Narbonne's Roman heritage, from milestones and parts of the original walls to an assemblage of domestic objects, coins, tools, and glassware. The **Chapelle de la Madeleine** is decorated with a 14th-century wall painting and houses a collection of Greek vases, sarcophagi, and mosaics.

In the archbishops' former apartments is the **Musée d'Art et d'Histoire**, which is as interesting for its luxurious furnishings and richly decorated ceilings as for its art collection. This includes some fine paintings by Canaletto, Brueghel, Boucher, and Veronese as well as a large selection of local earthenware.

South of the Canal de la Robine are a number of fine mansions, including the Renaissance **Maison des Trois Nourrices** on the corner of rue des Trois-Nourrices and

rue Edgard-Quinet. Nearby is the **Musée Lapidaire**, with architectural fragments from Gallo-Roman Narbonne, and the 13th-century Gothic **Basilique St-Paul-Serge**. The present building retains the crypt and some sarcophagi of an earlier church on this site.

Ⓝ Horreum
Rue Rouget-de-l'Isle. **Tel** 04 68 32 45 30. ◯ mid-Jul–mid-Oct: daily; Nov–mid-Jul: Wed–Mon. ● Jan 1, May 1, Nov 1 & 11, Dec 25. 🎫

血 Musée d'Archéologie et de Préhistoire/Musée d'Art et d'Histoire
Palais des Archevêques. **Tel** 04 68 90 30 65. ◯ mid-Jul–mid-Oct: daily; Nov–mid-Jul: Wed–Mon. ● Jan 1, May 1, Nov 1 & 11, Dec 25. 🎫

血 Musee Lapidaire
Eglise Notre-Dame de Lamourguié. **Tel** 04 68 90 30 65. ◯ mid-Jul–mid-Oct: daily; Nov–mid-Jul: Wed–Mon. ● Jan 1, May 1, Nov 1 & 11, Dec 25. 🎫 ♿

Environs
Southwest (8 miles/13 km), the Cistercian **Abbaye de Fontfroide** has an elegant cloister. The abbey is tucked away in a quiet valley, surrounded by cypress trees.

Golfe du Lion ⓮

Aude, Hérault. ✈ 🚌 🚆 Montpellier. ⛴ Sète. 🛈 La Grande Motte (04 67 56 42 00). www.ot-lagrandemotte.fr

Languedoc-Roussillon's shoreline (65 miles/100 km) forms an almost unbroken sweep of sandy beach. Only at its southern limits does it break into the rocky inlets of the Côte Vermeille. Purpose-built resorts created since the 1960s encourage eco-friendly, low-rise family accommodations, some in local styles, others with imaginative architecture.

La Grande Motte marina has distinctive ziggurat-style buildings (see p495). **Cap d'Agde** has Europe's largest naturist quarter. Inland **Agde**, founded by ancient Greek traders, is built of black basalt and has a fortified cathedral. **Port Leucate** and **Port Bacarès** are ideal for watersports. An older town is **Sète** (see p492). A feature of the flat Languedoc coast is its étangs – large shallow lagoons. Those nearest the Camargue are the haunt of thousands of wading birds.

A wide, sandy beach on the Cap d'Agde

Carcassonne **⑮**

The citadel of Carcassonne is a perfectly restored medieval town, and protected by UNESCO. It crowns a steep bank above the river Aude, a fairy-tale sight of turrets and ramparts overlooking the Basse Ville below. The strategic position of the citadel between the Atlantic and the Mediterranean and on the corridor between the Iberian peninsula and the rest of Europe led to its original settlement, consolidated by the Romans in the 2nd century BC. It became a key element in medieval military conflicts. At its zenith in the 12th century, it was ruled by the Trencavels who built the château and cathedral. Military advances and the Treaty of the Pyrenees in 1659, which relocated the French–Spanish border, hastened its decline. The attentions of architectural historian Viollet-le-Duc *(see p200)* led to its restoration in the 19th century.

The Restored Citadel
Restoration of La Cité has always been controversial. Critics complain it looks too new, favoring a more romantic ruin.

★ **Le Château**
A fortress within a fortress, the château has a moat, five towers, and defensive wooden galleries on the walls.

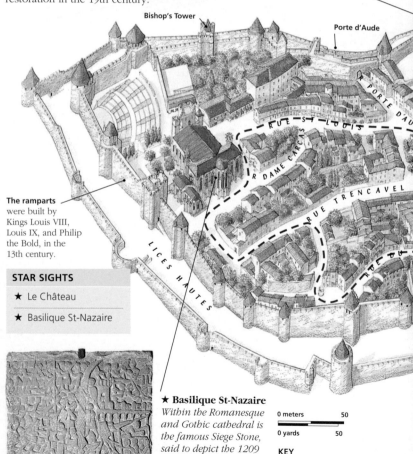

Bishop's Tower

Porte d'Aude

PORTE D'AUDE

RUE ST-LOUIS

R DAME CARCAS

RUE TRENCAVEL

The ramparts were built by Kings Louis VIII, Louis IX, and Philip the Bold, in the 13th century.

LICES HAUTES

STAR SIGHTS

★ Le Château

★ Basilique St-Nazaire

★ **Basilique St-Nazaire**
Within the Romanesque and Gothic cathedral is the famous Siege Stone, said to depict the 1209 Siege of Carcassonne by crusaders.

| 0 meters | | 50 |
| 0 yards | | 50 |

KEY

– – – Suggested route

RELIGIOUS PERSECUTION

Carcassonne's strategic position meant it was often at the center of religious conflict. The Cathars *(see p491)* were given sanctuary here in 1209 by Raymond-Roger Trencavel when besieged by Simon de Montfort in his crusade against heresy. In the 14th century the Inquisition continued to root out the Cathars. This painting depicts intended victims in the Inquisition Tower.

Les Emmurés de Carcassonne, JP Laurens

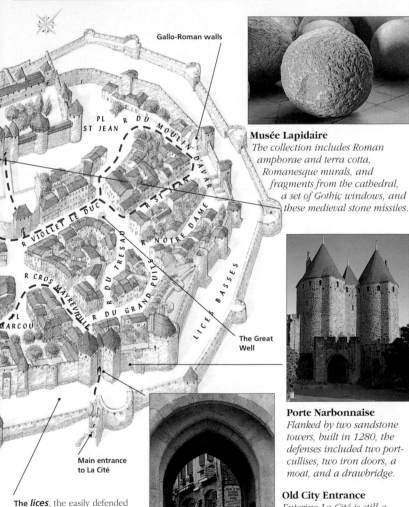

Gallo-Roman walls

PL ST JEAN
R DU MOULIN DAVAR
R ST JEAN
R VIOLLET LE DUC
R NOTRE DAME
R CROS MAYREVIEILLE
R DU TRESAU
R DU GRAND PUITS
LICES BASSES
PL MARCOU

The Great Well

Main entrance to La Cité

The *lices*, the easily defended spaces between the inner and outer ramparts, were also used for jousting, crossbow practice and for storage of timber and other materials.

Musée Lapidaire
The collection includes Roman amphorae and terra cotta, Romanesque murals, and fragments from the cathedral, a set of Gothic windows, and these medieval stone missiles.

Porte Narbonnaise
Flanked by two sandstone towers, built in 1280, the defenses included two portcullises, two iron doors, a moat, and a drawbridge.

Old City Entrance
Entering La Cité is still a step back in time, although it is one of France's top tourist destinations, filled with souvenir stores.

Béziers with its medieval cathedral, seen from Pont Vieux in the southwest

Minerve ⑯

Hérault. 🏠 120. 🛈 rue des Martyrs (04 68 91 81 43).
www.minerve-tourisme.fr

In the parched, arid hills of the Minervois, surrounded by vines and not much else, Minerve appears defiant on its rocky outcrop at the confluence of the rivers Cesse and Briant. It is defended by what the Minervois call the "Candela" (Candle), an octagonal tower which is all that remains of the medieval château. In 1210, the small town resisted the vengeful Simon de Montfort, scourge of the Cathars, in a siege lasting seven weeks. This culminated in the execution of 140 Cathars, who were burned at the stake.

Today visitors enter Minerve by a high bridge spanning the gorge. Turn right and follow the route of the Cathars past the Romanesque arch of the Porte des Templiers to the 12th-century **Eglise St-Etienne**. Outside the church is a crudely carved dove, symbol of the Cathars, and within is a 5th-century white marble altar table, one of the oldest artifacts in the region.

A rocky path follows the riverbed below the town, where the water has cut out caves and two bridges – the Grand Pont and the Petit Pont – from the soft limestone.

Béziers ⑰

Hérault. 🏠 73,000. ✈ 🚗 🚆 🛈 29 av Saint Saëns (04 67 76 84 00). 🌳 Fri. **www**.beziers-tourisme.fr

Famous for its bullfights and rugby, and the wine of the surrounding region, Béziers has several other points of interest. The town seems turned in on itself, its roads leading up to the massive 14th-century **Cathédrale St-Nazaire**, with its fine sculpture, stained glass, and frescoes. In 1209, several thousand citizens were massacred in the crusade against the Cathars. The papal legate's troops were ordered not to discriminate between Catholics and Cathars, but to "Kill them all. God will recognize his own!"

Statue of the engineer Paul Riquet in the allées Paul Riquet, Béziers

The **Musée du Biterrois** holds exhibitions on local history, wine, and the Canal du Midi, engineered in the late 17th century by Paul Riquet, Béziers' most famous son (*see p486*). His statue presides over the Allées Paul Riquet, which is lined by rows of plane trees and large cano-pied restaurants, a civilized focus to this otherwise business-like town.

🏛 **Musée du Biterrois**
Caserne St-Jacques. **Tel** 04 67 36 71 01. 🔵 Tue–Sun. 🔴 Jan 1, Easter, May 1, Dec 25. 🖾 🔥

Environs
Overlooking the Béziers plain and the mountains to the north is Oppidum d'Ensérune, a superb Roman site. The **Musée de l'Oppidum d'Ensérune** has a good archaeological collection, from Celtic, Greek, and Roman vases to jewelry and weapons.

The **Château de Raissac** (between Béziers and Lignan) houses an unusual 19th-century faïence museum in its stables.

🏛 **Musée de l'Oppidum d'Ensérune**
Nissan-lez-Ensérune. **Tel** 04 67 37 01 23. 🔵 daily; Sep–Apr: Tue–Sun. 🔴 public hols. 🖾 🔥 limited. http://enserune.monuments-nationaux.fr

🏛 **Château de Raissac**
Rte de Lignan sur Orr. **Tel** 04 67 49 17 60. 🔵 by appt. **www**.raissac.com

For hotels and restaurants in this region see pp588–90 and pp643–6

The Cathars

The Cathars (from Greek *katharos*, meaning pure) were a 13th-century Christian sect critical of corruption in the established church. Cathar dissent flourished in independent Languedoc as an expression of separatism, but the rebellion was rapidly exploited for political purposes. Peter II of Aragon was keen to annex Languedoc, and Philippe II of France joined forces with the pope to crush the Cathar heretics in a crusade led by Simon de Montfort in 1209. This heralded the start of over a century of ruthless killing and torture.

CATHAR CASTLES
The Cathars took refuge in the defensive castles of the Corbières and Ariège. Peyrepertuse is one of the most remote, difficult to reach even today: a long, narrow stone citadel hacked from a high, craggy peak over 2,000 ft (609 m) high.

Cathars *(also known as Albigensians) believed in the duality of good and evil. They considered the material world entirely evil. To be truly pure they had to renounce the world, and be non-violent, vegetarian, and sexually abstinent.*

The crusade *against the Cathars was vicious. Heretics' land was promised to the crusaders by the pope, who assured forgiveness in advance of their crimes. In 1209, 20,000 citizens were massacred in Béziers and, the following year, 140 were burned to death in Minerve. In 1244, 225 Cathars died defending one of their last fortresses at Montségur.*

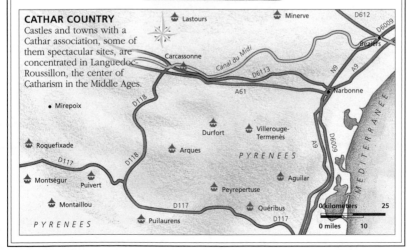

CATHAR COUNTRY
Castles and towns with a Cathar association, some of them spectacular sites, are concentrated in Languedoc-Roussillon, the center of Catharism in the Middle Ages.

Lastours
Minerve
D612
D6009
Béziers
Carcassonne
Canal du Midi
D6113
N9
A9
A61
Narbonne
• Mirepoix
D118
Durfort
Villerouge-Termenès
A9
D6009
Roquefixade
D118
Arques
PYRENEES
D117
Montségur
Puivert
Aguilar
Peyrepertuse
MEDITERRANÉE
Montaillou
D117
Quéribus
0 kilometers   25
PYRENEES
Puilaurens
D117
0 miles   10

The impressive Grand Hôtel *(see p590)* on quai de la Résistance, Sète

Sète ⑱

Hérault. 🏘 *43,500.* 🚉 🚌 ⛴
ℹ *60 grand' rue Mario Roustan*
(04 99 04 71 71) 🗓 *Wed & Fri.*
www.ot-sete.fr

Sète is a major fishing and
industrial port. It has a
gutsier, more raffish air than
much of the leisure-oriented
Mediterranean, with its stores

Cimetière Marin in Sète, burial
place of the poet Paul Valéry

selling ships' lamps and
propellers, and its quayside
restaurants full of hungry
sailors demolishing vast
platters of mussels, oysters,
and sea snails straight off the
boat. Most of Sète's restaurants can be found in a stroll
along the Grand Canal, with
its Italianate houses painted
in pastel colors and with
wrought iron balconies overlooking Sète's network of
canals and bridges. Boisterous
water jousting tournaments,
dating back to 1666, form part
of the patron saint's festival in
August *(see p37)*.

The **Musée International
des Arts Modestes** displays
everyday objects (including
some by well-known contemporary designers) in amusing
new contexts, within a renovated canalside warehouse.

Above the town is the
Cimetière Marin, where Sète's
most famous son, poet Paul
Valéry (1871–1945), is buried.
There is a small museum and
breathtaking views of the
coast and the mountains.

🏛 **Musée International des
Arts Modestes**
23 quai du Maréchal de Lattre de
Tassigny. **Tel** *04 99 04 76 44.*
◻ *Apr–Sep: daily; Oct–Mar:
Tue–Sun.* ⬤ *public hols.* 🚫 ♿
www.miam.org

Pézenas ⑲

Hérault. 🏘 *9,000.* 🚌
ℹ *pl des Etats de Languedoc
(04 67 98 36 40).* 🗓 *Sat.*
www.pezenas-tourisme.fr

Pézenas is a charming little
town easily appreciated in a
gentle stroll of its main sights,
and abounding in revealing
details, fragmentary evidence
of its past brilliance as the
seat of local government in
the 16th–17th centuries. Then
the town also played host to
many troupes of musicians
and actors, including Molière.

Best of all are the glimpses
of fine houses through courtyard doorways, such as the
Hôtel des Barons de Lacoste,
at 8 rue François-Oustrin, with
its beautiful stone staircase,
and the **Maison des Pauvres** at
12 rue Alfred Sabatier, with its
three galleries and staircase.

Look out for the medieval
store window on rue Triperie-
Vieille, and just within the
14th-century **Porte Faugères**,
the narrow streets of the
Jewish ghetto, which has a
chilling feeling of enclosure.
Stores selling antiques,
second-hand goods, and
books abound. All around
the town, vines stretch as
far as the eye can see.

The stone foyer of the Hôtel des
Barons de Lacoste in Pézenas

Parc Régional du Haut Languedoc ⑳

Hérault, Tarn. ✈ *Béziers*.
🚂 *Béziers, Bédarieux*. 🚌 *St-Pons-de-Thomières, Mazamet, Lamalou-les-Bains* 🅸 *St-Pons-de-Thomières (04 67 97 38 22).*
www.parc-haut-languedoc.fr

The high limestone plateaus and wooded slopes of upper Languedoc are a world away from the coast. From the Montagne Noire, a mountainous region between Béziers and Castres, up into the Cévennes is a landscape of remote sheep farms, eroded rock formations, and deep river gorges. Much of this area has been designated the Parc Régional du Haut Languedoc, the second largest of the French national parks after Ecrins.

St-Pons-de-Thomières is the entrance, with access to forest and mountain trails for walking and riding, plus a wildlife research center, where one can glimpse the mouflons (wild mountain sheep), eagles and wild boar which were once a common sight in the region.

If you take the D908 from St-Pons through the park you pass the village of **Olargues** with its 12th-century bridge over the river Jaur. **Lamalou-les-Bains**, on the park's eastern edge, is a small spa town with a restored Belle Epoque spa building and theater, and a soporifically slow pace.

Outside the park boundaries to the northeast there are spectacular natural phenomena. At the **Cirque de Navacelles**, the river Vis has joined up with itself, carving out an entire island. On it sits the peaceful village of Navacelles, visible from the road higher up. The **Grotte des Demoiselles** is one of the most magnificent in an area full of caves, where you walk through a calcified world. A funicular train takes visitors from the foot of the mountain to the top.

The **Grotte de Clamouse** is also an extraordinary experience, the reflections from underground rivers and pools flickering on the cavern roofs, with stalagmites resembling dripping candles.

🏛 **Grotte des Demoiselles**
St-Bauzille-de-Putois. **Tel** 04 67 73 70 02. ⬤ *daily.* ⬤ *Jan, Dec 25.* 📷
www.demoiselles.com

🏛 **Grotte de Clamouse**
Rte de St-Guilhem-le-Désert, St-Jean-de-Fos. **Tel** 04 67 57 71 05.
⬤ *Feb–mid-Nov: daily.* 📷
www.clamouse.com

Apse of St-Guilhem-le-Désert

St-Guilhem-le-Désert ㉑

Hérault. 🏠 *250.* 🚂 🅸 *Maison Communale (04 67 57 44 33).*
www.saintguilhem-valleeherault.fr

Tucked away in the Celette mountains, St-Guilhem-le-Désert is no longer as remote as when Guillaume of Aquitaine retired here as a hermit in the 9th century. After a lifetime as a soldier, Guillaume received a fragment of the True Cross from Emperor Charlemagne and established a monastery in this ravine above the river Hérault.

Vestiges of the first 10th-century church have been discovered but most of the building is a superb example of 11th–12th-century Romanesque architecture. Its lovely apsidal chapels dominate the heights of the village, behind which the carved doorway opens on to a central square.

Within the church is a somber barrel-vaulted central aisle leading to the sunlit central apse. Only two galleries of the cloisters remain: the rest are in New York, along with carvings from St-Michel-de-Cuxa *(see p481).*

Extraordinary limestone formations at the Grotte de Clamouse

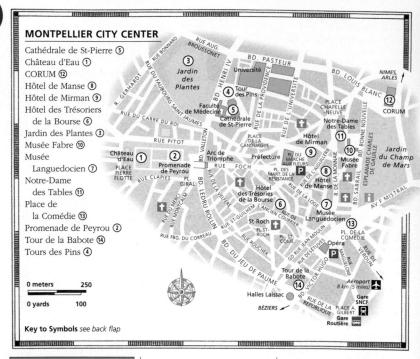

MONTPELLIER CITY CENTER

Cathédrale de St-Pierre ⑤
Château d'Eau ①
CORUM ⑫
Hôtel de Manse ⑧
Hôtel de Mirman ⑨
Hôtel des Trésoriers
de la Bourse ⑥
Jardin des Plantes ③
Musée Fabre ⑩
Musée
Languedocien ⑦
Notre-Dame
des Tables ⑪
Place de
la Comédie ⑬
Promenade de Peyrou ②
Tour de la Babote ⑭
Tours des Pins ④

0 meters   250
0 yards   100

Key to Symbols *see back flap*

Open-air café in the place de la Comédie, Montpellier

Montpellier ㉒

Hérault. 👥 256,000. 🚆 🚌 ✈️
🛈 30 allée Jean de Lattré de Tassigny
(04 67 60 60 60). 🛒 daily. 🎭 Festival
International Montpellier Danse
(Jun–Jul). **www**.ot-montpellier.fr

Montpellier is one of the
liveliest, most forward-looking
cities in the south, with a
quarter of its population under
25. Sometimes on a summer
evening during university
term time it resembles more a
rock festival than the capital
of Languedoc-Roussillon.

Center of the action is the
egg-shaped **place de la
Comédie**, known as "l'Oeuf"
("the egg"), with its 19th-cen-
tury opera house fronted by
the Fontaine des Trois Graces
and surrounded by buzzing
cafés. An esplanade of plane
trees and fountains leads to the
CORUM, an opera and conference center typical of the
city's brave new architectural
projects. The best of these is
Ricardo Bofill's Postmodern
housing complex known as
Antigone, which is modeled
on St. Peter's in Rome.

Montpellier was founded
relatively late for this region
of ancient Roman towns, developing in the 10th century
as a result of the spice trade
with the Middle East. The city's
medical school was founded
in 1220, partly as a result of
this cross-fertilization between the two
cultures, and remains one of
the most respected in France.

Most of Montpellier was
ravaged by the Wars of Religion in the 16th century. Only
the **Tour de la Babote** and the
Tours des Pins remain of the
12th-century fortifications. There
are few fine churches, the excep-

tions being the **Cathédrale de
St-Pierre** and the 18th-century
Notre-Dame des Tables.

Reconstruction in the 17th
century saw the building of
mansions with elegant courtyards, stone staircases, and
balconies. Examples open to
the public include **Hôtel de
Manse** on rue Embouque-
d'Or, **Hôtel de Mirman** near
place des Martyrs de la
Resistance and **Hôtel des
Trésoriers de la Bourse**. The
Hôtel des Lunaret houses the
Musée Languedocien which
exhibits Romanesque and
prehistoric artifacts.

Another 17th-century building houses the renovated
Musée Fabre with a collection
of mainly French paintings.

PONT DU GARD   ← To Uzès

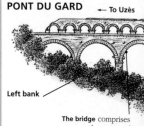

Left bank

The bridge comprises
three tiers of
continuous arches.

For hotels and restaurants in this region see pp588–90 and pp643–6

Highlights include Courbet's famous *Bonjour M. Courbet*, Berthe Morisot's *L'Eté*, and some evocative paintings of the region by Raoul Dufy.

A good place to view the city's position between mountains and sea is from the **Promenade de Peyrou**, a grand 18th-century square dominated by the **Château d'Eau** and the aqueduct which used to serve the city. North of here is the **Jardin des Plantes**, France's oldest botanical gardens (1593). Not to be missed is **Mare Nostrum**, the new aquarium in the Odysseum leisure zone, which has over 300 marine species.

🏛 **Musée Languedocien**
7 rue Jacques Coeur. **Tel** 04 67 52 93 03. ◯ Mon–Sat: pm only. ● public hols. 🖼

🏛 **Musée Fabre**
39 bd Bonne Nouvelle. **Tel** 04 67 14 83 00. ◯ Tue–Sun. 🖼 ▢ 🍴 ◑

Château d'Eau, Montpellier

La Grande-Motte ㉓

Hérault. 🏘 8,500. ▣ 🛈 pl du 1er Octobre 1974 (04 67 56 42 00). ▣ Sun (& Thu: mid-Jun–mid-Sep). www.ot-lagrandemotte.fr

The bizarre white ziggurats of this modern marina exemplify the development of the Languedoc-Roussillon coast.

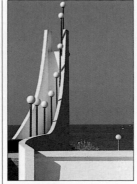

La Grande-Motte

One of several on the lagoons south of Montpellier, there are marinas and facilities for every kind of sport from tennis and golf to water sports, all flanked by golden beaches and pine forests. To the east are Le Grau-du-Roi, once a tiny fishing village, and Port-Camargue, with its big marina.

Aigues-Mortes ⓫

Gard. 🏘 8,000. ▣ ▣ 🛈 pl St-Louis (04 66 53 73 00). ▣ Wed & Sun. www.ot-aiguesmortes.fr

The best approach to this perfectly preserved walled town is across the salt marshes of the Petite Camargue. Now marooned 3 miles (5 km) from the sea, the imposing defenses of this once important port have become a tourist experience, worth visiting more for the effect of the ensemble than the tacky stores within. Aigues-Mortes ("Place of Dead Waters") was established by Louis XI in the 13th century to consolidate his power on the Mediterranean, and built according to a strict grid pattern. By climbing up the **Tour de Constance** you can walk out onto the rectangular walls, which afford a superb view over the Camargue.

Environs
To the northeast is **St-Gilles-du-Gard**, also once an important medieval port. Today it is worth a detour to see the superbly sculpted 12th-century façade of its abbey church. This was originally established by the monks of Cluny abbey as a shrine to St-Gilles, and a resting place on the famous pilgrimage route to Santiago de Compostela (*see pp400–1*).

Nîmes ㉕

See pp496-7.

Pont du Gard ㉖

Gard. 🛈 08 20 90 33 30. 🚉 from Nîmes. www.pontdugard.fr

No amount of fame can diminish the first sight of the 2,000-year-old Pont du Gard. The Romans considered it the best testimony to the greatness of their Empire, and at 160 ft (49 m) it was the highest bridge they ever built.

It is made from blocks of stone, hauled into place by slaves using an ingenious system of pulleys. The huge build-up of calcium in the water channels suggests the aqueduct was in continuous use for 400–500 years, carrying water to Nîmes along a 31-mile (50-km) route from the springs at **Uzès**. This charming town has an arcaded marketplace and several fine medieval towers.

Water channel

To Nîmes →

Right bank

Roman inscriptions include a damaged phallus carving as a good luck symbol.

Some stones weighed up to six tons.

Nîmes ㉕

Listed number one on the tourist map of Nîmes is the bus stop designed by Philippe Starck, who is also credited with reworking the city's pedestrian zone. Such innovations are part of the city's current design renaissance. Architectural projects range from imaginative housing to a glittering arts complex, under the guidance of a dynamic mayor. An important crossroads in the ancient world, Nîmes is equally well known for its Roman antiquities such as the amphitheater, the best preserved of its kind. The city is also famous for its festivals and bullfights (*feria*). These are good times to see the rest of Nîmes with its museums, archaeological collections and Old Town of narrow streets and intimate squares.

Arches of the Roman amphitheater

Historic Nîmes

Nîmes has had a turbulent history, suffering particularly during the 16th-century Wars of Religion when the Romanesque **Cathédrale Notre-Dame et St-Castor** was badly damaged. During the 17th and 18th centuries the town prospered from textile manufacturing, one of the most enduring products being denim or "de Nîmes." Many of the fine houses of this period have been restored and elegant examples can be seen on rue de l'Aspic, rue des Marchands and rue du Chapitre in the Old Town. Just outside the town center is the futuristic apartment building, **Nemausus I**.

The Roman gate, the **Porte Auguste**, built 20 years before

Jug from Musée Archéologique

the temple of **Maison Carrée**, was once part of one of the longest city walls in Gaul. Of the original arches still standing, two (large) were for carts and chariots and two (smaller) ones for pedestrians. The other major Roman remnant is the **Castellum**, where water used to arrive from the Pont du Gard (*see p495*). From the Castellum it was distributed around the city through thick pipes.

❧ Jardin de la Fontaine

Quai de la Fontaine. ☐ daily. ⓖ
When the Romans arrived in Nîmes, they found a town established by

① Tour Magne

② Mont Cavalier

Temple de Diane

③ Jardin de la Fontaine

ALÈS

0 meters   25
0 yards   250

RUE ROUGET DE L'ISLE
RUE DE LA TOUR MAGNE
BÉNÉDICTINS
RUE PASTEUR
RUE TRAJAN
QUAI DE LA FONTAINE
QUAI DE LA FONTAINE
RUE BOISSIER
RUE GRETRY
RUE DES CHASSAINTES
PLACE J. GUESTE
BOULEVARD
RUE FERNAND PELLOUTIER
RUE MARESCHAL
RUE EMILE JAMAIS
BOULEVARD
JEAN-JAURÈS
JEAN-JAURÈS
RUE DÉLON SOUBEYRAN
RUE BEC DE LIÈVRE
RUE DE LA
RUE DE L'HOTEL D
RUE RENAN
RUE LOUIS
RUE DU

Jardin de la Fontaine, with a view over the city

SIGHTS AT A GLANCE

For hotels and restaurants in this region see pp588–90 and pp643–6

the Gauls, centered on the source of a spring. They named the town Nemausus, after their river god. In the 18th century, formal gardens were constructed, and a network of limpid pools and cool stone terraces remains. High above the garden on **Mont Cavalier** is the octagonal **Tour Magne**, once a key part of the Roman walls, offering a great view of the city.

Arms of the city in a sculpture by Martial Raysse

VISITORS' CHECKLIST

Gard. 143,000. 7.5 miles (12 km) SSE Nîmes. bd Talabot (SNCF: 36 35). Rue St Félicité (0820 223 030). 6 rue Auguste (04 66 58 38 00). daily. Ferias: de Pentecôte (Pentecost), des Vendanges (Sep).
www.ot-nimes.fr

The Maison Carrée

venue for concerts, sporting events, and bullfights.

Maison Carrée
Pl de la Maison Carrée. *Tel* 04 66 21 82 56. daily.
Square House is a very prosaic name for this elegant Roman temple, the pride of Nîmes. Built around AD 2, it is one of the best preserved in the world, with finely fluted Corinthian columns and a sculpted frieze.

Musée des Beaux Arts
Rue Cité Foulc. *Tel* 04 66 67 38 21. Tue–Sun. Jan 1, May 1, Nov 1, Dec 25.
This fine arts museum houses an eclectic collection of Dutch, French, Italian and Flemish works, notably Jacopo Bassano's *Susanna and the Elders*, and the *Mystic Marriage of St. Catherine* by Michele Giambono. The Gallo-Roman mosaic of *The Marriage of Admetus*, discovered in 1882, is on the main floor.

Musée Archéologique
Musée d'Histoire Naturelle, 13 bis bd Amiral Courbet. *Tel* 04 66 76 74 80. Tue–Sun. Jan 1, May 1, Nov 1, Dec 25.
The museum's collection of Roman statues, ceramics, glass, coins, and mosaics is housed in Nîmes' natural history museum. The exhibits include important Iron Age menhir statues.

Carré d'Art/ Musée d'Art Contemporain
Pl de la Maison Carrée. *Tel* 04 66 76 35 35. Tue–Sun. Jan 1, May 1, Nov 1, Dec 25.
Nîmes' arts complex, by the British architect Sir Norman Foster, opened in 1993. Five floors of this glass and steel temple, which was built in tribute to the Maison Carrée opposite, lie underground. The complex has a library, a roof-terrace restaurant around a huge glass atrium, and the Musée d'Art Contemporain. Works cover the main European art movements from the 1960s onward, and include works by Raysse, Boltanski, and Lavier for France.

Bullfight at Les Arènes in Nîmes

Les Arènes
Bd des Arènes. *Tel* 04 66 21 82 56. daily. performance days.

All roads lead to the amphitheater, Les Arènes. Built at the end of the 1st century AD, the design of the oval arena and tiers of stone seats accommodated huge crowds of up to 20,000 spectators. Today it is in use again, a perfect
Key to Symbols *see back flap*

Map labels

Castellum
RUE GRAVEROL
RUE RANGUEIL
RUE BAUDIN
RUE BACHALAS
RUE CLERISSEAU
DE LA
OLUTION
ORT
PLACE
ST CHARLES
BOULEVARD GAMBETTA
AVIGNON
R DU MÉRIER D'ESPAGNE
R DU COUVENT
RUE NATIONALE
RUE DES ORANGERS
Porte Auguste
R DE L'HORLOGE
PERRIER
RUE DES LOMBARDS
RUE GENERAL
PL DU CHÂTEAU
Grand Temple
Cathédrale Notre-Dame et St-Castor
PL AUX HERBES
Musée du Vieux Nîmes
Musée Archéologique
RUE DORÉE
BD AMIRAL COURBET
RUE DE LA MADELEINE
RUE DE L'ASPIC
RUE DES GREFFES
RUE DE L'ÉTOILE
PLACE DE LA MADELEINE
Hôtel de Ville
SQ DE LA COURONNE
PLACE DU MARCHÉ
RUE RÉGALE
BD VICTOR-HUGO
Palais de Justice
BD DE LA LIBERATION
BD DES ARÈNES
Esplanade Charles de Gaulle
Les Arènes
RUE JEAN-REBOUL
PORTE DE FRANCE
PLACE DES ARÈNES
Gare SNCF, Gare Routière 200 m (420 yards)
ARLES, MONTPELIER Nemausus I
RUE BRIÇONNET
RUE DE LA RÉPUBLIQUE
RUE DE LA CITÉ
RUE BOURDALOUE
Aéroport 12 km (7.5 miles)
Musée des Beaux-Arts

PROVENCE AND THE COTE D'AZUR

BOUCHES-DU-RHONE · VAUCLUSE · VAR
ALPES-DE-HAUTE-PROVENCE · ALPES-MARITIMES

Fr-om its herb-scented hills to its yacht-filled harbors, no other region of France fires the imagination as strongly as Provence. The vivid landscape and luminous light have inspired artists and writers from Van Gogh to Picasso, F. Scott Fitzgerald to Pagnol.

The borders of Provence are defined by nature: to the west, the Rhône; south, the Mediterranean; and north, where the olive trees end. To the east are the Alps and a border which has shifted over the centuries between France and Italy. Within is a contrasting terrain of plummeting gorges, Camargue saltflats, lavender fields, and sun-drenched beaches.

Past visitors have left their mark. In Orange and Arles, the buildings of Roman *Provincia* are still in use. Fortified villages like Èze were built to withstand the Saracen pirates who plagued the coast in the 6th century.

In the 19th century, rich Europeans sought winter warmth on the Riviera; by the 1920s, high society was in residence all year, and their elegant villas remain. The warm sunlight nurtures intense flavors and colors. Peppers, garlic, and olives transform a netful of Mediterranean fish into that vibrant epitome of Provençal cuisine, *bouillabaisse*.

The image of Provence bathed in sunshine is marred only when the bitter Mistral wind scours the land. It has shaped a people as hardy as the olive tree, yet quick to embrace life to the full the moment the sun returns.

Cap Martin, seen from the village of Roquebrune

Lavender fields near the Gorges du Verdon

Exploring Provence

This sun-drenched southeastern region is France's most popular vacation destination. Sunworshippers cram the beaches in the summer months, and entertainment includes opera, dance, and jazz festivals, bullfights, casinos, and *boules* games. Inland is a paradise for walkers and nature lovers, with remote mountain plateaus, perched villages, and dramatic river gorges.

Promenade des Anglais, Nice

SIGHTS AT A GLANCE

For additional map symbols *see back flap*

GETTING AROUND
The largest airport in the region, and second
busiest in France, is Nice. Fly-drive packages
are popular, although mainly recommended for
touring inland. Traffic jams on coastal roads in
high season can usually be avoided by using
the autoroutes. Main coastal towns have good
bus and rail links, and bikes can be hired at
most train stations. The Chemin de Fer de
Provence rail line runs from Nice to
Digne-les-Bains through spectacular
mountain scenery. Mountain roads,
though tortuous, are good.

Saint-Paul

Le Lauzet-Ubaye

D900
Colle della
Maddalena
Barcelonnette

Motte-du-Caire   Seyne   Pra-Loup

Mont Pelat
3051m △

Allos

Saint-Étienne-
de-Tinée

La Javie   Colmars   Isola 2000

23 DIGNE-LES-BAINS   Valberg   Saint-Sauveur-
sur-Tinée   Saint-Martin-
Vésubie   Vallée des
Merveilles
Tende

eau-
oux

N85   Saint-André-
les-Alpes   Guillaumes   **41**   Roquebillière   D6204

Mézel   Barrême   Sénez   Annot   Puget-Théniers   Lantosque   Saorge

D953   Entrevaux   Breil-
sur-Roya

Moustiers-
Sainte-Marie   Castellane   Saint-Auban   Plan-du-Var   Sospel

D952   Saint-Auban   Mont Cheiron
△ 1777m   Escarène   Peille

D11   Gorges du
Verdon   Trigance   Le Logis-
du-Pin   D2   ROQUEBRUNE-
CAP-MARTIN   **42** MENTON

Lac de
Ste-Croix   GORGES DU LOUP **33**   VENCE   ÈZE   **39** **43** MONACO

L P E S   Comps-sur-Artuby   D6085   **34**   NICE **36** **37** VILLEFRANCHE-S.-MER

ST-PAUL-DE-
VENCE   **35**   **38** CAP FERRAT

Aups   Fayence   **17**   BIOT **31**   CAGNES-SUR-MER

ols   Draguignan   D955   VALLAURIS **30** **29** ANTIBES

D562   CANNES **27**   **28** CAP D'ANTIBES

'A Z U R   N7   A8   La Napoule   **KEY**

Argens   Carcès   Lorgues   FRÉJUS **24**   **25** SAINT-RAPHAËL

Brignoles   Vidauban   D25   Saint-Aygulf

sur-
ssole   Cannet-des-
Maures   Sainte-Maxime

D97   Le Garde-
Freinet   **22** SAINT-TROPEZ

A57   **21**   Cogolin   Ramatuelle

sollies-
Pont   Môle   Cavalaire-sur-Mer

D98   **19** HYÈRES   Lavandou

ges   Giens   Île du
Levant

Pòrquerolles   Île de Port Cros

Île de
rolles   **20**

ÎLES D'HYÈRES

MASSIF   DES   MAURES

Par National
du Mercantour

ALPES-MARITIMES

Var

═══	Highway
━━━	Major road
▬▬▬	Secondary road
═ ═ ═	Minor road
━ ━ ━	Scenic route
┅┅┅	Main railroad
───	Minor railroad
▬▬▬	International border
━━━	Regional border
△	Summit

0 kilometers   25

0 miles   25

Spectacular scenery near the quiet market town of Forcalquier

Mont Ventoux ❶

Vaucluse. ✕ *Avignon.* 🚉 *Avignon.*
🚌 *Carpentras.* ℹ *Av de la Prom
Saulten Provence (04 90 64 01 21).*

The name means "Windy
Mountain" in Provençal. A
variety of flora and fauna may
be found on the lower slopes
but only moss survives at the
peak, where the temperature
can drop to –17° F (–27°C).
The bare white scree at the
summit makes it look snow-
capped even during summer.
   Ventoux is the mountain on
which the legendary British
bicyclist Tommy Simpson died
during 1967's Tour de France.
Today, a road leads to the
radio beacon pinnacle, but the
trip should not be attempted
in bad weather. At other times,
spectacular views from the top
make the effort worthwhile.

**Roman mosaic from the Villa du
Paon in Vaison-la-Romaine**

Vaison-la-Romaine ❷

Vaucluse. 👥 *6,100.* 🚉
ℹ *pl du Chanoine Sautel
(04 90 36 02 11).* 🚌 *Tue.*
www.vaison-en-provence.com

This site has been settled
since the Bronze Age, but its
name stems from five
centuries as a Roman town.
   Although the upper town,
dominated by the ruins of a
12th-century castle, has some
charming narrow streets, stone
houses, and fountains, Vaison's
main attractions lie on the
opposite side of the river.
   The **Roman City** is split into
two districts: Puymin and La
Villasse. At Puymin, an
opulent mansion, the Villa du
Paon, and a Roman theater
have been uncovered.
   In 1992, the river Ouvèze
burst its banks, taking many

lives in Vaison and the nearby
area. Damage to some ruins,
such as the Roman bridge,
has since been repaired.
Also at Vaison is the fine
Romanesque **Cathédrale
Notre-Dame-de-Nazareth**,
with medieval cloisters.

🏛 Roman City
Fouilles de Puymin & Musée Théo
Desplans, pl du Chanoine Sautel.
Tel *04 90 36 0211.* ◯ *daily.* ●
Jan–mid-Feb. 🎟 🎫 ♿ *restr.* 🅿

Orange ❸

Vaucluse. 👥 *30,000.* 🚉 🚌 ℹ *5 cours
Aristide Briand (04 90 34 70 88).* 🚌 *Thu.*
www.otorange.fr

Orange is a thriving regional
center. The fields, orchards,
and great vineyards of the
Rhône Valley make it an
important marketplace for
produce such as grapes, olives,
honey, and truffles. Visitors
should explore the area around
the 17th-century Hôtel de Ville,
where attractive streets open
onto quiet, shady squares.
Orange has two of the greatest
Roman monuments in Europe.

🏛 Roman Theater
Rue Madeleine-Roch. **Tel** *04 90 51
17 60.* ◯ *daily.* 🎟 🎫 *entrance
also valid for Musée d'Orange.*
♿ *restricted.* 🅿 🅿
Dating from the 1st-century
AD reign of Augustus, the
well-preserved theater has
perfect acoustics. It is still used
for theater performances and
concerts. The back wall rises
to a height of 120 ft (36 m)
and is 338 ft (103 m) wide. In
2006 an immense glass roof,
built high above the theater
so as not to affect the acoustics, replaced the original roof
which was destroyed in a fire.

**Statue of Augustus Caesar in the
Roman Theater at Orange**

🏛 Triumphal Arch
Av de l'Arc de Triomphe.
The triple-arched monument
was built about AD 20. It is
elaborately decorated with
battle scenes, military
trophies, and inscriptions
to the glory of Tiberius.

🏛 Musée d'Orange
Rue Madeleine-Roch. **Tel** *04 90 51
17 60.* ◯ *daily.* 🎟
Relics here reflect the Roman
presence in Orange, including
400 marble fragments, the
earliest of which dates to
Emperor Vespasian's reign in
the 1st century BC.

Châteauneuf-du-Pape ❹

Vaucluse. 👥 *2,100.* 🚉 *Sorgues, then
taxi.* ℹ *pl du Portail (04 90 83 71
08).* 🚌 *Fri.* **www.**paysprovence.fr

Here, in the 14th century, the
popes of Avignon chose to
build a new castle (*château
neuf*) and plant the vineyards
from which one of the finest

View across the vineyards of Châteauneuf-du-Pape

wines of the Côtes du Rhône is produced. Now almost every doorway in this attractive little town seems to open into a *vigneron's* cellar.

After the Wars of Religion *(see pp54–55)*, all that remained of the papal fortress were a few fragments of walls and tower, but the ruins look spectacular and offer magnificent views across to Avignon and the Vaucluse uplands beyond.

Wine festivals punctuate the year, including the Fête de la Véraison in August *(see p38)*, when the grapes start to ripen, and the Ban des Vendages in September, when the grapes are ready to be harvested.

Avignon ❺

Vaucluse. 🏠 90,000. ✈ 🚆 🚍
ℹ️ 41 cours Jean Jaurès (04 32 74 32 74). 🗓️ Tue–Sun. 🎭 Festival d'Avignon (3 wks Jul).
www.avignon-tourisme.com

Massive ramparts enclose one of the most fascinating towns in southern France. The **Palais des Papes** *(see pp504–5)* dominates, but there are also other riches. North of the Palais is the 13th-century **Musée du Petit Palais**, once the Archbishop of Avignon's residence. Now a museum, it displays Romanesque and Gothic sculpture and medieval paintings, with works by Botticelli and Carpaccio.

Rue Joseph-Vernet and rue du Roi-René are lined with 17th- and 18th-century houses. There are also fine churches, such as the **Cathédrale de Notre-Dame-des-Doms**, and the 14th-century **Eglise St-Didier**. The **Musée Lapidaire** contains statues, mosaics, and carvings from pre-Roman Provence. The **Musée Calvet** features a superb array of exhibits, such as wrought-iron works and Roman finds. It also gives an overview of French art during the past 500 years, with works by Rodin, Utrillo, and Dufy.

Two major modern and contemporary art collections, the **Musée Anglardon** and **Collection Lambert**, have been added to the city's cultural

Pont St-Bénézet and the Palais des Papes in Avignon

repertoire. The former has works by Van Gogh, Cézanne, and Modigliani, while the latter features minimalist and conceptual art.

The place de l'Horloge is the center of Avignon's social life, with sidewalk cafés and a merry-go-round from 1900. One of the prettiest streets is the rue des Teinturiers. Until the 19th century, brightly patterned calico called *indiennes*

Open-air performance at the Avignon Festival

was printed here – inspiration for today's Provençal patterns. Avignon's renowned 12th-century bridge, the **Pont St-Bénézet**, was largely destroyed by floods in 1668. People danced on an island below the bridge but over the years, as the famous song testifies, *sous* has become *sur*.

Avignon hosts France's largest festival, which includes ballet, drama, and classical concerts. The "Off" festival features 600 companies from all areas of show business.

🏛 **Musée du Petit Palais**
Pl du Palais. **Tel** 04 90 86 44 58. ⭕
Wed–Mon. 🔴 Jan 1, May 1, Dec 25.
📷 🚻 📷 **www**.petit-palais.org

🏛 **Musée Lapidaire**
27 rue de la République. **Tel** 04 90
86 33 84. ⭕ Wed–Mon. 🔴 Jan 1,
May 1, Dec 25. 📷 🚻

🏛 **Musée Calvet**
65 rue Joseph Vernet. **Tel** 04 90 86
33 84. ⭕ Wed–Mon. 🔴 Jan 1,
May 1, Dec 25. 📷 🚻 ♿
restricted. **www**.musee-calvet.org

Palais des Papes

Confronted with factional strife in Rome and encouraged by the scheming of Philippe IV of France, Pope Clement V moved the papal court to Avignon in 1309. Here it remained until 1377, during which time his successors transformed the modest episcopal building into the present magnificent palace. Its heavy fortification was vital to defend against rogue bands of mercenaries. Today it is empty of the luxurious trappings of 14th-century court life, since virtually all the furnishings and works of art were destroyed or looted in the course of the centuries.

Pope Clement VI (1342–52)

Benedict XII's cloister incorporates the guest and staff wings, and the Benedictine chapel.

Trouillas tower

Belltower

Military Architecture
The palace and its ten towers were designed as an impregnable fortress. It eventually covered an area of 148,000 sq ft (15,000 sq m).

THE AVIGNON POPES

Seven "official" popes reigned in Avignon until 1376. They were followed by two "anti-popes," the last of whom, Benedict XIII, fled in 1403. Popes or anti-popes, few were known for their sanctity. Clement V died eating powdered emeralds, prescribed as an indigestion cure; Clement VI (1342–52) thought that the best way to honor God was through luxury. Petrarch was shocked by "the filth of the universe" at court. In 1367, Urban V tried to return the Curia (papal court) to Rome, a move that became permanent in 1377.

Benedict XII (1334–42)

La Gache tower

Corner tower

Champeaux gate

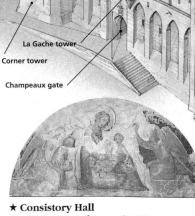

★ Consistory Hall
Simone Martini's frescoes (1340) were taken from the cathedral to replace works destroyed by fire in the papal reception hall in 1413.

For hotels and restaurants in this region see pp590–4 and pp646–50

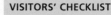

Papal Power
*More like a warlord's citadel than a
papal palace, the building's heavy
fortification reflects the insecure climate
of 14th-century religious life.*

★ Stag Room
*Fourteenth-century hunting
frescoes and ceramic tiles
adorn Clement VI's study,
making it the palace's
loveliest room.*

Angels' tower

Pope's chamber

Great courtyard

BUILDING THE PALACE

The palace comprises
Pope Benedict XII's simple
Palais Vieux (1334–42) and
Clement VI's flamboyant
Palais Neuf (1342–52). Ten
towers, some of which are
more than 164 ft (50 m)
high, are set in the walls
to protect its four
wings.

The Great Chapel is
66 ft (20 m) high and
covers an area of
8,400 sq ft (780 sq m).

The Great Audience Hall is
divided into two naves by
five columns with bestiary
sculpture on their capitals.

STAR FEATURES

★ Consistory Hall

★ Stag Room

KEY

☐ By Benedict XII (1334–42)

☐ By Clement VI (1342–52)

Carpentras ❻

Vaucluse. 🏠 *29,000.* 🚆 **ℹ** *Maison de Pays, 97 pl du 25 Août 1944 (04 90 63 00 78).* 🚩 *Fri.*
www.carpentras-ventoux.com

In 1320, Carpentras became capital of the papal county of Venaissin, and remained so until 1791. Modern boulevards trace the former ramparts, with only one original gate, the Porte d'Orange, surviving.

In the Middle Ages the town was home to a large Jewish community. The 1367 **Synagogue** is the oldest in France. The Sanctuary has been restored.

While not openly persecuted under papal rule, many Jews changed faith, entering **Cathédrale St-Siffrein** by the Porte Juive (Jews' Door).

The Law Courts were built in 1640 as the episcopal palace. The Criminal Court has 17th-century carved tablets of the local towns. In the pharmacy of the Hôtel-Dieu, the 18th-century cupboards are painted with quaint figures of monkey "doctors." More regional art and history is on show at the **Musée Sobirats**.

🕎 Synagogue
Pl de la Mairie. **Tel** *04 90 63 39 97.* ◯ *Mon–Fri.* ⬤ *Jewish feast days.*

🏛 Musée Sobirats
112 rue du Collège. **Tel** *04 90 63 04 92.* ◯ *Wed–Mon.* ⬤ *Oct–Mar & public hols.* 📷

Riverfront and watermill at Fontaine-de-Vaucluse

Fontaine-de-Vaucluse ❼

Vaucluse. 🏠 *650.* 🚆 **ℹ** *chemin du Gouffre (04 90 20 32 22).*
www.oti-delasorgue.fr

The main attraction here is the source of the river Sorgue. It is the most powerful spring in France, gushing at up to 19,800 gallons per second from an underground river at the foot of a cliff. It powers the Moulin à Papier Vallis Clausa (papermill), which produces handmade paper using the same methods as in the 15th century, and now sells maps, prints, and lampshades. There are also several museums. One is devoted to the poet Petrarch, who lived and wrote here, and another to the French Resistance of World War II.

Perched village of Gordes

Gordes ❽

Vaucluse. 🏠 *2,100.* **ℹ** *pl du Château (04 90 72 02 75).* 🚩 *Tue.*
www.gordes-village.com

Perched villages abound in Provence but Gordes is said to attract the most visitors. Dominated by a 16th-century château, the town forms such a harmonious whole that it might have been designed by an architect. The arcaded medieval lanes add to the attractive hilltop position.

Just south lies the **Village des Bories**, a bizarre, primitive habitat. Bories are tiny beehive-shaped huts built of overlapping dry stones. The construction techniques are thought to date back to Neolithic times. This group was inhabited from the 16th to the early 20th century.

The **Abbaye de Sénanque**, to the north, is a fine Romanesque Cistercian monastery.

♟Château de Gordes
Tel *04 90 72 02 75.* ◯ *daily.* ⬤ *Jan 1, Dec 25.* 📷

⌂ Village des Bories
Rte de Gorde. **Tel** *04 90 72 03 48.* ◯ *daily.* ⬤ *Jan 1, Dec 25, 31.* 📷

Luberon ❾

Vaucluse. ✈ *Avignon.* 🚆 *Cavaillon, Avignon.* 🚌 *Apt.* **ℹ** *Cavaillon (04 90 71 32 01).* **www**.cavaillon-luberon.fr

A huge limestone range, the Montagne du Luberon is one of the most appealing areas of Provence. Rising to 3,690 ft (1,125 m), it combines wild areas with picturesque villages. Almost the entire area is designated a regional nature park. Within it are more than 1,000 plant species and cedar and oak forests. The wildlife is varied, with eagles, vultures, snakes, beavers, wild boar, and the largest European lizards. The park headquarters are in **Apt**, the capital of the Luberon.

Once notorious as the haunt of highwaymen, the Luberon hills now hide sumptuous vacation homes. The major village is **Bonnieux**, with its 12th-century church and 13th-century walls. Also popular are **Roussillon**, with red ocher buildings, **Lacoste**, the site of the ruins of the Marquis de Sade's castle, and **Ansouis**, with its 14th-century Eglise St-Martin and 17th-century castle. **Ménerbes** drew to it the writer Peter Mayle, whose tales of life here brought this quiet region a worldwide audience.

Herb stall at St-Rémy-de-Provence

St-Rémy-de-Provence ⑩

Bouches-du-Rhône. 🏠 10,700. 🚌
ℹ pl Jean Jaurès (04 90 92 05 22).
🔄 Wed. www.saintremy-de-provence.com

For centuries St-Rémy, with its boulevards, fountains, and narrow streets, had two claims to fame. One was that Vincent Van Gogh spent a year here, in 1889–90, at the St-Paul-de-Mausole hospital. *Wheat Field with Cypress* and *Ravine* are among the 150 works he produced here. St-Rémy-de-Provence was also, in 1503,

the birthplace of Nostradamus, known for his prophecies. But, in 1921, St-Rémy found new fame when archaeologists unearthed the Roman ruins at **Glanum**. Little remains of the ancient city, sacked in AD 480 by the Goths, but the site impresses. Around the ruins of a Roman arch is a mausoleum, decorated with scenes such as the death of Adonis.

♫ Glanum
Tel 04 90 92 23 79. 🕐 Apr–Aug: daily; Sep–Mar: Tue–Sun. ● Jan 1, May 1, Nov 1 & 11, Dec 25. 🎫 🐾 🎁 🖼
www.glanum.monuments-nationaux.fr

Les Baux-de-Provence ⑪

Bouches-du-Rhône. 🏠 460. 🚌 Arles.
ℹ La Maison du Roy (04 90 54 34 39).
www.lesbauxdeprovence.com

One of the strangest places in Provence, the deserted citadel of Les Baux stands like a natural extension of a huge rocky plateau. The ruined castle and old houses overlook the Val d'Enfer (Infernal Valley), with its weird rocks.

In the Middle Ages Les Baux was home to powerful feudal lords, who claimed descent from the Magus Balthazar. It was the most famous of the Provençal Cours d'Amour, at which troubadours sang the praises of high-born ladies. The ideal of everlasting but unrequited courtly love contrasts with the war-like nature of the citadel's lords.

The glory of Les Baux ended in 1632. It had become a Protestant stronghold and Louis XIII ordered its destruction. The ruins of **Châteaux de Baux de Provence** are a reminder of a

Deserted medieval citadel of Les Baux-de-Provence

turbulent past and offer spectacular views. The living village below has a pleasant little square, the 12th-century **Eglise St-Vincent** and the **Chapelle des Pénitents Blancs**, decorated by local artist Yves Brayer, whose work can be seen in the **Musée Yves Brayer**.

In 1821 bauxite, a deep red mineral, was discovered here and named after the town. Deposits were intensely exploited until they ran out at the end of the 20th century.

To the southwest are the ruins of the **Abbaye de Mont-majour** with its 12th-century Romanesque church.

Parading the Tarasque, 1850

Tarascon ⑫

Bouches-du-Rhône. 🏠 14,000.
🚌 🚌 ℹ Les Panaromiques, av de la République (04 90 91 03 52).
🔄 Tue & Fri. www.tarascon.org

According to legend, the town takes its name from the Tarasque, a monster, half-animal and half-fish, which terrorized the countryside. It was tamed by Sainte Marthe, who is buried in the church here. An effigy of the Tarasque is still paraded through the streets each June *(see p37)*.

The striking 15th-century **Château du Roi René** on the banks of the Rhône is one of the finest examples of Gothic military architecture in Provence. Its somber exterior gives no hint of the beauties within: the Flemish-Gothic courtyard, the spiral staircase, and painted ceilings of the banqueting hall.

Opposite is Beaucaire, a ruined castle and gardens.

♣ Château du Roi René
Bd du Roi René. *Tel* 04 90 91 01 93.
🕐 daily. ● some public hols.
🎫 🎁

Arles ⑬

Few other towns in Provence combine all the region's charms so well as Arles. Its position on the Rhône makes it a natural, historic gateway to the Camargue *(see pp510–11)*. Its Roman remains, such as the arena and Constantine's baths, are complemented by the ocher walls and Roman-tiled roofs of later buildings. A bastion of Provençal tradition and culture, its museums are among the best in the region. Van Gogh spent time here in 1888–9, but Arles is no longer the industrial town he painted. Visitors are now its main business, and entertainment ranges from the Arles Festival to bullfights.

Emperor Constantine

Palais Constantine was once a grand imperial palace. Now only its vast Roman baths remain, dating from the 4th century AD. They are remarkably well preserved and give an idea of the luxury that bathers enjoyed.

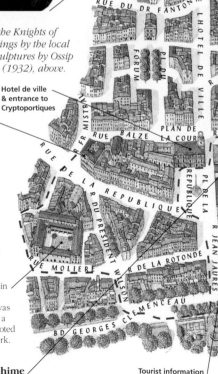

Musée Réattu
This museum, in the old Commandery of the Knights of Malta, houses witty Picasso sketches, paintings by the local artist Jacques Réattu (1760–1833), and sculptures by Ossip Zadkine, including La Grande Odalisque (1932), above.

Museon Arlaten
In 1904 the poet Frédéric Mistral used his Nobel Prize money to establish this museum devoted to his beloved native Provence. Parts of the collection are arranged in room settings, and even the museum attendants wear traditional Arles costume.

Hotel de ville & entrance to Cryptoportiques

Espace Van Gogh, in a former hospital where the artist was treated in 1889, is a cultural center devoted to his life and work.

Tourist information

★ Eglise St-Trophime
This church combines a noble 12th-century Romanesque exterior with superb Romanesque and Gothic cloisters. The ornate main portal is carved with saints and apostles.

| 0 meters | 100 |
| 0 yards | 100 |

LES ALYSCAMPS

A tree-lined avenue of broken medieval tombs is the focal point of these "Elysian Fields" to the southeast of Arles. It became Christian in the 4th century and was a prestigious burial ground until the 12th century. Some sarcophagi were sold to museums; others have been neglected. Mentioned in Dante's *Inferno*, painted by Van Gogh and Gauguin, it is a place for thought and inspiration.

Les Alyscamps by Paul Gauguin

★ Roman Amphitheater

This is one of the best-preserved monuments of Roman Provence. Each arch is supported by Doric and Corinthian columns. In summer there are bull contests in the 21,000-seat arena. The top tier provides a panoramic view of Arles.

Notre-Dame-de-la-Major is the church in which the *gardians* (cowboys) of the Camargue celebrate the feast day of their patron saint, St. George. Although the building dates from the 12th to 17th centuries, a Roman temple existed on this spot hundreds of years earlier.

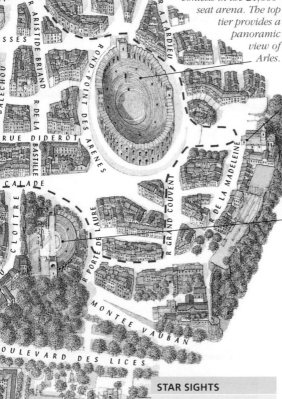

To train and bus stations

★ Roman Theater

Once a fortress, its stones were later used for other buildings. Today, the theater stages the Arles Festival. Its remaining columns are called the "two widows."

STAR SIGHTS

★ Roman Amphitheater

★ Roman Theater

★ Eglise St-Trophime

KEY

– – – Suggested route

The Camargue ⑭

Sunset over the Camargue

The Rhône delta was responsible for the formation of more than 280,000 acres (112,000 ha) of wetlands, pastures, dunes, and salt flats that make up the Camargue, but human efforts are needed to preserve it. The region now maintains a fragile ecological balance, in which a unique collection of flora flourishes, including tamarisk and narcisi, and fauna such as egrets and ibises. The pastures provide grazing for sheep, cattle, and small white Arab-type horses, ridden by the *gardians* or cowboys, a hardy community who traditionally lived in thatched huts *(cabanes)* and still play their part in keeping Camargue traditions alive.

Camargue gardian

Mas du Pont de Ro

D572

D570

Le Petit Rhône

Mêjanes ▪

PLAINE DE LA CAMARGUE

Etang de Vaccar

D37

Black Bulls

In a Provençal bull contest (known as a course*), the animals are not killed. Instead, red rosettes are plucked from between their horns with a small hook.*

PARC REGIONAL DE

PETITE CAMARGUE

Centre de Ginès

Stes-Maries-de-la-Mer

0 kilometers 5

0 miles 5

MEDITERRANEE

Les Stes-Maries-de-la-Mer

The May gypsy pilgrimage to this fortified church marks the legendary arrival by boat in AD 18 of Mary Magdalene, St. Martha, and the sister of the Virgin Mary. Statues in the church depict the event.

Flamingoes

These striking birds are always associated with the Camargue, but the region supports many other breeds, including herons, kingfishers, owls, and birds of prey. The area around Ginès is the best place to see them.

For hotels and restaurants in this region see pp590–4 and pp646–50

KEY

— Nature reserve boundary

– – Walking routes

– – Walking and cycling routes

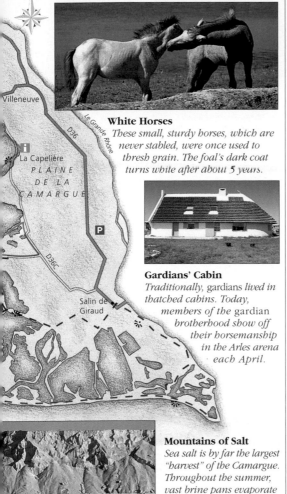

White Horses
These small, sturdy horses, which are never stabled, were once used to thresh grain. The foal's dark coat turns white after about 5 years.

Gardians' Cabin
Traditionally, gardians lived in thatched cabins. Today, members of the gardian brotherhood show off their horsemanship in the Arles arena each April.

Mountains of Salt
Sea salt is by far the largest "harvest" of the Camargue. Throughout the summer, vast brine pans evaporate and the crystals are heaped into shimmering camelles up to 26 ft (8 m) high.

Aix-en-Provence ⑮

Bouches du Rhône. 🏠 *135,000.*
🚌 🚌 ℹ *2 place du Général-de-Gaulle (04 42 16 11 61).* 🛍 *daily.*
www.aixenprovencetourism.com

Founded by the Romans in 103 BC, Aix was frequently attacked, first by the Visigoths in AD 477, later by Lombards, Franks, and Saracens. Despite this, the city prospered. By the end of the 12th century it was capital of Provence. A center of art and learning, it reached its peak in the 15th century during the reign of "Good King" René. He is shown in Nicolas Froment's *Triptych of the Burning Bush* in the 13th-century Gothic **Cathédrale de St-Sauveur**, also noted for its 16th-century walnut doors, Merovingian baptistry, and Romanesque cloisters.

Aix is still a center of art and learning, and its many museums include the **Musée Granet** of fine arts and arch-eology, and the **Musée des Tapisseries** (tapestries), in the Palais de l'Archevêché.

Aix has been called "the city of a thousand fountains." Three of the best are situated on cours Mirabeau. On one side are 17th- and 18th-century buildings with wrought-iron balconies; on the other are cafés. The Old Town centers on place de l'Hôtel de Ville, with its colorful flower market. In the northwest of town is the **Pavillon de Vendôme**, housing furniture and works of art by Van Loo.

Aix's most famous son is Paul Cézanne. The **Atelier Cézanne** is kept as it was when he died in 1906. Montagne Ste-Victoire, inspiration for many of his paintings, is 9 miles (15 km) east of Aix.

🏛 **Musée Granet**
Pl St-Jean de Malte. **Tel** 04 42 52 88 32. ⬤ *Tue–Sun.* ⬤ *Jan 1, May 1, Dec 25.* 🎫 🚻 ♿
🏛 **Musée des Tapisseries**
28 pl des Martyrs de la Résistance. **Tel** 04 42 23 09 91. ⬤ *Wed–Mon.*
⬤ *Jan.* 🎫 🚻
🏺 **Atelier Cézanne**
9 av Paul Cézanne. **Tel** 04 42 21 06 53. ⬤ *daily.* ⬤ *Dec–Feb: Sun; some public hols.* 🎫 🚻
www.atelier-cezanne.com

Old harbor of Marseille, looking toward the quai de Rive Neuve

Marseille ⑯

Bouches-du-Rhône. 👥 900,000.
✈ 🚉 🚌 ❓ ℹ 4 La Canebière
(0826 500 500). 🅿 daily.
www.marseille-tourisme.com

A Greek settlement, founded
in the 7th century BC, then
called Massilia, Marseille was
seized by the Romans in 49
BC. It became the "Gateway
to the West" for most Oriental
trade. France's largest port and
lively second-largest city has
close links with the Middle
East and North Africa.

In Marseille, narrow stepped
streets, quiet squares, and fine
18th-century façades contrast
with the bustle of boulevard
Canebière and the Cité
Radieuse, Le Corbusier's post-
war radical housing complex.

The old harbor now only
handles small boats, but its
daily fish market is renowned.

Marseille has many
excellent museums. Those in
the old harbor area include
the **Musée des Docks
Romains**, the **Musée d'Histoire de Marseille**, the **Musée
du Vieux Marseille**, and the
upbeat **Musée de la Mode**.

The **Musée Cantini**, to the
south, houses the 20th-century
art collection of sculptor Jules
Cantini. It includes Surrealist,
Cubist, and Fauve paintings.

On the other side of the city is
the **Musée Grobet-Labadié**, with
its fine furniture, tapestries,
and rare musical instruments.

Marseille has an extensive
tramway system and has
introduced a bike rental
program that allows people to
rent a bike in one part of
town and return it in another.

🏛 Musée des Beaux-Arts

Palais Longchamp, pl Aile Gauche.
Tel 04 91 14 59 30. 🕐 Tue–Sun.
🔴 until late 2012. 🎫 ♿
This museum is housed in the
handsome 19th-century Palais
Longchamp. Works include
Michel Serre's graphic views
of Marseille's plague of 1721,
Pierre Puget's town plans for
the city, and murals depicting
it in Greek and Roman times.

⚓ Château d'If

Tel 04 91 59 02 30. 🕐 Apr–Aug:
daily; Sep–Mar: Tue–Sun. 🎫 🖥

The Château d'If (Castle of
Yew) stands on a tiny island
1 mile (2 km) southwest of
the port. A formidable
fortress, it was built in 1529 to
house artillery, but never put
to military use and later
became a prison. Alexandre
Dumas' fictional "Count of
Monte Cristo" was supposed
to have been imprisoned here,
and visitors can see a special
cell, complete with escape
hole. Most real-life inmates
were either common criminals
or political prisoners.

🔒 Notre-Dame-de-la-Garde

Built between 1853 and 1864,
this Neo-Byzantine basilica
dominates the city. Its belfry,
151 ft (46 m) high, is capped
by a huge gilded statue of the
Virgin. The lavishly decorated
interior has colored marble
and mosaic facings.

🔒 Abbaye de St-Victor

Similar to a fortress in
appearance, the abbey was
rebuilt in the 11th century
after destruction by the
Saracens. In the French
Revolution, the rebels used
it as a barracks and prison.

There is an intriguing crypt
in the abbey's church, with
an original catacomb chapel
and a number of pagan and
Christian sarcophagi.

On February 2 each year,
St-Victor becomes a place of
pilgrimage. Boat-shaped cakes
are sold to commemorate the
legendary arrival of St. Mary
Magdalene, Lazarus, and St.
Martha nearly 2,000 years ago.

🔒 Cathédrale de la Major

Built in Neo-Byzantine style,
this is the largest 19th-century
church in France, 463 ft (141
m) long and 230 ft (70 m) high.
In the crypt are the tombs of
the bishops of Marseille. By it

Le Corbusier's innovative Cité Radieuse in Marseille

For hotels and restaurants in this region see pp590–4 and pp646–50

Fish market at Marseille

is the small and beautiful Ancienne Cathédrale de la Major.

⊞ Vieille Charité

Rue de la Charité. *Tel 04 91 14 58 80.*
☐ Tue–Sun. ● pub hols. 🈂️ 🚻 🔅
In 1640, the construction of a shelter "for the poor and beggars" of Marseille was begun by royal decree. 100 years later, Pierre Puget's hospital and domed church were opened. Now, the restored building houses the Musée d'Archéologie Egyptienne, with its fine collection of Egyptian artifacts; the Musée des Arts Africains is on the second floor.

Cassis ⑰

Bouches-du-Rhône. 🏠 *8,000.*
🚉 🚌 🛈 *quai Moulins, Le Port (08 92 25 98 92).* 🛒 *Wed & Fri.*
www.ot-cassis.com

Many of the villages along this coast have lost their original charm to development, but Cassis is still much the same little fishing port that attracted artists such as Dufy, Signac, and Derain. This is a place in which to relax at a waterside café, watching the fishermen or street performers while enjoying the seafood and a bottle of the local dry white wine for which Cassis is famous.

From Marseille to Cassis the coastline forms narrow inlets, the **Calanques**, their jagged white cliffs (some as much as 1,312 ft/400 m high) reflected in dazzling turquoise water. Wildlife abounds here, with countless seabirds, foxes, stone martens, bats, large snakes, and lizards. The flora is no less impressive, with more than 900 plant species, of which 50 are classified as rare. The En-Vau and Sormiou Calanques are especially lovely.

Toulon ⑱

Var. 🏠 *170,000.* ✈ 🚉 🚌 🚢
🛈 *pl Louis-Blanc (04 94 18 53 00).*
🛒 *Tue–Sun.* **www**.toulon tourisme.com

In 1793 this naval base was captured by an Anglo-Spanish fleet, but was retaken by the young Napoleon Bonaparte. The **Musée National de la Marine** is a focus for history. The **Musée d'Art de Toulon**, housed in an Italian Renaissance building, has a collection representing Fauvism, Minimalism, and Realism. The tower of the former town hall is all that remains of pre-war Quai Cronstadt (rebuilt and renamed Quai Stalingrad). The war-damaged Old Town has a few original buildings, and the fish market is worth a visit.

🏛 Musée National de la Marine

Pl Monsenergue. *Tel 04 94 02 02 01.* ☐ daily. ● Tue (Sep–Jun), May 1, Dec 25. 🈂️ 🔅 restr. 🛈 **www**.musee-marine.fr

🏛 Musée d'Art de Toulon

113 bd Marc Leclerc. *Tel 04 94 36 81 00.* ☐ Tue–Sun. ● Jan, public hols. 🈂️

Paul Signac's *Cap Canaille,* **painted at Cassis in 1889**

Tour of the Gorges du Verdon

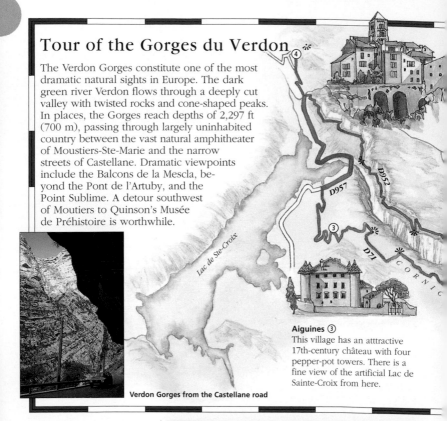

The Verdon Gorges constitute one of the most dramatic natural sights in Europe. The dark green river Verdon flows through a deeply cut valley with twisted rocks and cone-shaped peaks. In places, the Gorges reach depths of 2,297 ft (700 m), passing through largely uninhabited country between the vast natural amphitheater of Moustiers-Ste-Marie and the narrow streets of Castellane. Dramatic viewpoints include the Balcons de la Mescla, beyond the Pont de l'Artuby, and the Point Sublime. A detour southwest of Moutiers to Quinson's Musée de Préhistoire is worthwhile.

Aiguines ③
This village has an atttractive 17th-century château with four pepper-pot towers. There is a fine view of the artificial Lac de Sainte-Croix from here.

Verdon Gorges from the Castellane road

Hyères ⑲

Var. 54,000. ⊠ ▣ ▣ ▣
🛈 Av Ambroise Thomas (04 94 01 84 50). www.hyeres-tourisme.com
📅 Tue–Sun.

Toward the end of the 18th century, Hyères became one of the first health resorts of the Côte d'Azur. Among its subsequent visitors were Queen Victoria and writers Robert Louis Stevenson and Edith Wharton.

The main sights are found in the medieval streets of the Vieille Ville, which lead past the spacious, flagstoned place Massillon to a ruined castle and views over the coast.

Modern Hyères is imbued with a lingering Belle Epoque charm which has become popular with experimental film-makers. It continues to attract a health-conscious crowd and is a major center for aquatic sports.

Fishing off Porquerolles, the largest of the Iles d'Hyères

For hotels and restaurants in this region see pp590–4 and pp646–50

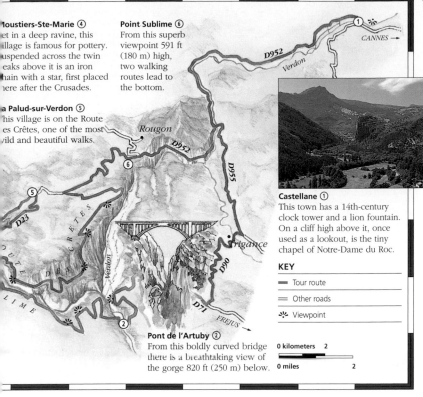

Moustiers-Ste-Marie ④
Set in a deep ravine, this
village is famous for pottery.
Suspended across the twin
peaks above it is an iron
chain with a star, first placed
here after the Crusades.

Point Sublime ⑥
From this superb
viewpoint 591 ft
(180 m) high,
two walking
routes lead to
the bottom.

La Palud-sur-Verdon ⑤
This village is on the Route
des Crêtes, one of the most
wild and beautiful walks.

Rougon

Trigance

Castellane ①
This town has a 14th-century
clock tower and a lion fountain.
On a cliff high above it, once
used as a lookout, is the tiny
chapel of Notre-Dame du Roc.

KEY

━━ Tour route

══ Other roads

☼ Viewpoint

Pont de l'Artuby ②
From this boldly curved bridge
there is a breathtaking view of
the gorge 820 ft (250 m) below.

0 kilometers   2

0 miles   2

Îles d'Hyères ❸

Var. ✈ Toulon-Hyères. 🚆 🚌 ⛴
Hyères. 🛈 Hyères (04 94 01 84 50).
www.hyeres-tourisme.com

Locally known as the Îles
d'Or, after the gold color of
their cliffs, this glamorous trio
of islands can be reached by
boat from Hyères, Le
Lavandou, and, in summer,
Cavalaire and Port-de-Miramar.
   Porquerolles, the largest of
the three, measures 4.5 miles
(7 km) by 2 miles (3 km). It
is covered in rich vegetation,
much of which, for instance
the Mexican bellombra tree,
was introduced from a variety
of exotic foreign climes.
   The island's main town,
also known as Porquerolles,
looks more like a north
African colonial settlement
than a Provençal village. It
was established in 1820 as a
retirement town for Napoleon's
most honored troops. All the

island's beaches lie along the
northern coastline. The best,
the long, sandy Plage Notre-
Dame, one of the finest
beaches in Provence, sits in a
sheltered bay about an hour's
walk from Porquerolles.
   A stroll around lush, hilly
Port-Cros, covering just 1 sq
mile (2.5 sq km), takes the
best part of a day. It rises to
640 ft (195 m), the highest
point on any of the islands.
   Port-Cros has been a national park since 1963. A unique
preserve of flora and fauna, its
waters are also protected.
There is even a 984-ft (300-m)
scenic swimming route. You
can buy a waterproof guide
to the underwater wildlife.
   The wild, virtually treeless
Île du Levant is reached by
boat from Port-Cros. Its main
draw is the oldest naturist
resort in France, Héliopolis,
founded in 1931. The eastern
half of the island, controlled
by the French navy, is permanently closed to the public.

Massif des Maures ㉑

Var. ✈ Toulon-Hyères. 🚆 Hyères,
Toulon or Fréjus. 🚌 Bormes-les-
Mimosas. ⛴ Toulon. 🛈 1 pl
Gambetta, Bormes-les-Mimosas
(04 94 01 38 38).
www.bormeslesmimosas.com

The dense wilderness of pine,
oak, and sweet chestnut
covering the Maures mountains
probably gave rise to its name,
meaning dark or gloomy. It
extends nearly 40 miles (65
km) between Hyères and
Fréjus. The D558 north of
Cogolin leads to the heart of
the Maures. Along the way is
La Garde-Freinet, well known
for its bottle-cork industry.
   Northwest of Cannet-des-
Maures lies the Abbaye de
Thoronet. With the abbeys at
Sénanque, in Vaucluse, and
Silvacane, in the Bouches-du-
Rhône, it is known as one of
the "Three Sisters" of Provence.

Harborside at St-Tropez

St-Tropez ⊕

Var. 🏛 6,000. 🚗 ℹ *quai Jean Jaurès (04 94 97 45 21).* 🚌 *Tue & Sat.* **www**.ot-saint-tropez.com

The geography of St-Tropez kept it untouched by the earliest development of the Côte d'Azur. Tucked away at the tip of a peninsula, it is the only north-facing town on the coast and so did not appeal to those seeking a warm and sheltered winter resort. In 1892 the painter Paul Signac was among the first outsiders to respond to its unspoiled charm, encouraging friends, such as the painters Matisse and Bonnard, to join him. In the 1920s the Parisian writer Colette also made her home here. St-Tropez also began to attract star-spotters, hoping for a glimpse of celebrities such as the Prince of Wales.

During World War II the beaches around St-Tropez were the scene of Allied landings, and part of the town was heavily bombed. Then, in the 1950s, young Parisians began to arrive, and the Bardot-Vadim movie helped to create the reputation of modern St-Tropez as a playground for gilded youth. The wild public behavior and turbulent love affairs of Roger Vadim, Brigitte Bardot, Sacha Distel, and others left fiction far behind. Mass tourism followed, with visitors once again more interested in spotting a celebrity than in visiting the **Musée de l'Annonciade** with its outstanding collection of works by Signac, Derain, Rouault,

Bonnard and others. Bardot had a villa at La Madrague, but tourists invaded her privacy, so she left.

Today, there are far more luxury yachts than fishing boats moored in St-Tropez harbor. Its cafés make ideal bases for people- and yacht-watching. Another center of the action is place des Lices, both for the Harley-Davidson set and the morning market. The tiny **Maison des Papillons** (Butterfly House), with its collection of more than 20,000 species, is an increasingly popular attraction.

The best beaches are found outside the town, including the golden curve of Pampelonne, jammed with beach clubs and restaurants. This is the beach on which to see and be seen. St-Tropez has no train station, so driving and parking can be a nightmare in summer.

It is said that St-Tropez takes its name from a Roman soldier martyred as a Christian

by the Emperor Nero. Each year in May a *bravade* in his honor takes place when an effigy of the saint is carried through the town to the accompaniment of musket fire.

Nearby are two small towns of differing character but equal charm. **Port-Grimaud** was only built in 1966 but the sensitive use of traditional architecture makes it seem older. Most of its "streets" are canals. Up in the hills, the winding streets of **Ramatuelle** have been restored to perfection by the largely celebrity population.

🏛 **Maison des Papillons**
9 rue Etienne Berny. **Tel** *04 94 97 63 45.* 🕐 *Apr–Oct, public & school hols: Mon–Sat.* 📷

🏛 **Musée de l'Annonciade**
Pl Grammont. **Tel** *04 94 17 84 10.* 🕐 *Wed–Mon.* ● *Jan 1, May 8, Nov 1.* 📷 🚫 🏛 📷

Stylish solution to the traffic problems in St-Tropez

BRIGITTE BARDOT

In 1956, Brigitte Bardot's film, *And God Created Woman*, was shot in St-Tropez by her new husband, Roger Vadim. By settling in St-Tropez, "BB" the sex-goddess changed the fortunes of the sleepy little fishing village and ultimately the Côte d'Azur, making it the center of her hedonistic lifestyle. In 1974, on her 40th birthday, she celebrated her retirement from movies at Club 55 on Pampelonne Beach, and now devotes her time to her animal sanctuary.

Brigitte Bardot in 1956

Digne-les-Bains ㉓

Alpes-de-Haute-Provence. 👥 *17,500.* 🚌 🚃 ℹ *pl de Tampinet (04 92 36 62 62).* 🛍 *Wed, Sat.* **www.ot-dignelesbains.fr**

This charming spa town in the foothills of the Alps features in Victor Hugo's *Les Misérables*. A trip on the *Train des Pignes* from Nice offers superb views. Apart from the spa, Digne also offers a lavender festival (*see p38*) and **Le Jardin des Papillons**, France's only butterfly garden.

🏛 **Le Jardin des Papillons**
St Benoît. **Tel** *04 92 31 83 34.* ⭕ *Apr–Sep: by appt only.* 🎫 ♿ 📷 *in summer.* 🅿 **www.proserpine.org**

Fréjus ㉔

Var. 👥 *53,000.* 🚌 🚃 ℹ *249 rue Jean Jaurès (04 94 51 83 83).* 🛍 *Wed, Fri–Sun.* **www.frejus.fr**

The modern town of Fréjus is dwarfed in importance by two impressive historic sites. The remains of the Roman port of **Amphithéâtre** (founded by Julius Caesar in 49 BC) may not be as complete as those at Orange or Arles but they are of exceptional variety. A great amphitheater, fragments of an aqueduct, a theater, and part of a rampart gateway remain. The sea has receded over the centuries and there are few traces of the original harbor.

The cathedral on place Formigé marks the entrance to the **Cité Episcopale**. The fortified enclave includes the 5th-century baptistry, one of the oldest in France, and the cathedral cloister, its coffered medieval roof decorated with scenes from the Apocalypse.

In 1959 Fréjus was hit by a wall of water as the Malpasset Barrage burst. To the north the ruined dam can still be seen.

🏛 **Amphithéâtre**
Rue Henri Vadon. **Tel** *04 94 51 34 31.* ⭕ *Tue–Sun.* ⭕ *Jan 1, May 1, Dec 25.* 🎫 📷 📷

🏛 **Cité Episcopale**
58 rue de Fleury. **Tel** *04 94 51 26 30.* ⭕ *Jun–Sep: daily.* ⭕ *Jan 1, May 1, Nov 1 & 11, Dec 25.* 🎫 *cloisters.* ♿ 📷 📷

THE CREATION OF A PERFUME

The best perfumes begin as a formula of essential oils extracted from natural sources. The blend of aromas is created by a perfumer called a "nose" because of his or her exceptional sense of smell. A perfume may use as many as 300 essences, all painstakingly extracted from plants by various methods: steam distillation, extraction by volatile solvents, and *enfluerage a froid* (for costly or potent essences). With this process, pungent blossoms are placed onto layers of fats for several days until the fats are saturated. The oils are then "washed" out with alcohol, and when this evaporates, it leaves the "pure" perfume essence behind.

Lavender water

Grasse flowers

St-Raphaël ㉕

Var. 👥 *40,000.* 🚌 🚃 ℹ *99 quai Albert 1er (04 94 19 52 52).* **www.saint-raphael.com**

Delightfully situated, St-Raphaël is a charming, old-style Côte d'Azur resort with Art Nouveau architecture and a palm-fronded promenade. Aside from its beaches, it offers a marina, a casino, Roman ruins, a 12th-century church, and a museum with treasures from a Roman wreck found by Jacques Cousteau.

It was here that Napoleon Bonaparte landed in 1799 on his return from Egypt.

Grasse ㉖

Alpes-Maritimes. 👥 *50,000.* 🚌 ℹ *Palais des Congrès, 22 cours Honoré Cresp (04 93 36 66 66).* **www.grasse.fr**

Cradled by hills, with views out to sea, Grasse is surrounded by fields of lavender, mimosa, jasmine, and roses. Grasse has been the center of the world's perfume industry since the 16th century, when Catherine de' Médici set the fashion for scented leather gloves. At that time, Grasse was also known

as the center for leather tanning. The tanneries have gone, but the perfume houses founded in the 18th and 19th centuries are still in business, although today Grasse perfumes are made from imported flowers or chemicals. Fragonard and Molinard have museums, but the best place to learn is at the **Musée Internationale de la Parfumerie**, which has a garden of fragrant plants.

Grasse was the birthplace of Jean-Honoré Fragonard, the artist. The **Villa-Musée Fragonard** is decorated with murals by his son. Fragonard's only religious work is in the **Cathédrale de Notre-Dame-du-Puy** in the Old Town, with three paintings by Rubens. The place aux Aires and the place du Cours typify Grasse's charm, surrounded by streets with Renaissance staircases and balconies.

🏛 **Musée International de la Parfumerie**
2 bd de Jeu du Ballon. **Tel** *04 97 05 58 00.* ⭕ *Mon, Wed–Sun.* ⭕ *Nov; public hols.* 🎫 ♿ 📷 📷 **www.museesdegrasse.com**

🏛 **Villa-Musée Fragonard**
23 bd Fragonard. **Tel** *04 93 36 80 20.* ⭕ *Wed–Mon.* ⭕ *Nov; public hols.* 🎫 📷

Statue honoring Jean-Honoré Fragonard in Grasse

Lavender fields near Puimoisson, Alpes-de-Haute-Provence ▷

High summer on the beach at Cannes, overlooked by the Carlton Hotel

Cannes ㉗

Alpes-Maritimes. 🏛 70,000. ✈ 🚌
🚆 ℹ Palais des Festivals, 1 La
Croisette (04 92 99 84 22). 🌐 Tue–
Sun. www.palaisdesfestivals.com

Just as Grasse is synonymous with the perfume industry, the first thing that most people associate with Cannes is its many festivals, especially the International Film Festival. There is much more to the city than these glittering events. It was Lord Brougham, the British Lord Chancellor, who put Cannes on the map, although Prosper Mérimée, Inspector of Historic Monuments, allegedly visited Cannes two months before him. Lord Brougham stopped here in 1834, unable to reach Nice due to a cholera outbreak there. Struck by the beauty and mild climate of what was then just a small fishing port,

he built a villa here. Other foreigners followed and Cannes became established as a top Mediterranean resort.

The Old Town which Lord Brougham knew is centered in the Le Suquet district, on the slopes of Mont Chevalier. Part of the old city wall can still be seen on place de la Castre, which is dominated by the **Notre-Dame de l'Espérance**, built in the 16th and 17th centuries in the Provençal Gothic style. An 11th-century watch tower is another attractive feature of the quarter, and the castle keep houses the **Musée de la Castre**, the eclectic finds of a 19th-century Dutch explorer, Baron Lycklama.

The famed **boulevard de la Croisette** is lined with gardens and palm trees. One side is occupied by luxury boutiques and hotels such as the Carlton, built in Belle Epoque style, whose twin cupolas were modeled on the breasts of La Belle Otero, a famous member of the 19th-century *demi-monde*. Opposite are some of the finest sandy beaches on this coast. The glamor of the Croisette, once one of the world's grandest thoroughfares, seems faded in the noise and fumes of summer.

🏖 Îles de Lérins

🚤 depart from: le Quai des Îles.
ℹ Horizon (04 92 98 71 36 for Île
Ste-Marguerite), Planaria (04 92 98
71 38 for Île St-Honorat).

Just off the coast from Cannes are the Îles de Lérins. The fort on **Île Sainte-Marguerite** is where the mysterious Man in the Iron Mask was imprisoned in the late 17th century. A

CANNES FILM FESTIVAL

The first Cannes Film Festival took place in 1946 and, for almost 20 years, it remained a small and exclusive affair, attended by the artists and celebrities who lived or were staying on the coast. The arrival of the "starlet," especially Brigitte Bardot, in the mid-1950s marked the change from artistic event to media circus, but Cannes remains the international marketplace for film-makers and distributors, with the *Palme d'Or* award conferring high status on its winner. The annual film festival is held in the huge Palais des Festivals, opened in 1982. It has three auditoriums, two exhibition halls, conference rooms, a casino, nightclub, and restaurant.

Gérard Depardieu and family arriving at the festival

For hotels and restaurants in this region see pp590–4 and pp646–50

popular theory is that his face had to be hidden because he resembled someone very important indeed – possibly even Louis XIV. Visitors can see the tiny cell that held him for more than ten years.

Ile Saint-Honorat has an 11th-century tower in which the resident monks took refuge during raids by the Saracens. There are also five ancient chapels. Both islands offer peaceful woodland walks, fine views, and quiet coves for swimming.

Beside the Boulevard de la Croisette

Cap d'Antibes ❷⑧

Alpes-Maritimes. 🛫 Nice. 🚊 🚌 Antibes. 🚢 Nice. 🅸 11 pl du Gén de Gaulle, Antibes (04 97 23 11 11). **www**.antibesjuanlespins.com

With its sumptuous villas in their lush grounds, this rocky, wooded peninsula, known as "the Cap" to regulars, has been a symbol of luxury life on the Riviera since it was frequented by F. Scott Fitzgerald and the rich American set in the 1920s. One of the wealthiest of all, magnate Frank Jay Gould invested in the resort of Juan-les-Pins and it became the focus of high life on the Cap. Today, memories of the Jazz Age live on at the Jazz Festival, when international stars perform *(see p37)*.

At the highest point of the peninsula, the sailors' chapel of **La Garoupe** has a collection of votive offerings and a 14th-century Russian icon. Nearby is the **Jardin Thuret**, created in 1856 to acclimatize

tropical plants. Much of the exotic flora of the region began its naturalization here.

🌺 **Jardin Thuret**
90 chemin Raymond. **Tel** 04 97 21 25 03. ⭘ Mon–Fri. ⬤ public hols.

Antibes ❷⑨

Alpes-Maritimes. 🏠 70,000. 🚊 🚌 🚢 🅸 11 pl du Général de Gaulle (04 97 23 11 11). 🚩 Tue–Sun. **www**.antibesjuanlespins.com

The lively town of Antibes was founded by the Greeks as Antipolis and settled by the Romans. In the 14th century, Savoy's possession of the town was contended by France until it fell to them in 1481, after which **Fort Carré** was built and the port, now a center of Mediterranean yachting, was remodeled by Vauban.

The Château Grimaldi, formerly a residence of Monaco's ruling family, was built in the 12th century. It now houses the **Musée Picasso**. In 1946 the artist used part of the castle as a studio and, in gratitude, donated all 150 works completed during his

The Goat (1946) by Pablo Picasso

stay, including *The Goat*. Most are inspired by his love of the sea, including *La Joie de Vivre*.

The pottery in the **Musée d'Histoire et d'Archéologie** includes objects salvaged from shipwrecks from the Middle Ages to the 18th century.

🏛 **Musée Picasso**
Château Grimaldi. **Tel** 04 92 90 54 20. ⭘ Tue–Sun. 🎟 ♿ 🏛 ⬜

🏛 **Musée d'Histoire et d'Archéologie**
1 Bastion St-André. **Tel** 04 92 90 56 87. ⭘ Tue–Sun. ⬤ public hols. 🎟 ♿ 🏛

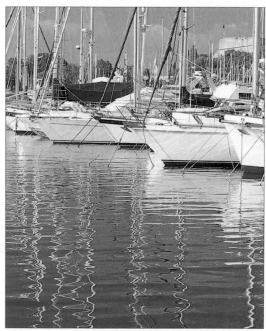

Sailing boats in the harbor at Antibes

Vallauris 30

Alpes-Maritimes. 🏠 31,000.
🚊 🚌 🛈 square 8 mai 1945
(04 93 63 82 58). 🛒 Tue–Sun.
www.vallauris-golfe-juan.fr

Vallauris owes its fame to the influence of Pablo Picasso, who rescued the town's pottery industry. In 1951, the village authorities commissioned Picasso to paint a mural in the deconsecrated chapel next to the castle, and his *War and Peace* (1952) is the chief exhibit of the **Musée National Picasso**. In the main square is a bronze statue, *Man with a Sheep*, donated by Picasso.

🏛 **Musée National Picasso**
Place de la Libération. **Tel** 04 93 64
71 83. 🕐 Wed–Mon. 🔴 Jan 1,
May 1, Nov 1 & 11, Dec 25. 📷 ♿
ground floor only. 📷
www.musee-picasso.vallauris.fr

Biot 31

Alpes-Maritimes. 🏠 9,000. 🚊 🚌
🛈 46 rue St-Sebastien (04 93 65
78 00). 🛒 Tue. **www**.biot.fr

A typical little hill village, Biot has retained its charm and has always attracted artists and artisans. The best known is Fernand Léger, who made his first ceramics here in 1949. Some of these and other works by him are in the **Musée Fernand Léger** outside town.
The town is also famous for its bubble-flecked glassware. The craft of the glassblowers can be seen (and purchased) at the **Verrerie de Biot**.

🏛 **Musée Fernand Léger**
255 chemin du Val-de-Pome.
Tel 04 92 91 50 20. 🕐 Wed–Mon.
🔴 Jan 1, May 1, Dec 25. 📷 ♿
📷 💻 **www**.musee-fernand
leger.fr
📷 **La Verrerie de Biot**
5 ch des Combes. **Tel** 04 93 65 03 00.
🕐 daily. 🔴 Jan 1, Dec 25. ♿ 📷 🍴

Renoir's studio at the Musée Renoir, Les Collettes in Cagnes-sur-Mer

Cagnes-sur-Mer 32

Alpes-Maritimes. 🏠 50,000. 🚊
🚌 🛈 6 bd Maréchal Juin
(04 93 20 61 64). 🛒 Tue–Fri.
www.cagnes-tourisme.com

Cagnes-sur-Mer is divided into three districts. The oldest and most interesting is Haut-de-Cagnes, with its steep streets, covered passageways, and ancient buildings, including a number of Renaissance arcaded houses. The other districts are Cagnes-Ville, the modern town where hotels and stores are concentrated, and Cros-de-Cagnes, a seaside fishing resort and yachting harbor. The **Château Grimaldi** in Haut-de-Cagnes was built in the 14th century and reworked in the 17th by Henri Grimaldi. Behind the fortress walls is a shady courtyard. The surrounding marble columns conceal a museum devoted to the olive tree and a small collection of modern Mediterranean art. There is also a group of paintings bequeathed by *chanteuse* Suzy Solidor. The 40 works, all portraits of her, are by artists including Marie Laurencin and Cocteau. On the ceiling of the banqueting hall is a vast illusionistic fresco of the *Fall of Phaeton* attributed to Carlone in the 1620s.
The last 12 years of Pierre Auguste Renoir's life were spent in Cagnes, at the **Musée Renoir, Les Collettes**. The house has been kept almost exactly as it was when he

Exterior of the Musée Fernand Léger in Biot, with a mural by the artist

d in 1919 and contains ten
his paintings. It is set in an
ive grove, along with his
reat bronze *Venus Victrix*.

♣ **Château Grimaldi**
Tel 04 92 02 47 30. ☐ Dec–mid-
Nov: Wed–Mon. ⬤ Jan 1, May 1,
mid-Nov–Dec 2, Dec 25. ✎

🏛 **Musée Renoir, Les
Collettes**
Tel 04 93 20 61 07. ☐ Wed–Mon.
⬤ Nov 1. ✎ ▯

La Ferme des Collettes (1915) by
Renoir, in Cagnes-sur-Mer

Gorges du Loup ㉝

Alpes-Maritimes. 🚉 Nice. 🚌
Cagnes-sur-Mer. 🚌 Grasse. 🚌 Nice.
ℹ️ Tourrettes-sur-Loup (04 93 24 18
93). **www**.tourrettessurloup.com

The river Loup rises in the
Pre-Alps behind Grasse and
cuts a deep path down to the
Mediterranean. Along its route
are dramatic cascades and
spectacular views. The superb
countryside is crowned by the
perched villages for which the
region is famous.

Gourdon owes much of its
appeal to its ancient houses,
grouped round a 12th-century
Château built on the site of a
Saracen stronghold and
perched high on the cliffside.
Its terraced gardens were laid
out by Le Nôtre *(see p179)*.

Tourrettes-sur-Loup is a
fortified village in which the
ramparts are formed by the
outer houses. It is famous for
its fields of violets, grown for
use in perfume and candies.
The **Bastide aux Violettes**
museum explores the role of
the flower in the village's
history and economy.

🏛 **Bastide aux Violettes**
Tel 04 93 59 06 97. ☐ Tue–Sat
& Sun pm. ▯ ♿ ▯
www.tourrettessurloup.com

Vence ㉞

Alpes-Maritimes. 🏘 20,000. 🚉
ℹ️ pl du Grand Jardin (04 93
58 06 38). 🛒 Tue & Fri.
www.vence.fr

Vence's gentle climate has
always been its main attraction; today it is surrounded by
vacation villas. It was an important religious center in the
Middle Ages. The **Cathédrale**
was restored by Vence's most
famous bishop, Antoine
Godeau. A 5th-century Roman
sarcophagus serves as its altar
and there are Carolingian
wall carvings. Note, too, the
15th-century carved choir
stalls and Godeau's tomb.

Just within the ramparts of
the Old Town, which retains
its 13th–14th-century town
gates, is place du Peyra, once
a Roman forum. Its urn-
shaped fountain, built in
1822, still provides fresh
water. On the edge of town,
the **Chapelle du Rosaire** was
built from 1947–51 and
decorated by Henri Matisse,

Domed roof in Vence

in gratitude to the nuns who
nursed him during an illness.
On its white walls, biblical
scenes are reduced to simple
black lines tinted by splashes
of light from the blue and
yellow stained-glass windows.

⛪ **Chapelle du Rosaire**
466 av Henri Matisse. *Tel* 04 93 58
03 26. ☐ Mon–Thu (Mon–Sat
school hols). ⬤ mid-Nov– mid-Dec,
and public hols. ✎ ▯

Market day in the Old Town of Vence

Street by Street: St-Paul-de-Vence ㉟

Restaurant sign, St-Paul-de-Vence

One of the most famous and visited hill villages of the Nice hinterland, St-Paul-de-Vence was once a French frontier post facing Savoy. Its 16th-century ramparts offer views over a landscape of cypress trees and red-roofed villas with palm trees and swimming pools. The village has been heavily restored but its winding streets and medieval buildings are authentic. It has proved a magnet for artists, both established and aspiring, throughout the 20th century. Today galleries and studios dominate the village.

View of St-Paul-de-Vence
The local landscape is a favorite subject for artists. Neo-Impressionist Paul Signac (1863–1935) painted this view of St-Paul.

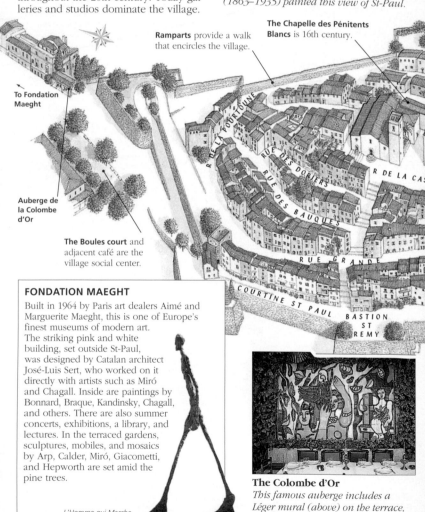

Ramparts provide a walk that encircles the village.

The Chapelle des Pénitents Blancs is 16th century.

To Fondation Maeght

Auberge de la Colombe d'Or

The Boules court and adjacent café are the village social center.

R DE LA PORTOUNE
RUE DES DORIERS
RUE DES BAUQUES
R DE LA CAS
RUE GRANDE
COURTINE ST PAUL
BASTION ST REMY

FONDATION MAEGHT

Built in 1964 by Paris art dealers Aimé and Marguerite Maeght, this is one of Europe's finest museums of modern art. The striking pink and white building, set outside St-Paul, was designed by Catalan architect José-Luis Sert, who worked on it directly with artists such as Miró and Chagall. Inside are paintings by Bonnard, Braque, Kandinsky, Chagall, and others. There are also summer concerts, exhibitions, a library, and lectures. In the terraced gardens, sculptures, mobiles, and mosaics by Arp, Calder, Miró, Giacometti, and Hepworth are set amid the pine trees.

L'Homme qui Marche by Giacometti

The Colombe d'Or
This famous auberge includes a Léger mural (above) on the terrace, a Braque dove by the pool, a Picasso, and a Matisse in the dining room.

The **Musée d'Histoire de Saint-Paul** has local waxwork scenes from the town's past.

Le Donjon, a grim medieval building, was used as a prison until the 19th century.

Eglise Collégiale
Begun in the 12th century, the church's treasures include a painting of St. Catherine, attributed to Tintoretto.

Grand Fountain
This charming cobble-stoned place has a pretty urn-shaped fountain.

VISITORS' CHECKLIST

Alpes-Maritimes. 2,900. 840 ave Emile Hugues, Vence (04 93 58 37 60). 2 rue Grande (04 93 32 86 95). www.saint-pauldevence.com **Fondation Maeght Tel** 04 93 32 81 63. www.fondation-maeght.com

Rue Grande
The doors of the 16th- and 17th-century houses bear coats of arms.

CELEBRITY VILLAGE

The Colombe d'Or (Golden Dove) auberge *(see p574)* was popular with many of the artists and writers who flocked to the Riviera in the 1920s. Early patrons included Picasso, Soutine, Modigliani, Signac, Colette, and Cocteau. They often paid for their rooms and meals with paintings, resulting in the priceless collection that can be seen by diners today. The rich and famous have continued to come to St-Paul: Zelda and F. Scott Fitzgerald had a dramatic fight over Isadora Duncan at dinner here one night, and Yves Montand married Simone Signoret on the terrace. A photo display of celebrity visitors in St-Paul museum features Sartre and de Beauvoir, Greta Garbo, Sophia Loren, Burt Lancaster, and Catherine Deneuve.

Artist Marc Chagall (1887–1985), who moved to St-Paul-de-Vence in 1950

Nice ❸⓺

The largest resort on the Mediterranean coast and the fifth biggest city in France, with its second busiest airport, Nice was founded by the Greeks and colonized by the Romans. Its temperate winter climate and verdant subtropical vegetation have long attracted visitors. Until World War II it was favored by aristocrats, including Tsar Nicholas I's widow who visited in 1856 and Queen Victoria who stayed in 1895. This glittering past has contributed to Nice becoming capital of the Côte d'Azur, and today it is also a center for business conferences and package vacations. Nice has worthy museums, good beaches, and an atmospheric street life. Best of all is Carnival: 18 days of celebrations finishing on Shrove Tuesday in a fireworks display and the Battle of the Flowers *(see p39)*.

Nice's Old Quarter

Yachts at anchor in Nice harbor

Exploring Nice

The promenade des Anglais, running right along the seafront, was built in the 1830s with funds raised by the English colony. Today it is an eight-lane, 5-mile (8-km) highway, with galleries, stores, and grand hotels like the **Negresco**, reflecting Nice's prosperity.

Nice was Italian until 1860, and the pastel façades and balconies of the Old Town have a distinctly Italianate feel. It lies at the foot of a hill still known as the Château for the castle which once stood there. The district is largely restored and its tall, narrow buildings house artists and galleries, boutiques and restaurants. The daily flower market in the cours Saleya should not be missed.

The **Cimiez** district, on the hills overlooking the town, is the fashionable quarter of Nice. The old monastery of Notre-Dame-de-Cimiez is well worth a visit. Lower down the hillside are Les Arènes, remains of an extensive Roman settlement

with vestiges of the great baths and an amphitheater. Excavated artifacts are on show at the archeological museum, next to the Musée Matisse. At the foot of the Cimiez hill is the **Musée Chagall**.

Discover Nice by night on a guided tramway tour. The circuit takes in 14 works of art by some of the most celebrated creators of the contemporary art scene. Tickets can be reserved in advance at the tourist office.

⛫ Musée Matisse

164 av des Arènes de Cimiez. *Tel 04 93 81 08 08.* ◯ *Wed–Mon.* ◉ *some public hols.* ♿ ▯
www.musee-matisse-nice.org
Inspired by the Mediterranean light, Matisse spent many years in Nice. The museum, housed in and below the 17th-century Arena Villa, displays drawings, paintings, bronzes, fabrics, and artifacts. Highlights include *Still Life With Pomegranates* and his last completed work, *Flowers and Fruits*.

⛫ Palais Lascaris

15 rue Droite. *Tel 04 93 62 72 40.* ◯ *Wed–Mon.* ◉ *some public hols.*
This stuccoed 17th-century palace is decorated with ornate woodwork, Flemish tapestries, and illusionistic ceilings thought to be by Carlone. Its small but delightful collection includes a reconstruction of an 18th-century apothecary's store.

⛫ Musée d'Art Moderne et d'Art Contemporain

Promenade des Arts. *Tel 04 97 13 42 01.* ◯ *Tue–Sun.* ◉ *Jan 1, Easter, May 1, Dec 25.* ♿ ▯
www.mamac-nice.org
The museum occupies a strikingly original complex of four marble-faced towers linked by glass passageways. The collection is particularly strong in Neo-Realism and Pop Art, with works by Andy Warhol, Jean Tinguely, and Niki de Saint-Phalle. Also well-represented are such Ecole de Nice artists as César, Arman, and Yves Klein.

Blue Nude IV (1952) by Henri Matisse

An azure view – relaxing on the promenade des Anglais

VISITORS' CHECKLIST

Alpes-Maritimes. 🏠 349,000.
✈ 4.5 miles (7 km) SW. 🚃 av
Thiers (36 35). 🚌 5 bd Jean
Jaurès (04 93 85 61 81). 🚢 quai
du Commerce (3260). 🛈 5 prom
des Anglais (08 92 70 74 07).
🏪 Tue–Sun. 🎭 Carnival.
www.nicetourism.com

🛕 Cathédrale Ste-Réparate
This 17th-century Baroque building is surmounted by a handsome tiled dome. Its interior is lavishly decorated with plasterwork, marble, and original paneling.

🏛 Musée Chagall
36 av du Docteur Ménard. **Tel** 04 93 53 87 20. ◯ Wed–Mon. ● Jan 1, May 1, Dec 25. 🎟 🛗 ✏ 🎦 📷 📱
This is the largest collection of works by Marc Chagall, with paintings, drawings, sculpture, stained glass, and mosaics. Best of all are the 17 canvases of the artist's *Biblical Message*.

🏛 Musée des Beaux-Arts
33 av des Baumettes. **Tel** 04 92 15 28 28. ◯ Tue–Sun. ● Jan 1, Easter, May 1, Dec 25. 🛗 restr. 📷 Thu. 📱
www.musee-beaux-arts.org
The 19th-century home of a Ukrainian princess displays works sent to Nice by Napoleon III after Italy ceded the city to France in 1860, as well as paintings by Renoir, Monet, and Dufy.

🏛 Palais Masséna
65 rue de France. **Tel** 04 93 91 19 10. ◯ Wed–Mon. 🛗 📱
Housed in a 19th-century Italianate villa, the Palais

Masséna exhibits trace the history of Nice from 1800 to the 1930s.

🛕 Cathédrale Orthodoxe Russe St-Nicolas
Completed in 1912, the cathedral was built in memory of a young Tsarevitch who died here in 1865. The exterior is of pink brick and gray marble with elaborate mosaics. The interior is resplendent with icons.

🏛 Musée des Arts Asiatiques
405 prom des Anglais. **Tel** 04 92 29 37 00. ◯ Wed–Mon. ● Jan 1, May 1, Dec 25. 🛗 📷 📱
www.arts-asiatiques.com
Exhibits of ancient and contemporary art from across Asia, in Kenzo Tange's uncluttered white marble and glass setting.

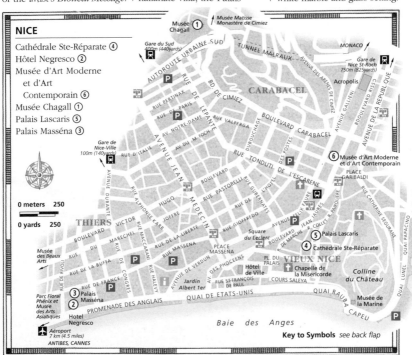

NICE

Cathédrale Ste-Réparate ④
Hôtel Negresco ②
Musée d'Art Moderne
  et d'Art
  Contemporain ⑥
Musée Chagall ①
Palais Lascaris ⑤
Palais Masséna ③

0 meters   250
0 yards   250

Chapelle de St-Pierre, Villefranche

Villefranche-sur-Mer ®

Alpes-Maritimes. 🏘 6,649. 🚆 🚌 🛈 Jardin François Binon (04 93 01 73 68). 🗓 Sat & Sun. www.villefranche-sur-mer.com

One of the most perfectly situated towns on the coast, Villefranche lies at the foot of hills forming a sheltered amphitheater. The town overlooks a beautiful natural harbor, which is deep enough to be a naval port of call.

The bright and animated waterfront is lined by Italianate façades, with cafés and bars from which to watch the fishermen. Here, too, is the medieval **Chapelle de St-Pierre**, which, after years of service storing fishing nets, was restored in 1957 and decorated by Jean Cocteau. His frescoes depict non-religious images and the life of St. Peter.

Also worth a visit is the 16th-century **Citadelle St-Elme**, incorporating the town hall and two art galleries.

Behind the harbor, the streets are narrow, winding, and often stepped. Walking through them, you get the odd glimpse of the harbor. The vaulted 13th-century rue Obscure has always provided shelter from bombardment, right up to World War II.

🛈 Chapelle de St-Pierre
Quai Amiral Courbet. **Tel** 04 93 76 90 70. 🗓 mid-Dec–mid-Nov: Tue–Sun. 🔴 Dec 25. 🖼

Cap Ferrat ®

Alpes-Maritimes. 🏘 2,000. 🛫 Nice. 🚆 Nice. 🚌 Beaulieu-sur-Mer. 🛈 59 av Denis Femeria (04 93 76 08 90). www.saintjeancapferrat.fr

The peninsula of Cap Ferrat boasts some of the most sumptuous villas found on the Riviera. From 1926 until the author's death, the best-known was Somerset Maugham's Villa Mauresque, where he received celebrities from Noël Coward to Winston Churchill.

High walls shield most of the exclusive villas, but possibly the best one is open to the public. The **Villa Ephrussi de Rothschild** is a terra cotta and marble mansion set in themed gardens on the crest of the cape. It belonged to the Baroness Ephrussi de Rothschild, who bequeathed it to the Institut de France in 1934. It is furnished as she left it, with her collections of priceless porcelain, items t[...] belonged to Marie Antoine[...] and a unique collection of drawings by Fragonard.

The town of **Beaulieu** lies where the cape joins the mainland. A pleasant marina with an exceptionally mild climate and very fine hotels, it is the site of another unique house, the extraordinary **Villa Kerylos**. Built between 1902 and 1908 for archeologist Theodore Reinach in imitation of an ancient Greek residence, it contains lovingly reproduced mosaics, frescoes, and furniture.

🏛 Villa Ephrussi de Rothschild
Cap Ferrat. **Tel** 04 93 01 33 09. 🗓 Feb–Oct: daily; Nov–Jan: Mon–Fri pms, w/e & school & public hols: daily. 🖼 🎥 🛈 🛈 www.villa-ephrussi.com

🏛 Villa Kerylos
Imp Gustave Eiffel, Beaulieu. **Tel** 04 93 01 01 44. 🗓 as above. 🖼 🎥 🛈 www.villa-kerylos.com

Greek-style Villa Kerylos at Beaulieu on Cap Ferrat

Louis XV salon at the Villa Ephrussi de Rothschild, Cap Ferrat

Eze ③⑨

Alpes-Maritimes. 🚶 3,100. 🚉 🚌
ℹ️ pl Général de Gaulle (04 93 41 26 00). www.eze-riviera.com

For many, Eze is the ultimate perched village, balancing on a rocky pinnacle high above the Mediterranean. Every summer, thousands of visitors stream through the 14th-century fortified gate. The flower-decked buildings are almost all stores, galleries, and craft workshops. At the top of the village, the château is surrounded by the lush tropical plants of the **Jardin Exotique**. The view from here is superb.

Farther along the Upper Corniche is the Roman Alpine Trophy **La Turbie** *(see pp46–7)*. This vast 6 BC structure dominates the surrounding village, with magnificent views towards Monaco and Italy.

🌿 **Jardin Exotique**
Rue du Château. **Tel** 04 93 41 10 30. 🔲 daily. 🔵 Dec 25. 🖼️

🏛️ **La Turbie**
🔲 Apr–mid-Sep: daily; mid-Sep–Mar: Tue–Sun. 🔵 public hols. 🖼️📷📷
www.ville-la-turbie.fr

Roquebrune-Cap-Martin ④⓪

Alpes-Maritimes. 🚶 12,000. 🚉
Nice. 🚉 🚌 ℹ️ 218 av Aristide Briand (04 93 35 62 87). 🏛️ Wed.
www.roquebrune-cap-martin.com

The medieval village of Roquebrune overlooks the wooded cape where the villas of the rich and famous still abound. Visitors here have included Coco Chanel and Greta Garbo. The cape has not always been kind – poet W.B. Yeats died here in 1939 and architect Le Corbusier was drowned off the coast in 1965.

In 1467 Roquebrune believed that by performing scenes from the Passion it escaped the plague, and every August it continues this tradition.

View from Roquebrune

Alpes-Maritimes ④①

Alpes-Maritimes. 🛫 Nice. 🚉 Nice.
🚉 Peille. 🚌 Nice. ℹ️ La Mairie, Peille (04 93 91 71 71). www.peille.fr

In the hinterland of the Côte d'Azur, it is still possible to find quiet, unspoiled villages off the tourist track. The tiny twin villages of **Peille** and **Peillon** are typical. Both have changed little since the Middle Ages, perched on outcrops over the Paillon river, their streets a mass of steps and arches. Peille, the more remote, even has its own dialect. The Alpes-Maritimes countryside is also unspoiled, its craggy gorges, tumbling rivers, and windswept plateaus just a few hours from the coast. Of note are the ancient rock carvings of the **Vallée des Merveilles** and rare wildlife in the **Parc National du Mercantour**.

Menton ④②

Alpes-Maritimes. 🚶 30,000. 🚉 🚌
ℹ️ Palais de l'Europe, 8 av Boyer (04 92 41 76 76). 🏛️ daily.
www.menton.fr

Menton's beaches, with the Alps and the golden buildings and Belle Epoque villas of the Old Town as a backdrop, would be enough to lure most visitors. In the 19th century, Queen Victoria and famous writers and poets often vacationed here. Tropical gardens and citrus fruits thrive in the town's perfect climate, mild even in February for the lemon festival *(see p39)*.

The **Basilica St-Michel** is a superb example of Baroque architecture in yellow and pink stone. The square before it is paved with a mosaic of the Grimaldi coat of arms. The **Salle des Mariages** in the Hôtel de Ville was decorated in 1957 by Jean Cocteau. Drawings, paintings, ceramics, and stage designs by the renowned artist are displayed in the **Musée Jean Cocteau**, housed in a 17th-century fort. Inside the Palais Carnolès, the **Musée des Beaux-Arts** features works from the Middle Ages to the 20th century.

🏛️ **Salle des Mariages**
Hôtel de Ville. **Tel** 04 92 10 50 00.
🔲 Mon–Fri. 🔵 public hols. 🖼️

🏛️ **Musée Jean Cocteau**
Vieux Port. **Tel** 04 93 57 72 30.
🔲 Wed–Mon. 🔵 public hols. 🖼️

🏛️ **Musée des Beaux-Arts**
3 av de la Madone. **Tel** 04 93 35 49 71. 🔲 Wed–Mon. 🔵 public hols.

Mosaic at the Musée Jean Cocteau in Menton

Monaco

Travelers to Monaco by car would do well to take the Moyenne Corniche, one of the most beautiful highways in the world, with incomparable views of the Mediterranean coastline. Arriving among the skyscrapers of Monaco today, it is hard to envisage the turbulence of its history. At first a Greek settlement, later taken by the Romans, it was bought from the Genoese in 1297 by the Grimaldis who, in spite of bitter family feuds and at least one political assassination, still rule as the world's oldest ruling dynasty. Monaco covers 0.74 sq miles (1.9 sq km) and, although its size has increased by one-third in the form of landfills, it still occupies an area smaller than that of New York's Central Park.

Aerial view of Monaco

Grand Casino

Exploring Monaco

Monaco owes its renown principally to its Grand Casino. Source of countless legends, it was instituted in 1878 by Charles III to save himself from bankruptcy. The first casino was opened in 1865 on a barren promontory (later named Monte-Carlo in his honor) across the harbor from ancient Monaco-Ville. So successful was Charles's money-making venture that, by 1870, he was able to abolish taxation for his people. Today, Monaco is a tax haven for thousands, and its residents have the highest per capita income in the world.

Visitors come from all over the world for the Grand Prix de Monaco in May and the Monte-Carlo Rally in January (*see p39*). Many of the greatest singers perform in the opera season. There is a fireworks festival (July–August), and an international circus festival at the end of January as well as world-class ballet and concerts. Facilities exist for every sort of leisure activity, and there is much else to enjoy without breaking the bank, including **Fort Antoine** and the Neo-Romanesque **Cathédrale**.

Grand Casino
Place du Casino. **Tel** *00 377 98 06 76 76*. daily, from noon. www.montecarloresort.com
Designed in 1878 by Charles Garnier, architect of the Paris Opéra (*see p97*), and set in formal gardens, the Casino gives a splendid view over Monaco. The lavish interior is still decorated in Belle Epoque style, recalling an era when this was the rendezvous of Russian Grand Dukes. Anyone can play the odds on the one-armed bandits of the Salon

Blanc or the roulette wheels of the Salons Européens. Even the most exclusive of the gaming rooms can be visited at a price, but their tables are for the big spenders only.

Palais Princier
Place du Palais. **Tel** *00 377 93 25 18 31*. Apr–Nov: daily.
Monaco-Ville, the seat of government, is the site of the 13th-century Palais Princier. The interior, with its priceless furniture and carpets and its

Skyscrapers and apartment blocks of modern Monte-Carlo

For hotels and restaurants in this region see pp590–4 and pp646–50

MONACO'S ROYAL FAMILY

Prince Albert II officially assumed the Monaco throne in July 2005, 3 months after his father, aged 81, died, ending a reign of over 55 years. Prince Rainier III was an effective ruler, descended from a Grimaldi who entered the Monaco fortress in 1297. His wife, former film star Grace Kelly, died tragically in 1982. Prince Albert and his sisters, Caroline and Stephanie, remain a focus of media attention.

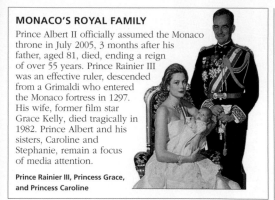

Prince Rainier III, Princess Grace, and Princess Caroline

VISITORS' CHECKLIST

Monaco. 🏛 37,000. ✈ 4.5 miles (7 km) SW Nice. 🚉 av Prince Pierre (SNCF: 36 35). 🛈 2a bd des Moulins (00 377 92 16 61 66). 🎭 daily. 🎪 Festival du Cirque (Jan–Feb); International Fireworks Festival (Jul–Aug); Fête Nationale Monégasque (Nov 19). www.visitmonaco.com

magnificent frescoes, is only open to the public in the summer. The changing of the guard is at 11:55am.

🏛 Musée des Souvenirs Napoléoniens et Archives Historiques du Palais

Pl du Palais. **Tel** 00 377 93 25 18 31. 🎭 daily. 🔴 Jan 1, May 1, Grand Prix, Nov, Dec 25. 📷

A genealogical tree on the wall traces the family links between the Grimaldis and Bonapartes. Also on

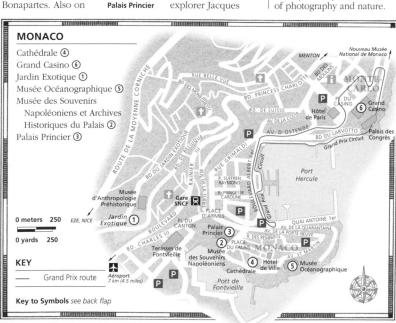

Guard outside the Palais Princier

show are Napoleon's personal effects and numerous portraits.

🐟 Musée Océanographique

Av Saint-Martin. **Tel** 00 377 93 15 36 00. 🎭 daily. 📷 🔇 🍴 🛍 www.oceano.mc

This museum was founded in 1910 by Prince Albert I. Its aquarium, fed with sea water, holds rare species of marine plants and animals. The museum houses an important scientific collection, diving equipment, and model ships. Marine explorer Jacques

Cousteau established his research center here.

🌺 Jardin Exotique

62 bd du Jardin Exotique. **Tel** 00 377 93 15 29 80. 🎭 daily. 🔴 Nov 19, Dec 25. 📷 🛍 www.jardin-exotique.mc

These gardens are considered to be the finest in Europe, with a huge range of tropical and subtropical plants. A museum of anthropology offers evidence of mammoths once living on the coast here.

🏛 Nouveau Musée National de Monaco

17 av Princesse Grace. **Tel** 00 377 98 98 91 26. 🎭 daily. 🔴 Jan 1, May 1, Grand Prix, Nov 19, Dec 25. 📷 🛍

This museum, housed in two adjoining villas and surrounded by lush gardens, hosts temporary exhibitions. There are usually two a year, on themes of photography and nature.

MONACO

Cathédrale ④
Grand Casino ⑥
Jardin Exotique ①
Musée Océanographique ⑤
Musée des Souvenirs Napoléoniens et Archives Historiques du Palais ②
Palais Princier ③

0 meters 250
0 yards 250

KEY

—— Grand Prix route

Key to Symbols see back flap

Map labels: MENTON, Nouveau Musée National de Monaco, RUE BELLE VUE, BD DES MONEGHETTI, ROUTE DE LA MOYENNE CORNICHE, BD PRINCESS CHARLOTTE, BD DES MOULINS, MONTE CARLO, BD DU JARDIN EXOTIQUE, BD. DE SUISSE, PL DU CASINO, Grand Casino ⑥, Hôtel de Paris, AV DE LA COSTA, AV. D'OSTENDE, BD DU LARVOTTO, Palais des Congrès, RUE GRIMALDI, Grand Prix Circuit, R. SUFFREN RAYMOND, R. PRINCESSE CAROLINE, Port Hercule, Musée d'Anthropologie Préhistorique, Gare SNCF, BOULEVARD ALBERT 1er, PLACE D'ARMES, EZE, NICE, Jardin Exotique ①, BOULEVARD CHARLES III, PL DU CANTON, Palais Princier ③, PLACE DU PALAIS ②, QUAI ANTOINE 1er, AV. DE LA QUARANTAINE, R. DES REMPARTS, AV. DE LA PORTE NEUVE, MONACO, AV. ST MARTIN, Terrasses de Fontvieille, Musée des Souvenirs Napoléoniens, Cathédrale ④, Hôtel de Ville, Musée Océanographique ⑤, Port de Fontvieille, Aéroport 7 km (4.5 miles)

CORSICA

HAUTE-CORSE · CORSE-DU-SUD

orsica, where the people speak their own language, has all the attributes of a mini-continent. There are tropical palm trees, vineyards, olive and orange groves, forests of chestnut and indigenous pine, alpine lakes, and cool mountain torrents filled with trout. Most distinctive of all is the parched maquis (scrub), heavy with the scent of myrtle, which Napoleon swore he could smell from Elba.

The fourth largest island in the Mediterranean after Sicily, Sardinia, and Cyprus, Corsica has been a problem and a bafflement to mainland France ever since 1769, when it was "sold" to Louis XV by the Genoese for 40 million francs. Before that, following years of struggle, the Corsican people had enjoyed 14 years of independence under the revered leadership of Pasquale Paoli. They understandably felt cheated by the deal with the French, and have resented them ever since. To vacationers visiting the island – in July and August tourists outnumber the inhabitants six to one – the Corsican–French relationship may be a matter of indifference. However, there is a strong (and sometimes quite violent) separatist movement, which does deter some tourists. As a result, Corsica's wild beauty has been preserved to an extent not seen in the rest of the Mediterranean.

For 200 years, from the 11th to the 13th century, Corsica was a colony of the old Tuscan republic of Pisa, whose builders founded beautifully proportioned Romanesque churches. These buildings are, along with the megalithic stone warriors in Filitosa, the noblest monuments to be seen here. For the rest, the birthplace of Napoleon is a place of wild seacoasts and mountain peaks, one of the last unspoiled corners of the Mediterranean: poor, depopulated, beautiful, old-fashioned, and doggedly aloof.

The village of Oletta in the Nebbio region around St-Florent

◁ A fisherman with feline friends in Bastia

Exploring Corsica

Corsica's main appeal is its scenery: a wildly beautiful landscape of mountains, forests, myrtle-scented maquis, and countless miles of sandy beaches. Late spring (when the wild flowers are in bloom) and early fall are the best times to visit – the temperature is moderate and there aren't too many visitors. The island is renowned for its superb hiking trails, some of which become cross-country skiing trails during the winter. Downhill skiing is also possible in February and March.

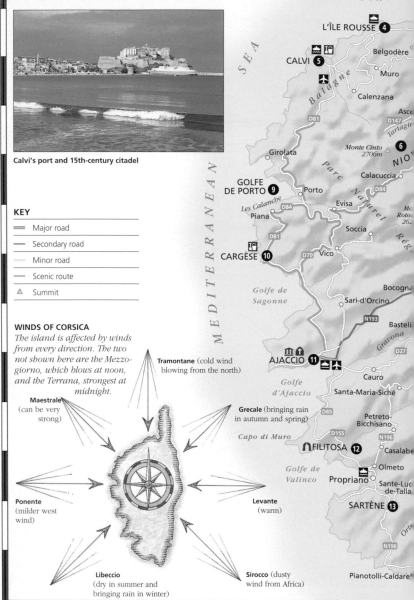

Calvi's port and 15th-century citadel

KEY

▬▬	Major road
▬▬	Secondary road
═══	Minor road
▬▬	Scenic route
△	Summit

WINDS OF CORSICA

The island is affected by winds from every direction. The two not shown here are the Mezzo-giorno, which blows at noon, and the Terrana, strongest at midnight.

Maestrale (can be very strong)

Ponente (milder west wind)

Libeccio (dry in summer and bringing rain in winter)

Tramontane (cold wind blowing from the north)

Grecale (bringing rain in autumn and spring)

Levante (warm)

Sirocco (dusty wind from Africa)

Ligurian Sea

L'ÎLE ROUSSE 4

Belgodère

CALVI 5

Muro

Calenzana

Asco

Balagne

Tartagin

Monte Cinto 2706m 6

Girolata

Calacuccia

NIO

GOLFE DE PORTO 9

Porto

Parc

Les Calanche

Evisa

Piana

Mo Roto 26

Soccia

Naturel

CARGÈSE 10

Vico

Golfe de Sagonne

Bocogna

Sari-d'Orcino

Régio

Basteli

Gravona

AJACCIO 11

Cauro

Golfe d'Ajaccio

Santa-Maria-Siché

Grecale

Petreto-Bicchisano

Capo di Muro

FILITOSA 12

Casalab

Golfe de Valinco

Olmeto

Propriano

Sante-Luc-de-Talla

SARTÈNE 13

Ort

Pianotolli-Caldare

The Calanche cliffs in the Golfe de Porto

GETTING AROUND

Car ferries (which should be reserved well in advance) depart from Marseille, Nice, and Toulon, arriving at Bastia, L'Île Rousse, Calvi, Ajaccio, Propriano, and Porto-Vecchio. There are also ferries from Sardinia to Bonifacio, and from Genoa, Livorno, and La Spezia to Bastia. Small airports are at Ajaccio, Bastia, Calvi, and Figari. Corsica's roads are narrow, twisting, and often tortuously slow, though breathtaking views reward the effort. A car is a must for exploring the island, since public transportation is limited. Carry spare gas – gas stations are few and far between.

| 0 kilometers | | 20 |
| 0 miles | 10 | |

Corte's Old Town, with its citadel high up on a rocky outcrop

Cap Corse ❶

Haute-Corse. 🚋 Bastia. 🚌 Bastia.
🚌 Bastia. 🛈 pl St-Nicolas, Bastia
(04 95 54 20 40). www.bastia-
tourisme.com

Cap Corse is the northern
tip of Corsica, 25 miles (40
km) in length but seldom
more than 7.5 miles (12 km)
wide, pointing like an accus-
atory finger toward Genoa.

There are two roads out of
Bastia to the cape: the D81
leading west across the mountains and joining up with the
D80 after the wine village of
Patrimonio; and the D80 traveling north along the eastern
shore to **Erbalunga** and
Macinaggio. The road is
narrow and twisting, a taste of
what awaits you in Corsica.

From the coastal village of
Lavasina, the D54 leads left off
the D80 to Pozzo; from here it
is a 5-hour round trip on foot
to the 4,300-ft (1,307-m)
summit of **Monte Stello**, the
highest peak on the cape. The
360-degree view from the top
takes in St-Florent to the west,
the massif of central Corsica
to the south, and the Italian
island of Elba to the east.

Farther up the coast, the
restored **Tour de Losse** is one
of many 16th-century Genoese
towers along the coast – part
of an elaborate system which
enabled all Corsican towns to
be warned within two hours
of impending barbarian raids.

The charming 18th-century
fishing port of **Centuri**, near
the tip of the peninsula on the
west coast, is an ideal spot
for a delicious seafood feast.
Pino, a pretty little village

The village of Erbalunga on the east coast of Cap Corse

straggling down the green
mountainside farther to the
south, has no hotel, only a
lovely little church dedicated
to the Virgin, full of model
ships placed there by mariners
grateful for her protection.

On the way south along the
vertiginous lower corniche,
be sure to turn left up the hill
to **Canari**. One of the larger
villages in this area, Canari has
a jewel of a 12th-century Pisan
church, Santa Maria Assunta,
a magnificent view across the
sea, and a thoroughly convivial
hotel-restaurant. All the by-
roads in this thickly wooded
area seem to lead somewhere
interesting. There are dozens
of picturesque hamlets in the
vicinity, and it should be borne
in mind that from this point
onward the landscape becomes
steadily less attractive as the
road winds on past the old
asbestos workings and
beaches of black sand below
the village of **Nonza**.

Bastia ❷

Haute-Corse. 🏙 39,000. ✈ 🚋
🚌 🚆 🛈 pl St-Nicolas
(04 95 54 20 40). 🛒 Tue–Sun.
www.bastia-tourisme.com

A thriving port and the
administrative capital of
Upper Corsica, Bastia is utterly
different in style from its sedate
west coast rival, Ajaccio. The
Genoese citadel and colorful
19th-century Italianate buildings around the old port are for
many people their first taste of
the authentic Mediterranean –
as it was half a century ago,
and as it stubbornly remains
in our imagination.

The center of Bastia's life is
the **place St-Nicolas**, facing
the wharf where ferries from
the mainland and Italy arrive.
Heading south along the
waterfront you come to the
place de l'Hôtel de Ville, site
of a daily food market.
Bordering the square are the
early 17th-century **Chapelle
de l'Immaculée Conception**,
with its ornate 18th-century
interior, and the mid-17th-
century **Eglise de St-Jean-
Baptiste**, whose façade
dominates the Vieux Port.

From here it is a short walk
up to the 16th-century **citadel**,
where there are two more
churches worth seeing: the
Rococo **Chapelle Sainte-Croix**,
with its striking *Black Christ*,
fished out of the sea by
Bastiais fishermen in 1428;
and the 15th-century **Sainte-
Marie**, which has a *Virgin*
made of a ton of solid silver.

Bastia's Vieux Port seen from the Jetée du Dragon

St-Florent ❸

Haute-Corse. 🏘 *1,500.* ▣ ▪
*Bâtiment Administratif (04 95 37
06 04).* 🚌 *1st Wed of month.*
www.corsica-saintflorent.com

St-Florent is almost a
Corsican St-Tropez – chic,
affluent, and packed with
yachts. Its citadel, which
houses photography
exhibitions, dates from 1439,
and is a fine example of
Genoese military architecture.
The town itself is pleasant to
wander around; its main
attraction, the 12th-century
Pisan **Cathédrale de Santa
Maria Assunta**, lies just inland
on the road to Poggio-d'Oletta.

Environs
A leisurely 4-hour circuit by car
of the **Nebbio** region, which
extends in an amphitheater
around St-Florent, might take
in the following: **Santo Pietro
di Tenda**; **Murato**, famous for
its magnificent **Eglise de San
Michele de Murato**, a 12th-
century Pisan Romanesque
construction built of white and
green stone; the **San Stefano**
pass, with the sea on either
side; **Oletta**, which produces a
special blue cheese made from
ewes' milk; the **Teghime** pass;
and finally the wine village of
Patrimonio, where there is
a strange, big-eared menhir
dating from 900–800 BC.
 Along the coast to the west
of St-Florent lies the barren, uninhabited **Désert des Agriates**.
If you can face the 6-mile (10-
km) haul to the sea – on foot,
by bike, or by motorbike –
the Saleccia beach is the most
beautiful on the island.

San Michele de Murato

L'Île Rousse ❹

Haute-Corse. 🏘 *2,400.* ▣ ▣ ▤
▪ *av Calizzi (04 95 60 04 35).*
🚌 *Summer: daily; winter: Tue & Fri.*
www.balagne-corsica.com

Founded in 1758 by
Pasquale Paoli, leader of
independent Corsica,
L'Île Rousse is today a
major vacation resort
and ferry terminal.
The town center is
dominated by a
marble statue of
Corsica's national hero,
Paoli. On the north side
of the square is the
covered market, with the
Old Town just beyond.
 In the summer months
L'Île Rousse becomes
overcrowded, its
beaches a mass of
bodies. It is worth
traveling 6 miles (10 km) up
the coast to **Lozari**, which
offers a magnificent, virtually
unspoiled stretch of sand.

Environs
One very pleasant way to
discover the **Balagne** region is
to take the tram-train from
L'Île Rousse to Calvi and
back. This odd little service
runs all year (more frequent
in summer), roughly keeping
to the coastline and stopping
at Algajola, Lumio, and various
villages along the way.

Calvi ❺

Haute-Corse. 🏘 *5,500.* ▣ ▣ ▤
▪ *Port de Plaisance (04 95 65 16 67).*
🚌 *daily.* **www**.balagne-corsica.com

Calvi, where Nelson lost his
eye in an "explosion of
stones" in 1794, is today half
military town, half cheap vacation resort. Its 15th-century
citadel is garrisoned by a
crack French regiment of the
foreign legion; while beyond
the ferry port is a seedy,
apparently endless camp-
site and trailer park.
 The town makes a
half-hearted case for
being the birthplace of
Christopher Columbus,
but there is no real evi-
dence to support this.
A much better claim to
fame is the food, which is
very good and reasonably
priced by Corsican stan-
dards. There is also a very
respectable jazz festival
at Calvi toward the
end of June.
 Outside town, the
19th-century **Chapelle
de Notre-Dame de la Serra** is
gloriously sited on a hilltop
commanding extensive views
in all directions.

**French foreign
legionnaire**

The Chapelle de Notre-Dame de la Serra, 3.5 miles (6 km) southwest of Calvi

Corte's 15th-century citadel seen at dawn

The Niolo ❻

Haute-Corse. 🚌 *Corte.* 🛈 *route de Cuccia (04 95 48 05 22).*

The Niolo, west of Corte, extends westward to the Vergio pass and the upper Golo basin, and to the east as far as the Scala di Santa Regina. It includes Corsica's highest mountain, the 8,859-ft (2,700-m) **Monte Cinto**, and its biggest river, the **Golo**, which meets the sea south of Bastia.

Alone of the various regions of Corsica, the Niolo persists in the cultivation of livestock as its economic mainstay.

The main town, **Calacuccia**, is suitable for excursions to Monte Cinto. The nearby ski resort of **Haut Asco** is best reached by the D147 from **Asco**, but enthusiasts can walk from Calacuccia (8–9 hours). To the south is the huge forest of **Valdu Niello**.

Corte ❼

Haute-Corse. 🏠 *6,700.* 🚌 🚌
🛈 *la Citadelle (04 95 46 26 70).*
🛒 *Fri.* **www.**centru-corsica.com

In the geographical center of Corsica, Corte was the chosen capital of the independence leader Pasqual Paoli from 1755–69, and today is the seat of the island's university.
In the Old Town is the 15th-century citadel, housing the **Museu di a Corsica**. Its exhibits relate to traditional Corsican life and anthropology.

Corte is the best base for exploring nearby mountain areas, especially since it stands exactly halfway along the GR20, the legendary 137-mile (220-km) trail from Calenzana to Conca.

🏛 **Museu di a Corsica**
La Citadelle. **Tel** 04 95 45 25 45.
⬜ *Apr–Jun & Oct: Tue–Sun; Jul–Sep: daily; Nov–Mar: Tue–Sat.*
⬛ *public hols.* 🖼 🗅 🏠 🏠
www.musee-corse.com

Environs

Don't miss the wildly beautiful **Gorges de la Restonica**, about 7.5 miles (12 km) out of town via the D623. Above these gorges adventurous walkers may wish to make the well-marked climb to the snow-fed **Lac de Melo** (allow 60–90 minutes); or the **Lac de Capitello**, 30 minutes farther on, where the snow stays as late as early June. The path – in winter a cross-country ski trail – follows the river.

South of Corte, the **Forêt de Vizzavona** features beech and pine woodland crisscrossed by trout-filled streams and walking trails (notably the GR20). It is a perfect refuge from the summer heat and is also an excuse to take the small-gauge train up from Ajaccio or Bastia, which stops at Vizzavona.

The Castagniccia ❽

Haute-Corse. 🚢 *Bastia.* 🚌 *Corte, Ponte Leccia.* 🚌 *Piedicroce, La Porta, Valle-d'Alesani.* 🛈 *Folelli (04 95 35 82 54).* **www.**castagniccia.fr

East of Corte is the hilly, chestnut-covered region of Castagniccia (literally "small chestnut grove"), which most Corsicans agree is the very heart and kernel of the island. It was here that independence leader Pasquale Paoli was born in 1725, and that the revolts against Genoa and later France began in earnest in 1729. Alas, many of the villages in this beautiful, remote area are nearly empty, their inhabitants having joined the 800,000 or so Corsicans (almost three times the present population) who live and work in mainland France or Italy. It seems hard to believe that in the 17th century, when the great chestnut forests introduced here by the Genoese were at the height of their production, this was the most prosperous and populated region in Corsica.

The D71 from Ponte Leccia (north of Corte) to the east coast winds through the center of the Castagniccia region, and to see it at a leisurely pace will take the best part of a day. Arm yourself with a picnic before you start, since there is little to be had in the way of supplies en route.

◁ Limestone cliffs of Bonifacio *(see p543)*

Golfe de Porto ❾

Corse-du-Sud. 🚶 🚌 ⛴ Ajaccio.
⛴ Porto. 🛈 Porto (04 95 26 10
55). www.porto-tourisme.com

Porto is sited at the head of
the Golfe de Porto, one of
the most beautiful bays in the
Mediterranean, which for the
sake of its fauna and flora has
been included in UNESCO's list
of the world's common cultural
heritage sites. The town has a
magnificent Genoese watchtower – the perfect spot for
admiring the sunset – and
regular boat excursions
(Apr–Oct) to the Calanche,
Scandola, and Girolata.

The **Calanche** begin 1.2
miles (2 km) out of Porto, on
the road to Piana. These 1,000-
ft (300-m) red granite cliffs
plunge sheer to the sea, and
are quite simply breathtaking.
They are accessible only by
boat or on foot: well-defined
trails start from the Tête du
Chien and the Pont de Mezanu,
while boat tickets are available
at Porto's Hôtel Le Cyrnée.

East of Porto are the Gorges
de la Spelunca, accessed by a
mule route punctuated by
Genoese bridges.

Just south of Porto along a
spectacular corniche drive
passing under granite archways, lies the pretty village of
Piana, a good base for
visiting this whole area, with
information on recommended
walks. One particularly
worthwhile destination is the
cove at **Ficajola** just below
Piana – a truly delightful beach.

Porto's marina and Genoese watchtower

Environs

The road over the mountains
from Porto to Calvi offers no
more than a taste of this
grandiose corner of
Corsica – you have to take
to the sea to view it
properly (ferries from Porto
and Galéria). **Girolata**, a tiny
hamlet north of Porto, can be
reached only by sea or via a
mule track (4 hours round
trip on foot) from a clearly
marked point 14 miles (23 km)
north of Porto on the D81.

At the mouth of the Golfe
de Girolata, the **Réserve
Naturelle de Scandola**, instituted in 1975, is the first land-
and-sea preserve in France,
covering over 2,500 acres
(1,000 hectares) of sea, and a
similar area of cliffs, caves, and
maquis. Marine life is abundant in these clear, protected
waters; the birds include
ospreys, puffins, and falcons.

CORSICAN FLOWERS

**Rock-
rose**

For lovers of wild
flowers, Corsica is a
Mediterranean
jewel. Much of the
island is covered
with maquis, a
tangle of aromatic
shrubs and low
trees which
flowers from late
winter onward.
Among its dense
variety are the
showy rockroses,
which shower the
ground with short-
lived pink or white petals,
and brilliant yellow
broom. Grassy and rocky
slopes are good places to
spot the widespread tassel
hyacinth and the Illyrian
sea lily which grows only
in Corsica and Sardinia.

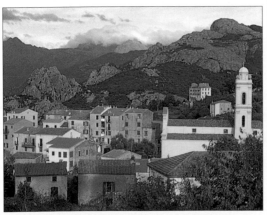
The town of Piana with the Calanche in the background

**Spanish
broom**

Illyrian sea lily

Tassel hyacinth

For hotels and restaurants in this region see pp594–5 and pp650–1

Cargèse's Greek rite church

Cargèse ⑩

Corse-du-Sud. 🏛 *1,000.* 🚌 ℹ️ *rue du Docteur Dragacci (04 95 26 41 31).* www.cargese.net

Cargèse overlooks the sea from a promontory between the bays of Sagone and Pero. It is a small town with an odd history: many of the people who live here are the descendants of 17th-century Greek refugees from Turkish rule, given asylum in Corsica.

A few Cargèsiens still speak Greek, and their icon-filled Eastern (Greek) rite church faces its Catholic counterpart in an attitude that must once have seemed confrontational. Nowadays the old rivalries have vanished, and the Orthodox priest and Catholic *curé* often stand in for one another.

There are many splendid beaches in the vicinity, notably at **Pero** and **Chiuni** just to the north, and at **Ménasina** and **Stagnoli** to the south.

Ajaccio ⑪

Corse-du-Sud. 🏛 *60,000.* 🚆 🚌 🛥️ ℹ️ *3 bd du Roi Jérôme (04 95 51 53 03).* 🕐 *Tue–Sun.* www.ajaccio-tourisme.com

Ajaccio, a noisy, busy town by Corsican standards, was the birthplace of Napoleon Bonaparte in 1769. Napoleon never returned to Corsica after crowning himself emperor of the French in 1804, but the town – modern capital of nationalist Corsica – celebrates his birthday every August 15.

The 16th-century **Cathédrale Notre-Dame de la Miséricorde**, where Napoleon was baptized in 1771, houses Delacroix's painting *Vierge du Sacré-Coeur*.

A few streets away, the **Maison Bonaparte**, where Napoleon was born and spent his childhood, contains family portraits, period furniture, and assorted memorabilia.

Much more interesting is the art collection assembled by Napoleon's unscrupulous uncle, Cardinal Fesch, who merrily looted churches, palaces, and museums during the Italian campaign and brought the swag home to Ajaccio. Housed in the 19th-century Palais Fesch, the **Musée Palais Fesch** contains the finest collection of Italian primitive art in France after the Louvre. Among its masterpieces are works by Bellini, Botticelli, Titian, Veronese, Bernini, and Poussin. Next to the Palais Fesch stands the **Chapelle Impériale**, built in 1855 by Napoleon III to accommodate the tombs of the Bonapartes.

From here, walk back along the quay to the Jetée de la Citadelle, which offers superb views of the town, the marina, and the Golfe d'Ajaccio. The adjacent 16th-century **citadel** is occupied by the army.

🏛 **Maison Bonaparte**
Rue St-Charles. **Tel** 04 95 26 26 26. 🕐 *Tue–Sun.* 🎫 🛈
www.musee-maisonbonaparte.fr

🏛 **Musée Palais Fesch**
50 rue Cardinal Fesch. **Tel** 04 95 21 48 17. 🕐 *Wed–Mon.* 🎫 ♿
www.musee-fesch.com

Environs
From the Quai de la Citadelle there are daily excursions to the **Îles Sanguinaires** at the mouth of the Golfe d'Ajaccio.

At Vero, 13 miles (21 km) northeast on the N193, is an unusual park, **A Cupulatta**, with over 150 species of tortoises and turtles (Apr–Oct).

A statue-menhir at Filitosa

Filitosa ⑫

Centre Préhistorique de Filitosa, Corse-du-Sud. **Tel** 04 95 74 00 91. 🕐 *Apr–Oct: daily.* 🎫 🛈
www.filitosa.fr

The 4,000-year-old, life-sized stone warriors of Filitosa are the most spectacular relics of megalithic man in Corsica. Discovered in 1946, these phallus-like granite menhirs represent an interesting progression from mere silhouettes to more detailed sculpture, etched with human features.

The five most recent and most sophisticated figures (about 1500 BC) stand around a thousand-year-old olive

Statue of Napoleon by Laboureur in place Maréchal Foch, Ajaccio

For hotels and restaurants in this region see pp594–5 and pp650–1

The fortified Old Town of Bonifacio, with the harbor in the foreground

tree, in the field below a tumulus. Other finds, which include a heavily armed warrior with shield, helmet, and sword, can be seen in the site's archeological museum.

Sartène ⓭

Corse-du-Sud. 🏠 3,600. 🚍
🛈 cours Soeur Amélie (04 95 77 15 40). 🚃 summer: daily; winter: Sat.

Sartene is a medieval fortified town of narrow cobbled streets and gray granite houses rising above the Rizzanese valley. Founded by the Genoese in the early 16th century, it has survived attacks by Barbary pirates and centuries of bloody feuding among the town's leading families.

Despite all this, Sartène has a reputation for deep piety, reinforced each year by the oldest and most intense Christian ceremony in Corsica, the Good Friday Catenacciu (literally, the "chained one"). A red-hooded penitent, bare-foot and in chains, drags a wooden cross through the Old Town in a re-enactment of Christ's ascent to Golgotha.

Environs
In the town center, the **Musée de la Préhistoire Corse** has a collection of Neolithic, Bronze, and Iron Age artifacts.

🏛 **Musée de la Préhistoire Corse**
Bd Jaques Nicolai. *Tel* 04 95 77 01 09. ⬜May–Sep: daily; Oct–Apr: Mon–Fri. 🈂 🈺
www.prehistoire-corse.org

Bonifacio ⓮

Corse-du-Sud. 🏠 2,700. 🚍 🚢
🛈 rue Fred Scamaroni (04 95 73 11 88).
🚃 Wed. www.bonifacio.fr

Bonifacio is the southern-most town in Corsica, dramatically sited on a limestone and granite cliff peninsula with stunning views *(see pp538–9)*. Its handsome harbor at the foot of the cliffs is the focus of life: cafés, restaurants, and boutiques abound and boats depart regularly for neighboring Sardinia and the uninhabited island of Lavezzi.

From the harbor, steps lead up to Bonifacio's fortified Old Town. The citadel, which was built by the conquering Genoese at the end of the 12th century, has long been the town's main defensive post, and from 1963–83 was the headquarters of the French foreign legion. From here, wander down to the tip of the promontory to see the three old windmills and the ruins of a Franciscan monastery.

Côte Orientale ⓯

Haute-Corse & Corse-du-Sud.
🛫 Bastia. 🛈 Aléria, Salenzara, Porto-Vecchio. 🚢 Bastia, Porto-Vecchio. 🛈 Aléria (04 95 57 01 51), Porto-Vecchio (04 95 70 09 58).

The flat, rather dreary alluvial plain stretching from Bastia to Solenzara has been rich farmland since 1945, the year it was finally drained and rid of malaria. More recently, vacation resorts and even high-rise hotels have mushroomed along the coast, cashing in on its long, sandy beaches.

The best sight in **Mariana**, which is otherwise uncomfort-ably close to the Bastia-Poretta airport, is the early 12th-century cathedral of Mariana known as **La Canonica**. A short distance away is the slightly older **Eglise de San Perteo**, surrounded by meadows.

About halfway down the coast, the port of **Aléria**, originally a Greek colony and the base for Rome's conquest of Corsica in 259 BC, is interesting for its rich archeological heritage. Just outside town, a museum housed in the 16th-century Fort de Matra chronicles daily life in Roman Aléria.

Toward the southern tip of the island, the fortified town of **Porto-Vecchio**, built by Corsica's Genoese conquerors, is now an extremely popular seaside resort. The setting is perfect for the conventional seaside vacation, with umbrella pines, cork oak forests, and glorious white sandy beaches within easy reach of the town, especially at **Palombaggia** and **Pinarello**.

The Golfe de Porto-Vecchio

TRAVELERS' NEEDS

WHERE TO STAY

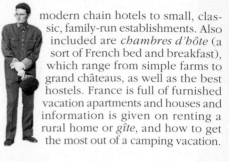

Many of France's 22,000 registered hotels are charming, idiosyncratic, and good value. On these four pages, the types of hotel on offer are summarized and tips provided on what to expect from French hotels. The hotel listings pages *(see pp550–95)* describe some of the best hotels around the country in every price category and style, from slick, modern chain hotels to small, classic, family-run establishments. Also included are *chambres d'hôte* (a sort of French bed and breakfast), which range from simple farms to grand châteaus, as well as the best hostels. France is full of furnished vacation apartments and houses and information is given on renting a rural home or *gîte*, and how to get the most out of a camping vacation.

The Hôtel Euzkadi at Espelette in the Pyrenees *(see p586)*

THE CLASSIC FAMILY HOTEL

If you're touring on a budget, the small, family-run, family-oriented hotel lurking in virtually every village and town is for you. It's likely to be the focal point of the village, with the bar and dining-room (if the food is up to standard) full of locals. The atmosphere is entirely informal, with children, cats, and dogs happily at home. In the hotel's dozen or so bedrooms, old-fashioned charm will make up for a lack of sprightliness and, perhaps, the mere trickle of hot water from the shower.

The annual *Logis de France* guide details over 4,000 of these family-run, mainly one- and two-star hotel-restaurants. They tend to be located in small towns or rural locations; there are none in Paris. Most are no more than roadside inns, but off the beaten track you will discover many converted farmhouses and inexpensive seaside hotels. While the *Logis* is a useful reference source, the quality of places listed can be uneven.

THE CHATEAU HOTEL

Many of France's châteaus and mansions have been converted into luxury hotels. They include everything from Renaissance piles with sweeping lawns to medieval castles with battlements and keeps. Grand hotels can be found all over France, with rich pickings in the Loire, the Savoie, the Haute-Savoie, and the Rhône delta. The properties included in the **Relais et Châteaux** brochure are recommended.

Typically, rooms are beautifully designed and the food is *haute cuisine*. Bedrooms range from grand suites to more simple abodes, often in converted farm-buildings, making it possible, if you're willing to forgo four-poster beds and antiques, to live in luxury without breaking the bank.

THE CITY HOTEL

Every big city has a clutch of hotels close to the train station or port. They range from cheap accommodations to a grand hotel or two. The most famous city hotels are the palace hotels in Paris and the Riviera resorts such as Nice and Cannes. Note that many city hotels do not have a restaurant or a salon and it is always worth checking the quality of the bedroom before you officially check in.

THE MODERN CHAIN HOTEL

Outlets of modern hotel chains are useful for inexpensive pitstops if you're traveling through France. Many are situated on the outskirts of towns near highways or main roads. The cheapest are the one-star, no-frills **Formule 1** motels, offering bedrooms with a double and single bed and no en suite facilities.

Two-star chains include **Ibis/Campanile, Hotels Première Classe**, and **Etap**. Three-star chains include **Novotel** and **Mercure**; both offer en suite accommodations and usually allow one child to stay with no charge, provided the

Le Négresco in Nice on the Côte d'Azur *(see p593)*

The Meurice hotel in the Tuileries Quarter of Paris *(see p555)*

whole family sleeps in one room (Novotel has free accommodations for two under-16s).

THE RESTAURANT-WITH-ROOMS

Throughout France, many upmarket restaurants also offer accommodations. Usually, the bedrooms match the restaurant's quality and are priced accordingly. Sometimes, though, gourmet restaurants have simple bedrooms hidden away upstairs – great finds for those who like to splash out on food while saving on lodging. Refer to the restaurant listings on pages 600–51.

MEALS AND FACILITIES

In high season, many resort hotels insist on half board or *demi-pension* (a per person rate for the room, dinner, and breakfast). There is also full board or *pension*, which covers lunch, too. While it is cheaper to opt for inclusive rates, meals come from set or limited-choice menus, which often omit the more interesting dishes.

Many smaller family-run hotels do not provide meals on Sunday evenings and often stop serving dinner as early as 9pm on other days.

Rooms usually have double beds; twin or single beds must be requested when reserving. All mid-range hotels have a choice of bathroom facilities. A short walk down the corridor to a separate bathroom can reduce the room rate considerably. A bathroom with a bath *(un bain)* is usually more expensive than one with a shower *(une douche); un cabinet de toilette* has a basin and bidet, without a bath, shower, or toilet. If you do not have *pension* or *demi-pension* accommodation, breakfast is often charged as an extra. Go instead to the local café, which may be cheaper and more filling.

Hôtel de l'Abbaye at Talloires in the French Alps *(see p580)*

GRADINGS

French hotels are graded from one star to five stars (the top five-star hotels are labeled "palace"). Hotels with two or more stars must have an elevator where appropriate, a phone in every room, and at least 40 percent of their bedrooms en suite. Three-star hotels must offer breakfast in the room and have 80 percent en suite rooms. Four- and five-star hotels must have room service, air conditioning, and all of their rooms en suite.

PRICES

Rates, inclusive of tax and service, are quoted per room (apart from *pension* and *demi-pension* arrangements). There is usually a small supplement for a third person in a room for two, and little reduction for single travelers.

As a rule, the higher the star rating the more you pay. Rates for a double room start from about €40 per night for a one-star hotel and go up to €100 or more for a four-star hotel. Costs also vary geographically with remote rural areas like Brittany being the cheapest. For equivalent accommodations in fashionable areas like the Dordogne and Provence expect to pay 20 percent more, and a further 20 percent again for Paris and the Côte d'Azur. Prices vary seasonally, too, with coastal and alpine areas raising rates by up to 50 percent in peak periods.

RESERVATIONS

Always reserve well in advance for Paris, and for hotels in popular tourist areas in July and August.

In seaside resorts, most hotels close from October to March, and ski resort hotels often close in April, so call ahead when traveling out of season to make sure a place is open.

Reservations can normally be held with a credit card. If you want to make a reservation while you are in France, there are tourist offices in all main cities, offering reservations up to eight days in advance.

The dining room of the Hôtel de la Cité, Carcassonne *(see p589)*

BED AND BREAKFAST

French bed and breakfasts, called *chambres d'hôte,* come in all shapes and sizes, from tiny cottages to elaborate châteaux full of family portraits and antiques, plus some *fermes-auberges (see p597).* In all cases you will stay in a private home, and should not expect hotel services or amenities. Many offer dinner – *table d'hôte* – on request, where you usually dine *en famille.* Over 25,000 rural *chambres d'hôte* are registered and inspected by **Gîtes de France**. Look out for the yellow and green *chambres d'hôte* signs on the roadside.

Roadside signs also lead to many B&Bs that are not registered. Information on these is available from local tourist offices.

The Gîtes de France logo

HOUSE RENTALS

The *gîte* is a rural vacation home, often converted from a farmhouse or its outbuildings. A *gîte* vacation is a popular and relatively cheap way to see France, particularly out of season, but you must book many months in advance for the best *gîtes*.

Gîtes de France registers some 45,000 *gîtes*, all inspected and graded to indicate the level of facilities. You can choose from a selection of 2,500 in the company's main brochure (available from the London office), or direct. Each of its 95 regional offices produces a booklet with all the *gîtes* in its *département*. These are also available through the head office in Paris, **Maison des Gîtes de France**, which itself publishes a series of listings catering for those with more specialized requirements. **Clévacances**, another reliable organization, has listings of good-quality *gîtes* throughout France.

France has plenty of other kinds of self-catering accommodations: expensive south-coast villas, ski resort chalets, city and coastal apartments. The *Allo Vacances* website (www.allovacances.com) provides a reservation service for vacation rentals throughout the different regions.

CAMPING

Eleven thousand official sites are spread around France's diverse countryside. The **Fédération Française de Camping et de Caravaning (FFCC)** publishes a comprehensive list, updated every year. Gîtes de France's *Camping à la Ferme* guide covers some simpler sites on farm land.

Campsites are graded from one to four stars. Three- and four-star sites are usually impressively spacious with plenty of amenities and electricity connections for a percentage of tents and campers. One- and two-star sites always have toilets, a public phone, and running water (though in one-star sites sometimes only cold water). What they lack in facilities they often make up for in peacefulness and rural charm.

Note, some sites only accept visitors with a **camping carnet**. *Carnets* are available from the RAC, and the clubs listed on the facing page.

HOSTELS

Hostels are a money-saving option for single travelers, though cheap hotels are often no more expensive for those travelling with a partner.

The IYHF's Hostelling guide details the **FUAJ**'s (Fédération Unie des Auberges de Jeunesse) 220 hostels around France, open to all ages and offering dormitory accommodation. If you are not a member of the **YHA** (Youth Hostel Association) in your home

Vacationers enjoying the pool at a campsite in high season

country, you have to pay a small surcharge each time you stay in a French youth hostel. **UCRIF** (Union des Centres de Rencontres Internationales de France) has 50 centers with a cultural bent scattered around France. All have single, shared, and dormitory accommodations and a restaurant.

In summer, you can stay in university rooms. Contact **CROUS** (Centre Régional des Oeuvres Universitaires et Scolaires) for details. *Gîtes d'étape* are usually large farmhouses with dormitories near walking, bicycling, and horse riding trails. Gîtes de France's *Gîtes d'Etape et de Séjour* guide details 1,600 sites.

DISABLED TRAVELERS

A number of associations publish information on accommodations throughout France with wheelchair access: the **Association des Paralysés de France (APF)**, the **Groupement pour l'Insertion des Personnes Handicapées Physiques (GIHP)**, and Gîtes de France's guide

The Carlton Intercontinental in Cannes *(see p592)*

Accessibles. APF has its own travel company, APF Evasion, to help arrange a vacation. **Les Compagnons du Voyage** (part of SNCF/ RATP), can arrange transportation, escorted or not, on all public transportation networks throughout France. There is also a useful website, www.guide-accessible.com, that lists, region by region, transportation companies adapted for wheelchair access.

FURTHER INFORMATION

A selection of brochures can be obtained from **Maison de la France**, including *City Breaks in France* and *France's Cultural Sites*, as well as the magazine *Traveler in France*. The French Government Tourist Office distributes *Logis de France* guides, and all the booklets for château-hotels and château-B&Bs. However, it only distributes the *Relais et Châteaux* guide over the counter.

The first port of call for all non-hotel accommodations in the French countryside should be Gîtes de France, including for B&B (brochures available from their Paris shop).

When in France, local tourist offices are the best source of information for B&Bs and furnished rentals.

Loisirs Accueil are special booking agencies that offer information on hotels, campsites, *gîtes*, and B&Bs in their area. A list of all 53 offices in France is available from the UK French Tourist Office.

DIRECTORY

CHAIN HOTELS

Campanile
Tel 0825 00 30 03 France.
www.campanile.com

Etap
Tel 0892 68 89 00 France.
www.etaphotel.com

Formule 1
Tel 0892 68 56 85 France.
www.hotelformule1.com

Hotel Première Classe
Tel 0892 68 81 23 France.
www.premiereclasse.com

Ibis
Tel 0870 609 0963 UK.
Tel 0892 68 66 86 France.
www.ibishotel.com

Novotel
Tel 0870 609 0962 UK.
Tel 0825 88 44 44 France.
www.novotel.com

Relais et Châteaux
Tel 0825 82 51 80 France.
www.relaischateaux.com

HOUSE RENTALS & B&B

Clévacances
Tel 02 51 47 71 07.
www.clevacances.com

Gîtes de France
59 St-Lazare, 75009 Paris.
Tel 01 49 70 75 85 or
0891 16 22 22 (chambre
d'hôte). www.gites-de-france.com

CAMPING

Fédération Française de Camping et de Caravaning (FFCC)
78 rue de Rivoli, 75004
Paris. *Tel* 01 42 72 84 08.
Fax 01 42 72 70 21.
www.ffcc.fr

HOSTELS

American Youth Hostel Association
8401 Colesville Road,
Suite 60, Silver Spring,
MD 20910. *Tel* (301) 495
1240. www.hiusa.org

CROUS

39 av G-Bernanos,
75231 Paris Cedex 05.
Tel 01 40 51 36 00.
www.crous-paris.fr

FUAJ (Féderation Unie des Auberges de Jeunesse)
27 rue Pajol, 75018 Paris.
Tel 01 44 89 87 27.
www.fuaj.fr

UCRIF
27 rue de Turbigo, 75002
Paris. *Tel* 01 40 26 57 64.
www.ethic-etapes.fr

YHA (Youth Hostel Association)
Trevelyan House, Matlock
Derbyshire DE4 3YH, UK.
Tel 0800 019 1700.
www.yha.org.uk

DISABLED TRAVELERS

APF
17 bd August Blanqui,
75013 Paris. *Tel* 01 40 78

69 00. *Fax* 01 45 89 40
57. www.apf.asso.fr

GIHP
32 rue de Paradis, 75010
Paris. *Tel* 01 43 95 66 36.
Fax 01 45 40 40 26.
www.gihpnational.org

Les Compagnons du Voyage
34 rue Championnet,
LAC CG25, 75018 Paris.
Tel 01 58 76 08 33.
www.compagnons.com

FURTHER INFORMATION

Loisirs Accueil
www.loisirs-accueil.fr

Maison de la France
Lincoln House, 300 High
Holborn, London W1V
7JH, UK. *Tel* 090 6824
4123 (within UK only).
www.uk.franceguide.com

Choosing a Hotel

Hotels have been selected across a wide price range for facilities, good value, and location. All rooms have private bath, TV, air conditioning, and are wheelchair accessible unless otherwise indicated. Most have Internet access, and in some cases, fitness facilities may be offsite. The hotels are listed by area. For map references, *see pp154-169.*

PRICE CATEGORIES
The following price ranges are for a standard double room and taxes per night during the high season. Breakfast is not included, unless specified:

€ under €80
€€ €80–€130
€€€ €130–€180
€€€€ €180–€250
€€€€€ over €250

PARIS

BEAUBOURG AND LES HALLES Hôtel Britannique €€€€
20 av Victoria, 75001 **Tel** *01 42 33 74 59* **Fax** *01 42 33 82 65* **Rooms** *40*   **Map** *13 A3*

The Britannique has many repeat visitors, who return for the central location beside Châtelet, as well as the Grand Tour atmosphere and helpful staff. A real *hôtel de charme*, with beautiful, characterful rooms and an abundance of old-fashioned charm. **www.hotel-brittanique.fr**

CHAILLOT QUARTER Hameau de Passy €€€
48 rue de Passy, 75016 **Tel** *01 42 88 47 55* **Fax** *01 42 30 83 72* **Rooms** *32*   **Map** *5 B3*

In the heart of the residential quarter of Passy, a stone's throw from the Eiffel Tower and the Trocadero, Hameau de Passy lies in a private lane, which is an oasis of green. Guest rooms overlook the garden. Breakfast is included and can be served in your room, upon request. Wi-Fi access available. **www.paris-hotel-hameaudepassy.com**

CHAILLOT QUARTER Concorde La Fayette €€€€
3 pl du Général Koenig, 75017 **Tel** *01 40 68 50 68* **Fax** *01 40 68 50 43* **Rooms** *1000*   **Map** *1 C2*

The formulaic Concorde La Fayette with its fascinating tower (one of the few in Paris) is thoroughly high-tech. Its facilities include a fitness club, a bar on the 33rd floor, restaurants, and a shopping gallery. The guest rooms afford truly splendid views over Paris and the Bois de Boulogne. **www.concorde-lafayette.com**

CHAILLOT QUARTER Hôtel du Bois €€€€
11 rue du Dôme, 75016 **Tel** *01 45 00 31 96* **Fax** *01 45 00 90 05* **Rooms** *41*   **Map** *2 D5*

Two minutes from the Arc de Triomphe and the Champs Elysées, Hôtel du Bois is ideal for haute-couture boutique-lovers. Behind a typically Parisian façade lies an interior rejuvenated in 2008 by the designer Michel Jouannet. The decor is light and airy, with bold fabrics and bright art on the walls. **www.hoteldubois.com**

CHAILLOT QUARTER Costes K €€€€€
81 av Kléber, 75016 **Tel** *01 44 05 75 75* **Fax** *01 44 05 74 74* **Rooms** *83*   **Map** *2 D5*

Not to be confused with the more expensive Hôtel Costes, this hotel is located just steps from the Eiffel Tower. It was designed and decorated by Spanish architect Ricardo Bofill, who used sycamore, stucco, marble, and stainless steel to create a feel of luxury. Cool Asian-style guest rooms.

CHAILLOT QUARTER Hôtel Elysées Regencia €€€€€
41 av Marceau, 75016 **Tel** *01 47 20 42 65* **Fax** *01 49 52 03 42* **Rooms** *43*   **Map** *2 E4*

Color is the central theme at this modishly decorated hotel right in the heart of the designer shopping district. Choose your room from a palette of blue, fuschia, aniseed (lime green), or lavender. The hotel also boasts a grand piano in the reception area, a paneled bar, and a massage room. **www.regencia.com**

CHAILLOT QUARTER Hôtel Keppler €€€€€
10 rue Kepler, 75016 **Tel** *01 47 20 65 05* **Fax** *01 47 23 02 29* **Rooms** *39*   **Map** *2 E5*

After extensive renovations, the Keppler is a chic and refined 4-star hotel. High ceilings throughout add to the sense of space, while the new facilities in the guest rooms, such as plasma screens, satellite TV, and allergy-free pillows, are welcome innovations. **www.keppler.fr**

CHAMPS-ELYSEES Royal Magda Etoile €€€
7 rue Troyon, 75017 **Tel** *01 47 64 10 19* **Fax** *01 47 64 02 12* **Rooms** *37*   **Map** *2 D3*

Just minutes from the Etoile in a quiet cobbled street, the Royal Magda Etoile is tastefully decorated in varying tones of cream. Rooms are on the small side, but the staff are exceptionally helpful and friendly and will go out of their way to help guests, especially families. **www.paris-hotel-magda.com**

CHAMPS-ELYSEES Claridge-Bellman €€€€€
37 rue François 1er, 75008 **Tel** *01 47 23 54 42* **Fax** *01 47 23 08 84* **Rooms** *42*   **Map** *2 F5*

The Claridge-Bellman is a miniature version of the old Claridge Hotel and is managed by its former directors. The hotel has a truly traditional feel. It is quiet, sober, and efficiently run, and is furnished throughout with tapestries and antiques. **www.hotelclaridgebellman.com**

Key to Symbols *see back cover flap*

CHAMPS-ELYSEES Four Seasons George V
31 av George V, 75008 **Tel** *01 49 52 70 00* **Fax** *01 49 52 71 10* **Rooms** *245*   **Map** *2 E5*

This legendary hotel, dotted with salons, old furniture, and art, lost a little of its charm when it was renovated. But it gained a stunning restaurant, Le Cinq, which boasts an award-winning chef and sommelier. There is also a great spa. Sheer opulence. **www.fourseasons.com/paris**

CHAMPS-ELYSEES Hotel Chambiges
8 rue Chambiges, 75008 **Tel** *01 44 31 83 83* **Fax** *01 40 70 95 51* **Rooms** *34*   **Map** *6 F1*

An elegant, cozy hotel on a quiet street just 5 minutes' walk from the Champs-Elysées. Warm colors and a classically Parisian atmosphere suffuse the whole place. In warm weather, enjoy breakfast on the flowery patio. **www.hotelchambiges.com**

CHAMPS-ELYSEES Hôtel Vernet
25 rue Vernet, 75008 **Tel** *01 44 31 98 00* **Fax** *01 44 31 85 69* **Rooms** *50*   **Map** *2 E4*

Gustave Eiffel (architect of the Eiffel Tower) created the dazzling glass roof of the dining room here. The impressive lobby has white and gold paneling, sumptuous red velvet curtains, antiques, and marble flooring. The rooms are large and quiet with flat screen TVs and Wi-Fi access. **www.hotelvernet.com**

CHAMPS-ELYSEES Le Bristol
112 rue du Faubourg-St-Honoré, 75008 **Tel** *01 53 43 43 00* **Fax** *01 53 43 43 01* **Rooms** *187*   **Map** *3 A4*

One of Paris's finest hotels, first opened in 1925, the Bristol's large rooms are sumptuously decorated with antiques and have magnificent marble bathrooms. The restaurant offers outstanding cuisine by chef Eric Frechon, winner of three Michelin stars. **www.lebristolparis.com**

CHAMPS-ELYSEES Plaza Athénée
25 av Montaigne, 75008 **Tel** *01 53 67 66 65* **Fax** *01 53 67 66 66* **Rooms** *191*   **Map** *6 F1*

The last word in luxury, the legendary Plaza Athénée is popular with honeymooners, aristocracy, and haute couture shoppers. The restaurant by Alain Ducasse is wonderfully romantic, while Le Bar du Plaza is now the hottest address in Paris for cocktails. **www.plaza-athenee-paris.fr**

CHAMPS-ELYSEES San Régis
12 rue Jean-Goujon, 75008 **Tel** *01 44 95 16 16* **Fax** *01 45 61 05 48* **Rooms** *44*   **Map** *7 A1*

Since it opened in 1923 the opulent San Régis has been popular with the jet set, who are drawn to its quiet, central location. A particularly welcoming, intimate luxury hotel, it is full of antiques and overstuffed sofas. Some rooms have wonderful balcony views over the rooftops. **www.hotel-sanregis.com**

INVALIDES AND EIFFEL TOWER QUARTER Grand Hôtel Levêque
29 rue Cler, 75007 **Tel** *01 47 05 49 15* **Fax** *01 45 50 49 36* **Rooms** *50*   **Map** *6 F3*

The Levêque lies between the Eiffel Tower and the Invalides on a pedestrianized street with a quaint fruit-and-vegetable market. The great location isn't the only attraction – guest rooms are well kept and the hotel also provides Internet access. **www.hotel-leveque.com**

INVALIDES AND EIFFEL TOWER QUARTER Hôtel Bourgogne et Montana
3 rue de Bourgogne, 75007 **Tel** *01 45 51 20 22* **Fax** *01 45 56 11 98* **Rooms** *32*   **Map** *7 B2*

Situated in front of the Assemblée Nationale, this hotel has an air of sobriety. Its features include an old-fashioned elevator and an all-white circular hall with brightly colored sofas. The guest rooms are decorated in a classical, aristocratic style. Extremely stylish. **www.bourgogne-montana.com**

INVALIDES AND EIFFEL TOWER QUARTER Hôtel de Suède St-Germain
31 rue Vaneau, 75007 **Tel** *01 47 05 00 08* **Fax** *01 47 05 69 27* **Rooms** *39*   **Map** *7 B4*

Located near the Orsay and Rodin museums, Hôtel de Suède St-Germain offers elegant rooms, decorated in late 18th-century style with pale colors. Guests receive an exceptionally warm welcome. The deluxe rooms offer a view over the park. A lovely little garden to breakfast in completes the picture. **www.hoteldesuede.com**

INVALIDES AND EIFFEL TOWER QUARTER Hôtel de Varenne
44 rue de Bourgogne, 75007 **Tel** *01 45 51 45 55* **Fax** *01 45 51 86 63* **Rooms** *25*   **Map** *7 B2*

Hidden beyond the hotel's severe façade is a narrow courtyard garden where guests breakfast in the summer. The bedrooms, furnished in elegant Louis XVI or Empire style, are impeccable. The hotel is popular with French government officials. **www.varenne-hotel-paris.com**

INVALIDES AND EIFFEL TOWER QUARTER Duc de St-Simon
14 rue de St-Simon, 75007 **Tel** *01 44 39 20 20* **Fax** *01 45 48 68 25* **Rooms** *34*   **Map** *7 C3*

The Hôtel Duc de St-Simon is justifiably one of the most sought-after hotels on the south side of the Seine. This is a charming 18th-century mansion, furnished with antiques, which lives up to its aristocratic pretensions. **www.hotelducdesaintsimon.com**

LATIN QUARTER Hôtel des Grandes Ecoles
75 rue Cardinal Lemoine, 75005 **Tel** *01 43 26 79 23* **Fax** *01 43 25 28 15* **Rooms** *51*   **Map** *9 B5*

This hotel is a cluster of three small houses around a beautiful garden, where you can breakfast in good weather. The rooms are all comfortable and furnished with traditional 18th-century-style floral wallpaper; some open onto the courtyard. Internet and Wi-Fi access are available. **www.hotel-grandes-ecoles.com**

LATIN QUARTER Hôtel Esmeralda
€€ Map 9 A4

4 rue St-Julien-le-Pauvre, 75005 **Tel** *01 43 54 19 20* **Fax** *01 40 51 00 68* **Rooms** *19*

The much-loved bohemian Hôtel Esmeralda lies in the heart of the Latin Quarter. With old stone walls and beamed ceilings, its charm has seduced the likes of Terence Stamp and Serge Gainsbourg. The best rooms overlook Notre-Dame cathedral. Breakfast is not provided here. **www.hotel-esmeralda.fr**

LATIN QUARTER Hôtel des Grands Hommes
€€€ Map 13 A1

17 pl du Panthéon, 75005 **Tel** *01 46 34 19 60* **Fax** *01 43 26 67 32* **Rooms** *31*

Teachers at the Sorbonne frequent this quiet family hotel close to the Jardin du Luxembourg. It boasts a great view of the Panthéon from the attic rooms on the upper floor. The guest rooms are comfortable. Wi-Fi service is available. **www.hoteldesgrandshommes.com**

LATIN QUARTER Hôtel les Degrès de Notre Dame
€€€ Map 9 B4

10 rue des Grands Degrès, 75005 **Tel** *01 55 42 88 88* **Fax** *01 40 46 95 34* **Rooms** *10*

An exceptionally friendly place to stay. The staff are genuinely welcoming and the wood paneling and oak beams around the building make it even more special. Lovely, clean bedrooms with Internet access available. The Bar Restaurant and Tea Room serves great food at a low price. **www.lesdegreshotel.monsite-orange.fr**

LATIN QUARTER Hôtel de Notre-Dame
€€€€ Map 9 B5

19 rue Maître Albert, 75006 **Tel** *01 43 26 79 00* **Fax** *01 46 33 50 11* **Rooms** *34*

The picturesque Hôtel de Notre-Dame overlooks Notre-Dame cathedral and the Seine on one side, and the Panthéon on the other. The furnishings are functional, but some rooms have beams or an old stone wall. The main appeal here is the location. The hotel has its own sauna and Wi-Fi access. **www.hotel-paris-notredame.com**

LATIN QUARTER Hôtel du Panthéon
€€€€ Map 13 A1

19 pl du Panthéon, 75005 **Tel** *01 43 54 32 95* **Fax** *01 43 26 64 65* **Rooms** *36*

This hotel is managed by the same family as the Hôtel des Grands Hommes: the welcome is equally warm and the decor similarly Classical. Extra romance and luxury can be found in room 34 with its divine four-poster bed. Wi-Fi is available throughout the hotel. **www.hoteldupantheon.com**

LUXEMBOURG QUARTER Hôtel du Globe
€€€ Map 8 F4

15 rue des Quatre-Vents, 75006 **Tel** *01 43 26 35 50* **Fax** *01 46 33 62 69* **Rooms** *14*

Occupying a 17th-century building by the Jardin du Luxembourg, the popular Hôtel du Globe provides excellent accommodation. The guest rooms are decorated with antique furniture and colorful fabrics. Breakfast is brought to your room. Reserve in advance. **www.hotelduglobeparis.com**

LUXEMBOURG QUARTER Aviatic
€€€€ Map 8 E5

105 rue de Vaugirard, 75006 **Tel** *01 53 63 25 50* **Fax** *01 53 63 25 55* **Rooms** *43*

True to its Parisian past and long-standing family hotel tradition, the much-loved Aviatic combines bohemian style with modern comforts. The rooms are individually decorated with charming pieces found at local flea markets and warm, bright textiles. Parking is available for an additional fee. **www.aviatic.fr**

LUXEMBOURG QUARTER Hôtel Louis II
€€€€ Map 8 E4

2 rue St-Sulpice, 75006 **Tel** *01 46 33 13 80* **Fax** *01 46 33 17 29* **Rooms** *22*

The charming, light-filled rooms of the Louis II are all individually styled. Each is characterized by exposed wooden beams, tasteful decor, and great attention to detail. Rooms overlook rue St-Sulpice or rue de Condé. The suites in the roof are particularly appealing. **www.hotel-louis2.com**

MONTMARTRE Regyn's Montmartre
€€ Map 4 E1

18 pl des Abbesses, 75018 **Tel** *01 42 54 45 21* **Fax** *01 42 23 76 69* **Rooms** *22*

Near Sacré-Cœur, this is an impeccably kept budget hotel. All the rooms are decorated with pastoral *toile de Jouy* patterns, and those on the top floor have views of the Eiffel Tower. Around the corner is Café des Deux Moulins at 15 rue Lepic, where Amélie worked in the film *Amélie*. **www.paris-hotels-montmartre.com/regyns**

MONTMARTRE Relais Montmartre
€€€ Map 4 E1

6 rue Constance, 75018 **Tel** *01 70 64 25 25* **Fax** *01 70 64 25 00* **Rooms** *26*

In the heart of Montmartre's network of steep winding streets, this charming hotel is all femininity with delicate floral fabrics, antique furniture, and painted beams. Quiet, intimate, and romantic with the added bonus of being well situated for neighborhood restaurants. **www.hotel-relais-montmartre.com**

MONTMARTRE Terrass Hôtel
€€€€€ Map 4 E1

12-14 rue Joseph-de-Maistre, 75018 **Tel** *01 46 06 72 85* **Fax** *01 42 92 34 30* **Rooms** *98*

Montmartre's most luxurious hotel, the rooms here are comfortable and airy with neo Art-Deco touches and, in some classic rooms, bold stripes. The big draw is the restaurant, where in the summer fashionable Parisians take in a world-class view over the city. **www.terrass-hotel.com**

MONTPARNASSE Hôtel Apollon Montparnasse
€€ Map 11 C3

91 rue Ouest, 75014 **Tel** *01 43 95 62 00* **Fax** *01 43 95 62 10* **Rooms** *33*

Close to the Parc des Expositions of the Porte de Versailles, the Apollon Montparnasse is decorated with Grecian statues and fine furnishings. The guest rooms are simple, but well equipped. Parking is available for an additional fee. The hotel also provides Wi-Fi facilities. **www.paris-hotel-paris.net**

Key to Price Guide *see p550* **Key to Symbols** *see back cover flap*

MONTPARNASSE Hôtel Delambre Montparnasse 🔲🟦 €€€
35 rue Delambre, 75014 **Tel** *01 43 20 66 31* **Fax** *01 45 38 91 76* **Rooms** *30*   **Map** *12 D2*

Located a few steps from Montparnasse cemetery, and close to the Jardin de Luxembourg and the Latin Quarter, this hotel mixes modern and classical styles. Guest rooms are simply furnished, with all modern conveniences. **www.delambre-paris-hotel.com**

MONTPARNASSE Hôtel Le Ste Beuve 🔲🟦 €€€€
9 rue Ste Beuve, 75006 **Tel** *01 45 48 20 07* **Fax** *01 45 48 67 52* **Rooms** *22*   **Map** *12 D1*

The Ste-Beuve is a small, carefully restored hotel for aesthetes and habitués of the Rive Gauche galleries. There is a fireplace in the hall, the rooms are pleasantly decorated in pastel shades, and several modern paintings add to the atmosphere. **www.hotel-sainte-beuve.fr**

MONTPARNASSE Villa des Artistes 🔲🟦 €€€€
9 rue de la Grande Chaumière, 75006 **Tel** *01 43 26 60 86* **Fax** *01 43 54 73 70* **Rooms** *55*   **Map** *12 D2*

The Villa des Artistes aims to recreate Montparnasse's artistic heyday when Modigliani, Beckett, and Fitzgerald were all visitors here. The guest rooms are clean, but the main draw is the large patio garden and fountain, where you can breakfast in peace. **www.villa-artistes.com**

MONTPARNASSE Le St-Grégoire 🔲🅿🟦 €€€€€
43 rue de l'Abbé Grégoire, 75006 **Tel** *01 45 48 23 23* **Fax** *01 45 48 33 95* **Rooms** *20*   **Map** *7 C5*

Le St-Grégoire is a fashionable townhouse hotel with immaculately decorated guest rooms with 19th-century furnishings. Reserve a room with a delightful private terrace. At the center of the drawing room is a charming fireplace. Parking is available for an additional fee. **www.paris-hotel-saintgregoire.com**

OPERA QUARTER Ambassador 🔲🟦🟦🟦 €€€€€
16 bd Haussmann, 75009 **Tel** *01 44 83 40 40* **Fax** *01 42 46 19 84* **Rooms** *297*   **Map** *4 E4*

One of Paris's best Art Deco hotels, the Ambassador has been restored to its former glory with plush carpeting and antique furniture. The ground floor has pink marble columns, Baccarat crystal chandeliers, and Aubusson tapestries. The restaurant, 16 Haussmann, is popular with Parisian gourmets. **www.ambassador.paris.radissonsas.com**

OPERA QUARTER Edouard VII Hotel 🔲🟦🟦🟦 €€€€€
39 av de l'Opéra, 75002 **Tel** *01 42 61 56 90* **Fax** *01 42 61 47 73* **Rooms** *70*   **Map** *4 E5*

The only hotel on the impressive Avenue de l'Opéra, the Edouard VII is centrally located between the Louvre and the Opéra Garnier, which makes it perfect for sightseeing. Request a room at the front for a breathtaking view over the Opéra House. **www.edouard7hotel.com**

OPERA QUARTER Le Grand Hôtel Intercontinental 🔲🅿🟦🟦🟦🟦 €€€€€
2 rue Scribe, 75009 **Tel** *01 40 07 32 32* **Fax** *01 42 66 12 51* **Rooms** *470*   **Map** *4 D5*

Directly next to the Opéra Garnier, this hotel is a sumptuous example of good taste. The rooms all have pictures with a musical theme reflecting the hotel's location. The opulent restaurant, the Café de La Paix, is renowned in the Opéra Quarter. **www.IHG.com**

ST-GERMAIN-DES-PRES Grand Hôtel des Balcons 🔲 €€
3 rue Casimir Delavigne, 75006 **Tel** *01 46 34 78 50* **Fax** *01 46 34 06 27* **Rooms** *50*   **Map** *8 F5*

Embellished with Art Nouveau features, this hotel has a beautiful hall with stained-glass windows and striking 19th-century-style lamps and wood paneling. Most guest rooms, quiet and well-decorated, enjoy a balcony. High-speed Internet access with Wi-Fi is available. **www.hotelgrandsbalcons.com**

ST-GERMAIN-DES-PRES Hôtel des Marronniers 🔲🟦 €€€
21 rue Jacob, 75006 **Tel** *01 43 25 30 60* **Fax** *01 40 46 83 56* **Rooms** *37*   **Map** *8 E3*

Situated between a courtyard and a garden, this hotel provides perfect tranquility. The cozy rooms are decorated with country fabrics. Those on the fourth floor garden side provide memorable views over the Parisian rooftops and the St-Germain-des-Prés church steeple. **www.hotel-marronniers.com**

ST-GERMAIN-DES-PRES Hôtel du Quai Voltaire 🔲🟦 €€€
19 quai Voltaire, 75007 **Tel** *01 42 61 50 91* **Fax** *01 42 61 62 26* **Rooms** *33*   **Map** *8 D2*

Overlooking the river, this hotel was once the favorite of Blondin, Baudelaire, and Pissarro, and has featured in several movies. It is best to avoid the rooms facing the quay, as they suffer from traffic noise. Higher floors are quieter, though, and the views are superb. **www.quaivoltaire.fr**

ST-GERMAIN-DES-PRES Hôtel d'Angleterre 🔲 €€€€
44 rue Jacob, 75006 **Tel** *01 42 60 34 72* **Fax** *01 42 60 16 93* **Rooms** *27*   **Map** *8 E3*

Once the British Embassy, the Hôtel d'Angleterre has retained many of the original features, including the fine old staircase, the exquisite garden, and the salon mantelpiece. The guest rooms are individually decorated; many have exposed beams and wonderful four-poster beds. **www.hotel-dangleterre.com**

ST-GERMAIN-DES-PRES Hôtel des Sts-Pères 🔲🟦 €€€€
65 rue des Sts-Pères, 75006 **Tel** *01 45 44 50 00* **Fax** *01 45 44 90 83* **Rooms** *39*   **Map** *8 E3*

Situated in one of the old aristocratic mansions of St-Germain-des-Prés, this hotel has quiet, large rooms – the best has an outstanding fresco on the ceiling. The lounge bar is popular with authors from the nearby publishing houses. **www.paris-hotel-saints-peres.com**

ST-GERMAIN-DES-PRES Hôtel de l'Abbaye St-Germain
10 rue Cassette, 75006 **Tel** *01 45 44 38 11* **Fax** *01 45 48 07 86* **Rooms** *44* **Map** *8 D5*

A 17th-century abbey, just steps from the Jardin du Luxembourg, this charming hotel has a history as a preferred hideout for artists and writers. Its finely furnished guest rooms and apartments have been tastefully done up and provided with modern facilities. For a real splurge, there are four duplex apartments. **www.hotelabbayeparis.com**

ST-GERMAIN-DES-PRES L'Hôtel
13 rue des Beaux-Arts, 75006 **Tel** *01 44 41 99 00* **Fax** *01 43 25 64 81* **Rooms** *20* **Map** *8 E3*

A riot of exuberance and opulence, this Jacques Garcia-designed hotel is gloriously decadent. Each room is unique; the Oscar Wilde suite, where the Irish author died and which boasts period furnishings, is the most famous. There's also a beautiful spa and a restaurant with one Michelin star. **www.l-hotel.com**

ST-GERMAIN-DES-PRES Lutétia
45 bd Raspail, 75006 **Tel** *01 49 54 46 46* **Fax** *01 49 54 46 00* **Rooms** *230* **Map** *8 D4*

The Lutétia is a mainstay of glamor on the south side of the river. The building's style is partly Art Nouveau and partly Art Deco, and has been restored throughout. Publishers and chic shoppers are regular customers in the restaurant. The location is convenient. **www.lutetia-paris.com**

ST-GERMAIN-DES-PRES Relais Christine
3 rue Christine, 75006 **Tel** *01 40 51 60 80* **Fax** *01 40 51 60 81* **Rooms** *51* **Map** *8 F4*

Always full, the Relais Christine is the epitome of the *hôtel de charme*. Part of a cloister from a 16th-century abbey, the hotel is a romantic, peaceful haven. The guest rooms, especially the deluxe rooms, are bright and spacious. Wi-Fi facilities are available. Reserve in advance. **www.relais-christine.com**

THE MARAIS Hôtel Caron de Beaumarchais
12 rue Vieille du Temple, 75004 **Tel** *01 42 78 14 15* **Fax** *01 40 29 06 82* **Rooms** *19* **Map** *9 C3*

Pretty 18th-century-style fabrics and crystal chandeliers adorn this elegant boutique hotel. The rooms are cozy, yet not too small, with wooden beams and oodles of character. There are also 21st-century touches, such as Internet access and air conditioning. **www.carondebeaumarchais.com**

THE MARAIS Hôtel de la Bretonnerie
22 rue Ste-Croix de la Bretonnerie, 75004 **Tel** *01 48 87 77 63* **Fax** *01 42 77 26 78* **Rooms** *29* **Map** *9 C3*

Carved stone walls and an arched dining room in the basement are some of the charming features of Hôtel de la Bretonnerie, housed in a 17th-century mansion. Its spacious rooms, with beams and antique furniture, are each decorated differently. Service is warm and friendly. **www.hotelbretonnerie.com**

THE MARAIS Hôtel des Deux-Iles
59 rue St-Louis-en-l'Ile, 75004 **Tel** *01 43 26 13 35* **Fax** *01 43 29 60 25* **Rooms** *17* **Map** *9 C4*

It's a privilege to be able to stay on the Ile St-Louis, and this converted 17th-century mansion offers an affordable way to do so. Here the atmosphere is peaceful, the small bedrooms are attractive, and the lounge has a real fire. **www.deuxiles-paris-hotel.com**

THE MARAIS Hôtel du Bourg Tibourg
19 rue du Bourg-Tibourg, 75004 **Tel** *01 42 78 47 39* **Fax** *01 40 29 07 00* **Rooms** *30* **Map** *9 C3*

This stylish spot was decorated by top interior designer Jacques Garcia and is extremely popular with fashionable visitors to Paris. The rooms are opulent and all bathrooms are fully clad in black marble. The beautiful interior courtyard is a pleasant feature. **www.bourgtibourg.com**

THE MARAIS Hôtel Duo
11 rue du Temple, 75004 **Tel** *01 42 72 72 22* **Fax** *01 42 72 03 53* **Rooms** *58* **Map** *9 B3*

A family-run hotel for three generations, the former Axial Beaubourg is still in the same hands, but has been given a trendy makeover. The stylish, contemporary decor features teal and brown, and there is a bijou bar and Japanese garden – all just steps from the Pompidou Center. **www.duo-paris.com**

THE MARAIS St-Paul-le-Marais
8 rue de Sévigné, 75004 **Tel** *01 48 04 97 27* **Fax** *01 48 87 37 04* **Rooms** *28* **Map** *10 D3*

Close to the historic place des Vosges, this hotel has wooden beams and old stone, with simple and modern furniture. Request a room facing the courtyard to avoid the noise of traffic coming from the rue de Sévigné. **www.hotelparissaintpaullemarais.com**

THE MARAIS Murano Urban Resort
13 bd du Temple, 75003 **Tel** *01 42 71 20 00* **Fax** *01 42 71 21 01* **Rooms** *52* **Map** *10 D1*

The über-hip and sleek Murano is the Marais' most luxurious hotel. Rooms feature huge Pop Art representations of 20th-century idols and have colored lighting that changes to suit your every mood. An equally cool bar and restaurant completes the glamorous scene. **www.muranoresort.com**

THE MARAIS Pavillon de la Reine
28 pl des Vosges, 75003 **Tel** *01 40 29 19 19* **Fax** *01 40 29 19 20* **Rooms** *56* **Map** *10 D3*

Set back from the marvelous place des Vosges, the Pavillon de la Reine is the best hotel in the Marais. Incredibly romantic, the hotel has a peaceful courtyard and sumptuous guest rooms, furnished with excellent reproduction antiques. **www.pavillon-de-la-reine.com**

Key to Price Guide *see p550* **Key to Symbols** *see back cover flap*

TUILERIES QUARTER Hôtel Louvre Ste Anne

32 rue Ste Anne, 75001 **Tel** *01 40 20 02 35* **Fax** *01 40 15 91 13* **Rooms** *20* **Map** *8 E1*

A small pleasant hotel located 5 minutes from the Louvre and Opéra. The hotel may be due for a makeover, but the rooms are clean, the staff are helpful, and there is a splendid reception area with a *trompe l'oeil* painting. A popular hotel with Japanese guests who frequent the nearby sushi restaurants. **www.paris-hotel-louvre.com**

TUILERIES QUARTER Brighton

218 rue de Rivoli, 75001 **Tel** *01 47 03 61 61* **Fax** *01 42 60 41 78* **Rooms** *65* **Map** *8 D1*

A real insiders' location, the Brighton provides a much-sought-after Rivoli address without the sky-high prices. The guest rooms have beautiful, high ceilings and large windows that look out either over the Jardin des Tuileries or over the courtyard. **www.espritdefrance.com**

TUILERIES QUARTER Hôtel du Louvre

Pl André Malraux, 75001 **Tel** *01 44 58 38 38* **Fax** *01 44 58 38 01* **Rooms** *177* **Map** *8 E1*

This, the first luxury hotel in France, was built in 1855 by order of Napoleon III. The lavish rooms have spectacular views: the Pissarro Suite is where the artist painted his view of the place du Théâtre Français. Parisians regularly visit the buzzing brasserie for lunch. **www.hoteldulouvre.com**

TUILERIES QUARTER Hôtel de Crillon

10 pl de la Concorde, 75008 **Tel** *01 44 71 15 00* **Fax** *01 44 71 15 02* **Rooms** *147* **Map** *7 C1*

With its magnificent location on the glittering place de la Concorde, the Crillon offers unsurpassed elegance. The hotel has a fine Royal Suite and terrace, a sublime dining room, and a fashionable bar designed by French fashion designer, Sonia Rykiel. **www.crillon.com**

TUILERIES QUARTER Meurice

228 rue de Rivoli, 75001 **Tel** *01 44 58 10 10* **Fax** *01 44 58 10 15* **Rooms** *150* **Map** *8 D1*

The Meurice is a perfect example of successful restoration, with excellent replicas of the original plasterwork and furnishings. The staff here are unfailingly helpful and the hotel offers personalized shopping and art-buying tours. The hotel's spa is first rate and the only place in Paris to offer Valmont products. **www.lemeurice.com**

TUILERIES QUARTER Ritz

15 pl Vendôme, 75001 **Tel** *01 43 16 30 70* **Fax** *01 43 16 45 38* **Rooms** *162* **Map** *4 D5*

A legendary address, the Ritz still lives up to its reputation, combining elegance and decadence. The Louis XVI furniture and chandeliers are all original, and the floral arrangements are works of art. The Hemingway Bar is home to the glitterati. **www.ritzparis.com**

ILE DE FRANCE

BARBIZON Hostellerie La Dague

5 grande rue, 77630 **Tel** *01 60 66 40 49* **Fax** *01 60 69 24 59* **Rooms** *25*

Located in an artists' village in the heart of the forest, this rustic ivy-clad manor house has a romantic setting. It is popular with Parisians, so reserve early. The bright rooms have pretty floral furnishings; there is also a modern annex. The traditional French restaurant is charming. **www.inter-hotel.fr**

BELLEVILLE MamaShelter

109 rue de Bagnolet, 75020 **Tel** *01 43 48 48 48* **Fax** *01 43 48 49 49* **Rooms** *170*

This concept hotel designed by Philippe Starck offers exceptionally low prices for nonrefundable reservations; if you require flexibility, the prices increase. The contemporary rooms all have iMacs, satin-cotton sheets, and microwaves. There is a trendy lounge bar and restaurant, too. **www.mamashelter.com**

ENGHIEN-LES-BAINS Grand Hôtel Barrière

85 rue Général de Gaulle, 95880 **Tel** *01 39 34 10 00* **Fax** *01 39 34 10 01* **Rooms** *43*

In the heart of this bustling spa town overlooking a lake, the Grand Hôtel lives up to its name. The interior was designed by Jacques Garcia. The rooms are luxurious, some in Louis XV style. The hotel has a traditional gourmet restaurant, a theater, and a casino. **www.lucienbarriere.com**

FONTAINBLEAU Grand Hôtel de l'Aigle Noir

27 pl de Napoléon Bonaparte, 77300 **Tel** *01 60 74 60 00* **Fax** *01 60 74 60 01* **Rooms** *18*

This prestigious mansion overlooks Fontainebleau château and its vast park. The elegant rooms are decorated in styles ranging from Louis XIII to Napoléon III. The conciergerie can arrange a host of activities in the area, and the bar serves snacks all day. **www.hotelaiglenoir.com**

MAFFLIERS Château de Maffliers

Allée des Marronniers, 95560 **Tel** *01 34 08 35 35* **Fax** *01 34 08 35 00* **Rooms** *99*

This 19th-century château lies in the heart of the L'Isle d'Adam forest, surrounded by a huge private park. The contemporary guest rooms have all modern conveniences including Wi-Fi. Some nonsmoking and wheelchair-accessible rooms. Bikes available to explore the forest. **www.accorhotels.com**

ROISSY-CHARLES-DE-GAULLE Sheraton Paris Airport

⊞ P ⊓ ⊼ ⊓ ▤ ⅃ €€€€

Terminal 2, Charles de Gaulle airport, Roissy, 95716 **Tel** *01 49 19 70 70* **Fax** *01 49 19 70 71* **Rooms** *252*

This state-of-the-art Sheraton is actually built into Terminal 2 and guarantees the longest sleep-in to anyone with a morning flight. Its neat and comfortable rooms have plenty of amenities and insulated windows, which means you can watch the planes taxiing by without hearing a thing. **www.sheratonparisairport.fr**

ST-GERMAIN-EN-LAYE Pavillon Henri IV

⊞ P ⊓ ⊼ €€€

19-21 rue Thiers, 78100 **Tel** *01 39 10 15 15* **Fax** *01 39 73 93 73* **Rooms** *42*

This sumptuous hotel is housed in a historic lodge built by Henri IV. It was here in 1638 that Louis XIV was born, and later where Dumas wrote *The Three Musketeers*. There is a wonderful panorama of Paris, and a gourmet restaurant. The rooms are stylish. **www.pavillon-henri-4.com**

ST PRIX Hostellerie du Prieuré

P ⊼ €€€

74 rue Auguste Rey, 95390 **Tel** *01 34 27 51 51* **Fax** *01 39 59 21 21* **Rooms** *8*

Located just 15 minutes by train from the Gare du Nord, this former *bistrot* now houses 8 spacious bedrooms, all individually furnished. The "Pompadour" is particularly grand and has a view of Paris in the distance. A copious breakfast is served and there are restaurants nearby. Friendly, helpful staff. **www.hostelduprieure.com**

ST-SYMPHORIEN LE CHATEAU Château d'Esclimont

⊞ P ⊓ ≅ ⊼ ⊓ ▤ €€€€

28700 **Tel** *02 37 31 15 15* **Fax** *02 37 31 57 91* **Rooms** *53*

This magnificent 16th-century fairytale château has a private forest, tennis courts, a golf course and a fitness circuit. This turreted building offers meticulously kept, comfortable rooms. The gourmet restaurant provides impeccable service. Dogs are welcome. **www.grandesetapes.fr**

VERSAILLES Hôtel de Clagny

€€

6 impasse de Clagny, 78000 **Tel** *01 39 50 18 09* **Fax** *01 39 50 85 17* **Rooms** *18*

The welcome in this quiet hotel near the train station is genuinely friendly. The rooms are furnished simply and clean, but unremarkable. There are numerous restaurants in the vicinity, and the owners of the Hôtel de Clagny are only too pleased to offer guidance.

VERSAILLES Trianon Palace

⊞ P ⊓ ≅ ⊼ ⊓ ▤ €€€€€

1 bd de la Reine, 78000 **Tel** *01 30 84 50 00* **Fax** *01 30 84 50 01* **Rooms** *199*

This is undoubtedly the most splendid hotel in the region. Built in Regency style, the hotel offers gorgeous, luxury guest rooms. The gourmet restaurant, run by Brit chef Gordon Ramsey, is the jewel in the crown. There is also a spa and a *hammam* (Turkish bath) for guests. **www.trianonpalace.fr**

LE NORD & PICARDY

AMIENS Hôtel de Normandie

P €

1bis rue Lamartine, 80000 **Tel** *03 22 91 74 99* **Fax** *03 22 92 06 56* **Rooms** *28*

This pleasant hotel with a red brick and stucco façade stands in a quiet street near the cathedral and train station. The rooms are spacious, with modern furnishings. The hotel has an arrangement with Le T'Chiot Zinc, an inexpensive traditional restaurant where meals can be eaten. Parking is extra. **www.hotelnormandie-80.com**

AMIENS Victor Hugo

€

2 rue de l'Oratoire, 80000 **Tel** *03 22 91 57 91* **Rooms** *10*

This friendly family hotel near the famous Gothic cathedral has a stone Bible carved into the façade. An old wooden staircase leads to the guest rooms. It makes an ideal base for exploring the city and is within easy walking distance of stores, restaurants, and bars. **www.hotel-a-amiens.com**

BERCK-SUR-MER Hôtel Neptune

⊞ P ⊓ ⊼ €

Esplanade Parmentier, 62600 **Tel** *03 21 09 21 21* **Fax** *03 21 09 29 29* **Rooms** *63*

This excellent, ultramodern hotel is right on the seafront. The guest rooms are airy, many with a view. The rooms are fully adapted for disabled guests. The restaurant, with its impressive view, serves traditional local food, including seafood and steak. **www.hotelneptuneberck.com**

BOULOGNE-SUR-MER Hôtel Hamiot

⊞ P ⊓ €€

1 rue Faidherbe, 62200 **Tel** *03 21 31 44 20* **Fax** *03 21 83 71 56* **Rooms** *12*

This lively portside hotel-restaurant has refurbished but somewhat old-fashioned rooms with plain walls, colored bedspreads, and dark furniture. The soundproofing is good. The Grand Restaurant has an excellent menu and a view; the less expensive Brasserie has a busy terrace. **www.hotelhamiot.com**

CALAIS Kyriad

P ⊓ ⊼ €

Digue G Berthe, 62100 **Tel** *03 21 34 64 64* **Fax** *03 21 34 35 39* **Rooms** *45*

Right on the beach, behind lines of old-fashioned bathing huts, is this modern hotel-restaurant. The guest rooms accommodate up to three people and are wheelchair-accessible. The restaurant has a changing menu. **www.hotel-plage-calais.com**

CAMBRAI Château de la Motte Fénélon `P` `11` `🌳` €€
Square Château, 59400 **Tel** *03 27 83 61 38* **Fax** *03 27 83 71 61* **Rooms** *40*

Set in its own gardens, this 1850s château is handsomely decorated with grand guest rooms in the main building, and more modest rooms in the annexes. There is also a tennis court. The restaurant serves excellent traditional cuisine in a brick-vaulted cellar. **www.cambrai-chateau-motte-fenelon.com**

CHANTILLY-GOUVIEUX Château de la Tour `P` `11` `🏊` `🌳` `🌳` €€€€
Chemin de la Chaussée, 60270 **Tel** *03 44 62 38 38* **Fax** *03 44 57 31 97* **Rooms** *41*

Just 20 minutes' drive from Charles de Gaulle airport, this imposing *fin-de-siècle* residence and its matching extension is a haven of luxury set in 12 acres (5 ha) of grounds. The dining room has beautiful wood flooring. There is a pleasant terrace, and facilities for disabled guests. **www.lechateaudelatour.fr**

DOUAI La Terrasse `P` `11` `♿` €€
36 Terrasse St Pierre, 59500 **Tel** *03 22 85 04 43* **Fax** *03 22 8506 69* **Rooms** *24*

This charming hotel has a sophisticated low-key interior, and the owners' passion for painting is evident in the many canvases that grace the walls. The excellent restaurant offers a wide range of fish dishes according to the catch of the day, and the cellar is stocked with a fine selection of vintage wines. **www.laterrasse.fr**

DUNKIRK Hôtel La Réserve `11` €
82 quai des Hollandais, 59140 **Tel** *03 28 66 50 21* **Fax** *03 28 66 74 44* **Rooms** *7*

This small, reliable hotel in the center of the town provides a good base from which to explore the area. The attractive rooms overlook the Yacht basin, and on the ground floor there is a popular, reasonably priced restaurant serving a wide range of fish dishes.

FERE-EN-TARDENOIS Château de Fère `P` `11` `🏊` `🌳` `🌳` €€€€
Rte de Fismes, 02130 **Tel** *03 23 82 21 13* **Fax** *03 23 82 37 81* **Rooms** *19 (plus 7 suites)*

In the background of this 16th-century hotel, set in vast grounds, are the ruins of the medieval castle of Anne de Montmorency. Each guest room here is unique, and the two dining rooms are splendid – with an amazing wine cellar, which can be visited. There are full facilities for disabled visitors. **www.chateaudefere.com**

GOSNAY La Chartreuse du Val de St Esprit `P` `11` `🌳` `🌳` `📺` `▤` €€€€
1 rue de Fouquières, 62199 **Tel** *03 21 62 80 00* **Fax** *03 21 62 42 50* **Rooms** *63*

On the outskirts of Béthune, this hotel is housed in an elegant château dating from 1764. Spacious guest rooms overlook the tree-filled park. There are three restaurants: the Chartreuse for the gourmet, Robert II for traditional cuisine, and Le Vasco for trendier guests. **www.lachartreuse.com**

HARDELOT PLAGE Hôtel du Parc `📺` `P` `11` `🏊` `🌳` `♿` €€€
111 av François Ier, 62152 **Tel** *03 21 33 22 11* **Fax** *03 21 83 29 71* **Rooms** *81*

A bright, airy, and contemporary hotel with rooms that have balconies or terraces overlooking extensive grounds. The hotel is located less than 30 minutes' drive from fashionable Le Touquet and within easy reach of the coast and two neighboring golf courses. There is also a good restaurant. **www.hotelduparc-hardelot.com**

LAON-VILLE HAUTE Hôtel La Bannière de France `P` `11` `♿` €€
11 rue Franklin Roosevelt, 02000 **Tel** *03 23 23 21 44* **Fax** *03 23 23 31 56* **Rooms** *18*

Housed in a coaching inn dating from 1685, this hotel provides a good base for exploring the ancient city of Laon. The excellent guest rooms have been fitted with all the modern conveniences. The dining room combines classic cuisine with Old-World charm. **www.hoteldelabannieredefrance.com**

LE TOUQUET Hôtel Be Cottage `P` `11` €€
41 rue Jean Monnet, 62520 **Tel** *03 21 05 15 33* **Fax** *03 21 05 41 60* **Rooms** *25*

This contemporary hotel stands in the center of town, near the beach. It is close to the covered market and the lively rue St Jean. The rooms are spacious and modern; nonsmoking rooms are also available. The restaurant rotates its menu daily, with a buffet in the evenings. **www.hotelbecottage.com**

LILLE Hôtel Kanai `▤` €€
10 rue de Bethune, 59000 **Tel** *03 20 57 14 78* **Fax** *03 20 57 06 01* **Rooms** *31*

An elegant arcaded front marks the entrance to this entirely refurbished hotel situated next to the excellent Christmas market. The moderately priced rooms are decorated in a pleasingly modern style. A library offers the day's newspapers. Children under 13 stay free. **www.hotelkanai.com**

LILLE Alliance Couvent des Minimes `📺` `P` `11` `▤` €€€€
17 quai du Wault, 59000 **Tel** *03 20 30 62 62* **Fax** *03 20 42 94 25* **Rooms** *83*

This converted 17th-century convent combines ancient and modern elements. Traditional Flemish brick arches surround the dining room with its sensational roof, while the guest rooms have benefited from the best of modern design. Some rooms are equipped for disabled guests. **www.alliance-lille.com**

LONGPONT Hôtel de l'Abbaye `P` `11` €€
8 rue des Tourelles, 02600 **Tel** *03 23 96 02 44* **Rooms** *11*

Located between Soissons and Villers-Cotterets, this hotel is named after the 12th-century abbey opposite, and is nearly as old. The guest rooms are old-fashioned and comfortable. The popular restaurant serves *cuisine du terroir*, grillades, and game in winter. **www.hotel-abbaye-longpont.fr**

LUMBRES Moulin de Mombreux
Chemin de Mombreux, 62380 **Tel** *03 21 39 62 44* **Fax** *03 21 93 61 34* **Rooms** *24*

This romantic 18th-century mill, hidden in its own grounds on the banks of the river Bléquin, works its charm on all who visit. Guests fall asleep to the sound of a waterfall. The restaurant is furnished with antiques and fine exposed beams. **www.moulindemombreux.com**

MAUBEUGE Hôtel Shakespeare
3 rue du Commerce, 59600 **Tel** *03 27 65 14 14* **Fax** *03 27 64 04 66* **Rooms** *35*

This is a functional and efficiently run hotel with friendly staff where you can stay without breaking the bank. It has an old-style exterior with a covered terrace for the bistro restaurant, which features a selection of grilled food. **www.shakespearemaubeuge.fr**

MONTREUIL Le Darnétal
Pl Poissonerie, 62170 **Tel** *03 21 06 04 87* **Fax** *03 21 86 64 67* **Rooms** *4*

A small hotel in the upper town of Montreuil, the rooms here are old-fashioned. The auberge is decorated with a host of pictures, knick knacks, and copper ornaments. It also has a popular traditional restaurant, which specializes in fresh fish; reserve ahead. **www.darnetal-montreuil.com**

MONTREUIL Château de Montreuil
4 chaussée des Capucins, 62170 **Tel** *03 21 81 53 04* **Fax** *03 21 81 36 43* **Rooms** *18*

The only relais château in Nord Pas de Calais, this elegant manor house is located inside the ramparts of the Montreuil that was once on the sea, before the sea retreated. There are lovely gardens, and a fine restaurant with an excellent wine list. **www.chateaudemontreuil.com**

REUILLY-SAUVIGNY L'Auberge le Relais
2 rue de Paris, 02000 **Tel** *03 23 70 35 36* **Fax** *03 23 70 27 76* **Rooms** *7*

A good base for visiting the champagne cellars just over the border, as well as in Epernay and Reims, this hotel-restaurant has pretty, brightly colored rooms and a pleasant conservatory overlooking a lovely garden. There is also an excellent gourmet restaurant. **www.relaisreuilly.com**

SARS-POTERIE Hôtel du Marquais
65 rue Général de Gaulle, 59216 **Tel** *03 27 61 62 72* **Fax** *03 27 57 47 35* **Rooms** *11*

Originally part of a series of farm buildings, this is now a friendly, family-run hotel. The modern color scheme complements the antique furniture and photographs. On sunny days, breakfast is served in the garden. There is also a private tennis court. **www.hoteldumarquais.com**

ST OMER Hôtel St-Louis
25 rue d'Arras, 62500 **Tel** *03 21 38 35 21* **Fax** *03 21 38 57 26* **Rooms** *30*

At this stone-built former coaching inn you can see the arches where horses and carriages were led through to the stables. The hotel, which is well placed to visit St Omer, has disabled access, and the rooms in the annex have been refurbished. There is also a brasserie. **www.hotel-saintlouis.com**

ST QUENTIN Hôtel des Canonniers
15 rue des Canonniers, 02100 **Tel** *03 23 62 87 87* **Fax** *03 23 62 87 86* **Rooms** *7*

An old townhouse has been elegantly converted into a comfortable, family hotel. It is surprisingly quiet despite being in the center of St Quentin. Large spacious individual rooms with period features and some suites for families. Breakfast is served in a courtyard garden on fine days. **www.hotel-canonniers.com**

VERVINS La Tour du Roy
45 rue du Général Leclerc, 02140 **Tel** *03 23 98 00 11* **Fax** *03 23 98 00 72* **Rooms** *22*

Steeped in history, this prestigious 17th-century château with its three towers was the site of German army headquarters in 1870, 1914, and 1940. General de Gaulle stayed here in 1956. The château has stately bedrooms, and a fine restaurant. **www.latourduroy.com**

WIMEREUX Hôtel St Jean
1 rue Georges Romain, 62930 **Tel** *03 21 83 57 40* **Rooms** *24*

Located in the city center, this hotel is situated within an attractive old building. Rooms are well decorated and brightly colored. There is a spa and sauna for hotel guests and a golf course 1.5 miles (3 km) away. The bar is available 24 hours a day to residents. Space for parking is limited, so reserve in advance. **www.hotel-saint-jean.fr**

CHAMPAGNE

BAZEILLES L'Auberge du Port
Rue de la Gare, 08140 **Tel** *03 24 27 13 89* **Fax** *03 24 29 35 58* **Rooms** *20*

This quiet country hotel just outside the historic city of Sedan has pleasing flower-filled gardens by the river Meuse, a theme reflected by the flowery fabrics in the guest rooms. The restaurant overlooks the river and surrounding countryside, and there is a lovely veranda. Closed Jul 30–Aug 29. **www.auberge-du-port.fr**

Key to Price Guide *see p550* **Key to Symbols** *see back cover flap*

CHALONS-EN-CHAMPAGNE Hôtel du Pot d'Etain ⊠ P €€

18 pl de la République, 51000 **Tel** *03 26 68 09 09* **Fax** *03 26 68 58 18* **Rooms** *30*

Right in the center of Châlons-en-Champagne in the heart of the champagne vineyards, this hotel is housed in an attractive building dating from the 15th century. The pleasant, renovated bedrooms are furnished with antiques. Enjoy homemade pastries and croissants for breakfast. **www.hotel-lepotdetain.com**

CHAMPILLON Royal Champagne P ⊞ ⚹ 🗏 🕹 €€€€€

Bellevue, 51160 **Tel** *03 26 52 87 11* **Fax** *03 26 52 89 69* **Rooms** *25*

The ideal retreat for Champagne enthusiasts, this former coaching inn is now a relais château with a first-class reputation as a hotel and restaurant. The elegant bedrooms offer superb views over the vineyards and the Valley of the Marne. The wine list is outstanding. **www.royalchampagne.com**

CHARLEVILLE-MEZIERES Hôtel de Paris P €

24 av Georges Corneau, 08000 **Tel** *03 24 33 34 38* **Fax** *03 24 59 11 21* **Rooms** *27*

Le Paris is just 5 minutes' walk from the center of the capital of the French Ardennes and its fine main square – the place Ducale. Fronted by a bourgeois residence, the hotel occupies three separate buildings. The modern rooms have been insulated for sound. Nearby are restaurants. **www.hoteldeparis08.fr**

COLOMBEY-LES-DEUX-EGLISES La Grange du Relais P ⊞ 🕸 🕹 €

26 route Nationale 19, 52330 **Tel** *03 25 02 03 89* **Fax** *03 25 01 51 81* **Rooms** *10*

Excellent refurbished country auberge, located just a short walk from the home of Charles de Gaulle and the memorial in his honor. This is a good base to visit Clairvaux abbey and the General's favorite champagne house, Drappier, in Urville. The quiet, spacious rooms are housed in the ancient stables. **www.lagrangedurelais.fr**

COURCELLES-SUR-VESLE Château de Courcelles P ⊞ 🕸 ⚹ 🖼 🗏 €€€€

8 rue du Château, 02220 **Tel** *03 23 74 13 53* **Fax** *03 23 74 06 41* **Rooms** *18*

A very special hotel, this perfect Louis XIV château was built in the 1690s. The buildings have been splendidly restored, with a fine restaurant, a special wine list, 50 acres (20 ha) of parkland, good sports facilities, and disabled access. The trees still display shrapnel from World War I. **www.chateau-de-courcelles.fr**

EPERNAY Hôtel de la Cloche ⊞ €

3 pl Mendès-France, 51200 **Tel** *03 26 55 15 15* **Fax** *03 26 55 64 88* **Rooms** *19*

The best value inexpensive hotel in Epernay, the Hôtel de la Cloche is just a few meters from the church of Notre Dame and a short walk to the avenue de Champagne, where the famous names have their establishments. Guest rooms are bright with modern furnishings. **www.hotel-la-cloche.com**

EPERNAY Hôtel Villa Eugène ⊠ P 🕸 ⚹ 🗏 €€€

82–84 av de Champagne, 51200 **Tel** *03 26 32 44 76* **Fax** *03 26 32 44 98* **Rooms** *15*

This elegant 19th-century residence lies close to the famous Epernay champagne houses. The hotel has been sensitively refurbished with individually styled rooms; all are handsome, spacious, and luxurious. Breakfast can be enjoyed in the luminous conservatory. **www.villa-eugene.com**

ETOGES Château d'Etoges P ⊞ ⚹ 🗏 🕹 €€€

4 rue Richebourg, 51270 **Tel** *03 26 59 30 08* **Fax** *03 26 59 35 57* **Rooms** *28*

Now a grand private hotel *(chambre d'hôte)*, the original medieval fortress was converted to a fairytale castle in the 17th century with fountains, much admired by Louis XIV. The building is protected by the *monuments historiques*. There is an excellent restaurant, and guests may use a boat on the moat. **www.etoges.com**

FAGNON Abbaye des Sept Fontaines P ⊞ ⚹ €€€

Fagnon, 08090 **Tel** *03 24 37 38 24* **Fax** *03 24 37 58 75* **Rooms** *23*

Originally a 12th-century monastery, rebuilt in 1693, this château hotel has the distinction of having hosted Marshal Foch, Emperor William II of Germany, and General de Gaulle. There is a huge lawn and a childrens' play area, an 18-hole golf course, a restaurant, and a quiet terrace. **www.abbayeseptfontaines.fr**

GIVET Les Reflets Jaunes ⊠ P ⚹ 🗏 €

2 rue Général de Gaulle, 08600 **Tel** *03 24 42 85 85* **Fax** *03 24 42 85 86* **Rooms** *17*

Located near a forest in the Meuse Valley, Les Reflets Jaunes stands in the center of this frontier town near Belgium. The city was fortified by Vauban and was the birthplace of Etienne Méhul, composer of the revolutionary song *Le Chant du Départ*. Restaurants are nearby. **www.les-reflets-jaunes.com**

HAYBES SUR MEUSE l'Ermitage Moulin Labotte P ⊞ €

52 rue Edmond Dromart, 08170 **Tel** *03 24 41 13 44* **Fax** *03 24 40 46 72* **Rooms** *10*

In the heart of the Ardennes forest, this mill dating from the end of the 18th century houses a hotel and restaurant. The great cogs from the mill still adorn the dining room. Comfortable guest rooms are furnished in traditional style. The restaurant serves local cuisine. **www.moulin-labotte.com**

LANGRES Grand Hôtel de l'Europe P ⊞ €€

23 rue Diderot, 52200 **Tel** *03 25 87 10 88* **Fax** *03 25 87 60 65* **Rooms** *26*

An old coaching inn on the main street of this attractive town, the Grand Hôtel de l'Europe has simple refurbished guest rooms, which are quieter at the back. The restaurant serves typical country food. Langres was the birthplace of Diderot, editor of the famous encyclopedia. **www.grand-hotel-europe-langres.federal-hotel.com**

MAGNANT Le Val Moret
P 🍴 🚶 ♿   €

Rue Maréchal Leclerc, 10110 **Tel** *03 25 29 85 12* **Fax** *03 25 29 70 81* **Rooms** *42*

This pretty, flower-bedecked modern motel on the A5 from Troyes to Dijon is ideally placed to explore the Champagne route in Aube and Nigloland entertainment park for children. There is secure parking. The restaurant is good, with a recognized chef and quality wine list. **www.le-val-moret.com**

MESNIL-ST-PERE Auberge du Lac - Au Vieux Pressoir
P 🍴 ▤ ♿   €€

5 rue du 28 Août 1944, 10140 **Tel** *03 25 41 27 16* **Fax** *03 25 41 57 59* **Rooms** *21*

A typical half-timbered Champagne house in a village on the edge of the Lac d'Orient, Europe's biggest manmade lake, this hotel provides fantastic bird-watching opportunities, especially in April and September. The hotel is accessible for disabled guests, with a good restaurant. **www.auberge-du-lac.fr**

MOUSSEY Domaine de la Creuse
P   €€€

10800 **Tel** *03 25 41 74 01* **Rooms** *5*

Stunning rural *chambre d'hôte* in a beautifully modernized 18th-century courtyard-style farm, typical of this part of the Aube-en-Champagne. It is a 10-minute drive from the Michelin-starred restaurant, La Parentale. The combination is hard to beat as a base to explore this attractive area. **www.domainedelacreuse.com**

REIMS Hôtel Crystal
P   €€

86 place Drouet d'Erlon, 51100 **Tel** *03 26 88 44 44* **Fax** *03 26 47 49 28* **Rooms** *31*

This 1920s hotel in the busiest part of Reims is surprisingly quiet, with pleasantly decorated rooms. The lobby and elevator retain their Art Deco style, and there is a garden, where breakfast is served in summer. The nearby place Drouet Derlon has a choice of restaurants. **www.hotel-crystal.fr**

REIMS Hôtel de la Paix
P ⛲ 🚶 📺 ▤ ♿   €€€

9 rue de Buirette, 51100 **Tel** *03 26 40 04 08* **Fax** *03 26 47 75 04* **Rooms** *169*

This fine hotel is in the heart of the city, within walking distance of the cathedral, the best restaurants, and the high-speed rail station. The elegant central courtyard blends 15th-century architecture with modern touches, and is ideal for a drink or breakfast in fine weather. Spacious lounge and Champagne bar. **www.bestwestern-lapaix-reims.com**

REIMS Château Les Crayères
P 🍴 🚶 ▤ ♿   €€€€€

64 bd Henry Vasnier, 51100 **Tel** *03 26 82 80 80* **Fax** *03 26 82 65 52* **Rooms** *20*

Superbly aristocratic château with every luxury set in an English-style park next to the Roman *crayères* – the wine cellars of the Champagne houses which have been cut into the chalk. There is a superb restaurant, one of the best in France. **www.lescrayeres.com**

SEDAN Le Château Fort
P 🍴   €€

Port des Princes, 08200 **Tel** *03 24 26 11 00* **Fax** *03 24 27 19 00* **Rooms** *54*

For years no one knew what to do with Europe's largest fortress. Now it hosts an exceptional hotel, under the banner of France Patrimoine, restored to the highest standards of the *monuments historiques*. Some rooms have disabled access, and there is a good restaurant. **www.hotelfp-sedan.com**

SEPT SAULX Le Cheval Blanc
P 🍴   €€

2 rue Moulin, 51400 **Tel** *03 26 03 90 27* **Fax** *03 26 03 97 09* **Rooms** *24*

Between Reims and Chalons en Champagne in the middle of prestigious vineyards, this excellent hotel is attractively furnished. The rooms open on to the delightful gardens on the river Vesle. The beautifully presented restaurant has a terrace with flowers. Hotel is closed Feb 14–28 & Mon–Tue from Jan–Apr. **www.chevalblanc-sept-saulx.com**

ST-DIZIER Hôtel de Champagne
P 🍴 ♿   €

19 av Jean-Pierre Timbaud Marnaval, 52100 **Tel** *03 25 04 49 61* **Fax** *03 25 07 11 91* **Rooms** *30*

This welcoming hotel, located in the outskirts of the town, has a cheerful breakfast room with a grand piano. Bedrooms are simply furnished but are clean, peaceful, and have Wi-Fi access. Special rates apply on weekends. Facilities include a bar and a restaurant. **www.hotel-de-champagne.fr**

TROYES Champs des Oiseaux
P   €€€

20 rue Linard Gonthier, 10000 **Tel** *03 25 80 58 50* **Fax** *03 25 80 98 34* **Rooms** *12*

The finest hotel in Troyes, this is located by the cathedral in the town center. The sheer charm of the restored 15th- and 16th-century buildings as well as top service never fail to impress. The planted courtyards and brick half-timbered walls make for a memorable stay. Snacks are served. **www.champdesoiseaux.com**

TROYES La Maison de Rhodes
P ♿   €€€€

18 rue Linard Gonthier, 10000 **Tel** *03 25 43 11 11* **Fax** *03 25 43 10 43* **Rooms** *11*

A sister hotel to the Champ des Oiseaux, this is almost as grand, with stunningly restored 16th-century architecture, including brick and timber galleries and stairways. Though a newer hotel, it is just as popular. The hotel has disabled access, and an organic restaurant for guests who reserve a table. **www.maisonderhodes.com**

VIGNORY Le Relais Verdoyant
P 🍴 🚶   €

Quartier de la Gare, 52320 **Tel** *03 25 02 44 49* **Fax** *03 25 01 96 89* **Rooms** *7*

Just outside the village of Vignory, this converted farm in a peaceful hamlet makes for a relaxing stay. It is a few kilometers from Colombey les Deux Eglises, where the great cross of Lorraine marks the resting place of Général de Gaulle. Excellent, reasonably priced restaurant. **www.le-relais-verdoyant.fr**

Key to Price Guide *see p550* **Key to Symbols** *see back cover flap*

WILLIERS Chez Odette
Rue Principale, 08110 **Tel** *03 24 55 49 55* **Fax** *03 24 55 49 59* **Rooms** *9*

Right by the Belgian border, this hotel is an exercise in contrasts – on the outside it looks like a country family hotel and bistro, but inside it is startlingly elegant, with ultramodern decor and furnishings. There is a gastronomic restaurant, a bistro, and a bar. **www.chez-odette.com**

ALSACE & LORRAINE

COLMAR Hôtel St Martin
38 grand' rue, 68000 **Tel** *03 89 24 11 51* **Fax** *03 89 23 47 78* **Rooms** *40*

Near the Schwendi fountain in the middle of Alsace's most picturesque spot, this hotel comprises three houses dating from the 14th and 17th centuries and an inner courtyard with a Renaissance stair turret. There are a number of good restaurants on the doorstep. **www.hotel-saint-martin.com**

COLMAR Hostellerie Le Marechal
4 pl Six Montagnes Noires, 68000 **Tel** *03 89 41 60 32* **Fax** *03 89 24 59 40* **Rooms** *30*

This luxurious 16th- and 17th-century house, by the river Lauch in the old part of the city, is home to the Hostellerie Le Marechal. Some of the guest rooms have four-poster beds and views of the canal. The candlelit restaurant, A L'Echevin, faces the canal. **www.le-marechal.com**

DIEVE Hostellerie du Château des Monthairons
26 rte de Verdun, Les Monthairons, 55320 **Tel** *03 29 87 78 55* **Fax** *03 29 87 73 49* **Rooms** *25*

This grand 19th-century château is in its own walled grounds, south of Verdun. Its features include two chapels, a heronry, and a private beach on the Meuse. First-floor rooms are furnished with antiques; the others are modern. The restaurant has a terrace overlooking the countryside. **www.chateaudesmonthairons.com**

DRACHENBRONN Auberge du Moulin des 7 Fontaines
1 sept Fontaines, 67160 **Tel** *03 88 94 50 90* **Fax** *03 88 94 54 57* **Rooms** *10*

Hidden in the forest, this auberge is run by the Finck family in typical rural Alsace style. The old-style bedrooms are situated in the converted 18th-century mill. There are exceptional-value meals on the terrace in summer. It is a great favorite with hikers. **www.auberge7fontaines.com**

EGUISHEIM Hostellerie du Pape
10 grand rue, 68420 **Tel** *03 89 41 41 21* **Fax** *03 89 41 41 31* **Rooms** *44*

This hotel is a former *maison de vigneron*, a wine-grower's house with vine-covered balconies. It is named in honor of Pope Leon IX, who was born in the village in 1002. His statue is nearby. The restaurant serves traditional local dishes. **www.hostellerie-pape.com**

GERARDMER Le Grand Hôtel
Place du Tilleul, 88400 **Tel** *03 29 63 06 31* **Fax** *03 29 63 46 81* **Rooms** *90*

This may be the oldest hotel in Gerardmer but it has a thoroughly modern luxury feel. The charming decor chimes perfectly with the traditional Vosges setting. There is a relaxing garden, two pools, and three restaurants. Nearby you'll find the famous lake, mountain scenery, and low-land skiing. **www.grandhotel-gerardmer.com**

GUNDERSHOFFEN Le Moulin
7 rue du Moulin, 67110 **Tel** *03 88 07 33 30* **Fax** *03 88 72 86 47* **Rooms** *12*

A really beautiful conversion of a picturesque water mill has resulted in this unexpected *hotel de charme* on the edge of the northern Vosges. Rooms are authentic and comfortable and the hotel also has a very popular Michelin-starred restaurant, Le Cygne. Convenient for Strasbourg and the Maginot Line. **www.hotellemoulin.com**

JUNGHOLZ Les Violettes
Route de Thierenbach, 68500 **Tel** *03 89 76 91 19* **Fax** *03 89 74 29 12* **Rooms** *22*

This is an imaginative and luxurious reconstruction of a charming sandstone Alsacien hotel. It has the feel and welcome of a large family home. A conservatory overlooks the surrounding countryside and there is a huge spa with saunas, hammams, two pools, and a Jacuzzi. The restaurant is highly recommended. **www.les-violettes.com**

KAYSERSBERG Hôtel Constantin
10 rue Père Kohlman, 68240 **Tel** *03 89 47 19 90* **Fax** *03 89 47 37 82* **Rooms** *20*

A beautifully restored 17th-century house in the center of the old town conceals a hotel that has been modernized to create stylish rooms. Breakfast is served in the conservatory; other meals are available next door at the Relais du Château, owned by the same family. **www.hotel-constantin.com**

LA PETITE PIERRE Aux Trois Roses
19 rue Principale, 67290 **Tel** *03 88 89 89 00* **Fax** *03 88 70 41 28* **Rooms** *40*

This hotel is in an 18th-century house in the middle of this attractive hilltop village. Some of the pleasant rooms have balconies, and there is a guest lounge with an open fire. Excellent value for money. The dining room serves traditional Vosgien dishes. The village is home to the Maison du Parc. **www.aux-trois-roses.com**

LAPOUTROIE Les Alisiers 🅿️ 🍽️ €€
5 rue du Faudé, 68650 **Tel** *03 89 47 52 82* **Fax** *03 89 47 22 38* **Rooms** *16*

This attractive hotel has grown out of a pretty converted farm dating from 1819. The refurbished guest rooms are decorated in country style. The terrace has fabulous views of the hills and valleys. From the dining room you can enjoy the excellent food and the view at the same time. **www.alisiers.com**

LUNEVILLE Château d'Adoménil 🅿️ 🍽️ ⛱️ 🏃 📋 €€€€
54300 **Tel** *03 83 74 04 81* **Fax** *03 83 74 21 78* **Rooms** *14*

This imposing Relais Château in an extensive park on the river Meurthe is not far from the 18th-century splendors of Nancy. The guest rooms are splendidly bourgeois in the château itself or Provençal in theme in the beautiful outbuildings. The restaurant is a gourmet rendezvous. **www.adomenil.com**

METZ Grand Hôtel de Metz 📺 🅿️ €€
3 rue des Clercs, 57000 **Tel** *03 87 36 16 33* **Fax** *03 87 74 17 04* **Rooms** *62*

A stylish hotel on a pedestrianized street in the center of this fine, underrated city, with French and Prussian architecture. The hotel is an interesting combination of Baroque entrance hall and rustic rooms, near the cathedral and the covered market. Good restaurants are nearby. **www.hotel-metz.com**

NANCY Grand Hôtel de la Reine 📺 🅿️ 🍽️ 📋 €€€
2 pl Stanislas, 54000 **Tel** *03 83 35 03 01* **Fax** *03 83 32 86 04* **Rooms** *43*

Experience the Ancien Régime in Europe's finest Neoclassical square – the stunningly restored place Stanislas. The hotel occupies the house originally built in 1752 for the steward to Stanislas, Duke of Lorraine, the last king of Poland. A host of famous visitors includes Tsar Alexander I of Russia. **www.hoteldelareine.com**

OBERNAI Hôtel Restaurant des Vosges 📺 🍽️ €
5 pl de la Gare, 67210 **Tel** *03 88 95 53 78* **Fax** *03 88 49 92 65* **Rooms** *20*

A cheerful and welcoming small hotel by the train station, this is a mixture of old and modern buildings with a pleasant, traditional atmosphere. The rooms are exceptionally well kept. The restaurant is a cross between traditional Alsace and bistro style. **www.hotel-obernai.com**

REMIREMONT Hôtel du Cheval de Bronze 🏃 €
59 rue Charles de Gaulle, 88200 **Tel** *03 29 62 52 24* **Fax** *03 29 62 34 90* **Rooms** *35*

A former coaching inn, set behind the 17th-century arcades of this attractive town in the foothills of the Vosges, this simple provincial hotel is ideal for visiting the Vosges mountains. The Ballon d'Alsace is an easy drive, as is the World War I mountain battlefield Hartmannswillerkopf. **www.hotelchevalbronze.com**

SAVERNE Chez Jean 📺 🅿️ 🍽️ €€
3 rue Gare, 67700 **Tel** *03 88 91 10 19* **Fax** *03 88 91 27 45* **Rooms** *25*

A four-story traditional Alsace house in the center of town, this was once a convent. The rooms are tastefully decorated in local style. There are good views of the surrounding hills. There is a sauna for guests' use. The Winstubs' Rosestiebele restaurant is on the ground floor. **www.chez-jean.com**

SELESTAT Auberge des Alliés 🍽️ €
39 rue des Chevaliers, 67600 **Tel** *03 88 92 09 34* **Fax** *03 88 92 12 88* **Rooms** *17*

Set in the old town, part of this hotel-restaurant occupies a house dating from 1537. The city contained one of the finest schools in Europe; its unique library holds the *Cosmographiae Introductio*, with the first reference to America in print. Rooms are small and simple, with old-fashioned decor.

SELESTAT Hostellerie Abbaye de la Pommeraie 📺 🅿️ 🍽️ 📋 €€€
8 av Maréchal Foch, 67600 **Tel** *03 88 92 07 84* **Fax** *03 88 92 08 71* **Rooms** *13*

In the old city of Selestat, famous for its centuries-old library, this fine 17th-century building was once part of the medieval Baumgarten Abbey. The guest rooms are everything you would expect of a Relais Château, and there are two very good restaurants. **www.pommeraie.fr**

STRASBOURG Au Cerf d'Or 📺 🍽️ ⛱️ 🏃 📋 €€
6 pl de l'Hôpital, 67000 **Tel** *03 88 36 20 05* **Fax** *03 88 36 68 67* **Rooms** *43*

An inexpensive base for visiting the sights of old Strasbourg, this old-style, half-timbered Alsace family hotel has refurbished rooms throughout. The main hotel has more charming rooms, but the annex has a small pool and a sauna. There are several restaurants on the nearby waterfront. **www.cerf-dor.com**

STRASBOURG Hôtel Chut 🍽️ ♿ €€€
4 rue du Bain aux Plantes, 67000 **Tel** *03 88 32 05 06* **Fax** *03 88 32 05 50* **Rooms** *8*

Two picturesque 16th-century half-timbered houses make up this hotel in the historic Petite France quarter of old Strasbourg. Within, old and contemporary have been successfully blended and a Zen ambience pervades. There is a good restaurant, and parking is possible by arrangement. One room has wheelchair access. **www.hote-strasbourg.fr**

VENTRON Les Buttes - L'Ermitage 📺 🅿️ 🍽️ ⛱️ 🏃 ♿ €€
L'Ermitage Frère Joseph, 88310 **Tel** *03 29 24 18 09* **Fax** *03 29 24 21 96* **Rooms** *62*

Two hotels in one in the Parc Naturel Régionale des Ballons des Vosges, a protected part of the Vosges at the foot of the mountains. Les Buttes has a gastronomic restaurant, while simpler, traditional food is served at the Ermitage. These hotels make an ideal base for skiing in winter or mountain walking in summer. **www.frerejo.com**

Key to Price Guide *see p550* **Key to Symbols** *see back cover flap*

NORMANDY

AGNEAUX Château d'Agneaux

P 🍴 ♿ €€€

Av Ste Marie, 50180 **Tel** *02 33 57 65 88* **Fax** *02 33 56 59 21* **Rooms** *13*

A 13th-century château hotel nestled in the intensely rural Vire Valley. Individual rooms preserve the character of the hotel with period furniture, parquet flooring, and wooden paneling. Two restaurants are housed in the medieval farm buildings. Equidistant from Mont-St-Michel, the Cotentin Peninsula, and the Normandy beaches. **www.chateau-agneaux.fr**

ALENÇON Hôtel des Ducs

P €

50 av Wilson, 61000 **Tel** *02 33 29 03 93* **Fax** *02 33 29 28 59* **Rooms** *24*

Centrally located opposite the train station, this hotel is comfortable and well maintained. The bedrooms are modern in style and have simple, unfussy furnishings. Bathrooms are clean and functional. The pretty garden is a nice place to have breakfast in fine weather. **http://hotel-centre-ville.hoteldesducs-alencon.fr**

AUDRIEU Château d'Audrieu

P 🍴 ≋ 🎋 €€€

Le Château, 14250 **Tel** *02 31 80 21 52* **Fax** *02 31 80 24 73* **Rooms** *25*

This 18th-century château was transformed into a luxurious hotel in 1976. A short distance from Bayeux, it has an immense park, providing wonderful views. The stunning guest rooms are elegantly furnished with period pieces. There is an excellent gourmet restaurant. The hotel is closed mid-Dec–mid-Feb. **www.chateaudaudrieu.com**

BAGNOLES-DE-L'ORNE Le Manoir du Lys

🌐 P 🍴 ≋ 🎋 🔲 ♿ €€

Route de Juvigny, 61140 **Tel** *02 33 37 80 69* **Fax** *02 33 30 05 80* **Rooms** *30*

A family *hotel de charme* offering childrens' breakfast, baby-sitting services (48 hours' notice), and transportation to the station at Bagnoles sur Orne. There is plenty to do for the active – bike riding, climbing, and tennis; and for the not so active there's billiards, ping pong, golf, cooking weekends, and a local casino. **www.manoir-du-lys.fr**

BAYEUX Hôtel Bellefontaine

🌐 P 🎋 🔲 ♿ €€

49 rue de Bellefontaine, 14400 **Tel** *02 31 22 00 10* **Fax** *02 31 22 19 09* **Rooms** *20*

Situated a few minutes from the city center, and within sight of the town's magnificent cathedral, this lovely 18th-century château is surrounded by a vast park. The rooms are spacious, and those in the converted stables are particularly suitable for families. **www.hotel-bellefontaine.com**

CABOURG Castel Fleuri

€€

4 av Alfred Piat, 14390 **Tel** *02 31 91 27 57* **Fax** *02 31 24 03 48* **Rooms** *22*

A welcoming, unsophisticated *hotel de charme* with smallish but nicely decorated rooms and some family suites. Well placed in the town center just 650 ft (200 meters) from the beach in this fashionable seaside resort. The pleasant garden is an added bonus. **www.castel-fleuri.com**

CAEN Best Western Le Dauphin

🌐 P 🍴 🎋 📺 ♿ €€

29 rue Gémare, 14000 **Tel** *02 31 86 22 26* **Fax** *02 31 86 35 14* **Rooms** *37*

In a quiet but central location, this old priory has been tastefully renovated, retaining original features such as the arched windows and stone walls. The rooms are comfortable; nonsmoking and family rooms are available. There is a breakfast buffet, and a gourmet restaurant. **www.le-dauphin-normandie.com**

CAEN Hôtel Mercure Porte de Plaisance

🌐 P 🍴 🎋 🔲 ♿ €€

1 rue Courtonne, 14000 **Tel** *02 31 47 24 24* **Fax** *02 31 47 43 88* **Rooms** *126*

An atmosphere of quiet elegance pervades, with every attention paid to the guests' comfort. The rooms of this chain hotel, centrally located opposite the harbor, are cozy and tastefully furnished. Disabled guests are catered for, and there is parking for an additional charge. **www.accorhotels.com**

CAMBREMER Château les Bruyères

P 🍴 ≋ ♿ €€

Route du Cadran, 14340 **Tel** *02 31 32 22 45* **Fax** *02 31 32 22 58* **Rooms** *13*

This beautiful château, set in a large tree-filled park, is a prime example of First Empire architecture. Rooms – some housed in a neighboring 18th-century house – are individually-styled. Marcel Proust is among the guests to have stayed here. The excellent restaurant serves a varied menu and specializes in local cider. **www.chateaulesbruyeres.com**

CEAUX Le Relais du Mont

P 🍴 🎋 €

La Buvette, 50220 **Tel** *02 33 70 92 55* **Fax** *02 33 70 94 57* **Rooms** *28*

South of Avranches, this hotel faces west and enjoys splendid sunsets over the bay of Mont-St-Michel. Le Relais du Mont offers decent-sized, well-maintained rooms. There are good facilities, family rooms, and an excellent restaurant. **www.relais-du-mont.fr**

CHERBOURG Hôtel Renaissance

P €

4 rue de l'Eglise, 50100 **Tel** *02 33 43 23 90* **Fax** *02 33 43 96 10* **Rooms** *12*

Good-value, well-maintained hotel with attractive rooms, each named after different flowers. The hotel is well located overlooking the harbor, and conveniently placed for the cross-Channel ferries and for the Cité de la Mer museum. The staff are very friendly. Limited parking is available. **www.hotel-renaissance-cherbourg.com**

CREPON La Ferme de la Rançonnière

Route d'Arromanches, 14480 **Tel** *02 31 22 21 73* **Fax** *02 31 22 98 39* **Rooms** *35*

An attractive fortified stone farm dating from the 13th century, featuring a typical closed courtyard with arched gateways. The rooms and the restaurant have been decorated in the same historic style. Only 1.5 miles (3 km) from the sea with golf courses all around and plenty of opportunities for sailing and bike riding. **www.ranconniere.fr**

DEAUVILLE Hôtel Normandy Barrière

38 rue J Mermoz, 14800 **Tel** *02 31 98 66 22* **Fax** *02 31 98 66 23* **Rooms** *290*

Deauville's landmark, this Anglo-Normandy manor house is a luxury hotel with beautiful, spacious rooms and fitness facilities. The large Belle Epoque dining room serves classic, traditional Normandy fare. Although it has been modernized, the hotel retains its 1920s charm. **www.lucienbarriere.com**

DOUAINS-PACY-SUR-EURE L'Etape de la Vallée

1 rue Edouard Isambard, 27120 **Tel** *02 32 36 12 77* **Fax** *02 32 36 22 74* **Rooms** *15*

A lovely villa set on the banks of the Eure river, this makes an ideal stopover for visiting nearby Giverny. Choose from cozy rooms with river views in the main building, or from the more modern and spacious rooms at the back. A pretty terrace overlooks the ornamental gardens. Restaurant serves good, classic dishes. **www.etapedelavallee.com**

ETRETAT Domaine St Clair

Chemin de St Clair, 76790 **Tel** *02 35 27 08 23* **Fax** *02 35 29 92 24* **Rooms** *21*

Stunningly situated with panoramic views of the village and cliffs of Etretat, this 19th-century Anglo-Norman château has comfortable rooms, some with private spa baths. The rooms are individually decorated with four-poster beds and period furniture. **www.hoteletretat.com**

FECAMP Le Grand Pavois

15 quai Vicomté, 76400 **Tel** *02 35 10 01 01* **Fax** *02 35 29 31 67* **Rooms** *35*

Built on the quay, this modern hotel has an attractive marine-themed interior. The bedrooms are bright and spacious, and those at the front have balconies overlooking the port. There is a piano bar with live music on some nights. Good choice of restaurants within easy walking distance. **www.hotel-grand-pavois.com**

FONTENAI-SUR-ORNE Le Faisan Doré

Rte Paris, 61200 **Tel** *02 33 67 18 11* **Fax** *02 33 35 82 15* **Rooms** *16*

This decent-sized hotel is located in the Suisse Normande region, close to Argentan. The quieter rooms overlook the pretty garden. There is a well-stocked bar with over 140 different wines. Meals can be eaten in the brightly decorated restaurant, or outside in summer. **www.lefaisandore.com**

GRANDCHAMP MAISY Hôtel Duguesclin

4 quai Henri Crampon, 14450 **Tel** *02 31 22 64 22* **Fax** *02 31 22 34 79* **Rooms** *25*

This friendly modern hotel is located on the seafront promenade. The rooms are simply furnished and well maintained. The excellent restaurant specializes in seafood. Parking is available. This fishing port is a good base for visiting the D-Day landing beaches at Pointe du Hoc. **www.leduguesclin.eu**

GRANVILLE Hôtel Michelet

5 rue Jules Michelet, 50400 **Tel** *02 33 50 06 55* **Fax** *02 33 50 12 25* **Rooms** *19*

The hotel is close to the stores, restaurants, and the casino in this charming historic port. An attractive Colonial-style building, tastefully renovated, with simply furnished, well-kept rooms, some with a view. Convenient for the beach and thalasso center. Free parking. **www.hotel-michelet-granville.com**

HONFLEUR La Ferme Siméon

Rue Adolphe Marais, 14600 **Tel** *02 31 81 78 00* **Fax** *02 31 89 48 48* **Rooms** *34*

Ancient farmhouse mansion that was the haunt of the Impressionist artists from the Honfleur school. Now a luxury hotel, restaurant, and spa center. Beautifully converted guest rooms; spacious and charmingly furnished. The oak-beamed restaurant serves excellent food. **www.fermesaintsimeon.fr**

L'AIGLE Hôtel du Dauphin

Pl de la Halle, 61300 **Tel** *02 33 84 18 00* **Fax** *02 33 34 09 28* **Rooms** *30*

This stone-built inn has a lot of history. Established in 1618, the original stables were razed during the bombardment of L'Aigle in 1944. Now a hotel that has been in the same family for over 60 years, it has a restaurant, a brasserie, and a store. The rooms are functional, and there is a comfy lounge. **www.hotel-dauphin.free.fr**

MACE Hôtel Île de Sées

Vandel, 61500 **Tel** *02 33 27 98 65* **Fax** *02 33 28 41 22* **Rooms** *16*

A rural hotel surrounded by a large park set in the heart of Normandy studfarm country. This traditional half-timbered former dairy is a friendly hotel with pleasant, cozy rooms in soft pastel tones. An ideal place to unwind and relax. Delicious food served in the comfortable restaurant. **www.ile-sees.fr**

MESNIL-VAL Hostellerie de la Vieille Ferme

23 rue de la Mer, 76910 **Tel** *02 35 86 72 18* **Fax** *02 35 86 12 67* **Rooms** *34*

An 18th-century farmhouse with several attractively converted outbuildings make up this Anglo-Norman hotel complex set in its own park near the beach. The guest rooms are romantically old-fashioned, with oak beams and great views. Rustic-style seafood restaurant. **www.vielle-ferme.net**

Key to Price Guide *see p550* **Key to Symbols** *see back cover flap*

MONT-ST-MICHEL Terrasses Poulard 🏨 €€€
BP 18, 50170 **Tel** *02 33 89 02 02* **Fax** *02 33 60 37 31* **Rooms** *29*

An old stone building at the heart of Mont-St-Michel with magnificent views over the bay, as well as the abbey and the gardens. The rooms are small but clean and comfortable. The hotel is under the same ownership as the famous omelette restaurant La Mère Poulard. **www.terrasses-poulard.fr**

MORTAGNE AU PERCHE Le Tribunal 🏨🏃♿ €€
4 pl Palais, 61400 **Tel** *02 33 25 04 77* **Fax** *02 33 83 60 83* **Rooms** *21*

Some rooms in this pretty hotel date back to the 13th century. It is a well-kept establishment with plush guest rooms and great baths. A stay here gives an experience of pleasant simplicity. The restaurant serves local dishes, on an outside terrace in summer. **www.hotel-tribunal.fr**

MORTAIN Hôtel de la Poste 🅿🏨♨🏃 €
1 pl des Arcades, 50140 **Tel** *02 33 59 00 05* **Fax** *02 33 69 53 89* **Rooms** *25*

On the spectacular Cherbourg peninsula, this attractive 19th-century house overlooks the lovely river in Mortain. A pleasant family-run hotel with comfortable, quiet rooms and good service. Fine restaurant with an excellent wine list. Disabled facilities and a private garage. **www.hoteldelaposte.fr**

OUISTREHAM Hôtel de la Plage 🅿 €
39–41 av Pasteur, 14150 **Tel** *02 31 96 85 16* **Fax** *02 31 97 37 46* **Rooms** *16*

The owners have refreshed this pleasing family hotel, which lies a short walk from the expansive beach. The rooms are large and comfortable, and there's an in-house sauna. To the west you'll find wartime sites like Pegasus Bridge; to the east the beaches with family activities such as kite surfing, sand yachting, and sailing. **www.hotel-ouistreham.com**

PONT AUDEMER Belle-Île-sur-Risle 🅿🏨♨🏃🖼 €€
112 rte de Rouen, 27500 **Tel** *02 32 56 96 22* **Fax** *02 32 42 88 96* **Rooms** *24*

Set on an island in its own large garden of ancient trees and roses, the hotel has a fitness center, sauna, and two pools (outdoor and indoor). The rooms are comfortable and elegant, ideal for a relaxing stay. Superb cuisine in the 19th-century rotunda. Closed mid-Nov–mid-Mar. **www.bellile.com**

PONT DE L'ARCHE Hôtel de la Tour 🅿 €
41 quai Foch, 27340 **Tel** *02 35 23 00 99* **Fax** *02 35 23 46 22* **Rooms** *18*

This attractive 18th-century Norman house sits at the river's edge, backing onto the village's ramparts. The interior reveals typical Normandy architecture with timber and brick walls. The good-sized rooms are individually decorated. Patio garden. Restaurants nearby. **www.hoteldelatour.org**

ROUEN Hôtel Notre-Dame 🅿 €
4 rue de la Savonnerie, 76000 **Tel** *02 35 71 87 73* **Fax** *02 35 89 31 52* **Rooms** *28*

This was the home of Bishop Cauchon, Joan of Arc's accuser, until his death in 1442. This hotel located between the cathedral and the Seine has spacious rooms decorated in contemporary colors. The staff are friendly. Good buffet breakfast. Choice of restaurants nearby. **www.hotelnotredame.com**

ROUEN Le Vieux Carré €
34 rue Ganterie, 76000 **Tel** *02 35 71 67 70* **Fax** *02 35 71 19 17* **Rooms** *14*

City-center hotel near the Musée des Beaux Arts and a short walk from the cathedral. This charming timbered 18th-century building hides prettily decorated, intimate guest rooms. Cozy atmosphere and attentive service. There is a shaded cobbled courtyard and tearoom. **www.vieux-carre.fr**

ST-LO Hôtel Mercure 🅿🏨🏃♿ €€
5–7 av de Briovère, 50000 **Tel** *02 33 05 08 63* **Fax** *02 33 05 15 15* **Rooms** *67*

Opposite the town's ramparts, this modern hotel is attractive and quiet and has comfortable and well-proportioned guest rooms. The restaurant "Le Tocqueville" is in a large room with lovely views of the Vire river and serves regional specialties. There is also a cozy bar. **www.mercure.com**

ST-PATERNE Château de St-Paterne 🅿🏨♨🏃 €€€
Le Château, 72610 **Tel** *02 33 27 54 71* **Rooms** *10*

Henry IV's 15th-century love-nest is set in a private park just on the outskirts of Alençon. This is not so much a hotel as a family château, where a fixed menu is served *en famille* to guests in the candlelit dining room. Magnificent rooms with stately furnishings. Closed mid-Dec–mid-Mar. **www.chateau-saintpaterne.com**

ST-VAAST-LA-HOUGUE Hôtel de France et Fuchsias 🅿🏨🏃 €€
20 rue de Maréchal Foch, 50550 **Tel** *02 33 54 40 41* **Fax** *02 33 43 46 79* **Rooms** *35*

A lovely country house hotel near the fishing harbor of St-Vaast, renowned for its oysters. Country-style cozy rooms, most overlooking the exotic garden. The restaurant "Des Fuchsias" is set in a conservatory and serves delicious warm oyster dishes. Good buffet breakfast, too. Closed Jan–Feb. **www.france-fuchsias.com**

ST-VALERY-EN-CAUX La Maison des Galets 🏨📋 €€
22 cour Le Perrey, 76460 **Tel** *02 35 97 11 22* **Fax** *02 35 97 05 83* **Rooms** *14*

Sited between the port and the cliffs, some of the rooms in this comfortable hotel overlook the harbor. Inside, old and new combine to create a pretty, relaxed ambience. The "chambre bleu" has a glorious view of the sea from the bathroom, and there are panoramic views of the waterfront from the restaurant. **www.lamaisondesgalets.com**

VERNON Hôtel d'Evreux   P ⅱ ⅋   €
11 pl d'Evreux, 27200 **Tel** *02 32 21 16 12* **Fax** *02 32 21 32 73* **Rooms** *12*

This typical Norman building in the center of Vernon, behind magnificent lime trees, is a former coaching inn with bright, sunny rooms and old-fashioned furniture. The restaurant, with its giant fireplace, serves innovative traditional fare. Parking is available. **www.hoteldevreux.fr**

BRITTANY

AUDIERNE Hôtel de la Plage   ⌕ ⅱ ⅋   €
21 bd Emmanuel Brusq, 29770 **Tel** *02 98 70 01 07* **Fax** *02 98 75 04 69* **Rooms** *22*

Agreeable, modern, good-value, family hotel situated on the beach. The rooms are characterized by cheerful marine decor and great views of the Bay of Audierne. Billiards can be played in the bar. Excellent seafood restaurant. Well placed for a tour of the sites of Finistère. **www.hotel-finistere.com**

BENODET Domaine de Kereven   P   €
Bénodet, 29950 **Tel** *02 98 57 02 46* **Fax** *02 98 66 22 61* **Rooms** *12*

A number of buildings attractively built in traditional style on the site of an 18th-century cider farm. Pleasantly furnished, characterful rooms overlook the expansive grounds. Just 1 mile (1.5 km) from the popular beaches at Bénodet and not far from the cathedral city of Quimper. Closed Dec–Mar.

BREST Hôtel de la Corniche   P ⅱ ⅌   €€
1 rue Amiral-Nicol, 29200 **Tel** *02 98 45 12 42* **Fax** *02 98 49 01 53* **Rooms** *16*

This modern hotel, built of local stone in the Breton style, is on the west side of the city near the naval base. It is conveniently located for walks along the scenic coastline. The rooms are simply furnished. The hotel restaurant offers a set evening menu four nights per week; reservations required. **www.hotel-la-corniche.com**

CARNAC Hôtel Tumulus   ⌕ P ⅱ ≋ ⅋   €€
Route du Tumulus, 56340 **Tel** *02 97 52 08 21* **Fax** *02 97 52 81 88* **Rooms** *23*

This hotel is located near the prehistoric sights that make Carnac world famous. Refurbished, elegant rooms mix a Gustavian style with a touch of the Orient. There are fine views across the grounds onto Quiberon Bay. The pool, lush gardens, wellness center, and restaurant add to this hotel's appeal. Closed Dec–Feb. **www.hotel-tumulus.com**

CHATEAUBOURG Moulin Ar Milin   ⌕ P ⅱ ⅋   €€
30 rue due Paris, 35221 **Tel** *02 99 00 30 91* **Fax** *02 99 00 37 56* **Rooms** *32*

Attractive water mill converted into a *hotel de charme* with two parts: the Hôtel de Moulin in the original mill and the more recent Hôtel du Parc. There are 100 different types of trees in the park, which has a river running through it and a tennis court. The first-class restaurant has a noted wine list. Closed Dec 25–early Jan. **www.armilin.com**

DINAN Moulin de la Fontaine des Eaux   P ⅋   €
Vallée de la Fontaine des Eaux, 22100 **Tel** *02 96 87 92 09* **Fax** *02 96 87 92 09* **Rooms** *5*

Set in a wooded valley 5 minutes from the port of Dinan, this converted 18th-century watermill overlooks its own lake and grounds. This is a *chambre d'hôte* only; there is no restaurant, but breakfast is provided. Simply furnished rooms, with disabled access. Private parking. **www.dinanbandb.com**

DINARD Hôtel de la Vallée   ⌕ P ⅱ ⅋   €€
6 av Georges V, 35801 **Tel** *02 99 46 94 00* **Fax** *02 99 88 22 47* **Rooms** *24*

A completely refurbished and modernized hotel centrally located on the harborfront but away from the hustle and bustle of the resort. Choose one of the front rooms, as they have lovely views. The restaurant is the rising star of Dinard cuisine; excellent seafood as well as a choice of beef or duck. Closed Jan. **www.hoteldelavallee.com**

DOL DE BRETAGNE Domaine des Ormes   ⌕ P ⅱ ≋ ⅋ ⅌ ▤   €
35120 **Tel** *02 99 73 53 00* **Fax** *02 99 73 53 55* **Rooms** *45*

This is part of a privately owned vacation resort with an 18-hole golf course, aquaparc, horse-riding school, and adventure park. The guest rooms are charming – there are even 18 cozy tree houses with rooms, accessible by rope ladder! The restaurant serves classic French food. **www.lesormes.com**

FOUESNANT Hôtel l'Orée du Bois   €
4 rue Kergoadig, 29170 **Tel** *02 98 56 00 06* **Fax** *02 98 56 14 17* **Rooms** *15*

Simple, well-furnished rooms with en suite showers are excellent value; the rooms with just a sink are a bargain. A cheerful breakfast room is decked out in bright marine decor and there's a terrace for breakfast on fine days. The hotel is just a few minutes' walk from the beach at Cape Coz and the coast paths. **www.hotel-oreedubois.com**

ILE DE GROIX Hôtel de la Marine   ⅱ ⅋   €€
7 rue du Général de Gaulle, 56590 **Tel** *02 97 86 80 05* **Fax** *02 97 86 56 37* **Rooms** *22*

Expect a warm welcome at this hotel in the middle of the beautiful island of Groix. This relaxing hideaway has charming guest rooms that overlook either the sea or the garden terrace. At the restaurant, great care is taken in the preparation of fine fish dishes. **www.hoteldelamarine.com**

Key to Price Guide *see p550* **Key to Symbols** *see back cover flap*

LOCQUIREC Le Grand Hôtel des Bains 🏖🅿️🍴♨️📺 €€€

15 rue de L'Eglise, 29241 **Tel** *02 98 67 41 02* **Fax** *02 98 67 44 60* **Rooms** *36*

Convenient for visiting the Armorique Regional Park, this Belle Epoque spa hotel has gardens that lead to a sandy beach. Rooms have stylish contemporary furnishings, most with balconies. Beauty and health treatments are available. Restaurant open evenings only. The chef uses fresh, local produce. **www.grand-hotel-des-bains.com**

MORLAIX Hôtel de l'Europe 🏖🍴 €€

1 rue d'Aiguillon, 29600 **Tel** *02 98 62 11 99* **Fax** *02 98 88 83 38* **Rooms** *60*

This Second Empire hotel, located in the city center, has an elegant and richly decorated interior. The guest rooms are well equipped and soundproofed. Each room is different, from traditional to modern. Service is attentive. Buffet breakfast. The brasserie is good value. **www.hotel-europe-com.fr**

PENESTIN SUR MER Hôtel Loscolo 🅿️🍴 €€

La Pointe de Loscolo, 56760 **Tel** *02 99 90 31 90* **Fax** *02 99 90 32 14* **Rooms** *13*

A traditional building with slate roof, on a cape with magnificent sea views to both sides, and good walking nearby. The rooms are comfortable; some have a private terrace. The breakfast is copious; half-board rates (which include two meals) are good value. The restaurant serves rich cuisine. Closed Dec–Mar. **www.hotelloscolo.com**

PLEVEN Manoir du Vaumadeuc 🅿️🧍 €€

Le Vaumadeuc, 22130 **Tel** *02 96 84 46 17* **Fax** *02 96 84 40 16* **Rooms** *13*

This grand old manor house nestles in the Fôret de la Hunaudaye. The building dates from the 15th century, and inside, the magnificent granite staircase leads you to the first-floor guest rooms. The wooded park around it has a beautiful rose garden and lake. Heliport and parking. **www.vaumadeuc.com**

PLOUBAZLANEC Les Agapanthes 🅿️🧍🍴 €

1 rue Adrien Rebours, 22620 **Tel** *02 96 55 89 06* **Fax** *02 96 55 79 79* **Rooms** *21*

On the village square, this 18th-century hotel reveals a bright, modern interior. The rooms are clean and comfortable and prettily decorated in a maritime theme. There is an extension with more spacious rooms that are ideal for families. Most rooms have a view of Paimpol Bay, as does the terrace. **www.hotel-les-agapanthes.com**

PLOUGONVELIN Hostellerie de la Pointe de St-Mathieu 🏖🅿️🍴♨️📺 €€

Pointe de St-Mathieu, 29217 **Tel** *02 98 89 00 19* **Fax** *02 98 89 15 68* **Rooms** *23*

Situated near a lighthouse and ancient abbey ruins, this hotel was once a traditional farm but has grown into a modern hotel. The farmhouse now houses a restaurant serving sophisticated seafood dishes. The hotel makes a great base from which to explore the dramatic Atlantic coastline. **www.pointe-saint-mathieu.com**

QUIBERON Hôtel Bellevue 🅿️🍴♨️🧍 €

Rue de Tiviec, 56173 **Tel** *02 97 50 16 28* **Fax** *02 97 30 44 34* **Rooms** *38*

Located near the seafront, casino, and thalassotherapy center, this modern hotel forms an L-shape around the heated swimming pool. The guest rooms are comfortable; the restaurant is airy and bright. Poolside buffet breakfast or Continental breakfast in your room. Demi-*pension* (half board) only. Private parking. **www.bellevuequiberon.com**

QUIMPER Hôtel Gradlon 🅿️🧍 €€

30 rue de Brest, 29000 **Tel** *02 98 95 04 39* **Fax** *02 98 95 61 25* **Rooms** *20*

Just 2 minutes' walk from the historic city center, this hotel has charming, peaceful rooms – a few overlooking the enclosed flower garden and fountain. Some disabled access. Continental breakfast is served on the pretty veranda. Cozy salon bar with open fire. **www.hotel-gradlon.com**

RENNES Le Coq-Gadby 🏖🅿️🍴🧍 €€€€

156 rue d'Antrain, 35700 **Tel** *02 99 38 05 55* **Fax** *02 99 38 53 40* **Rooms** *24*

An elegant 17th-century building just 5 minutes' drive from the city center. Calm and intimate with classic period furnishings, polished parquet floors, and ornate mirrors. The guest rooms "Olympe," "Louis XV," "Louis XVI," and "Anglaise" are vast and elegant. Spa and sauna next door to hotel. **www.lecoq-gadby.fr**

ROSCOFF Hôtel Bellevue 🅿️🧍 €

Bd Ste Barbe, 29681 **Tel** *02 98 61 23 38* **Fax** *02 98 61 11 80* **Rooms** *18*

This old Breton house, just a few minutes from the ferry terminal, enjoys fine views of the sea and old port. The guest rooms are a little cramped, but bright and quiet. At the back of the building is a pleasant patio garden where Continental breakfast is served on warm days. **www.hotel-bellevue-roscoff.fr**

ST MALO Hôtel Elizabeth 🅿️🧍 €€

2 rue des Cordiers, 35400 **Tel** *02 99 56 24 98* **Fax** *02 99 56 39 24* **Rooms** *17*

This hotel is located within the ramparts of the old town, just 2 minutes' drive from the ferry terminal. The building has a 16th-century stone façade. The interior is classic in style, if a little somber. Rooms are comfortable and well equipped. Friendly owners, and private garage. Closed Jan. **www.hotel-elizabeth.fr**

ST THEGONNEC Ar Presbital Koz 🅿️🍴 €

18 rue de Gividic, 29410 **Tel** *02 98 79 45 62* **Fax** *02 98 79 48 47* **Rooms** *6*

Rustic, comfortable bed and breakfast. This 18th-century building, once a presbytery, has six spacious guest rooms. No television. Breakfast can be enjoyed outside on the terrace. Mme Prigent, the owner, will prepare a three-course dinner if you reserve before noon. Large garden with parking. **http://ar.presbital.koz.free.fr**

VANNES Villa Kerasy   `P` `🗏` `♿`   €€

20 av Favrel et Lincy, 56000 **Tel** *02 97 68 36 83* **Fax** *02 97 68 36 84* **Rooms** *15*

A hotel with plenty of charm, the Asian-inspired Villa Kerasy takes the French East India Company and the spice route as its theme. Each room represents a different port. The spa specializes in Ayurvedic treatments, which promise revitalization, an end to stress, and a spiritual awakening. Closed mid-Nov–mid-Dec & Jan. **www.villakerasy.com**

THE LOIRE

AMBOISE Le Choiseul   `P` `🍴` `≈` `大` `🗏`   €€€

36 quai Charles-Guinot, 37400 **Tel** *02 47 30 45 45* **Fax** *02 47 30 46 10* **Rooms** *32*

An ivy-covered 18th-century manor house set in elegant grounds, with views of the Loire. The comfortably sized guest rooms are traditionally decorated. The airy restaurant serves sophisticated cuisine. There are pretty flower-filled walks, and tennis courts. **www.grandesetapes.fr**

ANGERS Hôtel Mail   `P`   €

8 rue des Ursules, 49100 **Tel** *02 41 25 05 25* **Fax** *02 41 86 91 20* **Rooms** *26*

A charming hotel in a quiet corner of the city center, this 17th-century building was once part of a convent. The bedrooms are tastefully decorated. A particularly good breakfast is served in the dining room. There is also a shaded courtyard with tables. Friendly owners. **www.hotel-du-mail.com**

ANGERS Hôtel Anjou   `📺` `P` `🍴` `大` `🗏`   €€

1 bd de Maréchal Foch, 49100 **Tel** *02 41 21 12 11* **Fax** *02 41 87 22 21* **Rooms** *53*

The interior of this city-center hotel has eclectic decoration, with Art Deco mosaics, 17th- and 18th-century fixtures, ornate ceilings, and stained-glass windows. The rooms are spacious and elegantly furnished. "Le Salamandre" restaurant is recommended. Parking available. **www.hoteldanjou.fr**

AZAY LE RIDEAU Le Grand Monarque   `P` `🍴`   €

3 pl de la République, 37190 **Tel** *02 47 45 40 08* **Fax** *02 47 45 46 25* **Rooms** *24*

In a peaceful setting, this hotel comprises two buildings, one an ancient staging post, the other a *hôtel particulier*, separated by a tree-lined courtyard. The rooms are traditionally furnished and the bathrooms functional. There's a rustic dining room and an attractive terrace overlooking the park. Closed Dec–Feb. **www.legrandmonarque.com**

AZAY LE RIDEAU Manoir de la Rémonière   `🏊` `P` `≈` `大` `🖥`   €€

La Chapelle Ste Blaise, 37190 **Tel** *02 47 45 24 88* **Fax** *02 47 45 45 69* **Rooms** *6*

A 15th-century château built on the sight of a Roman villa by the River Indre not far from the Château d'Azay-le-Rideau. The stately bedrooms have an old-world feel and views onto the grounds and the Gallo-Roman ruins. There is a large pool and ample sporting possibilities, including archery and fishing. **www.manoirdelaremoniere.com**

BEAUGENCY Hôtel de la Sologne   `P` `大`   €

6 pl St Firmin, 45190 **Tel** *02 38 44 50 27* **Fax** *02 38 44 90 19* **Rooms** *16*

This typical Sologne stone building on the main square overlooks the ruined castle keep of St Firmin. The bedrooms are small, but cozy, bright, and simply furnished. There is a pretty flower-decked patio where breakfast can be eaten. Private parking available. **www.hoteldelasologne.com**

BOURGES Le Bourbon   `📺` `P` `🍴` `大` `🗏`   €€€

Bd République, 18000 **Tel** *02 48 70 70 00* **Fax** *02 48 70 21 22* **Rooms** *58*

An ancient 17th-century abbey building in the center of Bourges now houses this comfortable hotel. The bright, spacious rooms are furnished in a modern, elegant style. Impressive salon bar and gastronomic restaurant in the former chapel St Ambroix. Parking available. **www.alpha-hotellerie.com**

CHAMPIGNE Château des Briottières   `P` `🍴` `≈` `大`   €€€

Rte Marigné, 49330 **Tel** *02 41 42 00 02* **Fax** *02 41 42 01 55* **Rooms** *14*

Family-run 18th-century château set in the 125-acre park à l'Anglaise. The rooms have luxurious furnishings with canopied beds and rich fabrics. There is also a charming cottage with double rooms for families. Romantic dinners as well as cooking classes for groups are on offer; reservations required. **www.briottieres.com**

CHARTRES Le Grand Monarque   `📺` `P` `🍴` `🗏`   €

22 place des Epars, 28005 **Tel** *02 37 18 15 15* **Fax** *02 37 36 34 18* **Rooms** *55*

This converted 16th-century staging post, with massively thick stone walls, has been managed by the same family since the 1960s. Part of the Best Western network. The rooms are simple. There is a pleasant bistro, and a gastronomic restaurant, "Le Georges." Spa for guests. **www.bw-grand-monarque.com**

CHÊNEHUTTE-LES-TUFFEAUX Le Prieuré   `P` `🍴` `≈` `大`   €€€

Le Prieuré, 49350 **Tel** *02 41 67 90 14* **Fax** *02 41 67 92 24* **Rooms** *36*

This former priory, dating from the 12th century, has magnificent views over the Loire. The bedrooms in the priory have a romantic, refined decor, two with fireplaces. More modern bedrooms are found in the bungalows scattered in the park.The elegant restaurant serves gourmet cuisine with the best regional produce. **www.grandesetapes.fr**

Key to Price Guide *see p550* **Key to Symbols** *see back cover flap*

CHENONCEAUX Hostel du Roy   P ⑪ 🛅   €

9 rue du Dr Bretonneau, 37150 **Tel** *02 47 23 90 17* **Fax** *02 47 23 89 81* **Rooms** *30*

A sprawling hotel-restaurant, with a 16th-century fireplace and a dining room hung with hunting trophies. The well-equipped rooms are simple and appealing, and the atmosphere relaxing. There is a garden and pretty terrace. The restaurant serves classic dishes, including game in season. **www.hostelduroy.com**

CHENONCEAUX Hôtel du Bon Laboureur   P ⑪ 🛅🛅🛅🛅   €€

6 rue de Dr Bretonneau, 37150 **Tel** *02 47 23 90 02* **Fax** *02 47 23 82 01* **Rooms** *25*

Near the famous château, this inn is set in its own park. The bedrooms are located in the collection of 18th-century stone dwellings. They are small but well equipped and have designer bathrooms. Some are suitable for disabled guests. The oak-beamed restaurant is good. Closed Jan–mid-Feb. **www.bonlaboureur.com**

CHINON Hostellerie Gargantua   P ⑪   €

73 rue Voltaire, 37500 **Tel** *02 47 93 04 71* **Fax** *02 47 93 08 02* **Rooms** *8*

This hotel, in the ancient Palais du Boulliage with its pointed roof and turret, is a local landmark. The guest rooms are comfortable, if cramped. Each has a theme, from Jeanne d'Arc and Richelieu to the Empire period. Pleasant dining room and terrace. Modern and classic cuisine. Closed Dec. **www.hotel-gargantua.com**

CHINON Hôtel Diderot   P   €

4 rue Buffon, 37500 **Tel** *02 47 93 18 87* **Rooms** *26*

The palm and olive trees that grow around the 18th-century building testify to the mild climate. This elegant creeper-clad hotel is found on a quiet street near Chinon city center. The rooms are calm, simple, and well-maintained. Breakfast served in a rustic dining room. Free municipal parking nearby. **www.hoteldiderot.com**

CHINON Château de Marçay   🛅 P ⑪ 🛅🛅🛅🛅🛅   €€

Le Château, 37500 **Tel** *02 47 93 03 47* **Fax** *02 47 93 45 33* **Rooms** *39*

Elegant hotel in this restored 15th-century fortified château. Enjoy the lovely views over the surrounding parkland and vineyards from the well-appointed bedrooms. Refined and aristocratic atmosphere, impeccable service and cuisine. Closed mid-Jan–mid-Mar. **www.chateaudemarcay.com**

COUR-CHEVERNY Hôtels des Trois Marchands   P ⑪   €

Pl de l'Eglise, 41700 **Tel** *02 54 79 96 44* **Fax** *02 54 79 25 60* **Rooms** *24*

Just half a mile (1 km) from the château, this ancient coaching inn with a garden has been in the same family since 1865. The bedrooms are comfortably furnished in a rustic style. Have breakfast in one of the three Louis XIII dining rooms. Excellent restaurant. Parking available.

FONTEVRAUD-L'ABBAYE Le Prieuré St-Lazare   🛅 P ⑪ 🛅   €

38 rte St Jean de l'Habit, 49590 **Tel** *02 41 51 73 16* **Fax** *02 41 51 75 50* **Rooms** *52*

The surroundings of this hotel, housed in the former St Lazare priory within the famous royal abbey complex, are stunning. The rooms are elegantly decorated in a modern, contemporary style. The restaurant, in the ancient cloister, is a gourmet's delight. Closed mid-Nov–Mar. **www.hotels-francepatrimoine.com**

GENNES Aux Naulets d'Anjou   P ⑪ 🛅🛅   €

18 rue Croix de la Mission, 49350 **Tel** *02 41 51 81 88* **Fax** *02 41 38 00 78* **Rooms** *19*

At the edge of the village in private grounds, this hotel is quiet and comfortable. The warm welcome compensates for the lack of architectural interest. The rooms are simple and bright. The restaurant serves traditional cuisine with no frills. Reading room and lounge. Closed mid-Dec–Jan. **www.hotel-lesnauletsdanjou.com**

GIEN La Poularde   ⑪   €

13 quai de Nice, 45500 **Tel** *02 38 67 36 05* **Fax** *02 38 38 18 78* **Rooms** *9*

On the banks of the river Loire, just steps away from the Musée de la Faïencerie, this hotel is functional and somewhat lacking in charm. The 19th-century bourgeois house has pleasant rooms simply furnished with Louis-Philippe furniture. The restaurant serves excellent food. **www.lapoularde.fr**

LA CHARTRE SUR LE LOIR Hôtel de France   P ⑪ 🛅🛅   €

20 pl de la République, 72340 **Tel** *02 43 44 40 16* **Fax** *02 43 79 62 20* **Rooms** *21*

This ivy-clad hotel in the city center has a delightful garden bordering the river. Good value standard-sized bedrooms. Simply furnished, but comfortable. The bar and the brasserie are basic, but the dining room is pleasant. Generous portions of good food. Pretty garden terrace. Closed Dec 25–end Jan. **www.hoteldefrance-72.fr**

LA FERTE ST AUBIN Orée des Chênes   P ⑪ 🛅🛅   €€

Rte de Marchily, 45240 **Tel** *02 38 64 84 00* **Fax** *02 38 64 84 20* **Rooms** *26*

This hotel-restaurant complex was built to reflect the local Solange architecture. Situated in a vast park, a peaceful stay is ensured. The comfortable rooms are furnished with style. Regional dishes are served in the excellent restaurant. Good base for fishing and walking holidays. **www.chateaux-france.com/plessisbeauregard/**

LE CROISIC Fort de l'Océan   P ⑪ 🛅🛅🛅   €€€€

Pointe du Croisic, 44490 **Tel** *02 40 15 77 77* **Fax** *02 40 15 77 80* **Rooms** *9*

A Vauban construction, 17th-century ramparts enclose this former fortress facing the sea. Nothing remains of the harsh military lifestyle. The guest rooms are stylish and comfortable, with some equipped for disabled visitors. The restaurant serves wonderful seafood. **www.hotelfortocean.com**

LE MANS Auberge de la Foresterie

Route de Laval, 72000 **Tel** *02 43 51 25 12* **Fax** *02 43 28 54 58* **Rooms** *40*

Elegant and welcoming hotel with pleasant gardens and a pool-side terrace for meals when the weather is fine. Easy access by tram to the historic center of Le Mans and the cathedral. One child under 13 stays free, in the same room. **www.aubergedelaforesterie.com**

LOCHES Hôtel de France

6 rue Picois, 37600 **Tel** *02 47 59 00 32* **Fax** *02 47 59 28 66* **Rooms** *19*

In an elegant former staging post built of local tuffeau stone with a traditional slate roof, this hotel is situated near the historic medieval gate. The rooms are simply furnished, comfortable and well maintained. Restaurant serves good regional dishes such as home-smoked salmon. **http://h.france.loches.free.fr**

LOUE Hôtel Ricordeau

13 rue de la Libération, 72540 **Tel** *02 43 88 40 03* **Fax** *02 43 88 62 08* **Rooms** *13*

A former coaching inn, this lovely stone building has comfortable rooms, each decorated in a different style. Some bedrooms overlook the pretty garden that leads down to the river, where boats are moored for guests' use. Copious breakfasts with cold meats, cheese, cake, fruit, and homemade jams are available. **www.hotel-ricordeau.fr**

LUYNES Domaine de Beauvois

Rte de Cléré-les-Pins, 37230 **Tel** *02 47 55 50 11* **Fax** *02 47 55 59 62* **Rooms** *36*

This Renaissance manor house built around a 15th-century tower overlooks its own lake. The park is so vast that the pathways are signposted. Rooms are large and comfortable, with luxurious marble bathrooms. Enjoy a candlelit dinner in the acclaimed restaurant. **www.grandesetapes.fr**

MONTBAZON Château d'Artigny

Rte de Monts, 37250 **Tel** *02 47 34 30 30* **Fax** *02 47 34 30 39* **Rooms** *65*

This 20th-century château has grounds overlooking the River Indre. The grandiose classical exterior is matched by a formal Empire-style interior. The Baroque-style guest rooms are sumptuous. The splendid rotunda restaurant serves gourmet regional specialties. Superb wine list. **www.grandesetapes.fr**

MONTLOUIS SUR LOIRE Château de la Bourdaisière

25 rue de la Bourdaisière, 37270 **Tel** *02 47 45 16 31* **Fax** *02 47 45 09 11* **Rooms** *22*

A magnificent château refurbished as luxury accommodations. Gabrielle d'Estrées, mistress of Henri IV, was born here in 1565. Some of the elegant, luxurious guest rooms have period furniture. The pavilion in the grounds houses six bedrooms. The gardens are open to the public. Closed Jan–Feb. **www.chateaulabourdaisiere.com**

MONTREUIL-BELLAY Relais du Bellay

96 rue Nationale, 49260 **Tel** *02 41 53 10 10* **Fax** *02 41 38 70 61* **Rooms** *43*

The 17th-century main building and stylishly furnished annex house the guest rooms. All are calm and quiet, some with disabled access. Heated pool, sauna, Turkish bath, Jacuzzi, and gym available. The Splendid hotel, which shares the hotel grounds, has a restaurant. **www.hotelrelaisdubellay.fr**

MUIDES SUR LOIRE Château de Colliers

41500 **Tel** *02 54 87 50 75* **Fax** *02 54 87 03 64* **Rooms** *6*

This château, a short drive east of Blois in the woods, is both rustic and grand. In the 18th century it belonged to a governor of Louisiana. There is a delightfully romantic room, at the top of the building, with Empire period furniture and a roof terrace. Dinner is by reservation only. **www.chateau-colliers.com**

NANTES All Seasons

3 rue de Couëdic, 44000 **Tel** *02 40 35 74 50* **Fax** *02 40 20 09 35* **Rooms** *65*

Part of the Accor group, this modern hotel is functional rather than attractive. It stands in a busy pedestrian square in the city center, well placed for visiting the sights. Reasonably sized, comfortable rooms, some with disabled access. Good buffet breakfast. Parking for a fee. **www.accorhotels.com**

NANTES Amiral

26 bis rue Scribe, 44000 **Tel** *02 40 69 20 21* **Fax** *02 40 73 98 13* **Rooms** *49*

Movie theaters, theaters, restaurants, and Passage Pommeraye are on the doorstep of this city center hotel. The soundproofing in the bedrooms is good. The façade is modern and bright, and the guest rooms are fully equipped and comfortable. Continental breakfast. **www.hotel-nantes.fr**

NANTES Hôtel La Pérouse

3 allée Duquesne, 44000 **Tel** *02 40 89 75 00* **Fax** *02 40 89 76 00* **Rooms** *46*

Named after a French navigator, this chic hotel with its zen atmosphere opened in 1993. The rooms have glossy wooden flooring and crisp contempory furniture. Reasonably quiet. The breakfast buffet is good. Free access to nearby gym for guests. **www.hotel-laperouse.fr**

NOIRMOUTIER EN L'ILE Hotel Fleur de Sel

Rue des Sauliniers, 85330 **Tel** *02 51 39 09 07* **Fax** *02 51 39 09 76* **Rooms** *35*

This hotel stands in the middle of a vast landscaped Mediterranean-style garden with a swimming pool. Some guest rooms are decorated with English-style pine and face the pool; others have a marine theme and private terrace. The chef serves the best cuisine in the Vendée. Closed Nov–mid-Mar. **www.fleurdesel.fr**

Key to Price Guide *see p550* **Key to Symbols** *see back cover flap*

ONZAIN Domaine des Hauts de Loire

P ⅏ ≅ ⛱ ▤   €€€

Rte d'Herbault, 41150 **Tel** *02 54 20 72 57* **Fax** *02 54 20 77 32* **Rooms** *32*

This former hunting lodge with large grounds retains its grandeur, with richly furnished, bright, comfortable guest rooms. This is an unashamedly expensive place to relax. The chef prepares cutting-edge and classic food, served with superb local wines. There is a tennis court. Closed Dec–Feb. **www.domainehautsloire.com**

ORLEANS Hôtel de l'Abeille

€

64 rue Alsace Lorraine, 45000 **Tel** *02 38 53 54 87* **Fax** *02 38 62 65 84* **Rooms** *31*

Named in honor of Napoleon and his emblem the bee, this hotel has been run by the same family since 1920. It is something of a shrine to Joan of Arc. The grand Neo-Classical building houses well decorated, old-style rooms and a good library. There is a terrace looking onto the cathedral. **www.hoteldelabeille.com**

RESTIGNE Manoir de Restigné

P ⅏ ≅ ⛶   €€€€

15 rte de Tours, 37140 **Tel** *02 47 97 00 06* **Fax** *02 47 97 01 43* **Rooms** *10*

Sitting among vineyards near Bourgueil is this tastefully restored 17th-century manor house, offering spacious, elegantly furnished bedrooms named after grape varieties. Meals are served in the former wine cellar and there is a lovely 18th-century orangerie in the grounds. Closed Jan–mid-Feb. **www.manoirderestigne.com**

ROCHECORBON Domaine des Hautes Roches

▣ P ⅏ ≅ ⛱   €€€

86 quai de la Loire, 37210 **Tel** *02 47 52 88 88* **Fax** *02 47 52 81 30* **Rooms** *14*

Surrounded by Vouvray vineyards, near Tours, this was once a monks' residence. Fully restored, it has all modern comforts. The underground rooms, hewn into the tuffeau chalk in this "troglodyte" hotel, are spacious and characterful. Dine in the château, or on the terrace. Closed Feb–Mar. **www.leshautesroches.com**

ROMORANTIN-LANTHENAY Grand Hôtel du Lion d'Or

▣ P ⅏ ▤   €€€

69 rue Georges Clémenceau, 41200 **Tel** *02 54 94 15 15* **Fax** *02 54 88 24 87* **Rooms** *16*

This former Renaissance mansion house is now a gastronomic halt in a historic town. From the outside the building is unimpressive, but the interior has instant charm. The luxury bedrooms lead off from a cobbled courtyard. The decor is authentic Napoléon III. Formal gardens. **www.hotel-liondor.fr**

SALBRIS Domaine de Valaudran

P ⅏ ≅ ♿   €€

Route de Romorantin, 41300 **Tel** *02 54 97 20 00* **Fax** *02 54 97 12 22* **Rooms** *32*

This big family house set in 5 acres (2 ha) of gardens in the heart of the Sologne has been transformed into a pleasant country-house hotel. The stylish, contemporary rooms contrast with the stately home exterior. A billiard table is available. The good, traditional restaurant uses home-grown vegetables. **www.hotelvalaudran.com**

SAUMUR La Croix de la Voulte

▤ P ≅   €

Rte de Boumois, 49400 **Tel** *02 41 38 46 66* **Fax** *02 41 38 46 66* **Rooms** *4*

This manor house, outside Saumur, dates from the 15th century. Built at a crossroads or *croix*, it was the turning point for the royal huntsmen. The bedrooms are all different, two with original Louis XIV fireplaces, and classic furnishings. Breakfast served at poolside in fine weather. **www.lacroixdelavoulte.com**

SAUMUR Hôtel Anne d'Anjou

▣ P ⅏ ⛱   €€

32-34 quai Mayaud, 49400 **Tel** *02 41 67 30 30* **Fax** *02 41 67 51 00* **Rooms** *44*

The decor in this elegant mansion, sitting between the river Loire and the château, is sophisticated and romantic. This fine building with its impressive façade, grand staircase, and painted ceiling has guest rooms decorated in Empire or contemporary style. Breakfast in the courtyard. **www.hotel-anneanjou.com**

SILLE-LE-GUILLAUME Relais des Etangs de Guibert

P ⅏   €

Neufchâtel-en-Saosnois, 72600 **Tel** *02 43 97 15 38* **Fax** *02 43 33 22 99* **Rooms** *15*

North of Le Mans, this beautiful stone-built country house is situated at the edge of the forest in a charming and romantic setting, with a turret overlooking the flower-filled grounds and lake. Individually decorated rooms in warm tones, some with original beamed ceilings. Friendly. **www.lesetangsdeguibert.com**

SOUVIGNY-EN-SOLOGNE Ferme des Foucault

P   €

Ménestreau-en-Villette, 45240 **Tel** *02 38 76 94 41* **Fax** *02 38 76 94 41* **Rooms** *3*

Deep in the forest in the Sologne countryside is this attractive redbrick and timber farmhouse. The immense bedrooms are cozy, with superb bathrooms. One even has a fireplace. The other rooms are decorated with paintings by the owner's daughter. Friendly, relaxed atmosphere. **www.ferme-des-foucault.com**

ST LAURENT NOUAN Hôtel Le Verger

P ⛱   €

14 rue du Port-Pichard, 41220 **Tel** *02 54 87 22 22* **Fax** *02 54 87 22 82* **Rooms** *14*

Ideally placed for visiting the famous Loire châteaux, and only 5 miles (8 km) from Chambord, this 19th-century bourgeois house has an interior courtyard and fountain. The rooms are well maintained, spacious, and calm. The wooded park ensures a peaceful stay. **www.hotel-le-verger.com**

ST NAZAIRE Au Bon Acceuil

⅏ ⛱   €€

39 rue Marceau, 44600 **Tel** *02 40 22 07 05* **Fax** *02 40 19 01 58* **Rooms** *17*

This enchanting hotel in a peaceful corner of the city center had the fortune to escape the destruction of World War II. The guest rooms are simple, modern, and functional. The dining room is a little gloomy, but serves good seafood. Friendly and welcoming atmosphere. Closed last 2 weeks Jul. **www.au-bon-accueil44.com**

ST PATRICE Château de Rochecotte · P ¶ ≈ ★ · €€€
St Patrice, Langeais, 37130 **Tel** *02 47 96 16 16* **Fax** *02 47 96 90 59* **Rooms** *35*

Situated a short way from Langeais, Prince Talleyrand's château was completely renovated and opened as an elegant hotel in 1986. It is set in a charming, tranquil 19-acre (8 ha) park and woodland. The guest rooms are large, each with a view. The interior is decorated sumptuously. Closed mid-Feb–mid-Mar. **www.chateau-de-rochecotte.fr**

TOURS Hôtel L'Adresse · ★ 目 · €€
12 rue de la Rôtisserie, 37000 **Tel** *02 47 20 85 76* **Rooms** *17*

A completely refurbished hotel concealed behind a discreet but elegant façade of an 18th-century townhouse. The rooms offer an appealing blend of minimalist modern and 18th-century architecture. Located right in the city center, it is ideal for restaurants, the conference center, and the train station. **www.hotel-ladresse.com**

VOUVRAY Château de Jallanges · P ¶ ≈ ★ · €€€
9 Jallange, Vernou sur Brenne, 37210 **Tel** *02 47 52 06 66* **Fax** *02 47 52 11 18* **Rooms** *7*

An imposing Renaissance brick château, and now a family home, the comfortable guest rooms are furnished with style. Guests are taken on a guided tour from the private chapel to the top of the turrets from where there is a superb view. A good base for exploring Touraine. **www.jallanges.com**

BURGUNDY & FRANCHE-COMTE

ALOXE-CORTON Hôtel Villa Louise · P ≈ ★ · €€
9 rue Franche, 21420 **Tel** *03 80 26 46 70* **Fax** *03 80 26 47 16* **Rooms** *11*

The finest Corton-Charlemagne vines provide a magnificent backdrop to this 17th-century wine-makers' domaine. Cozy bedrooms have well-equipped bathrooms. The rustic interior includes a living room with open fireplace. Wine-tasting evenings for guests. There are Turkish baths, a solarium, and a heated pool. Closed Jan–Feb. **www.hotel-villa-louise.fr**

ARC-ET-SENANS La Saline Royale · P · €
Arc-et-Senans, 25610 **Tel** *03 81 54 45 00* **Rooms** *30*

To stay in this World Heritage site and architectural museum is a unique experience combining high-class dormitory accommodation with Louis XVI magnificence. The breathtaking salt works, an 18th-century masterpiece by Nicolas Ledoux, accepts guests, but you must reserve well in advance. Closed Nov–Feb. **www.salineroyale.com**

AUXERRE Le Parc des Maréchaux · ★ P ≈ ★ 目 · €€
6 av Foch, 89000 **Tel** *03 86 51 43 77* **Fax** *03 86 51 31 72* **Rooms** *25*

Close to the town center is this elegant, renovated Napoleon III building. The pretty bedrooms, each named after a famous French *maréchal*, are decorated in soft golden tones and furnished in the Empire style. The quietest rooms overlook the lovely park planted with century-old trees. Cozy bar for guests. **www.hotel-parcmarechaux.com**

BEAUNE Hôtel Grillon · P ≈ 目 · €
21 rte de Seurre, 21200 **Tel** *03 80 22 44 25* **Fax** *03 80 24 94 89* **Rooms** *20*

Charming hotel sitting in a walled garden, just 15 minutes' walk from Beaune town center. The rooms in the main building are cozy, with traditional furnishings. There are more spacious, modern-style rooms in the extension. Breakfast is served in the conservatory, or on the garden terrace in summer. **www.hotel-grillon.fr**

BEAUNE Hôtel Le Cep · ★ P ¶ ★ 目 · €€€
27 rue Maufoux, 21200 **Tel** *03 80 22 35 48* **Fax** *03 80 22 76 80* **Rooms** *64*

In the heart of the Old Town is this elegant hotel, renovated in a Renaissance style. Legend has it that Louis XIV preferred to stay here rather than at the hospice. The rooms, some with Baroque decor, are ornately furnished with antiques. Each is named after local wine. **www.hotel-cep-beaune.com**

BESANÇON Hôtel Charles Quint · P ≈ · €€
3 rue du Chapitre, 25000 **Tel** *03 81 82 05 49* **Fax** *03 81 82 61 45* **Rooms** *9*

A charming hotel situated in the historic center. The tastefully decorated interior combines 18th-century architecture with modern amenities. The rooms are elegant without being ostentatious, the best are those with a small terrace overlooking the garden. Breakfast is served in a wood-paneled salon, or outside in fine weather. **www.hotel-charlesquint.com**

BOUILLAND Le Vieux Moulin · P ¶ ≈ ★ ★ · €€
Le Village, 21420 **Tel** *03 80 21 51 16* **Fax** *03 80 21 59 90* **Rooms** *26*

A renovated watermill in this spectacular Burgundy village set in the Rhône valley. Modern, comfortable rooms with simple, stylish furnishings. Views of either the river or the surrounding countryside. Sauna, Jacuzzi, and fitness center. Renowned contemporary restaurant. Closed Jan–mid-Mar. **www.le-moulin-de-bouilland.com**

CHABLIS Le Bergerand's · P ★ · €
4 rue des Moulins, 89800 **Tel** *03 86 18 96 08* **Fax** *03 86 18 96 09* **Rooms** *18*

This popular bed & breakfast on the edge of the River Serein is the perfect place to stop over and sample the local wines. The rooms are bright and gaily decorated and there is a comfortable lounge bar, a tea room, a hammam, and a Jacuzzi. A buffet breakfast is available, and picnic baskets are prepared on request. **www.chablis-france.fr**

...IS Hostellerie des Clos

...es-Rathier, 89800 **Tel** *03 86 42 10 63* **Fax** *03 86 42 17 11* **Rooms** *36*

...wner has renovated a medieval convent in this famed wine village. There are comfortable, modern rooms and ...of the best restaurants in the region (Michelin starred). The terrace overlooks a delightful garden and vineyards. ...e rooms have wheelchair access. Closed mid-Dec–mid-Jan. **www.hostellerie-des-clos.fr**

...AGNY Lameloise

...5 pl d'Armes, 71150 **Tel** *03 85 87 65 65* **Fax** *03 85 87 03 57* **Rooms** *16*

...uxury hotel and gastronomic restaurant situated in an elegant Burgundian house, which has stood for nearly a century in the small town square. Ample rooms have impeccable bathrooms. The refined classic decor includes oak beamed ceilings and period furniture. The restaurant is excellent. Closed mid-Dec–end-Jan. **www.lameloise.fr**

CHAILLY-SUR-ARMANÇON Château de Chailly

Rue Dessous, 21320 **Tel** *03 80 90 30 30* **Fax** *03 80 90 30 00* **Rooms** *45*

One façade of this beautifully restored château is ornately Renaissance, while another recalls the building's medieval heritage. Luxury accommodations with spacious, meticulously maintained rooms. Facilities include a golf course, tennis, Jacuzzi, Turkish bath, and four eateries. **www.chailly.com**

DIJON Le Jacquemart

32 rue Verrerie, 21000 **Tel** *03 80 60 09 60* **Fax** *03 80 60 09 69* **Rooms** *31*

In the heart of the city, near the Palais des Ducs, the Musée des Beaux Arts, and the lucky owl. An attractive 18th-century bourgeois house with decent-sized rooms and antique-style furniture. The decor is somber, but characterful. Quiet and comfortable. Continental breakfast. **www.hotel-lejacquemart.fr**

DIJON Hostellerie du Chapeau Rouge

5 rue Michelet, 21000 **Tel** *03 80 50 88 88* **Fax** *03 80 50 88 89* **Rooms** *30*

Charming 16th-century hotel located in the heart of the city. The well-worn floorboards and period fireplaces still exist, but the decor is contemporary. Chic, individually decorated rooms vary in style from Asiatic to Baroque, romantic to feng shui. Creative, gastronomic cuisine is served in the glass-domed dining room. **www.chapeau-rouge.fr**

DOLE La Chaumière

346 av du Maréchal-Juin, 39100 **Tel** *03 84 70 72 40* **Fax** *03 84 79 25 60* **Rooms** *19*

This ancient farmhouse, outside the city center of the charming former capital of Comté, has authentic furniture that matches the ambience. Elegant and comfortable, well-maintained and soundproofed rooms ensure a tranquil night. Exceptional restaurant with Michelin-starred creative cuisine. **www.la-chaumiere.info**

GEVREY-CHAMBERTIN Hôtel les Grands Crus

Rte des Grands Crus, 21220 **Tel** *03 80 34 34 15* **Fax** *03 80 51 89 07* **Rooms** *24*

A light, airy hotel with wonderful views over the grands crus vineyards. Located in the heart of the Côte de Nuits, this country house built in a typical Burgundian style has traditionally furnished rooms that overlook the garden. The comfy lounge centers around an open fireplace. **www.hoteldesgrandscrus.com**

JOIGNY La Côte St Jacques

14 faubourg de Paris, 89300 **Tel** *03 86 62 09 70* **Fax** *03 86 91 49 70* **Rooms** *31*

Smartly renovated hotel overlooking the River Yonne, with a delightful garden leading to the water's edge. Soft, harmonious colors and contemporary furniture create a pleasing ambience. Superb facilities: spa, private boat for guests, winter lounge with open fire, and summer lounge with terrace. The restaurant is outstanding. **www.cotesaintjacques.com**

LA BUSSIÈRE-SUR-OUCHE Abbaye de la Bussière

La Bussière-sur-Ouche, 21360 **Tel** *03 80 49 02 49* **Fax** *03 80 49 05 23* **Rooms** *15*

A superb conversion of a 12th-century abbey surrounded by a tranquil park. Each room has a view of the grounds with its 52 types of tree and ornamental lake. Two fine Michelin-starred restaurants are presided over by award-winning chef Olivier Elzer. A perfect base for visiting the Burgundy vineyards. **www.abbaye-dela-bussiere.com**

LEVERNOIS Hostellerie de Levernois

Rue du Golf, 21200 **Tel** *03 80 24 73 58* **Fax** *03 80 22 78 00* **Rooms** *26*

Not far from Beaune, in the heart of the Burgundy countryside nestles this classic 19th-century manor house. Set in a park with a small river running through it, a relaxing stay is guaranteed. The rooms retain traces of the era, with parquet floors and Burgundy tiles, yet the facilities are up to date. A converted barn houses an authentic bistro. **www.levernois.com**

MALBUISSON Hôtel Le Lac

31 Grand Rue, 25160 **Tel** *03 81 69 34 80* **Fax** *03 81 69 35 44* **Rooms** *54*

Perched above the lake of St-Point in the Jura mountains, this imposing, elegant 1930s building has prettily decorated rooms, some with a lake view. The atmosphere is comfortable and pleasant, although service is abrupt – but that's normal for the region. Great buffet breakfast. **www.hotel-le-lac.fr**

MALBUISSON Le Bon Acceuil

Rue de la Source, 25160 **Tel** *03 81 69 30 58* **Fax** *03 81 69 37 60* **Rooms** *12*

Situated between the forest and the shores of Lac St Point is this friendly hotel. Rooms are spacious and comfortable, with simple pinewood furniture and homely fabrics. The restaurant serves outstanding contemporary cuisine, remaining faithful to the local produce. Closed mid-Dec–mid-Jan & 2 weeks Mar. **www.le-bon-accueil.fr**

MARTAILLY-LES-BRANCION La Montagne de Brancion   🅿 🍴 ♨

Col de Brancion, 71700 **Tel** *03 85 51 12 40* **Fax** *03 85 51 18 64* **Rooms** *19*

East of Tournus, perched on a hillside a few steps away from the medieval village, this hotel has a panoramic v
the surrounding countryside. All rooms face east looking out over the Mâconnais mountains and the vineyards.
bright, prettily-decorated rooms have modern furnishings. The restaurant is highly recommended. **www.brancion.c**

NANS-SOUS-STE-ANNE A l'Ombre du Château   📑 🅿 ♿   €

6 rue du Château, 25330 **Tel** *03 81 86 54 72* **Fax** *03 81 86 43 29* **Rooms** *4*

Located southwest of Ornans, this converted 18th-century stone outbuilding of a château is set in a vast wooded
park. Well-kept rooms have been carefully and tastefully restored. There is a generous breakfast with homemade
pastries. The American owners aim to please. Closed Nov–Apr. **www.frenchcountryretreat.com**

NANTOUX Domaine de la Combotte   🅿 ♨ ♿   €€

2 La Combotte, 21190 **Tel** *03 80 26 02 66* **Fax** *03 80 26 07 84* **Rooms** *5*

Near Beaune, this family-run wine estate offers *chambres d'hôte*. Large comfortable rooms, one with wheelchair
access and one family room. Well-equipped, with modern decor. The owners delight in sharing their passion for wine
and truffles. **www.lacombotte.com**

NEVERS Clos Ste Marie   🅿   €

25 rue du Petit-Mouësse, 58000 **Tel** *03 86 71 94 50* **Fax** *03 86 71 94 69* **Rooms** *17*

After visiting the sights of Nevers, unwind in this attractive, calm hotel just five-minutes from the pedestrianized
center. Pretty, bright, and well-proportioned rooms are furnished with quaint fabrics and antique furniture. The
flower-filled garden can be enjoyed while having breakfast on the shady terrace. **www.clos-sainte-marie.fr**

NITRY Auberge de la Beursaudière   🅿 🍴 ♿   €

5 & 7 rue Hyacinthe-Gautherin, 89310 **Tel** *03 86 33 69 70* **Fax** *03 86 33 69 60* **Rooms** *11*

Midway between Auxerre, Chablis, and Vézelay, this hotel stands in a 12th-century former priory. The attractive bedrooms
are each named after ancient trades: *Le Sabotier, La Dentellière, La Repasseuse*. The best, *Le Vigneron* and *L'Ecrivain*,
are roomy and elegant. Buffet breakfast is served in a former wine cellar. Closed Jan. **www.bersaudiere.com**

NUITS-ST-GEORGES Hôtel la Gentilhommière   🅿 🍴 ♨ 🛏 🍽   €€

13 vallée de la Serrée, 21700 **Tel** *03 80 61 12 06* **Fax** *03 80 61 30 33* **Rooms** *41*

This former 16th-century hunting lodge with its typical Burgundy tiled roof is now a beautiful hotel and renowned
restaurant. The bedrooms are classically furnished, and the suites are decorated in styles from colonial to zen. Well-
mastered cuisine. Terrace overlooks the river. Closed Jan. **www.lagentilhommiere.fr**

POLIGNY Hostellerie des Monts de Vaux   🅿 🍴 🍽   €€€

Monts Vaux, 39800 **Tel** *03 84 37 12 50* **Fax** *03 84 37 09 07* **Rooms** *10*

Run by the Carrion family since 1967, this hotel occupies an elegant coaching inn on the outskirts of Poligny, in
lovely gardens. The rooms are decorated in a bourgeois style with antique furniture. Refined atmosphere. Good Jura
cuisine and wine in the restaurant. Tennis. **www.hostellerie.com**

PORT-LESNEY Château de Germigney   🌊 🅿 🍴 ♨ 🍽   €€€

Le Parc, 39600 **Tel** *03 84 73 85 85* **Fax** *03 84 73 88 88* **Rooms** *19*

This hotel is located just 4 miles (6 km) from Arc-et-Senans in its own grounds bordering the Loue river. This exquisite
château has tastefully decorated rooms with modern facilities. Smaller, less expensive rooms are in the annex.
Exceptional restaurant and natural water pool. Relaxed and unstuffy service. **www.chateaudegermigney.com**

SAULIEU Le Relais Bernard Loiseau   🅿 🍴 ♨ ♿ 🛏 🍽   €€€€€

2 rue d'Argentine, 21210 **Tel** *03 80 90 53 53* **Fax** *03 80 64 08 92* **Rooms** *33*

A renowned hotel and acclaimed restaurant established by the late Bernard Loiseau. Modern comfort and traditional
Burgundy furnishings – wood-paneled walls, red floor tiles. The refined rooms have either a fireplace or balcony
overlooking the gardens à l'Anglaise. Fine service. Closed Jan. **www.bernard-loiseau.com**

ST-AMOUR-BELLEVUE L'Auberge du Paradis   🅿 🍴 ♨ 🍽   €€

Le Plâtre-Durand, 71570 **Tel** *03 85 37 10 26* **Rooms** *8*

A young dynamic couple have tastefully renovated this auberge. The bedrooms take their names from different spices
and are decorated with style and originality. Chic, contemporary decor with open-plan bathrooms. Some rooms have
balconies overlooking the garden. Breakfast is copious. Good restaurant. Closed Jan. **www.aubergeduparadis.fr**

ST-GERVAIS-EN-VALLIERE Moulin d'Hauterive   🅿 🍴 ♨ ♿ 🛏   €

Hameau de Chaublanc, 71350 **Tel** *03 85 91 55 56* **Fax** *03 85 91 89 65* **Rooms** *20*

Not far from Beaune, in a secluded setting on the bank of the Dheune river, this converted watermill was built in the
12th century by the monks of Citeaux abbey. Each room is unique, tastefully furnished with antiques. The owner-
chef serves inventive home cooking. One room has wheelchair access. **www.moulinhauterive.com**

VALLÉE DE COUSIN Hostellerie du Moulin des Ruats   🅿 🍴 ♿   €€

9 rue des Isles Labaumes, 89200 **Tel** *03 86 34 97 00* **Fax** *03 86 31 65 47* **Rooms** *25*

A few kilometers from the old fortified town of Avallon, in the valley formed by the River Cousin, lies this former flour
mill, now a classic hotel-restaurant. Comfortable, charming rooms with traditional furnishings have views over the garden
or the river; some with a terrace. Restaurant serves classic cuisine. Closed mid-Nov–mid-Feb. **www.moulindesruats.com**

Key to Price Guide *see p550* **Key to Symbols** *see back cover flap*

...ELAY L'Espérance 🅿🍴♨🏃🖥 €€€€€

...ère-sous-Vézelay, 89450 **Tel** *03 86 33 39 10* **Fax** *03 86 33 26 15* **Rooms** *34*

...e guest rooms here are in three buildings: the main building has classic furnishings, Moulin has rustic charm, and ...e des Marguerites is contemporary, with terraces overlooking the garden. Wonderful restaurant, excellent but ...pensive wines, and impeccable service. Closed mid-Jan–mid-Mar. **www.marc-meneau-esperance.com**

...ILLENEUVE-SUR-YONNE La Lucarne aux Chouettes 🍴 €

7 quai Bretoche, 89500 **Tel** *03 86 87 18 26* **Fax** *03 86 87 18 26* **Rooms** *4*

On the riverbank, four typical Burgundian 17th-century houses have been converted into sophisticated *chambres d'hôtes*, all with a river view. The individually decorated rooms have oak beams, four-poster beds, *toile de Jouy* fabric, antique furniture, and hand-painted bathroom tiles. Charming dining room and terrace. **www.lalucarneauxchouettes.fr**

VONNAS Georges Blanc 🅿🍴♨🏃🖥 €€€€

Pl Marché, 01540 **Tel** *04 74 50 90 90* **Fax** *04 74 50 08 80* **Rooms** *41*

Sumptuous hotel-restaurant in an ancient timbered and brick mansion, surrounded by a garden. The luxurious rooms were decorated by Pierre Chaduc. The atmosphere sways between refinement and opulence; the decor mixes Louis XIII and rustic styles. Most bathrooms have Jacuzzis. Spa with sauna. **www.georgesblanc.com**

YONNE Hôtel d'Avallon Vauban 🅿🖥 €

53 rue de Paris, 89200 **Tel** *03 86 34 36 99* **Fax** *03 86 31 66 31* **Rooms** *26*

This charming, ivy-clad house, on the main road into Yonne, is a great base for exploring the area. The bedrooms are simply furnished, and those at the back are quieter and have views directly over the pretty garden. The shady courtyard is a great place to enjoy breakfast in fine weather. **www.avallonvaubanhotel.com**

THE MASSIF CENTRAL

BEAULIEU-SUR-DORDOGNE Manoir de Beaulieu 🅿🍴🏃 €€

4 pl Champ de Mars, 19120 **Tel** *05 55 91 01 34* **Fax** *05 55 91 23 57* **Rooms** *25*

Situated in the main square of this pretty village, this traditional hotel was founded in 1913. The rooms have been nicely renovated and are decorated in different styles; whether rustic or modern each one is comfortably sized with a well-maintained bathroom. The lounge bar has comfy leather chairs. **www.manoirdebeaulieu.com**

BELCASTEL Du Vieux Pont 🅿🍴🖥 €€

Le Bourg, 12390 **Tel** *05 65 64 52 29* **Fax** *05 65 64 44 32* **Rooms** *7*

Being lulled to sleep by the murmuring of the river is just one of the attractions of this unpretentious hotel. Rooms are spacious, light, and airy, and all have river views. Across the medieval cobbled bridge, the same family also runs an imaginative but affordable restaurant. Closed Jan–mid-Mar. **www.hotelbelcastel.com**

BÉNÉVENT L'ABBAYE Le Cèdre 🅿🍴♨🍴♿ €

Rue de l'Oiseau, 23210 **Tel** *05 55 81 59 99* **Fax** *05 55 81 59 98* **Rooms** *16*

In the lush countryside northwest of Aubusson lies this classic hotel and restaurant. Behind the 18th-century granite façade hides a contemporary interior. Rooms range from romantic, with four-poster beds, to plainly furnished. The beautiful garden has a terrace shaded by a monumental cedar tree. Closed Jan–Feb. **www.hotelducedre.fr**

CHAMALIERES Hôtel Radio 📶🅿🍴🖥 €€

43 av Pierre et Marie Curie, 63400 **Tel** *04 73 30 87 83* **Fax** *04 73 36 42 44* **Rooms** *26*

Built in the 1930s, this Art Deco hotel on a hill overlooking Clermont-Ferrand retains its original mosaics, mirrors, and decorative ironwork, alongside radio memorabilia. Spacious rooms have period furnishings, some with balconies. First-class restaurant and attentive service. **www.hotel-radio.fr**

CONQUES Hôtel Ste Foy 📶🅿🍴🏃🖥 €€

Le Bourg, 12320 **Tel** *05 65 69 84 03* **Fax** *05 65 72 81 04* **Rooms** *17*

Facing the much-visited abbey in one of the most charming Aveyron villages, this ancient 17th-century inn retains traces of its rustic past. Old stone walls, low ceilings and oak beams are complemented by elegant furniture and modern amenities. Idyllic interior courtyard, and shady terrace. Restaurant recommended. Closed Nov–Easter. **www.hotelsaintefoy.fr**

LAGUIOLE Michel Bras 📶🅿🍴🏃🖥♿ €€€€€

Route de l'Aubrac, 12210 **Tel** *05 65 51 18 20* **Fax** *05 65 48 47 02* **Rooms** *15*

Built on a hillside with a spectacular view of the Aubrac plain houses, this futuristic construction is one of France's most acclaimed hotel-restaurants. The amply-sized rooms, with floor-to-ceiling windows, are contemporary and minimalist with modern facilities. The restaurant is a gourmet's paradise. Closed Nov–Easter. **www.michel-bras.fr**

LIMOGES Hôtel Jeanne d'Arc 📶🅿 €€

17 av du Général-de-Gaulle, 87000 **Tel** *05 55 77 67 77* **Fax** *05 55 79 86 75* **Rooms** *50*

A surprisingly atmospheric hotel near Limoges train station and within walking distance of the center. The building has been tastefully renovated without losing its 19th-century feel. The rooms are stylish and equipped with all the three-star comforts you'd expect. **www.hoteljeannedarc-limoges.fr**

LIMOGES Domaine de Faugeras 🖼️ 🅿️ 🍴 🛏️ 📺 📋 ♿ €

Allée de Faugeras, 87000 **Tel** *05 55 34 66 22* **Fax** *05 55 34 18 05* **Rooms** *9*

Located in its own park on the edge of the city center, this 18th-century manor house is a peaceful place to stay. Cultural heritage blends successfully with modernity. The rooms are contemporary in style, and well-equipped. Th' pleasant lounge has an open fireplace and there is a spa and brasserie. **www.domainedefaugeras.com**

MENDE Hôtel de France 🅿️ 🍴 🏃 📋 ♿ €

9 bd Lucien-Arnault, 48000 **Tel** *04 66 65 00 04* **Fax** *04 66 49 30 47* **Rooms** *27*

This entirely renovated staging post, dating from 1856, offers rooms that are cozy, comfortable, and stylish; the quietest ones overlook the gardens. Relax in front of a roaring fire in winter, or enjoy breakfast on the pretty terrece in summer. A friendly family-run hotel. **www.hoteldefrance-mende.com**

MILLAU Château de Creissels 🅿️ 🍴 🛏️ €

Rte de St-Afrique, 12100 **Tel** *05 65 60 16 59* **Fax** *05 65 61 24 63* **Rooms** *30*

A short distance from Millau is this 12th-century château with stunning views over the Tarn valley and the Millau viaduct. Rooms in the 1970s extension are comfortable and quiet, with balconies overlooking the gardens. Enjoy local dishes in the stone-vaulted restaurant. Closed Jan–Feb. **www.chateau-de-creissels.com**

MONTSALVY Auberge Fleurie 🍴 €

Pl du Barry, 15120 **Tel** *04 71 49 20 02* **Fax** *04 71 49 29 65* **Rooms** *7*

This ivy-clad village inn situated in the south of Auvergne, offers excellent value for money. The rustic charm of the original building is complemented by pretty, colorful fabrics in the individually decorated rooms. The largest rooms have canopied beds. Creative cuisine is served in the restaurant. Closed mid-Jan–mid-Feb. **www.auberge-fleurie.com**

MOUDEYRES Le Pré Bossu 🅿️ 🍴 €€

43150 **Tel** *04 71 05 10 70* **Fax** *04 71 05 10 21* **Rooms** *6*

Authentic low, stone cottage with a thatched roof in the heart of the Auvergne countryside. The bedrooms, named after birds, are modern and comfortable with relaxing decor and furniture imported from Asia. There are homemade jams for breakfast and home-grown vegetables for dinner. Closed Nov–Easter. **www.auberge-pre-bossu.com**

PAILHEROLS Auberge des Montagnes 🅿️ 🍴 🛏️ 🏃 📺 €

Le Bourg, 15800 **Tel** *04 71 47 57 01* **Fax** *04 71 49 63 83* **Rooms** *23*

On the flanks of the Monts du Cantal, it's worth seeking out this cozy mountain auberge. In winter there are log fires; in summer head for the large garden with a children's play area. The restaurant attracts locals from miles around with its good-value country cooking. Treatments available in the spa. **www.auberge-des-montagnes.com**

PERIGNAT-LES-SARLIEVE Hostellerie St Martin 🖼️ 🅿️ 🍴 🛏️ 🏃 📺 €€

Allée de Bonneval, 63170 **Tel** *04 73 79 81 00* **Fax** *04 73 79 81 01* **Rooms** *32*

Located a few kilometers south of Clermont-Ferrand, this splendid Cistercian abbey dates from the 14th century. It now houses a comfortable hotel surrounded by a peaceful park. There are three styles of rooms: standard (in the modern annex), and superior and deluxe in the ancient building. **www.hostelleriestmartin.com**

PEYRELEAU Grand Hôtel de la Muse et du Rozier 🅿️ 🍴 🛏️ 🏃 €€

Rue des Gorges du Tarn, 12720 **Tel** *05 65 62 60 01* **Fax** *05 65 62 63 88* **Rooms** *38*

This century-old hotel sits in an idyllic spot among the trees at the water's edge. The quaint exterior contrasts with the contemporary design inside; natural materials, white walls, and light create a purist atmosphere. The rooms all have river views. There is a mini-beach at the riverside, and a good restaurant. Closed mid-Nov–Apr. **www.hotel-delamuse.fr**

PONTGIBAUD Hôtel Saluces 🅿️ 🏃 €

Rue de la Martille, 15140 **Tel** *04 71 40 70 82* **Fax** *04 71 40 71 70* **Rooms** *8*

Located in the center of this beautiful Renaissance town, this 15th–16th-century house looks like a small château. It is family-run and offers a warm welcome. The rooms are large, attractively decorated, and each has its own bath/ shower. There is a bar, and afternoon teas are served in the salon. **www.hotel-salers.fr**

RODEZ La Ferme de Bourran 🖼️ 🅿️ 📋 ♿ €€

Quartier de Bourran, 12000 **Tel** *05 65 73 62 62* **Fax** *05 65 72 14 15* **Rooms** *7*

This small hotel with modern bedrooms occupies a renovated farmhouse, which sits on a hillock in a secluded spot near Rodez. Bright contemporary and comfortable rooms are painted in white, gray, and ivory tones. The relaxing lounge has a lovely open fireplace, and there is a large terrace for breakfast in summer. **www.fermedebourran.com**

SALERS Le Bailliage 🅿️ 🍴 🛏️ 🏃 €

Rue Notre-Dame, 15410 **Tel** *04 71 40 71 95* **Fax** *04 71 40 74 90* **Rooms** *27*

The Bailliage is one of the nicest places to stay in this attractive mountain town. Cheaper rooms occupy a separate annex, but all are comfortable and some particularly jolly. There's a garden and a restaurant in which to sample Salers cheese. Closed mid-Nov–mid-Mar. **www.salers-hotel-bailliage.com**

ST-ALBAN-SUR-LIMAGNOLE Relais St Roch 🅿️ 🛏️ 🏃 📋 €€€

Château de la Chastre, chemin du Carreirou, 48120 **Tel** *04 66 31 55 48* **Fax** *04 66 31 53 26* **Rooms** *9*

The pretty granite pink stone building contrasts with the lush green of the surrounding countryside. The rooms in this 18th-century mansion are classically decorated and elegantly furnished with antiques and tapestries. Cozy lounge bar with over 300 whiskies. The owners have a delightful restaurant nearby. Closed Nov–Easter. **www.relais-saint-roch.fr**

ST-ARCONS-D'ALLIER Les Deux Abbesses

Le Château, 43300 **Tel** *04 71 74 03 08* **Fax** *04 71 74 05 30* **Rooms** *6*

An entire tiny hamlet has been restored to form this outstanding hotel. Four cottages house the rooms, cobbled streets serve as corridors, and the château houses a reception and dining room. Romantic rooms, and fantasy-style bathrooms: an old wine *cuve* serves as a bathtub, an animal's trough as a sink. Closed Nov–Easter. **www.lesdeuxabbesses.com**

ST-BONNET-LE-FROID Le Clos des Cimes

Le Bourg, 43290 **Tel** *04 71 59 93 72* **Fax** *04 71 59 93 40* **Rooms** *12*

Gourmet pilgrims compete for rooms at this fabulous auberge deep in the countryside. The prize is a luxurious room with original artworks and stunning views over the valley. The Marcon family runs the place with tremendous attention to detail. Prepare to be pampered. Cooking lessons available. Closed Jan–Easter. **www.regismarcon.fr**

ST GERVAIS D'AUVERGNE Castel-Hôtel 1904

Rue de Castel, 63390 **Tel** *04 73 85 70 42* **Fax** *04 73 85 84 39* **Rooms** *15*

Rooms are surprisingly affordable in this turreted château where period furniture, oak beams, and highly polished floors ensure a homely atmosphere. Guest rooms are set round an attractive courtyard. There are two good restaurants: one rustic, the other grand. Closed Nov–Easter. **www.castel-hotel-1904.com**

ST-MARTIN-VALMEROUX Hostellerie de la Maronne

Le Theil, 15140 **Tel** *04 71 69 20 33* **Fax** *04 71 69 28 22* **Rooms** *21*

Not far from Salers, encircled by the Auvergne volcanoes, is this 19th-century manor house. Renovated with taste, it houses sunny, prettily decorated rooms with stylish classic furnishings. Discover the park by following one of the suggested walks, or take a siesta in the tree house. The restaurant is one of the best in the region. **www.maronne.com**

ST-PRIEST-BRAMEFANT Château de Maulmont

Maulmont, 63310 **Tel** *04 70 59 14 95* **Fax** *04 70 59 11 88* **Rooms** *18*

Superb 19th-century château surrounded by parkland and lovely gardens. Well-equipped, spacious bedrooms feature elegant, classic decor, and period furniture. The oak-paneled dining room serves delicious traditional fare. Boating and golf are nearby. Closed mid-Nov–Apr. **www.château-maulmont.com**

VICHY Aletti Palace Hotel

3 pl Joseph-Aletti, 03200 **Tel** *04 70 30 20 20* **Fax** *04 70 98 13 82* **Rooms** *129*

Vichy's top hotel oozes Belle-Epoque grandeur from its stately reception hall to the crystal chandeliers. Guest rooms have been modernized but are tranquil and well proportioned. Fine restaurant and a terraced pool. In World War II, the Aletti was home to Vichy's Minister of War. **www.hotel-aletti.fr**

VITRAC Auberge de la Tomette

Le Bourg, 15220 **Tel** *04 71 64 70 94* **Fax** *04 71 64 77 11* **Rooms** *16*

A lovely country retreat set in huge gardens with a games area for children. Recent enhancements include a heated pool, sauna, and *hammam*. The rooms are restful and spacious; six designed for families. Equal thought and attention goes into the cooking. Closed Nov–Easter. **www.auberge-la-tomette.com**

YGRANDE Château d'Ygrande

Le Mont, 3320 **Tel** *04 70 66 33 11* **Fax** *04 70 66 33 63* **Rooms** *19*

A meticulously renovated, quality hotel is housed in this grand 19th-century building. The rooms are beautiful, bright, and elegant. A vast park offers walking, bicycling, horseback riding, and boating. Inside there is a *hammam*, fitness center, sauna, and billiards. Good restaurant serving local produce. Closed Jan–Mar. **www.chateauygrande.fr**

THE RHONE VALLEY & FRENCH ALPS

ANNECY Hôtel Palais de l'Isle

13 rue Perrière, 74000 **Tel** *04 50 45 86 87* **Rooms** *33*

Opposite the Palais de l'Isle, this hotel sits like a Venetian *palazzo* on the edge of the Thouin canal. The renovated rooms in the 18th-century house are comfortable and well-equipped, with modern decor using neutral colors. The best rooms are found on the canal side. **www.hoteldupalaisdelisle.com**

BAGNOLS Château de Bagnols

Le Bourg, 69620 **Tel** *04 74 71 40 00* **Fax** *04 74 71 40 49* **Rooms** *21*

In 1987 Lady Hamlyn restored this château north of Lyon, surrounded by Beaujolais vineyards, and created a luxury hotel. The 13th-century building has turrets, moat, and drawbridge. The rooms are richly decorated in velvet, silk, and antiques. Michelin-starred restaurant. **www.chateaudebagnols.com**

BRIANÇON Hôtel Cristol

6 rte d'Italie, 05100 **Tel** *04 92 20 20 11* **Fax** *04 92 21 02 58* **Rooms** *24*

Well-kept, traditional hotel. The attractive bedrooms are modern, airy, and bright; some have balconies with a view of the Vauban fortifications. Friendly service, and children are well catered for here. Charming dining room serves interesting themed menus. **www.hotel-cristol-briancon.fr**

CHALMAZEL Château de Marcilly Talaru 🗂 P €€
42920 **Tel** *04 77 24 88 09* **Fax** *04 77 24 87 07* **Rooms** *5*

Situated at an altitude of 3,000 ft (900 m), Chalmazel becomes a small ski resort in winter. The bedrooms at this hotel reflect the overall grandeur of the magnificent fortified medieval château, with four-poster beds and classic furnishings. There are well-equipped bathrooms, too. Breakfast included. *Table d'hôte* on request. **www.chateaudechalmazel.com**

CHAMBERY Hôtel des Princes 🗒📧 €€
4 rue de Boigne, 73000 **Tel** *04 79 33 45 36* **Fax** *04 79 70 31 47* **Rooms** *45*

Situated in the grandest section of the Old Town, near La Fontaine des Elephants, this charmingly old-fashioned hotel has quiet, comfortable rooms, though not very spacious. The service is welcoming and friendly. There are several restaurants nearby to choose from. **www.hoteldesprinces.eu**

CHAMBERY Château de Candie 🗒P🍽≋🏃♿ €€€
Rue du Bois de Candie, 73000 **Tel** *04 79 96 63 00* **Fax** *04 79 96 63 10* **Rooms** *35*

Dominating the valley of Chambèry, this splendid hotel has a panoramic view of the mountains. A 14th-century Savoyard house has been beautifully transformed and offers sumptuous bedrooms decorated with refinement. A tranquil spot surrounded by its own park. Excellent restaurant serving classic gourmet cuisine. **www.chateaudecandie.com**

CHAMONIX MONT BLANC Le Hameau Albert 1er 🗒P🍽≋📺📧 €€€€
119 impasse du Montenvers, 74402 **Tel** *04 50 53 05 09* **Fax** *04 50 55 95 48* **Rooms** *36*

Part of a hotel complex including the traditional hotel Albert 1er, the authentic and unusual Chalet Soli, and the chic La Ferme. The large chalet-hotel has stunning views of Mont Blanc. The well-proportioned rooms have elegant designer furniture. Two good restaurants, one with two Michelin stars. There is also a sauna. **www.hameaualbert.fr**

CHANTERMERLE-LES-GRIGNAN Le Parfum Bleu P≋ €€
26230 **Tel** *04 75 98 54 21* **Fax** *04 75 98 54 21* **Rooms** *5*

The sound of cicadas and aroma of lavender – this is quintessential Drôme-Provençale. A beautifully restored stone farmhouse with bright blue shutters offers comfortable *chambres d'hôtes*, each with a private entrance. The rooms have original stone floors and simple, modern furnishings. Buffet breakfast. *Table d'hôte* on request. **www.parfum-bleu.com**

CHONAS L'AMBALLAN Domaine de Clairefontaine P🍽🏃 €€
Chemin des Fontanettes, 38121 **Tel** *04 74 58 81 52* **Fax** *04 74 58 80 93* **Rooms** *28*

Set in a magnificent park in a small village south of Vienne, among ancient trees, this former manor house has impeccably furnished rooms. The modern annex has more chic rooms with balconies. The restaurant has a good reputation but can be inconsistent. **www.domaine-de-clairefontaine.fr**

CLIOUSCLAT La Treille Muscate P🍽 €
Le Village, 26270 **Tel** *04 75 63 13 10* **Rooms** *12*

A pleasant Provençale inn in a village renowned for its pottery. The bedrooms are individually decorated: choose from Basque red, pastel blue, or African. Some rooms have south-facing balconies. The vaulted dining room serves local cuisine. Breakfast is served in the garden on sunny days. Closed Jan–mid-Feb. **www.latreillemuscate.com**

CORDON Le Cordonant P🍽📺📧 €
Les Darbaillets, 74700 **Tel** *04 50 58 34 56* **Fax** *04 50 47 95 57* **Rooms** *16*

A friendly family-run hotel at this ski resort west of Chamonix, the trim, well-kept chalet has a garden. The rooms are comfortable, with pretty rustic furniture. The best rooms have great views of Mont Blanc. The restaurant serves hearty alpine cuisine. Good value. **www.lecordonant.fr**

DIVONNE-LES-BAINS Château de Divonne 🗒P🍽≋🏃 €€€
115 rue des Bains, 01220 **Tel** *04 50 20 00 32* **Fax** *04 50 20 03 73* **Rooms** *34*

From this charming 19th-century mansion set in a large park, not far from Geneva, there are panoramic views of Mont Blanc and Lake Geneva. Inside is a monumental staircase. The rooms are richly furnished. Tennis courts on site, and golf course nearby. Classic cuisine. **www.chateau-divonne.com**

EVIAN-LES-BAINS Hôtel Royal Palace 🗒P🍽≋🏃♿ €€€€€
Rive Sud du Lac de Genève, 74500 **Tel** *04 50 26 85 00* **Fax** *04 50 75 38 40* **Rooms** *144*

An imposing hotel situated on the water's edge by Lake Geneva. Four restaurants, jogging trails, spa treatments, a private garden, and a children's club are all on offer. Rooms and suites are tastefully decorated and most have impressive views over the lake. **www.evianroyalresort.com**

GRENOBLE Splendid Hôtel 🗒P🏃📧 €
22 rue Thiers, 38000 **Tel** *04 76 46 33 12* **Fax** *04 76 46 35 24* **Rooms** *45*

Chic, centrally located hotel in a quiet location, with a walled garden. The guest rooms range from classical to modern, with gaily painted frescoes. Efficient service and amenities. Continental and *à la carte* breakfast served in the dining room, or garden terrace. **www.splendid-hotel.com**

GRESY-SUR-ISÈRE La Tour de Pacoret P🍽≋ €
Montailleur, 73460 **Tel** *04 79 37 91 59* **Fax** *04 79 37 93 84* **Rooms** *11*

The tower has been here since 1283 when it was erected to guard the Combe de Savoie. Beside it, this quality hotel with stylish rooms has developed. The bedrooms, each named after a flower, are decorated in warm tones. The mountain scenery can be enjoyed from the terrace. Traditional dishes served. **www.hotel-pacoret-savoie.com**

Key to Price Guide *see p550* **Key to Symbols** *see back cover flap*

LE POET LAVAL Les Hospitaliers
Vieux Village, 26160 **Tel** *04 75 46 22 32* **Fax** *04 75 46 49 99* **Rooms** *20*

A beautifully restored hotel in the center of a tiny hilltop medieval village east of Montélimar. The elegantly furnished bedrooms, in the old stone buildings, are spacious and quiet. The restaurant offers first-class service, excellent cuisine, and a wide range of good Rhône valley wines. **www.hotel-les-hospitaliers.com**

LES DEUX ALPES Chalet Hôtel Mounier
2 rue de la Chapelle, 38860 **Tel** *04 76 80 56 90* **Fax** *04 76 79 56 51* **Rooms** *46*

Now a quality hotel, this former alpine farm has plenty of character. Contemporary, yet ultracozy rooms have a chic, authentic chalet atmosphere. Well-equipped with up-to-date amenities, the hotel is constantly being upgraded. The lounge features an open fireplace. Good restaurant. Closed May–Jun & Sep–mid-Dec. **www.chalet-mounier.com**

LYON Hôtel des Artistes
8 rue Gaspard-André, 69002 **Tel** *04 78 42 04 88* **Fax** *04 78 42 93 76* **Rooms** *45*

Close to the place Bellecour, the Saône River and next door to the Theâtre des Célestins, this delightful hotel is a favorite haunt of actors. Pleasant, bright, airy rooms. Breakfast is served in an attractive room that is decorated with a Jean Cocteau-style fresco. **www.hotel-des-artistes.fr**

LYON La Maison du Greillon
12 Montée du Greillon, 69009 **Tel** *04 72 29 10 97* **Rooms** *5*

This large building was once home to Lyon sculptor Joseph Chinard. Now a small and tranquil bed and breakfast with its own garden, fountain, and terrace, and great views of the Croix-Rousse and the Saône. The well-kept rooms have elegant classic furnishings. There is a roomy dining room and a kitchen for guests to use. **www.legreillon.com**

LYON Cour des Loges
6 rue du Bœuf, 69005 **Tel** *04 72 77 44 44* **Fax** *04 72 40 93 61* **Rooms** *62*

This luxury hotel occupies four renovated Renaissance mansions around a central galleried courtyard in Vieux Lyon. The reception area has a stunning glass roof. The elegant rooms blend Renaissance and contemporary decor. The restaurant serves classic cuisine. **www.courdesloges.com**

MANIGOD Hôtel-Chalets de la Croix-Fry
Rte du Col de la Croix-Fry, 74230 **Tel** *04 50 44 90 16* **Fax** *04 50 44 94 87* **Rooms** *10*

High on a mountain pass east of Annecy, this delightful chalet-style hotel combines Alpine rustic with comfort in a friendly atmosphere. The wooden interior is charming, decorated with Savoyard furniture. The guest rooms are cozy. Closed May and October–November. **www.hotelchaletcroixfry.com**

MEGÈVE Les Fermes de Marie
163 chemin de Riante Colline, 74120 **Tel** *04 50 93 03 10* **Fax** *04 50 93 09 84* **Rooms** *71*

Lovingly restored chalets with chic country-style rooms. The bedrooms reflect Savoyard charm with rustic furniture and decor in natural colors. The ambience is professional, yet relaxed and friendly. The facilities are superb: spa, sauna, Jacuzzi, hairdresser, games room, fitness center, and a good restaurant. Closed May–Jun. **www.fermesdemarie.com**

MONTELIMAR Sphinx
19 bd Desmarais, 26200 **Tel** *04 75 01 86 64* **Fax** *04 75 52 34 21* **Rooms** *24*

Old-fashioned charm greets visitors to this former 17th-century *hôtel particulier*. Situated in the historic city center, it is surprisingly calm, with a private courtyard and delightful shady terrrace. Relax and enjoy the restful atmosphere of the comfortable, homely ambience. **www.sphinx-hotel.fr**

PEROUGES Hostellerie du Vieux Pérouges
Pl du Tilleul, 01800 **Tel** *04 74 61 00 88* **Fax** *04 74 34 77 90* **Rooms** *28*

This historic inn is a filmmaker's dream, converted from 13th-century buildings and set in a medieval hilltop village. The four ancient houses are clustered around the main square. The decor is different in each house. Ultraclassic cuisine serving regional dishes with precision. **www.hostelleriedeperouges.com**

ROMANS SUR ISERE Hôtel l'Orée du Parc
6 av Gambetta, 26100 **Tel** *04 75 70 26 12* **Fax** *04 75 05 08 23* **Rooms** *10*

After visiting le Palais Idéal du Facteur Cheval, head 16 miles (25 km) south to Romans, and relax in this charming hotel. A tastefully renovated 20th-century manor house in its own park, all the rooms are nonsmoking and filled with modern, elegant furnishings. **www.hotel-oreeparc.com**

SERVAS Le Nid à Bibi
Lalleyriat, 1960 **Tel** *04 74 21 11 47* **Fax** *04 74 21 02 83* **Rooms** *5*

A peaceful night's sleep awaits at this adorable *chambre d'hôtes* next to Bourg. Cozy, comfortable, and well-equipped rooms each have a private bathroom. Guests enjoy a homely atmosphere and have use of the living area and garden. Hearty breakfast with homemade jams, pastries, and cold meats. *Table d'hôte* on request. **http://lenidabibi.com**

ST-CYR-AU-MONT-D'OR L'Ermitage Hôtel
Chemin de l'Ermitage Mont Cindre, 69450 **Tel** *04 72 19 69 69* **Fax** *04 72 19 69 71* **Rooms** *29*

Just 15-minutes from Lyon city center, this design establishment harmonizes different materials with success: concrete, wood, glass, aluminum, and stone. The rooms are luminous with quirky accessories, ultramodern equipment, and a view of Fourvière. Lyon specialties are served in the terrace restaurant. **www.ermitage-college-hotel.com**

ST-ETIENNE Mercure Parc de l'Europe

Rue Wuppertal, 42000 **Tel** *04 77 42 81 81* **Fax** *04 77 42 81 89* **Rooms** *120*

This large, practical, modern building lacks charm, but is conveniently situated for the city center. The bedrooms are bright and well maintained, with fully equipped bathrooms. The interior has a theatrical theme. There is also a cozy bar and a contemporary restaurant serving local produce. **www.mercure.com**

TALLOIRES Hôtel l'Abbaye

Chemin des Moines, 74290 **Tel** *04 50 60 77 33* **Fax** *04 50 60 78 81* **Rooms** *33*

This elegant hotel occupying a former 17th-century Benedictine abbey is beautifully situated on the shores of Lac d'Annecy. Cézanne used to be a regular guest. The large rooms have wonderfully decorated period ceilings and antique furniture. Attractive garden and good restaurant. Closed Jan–mid-Feb. **www.abbaye-talloires.com**

VAL D'ISERE Christiania

Chef Lieu, 73152 **Tel** *04 79 06 08 25* **Fax** *04 79 41 11 10* **Rooms** *70*

Splendid modern chalet with a magnificent view of the ski slopes at this popular resort for the rich and famous. Luxurious fully equipped rooms, all with balconies, are decorated in an elegant Alpine theme. Pamper yourself in the health and fitness center. Superb buffet breakfast. **www.hotel-christiania.com**

VALLON PONT D'ARC Le Clos des Bruyères

Rte des Gorges, 07150 **Tel** *04 75 37 18 85* **Fax** *04 75 37 14 89* **Rooms** *32*

Situated in the Gorges d'Ardèche, this modern hotel, built in a Provençal style, has bedrooms that open onto the pool via a balcony or terrace. Family rooms are available. Rent a canoe or quad and take a picnic to explore the river and countryside. Nautical-themed restaurant. **www.closdesbruyeres.net**

POITOU & AQUITAINE

ARCACHON Hôtel Le Dauphin

7 av Gounod, 33120 **Tel** *05 56 83 02 89* **Fax** *05 56 54 84 90* **Rooms** *50*

This well-run hotel dating from the late 19th century is instantly recognizable from its red-and-white brickwork. It's located a few blocks back from the sea in a quiet residential district. Spick-and-span rooms have simple pine furnishings and white walls. **www.dauphin-arcachon.com**

BONNEUIL-MATOURS L'Olivier

11 rue du petit Bornais, 86210 **Tel** *05 49 02 73 53* **Rooms** *4*

This delightful bed and breakfast is on the edge of the Forêt de Moulière, close to Futuroscope, Chauvigny, Châtellerault, and Poitiers. The four bedrooms are homely and individually styled. One is in the attic and two have canopied beds. There is a living room and dining room for communal use and a delightful garden. **www.vienne-hotes-lolivier.com**

BORDEAUX La Maison du Lierre

57 rue Huguerie, 33000 **Tel** *05 56 51 92 71* **Fax** *05 56 79 15 16* **Rooms** *12*

Close to Bordeaux's chic Golden Triangle, this small hotel – its homely atmosphere more like a *chambre d'hôte* - has been renovated with flair. Rooms are stylish. Generous homemade breakfasts may be served in the interior courtyard. It is wise to reserve ahead. **www.maisondulierre.com**

BORDEAUX La Maison Bord'Eaux

113 rue Docteur Albert Barraud, 33000 **Tel** *05 56 44 00 45* **Fax** *05 56 44 17 31* **Rooms** *6*

Wine lovers will enjoy this small boutique hotel where a large range of wines is available by the glass or bottle. The owners can also arrange wine-tasting visits to châteaux. Rooms look onto a garden where breakfast and meals are often served. Parking is available, which is rare for a city hotel. **www.lamaisonbord-eaux.com**

CAP-FERRET La Maison du Bassin

5 rue des Pionniers, 33950 **Tel** *05 56 60 60 63* **Fax** *05 56 03 71 47* **Rooms** *7 (plus 4 annex rooms)*

Ultrachic and highly sought-after address at the end of the Cap-Ferret peninsula. A colonial ambience is achieved with highly polished wood, cane chairs, and arty knick-knacks. Try one of the tasty tropical rums as an aperitif, before dining on the tropical veranda. Reservations by phone only. **www.lamasiondubassin.com**

CARSAC La Villa Romaine

Saint Rome, 24200 **Tel** *05 53 28 52 07* **Fax** *05 53 28 58 10* **Rooms** *17*

This plush hotel occupies a group of beautifully restored stone buildings that stand on the site of a Gallo-Roman villa, next to some magnificent water gardens and in the heart of the Périgord Noir. Rooms are equipped with all the luxury modern comforts, and the bedrooms are all spacious and peaceful. **www.lavillaromaine.com**

CIERZAC Le Moulin de Cierzac

Rte de Cognac, 17520 **Tel** *05 45 83 01 32* **Fax** *05 45 83 03 59* **Rooms** *7*

A short drive south of Cognac is this hotel-restaurant in a 17th-century mansion set in extensive grounds. Pleasant rooms contain exposed beams; some have river views. The restaurant serves local specialties. Afterwards, choose your *digestif* from a vast array of cognacs. **www.moulindecierzac.com**

COGNAC Les Pigeons Blancs
[P] [🍴] [🏃] €€

110 rue Jules-Brisson, 16100 **Tel** *05 45 82 16 36* **Rooms** *6*

In the heart of the cognac vineyards, this 17th-century auberge offers a warm welcome and a handful of elegantly decorated rooms decked out with period furniture. Two are nonsmoking. Other facilities include an excellent restaurant and a garden. Baby-sitting available. **www.pigeons-blancs.com**

COULON Le Central
[P] [🍴] [▤] €

4 rue d'Autremont, 79510 **Tel** *05 49 35 90 20* **Fax** *05 49 35 81 07* **Rooms** *13*

Situated in the mysterious fens of the Marais Poitevin, this traditional village hotel has been in the same family for three generations. The guest rooms are bright, clean, and tasteful. Downstairs is a deservedly popular restaurant. You'll need to reserve well ahead. Disabled access. **www.hotel-lecentral-coulon.com**

EUGENIE-LES-BAINS La Maison Rose
[P] [🍴] [≈] [▦] €€€€

334 rue René Vielle, 40320 **Tel** *05 58 05 06 07* **Fax** *05 58 51 10 10* **Rooms** *31*

The illustrious chef Michel Guérard draws worshippers to Eugénie, a thermal spa dating back to the 18th century. This, the most modest of his five hotels, feels like a country house, from the rose-filled garden to the pretty guest rooms – not lavish but absolutely immaculate. Closed Dec–Jan. **www.michelguerard.com**

EUGENIE LES BAINS Les Prés d'Eugénie
[P] [🍴] [≈] [▦] [▤] €€€€€

334 rue René Vielle, 40320 **Tel** *05 58 05 06 07* **Fax** *05 58 51 10 10* **Rooms** *32*

Michel Guérard's highly acclaimed hotel has six gorgeous suites in addition to its simple but luxurious bedrooms. The 19th-century manor is famed for its *cuisine minceur* restaurants, which offer residents the option of losing weight while reveling in some of France's finest cooking. **www.michelguerard.com**

GRENADE-SUR-L'ADOUR Pain Adour et Fantaisie
[🍴] [🏃] [▤] [♿] €€

14-16 pl des Tilleuls, 40270 **Tel** *05 58 45 18 80* **Fax** *05 58 45 16 57* **Rooms** *11*

This elegant hotel overlooking Grenade's arcaded central square on one side, and the river on the other, is home to one of the region's best restaurants. In keeping with the hotel's 17th-century architecture, antiques, oak paneling, and parquet predominate. Spacious rooms. **www.chateauxhotels.com/fantaisie**

HOSSEGOR Les Hortensias du Lac
[P] [≈] €€

1578 av du Tour du Lac, 40150 **Tel** *05 58 43 99 00* **Fax** *05 58 43 42 81* **Rooms** *24*

This hotel, set in pine forests not far from the ocean and overlooking Hossegor lake, provides a peaceful retreat. Guest rooms in the 1930s villa are tranquil, with their neutral tones offset against dark wood, all with a terrace or balcony. Splendid champagne buffet breakfast. Closed mid-Nov–Easter. **www.hortensias-du-lac.com**

LA ROCHELLE Les Brises
[🔲] [P] €€

Chemin de la Digue-Richelieu, rue Philippe Vincent 17000 **Tel** *05 46 43 89 37* **Fax** *05 46 43 27 97* **Rooms** *48*

A comfortable and popular hotel within walking distance of the vieux port and the bustling city center. It's worth paying extra for a seafront room. Not only are they more spacious, but they also benefit from balconies with wonderful views out to sea and the offshore islands. **www.hotellesbrises.eu**

LE BOIS-PLAGE-EN-RE Hôtel L'Océan
[P] [🍴] [≈] €€€

172 rue St-Martin, 17580 **Tel** *05 46 09 23 07* **Fax** *05 46 09 05 40* **Rooms** *29*

There's a real seaside feel to this hotel on the southern coast of the Île de Ré. Potted palms, giant parasols, and sun-bleached wooden decking outside; inside, pretty pastels and marine motifs for the rooms. Not surprisingly, ultrafresh fish dominates the restaurant menu. Massage and beauty treatments are available. **www.re-hotel-ocean.com**

MAGESCQ Relais de la Poste
[P] [🍴] [≈] [🏃] [▦] [▤] €€€€

24, av de Maremne, 40140 **Tel** *05 58 47 70 25* **Fax** *05 58 47 76 17* **Rooms** *24*

This small and wonderfully relaxed hotel set in a 19th-century coaching inn has a garden and nicely landscaped pools. It combines comfort, celebrated cuisine, fine wines, and family tradition. You're not far from the sea here, with Bayonne and Biarritz within easy striking distance. Closed mid-Nov–Christmas. **www.relaisposte.com**

MARGAUX Le Pavillon de Margaux
[P] [🍴] [≈] €€

3 rue Georges-Mandel, 33460 **Tel** *05 57 88 77 54* **Fax** *05 57 88 77 73* **Rooms** *14*

In the center of Margaux village, this handsome hotel provides a comfortable base for exploring the Médoc vineyards. Guest rooms, which are "sponsored" by local wine châteaux, are individually styled. Some have antiques and four-posters, others rattan and floral fabrics. **www.pavillonmargaux.com**

MARTHON Château de la Couronne
[P] [≈] €€€€€

Château de la Couronne, 16380 **Tel** *05 45 62 29 96* **Rooms** *5*

A boutique château hotel and sometime film and TV location offering five suites decorated in a bold, contemporary style with original artworks. Everything is supplied for relaxation: three sitting rooms, a private movie theater, a billiard room, a music room, and a large expanse of private parkland. **www.chateaudelacouronne.com**

NIEUIL Château de Nieuil
[P] [🍴] [≈] [🏃] [▤] €€€

16270 **Tel** *05 45 71 36 38* **Fax** *05 45 71 46 45* **Rooms** *14*

King François I hunted in the extensive park surrounding this superb Renaissance château with its pepper-pot towers and sweeping staircase. A quiet night is assured in the elegant, comfortable rooms. The stables now house an excellent restaurant. **www.chateaunieuilhotel.com**

POITIERS Château du Clos de la Ribaudière   🍴 ⚏   €€

Chasseneuil Center, Chasseneuil du Poitou, 86360 **Tel** *05 49 52 86 66* **Fax** *05 49 52 86 32* **Rooms** *39*

Close to Poitiers, this magnificent hotel and restaurant is housed in a château dating back to the 18th century. The bedrooms are spacious and sophisticated. Special-price breaks are available for two people including a night's stay, meals, and either a game of golf or a visit to nearby Futuroscope. **www.ribaudiere.com**

ROCHEFORT-SUR-MER La Corderie Royale   🅿 🍴 ⚏ 🖿 🗏   €€€

Rue Audebert, 17300 **Tel** *05 46 99 35 35* **Fax** *05 46 99 78 72* **Rooms** *50*

The best place to stay in Rochefort, both for comfort and convenience, this hotel-restaurant stands on the leafy banks of the River Charente between the yacht harbor and the royal rope-making factory (after which the hotel is named). The restaurant is a good place for lunch. **www.corderieroyale.com**

ROYAN Domaine de St Palais   🅿   €€

50 rue du Logis, St Palais sur Mer, 17420 **Tel** *05 46 39 85 26* **Rooms** *4*

This elegant haven is discreetly set back from the bustling coast near Royan. It occupies a building that is largely 18th century but has a history dating back even earlier. Two of the stylish rooms overlook the garden and two look toward woods. There are also eight apartments and one suite. **www.domainedesaintpalais.eu**

SABRES Auberge des Pins   🅿 🍴 🕴   €€

Rte de la Piscine, 40630 **Tel** *05 58 08 30 00* **Fax** *05 58 07 56 74* **Rooms** *25*

From the moment you enter this attractive farmhouse, deep in the forests of the Landes Regional Park, you know you're in for a treat. This is country living at its best: old-style hospitality, homely rooms, open fires in winter, and quiet corners to curl up in with a book. Fine restaurant. **www.aubergedespins.fr**

SEIGNOSSE La Villa de l'Etang Blanc   🅿 🍴   €€€

2265 rte de l'Etang Blanc, 40510 **Tel** *05 58 72 80 15* **Fax** *05 58 72 83 67* **Rooms** *10*

This charming hotel is set in a park with direct access to the Etang Blanc. The elegant rooms are individually decorated in a romantic style. There's a good restaurant with a wonderful view of the lake. It serves traditional seasonal dishes with discreet, professional service. Closed mid-Nov–Apr. **www.villaetangblanc.fr**

ST-EMILION Au Logis des Remparts   🅿 ⚏ 🗏   €€€

18 rue Guadet, 33330 **Tel** *05 57 24 70 43* **Fax** *05 57 74 47 44* **Rooms** *17*

Outside peak season, when prices drop, this modest hotel provides a comfortable overnight stop. Its main draws are the sizeable terraced garden and swimming pool. The rooms lack character, but those on the back benefit from views over the vineyards. **www.logisdesremparts.com**

ST-EMILION Hostellerie de Plaisance   📶 🅿 🍴 🗏   €€€€€

Pl du Clocher, 33330 **Tel** *05 57 55 07 55* **Fax** *05 57 74 41 11* **Rooms** *17 (plus 4 suites)*

Upscale hotel in an exceptional location overlooking St-Emilion and its famous vineyards. Luxurious rooms boast the full range of amenities, including magnificent bathrooms. Some have private terraces. The service is top-notch and the restaurant one of the region's best. **www.hostelleriedeplaisance.com**

ST-LOUP-LAMAIRE Château de St Loup sur Thouet – The Keep   🅿   €€€€

Château de St-Loup, 79600 **Tel** *05 49 64 81 73* **Fax** *05 49 64 82 06* **Rooms** *13*

This moated medieval château is owned by a count. The keep houses bed and breakfast rooms, many with four-poster beds; the best is the Suite of the Black Prince. There are other stately rooms in the main château, which is open to visitors during the day. The extensive grounds include parkland and an orangery. **www.chateaudesaint-loup.com**

ST-SEURIN-D'UZET Blue Sturgeon   🅿 🍴 ⚏   €€

3 rue de la Cave, 17120 **Tel** *05 46 74 17 18* **Rooms** *4*

A calm, chic, eclectically furnished bed and breakfast in the small village of St-Seurin-d'Uzet, which is alleged to be the first place in Europe to have produced caviar in the 1920s (hence the hotel's name). Good beaches nearby and the famous vineyards of the Médoc are just across the Gironde estuary. Dinner is served on request. **www.bluesturgeon.com**

TRIZAY Les Jardins du Lac   🅿 🍴 ⚏ 🕴   €€

3 chemin de Fontchaude, 17250 **Tel** *05 46 82 03 56* **Fax** *05 46 82 03 55* **Rooms** *8*

A well-run hotel midway between Rochefort and Saintes. The modern buildings are surrounded by landscaped gardens with a trout lake and woodland. Airy and well-maintained rooms all offer lake views. Meals are served outside in fine weather. A lovely, relaxing place to stay. **www.jardins-du-lac.com**

PERIGORD, QUERCY, & GASCONY

AGEN Hôtel Château des Jacobins   🅿 🗏   €€€

1 pl des Jacobins, 47000 **Tel** *05 53 47 03 31* **Fax** *05 53 47 02 80* **Rooms** *15*

Built in the early 19th century, this small, ivy-clad château with a walled garden is an oasis of calm in the city center. The rooms are elegantly decorated with period furniture and chandeliers. There's secure parking and you'll find plenty of fine restaurants within easy walking distance. **www.chateau-des-jacobins.com**

Key to Price Guide *see p550* **Key to Symbols** *see back cover flap*

ALBI La Regence George V €

27–29 av Maréchal Joffre, 81000 **Tel** *05 63 54 24 16* **Fax** *05 63 49 90 78* **Rooms** *20*

This comfortable, inexpensive hotel near the train station and not far from the city center offers a choice of standard rooms or larger junior suites. All are decorated in warm and bright colors. Outside there is a terrace and a small garden. Breakfast only but there are plenty of restaurants nearby. **www.laregence-georgev.fr**

ALBI Hostellerie du Grand St Antoine €€€

17 rue St-Antoine, 81000 **Tel** *05 63 54 04 04* **Fax** *05 63 47 10 47* **Rooms** *44*

Owned by the same family for five generations, the Grand St Antoine claims to be one of the oldest hotels in France. Guests have the use of a swimming pool and a tennis court 2-miles (3-km) away. Parking is available for an extra charge. The restaurant serves traditional southwestern cuisine. **www.hotel-saint-antoine-albi.com**

BEYNAC-ET-CAZENAC Café de la Rivière €

Bourg, 24220 **Tel** *05 53 28 35 49* **Rooms** *3*

This renowned restaurant situated above the River Dordogne has three simple bed and breakfast rooms. There is one double and two twins; all have wooden floors, white linen bedspreads, and en-suite bathrooms. Free Wi-Fi Internet access is also available. Closed Nov–Apr. **www.cafedelariviere.com**

BOURDEILLES Hostellerie Les Griffons €€

24310 **Tel** *05 53 45 45 35* **Fax** *05 53 45 45 20* **Rooms** *10*

All of the rooms in this 16th-century mansion have plenty of character, with exposed beams and vividly colored paints and fabrics. Some rooms are in the attic and others have views over the river. The restaurant serves dinner plus Sunday lunch. Closed Nov–mid-Apr. **www.griffons.fr**

BRANTOME Le Moulin de l'Abbaye €€€€€

1 rte de Bourdeilles, 24310 **Tel** *05 53 05 80 22* **Fax** *05 53 05 75 27* **Rooms** *19*

Treat yourself to a night of luxury in this romantic, creeper-covered mill on the River Dronne. Rooms are in the mill and in two handsome old houses nearby, but all share the same fresh yet sophisticated decor. Terraced waterside gardens proivde the perfect breakfast spot. Closed mid-Nov–Apr. **www.moulinabbaye.com**

CHAMPAGNAC-DE-BELAIR Le Moulin du Roc €€€€

Av Eugène le Roy, 24530 **Tel** *05 53 02 86 00* **Fax** *05 53 54 21 31* **Rooms** *13*

In a magical setting on the river Dronne, just outside Brantôme, is this luxury hotel hidden under swathes of greenery in a converted 17th-century watermill. In addition to the sumptuous, individually styled rooms, there is a superb restaurant, an indoor pool, and tennis court. Closed Dec–Mar. **www.moulinduroc.com**

CHANCELADE Château des Reynats €€€

Av des Reynats, 24650 **Tel** *05 53 03 53 59* **Fax** *05 53 03 44 84* **Rooms** *50*

Just west of Périgueux, this charming 19th-century château makes for an agreeable night's stay. Standard rooms in the "Orangerie" annex are bright and breezy, but for real atmosphere upgrade to the château rooms. There's a top-notch resturant, too, and spacious grounds. **www.chateau-hotel-perigord.com**

COLY Manoir d'Hautegente €€€€

Haute Gente, 24120 **Tel** *05 53 51 68 03* **Fax** *05 53 50 38 52* **Rooms** *17*

Not far from Sarlat and the Lascaux caves is this picturesque manor house, once the mill and forge of an abbey. It is now a family-run, friendly hotel with log fires, private fishing, and well-tended riverside gardens. Half-board mandatory in high-season; the food is excellent. Closed Nov–Apr. **www.manoir-hautegente.com**

CONDOM Le Logis des Cordeliers €

Rue de la Paix, 32100 **Tel** *05 62 28 03 68* **Fax** *05 62 68 29 03* **Rooms** *21*

Modern hotel offering modest but well priced rooms in the center of Condom. Picture windows lend space and light and many rooms have balconies overlooking the pool. There is no in-house restaurant, but you can eat in the highly rated Table des Cordeliers next door. Closed Jan. **www.logisdescordeliers.com**

CORDES SUR CIEL Hostellerie du Vieux Cordes €€

21 rue St-Michel, 81170 **Tel** *05 63 53 79 20* **Fax** *05 63 56 02 47* **Rooms** *21*

At the top of the medieval town, with lovely views over the valley, this hotel occupies a three-story stone building with vaulted ceilings. Prices of the rooms vary according to their size and style. Some are quite elaborately decorated, while others, labeled "eco," are simpler. The restaurant serves dishes based on local produce. **www.vieuxcordes.fr**

CUQ-TOULZA Cuq en Terrasses €€€

Cuq le Château, 81470 **Tel** *05 63 82 54 00* **Fax** *05 63 82 54 11* **Rooms** *7*

A renovated 18th-century hilltop house in the Cocagne region, midway between Toulouse and Castres. The rooms have overhead beams and varnished flagstone floors. Nestling in the lovely gardens is an inviting pool. The restaurant menu draws on the produce of local farms. **www.cuqenterrasses.com**

DOMME L'Esplanade €€

Rue du Pont Carrel, 24250 **Tel** *05 53 28 31 41* **Fax** *05 53 28 49 92* **Rooms** *15*

Perched on the edge of a cliff, the best rooms in this elegant hotel offer panoramic views of the Dordogne valley. Some have canopied four-poster beds to match the refined, opulent decor. Less dramatic but very comfortable rooms are among the streets of the medieval bastide. Closed mid-Nov–Mar. **www.esplanade-perigord.com**

FIGEAC Château du Vigier du Roy

52 rue Emile Zola, 46100 **Tel** *05 65 50 05 05* **Fax** *05 65 50 06 06* **Rooms** *9*

Centuries ago, this mansion with its 14th-century tower was once the residence of a judge, the King's representative in Figeac. The rooms all have a medieval flavor, with four-poster or canopied beds. The restaurant is in the former guards' room. **www.chateau-viguier-figeac.com**

GOUDOURVILLE Château de Goudourville

82400 **Tel** *05 63 29 09 06* **Fax** *05 63 39 7 5 22* **Rooms** *6*

This château betweeen Agen and Moissac dates back to the 11th century and the guest rooms are redolent with history. The rooms – some of them enormous – are decorated with 18th-century furniture and tapestries and have views over the valley, the village, or the battlements. **www.chateau-goudourville.fr**

LACAVE Le Pont de l'Ouysse

Le Pont de l'Ouysse, 46200 **Tel** *05 65 37 87 04* **Fax** *05 65 32 77 41* **Rooms** *14*

There's a Provençal air to this chic restaurant-with-rooms in riverside gardens not far from Rocamadour. Inside, cool creams blend with ocher hues, and the rooms and two apartments are fabulously quiet. In their fourth generation, the Chambon family has created a real hideaway. Inventive cuisine. **www.lepontdelouysse.fr**

LE BUGUE SUR VEZERE Domaine de la Barde

Route de Périgeux, 24260 **Tel** *05 53 07 16 54* **Fax** *05 53 54 76 19* **Rooms** *18*

Elegant guest rooms are housed within an 18th-century manor house (nine rooms), an old mill (eight rooms), and the forge (one room). The large grounds include classical gardens and a jet-stream swimming pool. If you want to get away from it all, there are riverside paths and meadow walks nearby. **www.domainedelabarde.com**

LECTOURE Hôtel de Bastard

Rue Lagrange, 32700 **Tel** *05 62 68 82 44* **Fax** *05 62 68 76 81* **Rooms** *31*

Despite its name, this elegant hotel is one of the best in the Gers. Antique furnishings are coupled with modern comforts in an 18th-century townhouse. Facilities include a small garden, sun deck, and swimming pool. Refined regional cuisine makes the restaurant perennially popular. Closed Dec 22–Feb 1. **www.hotel-de-bastard.com**

LES-EYZIES-DE-TAYAC Les Glycines

24620 **Tel** *05 53 06 97 07* **Fax** *05 53 06 92 19* **Rooms** *24*

A charming and luxurious small hotel in Périgord Noir, which is particularly convenient for visiting the prehistoric painted caves nearby. The best rooms (junior suites) have their own private terraces and direct access to the garden. A choice of picnics can be ordered from the reception desk. **www.les-glycines-dordogne.com**

MARTEL Relais Ste-Anne

Rue du Pourtanel, 46600 **Tel** *05 65 37 40 56* **Fax** *05 65 37 42 82* **Rooms** *21*

Behind the discreet entrance hides a lovely old building, once a girls' boarding school complete with chapel, in spacious grounds. Everything is designed for a relaxing stay, from the beautifully appointed rooms – some with private terrace – to the heated pool. Hearty breakfasts. Closed mid-Nov–Mar. **www.relais-sainte-anne.com**

MAUROUX Hostellerie Le Vert

46700 **Tel** *05 65 36 51 36* **Fax** *05 65 36 56 84* **Rooms** *6*

Ancient cedar trees shade the grounds of this 17th-century house, part of a former wine estate at the heart of the Cahors wine region. The rooms are spacious and exposed stone walls give them great character. Reserve for dinner in the cool dining room or on the flower-filled terrace. Closed Nov–Mar. **www.hotellevert.com**

MERCUES Château de Mercuès

46090 **Tel** *05 65 20 00 01* **Fax** *05 65 20 05 72* **Rooms** *30*

Dominating the Lot valley is this turreted 13th-century château where the bishops of nearby Cahors once lived. It is now a luxury hotel offering rooms on a suitably grand scale, gourmet dining among chandeliers or in the courtyard, tennis courts, and extensive parkland. **www.chateaudemercues.com**

MOISSAC Le Moulin de Moissac

Esplanade du Moulin, 82200 **Tel** *05 63 32 88 88* **Fax** *05 63 32 02 08* **Rooms** *36*

Though not the most attractive building, this hotel in a former mill more than compensates with its quiet, riverside location, efficient service, and well-equipped rooms. All come with DVD/CD player, Wi-Fi Internet, and coffee machine. Central Moissac is a stroll away. **www.lemoulindemoissac.com**

MONTCUQ EN QUERCY Domaine de St Géry

46800 **Tel** *05 65 31 82 51* **Fax** *05 65 22 92 89* **Rooms** *5*

The carefully maintained grounds of this hotel yield costly truffles, which have pride of place on the dining room menu. All the rooms are different, the most unusual is a vaulted cellar with two terraces. The others have either a private terrace or direct access to the garden. **www.saint-gery.com**

NONTRON La Maison des Beaux Arts

7 av du Général Leclerc, 24300 **Tel** *05 53 56 39 77* **Rooms** *5*

The "House of Fine Arts" is a restored 19th-century townhouse in pleasant Nontron. Inside, it is light and brightly decorated and there are magnificent views from the windows. Drawing and painting courses are sometimes held here. There is also a self-contained apartment available for rent. **www.la-maison-des-beaux-arts.com**

ROCAMADOUR Domaine de la Rhue
P ☷ €€€

46500 **Tel** *05 65 33 71 50* **Fax** *05 65 33 72 48* **Rooms** *14*

A short drive from Rocamadour is this peaceful hotel in beautifully converted 19th-century stables. Exposed beams and stonework give the spacious rooms an upscale rustic charm. Some come with a terrace, others with a kitchenette. The nearest restaurants are in Rocamadour. **www.domainedelarhue.com**

SARLAT Le Moulin Pointu
⊞ ☷ €

Ste Nathalene, 24200 **Tel** *05 53 28 15 54* **Fax** *05 53 28 15 54* **Rooms** *5*

Conveniently located on the outskirts of Sarlat, this bed and breakfast has cozy rooms with direct access to the garden, which has a pond and a small river. Breakfast can be enjoyed on the terrace near the swimming pool. Dinner (available on request) is shared with the family and other guests. **www.moulinpointu.com**

SEGUENVILLE Château de Seguenville
€€

Cabanac Seguenville, 31480 **Tel** *05 62 13 42 67* **Fax** *05 62 13 42 68* **Rooms** *5*

Perched on a hill near Toulouse, this château has great views of the surrounding countryside. A monumental staircase leads to the bedrooms, which are decorated with warm and bright colors; some have antique baths and sinks. The panoramic terrace doubles as a dining room for breakfast and dinner in summer. **www.chateau-de-seguenville.com**

ST-AFFRIQUE-LES-MONTAGNES Domaine de Rasigous
P ⊞ ☷ €€

Domaine de Rasigous, 81290 **Tel** *05 63 73 30 50* **Rooms** *8*

This genteel estate offers a peaceful spot within easy reach of Albi, Castres, Toulouse, and Carcassonne. Three of the spacious rooms are suites and there is a large warm lounge where you can enjoy tea by the fireside. Outside, the park is shaded by ancient trees. Free bike rental is available. Closed mid–Nov–mid–Mar. **www.domainederasigous.com**

ST-CIRQ-LAPOPIE Le Château de St-Cirq Lapopie
☷ €€€€

Le Bourg, 46330 **Tel** *05 65 31 27 48* **Rooms** *5*

An exquisitely restored château in the middle of one of the prettiest villages in France. The most original feature is the heated indoor swimming pool carved out of the rock on which the village stands. Rooms are beautifully decorated. Meals are not available. Closed Oct–May. **www.longitudehotels.com/chateau-st-cirq-lapopie/en**

ST-JEAN DE CORNAC Le Manoir de Saint Jean
P ⊞ ☷ ⌂ €€€

82200 **Tel** *05 63 05 02 34* **Fax** *05 63 05 07 50* **Rooms** *10*

A 19th-century manor house in the Quercy Blanc has been converted into Le Manoir de Saint Jean. The hotel is surrounded by orchards, vineyards, and ancient parkland, and has a pretty terrace giving onto the garden. The restaurant is noted for its fine cuisine. Each room is allocated its own covered parking space. **www.manoirsaintjean.com**

ST-VIVIEN Auberge du Moulin de Labique
P ⊞ ☷ €€€

St Eutrope de Born, Villeréal, 47210 **Tel** *05 53 01 63 90* **Fax** *05 53 01 73 17* **Rooms** *6*

This welcoming 18th-century country residence is decorated with antique furniture, paintings, and patterned wallpaper. Enjoy breakfast or a glass of local wine on the terrace while listening to the babbling mill stream. The excellent dinners are created with home-grown food and local produce. **www.moulin-de-labique.fr**

TEYSSODE Domaine d'en Naudet
P ☷ ▥ €€

81220 **Tel** *05 63 70 50 59* **Rooms** *4*

One singular room here is in a converted watchtower; the others are in the old barn and stables facing south over the garden and a nearby Roman road. Breakfast can be enjoyed on the upper terrace with views of the countryside. There are tennis courts and a golf course nearby. Wi-Fi Internet access is also available. **www.domainenaudet.com**

TOULOUSE Les Loges de St Sernin
▧ ▤ €€

12 rue St Bernard, 31000 **Tel** *05 61 24 44 44* **Rooms** *4*

This renovated private city house with guest bedrooms on the upper floors offers superb comfort. On a street near Toulouse's principal monument, Basilique St-Sernin, and within easy walking distance from the main square, it could not be more conveniently located. The owner is welcoming and obliging. **www.dormiratoulouse.net**

TOULOUSE Hôtel des Beaux Arts
▧ P ⊞ ▤ €€€€

1 pl du Pont Neuf, 31000 **Tel** *05 34 45 42 42* **Fax** *05 34 45 42 43* **Rooms** *19*

Behind a beautiful Belle Epoque façade, beside the Pont Neuf, lies a chic hotel with modern comforts. The less expensive rooms are on the small side – better to upgrade for river views and more space. For a special occasion, opt for room 42 with its own tiny terrace among the roof tiles. **www.hoteldesbeauxarts.com**

THE PYRENEES

AINHOA Ithurria
P ⊞ ☷ ▤ €€€

Pl du Fronton, 64250 **Tel** *05 59 29 92 11* **Fax** *05 59 29 81 28* **Rooms** *28*

This pretty 17th-century Basque inn was a stop on the pilgrimage route to Compostela. Opposite is the village's *pelota* court. Rooms are comfortable and prettily decorated, and the cozy dining room has an open fireplace, oak beams, and a menu with local specialties. Closed Dec–mid-Apr. **www.ithurria.com**

ANGLET Château de Brindos

1 allée du Château, 64600 **Tel** *05 59 23 89 80* **Fax** *05 59 23 89 81* **Rooms** *29*

Set in extensive, wooded grounds, this luxurious country house hotel offers gracious living beside a peaceful lake. Modern facilities include a weight room, sauna, and *hammam*, with the beach and a golf course a short drive away. Enjoy breakfast on the jetty over the lake. **www.chateaudebrindos.com**

ARBONNE Laminak

Route de St Pée, 64210 **Tel** *05 59 41 95 40* **Fax** *05 59 41 87 65* **Rooms** *12*

A cozy hotel in a big, beautifully furnished Basque house with countryside and mountain views from the windows. Three of the rooms have private terraces, and outside there is a large garden. Light evening meals are available on request. Within reach of eight golf courses. **www.hotel-laminak.com**

ARGELES GAZOST Hôtel le Miramont

44 av des Pyrénées, 65400 **Tel** *05 62 97 01 26* **Fax** *05 62 97 56 67* **Rooms** *27*

This stylish hotel harking back to the 1930s is set amid manicured gardens in an attractive spa town. Eight rooms, furnished with antiques, are in a separate villa in the gardens, sharing the facilities of the main wing. Chef Pierre Pucheu serves Atlantic-Pyrenees delicacies. **www.hotelmiramont.com**

ARREAU Hôtel d'Angleterre

Rte Luchon, 65240 **Tel** *05 62 98 63 30* **Fax** *05 62 98 69 66* **Rooms** *17*

This 17th-century inn, set in a pretty village of slate-roofed houses in the foothills of the Pyrenees, offers a good restaurant, plainly furnished but comfortable rooms, a garden, swimming pool, terrace, and children's games area. A great base for exploring the stunning countryside. **www.hotel-angleterre-arreau.com**

AURIGNAC Le Moulin

Samouillan, 31420 **Tel** *05 61 98 86 92* **Rooms** *2*

A restored mill in a quiet tributary valley of the Garonne. Choose your room by theme: Zen, elephants, or French country house. There is a minimum two-night stay and discounts are available for longer stays. Meditation and other spiritual workshops are often held here, or you can relax in the large garden. **www.moulin-vert.net**

BEAUCENS Eth Berye Petit

15 route de Vielle, 65400 **Tel** *05 62 97 90 02* **Rooms** *3*

Family-run bed and breakfast in an 18th-century farmhouse situated in a quiet hamlet south of Lourdes. Two of the rooms are cozy spaces in the attic; the third room is larger and has its own balcony with mountain views. *Table d'hôte* dinner on Friday and Saturday evenings by prior arrangement. **www.beryepetit.com**

BIARRITZ Villa Le Goëland

12 plateau d'Atalaye, 64200 **Tel** *05 59 24 25 76* **Rooms** *4*

This grand old villa is close to both the town center and the beach. There are magnificent views over the Port Vieux, the Rocher de la Vierge, and the distant coast of Spain. One room has its own large private terrace. Because it is a family home, no meals are available, but there are a number of good restaurants nearby. **www.villagoeland-biarritz.com**

BIARRITZ Hôtel du Palais

1 av de l'Impératrice, 64200 **Tel** *05 59 41 64 00* **Fax** *05 59 41 67 99* **Rooms** *132*

The grande dame of Biarritz's hotel scene, with an ambience harking back to the resort's Belle Epoque heyday. A magnificent heated seawater pool, direct beach access, a putting green, a playground, and kids' pool complement the lovely rooms and outstanding restaurants. **www.hotel-du-palais.com**

CAMON Château de Camon

Camon, 9500 **Tel** *05 61 60 31 23* **Rooms** *9*

This massive abbey, dating back to the 10th century, dominates a pretty fortified village within easy reach of Mirepoix and Montségur. Classically French rooms are sumptuous and spacious. The restaurant (dinner only) draws on local and seasonal ingredients. In summer, tables are set in the abbey cloister. Closed Nov–mid-Mar. **www.chateaudecamon.com**

ESPELETTE Hôtel Euzkadi

285 rte Karrika Nagusia, 64250 **Tel** *05 59 93 91 88* **Fax** *05 59 93 90 19* **Rooms** *27*

Set in quiet countryside not far from the Atlantic beaches, this small and friendly family-run hotel has a pretty terrace, well-appointed rooms, a large swimming pool, tennis courts, and secure parking. Owners Michèle and André Darriadou's restaurant serves Basque-influenced dishes. **www.hotel-restaurant-euzkadi.com**

ISSOR Les 3 Baudets

64570 **Tel** *05 59 34 41 98* **Rooms** *5*

An 18th-century former farmhouse in a peaceful location surrounded by woods and meadows between Arette and Oloron-Ste-Marie. A good base from which to explore the central-western Pyrenees. It has five spacious rooms and a restaurant in the old sheep barn where grilled meats and homemade desserts are served. **www.3baudets-pyrenees.com**

LASSEUBE Maison Rancésamy

Quartier Rey, 64290 **Tel** *05 59 04 26 37* **Rooms** *5*

This delightful rural retreat in the undulating countryside northwest of Oloron-Ste-Marie is run by charming and hospitable owners. The rooms are cozy and meals (*table d'hôte* dinner only) are exquisitely prepared. A place to unwind and enjoy the peace, or to use as a base while exploring the Pyrenees. **www.missbrowne.com**

LOUHOSSOA Domaine de Silencenia
64250 Tel 05 59 93 35 60 Rooms 5

Just off the road between St-Jean-Pied-de-Port and Cambo-les-Bains lies this bed and breakfast in its own grounds with a swimming pool and small lake. The cozy bedrooms are individually decorated and equipped with four-poster beds. Breakfast and an excellent *table d'hôte* dinner are available. **www.domaine-silencenia.com**

LOURDES Grand Hôtel de la Grotte
66 rue de la Grotte, 65100 Tel 05 62 94 58 87 Fax 05 62 94 20 50 Rooms 83

One of the grandest hotels in the historic pilgrimage town of Lourdes, close to the famous grotto and fortress, with large rooms furnished opulently in Louis XVI style – some with views of the cathedral. The restaurants offer a choice of buffet or brasserie dining. Closed Nov–mid-Apr. **www.hotel-grotte.com**

MAUBOURGUET La Maison at Maubourguet
40 rue de l'hotel de ville, 65700 Tel 05 62 31 71 19 Fax 05 62 31 71 19 Rooms 3

This small English-run bed and breakfast in an untouristy town north of Tarbes is an ideal base for exploring western Gascony. The owners couldn't be more welcoming and obliging. The rooms are decorated with warmth and charm. Private, secluded garden with swimming pool. Parking in the square nearby. **www.maisonatmaubourguet.com**

MIREPOIX La Maison des Consuls
6 pl Maréchal Leclerc, 09500 Tel 05 61 68 81 81 Fax 05 61 68 81 15 Rooms 8

Housed in a charming 14th-century building that was once the district's courtroom, this hotel is located on a renowned medieval square in the heart of this picturesque little town. The rooms are filled with an eclectic array of antiques. The café-bar serves breakfast and snacks. **www.maisondesconsuls.com**

MONEIN Maison Canterou
Quartier Laquidée, 64360 Tel 05 59 21 41 38 Rooms 5

A traditional farmhouse with inner courtyard on a wine estate producing Jurançon wines, sitting on the rolling Béarn hills. All the rooms are prettily decorated. "Palombière" under the eaves is spacious, while "Mansengou" has a balcony opening out to face the Pyrenees. "Cupidon" is for romantics. *Table d'hôte* is available on request.

ORTHEZ Reine Jeanne
44 rue Bourg Vieux, 64300 Tel 05 59 67 00 76 Fax 05 59 69 09 63 Rooms 30

Occupying an 18th-century building in this historic Béarnaise town straddling the Gave de Pau river, this pleasant hotel has small guest rooms around a sheltered courtyard, as well as a modern wing with larger rooms. Country-style restaurant with traditional cooking. **www.reine-jeanne.fr**

PAU Bristol
3 rue Gambetta, 64000 Tel 05 59 27 72 98 Fax 05 59 27 87 80 Rooms 22

This longstanding hotel (founded in 1903) is centrally located making it ideal for exploring Pau on foot. The rooms are tastefully decorated and varied, some have a balcony while others have a view of the Pyrenees. The bathrooms are equipped with large baths and showers. Free Wi-Fi is available. **www.hotelbristol-pau.com**

PAU Hôtel du Parc Beaumont
1 av Edouard VII, 64000 Tel 05 59 11 84 00 Fax 05 59 11 85 00 Rooms 80

This luxurious modern hotel, part of the Concorde group, stands in beautiful grounds next to Pau's casino and palm-lined boulevard with great views of the Pyrenees. Rooms are lavishly furnished, and there is a heated pool, whirlpool, sauna, and *hammam* (Turkish bath). **www.hotel-parc-beaumont.com**

SARE Ttakoinenborda
Maison Ttakoinenborda, 64310 Tel 05 59 47 51 42 Rooms 4

A traditional 17th-century farmhouse near the beautiful town of Sare, surrounded by fields and woods. *Table d'hôte* dinner includes Basque specialties and homemade bread. A useful base from which to explore the inland Basque Country and the coast or to hop over the border into Spain. **http://guesthouse.sare.france.com**

SARE Hôtel Arraya
Pl du Village, 64310 Tel 05 59 54 20 46 Fax 05 59 54 27 04 Rooms 20

Modern facilities blend with old-world character at this half-timbered hotel on the pilgrimage route to Compostela. Whitewashed stone walls are half-covered in foliage, bedrooms are rustic and decorated in Basque colors, and the restaurant serves regional specialties. Closed Nov–Mar. **www.arraya.com**

SAUVETERRE DE BEARN La Maison de Navarre
Quartier St Marc, 64390 Tel 05 59 38 55 28 Fax 05 59 38 55 71 Rooms 7

This pink mansion house in a beautiful medieval village has bright, airy guest rooms. Comfortable, good value for money, and child friendly. The family donkey, Zebulon, lives in the garden. The beaches of the Atlantic coast are not too far away. Excellent restaurant. Closed Nov–Apr. **www.lamaisondenavarre.com**

ST-ETIENNE DE BAÏGORRY Hôtel Arcé
Rte Col d'Ispeguy, 64430 Tel 05 59 37 40 14 Fax 05 59 37 40 27 Rooms 20

This welcoming Basque inn is set in the Aldudes valley, in the foothills of the Pyrenees, ideal for exploring the Basque country. The pool is on the opposite bank of the river, along with a tennis court. There is a pleasant restaurant terrace and guest rooms with modern styling. Closed mid-Nov–mid-Mar. **www.hotel-arce.com**

ST GIRONS Hôtel Eychenne `P ⑪ ≈`   €€€
8 av Paul Laffont, 09200 **Tel** *05 61 04 04 50* **Fax** *05 61 96 07 20* **Rooms** *35*

The former coaching inn has been run by the same family for seven generations, and the light, airy bedrooms and gracious public areas are filled with antiques and heirlooms. The facilities are modern, however, and there is a pretty garden where you can lunch in the open air. **www.ariege.com/hotel-eychenne/**

ST JEAN-DE-LUZ La Devinière `P`   €€€
5 rue Loquin, 64500 **Tel** *05 59 26 05 51* **Fax** *05 59 51 26 38* **Rooms** *10*

The bedrooms in this charming 18th-century building are all different, prettily decorated, and furnished with antiques, artworks, and rare books. There is a cozy lounge-library with an open fireplace and a grand piano, and a breakfast-tea room. There is also a tiny garden, but no restaurant. **www.hotel-la-deviniere.com**

ST JEAN-PIED-DE-PORT Hôtel les Pyrénées `⚀ P ⑪ ≈ ♣ ⛾ 目`   €€€
19 pl du Général-de-Gaulle, 64220 **Tel** *05 59 37 01 01* **Fax** *05 59 37 18 97* **Rooms** *20*

This 18th-century coaching inn stands at the French end of the Roncevaux pass, where the pilgrims' route to Santiago de Compostela crosses the Pyrenees. Immaculate rooms, health club with heated outdoor pool, and a restaurant offering both gastronomic and budget menus. **www.hotel-les-pyrenees.com**

ST-LIZIER Villa Belisama `⑪ ≈`   €€
Rue Notre Dame, 09190 **Tel** *05 61 02 83 24* **Rooms** *3*

In a historic village above St-Girons lies this charming bed and breakfast in a restored house (parts of which date to the 12th century). Guest rooms are large and there is a garden, a small pool, and a library with an esoteric collection of books. Breakfast as well as *table d'hôte* dinner on request. **www.ariege.com/belisama**

LANGUEDOC-ROUSSILLON

AIGUES-MORTES Hôtel des Croisades `P ⑪ 目`   €
2 rue du Port, 30220 **Tel** *04 66 53 67 85* **Fax** *04 66 53 72 95* **Rooms** *15*

Just outside the ramparts, beside the canal, this appealing hotel has a pretty garden, modern and well-equipped rooms, and helpful staff. The sights of historic Aigues Mortes are a short walk away, and the wetlands and beaches of the Camargue are nearby. Parking for a fee. **www.lescroisades.fr**

AIGUES-MORTES Hôtel St Louis `P ⑪`   €€
10 rue Amiral Courbet, 30220 **Tel** *04 66 53 72 68* **Fax** *04 66 53 75 92* **Rooms** *22*

Spacious rooms with modern comforts and a location next to the famous Constance Tower make this friendly hotel in an 18th-century building one of the better places to stay in Aigues-Mortes. Good restaurant, pretty patio, and garage parking available for a fee. Closed mid-Oct–Easter. **www.lesaintlouis.fr**

BARJAC Hôtel Le Mas du Terme `P ⑪ ≈ ♣ 目`   €€
Rte de Bagnoles sur Ceze, 30430 **Tel** *04 66 24 56 31* **Fax** *04 66 24 58 54* **Rooms** *23*

Set among its own vineyards and lavender fields, this sturdy old stone farmhouse-hotel in the heart of the Ardèche has plenty of character, lovely surroundings, charming bedrooms and public areas, and a fine restaurant. Activities for children include riding, ping-pong, and *boules*. **www.masduterme.com**

BEZIERS Hôtel le Champ-de-Mars `P`   €
17 rue de Metz, 34500 **Tel** *04 67 28 35 53* **Fax** *04 67 28 61 42* **Rooms** *10*

This family-run establishment offers comfortable, good-sized bedrooms. Located in a quiet side street, it is close to the sights, restaurants, and cafés of historic Béziers. Baskets filled with geraniums adorn the front, while most rooms overlook the small, flower-filled back garden. **www.hotel-champdemars.com**

BEZIERS Clos de Moussanne `P ≈`   €€
Route de Pezenas, 34500 **Tel** *04 67 39 31 81* **Rooms** *4*

The imposing entrance to this *chambre d'hôtes,* sheltered by two plane trees, is at the end of a leafy alley. The sophisticated bedrooms in this former convent have parquet floors, contemporary furnishings, and modern bathrooms. The best also have a terrace overlooking the pool. *Table d'hôte* on request. **www.leclosdemoussanne.com**

BIZE-MINERVOIS La Bastide Cabezac `P ⑪ ≈ 目 ♿`   €€
18–20 Hameau Cabezac, 11120 **Tel** *04 68 46 66 10* **Fax** *04 68 46 66 29* **Rooms** *12*

A relaxing stay awaits at this charming bastide, which nestles among olive trees and vines. Outside there are typical ocher-colored walls and shuttered windows; inside, the rooms are modern and comfortable with warm, sunny colors and regional furniture. The restaurant is excellent, and wine tastings can be arranged. **www.la-bastide-cabezac.com**

BOUZIGUES La Côte Bleue `P ⑪ ≈`   €€
Av Louis Tudesq, 34140 **Tel** *04 67 78 31 42* **Fax** *04 67 78 35 49* **Rooms** *31*

This modern hotel close to the charming fishing village of Meze, on the inner shore of the calm Thau lagoon, has somewhat bland rooms but fantastic sea views from the balconies. Its highly regarded restaurant specializes in plump, tasty oysters, shellfish, and crustaceans. **www.la-cote-bleue.fr**

Key to Price Guide *see p550* **Key to Symbols** *see back cover flap*

BRIGNAC La Missare

9 rue de Clermont, 34800 **Tel** *04 67 96 07 67* **Rooms** *4*

Sculptured balconies and carved stone walls contrast with the original role of this 19th-century farmhouse. The former outhouses have been converted into delightful *chambres d'hôtes*; each room individually decorated with Louis XV beds and eclectic *objets d'art* collected by the owners. **www.la.missare.free.fr**

CARCASSONNE Des Trois Couronnes

2 rue Trois Couronnes, 11000 **Tel** *04 68 25 36 10* **Fax** *04 68 25 92 92* **Rooms** *69*

This businesslike hotel looks across the river Aude towards the battlements of medieval Carcassonne, and its fourth-floor restaurant has unbeatable views of the floodlit ramparts at night. Very good value, with much better facilities than most local hotels in its price bracket. **www.hotel-destroiscouronnes.com**

CARCASSONNE Hôtel de la Cité

Pl August-Pierre Pont, 11000 **Tel** *04 68 71 98 71* **Fax** *04 68 71 50 15* **Rooms** *61*

The finest hotel in the Languedoc-Roussillon region, with immaculate service, opulent rooms, a glorious pool, formal gardens, superb restaurants, and an unbeatable location within Carcassonne's medieval town, La Cité. Golf, canoeing, and white-water rafting are available nearby. **www.hoteldelacite.com**

CASTILLON DU GARD Le Vieux Castillon

Rue Turion Sabatier, 30210 **Tel** *04 66 37 61 61* **Fax** *04 66 37 28 17* **Rooms** *32*

Restored buildings in a medieval village have been converted into a stylish, discreet, and prestigious hotel with fine facilities and wonderful food. Le Vieux Castillon is part of the prestigious Relais et Châteaux consortium, living up to demanding standards. Reserve well in advance. **www.vieuxcastillon.com**

CERET La Terrasse au Soleil

1500 rte de Fontfrede, 66400 **Tel** *04 68 87 01 94* **Fax** *04 68 87 39 24* **Rooms** *41*

This hotel is perched on the slopes above the village of Céret (where Picasso lived and worked) and has great views of Mt. Canigou and the Pyrenees. The restaurant is renowned for its regional cuisine. This is a great place for an active family, with pretty rooms and good facilities. Closed Dec–Mar. **www.terrasse-au-soleil.com**

COLLIOURE Relais des Trois Mas

Rte de Port-Vendres, 66190 **Tel** *04 68 82 05 07* **Fax** *04 68 82 38 08* **Rooms** *23*

This lovely hotel comprises several restored old buildings in pine-shaded gardens, with superb views of the Côte du Vermeille and the port and town of Collioure. Most rooms have terraces or verandas, and all have sea views. La Balette restaurant has a fine traditional menu. **www.relaisdestroismas.com**

FERRIERES-LES-VERRERIES Mas de Baumes

34190 **Tel** *04 66 80 88 80* **Fax** *04 66 80 88 82* **Rooms** *7*

This converted glassworks hides in an isolated location. Bedrooms each reveal a different theme – Barbara Cartland, Oriental, or 18th century – with contemporary decor that blends elegantly with the ancient stone building. Refined, yet relaxed ambience. Original cuisine served in the restaurant. Closed Nov–Easter. **www.oustaldebaumes.com**

MOLITG-LES-BAINS Château de Riell

66500 **Tel** *04 68 05 04 40* **Fax** *04 68 05 04 37* **Rooms** *22*

Exuberant Baroque-style château rising out of the pine trees. The interior is very contemporary with stone floors, ocher tones, and a flamboyant jungle-lounge. Stylish, comfortable rooms, some located in maisonettes in the park. Generous, creative cuisine is served in the *bodega*-type restaurant. Closed Nov–Easter. **www.chateauderiell.com**

MONTPELLIER Hôtel du Palais

3 rue Palais des Guilhem, 34000 **Tel** *04 67 60 47 38* **Fax** *04 67 60 40 23* **Rooms** *26*

The Hôtel du Palais is in an attractive, century-old building in the heart of the old quarter of Montpellier. Bedrooms are on the small side, but with welcoming personal touches such as fresh flowers. A good choice for a budget short break. Plenty of restaurants nearby. **www.hoteldupalais-montpellier.fr**

MONTPELLIER New Hotel du Midi

22 bd Victor Hugo, 34000 **Tel** *04 67 92 69 61* **Fax** *04 67 92 73 63* **Rooms** *44*

A Hausmann-style building, with *belle époque* touches, situated on the bustling Place de la Comèdie. The refurbished and spacious rooms have modern amenities and are decorated in warm tones such as chocolate and caramel, raspberry, and *pistache*. Centrally located with a choice of restaurants nearby. **www.new-hotel.com**

NARBONNE Grand Hôtel du Languedoc

22 bd Gambetta, 11100 **Tel** *04 68 65 14 74* **Fax** *04 68 65 81 48* **Rooms** *40*

This stylish hotel in a 19th-century building is a short walk from Narbonne's cathedral, city-center shopping, markets, and museums. The popular restaurant retains traces of its Belle Epoque elegance. Spacious rooms with high ceilings, air conditioning, and soundproofing. **www.hoteldulanguedoc.com**

NIMES Imperator-Concorde

Quai de la Fontaine, 30000 **Tel** *04 66 21 90 30* **Fax** *04 66 67 70 25* **Rooms** *60*

Built in 1929, this hotel has been frequented by the rich and famous, including Ava Gardner and Hemingway. The well-equipped rooms, some with a 1930s decor and others more modern, overlook an enchanting garden planted with cedars and palm trees. The restaurant is recommended for its imaginative regional dishes. **www.hotel-imperator.com**

NIMES New Hôtel la Baume

21 rue Nationale, 30000 **Tel** *04 66 76 28 42* **Fax** *04 66 76 28 45* **Rooms** *34*

Housed in an elegant 17th-century townhouse, la Baume is one of the most pleasant places to stay in Nîmes. A short step from the sights, it blends old-world charm with modern facilities. Some rooms are even listed as historic monuments. No restaurant, but a welcoming café-bar. **www.new-hotel.com**

PERPIGNAN Hôtel de la Loge

1 rue des Fabriques d'en Nabot, 66000 **Tel** *04 68 34 41 02* **Fax** *04 68 34 25 13* **Rooms** *22*

This affordable hotel in the heart of Perpignan's medieval quarter is housed within the walls of a 16th-century Catalan mansion with a mosaic forecourt and fountain. Its comfortable rooms all have en-suite facilities. Unassuming and cozy, ideal for a short break. **www.hoteldelaloge.fr**

PERPIGNAN Villa Duflot

Rond point Albert Donnezan, 66000 **Tel** *04 68 56 67 67* **Fax** *04 68 56 54 05* **Rooms** *25*

An Italian villa enclosed in its own vast park at the edge of a busy urban area. The elegant interior, bathed in light from large bay windows, has Art-Deco touches and contemporary sculptures. Well-sized, renovated rooms are chic and comfortable. The pleasant restaurant opens out onto the pool and serves regional cuisine. **www.villa-duflot.com**

PRADES Castell Rose

Chemin de la Litera, 66500 **Tel** *04 68 96 07 57* **Rooms** *5*

A charismatic hacienda-style *chambre d'hôtes* ideally situated for visiting the abbey of St-Martin-du-Canigou. The imposing pink marble building has a grand arcaded gallery and tower overlooking Spanish gardens and an immense park. The pleasant rooms are furnished with period furniture. Stylish and refined. **www.castellrose-prades.com**

QUILLAN Hôtel Cartier

31 bd Charles de Gaulle, 11500 **Tel** *04 68 20 05 14* **Fax** *04 68 20 22 57* **Rooms** *28*

The family-run Hôtel Cartier is housed in a 1950s Art Deco building in the center of Quillan. The clean, comfortable rooms are simple, almost Spartan, with neutral colors. The restaurant is similarly unassuming, but friendly, affordable, and as popular with locals as it is with visitors. **www.hotelcartier.com**

SAILLAGOUSE L'Atalaya

Llo, 66800 **Tel** *04 68 04 70 04* **Fax** *04 68 04 01 29* **Rooms** *13*

Clinging to a hillside in the Cerdagne region, this pretty stone auberge has a spectacular view towards Spain – which is most impressive from the edge of the pool. Comfortable, well-maintained bedrooms are individually, tastefully decorated. Quality fabrics and stylish furniture create a luxury feel. Closed Nov & Jan–Mar. **www.atalaya66.com**

SETE Grand Hôtel

17 quai de Tassigny, 34200 **Tel** *04 67 74 71 77* **Fax** *04 67 74 29 27* **Rooms** *43*

Set beside Sète's famous canal, this 19th-century building has been restored to its former grandeur, and its conservatory-restaurant is one of the finest in Sète. Rooms are freshly decorated and well equipped – the best have balconies overlooking the canal. Service is extremely professional. **www.legrandhotelsete.com**

SOMMIERES Hôtel de l'Orange

7 rue des Beaumes, 30250 **Tel** *04 66 77 79 94* **Rooms** *7*

Located in the Cévennes region, this charming *hôtel particulier* dating from the 17th century is situated on the terraces looking down to the village. Well-proportioned bedrooms vary in style, from traditional to modern with colorful furnishings. Carefully tended ornamental gardens are pleasant to stroll in. **www.hotel.delorange.free.fr**

ST CYPRIEN L'Ile de La Lagune

Bd de l'Almandin, Les Capellans, 66750 **Tel** *04 68 21 01 02* **Fax** *04 68 21 06 28* **Rooms** *22*

One of the most luxurious hotels in the region, this building was constructed in the 1990s on an island in the middle of a lagoon. The impressive white structure, reminiscent of Spanish architecture, houses chic, airy, contemporary rooms with balconies. The excellent restaurant has a pleasant terrace. Private beach. **www.hotel-ile-lagune.com**

UZES Hostellerie Provençale

1–3 rue Grande Bourgade, 30700 **Tel** *04 66 22 11 06* **Fax** *04 66 75 01 03* **Rooms** *9*

A small friendly hotel ideally situated for exploring this lovely old town, especially on market day. While the old stone building with its *tommete* tiled floors and rustic furniture recalls the past, amenities are up to date. Some rooms have Jacuzzis. The dining room is gaily decorated and serves typical Provençale fare. **www.hostellerieprovencale.com**

PROVENCE AND THE COTE D'AZUR

AIX EN PROVENCE Hôtel St Christophe

2 av Victor Hugo, 13100 **Tel** *04 42 26 01 24* **Fax** *04 42 38 53 17* **Rooms** *67*

This superb town house hotel has bedrooms with all modern facilities – reserve in advance to secure a room with a tiny balcony. Decorated in Art Deco style, the ground floor is a bustling old-fashioned brasserie of the best kind, with tables indoors and out. Very central location. **www.hotel-saintchristophe.com**

Key to Price Guide *see p550* **Key to Symbols** *see back cover flap*

AIX EN PROVENCE Hôtel des Augustins

3 rue de la Masse, 13100 **Tel** *04 42 27 28 59* **Fax** *04 42 26 74 87* **Rooms** *29*

In a converted 12th-century convent, with the reception housed in a 15th-century chapel, the Hôtel des Augustins offers a haven of peace in the heart of bustling Aix. The rooms are large and comfortable in traditional Provençal style. No restaurant, but places to eat nearby. **www.hotel-augustins.com**

ANTIBES La Bastide de la Brague

55 av No. 6 La Brague, 06600 **Tel** *04 93 65 73 78* **Rooms** *5*

A welcoming, family-run bed and breakfast, serving meals on request. This large Provençal house offers five comfortable, well-decorated, and spacious bedrooms, some with their own private patios. Breakfast can be taken outside, under the olive trees on the terrace, in fine weather. **www.bbchambreantibes.com**

ANTIBES Mas Djoliba

29 av Provence, 06600 **Tel** *04 93 34 02 48* **Fax** *04 93 34 05 81* **Rooms** *13*

Mas Djoliba is a big, old-fashioned farmhouse set among lots of greenery, with palm trees surrounding the pool terrace. Convenient for old Antibes and the beaches nearby, it is perfect for a romantic weekend or a longer stay. Closed end Oct–Mar. Half-board (which includes two meals) obligatory May–Sep. **www.hotel-djoliba.com**

ARLES Hotel de Amphithéâtre

5–7 rue Diderot, 16200 **Tel** *04 90 96 10 30* **Fax** *04 90 93 98 69* **Rooms** *33*

This bargain hotel has plenty of character and a perfect location next to Arles' amphitheater. Some of the rooms are on the small side, but the decor is charmingly Provençal. The public areas are pleasant, the service is helpful, and there is discounted parking available nearby. A good choice for families. **www.hotelamphitheatre.fr**

ARLES Hôtel Calendal

5 rue Porte de Laure, 13200 **Tel** *04 90 96 11 89* **Fax** *04 90 96 05 84* **Rooms** *38*

This relaxing hotel in the historic center of Arles, near the Roman arena, has charmingly decorated and air conditioned rooms, a few with balconies overlooking the arena or the Roman theater. Breakfast is served in the garden, which is shaded by palm trees. **www.lecalendal.com**

ARLES Hôtel d'Arlatan

26 rue du Sauvage, 13200 **Tel** *04 90 93 56 66* **Fax** *04 90 49 68 45* **Rooms** *47*

The former 15th-century town residence of the Comtes d'Arlatan, this is one of the most beautiful historic hotels in the region. The rooms are furnished with antiques. Glass panels in the salon floor reveal 4th-century Roman foundations. Walled garden and stone terrace. **www.hotel-arlatan.fr**

BEAULIEU SUR MER La Réserve de Beaulieu

5 bd du Général Leclerc, 06310 **Tel** *04 93 01 00 01* **Fax** *04 93 01 28 99* **Rooms** *39*

A luxury hotel right on the seafront, in the heart of Beaulieu near the sailing harbor. The elegant rooms are decorated in warm pastel tones, and there is a magnificent pool next to the sea. The gastronomic restaurant has two Michelin stars. Closed mid-Oct–mid-Dec. **www.reservebeaulieu.com**

BIOT Hôtel les Arcades

16 pl des Arcades, 06410 **Tel** *04 93 65 01 04* **Fax** *04 93 65 01 05* **Rooms** *12*

This 15th-century inn is a quirky haven of tranquility. The rooms are small (even poky) but undeniably atmospheric. Top-floor rooms have terraces with views to the sea. The bar serves as breakfast room and restaurant, which you share with the local bohemian set and their dogs. **www.hotel-restaurant-les-arcades.com**

BORMES-LES-MIMOSAS Domaine du Mirage

38 rue de la Vue des Iles, 83230 **Tel** *04 94 05 32 60* **Fax** *04 94 64 93 03* **Rooms** *33*

Perched above the bay of Le Lavandou and a 10-minute drive from one of the Riviera's best beaches, this Victorian-style hotel has spectacular views from its balconies and a beautiful pool. Light dishes are served by the pool at lunch, while in the evening you can choose from a short seasonal menu. Attentive staff. **www.domainedumirage.com**

CANNES La Villa Tosca

11, rue Hoche, 06400 **Tel** *04 93 38 34 40* **Fax** *04 93 38 73 34* **Rooms** *22*

A large Beaux-Art-style hotel, ideally located for the beach, train station, and the Palais des Festivals. In the rooms, there's a mix of contemporary and antique furniture with plenty of original features. It is well worth paying a little extra for one of the larger rooms, some of which have balconies. **www.villa-tosca.com**

CANNES Hôtel Molière

5 rue Molière, 06400 **Tel** *04 93 38 16 16* **Fax** *04 93 68 29 57* **Rooms** *24*

This 19th-century building is very close to la Croisette, Cannes' sea-front esplananade, with bright and comfortable rooms and balconies overlooking an attractive garden where breakfast is served. Good value and very much in demand – reserve well in advance. **www.hotel-moliere.com**

CANNES Hôtel Splendid

4 av Felix Faure, 06400 **Tel** *04 97 06 22 22* **Fax** *04 93 99 55 02* **Rooms** *62*

This white wedding-cake of a hotel with its Belle Epoque façade right in the center of Cannes has fantastic views of the yacht harbor from the rooftop restaurant, and some sea-facing rooms have great balconies. Very good service, and a warm, friendly atmosphere. **www.splendid-hotel-cannes.fr**

CANNES Eden Hôtel

133 rue d'Antibes, 06400 **Tel** *04 93 68 78 00* **Fax** *04 93 68 78 01* **Rooms** *115*

This new boutique hotel is bright, colorful, and trendy, with a hint of 1960s retro complementing the modern feel. Close to the town's fashionable shopping streets, its facilities are enhanced with the addition of a heated pool, whirlpool, massage room, and fitness center. **www.eden-hotel-cannes.com**

CANNES Carlton Inter-Continental

58 la Croisette, 06414 **Tel** *04 93 06 40 06* **Fax** *04 93 06 40 25* **Rooms** *341*

The grandest of the grand, this is where the stars come to stay. During the film festival, there is a long waiting list for reservations. Art Deco surroundings, with discreetly luxurious facilities in the rooms and public areas, and a private beach with deck chairs and sun umbrellas. **www.intercontinental.com/cannes**

CAP D'ANTIBES La Garoupe et Gardiole

60–74 chemin de la Garoupe, 06160 **Tel** *04 92 93 33 33* **Fax** *04 92 67 61 87* **Rooms** *37*

Pines and cypresses surround the pink 1920s buildings of this delightful (and delightfully affordable, by Cap d'Antibes standards) hotel. Tiled floors, beamed ceilings, and whitewashed walls perpetuate the rural image. Bedrooms are light and airy. Shady terrace and pretty pool. **www.hotel-lagaroupe-gardiole.com**

CAP D'ANTIBES La Jabotte

13, av Max Maurey, 06160 **Tel** *04 93 61 45 89* **Rooms** *10*

A small hotel with a bed-and-breakfast feel, La Jabotte is fully booked weeks ahead in summer thanks to the tastefully decorated rooms, warm welcome, and incredibly reasonable prices. A house *apéritif* is served every evening in the courtyard. The beach is just steps away. Closed Nov. **www.jabotte.com**

CAP D'ANTIBES Hôtel du Cap (Eden Roc)

Bd Kennedy, 06600 **Tel** *04 93 61 39 01* **Fax** *04 93 67 76 04* **Rooms** *120*

Built in 1870, this is the ultimate Antibes palace, and a hideaway for the rich and famous. Most accommodation is in luxury suites or apartments. Seaside cabanas are available and there is a huge heated seawater pool. Superb food, obsequious service, and state-of-the-art facilities. **www.hotel-du-cap-eden-roc.com**

CASSIS Les Jardins de Cassis

Rue Auguste Favier, 13260 **Tel** *04 42 01 84 85* **Fax** *04 42 01 32 38* **Rooms** *36*

The most pleasant place to stay in the picturesque port of Cassis, this hotel is much in demand, so reserve early. The guest rooms, in a cluster of buildings painted in pastel shades, are small but well planned. Good facilities include a Jacuzzi and a pool in a garden of lemon trees and bougainvillea. Closed Dec–Mar. **www.lesjardinsdecassis.com**

CASTELLANE Nouvel Hôtel du Commerce

Pl de l'Eglise, 04120 **Tel** *04 92 83 61 00* **Fax** *04 92 83 72 82* **Rooms** *34*

This hotel, in the picturesque small town of Castellane, makes a good base for exploring the surrounding area. The pretty, well-equipped, and immaculate rooms overlook the market square or the crag that surmounts Castellane. The dining room veranda is a lovely, airy spot. Closed Nov–Mar 1. **www.hotel-fradet.com**

EZE Château Eza

Rue de la Pise, 06360 **Tel** *04 93 41 12 24* **Fax** *04 93 41 16 64* **Rooms** *11*

This remarkable building is a collection of medieval houses perched at the summit of Eze's "eagle's nest." Once home to Prince William of Sweden, it has been converted into a tiny jewel of a luxury hotel with elegant rooms and utterly breathtaking views from its terraces. Closed Nov–mid-Dec. **www.chateaueza.com**

FONTVIEILLE Hôtel La Peiriero

36 av des Baux, 13990 **Tel** *04 90 54 76 10* **Fax** *04 90 54 62 60* **Rooms** *42*

This welcoming family hotel has been created in a traditional Provençal farm, known as a *mas*. The food, the colors, and the atmosphere are all typically Provençal. In summer it is cool and relaxing and in winter warm and cozy. Children are well catered for with a specially designed play area. **www.hotel-peiriero.com**

JUAN LES PINS Hôtel des Mimosas

Rue Pauline, 06160 **Tel** *04 93 61 04 16* **Fax** *04 92 93 06 46* **Rooms** *34*

Palm trees surround this gracious hotel, built at the turn of the 19th century and offering character and style at a reasonable rate. The hotel is beautifully presented, with comfortable, cool, simply furnished rooms. Request a quieter room overlooking the swimming pool. Closed Sep–May. **www.hotelmimosas.com**

LES ARCS SUR ARGENS Logis du Guetteur

Pl du Château, 83460 **Tel** *04 94 99 51 10* **Fax** *04 94 99 51 29* **Rooms** *13*

Within the tower of an 11th-century castle – a prominent landmark overlooking the small village – this cozy hotel is a fine place to stay in summer or winter, almost equidistant between Mediterranean beaches and Alpine ski slopes. Views from the ramparts are epic. **www.logisduguetteur.com**

LES BAUX DE PROVENCE L'Hostellerie de la Reine Jeanne

Grande rue, 13520 **Tel** *04 90 54 32 06* **Fax** *04 90 54 32 33* **Rooms** *10*

This old house in the center of one of Provence's most charming – and most-visited – villages has a dozen rooms, each different and attractively decorated and simply furnished. Not ideal for small children, and parking nearby is always a challenge. **www.la-reinejeanne.com**

Key to Price Guide *see p550* **Key to Symbols** *see back cover flap*

LES BAUX DE PROVENCE Auberge de la Benvengudo

Vallon de l'Arcoule, 13520 **Tel** *04 90 54 32 54* **Fax** *04 90 54 42 58* **Rooms** *28*

With comfortable, lavishly decorated bedrooms, a large garden, and tennis court, this attractive country house near the hilltop village of Les Baux is one of the most charming places to stay on the fringes of the Bouches du Rhône. It is a good base for exploring the region. Closed Nov–Mar. **www.benvengudo.fr**

MARSEILLE Sofitel Marseille Vieux Port

36, bd Charles Livon, 13007 **Tel** *04 91 15 59 00* **Fax** *04 91 15 59 50* **Rooms** *134*

Decorated in minimalist style with dark wood and streamlined furniture, this luxury hotel is most remarkable for its spectacular views of the Vieux Port. Opt for one of the 28 rooms with terraces. The major sights are all nearby and the top-floor restaurant has panoramic views. **www.accorhotels.com**

MENTON Hôtel Aiglon

7 av de la Madone, 06500 **Tel** *04 93 57 55 55* **Fax** *04 93 35 92 39* **Rooms** *28*

Not far from the seafront, the Aiglon offers every comfort, including a heated swimming pool and a luxuriant garden. Housed in a charming 19th-century town house, it is nicely decorated and has a good restaurant with tables on a terrace shaded by palms. **www.hotelaiglon.net**

MOUSTIERS STE MARIE La Bastide de Moustiers

Chemin de Quinson, 04360 **Tel** *04 92 70 47 47* **Fax** *04 92 70 47 48* **Rooms** *12*

Outside one the region's prettiest villages, La Bastide de Moustiers is housed in a 17th-century building, but contains the latest facilities. Surrounded by a gorgeous garden, the hotel has sweeping views of the surrounding mountains and a good restaurant. There is a room with disabled access. **www.bastide-moustiers.com**

NICE Hôtel Windsor

11 rue Dalpozzo, 06000 **Tel** *04 93 88 59 35* **Fax** *04 93 88 94 57* **Rooms** *57*

The Hôtel Windsor provides a wide array of services and facilities, including a pool in an exotic palm garden, a children's play area, and a health and beauty center offering massage and a sauna. Some rooms are individually decorated by local artists. Snack bar and restaurant. **www.hotelwindsornice.com**

NICE Hôtel Suisse

15, Quai Rauba Capéu, 06300 **Tel** *04 92 17 39 00* **Fax** *04 93 85 30 70* **Rooms** *42*

When it comes to value for money in Nice, it is hard to beat this sleek hotel a few steps from the food market in the cour Saleya. There is no swimming pool, but the beach is just across the street and there are balconies with views of the Baie des Anges. The staff are friendly and helpful. **www.hotel-nice-suisse.com**

NICE La Pérouse

11 quai Rauba-Capeu, 06300 **Tel** *04 93 62 34 63* **Fax** *04 93 62 59 41* **Rooms** *60*

La Pérouse has the best view in Nice. At the eastern end of the Baie des Anges, it perches on a clifftop site between the Promenade des Anglais and the port. Sea-facing rooms have small terraces, which are very peaceful. In summer the restaurant has tables beneath lemon trees. **www.hotel-la-perouse.com**

NICE Le Negresco

37 promenade des Anglais, 06000 **Tel** *04 93 16 64 00* **Fax** *04 93 88 35 68* **Rooms** *120*

The Negresco is the grande dame of Riviera hotels and has been a landmark on the promenade des Anglais since it opened in 1913, with a seemingly endless list of rich and famous guests. Superbly decorated and furnished with works of art. Flawless service and modern facilities. **www.hotel-negresco-nice.com**

SEILLANS Hôtel des Deux Rocs

Place Font d'Amont, 83440 **Tel** *04 94 76 87 32* **Fax** *04 94 76 88 68* **Rooms** *13*

This 17th-century Provençal mansion on the village square has a strong family atmosphere, decorated with antiques and traditional fabrics. Rooms at the front are the biggest and brightest. Mediterranean cuisine is served beside the square's fountain in summer. Closed Jan–mid-Feb. **www.hoteldeuxrocs.com**

ST-JEAN-CAP-FERRAT Hôtel Brise Marine

58 av Jean-Mermoz, 06230 **Tel** *04 93 76 04 36* **Fax** *04 93 76 11 49* **Rooms** *16*

If you are looking for a calm place to relax, this small hotel is ideal. Facing the sea on one side and the Alpes-Maritime on the other, the views are magnificent. The lack of a swimming pool is made up for by the fact that the beach is 160-feet (50-meters) away. Closed Nov–Feb. **www.hote-brisemarine.com**

ST-JEAN-CAP-FERRAT Royal Riviera

3 av Jean Monnet, 06230 **Tel** *04 93 76 31 00* **Fax** *04 93 01 23 07* **Rooms** *96*

This luxury hotel in the glitzy resort of St-Jean-Cap-Ferrat has an enviable asset – its own private sandy beach. Some of the rooms seem small for the price, but service aims to satisfy every whim. The L'Orangerie, a smaller building facing the swimming pool, houses 16 pleasant rooms. **www.royal-riviera.com**

ST PAUL DE VENCE Hostellerie des Remparts

72 rue grande, 06570 **Tel** *04 93 32 09 88* **Fax** *04 93 24 10 47* **Rooms** *9*

In the heart of this picturesque village, the Hostellerie des Remparts offers modern comforts in a medieval setting. Its rooms are furnished with antiques, and have marvelous views. There is a small garden terrace. The village is car-free and parking is some distance away. Closed Mondays out of season. **www.hostellerielesremparts.com**

ST PAUL DE VENCE La Colombe d'Or

`P` `TI` `≅` `★` `目` `&`   €€€€€

Pl de Gaulle, 06570 **Tel** *04 93 32 80 02* **Fax** *04 93 32 77 78* **Rooms** *25*

The most luxurious place to stay in St Paul, this former farmhouse in a fabulous setting once hosted Impressionist painters, and originals by Picasso and Matisse grace its walls. The guest list is still impressive, and early reservations are necessary. The restaurant is highly rated. **www.la-colombe-dor.com**

ST TROPEZ Lou Cagnard

`P`   €€

Av Paul Roussel, 83990 **Tel** *04 94 97 04 24* **Fax** *04 94 97 09 44* **Rooms** *19*

Occupying an old town house, this small hotel is only a minute's walk away from St Tropez's lively square, the place des Lices. Request a room overlooking the small garden with its shady mulberry trees; there is no air conditioning, and rooms in the front are noisy with open windows. Closed Dec & Jan. **www.hotel-lou-cagnard.com**

ST TROPEZ Pastis Hôtel St Tropez

`P` `≅` `Ψ` `目` `&`   €€€€

61 av du Général Leclerc, 83990 **Tel** *04 98 12 56 50* **Fax** *04 94 96 99 82* **Rooms** *9*

St-Tropez attracts more than its fair share of ostentation, but this nine-room inn decorated with contemporary art and a judicious mix of modern and antique furniture is for those who prefer a more discreet charm. The heated pool is surrounded by centuries-old palm trees. There is a strict "no dress code" policy. **www.pastis-st-tropez.com**

ST TROPEZ La Ponche

`P` `TI` `★` `目`   €€€€€

Port des Pêcheurs, 83990 **Tel** *04 94 97 02 53* **Fax** *04 94 97 78 61* **Rooms** *18*

For those looking for a boutique hideaway in St Tropez, this cluster of one-time fishermen's cottages may fit the bill. The bedrooms are large and artfully chic, and include two family-size rooms. Among the famous guests have been Pablo Picasso and 1950s film star Romy Schneider. Closed Nov–mid-Feb. **www.laponche.com**

VENCE Mas de Vence

`⊡` `P` `TI` `≅` `★` `目` `&`   €€

539 av Emile Hugues, 06140 **Tel** *04 93 58 06 16* **Fax** *04 93 24 04 21* **Rooms** *41*

This modern establishment may not appeal to those looking for somewhere quaint, but its architecture and colors are in keeping with Provençal tradition and it has excellent facilities including air-conditioned, insulated rooms, a small garden, and a terrace restaurant. **www.azurline.com**

VILLEFRANCHE-SUR-MER Hôtel La Flore

`⊡` `P` `≅` `★` `目` `&`   €€€

5 bd Princess Grace de Monaco, 06230 **Tel** *04 93 76 30 30* **Fax** *04 93 76 99 99* **Rooms** *31*

This traditional hotel dating from the beginning of the 20th century has been completely renovated in a Provençal style. The rooms are calm and overlook the sea and Villefranche's famous port. The Citadelle and a myriad of different restaurants are a few minutes' walk away. **www.hotel-la-flore.fr**

VILLEFRANCHE-SUR-MER Hôtel Versailles

`⊡` `P` `TI` `≅` `目`   €€€€

7 bd Princesse Grace, 06230 **Tel** *04 93 76 52 52* **Fax** *04 93 01 97 48* **Rooms** *46*

This modern hotel has enough facilities for a longer stay, including a swimming pool, a restaurant specializing in Provençal cuisine, a large terrace, and bedrooms with great views. Perhaps its only (slight) drawback is its location on a busy thoroughfare. Secure parking. Closed Nov–mid-Mar. **www.hotelversailles.com**

CORSICA

AJACCIO Hôtel Kallisté

`P` `目` `&`   €€

51 cours Napoléon, 20000 **Tel** *04 95 51 34 45* **Fax** *04 95 21 79 00* **Rooms** *48*

Right in the middle of the busy Cours Napoléon, the rooms are surprisingly quiet in this well-run, clean hotel. Wrought-iron banisters and exposed stone walls add a rustic touch to the building, which dates back to 1864. Just a few minutes' walk to the train and bus stations. **www.cyrnos.net**

AJACCIO Hôtel Les Mouettes

`P` `≅` `★` `目` `&`   €€€€

9, cours Lucien Bonaparte, 20000 **Tel** *04 95 50 40 40* **Fax** *04 95 21 71 80* **Rooms** *28*

This hotel not far from the center of town has its own stretch of sandy beach – and a pool. The spacious rooms are decorated in classic style, reflecting the building's 19th-century façade. There's no restaurant, but a hearty breakfast and snack plates are served. Closed mid-Nov–mid-Mar. **www.hotellesmouettes.fr**

BASTIA Hôtel Posta Vecchia

`⊡` `★` `目`   €€

Quai des Martyrs de la Libération, 20200 **Tel** *04 95 32 32 38* **Fax** *04 95 32 14 05* **Rooms** *50*

Conveniently situated in the heart of the city, this busy hotel is next to the bustling, colorful, old port with its lively restaurants. Ask for a room in the front so that you can watch the evening promenade along the tree-lined quay. Public parking in front. **www.hotel-postavecchia.com**

BASTIA Hôtel Pietracap

`P` `≅` `目`   €€€€

Rte San Martino, San Martino di Lota, 20200 **Tel** *04 95 31 64 63* **Fax** *04 95 31 39 00* **Rooms** *39*

Supremely comfortable hotel in a beautiful setting along the coast road from Bastia. A large park with olive trees that are over 100 years old separates the hotel from the sea. Large outdoor swimming pool. Private parking lot. Closed Dec–Apr. **www.hotel-pietracap.com**

Key to Price Guide *see p550* **Key to Symbols** *see back cover flap*

BONIFACIO Hôtel le Royal
P ⑪ ▤ €€

8 rue Fred Scamaroni, 20169 **Tel** *04 95 73 00 51* **Fax** *04 95 73 04 68* **Rooms** *14*

Busy hotel in the old town with views over the cliffs and sea. Freshly painted, pastel-colored rooms. The cathedral is a few minutes' walk away, and steps lead down to the lively quayside. The little tourist train stops just outside. The restaurant serves mainly local dishes. **www.hotel-leroyal.com**

BONIFACIO Hôtel Résidence du Center Nautique
P ⑪ ⭍ ▤ €€€

Quai Nord, Port de Plaisanc, 20169 **Tel** *04 95 73 02 11* **Fax** *04 95 73 17 47* **Rooms** *11*

With its nautical-themed decor, this is the only hotel in Bonifacio that overlooks the harbor. Duplex rooms – some facing the port – are spacious and comfortable. The restaurant serves delicious food, though the service can be abrupt. The private parking is a bonus for the center of town location. Closed Oct–Mar. **www.center-nautique.com**

CALVI Hostellerie l'Abbaye
▧ P ≈ ▤ €€€€

Rte Santore, 20260 **Tel** *04 95 65 04 27* **Fax** *04 95 65 30 23* **Rooms** *43*

This pretty ivy-covered hotel was built on the walls of a 16th-century abbey. Ideally positioned on a slight incline, just above the port, it is set back from the road and is surrounded by an immaculate garden. A 5-minute walk takes you to the town center. Closed Nov–Apr. **www.hostellerie-abbaye.com**

CORTE Hôtel Dominique Colonna
P ≈ ⭍ ▤ ⑆ €€

Vallée de la Restonica, 20250 **Tel** *04 95 45 25 65* **Fax** *04 95 61 03 91* **Rooms** *29*

It would be hard to imagine a more idyllic location than this lush green valley, with a small waterfall. Rooms are tastefully decorated in contemporary style and the service is impeccable. There is an excellent traditional restaurant next door, or the village restaurants are just 20-minutes' walk away. **www.dominique-colonna.com**

ÎLE ROUSSE Best Western Hôtel Santa Maria
P ≈ ⭍ ▤ €€€€

Rte du Port, 20220 **Tel** *04 95 63 05 05* **Fax** *04 95 60 32 48* **Rooms** *56*

Superbly situated on the road to the islet of Île Rousse, this charming hotel has its own little beach and is just a short walk to the main square, with its stores and restaurants. All rooms have a terrace with sea views. Restaurant serves lunch in July and August. **www.hotelsantamaria.com**

PIANA Les Roches Rouges
P ⑪ ⭍ €€€

Rte Porto, 20115 **Tel** *04 95 27 81 81* **Fax** *04 95 27 81 76* **Rooms** *30*

Built in 1912, this splendid hotel retains all the charm of that era. Large, simply furnished rooms look out onto the bay of Porto, nominated by UNESCO as one of the world's five most beautiful bays. Excellent dining room with terrace and garden. Closed Nov–Mar. **www.lesrochesrouges.com**

PORTO Le Maquis
P ⑪ €€

Porto, 20150 **Tel** *04 95 26 12 19* **Fax** *04 95 26 18 55* **Rooms** *6*

Quiet family-run hotel on the outskirts of town, on the coast road to Calvi. Surprisingly sophisticated menu in the charming restaurant. Dramatic views over the mountains. Comfortable rooms, pretty garden, and parking available. Closed Dec–Jan. **www.hotel-lemaquis.com**

PORTO-VECCHIO Chez Franca
P ▤ €€€€

Rte de Bonifacio, 20137 **Tel** *04 95 70 15 56* **Fax** *04 95 72 18 41* **Rooms** *14*

This modern hotel is conveniently situated between the town and the port. A lot of care has gone into the renovation of the rooms. The superb beaches of Guilia and Palombaggia are a few kilometers away. Good base for excursions to Zonza and Bavella. Closed Dec. **www.francahotel.com**

PROPRIANO Le Lido
⑪ ▤ ⑆ €€€€

Av Napoléon, 20110 **Tel** *04 95 76 06 37* **Fax** *04 95 76 31 18* **Rooms** *11*

Le Lido has a unique location on a rocky peninsula with a beach. The simple decor doesn't aim to compete with the setting, but terra cotta tiles, mosaics, and wood beams lend charm. Opt for a main floor room opening onto the beach. The very good restaurant specializes in oven-baked lobster. Closed Nov–mid-Apr. **www.le-lido.com**

SARTENE Hôtel St Damianu
▧ P ⑪ ≈ ⭍ ⑰ ▤ ⑆ €€

Quartier San Damien, 20100 **Tel** *04 95 70 55 41* **Fax** *04 95 70 55 78* **Rooms** *28*

A gem of a hotel. Large airy rooms have terraces with fabulous views of the gulf of Valinco or the mountains. Facilities include a huge swimming pool surrounded with teak decking, a garden, *hammam*, disabled access, secure parking, and an excellent dining room. Closed Nov–Apr. **www.sandamianu.fr**

ST FLORENT Hôtel Maxime
P €€

Rte La Cathédrale, 20217 **Tel** *04 95 37 05 30* **Fax** *04 95 37 13 07* **Rooms** *19*

Set back from the street on the way to the 12th-century cathedral of Santa Maria Assunta, this modern hotel is an oasis of calm only a minute's walk from the hurly-burly of the fashionable port. Pleasant, airy rooms with sea views from the top floor.

VIZZAVONA Hôtel du Monte D'Oro
P ⑪ ⭍ ⑆ €€

Col de Vizzavona RN 193, 20219 **Tel** *04 95 47 21 06* **Fax** *04 95 47 22 05* **Rooms** *24*

You'll feel as though you are in an Agatha Christie novel the moment you walk into this charming hotel, built in 1880 and set in the forest on the road between Ajaccio and Bastia. Wood-paneled corridors, large living room, and elegant dining room serving organic food. A *gite* is also available for rent. Closed Nov–Apr. **www.monte-oro.com**

WHERE TO EAT

The French consider eating well an essential part of their national birthright. There are few other places where people are as passionately knowledgeable about their cuisine and their wine. Restaurant reviews, as well as cooking and food shows on television, are avidly followed and the general quality of both fresh food and restaurant offerings is vastly better in France than it is in most other European countries.

This introduction to the restaurant listings, which are arranged by region and town *(see pp600–51)*, looks at the different types of restaurant in France and gives practical tips on eating out, reading menus, ordering, and service – everything you need to know to enjoy your meal. At the front of the book is a guide to a typical menu and an introduction to French wine *(see pp24–7)*. The main food and wine features are at the beginning of each of the five regional sections.

FRENCH EATING HABITS

The traditional large meal at noon survives mainly in rural regions. In cities, lunch is increasingly likely to consist of a sandwich, salad, or a steak in a café, while dinner is the main meal of the day. Usually, lunch is from noon to 2pm and dinner is from 8 to 10pm, with last orders taken 30 minutes before closing time.

Some family-owned places are closed at weekends, so it may be difficult to find a meal anywhere outside your hotel on Sundays, except in large cities. Off the beaten track and in resort towns, restaurants and hotels are often closed out of season, so it is advisable to telephone ahead.

Over the past few decades, French eating habits have changed dramatically. The growing popularity of the cuisine of former French colonies means that North African and Vietnamese places are now easy to find, as are Chinese restaurants. Burger and Tex-Mex joints are also popular with young people. As city-dwellers and suburbanites in France have become almost as health-conscious as other Europeans, there has been an explosion of "light" foods; and the rise of the *hypermarchés* (hypermarkets) has resulted in less fresh produce on the menu as more frozen and prepared food is eaten.

REGIONAL COOKING

One of the great pleasures of traveling in France is sampling the country's regional

Typical elegant terrace restaurant in Provence

cuisine. In every *département* of France, menus will nearly always include local specialties, which reflect predominant local products and agriculture. A good way to divide France gastronomically is the butter/olive oil divide. In the north, butter is generally used in cooking; in the south, olive oil; and in the southwest, goose and duck fat predominate.

Each region takes great pride in its own cuisine. Nationally, the best-known dishes come from four regions: Alsace, a province with close German ties; the southwest, where *cassoulet*, a rich stew of white beans, tomatoes, sausage, and duck is a well-loved dish; the Alps, which gave *fondue* to the nation; and Provence, famed for *bouillabaisse*, a rich fish soup from Marseille.

The gastronomic capital of France is, however, considered to be Lyon, which is home to a significant proportion of France's best restaurants and many superb no-nonsense bistros known as *bouchons*.

La Cigale, a Belle Epoque brasserie in Nantes *(see p623)*

RESTAURANTS

Encompassing the whole alphabet of French cuisine, restaurants in France range from tiny whitewashed places with rush-bottomed chairs to stately, wood-paneled château dining rooms and the top kitchens of famous chefs. Many hotels have fine restaurants open to non-residents, a selection of which can be found in the hotel listings *(see pp550–95)*.

Prices for restaurants of the same rating are more or less consistent throughout France except in large cities, where they can be more expensive. The quality of the food and service, though, is the most significant price factor and you can easily spend over €150 per head to eat at one of the top establishments.

There are several different kinds of French cuisine that you may come across. *Haute cuisine* is the traditional cooking method, where the flavor of the food is enhanced with rich sauces. *Nouvelle cuisine* challenged this method, especially for the diet-conscious, in using light rather than creamy sauces which bring out the texture and color of the ingredients. *Cuisine bourgeoise* is French home cooking. *Cuisine des Provinces* uses high-quality ingredients to prepare traditional rural dishes. *Jeune Cuisine Fran-çaise* is the latest trend, where young chefs have rebelled against Michelin traditions to create their own cooking style.

BISTROS

When the French go out to eat, they are most likely to visit the broadest class of restaurant, the bistro. Bistros vary enormously – some urban bistros are formally decorated, while those in smaller cities and in the country tend to be more casual. They offer a good, moderately priced meal

The restaurant L'Excelsior at Nancy in Lorraine *(see p614)*

from a traditional menu of an *entrée* or *hors d'oeuvre* (appetizer), *plats mijotés* (simmered dishes) and *grillades* (grilled fish and meats), followed by cheese and dessert.

BRASSERIES

Brasseries have their origin in Alsace and were originally attached to breweries; the name brasserie actually means brewery. Usually found in larger cities, they are big, bustling places, many with fresh shellfish stands outside. They serve beer on tap as well as a *vin de la maison* (house wine) and a variety of regional wines. Menus include simple fish and grilled meat dishes along with Alsatian specialties like *choucroute garnie* (sauerkraut with sausage and pork). Prices are very much on a par with those you would pay at bistros. Like cafés, brasseries are usually open from morning until night and serve food all day long.

Camembert

FERME-AUBERGES

In the country you may eat at a simple "farm inn," where good, inexpensive meals, often made with fresh farm produce, are eaten with your host's family as part of your room and board. For more details on *ferme-auberges*, see under Bed and Breakfast on page 548.

CAFES

Cafés represent the soul of France. Every place but the tiniest hamlet can be counted on to have a café, open as a rule from early in the morning until 10pm or so. They serve drinks, coffee, tea, simple meals, and snacks such as salads, omelets, and sandwiches throughout the day, and usually provide a cheaper breakfast than most hotels.

As well as serving refreshments, cafés are a good source of information and provide the traveler with endless opportunities to observe the French at their most relaxed.

In villages, almost the entire population might drift in and out of the single café during the course of a day, while large cities have cafés that cater for a specific clientele, such as workers or students. Paris's most famous cafés were traditional meeting places for intellectuals and artists to exchange ideas *(see p152)*.

Auberge du XII Siècle at Saché in the Loire Valley *(see p624)*

Tables outside a café in the Old
Town of Nice on the Côte d'Azur

BISTRO ANNEXES

Over the past few years,
baby-bistros or bistro annexes
have appeared in larger cities,
especially Paris and Lyon, as a
new category of restaurant.
They are lower-priced sister
eateries of famous – and much
more expensive – restaurants
run by well-known chefs.
Many of them offer *formule
prix-fixe* (fixed-price) menus
and the chance to sample the
cooking of a celebrated kitchen
in relaxed surroundings.

FAST FOOD

If you want to avoid the
American fast food chains,
wine bars and *salons du thé*
are also good value for light
meals. Cafeterias, found in
some shopping centers, serve
tasty food at reasonable prices.

RESERVATIONS

In cities and larger towns it is
always best to make a reservation, especially from May to
September. This rarely applies
to cafés or in the country,
where you can walk into
most places without a
reservation. However, if you
are traveling in remote rural
and resort areas off season, it
is worth checking first that the
restaurant is open all year.

   If you have a reservation and
your plans change, then you
should call and cancel. Smaller
restaurants, in particular, must
fill all their tables to make a
profit, and "no-shows"
threaten their livelihood.

READING THE MENU AND ORDERING

When the menu is presented,
you'll usually be asked if
you'd like an aperitif. Since
many French people do not
drink spirits before a meal, this
could be Kir (white wine
mixed with a dash of black-
currant liqueur), vermouth,
light port (drunk in France as
a cocktail), or a soft drink.

   Opening the menu, *les
entrées* or *hors d'oeuvre* are
starters. *Les plats* are the main
courses, and most restaurants
will offer a *plat du jour*, or
daily special; these are often
seasonal or local dishes of
particular interest. A selection
of dishes from a classic French
menu is given on pages 24–5.

   Cheese is served as a separate course between the main
course and dessert. Coffee is
served black, unless you specify
"*crème.*" Alternatively, you can
ask for a *tisane*, or herbal tea.

WINE

Restaurants mark up wine
considerably, so it can be better
to further your connoisseur-
ship with bottles purchased in
stores than when dining out.
Local wine, however, is often
served in carafes. Ordering a
demi (50 cl) or *quart* (25 cl)
carafe is a cheap way to try
out a region's wines.

   French law divides the country's wines into three classes,
in ascending order of quality:
Vin de France, Indication
Géographique Protégée (IGP),
and Appellation d'Origine
Contrôlée (AOC). The Vin de

France wines are rarely found
in restaurants, but for help
in choosing a regional wine
(IGP upward), refer to the
wine features in the regional
sections of this book. For an
introduction to French wine,
see pages 26–7.

   When in doubt, order the
house wine. Few restaurants
will risk their reputation on an
inferior house wine, and they
often provide value for money.

WATER

Tap water is supplied on
request free of charge, and is
perfectly safe to drink. The
French also pride themselves
on their wide range of mineral
waters. Favourite mealtime
brands include Evian and the
slightly fizzy Badoit.

Le Moulin de Mougins *(see p650)*

HOW TO PAY

Visa/Carte Bleue (V) is the
most widely accepted credit
card in France. Master-
card/Access (MC) is also
commonly accepted, while
American Express (AE) and
Diners Club (DC) tend to be
accepted only in upmarket
establishments. However, you
should always carry plenty of

La Tour d'Argent in the Latin Quarter of Paris *(see p603)*

cash, especially when touring the countryside, as many smaller restaurants still do not accept any credit cards. If in doubt, ask when you make a reservation.

SERVICE AND TIPPING

The pace of a French meal is generally leisurely. People think nothing of spending 4 hours at the table, so if you are pressed for time, go to a café or brasserie. A service charge of 12.5 to 15 percent is almost always included in the price of your meal, but most French people leave a few euro cents behind in a café, and an additional 5 percent or so of the total bill in other restaurants. In the grander restaurants, which pride themselves on their service, an additional tip of 5 to 10 percent is correct.

Thirty euro cents is sufficient for restroom attendants, and 50 or 70 euro cents an item is appropriate for the cloakroom attendant.

DRESS CODE

Even when dressed casually, the French are generally well turned out; visitors should aim for the same level of presentable comfort. Running shoes, shorts, beach clothes, or active sportswear are unacceptable everywhere except cafés or beachside places.

The restaurant listings indicate which restaurants require men to wear a jacket and tie *(see pp600-51)*.

CHILDREN

French children are introduced early to restaurants and as a rule are well behaved. Consequently, children are well received almost everywhere in France. However, few restaurants provide special facilities like high chairs or baby seats, as children are expected to behave sensibly, and there is often not much room for strollers.

PETS

Dogs are usually accepted at all but the most elegant restaurants. As the French

The Eychenne hotel-restaurant at St-Girons in the Pyrenees *(see p588)*

are great dog lovers, do not be surprised to see your neighbor's lapdog sitting on the next-door *banquette*.

SMOKING

Despite all attempts to circumvent the no-smoking laws, especially in restaurants and cafés, the French have had to bow to the inevitable and should now adhere to government regulations about smoking in public.

Therefore, in line with other European countries, since 2007 smoking has been banned in all public places throughout France.

An elegant dining room in a hotel in Evian-les-Bains

WHEELCHAIR ACCESS

Though the restaurants of newer hotels usually provide wheelchair access, it is often restricted elsewhere. A word when you are booking your table should ensure that you are given a conveniently located table and assistance, if needed, when you arrive.

The listings show restaurants with wheelchair access.

Refer also to page 549 of this book, which gives the names and addresses of some organizations that provide advice to disabled travelers in France.

VEGETARIAN FOOD

France remains difficult for vegetarians, although some progress has been made in recent years. In most nonvegetarian restaurants the main courses are firmly oriented toward meat and fish. However, you can often fare well by ordering from the *entrées* and should never be timid about asking for a dish to be served without its meat content. Provided you make your request in advance, most smart restaurants will prepare a special vegetarian dish.

Only larger cities and university towns are likely to have fully fledged vegetarian restaurants. Otherwise cafés, pizzerias, crêperies and Oriental restaurants are good places to find vegetarian meals.

PICNICS

Picnicking is the best way to enjoy the wonderful fresh produce, local bread, cheeses, and *charcuterie* from the markets and enticing shops to be found all over France. For more details see pages 652–5.

Picnics are also a good way to eat cheaply and enjoy the French countryside. Picnicking areas along major roads are well marked and furnished with tables and chairs, but country lanes are better still.

Choosing a Restaurant

The restaurants in this guide have been selected across a wide range of price categories for their good value, exceptional food, and interesting location. This chart lists the restaurants by region, in chapter order. Map references for Paris restaurants correspond with the Paris Street Finder, *see pp154–69*.

PRICE CATEGORIES
The following price ranges are for a three-course meal for one, including a half-bottle of house wine, tax, and service:
€ under €30
€€ €30–€45
€€€ €45–€60
€€€€ €60–€90
€€€€€ over €90

PARIS

BASTILLE Bistrot du Peintre €€
116 ave Ledru Rollin, 75011 **Tel** *01 47 00 34 39*   **Map** *10 F5*

This laid-back bistro, in a turn-of-the-century building with Art Deco moldings, is popular with local artists and media types who come for the decent prices and the busy terrace. The food is simple but decent, such as steak and excellent fish dishes, all served with *frites* and vegetables.

BASTILLE Le Bistrot Paul Bert €€
18 rue Paul Bert, 75011 **Tel** *01 43 72 24 01*

This bistro's popularity is not surprising, given its combination of vintage decor – complete with zinc bar – and classic bistro cooking. Staff are welcoming, the steak-*frites* is one of the best in town, and the dining room is always buzzing with a mix of Parisians and international gourmets. The wine list is exceptional.

BASTILLE Le Repaire de Cartouche €€€
8 bd Filles du Calvaire, 75011 **Tel** *01 47 00 25 86*   **Map** *10 D2*

Rodolphe Paquin might not get as much press as some other Parisian chefs, but his two-level, country style restaurant continues to offer some of the best value for money in town. There's a bargain lunch menu and sophisticated *à la carte* offerings, such as *lièvre à la royale* (hare in wine sauce) and "crispy pig's head."

BEAUBOURG AND LES HALLES Le Tambour €
41 rue Montmartre, 75002 **Tel** *01 42 33 06 90*   **Map** *9 A1*

This Les Halles institution, decorated with wacky Parisian memorabilia, serves food until 3:30am (until 1am Sun and Mon), making it a prized destination for Paris' night-owls. Its late-night hours do not reduce the quality of the fare, which is consistently restorative, hearty bistro food along the *steak-frites* line.

BEAUBOURG AND LES HALLES Au Pied du Cochon €€
6 rue Coquillière, 75004 **Tel** *01 40 13 77 00*   **Map** *8 F1*

This colorfully restored brasserie was once popular with high society, who came to observe the workers in the old market and to savor the onion soup. Although touristy, this huge place is fun, and its menu has something for everyone (including excellent shellfish). Still one of the best places after a night out.

BEAUBOURG AND LES HALLES Aux Tonneaux des Halles €€
28 rue Montorgueil, 75001 **Tel** *01 42 33 36 19*   **Map** *9 A1*

A genuine Parisian bistro, Aux Tonneaux des Halles is one of the last surviving bistros of its kind, with its real zinc bar and one of the tiniest kitchens in Paris. Service is not particularly quick, but when the food is this good, who cares! The wine list offers good value.

BEAUBOURG AND LES HALLES Café Beaubourg €€
43 rue Saint-Merri, 75004 **Tel** *01 48 87 63 96*   **Map** *9 B2*

With views of the animated piazza of the Beaubourg museum, Café Beaubourg has elegant and contemporary decor. Simple and reliable, if slightly overpriced, fare is guaranteed – a variety of tartares, grilled meats, and fish. The menu even offers a light and tasty Thai salad.

BEAUBOURG AND LES HALLES Le Hangar €€
12 impasse Berthaud, 75003 **Tel** *01 42 74 55 44*   **Map** *9 B2*

Anyone who has found this locals' favorite in its quiet spot next door to the doll museum is sure to go back for the simple yet seductive cooking. Two trademark dishes are the panfried *foie gras* on olive oil mash and the runny chocolate cake. There isn't much in the way of decor, but the food more than makes up for it.

BEAUBOURG AND LES HALLES Chez la Vieille €€€
1 rue de Bailleul, 75001 **Tel** *01 42 60 15 78*   **Map** *8 F2*

Portions are getting smaller in Paris restaurants, but not in this old-fashioned bistro where diners are encouraged to help themselves to pâtés, salads, and desserts, such as chocolate mousse and homemade tarts. Main dishes are equally hearty; think tripe stew or *blanquette de veau* (veal in white sauce).

Key to Symbols *see back cover flap*

BEAUBOURG AND LES HALLES Georges
19 rue Beaubourg, 75004 **Tel** *01 44 78 47 99*   **Map** *9 B2*

On the top floor of the Pompidou Center, the Georges offers stunning views from its immense terrace. This trendy restaurant serves light and inspired cuisine, such as *mille-feuilles* of crab and mushrooms. Minimalist decor, with lots of steel and aluminum.

CHAILLOT AND PORTE MAILLOT Bistro le Goupil
4 rue Claude Debussy, 75017 **Tel** *01 45 74 83 25*   **Map** *1 C1*

This vintage bistro on the edge of Paris has a loyal following among locals, who come for the perfectly cooked entrecôte or more sophisticated dishes, such as monkfish with artichokes and wild mushrooms. The young chef surveys the lively scene from his open kitchen. Reservations are essential.

CHAILLOT AND PORTE MAILLOT La Plage
Port Javel, 75015 **Tel** *01 40 59 41 00*   **Map** *5 B5*

A spectacular site facing the Statue of Liberty on the Ile aux Cignes, the French and Mediterranean cuisine here is as good as the view. The huge terrace is the place to be seen at lunchtime, as well as an idyllic spot for a summer candlelit dinner. The decor is an attractive mix of wood and pastel tones. Service can be slow.

CHAILLOT AND PORTE MAILLOT Chez Géraud
31 rue Vital, 75016 **Tel** *01 45 20 33 00*   **Map** *5 B3*

Géraud Rongier, the jovial owner, is a scrupulous observer of *cuisine du marché*, using what's fresh at the market each day to create dishes like shoulder of lamb cooked on a spit, *sabodet* sausage in red wine sauce, skate with mustard, or roast pigeon with port sauce. The mural was specially created for the restaurant.

CHAILLOT AND PORTE MAILLOT Oum El Banine
16 bis rue Dufrenoy, 75016 **Tel** *01 45 04 91 22*   **Map** *5 A1*

The owner of this small, Moroccan restaurant in the chic residential quarter learned her art from her mother. Good *harira* (a thick, spicy soup), flavorful tagines, *pastilla* (a savory puff-pastry tart), and *brik* (stuffed pastry triangle). *Cous cous* is served with five choices of *ragoût*.

CHAILLOT AND PORTE MAILLOT Le Timgad
21 rue Brunel, 75017 **Tel** *01 45 74 23 70*   **Map** *1 C3*

Because this has been Paris's best-known, most elegant Maghrebian restaurant for years, it's essential to reserve ahead. The menu has many different *briks*, *tagines*, and *cous cous* dishes, as well as specialties like grilled pigeon, *pastilla*, and *méchoui* (whole roast lamb), which needs to be ordered in advance.

CHAILLOT AND PORTE MAILLOT Zébra Square
3 pl Clément Ader, 75016 **Tel** *01 44 14 91 91*   **Map** *5 B4*

Part of the Hotel Square complex, this modern building has stylish, minimalist decor that has been spiced up by splashes of zebra print. The equally innovative, modern cuisine is also served in great style. Brunch on Sundays is especially popular. A hit with the fashion and media crowd.

CHAMPS-ELYSEES Granterroirs
30 rue Miromesnil, 75008 **Tel** *01 47 42 18 18*   **Map** *2 B4*

In the modish Champs-Elysées area it is a surprise to come across this *épicerie*-restaurant decorated like a country kitchen, with long, shared wooden tables. More than 800 products line the shelves, many of which can be tasted in salad and open sandwich plates; a different hot dish is served every day. Lunch only.

CHAMPS-ELYSEES Le Bœuf sur le Toit
34 rue du Colisée, 75008 **Tel** *01 53 93 65 55*   **Map** *3 A4*

This Art Deco brasserie run by the Flo group, which owns many historic brasseries in Paris, is one of the more reliable places to eat around the Champs-Elysées. Alongside classic steak-*frites*, sole *meunière*, and seafood platters, you will find more adventurous specials such as lobster soup and monkfish cooked with Sauterne.

CHAMPS-ELYSEES Savy
23 rue Bayard, 75008 **Tel** *01 47 23 46 98*   **Map** *2 F1*

Opened in 1923, this Art-Deco restaurant with cozy booths in the front room is dedicated to the hearty cooking of the Aveyron region in central France. Order a marbled steak or the lamb shoulder for two, served with crisp shoestring *frites*, with one of the excellent wines from the cellar, perhaps a Mercury from Burgundy.

CHAMPS-ELYSEES Sens
23 rue Ponthieu, 75008 **Tel** *01 42 25 95 00*   **Map** *3 A5*

This concept restaurant, clad in soft grays and silvers, makes clever use of lighting to create the urban-chic feel that attracts the trendy crowd. Plastic, trunk-like pillars prop up the mezzanine. The menu features interesting Asian-influenced dishes such as grilled sea bream with wok-fried vegetables.

CHAMPS-ELYSEES Mini Palais
Grand Palais, 1 av Winston Churchill, 75008 **Tel** *01 42 56 42 42*   **Map** *3 A5*

Michelin-starred chef Eric Fréchon presides over the kitchen at this brasserie, housed in the Grand Palais. The cuisine focuses on well-sourced, top-quality seasonal produce. Be sure not to miss the special house dessert of a giant rum baba, served with vanilla cream.

CHAMPS-ELYSEES La Fermette Marbeuf 1900

5 rue Marbeuf, 75008 **Tel** *01 53 23 08 00*

Map *2 F5*

Fabulous Belle Epoque mosaics, tiles, and ironwork were discovered beneath the formica walls of this Champs Elysées bistro. La Fermette Marbeuf also serves good classic food, including a tasting menu with a wide range of *appellations contrôlées* wines.

CHAMPS-ELYSEES Lasserre

17 av Franklin Roosevelt, 75008 **Tel** *01 43 59 02 13*

Map *7 A1*

Built for the 1937 World Fair to imitate the interior of a luxury liner, this restaurant, once favored by Marc Chagall and Dalí, combines opulent decor with exceptional wines and deliciously refined cuisine by chef Christophe Moret. His dishes are inspired by 19th-century recipes such as macaroni with black truffles. Service is faultless.

CHAMPS-ELYSEES Le Cinq

31 av George V, 75008 **Tel** *01 49 52 70 00*

Map *2 E5*

For a rare splurge, it's hard to do better than this sumptuous, Michelin-starred restaurant in the George V. The technically stunning food is not stuck in a time warp; ingredients such as wasabi and harissa make their way into some dishes. The €85 lunch menu is something of a bargain, given the quality of the food.

CHAMPS-ELYSEES Pavillon Ledoyen

1 av Dutuit, 75008 **Tel** *01 53 05 10 01*

Map *7 B1*

The cuisine at Pavillon Ledoyen is refined. Delicacies are skillfully prepared with meticulous care and innovation, and include many fish and seafood specialties. Ask for a table in the dining room – a re-creation of a 1950s grill room – or one on the terrace.

ILE DE LA CITE AND ILE SAINT-LOUIS Isami

4 quai Orléans, 75004 **Tel** *01 40 46 06 97*

Map *9 C4*

As you walk through the door of this little Seine-side restaurant the hostess will warn you that they "serve only raw fish here," which is why this restaurant is so popular with Japanese expats and locals who come here for sushi of a quality rarely found in Paris. There is also a carefully chosen selection of fine sakes.

ILE DE LA CITE AND ILE SAINT-LOUIS Mon Vieil Ami

69 rue St Louis en l'Ile, 75004 **Tel** *01 40 46 01 35*

Map *9 B4*

Star Alsatian chef Antoine Westermann runs this modern bistro with stone walls, frosted glass partitions, and a long shared table on one side. Vegetables from market gardener Joël Thiébault feature in inventive dishes, which occasionally draw on North African ingredients such as preserved lemon or *cous cous*.

INVALIDES AND EIFFEL TOWER QUARTER Le Troquet

21 rue François Bonvin, 75015 **Tel** *01 45 66 89 00*

This is a jewel in an unlikely residential street with a view of the Eiffel Tower. Locals soak up the friendly atmosphere and devour Basque chef Christian Etchebest's fabulous cooking. The menu is chalked up on a blackboard each day in the retro-style dining room.

INVALIDES AND EIFFEL TOWER QUARTER Au Bon Accueil

14 rue Montessuy, 75007 **Tel** *01 47 05 46 11*

Map *6 E2*

Au Bon Accueil looks like a bistro from the outside with its terrace overlooking the Eiffel Tower but, once inside, the quality of the food and chic contemporary decor make it feel like a mini *haute cuisine* restaurant. If you are on a budget, try the amazing-value *prix fixe* menus at lunch and dinner, which don't skimp on ingredients.

INVALIDES AND EIFFEL TOWER QUARTER La Villa Corse

164 bd de Grenelle, 75015 **Tel** *01 53 86 70 81*

Map *6 E5*

In a pleasant neighborhood, La Villa Corse is one of the city's best restaurants for fresh and strongly flavored Corsican-Mediterranean cuisine. The menu features wild boar stew, olive veal, Brocciu cheese, and chestnut bread – a specialty from the city of Bonifacio. Good choice of Corsican wines.

INVALIDES AND EIFFEL TOWER QUARTER L'Arpège

84 rue de Varenne, 75007 **Tel** *01 47 05 09 06*

Map *7 B3*

Alain Passard's three-star restaurant near the Musée Rodin is one of the most highly regarded in Paris. It has striking pale-wood decor, sprightly service, and excellent food. The menu is based on the very best seasonal produce, with creative and harmonious pairings of ingredients. Don't miss the apple tart.

INVALIDES AND EIFFEL TOWER QUARTER Le Jules Verne

2nd platform, Eiffel Tower, 75007 **Tel** *01 45 55 61 44*

Map *6 D3*

This is no tourist trap: reservations at the Jules Verne on the second platform of the Eiffel Tower are among the hardest to obtain in Paris. The sleek, all-black decor suits the monument perfectly and the pretty, flavorful cuisine is very good, indeed.

JARDIN DES PLANTES QUARTER Marty Restaurant

20 av des Gobelins, 75005 **Tel** *01 43 31 39 51*

Map *13 B3*

The Marty was established by E. Marty in 1913 and is still family run. The interior is authentic Art Deco in style, but the cuisine steals the show. The menu features hearty fare, such as roast duck or rabbit casserole, and seasonal dishes, such as gazpacho. Excellent *crème brûlée*.

...ARTER Le Grenier de Notre Dame
... Bûcherie, 75005 **Tel** *01 43 29 98 29* | Map 9 A4 | €

... de Notre Dame opened in the 1970s and still exudes its original hippie atmosphere. Mostly organic ...ts go into the filling, predominantly macrobiotic meals such as vegetarian casserole, or vegetarian escalope ...crumbs. Good choice of reasonably priced wines, including some vintage Bordeaux wines.

... QUARTER Le Balzar
...ue des Ecoles, 75005 **Tel** *01 43 54 13 67* | Map 9 A5 | €€

...re's a fair choice of brasserie food here but the main attraction is the Left Bank ambience. Traditionally dressed ...iters weave their way among the hustle and bustle, providing express service, with archetypal brasserie decor to ...atch: there are large mirrors and comfortable leather seats.

LATIN QUARTER Perraudin
157 rue St-Jacques, 75005 **Tel** *01 46 33 15 75* | Map 12 F1 | €€

From the red-and-white tablecloths to the zinc-topped bar and the cuisine, everything at Perraudin looks and feels like a genuine 1900s bistro. On the menu are staples like *carré* of lamb and *frites*, carpaccio of beef with Parmesan, and creamy *riz au lait* (rice pudding). Reservations for 7–8pm only – or wait at the bar (tables turn over quickly.)

LATIN QUARTER Le Petit Pontoise
9 rue Pontoise, 75005 **Tel** *01 43 29 25 20* | Map 9 B5 | €€

This is a popular neighborhood venue, where herbs and spices are used inventively on the daily changing menu. A typical menu will probably be composed of *foie gras* with figs, followed by a whole vanilla roasted sea-bass, and, finally, pineapple roasted in ginger. Reservations recommended.

LATIN QUARTER Le Pré Verre
8 rue Thénard, 75005 **Tel** *01 43 54 59 47* | Map 9 A5 | €€

The brothers Marc and Philippe Delacourcelle run this plum-walled bistro whose cooking draws liberally on Asian ingredients – a signature dish is salt cod roasted with cassia bark and served with smoked potato purée. Wines come from small producers. The dining room is always lively.

LATIN QUARTER La Tour d'Argent
15–17 quai de la Tournelle, 75005 **Tel** *01 43 54 23 31* | Map 9 B5 | €€€€€

Established in 1582, originally in a stone tower, the Tour appears to be eternal. The young chefs hired by patrician owner Claude Terrail have rejuvenated the classic menu at this luxurious panoramic restaurant, with one of the finest wine cellars. The ground-floor bar is also a gastronomic museum. There's a cheaper set menu at lunchtime.

MONTMARTRE Au Grain de Folie
24 rue la Vieuville, 75018 **Tel** *01 42 58 15 57* | Map 4 F1 | €

Paris has few vegetarian restaurants, and this one has a truly cozy feel. The main courses consist of salads with interesting combinations of vegetables and grains (most of which are organic). Au Grain de Folie's apple crumble is highly recommended, so be sure to leave room for it.

MONTMARTRE Hotel Amour
8 rue de Navarin, 75009 **Tel** *01 48 78 31 80* | Map 4 F2 | €

Food at this low-key but trendy bistro, with vintage decor below Montmartre in the fashionable 9th *arrondissement*, is a cross between all things French and Anglo Saxon. Think macaroni and cheese, burgers, and *crème brulée*. In summer request a table in the pretty courtyard.

MONTMARTRE La Famille
41 rue des Trois Frères, 75009 **Tel** *01 42 52 11 12* | Map 4 F1 | €€

The contemporary French cuisine at La Famille is as delicious as it is avant-garde. Don't be surprised if your meal is presented with a smiley face drawn in the sauce! Dishes such as marinated salmon in a thyme and rosemary crust are excellent. The decor borders on minimalist.

MONTMARTRE Le Wepler
14 pl de Clichy, 75018 **Tel** *01 45 22 53 24* | Map 6 D1 | €€

Established in 1892, this retro-style brasserie is open until late into the night. Good for afternoon tea, early evening cocktails, and pre- or post-show dinners. Le Wepler serves appetizing large shellfish platters as well as sauerkraut, *andouillette* (sausage), and *confit de canard*.

MONTMARTRE Table d'Eugène
18 rue Eugène Sue, 75018 **Tel** *01 42 55 61 64* | Map 6 D1 | €€€

Slightly off the beaten track, this tiny restaurant is considered by many locals to be one of the best in Montmartre. Chef Geoffroy Maillard proves his worth with innovative cuisine, based around high-quality, carefully sourced seasonal produce. There is also an excellent selection of wines from independent producers. Book ahead.

MONTPARNASSE Port Manech
52 rue du Montparnasse, 75014 **Tel** *01 43 21 96 98* | Map 12 D2 | €

Port Manech is just like a little piece of Brittany right here in Paris. Try the tasty pancakes such as Provençal (mushrooms and snail butter) washed down perfectly with a cup of cider. There is a large choice of flambéed pancake varieties for dessert.

MONTPARNASSE La Régalade

49 av Jean Moulin, 75014 Tel 01 45 45 68 58

Gourmet fare for a bargain at this traditional bistro. Try dishes such as duck *foie gras* casserole or panfried ▢ leek vinaigrette for a main course, and the chef's specialty Grand Marnier soufflé for dessert. The seasonal r▢ based on a *cuisine du marché*. Reservations essential.

MONTPARNASSE Le Timbre

3 rue Sainte Beuve, 75006 Tel 01 45 49 10 40

Map 12

British native Chris Wright runs this postage-stamp-sized bistro with an open kitchen near the Luxembourg garden If the blackboard menu is resolutely French with neo-bistro dishes such as lentil salad with pork cheek or sea bream with olives, the plate of British cheese does pay tribute to his origins.

MONTPARNASSE Restaurant l'Assiette

€€€

181 rue du Château, 75014 Tel 01 43 22 64 86

Map 11 C4

Long run by cigar-smoking chef Lulu and frequented by socialist politicians, this insider's bistro was taken over by the young, Alain Ducasse-trained David Rathgeber in 2008. His menu of bistro classics such as marinated herrings with warm potato salad and crème caramel "revisited" is attracting a younger set of celebrities.

MONTPARNASSE La Cagouille

€€€

10–12 pl Constantin Brancusi, 75014 Tel 01 43 22 09 01

Map 11 C3

This large venue, on the stark new place Brancusi in the rebuilt Montparnasse district, is one of Paris's best fish restaurants. Fish is served simply with few sauces or adornments. Unusual seasonal delicacies might include black bay scallops and *vendangeurs* (tiny red mullet).

MONTPARNASSE La Coupole

€€€

102 bd du Montparnasse, 75014 Tel 01 43 20 14 20

Map 12 D2

This famous brasserie has been popular with the fashionistas, artists, and thinkers since its creation in 1927. Under the same ownership as Brasserie Flo, it has a similar menu: shellfish, smoked salmon, and good desserts. Flambéed beef is a specialty. Open from breakfast until 2am.

OPERA QUARTER Chartier

€

7 rue du Faubourg Montmartre, 75009 Tel 01 47 70 86 29

Map 4 F4

Despite its impressive 1900s decor, Chartier caters to people on a budget, mostly students and tourists, though some of the old *habitués* still come back for the basic cuisine (hard-boiled eggs with mayonnaise, house pâté, roast chicken, and pepper steak). Expect no-frills service; the waiters are very busy.

OPERA QUARTER La Bourse ou la Vie

€€

12 rue Vivienne, 75002 Tel 01 42 60 08 83

Map 10 F5

Looking for the best steak-*frites* in Paris? You may well find it at this restaurant with a red-and-yellow 1940s decor near the old stock exchange. The secret here is top-quality meat and the animal fat that is used to cook the *frites*; order it doused in creamy cracked-peppercorn sauce. A soundtrack of French chanson adds to the atmosphere.

OPERA QUARTER La Vaudeville

€€

29 rue Vivienne, 75002 Tel 01 40 20 04 62

Map 4 F5

This is one of seven brasseries owned by Paris's reigning brasserie king, Jean-Paul Bucher. Good shellfish, Bucher's famous smoked salmon, many fish dishes as well as classic brasserie standbys like pig's trotters and *andouillette* (tripe sausage). Quick, friendly service and a noisy ambience make it fun.

OPERA QUARTER Willi's Wine Bar

€€

13 rue des Petits-Champs, 75001 Tel 01 42 61 05 09

Map 8 F1

This charming, cozy wine bar has been offering a range of over 250 kinds of wine since 1980. The menu includes cream of asparagus soup with tarragon, salt-roasted lamb, and, of course, an excellent wine list. The bar also sells an array of examples of "wine art."

OPERA QUARTER Un Jour à Peyrassol

€€€

13 rue Vivienne, 75002 Tel 01 42 60 12 92

Map 10 F5

The Commanderie de Peyrassol, one of the best vineyards in Provence, runs this restaurant dedicated to truffles, wine, and other products from the area. The two rustic-meets-modern dining rooms have a warm Provençal atmosphere, reinforced by the earthy aroma of dishes such as truffle-laced scrambled eggs.

OPERA QUARTER Drouant

€€€€

16–18 pl Gaillon, 75002 Tel 01 42 65 15 16

Map 4 E5

This former Alsatian brasserie founded in 1880 is now a contemporary restaurant run by Antoine Westermann (who is also behind the bistro Mon Vieil Ami *see p602*). Order *à la carte* to sample his generous *hors d'oeuvres*, which fill the table with little bowls and plates. Upstairs are several private salons for groups.

OPERA QUARTER La Fontaine Gaillon

€€€€

1 rue de la Michodière, 75002 Tel 01 47 42 63 22

Map 4 E5

Housed in a 17th-century mansion, Fontaine Gaillon is partly owned by legendary film actor Gérard Depardieu. The menu changes daily and might include *confit de canard* or lamb chops and strawberries in Anjou wine. The interiors are comfortable, and there is a good wine list.

Key to Price Guide *see p600* **Key to Symbols** *see back cover flap*

SAINT-GERMAIN-DES-PRES Chez les Filles

64 rue du Cherche Midi, 75006 **Tel** *01 45 48 61 54*

Map 7 C5

Moroccan sisters run this small, lively restaurant, with exotic afternoon tea breaks. Tagines, salads, and *cous cous* are on the lunch menu, while teatime treats include great pastries washed down with lots of mint tea. The interior features wrought-iron work and *kilims* bearing Moroccan accents. Closed Sun.

SAINT-GERMAIN-DES-PRES La Crèmerie

9 rue Quatre Vents, 75006 **Tel** *01 43 54 99 30*

Map 8 E4

A former dairy store dating from 1880, this little store with a painted glass ceiling has been a wine bar since the 1950s. The current owners, a pair of former architects, focus on "natural" wines served with bread and butter from Brittany, hams from Spain, sausage from the Ardèche, and burrata cheese from Puglia in Italy.

SAINT-GERMAIN-DES-PRES J'Go

Rue Clement, 75006 **Tel** *01 43 26 19 02*

Map 8 E4

This lively Toulousian wine bar doubles as a *rotisserie* serving juicy spit-roasted lamb from Quercy, whole-roasted chicken, and black pig from Bigorre. The set menu is excellent value, offering pâté, a giant salad, and delicious lamb with creamy white beans. *Tapas* are also served and the wine (by the bottle or the glass) is consistently excellent.

SAINT-GERMAIN-DES-PRES L'Epigramme

9 rue de l'Eperon, 75006 **Tel** *01 44 41 00 09*

Map 8 F4

With terra cotta tiles, wood beams, and windows looking onto a leafy courtyard, L'Epigramme has plenty of Left Bank charm. The glassed-in kitchen turns out impeccable modern bistro food such as Basque farmer's pork on a bed of turnip *choucroute*; also look out for game in season. Service is equally polished.

SAINT-GERMAIN-DES-PRES Polidor

41 rue Monsieur le Prince, 75006 **Tel** *01 43 26 95 34*

Map 8 F5

Once frequented by Verlaine and Rimbaud, this is bohemian Paris incarnate. The place has kept its reputation by sticking to traditional cuisine at rock-bottom prices. Grilled steak, *daube de bœuf*, veal, and various dessert tarts feature on the menu.

ST-GERMAIN-DES-PRES Joséphine Chez Dumonet

117 rue du Cherche-Midi, 75006 **Tel** *01 45 48 52 40*

Map 11 C1

Pre-World War II bistros with old-fashioned menus have become a rarity in Paris, which explains the popularity of Joséphine. Start with the help yourself marinated herring before superb steak tartare or perhaps a rib-sticking cassoulet; desserts are equally gargantuan. The wine list is lengthy and expensive.

SAINT-GERMAIN-DES-PRES Le Procope

13 rue de l'Ancienne Comédie, 75006 **Tel** *01 40 46 79 00*

Map 8 F4

Opened in 1686, Paris's oldest café welcomed literary and political figures such as Voltaire and Diderot. Nowadays, it's still a hub for the intelligentsia, who sit alongside those curious about this historical place. *Coq au vin* (chicken cooked in wine) is the specialty. Shellfish platters are also popular.

THE MARAIS Chez Hannah

54 rue des Rosiers, 75004 **Tel** *01 42 74 74 99*

Map 9 C3

L'As du Fallafel may be better known, but Chez Hannah serves falafel sandwiches to rival any in this street filled with Jewish delis. They come packed with crunchy garbanzo bean balls, tahini sauce, melting aubergine (eggplant) and chilli, to be eaten in the lively dining room or standing in the street. A locals' favorite.

THE MARAIS Bistrot de L'Oulette

38 rue des Tournelles, 75004 **Tel** *01 42 71 43 33*

Map 10 E3

A tiny restaurant with good-quality food at reasonable prices. The fixed-price menu is particularly good value. Southwestern cuisine includes delicious *confit de canard* and cassoulet, followed by white chocolate soup for dessert. There is also superb homemade chestnut bread.

THE MARAIS Chez Jenny

39 bd du Temple, 75003 **Tel** *01 44 54 39 00*

Map 10 D1

This huge brasserie on the place de la République, with waitresses in traditional dress, has been a bastion of Alsatian cooking since it was founded more than 60 years ago. The *choucroute* (sauerkraut) *spéciale Jenny* makes a hearty meal, followed by a sorbet and a fruit liqueur.

THE MARAIS Le Colimaçon

44 rue Vieille du Temple, 75004 **Tel** *01 48 87 12 01*

Map 9 C3

Le Colimaçon (snail) refers to the restaurant's centerpiece: a corkscrew staircase. A historically preserved building dating from 1732, it has period wooden beams in the ceiling. Snails are also on the menu, along with frogs' legs in parsley and tomato sauce and *blanquette* of veal, the house specialty.

THE MARAIS Les Philosophes

28 rue Vieille du Temple, 75003 **Tel** *01 48 87 49 64*

Map 9 C3

Among the many cafés run by Xavier Denamour in this street, Les Philosophes is the most popular at meal times for its above-average bistro fare: the steak-*frites* are just as they should be, and tomato *tarte tatin* is a specialty. The terrace is perfect for people-watching, and service is jovial if rushed.

THE MARAIS Le 404
€€€

69 rue des Gravilliers, 75003 **Tel** *01 42 74 57 81*

Map 9 B1

It's a party every night at this North African restaurant lined with low tables and ottomans (there is also seating in the mezzanine). The later the hour, the higher the volume, and by the end of the night everyone is on their feet. The food is good, too: try one of the tagines, or the house specialty, couscous.

THE MARAIS Le Gaigne
€€€

12 rue Pecquay, 75004 **Tel** *01 44 59 86 72*

Map 9 C2

Chef Mickaël Gaignon had years of *haute cuisine* training under his belt before opening this intimate ivory-and-plum dining room with paintings of food on the walls. His inventive seasonal cooking focuses on the quality of the ingredients, such as scallop tartare flavored with lemon and served with red chicory.

THE MARAIS L'Ambroisie
€€€€€

9 pl des Vosges, 75004 **Tel** *01 42 78 51 45*

Map 10 D3

In a former jewelry store restored by Chef Bernard Pacaud, this is one of only a handful of Parisian restaurants with three Michelin stars. The cuisine includes a langoustine *feuillantine* (langoustines wrapped in very thin pastry) flavored with sesame seeds, and veal escalope served with minced artichokes. Reservations accepted one month in advance.

TUILERIES Le Fumoir
€€

6 rue de l'Amiral Coligny, 75001 **Tel** *01 42 92 00 24*

Map 4 F2

A café by day and a rather sultry restaurant-bar at night, Le Fumoir serves remarkably good food with a Scandinavian touch that often appears in condiments such as cranberries or horseradish. Cocktails are good and there is an intimate library at the back with big leather armchairs.

TUILERIES QUARTER Café Marly
€€€

93 rue de Rivoli, 75001 **Tel** *01 49 26 06 60*

Map 8 E2

In a wing of the Louvre, this is a handy restaurant when feet ache and bellies rumble after trekking round the galleries. You'll find everything from salads and burgers to traditional and contemporary French cusine. It's also in a top spot for a coffee on the terrace overlooking the Louvre's main thoroughfare.

TUILERIES QUARTER Le Grand Véfour
€€€€€

17 rue de Beaujolais, 75001 **Tel** *01 42 96 56 27*

Map 12 F1

This 18th-century restaurant has two Michelin stars and is considered by many to be Paris's most attractive. Chef Guy Martin's creative dishes include *foie gras* ravioli with a truffle sauce, and hazelnuts and chocolate with caramel ice cream and sea salt.

ILE DE FRANCE

BARBIZON Hôtellerie du Bas-bréau
€€€€

22 Grande Rue, 77630 **Tel** *01 60 66 40 05*

Author Robert Louis Stevenson has been among the celebrated guests at this hotel-restaurant with its classic menu and enormous wine list. The much-praised cooking includes sole with caviar, wild boar, and venison in season, and, for dessert, Grand Marnier soufflé.

BOULOGNE-BILLANCOURT Le Pré Catelan
€€€€€

Bois de Boulogne, Rte de Suresnes, 75016 **Tel** *01 44 14 41 14*

Housed in a chic Napoleon III villa, in a charming setting by the Bois de Boulogne, this Michelin-starred restaurant serves *haute cuisine* fit for a king. Chef Frédéric Aton strives for perfection, with dishes such as *foie gras* in port, fried with lentils and served in a cream of *foie gras* and black truffle sauce.

DAMPIERRE Auberge Saint-Pierre
€€

1 rue de Chevreuse, 78720 **Tel** *01 30 52 53 53*

This half-timbered inn facing the grand château de Dampierre has a rustic, convivial dining room. The gourmet menu has fine dishes such as tartare of potatoes with *foie gras*, salad of baby scallops with white radish, stuffed quail with lentils, and chicken leg with *foie gras* stuffing.

ISSY-LES-MOULINEAUX L'Ile
€€€

Parc Ile Saint-Germain, 170 quai Stalingrad, 92130 **Tel** *01 41 09 99 99*

Set in the heart of the Ile St-Germain Park, with its vast terrace shaded by chestnut trees, this restaurant is a great place for outdoor dining in the warmer months. The setting can also be admired from the conservatory in cooler weather. Fine traditional cuisine includes revisited classics such as salmon and scallop tartare with mango and ginger.

ISSY-LES-MOULINEAUX Les Symples de l'Os à Moelle
€€

18 av de la République, 92130 **Tel** *01 41 08 02 52*

This restaurant replicates the winning formula of La Cave de l'Os à Moelle, an annex of the gourmet bistro L'Os à Moelle in the 15th arrondissement. Seated at long tables, diners help themselves to a multitude of pâtés, soups, and salads which are followed by a hearty main course and a buffet of cheeses and desserts... all for €25.

Key to Price Guide *see p600* **Key to Symbols** *see back cover flap*

LE-PERREUX-SUR-MARNE Les Magnolias 目 T P €€€€
48 av de Bry, 94170 **Tel** *01 48 72 47 43*

After working in a series of *haute-cuisine* restaurants, young chef Jean Chauvel went out on a limb and opened this wildly creative restaurant in a little-known suburb of Paris. The risk has paid off: food-lovers come from far and wide for his graphically presented dishes, each of which comes with a whimsical menu description.

MAISONS-LAFFITTE Les Jardins de la Vieille Fontaine 🖼 €€€
8 av Grétry, 78600 **Tel** *01 39 62 01 78*

An elegant setting inside a beautiful white mansion near the Maisons-Laffitte Park. Seasonal menus offer gastronomic cuisine in an unpretentious manner. Delicious, well-presented dishes like a *mille-feuille* of goat's cheese and aubergine (eggplant) or caramelized pan-fried cod. Irresistible desserts. Reasonably priced wine.

NEUILLY-SUR-SEINE Le Zinc Zinc P €€
209 ter av du Général-de-Gaulle, 92200 **Tel** *01 40 88 36 06*

Le Zinc Zinc has reinvented the bistro for the 21st century, serving breakfast, lunch, *tapas*, and dinner with a huge choice of dishes for every appetite. You can sit at the bar for a simple meal of steak-*frites* or Spanish ham, or have a three-course dinner of contemporary bistro fare in the bordeaux-and-cream dining room.

PROVINS Aux Vieux Remparts 🛠 👤 🖼 €€€€
3 rue Couverte, 77160 **Tel** *01 64 08 94 00*

In the medieval part of town, this timbered building boasts a restaurant and a hotel. The Aux Vieux Remparts is a gastronomic restaurant serving creative fare such as prawns with eggplant caviar, carpaccio of monkfish, and chocolate cake made with salt and served with caramelized lemon.

RAMBOUILLET Le Cheval Rouge 目 €€
78 rue du Général de Gaulle, 78120 **Tel** *01 30 88 80 61*

This intimate restaurant is close to the Château de Rambouillet. The good-humored chef serves up an array of delicious traditional fare such as *foie gras*, snails, and steak tartare. A great-value buffet is available at lunchtime. Some of the tables are in the conservatory.

RUEIL-MALMAISON Relais de St-Cucufa 👤 🖼 P €€€
114 rue Générale-de-Miribel, 92500 **Tel** *01 47 49 79 05*

Combining Breton and Italian flair, the chefs present a traditional menu that includes *morille fricassée* with poached egg; lobster, grapefruit, and avocado salad; platter of grilled shellfish; fillet of beef; and roast lamb. Enjoy lunch in the attractive garden, or dinner in front of the fire. Classic wine selection.

ST-GERMAIN-EN-LAYE Le Saint Exupéry 👤 P 🖼 P €€€
11 av des Loges, 78100 **Tel** *01 39 21 50 90*

In an elegant setting in the Ermitage des Loges hotel near the château, this restaurant is frequented by locals. The young chef enlivens classic dishes, such as entrecôte steak with panfried Jerusalem artichokes, gratin of scallops and braised chicory, and stuffed-squid risotto. The children's menu is excellent value.

ST-OUEN Le Soleil P €€€
109 av Michelet, 93400 **Tel** *01 40 10 08 08*

Steps away from the St-Ouen flea market and a short drive from the Stade de France, this charming bistro has a vibrant interior. The menu includes duck confit with spicy aubergine (eggplant) or more classic dishes such as a Charolais entrecôte. Superb Rum baba for dessert. Good, slightly expensive wine. Reserve ahead.

VERSAILLES La Terrasse 🖼 €€€
11 rue St-Honoré, 78000 **Tel** *01 39 50 76 00*

A fun restaurant specializing in southwestern cuisine. On a warm day the large, shaded terrace is a godsend. The decor inside is bright and kitsch. Specialties include some intriguing *foie gras* combinations, such as *foie gras* with gingerbread, as well as duck with honeyed peaches.

VERSAILLES Le Valmont 👤 目 🖼 P €€€€
20 rue au Pain, 78000 **Tel** *01 39 51 39 00*

Refined cuisine at this yellow-and-blue bistro tucked behind the market hall. Chef Philippe Mathieu presents an ambitious menu with dishes such as escalope of veal deglazed with Banyuls vinegar, John Dory with fennel and ginger, and *fondant au chocolat* for dessert. Good wines by the glass.

LE NORD & PICARDY

AIRE-SUR-LA-LYS Hostellerie des Trois Mousquetaires 👤 P 🖼 €€€
Château de la Redoute, rte de Béthune, 62120 **Tel** *03 21 39 01 11*

Rural peace and the charm of a 19th-century mansion in its own grounds with a lake. Unusually, the kitchens are visible, and serve imaginative classic cuisine. The varied menu includes regional dishes. A popular destination with visitors from the UK; reserve ahead.

AMIENS Le Pré Porus
`P 🏃 ♿ 🖼` €€

95 rue de Voyelle, 80000 **Tel** *03 22 46 25 03*

Attractive and popular riverside restaurant by the Somme. The very varied menu specializes in all sorts of fish dishes as well as grilled meat according to the season and panfried *foie gras* with mango. A good place to stop for lunch while visiting the nearby historic Roman waterways and market gardens.

AMIENS L'Aubergade
`P 🏃 🖼 🍷` €€€€€

78 rte Nationale, 80480 **Tel** *03 22 89 51 41* **Fax** *03 22 95 44 05*

Mediterranean-looking restaurant run by Eric Boutte, a young chef who won his first star and is making a name for himself. After working in top Paris restaurants, he returned to his native Amiens with a vision for his restaurant. His favorite ingredient is duck. Other dishes include panfried scallops with *foie gras* and lime soufflé with prunes.

ARRAS La Faisanderie
`🏃` €€€

45 grand place, 62000 **Tel** *03 21 48 20 76*

Also on the magnificent Grand Place, with its spectacular scrolled gable façades, this restaurant is housed in a 17th-century building with a splendid brick vaulted dining room. The cuisine is dictated by what the chef finds at the market. The best of several restaurants on the square, by far.

BEAUVAIS La Table de Céline
`🏃` €€

6 bis rue Antoine Caron, 60000 **Tel** *03 44 45 79 79*

This traditional restaurant is decorated in soothing tones, and has an open fire in winter, with an agreeable terrace for outdoor dining in the warmer months. Choice dishes include ingredients such as scallops, prawns, duck *foie gras*, salmon, and local lamb. Closed Mon, and Tue, Thu, Fri, and Sat lunch.

BERGUES Le Bruegel
`🏃 🖼` €

1 rue du Marché aux Fromages, 59380 **Tel** *03 28 68 19 19* **Fax** *03 28 68 67 12*

Bergues is just outside Dunkirk and is a pleasant surprise. This is a very popular restaurant for families, with long tables and waiters in medieval dress. The picturesque building by the canal dates from 1597, when Spain ruled Flanders. Pork cheeks and lentils and other Flemish dishes with beer are the order of the day.

BOULOGNE-SUR-MER La Matelote
`P 🏃 📋 ♿ 🍷` €€€€

80 bd Ste Beuve, 62200 **Tel** *03 21 30 17 97* **Fax** *03 21 83 29 24*

One of the rising gastronomic stars, this is a top-notch seafood restaurant on the seafront, opposite the National Marine center. The interior is fancy, with sea-going ornaments and a red-and-gold Louis XVI motif. Try the warm lobster with artichoke hearts and basil or monkfish in Parmesan.

CALAIS Histoire Ancienne
`🏃 📋` €€

20 rue Royale, 62100 **Tel** *03 21 34 11 20* **Fax** *03 21 96 19 58*

This is a modernized restaurant that has managed to preserve its image as an old-fashioned bistro, with a zinc counter and the old-style bench seating. It is located opposite the Parc Richelieu. The well prepared menu is split between grilled meats and traditional local dishes.

CALAIS Le Channel
`🏃 📋 🍷` €€€

3 bd de la Résistance, 62100 **Tel** *03 21 34 42 30* **Fax** *03 21 97 42 43*

A good fish restaurant right next to the harbor, the yacht club, and the Bassin du Paradis, with a fine view of the boats coming and going. The restaurant is bright and nicely decorated with painted woodwork. It has a wine list to be proud of. An ideal spot to wait for the ferry.

CAMBRAI Le Jolly Sailor
`🏃 🖼` €

11 rue de Douai, 59400 **Tel** *03 27 81 29 66*

Simple, good-value traditional cuisine is offered at this restaurant housed in a bright-yellow building, with a terrace overlooking a canal. The menu draws on market availability and changes daily. The atmosphere is warm and welcoming, and there is often live music.

CASSEL Estaminet T'Kasteel Hof
`🏃 🖼` €

Rue St-Nicolas, 59670 **Tel** *03 28 40 59 29*

There are sweeping views of the flat countryside from this Flemish-style *estaminet* (no-frills café) which serves local dishes, often with local cheeses, accompanied by beer. It was at Cassel that the "Grand Old Duke of York," son of George III, marched his 10,000 men up to the top of the hill (as popularized in a British song).

COMPIEGNE Bistro des Arts
`🏃 📋 🖼` €

35 cours Guynemer, 60200 **Tel** *03 44 20 10 10*

A lively bistro serving sophisticated, good-value fare. Located in the center of town, with an artistic atmosphere. Chairs and red leather benches, but no tablecloths. Each day's menu is put up on the slate according to the market. The cuisine is traditional French, and usually includes a meat and a fish dish.

COMPIEGNE Alain Blot
`P 🏃 ♿ 🖼 🍷` €€€€

21 rue Maréchal Foch, Rethondes, 60153 **Tel** *03 44 85 60 24* **Fax** *03 44 85 92 35*

The proprietor's motto is that seafood should be "a simple expression of the sea." This starred restaurant, with a delightful dining room and veranda opening onto an immaculate garden, is known for its range of classic dishes, such as grilled bass with caramelized red onion. Reserve ahead.

Key to Price Guide *see p600* **Key to Symbols** *see back cover flap*

DOUAI La Terrasse

36 terrasse St-Pierre, 59500 **Tel** *03 27 88 70 04* **Fax** *03 27 88 36 05*

An excellent hotel and restaurant in a lane next to the Collégiale St Pierre, with an extensive wine list of over 1,000 references. The opulent restaurant is decorated with paintings. Try the chef's inspiration – smoked salmon stuffed with asparagus and grilled scallops with blood sausage.

DUNKIRK Estaminet Flamand

6 rue des Fusiliers-Marins, 59140 **Tel** *03 28 66 98 35*

Having suffered from many wars, Dunkirk is not a scenic tourist destination. It has, however, retained its culinary traditions, exemplified here in this pleasant *estaminet* (simple café). Delicious and authentic Flemish cuisine including marrow bones, *Maroilles* cheese, beer tart, and sugar tart.

DUNKIRK L'Estouffade

2 quai de la Citadelle, 59140 **Tel** *03 28 63 92 78* **Fax** *03 28 63 92 78*

A small, popular restaurant specializing in seafood, with views of the port. In summer there is a quiet terrace onto the quay that runs alongside the commercial basin. Turbot is a specialty here. Desserts include chocolate and fruit specialties.

LAON La Petite Auberge

45 bd Brossolette, 02000 **Tel** *03 23 23 02 38*

Chef Willy Marc Zorn serves a creative and exotic menu, with distinct Oriental influences. His specialties include hot *foie gras de canard* and local pork with polenta and Espelette peppers. The extensive wine list has more than 200 prestige vintages, and each dish is complemented by a selected bottle.

LILLE Au Bout des Doigts

5 rue St-Joseph, 59000 **Tel** *03 20 74 55 95*

A different concept for the French in dining out, meals at this restaurant comprise a selection of 8–10 small dishes. There are no knives and you can eat with your fingers. The cooking is based on mixing flavors, and the wine is drawn from all over the world. The decor is contemporary.

LILLE La Ducasse

95 rue de Solferino, 59000 **Tel** *03 20 57 34 10*

This traditional brasserie in the lively Halles district is something of an institution in Lille. Regional cuisine and beer from a local microbrewery are the highlights, but there is also a mechanical musical box and an accordionist who plays on Friday evenings for the diners who like to sing. Choose a table on the terrace in fine weather.

LILLE Le Compostelle

4 rue Saint-Etienne, 59800 **Tel** *03 28 38 08 30* **Fax** *03 28 38 08 39*

Just off the Grand Place is this former 16th-century hostel on the route to the shrine of St-Jacques de Compostelle (Santiago de Compostela) in northwest Spain. Today the hostel combines old-fashioned charm with contemporary decor. The chef provides a nice blend of regional and traditional cuisine.

MONTREUIL-SUR-MER Auberge de la Grenouillère

Rue de la Grenouillère, La Madeleine-sous-Montreuil **Tel** *03 21 06 07 22* **Fax** *03 21 86 36 36*

Three kilometers from Montreuil, this Picardy farm on the banks of the Canche is furnished traditionally with copper, antique sideboards, and wall paintings of frogs enjoying a good meal. The modern menu is backed up by a good wine list. Tasty crayfish and frogs' legs. The restaurant gained its first Michelin star in 2008.

POIX DE PICARDIE L'Auberge de la Forge

14 rue du 49ème Régiment BCA, Caulières, 80290 **Tel** *03 22 38 00 91* **Fax** *03 22 38 08 48*

A former staging post on the way from Amiens to Neufchatel, this half-timbered Picardy inn serves old-fashioned hearty fare. The restaurant is stylish and attractive. The chef's specialty is duck, in various forms. The *endives gratinées*, ham with *Maroilles* cheese, and endive and scallops are also good.

RECQUES-SUR-HEM Château de Cocove

Av de Cocove **Tel** *03 21 82 68 29* **Fax** *03 21 82 72 59*

This fine 18th-century château, halfway between Calais and St-Omer, is a real rural retreat. Napoleon had parties here while waiting to invade England. The restaurant is in the beautifully restored old stone stables. Trays of shellfish can be specially prepared if ordered in advance.

ROEUX Le Grand Bleu

41 rue Henri-Robert, 62118 **Tel** *03 21 55 41 74*

A wooden chalet houses this popular establishment where fish dishes, such as turbot with aubergine (eggplant) fries, are the specialty. Wine is served either by the glass or by the bottle. Choose a window table and enjoy the view of Le Grand Bleu lake, which turns a beautiful shade of blue in the sunshine.

ROYE La Flamiche

20 pl de l'Hôtel de Ville, 80700 **Tel** *03 22 87 00 56* **Fax** *03 22 78 46 77*

Known as a prestige gastronomic restaurant throughout the area (with a Michelin star since 1964), Madame Klopp has run this impeccable establishment for many years. Try the panfried scallops, the tajine of Somme eels, or local *flamiche* with leeks. The dining room is filled with an exhibition of sculpture and paintings.

SANGATTE Les Dunes
P 🏃 €€
Rte Nationale 48, Blériot Plage, 62231 **Tel** *03 21 34 54 30* **Fax** *03 21 97 17 63*

This hotel and restaurant is located at Blériot Plage where, in 1909, an intrepid Frenchman set out on his successful attempt to be the first man to cross the Channel in powered flight. Today this establishment is very handy for the Channel Tunnel. Great seafood: try the cassoulet of mussels.

SARS-POTERIES L'Auberge Fleurie
P 🏃 🎴 €€€€
67 rue Général de Gaulle, 59216 **Tel** *03 27 67 38 22* **Fax** *03 27 65 88 73*

This grand farmhouse with pretty gardens has been converted into a restaurant serving classic French cooking at its best. The pike-perch on a bed of cabbage and bacon is good, as is the shellfish. In winter, venison, wild boar, and partridge feature regularly on the menu.

STEENVOORDE Auprès de mon Arbre
🏃 🎴 €€
932 rte d'Ecke, 59114 **Tel** *03 28 49 79 49*

In this town, famous for its carnival giants that parade each year through the center, and for its church steeple with its high belfry, this restaurant is well regarded. The owner was the chef at a well-known Lille restaurant before settling here in the late 1990s. Classic French as well as traditional Flemish cuisine.

WIMEREUX Hôtel Atlantique
P 🏃 🎴 €€€€
Digue de mer, 1st floor, 62930 **Tel** *O3 21 32 41 01* **Fax** *03 21 87 46 17*

Right on the promenade, with a great view of the sea, as you would expect. The chef Alain Delpierre comes as something of a surprise in this old-fashioned setting. Red mullet in a salad with balsamic vinegar is one specialty. There are also 18 refurbished guest rooms – ask for one facing the Channel.

CHAMPAGNE

AIX-EN-OTHE Auberge de la Scierie
P 🏃 ♿ 🎴 🍽 €€€
La Vove, 10160 **Tel** *03 25 46 71 26.* **Fax** *03 25 46 65 69*

Auberge de la Scierie is run by a Franco-Australian-British couple, who worked together at the Savoy in London, and together speak five languages. They specialize in shellfish with a distinctly Oriental flavor. This auberge, set in 8 acres (3 ha) of grounds with a swimming pool, also has guest rooms, and cooking courses are offered.

ARSONVAL Hostellerie de la Chaumière
P 🏃 ♿ 🎴 €€€
Arsonval, 10200 **Tel** *03 25 27 91 02* **Fax** *03 25 27 90 26*

For many years now this hospitable Anglo-French couple have been welcoming guests to their restaurant and hotel overlooking the Aube. It is close to the route de Champagne. Dishes include homemade *foie gras*, and some of the best kidneys and bacon in France. Rustic dining room with wooden beams.

BAR-SUR-AUBE Le Cellier aux Moines
🏃 €€
Rue Général Vouillemont, 10200 **Tel** *03 25 27 08 01* **Fax** *03 25 01 56 22*

As the name implies, this huge 12th-century cellar in the center of this pleasant old town (once the main route to Switzerland) has been converted into a restaurant with a vineyard theme. The staff wear *vignerons'* outfits for groups. Try the *andouillette* (tripe sausage) with excellent local Chaource cheese.

BREVONNES Au Vieux Logis
P 🏃 ♿ 🎴 €€
1 rue de Piney, 10220 **Tel** *03 25 46 30 17*

This first-class restaurant is part of a completely refurbished traditional hotel. The menu features classic French cuisine, including dishes such as snails in garlic cream with local Chaource cheese. This is a good choice for those visiting the artificial lakes nearby as well as the Fôret de L'Orient.

CHALONS-EN-CHAMPAGNE Les Temps Changent
P 🏃 📋 ♿ €€
1 rue Garinet, 51000 **Tel** *03 26 66 41 09*

Head to the Hôtel d'Angleterre in the town center to dine at this popular bistro. There is a different menu every day that focuses on seasonal produce. Try the roast shoulder of lamb with basil or the delicious passion fruit soufflé accompanied by wine served either by the glass or bottle.

CHALONS-EN-CHAMPAGNE Au Carillon Gourmand
🏃 📋 🎴 €€€
15 bis pl Monseigneur Tissier, 51000 **Tel** *03 26 64 45 07*

In the center of the old town in the Notre-Dame-de-Vaux quarter, this welcoming restaurant has a pleasant covered terrace that opens onto the street. The *plat du jour* (dish of the day) is chosen according to what is best at the market. Try carpaccio of salmon or spiced duck pâté.

CHAUMONT Les Remparts
P 🏃 📋 ♿ 🎴 €€€
72 rue de Verdun, 52000 **Tel** *03 25 32 64 40*

This coaching inn has a restaurant, brasserie, and hotel, all on-site. The restaurant specializes in dishes that include truffles and the local Langres cheese. Much cheaper meals are available in the Brasserie 1-2-3, located in the same building. Both restaurants look out over the attractive grounds.

Key to Price Guide *see p600* **Key to Symbols** *see back cover flap*

COMBEAUFONTAINE Le Balcon
1 pl 15 Juin 1940, 70120 **Tel** *03 84 92 11 13* **Fax** *03 84 92 15 89*

This good old-fashioned provincial restaurant, half an hour from Langres, deserves recognition. Try the chef's recommendation – the *menu gourmand* – and you will come away more than satisfied in body and wallet. The brasserie offers good weekday lunches. Rooms are also available.

EPERNAY La Table Kobus
3 rue Dr Rousseau, 51200 **Tel** *03 26 51 53 53* **Fax** *03 26 58 42 68*

An excellent brasserie near the center of this town that is all about champagne. Uniquely, you can bring your own bottle of champagne to drink with your meal. The menu is classic French cuisine. The homemade terrine of *foie gras fait maison* is particularly recommended.

FOUCHERES Auberge de la Seine
1 faubourg de Bourgogne, 10260 **Tel** *03 25 40 71 11* **Fax** *03 25 40 84 09*

A picturereserve posting inn halfway between the Côte des Bar and the Champagne vineyards. The restaurant in Louis XIII-style opens onto a pretty riverside terrace. The chef, who has run the kitchens of other starred restaurants in the area, specializes in lobster.

JOINVILLE Le Soleil d'Or
9 rue Capucins, 52300 **Tel** *03 25 94 15 66* **Fax** *03 25 94 39 02*

This 17th-century house, with elegant guest rooms and a restaurant, was the home of the Guise family. The dining room is decorated with statues from a 14th-century convent, and there is an agreeable covered terrace. An original menu changes every day.

LANGRES La Pignata
59 rue Diderot, 52200 **Tel** *03 25 87 63 70*

Italian restaurant serving pizzas and other tasty dishes, such as veal with Milanese sauce or seafood tagliatelle, with house wine. It is located in the center of this historic fortress town. Wander the old cramped streets and try to spot the first barracks allocated to the Foreign Legion, in 1832.

LANGRES L'Auberge des Voiliers
Lac de la Liez, 52000 **Tel** *03 25 87 05 74*

Hidden away from the historic city of Langres, this auberge overlooks a good-sized lake with views of the city walls. The main restaurant serves "modernized" traditional dishes – *foie gras* with rhubarb or fillet of pike with nettle soufflé. There is also a cheaper brasserie if you prefer more simple cuisine.

LE MESNIL-SUR-OGER Le Mesnil
2 rue Pasteur, 51190 **Tel** *03 26 57 95 57* **Fax** *03 26 57 78 57*

In a pretty wine-growing village in the heart of the Champagne vineyards is this gourmet restaurant, set in an attractive old house. The restaurant owner is happy to show patrons around his fine wine cellars. The village is the home of the museum of the vine and wine in the Maison Launois.

L'EPINE Aux Armes de Champagne
31 av de Luxembourg, 51460 **Tel** *03 26 69 30 30* **Fax** *03 26 69 30 26*

A top-class establishment, with a restaurant and hotel rooms, next to the majestic 15th-century basilique Notre Dame. Classic French cuisine is prepared with vegetables from the restaurant's garden, such as asparagus with truffle sauce and flakes of *foie gras* or lobster with apricots. Good vegetarian selection.

NOGENT-SUR-SEINE Au Beau Rivage
20 rue Villiers-aux-Choux, 10400 **Tel** *03 25 39 84 22* **Fax** *03 25 39 18 32*

This riverside hotel and restaurant comes highly recommended, particularly since the bedrooms have been refurbished. An attractive terrace looks out from the dining room onto the Seine. French traditional *cuisine gastronomique*, with *foie gras* and rabbit on a menu that will make your mouth water.

REIMS La Brasserie Boulingrin
48 rue Mars, 51100 **Tel** *03 26 40 96 22* **Fax** *03 26 40 03 92*

This famous Reims brasserie and a regular meeting place for locals has kept its Art Deco mosaics of jolly grape harvesters *vendangeurs en Champagne*. Good value and a lively place to dine, near the covered market. Oysters and *steak tartare* are specialties. There is also a large selection of champagnes.

REIMS Le Café du Palais
14 pl Myron Herrick, 51100 **Tel** *03 26 47 52 54*

An Aladdin's cave of paintings, photos, and a famous Art-Deco, stained-glass roof by Jacques Simon have been assembled over the years by owner Jean-Louis Vogt. This is a much-loved family run brasserie in the heart of Reims, which has been in existence since 1930. Excellent main dishes, great desserts, and a fine selection of champagne.

REIMS L'Assiette Champenoise
40 av Paul Vaillant-Couturier, Tinqueux, 51430 **Tel** *03 26 84 64 64* **Fax** *03 26 04 15 69*

A well-established gastronomic star, which is reflected in the price. Lobster dishes are a specialty, and pigeon and lamb are other favorites of chef Arnaud Lallement. Housed in an elegant *maison de maitre*, the restaurant has two rosettes. Attractions include a beautiful flower garden and terrace.

ROCROI Hôtel-Restaurant le Commerce
5 pl d'Armes, 08230 **Tel** *03 24 54 11 15*

This pleasantly old-fashioned, good-value restaurant is set in the central square of an amazingly well preserved and unique star-shaped fortress rebuilt by Vauban in 1675. It serves traditional and local dishes such as *escargots*, *coq au vin*, or rabbit in cider, and for dessert *île flottante* (poached meringues), chocolate mousse, or *profiteroles*.

SEDAN Le Saint-Michel
3 rue Saint-Michel, 08200 **Tel** *03 24 29 04 61*

Situated beneath the Château Fort de Sedan, this restaurant is combined with a hotel and a gift shop stocked with local crafts and culinary produce. The traditional menu includes Ardennes specialties, such as wild boar, pork kidneys, and a variety of cured meats and hams.

SIGNY LE PETIT Au Lion d'Or
Pl de l'Eglise, 08380 **Tel** *03 24 53 51 76* **Fax** *03 24 53 36 96*

On the circuit of fortified churches, this restaurant and hotel is housed behind an 18th-century red-brick façade. The nonsmoking Louis XIII restaurant serves a delicious *foie gras* with a wild rose jam. Skilfully prepared fish is another specialty of this well-run dining establishment.

ST IMOGES La Maison du Vigneron
Rte Départamentale 951, 51160 **Tel** *03 26 52 88 00* **Fax** *03 26 52 86 03*

Between Reims and Epernay, in a village in the heart of the Parc Régionale de la Montagne Noire et de Reims, is this good restaurant and champagne house. Excellent regional dishes imaginatively prepared and, if you wish, accompanied by the owner's champagne vintages.

STE MENEHOULD Le Cheval Rouge
1 rue Chanzy, 51800 **Tel** *03 26 60 81 04* **Fax** *03 26 60 93 11*

Two places to eat in one establishment: the restaurant, with its distinctive fireplace, or in the much cheaper brasserie, which specializes in pigs' trotters. Monsieur Fourreau, the owner of the establishment, sends pigs' trotters all over Europe.

TROYES Les Crieurs de Vin
4 pl Jean Jaurès, 10000 **Tel** *03 25 40 01 01*

An inexpensive wine bar with an agreeably raffish air run by two wine fanatics. In the front they sell wine to take out, and in the back they sell it to accompany their bistro-style menu. Lots of exposed beams and bare wooden tables. The traditional French menu is on a blackboard.

TROYES Tartines et Bulles
31 rue de la Cité, 10000 **Tel** *03 25 80 58 23*

In attractive premises, this restaurant uses local produce to turn out good, cheap dishes. The specialty is *tartines gratinées* (toasted sandwiches) made with local Chaource cheese. There are copious salads, as well as delicious desserts. Wine is served by the glass or jug, and there's a choice of two champagnes by the glass.

TROYES Au Jardin Gourmand
31 rue Paillot de Montabert, 10000 **Tel** *03 25 73 36 13* **Fax** *03 25 73 36 13*

In the heart of the old town, with its forest of half-timbered houses, this charming restaurant quietly pleases all who come here. The specialty is the local delicacy, *andouillette* (tripe sausage). Pleasant small paneled dining room and delightful terrace for eating out in summer. Try the lavender ice cream.

VILLEMOYENNE La Parentele
32 rue Marcelin Lévêque, 10260 **Tel** *03 25 43 68 68* **Fax** *03 25 43 68 69*

This restaurant has made a name for itself with crayfish cooked in coconut cream and ravioli *au foie gras*. In a short time the owners, two brothers who took over the family business, won their first Michelin star. Experts say the champagne wine list is perfect.

ALSACE & LORRAINE

BAERENTHAL L'Arnsbourg
18 untermuhlthal, 57230 **Tel** *03 87 06 50 85* **Fax** *03 87 06 57 67*

One of the few three-rosette restaurants in France, hidden in a pretty glade in the forest of the northern Vosges. Brother and sister team Jean-Georges and Cathy Klein conjure up light, imaginative dishes, such as *grillade de foie gras* of duck with crystalized lemon, accompanied by great wines.

BITCHE Le Strasbourg
24 rue Col. Teyssier, 57230 **Tel** *03 87 96 00 44* **Fax** *03 87 96 11 57*

Excellent hotel restaurant in the shadow of Vauban's fascinating citadelle, which contains a memorial to the American infantry that liberated the town. Le Strasbourg has a big traditional dining room, with a beautiful white molded fireplace. The cuisine here is traditional, with *foie gras* and a range of fish dishes.

Key to Price Guide *see p600* **Key to Symbols** *see back cover flap*

COLMAR La Table de Louise

2 rue Edouard-Richard, 68000 **Tel** *03 89 24 00 00*

Austere but fashionable decor in this attractive brasserie brings a touch of 1900s Parisian style to comfortable, old-fashioned Colmar. The wide ranging traditional menu includes terrine of goose *foie gras* with pumpkin chutney. Situated just 2-minutes from the very beautiful half-timbered Renaissance town center.

COLMAR Le Caveau de St Pierre

24 rue de la Herse, 68000 **Tel** *03 89 41 99 33*

Built in 1568 into the medieval fortifications, this restaurant stands in the Little Venice quarter, reached by a boardwalk along the canal. Warm traditional decor with painted beams. Specialties include fillet of beef cooked in a sauce of local Munster cheese, fish dishes, and *choucroute* (pickled cabbage served with sausage and bacon).

ILLHAEUSERN L'Auberge de l'Ill

2 rue de Collonges, 68970 **Tel** *03 89 71 89 00* **Fax** *03 89 71 82 83*

The Mecca of Alsacien cuisine, and still a Haeberlin family affair, this restaurant has held three rosettes for over 40 years! Set on the banks of the river Ill in the heart of the village, with gardens and storks nesting. Lobster with quinoa and Oriental spices, salmon soufflé, terrine of goose *foie gras* with truffles.

KAYSERSBERG Restaurant Saint Alexis

Restaurant Saint Alexis, 68240 **Tel** *03 89 73 90 38*

Hidden in the hills above the vineyards of Kaysersberg and Riquewihr, this old farm, set in cherry orchards near a chapel dating in part from the 5th century, houses a popular restaurant. Every menu starts with soup, followed by meat pie or stewed cockerel or game and omelet. Reserve ahead.

KAYSERSBERG Au Lion d'Or

66 rue Général de Gaulle, 68240 **Tel** *03 89 47 11 16* **Fax** *03 89 47 19 02*

Right in the old town, a lot of history surrounds this excellent, unpretentious institution built in 1521 and run by the same family since 1724. A carved lion's head decorates the door into the restaurant. The characterful dining room has a big open fire in winter. Traditional dishes include wild game, *foie gras*, and sauerkraut.

LEMBACH Gimbelhof

Rte Forestière, 67510 **Tel** *03 88 94 43 58*

Upgraded Alsacien farm lost in the hills right on the German frontier, 6 miles (10 km) north of Lembach and only an hour from Strasbourg. Across the valley is the magnificent ruined château de Fleckenstein. Excellent local dishes. This very professional and modestly priced establishment is well supported by both Germans and locals. Reserve ahead.

LEMBACH Auberge du Cheval Blanc

4 rue de Wissembourg, 67510 **Tel** *03 88 94 41 86* **Fax** *03 88 94 20 74*

In an 18th-century coaching inn, this restaurant in the village of Lembach is the best in the north of Alsace. The owner was the Gault Millau's most promising chef 2009 and serves truly excellent traditional regional dishes as well as the best French *haute cuisine*. Cheaper set menus are also available.

LES THONS Le Couvent des Cordeliers

Les Thons, 88410 **Tel** *03 29 07 90 84*

A fine ramshackle collection of 15th-century monastery buildings north of Renaissance Châtillon-sur-Saône is home to this unusual restaurant. The owner roasts slices of gammon over an open fire. Very popular; reserve ahead and ask to be seated downstairs, *"en bas."* There is a free museum.

MARLENHEIM Le Cerf

30 rue Général de Gaulle, 67520 **Tel** *03 88 87 73 73* **Fax** *03 88 87 68 08*

At the northern end of the Route des Vins, this old coaching inn, owned by the same family since 1930, serves modernized traditional Alsace dishes. It has a reputation for serving a good square meal, even second helpings. *Choucroute* with suckling pig and panfried *foie gras*. Rooms available.

METZ Le Bistrot des Sommeliers

10 rue Pasteur, 57000 **Tel** *03 87 63 40 20* **Fax** *03 87 63 54 46*

A gastronomic experience wrapped up in brasserie clothing. The chef was formerly second in one of France's top restaurants. The wine list is outstanding, with 400 different labels covering the whole country. Excellent bistro-style food, with a mostly business clientele. Crayfish *vol au vent* is a specialty.

METZ Restaurant des Roches

29 rue Roches, 57000 **Tel** *03 87 74 06 51* **Fax** *03 87 75 40 04*

Set on the ground floor of an 18th-century building opposite France's oldest theater, this restaurant specializes in fish – bass, daurade and turbot – and shellfish. You can pick your own live lobster from the glass tank. In summer there is a terrace for dining alongside the Moselle.

NANCY Chez Tanesy

223 Grande Rue, 54000 **Tel** *03 83 35 51 94*

A discreet 18th-century façade conceals what is reputed to be the best restaurant in Nancy and certainly the most reasonably priced. The restaurant is named after the well-known local chef who owns and runs the establishment. *Coquilles St Jacques* (scallops) with truffle sauce is recommended. Close to Place Stanislas.

NANCY L'Excelsior

50 rue Henri Poincaré, 54000 **Tel** *03 83 35 24 57*

This classic Nancy brasserie with Belle Epoque decor and stained-glass windows is a famous rendezvous spot for artists. In continuous use since 1911, it has excellent service, and you can also reserve your table over the Internet. L'Excelsior serves refined dishes with *foie gras* and *choucroute garnie*.

OBERNAI La Cloche

90 rue Général Gouraud, 67210 **Tel** *03 88 49 90 43*

In a 14th-century house with original paneling and windows, is this tavern-style restaurant. Located in the heart of the old town, it offers traditional Alsace cuisine with Munster cheese in the sauces. Always two different fish on the menu, and *tarte flambée* in the evenings. Excellent service. Reserve ahead.

RIEDISHEIM Restaurant de la Poste

7 rue Général de Gaulle, Riedisheim, 68400 **Tel** *03 89 44 07 71* **Fax** *03 89 64 32 79*

A coaching inn since 1850, six generations of the Kieny family have maintained this restaurant with its elegant dining rooms. You will find traditional Alsace cooking with suckling pig a specialty, according to the season. They are also great experts in cooking with chocolate.

RIQUEWIHR Le Sarment d'Or

4 rue du Cerf, 68340 **Tel** *03 89 86 02 86* **Fax** *03 89 47 99 23*

In a beautiful 16th-century house, tucked away in a quiet Renaissance street of this wonderfully preserved village, this restaurant's beamed dining room is elegantly decorated. The cooking combines invention and tradition. Warm *kugelhopf* cake for breakfast from the family store just nearby. Rooms available.

SAVERNE Taverne Katz

80 grand rue, 67700 **Tel** *03 88 71 16 56*

In the center of the town opposite the huge château, this taverne was built in 1605 and is still beautifully preserved inside and out with a traditonal flowered terrace and polished wood in the dining room. The food is French with a regional slant, and includes duck with *foie gras* and medallions of rabbit.

STRASBOURG Pâtisserie Winter

25 rue du 22 Novembre, 67000 **Tel** *03 88 32 85 40* **Fax** *03 88 22 04 28*

This is a good place for the ordinary visitor to Strasbourg, who does not have the expense account of a Member of the European Parliament. Simple meals at reasonable prices at this location in the city center. Good salads and *pâtisseries* with beer or wine.

STRASBOURG Au Crocodile

10 rue Outre, 67000 **Tel** *03 88 32 13 02* **Fax** *03 88 75 72 01*

One of the finest restaurants in France's other capital. Splendid polished woodwork, elegant decor, and the famous crocodile brought back from a campaign in Egypt by an Alsatian Captain in the French army. Super service and light, original cusine. A truly great wine list that covers the world.

VERDUN Hostellerie le Coq Hardi

Av de la Victoire, 55100 **Tel** *03 29 86 36 36* **Fax** *03 29 86 09 21*

This traditional, classic French provincial hotel and restaurant has good food, a great wine list, and an elegant dining room. Try the langoustine lasagne and snails. The bistro option provides cheaper, quick meals, such as steak and fries. There is a pleasant summer terrace.

WINDSTEIN Auberge des Deux Châteaux

33 rue des Châteaux, 67110 **Tel** *03 88 09 24 41*

An exceptional little hotel-restaurant between two ruined medieval castles in the regional park. On the D53 between Jaegerthal and Dambach, turn up the valley of the Windstein and keep going until you get to the top. The food is traditional Alsatian, and specialties are game and *tarte flambée*. There are great views. Closed Dec–Jan.

WISSEMBOURG Daniel Rebert

7 pl du Marché aux Choux, 67100 **Tel** *03 88 94 01 66* **Fax** *03 88 54 38 78*

Daniel Rebert is one of the best chocolatiers and pâtissiers in France. In the shadow of his luxury production of cakes and chocolates there is a discreet *salon de thé*, serving light lunches. Afterwards, you can choose the cakes and chocolates from the dizzying display to take home.

NORMANDY

ACQUIGNY Hostellerie d'Acquigny

1 rue d'Evreux, 27400 **Tel** *02 32 50 20 05*

This former coaching inn houses a charming restaurant. The regulars appreciate the inexpensive set menus, but it is worth choosing *à la carte*: pan-fried *foie gras* with dried fruit or roast cod steak served with chorizo and a creamy garlic sauce are both good choices. Expect an eclectic wine list and animated service.

Key to Price Guide *see p600* **Key to Symbols** *see back cover flap*

ALENCON Le Bistrot

21 rue de Sarthe, 61000 **Tel** *02 33 26 51 69*

Classic French bistro with the distinctive old-fashioned, green-painted front, red-checkered tablecloths, and old movie posters. The regularly changing menu includes blood sausage and *filet mignon* of pork in cream, which are local favorites. A well-stocked, sensibly priced wine list complements the food.

AUMALE La Villa des Houx

6 av Général de Gaulle, 76390 **Tel** *02 35 93 93 30* **Fax** *02 35 93 03 94*

A former *gendarmerie* (police station), this is an ideal place to stop along the route from Rouen to Amiens. The menu offers the refined taste of real Normandy cuisine with a modern twist. Try the *foie gras* with fruit crumble as an appetizer, followed by stuffed, boned quail and Calvados soufflé.

BARNEVILLE-CARTERET Marine

11 rue de Paris, 50270 **Tel** *02 33 53 83 31* **Fax** *02 33 53 39 60*

At this restaurant near the port, chef Laurent Cesne prepares inventive dishes such as tartare of scallops perfumed with fresh ginger, and lamb roast served with tomatoes, olives, arugula, and Parmesan cheese. Modern, comfortable dining room; precise and attentive service. Wine list matches food.

BAYEUX La Coline d'Enzo

4 rue des Bouchers, 14400 **Tel** *02 31 92 03 01*

The focus here is on fish: sea bass cooked in clay is a specialty. The dishes are creative and innovative. At lunchtime opt for the *suggestion du jour* (daily special), which is particularly good value. The restaurant has a modern feel with bright decor that successfully combines the old with the new. Reserve ahead.

BEUVRON EN AUGE Le Pavé d'Auge

Les Halles, 14430 **Tel** *02 31 79 26 71* **Fax** *02 31 39 04 45*

The talented chef serves food made from locally sourced produce. The dining room, in the renovated ancient village market hall, has lots of charm. The menus focus on fish, with a small choice of meat and poulty. Choose from Isigny oysters or grilled langoustines, and then braised hake or *rascasse*.

BRIQUEVILLE-SUR-MER Couleurs Saveurs

2 rte de Brettonnière, 50290 **Tel** *02 33 61 65 62*

This coastal restaurant, north of Granville, serves a menu of surprising flavor combinations in its bright, modern dining room. Expect to find dishes such as fillet of fish roasted with *demi-sel* butter and served with citrus fruits and wasabi, or spicy local lamb with turmeric sauce, and sponge cake with grapefruit marmalade for dessert.

CAEN Le Pressoir

3 ave Henri-Chéron, 14000 **Tel** *02 31 73 32 71* **Fax** *02 31 26 76 64*

Award-winning chef Ivan Vautier and his wife Sandrine run this excellent, contemporary restaurant that uses the best local ingredients in an innovative take on Norman cuisine. The à la carte menu offers a wide range of dishes and there are sensibly priced set menus, too. Closed Mon, Sun dinner, Feb school hols, & Jul 23–Aug 21.

CHERBOURG Le Faitout

2 rte de Bretonnière, 50290 **Tel** *02 33 61 65 62*

A bastion of tradition, Le Faitout is located in an old quarter of the city. This animated bistro-style restaurant serves family-style dishes *par excellence*. Sample the delicious red mullet, fresh Barfleur mussels, grilled sardines, and a wonderfully crispy confit of duck.

COSQUEVILLE Au Bouquet de Cosqueville

Hameau Remond, 50330 **Tel** *02 33 54 32 81* **Fax** *02 33 54 63 38*

Good portions of fresh seafood, such as lobster cooked in cider, local fish, and shellfish, served at this elegantly rustic restaurant in an ivy-clad house in the village center. Freshest local produce chosen with care. Tasty crêpes and *crème brulée* for dessert. Impressive wine list.

COURSEULLES SUR MER Paris

Pl 6-Juin, 14470 **Tel** *02 31 37 45 07* **Fax** *02 31 37 51 63*

A good-value-for-money restaurant in this relaxed seaside resort, north of Caen, on the Côte Nacre. Friendly service in the simply furnished dining room, where simple seafood and meat dishes are prepared with care. The terrace and veranda outside are protected from the gusty sea breezes.

DEAUVILLE Le Spinnaker

52 rue Mirabeau, 14800 **Tel** *02 31 88 24 40* **Fax** *02 31 88 43 58*

After a stroll along the seafront promenade, make your way to one of Normandy's finest fish restaurants. An attractive modern dining room specializes in fish and seafood, and also grilled meat dishes. Delicious cannelloni of langoustine and chestnut is an innovative choice. Friendly, attentive service. Closed Jan.

DIEPPE Bistrot de Pollet

23 rue Tête de Bœuf, 76200 **Tel** *02 35 84 68 57*

Small, friendly bistro-style restaurant with chef's daily suggestions, depending on the catch of the day, in the old fishing quarter of the port. Simple unfussy fish dishes: haddock salad, grilled sardines, poached sole, and bass. Limited selection of wines. Packed with locals and regulars; reserve ahead.

DOMFRONT Auberge Grand Gousier

1 pl Liberté, 61700 **Tel** *02 33 38 37 25*

Domfront escaped destruction during the bombardments of 1944, and this family-run auberge is testimony to this, standing in the medieval town center with its authentic fireplace. The specialty is warm oysters with a creamy Camembert sauce. The portions are generous and the welcome genuine.

DRUBEC La Haie Tondue

La Haie Tondue RN175, 14130 **Tel** *02 31 64 85 00*

This handsome, old, vine-clad restaurant out in the countryside has an attractive terrace and plenty of Norman beams and half timbering. Authentic, traditional cuisine includes panfried crayfish with aubergine (eggplant) "caviar" and veal with a cheese sauce. Good value for money.

EVREUX La Croix d'Or

3 rue Josephine, 27000 **Tel** *02 32 33 06 07*

A lively and popular brasserie in this pleasant cathedral town. The locals say that the Empress Josephine used to eat here. The menu today focuses on huge platters of oysters and other seafood, as well as a range of simply prepared, delicious fresh fish dishes.

FALAISE l'Attache

Rte de Caen, 14700 **Tel** *02 31 90 05 38* **Fax** *02 31 90 57 19*

Reservations recommended for this restaurant in the heart of Calvados. A beautifully renovated former staging post, with the dining room decorated in relaxing tones. The classic repertoire has an added dimension – the chef uses long-forgotten plants and aromatic herbs to flavor his cuisine. Impeccable service. Reservation recommended.

FECAMP La Marée

77 quai Bérigny, 76400 **Tel** *02 35 29 39 15*

This lively restaurant on the harbor is frequented by both locals and tourists, who come to feast on the wonderfully fresh seafood and fish dishes. The entire menu is dedicated to fish, and specialties include homemade fish soup, smoked fish, and huge seafood platters. There is a small, sunny terrace and a good range of wines.

FOURGES Moulin de Fourges

38 rue du Moulin, 27630 **Tel** *02 32 52 12 12* **Fax** *02 32 52 92 56*

A beautiful riverside watermill that would no doubt have pleased Monet, who lived at nearby Giverny. Local produce innovatively used to achieve astonishing results. During the winter months the Moulin is transformed into a mountain chalet-style restaurant serving mainly *fondue*. Pleasant dining area, and decent wines. Closed Jan.

GISORS Le Cappeville

17 rue Cappeville, 27410 **Tel** *02 32 55 11 08* **Fax** *02 32 55 93 92*

Rustic restaurant in the oldest part of town, serving traditional Normandy cuisine. The chef Pierre Potel shows his skill in creating tasty dishes using local produce. Try the succulent veal or the ravioli with snails. Impressive cheese board. Le Cappeville has a friendly, relaxed atmosphere.

GRANVILLE La Citadelle

34 rue du Port, 50406 **Tel** *02 33 50 34 10* **Fax** *02 33 50 15 36*

Overlooking the bay of St-Michel, the reliable cooking and the view over the fishing port from the terrace is enough to draw anyone over the bridge. Elegant, modern dining room serves generous portions. The freshest seafood platter in town, the biggest portion of sole, and Norman scallops. Closed Jan.

HONFLEUR Côte Resto

8 pl Saint-Catherine, 14600 **Tel** *02 31 89 31 33* **Fax** *02 31 89 90 17*

Attractive traditional timber-and-brick building with a terrace opposite the church. Wonderfully fresh seafood dishes. Simplicity is the key, using the best produce. Savor the *mille-feuille* of beets and sardines, or the *choucroute* of haddock with saffron cream sauce. You can also compose your own seafood platter. Good white wine selection.

HONFLEUR La Ferme St Siméon

Rue A.Marais, 14600 **Tel** *02 31 81 78 00* **Fax** *02 31 89 48 48*

A luxurious place to eat in this pretty fishing port. The restaurant of this spa hotel is known for elaborate fish dishes such as stuffed red mullet with jellied cauliflower consommé and *croque en bouche bouillabaisse*. The elegant dining room has an Old-World charm and a wonderful beamed ceiling. There is also an excellent wine list.

LA FERRIERE AUX ETANGS Auberge de la Mine

Le Gué-Plat, 61450 **Tel** *02 33 66 91 10* **Fax** *02 33 96 73 90*

At this former mine-workers' cantine, traditional Norman dishes are produced with originality, such as veal sweetbreads with Vire *andouille*, and roast pollock with herbs. Delicious desserts include *savarin* (alcohol-soaked yeast cake) with Calvados and caramelized apples on a skewer, plus an excellent cheese board. Closed Jan.

LES ANDELYS La Chaine d'Or

27 rue Grande, 27700 **Tel** *02 32 54 00 31* **Fax** *02 32 54 05 68*

Book a table in this restaurant to taste such delicacies as langoustines accompanied by citrus-fruit chutney, a *foie gras* trio, roast sole with black-olive risotto, or a confit of Limousin lamb. Romantic setting on the banks of the Seine in an 18th-century auberge. Rooms available. Closed Jan.

Key to Price Guide *see p600* **Key to Symbols** *see back cover flap*

LYONS LA FORET Restaurant de la Halle

Pl Benserade, 27480 **Tel** *02 32 49 49 92*

An attractive, traditional Norman village surrounded by the largest beech forest in Europe merits this good local restaurant, located opposite the ancient market hall. Simple, straightforward, delicious cuisine, especially the lamb cooked with rosemary. Starchy service.

MONT-ST-MICHEL Auberge St Pierre

Grande rue, 50170 **Tel** *02 33 60 14 03* **Fax** *02 33 48 59 82*

Lamb grazed on the surrounding salt marshes, known as *agneau pré salé*, features on the menu in this charming timbered 15th-century building. Seafood is also a house specialty. Try the favorites such as crab or salmon. Fresh local produce is used in the preparation of traditional dishes.

MONT-ST-MICHEL La Mère Poulard

Grande rue, 50170 **Tel** *02 33 89 68 68*

A deluxe brasserie on the famous Mont St-Michel, where visitors come from all over the world to sample the famous omelet *Mère Poulard* cooked in a long-handled pan over a fire. Also delicious are the *pré-salé* lamb (lamb fed on the surrounding salt marshes), and spit-roasted pig.

PONT AUDEMER Belle Isle sur Risle

Belle Isle sur Risle, 27500 **Tel** *02 32 56 96 22*

Part of the Relais du Silence chain, this gracious hotel and restaurant is housed in an elegant, ivy-covered, 19th-century gentleman's residence. The menu balances fish and meat dishes and demonstrates an original use of spices. On Saturdays and public holidays a pianist plays while you dine.

PONT L'EVEQUE Auberge de l'Aigle d'Or

68 rue de Vaucelles, 14130 **Tel** *02 31 65 05 25* **Fax** *02 31 65 12 03*

A well-maintained 16th-century coaching inn with a pretty courtyard provides an attractive setting for a good-value meal of *escargots Pays d'Auge* and free-range chicken cooked in a cider sauce. The menu changes seasonally and ensures the best local produce. Attentive service.

PONT SAINT-PIERRE Hostellerie La Bonne Marmite

10 rue René Raban 27300 **Tel** *02 32 49 70 24* **Fax** *02 32 48 12 41*

A top Logis de France not too far from Rouen in an old coaching inn. The dining room is as elegant as the building, with a *caisson* ceiling. Try the *foie gras de canard à l'ancienne* and the warm lobster salad. This is Norman cooking at its best. The wine cellar boasts some fine old Bordeaux.

PUTANGES PONT ECREPIN Hôtel du Lion Verd

Pl de l'Hôtel de Ville, 61210 **Tel** *02 33 35 01 86* **Fax** *02 33 39 53 32*

This welcoming hotel-restaurant sits on the riverside of the Orme. The menu offers local Normandy produce with pride and a refreshing approach. The result is wonderful: hearty terrines, Auge Valley *cochon de lait* (suckling pig), good homemade desserts such as strawberry tart. Good-value lunch menu.

ROUEN Le 37

37 rue St-Etienne-des-Tonneliers, 76000 **Tel** *02 35 70 56 65*

Attractive city center bistro, chic and zen, presents a cuisine that is a touch more modern than its celebrated parent, Restaurant Gill. Enjoy savory dishes such as crab tortilla with arugula salad, and duck leg served with vegetables seasoned with Thai spices. For dessert try the citrus-fruit gratin served with mandarin sorbet. Reservations recommended.

ROUEN La Couronne

31 pl Vieux Marché, 76000 **Tel** *02 35 71 40 90* **Fax** *02 35 71 05 78*

In the oldest auberge in France, dating from 1345, the experienced, talented chef ensures that you pass a memorable moment here with classic gourmet dishes such as pan-fried escalope of *foie gras*, lobster with champagne sauce, and duck *à la Rouennaise*. Great Normandy cheeses.

ROUEN Restaurant Gill

8-9 quai de la Bourse, 76000 **Tel** *02 35 71 16 14* **Fax** *02 35 71 96 91*

A highly recommended restaurant on the Seine quays. For over 20 years chef Gilles Tournadre has been creating sophisticated dishes in this elegant dining room. Specialties include langoustines served with fresh tomato chutney, pigeon *à la rouennaise*, and fillet of bass with onion marmalade. Remarkable wine list.

STE CECILE Le Manoir de l'Acherie

Acherie, 50800 **Tel** *02 33 51 13 87* **Fax** *02 33 51 33 69*

In this old-fashioned manor house, with rooms in a converted chapel, the produce of Normandy features highly, such as cream, apples, calvados, and cider. Expect to find ham and lamb either braised in calvados, or served in a cider-flavored sauce. Even the apple tart is flambéed in this apple brandy. Good cheese board.

TROUVILLE SUR MER Régence

132 bd Fernand Moureaux, 14360 **Tel** *02 31 88 10 71* **Fax** *02 31 88 10 71*

Beautiful interior with mirrors and 19th-century wood paneling decorated by hungry Impressionist painters. The charming service and refined ambience lend to the feeling of elegance and good value. Not far from the shore, the seafood and shellfish are the house specialties. Well-presented dishes.

VEULES LES ROSES Les Galets   P 🚶 ♿   €€€
3 rue Victor Hugo, 76980 **Tel** *02 35 97 61 33* **Fax** *02 35 57 06 23*

Traditional brick-built restaurant close to the pebbly beach, which is typical of the Côte d'Albâtre. Comfortable dining area inside, and lovely terrace outside. If you want to have a meal by the sea, this is just the place, but reserve ahead. Classic dishes prepared with care.

VILLERS BOCAGE Les Trois Rois   P 🚶   €€€
2 pl Jeanne d'Arc, 14310 **Tel** *02 31 77 00 32* **Fax** *02 31 77 93 25*

In a vast square surrounded by a garden and vegetable patch, this restaurant flaunts all the characteristics of a traditional Norman restaurant. Spacious, elegant dining area serving generous portions of well-prepared local dishes, such as tripe and fresh fish dishes. Efficient service.

BRITTANY

AUDIERNE Le Goyen   P 🚶 ♿ 🍴 🍷   €€€
Pl Jean-Simon, 29770 **Tel** *02 98 70 08 88* **Fax** *02 98 70 18 77*

Classic seafood is served at this hotel-restaurant facing the sea. Deliciously fresh oysters and seafood platters are a good choice. The menu also includes pollock accompanied by a vegetable risotto and green-pea sauce, and pan-fried *Coquilles St-Jacques* (scallops) in an Arabica-bean crust, accompanied by *endive à l'orange*.

AURAY L'Eglantine   🚶 🍴   €€
17 place St-Saveur, 56400 **Tel** *02 97 56 46 55*

Sitting on the quay of the pretty Saint-Goustan port, this restaurant offers a selection of both fish and meat options. Freshly caught sole and turbot are simply prepared, and seafood platters are excellent, while other fish dishes are accompanied by elaborate sauces. Meat-lovers will appreciate the succulent pigeon and steak.

BELLE ILE EN MER La Désirade   🚶 🍷 🍴   €€€€
Le Petit Cosquet, 56360 **Tel** *02 97 31 70 70*

This family hotel and restaurant is in an attractive, traditional Brittany farmhouse only a few minutes from the beach. The chef specializes in fresh ingredients, with fish and seafood to the fore. Picnics can be ordered for a day's outing on the shore of this wonderful island. Closed Jan–Apr.

BREST Da Vinci   🚶 🍷   €
6 rue Louis Pasteur, 29200 **Tel** *02 98 46 90 90*

This Italian restaurant offers a pleasant alternative to the many local seafood restaurants. It is run in tandem with an Italian grocery store by the Halles food market. Ravioli, pasta, and risotto are prepared on the premises and there is a selection of Italian wine to accompany it. A popular local spot so reserve in advance.

BREST La Fleur de Sel   🍷   €€€€
15 bis rue de Lyon, 29200 **Tel** *02 98 44 38 65* **Fax** *02 98 44 38 53*

A modern, bright city center restaurant, with simple, comfortable furnishings. The dishes are prepared with precision. Try the skate fish with black-olive tapenade and pesto, or a parmentier of lamb. Good value for money, especially the *formule* at lunchtime. Service can sometimes be a little stuffy.

CARANTEC Restaurant Patrick Jeffroy   P 🚶 ♿ 🍴 🍷   €€€€€
20 rue Kélénn, 29660 **Tel** *02 98 67 00 47* **Fax** *02 98 67 08 25*

A magnificent view over Kélénn beach from the restaurant in this fabulous 1930s manor-house hotel. Shellfish in abundance. Classic and modern cuisine combine to perfection. Terrine of crab is served with artichoke and accompanied by a vinaigrette of shallots, coconut milk, and Thai curry. Extensive choice of Loire valley wines.

CARNAC La Calypso   🚶 P ♿   €€€
158 rte du Pô, 56340 **Tel** *02 97 52 06 14*

Overlooking the oyster beds of the Anse du Pô, this popular seafood restaurant is all the more charming for the colorful character that runs it. The house specialty is lobster or steak cooked over a wood fire in the hearth. A choice of fish of the day is offered as well as the usual seafood platters. Reservations are essential.

CONCARNEAU Le Petit Chaperon Rouge   🚶 🍴   €
7 pl Duguesclin, 29900 **Tel** *02 98 60 53 32*

Following the "Little Red Riding Hood" theme with its wicker baskets and red tablecloths, this crêperie near the harbor has a delicious choice of savory and sweet fillings, such as La Blandette (goat's cheese, spinach, ham, and cream) and Mère Grande (banana and honey flambéed with rum).

DINAN La Mère Pourcel   🍴 🍷   €€€
3 pl des Merciers, 22100 **Tel** *02 96 39 03 80* **Fax** *02 96 39 49 91*

This restaurant in a stunning timbered Gothic building is a Dinan landmark, serving generous portions of seasonal gourmet cuisine. Locally reared lamb is on offer, along with more innovative dishes. There is a good selection of fine wines. The tables are on the cobbled street. Closed Jan.

GUIMILIAU Ar Chupen
43 rue de Calvaire, 29400 **Tel** *02 98 68 73 63*

After admiring the richly decorated church, step down the road to this restaurant in a renovated Breton farmhouse. Traditional lacy galettes, made with sarrazin flour, and crêpes are prepared to order. The choice of fillings seems endless. Good place for children, and vegetarians. Friendly staff.

HEDE L'Hostellerie du Vieux Moulin €€
Ancienne rte de St Malo, 35630 **Tel** *02 99 45 45 70* **Fax** *02 99 45 44 86*

Built in the 19th century as part of a complex to supply water power, the restaurant overlooks the Hédé castle, with the ruins of the old watermill in the grounds. Good-value lunchtime menus, including panfried scallops, lightly grilled langoustines, and succulent duck. Rooms available.

LE CONQUET Le Relais de Vieux Port €
1 quai Drellach, 29217 **Tel** *02 98 89 15 91*

You can almost dangle your feet in the water as you sit to choose the fillings for your crêpe. Seafood is the house specialty. Try a crêpe filled with fresh scallops or prawns accompanied by a green salad. Leave room for dessert, especially the Bonne Maman with caramelized apples and whipped cream.

LORIENT Le Neptune €€
15 av de la Perrière, 56100 **Tel** *02 97 37 04 56* **Fax** *02 97 87 07 54*

The haul at the nearby fishing port of Keroman determines the dish of the day at this restaurant. Modern interior, with some tables in a pretty conservatory at the rear of the dining room. The menu includes flambéed lobster and fricassée of monkfish. Generous portions and friendly service.

MORLAIX Brasserie de l'Europe €€
1 rue d'Aiguillon, 29600 **Tel** *02 98 88 81 15*

An authentic brasserie in the town center next to the hotel of the same name. Everything from breakfast to sandwiches and cooked dishes is served right through the day from 8am until 9:30pm. There is a conservatory for winter and a pleasant terrace for summer.

NOYAL-SUR-VILAINE Auberge du Pont d'Acigné €€€
Le Pont d'Acigné, 35530 **Tel** *02 99 62 52 55*

Not far from Rennes, overlooking the Vilaine river and an attractive water mill, is this delightful gourmet restaurant. The creative menu is based on seasonal market produce; dishes include roast veal flavored with licorice, and a warm lobster, beet, and tarragon starter. There is also a fine selection of desserts.

PAIMPOL L'Islandais €
19 quai Morand, 22500 **Tel** *02 96 20 93 80* **Fax** *02 96 20 72 68*

A popular crêperie overlooking the lively Paimpol harbor. The chef presents a good selection of traditional Breton galettes, always a favorite with children and a good option for vegetarians. Shellfish is abundant, with fresh oysters, mussels, lobsters, and langoustines. Expect to pay more for seafood.

PERROS-GUIREC Le Gulf Stream €€
26 rue des Sept-Iles 22700 **Tel** *02 96 23 21 86* **Fax** *02 96 49 06 61*

An excellent and reasonably priced hotel-restaurant with a warm, family feel. There are fine views of the coast from the dining room. As well as the expected fish and other seafood, the restaurant serves traditional French food according to the season. There is also a good wine list.

PLOUBALAY Le Gare €€€
4 rue des Ormelet, 22650 **Tel** *02 96 27 25 16*

Thomas Mureau, the former owner of the renowned Fleur de Sel at St Malo, concocts dishes with a touch of personality in this rustic restaurant. Of particular note are the brochettes of St. Jacques accompanied by a truffle-flavored vinaigrette, and the Breton *sablé* served with pineapple and coriander. The best tables overlook the garden.

QUIBERON Le Relax €€€
27 bd Castéro, 56170 **Tel** *02 97 50 12 84*

With lovely sea views and a pretty garden, this restaurant is guaranteed to make you relax. A wide selection of superbly cooked seasonal fish, as well as mussels, langoustines, crab, and oysters. Tasty seafood sauerkraut. Good wine cellar and a sommelier who knows his stuff, but is not stuffy.

QUIMPER L'Ambroisie €€€
49 rue Elie Fréron, 29000 **Tel** *02 98 95 00 02*

Located just at the end of one of the tiny streets in the center of Quimper, a short walk from the cathedral, L'Ambroise offers good, simple cuisine using quality produce. Try the roast monkfish in a spicy crust, smoked salmon roulade with asparagus and poached eggs, and the tartare of fresh fruit with ice cream.

RENNES Léon le Cochon €
1 rue du Maréchal Joffre, 35000 **Tel** *02 99 79 37 54*

A popular restaurant with a pig theme that has mellowed somewhat over time. Pork sausage from Morteau and pig's trotters are still on the menu, but you can also try terrine of *foie gras* marinated in Jurançon, beef, duck, prawns, and fish. It is possible to order take-out of most dishes, including the *foie gras*.

RENNES Le Tire-Bouchon   €€
2 rue du Chapitre, 35000 **Tel** *02 99 79 43 43*

This relaxed friendly restaurant offers unpretentious home cooking. Mackerel pâté, braised beef and carrots, and rice pudding are just some of the dishes on offer. The wines are selected by the owner, who has a preference for *"vins naturels."* Ideally located just around the corner from the tourist office.

ROSCOFF Le Surcouf   €€
14 rue Amiral Révellière, 29680 **Tel** *02 98 69 71 89* **Fax** *02 98 69 71 89*

Near the church, this brasserie-style restaurant serves regional cuisine. The fixed-price menus have a wide choice of local coastal produce. Start with a plate of mussels, sea snails, whelks, and a half-dozen oysters. For the main course, choose a lobster from the tank, or the delicious seafood casserole.

ROSCOFF Le Temps de Vivre   €€€€
17-19 pl Lacaze-Douthiers, 29680 **Tel** *02 98 61 27 28* **Fax** *02 98 61 19 46*

The acclaimed chef Jean-Yves Crenn does wonderful things with vegetables in this restaurant facing the sea. Seafood is the specialty: pan-fried scallops served with braised chicory; fruit chutney; and lemon, ginger, and coconut milk sauce. Good selection of wines. Friendly staff.

ST-BRIEUC Amadeus   €€
22 rue de Gouët, 22000 **Tel** *02 96 33 92 44* **Fax** *02 96 33 92 44*

In one of this historic town's oldest buildings, this elegant gourmet restaurant specializes in fish – a carpaccio of scallops with vanilla olive oil dressing, and fillet of sole are outstanding. The wide range of tempting desserts includes Amaretto chocolate cake and Breton butter cookies with fruit.

ST-BRIEUC L'Air du Temps   €€€
4 rue du Gouët, 22000 **Tel** *02 96 68 58 40*

A welcome addition to the local culinary scene, this pleasant bistro-style restaurant is fast establishing a good reputation. The interior combines 200-year-old stone walls with modern decor. Dishes are served in caste-iron Staub ware. Coquilles St-Jacques (scallops) are cooked at your table.

ST-MALO La Corderie   €€
9 chemin de la Corderie, 35400 **Tel** *02 99 81 62 38*

A fish restaurant in an attractive old house. The menu changes according to whatever the fishing boats bring in. Coquilles St-Jacques (scallops) are served with a seaweed flavored cream sauce. Meat dishes such as duck breast in honey are also on offer. A quiet spot with fine views over the moorings and the Tour Solidor.

ST-MALO Le Chalut   €€€€
8 rue de la Corne de Cerf, 35400 **Tel** *02 99 56 71 58* **Fax** *02 99 56 71 58*

One of St Malo's best restaurants, the chef excels in fish dishes and well-chosen produce simply prepared. A platter of fish served with a saffron-flavored sauce, and St-Pierre with coriander are examples of the delicious dishes on offer. Good selection of cheese, too. Reservations recommended.

VANNES Les Remparts   €€€
6 rue Alexandre-le-Pontois, 56000 **Tel** *02 97 47 52 44*

Tasty meals at reasonable prices are served in this restaurant opposite the ramparts. The chef uses regional ingredients with originality. Try the gravlax of salmon with horseradish or one of the vegetarian options. Good selection of wines by the glass, many from organic producers.

VITRE La Taverne de l'Ecu   €€€
12 rue Baudairie, 35500 **Tel** *02 99 75 11 09* **Fax** *02 99 75 82 97*

This half-timbered Renaissance house provides a historic ambience for a meal in one of two dining rooms. Menu changes seasonally. Try the venison served with a chestnut flan, fish with sorrel sauce, or roast leg of rabbit. Homemade bread accompanies your meal.

THE LOIRE VALLEY

AMBOISE Le Choiseul   €€€€€
36 quai C.Guinot, 37400 **Tel** *02 47 30 45 45* **Fax** *02 47 30 46 10*

Elegant 18th-century hotel with a pretty garden and views of the Loire from the airy dining room. The sophisticated menu changes seasonally; in spring a meal might include spicy roast pig, and in summer roast pollock served with gnocchi. Good Touraine wines and many other regional wines.

ANGERS Ma Campagne   €
14 promenade de la Reculée, 49000 **Tel** *02 41 48 38 06*

A traditional, country-style auberge just a few minutes' walk along the river from the center of town. The terrace has great views overlooking the River Maine. The cheaper menus are particularly good value for money. For dessert, the pear coated in chocolate is recommended.

Key to Price Guide *see p600* **Key to Symbols** *see back cover flap*

ANGERS Le Lucullus
5 rue Hoche, 49000 **Tel** *02 41 87 00 44* **Fax** *02 41 87 00 44*

This pretty restaurant carved into the tuffeau rock has two lovely vaulted dining rooms. Classic dishes and regional specialties served with an added touch from the chef. Try the lobster flan with basil sorbet accompanied by a lobster velouté, and the classic fillet of beef with *morille* mushrooms.

BEAUGENCY Le P'tit Bateau
54 rue du Pont, 45190 **Tel** *02 38 44 56 38* **Fax** *02 38 46 44 37*

Near the château, the P'tit Bateau is the most appealing restaurant in town. Popular with locals, it offers traditional cuisine in a rustic dining room with exposed beams and open fireplace. Fresh fish, game in season, and wild mushrooms feature on the menu. There is a courtyard terrace for sunny days.

BLOIS Hôtel Restaurant Coté Loire
2 pl de la Grève, 41000 **Tel** *02 54 78 07 86*

A good old fashioned 16th-century restaurant and hotel overlooking the River Loire. The simple but reasonably-priced menu changes regularly and there is sometimes a *menu unique* at lunch time. The Coté Loire is a good place to break while visiting the château and neighboring sites on the Loire.

BLOIS L'Orangerie du Château
1 av Jean Laigret, 41000 **Tel** *02 54 78 05 36* **Fax** *02 54 78 22 78*

Housed in the 15th-century château's former winter garden, the fine setting is matched by the food and wine here. The menu features regional favorites with an innovative approach, such as pan-fried scallops with goat's cheese gnocchi, or escalope of *foie gras* served with beet sauce. A dependable wine list with good Touraine producers.

BOUCHEMAINE La Terrasse
4 pl Rouzebouc, 49080 **Tel** *02 41 77 11 96* **Fax** *02 41 77 25 71*

Located in a hamlet on the confluence of the rivers Loire and Maine, this restaurant has a panoramic view. The menu features freshly caught eel, pike-perch, salmon, and other freshwater fish. Classic dishes are excellently prepared, such as *sandre au beurre blanc* (pike-perch in butter). Ironically, there is no terrace.

BOURGES La Courcillière
Rue de Babylone, 18000 **Tel** *02 48 24 41 91*

By the marshes overlooking the river Yèvre, it's worth the 20-minute walk from the city center for freshwater fish and local cooking – classic dishes such as pike-perch fillet, eel in red wine, or delicious salmon. Traditional dining area with modern bright decor and delightful terrace. Attentive service.

BOURGES Le Jacques Coeur
3 pl Jacques Coeur, 18000 **Tel** *02 48 26 53 01*

This restaurant, with its small dining room, offers a menu of classic dishes based on the very best local produce. Choices include fillet of salmon served with saffron-infused chicory and a creamy langoustine sauce, and pigeon *en croute* with *foie gras* accompanied by artichoke purée. There is a good selection of local cheeses.

BOURGUEIL Le Moulin Bleu
7 rue du Moulin-Bleu, 37140 **Tel** *02 47 97 73 13* **Fax** *02 47 97 79 66*

The house at the foot of this pretty blue mill has two vaulted dining rooms serving traditional dishes in a friendly atmosphere. The cuisine remains faithful to the region, with Touraine-reared veal served with a Vouvray butter sauce. Good Bourgeuil producers on the wine list. In the off-season only open Friday and Saturday evenings.

BRACIEUX Le Rendez-vous des Gourmets
20 rue Roger Brun, 41250 **Tel** *02 54 46 03 87*

This auberge was taken over and completely renovated by Didier Doreau, the former second chef from the nearby luxury Relais. He has sucessfully created his own place offering traditional and regional cuisine at an affordable price. The restaurant has become very popular so it is best to reserve ahead.

CHARTRES Le Grand Monarque – Le Georges
22 pl des Epars, 28000 **Tel** *02 37 18 15 15* **Fax** *02 37 36 34 18*

Within this magnificent 17th-century staging post are both a gourmet "Le Georges" restaurant, and a brasserie serving traditional food. The cuisine is ambitious and flavorful, with dishes such as crayfish served with beets and chanterelles, and sea bass with onion confit and porcini mushrooms. Excellent desserts. First-rate wine cellar.

CHENONCEAUX Hôtel Restaurant la Roseraie
7 rue du Docteur Bretonneau, 37150 **Tel** *02 47 23 90 09*

A pleasant 18th-century *hotel de charme* close to the château. The traditional restaurant serves classic French cuisine. The "dégustation" menu offers particularly good value for money and includes dishes such as fish terrine with garden vegetables, rissolé of lamb with mushrooms, and a delicious crème caramel.

CHINON Les Années 30
78 rue Haute St-Maurice, 37500 **Tel** *02 47 93 37 18* **Fax** *02 47 93 33 72*

This elegant little eatery on the way up to the château has a chef who has brought back the spark to this menu. Stéphane Charles presents dishes such as poached langoustines with Mexican spices, and sea bass served with an exotic fruit sauce, roast pineapple, and sweet potato. Good local wines.

CLISSON La Bonne Auberge
€€€€

1 rue Olivier de Clisson, 44190 **Tel** *02 40 54 01 90* **Fax** *02 40 54 08 48*

A comfortable auberge in the city center with three attractive dining rooms, one set in a conservatory with garden views. The specialties here include lobster gratin, *paupiettes* of sea bass, scallops with truffles, and pigeon breast in red Chinon sauce. The desserts are delicate, and the selection of Muscadets is good.

CONTRES La Botte d'Asperges
€€

52 rue Pierre-Henri Mauger, 41700 **Tel** *02 54 79 50 49* **Fax** *02 54 79 08 74*

Locally grown asparagus features prominently on the menu, in season. Behind the rustic atmosphere is an inspirational chef who prepares such delights as leg of rabbit stuffed with mushrooms and cured ham, and for dessert crème brûlée perfumed with basil and thyme. Small, well-chosen wine list. You can also take food out.

DOUE-LA-FONTAINE Auberge de la Bienvenue
€€€

104 rte de Cholet, 49700 **Tel** *02 41 59 22 44* **Fax** *02 41 59 93 49*

A pretty inn situated in this town of roses. The menu offers elaborate, savory preparations using welcome favorites, such as calf's liver in port and pepper sauce, terrine of *foie gras* flavored with local Coteaux du Layon wine, or saddle of Aveyron lamb. Other dishes include local products such as pike-perch, crayfish, and wild mushrooms.

FONTEVRAUD-L'ABBAYE La Licorne
€€€€

Allée Sainte-Catherine, 49590 **Tel** *02 41 51 72 49* **Fax** *02 41 51 70 40*

Next to the splendid abbey, this popular restaurant has a pretty courtyard terrace and elegant dining room. The menu includes creations such as langoustine ravioli in morel sauce and, for dessert, strawberries flavored with roses. Good Saumur wines. Reserve ahead.

GENNES Auberge du Moulin de Sarré
€

Rte de Louerre, 49350 **Tel** *02 41 51 81 32*

After taking a tour of the 16th-century watermill (the only working one in the region), try either the menu of *fouées* (warm bread puffs, made from flour ground at the mill) with fillings such as goat's cheese, or *rillettes* (duck pâté), or the fresh trout menu (fished on the spot). Reservations are required.

GIEN Restaurant la Poularde
€€€€

13 quai de Nice, 45500 **Tel** *02 38 67 36 05* **Fax** *02 38 38 18 78*

A classic restaurant on the banks of the Loire, serving traditional cuisine in an elegant dining room, with Gien tableware. The menu includes roast pike-perch served with a Chinon wine sauce, or eel accompanied by a saffron-infused sauce, and seasonal red fruit with mango cream. Game appears on the menu in season.

LA FERTE IMBAULT Auberge à la Tête de Lard
€€

13 pl des Tilleuls, 41300 **Tel** *02 54 96 22 32*

An authentic, completely refurbished country hotel in the heart of the Sologne houses a delightful restaurant, which offers a traditional menu with choices such as wild boar and other seasonal country dishes. This is a good place to stop when visiting the Loire Châteaux. Closed Sun dinner; Tue lunch; Mon.

LAMOTTE BEUVRON Hôtel Tatin
€€€

5 av de Vierzon, 41600 **Tel** *02 54 88 00 03* **Fax** *02 54 88 96 73*

This elegant hotel-restaurant serves traditional fare made with fresh local produce. The menu includes *foie gras*, salad of homemade pâté and warm goat's cheese, pike-perch, pigeon, steak, and the famous *tarte Tatin*. There is a good selection of quality Sancerre and Cheverny wines.

LANGEAIS Au Coin des Halles
€€

9 rue Gambetta, 37120 **Tel** *02 47 96 37 25*

This restaurant is the venture of Pascal Bouvier, former chef of the illustrious Choiseul at Amboise. It successfully combines a Zen interior with excellent cuisine and affordable prices. The menu is varied – mullet and sandre (pike-perch) from the Loire, shoulder of lamb, duck, Brittany sardines, and *foie gras*. Next to the Château de Langeais.

LE MANS Le Bistrot du Mans
€

12 rue Hippolyte Lecornué, 72000 **Tel** *02 43 87 51 00*

Cheerful, busy, traditional brasserie, beautifully decorated in early 1900s style. The wide ranging menu features such classic dishes as fresh asparagus wrapped in smoked salmon and served with Hollandaise sauce, or steak with blue cheese sauce. Breakfast is served until noon. Great value.

LE MANS Le Nez Rouge
€€

107 grande rue, 72000 **Tel** *02 43 24 27 26*

A charming timbered restaurant in the medieval part of Le Mans. The young chef has trained in some of the best restaurants in France. His dishes are based on the freshest produce, such as lobster and veal sweetbreads. The dining room is cozy and intimate, and there is a terrrace across the road. Reserve ahead.

LEMERE L'Auberge de Jable
€€

le Clos de Jable, 37120 **Tel** *02 47 95 47 95*

A delightful country restaurant in a huge 15th-century farm, set in 50 acres (20 ha) of fields and vineyards. The auberge is run by a Franco-American couple who have plans for *chambres d'hôtes*. The chic decor is matched by the elegant food. Sweetbreads and panfried *foie gras* are served outside in fine weather and by an open fire in winter.

Key to Price Guide *see p600* **Key to Symbols** *see back cover flap*

LES SABLES D'OLONNE L'Affiche
21 Quai Giné, 85100 **Tel** *02 51 95 34 74*

Diners crowd in to this Intimate little fish restaurant: the food is excellent, the menu is varied, and the wine is good. Make sure you get the right restaurant on the busy Quai – there are several but this one serves the best seafood platters, which is why it is so popular with the locals. Reservations are essential.

MALICORNE-SUR-SARTHE La Petite Auberge
5 pl du Guesclin, 72270 **Tel** *02 43 94 80 52* **Fax** *02 43 94 31 37*

In summer dine on the riverside terrace and watch the boats go by; in winter take refuge around the magnificent medieval fireplace. Enjoy classic cuisine with an innovative twist, such as delicious tartare of scallops accompanied by beets, or perfectly cooked venison with blueberry jam.

MONTBAZON La Chancelière Jeu de Cartes
1 pl des Marronniers, 37250 **Tel** *02 47 26 00 67* **Fax** *02 47 73 14 82*

Modern, sophisticated cuisine prepared with precision. This restaurant proposes savory but uncomplicated dishes such as creamy Richelieu truffle risotto, or escalope of *foie gras* served with polenta flavored with figs and lemon. Well-selected wine list with good Vouvray and Bourgueil producers.

MONTOIRE-SUR-LE-LOIR Le Cheval Rouge
Pl Foch, 41800 **Tel** *02 54 85 07 05* **Fax** *02 54 85 17 42*

After visiting the chapel and prior's lodging where Ronsard (16th-century French poet) spent his last years, stop off and dine on classic cuisine in this antiquated staging post. Enjoy well-prepared regional dishes in the attractive dining room or outside on the shady terrace with its ancient plane trees.

MONTSOREAU Diane de Méridor
12 quai Philippe de Commines, 49730 **Tel** *02 41 51 71 76* **Fax** *02 41 51 17 17*

While dining you have a view of the château that was the movie setting for the interpretation of la Dame de Montsoreau by Alexandre Dumas. Carved out of tuffeau rock, in this town perched above the Loire, this restaurant is rustic with exposed beams and an open fireplace. It specializes in freshwater fish dishes cooked to perfection.

NANTES La Cigale
4 pl Graslin, 44000 **Tel** *02 51 84 94 94* **Fax** *02 51 84 94 95*

This ornate Belle Epoque brasserie dates from 1895 when it was frequented by celebrated writers and Nantes elite. The quality of the cuisine matches the exceptional interior. Oysters, carpaccio of salmon, and beef *à la plancha* (cooked on a hot plate). Open all day. Extensive wine list.

NANTES Les Temps Changent
1 pl Aristide-Briand, 44000 **Tel** *02 51 72 18 01*

Excellent chef with a vision of modern cuisine. This welcoming venue provides quality French dishes that combine classic produce and inventive cooking. Menu includes sea bream served with a green pea sorbet, and confit of lamb accompanied by eggplant)and curry sauce. Interesting wines.

NANTES Le Pressoir
11 quai de Turenne, 44000 **Tel** *02 40 35 31 10*

More than a simple bistro, this restaurant is a newcomer on the quays. The young chef presents interesting dishes such as *foie gras* and oxtail terrine, *pot au feu* of goose, and wild duck served with shallots. The wine list is extensive, many available by the glass. Reserve ahead.

NANTES L'Océanide
2 rue Paul Bellamy, 44000 **Tel** *02 40 20 32 28*

A first-class seafood restaurant and one of the best in Nantes. It was designed in World War II – when it was impossible to travel – to resemble the interior of an ocean liner. Being next to the Talensac market with its 14 fishmongers, 10 butchers, and 16 *charcutiers* means the fresh ingredients change daily.

NOUAN-LE-FUZELIER Le Dahu
14 rue Henri Chapron, 41600 **Tel** *02 54 88 72 88*

This rustic dining room in a converted barn is set in a lovely garden in the heart of the Solange countryside. This is prime hunting territory, and the menu features not only game in season, but also a selection of fish dishes, such as brill served with local asparagus. Well-chosen wine list, with organic vintages from Quenioux.

ONZAIN Domaine des Hauts de Loire
Rte de Herbault, 41150 **Tel** *02 54 20 72 57* **Fax** *02 54 20 77 32*

Gastronomic cuisine is served in this former hunting lodge, set within its own park. Superb dishes are presented by chef Rémy Giraud, such as potatoes stuffed with caviar d'Aquitaine, guinea fowl accompanied by chestnut ravioli and a coffee-flavored sauce, and lobster served with rum and cinnamon sauce. Classic wine list.

ORLEANS La Chancellerie
27 pl du Martroi, 45000 **Tel** *02 38 53 57 54*

This lively brasserie-restaurant is located on the town's main square. Built by order of the Duke of Orléans in 1754, it was used to keep the carriages, and later became the omnibus station. The interior has high ceilings, a marble bar, leather banquettes, and brass trimmings. Staple fare enlivened by good wines. Snacks and salads are also available.

ORLEANS La Dariole

25 rue Etienne Dolet, 45000 **Tel** *02 38 77 26 67*

A surprising little restaurant and tearoom in a 15th-century, half-timbered building in the narrow streets of the city center. Open during the day and on Friday and Tuesday evenings, the menu includes meat and seafood and changes every two weeks, with dishes like Coquilles St-Jacques (scallops) with rosemary on a skewer. Excellent value.

ORLEANS La Terrasse du Parc

Av du Parc Floral, 45100 **Tel** *02 38 25 92 24*

When the prestigious Les Antiquaires in the city center was closed for redevelopment work, owner Philippe Bardau opened this elegant establishment in the park. A super-modern conservatory with huge bay windows overlooks the park and a terrace. Refined gourmet menu. Ideally reserve 48 hours ahead.

ROCHECORBON Les Hautes Roches

86 quai Loire, 37210 **Tel** *02 47 52 88 88* **Fax** *02 47 52 81 30*

The dining room in this château is decorated in contemporary tones and serves meticulously prepared classic cuisine. The chef concocts irresistible dishes, such as salad of warm *foie gras* and figs, Racan pigeon, Charolais beef, and fillet of John Dory with a classic Béarnaise sauce. The cellar has wonderful wines from the best local producers.

SACHE Auberge du XII siècle

1 rue du Château, 37190 **Tel** *02 47 26 88 77* **Fax** *02 47 26 88 21*

In an historic building, a stone's throw from the Balzac museum, the dining room of this restaurant has a rustic atmosphere, with exposed beams. There is a good choice of fixed-price menus with classic dishes, such as pigeon roast with scallops and poached turbot, and raspberry *feuillantine* for dessert.

SANCERRE Auberge la Pomme d'Or

Pl de la Mairie, 18300 **Tel** *02 48 54 13 30* **Fax** *02 48 54 19 22*

This small restaurant in a former coaching inn serves classic dishes. The savory cuisine uses seasonal produce from the region. Enjoy the simplicity of the Chavignol goat's cheese, breast of guinea fowl with asparagus, or pike-perch, complemented by a glass of Sancerre.

SAUMUR Auberge St Pierre

6 pl St Pierre, 49400 **Tel** *02 41 51 26 25* **Fax** *02 41 59 89 28*

On a square near the château in a former 15th-century monastery, this convivial restaurant serves regional specialties prepared with care. Dishes include pike-perch fillet and chicken cooked in Loire wine. Accompany a regional cheese with a glass of fruity red wine, such as St Nicolas de Bourgueil.

ST-OUEN LES VIGNES L'Aubinière

29 rue Jules Gautier, 37530 **Tel** *02 47 30 15 29* **Fax** *02 47 30 02 44*

North of Amboise, this small rustic restaurant opens onto a pretty garden that leads down to the river. Enjoy the creations of chef Jacques Arrayet, who serves outstanding dishes including steamed pollock on a fennel purée, and breast of guinea fowl stuffed with chorizo and served with a gratin of Jerusalem artichoke.

THOUARCE Le Relais de Bonnezeaux

Rte Angers, 49380 **Tel** *02 41 54 08 33* **Fax** *02 41 54 00 63*

This large, pleasant dining room is located in a converted train station overlooking the vineyards – this is sweet wine country. Imaginative cuisine with regional produce in dishes such as pigeon with an Anjou sauce and the specialty, eel braised in Coteaux del Layon wine.

TOURS L'Atelier Gourmand

37 rue Etienne Marcel, 37000 **Tel** *02 47 38 59 87* **Fax** *02 47 50 14 23*

A charming small restaurant in a 15th-century building in the old part of Tours. Fabrice Bironneau presents a competitively priced, interesting menu. Dishes include braised beef, and lamb cassoulet. Warm, homely ambience. Good wine selection. Book ahead.

TOURS L'Odéon

10 pl de la Gare, 37000 **Tel** *02 47 20 12 65*

Just a short walk from Tours' station, this Art Deco-style restaurant provides high-quality French regional dishes such as smoked salmon, duck, or pigeon, and a special all-lobster menu. There is a good selection of classic French desserts, and the wine list is particularly extensive.

TOURS L'Arche de Meslay

14 rue Ailes in Parçay Meslay, 37210 **Tel** *02 47 29 00 07* **Fax** *02 47 29 04 04*

Worth the 6-mile (9-km) detour from the city center, this refined, contemporary restaurant has a sunny terrace and a kitchen in full view. Watch the chef prepare a delicious roast langoustine, or *bouillabaisse tourangelle* (regional fish stew). A good selection of wines is available by the half bottle.

TOURS La Rive Gauche

23 rue du Commerce, 37000 **Tel** *02 47 05 71 21*

This restaurant has gained national recognition within a very short space of time. A varied menu features dishes with imaginative combinations such as Racan pigeon cooked with Lapsang Souchong tea. Prices remain reasonable, with a lunchtime discovery menu for just €35. Themed cookery workshops are also held here.

Key to Price Guide *see p600* **Key to Symbols** *see back cover flap*

TOURS La Roche Le Roy

`P 🏠 ▤ ⑪ 🛒 ♟`   €€€€

*55 rte de St-Avertin, 37000 **Tel** 02 47 27 22 00 **Fax** 02 47 28 08 39*

On the edge of the city center, in an elegant 18th-century manor, is this Michelin-starred restaurant serving classic, quality French cuisine. Specialties include creamed lentils with *foie gras* and a distinctive version of steak Rossini. There is a good selection of wines from the Loire and Bordeaux.

VALAIRE L'Herbe Rouge

`P 🏠 🛒`   €

*le Bourg, 41120 **Tel** 02 54 44 98 14*

Hidden away in tiny Valaire, a few kilometers from Chaumont-sur-Loire, is this excellent country bistro. The decor is somewhat stuck in the 1950s with plastic stools and other kitsch touches, but there is a pleasant terrace for fine days. Simple traditional cooking includes chicken liver pâté, *paupiette de veau* (stuffed veal), and *clafouti*. Good local wines.

VENDOME La Vallée

`P 🏠 ♿ 🛒 ♟`   €€

*34 rue Barré-de-St-Venant, 41100 **Tel** 02 54 77 29 93*

This restaurant serves well-prepared traditional dishes by chef Marc Georget, who is respectful of the quality of the produce. Offerings include Loire valley asparagus in season, fish from Brittany, and well-sourced veal. Classic, rustic dining room. Good regional wines, too.

VIGNOUX SUR BARANGEON Le Prieuré

`P 🏠 ♿ 🛒`   €€€

*2 rte de St Laurent, 18500 **Tel** 02 48 51 58 80 **Fax** 02 48 54 56 01*

Near to Vierzon, this lovely hotel-restaurant was built in 1862 to serve as the village presbytery. High-quality gourmet cuisine is served in the elegant dining room or on the covered terrace by the pool. Expect to find dishes such as duck confit with sautéed potatoes, and pan-fried monkfish with a lobster sauce.

VOUVRAY La Cave Martin

`🏠 🛒 ♟`   €

*66 vallée Coquette, 37210 **Tel** 02 47 52 62 18*

In this wine village, this restaurant carved into the tuffeau rock has a rustic menu with *andouillettes* (tripe sausages), duck breast and confit, and a decent choice of salads. Start with a glass of local fizzy wine, and finish with an unctuous sweet Vouvray with dessert. Reserve ahead.

BURGUNDY & FRANCHE-COMTE

ARBOIS Jean-Paul Jeanet

`P ▤ 🏨 ⑪ ♟`   €€€€

*9 rue de l'Hôtel de Ville, 39600 **Tel** 03 84 66 05 67*

In the center of picturesque Arbois, this ancient convent houses an impressive hotel and restaurant. The dining room is elegant and rustic with a pretty terrace. Staff are attentive and enthusiastic. The cuisine of Jean-Paul Jeanet constantly evolves, and his dishes are created with passion and harmony. Exciting desserts, too.

ARNAY LE DUC Chez Camille

`P 🏠 ♿`   €€€€

*1 pl Edouard Herriot, 21230 **Tel** 03 80 90 01 38*

This former vacation residence of a Marechal de France has a modern dining room serving traditional Burgundy fare, where game takes pride of place. Hearty, rustic dishes that eschew contemporary trends. Specialties include a marvelous rabbit pâté, guinea fowl with pheasant, and confit of cabbage.

AUTUN Les Ursulines

`🛒`   €€€€

*14 rue de Rivault, 71400 **Tel** 03 85 86 58 58*

Situated above the ramparts of the old town, with superb views of the Morvan countryside, this elegant, gastronomic restaurant serves up classic gourmet cuisine. Dishes include turbot served with a squid sauce, duck fillet with honey, and a melt-in-the-mouth chocolate fondant. The vast courtyard is good for outdoor dining in summer.

AUXERRE Le Jardin Gourmand

`P 🏠 ♿ 🛒`   €€€€€

*56 bd Vauban, 89000 **Tel** 03 86 51 53 52 **Fax** 03 86 52 33 82*

Adventurous and inventive dishes are on offer at this attractive dining room in a former wine-grower's house. Try the puff pastry parcel of green asparagus with poached egg and white Alba truffles. The menu changes with the season, and with the chef's vegetable garden. Wonderful cheeses. Pleasant patio. Reserve ahead.

AVALLON Relais des Gourmets

`P 🏠 ♿ 🛒`   €€

*45–47 rue de Paris, 89200 **Tel** 03 86 34 18 90*

A traditional auberge with two dining rooms in the fine fortified town of Avallon. The glass-domed, light and airy Salle des Oliviers does indeed have olive trees planted in it. The set menus offer a good selection of both fish and meat dishes, and a vegetarian choice. The bistro, La Salle Bourguignonne, has simple good-value, fixed-priced menus.

BEAUNE La Ciboulette

`🏠 ▤ ♿ ♟`   €

*69 rue Lorraine, 21200 **Tel** 03 80 24 70 72 **Fax** 03 80 22 79 71*

A delightful little bistro frequented by locals; always a good sign. The basic decor is in contrast with the high standard of cooking. Hearty dishes, such as steak with pungent Epoisses cheese. The best value in town. Local wine merchants come here to choose from the excellent wine list.

BEAUNE Le Bistro de L'Hôtel

3 rue Samuel Legay, 21200 **Tel** *03 80 25 94 10*

Expect a friendly welcome at this restaurant and the adjacent L'Hôtel de Beaune, both within the city walls. High quality ingredients are sourced from local suppliers. The menu varies depending on the season, but most dishes are French with Italian influences. Excellent wine list and lovely terrace. Cooking courses and *domaine* visits are available.

BEAUNE L'Ecusson

Pl Malmedy, 21200 **Tel** *03 80 24 03 82*

Wooden floors and oak beams give a rustic look to this restaurant. The cuisine is daring and stamped with the chef's personality. Trademark dishes include fillet of Charolais beef with cannelloni stuffed with Bourgogne truffle. To finish, why not try the Epoisse-flavored ice cream? There are several good Burgundies on the wine list.

BEAUNE Hostellerie de Levernois

Rte de Cobertault, Levernois, 21200 **Tel** *03 80 24 73 58* **Fax** *03 80 22 78 00*

This beautiful old mansion with formal gardens occupies an idyllic country setting. The classic restaurant serves up "serious" cuisine, such as snail and frogs' leg risotto, Charolais beef with a Pinot Noir sauce, shoulder of lamb *de sept heures*, or salmon smoked over vine cuttings. Vast wine list. Faultless service.

BELFORT Le Pot au Feu

27 bis grand' rue, 90000 **Tel** *03 84 28 57 84* **Fax** *03 84 58 17 65*

This bustling restaurant in a 17th-century vaulted cellar serves homely dishes alongside modern, innovative cuisine. Opt for the *pot au feu*, which is a braised beef and vegetable stew, or panfried veal kidneys with morille mushrooms, or salmon sushi with wasabi and horseradish sauce.

BONLIEU La Poutre

25 Grande Rue, 39130 **Tel** *03 84 25 57 77*

A charming farmhouse dating from 1740 houses this rustic dining room with stone walls and oak beams. Relax in the friendly atmosphere, and delight in the good home cooking based on regional specialties. Well-presented dishes include pan-fried *foie gras* and crayfish *ragoût*. Ideally situated for visits to the spectacular Cascades du Hérisson.

CHABLIS La Cuisine au Vin

16 rue Auxerroise, 89800 **Tel** *03 86 18 98 52*

Proprietor Daniel Etienne Defaix, largely responsible for the development of Chablis, has also launched this attractive restaurant. Traditional Burgundy recipes are given a contemporary makeover. An interesting range of well-prepared dishes are on the menu and include ham on the bone and parsley-imbibed snails.

CHAGNY Lameloise

36 pl d'Armes, 71150 **Tel** *03 85 87 65 65* **Fax** *03 85 87 03 57*

Family owned for more than a century, Lameloise is known for its reassuringly classic French dishes. Well-mastered Burgundian cooking: guinea fowl and *foie gras*, poached in a consommé and served with caramelized salsify and quince, and vanilla macaroon with pistachio cream. Pure, powerful flavors done to perfection.

CHAINTRE La Table de Chaintré

Le Bourg, 71570 **Tel** *03 85 32 90 95* **Fax** *03 83 32 91 04*

Not far from Mâcon, this well-established restaurant comes highly recommended, with a menu that changes weekly. Try the *menu découverte*, with four small main dishes, cheese, and dessert, or order *à la carte* favorites like sea bass, Bresse chicken, or Erquy scallops. Great desserts are also available.

CHALON-SUR-SAONE L'Air du Temps

7 rue de Strasbourg, 71100 **Tel** *03 85 93 39 01* **Fax** *03 85 93 39 01*

Plainly furnished restaurant, with flavors and colors that explode on the palate. The regional menu changes every 15 days and uses seasonal ingredients. The chef simplifies classic dishes, and delicacies include *escargots* and roasted veal fillet. Friendly service.

CHAROLLES Restaurant Fédéric Doucet

2 av de la Libération, 71120 **Tel** *03 85 24 11 32*

Where better to enjoy a Charolais steak than at Charolles? This beautiful, chic, provincial restaurant, near the village church, serves modern cuisine with a nod to the traditional. The chef's talent shines in dishes such as the sole with Collioure anchovies and beef with goat's cheese. Desserts also reveal careful preparation. Good Maçon wines.

CHASSAGNE-MONTRACHET Le Chassagne

4 impasse Chenevottes, 21180 **Tel** *03 80 21 94 94* **Fax** *03 80 21 97 77*

Definitely the right place to enjoy a glass of Chassagne – at the Chassagne restaurant. Try the deliciously fresh lobster, or John Dory with anchovies served with Paimpol beans, accompanied by the local Chardonnay, or the venison with pumpkin with a good red Pinot. The quality outweighs the price.

DIJON D'Zenvies

12 rue Odebert, 21000 **Tel** *03 80 50 09 26*

A contemporary bistro situated near Les Halles serving simple gourmet cuisine. The chef is part of the new generation who remain faithful to quality produce and present unfussy dishes. Specialties include *foie gras* served with a chutney, steak with a "real" Béarnaise, cod with crushed potatoes, and a rich chocolate tart. Good choice of wines by the glass.

Key to Price Guide *see p600* **Key to Symbols** *see back cover flap*

e Bistrot des Halles

P 🗐 & 🏠 €€

nnelier, 21000 **Tel** *03 80 49 94 15*

time this 1900s-style bistro is roaring. Located next to the market, it attracts food merchants and local s people with its meat pie, *jambon persillé*, and *bœuf bourguignon*. Well-known Dijon chef Jean-Pierre Billoux, as an upmarket restaurant in Dijon center, oversees this bistro.

ON Le Chabrot

🗐 🏠 🍷 €€

rue Monge, 21000 **Tel** *03 80 30 69 61* **Fax** *03 80 50 02 35*

ie cozy interior, chatty owner, and regional specialties make this restaurant very popular. Le Chabrot presents traditional dishes with an innovative twist, such as the snail ravioli. There is a good selection of Burgundy wines, and some of them are sold by the glass.

DIJON Hostellerie du Chapeau Rouge

🗐 🍴 🍷 €€€€€

5 rue Michelet, 21000 **Tel** *03 80 50 88 88*

Simply the best place to eat in town. The methodical and determined chef invites diners to travel the world with compositions like monkfish in a sesame crust. Many of the dishes reflect an Asiatic note. The quality of the meat is also impressive: black pig from Bigorre and Bresse chicken. Luscious desserts.

DOLE La Chaumière

P 🀄 🏠 €€€€

346 mal-Juin, 39100 **Tel** *03 84 70 72 40* **Fax** *03 84 79 25 60*

You need an open mind and a curious nature to enjoy the cuisine at this delightful, elegant restaurant. There are creative, unusual dishes such as fillets of whiting with Jerusalem artichokes, spinach, lemon, and coriander, or turnips flavored wtih Campari and seared duck breast, and olive sorbet. Take the plunge. Rooms available.

FONTANGY Ferme Auberge de la Morvandelle

P 🀄 & €

Précy-sous-Thil, 21390 **Tel** *03 80 84 33 32*

This is a working farm, open to guests only at the weekend. The dining area is in a converted barn, providing an authentic countryside experience. The farm supplies many of the ingredients for its homemade dishes such as chicken liver salad, roast guinea fowl, and fruit tarts. Reserve ahead.

GEVREY-CHAMBERTIN Chez Guy

🗐 🏠 🍷 €€€

3 pl de la Mairie, 21220 **Tel** *03 80 58 51 51* **Fax** *03 80 58 50 39*

A charming little restaurant with exposed oak beams, and a terrace for fine days. Simple local cuisine such as *coq au vin* and hearty *joue de bœuf*; both cooked slowly in red wine. More contemporary dishes include bream with a parsnip and hazelnut purée and lobster sauce. A good selection of fairly priced wines. Good service.

IGUERANDE La Colline du Colombier

P 🀄 & 🏠 €€€

Colombier, 71340 **Tel** *03 85 84 07 24*

Michel and Marie-Pierre Troisgros have renovated this ancient farmhouse, which looks down over the surrounding countryside and village. The cuisine focuses on local beef and veal, and organic produce. Simple, modern dishes are prepared with care and served in a charmingly rustic dining room.

LONS-LE-SAUNIER Le Relais des Salines

🀄 €

26 rue des Salines, 39000 **Tel** *03 84 43 01 57*

In the heart of the Jura lies this lively brasserie dishing up hearty mountain favorites in a friendly animated dining room. Satisfying dishes focus on meat, cheese, and potatoes. There is a good selection of salads, too. The Jura Chardonnays, Poulsards, and Savagnins make a welcome appearance, sold by the pitcher or glass.

MAGNY-COURS Absolue Renaissance

P 🀄 🗐 & 🏠 €€

2 rue de Paris, 58470 **Tel** *03 86 58 10 40*

Paces away from the Formula One circuit, this restaurant sits in a vast garden, with its own vegetable patch. Menus consist of classic dishes that have been revived with a contemporary flourish. Expect to find tasty options such as a *trilogie* of salmon, marinated, tartare, and smoked.

MALBUISSON Le Bon Acceuil

P 🀄 €€€

Rue de la Source, 25160 **Tel** *03 81 69 30 58*

This colorful restaurant is one of the most inventive kitchens in the Haut-Doubs, and very reasonably priced, too. The menus change seasonally, but expect to find creative dishes like oyster tempura with an emulsion of beets, and roast lamb with gnocchi. The sommelier is knowledgeable about Jura wines. Reservations recommended.

MONTFAUCON La Cheminée

P 🀄 & 🏠 €€

3 rue de la Vue des Alpes, 25660 **Tel** *03 81 81 17 48*

As the address suggests the Alpine scenery around the restaurant is spectacular. Located just a few kilometers from Besançon, this auberge with its comfortable rustic dining room is full of charm. Tasty dishes are based on local produce. Specialties include pan-fried lamb and a *fricassée* of lobster.

NEVERS Jean-Michel Couron

🗐 🍷 €€€€

21 rue St-Etienne, 58000 **Tel** *03 86 61 19 28* **Fax** *03 86 36 02 96*

Intimate, elegant restaurant, attentive service, and remarkable cuisine. Well-mastered dishes using the best produce to create perfectly balanced flavors in dishes such as fillet of Charolais beef on lentils, accompanied by hazelnut pasta and Parmesan. Inventive desserts and good wines by the glass, too.

NITRY Auberge de la Beursaudière

Chemin de Ronde, 89310 **Tel** *03 86 33 69 69* **Fax** *03 86 33 69 60*

A typical Morvan welcome awaits here, where the staff wear peasant costume. The portions are generous. Th [...] includes *andouillette de Clamecy* (tripe sausage), veal hock, *corniotte Morvandelle* (cheese filled pastry), *côte d[...] bœuf*, and *tournedos* (thick medallion of beef). Rooms available.

NUITS-ST-GEORGES L'Alambic

Rue de Général de Gaulle, 21700 **Tel** *03 80 61 35 00*

In this celebrated wine village lies L'Alambic, with a menu of 450 different wines, 75 of which are Nuits-St-Georges. On the culinary front no real surprises; classic Burgundy dishes are on offer in the attractive vaulted Cisterian dining room. The menu includes *fricassée* of snails, *oeuf en meurette*, and quails with prunes and polenta.

PORT LESNEY Le Bistro Pontarlier

Port Lesney, 39600 **Tel** *03 84 37 83 27* **Fax** *03 84 73 88 88*

One of the best-value restaurants in the region, this bistro is well established in the old schoolhouse of a pretty wine-growing village in the Arbois area. It is associated with the luxury hotel, Château de Germigny, in the same village, with the same chefs and cuisine – but simpler and less expensive. Excellent bistro atmosphere.

PULIGNY-MONTRACHET La Table d'Olivier Leflaive

Pl du Monument, 21190 **Tel** *03 80 21 37 65* **Fax** *03 80 21 33 94*

Located in a famous wine village, this rustic restaurant is named after its founder, who makes all the wines himself. The restaurant specializes in wine-tasting lunches in which cold meats, Bresse chicken, and Burgundy cheeses are offered alongside wines to taste, such as St-Aubin, Bourgogne Blanc, and Puligny-Montrachet. Reservations required.

QUARRE LES TOMBES Auberge de l'Atre

Les Lavaults, 89630 **Tel** *03 86 32 20 79* **Fax** *03 86 32 28 25*

The decorative interior of this restaurant in the Morvan region contrasts with the rustic simplicity of the building. The dining room has an authentic hearth, or *âtre*, and there is an attractive terrace. There are classic dishes, such as roast lamb with rosemary and soufflé flavored with *marc de bourgogne*.

SAULIEU Le Relais Bernard Loiseau

2 rue d'Argentine, 21210 **Tel** *03 80 90 53 53* **Fax** *03 80 64 08 92*

This restaurant remains one of France's best. The chef Patrick Bertron has successfully taken on the challenge, motivated by Mme. Loiseau. There are well-mastered, imaginative interpretations of traditional dishes such as pan-fried scallops served with a *palet* of pumpkin and cockles. Delicious desserts. Extensive wine list.

SENS La Madeleine

1 rue Alsace-Lorraine, 89100 **Tel** *03 86 65 09 31* **Fax** *03 86 95 37 41*

With the two-Michelin-star rating, here you will find elegant, refined cuisine with great attention to the ingredients. Seasonal menus offer specialties such as *foie gras* with apple and saffron compote, sea bass, and a gorgeously gooey chocolate mousse with raspberry sauce. Good Chablis and local Irancy wines. Reserve ahead.

ST-AMOUR BELLEVUE L'Auberge du Paradis

Le Plâtre Durand, 71570 **Tel** *03 85 37 10 26*

Once a bakery, then a grocer's, now one of the most dynamic restaurants in Burgundy. The chef here oozes enthusiasm and personality. Daring combinations of spices result in exciting dishes including bold desserts such as spicy *crème au chocolat* with apple cream. The pretty dining room is decorated with bright, checkered fabrics and Moroccan rugs.

ST PERE SOUS VEZELAY L'Espérance

St Père sous Vézelay, 89450 **Tel** *03 86 33 39 10* **Fax** *03 86 33 26 15*

L'Espérance serves perhaps the greatest food in Burgundy, in an elegant dining room that opens out onto a terrace with superb views. Marc Meneau, one of France's finest chefs, presents modern classics, such as scallops with lemon or fresh truffles, and tender, succulent Quercy lamb. Classic wine list.

ST-ROMAIN Les Roches

Pl de la Mairie, 21190 **Tel** *03 80 21 21 63*

Small hotel-restaurant sitting on the main square of this village well known to wine connoisseurs. Plain, no-frills cooking in a dining room to match. Relax with a chilled glass of St-Romain Blanc accompanied with homemade nibbles, then dig into hearty, homely dishes such as the veritable *haché parmentier*. One of the best value places in the region.

TOURNUS Le Restaurant Greuze

1 rue A Thibaudet, 71700 **Tel** *03 85 51 13 52* **Fax** *03 85 51 75 42*

Ultraclassic cuisine and decor, the restaurant itself is a monument to a bygone era. Here's the place to enjoy some of the best classic cooking in France, such as scallops with vegetable *pot au feu* perfumed with citronelle, Bresse chicken, or a succulent steak of Salers-Charolais beef. Good Mâcon and Beaujolais wines.

VERDUN-SUR-LE-DOUBS L'Hostellerie Bourguignonne – Didier Denis

2 av Pdt-Borgeot, 71350 **Tel** *03 85 91 51 45* **Fax** *03 85 91 53 81*

On the riverbank, in the heart of the countryside, this rustic establishment serves unpretentious, straightforward cooking with local ingredients. They do a very good local Charolais beef fillet, and a seafood couscous with lobster, scallops, and king prawns, flavored with star anise and peppery mint. Excellent wine list.

Key to Price Guide *see p600* **Key to Symbols** *see back cover flap*

VENOY Le Moulin de la Coudre
*2 rue des Gravottes, La Coudre, 89290 **Tel** 03 86 40 23 79*

Near to Auxerre in the heart of the Yonne lies this restored watermill housing a hotel and restaurant. Classic cuisine is prepared with touches of originality; menus change weekly according to seasonal produce and the whim of the chef. In winter, relax with coffee in front of the open fireplace; in summer, enjoy the flower-filled garden.

VILLENEUVE SUR YONNE Auberge La Lucarne aux Chouettes
*7 quai Bretoche, 89500 **Tel** 03 86 87 18 26 **Fax** 03 86 87 22 63*

Renovated by actress Leslie Caron, this 17th-century inn has a lovely setting by the river Yonne. Dining outside on the terrace is delightful in summer. The dining room is cozy with exposed beams. The menu presents traditional dishes, such as snails and wild mushroom salad.

VILLERS-LE-LAC Le France
*8 pl Cupillard, 25130 **Tel** 03 81 68 00 06 **Fax** 03 81 68 09 22*

The cuisine here is fine and inventive, full of contrasts but still simple. The chef has his own herb garden outside and an expansive selection of spices collected during his travels. The dining room is airy and bright. Try the pigeon breast accompanied by a chocolate sauce and served with licorice-perfumed salsify. Refreshing sorbets.

VINCELOTTE Auberge des Tilleuls
*12 quai de l'Yonne, 82290 **Tel** 03 86 42 22 13*

This attractive auberge on the banks of the river serves cuisine that is packed with flavors, not only from Burgundy, but from other French regions, too. Dishes include garlic from Arleux, lentils from Puy, and *andouille* from Vire. Try succulent entrecôte steak, pan-fried in Bordier butter. Good selection of Burgundy wines, especially Irancy.

VONNAS Georges Blanc
*Pl Marché, 01540 **Tel** 04 74 50 90 90 **Fax** 04 74 50 08 80*

A popular shrine of cooking with smooth service in a dining room crammed with antiques. The ambience wavers between the refined and the rustic. Inventive cuisine is prepared by M. Blanc's two sons, including Bresse chicken with *foie gras* and lobster ravioli with sorrel. Excellent wines.

THE MASSIF CENTRAL

ALLEYRAS Le Haut Allier
*Pont d'Alleyras, 43580 **Tel** 04 71 57 57 63 **Fax** 04 71 57 57 99*

This hotel-restaurant nestled in the Allier gorge is well worth seeking out for its warm welcome and inventive cuisine. Local produce features in traditional dishes such as saddle of Saugues lamb, or more imaginative dishes such as a crumble of Auvergne ham. The set menus represent excellent value.

AUMONT-AUBRAC Restaurant Prouhèze
*2 rte du Languedoc, 48130 **Tel** 04 66 42 80 07 **Fax** 04 66 42 87 78*

The award-winning chef uses only the freshest ingredients to create elegant and unusual flavors. Menu highlights include an *aligot* (potatoes with cheese) casserole and pan-fried fillet of Aubrac beef with *vin jaune*. Good selection of Languedoc wines. Its sister restaurant, Le Compostelle, serves less expensive country fare.

BELCASTEL Vieux Pont
*Le Bourg, 12390 **Tel** 05 65 64 52 29*

This imaginative restaurant lies across a medieval cobbled bridge: the air is fresh, and the river burbles beside the stylishly rustic dining room. Dishes are prepared with talent and modernism. Quality produce is used to create dishes such as Mont Royal pigeon with porcini mushrooms and Aveyron veal. Reservation recommended.

BOUDES La Vigne
*Pl de la Mairie, 63340 **Tel** 04 73 96 55 66*

In the main square of this small wine-making village lies one of the few truly creative restaurants in the region. The chef is constantly seeking out new ideas. Menus change regularly; expect to find dishes such as cod and scallop mousse. The cheeses and desserts are treated with the same attention. Good-value set menus.

BOUSSAC Le Relais Creusois
*40 Maison Dieu, rte de la Châtre, 23600 **Tel** 05 55 65 02 20 **Fax** 05 55 65 13 60*

Do not be put off by the incongruous exterior or the downbeat decor – this is award-winning cuisine. The chef seeks inspiration from far and wide to deliver original dishes, such as pike-perch with parsnip purée, and duck with elderberries. Some tables afford views over the beautiful Petite Creuse valley. Phone to make sure it is open. Closed Jan–mid-Mar.

BRIVE-LA-GAILLARDE Chez Francis
*61 av de Paris, 19100 **Tel** 05 55 74 41 72*

Reminiscent of an authentic Parisien bistro, this retro pub has become an institution in Brive. The cuisine is generous and well prepared. Regional favorites are revisited such as baby squid, Jerusalem artichokes, or veal *pot au feu*. Good selection of southern French wines. Reservations recommended.

CLERMONT-FERRAND Le Caveau

9 rue Philippe Marcombes, 63000 **Tel** *04 73 14 07 03*

Don't be deterred by the uninviting entrance; at the bottom of the simple staircase is a delightful vaulted dining room. Dishes are rustic and traditional. Huge chunks of Salers or Aubrac beef and *coq au vin* make this a meat eater's paradise. Luckily the desserts are not of the same gargantuan proportions. Reserve ahead.

CLERMONT-FERRAND Amphitryon Capucine

50 rue Fontgiève, 63000 **Tel** *04 73 31 38 39*

In this small, wooden-fronted restaurant guests can enjoy the best seasonal local ingredients in a dining room complete with a fireplace and oak beams. Simple dishes, well-prepared without pretention, include *gnocchi* with roast langoustine and truffles, and potted chocolate pudding. Good wines from Languedoc and Auvergne.

CLERMONT-FERRAND Goûts et Couleurs

6 pl Champgil, 63000 **Tel** *04 73 19 37 82*

The geometric 1980s decor is softened by an ancient vaulted ceiling in this former mirror workshop. Modern, inventive cuisine using quality ingredients offers the best value in town. Good choice of both meat and fish dishes. Leave room for delicious desserts, such as warm lemon madeleines with citrus-fruit jelly and margarita sorbet.

COLLONGES-LA-ROUGE Auberge Le Prieuré

Pl de l'Eglise, 19500 **Tel** *05 55 25 41 00*

Typical 18th-century auberge built in the local red stone, with a pretty terrace. Simple, well-prepared classic dishes such as the *foie gras* with onion confit, pan-fried duck breast, and pike-perch with lemon butter sauce. If you are in a rush, there is a *casse croûte* menu, where the appetizer and main course are served at the same time.

FLORAC La Source du Pêcher

Rue Remuret, 48400 **Tel** *04 66 45 03 01* **Fax** *04 66 45 28 82*

Charming little restaurant in a converted mill where you can watch the fish jumping while you eat. Regional produce takes pride of place – duck with bilberries, local lamb, Lozère trout, and chestnut-flower honey, depending on the season. Excellent choice of Languedoc wines. Closed from November to Easter.

LAGUIOLE Michel Bras

Rte de l'Aubrac, 12210 **Tel** *05 65 51 18 20* **Fax** *05 65 48 47 02*

A wall of glass overlooks the Aubrac countryside from this three-star hilltop restaurant. Michel and Sebastien Bras are renowned for their cutting-edge cuisine. The pan-fried pigeon, flavored with asafetida and served with Cévenne onions and a juniper and orange sauce, is out of this world. Closed Nov–Easter.

LE PUY-EN-VELAY Tournayre

12 rue Chênebouterie, 43000 **Tel** *04 71 09 58 94*

The delightful restaurant is located in one of the oldest *hôtels particuliers* in Le Puy-en-Velay, which dates from the 12th century. The dining room has vaulted ceilings and stone walls. The chef prepares typical Auvergne cuisine, as well as more elaborate dishes like warm lobster tart, and langoustine crumble with *morille* mushrooms.

LE PUY-EN-VELAY François Gagnaire

4 av Clément Charbonnier, 43000 **Tel** *04 71 02 75 55*

Sophisticated restaurant housed in the Hôtel du Parc. The dining room is simply furnished with colorful Raoul Dufy prints lining the walls. The chef is an old master who knows exactly where he's going. He creatively treats local ingredients with a modern twist. Dishes include pan-fried *foie gras* on a bed of artichokes, and turbot with wild mushrooms.

LE ROUGET Hôtel des Voyageurs

20 av de 15 septembre 1945, 15290 **Tel** *04 71 46 10 14* **Fax** *04 71 46 93 89*

Situated 16 miles (25 km) southwest of Aurillac is this stone-built Cantal hotel-restaurant serving well-prepared traditional dishes. The reasonably priced *menu du terroir* includes choices such as the risotto with prawns, and pan-fried sea bream served with citrus-fruit-flavored quinoa. Good selection of wines.

LIMOGES Chez Alphonse

5 pl de la Motte, 87000 **Tel** *05 55 34 34 14* **Fax** *05 55 34 34 14*

This lively bistro serves regional cuisine made with fresh ingredients that the chef himself sources daily from the local market. The traditional Limousin dishes are usually meat or fish based; the *prix-fixe* menus are great. Generous cheese platter and good chocolate mousse. Reservations recommended. Closed Jul 27–Aug 10; Dec 29–Jan 12; Sun.

LIMOGES Chez François

Pl de la Motte, 87000 **Tel** *05 55 32 32 79* **Fax** *05 55 32 87 39*

Unbeatable value and a convivial atmosphere at this restaurant inside Limoges' covered market hall. It is only open at lunchtime. Be sure to get here early for a place at the communal tables – or prepare to wait in line. The food is nothing fancy, but well cooked and tasty. The single, three-course menu changes daily.

LIMOGES L'Amphitryon

26 rue de la Boucherie, 87000 **Tel** *05 55 33 36 39* **Fax** *05 55 32 98 50*

Chic contemporary dining space in the heart of old Limoges. The food is sophisticated and the flavors delicate, in keeping with the Limoges porcelain on which it is served. A regular favorite is the fillet of Limousin beef, while desserts center around seasonal fruits.

Key to Price Guide *see p600* **Key to Symbols** *see back cover flap*

MILLAU La Braconne
7 pl Maréchal Foch, 12100 **Tel** *05 65 60 30 93*

Under the arcades of a picturesque square is this friendly restaurant with an authentic 13th-century vaulted dining room. The terrace is also attractive with comfy wicker chairs. Classic savory cuisine with specialties like succulent flambéed leg of lamb. The homely atmosphere makes this a relaxing place to stop for a meal.

MONTLUCON Le Grenier à Sel
10 rue Ste-Anne, 03100 **Tel** *04 70 05 53 79* **Fax** *04 70 05 87 91*

This ivy-covered 16th-century mansion has huge fireplaces and an elegant dining room decked out in restful pastel tones. In fine weather, meals may be served on the enchanting terrace. Try cannelloni filled with whiting and crayfish and served with seasonal vegetables. Good-value set menus.

MONTSALVY L'Auberge Fleurie
Pl du Barry, 15120 **Tel** *04 71 49 20 02*

A charming ivy-clad auberge with oak beams, an open fireplace, and a rustic feel. The chef emphasizes presentation for his creative dishes. The menus change according to seasonal produce with specialties such as carpaccio of hare served with fennel and basil-flavored butter. Delicious desserts include chocolate meringue pudding.

MOUDEYRES Le Pré Bossu
Le Bourg, 43150 **Tel** *04 71 05 10 70* **Fax** *04 71 05 10 21*

Restaurant-with-rooms that is well worth seeking out for the peaceful location and expertly executed cuisine. Many of the herbs and vegetables – including old-fashioned varieties – come from the garden. There is even a vegetarian menu – a rare treat in this corner of France. Dinner only. Closed Nov–Apr.

MOULINS Le Trait d'Union
16 rue Gambette, 3000 **Tel** *04 70 34 24 61*

Upmarket contemporary bistro in the city center serving cuisine that balances classicism and modernism. The chef, who has worked with some of the country's best, pays homage to the region with dishes such as Monts du Forez veal and classic steak Rossini. There is a selection of local goat's cheeses.

MURAT Le Jarrousset
Rte de Clermont-Ferrand, 15300 **Tel** *04 71 20 10 69* **Fax** *04 71 20 15 26*

Surrounded by attractive gardens, just east of Murat, is this discreet restaurant. The chef seeks inspiration from top-quality ingredients, most of them sourced locally. The gastronomic menu changes every season, allowing for lots of creativity.

RODEZ Goûts en Couleurs
38 rue Bonald, 12000 **Tel** *05 65 42 75 10*

Situated in the old town, looking out onto Embergues Square, this charming dining room is decorated with the owner's colorful paintings. Dishes such as an *île flottante* of truffles with licorice, and Brill with Nadaillac snails bear witness to the imaginative cuisine of the chef. Good wine selection and friendly service.

ST-BONNET-LE-FROID Auberge des Cimes
Le Bourg, 43290 **Tel** *04 71 59 93 72* **Fax** *04 71 59 93 40*

The restaurant at the Clos des Cimes hotel has been awarded its third Michelin star. Depending on the season, you'll feast on roast lamb, suckling pig perfumed with sage, or fragrant mushrooms. Wonderful selection of Auvergne and Ardeche cheeses, matured on the premises. Delicious desserts, too. Closed Jan–mid-March.

ST-JULIEN-CHAPTEUIL Vidal
Pl du Marché, 43260 **Tel** *04 71 08 70 50* **Fax** *04 71 08 40 14*

In a sleepy village surrounded by mountain peaks, the Vidal family runs a convivial restaurant decorated with murals depicting local scenery. Dishes include *foie gras* served with toasted blueberry gingerbread, stuffed fillet of beef, and Velay lamb. Closed mid-Jan–Feb.

UZERCHE Restaurant Jean Teyssier
Rue du Pont-Turgot, 19140 **Tel** *05 55 73 10 05* **Fax** *05 55 98 43 31*

A taste of the Mediterranean has come to the Corrèze with dishes such as *vol-au-vent* with Roquefort sauce, braised lamb with parsnip purée, and trout with zucchini gratin. Wonderful panoramic restaurant with views of the Vezère. Closed mid-Feb–mid-Mar.

VICHY Brasserie du Casino
4 rue du Casino, 03200 **Tel** *04 70 98 23 06* **Fax** *04 70 98 53 17*

A veritable institution on the Vichy restaurant scene, across the road from the Grand Casino. Dine in stylish Art Deco surroundings – all wood and mirrors and big bench-seats – on upscale brasserie fare. *Foie gras* served warm with balsalmic vinegar and raspberry charlotte are among the classics on offer.

VICHY Jacques Decoret
15 rue du Parc, 3200 **Tel** *04 70 97 65 06*

This restaurant is continuously improving. Imaginative dishes are prepared with precision. Pan-fried *foie gras* with *Bonite* bouillon, and langoustines coated with dill and horseradish are just some of the dishes that testify to the chef's creativity and culinary talent.

THE RHONE VALLEY AND FRENCH ALPS

ANNECY Le Belvédère
7 chemin Belvédère, 74000 **Tel** *04 50 45 04 90*

This dining room has comfy leather chairs, a wonderful view of the lake and a pretty terrace. Appetizing contemporary recipes are prepared with finesse. Dishes such as *foie gras* perfumed with vanilla and served with fig compote explode with flavors. Divine desserts too, such as creamed apple with saffron and homemade sorbet.

BOURG-EN-BRESSE Les Quatres Saisons
6 rue de le République, 1000 **Tel** *04 74 22 01 86*

Friendly, convivial restaurant serving traditional dishes jazzed up with a modern touch. The chef, passionate about both wines and local produce, livens up old favorites: tartare of scallops, crab, and prawns with a wasabi coulis, or fillet of pork with honey, Szechuan pepper, and kumquat. Good Rhône and Burgundy wine selection.

CHAMBERY Château de Candie – L'Orangerie
Rue de Bois de Candie, Chambéry le Vieux, 73000 **Tel** *04 79 96 63 00* **Fax** *04 79 96 63 10*

A 14th-century château in its own grounds is the beautiful setting for this elegant restaurant. Classic produce is prepared with a contemporary touch in such dishes as tartare of scallops with crushed cashew nuts, or more rustic hare with lemon confit. Closed 2 weeks Apr & 2 weeks Nov.

CHAMONIX La Calèche
Rue Dr. Paccard, 74400 **Tel** *04 50 55 94 68*

A traditional Chamonix mountain restaurant that has been run by the same family since 1946. Enjoy typical Savoyard specialties such as *tartiflette*, fondue, and *raclette*, as well as grilled meat, in the dining room crammed with old skis, Swiss clocks, copper pans, and a bobsled from the 1924 Winter Olympics. Good Savoie wines.

CHAMONIX Les Jardins du Mont Blanc
62 Allée du Majestic, 74400 **Tel** *04 50 55 35 42*

A mountain hotel offering savory modern Alpine cuisine using the best produce the region can offer. The chef revisits classic dishes, such as salt cod, and prepares them with subtlety and faultless precision. Magnificent desserts, too. It tends to be noisy when there are large groups. Good-value menu at lunchtime.

CHAMONIX Le Hameau Albert 1er
119 impasse Montenvers, 74402 **Tel** *04 50 53 05 09* **Fax** *04 50 55 95 48*

Luxury Savoyard hotel-restaurant in the mountains, with a view of Italy. The superb cooking of Pierre Carrier tempts the palate. The vegetable patch next door provides seasonal inspiration for dishes such as fish accompanied by *ratte* potatoes and violet artichokes with a Château Chalon sauce, or a gratin of salsify. Good cheese board.

COLLONGES AU MONT D'OR Paul Bocuse
40 quai de la Plage, 69660 **Tel** *04 72 42 90 90* **Fax** *04 72 27 85 87*

Paul Bocuse has become an institution for French cooking, and is simply irreplaceable. Try delicacies such as black truffle soup with pastry, the cooked-to-perfection turbot with its *beurre blanc* sauce, or the legendary gratin of crayfish. The wines are also superb. Reserve a table well in advance.

COURCHEVEL Le Genépi
Courchevel 1850, 73120 **Tel** *04 79 08 08 63*

This restaurant is one of the best value-for-money places at the luxury ski resort of Courchevel 1850. Both traditional mountain fare and classic dishes are prepared with finesse, such as carpaccio of duck with basil, lobster ravioli, and stuffed rabbit, and are served in the elegant rustic dining room.

COURCHEVEL Le Chabichou
Quartier des Chenus, 73120 **Tel** *04 79 08 00 55* **Fax** *04 79 08 33 58*

Reserve a table by the huge windows to enjoy views of the mountains. With two Michelin stars, Le Chabichou offers exotic and creative cuisine at one of the most popular restaurants in this extensive resort. Refined ambience and old-school favorites with an elaborate touch, such as Bresse pigeon stuffed with *foie gras*, pear, and cloves.

EVIAN LES BAINS Histoire de Goût
1 av Général Dupas, 74500 **Tel** *04 50 70 09 98*

Restaurant and wine bar serving gourmet bistro food. Perch at the zinc-topped bar and choose from over 200 wines, or settle in the elegant vaulted dining room adorned with wrought-iron chandeliers. Good-value menus include a vegetarian option – the *découverte* menu is particularly recommended.

GRENOBLE Le Mas Bottero
168 Cours Berriat, 38000 **Tel** *04 76 21 95 33*

Dishes here reflect the Provençal roots of the young chef, as well as his devotion to organic produce. Tasty offerings include artichokes served with arugula *pistou*, pigeon in a hazelnut crust, and organic salmon with celery and green apple. In summer, tables are set up outside, under the ancient wisteria.

Key to Price Guide *see p600* **Key to Symbols** *see back cover flap*

GRENOBLE A Ma Table
92 cours Jean-Jaurès, 38000 **Tel** *04 76 96 77 04* **Fax** *04 76 96 77 04*

There are regular changes to the menu, depending on seasonal local produce, at this small prettily decorated restaurant. Well-mastered classic cuisine includes dishes such as caramelized pear and gorgonzola tart with smoked duck breast, Vercors trout in mustard sauce, and duck cassoulet with almonds and coconut. Reserve ahead.

GRENOBLE Le Fantin Latour
1 rue Général Beylié, 38000 **Tel** *04 76 01 00 97*

The presentation at this chic restaurant is extravagant: apéritifs are presented on a bed of wild plants, and the dessert comes decorated with pebbles. The cuisine also breaks down traditional boundaries in using creative combinations of herbs and spices, as in pigeon served with a lichen and sage sauce. Dynamic staff, too.

LA CLUSAZ La Scierie
321-331 rte du Col des Aravis, 74220 **Tel** *04 50 63 34 68*

This restaurant is located in a former sawmill in the bustling center of this popular ski resort. The chef has created an extensive menu at reasonable prices, with dishes ranging from local mountain charcuterie and salad to more elaborate affairs such as John Dory fillet served with a sage and Parmesan risotto.

LAMASTRE Restaurant Barattéro
Pl Seignobos, 07270 **Tel** *04 75 06 41 50* **Fax** *04 75 06 49 75*

This is an elegant restaurant with an attractive garden at the Hotel Midi in the lovely Ardèche town of Lamastre. Classic cuisine such as panfried *foie gras* salad, Bresse chicken, crayfish with a richly flavored sauce, and Ardèche chestnut soufflé. The wine list focuses on St-Joseph and St-Péray. Reserve ahead.

LARGENTIÈRE Le Chêne Vert
Rocher, 7110 **Tel** *04 75 88 34 02*

Traditional Ardèchois hotel and restaurant situated in the countryside, near Aubenas. Choose from well-prepared regional classics such as *foie gras* served with a fig confit or roast rabbit flavored with thyme, accompanied by a *tartiflette* Ardèchoise. To finish, a fruit salad topped by a frothy cream infused with Bourbon vanilla.

LE BOURGET-LE-LAC Beaurivage
Boulevard du Lac, 73370 **Tel** *04 79 25 00 38*

Superbly situated on the banks of the lake, this typical auberge has a dining room opening out onto a lovely terrace overhung with plantain trees. Enjoy classic Savoyard cuisine, grilled lobster, and a risotto flavored with *bouillabaisse*, or the chicken breast stuffed with *foie gras* and served with risotto, while enjoying the view.

LYON Brasserie Georges
30 cour Verdun, 69002 **Tel** *04 72 56 54 54* **Fax** *04 78 42 51 65*

Huge, bustling city-center bistro with fast service and a splendid Art Deco interior. The extensive menu includes a choice of Lyonnais specialties such as *andouillette* (tripe sausage) and Dauphinoise potatoes, but also a variety of seafood dishes, sauerkraut, and omelet. Good choice for children and vegetarians.

LYON La Gargotte d'Ivan
15 rue Royale, 69001 **Tel** *04 78 28 79 20*

Just north of the Grand Théâtre lies "Ivan's Canteen," a friendly restaurant with retro decor, Rococo gilding, and mirror-lined walls. The young and talented chef prepares semi-gastronomic dishes at bistro prices. The menus include dishes based on grand classics enlivened with a touch of originality. Small selection of good wines at reasonable prices, too.

LYON 33 Cité
33 quai Charles de Gaulle, 69006 **Tel** *04 37 45 45 45*

Modern city center brasserie facing the Cité Internationale. This stylish dining room offers classic and contemporary cuisine prepared with care; dishes include a *mille-feuille* of crab, lightly cooked tuna with sesame seeds, and Dombe duck breast "Rossini." Wines can be ordered by the glass or bottle.

LYON L'Alexandrin
83 rue Moncey, 69003 **Tel** *04 72 61 15 69*

The young, gifted chef here creates gourmet Lyonnais dishes. Faultless preparation results in cooked-to-perfection dishes with personality. These include pike mousse with a creamy crayfish sauce, and Bresse chicken cooked in vinegar. The same care is taken with the vegetables, including the *cocotte* of vegetables with chestnuts.

LYON Nicolas le Bec et Taka
14 rue Grolée, 69002 **Tel** *04 78 42 15 35* **Fax** *04 72 40 98 97*

Cutting-edge, inventive cuisine with audacious touches shows in dishes such as caramelized Bresse pigeon with a pomegranate reduction. The setting is elegant and contemporary, and there's an excellent wine list with a particularly good range of Burgundies, but at a price. Closed 2 weeks Jan & 2 weeks Aug.

MEGEVE La Petite Ravine
743 chemin de la Ravine, Demi Quartier Combloux, 74120 **Tel** *04 50 21 38 67*

Typical alpine chalet restaurant with a homely, convivial ambience. In winter, skiers stop off to relax and have a bite, in summer hikers settle back to admire the view. The selection of dishes is limited but tasty regional favorites are included: cheese fondue, *croûte au* Beaufort cheese, and salads. Ideal for all the family.

MEGEVE La Taverne du Mont d'Arbois   🅿️ 🖼️   €€€€

3001 rte Edmond de Rothschild, 74120 **Tel** *04 50 21 03 53*

Once a tavern frequented by locals, this authentic chalet now attracts a chic Megève crowd. The chef prepares dishes based on traditional recipes; carpaccio of bream and crayfish gratin are on the menu alongside old favorites such as *raclette* and fondue. The desserts are excellent.

MORZINE La Chamade   🛗 ♿ 🖼️   €€

Morzine, 74110 **Tel** *04 50 79 13 91* **Fax** *04 50 79 27 48*

Traditional Alpine family-run restaurant with a wide menu. Pizzas cooked in wood-fired ovens, cheese platters, and regional fare such as piglet and charcuterie (cold meats). Good selection of appetizers including Motzinoise tomme salad, rabbit with lentils, mixed grill, and a superb cheese selection including several local tommes. Vegetarian dishes.

ROANNE La Troisgros   🅿️🛗📋♿🍴🍷   €€€€€

Pl Jean Troisgros, 42300 **Tel** *04 77 71 66 97* **Fax** *04 77 70 39 77*

La Troisgros is one of the most prestigious restaurants in France, with elegant contemporary decor. Sit in the dining room with its pure lines and zen atmosphere and feast on delights such as duck fillet with cherries. There is also a specialized food library.

ST-AGREVE Domaine de Rilhac   🅿️🛗♿   €€€€

Rilhac, 07320 **Tel** *04 75 30 20 20* **Fax** *04 75 30 20 00*

Located in a peaceful corner of the Ardèche, in this renovated farmhouse, chef Ludovic Sinz creates classic dishes with an innovative approach. On the menu, there is a choice of dishes such as pumpkin soup with snails, pan-fried chicory with scallops and chestnut sauce, and to finish, a warm chocolate tart.

ST-ETIENNE Le Bistrot de Paris   🖼️   €

7 pl Jean Jaurès, 42000 **Tel** *04 77 32 21 50*

This convivial bistro is located on an attractive square in the city center. The menu changes daily, according to whatever is available and freshest at the local market. Dishes here are all excellent value for money, and there is a pleasant terrace for summer dining and watching the rest of the world pass by.

ST-MARTIN-DE-BELLEVILLE La Bouitte   🅿️🛗🖼️🍷   €€€€€

St Marcel, 73440 **Tel** *04 79 08 96 77* **Fax** *04 79 08 96 03*

In a charming Alpine chalet, this restaurant serves inventive dishes using regional Alpine herbs. Try the local fish, such as the tantalizing *féra du lac Léman* served with artichoke-filled cannelloni. There is also a very good selection of cheese and desserts. Cooking courses are available.

TAIN L'HERMITAGE Lycée Hotelier de l'Hermitage   📝🅿️   €

Rue Jean Monnet, 26600 **Tel** *04 75 07 57 14*

On the outskirts of this famous wine-making town lies this training college for aspiring chefs, waiters, and sommeliers. The students run two restaurants serving classic gourmet dishes. Each Thursday, the evenings have a chosen theme. The menu changes constantly and the prices include an apéritif and wine. Only open when school is in session.

TALLOIRES La Villa des Fleurs   🅿️🛗🖼️   €€€

Rte du Port, 74290 **Tel** *04 50 60 71 14* **Fax** *04 50 60 74 06*

The cuisine at this charming stone-built house set in its own grounds focuses on fish caught in Lake d'Annecy, a stone's throw away. Try the succulent local féra fish, or the poached trout. Traditional regional dishes are also served. Dine outside with a view of the lake in fine weather. Pleasant service. Rooms available.

TOURNON Le Tournesol   🛗🖼️🍷   €€

44 av Maréchal Foch, 07300 **Tel** *04 75 07 08 26* **Fax** *04 75 07 08 26*

Chic restaurant near the riverside with a panoramic view of the Hermitage vineyards. The interior is smart and contemporary, and the young chef shows his originality in dishes such as *foie gras* with apple coulis, or salmon cooked in maple syrup and flavored with fresh ginger. Homemade desserts. Well-chosen wines.

URIAGE-LES-BAINS Les Terrasses d'Uriage   🅿️📋🍴🍷   €€€€€

Pl de la Déesse-Hygie, 38410 **Tel** *04 76 89 10 80*

Located in a typical thermal resort is this dynamic restaurant offering interesting, innovative dishes with a touch of eccentricity. The elegant dining room in a Napoleon III building opens out onto a lovely park. Savor dishes such as guinea fowl served with sorrel and dill *fromage blanc*. Desserts are wonderful, and there's a vast choice of wines.

VALENCE Restaurant Pic   🅿️🛗📋♿🖼️🍴🍷   €€€€

285 av Victor Hugo, 26000 **Tel** *04 75 44 15 32* **Fax** *04 75 40 96 03*

Refined restaurant with inspirational cuisine in a luxurious hotel. Lobster with red fruit and berries, celery and green pepper has enhanced the reputation of this constantly evolving, nonconventional establishment. Great Rhône wines. The restaurant runs cooking courses.

VIENNE La Pyramide   🅿️📋♿🖼️🍴🍷   €€€

14 bd Fernand Point, 38200 **Tel** *04 74 53 01 96*

One of France's classic Michelin-starred hotel-restaurant establishments. Professionalism reigns supreme. Gastronomic creations are based on regional produce; choices include pan-fried *foie gras* flavored with Madagascar pepper, *féra du lac* fish with a pea purée, and emulsion of Shimeji mushrooms. Superb selection of Rhône wines.

Key to Price Guide *see p600* **Key to Symbols** *see back cover flap*

POITOU & AQUITAINE

ANGOULEME Le Terminus
3 pl de la Gare, 16000 **Tel** *05 45 95 27 13*

Chic, modern restaurant where good food, prompt service, and well-priced menus make up for the location on a busy main road. Ultrafresh seafood takes pride of place, with particular mention of the mixed fish grill and Spanish *fricassée* of monkfish. Leave room for one of the wicked desserts.

ARCACHON Chez Yvette
59 bd du Général Leclerc, 33120 **Tel** *05 56 83 05 11*

Seafood doesn't come much fresher than at this venerable Arcachon restaurant run by former oyster farmers. Success stories include lamprey *à la bordelaise* (eel-like fish cooked in wine) and roast turbot, but it is hard to resist the spectacular seafood platters. It's wise to reserve a table.

ARCINS Le Lion d'Or
11 rte de Pauillac, 33460 **Tel** *05 56 58 96 79*

A small and welcoming village auberge in the heart of the Médoc vineyards north of Margaux. Loved by locals who appreciate the traditional seasonal cooking. Local Pauillac lamb is a springtime favorite, while in fall the accent is on game. No fixed menus, but prices remain reasonable.

BORDEAUX Bistrot d'Edouard
16 pl du Parlement, 33000 **Tel** *05 56 81 48 87*

On one of Bordeaux's prettiest squares, this fuss-free bistro offers a broad range of inexpensive fixed-price menus. Don't expect gourmet dining, but the food is reliable, covering everything from salads, omelets, vegetarian dishes, and fish to regional specialties. Outside dining in summer.

BORDEAUX Le Café du Musée
Musée d'Art Contemporain, 7 rue Ferrère, 33000 **Tel** *05 56 44 71 61*

Splendid lunch spot on top of the contemporary art museum. Modern decor complements stylish dishes ranging from *foie gras* and oysters to duck spring rolls and sashimi. The Sunday buffet is a must on the Bordeaux scene. Also serves coffee, desserts, and light meals until 6pm.

BORDEAUX La Tupina
6 rue Porte de la Monnaie, 33800 **Tel** *05 56 91 56 37* **Fax** *05 56 31 92 11*

The heart of La Tupina is the open fire over which succulent meats are grilled and in winter a cauldron of soup bubbles away. This is an excellent place to try bordelais specialties such as lamprey in wine, grilled shad, or baby eels cooked in olive oil with garlic and hot pepper. Simple, old-fashioned desserts.

COGNAC Les Pigeons Blancs
110 rue Jules-Brisson, 16100 **Tel** *05 45 82 16 36*

Owned by the same family since the 17th century, this former post house is renowned for its excellent service, wine, and food. The popular daily menu really does change every day. Veal sweetbreads with an aged red Pineau sauce and a glass of VSOP cognac is a sure-fire winner. Fabulous dessert trolley.

COULON Le Central
4 rue d'Autremont, 79510 **Tel** *05 49 35 90 20* **Fax** *05 49 35 81 07*

A deservedly popular hotel-restaurant in the Marais. Indulge yourself with original dishes such as snail cassoulet or rabbit lasagne. More traditional fare includes *foie gras* and lamb with lashings of herbs and garlic – an absolute classic. Portions are generous. Reserve ahead. Closed Feb.

EUGENIE-LES-BAINS La Ferme aux Grives
111 rue Thermes, 40320 **Tel** *05 58 05 05 06* **Fax** *05 58 51 10 10*

The more "rustic" of Michel Guérard's much acclaimed restaurants still serves sublime food. Normally heavy southwestern dishes are reinvented for a modern palate, such as oysters served with ginger shavings and fresh cilantro accompanied by a "chantilly" of green tea.

GRENADE-SUR-L'ADOUR Pain Adour et Fantaisie
14-16 pl des Tilleuls, 40270 **Tel** *05 58 45 18 80* **Fax** *05 58 45 16 57*

Elegant, Michelin-starred restaurant run by a former pupil of Michel Guérard. Trademark dishes include duck *foie gras* flavored with local *jurançon* wine and juniper. Fish and seafood changes with the seasons. Good-value lunch menu, and a romantic riverside terrace for summer dining.

ILE D'OLORON L'Ecailler
65 rue du Port, La Cotiniere, 17310 **Tel** *05 46 47 10 31*

On the west coast of the island, looking toward La Cotinière harbor is this hotel and restaurant, which inevitably specializes in seafood, including lobster from its own tank. Other choices on the menu include grilled fish and meat dishes such as the rib steak with coarse sea salt. A terrace and patio-garden allow for outdoor dining.

JARNAC Restaurant du Château   🅿🏃📋♿🍴🍷   €€€€

*15 pl du Château, 16200 **Tel** 05 45 81 07 17 **Fax** 05 45 35 35 71*

This restaurant near Château Courvoisier is renowned throughout the Cognac region for producing quality regional cuisine. Highlights are the tartare of langoustines and scallops with a mango vinaigrette, guinea fowl with a morille stuffing served with eggplant caviar, and a Cognac-laced soufflé for dessert with a Cognac digestif to round things off.

LA ROCHELLE Le Boute en Train   🏃♿�️   €€

*7 rue des Bonnes Femmes, 17000 **Tel** 05 46 41 73 74 **Fax** 05 46 45 90 76*

You are assured a warm welcome at this lively French bistro where all the fresh foodstuffs come from the nearby market. This means a great choice of daily dishes and a menu that changes with the seasons. Fortunately, the chocolate mousse is a standard. Reserve ahead.

LA ROCHELLE Le Comptoir des Voyages   🍽🚆🍴🍷   €€

*22 rue St-Jean du Perot, 17000 **Tel** 05 46 50 62 60 **Fax** 05 46 41 90 80*

Another addition to the Coutanceau stable, this time with a colonial theme – potted palms, rattan chairs, and flavors from around the world. From the single menu you might start with a carpaccio of red tuna with a tartare of vegetables, followed by saddle of lamb cooked in Guinness, and, for dessert, chocolate pizza. Simply sublime.

LANGON Claude Darroze   🅿🏃🚆🍴🍷   €€€€

*95 cours du Général-Leclerc, 33210 **Tel** 05 56 63 00 48 **Fax** 05 56 63 41 15*

Inside this unassuming hotel-restaurant you'll find wonderfully over-the-top decor and some of the region's best food and wine. Depending on the season, you might be regaled with a hearty stew of lamprey eels served with leeks and a stunning Grand Marnier soufflé, light as air. There's an extensive wine list with a choice of more than 600 wines.

MARGAUX Le Pavillon de Margaux   🅿🚆   €€€

*3 rue Georges Mandel, 33460 **Tel** 05 57 88 77 54*

This wine bar (serving cheese, charcuterie, and other tapas) is located in a hotel in one of the principal towns of the Médoc wine-producing region. Full meals *table d'hôte*-style are also served, strictly by reservation only, in the elegant surroundings of the nearby Château Marojallia.

MIMIZAN Hôtel Atlantique   🏃   €€

*38 av de la Côte d'Argent, 40200 **Tel** 05 58 09 09 42 **Fax** 05 58 82 42 63*

Very popular, modestly priced restaurant in a hotel on the seafront at the north end of the beach. Seafood is a specialty, with good *soupe de poisson* as well as regional gastronomic favorites such as *magret de canard*, *confit de canard*, and wild boar with prunes.

MONT-DE-MARSAN Didier Garbage   🅿🏃🍽♿🚆🍴🍷   €€€€

*RN 134, Uchacq-et-Parentis, 40090 **Tel** 05 58 75 33 66 **Fax** 05 58 75 22 77*

One of France's up-and-coming chefs turns out authentic landaise cuisine in his convivial, slightly rustic restaurant outside Mont-de-Marsan. Look forward to lamprey, elvers (freshwater eels), and expertly crafted fish dishes, in addition to meats and luscious desserts. There's also a bistro for casual dining.

MONTMORILLON Le Lucullus   🏃🍽♿   €€€

*4 bd de Strasbourg, 86500 **Tel** 05 49 84 09 09 **Fax** 05 49 84 58 68*

A traditional country auberge where the food takes precedence. The set menus change frequently and present plenty of choice, including a vegetarian option. Sample crab and asparagus flan or pork with *foie gras* sauce. The attached brasserie offers cheaper, less formal dining.

NIORT La Table des Saveurs   🏃🍽♿   €€

*9 rue Thiers, 79000 **Tel** 05 49 77 44 35 **Fax** 05 49 16 06 29*

Despite its town-center location and classy cuisine, this popular restaurant offers excellent value for money. Even the cheapest menu includes three courses. This is regional cooking, which means plenty of fish dishes, such as a langoustine crumble or duo of pike-perch and red mullet.

PAULLIAC Château Cordeillan-Bages   🅿🏃🍽♿🚆🍴🍷   €€€€€

*Rte des Châteaux, 33250 **Tel** 05 56 59 24 24 **Fax** 05 56 59 01 89*

This popular restaurant in the heart of Bordeaux's vineyards is aspiring to its third Michelin star. The Pauillac lamb is a signature dish, representing traditional cuisine; the molecular cuisine proposes dishes such as hot oyster soufflé and crispy sea water. Well worth a splurge.

POITIERS Le Pince Oreille   🍷   €€

*11 rue des trois rois, 8600 **Tel** 05 49 60 25 99*

Live music – including jazz, blues, and swing – is as much of an attraction as the food and drink in this city-center "café-concert-restaurant." The menu concentrates on straightforward specialties, notably meat, fish, and vegetables grilled *à la plancha*, Brazilian-style to make them crusty and caramelized. Wine tasting events are also held here.

POITIERS Les Bons Enfants   €€

*11 bis rue Cloche-Perse, 86000 **Tel** 05 49 41 49 82 **Fax** 05 49 46 05 38*

A charming restaurant decorated with souvenirs from the classroom and old school photographs. The cuisine is traditional with favorites such as veal with chanterelles and shallots, and chocolate mousse. The portions are generous and service is cheerful, but the tables are packed close together in the small dining room. Reserve ahead.

Key to Price Guide *see p600* **Key to Symbols** *see back cover flap*

ROCHEFORT La Belle Poule

102 av du 11 Novembre, 17300 **Tel** *05 46 99 71 87* **Fax** *05 46 83 99 77*

A modern building made more agreeable thanks to a massive fireplace and lots of greenery. The chef uses herbs and spices to splendid effect in his regionally inspired dishes. Favorites include roast pigeon with stuffed cabbage, and roast scallops perfumed with vanilla.

ROYAN La Jabotière

Esplanade de Pontaillac, 17200 **Tel** *05 46 39 91 29* **Fax** *05 46 38 39 93*

Modern cuisine in a renovated beachfront restaurant. Sample carpaccio of scallops marinated in lime juice and orange confit or fricassée of veal sweetbreads served with a sweet potato gratin, finishing with an apple and apricot soufflé. In summer, the terrace is packed with customers enjoying the excellent lunch deals. Closed Jan.

SABRES Auberge des Pins

Rte de la Piscine, 40630 **Tel** *05 58 08 30 00*

Gorgeous landaise farmhouse run by an adorable family. The oak-lined dining room provides the perfect setting for typical landaise cuisine, ranging from flavorful asparagus and fresh fish to duck in all its guises. Best of all, though, is the boned pigeon stuffed with *foie gras*. Good selection of local wines and armagnac.

SAINTES Relais du Bois St-Georges

Parc Atlantique, 132 Cours Genet, 17100 **Tel** *05 46 93 50 99* **Fax** *05 46 93 34 93*

Two first-class restaurants, part of a hotel on the outskirts of Saintes in big, beautiful grounds with lawns, a tennis court, an indoor pool, a lake, a croquet lawn, and piano bar. The gastronomic restaurant serves excellent seafood. The bistro, La Table du Bois, is much cheaper, serving good local dishes.

ST-EMILION L'Envers du Décor

11 rue du Clocher, 33330 **Tel** *05 57 74 48 31* **Fax** *05 57 24 68 90*

Local vignerons rub shoulders with tourists in this delightful little bistro-cum-wine bar. The menu runs the gamut from omelets and salads to more elaborate regional dishes, or you can choose from daily specials on the chalkboard. Winner of the award for the best wine list in France in its class.

ST-MARTIN-DE-RE La Baleine Bleue

Quai Launay Razilly, Ilot du Port, 17410 **Tel** *05 46 09 03 30* **Fax** *05 56 09 30 86*

The fish couldn't be much fresher at this celebrated portside restaurant. Menus change daily depending on the catch, but typical offerings are scallop carpaccio, home-smoked salmon, and cod with lemon confit. For dessert, try the roast figs with spicy ice cream. Closed Jan.

TALMONT L'Estuaire

1 av de L'Estuaire, 17120 **Tel** *05 46 90 43 85*

Situated beside the Gironde estuary (as the name suggests), this restaurant is a short way from the preserved old village of Talmont and its remarkable clifftop church. The menu is particularly strong on traditional fish and seafood dishes. It is also a bar, tearoom, and seven-room hotel.

PERIGORD, QUERCY, & GASCONY

AGEN Mariottat

25 rue Louis-Vivent, 47000 **Tel** *05 53 77 99 77* **Fax** *05 53 77 99 79*

It comes as a surprise to find this elegant restaurant tucked down a very ordinary backstreet, but inside the 19th-century mansion, with its chandeliers and high ceilings, you're in for a treat. Duck reigns supreme – *assiette tout canard* is the signature dish, alongside succulent Agen prunes and summer fruits.

ALBI Le Jardin des Quatre Saisons

19 bd de Strasbourg, 81000 **Tel** *05 63 60 77 76* **Fax** *05 63 60 77 76*

A gourmet restaurant that won't break the bank, here there are just three menus at lunchtime, each with a wide selection of dishes. At Le Jardin des Quatre Saisons the cooking is very much seasonal, but among the regular favorites you'll find *foie gras* in various guises, seafood *pot au feu*, and roast pigeon.

ALBI Le Vieil Alby

23-25 rue Toulouse-Lautrec, 81000 **Tel** *05 63 38 28 23*

This welcoming and well-priced hotel-restaurant is a good place to try typical local dishes, such as a raddish and pork liver salad, followed by cassoulet, or perhaps tripe cooked Albi-style. All desserts are homemade. In warm weather, dine in the lovely interior courtyard with its retractable roof.

AUCH Le Papillon

Carrefour de l'Arçon "Au Petit Guilhem", Montaut-les-Creneaux, 32810 **Tel** *05 52 65 51 29*

There are some lovely after-lunch walks to be had from this restaurant, which sits in a small village northeast of Auch. Choose from four set menus or *à la carte*, which offers homemade cassoulet, *foie gras*, and good fish and seafood options. A small garden has swings for children.

BERGERAC La Flambée

Rte de Périgeux, 49 av Marceau-Fevry, 24100 **Tel** *05 53 57 52 23*

Depending on which of the three set menus you choose, you could opt for smoked herring, smoked salmon, oysters, *foie gras, escargot,* or frog's legs for an appetizer. A good entree to select is the *magret de canard*. Desserts include apple crumble. Also a very relaxing hotel with swimming pool.

BRANTOME Les Frères Charbonnel

57 rue Gambetta, 24310 **Tel** *05 53 05 70 15* **Fax** *05 53 05 71 85*

The restaurant of the Hôtel Chabrol has a well deserved reputation for its upscale regional cuisine and excellent service. Black périgord truffles add style to omelets and to the house special, pike-perch *vol-au-vent*. These can be enjoyed in the dining room, or on the riverside terrrace. Closed Feb.

BRANTOME Le Moulin de l'Abbaye

1 rte de Bourdeilles, 24310 **Tel** *05 53 05 80 22* **Fax** *05 53 05 75 27*

Dine in luxury on innovative dishes such as duck *foie gras* poached in walnut liqueur in this converted mill, in a romantic setting on the bank of the Dronne river. Luscious desserts might include a gratin of strawberries with white chocolate. A magical setting and impeccable service. Closed Nov–Apr.

CAHORS Auberge du Vieux Cahors

144 rue St Urcisse, 46000 **Tel** *05 65 35 06 05*

Regional cuisine is the focus of the menu in this 15th-century auberge in the historical town center of Cahors. Specialties include duck *foie gras*, beef carpaccio flavored with truffle, Burgundy snails, and a wide choice of fish dishes. There are a few terrace tables for outdoor dining.

CAHORS Le Balandre

5 av Charles-de-Freycinet, 46000 **Tel** *05 65 53 32 00* **Fax** *05 65 53 32 26*

For fine dining in Cahors, head for the restaurant in the Hôtel Terminus, where 1930s decor complements refined Quercy cuisine. Rustic dishes, such as roast Quercy lamb laced with juniper juice, are given a modern twist. Or try duck cannelloni served with walnut *rillette*. Cahors wines feature strongly.

CASTRES Café du Pont

Les Salvages, 81100 **Tel** *05 63 35 08 21*

Les Salvages lies about 4-miles (6-km) northeast of Castres *en route* to the scenic rock formations of the Sidobre. This restaurant has a shady terrace on the bank of the River Agout. Seasonal ingredients and local produce predominate on the menu. Upstairs there are five guest bedrooms.

CHAMPAGNAC-DE-BELAIR Le Moulin du Roc

Champagnac-de-Belair, 24530 **Tel** *05 53 02 86 00* **Fax** *05 53 54 21 31*

A romantic waterside setting plus top-notch cuisine make this gourmet restaurant stand out. The lunch menu (not served on Sundays) offers particularly good value. Iced garden herb soup and roast breast of guinea fowl with *foie gras* are just two of the treats in store.

CONDOM La Table des Cordeliers

1 rue des Cordeliers, 32100 **Tel** *05 62 68 43 82* **Fax** *05 62 28 15 92*

Modern cuisine using top-quality local produce is prepared with talent at this contemporary restaurant housed in the cloisters of a 13th-century convent. Depending on the season, enjoy porcini mushroom *tartelette*, succulent duck, and an apple dessert accompanied by iced nougat with prunes. Good choice of regional wines and armagnacs.

CORDES-SUR-CIEL Bistrot Tonin'ty

Hostellerie du Vieux Cordes, Haut de la Cité, 81170 **Tel** *05 63 53 79 20*

One of several restaurants and hotels in the medieval town of Cordes that are owned by master *pâtissier* Yves Thuries. There is an enchanting courtyard shaded by an ancient wisteria and, in summer, tables are also set out on the terrace overlooking the valley. The menu focuses on salmon and duck.

DOMME L'Esplanade

Le Bourg, 24250 **Tel** *05 53 28 31 41* **Fax** *05 53 28 49 92*

Welcoming and efficient service, well-presented dishes, and an unbeatable panorama of the Dordogne valley keep customers coming back to this hotel-restaurant. Ask for a window or terrace table. Signature dishes include *foie gras de canard* with truffles, in season, and the delectable chocolate gâteau.

FIGEAC La Cuisine du Marché

15 rue Clermont, 46100 **Tel** *05 65 50 18 55* **Fax** *05 65 50 18 55*

In a former wine cellar in the heart of Figeac's medieval core, this attractive restaurant takes pride in using only the freshest ingredients. Star billing goes to its wide range of fish dishes, though you'll also find plenty of local classics all prepared in the open kitchen. The set menus represent good value.

FOURCES Château de Fources

Fources, 32250 **Tel** *05 62 29 49 53*

Fources is one of Gascony's most delightful villages. Its Renaissance château, beside the river, is now a hotel-restaurant where you can dine in a magnificent dining room with broad stone walls or at shaded tables outside. The hotel boasts palatial rooms, some with four-poster beds. Reservations essential.

Key to Price Guide *see p600* **Key to Symbols** *see back cover flap*

FRANCESCAS Le Relais de la Hire
11 rue Porte-Neuve, 47600 **Tel** *05 53 65 41 59* **Fax** *05 53 65 86 42*

The chef of this upmarket village restaurant near Nérac makes full use of his herb garden and edible flowers to create dishes that are a feast for all the senses. Try the temping artichoke soufflé with *foie gras* or oriental-flavored roast turbot with caramelized onions, followed by desserts that look almost too good to eat.

GAILLAC Les Sarments
27 rue Cabrol, 81600 **Tel** *05 63 57 62 61* **Fax** *05 63 57 62 61*

The brick arches and exposed beams of this 14th-century wine vault in the heart of old Gaillac provide a striking setting for the beautifully presented food that tends toward the traditional, but with imaginative touches. Particularly fine desserts. Good opportunity to sample Gaillac wines at reasonable prices.

ISSIGEAC La Brucelière
Place de la Capelle, 24560 **Tel** *05 53 73 89 61*

In a charming village 9 miles (15 km) from Bergerac is this former coaching inn with a traditional dining room. The menu includes regional produce, with a particular emphasis on seafood such as lobster and crayfish. The dishes are creative, with a touch of exoticism, and the atmosphere is relaxed. A spacious, shady terrace overlooks the garden.

LACAVE Le Pont de l'Ouysse
Le Pont de l'Ouysse, 46200 **Tel** *05 65 37 87 04* **Fax** *05 65 32 77 41*

A chic restaurant-with-rooms not far from Rocamadour. It's in a lovely riverside setting, sheltered under an imposing cliff. Inventive variations on local dishes include casserole of duck liver with Paimpol beans. There are good-value lunch menus, but it is magical dining under the trees at night.

LES EYZIES-DE-TAYAC Au Vieux Moulin
2 rue du Moulin-Bas, 24620 **Tel** *05 53 06 94 33* **Fax** *05 53 06 98 06*

Dine on well-priced regional cuisine in a 17th-century mill, with its rustic interior, or beside the river in peaceful, flower-filled gardens. Among the simple but beautifully prepared dishes, choose from *escalope* of *foie gras* with truffle sauce or truffle risotto, with pigeon casserole to follow. Closed Nov–Apr.

MANCIET La Bonne Auberge
Pl du Pesquerot, 32370 **Tel** *05 62 08 50 04* **Fax** *05 62 08 58 84*

The same family has been running this small hotel-restaurant for over 40 years, and it shows in the quality of the creative southwestern cuisine. The platter of local specialties is a great introduction to Gascon fare, and menus change regularly. Fabulous armagnac list – some over 100 years old.

MARMANDE Le Moulin d'Ane
Virazeil, 47200 **Tel** *05 53 20 18 25*

Consistently excellent seasonal cuisine in this restored 18th-century watermill near Marmande. Typical southwestern dishes include succulent blonde d'Aquitaine beef, tender fillets of duck breast, and apple tart laced with armagnac. Be sure to try the exceptionally plump and juicy Marmande tomatoes.

MONBAZILLAC La Tour des Vents
Moulin de Malfourat, 24240 **Tel** *05 53 58 30 10* **Fax** *05 53 58 89 55*

Reserve a window or terrace table to enjoy the wonderful views over the Dordogne valley to Bergerac. Good-value menus offer local specialties, including *foie gras* and duck, but also fish and seafood. There is even a vegetarian option. Treat yourself to a glass of sweet Monbazillac with *foie gras* or dessert. Closed Jan.

MONTAUBAN Au Fil de l'Eau
14 quai de Dr Lafforgue, 82000 **Tel** *05 63 66 11 85* **Fax** *05 63 91 97 56*

An ancient building housing a spacious modern restaurant on the banks of the river. The menu is composed of traditional dishes such as panfried *foie gras* accompanied by gingerbread, *omelet aux truffes*, and duckling served with a rich red wine sauce. Good regional wines.

PERIGUEUX Le Clos Saint-Front
5 rue de la Vertu, 24000 **Tel** *05 53 46 78 58* **Fax** *05 53 46 78 20*

Reservations are recommended at this restaurant near Périgueux's prehistory museum, with its inventive, inexpensive cuisine and peaceful courtyard garden. According to the season, you could opt for lamb flavored with spices and rosemary, or sole served with an onion, thyme, and lemon compote. Reservations recommended.

PERIGUEUX L'Essentiel
8 rue de la Clarté, 24000 **Tel** *05 53 35 15 15* **Fax** *05 53 35 15 15*

Another city-center restaurant where it's wise to reserve. The dining room's sunny southern colors complement dishes such as roast *foie gras* with gnocchi. There's also a pretty, pocket-sized garden. The wine list offers more than 100 wines to choose from.

PUJAUDRAN Le Puits St-Jacques
Pl de la Mairie, 32600 **Tel** *05 62 07 41 11* **Fax** *05 62 07 44 09*

Michelin-starred restaurant where you can feast on panfried *foie gras* with gingerbread, or Limousin beef with shallot confit. Neither pretentious nor too pricey, if you opt for a set menu. Rustic chic ambience, with lots of red Toulousain brick work and a pleasant patio.

PUJOLS La Toque Blanche 🅿🕴📋♿🍷 €€€€
Pujols, 47300 **Tel** *05 53 49 00 30*

A renowned gourmet restaurant in a medieval village between Agen and Villeneuve-sur-Lot. The best place to eat is in the air-conditioned conservatory, which has panoramic views. The menu changes with the seasons but is always based on local products. Dessert choices include homemade ice creams and sorbets. A hotel adjoins the restaurant.

PUYMIROL Les Loges de l'Aubergade 🅿🕴📋♿🎴🍷 €€€€€
52 rue Royale, 47270 **Tel** *05 53 95 31 46* **Fax** *05 53 95 33 80*

One of the southwest's great restaurants is set in a beautiful medieval lodge on a hilltop. Here Michel Trama creates sublime dishes such as *foie gras* panfried and served with toasted hazelnuts. Equally theatrical setting with Baroque drapes and exposed stone, and a gorgeous Italianate courtyard.

ROCAMADOUR Sainte Marie 🕴🎴 €€
Pl des Senhals, 46500 **Tel** *05 65 33 63 07*

There is a splendid view over the Alzou valley from the terrace of this hotel-restaurant, which clings to the rock in the middle of Rocamadour. Local Quercy and southwestern dishes using fresh produce make up the menu – homemade cassoulet and *confit de canard* – with options for children available. Inexpensive "express" menu at lunchtimes.

SARLAT La Couleurvrine €
1 pl de la Bouquerie, 24200 **Tel** *05 53 59 27 80*

A hotel and restaurant housed in one of the towers of the town's old ramparts. Appetizers include duck *foie gras* and *pâté* of hare. Main courses include scallops, panfried monkfish, stuffed mushrooms, and venison. For less formal dining there is a bistro serving an inexpensive dish of the day and staging jazz recitals in the evening.

SORGES Auberge de la Truffe 🅿🕴📋🎴 €€€
Le Bourg, 24420 **Tel** *05 53 05 02 05* **Fax** *05 53 05 39 27*

Sorges is the self-proclaimed truffle "capital" of France, and this auberge is the perfect place to sample Périgord's "black diamond." The top-price menu features truffles with every course. Less expensive fare is on offer, too, and the set menus start at a reasonable price. Truffle-hunting weekends are offered.

ST-MEDARD Le Gindreau 🅿🕴📋🎴🍷 €€€€
Le Bourg, 46150 **Tel** *05 65 36 22 27* **Fax** *05 65 36 24 54*

In a hamlet northwest of Cahors, Alexis Pélissou has created one of the region's finest restaurants. Using top-quality local produce, he reinvents traditional standards for modern tastes. Meals are served in the former schoolhouse or on the terrace shaded by chestnut trees. Big choice of local wines. Closed Oct 18–26 & Dec 20–Jan 12.

TOULOUSE Brasserie Flo Les Beaux Arts 🕴📋🎴 €€€€
1 quai de la Daurade, 31000 **Tel** *05 61 21 12 12* **Fax** *05 61 21 14 80*

An authentic and bustling brasserie serving a broad range of dishes, from salads and seafood to southwestern favorites. To start, you could opt for a flavorsome dish of scallops baked with chanterelle mushrooms, followed by a seafood *pot-au-feu*, and prune-and-armagnac ice cream. The menu changes regularly.

TOULOUSE Les Jardins de l'Opéra 🕴📋🍷 €€€€
1 pl du Capitole, 31000 **Tel** *05 61 23 07 76* **Fax** *05 61 23 63 00*

Gourmet dining at its most refined in the restaurant of the Grand Hôtel de l'Opéra. Hushed tones and widely spaced tables create a suitably reverent atmosphere for dishes such as whole lobster garnished with a seaweed crust, or figs cooked in Banyuls wine and filled with vanilla ice cream. Impeccable service.

TURSAC La Source 🕴🎴 €€
Le Bourg, 24620 **Tel** *05 53 06 98 00*

If you're looking for somewhere to eat while exploring the Vézère valley, try this friendly little village restaurant. Simple, tasty dishes include wild mushroom soup and walnut pie. There's a vegetarian menu, using produce fresh from the garden, and some international options, for a change. Closed Tue & Wed.

VAREN Le Moulin de Varen 🅿🕴📋♿ €€
Le Bourg, 82330 **Tel** *05 63 65 45 10*

A converted mill in the Aveyron gorges, near the lovely town of St-Antonin-de-Noble-Val. There's no carte, but plenty of choice on the set menus, all of which offer excellent value for money. The food is beautifully presented and the atmosphere relaxed. Closed Sun dinner, Mon.

THE PYRENEES

AINHOA La Maison Oppoca 🎴 €€€
Le Bourg, 64250 **Tel** *05 59 29 90 72*

This hotel and restaurant is situated in the center of one ot the most beautiful villages in the French Basque country. *Foie gras* and suckling pig are on the menu with, of course, *gâteau basque* for dessert. Upstairs there are ten light and comfortable guest rooms with large beds.

Key to Price Guide *see p600* **Key to Symbols** *see back cover flap*

ASCAIN Atelier Gourmand
Place de Fronton, 64310 Tel 05 59 54 46 82

Sitting at the foot of a church in the picturesque Pyrenean village of Ascain is this lively, trendy restaurant. The menu includes Basque favorites. Take your pick from finger-licking *tapas*, *pipérade*, and *axoa* (a spicy Basque stew), or fillet of sea bream.

AUDRESSEIN L'Auberge d'Audressein
Castillon, 09800 Tel 05 61 96 11 80

This restaurant-with-rooms in a former blacksmith's forge has various set menus named after the local valleys. Dishes include typical Ariège recipes. There are seven guestrooms overlooking the river, the valley, or the village. A great place to come if you are in search of quiet countryside and the simple life.

AX-LES-THERMES L'Auzeraie
1 av Théophile Delcassé, 09110 Tel 05 61 64 20 70

A restaurant and 33-room hotel in a pleasant spa town, which makes a handy stop on the way from the Ariège to Andorra or Spain. At lunchtime from Monday to Friday you can take pot luck with an inexpensive menu of *entrée du jour* and *plat du jour*. A children's menu is also available.

BAGNERES DE LUCHON Les Caprices d'Etigny
30 bis allées d'Etigny, 31110 Tel 05 61 94 31 05

Fine mountain views from the tables in the conservatory-style dining room. The menu stresses local lamb and beef grilled over a wood fire, and trout from the nearby Lac d'Oo presented in a number of different styles. The good wine list emphasizes the finer wines of southwestern France.

BAREGES Auberge du Lienz (Chez Louisette)
Rte Lienz, 65120 Tel 05 62 67 17 Fax 05 62 92 65 15

A good choice for an *après-ski* meal, at the foot of the local pistes, with stunning views of the Pic du Midi de Bigorre. Menu mainstays include mutton stewed in Madeira wine, trout, and sumptuous soufflés. The *pièce de résistance* is the ham *garbure* – a hefty dish of ham, bacon, and cabbage.

BAYONNE Le Bayonnais
38 quai des Corsaires, 64100 Tel 05 59 25 61 19 Fax 05 59 59 00 64

With a handful of tables on the terrace and more inside, this small restaurant has a well-deserved reputation for imaginative dishes, such as baby lamb, sole with lentils, chestnut soup with *foie gras*, and pastilla with figs. Well-chosen wine list emphasizes regional wines and major names from elsewhere in France.

BAYONNE Auberge du Cheval Blanc
68 rue Bourgneuf, 64100 Tel 05 59 59 01 33

Stray from the set menu at this well-regarded hotel in the riverside Petit Bayonne quarter. The menu changes with the seasons, with local dishes, such as *xamano* (ham and mashed potatoes), fine Atlantic seafood, interesting soups and casseroles, and delicious desserts. Respectable wine list. Closed Feb, 2nd week Jul, 1st wk Aug, & 2nd wk Nov.

BIARRITZ Chez Albert
Port des Pêcheurs, 64200 Tel 05 59 24 43 84 Fax 05 59 24 20 13

From the terrace there are superb views of Biarritz's picturesque fishing harbor and surrounding cliffs and beaches, making this fine seafood restaurant popular. Arrive early for the best tables. Piled platters of seafood, freshly caught lobster, sole, sea bream, tuna, and sardines are among the treats here. Closed Jan.

BIARRITZ Le Sissinou
5 av Maréchal Foch, 64200 Tel 05 59 22 51 50

Managed by chef Michel Cassou-Debat – a veteran of some of France's top establishments – Sissinou is one of Biarritz's most talked-about restaurants. Elegant in a minimalist way. Wonderful food such as tuna carpaccio and a fricassée of veal sweetbreads served with carrots flavored with balsamic vinegar and desserts that invite indulgence.

FOIX Le Phoebus
3 rue Irénée Cros, 09000 Tel 05 61 02 87 87

This restaurant on the banks of the Ariège river has big windows overlooking the water toward the castle, which is floodlit at night. Roast pigeon, and iced tomato and raspberry soup are two of the specialties here. Closed Mon, Sat lunch, Sun dinner, & Jul 23–Aug 23.

LARRAU Etchemaïté
Larrau, 64560 Tel 05 59 28 61 45 Fax 05 59 28 72 71

This family-run mountain inn and restaurant has a spectacular location and a cozy dining room with open fireplace and great views. Favorites are lamb and duck dishes garnished with apples, porcini mushrooms, or *foie gras* and there is usually a good choice of Atlantic seafood, too. Varied wine list.

LOURDES Le Magret
10 rue des 4 Freres Soulas, 65100 Tel 05 62 94 20 55

One of the better places to eat in Lourdes city center. The menu varies according to the season with Gascon black pork, Pyrenean lamb, *magret de canard* (duck breast), veal, lamb, and duck as reliable specialties. Regional wines from the nearby Jurancon and Madiran regions accompany the meal. Vegetarians are catered for.

MIREPOIX Les Remparts
6 cours Louis Pons Tande, 09500 **Tel** *05 61 68 12 15*

Chef Nicolas Coutand serves inventive dishes inspired by traditional Pyrenean and Mediterranean cuisine. The restaurant has two dining rooms: one in a cozily converted cellar, the other with a wide wood-beamed ceiling and colorful paintwork. Robust classic dishes of the region. Children's menu is available.

MONTSEGUR Costes
Le Village, 09300 **Tel** *05 61 01 10 24*

This simple café-restaurant is part of a hotel beneath the crag that is home to Montségur's ruined castle. Organic ingredients are used in tasty local dishes, mostly prepared on the open wood fire – game, duck, wild mushrooms, pork, and, of course, cassoulet. Just the thing after the steep clamber to the castle. Phone to check winter opening.

ORTHEZ Au Temps de la Reine Jeanne
44 rue Bourg-Vieux, 64300 **Tel** *05 59 67 00 76* **Fax** *05 59 69 09 63*

This rustic eating-place is attached to a comfortable country inn. The menu is equally rustic, with plenty of local dishes, including offal and rich meaty dishes. Liver, blood sausage, suckling pig, *foie gras*, cassoulet, and monkfish all make an appearance. Good value.

PAU Chez Pierre
16 rue Louis Barthou, 64000 **Tel** *05 59 27 76 86* **Fax** *05 59 27 08 14*

Chez Pierre exudes 19th-century elegance and prides itself on the old-fashioned, clublike atmosphere that harks back to Pau's heyday as a British expatriate's hideaway. Classic French regional cooking along with some surprises, such as cod with Espelette peppers, and an extensive wine list.

ST-BERTRAND-DE-COMMINGES L'Oppidum
Rue de la Poste, 31510 **Tel** *05 61 88 33 50*

Located in the old town just below St-Bertrand's celebrated cathedral, is this small, friendly hotel and restaurant serving good, unpretentious food. Featuring on the menu are the local stew, *garbure*, *foie gras*, and trout. All accompanied by local wines. There are 15 simple guest bedrooms upstairs.

ST GAUDENS La Connivence
Chemin Ample, Valentine, 31800 **Tel** *05 61 95 29 31*

The outdoor terrace with its fine views is one of the main attractions of La Connivence. The bill of fare is traditional, as is the atmosphere, but helpings are generous and the wine list, though limited, is well chosen. Service is prompt and friendly. An unpretentious spot for lunch or dinner. Closed Mon, Sat lunch, & Sun dinner.

ST-JEAN-DE-LUZ Chez Pablo
5 rue Mlle. Etcheto, 64500 **Tel** *05 59 26 37 81*

One of the resort's oldest restaurants and run by the same family since 1932. It serves traditional Basque cuisine prepared with seasonal ingredients, specializing in fish and seafood. Good dishes to opt for are cod croquettes, cod-stuffed peppers, prawns with rice, and *chipirones* in their own ink. Homemade desserts. Closed Wed.

ST-JEAN-DE-LUZ Restaurant Txalupa
Pl Corsaires, 64500 **Tel** *05 59 51 85 52*

Txalupa is a favourite local restaurant. Expect the best catches of the Atlantic coast prepared in dishes such as king prawns in a hot vinegar dressing, sardines in tomato salsa, oysters and lots of other shellfish, tuna, cod and monkfish. Extensive wine list, and imaginative desserts. Book ahead.

ST-JEAN-DE-PIED-DE-PORT Relais de la Nive
4 pl Charles de Gaulle, 64220 **Tel** *05 59 37 04 22*

The most conspicuous place to eat in St-Jean-de-Pied-de-Port, and as a result always busy with passing pilgrim traffic, is this brasserie-creperie, which picturesquely overhangs the river between the new bridge and the old. It serves inexpensive meals as well as snacks such as pancakes, sandwiches, and ice cream.

ST-LARY SOULAN La Grange
13 rte Autun, 65170 **Tel** *05 62 40 07 14*

This old-fashioned farm building at St-Lary-Soulan in the high Pyrenees is a delightful place to stop for lunch. A well-appointed and attractively decorated restaurant, it exudes rustic charm. The traditional bill of fare includes robust meaty main dishes, with game, beef, and lamb grilled over a wood fire. Closed Nov–Apr.

ST-LIZIER De la Tour
Rue du Pont, 09190 **Tel** *05 61 66 38 01*

This place overhanging the River Salat is the most convenient place to eat while visiting the historic village of St-Lizier. On the menu is trout from the Couserans region, lamb, duck, and homemade pâtés and terrines. A good, inexpensive lunchtime menu is served on weekdays and there is also a children's menu.

ST-SULPICE-SUR-LEZE La Commanderie
Pl de l'Hôtel de Ville, 31410 **Tel** *05 61 97 33 61* **Fax** *05 61 97 32 60*

In a fortified *bastide* village famous for its medieval architecture, La Commanderie has fans all over the world for its innovative cooking. Chef Jean Pierre Crouzet creates dishes such as vegetable *ragoût* with morille mushrooms and ewe's cheese and roast pigeon with garlic and juniper. Lovely, spacious dining room. Closed 2 weeks in Dec.

SARE Baratxartea
J.B. Fagoaga, 64310 **Tel** *05 59 54 20 48*

An ancient Basque house is the setting for this hotel and restaurant in the exceptionally pretty town of Sare. The menu is rich in home produce: vegetables are from the garden, charcuterie is prepared over the winter months, hams are cured in the barn, and jams are homemade.

TARBES L'Ambroisie
48 rue Abbé Torné, 65000 **Tel** *05 62 93 09 34* **Fax** *05 62 93 09 24*

The top restaurant in Tarbes attracts plaudits for dishes ranging from roast pigeon to *foie gras* in peach compote. Housed in a 19th-century church building, the restaurant offers a changing menu, brisk service, and food worth lingering over. Wine list features the finer Madiran domains. Reserve ahead.

LANGUEDOC-ROUSSILLON

AIGUES-MORTES Le Café des Bouzigues
7 rue Pasteur, 30220 **Tel** *04 66 53 93 95*

It is usually easy to find a table in this large traditional bistro. The menu is strongly Mediterranean, with plenty of regional seafood, Provençal dishes, and reasonably priced wines from Provence and Languedoc. Lamb with thyme and garlic and peach salad are among the outstanding dishes.

AIGUES-MORTES Marie Rosé
13 rue Pasteur, 30220 **Tel** *04 66 53 79 84*

A delightful restaurant located in an ancient presbytery with a kitchen garden. The chef prepares Provençale dishes with a delicate touch. Talent and accomplishment shine through in dishes such as the violet flan, sea bream and *calamars à la plancha*, and baby lamb with artichokes. There is also a small selection of well-chosen wines.

ANDUZE Auberge Les Trois Barbus
Rte de Mialet, Generargargues, 20140 **Tel** *04 66 61 72 12*

Deep in the Cevennes above the Camisards valley, with spectacular views, this rustic hotel-restaurant has the added attraction of a pool that diners may use for an after-lunch dip. Traditional Cevennes and Languedoc dishes as well as more adventurous offerings. Delicious *foie gras* and truffles. Closed Feb–mid-Mar.

ARLES SUR TECH Les Glycines
Rue du Jeu de Paume, 66150 **Tel** *04 68 39 10 09* **Fax** *04 68 39 83 02*

Arles sur Tech is a place that beckons you to pause for a while, and this hotel-restaurant is an excellent place for a lunch stop. It is very good value for money, with a lovely wisteria-covered patio and a menu that emphasizes regional cuisine and local produce, with plenty of ham, pork, and sausage dishes. Closed Jan.

BEZIERS Octopus
12 rue Boiledieu, 34500 **Tel** *04 67 49 90 00* **Fax** *04 67 28 06 73*

Béziers has no shortage of quality places to eat, but Octopus stands out from the crowd. With fresh, chic decor, this restaurant feels very welcoming. The modern menu is balanced by a well-chosen list of wines from the Languedoc-Roussillon vineyards.

BIZE MINERVOIS La Bastide Cabezac
18-20 hameau Cabezac, 11120 **Tel** *04 68 46 66 10*

Attractive 18th-century staging post with an elegant restaurant. The chef is motivated and dynamic, producing outstanding dishes such as delicate crayfish tart, and monkfish roasted in a pinenut crust flavored with curry and served with Camargue rice and a light lemongrass sauce.

CAP D'AGDE Le Brasero
Port Richelieu, rue Richelieu, 34300 **Tel** *04 67 26 24 75* **Fax** *04 67 26 24 75*

Overlooking the port with its yachts and fishing boats, Le Brasero has a well-earned reputation for good-value seafood. Its seafood platters are generous and varied, and other marine delights include grilled fish of all kinds, fresh anchovies, squid, tuna, and swordfish. Grilled meat dishes also available. Reserve ahead.

CARCASSONNE Le Languedoc
32 allée d'Iéna, 11000 **Tel** *04 68 25 22 17* **Fax** *04 68 25 04 14*

This restaurant appeals to people who like their surroundings and cuisine to be traditionally French, even a little staid. The menu features all the regional classics, and Le Languedoc is one of the best places for cassoulet – the hearty bean and sausage casserole that is the Languedoc's most typical dish. Closed Jan.

CARCASSONNE Les Bergers d'Arcadie
70 rue Trivalle, 11000 **Tel** *04 68 72 46 01*

A friendly unpretentious little restaurant close to the ramparts of the magnificent citadel. Cuisine is based on Languedoc produce and combines old and new influences to create an interesting menu. Specialties include poached *foie gras*, and *cochon de lait* glazed with caramelized honey and served with seasonal mushrooms. Delicious desserts.

CARCASSONNE Le Parc Franck Putelat

P ▤ & ⌘ ♈ ♈ ⓔⓔⓔⓔ

80 chemin des Anglais, 11000 **Tel** *04 68 71 80 80*

The chef, with the help of his young kitchen team, has stamped his personality on this gastronomic restaurant in a comparatively short time. Contemporary food is served in a relaxed, yet refined atmosphere. Expect spectacular fish dishes such as spider crab, sea urchin, and caviar prepared with simplicity. Gourmet desserts. Good-value set menus.

COLLIOURE La Balette

P ⋔ ▤ ▤ ⌘ ⓔⓔⓔ

114 rte de Port-Vendres, 66190 **Tel** *04 68 82 05 07* **Fax** *04 68 82 38 08*

Specialties at this cheerful restaurant, part of the Relais des Trois Mas, include soused Collioure anchovies marinated in Banjul wine vinegar, terrine of *foie gras* and chestnuts, sea bass served with chicory crumble, and pigeon cooked in honey. Set above the picturesque bay of Collioure. Reserve ahead in summer.

COLLIOURE Le 5e Péché

ⓔⓔⓔ

18 rue Fraternité, 66190 **Tel** *04 68 98 09 76*

The best produce Catalogne has to offer combined with the skill of the Japanese chef make this small restaurant a great success. An original range of Japanese-inspired dishes include carpaccio of freshly caught fish, stir-fried tuna with a Banyuls-flavored sauce, and a *crème Catalane* of caramelized artichokes. Book ahead.

CUCUGNAN Auberge du Vigneron

⋔ ▤ ▤ ♈ ⓔⓔ

2 rue Achille Mir, 11350 **Tel** *04 68 45 03 00* **Fax** *04 68 45 03 08*

The dining room is in the cool wine cellar of a charming inn in the heart of an attractive Corbières village. The menu is Catalan-influenced, with fresh seafood and duck prepared in a variety of ways, even with figs or peaches. The wine list is unpretentious, with a good choice of the muscular reds of the Corbières domains.

FONTJONCOUSE L'Auberge du Vieux Puits

P ▤ & ♈ ♈ ⓔⓔⓔⓔ

Av St Victor, 11360 **Tel** *04 68 44 07 37*

The small village of Fontjoncouse in the Corbière countryside has been made famous by this superb restaurant. Chef Gilles Goujon is both energetic and ambitious. The menu ranges from a simple, *salade niçoise* to more complex dishes such as lobster-stuffed cannelloni. Game also features when in season. Excellent wines.

GIGNAC Restaurant Matthieu de Lauzun

⋔ ▤ & ♈ ⓔⓔⓔⓔ

3 bd de l'Esplanade, 34150 **Tel** *04 67 57 50 83*

At this restaurant, west of Montpellier, chef Matthieu de Lauzan prepares inventive Mediterranean cuisine. Dishes are carefully prepared and harmonious. Vegetables with prawn tempura and cucumber gazpacho is a sweet success. Desserts are delicious. Good wines from up-and-coming producers.

LE BOULOU L'Hostalet de Vivès

⋔ ⌘ ⓔⓔ

Rue de la Mairie Vivès, 66490 **Tel** *04 68 83 05 52*

Not far from the artist town of Céret lies this lovely auberge serving authentic Catalan cuisine. A favorite with the locals, it has a good choice of well-prepared dishes at reasonable prices – a real bonus in this region popular with tourists. Discover Catalan dishes such as *cargolade* (grilled snails), and rabbit served with *aioli*.

MARAUSSON Parfums de Garrigues

P ⋔ ▤ & ⌘ ⓔⓔⓔ

37 rue de l'Ancienne Poste, 34370 **Tel** *04 67 90 33 76*

Comfortable dining room with sunny tones and a pretty shady courtyard in the center of a sleepy village, near Beziers. The fine southwest cuisine includes the best regional produce and reflects the scents of the Garrigue. The menu includes a refreshing goat's milk *crème* with Bouzigues oysters, and veal served with grilled vegetables.

MINERVE Relais Chantovent

⌘ ♈ ⓔⓔⓔ

17 Grande Rue, 34210 **Tel** *04 68 91 14 18*

The terrace of this restaurant offers diners stunning panoramic views over the Gorges du Brian. There is a choice of menus, each with a different emphasis: regional menu, duck menu, aromatic herb menu, and truffle menu. The wine list is extensive and contains many high-quality vintages. Reservations are advised.

MONTPELLIER Petit Jardin

⋔ ⌘ ⓔⓔ

20 rue Jean-Jacques Rousseau, 34000 **Tel** *04 67 60 78 78*

The menu is locally inspired in this pretty restaurant in Montpellier's historic quarter. The "Little Garden" is tucked away from the street, and diners may eat indoors, looking out at its greenery, or in the garden among the flowers, fruit trees, and potted herbs. Dishes include fish soup and lamb with garlic and rosemary.

MONTPELLIER Chez Boris

& ⌘ ⓔⓔ

20 rue de l'Aiguillerie, 34000 **Tel** *04 67 02 13 22*

The most talked about bistro in town, and rightly so. Located near the Musée Fabre in the center of the city, the atmosphere here is friendly and relaxed. Classic dishes have been reinvented: think *cochon au lait* (pork in milk) cooked with spices. The portions are generous, and wine can be ordered by the glass.

MONTPELLIER La Diligence

⌘ ♈ ⓔⓔⓔ

2 pl Pétrarque, 34000 **Tel** *04 67 66 12 21*

A sophisticated restaurant in the city center, located on a historic square between the place de la Comédie and the place de la Préfecture. La Diligence occupies a 14th-century listed building with graceful stone vaulting. There is a choice of set menus: lunch, taster, or gourmet. Good wine list.

Key to Price Guide *see p600* **Key to Symbols** *see back cover flap*

MONTPELLIER Jardin des Sens

11 av St Lazare, 34000 **Tel** *04 99 58 38 38* **Fax** *04 99 58 38 39*

Probably the best restaurant in town. Continuously innovative, with regional specialties given a new twist, such as terrine of lobster with mango and melon, and some delicious juxtapositions such as pigeon with a cacao sauce. The wine list features finer wines of the Corbières slopes and the domaines of the Languedoc.

NARBONNE Le Table de St-Crescent

Domaine St-Crescent, 68 ave Général Leclerc, 11100 **Tel** *04 68 41 37 37*

An address to impress, with a superb, seasonally influenced menu that combines the best produce of the Mediterranean with that of the Languedoc hinterland, with wines to match. Ravioli of Leucate oysters roast duck with Collioure anchovies and more. Perfect for a special evening.

NARBONNE Restaurant Le H

Rte de Narbonne Plage, 11100 **Tel** *04 68 45 28 50*

Heading out of the town center toward the beach, you will come across this lovely restaurant. Surrounded by rows and rows of La Clape vines sits Gérard Bertrand's wine domaine. The room is rustic yet chic with stone walls and thick wooden beams, which provides the perfect setting for a carpaccio of duck or a chunk of beef.

NIMES Le Cheval Blanc

1 pl des Arènes, 30000 **Tel** *04 66 76 19 59*

A lively wine bar with a classic brasserie-style interior, comfy banquet seating, and some Art-Deco features in the historic center of Nîmes. The wine list is extensive, featuring established names as well as lesser known southern Rhône and Languedoc wines. Typical fare – *brandade* (smoked fish with cream), pig's trotters, and *côte de boeuf* – is well-prepared.

NIMES L'Orée du Parc

755 rue Tour de l'Evèque, 30000 **Tel** *04 66 84 50 57*

The restaurant of the L'Orangerie hotel stands in the middle of a park filled with ancient trees, about a 15-minute stroll from Nîmes' historic town center. A relaxed and comfortable setting, there is a conservatory with a cozy atmosphere and a terrace for summer dining. Dishes are traditional but sophisticated. Good wine list.

NIMES Aux Plaisirs des Halles

4 rue Littré, 30000 **Tel** *04 66 36 01 02* **Fax** *04 66 36 08 00*

With a particularly good regional wine list from the Languedoc, Corbières, Minervois, Provence, and Hérault, Aux Plaisirs des Halles is decorated with clean, modern lines. French cuisine with a Provençal influence by chef Sébastien Granier. Closed Sun, Mon; 2 wks Oct–Nov; & some public hols.

NIMES Le Lisita

2 bd des Arènes, 30000 **Tel** *04 66 67 29 15* **Fax** *04 66 67 25 32*

Le Lisita is not to be missed. This is one of the most popular restaurants in Nîmes, serving cutting-edge food and an outstanding wine list. The surroundings are attractive, too, with modern design set off by old stone walls in two rooms, plus an attractive terrace facing Les Arènes. Closed Sun, Mon.

PERPIGNAN La Galinette

23 rue Jean Payra, 66000 **Tel** *04 68 35 00 90*

The spacious, refined, modern dining room has a formal air. By contrast, in the kitchen is a chef passionate about food and prepared to take risks. Seafood is a specialty: prawns with coriander, red mullet tart and fillet of fish *à la plancha*. An expert sommelier is on hand to help you select from an impressive selection of regional wines.

PERPIGNAN Le Chap'

18 bd Jean Bourrat, 66000 **Tel** *04 68 35 14 14*

Gourmet restaurant in one of Perpignan's fancy hotels. The decor in the dining room is contemporary and the menu is equally chic and modern. Technically superb dishes include risotto *à la chlorophyll*, and fish crumble flavored with ginger and lemongrass. Some old favorites still feature for those feeling less adventurous.

PEZENAS L'Entre Pots

8 av Louis-Montagne, 34120 **Tel** *04 67 30 00 00*

Frequented by locals, this trendy restaurant housed in a former wine warehouse has a convivial, intimate atmosphere. Unpretentious gourmet cuisine is based on the regional produce and flavors of the Garrigue. The wine list is deliberately short with an emphasis on the best Languedocs. Reserve ahead.

PORT CAMARGUE Le Carré des Gourmets

Pointe de la presqu'ile, 30240 **Tel** *04 66 53 36 37*

This gourmet restaurant forms part of the Le Spinaker hotel complex. A contemporary dining room boasts a lovely terrace facing out over the marina. The chef successfully combines Camargue and Catalan influences with dishes like *pata negra* cured ham, and pigeon stuffed with pine nuts. Great Languedoc wines.

PORT-VENDRES La Cote Vermeille

Quai Fanal, 66660 **Tel** *04 68 82 05 71* **Fax** *04 68 82 05 71*

This super seafood restaurant has a great quayside location with views of the fishing harbor and coastline. Fishing nets, lobster pots, and stuffed fish adorn the walls, and fresh fish, shellfish, squid, and lobster adorn the menus. Closed Thu dinner, Sun dinner, & Mon.

PRADES Le Jardin d'Aymeric 📋 ♿ €€
3 av Général de Gaulle, 66500 **Tel** *04 68 96 53 38*

Refined Catalan cuisine prepared using fresh regional produce and perfumed with local mountain herbs. The menu revisits traditional dishes such as saddle of lamb with thyme accompanied by a light parsley-flavored sauce, and seasonal fruit gratin. Good selection of regional Roussillon wines at reasonable prices.

QUILLAN Cartier 🅿️ 🚶 🍷 €€
31 bd Charles de Gaulle, 11500 **Tel** *04 68 20 05 14*

A family-run restaurant and hotel in a town that serves as the crossroads for routes across the eastern Pyrenees. The menu concentrates on traditional dishes and ingredients of the region, including duck, *foie gras*, cassoulet, wild mushrooms, and truffles. Limoux, Fitou, and Corbières vintages dominate the wine list.

SAILLAGOUSE La Vieille Maison Cerdane 🚶 🏵 €€€
Pl de la Cerdagne, 66800 **Tel** *04 68 04 72 08*

This venerable restaurant and hotel, in an old coaching inn, has been run by the Planes family since 1895. The chef serves up Catalan specialties, including *caneton aux raisin* (duck casserole), *ollada* (rustic meat and vegetable stew), and *crème catalane* for dessert. There is also a good selection of tapas. Closed Sun dinner & Mon in winter.

SETE La Palangrotte 🚶 📋 €€€
Quai de la Marine, 34200 **Tel** *04 67 74 80 35* **Fax** *04 67 74 97 20*

In Sète there is nowhere more pleasant to sample the famous oysters and other shellfish of the Etang de Thau lagoon than this cheerful marine-themed restaurant. Some of the best seafood on the coast, better for lunch than dinner. Closed Mon, Sun dinner (except Jul, Aug).

SOURNIA Auberge de Sournia 🚶 🔲 €€
4 rte de Prades, 66730 **Tel** *04 68 97 72 82*

In the heart of the Pyrénées-Orientales is this quaint auberge run by an enthusiastic young couple. The food has regional flourishes, enlivened with a modern touch. Duck in all its guises is the specialty; try the savory duck breast stuffed with goat's cheese. Other dishes include scallops, red mullet, and king prawns.

ST MARTIN DE LONDRES Les Muscardins 🅿️ 🚶 📋 🍷 €€€€
19 rte Cevennes, 34380 **Tel** *04 67 55 75 90* **Fax** *04 67 55 70 28*

Surprising to find such a sophisticated dining experience in a little country town, but Les Muscardins is worth a special expedition for monkfish accompanied by risotto perfumed with yucca flowers, and carpaccio of smoked Aubrac veal. The surroundings are elegant. Good selection of regional wines.

UZES La Taverne 🚶 🔲 🍷 €€
Rue Sigalon, 30700 **Tel** *04 66 22 47 08*

Located in the pedestrian area in the center of the town, this atmospheric restaurant has a vaulted ceiling and a pretty terrace that is perfect for summer dining. It serves local specialties, such as *brandade de Nîmes* (salt-cod dip) and *filet de taureau de Camargue* (Camargue steak). There is an extensive wine list.

VILLEFRANCHE DE CONFLENT Auberge St-Paul 🚶 ♿ 🔲 🍷 €€€€€
7 pl Eglise, 66500 **Tel** *04 68 96 30 95* **Fax** *04 68 96 05 60 30*

Originally a 13th-century chapel, this village restaurant has an attractive terrace and a charming, rustic dining room. The menu is cosmopolitan, with fresh local produce and a sophisticated wine list, with fine Burgundy and Roussillon vintages. Closed Sun dinner, Mon, Tue.

PROVENCE AND THE COTE D'AZUR

AIX-EN-PROVENCE Brasserie Léopold 🚶 📋 ♿ 🔲 🍷 €€€
2 av Victor Hugo, 13090 **Tel** *04 42 26 01 24* **Fax** *04 42 38 53 17*

Classic French brasserie with dozens of tables and bustling waiters, on the ground floor of the comfortable Hôtel Saint-Christophe in the center of Aix. A great place for a full-scale meal, a snack, or just a drink at any time of day or year. Strong on regional cuisine and traditional brasserie fare.

AIX-EN-PROVENCE Mas d'Entremont 🅿️ 🚶 ♿ 🔲 🍷 €€€€
Quartier des Platrières, 13090 **Tel** *04 42 17 42 42* **Fax** *04 42 21 15 83*

The food is imaginative, the list of Provençal wines is good, and the setting in a lush park above Aix at Célony is delightful. Plenty of regional meat and fish. In summer, dine on a lovely terrace overlooking the gardens, with fine views. The dining room has huge picture windows overlooking the park. Closed Sun dinner, Mon lunch, Nov–Apr.

AIX-EN-PROVENCE Yamato 🅿️ 📋 ♿ 🔲 🍴 🍷 €€€€
21 av des Belges **Tel** *04 42 38 00 20*

Run by Koji and Yuriko Somaya, this is arguably the most authentic Japanese restaurant in Aix-en-Provence. Whether you dine in the Zen garden or in the airy dining room, you'll be transported far from France to the Orient. The sushi is superb, as are the less predictable dishes such as *chawanmushi* (grilled eel). Closed Mon–Tue lunch.

Key to Price Guide *see p600* **Key to Symbols** *see back cover flap*

AIX-EN-PROVENCE Le Clos de la Violette
10 av Violette, 13100 **Tel** *04 42 23 30 71* **Fax** *04 42 21 93 03*

This is an elegant address in a chic mansion standing in its own gardens: tranquil, intimate, and perfect for a romantic evening. People do dress up a little to eat here. The wine list is extensive (and very strong on local and Provençal wines) and the menu is Provençal with a modern edge. Closed Sun & Mon.

ARLES La Gueule du Loup
39 rue des Arènes, 13200 **Tel** *04 90 96 96 69* **Fax** *04 90 96 96 69*

La Gueule du Loup ("the Wolf's Maw") is more welcoming than its ferocious name implies, with a menu that changes virtually daily and serves up exquisite Provençal cuisine in charmingly rustic surroundings. Prompt service and a good choice of wines. Not cutting-edge cuisine, but good at what it does. Closed Sun, Mon lunch, & Jan.

ARLES Lou Marques
Bd Lices, 13631 **Tel** *04 90 52 52 52* **Fax** *04 90 52 52 53*

Lou Marques – the restaurant of the venerable Hôtel Jules César – is one of the best places to eat in Arles, with a central location, pleasant terrace with tables under white umbrellas, and a bill of fare that concentrates on classic Provençal dishes. Dignified surroundings. Closed Mon, Sat lunch, Sun dinner.

ARLES L'Atelier de Jean-Luc Rabanel
7 rue des Carmes, 13200 **Tel** *04 90 91 07 69*

Arrive with a large appetite at this small restaurant in the center of Arles; there is a minimum of seven courses at lunch and 13 at dinner. Jean-Luc Rabanel works almost exclusively with organic produce from his own vegetable garden and each dish is a miniature work of art. Reserve ahead or drop into the casual bistro next door. Closed Mon–Tue.

AVIGNON La Fourchette
17 rue Racine, 84000 **Tel** *04 90 85 20 93* **Fax** *04 90 85 57 60*

Much loved locally, La Fourchette is a quirky little place with walls adorned by antique forks and festival posters. The menu is traditional Provençal, with a modern take on dishes such as duck breast in garlic and vegetable crêpes. Excellent choice of cheeses. Closed Sat, Sun, Aug. Reservations required.

AVIGNON Le Petit Bedon
70 rue Joseph-Vernet, 84000 **Tel** *04 90 82 33 98* **Fax** *04 90 85 58 64*

Le Petit Bedon, just inside the walls of Avignon's old quarter, has a good reputation for tasty dishes such as poached vegetables with tapenade and *pistou*, *bourride de loup* (monkfish stew), and courgette (zucchini) purée with garlic. Amiable atmosphere. Provençal wines. Closed Sun lunch (all year), Mon lunch Nov–Apr.

AVIGNON Christian Etienne
10 rue Mons, 84000 **Tel** *04 90 86 16 50* **Fax** *04 90 86 67 09*

The wine list is strong on Provençal and Rhône Valley vintages, the location in the medieval heart of Avignon near the Papal Palace is hard to beat, and the food is equally unbeatable in this highly regarded restaurant, with menus that emphasize imaginatively treated local produce. Closed Sun, Mon (except in Jul).

AVIGNON La Mirande
4 pl de la Mirande, 84000 **Tel** *04 90 14 20 20* **Fax** *04 90 86 26 85*

One of the most delicious places to eat in Avignon, with tables outside beneath olive trees and the floodlit walls of the Palais des Papes or indoors in a grand dining room in what was once a cardinal's palace. Extensive, dazzling menu and wine list. Friendly service. Reserve in advance. Closed Tue, Wed; mid-Jan–mid-Feb.

BIOT Les Terraillers
11 rte Chemin Neuf, 06410 **Tel** *04 93 65 01 59*

Sophisticated restaurant serving dishes that are rich in every sense of the word, flavored with truffles and the herbs of surrounding hills. The *foie gras escalope* is not to be missed, and the lamb is a culinary triumph. The wine list highlights some of the better *vins de France* of Provence. Closed Wed, Thu, Nov.

BONNIEUX La Bastide de Capelongue Restaurant Edward Loubet
84480 **Tel** *04 90 75 89 78* **Fax** *04 90 75 93 03*

Two Michelin stars keep this fine restaurant ahead of the local competition. Reservations essential, especially during the Cannes Film Festival. The menu changes with the seasons and celebrates the produce and flavors of the Luberon hills and the Mediterranean coast, such as truffles *en-croûte* and roasted venison.

CAGNES Fleur de Sel
85 Montée de la Bourgade, 06800 **Tel** *04 93 20 33 33*

Delightful small restaurant serving unpretentious cooking at affordable prices – especially the set menus. Attractively rustic surroundings – the restaurant is in the heart of the village of Haut de Cagnes, next to the medieval church. Adequate choice of inexpensive wines. Closed Wed; Nov–Mar.

CAGNES Entre Cour et Jardin
102 Montée de la Bourgade, 06800 **Tel** *04 93 20 72 27*

At this small, charming restaurant in the medieval center of Cagnes, the chef/owner serves classic local dishes, which follow the seasons. The food is very tasty and portions are generous. Service is friendly. Changing exhibitions of paintings by local artists adorn the whitewashed walls.

CANNES Le Pastis   目 🖼   €€
28 rue du Commandandement André, 06400 **Tel** *04 92 98 95 40*

With an interior that feels like a cross between an American diner and a French bistro, Le Pastis is perfect for a casual meal at any time of day. The menu is mostly Mediterranean with dishes such as *daube à la niçoise* (beef stew), but you will also find Caesar salad and steak tartare. Near the main shopping street and beach. Closed Sun lunch.

CANNES Ondine   🖼 🍷   €€€
15 bd de la Croisette, 06400 **Tel** *04 93 94 23 15*

Beach restaurants usually have modest gastronomic aspirations, but Ondine is an exception. Chef Jean-Pierre Silva visits the market every day to hand-select the freshest ingredients. The focus is on fish with dishes such as crab salad and turbot with spring vegetables. Excellent wine list. Closed Wed.

CANNES La Cave   目 🍷   €€€€
9 bd de la République, 06400 **Tel** *04 93 99 79 87*

La Cave has been running since 1989 and is popular with both locals and tourists. Its large choice of traditional, Provençal dishes is made from fresh, locally sourced ingredients. The wine list has over 350 references, including an excellent selection from local producers. Closed Sat lunch, Sun.

CANNES Le 38   目 ♿ 🍷   €€€€
38 rue des Serbes, 06400 **Tel** *04 92 99 79 60* **Fax** *04 93 99 26 10*

It is difficult to eat more lavishly than in the posh surroundings of the Royal Gray, where diners can expect some of the finest cooking in Cannes – but at a surprisingly affordable price, and with courteous service. The accent is on Provençal flavors and Mediterranean seafood. Extensive wine list. Closed Sun, Mon.

CANNES La Palme d'Or   P 目 🍷 ♿   €€€€€
73 la Croisette, 06400 **Tel** *04 92 98 74 14*

Children are not actually barred from this restaurant of the stars, nor is it essential to wear a tie – but diners who are not dressed to impress may feel self-conscious here. The food is imaginative and superb, with an impressive, costly wine list. Reservations required. Closed Sun, Mon, Jan–Mar.

CARPENTRAS Chez Serge   🚶 🖼 🍷   €€€
90 rue Cottier, 84200 **Tel** *04 90 63 21 24* **Fax** *04 90 60 30 71*

Chez Serge is a surprising discovery in sleepy Carpentras – a mix of old and new that is reflected in its style and menu. There's inventive, refined international cooking and evening wine tastings. Fresh fish is cooked in imaginative ways and wild mushrooms feature often on the menu.

CASTELLANE Auberge du Teillon   🚶   €€€€
Rte Napoléon - la Garde, 04120 **Tel** *04 92 83 60 88* **Fax** *04 92 83 74 08*

Pleasant country inn 4 miles (6 km) from the busy tourist hot-spot of Castellane. The bill of fare is unprententious and changes according to the seasons, emphasizing traditional Provençal dishes, simply prepared including home-smoked salmon. Rooms available. Closed Nov–Mar; Sun dinner, Mon (except Jul & Aug).

CAVAILLON Restaurant Prévôt   🚶 目 ♿ 🍷   €€€€
353 av de Verdun, 84300 **Tel** *04 90 71 32 43*

A gastronomic treat in the heart of the pretty market town of Cavaillon, where chef Jean-Jacques Prévôt is mad about melons – his restaurant has them as a decorative motif and there is even a set menu dedicated to the gourd family. Melon and scallops are recommended. Good portfolio of wines. Closed Sun.

CHATEAU-ARNOUX La Bonne Etape   P 🚶 目 ♿ 🍷   €€€€€
Chemin du Lac, 04160 **Tel** *04 92 64 00 09* **Fax** *04 92 64 37 36*

This charming inn, located in a nondescript market town, has an outstanding array of dishes and emphasizes fresh local produce, especially lamb. The wine list is lengthy, featuring vintages from almost every French region. The dining room is decorated with paintings and tapestries. Closed Mon, Tue Sep–Jun, Jan–mid-Feb.

CHATEAUNEUF DU PAPE La Mère Germaine   P 🖼 🍷   €€
3 rue Commandant Lemaitre, 84230 **Tel** *04 90 83 54 37* **Fax** *04 90 83 50 27*

Surrounded by vineyards, this restaurant has an outstanding list of local and regional wines. The cooking is classic Provençal, servings are generous, and La Mère Germaine offers good value and friendly service. Go for lunch to enjoy the view.

COLLOBRIERES La Petite Fontaine   🍽 🚶 🖼   €€
1 pl de la Republique, 83610 **Tel** *04 94 48 00 12* **Fax** *04 94 48 03 03*

This simple restaurant is in the center of Collobrières, a sleepy hill village in the heart of the Massif des Moaures. Specialties include chicken and garlic *fricassée*, rabbit with fresh herbs, and duck with wild mushrooms, complemented by wines from the local wine co-operative. Closed Sun dinner, Mon, last two weeks Sep.

DIGNE-LES-BAINS La Chauvinière   🚶 🖼   €€
52 rue Hubac, 04000 **Tel** *04 92 31 40 03*

This small, traditional restaurant is situated in the old part of the town. The chef uses the very best seasonal ingredients, and the menu includes freshly prepared *foie gras* dishes and a range of homemade *pâtisserie*. The atmosphere is welcoming, and there is a pretty terrace for outdoor dining.

Key to Price Guide *see p600* **Key to Symbols** *see back cover flap*

DIGNE-LES-BAINS Le Grand Paris
19 bd Thiers, 04000 **Tel** *04 92 31 11 15* **Fax** *04 92 32 32 82*

This rather grand hotel-restaurant has an air of bourgeois respectability that may be a little off-putting to some – for a more relaxed atmosphere, sit outside on the terrace. Classic food, such as *brandade* (mashed potatoes) with peppers, lamb *mignonette*, and pigeon. Good choice of Rhône and Provençal wines. Closed lunch Mon–Thu, Dec–Mar.

EZE Troubadour
4 rue du Brec, 06360 **Tel** *04 93 41 19 03*

Pleasant, traditional restaurant in the center of Eze's labyrinth of stone buildings that can only be reached on foot. The Troubadour has three small dining rooms, tucked inside medieval walls and offering a respite from the summer sun. Set menus and à la carte options feature classic Provençal cooking. Closed Sun, Mon, mid-Nov–mid-Dec.

FAYENCE Le Moulin de la Camandoule
Chemin de Notre Dame, 83440 **Tel** *04 94 76 00 84* **Fax** *04 94 76 10 40*

In an ancient olive mill, this hotel-restaurant benefits from a peaceful and idyllic setting. Chef Philippe Choisy offers several menus and à la carte dishes of high quality; the flavors are Provençal and the ingredients all fresh and seasonal. Lunch is often served on the terrace. Closed Wed, Thu.

FAYENCE Le Castellaras
Rte de Seillans, 83440 **Tel** *04 94 76 13 80* **Fax** *04 94 84 17 50*

Le Castellaras serves dishes that balance tradition with innovation: lamb fillet with tarragon sauce; scampi marinated in olive oil, lemon, and tarragon; polenta in truffle oil. The wine list draws mainly from the Côtes de Provence vineyards. Closed Mon, Tue (except Jul–Aug). Reserve ahead. Closed Jan.

GIGONDAS Les Florets
Rte des Dentelles, 84190 **Tel** *04 90 65 85 01* **Fax** *04 90 65 83 80*

The terrace of this hotel-restaurant has fine views of the Dentelles de Montmirail. Well-presented regional cooking is complemented by the fine wines of the Gigondas region. The restaurant is popular, so arrive early or make a reservation. Closed Wed, Jan–mid-Mar.

GRASSE Bastide St Antoine
48 av H. Dunant, 06130 **Tel** *04 93 70 94 94* **Fax** *04 93 70 94 95*

Jacques Chibois's superb restaurant is attached to his delightful boutique-hotel in Grasse's quartier St-Antoine, with a menu that will excite gourmets and lovers of inventive French cuisine – duckling, truffles, and an inventive approach to vegetables. There is also an excellent, mainly Provençal, wine list.

JUAN LES PINS Les Pêcheurs
10 bd Maréchal Juin, Cap d'Antibes, 06160 **Tel** *04 92 93 13 30* **Fax** *04 92 93 15 04*

The Hotel Juana has recently exchanged its celebrated rooftop restaurant for this luxurious restaurant on the beach with high-tech touches and a vast terrace. Chef Francis Chauveau's cuisine is delicious and creative. Indulge in the grilled sea bass with lemons and marinated vegetables. Closed Tues, Wed (except Jul–Aug).

LA CADIERE D'AZUR Hostellerie Bérard
Av Gabriel Peri, 83740 **Tel** *04 94 90 11 43* **Fax** *04 94 90 01 94*

This renowned hotel-restaurant in the converted buildings of an 11th-century convent has a fine view over the Bandol vineyards. Owners and chefs Rene and Jean François Bérard do marvelous things with fish and shellfish, including a sublime mussel soup flavored with saffron. Local Bandol wines. Closed Mon, Tue, Jan.

MARSEILLE Chez Madie (Les Galinettes)
138 quai du Port, 13002 **Tel** *04 91 90 40 87* **Fax** *04 91 31 44 74*

A Marseillais institution for generations (it is now in the hands of the granddaughter of the eponymous founder). Legendary *bouillabaisse*, *bourride*, and other fish dishes are complemented by tripe and pigs' trotters. Definitely not for vegetarians, nor for picky children. Closed Sun.

MARSEILLE Toinou
3 cours Saint-Louis, 13001 **Tel** *04 91 33 14 94*

This is the place for seafood platters in Marseille. Set on a lively square, Toinou started over 40 years ago as a take-out counter. It still does a roaring take-out trade though many people now opt to dine in the simple dining room. For a taste of everything, try the Toinou Spécial for two people.

MARSEILLE Les Arcenaulx
25 cours d'Estienne d'Orves, 13000 **Tel** *04 91 59 80 30* **Fax** *04 91 54 76 33*

In the old warehouse district north of the Vieux Port, Les Arcenaulx is housed in the former premises of a 17th-century publisher. A great place to start or end an evening's bar-hopping in nearby streets. Dishes include scallops with grilled almonds, and steak tartare. Closed Sun.

MARSEILLE Restaurant Michel
6 rue des Catalans, 13007 **Tel** *04 91 52 30 63* **Fax** *04 91 59 24 05*

Bouillabaisse is the specialty of the house at this fine, busy brasserie. Other fish dishes include *bourride*, sardines, and the always reliable catch of the day, fresh and simply grilled. Popular with locals – get there early to be sure of a table. Wine list includes names from Bandol and Cassis.

MARTIGUES Le Miroir
4 rue Marcel Galdy, 13500 **Tel** *04 42 80 50 45*

Facing the fishing port of Martigues, with its colorful wooden boats, this restaurant specializes in fish. There is plenty of space, with six dining rooms and two terraces – choose an outside table for maximum charm. Cooking is simple yet tasty, with dishes such as mussels with fennel and saffron. Closed Sat lunch; Sun, Mon, & Wed dinner; & Jan.

MENTON Le Mirazur
30 av Aristide Briand, 06500 **Tel** *04 92 41 86 86*

Argentinian-born Mauro Colagreco is a promising chef who has settled in Menton, where his contemporary restaurant boasts its own tropical garden. Like a painter, he decorates his plates with dabs and flourishes, often using wild herbs and flowers picked from the mountains. There is a good-value lunch menu. Closed Mon–Tue & Dec–Feb.

MONACO Maya Bay
24 av Princesse Grace, 98000 **Tel** *00 37 7 97 70 74 67* **Fax** *00 37 7 97 77 58 10*

Chef Olivier Streiff's punk haircut and black eyeliner is a tribute to the Doors, and his cooking has an equally rock 'n' roll style. A typical dish is duckling with banana, dried fruits, confit apple, and roasted juniper berries. The dining room has a lush, tropical feel and the restaurant has a separate sushi bar. Closed Mon–Sun; Nov.

MOUGINS Le Moulin de Mougins
Notre-Dame-de-Vie, rte départementale 3, 06250 **Tel** *04 93 75 78 24* **Fax** *04 93 90 18 55*

Alain Llorca's 2-Michelin-star restaurant is the place for a special treat, with superb, imaginative cuisine that leans toward seafood prepared in new ways. The wines include some of the very best of Provence. The garden terrace is adorned by modern sculptures. Reservations are essential. Closed Mon & Tue lunch; Sun dinner.

MOUSTIERS La Treille Muscate
Pl de l'Eglise, 04360 **Tel** *04 92 74 64 31* **Fax** *04 92 74 63 75*

Excellent food such as *pistou* of vegetables in this lovely little Provençal bistro, with a great location on the main square of one of the region's prettiest villages. Good value, with a choice of set menus and a decent wine list, La Treille Muscate is especially pleasant for a relaxed alfresco lunch. Closed Wed & Dec–Feb.

NICE Bistrot d'Antoine
27 rue de la Préfecture, 06300 **Tel** *04 93 85 29 57*

Armand Crespo, formerly of Lou Cigalon in Valbonne, is the man behind the revival of this Niçoise bistro. He can often be seen buying produce at the nearby market. Meat off the grill is the main event: try the duck *magret* or the veal kidneys, which could make an offal-lover out of anyone. Well-chosen wines. Closed Sun–Mon; Aug.

VENCE Le Pigeonnier
3 pl du Peyra, 06140 **Tel** *04 93 58 03 00*

At this traditional restaurant serving local cuisine the menu includes a large selection of fish, seafood, and meat dishes. In summer diners can enjoy the sunny terrace, while in winter the dining room is warmed by a large open fire. Closed Mon, Sun dinner (except Jul & Aug); Jan; Nov.

VENCE Les Bacchanales
247 av de Provence **Tel** *04 93 24 19 19*

Christophe Dufau made his name in Tourrettes-sur-Loup before moving his restaurant into this slightly hard-to-find villa on the edge of Vence. His cooking is original without resorting to unnecessary flourishes. Typical of his style is an appetizer of caramelized melon with crumbled ricotta and spicy *soubressade* sauce. Closed Tue–Wed.

VILLEFRANCHE-SUR-MER L'Oursin Bleu
11 quai Courbet, 06230 **Tel** *04 93 01 90 12* **Fax** *04 93 01 80 45*

A bubbling aquarium in the foyer hints that this cheerful little eating place puts the accent on fresh fish. The location is delightful, on the quayside, with tables under umbrellas on the terrace and a dining room decorated with seafaring memorabilia. The ideal place for a long, lazy, summer lunch. Closed Tue; Nov–Mar.

CORSICA

AJACCIO Pampasgiolu
15 rue de la Porta, 20000 **Tel** *04 95 50 71 52.*

Reserve in advance at this popular eating place in the old city, with its attractive, rustic dining rooms and small terrace. Try the *spuntini* (snack) platters of fish or meat local specialties or go for the veal with olives. Good desserts, including chestnut fondant. Closed lunch, Sun.

AJACCIO Le 20123
2 rue su Roi du Rome, 2000 **Tel** *04 95 21 50 05*

Named for the tiny Corsican town of Pila-Canale, this restaurant aims to bring an authentic taste of the village to the city. You can eat on the lantern-lit terrace, in the dining room filled with bric-a-brac, or at a long shared table in the cellar. Try the charcuterie and hearty meat stews. Closed lunch; Mon.

Key to Price Guide *see p600* **Key to Symbols** *see back cover flap*

BASTIA Brasserie La Réserve
Port de Toga, 20600 **Tel** *04 95 31 05 35*

Overlooking the port, this modern brasserie is popular with local people, and is the ideal spot for a simple, leisurely lunch while watching the fishing boats drift in and out of the harbor. The chef and staff are very friendly, the food is good, and the portions are generous. Closed Sun.

BASTIA A Casarella
6 rue Ste Croix, 20600 **Tel** *04 95 32 02 32*

Hidden in the maze of streets in the citadel area, this is a reliable place to try Corsican cuisine with the occasional luxury touch, as in brocciu (the local fresh cheese) cooked with *foie gras*. Among the chef's other specialties are stuffed sardines, veal roasted with herbs, and Corsican *crème brûlée*. Closed Sat lunch; Sun; Oct–Apr.

BONIFACIO Le Goeland Beach
Plage de la Tonnara **Tel** *04 95 73 02 51*

In the middle of a nature preserve, Tonnara beach creates a breathtaking setting for this waterfront restaurant. The specialty is fish grilled over the wood fire (priced by weight), but you can also try typically Corsican dishes such as aubergines (eggplant) baked with tomato sauce. Drop into the snack bar at any time of day. Closed Nov–Apr.

CALVI Le Bout du Monde
Plage du Calvi, 20260 **Tel** *04 95 65 15 41*

Excellent food at this friendly but classy beach spot. You'll be spoiled for choice between seafood platters, langoustine ravioli, scallops in orange butter, grilled rib of beef, or huge salads, followed by caramelized apple tart or chestnut cream. Closed dinner in winter.

CORTE U Museu
13 Quart Quatre Fountains, 20250 **Tel** *04 95 61 08 36*

At the foot of the citadelle in the old town, this large restaurant has several dining rooms, including a tree-shaded terrace. There is a wide choice of dishes ranging from pizzas, pastas, and salads to traditional Corsican dishes of white beans and lamb, *brocciu*-stuffed lasagne (stuffed with a Corsican cheese), and grilled meats with herbs. Closed Nov–Apr.

ILE ROUSSE A Siesta
Promenade à Marinella, 20220 **Tel** *04 95 60 28 74* **Fax** *04 95 60 27 03*

Fresh seafood is the pride of this trendy beach restaurant. On hot nights they'll move the tables directly onto the beach so you can dine under the stars on spidercrabs, lobsters, or *bouillabaisse*. Other choices include seafood ravioli and carpaccio of fish. Excellent desserts and wine list. Closed Nov–Mar.

PORTO VECCHIO Le Lodge
Quai Pascal Paoli, Port de Plaisance, 20137 **Tel** *04 95 22 47 93*

This trendy restaurant next to the harbor attracts a young crowd, especially in the evenings when the atmosphere is very lively. The cooking is traditional and of good quality, with generous portions. Service is relaxed and friendly. Great cocktails are served at the bar. Closed Feb.

PORTO VECCHIO Le Bistro
4 Quai Pascal Paoli, Port de Plaisance, 20137 **Tel** *04 95 70 22 96*

Lively eating spot situated in the yachting harbor in the lower town. Pretty dining room and large terrace. Fresh seafood with a choice of red mullet with anchovies and tomatoes, sea bream, or grilled spiny lobster. Excellent *tartare* of beef or civet of wild boar. There's a new *tapas* bar and a good choice of *crêpes suzettes*. Closed Feb & Sun.

PORTO VECCHIO Casadelmar
Rte de Palombaggia **Tel** *04 95 72 34 34*

In a contemporary luxury hotel a few minutes from the center of Porto Vecchio, this restaurant makes luxurious use of seasonal, mostly local ingredients. Dishes often have an Italian slant, as in raviolini of beef tartare with aged pecorino and 25-year-old balsamic vinegar. The hotel also has a more casual restaurant. Closed Nov–Apr.

PROPRIANO Chez Parenti
10 av Napoléon **Tel** *04 95 76 12 14* **Fax** *04 95 76 27 11*

Run since 1935 by the Parenti family, this restaurant was originally a fisherman's shack – it still has a modest façade but the terrace overlooking the sea will soon make you forget it. The specialty is freshly caught seafood, though you will also find delicious meat dishes. Save room for the Corsican cheeses. Closed Mon lunch & Sun dinner, Nov–Apr.

SARTENE Auberge Santa Barbara
Alzone (2 miles [3km] out of Sartène on the road to Propriano), 20100 **Tel** *04 95 77 09 06* **Fax** *04 95 77 09 09*

Outdoor eatery in lovely gardens, owned by Corsica's foremost female chef, Gisèle Lovichi. Choose between homemade charcuterie or country soup with its vegetable salad, and stuffed leg of lamb or saddle of lamb with herb crust. Finish with *fiadone*, a dessert made with Corsican cheese, lemons, and eggs. Closed mid-Oct–Mar, Mon.

ST-FLORENT La Rascasse
Quai d'Honneur, 20217 **Tel** *04 95 37 06 99* **Fax** *04 95 35 00 08*

Inventive cooking in this stylish fish restaurant in a prime position on the port. Ensconce yourself on the terrace and study the yachts as you wait for your order of fish soup, seafood risotto, or grilled squid. Try the classic *bouillabaisse* or a grilled lobster, and leave room for one of the sublime desserts. Closed Wed (except Jul & Aug).

Shopping in France

Shopping in France is a delight. Whether you go to the hypermarkets and department stores, or seek out the small specialist stores and markets, you will be tempted by stylish French presentation and the quality of goods on offer. Renowned for its food and wine, France also offers world-famous fashion, perfume, pottery, porcelain, and crystal. This section provides guidelines on opening hours, and the range of goods stocked by the different types of stores. There are also details of quintessentially French products that are worth hunting down and a size conversion chart to aid clothes shopping.

Olive Oil from Baux

Fresh nectarines and melons on sale at a market stall

OPENING HOURS

Food stores open anywhere between 7–8am and close around noon for lunch. In the north, the lunch break generally lasts for 2 hours; in the south, it is 3–4 hours (except in resorts, where it is shorter). After lunch, most food stores re-open until 7pm or later.

Bakeries open early and close early, although many stay open until 1pm or later, to catch the late baguette buyers and to serve a range of lunchtime snacks.

Supermarkets, department stores, and most hypermarkets remain open all day, with no lunchtime closure.

General opening hours for non-food stores are 9am–6pm Monday through Saturday, often with a break for lunch. Many of these stores are closed on Monday mornings, and the smaller stores may stay closed all day. In the tourist regions, however, stores usually open every day in high season.

Sunday is by far the quietest shopping day, although most food stores (and news stands) are open in the morning. Virtually every store in France is closed on Sunday afternoon.

HYPERMARKETS AND DEPARTMENT STORES

Hypermarkets (*hypermarchés* or *grandes surfaces*) can be found on the outskirts of every sizeable town: look for signs indicating *centre commercial*. Much bigger than supermarkets, they sell mainly groceries, but their

other lines include clothing, home accessories, and electronic equipment. They also sell discount gasoline. **Carrefour**, **Casino**, **Auchan**, **Leclerc**, and **Intermarché** are the biggest.

Department stores (*grands magasins)*, such as **Monoprix** and **Franprix** are usually found in town centers. The more upmarket **Printemps** and **Galeries Lafayette** also have out-of-town locations.

A tempting local bakery

SPECIALIST STORES

One of the pleasures of shopping in France is that specialist food stores continue to flourish, despite the influx of supermarkets and hypermarkets. The *boulangerie* (bakery) is frequently combined with a *pâtisserie* selling cakes and pastries. The *traiteur* sells prepared foods. *Fromagers* (cheese shops) and other stores specializing in dairy products (*produits laitiers)* may be combined, but the *boucherie*

(butcher) and *charcuterie* (pork butcher-delicatessen) are often separate stores. For general groceries go to an *épicerie* or *alimentation*, but don't confuse this with an *épicerie fine*– a delicatessen.

Cleaning and household products are available from a *droguerie*, while hardware is bought from a *quincaillerie*. The term *papeterie* (stationer) covers both the expensive, specialist retailers and their hypermarket equivalents.

MARKETS

This guide lists the market day for every town featured in the Area by Area section. To find out where the market is, ask a passerby for *le marché*. Markets are held in the morning and usually finish promptly at noon. Look for local producers, including those with only one or two special items to sell, since their goods are often more reasonably priced and of better quality than stalls with multiple items. By law, price tags include the origin of all produce: *pays* means local. Chickens from Bresse are marketed wearing a red, white, and blue badge with the name of the producer. If you are visiting markets over several weeks, look for items just coming into season, such as fresh walnuts, the first wild asparagus, early artichokes, or wild strawberries. At the market, you can also buy spices and herbs, some offbeat peculiarities (such as decorative cabbages), shoes, and clothing.

The year is full of seasonal regional markets in France, specializing in such things as truffles, hams, garlic, *foie gras*, and livestock. *Foires artisanales* may be held at the same time as the seasonal markets, selling local produce and crafts.

Sausages and cheeses, regional specialties on offer in a Lyon market

REGIONAL PRODUCE

French regional specialties are available outside their area of origin, but it is more interesting to buy them locally since their creation and flavor reflect the traditions, tastes, and climate of the region.

Provence, in the south, prides itself on the quality of its olive oil, the best of which is made from the first cold pressing, lovingly decanted every day for a week. If you cannot get to a niche olive oil producer in Provence, head to **Oliviers et Co** which has branches throughout the country, and sells an excellent selection of oils. Be sure to indulge in a tasting session to sample the flavors. In the temperate north, the delicious Camembert cheese is the product of fresh Norman milk that has been cured for at least three weeks.

Popular drinks are also associated with particular regions. Pastis, made from aniseed, is popular in the south. Calvados, made in Normandy from apples, is popular in the north. Crème

Pastis 51, drunk in the south

de Fruit de Dijon, the secret ingredient to many a good cocktail or dessert, comes in many flavors (from peach to wild strawberry) in addition to the well-known black-currant – **Crème de Cassis**. Visit local producers to buy good versions of this thick, alcoholic syrup.

To a large extent, location determines the quality of regional produce. For example, the culinary tradition of Lyon *(see pp380–1)*, France's premier gastronomic city, stems from the proximity of Charolais cattle, Bresse chickens and pork, wild game from La Dombes, and the finest Rhône Valley wines.

Alongside sachets of dried herbs from Provence and braided strings of garlic and onions, be sure to buy the seasoning loved by all self-respecting francophile cooks – salt from the Ile de Ré *(see p416)* or Guerande. If you happen to be visiting the area, check out the salt flats and pick up the crumbly coarse grains at a local market. The Fleur de Sel is a delicate flaky variety and the Sel Marin is a gray, coarser type of salt.

BEAUTY PRODUCTS

French women are renowned for their beauty, and there is a plethora of good beauty products in France. The major French labels, such as **Chanel** and **Guerlain**, are available overseas, but die-

hard cosmetics fans should scour the local beauty counters to find special products that are only on sale in France.

While in Paris, beauty junkies must visit the Chanel store on the rue Cambon and the Guerlain store on the Champs Elysées to buy scent that is only available in those particluar stores. Throughout the rest of the country, supermarket brands such as Evian, Eau Thermale d'Avene, and Barbara Gould are huge hits with magazine beauty editors. In particular, the cold cream by Eau Thermale d'Avène, the foaming cleanser by Barbara Gould, and Evian's facial toning gel can be found in many a fashionista's make-up bag. Similarly many a groomed Parisian swears by Nuxe's cult body oil *Huile Prodigieuse*, Caudalie's *Vinotherapary Cabernet* body scrub (with grape extracts), and Elancyl's anti-cellulite toning cream.

Oenobiol tanning supplement capsules and Phytomer's hair care range are considered absolutely necessary by St-Tropez beach lovers looking to lessen sun damage to hair and skin.

A more traditional approach to French grooming can be found by buying *savon de marseilles* – good-quality traditional soap made with plenty of olive oil.

True scent aficionados should head for Grasse *(see p517)*, the perfume capital of the world. Be sure to visit the three largest scent factories, **Fragonard**, **Molinard**, and **Galimard**, all of which have scent available for purchase.

Provençal dried herbs for culinary use and for making teas

ACCESSORIES

French fashion is rightfully famous, but aside from the main couture labels and stores (see pp142–4), the best way to get the French look is to accessorize à la Français. In keeping with the French tradition of specialist local trades, there are certain regions that excel in producing accessories.

For a start, a hand-made umbrella from Aurillac (see p364) is guaranteed to chase away rainy-day blues in style. The best-known umbrella manufacturers are **L'Ondée au Parapluie d'Aurillac**, **Piganiol**, and **Delos**, who will customize one for you with a photograph of whomever you choose to chase away the storms.

Beautiful hands are easily available courtesy of the glove trade in Millau. Visit **L'Atelier Gantier** (the Glove Workshop) to pick up a stunning pair of expertly hand-stiched leather gloves in one of a seemingly endless array of colors.

More casual chic can be found with brightly colored wicker baskets from local markets and hardware stores. These quickly turn a casual ensemble into boho-chic outfit. Beachside boutiques are great places for picking up stylish sarongs, beads, and bracelets for any trip to *la plage* (the beach). **K Jacques** sandals from St-Tropez have long been must-have items among the fashion set.

When it is time to hit the slopes rather than the beach, French skiwear labels such as Rossignol can be a good buy, but only at the end of the season. At the height of *piste* time, ski resort stores are expensive. Once the snow starts to melt, however, ex-rental gear including skis and boots can be picked up relatively cheaply, while ski jackets, hats, and *après* ski wear tends to be gloriously cut-price.

HOUSEHOLD GOODS

If you are in the market for housewares, the best stores are Ikea, Alinea, and Habitat. Truffaut sells garden furniture, and Leroy Merlin is the hypermarket of the home improvement world.

It is surprisingly rare to see the whole range of kitchen goods in a specialist store. Instead, try the kitchen section of department stores. General hardware stores stock cast-iron cooking equipment. White china is sold in specialist shops.

Traveling through Normandy provides the perfect excuse for sampling many wonderful products, not least the *crème de chantilly*, but for tableware fans or lingerie lovers, the lace industry here is also guaranteed to please. While the **Alençon** lace is extremely expensive and mainly finds its way onto couture sold in top Parisian stores, hitting the stores in Argentan, Chantilly (see pp204–5), and Bayeux (see pp252–3) is likely to yield exquisite yet affordable pieces. It is worth hunting around for lace pieces which can be used to liven up an outfit: lace has made a fashion comeback in recent times and a customized delicate flower on a bag or blouse is à la mode.

Lace curtains are easy to come by, as are lovely table-cloths. The easiest way to be sure not to miss anything is to take "the lace road" and tour the lace museums and boutiques of Alençon, Argentan, Caen (see pp253–4), Courseulles, Villedieu-les-Poêles, and La Perrière.

With a beautiful tablecloth in place, you can proceed to pick up stunning crystal from which to sniff, swirl, and sip great French wine. The most famous French crystal maker, **Baccarat**, has a museum where you can take in some of their amazing creations and a store where you can buy a little Baccarat bauble to take home with you. A cheaper French crystal maker which is still elegant for every-day wear is **Crystal d'Arques**. You can tour the small museum in the factory and buy stemware at discount prices in the factory store.

Pottery is available at reasonable prices, especially near centers of production, such as Quimper (see p274) in Brittany, Aubagne near Marseille, and Vallauris (see p522) near Grasse.

Porcelain from Limoges (see p356) sets off any meal beautifully: a dinner set from the **Royal Limoges** factory store can be a great investment.

Similarly, stunning **Aubusson** tapestries are seriously expensive and unlikely to be an impulse vacation purchase. However, interior design fanatics could do worse than plan their tapestry or rug purchase

SIZE CHART

Women's dresses, coats, and skirts

French	36	38	40	42	44	46	48	
British	8	10	12	14	16	18	20	
American	4	6	8	10	12	14	16	

Women's shoes

French	36	37	38	39	40	41		
British	3	4	5	6	7	8		
American	5	6	7	8	9	10		

Men's suits

French	44	46	48	50	52	54	56	58
British	34	36	38	40	42	44	46	48
American	34	36	38	40	42	44	46	48

Men's shirts

French	36	38	39	41	42	43	44	45
British	14	15	$15\frac{1}{2}$	16	$16\frac{1}{2}$	17	$17\frac{1}{2}$	18
American	14	15	$15\frac{1}{2}$	16	$16\frac{1}{2}$	17	$17\frac{1}{2}$	18

Men's shoes

French	39	40	41	42	43	44	45	46
British	6	7	$7\frac{1}{2}$	8	9	10	11	12
American	7	$7\frac{1}{2}$	8	$8\frac{1}{2}$	$9\frac{1}{2}$	$10\frac{1}{2}$	11	$11\frac{1}{2}$

around a trip to the home of weaving in Aubusson (see pp356–7).

Finishing touches are fun to shop for and can certainly be more frivolous. Be sure to visit the local markets for gingham cotton napkins, linen cleaning cloths, and seafood accoutrements (such as lobster crackers and oyster forks). In Provence be sure to stock up on cheap, brightly colored cookware – tagines, terra cotta bowls, and painted plates are all in abundance.

WINE

To buy wine straight from the vineyards and wine co-operatives, follow the tasting (dégustation) signs to vineyards (domaines). You may be expected to buy at least one bottle, except where a small fee is charged for wine-tasting. Wine co-operatives make and sell the wine of small producers. Here you can buy wine in 5- and 10-liter containers (en tonneau), as well as in bottles. Wine sold en tonneau, once opened, needs to be consumed fairly quickly, as it will deteriorate within a few days. Wine sold in bottles travels better.

Nicolas is France's main wine retailer, with many branches.

FACTORY OUTLETS

The French sales system is very rigid (see p140) but true bargain hunters know that factory stores have some items on sale all year round. The biggest factory outlets in France can be found in and around Troyes in outlet malls called **Marques Avenue** (Brands Avenue), **Marques City** (Brands City), and **McArthur Glen**, a large American outlet. They sell everything from Yves Saint Laurent suits to Black and Decker drills, Cristofle silverware, and Bonpoint babygros. As different an experience as you can get from browsing around French markets and local specialist stores, what factory outlets lack in charm they make up for in bargains. If a whole new wardrobe is in order, it is definitely worth a trip.

DIRECTORY

HYPERMARKETS AND DEPARTMENT STORES

For details of addresses, visit the following websites

Auchan
www.auchan.fr

Carrefour
www.carrefour.fr

Casino
www.supercasino.fr

Franprix
www.franprix.fr

Galeries Lafayette
www.galerieslafayette.com

Intermarché
www.intermarche.com

Leclerc
www.e-leclerc.com

Monoprix
www.monoprix.fr

Printemps
www.printemps.com

REGIONAL PRODUCE

Crème de Cassis
Gabriel Boudier
14 rue de Cluj
21007 Dijon.
Tel 03 80 74 33 33.

Oliviers et Co
For details of addresses,
visit www.oliviers-co.com

BEAUTY PRODUCTS

Chanel
31 rue Cambon 75008
Paris. *Tel 01 42 86 26 00.*
www.chanel.com

Fragonard
20 bd Fragonard
06130 Grasse.
Tel 04 93 36 44 65.
www.fragonard.com

Galimard
73 route de Cannes
06130 Grasse.
Tel 04 93 09 20 00.
www.galimard.com

Guerlain
68 av des Champs
Elysées, 75008 Paris.
Tel 01 45 62 52 57.
www.guerlain.fr

Molinard
60 bd Victor Hugo
06130 Grasse.
Tel 04 93 36 01 62.
www.molinard.com

ACCESSORIES

L'Atelier Gantier
21 rue Droite
12100 Millau.
Tel 05 65 60 81 50.

Delos
14 rue Rocher
15000 Aurillac.
Tel 04 71 48 86 85.
www.delos-france.com

K Jacques
32 rte Plages
83990 St Tropez.
Tel 04 94 97 41 50.
www.kjacques.com

L'Ondée au Parapluie d'Aurillac
27 rue Victor Hugo
15000 Aurillac.
Tel 04 71 48 29 53.

Piganiol
9 rue Ampère
15000 Aurillac.
Tel 04 71 63 42 60.

HOUSEHOLD GOODS

Alençon Lace Museum
Cour carrée de la Dentelle
61000 Alençon.
Tel 02 33 32 40 07.

Alinea
www.alinea.fr

Aubusson
Manufacture Saint-Jean
3 rue Saint-Jean
23200 Aubusson.
Tel 05 55 66 10 08.

Baccarat
20 rue des Cristalleries
54120 Baccarat.
Tel 03 83 76 60 06.
www.baccarat.com

Cristal d'Arques
Zone industrielle, 62510
Arques. *Tel 03 21 95 46 96.*

Habitat
www.habitat.net

Ikea
www.ikea.com

Leroy Merlin
www.leroymerlin.fr

Royal Limoges
28 rue Donzelot
Accès par le quai du Port
du Naveix, 87000 Limoges.
Tel 05 55 33 27 37.
www.royal-limoges.fr

Truffaut
www.truffaut.com

WINE

Nicolas
www.nicolas.com

FACTORY OUTLETS

Marques Avenue
Av de la Maille, 10800
Saint Julien les Villas.
Tel 03 25 82 80 80.
www.marquesavenue.com

Marques City
35 rue Danton
10150 Pont Sainte Marie.
Tel 03 25 46 37 48.
www.marquescity.fr

McArthur Glen
ZI des magasin d'usines
du Nord 10150
Pont Sainte Marie.
Tel 03 25 70 47 10.
www.mcarthurglen.fr

Entertainment in France

Paris is one of the world's great entertainment cities, but France's reputation as a center of excellence in the arts extends well beyond the capital. Whether you prefer to attend theater or catch a movie, listen to jazz or techno, or watch modern dance, the country has a wide array of choices. The regional chapters in this guide will give you an insight into local gems, while these pages provide an overview of entertainment trends and events. Major festivals, such as Avignon and Cannes, occupy an important place in French hearts, so reserve well ahead if you plan to attend. For small festivals and local happenings, tourist office websites have up-to-the-minute listings.

The spectacular setting of Avignon Theater at night

THEATER

Going to the theater in France can be as formal or intimate as you choose. A trip to a major theater can involve dressing up, making special *souper* (late dinner) reservations at a nearby restaurant specializing in theater-goers, and quaffing exorbitantly priced champagne during the interval. On the other hand, a trip to a small-scale theater can be about casual dress, cheap tickets, and an intimate experience.

French movie stars frequently return to the stage, including Gérard Depardieu and Fanny Ardant in *The Beast in the Jungle*. This trend reflects the continuing popularity of the theater. Whatever the genre, the French love an evening *au théâtre,* be it a French farce or a festival of street theater.

France's biggest theater festival is at **Avignon** *(see p503)* which is held during three weeks in July and is mainly open-air. It also includes ballets, drama, and classical concerts. Many outdoor theaters operate in summer and are often free. Contact the town's tourist office for a program.

Circus is also dear to the French. In small towns, summertime is often heralded by the circus loudspeaker strapped to the top of a car cruising the streets and inviting adults and children alike to flock to the big top.

Large-scale *spectacles* or shows are another popular form of theater, be they massive musicals or *son et lumières* performances. Marionettes are also given due respect in France, where puppet shows go beyond traditional Punch and Judy territory.

MOVIES

La Septième Art, as the French refer to the movies, reveals the respect with which the genre is held. From the Lumière brothers and their innovative technology to contemporary critical smashes, such as *The Chorus* and *Amélie* to the *Nouvelle Vague,* France's influence on movies is undeniable. The French are supportive of local, independent movie theaters, and small towns are often fiercely protective of their screening center. So when visiting the movie theater, try to avoid the behemoths of UGC and Gaumont and instead head to a tiny *salle de cinéma.* If your

language skills won't stretch to seeing a French film while in France, be sure to catch the VO *(Version Originale)* of any other language films, which will be screened in the original language. VF *(Version Française)* denotes a dubbed screening in French. As any expatriate in France knows, hearing a strange French voice coming out of a Hollywood A-lister's mouth is likely to dull any enjoyment of a major blockbuster movie.

Another thing to bear in mind is the French attitude to snacking. Essentially it is only acceptable for children, and even then only at a designated time after school. While French movie theaters do have concession stands selling popcorn and candy, it is only the foreigners who can be heard munching throughout the tense parts of the film. On the other hand, some French theaters have bars and restaurants attached, so that movie goers can dissect the movie over a meal. Many theaters run mini directors' festivals with several movies shown back to back, attracting serious film buffs and those curious to learn more.

As the fame of **Cannes** *(see p520)* reflects, film festivals are taken seriously by the French. Cannes itself is a maelstrom of media hype, old-school glamor, and shiny new cash. It is an amazing experience if you can get tickets to any of the movies or parties, but these are notoriously hard to get since they are by invitation only.

Poster promoting La Rochelle international film festival

Red carpet and razzmatazz at the Cannes film festival

An easier way to experience the fabulous side of film is to attend the lower-key American and Asian film festivals in **Deauville** *(see p255)*. The former is seen as a major launch pad for U.S. independent films looking for European release and attracts big stars and cult directors alike. The competition section of the festival has ten films in the running each year. The chic town of Deauville is small and accessible and, while the chance of bumping into a huge star is slim, it feels possible.

The film festival in **La Rochelle** *(see p416)*, the second largest in France, does not attract big actors, but film fans will not be disappointed with the large selection of movies.

A truly great way to catch a movie in France is at an open-air festival. There are many such events throughout the country; check local listings so as not to miss out. And if you are lucky enough to be in Arles *(see pp508–9)*, an epic experience can be had at their annual showing of historical Roman block-busters, screened against the backdrop of a magnificent Roman amphitheater. Contact **Théâtre Antique** for details.

DANCE

Dancing is a way of life in France. From formal lessons to spontaneous outbreaks of grooving in the village square, moving to music is central to all types of celebration. Most foreigners' first experience with French dancers occurs in a nightclub and is, more often than not, accompanied by an expression of surprise. In even the most upscale nightclub, it is not unusual to see trendy twentysomethings jiving away to *le rock*, a formal form of rock and roll dancing. French teens are taught *le rock* before being unleashed on the party scene, and a basic understanding of its signature twirls and twists is considered vital to being a good dancer.

The love affair with formal dance sessions starts young, but lasts until late in life: tea dances are a major fixture of most older people's social calendars. Community centers, sports auditoriums, restaurants, and chic nightclubs often host *thé dansants* (tea dances), normally in the late afternoon or early evening.

Another way to experience French dance culture is to head to a *guingette*, a moored party boat with a convivial, old-fashioned atmosphere. People here dance the *quadrille* or the *musette* to accordion music, spinning around on the banks of the river. While the guingettes were traditionally clustered around the Marne river, they have now spread throughout France and are definitely worth seeking out if your travels take you close to a major tributary.

In general, lots of dancing takes place near to water in France. Those looking to get into the groove in the south should take their dancing shoes to the quays in Bordeaux and Marseille.

Of course, once a year, on July 13 and 14, a very unusual impromptu dancing venue springs up around the country with the *Bals des Pompiers*. The "Firemen's Balls" are a national institution when the French of all ages head down to their local fire station to celebrate Bastille day by dancing to everything from Piaf to hip hop until the early hours of the morning.

If you would prefer to watch rather than participate, there are several major dance festivals that celebrate the dance traditions of different regions. The **Gannat festival** held in the Auvergne *(see p353)* is a fine example of a regional dance extravaganza, as is the **Festival Interceltique de Lorient** *(see p270)* which celebrates Celtic music and dance. The main international dance festivals are held in **Montpellier** *(see pp494–5)* and **Lyon** *(see pp378–81)*. These provide a wonderful opportunity to enjoy major contemporary dance talent from around the world.

Wonderful costumes and choreography at the Montpellier dance festival

MUSIC

The French music scene is about far more than Johnny Hallyday, although it must be said that the ageing rocker still manages to sell stacks of records, concert tickets, and gossip magazines. It should also be pointed out that he is actually Belgian, but the French have taken him to their hearts anyway. Neither is the scene just about Bob Sinclair, Daft Punk, Air, and "Le French Touch." However, the fact that both dance music and rock happily coexist in the French charts reflects a truism of the music scene over here, which is that there is space for all kinds of tunes. *Chanson* has made a huge comeback over recent years as the success of the movement's poster boy Benjamin Biolay reveals. The new French *chanson* scene is dominated by Biolay, although other well-known artists in this genre include Vincent Delerm and Benabar.

Female crooners are also all the rage; listen to Lara Fabian or reality TV pop star Chimène Badi for confirmation of this.

The other recent musical phenomenon in France came off the back of a hit movie *The Chorus* (*Les Choristes*, 2004) which has seen impressive soundtrack sales, and one can at least speculate on the impact it might have had on attendance at evensong.

The event which best symbolizes this musical cornucopia is the Fête de la Musique. Every year on June 21, France resonates to the sound of this national music festival. Amateur and professional musicians alike set up their stages throughout villages and towns and peform. The best way to enjoy this is to walk around and try and take in as many different "concerts" as possible, but be aware that for some wannabe rock stars this is their only chance to shine, regardless of whether they can sing or not. Musical quality aside, what is most impressive about the Fête de la Musique is the sheer

number of genres that one can hear in a few streets. Ranging from full orchestras to one-man rap artists, you can expect to hear everything from accordion music to panpipes, *chanson*, hip hop and electro.

If you prefer your festivals a little more specialized, visit one of the events focusing on the very best of everything from chamber music to jazz. The July **Festival of Francofolies** in La Rochelle (*see p416*) brings together French music enthusiasts from around the world just as **Jazz in Antibes** draws top performers to this chic seaside town (*see p521*). The **Chorégies d'Orange**, France's oldest opera festival, takes place throughout July and August in the well-preserved Roman amphitheater, which retains perfect acoustics. The organ festival in **Aubusson** (*see pp356–7*) focuses around the amazing organ in the Sainte Croix church and **La Roque d'Anthéron** looks set to continue to pull in piano-loving crowds. The **Colmar international festival** (*see p227*) is a major draw for classical music buffs, and the **Aix festival** (*see p511*) is a must for any serious fan, while the **Montpellier** (*see pp494–5*) **and Radio France** event appeals to music lovers throughout the world.

CLUBS

Cool clubs and artful partying most definitely exist outside the capital city, despite what Parisians may believe. There are, of course, bars, clubs, and discos throughout the country, and night owls looking to dance are unlikely to be disappointed by the range of options on offer. Small local venues can be great fun, and community events such as open-air parties and festivals are almost always worth a look.

In general, nightclubs open late and even in small towns, don't really get going until after midnight. The French are more likely to nurse a few drinks rather than dash around buying multiple

rounds, and shots are almost unheard of over here. It is considered uncouth to drink wine outside of mealtimes, although champagne is always a good thing! The prevailing custom is to join together with friends and buy a bottle of spirits between you. The nightclub will present you with plenty of mixers and – the big benefit of going for this option – you will usually get a table all to yourselves. Tables are generally reserved for those in possession of a full bottle of spirits; a single gin and tonic does not warrant a seat. As extravagant as this may seem, it is generally cheaper than buying individual drinks for four or more people.

In terms of dress code, trainers are almost always forbidden, and the dressier the better could be seen as the rule. In house or hip-hop clubs strict dress codes tend to be relaxed. However, in more traditional *boites de nuit* (night clubs) getting glammed-up is the way to go. Clubs with difficult door policies can often be out-foxed by late diners. If you are worried about getting in, call ahead and make a dinner reservation. Alternatively flaunt designer labels at the doormen.

To experience one of France's most glamorous clubs head to **Les Planches** – an uber-chic spot outside Deauville (*see p255*). Aside from its swimming pool in which starlets frolick at 3am, vintage cars tear around town rounding up party goers with a generally hedonistic atmosphere, Les Planches offers a friendly, fun vibe.

Up in the mountains **Le Privilege** in Chamonix (*see p322*) and **Le Loft** in Méribel are jumping Alpine party places.

The Cote d'Azur (*see pp499–531*) is, of course, renowned for its hedonistic nightlife. **Les Caves du Roy** in the Hotel Byblos and **Nikki Beach** in St-Tropez (*see p516*) are perfect for the jet set, while **Jimmy'z** in Monaco (*see pp530–1*) is the place to hang out with highrollers.

SPECTATOR SPORTS

Sporting enthusiasts are spoiled for choice in France, with opportunities to indulge in spectator sports throughout the country. If you don't want to wait to see the *grande finale* of the **Tour de France** in Paris, why not see it start in Brittany *(see pp268–85)*. Alternatively, taking in the spectacle from a tiny village en route is a great experience (drivers beware: the Tour takes precedence and the traffic will be stopped for a very, very long time).

If football is more your thing, then head to the Olympic stadia to catch huge teams, such as **Lyon** and **Marseille**, in action.

Surfing fans should make for Biarritz *(see p452)*, Lacanau *(see p424)* and Hossegor *(see p424)* to watch the tournaments there, while ski aficionados might want to watch the European Cup in Les Trois Vallées *(see p322)*.

Golfers flock to the **PGA Open** held outside Paris and to the **LPGA in Evian**, which is the world's second most valuable tournament after the U.S. Open.

Riders will be drawn to one of France's national studs at the **Haras National de Pompadour** for dressage, show-jumping, and other competitions throughout the year. Similarly, equine enthusiasts should not miss out on exciting horse racing at the renowned **Chantilly Racecourse**.

The **Le Mans** 24-hour car race is an institution, as is the famous **Grand Prix** in Monaco *(see pp530–31)*. The **French Grand Prix** at Magny Cours, south of Nevers *(see pp339–40)*, is also well worth a visit.

No visitor to France in the summer should miss out on one of the greatest spectator sports of them all: head to the village square and take in a game of *petanque* (also known as *boules*).

DIRECTORY

THEATER

Avignon Theater Festival
www.festival-avignon.com
Tel 04 90 14 14 14.

MOVIES

Cannes Film Festival
www.festival-cannes.fr

Deauville Film Festival
www.festival-deauville.com

La Rochelle Film Festival
www.festival-larochelle.org

Théâtre Antique d'Arles
Association Peplum.
Tel 04 90 93 19 55.
www.festivalpeplum-arles.com

DANCE

Festival Interceltique de Lorient
Tel 02 97 64 03 20.
www.festival-interceltique.com

Gannat Festival
Tel 04 70 90 12 67.
www.gannat.com

Lyon Festival
Tel 04 72 07 41 41.
www.biennaledelyon.org

Montpellier Festival
Tel 08 00 60 07 40.
www.montpellierdanse.com

MUSIC

Aix Festival
Tel 04 42 17 34 00.
www.festival-aix.com

Aubusson Festival
Tel 05 55 66 32 12.
www.orgue-aubusson.org

Choregies d'Orange
Tel 04 90 34 24 24.
www.choregies.asso.fr

Colmar International Festival
Tel 03 89 20 68 97.
www.festival-colmar.com

Festival of Francofolies
Tel 05 46 28 28 28.
www.francofolies.fr

Jazz in Antibes
Tel 04 97 23 11 10.
www.antibesjuanlespins.com

Radio France and Montpellier Festival
Tel 04 67 02 02 01.
www.festivalradiofrancemontpellier.com

La Roque d'Antheron
Tel 04 42 50 51 15.
www.festival-piano.com

CLUBS

Les Caves du Roy
Av Paul Signac
83990 St-Tropez.
Tel 04 94 56 68 00.
www.byblos.com

Jimmy'z
Le Sporting Club,
Av Princesse Grace,
Monte Carlo.
Tel 00 377 98 06 73 73.

Le Loft
Parc Olympique,
La Chaudanne,
73550. Méribel.
Tel 04 79 00 36 58.
www.leloftmeribel.com

Nikki Beach
Route de Epi
Ramatuelle
83350 St-Tropez.
Tel 04 94 79 82 04.
www.nikkibeach.com

Les Planches
Les Longs Champs
14910 Blonville sur Mer.
Tel 02 31 87 58 09.

Le Privilege
Rue des Moulins
74400 Chamonix.
Tel 04 50 53 29 10.
www.barleprivilege.com

SPECTATOR SPORTS

Chantilly Racecourse
Rue Plaine des Aigles,
Chantilly, Oise.
Tel 03 44 62 44 00.
www.france-galop.com

French Grand Prix
Magny Cours, 58170.
Tel 03 86 21 80 00.
www.fia.com

Grand Prix
Automobile Club de Monaco.
Tel 00 377 93 15 26 00.
www.fia.com

Haras National de Pompadour
Tel 08 11 90 21 31.
www.haras-nationaux.fr

LPGA in Evian
www.evianmasters.com

Le Mans
Tel 02 43 40 24 24.
www.lemans.org

Olympique Lyon
350 av Jean Jaurès
69007 Lyon.
www.olweb.fr

Olympique de Marseille
3 bd Michelet
13008 Marseille.
www.om.net

PGA Open
www.pgafrance.net

Tour de France
www.letour.fr

Specialist Vacations and Outdoor Activities

France offers an amazing variety of leisure and sports activities, making it a wonderful choice for a specialist vacation. The French take great pride in the *art de vivre*, which entails not only eating and drinking well, but also pursuing special interests and hobbies. For the best in entertainment and spectator sports, festivals and annual events, see *France through the Year* on pages 36–9. Information on leisure and sporting activities in a particular region is available from the tourist offices listed for each town in this guide. The suggestions below cover the most popular, and also the more unusual, pursuits.

Students honing their culinary skills on a Hostellerie Bérard cooking course

SPECIALIST VACATIONS

French government tourist offices *(see p669)* have an extensive range of information on travel companies that offer special interest vacations. and can send you a copy of *The Traveler in France Reference Guide*.

If you want to improve your French, many language courses are available. These are very often combined with other activities, such as cooking or painting. For more information, request *Cours de français pour étudiants étrangers* (French courses for foreign students) from the **French Institute** in London.

Young people can enjoy a French-speaking vacation by working part time on the restoration of historic sites with **Union REMPART** *(Union pour la Réhabilitation et Entretien des Monuments et du Patrimoine Artistique)*.

A tantalizing array of gastronomic courses is on offer to introduce you to classical French cuisine or the cooking of a particular region. For experienced cooks, more advanced and specialist courses are available too. Wine-appreciation courses can also be found and are always very popular.

There are numerous art and crafts courses throughout the country, catering to everyone from the absolute beginner to the most accomplished artist.

Nature lovers can enjoy the national parks *(parcs nationaux)* and join organized bird-watching and botanical trips in many areas, including the Camargue, the Cévennes, and Corsica.

Le Guide des Jardins en France, published by Actes

Painting the picturesque French landscape

Sud, is a useful reference guide when visiting France's many beautiful gardens.

GOLF

There are golf courses all over France, especially along the north and south coasts and in Aquitaine. Players have to reach a minimum standard and obtain a licence in order to play, so be sure to take your handicap certificate with you. Top courses offer weekend or longer tutored breaks geared to all levels of experience. The **Fédération Française de Golf** will provide a list of all the courses throughout France.

Specialist golf packages, including deluxe hotel accommodations, can be ideal for serious golfers and their non-golfing partners alike. The spectacular Hotel Royal and its renowned **Evian Masters** golf course is a very exclusive, pampering option. The 18-hole course is guaranteed to appeal to fans. There is also a spa and five swimming pools, perfect for lazing. The climbing wall, squash, and tennis courts will appeal to more active visitors.

In the south, the **American Golf Academy** offers a team of golf pros who are adept at coaching children, beginners, and also experts through their eight different courses and private lessons. Their summer schools and master classes are highly sought after.

The **Hotel de Mougins**, with a lovely address on the "avenue du Golf," is situated close to ten prestigious golf courses, including the Golf Country Club Cannes, the Royal Mougins Golf Club, and the Golf d'Opio-Valbonne. The hotel can arrange rounds at the different clubs, and offers packages which include extras, such as lunch in the clubhouse.

The **Golf Hotel Grenoble Charmeil** can organize green fees for three courses, including the Grenoble International course. In Brittany, the **St-Malo Golf and Country Club** has a 19th-century manor house interior and an impressive 27-hole golf course, surrounded by the Mesnil forest.

TENNIS

Tennis is a very popular sport in France, and courts for hourly rental can be found in almost every town. It is a good idea to bring your own equipment, since rental facilities may not be available.

HIKING

In France, more than 38,000 miles (60,000 km) of long-distance tracks, known as *Grandes Randonnées* (GR), are clearly marked. There are also 50,000 miles (80,000 km) of the shorter *Petites Randonnées* (PR).

The routes vary in difficulty and include long pilgrim routes, alpine crossings, and tracks through national parks. Some *Grandes* and *Petites Randonnées* are open for mountain biking as well as horse riding.

Topo Guides, published by **Fédération Française de la Randonnée Pédestre**, describe the tracks, providing details of transportation, places for overnight stops, and food stores. A series geared specifically toward families is *Promenades et Randonnées*.

BICYCLING

For advice on bicycling in France, contact the British **CTC** (Cyclists' Touring Club) or the **Fédération Française de Cyclisme**.

Mountain biking - a great way to explore

Escaping into the forest at Fontainebleau *(see pp180–1)*

Serious bicyclists could live their dreams by joining up for a Tour de France stage vacation with the **Velo Echappe** *Etape du Tour* team. The company organizes two types of adventure – a fully guided program or a self-guided option. They handle all the registration forms and paperwork, and on the guided option they will put you up in a hotel a block away from the end of the stage. Applications to the tour company must be received by the end of March every year to have a chance to ride along with the Tour de France professionals.

At the other end of the scale, people who enjoy a gentle bike ride could opt for a wine bicycling tour through the vineyards of France. Freewheeling down the Route des Grands Crus in Burgundy may be more than enough vacation exercise for some.

Duvine Adventures organizes tours that take in famed vineyards such as La Tache, Romanée-Conti, and Nuit-St-Georges. The riding includes flat spells and hills, and there are excellent lunches.

Local tourist offices provide details about riding facilities in their areas. **Voies Vertes** offers information on "greenways," easy rides through some of France's loveliest countryside. *Gîtes de France (see p549)* offer dormitory accommodations in the vicinity of well-known tracks.

HORSE RIDING

There are many reputable companies that offer riding breaks from one-hour treks to long weekends or vacations of a week or more. The best way to choose is to decide which type of countryside you would prefer to see from the saddle. If the Mont St-Michel *(see pp256–61)* and the beaches of Brittany appeal, then **A La Carte Sportive** offer stables with horses trained in trekking, for beginners and intermediates. For more experienced riders, riding a Camargue mount through the countryside of Provence *(see pp510–11)* is a wonderful treat. **Ride in France** organizes rides through beautiful scenery, vineyards, and picturesque villages,

Hiking along the Gorges du Verdon in Provence *(see pp514–15)*

allowing riders to experience the flora and fauna of the area. Horse lovers with a taste for the historical, or those hankering after a little luxury, could do worse than to sign up for a break with the **Cheval et Chateaux** company which organizes horse-riding tours around chateaus in the Loire. Not only do riders get to take in the majesty of the chateaus of the region, the overnight accommodations also comes courtesy of a castle. It makes an ideal way to play lord or lady of the manor while indulging in a passion for trekking.

MOUNTAIN SPORTS

The French mountains, especially the Alps and the Pyrenees, provide a wide range of sporting opportunities. In addition to winter downhill skiing and *ski de fond* (cross-country), the mountains are enjoyed in the summer by rock-climbers and mountaineers, and by those skiers who can't wait for winter and so indulge in some of Europe's best glacier skiing.

Climbers should contact the **Féderation Française de la Montagne et de l'Escalade** for more information on the best climbing locations and other useful tips.

Winter sports fans should join the serious skiers and snowboarders who head to the French hills in droves every season. The mountains here have terrain to satisfy all levels of expertise from toddlers in the kids' club through to death-defying off-piste athletes, adrenalin junkie snowboarders, kite-surfers and middle-of-the-road snow fans who are happiest cruising blue runs and eating in slope-side restaurants.

SKIING

Undoubtedly, France has some of the best ski resorts anywhere in the world. The sheer scale of some of the larger areas can be quite daunting if you're on a week-long trip – especially to those who insist on covering all the trails on the map. The Trois Vallées ski area (*see p322*), for example, is made up of three valleys which include the resorts of Courchevel, Méribel, Val Thorens, and Les Ménuires. Added together, they comprise a staggering 375 miles (600 km) worth of pistes.

The Trois Vallées is an excellent example of how French ski resorts differ wildly in style. Super-chic stations such as Courchevel and Méribel draw skiers from around the world, often dressed in cutting-edge ski fashion and using the latest hi-tech equipment. In these resorts the hotels – especially those dubbed to be "in" – are expensive, and eating and drinking in the "see and be seen spots" here puts a significant dent in the most generous of vacation budgets. On the other hand, resorts which are considered less glamorous, such as Vals Thorens and Les Menuires, can be enjoyed without designer labels and huge credit card limits.

The main consideration when choosing a resort should be the percentage of terrain to suit your ability. For example, a beginner might be miserable in a resort aimed at experts and offering only a few green runs. Similarly, a confident intermediate looking to improve will be frustrated by a ski area full of easy cruising slopes over-run with beginners.

It is also important to think about whether or not it matters to you if the village is picturesque. Die-hard ski fans can overlook ugly concrete architecture in towns such as Flaine, while those looking for the bigger picture would be best off heading to somewhere pretty, such as La Clusaz or Megève (*see p322*).

The proximity of accommodations to piste is also very important; most people find it is worth paying a premium for accommodations near the slopes and lifts, rather than having to stagger back in heavy boots carrying your skis after a long day's schussing.

Aside from obvious concerns such as nightlife, children's crèches, and the efficiency of lift networks, it can also be useful to look at historic snow reports for the last few years for the time you are planning your trip. The weather can be unpredictable though so be sure to also check the resorts' snow-making capabilities. Armed with these details you should be in a good position to pick the right resort for you but remember, while the Alps get most of the attention, the Pyrenees can offer some seriously good skiing, too.

AERONAUTICAL SPORTS

Learning to fly in France can be relatively inexpensive. Information on the different flying schools is available from the **Fédération Nationale Aéronautique**. There are also plenty of opportunities to learn the exhilarating skills of gliding, paragliding, and hang gliding. For more information, contact the **Fédération Française de Vol Libre**.

If piloting a plane is a little too much, you can opt for ballooning instead. France has an illustrious ballooning history, being the birthplace of the Montgolfier brothers who pioneered the art in 1783. **Ballon de Paris** provides a tethered taste of adventure in Paris with a trip into the air in the **Parc André-Citroën**, but floating unfettered over the countryside can be arranged by several companies around the country. **France Balloons** can organize trips over Fontainebleau (*see pp180–1*) outside Paris or over the Burgundian vineyards. Alternatively, they offer the opportunity to appreciate the spectacular chateaus of the Loire from a balloon. In Provence **Hot Air Balloon Provence** can float you over the picturesque villages, cornfields and vines of the Lubéron (*see pp506–7*).

WATER SPORTS

Whitewater rafting, kayaking, and canoeing all take place on many French rivers, especially in the Massif Central. More information on these sports and the best places to take part can be obtained from the **Fédération Française de Canoë-Kayak**.

The Atlantic coast around Biarritz (*see p452*) offers some of the best surfing and windsurfing in Europe. Excellent windsurfing can also be found in Brittany, with **Wissant** in particular being a big draw. A charming small fishing village, Wissant is considered a decent stop on any windsurf tour.

Surfers who prefer to do it without the sail head to **Hossegor** outside Biarritz (*see* *p452*) for fantastic waves. The surfing here is world-class and perhaps not ideal for beginners, but the after-surf scene is great fun for anyone who is more interested in lying on the beach or paddling at the shore than carving up the water.

Similarly the town of **Lacanau** (*see p424*) plays host to international surf competitions, drawing wave fans from all over the world.

Sailing and waterskiing are also very popular in France. Contact the **Fédération Française de Voile** for more details. Training schools and equipment rental are found at places along the coast and on lakes.

If cruising on a boat is your kind of thing, there are many outlets that can help. One of the swankier options is to take a **Sunsail** bareboat tour around the Côte d'Azur, although this option is only available to those who have reached a certain level of boatmanship. The company also offers a range of skippered tours around the beautiful coastline.

Swimming facilities throughout the country are generally good, although beaches in the South of France can become very crowded in high season (*see pp474–5*).

HUNTING & FISHING

Although hunting is a popular sport in France, a *permis de chasse* is required, for which there is a fee. You will need a copy of your own national hunting licence and to pass an exam in French, which makes it difficult for visitors. There are regional variations on the season, depending on the type of hunting. Since the hunting ban came into force in England, many French hunts have found English hunters a welcome boost to their numbers.

All kinds of fishing, for both fresh and seawater fish, are available, depending on the individual area. Local fishing stores sell the *carte de pêche*, which gives details of regulations.

NATURISM

There are nearly 90 naturism centers in France. These are mostly located in the south and southwest of the country, as well as in Corsica. Information in English can be obtained from French Government Tourist Offices (*see p669*), or from the **Fédération Française de Naturisme**.

PUBLIC EVENTS

To join the French as they enjoy their spare time, look out for local soccer and rugby games, bike races, or other sporting events suited to spectators.

Special seasonal markets and local *fêtes* often combine antiques fairs and *boules* tournaments with rock and pop concerts, making an enjoyable day out.

SPA VACATIONS

France is renowned for its sea-water based thalasso-therapy spa techniques, with many centers, salons, and hotels offering "thalasso" treatments. The seaside towns and resorts seem to be the most logical place to head for ocean-based treatments, and not surprisingly there are some excellent spots dotted around the coastline.

Chic seaside town Deauville (*see p255*) plays host to upscale spa seekers in the **Algotherm Thalassotherapy Spa**. Similarly the **Sofitel Thalassa** in Quiberon (*see p278*) offers top-class water therapy. More water therapy can be found near the springs at Vichy (*see pp358–9*) at the **Les Celestins** spa and at the **Evian Royal Resort** (*see p391*).

Wine in France is considered to be almost as important as water, so it is not surprising that a spa specializing in "vinotherapy" or wine therapy has hordes of loyal fans. Head to **Les Sources de Caudalie** spa among the vines near Bordeaux and indulge in a vinosource grape facial and cabernet scrub.

If big name treatments are your thing, you should head to **Le Mas Candille** which

hosts the first Shiseido spa in continental Europe. The products used are as exceptional as one would expect from such a swanky brand, and the techniques are Oriental-based.

Finally, if a thoroughly indulgent approach to a spa session is your idea of vacation heaven, then splurge at the new **Four Seasons Terre Blanche** in Provence. The half-day retreat of total indulgence involves a salt and oil scrub, an aromatherapy massage, an acupressure facial, and an Oriental head massage. If you want to go *à la carte*, you can choose from a wide range of delights such as an eye-lifting facial, a body-toning massage, or an Oshadi clay wrap.

If you can't escape from the city, the Valmont spa at the **Hotel Meurice** and **Four Seasons** spa at the George V can provide the ultimate escape and spa break right in the center of Paris.

YOGA

The beautiful countryside in France provides the perfect backdrop for a restorative yoga retreat vacation. The **Manolaya Yoga Centre** offers relaxing and fun hatha yoga vacations throughout Provence and its Avignon-based center. For the more dynamic style of ashtanga yoga, try **The Shala** retreats held in the beautiful foothills of the Cevennes.

Another excellent option is a break at the **Domaine de la Grausse** in the foothills of the Pyrénees, where walking and visiting local waterfalls, chateaux, medieval villages, and even taking in some cave paintings are all on the agenda. Those with any energy left over can take advantage of options to go mountain biking, riding, playing golf, and fishing.

Beginners and experienced yoga fans alike are welcome at the **Europe Yoga Centre**, which specializes in hatha and also astanga yoga. Both individual retreats and group vacations can be arranged at the center.

GOURMET

For gourmets looking to learn how to recreate some of the stunning meals enjoyed in French restaurants, or wine buffs seeking to increase their knowledge and cellar at the same time, there are many excellent options. The sheer number of cooking classes available throughout the country may seem over-whelming, so the first step in choosing an activity vacation of this kind is to consider your initial skill level and what you wish to achieve from the break. From die-hard kitchen disasters to budding restaurateurs, there is a gourmet break in France that will suit.

Two options for beginner chefs are the "cookery holiday" from **Cook in France**, which emphasizes fun rather than serious hard work in the kitchen, and Rosa Jackson's cooking school, **Les Petits Farcis**, in Nice (see pp526–7), where she guides food-lovers around the town's glorious fresh produce stalls explaining how to spot the best melon, or how to cook the intimidating artichoke. The Cook in France team offers many specialized courses (such as matching wine to food) alongside their standard culinary classes, while Rosa Jackson's cooking school offers the opportunity to rustle up a menu based on whatever looks great in the market on that particular day.

Budding culinary stars might want to head to Alain Ducasse's **Ecole de Cuisine** in Paris, which organizes both cooking and wine courses. It offers day and evening courses, held in an ultra-modern, professionally equipped kitchen. Also in Paris is the **Ecole Ritz Escoffier**, which holds workshops for both adults and children, at the Ritz Hotel. Lessons last from an hour to half a day, and cover themes such as chocolate or making the perfect pastry.

Oenophiles, on the other hand, might like to join with the **French Wine Explorers** who offer tours around vineyards. Alternatively, arranging wine classes via the French tourist office can be an excellent idea. **Wine Travel Guides** has an informative website for independent travelers, listing vineyards that are recommended by regional wine experts.

ARTS AND CRAFTS

France is a top choice for creative people looking to get away from it all and to express themselves in beautiful surroundings. Whether your preferred method of expression is scribbling in a notebook by yourself on the banks of a river, or perfecting your pastel technique in an art master class, there is an outlet for you somewhere in France.

Mas Saurine offers residential and non-residential painting vacations in the Pyrenees, 30 minutes from Perpignan. Small group classes, geared to different levels of ability, are taught in an old stone barn by exhibiting artists.

Courses in stone and bronze sculpture are on offer in Normandy, near Honfleur, with experienced sculptor **Sally Hersh**. Some of the artist's pieces are also available for purchase.

Those with a passion for seeing life through a lens are well catered for with photography courses with **Graham and Belinda Berry** at their farmhouse in Lot, southwest France. Courses suitable for all ages and abilities are offered here.

DIRECTORY

SPECIALIST VACATIONS

French Institute
17 Queensberry Place, London SW7 2DT United Kingdom.
Tel 020 7073 1350.
www.institut-francais.org.uk

Union REMPART
1 rue des Guillemites, 75004 Paris.
Tel 01 42 71 96 55.
www.rempart.com

GOLF

American Golf Academy
Tel 06 81 54 96 42.
www.american-golf-academy.com

Fédération Française de Golf
68 rue Anatole France, 92300 Levallois Perret.
Tel 01 41 49 77 00.
www.ffgolf.org

Golf Hotel Grenoble Charmeil
38210 Saint Quentin sur Isère. **Tel** 04 76 93 67 28. www.golfhotel grenoble.com

Hotel de Mougins
205 av du Golf, 06250 Mougins. **Tel** 04 92 92 17 07. www.hotel-de-mougins.com

Hotel Royal and Evian Masters
South Shore Lake Geneva, 74500 Evian. **Tel** 04 50 26 85 00. www.evian royalresort.com

St-Malo Golf and Country Club
Domaine de St-Yvieux 35540 Le Tronchet.
Tel 02 99 58 96 69.
www.saintmalogolf.com

HIKING

Fédération Française de Randonnée Pédestre
64 rue du Dessous des Berges, 75013 Paris.
Tel 01 44 89 93 90.
www.ffrandonnee.fr

BICYCLING

CTC
Parklands, Railton Rd, Guildford, Surrey GU2 9JX United Kingdom.
Tel 0844 736 8450.
www.ctc.org.uk

Duvine Adventures
www.duvine.com

Fédération Française de Cyclisme
5 rue de Rome, 93561 Rosny-sous-Bois.
www.ffc.fr

Velo Echappe
www.veloechappe.com

Voies Vertes
www.voiesvertes.com

HORSE RIDING

A La Carte Sportive
www.carte-sportive.com
www.iowners.net

Cheval et Châteaux
www.cheval-et-chateaux.com

Ride in France
www.rideinfrance.com

DIRECTORY

MOUNTAIN SPORTS

Féderation Française de la Montagne et de l'Escalade
8–10 quai de la Marne, 75019 Paris.
Tel 01 40 18 75 50.
www.ffme.fr

SKIING

For information on the different resorts, visit the following websites:

www.flaine.com
www.laclusaz.com
www.megeve.com
www.les3vallees.com
www.courchevel.com
www.meribel.net
www.valthorens.com
www.lesmenuires.com

AERONAUTICAL SPORTS

Ballon de Paris
Parc André-Citroën
75015 Paris.
Tel 01 44 26 20 00.
www.ballondeparis.com

Fédération Française de Vol Libre
4 rue de Suisse,
06000 Nice.
Tel 04 97 03 82 82.
www.federation.ffvl.fr

Fédération Nationale Aéronautique
155 av Wagram,
75017 Paris.
Tel 01 44 29 92 00.
www.ff-aero.fr

France Balloons
Tel 08 10 60 01 53.
www.franceballoons.com

Hot Air Balloon Provence
www.montgolfiere-provence-ballooning.com

WATER SPORTS

Fédération Française de Canoë-Kayak
87 quai de la Marne,
94340 Joinville-le-Pont.
Tel 01 45 11 08 50.
www.ffck.org

Fédération Française de Voile
17 rue Henri Bocquillon,
75015 Paris.
Tel 01 40 60 37 00.
www.ffvoile.fr

Hossegor Tourist Office
Pl des Halles – B.P. 6
40150 Hossegor.
Tel 05 58 41 79 00.
www.hossegor.fr

Lacanau Tourist Office
Pl de l'Europe
33680 Lacanau.
Tel 05 56 03 21 01.
www.medococean.com

Sunsail
www.sunsail.com

Wissant Tourist Office
Pl de la Mairie
62179 Wissant.
Tel 08 20 20 76 00.
www.ville-wissant.fr

NATURISM

Fédération Française de Naturisme
www.ffn-naturisme.com

SPA VACATIONS

Algotherm
10 rue Alexander Fleming
14200 Herouville-Saint-Clair.
Tel 02 31 06 16 26.
www.algotherm.fr

Les Celestins Vichy
111 bd des Etats-Unis
03200 Vichy.
Tel 04 70 30 82 00.
www.vichy-spa-hotel.fr

Evian Royal Resort
Rive Sud du Lac de Génève,
74501 Evian-les-Bains.
Tel 04 50 26 85 00.
www.evianroyal
resort.com

Four Seasons Provence
Domaine de Terre Blanche 83440
Tourrettes Var.
Tel 04 94 39 90 00.
www.fourseasons.com

Hotel Four Seasons George V
31 av George V,
75008 Paris.
Tel 01 49 52 70 00.
www.fourseasons.com

Hotel Meurice
228 rue de Rivoli
75001 Paris.
Tel 01 44 58 10 10.
www.lemeurice.com

Le Mas Candille
Bd Clément Rebuffel
06250 Mougins.
Tel 04 92 28 43 43.
www.lemascandille.com

Sofitel Thalassa Quiberon
Pointe de Goulvars
BP 10802 Quiberon Cedex
56178 Quiberon.
Tel 02 97 50 20 00.
www.thalassa.com

Les Sources de Caudalie
Chemin de Smith Haut Lafitte
33650 Bordeaux–Martillac.
Tel 05 57 83 83 83.
www.sources-caudalie.com

YOGA

Domaine de la Grausse
09420 Clermont la Grausse, Ariège.
Tel 05 61 66 30 53.
www.yoga-in-france.com

Europe Yoga Centre
46800 St Matre Lot.
Tel 05 65 21 76 20.
www.europeyoga.com

Manolaya Yoga Centre
FFPY 39 rue de la Bonneterie, 84000 Avignon.
Tel 04 90 82 10 52.
www.manolaya.org

The Shala
Les Pauses, St André de Majencoules,
Gard 30570.
www.theshala.co.uk

GOURMET

Cook in France
Tel 05 53 30 24 05.
www.cookinfrance.com

Ecole de Cuisine
64 rue du Ranelagh,
75016 Paris.
Tel 01 44 90 91 00.
www.ecolecuisine-alainducasse.com

Ecole Ritz Escoffier
Tel 01 44 16 30 50.
www.ritzescoffier.com

French Wine Explorers
www.wine-tours-france.com

Les Petits Farcis
7 rue du Jésus
06300 Nice.
Tel 06 81 67 41 22.
www.petitsfarcis.com

Wine Travel Guides
www.winetravel
guides.com

ARTS AND CRAFTS

Graham and Belinda Berry
46800 Montcuq.
Tel 05 65 31 49 72.
www.imagefrance.co.uk

Mas Saurine
Comi de l'Estrada,
66320 Joch.
Tel 04 68 05 85 66.
http://mas-saurine.com

Sally Hersh
Tel 01798 861 2480 (UK).
www.sallyhersh.com

SURVIVAL
GUIDE

PRACTICAL INFORMATION

France is justifiably proud of its many attractions, for which it has excellent tourist information facilities. Both in France and abroad, French government tourist offices are an invaluable source of reference for practical aspects of your stay. Most towns and large villages have a tourist information office; the relevant address, telephone

FNOTSI
Tourist information logo

number, and website (if available) are provided for each town and area listed in this guide. Domestic tourism in France creates peak vacation migration periods, especially between July 14 and August 31. Consequently, the hotel and restaurant trades are seasonal. A little forward planning will allow you to avoid the pitfalls of seasonal closure.

VISAS AND PASSPORTS

Citizens of EU countries, apart from the UK and Ireland, can enter France with a national identity card. Visitors from the UK, Ireland, the US, Canada, Australia, and New Zealand need a full passport. Tourist trips may last up to 3 months, after this a *carte de séjour* (residency permit) is required. Like most EU countries (but not the UK and Ireland) France is part of the Schengen agreement for shared border controls. If you enter the Schengen area through a member country, you are free to cross into all member countries within your 90-day stay.

Non-EU nationals who wish to work or study in France, or stay longer than three months, should obtain a visa from a French consulate in their home country. For more information, check the website of your French embassy and your own country's state department.

CUSTOMS INFORMATION

EU residents are allowed to carry any amount of goods between EU countries without paying customs duties, as long as the goods are for personal use. Among the limits generally accepted as being for personal use are 800 cigarettes, 90 liters of wine, and 110 liters of beer.

Visitors from outside the EU can reclaim sales tax *(TVA)* on many French goods if more than €175 is spent in one store in one day. To claim the tax back you must get a *détaxe* form from the store and take your goods out of the EU within three months. Present the receipt at customs when

leaving the country, and mail the stamped receipt as instructed. The refund will then be sent to you or credited to your bank card. There are *détaxe* desks at all main airports and in big stores. Full information is available from **Direction Générale des Douanes**.

Office de Tourisme in the Vence region of France

TOURIST INFORMATION

All cities, towns, and many villages have *offices de tourisme*, which provide invaluable free maps and information on local attractions and accommodations. Tourist offices often produce useful guides covering walking and bike routes, bike rental, local gastronomy, traditional farm produce, and more. Some regional and *département* offices also offer well-priced hotel and tour packages, and many city offices have organized imaginative guided tours and themed routes.

Before traveling to France, you can get basic orientation information and advice from France's official tourist website

FranceGuide or from the French government tourist office (usually called **Atout France**) in your country. For in-depth regional planning it is best to use the websites of the relevant Regional Tourist Boards *(Comité Régional du Tourisme)* or those of the many *départements (Comités Départementaux du Tourisme)*. The latter provide a valuable range of detailed information. Nearly all websites are available in English. Links to these sites can be found on the FranceGuide website.

ADMISSION CHARGES

Most museums and monuments in France charge an entry fee, usually from €2 to €10. There are often family discounts, and those under 26 years old with an EU passport have free access to permanent exhibitions at state-owned sights.

Several multi-entry discount plans are available that reduce costs if you plan to visit a number of sights. Foremost, the Paris Museum Pass gives unlimited entry to over 60 museums and monuments in and around Paris, for either 2, 4, or 6 days. It can be bought in advance online (www. parismuseumpass.com). Other places have local plans, which often include unlimited use of local transportation. Check local tourism websites to see what is available.

Sign to monument of cultural importance

◁ Menton, Côte d'Azur with backdrop of the Alps

The Arc de Triomphe du Carrousel and the Musée du Louvre in Paris

OPENING HOURS

This guide lists which days of the week sights are open. National museums and sights normally close on Tuesdays, with a few exceptions that close on Mondays. Generally, the larger museums and sights are open from 9 or 10am–6pm, sometimes with one late evening a week, often Thursday. Note that smaller museums and churches may close from 12:30–2pm.

Opening times can also vary considerably by season, especially for country châteaux, estates, and gardens. Many are open daily in the peak July to August vacation season and then close completely from November to March, or are only open on weekends. Most sights are closed on Christmas and New Year's day.

See page 652 for details on opening hours for stores; page 674 for banks; and pages 596–7 for restaurants.

TAXES AND TIPPING

A service charge of 12.5 to 15 percent is included on all restaurant checks and it is customary to round up the check by a few euros in a restaurant, or a few cents in a café, especially if the service has been good. In grander restaurants, an extra tip of 5–10 percent is the norm.

For taxi drivers, the usual tipping rate is around 10 percent. For hotel porters, it is common to tip around 75 cents to €1.

TRAVELERS WITH SPECIAL NEEDS

France is working hard to improve access to all its services. There are disabled parking spaces in many streets and all public parking lots. These can be used free of charge with a European Blue Badge. SNCF (French railways) has introduced the *Accès Plus* plan, through which wheelchair users and others with mobility problems can reserve ahead to guarantee a space and free assistance. For information go to the "Everyday Life" (*Vie Pratique*) section on the SNCF website and look under *Services* + (*see p682*).

In Paris, some buses, some RER lines, and one Métro line (no. 14) are wheelchair accessible (*see pp688–9*). By law, all taxis must carry wheelchair users for no extra charge (*see p688*).

Much has been done to improve access to attractions, but access to smaller historic houses and country châteaux can be difficult at times. The blue *Tourisme & Handicap* label indicates attractions, hotels, restaurants, and other facilities that meet full disabled access criteria. Many hotels and *chambres-d'hôtes* (bed and breakfasts) have adapted rooms, and major reservation agencies such as *Logis de France* or *Gîtes de France* indicate this on their websites.

For information on disabled facilities in France, the best resource is the **Association des Paralysés de France** (*APF*),

which produces an annual *Guide Vacances* vacation booklet. The **Infomobi** website also has comprehensive information on transportation services for the disabled in and around Paris. Both these resources are in French only. Further information in English can be found on the FranceGuide website.

TRAVELING WITH CHILDREN

Families traveling in France benefit from a range of cost-cutting discounts including reduced or free admission to attractions for children. Children under 4 travel free on most public transportation and children aged 4 to 11 (4 to 9, in Paris) travel half price.

Some of the big French hotel chains (notably Novotel) specialize in catering for families, while many small country hotels and *chambres-d'hôtes* have cost-efficient family rooms (*chambres familiales*). If you base yourself in one area for two days or more, a self-contained *gîte*, with several rooms and a kitchen, can offer exceptional value for money (*see pp548–9*).

Virtually all French restaurants welcome children, and many have a children's menu (*menu d'enfants*) for €5–€8.

The FranceGuide website has information on attractions throughout France, while local tourism websites list regional-specific family attractions and activities. For more ideas, consult websites such as **France for Families** and **Kids in Tow**.

The Château de Versailles has excellent disabled access

SENIOR TRAVELERS

Senior visitors to France do not enjoy reduced admission fees at national museums and monuments although some privately-owned châteaux and attractions do offer lower prices for older people. Discounted travel on public transport is only available with multi-journey passes issued by some cities, and the SNCF *Carte Senior* for the over 60s *(see p682)*. However, these cards are not much use for short visits, as you'll only notice the discount if you make several journeys on each system. Railpasses (see p682) bought in advance outside France can be better value.

STUDENT INFORMATION

Students aged under 26 with a valid **International Student Identity Card** (ISIC) benefit from many discounts, as well as those available to everyone in France aged 25 or under. The Centre d'Information et de Documentation Jeunesse will provide you with further information (www.cidj.com).

GAY AND LESBIAN TRAVELLERS

France has prominent gay and lesbian communities that are becoming ever more part of the cultural mainstream. The Marais district of Paris is the country's foremost "gay village," but there are gay clubs and services all over the capital. There are gay communities in many other cities, especially in Toulouse, Nantes, Montpellier, and Nice. Tune into Radio FG (98.2 MHz) or consult listings in *Têtu* and *Lesbia* magazines for a wide range of gay-friendly information. For further help, contact **Centre Gai et Lesbien** in Paris.

TRAVELING ON A BUDGET

How much you spend on a holiday in France will vary enormously depending on what you do. However, in general, two people staying at a basic hotel (an average of €60 for a double room), eating both lunch and dinner in restaurants, visiting a few attractions, and using public transit can roughly expect to spend €160 per day in most parts of France, or €80 each.

Staying in Paris, the Côte d'Azur, and other fashionable resorts is expensive but less-visited rural regions such as Normandy, inland Brittany, and Lorraine can be more affordable. Traveling in peak season (July–mid-September) will also be costly with high

International Student Identity Card

hotel rates, particularly in the most popular regions. December and March, the winter sports season, can also be pricey, particularly in the Alps. If you want to keep costs down it is best to travel during the low season when hotel prices are much cheaper. City hotels, however, can be more reasonable between July and August when most French people head for the country.

Staying in a *chambre-d'hôtes* (bed and breakfast) is a good alternative to costly hotels. Traditionally, these are located in the countryside but they are now popping up in towns and the average price for a comfortable double room is around €40 including breakfast. Another option is a *gîte*, which offers cooking facilities, though these usually require a minimum stay of a weekend or a week.

When dining, opt for a set menu – ordering from the à la carte menu will be far more expensive. Eating your main

Waiting to travel at Marseille Gare St-Charles train station

meal at lunchtime rather than in the evening will mean you can make the most of the best-value set menus or *formules*. To keep costs down when sightseeing, opt for a City Pass that gives unlimited travel on local transportation as well as entry to local monu-ments *(see p689)*. If you intend to rent a car, book it in advance through an Internet rental agency to get the best rates.

FRENCH TIME

France is one hour ahead of Greenwich Mean Time (GMT) in both winter and summer.

ELECTRICAL ADAPTORS

The voltage in France is 220 volts. Plugs are the standard

Queueing for the Eiffel Tower

type used in most of Europe with two round pins, or three for applications that need to be grounded. Many hotels offer built-in adaptors for shavers.

CONVERSION CHART

Imperial to metric
1 inch = 2.54 centimeters
1 foot = 30 centimeters
1 mile = 1.6 kilometers
1 ounce = 28 grams
1 pound = 454 grams
1 pint = 0.6 liter
1 gallon = 4.6 liters

Metric to imperial
1 millimeter = 0.04 inch
1 centimeter = 0.4 inch
1 meter = 3 feet 3 inches
1 kilometer = 0.6 mile
1 gram = 0.04 ounce
1 kilogram = 2.2 pounds
1 liter = 1.8 pints

RESPONSIBLE TRAVEL

In France, as in many other countries, there has been a rapid growth in environmental awareness. **Echoway** is one of the leading French ecotourism organizations, encouraging heightened awareness of responsible travel. **Mountain**

Riders promotes sustainable winter tourism in the Alps, providing information on how to get to the mountains via public transit and arranging group walks to clean up mountain pistes each spring.

France has a long-running rural tourism network, with farmhouse accommodation available through the central Gîtes de France agency *(see p549)*. There are also smaller organizations with a more defined ecological stance such as **Accueil Paysan**, which is a network of small-scale farmers practicing low-impact, sustainable agriculture. Another alternative to staying in a hotel is camping, and there are over 9,000 fully-equipped campsites across the country to choose from *(see p548)*.

Information on local green tourism *(tourisme vert* or *eco)* initiatives and activities can be found through local tourist offices. Many towns have weekly markets selling only organic and traditional produce (usually called a *marché bio*), which allow visitors to give back to the local community. Market days have been provided throughout the guide.

DIRECTORY

EMBASSIES

Australia
4 Rue Jean Rey, 75015 Paris. **Map** 6 D3. **Tel** 01 40 59 33 06. **www.** france.embassy.gov.au

Canada
35 Ave Montaigne, 75008 Paris. **Map** 6 F1.
Tel 01 44 43 29 00.
www.canadainternational.
gc.ca

United Kingdom
35 Rue du Faubourg St-Honoré, 75383 Paris.
Map 3 C5.
Tel 01 44 51 31 00.
http://ukinfrance.fco.
gov.uk/fr

United States
2 Ave Gabriel, 75008 Paris. **Map** 3 A5.
Tel 01 43 12 22 22.
http://france.
usembassy.gov

FRENCH TOURIST OFFICES

Australia
Level 13, 25 Bligh St, Sydney NSW 2000.
Tel (2) 9231 52 44.
www.au.franceguide.com

Paris Convention and Visitors Bureau
25 Rue des Pyramides, 75001 Paris.
Tel 01 49 52 42 63.
www.parisinfo.com

United Kingdom
Lincoln House, 300 High Holborn, London WC1V 7JH. **Tel** 0906 824 4123.
www.uk.franceguide.com

United States
444 Madison Ave, New York, NY 10022.
Tel (1) 212 838 7800.
www.us.franceguide.com

CUSTOMS INFORMATION

Direction Générales des Douanes
Tel 08 11 20 44 44.
www.douane.gouv.fr

GAY AND LESBIAN TRAVELERS

Centre Gai et Lesbien
63 Rue Beaubourg, 75003 Paris.
Tel 01 43 57 21 47.

SPECIAL NEEDS

APF
www.apf.asso.fr

Infomobi
www.infomobi.com

Tourisme & Handicaps
www.tourisme-
handicaps.org

FAMILIES AND STUDENTS

France for Families
www.france4families.com

International Student Identity Card (ISIC)
www.isic.org
www.isiccard.com

Kids in Tow
www.kidsintow.co.uk

RESPONSIBLE TRAVEL

Accueil Paysan
Tel 04 76 43 44 83.
www.accueil-paysan.com

Echoway
www.echoway.org

FranceGuide
www.franceguide.com

Mountain Riders
www.mountain-
riders.org

Personal Security and Health

On the whole France is a safe place for visitors, but it is always a good idea to take the normal precautions of looking after your possessions and avoiding unfamiliar or unfrequented residential urban areas after dark. If you become sick during your stay, pharmacies generally offer good advice while the emergency services can be contacted for any serious medical problems. Consulates and consular departments *(see p671)* at your embassy can also provide assistance in an emergency.

French pharmacy sign

Gendarmes

POLICE

Violent crime is not a major problem in France, but as in any country it is advisable to be on your guard against petty theft, especially in cities. If you are robbed, lose any property, or are the victim of any other type of crime, report the incident as soon as possible at the nearest *commissariat de police* (police station). In an emergency, dialing 17 will also connect you to the police department, but you will still have to go to a station to make a statement. In small towns and villages, crime is reported to the *gendarmerie*, the force mainly responsible for rural policing. The *mairie* (town hall) is also a good place to go for help but this will only be open during office hours.

At all police stations you will be required to make a statement, called a *PV* or *procès verbal*, listing any lost or stolen items. You will need your passport, and, if relevant, your vehicle papers. It is important to keep a copy of your police statement for your insurance claim.

LOST AND STOLEN PROPERTY

The likelihood, and impact, of street theft can be considerably reduced by a few simple precautions. In the first instance, make sure that all possessions are covered by a comprehensive travel insurance policy before arrival. Once in France, avoid risky city neighborhoods, and beware of pickpockets, especially on the Paris Métro during rush hour (particularly just as the car doors are closing). When you sit at a sidewalk café table, always keep your bag within reach and in sight, preferably on your lap or on the table, and never leave it on the ground or hanging on the back of a chair. Keep bags zipped up and held close to you when walking along, and never leave luggage unattended at train stations or other travel centers. Keep valuables securely concealed and only carry with you as much cash as you think you will need for the day.

For lost or stolen property, it may be worth returning to the station where you reported the incident to check if the police have retrieved some of the items. In addition, all French town halls have a *Bureau d'Objets Trouvés* (lost property office), although they are often inefficient and finding items can take time. Lost property offices can also be found at larger train stations, which will be open during office hours.

If your passport is lost or stolen, notify your consulate immediately *(see p671)*. The loss of credit or debit cards should also be reported as soon as possible to your bank to avoid fraudulent use.

TRAVEL INSURANCE

All travelers in France should have a comprehensive travel insurance policy providing adequate cover for any eventuality, including potential medical and legal expenses, theft, lost luggage and other personal property, accidents, travel delays, and the option of immediate repatriation by air in the event of a major medical emergency. Winter sports are not covered by standard travel policies so if you are planning to ski or to undertake any other adventure sports in France you will need to pay an additional premium to make sure you are protected. All insurance policies should come with a 24-hour emergency number.

IN AN EMERGENCY

The phone number for all emergency services is 112, but in practice it is often quicker to call the relevant authority direct on their traditional two-digit numbers. In a medical emergency call the **Service d'Aide Médicale Urgence** (SAMU), who will send an ambulance. However, it can sometimes be faster to call

DIRECTORY

EMERGENCY NUMBERS

All Emergency Services
Tel 112.

Ambulance (SAMU)
Tel 15.

Fire (Sapeurs Pompiers)
Tel 18.

Police and Gendarmerie
Tel 17.

the **Sapeurs Pompiers** (fire service) who also offer first aid and can take you to the nearest hospital. This is particularly true in rural areas, where the fire station is likely to be much closer than the ambulance service based in town. The paramedics are called *secouristes*.

HOSPITALS AND PHARMACIES

All European Union nationals holding a European Health Insurance Card (EHIC) are entitled to use the French national health service. However, under the French system patients must pay for all treatments and then reclaim most of the cost from the health authorities. Therefore, non-French EU nationals who use health services in France will need to insure they keep the statement of costs (*feuille de soins*) that is provided by the doctor or hospital. This should include stickers for any prescription drugs, which must be stuck onto the statement by the pharmacist once you have made your purchase. Around 80 percent of the cost can be claimed back by following the instructions provided with your EHIC card. This can be a time-consuming process, and it can often be simpler to use private travel insurance. Non-EU nationals must have full private medical insurance while in France and pay for services in the same way, claiming their costs back in full from their insurance company.

Well-equipped public hospitals can be found throughout France. In all towns and cities there are hospitals with emergency departments (called *urgences* or *service des urgences*) that can deal with immediate medical problems. If your hotel cannot direct you to one, call the SAMU or fire service. Should you require an English-speaking doctor, your consulate should be able to recommend one in the area, and in Paris and some other cities in France, there are both American and British private hospitals.

Pharmacies, identified by an illuminated green cross sign, are plentiful and easy to find. French pharmacists are highly trained and can diagnose minor health problems and suggest appropriate treatments. When one is closed, a card in the window will give details of the nearest *pharmacie de garde* that is open on Sundays or during the night.

NATURAL HAZARDS

Forest fires are a major risk in many parts of France. High winds can mean fires spread rapidly in winter as well as in summer, so be vigilant about putting out all campfires and cigarette butts. Keep well away from any area where there is a fire, since its direction can change quickly.

Before exploring any of the country's seven national parks or its regional nature parks (*parcs naturels*), visit the relevant park information center to check the regulations and recommendations that apply within the area, and take care to observe them. When walking in mountains or sailing, inform the relevant authority – such as a park information center or a harbormaster – of your intended route and when you expect to return. Never try to walk in

Police car

Fire engine

Ambulance

remote mountain areas or across tidal marshes without an experienced guide, or against local advice.

During the hunting season (Sep–Feb and especially Sundays) dress in visible colors when out walking and avoid areas where hunters are staked out in hides (*see p663*).

SAFETY ON BEACHES

There are many good family beaches throughout France where bathing is rarely dangerous. Many beaches are guarded in summer by lifeguards (*sauveteurs*) – always heed their instructions and only swim in supervised areas. Also look out for the system of colored flags, indicating whether it is safe to swim. Green flags mean bathing is safe; orange flags warn that bathing may be dangerous and that only the part of the beach marked out by flags is guarded. Swimming outside this area is therefore not recommended. Red flags indicate dangerous conditions (high waves, shifting sands, strong undercurrents), so all bathing is forbidden. Many beaches also display blue flags, which are used throughout the European Union as a sign of cleanliness.

Fire hazard poster

Banking and Local Currency

You may bring any amount of currency into France, but anything over €7,500 (cash and checks) must be declared on arrival. The same applies when you leave. Travelers' checks are the safest way to carry money abroad, but credit or debit cards, which can be used to withdraw local currency, are by far the most convenient. Exchange bureaus are located at airports, large train stations, and in some hotels and stores, although banks usually offer the best rates of exchange.

ATM in Paris

USING BANKS

Most banks will exchange foreign currency and travelers' checks, but the commission rates vary, so it is worth looking around to make sure you get the best deal. Virtually all bank branches have ATMs (automatic teller machines), which accept major credit and debit cards. Most ATMs can give instructions in English.

Travelers' checks can be obtained from **American Express** (AmEx), **Travelex**, or your bank. American Express checks are widely accepted and no commission is charged if they are exchanged at their offices. In the case of theft, checks are replaced at once.

BANKING HOURS

In Paris, and many other cities, banks are generally open from 9 or 10am–5pm Mon–Fri, with some branches open on Saturdays. Elsewhere banks are usually closed on Mondays and generally open from 8 or 9am–12:30pm and 2–5pm Tue–Fri and 8 or 9am–12:30pm on Saturday. There are, however, many variations between banks, and individual

Credit card readers require you to enter your PIN

branches. All banks close on Sundays and public holidays, and many also close at noon on the working day before the holiday.

EXCHANGE BUREAUS

Outside Paris, independent exchange bureaus are rare except in major train stations and high-density tourist areas. Privately owned exchange bureaus can have variable rates: check commission and minimum charges first.

CREDIT AND DEBIT CARDS

Major credit cards such as **Visa** or **MasterCard** and debit cards such as Switch, Maestro, or Cirrus are widely used, and are essential for most large transactions such as renting a car. Many French businesses do not accept American Express credit cards.

French credit and debit cards operate on a chip-and-PIN system so you will need to know your PIN (code personnel). If you have a North American card that does not use chip-and-PIN technology, you must ask that your card be swiped.

Given the high commission rates often charged for exchanging travelers' checks, the most economical and convenient way to get local currency is just to withdraw it from an ATM with a debit card. Bear in mind, however, that ATMs may run out of bills during weekends. If an ATM is not working, you can also withdraw up to €300 per day on major credit cards at the foreign counter of a bank. The bank may need to obtain telephone authorization for such withdrawals first.

THE EURO

France was one of the twelve countries taking the euro (€) in 2002, with the original currency, the franc, phased out on the February 17, 2002.

EU members using the euro as sole official currency are known as the Eurozone. Several EU members have either opted out or have not met the conditions for adopting the single currency.

Euro bills are identical throughout the Eurozone countries, each one including designs of fictional monuments and architectural structures, and the 12 stars of the EU. The coins, however, have one side identical (the value side), and one side with an image unique to each country. Both bills and coins are exchangeable in any of the participating Euro countries.

Bank Bills

Euro bank bills have seven denominations. The €5 bill (gray in color) is the smallest, followed by the €10 bill (pink), €20 bill (blue), €50 bill (orange), €100 bill (green), €200 bill (yellow), and €500 bill (purple). All bills show the stars of the European Union.

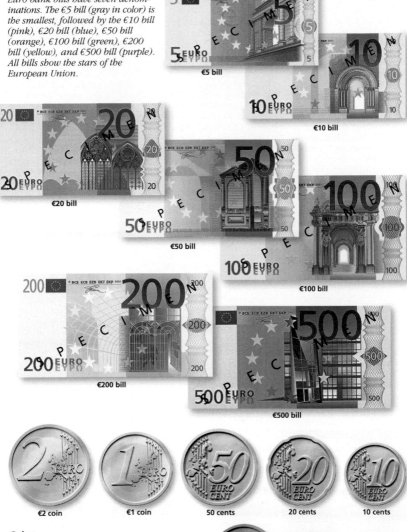

€5 bill

€10 bill

€20 bill

€50 bill

€100 bill

€200 bill

€500 bill

€2 coin

€1 coin

50 cents

20 cents

10 cents

Coins

The euro has eight coin denominations: €1 and €2; 50 cents, 20 cents, 10 cents, 5 cents, 2 cents, and 1 cent. The €2 and €1 coins are both silver and gold in color. The 50-, 20-, and 10-cent coins are gold. The 5-, 2-, and 1-cent coins are bronze.

5 cents

2 cents

1 cent

Communications and Media

French telecommunications are very efficient. Most landline telephones are provided by France Télécom, which also owns Orange, the international cell phone group. Public telephones can be found in most public places and usually require a phone card (*télécarte*). Post offices (*bureaux des postes*) are identified by the blue-on-yellow La Poste sign; the postal service was previously known as PTT and this is often still indicated on road signs. Foreign-language newspapers are available in most large towns, and some TV channels and radio stations broadcast foreign-language programs.

A distinctive yellow French mailbox

LOCAL AND INTERNATIONAL PHONE CALLS

All French telephone numbers have ten digits, and you must key in all the digits even if you are in the same area. In landline numbers the first two digits indicate the region: 01 is for Paris and the Ile de France; 02, the northwest; 03, the northeast; 04, the southeast; and 05, the southwest. French cell phone numbers begin with 06, and 08 indicates a special-rate number. All 0800 numbers are toll-free. For landline numbers, cheap rates operate on evenings, weekends, and public holidays. It is best to avoid making calls from hotels since most add hefty surcharges.

To call France from abroad, dial 00 33 and omit the initial zero from the 10-digit French number. You cannot call French 08 numbers from outside the country.

To call abroad from France, dial 00 and then the country code (Australia 61, USA and Canada 1, Irish Republic 353, New Zealand 64, and UK 44).

France Télécom public telephone

CELL PHONES

Cell phone coverage is generally good throughout France, although signals may be weak in some mountain areas. French cell phones use the European-standard 900 and 1900 MHz frequencies, so UK cell phones work if they have a roaming facility enabled. North American cell phones will only operate in France if they are tri- or quad-band. Check roaming charges with your service provider before traveling, since making and receiving calls can be expensive. Some companies offer "packages" for foreign calls.

If you expect to use your phone frequently it can be more economical to get a cheap pay-as-you-go French cell phone from one of the main local providers such as **Orange France**, **Bouygues Télécom**, or **SFR**. All three companies have stores in most towns. You can also insert a local SIM card into your own phone, but this will only work if your phone has not been blocked by your service provider.

PUBLIC TELEPHONES

Few pay phones (*cabine téléphonique*) now accept coins, so to use one you will need a phone card (*télécarte*). Sold in *tabacs*, post offices, train stations, and some newsstands, cards are available for 50 or 120 telephone units, and are simple to use. When you enter a phone box, the phone display will say "*Decrochez*," your signal to pick up the phone, followed

by "*Introduisez votre carte*," for you to insert your card. The display will then say "*Patientez SVP*," followed by "*Numérotez*," at which point you dial the number you wish to call. For local calls, one unit lasts up to six minutes. Don't forget to take your card with you when you finish the call.

Many phones also accept credit cards (with a PIN), and Travelex exchange bureaus (*see p674*) also sell an International Telephone Card that can be used in several countries and provides good value for money. There are still a few coin and token-operated pay phones left in some cafés. At some large train stations and post offices there are staffed telephone booths (*cabines*) where you pay after you have made your call. This can be a cheaper option when making long-distance calls.

INTERNET ACCESS

The Internet is widely used in France, but surprisingly, Internet cafés are a lot less common than in much of Europe. They are plentiful in Paris, and there are usually a few in most cities and resorts, but in small towns and rural areas, they can be hard to find. It is often much easier to get online if you travel with a laptop. In Paris there are free Wi-Fi hotspots in many Métro stations, public libraries, and other locations, and similar projects are being introduced in other major cities. Many hotels and even *chambres-d'hôtes* now offer Wi-Fi connections, but check that these are free. Most hotels use one of several subscription services such as Orange France and **Meteor**, with which you buy a certain amount of time-credit and are then given an access code. Any time-credit remaining can be used anywhere that uses the same service.

French Wi-Fi servers often use different frequencies from those in the UK and North America, so you may need to manually search for the network (for more details, see the Orange Wi-Fi website). If you need to use a cable connection, note that the French modem socket is incompatible with US and UK plugs. Adaptors are available, but it is often cheaper and easier to buy a French modem lead.

POSTAL SERVICES

The postal service in France is fast and usually reliable. There are post offices in most towns, and there are large main offices in all cities. Postage stamps *(timbres)* can be bought at post offices individually or in a *carnet* of seven or ten, although the most convenient place to buy stamps is often at a *tabac*, where phonecards can also be purchased.

Post offices usually open from 9am–5pm Mon–Fri, often with a break for lunch, and 9am–noon on Saturdays. Post offices in towns and cities are best avoided when they first open since this is when they are at their busiest.

Letters are mailed in yellow mailboxes that often have separate slots for mail within the town you are in, within the *département*, and for other destinations *(autres destinations)*. There are eight different price zones for international mail. Information on all mail services is provided on the **La Poste** website.

NEWSPAPERS AND MAGAZINES

Newspapers and magazines can be bought at newspaper stores *(maisons de la presse)* or newsstands *(kiosques)*. Regional newspapers tend to be more popular than the Paris-based national papers, such as the conservative *Le Figaro*, weighty *Le Monde*, or leftist *Libération*. The daily *International Herald Tribune* can be found throughout France. Other foreign papers are also often available on the day of publication in resorts and large cities.

The weekly listings magazines *Pariscope* (Thursday) and *L'Officiel des Spectacles* (Wednesday) give the latest on entertainment news in Paris. *Les Inrockuptibles* magazine has information on current music, movies, and the other arts from all over France. Many smaller cities have their own listings magazines, usually in French and often free, which can generally be found at tourist offices.

TV AND RADIO

All French television networks use Digital Video Broadcasting (DVB). There are 18 free channels, including the major national channels *TF1* and *France 2*. Canal Plus (or *Canal +*), a subscription-only channel, offers a broad mix of programs including live sports and movies in English with French subtitles. A film shown in its original language is listed as *VO (Version Originale)*; a film dubbed into French is indicated as *VF (Version Française)*. Most hotels subscribe to *Canal +,* and many also have cable and satellite TV, including English-language stations such as CNN, MTV, Sky, and BBC World.

It is easy to pick up UK radio stations in France, including *Radio 4* (198 long wave). *BBC World Service* broadcasts all night on the same wavelength. *Voice of America* can be found at 90.5, 98.8, and 102.4 FM. *Radio France International* (738 AM) gives daily news in English from 3–4pm.

Newspapers sold in France

DIRECTORY

TELEPHONE AND INTERNET SERVICE

Bouygues Télécom
Tel 1064 (from a landline).
www.bouyguestelecom.fr

Meteor
www.meteornetworks.com

Orange France
Tel 0810 555 421.
www.orange.fr
www.orange-wifi.com

SFR
Tel 1026 (from a landline phone in France).
www.sfr.fr

POST OFFICE

La Poste
www.laposte.fr

USEFUL TELEPHONE NUMBERS AND CODES

- **Directory information**
  118 712.
- **International directory information**
  118 700.
- **France Telecom/Orange**
  0800 36 47 75.
  0969 36 39 00 (in English).
- **Toll-free, reduced, and premium numbers**
  0800; 0810, 0820, 0825 (toll-free and reduced rate); 0890, 0891, 0892 (premium rate).
- **In case of emergencies**
  17.

La Poste road sign

TRAVEL INFORMATION

France enjoys sophisticated air, road, and rail travel. Direct flights from all over the world serve Paris and some regional airports. Paris is the hub of a vast internal rail network and of Europe's high-speed train network, with the Euro-star to London, Thalys to Brussels, and TGVs to Geneva and other destinations. Highways cross into all surrounding countries, including, via the Eurotunnel, the UK. France is also served by frequent Channel and Mediterranean ferries.

Getting to or from France on the national carrier, Air France

ARRIVING BY AIR

France is served by nearly all international airlines. Most long-haul flights arrive at Paris Charles de Gaulle airport, but there are flights from Europe and North Africa to many other airports around the country.

Airlines with regular flights between the UK and France include **British Airways**, **Air France**, and low-cost airlines such as **bmibaby**, **Flybe**, **Jet2**, **Ryanair**, and **easyJet**. From North America there are direct flights to Paris from about 20 cities, mainly on **Air Canada**, **American Airlines**, **Delta**, **United**, and Air France. **Qantas** provides connecting flights from Australia and New Zealand.

PARIS AIRPORTS

Paris' Charles-de-Gaulle airport (CDG), about 19 miles (30 km) from the city, is the main hub airport in France. Access to central Paris is by RER line B from CDG2, which takes 40 minutes to Gare du Nord and 45 minutes to Châtelet-Les Halles. Regular bus services run from the airport to different parts of Paris, and to Disney-land Paris theme park. Air France buses run to the Arc de Triomphe and western Paris,

and to Montparnasse; each journey takes about 45 minutes. RATP buses (Roissybus) depart every 20 minutes for L'Opéra and take about 50 minutes. Taxis into central Paris cost around €30–€45 and can take up to an hour.

Paris' other main airport, Orly, in the south of the city, serves mainly domestic and short-haul international flights. Shuttle buses link the airport with RER line C at Pont de Rungis and an automatic train, Orlyval, links the airport with RER line B at Antony, from where trains run to Châtelet-Les Halles in 35 minutes. Air France buses for central Paris depart every 30 minutes; RATP Orlybus runs to Denfert-Rochereau Métro; and the Jetbus connects Orly to Châtelet-Les Halles, departing every 15–20 minutes. Taxis take 25–45 minutes to the city center, and cost about €25.

ARRIVING BY SEA

Several regular ferry services operate between the UK and Ireland and France. Dover–Calais is the quickest route: **P&O Ferries** has up to 25 crossings daily, with a journey time of 90 minutes or less. **Seafrance** also offers several crossings a day. **Norfolkline** runs from Dover to Dunkerque in about two hours and has some of the lowest fares. Farther west, French operator **Transmanche Ferries/LD Lines** has crossings between Newhaven and Dieppe (about 4 hrs) and Portsmouth and Le Havre (8 hrs overnight). The biggest operator in the western Channel is **Brittany Ferries**, which sails from Portsmouth to Caen (7 hrs overnight), Poole to Cherbourg (6 hrs overnight), Portsmouth to St-Malo (10 hrs overnight), Plymouth to Roscoff (8 hrs overnight), and weekly between Cork and Roscoff (14 hrs). From April/May to September/October Brittany Ferries also runs high-speed services on the

Plying the Mediterranean with SNCM Ferryterranée

Poole–Cherbourg and Portsmouth–Cherbourg routes (4 hrs 30 mins). **Condor Ferries** sail from Portsmouth to Cherbourg in 5 hours (July–September only) and from Poole and Weymouth to St-Malo via Jersey or Guernsey (May–September only).

Irish Ferries runs between Rosslare and Cherbourg (17 hrs overnight), and to Roscoff (15 hrs 30 mins overnight) from mid-May to September. SNCM run ferries from a range of European ports *(see p683)*.

ARRIVING BY TRAIN

There are at least 20 **Eurostar** trains daily between London St. Pancras and the Gare du Nord in Paris. The journey via the Channel Tunnel takes 2 hrs 15 mins. Several trains also stop at Ebbsfleet or Ashford in Kent, Calais–Frethun, Lille (1 hr 30 mins from London), and Disneyland Paris.

Paris and its six main stations are the great hub of the French rail network. Traveling from Belgium, Holland, and north

EURO TUNNEL

Eurotunnel logo

Germany, you arrive at the Gare du Nord; from other parts of Germany you come into the Gare de l'Est. Trains from Switzerland and Italy arrive at the Gare de Lyons. From Spain you come into the Gare d'Austerlitz. Outside Paris, other major rail hubs include Lille, Tours, Bordeaux, and Lyon. For more information on French rail services and traveling to France by train *see pp680–82*.

ARRIVING BY ROAD

Passengers from the UK can travel to France with their vehicle either by ferry or on the **Eurotunnel** shuttle through the Channel Tunnel. Eurotunnel runs at least four trains an hour during the day, and the trip takes about 35 minutes. Fares compete with those of the ferry companies, and similarly vary by season, day, and time of travel. For Eurotunnel crossings, it is possible to turn up and wait for the next available space.

Long-distance bus travel is a good value alternative and

Eurolines runs three to five departures daily from Victoria Coach Station in London to Bagnolet in eastern Paris. Buses also run from London and other parts of the UK to Lille, Lyon, Marseille, and several other French towns and cities.

GREEN TRAVEL

Traveling in France without flying or driving is relatively easy thanks to the high quality of public transportation, particularly the SNCF rail network. There are daily train services from across Europe, ferries to the UK, Ireland, and Mediterranean destinations, and the Eurostar connection with London *(see pp680–85)*.

The French government has introduced an "Ecomobility" program, which aims to make it easier to transfer from trains to local buses, bicycles, or other non-car forms of transportation. This includes free-bicycle programs like the *Vélib'* now in use in Paris and other cities *(see p689)*. Many regions have also developed **Voies Vertes**, long-distance paths for biking or walking, such as the one along the Loire from Orléans to St-Nazaire.

DIRECTORY

AIRLINES

Air Canada
Tel 01 888 247 2262 (Canada),
0825 880 881 (France).
www.aircanada.com

Air France
Tel 0820 320 820 (France).
www.airfrance.com

American Airlines
Tel 01 800 433 7300 (USA), 0826 460 950 (France). www.aa.com

British Airways
Tel 0844 490 0787 (UK), 0825 825 400 (France).
www.britishairways.com

bmibaby
www.bmibaby.com

Delta
Tel 01 800 221 1212 (USA),
08 11 64 00 05 (France).
www.delta.com

easyJet
Tel 0871 244 2366 (UK), 0826 103 320 (France).
www.easyjet.com

Flybe
www.flybe.com

Jet2
Tel 0871 226 1737 (UK), 0821 230 203 (France).
www.jet2.com

Qantas
Tel 13 13 13 (Australia), 08 11 98 00 02 (France).
www.qantas.com

Ryanair
Tel 0871 246 000 (UK), 0892 780 270 (France).
www.ryanair.com

United
Tel 01 800 864 8331 (USA),
0810 72 72 72 (France).
www.united.com

FERRY SERVICES

Brittany Ferries
www.brittany-ferries.com

Condor Ferries
www.condorferries.co.uk

Irish Ferries
www.irishferries.com

Norfolkline
www.norfolkline.com

P&O Ferries
www.poferries.com

Seafrance
www.seafrance.com

Transmanche Ferries/LD Lines
www.transmanche
ferries.com

RAIL TRAVEL

See also *p682*

Eurostar
Tel 08705 186 186 (UK), 0892 35 35 39 (France).
www.eurostar.com

ROAD TRAVEL

Eurolines
Tel 0871 781 8181 (UK), 0892 899 091 (France).
www.eurolines.com

Eurotunnel
Tel 08705 35 35 35 (UK), 0810 630 304 (France).
www.eurotunnel.com

GREEN TRAVEL

Train+Bicycle Travel
www.velo.sncf.com

Voies Vertes
www.voiesvertes.com

Traveling by Train

SNCF logo

The French state railway, Société Nationale des Chemins de Fer (**SNCF**), runs Europe's most comprehensive national rail network. Its services include high-speed long-distance TGVs and mainline expresses, overnight sleepers, Motorail, and rural branch lines that reach every corner of the country. Lines closed for economic reasons are replaced by SNCF's modern buses, free to railpass holders. Travel off the main lines can be slow, though some cross-country journeys are quicker if you change trains in Paris.

TRAVELING AROUND FRANCE BY TRAIN

France has always been known for the punctuality of its trains, and has maintained a high level of investment in the state-owned rail system, SNCF. The pride of the SNCF is its TGV high-speed trains, with journey times such as Lille–Lyon or Paris–Marseille in just 3 hours. In addition, frequent, fast, and comfortable main-line express trains provide a comprehensive city-to-city service, while regional lines provide connections to smaller towns and villages. SNCF is also the largest bus operator in France, filling in the gaps where railroad lines have been closed.

Sleeper trains are a convenient way to travel long distances at night, and motorists can travel with their cars on **AutoTrain** trains. Most (but not all) long-distance trains have restaurant cars.

Further information on French railways is provided on the main SNCF website (*see p682*) where reservations can also be made. To book

a long-distance train from abroad, visit www.voyages-sncf.com. **Rail Europe** also offers a comprehensive information and booking service for travel throughout Europe. For useful links and an invaluable guide to every aspect of using French and other European railways, visit **The Man in Seat 61** website.

LOCAL AND SCENIC RAILWAYS

Alongside the national rail network are several special railroads that operate around France. On Corsica, the **Chemins de Fer de la Corse** has narrow-gauge lines between Calvi, Bastia, and Ajaccio. Particularly spectacular is the train trip along the northwest coast between L'Ile-Rousse and Calvi. In summer, old-style *trains touristiques* run on this and other lines. In Provence, the privately-run **Chemins de Fer de Provence** runs the *Train des Pignes*

The train to Le Montenvers is a particularly scenic route

over a magnificent 90-mile (150-km) mountain route from Nice to Digne-les-Bains. SNCF also runs many more *trains touristiques* on particularly scenic sections of its regional network. These are usually in mountainous areas during the winter months and in summer on the coast and in the countryside. *Gentiane Bleu* trains run from Dijon to the winter snows in the Jura, and the *Train des Merveilles* runs from Nice into the Alps at Tende. For a guide to all these routes visit www.trainstouristiques-ter.com.

RER

Symbol for Paris suburban trains

Several privately or locally owned rail lines around France are kept going by enthusiasts who offer excursions for part of the year, often using steam trains. The *Chemin de Fer de la Baie de la Somme* travels around the Somme Bay in Picardy and the *Chemin de Fer Touristique du Tarn* operates in the Tarn hills near Albi. Nearly all of these companies are members of the **UNECTO** association.

TYPES OF TRAIN

SNCF trains are divided into several types. TGV (*Train à Grande Vitesse*) trains are the flagships of the network, traveling on specially built track at around 186 mph (300 km/h). There are four main TGV route networks; to the north, west, east, and south-east from Paris, with additional hubs at Lille, Lyon, Bordeaux, and Marseille. In some places, TGVs have separate stations built outside town centers. The trains have first- and second-class carriages, and some of them offer Internet access. Seat reservations are obligatory for all TGV trains: tickets can be bought at stations until shortly before departure time, or booked ahead online.

Within the TGV network there are several international services including Eurostar, linking France with the UK;

Thalys, which runs between Paris and Belgium, and Holland and Germany; and Lyria, serving Switzerland and Artesia, which runs a TGV service to Turin and Milan, and a conventional train from Paris to Rome. Non-TGV international trains also operate, notably the nightly Elipsos from Paris to Madrid and Barcelona.

Corail trains are conventional long-distance express trains with modern carriages; Corail Téoz trains run by day; Corail Lunéa trains are overnight with sleepers. Corail Intercités trains are slightly faster with fewer stops. Reservations are obligatory for all Corail trains and can be made through Rail Europe or SNCF.

Motorail trains allow drivers to cut out long distances by traveling overnight with their car on the same train. Routes

The TGV, with its distinctive-looking "nose"

run from Calais to Nice via Avignon, and Calais to Narbonne. AutoTrains run from Paris to Nice, Narbonne, and Bordeaux. Reservations are essential.

TER trains are regional services that usually stop at every station. Reservations are not required and tickets can generally not be bought in

advance. Route maps and information (in French only) for each region are available at stations and on the TER website *(see p682)*. Transilien is the TER network for the Ile-de-France around Paris, which is integrated with the RER suburban trains and the Métro.

TGV RAIL SERVICE

Trains à Grande Vitesse, or high-speed trains, travel at speeds up to 186 mph (300 km/h). There are four routes: TGV Nord from Paris Gare du Nord, TGV Atlantique from Paris Gare Montparnasse, TGV Sud-Est from Paris Gare de Lyon and TGV Est from Paris Gare de l'Est.

KEY

- Nord
- Atlantique
- Sud-Est
- Est

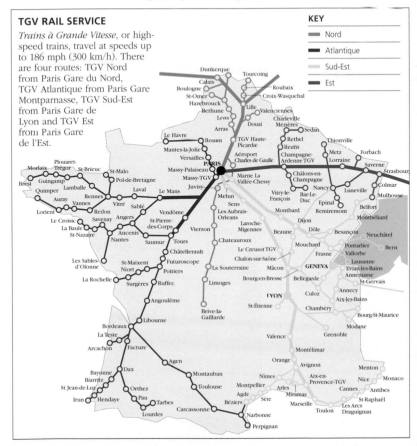

The automatic ticket machines at the Gare de Lyon in Paris

FARES AND PASSES

Fare rates vary according to the type of train. For all trains that can be reserved online (TGV, Corail, Motorail), there are two or three basic fare rates for each class. The cheapest tickets are called Prem's, which must be bought well in advance and cannot be altered after payment. On most TER and some Corail trains, fares are cheaper at off-peak times *(périodes bleues)*; peak times *(périodes blanches)* are 5–10am Monday and 3–8pm Friday and Sunday.

SNCF sells several travel cards that give fare reductions of around 50 percent. Examples are the *Carte 12–25* for young people, *Carte Senior* for over-60s, *Carte Escapades* for frequent travelers, and *Carte Enfant +* for parents with small children. Further details are available on the SNCF website.

For visitors intending to make several train journeys around France it is worth investing in a multi-journey rail pass, which can only be bought outside the country. The **Inter-Rail** pass, for UK and other European residents, is valid for several European countries, giving unlimited travel for 3, 4, 6, or 8 days (not necessarily consecutively) within one month. Visitors from outside Europe can buy a France Railpass, permitting 3 to 9 days of unlimited travel within one month, or a **Eurail** Select Pass that covers France and neighboring countries. Be aware that some trains, including the TGV, charge additional supplements, which are usually included in the price. For more information visit the Rail Europe website.

BUYING TICKETS

Train tickets can be bought at any SNCF station and by phone or online. At most stations there are both staffed counters and automatic ticket machines *(billetterie automatique),* which accept cash or credit cards and have instructions in English. Tickets for trains that require a reservation (TGV, Corail) can be bought up to 90 days in advance and up until 5 minutes before departure. Tickets bought in advance can be collected from the station, or sent to your address.

From outside France you can buy TGV and Corail tickets through www.voyages-sncf. com, the English arm of the SNCF website, although it can be easier to use Rail Europe. Travelers with mobility problems can arrange assistance through the *Accès Plus* program; more information is available online or from FranceGuide *(see pp668–71).*

Note that before any train journey in France, you must validate your ticket in a *composteur* machine.

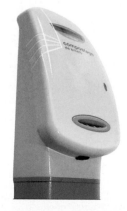

TIMETABLES

French train timetables change twice a year, in May and September, and all of them can be consulted on the SNCF website. Stations have free regional TER timetables available and information on the TGV network. Other free leaflets provide information on topics such as traveling with children, reduced fares, and travel for the disabled.

DIRECTORY

RAIL INFORMATION

Autotrain
www.autotrain-voyages-sncf.com

Corail
www.coraillunea.com
www.corailteoz.com

Eurail
www.eurail.com

Inter-Rail
www.interrail.net

Rail Europe
www.raileurope.com

SNCF
www.sncf.com

TER
www.ter-sncf.com

The Man in Seat 61
www.seat61.com

LOCAL RAILROADS

Chemins de Fer de la Corse
www.train-corse.com

Chemins de Fer de Provence
www.trainprovence.com

UNECTO
www.trains-fr.org

Composteur Machine
Yellow composteur *machines (left) are located in station halls and at the head of each platform. You must validate passes by inserting tickets and reservations separately, printed side up. The* composteur *will punch your ticket, printing the time and date on the back. The train inspector may impose a penalty if you fail to do this.*

Traveling by Boat

With both Mediterranean and Atlantic coastlines, France offers excellent opportunities for sailing and has very good facilities. Inland, there is an extensive network of rivers, canals, and other waterways. Cruising through them is an ideal way to discover some of the country's most charming countryside. Frequent scheduled ferries also connect mainland France to Corsica and other parts of the Mediterranean as well as to the British Channel Islands off Normandy.

Boats moored along the Canal du Midi, Roussillon

TRAVELING BY FERRY

Car ferries sail to Corsica from Marseille, Nice, and Toulon, the main operators being **SNCM** and **Corsica Ferries**. **La Méridionale** sails between Corsica and Sardinia, and **Moby Lines** also connects Corsica with Livorno and Genoa in mainland Italy. **Grimaldi Ferries** sails from France to Morocco and Italy. Regular ferries also connect France and North Africa; SNCM runs to Algeria and Tunisia, while **Comanav** has a luxury service from Sète to Morocco.

In the Atlantic, **Manche-Iles Express** and **Compagnie Corsaire** sail from St-Malo and the Normandy ports of Granville, Barneville-Carteret, and Diélette to the British Channel Islands. For a guide to all European ferry services visit www.ferrylines.com.

SAILING IN FRANCE

France has excellent sailing facilities, with marinas all around its coast. On the Atlantic coast, well-equipped ports include Honfleur and St-Vaast-la-Hougue in Normandy, St-Malo and Pleneuf-St-André in Brittany, and La Rochelle and Arcachon on the west

coast. Among the best in the Mediterranean are St-Cyprien near the Spanish border, Antibes on the Cote d'Azur, and the small harbors of Corsica. Boats for charter or short-term rental are available at most marinas and information on rules and permits is available from the **Ministère de l'Ecologie**. The **Fédération Française de Voile** provides updates on sailing conditions.

CANAL AND RIVER TRIPS

There are many options for exploring French waterways, from short boat trips to cruises of several days. The official guide to the system is provided by **Voies Navigables de France**. Many companies offer cruises around France; among the best are **En Peniche**, which uses traditional barges or *peniches*, **Locaboat**, and **Crown Blue Line**. For narrow boats on the Canal du Midi, try **Minervois Cruisers**.

Short excursions are popular around the Marais Poitevin wetlands between La Rochelle and Poitiers, and along the Canal de Bourgogne from Dijon. **Les Caminades** runs trips along the Dordogne in traditional *gabarre* boats. For rides on the River Seine in Paris *see p689*.

DIRECTORY

FERRY SERVICES

Comanav
Tel 04 67 46 68 00.
www.aferry.fr

Compagnie Corsaire
Tel 0825 138 100.
www.compagniecorsaire.com

Corsica Ferries
Tel 0825 095 095.
www.corsica-ferries.fr

Grimaldi Ferries
Tel 04 94 87 11 45 (in France).
www.grimaldi-lines.com

Manche-Iles Express
Tel 0825 133 050 (in France),
01418 7013 (in Jersey).
www.manche-iles-express.com

La Méridionale
Tel 0810 201 320.
www.lameridionale.fr

Moby Lines
Tel 00 49 (0)611 14020.
www.mobylines.com

SNCM
Tel 3260 (24-hrs for all ports).
www.sncm.fr

SAILING INFORMATION

Fédération Française de Voile
www.ffvoile.fr

Ministère de l'Ecologie
www.developpement-durable.gouv.fr

CANAL AND RIVER TRIPS

Les Caminades
Tel 05 53 29 40 95.
www.best-of-perigord.tm.fr

Crown Blue Line
Tel 04 68 94 52 72.
www.crownblueline.com

En-Peniche
Tel 04 67 13 19 62.
www.en-peniche.com

Locaboat
Tel 03 86 91 72 72.
www.locaboat.com

Minervois Cruisers
Tel 01926 811842 (in UK).
www.minervoiscruisers.com

Voies Navigables de France
www.vnf.fr

On the Road

France's network of modern highways (autoroutes) allow quick and easy access to all parts of the country. However, you can save money on tolls and explore France in a more leisurely way by using some of the other high-quality roads that dissect the country. This section outlines both alternatives and gives instructions on how to use highway toll booths (*péage*) and French parking meters (*horodateurs*), as well as some of the rules governing driving in France. There are also tips on how to get weather and traffic forecasts, where to rent a car, and how to get the best road maps.

Highway and main road signs

WHAT TO TAKE

Effective insurance is essential when taking a car to France. All car insurance policies in the EU automatically include minimum third-party insurance cover, which is valid in any EU country. However, the extent of cover provided beyond the legal minimum varies between insurance companies, so it is best to check your policy before you travel, and, if necessary, procure additional cover. For holders of fully comprehensive car insurance, most companies provide full European cover for a small extra premium; some do not charge for this, but still require you to notify them before traveling. It is also advisable to have breakdown cover with one of the Europe-wide networks with English-speaking phonelines.

While driving in France you must carry in the car your driver's licence, passport, the vehicle registration document, and a certificate of insurance. You must also have a set of spare light bulbs, at least one red warning triangle, and a luminous reflecting jacket to be worn if you ever have to stop on a highway because of a breakdown or other emergency. You can be fined if you are stopped by the police and do not have this equipment. The car's country of registration should be displayed on a sticker or as part of the license plate, and right-hand drive cars need headlamp deflectors for driving on the right – kits are available at most ports.

BUYING GAS

All fuel stations have unleaded gas and diesel fuel (*gazole* or *gas-oil*, or a high-grade *gas-oil +*). Many stations also have LPG (*GPL*). The cheapest are attached to big supermarkets, and many major service stations have 24-hr pumps, with payment by credit card.

RULES OF THE ROAD

Wearing seat belts, in the front and back of the car, is compulsory in France, as is the use of booster seats for children under 10. It is illegal to use a cell phone while driving, even if it's on hands-free mode. Dipped headlights must be used in poor visibility, and motorcyclists must have dipped headlights lit at all times. Unless road signs indicate otherwise, *Priorité à droite* means that you must give way to any vehicle joining the road from the right except on traffic circles. Flashing head-lights mean that the driver is claiming the right of way. For further details consult AA or RAC websites (*see p687*).

SPEED LIMITS AND FINES

Speed limits in France are as follows:
• On autoroutes: 80 mph (130 kph); 68 mph (110 kph) when it rains.
• On divided highways: 68 mph (110 kph); 56–62 mph (90–100 kph) when it rains.
• On other roads: 56 mph (90 kph); 49 mph (80 kph) when it rains.
• In towns and villages: 31 mph (50 kph).

There are also lower speed limits on all roads for vehicles towing a trailer or camper.

On-the-spot fines are levied for speeding, not stopping at a Stop sign, for overtaking where forbidden, and exceeding the speed limit by over 25 mph (40 kph). Driving with over 0.05 percent alcohol in the blood is illegal.

HIGHWAYS

Most highways in France are toll roads (*autoroutes à péage*). The **Societé d'Autoroutes** website (*see p687*) lists the rates charged for each journey. There are also toll-free auto-routes, notably those around big cities like Paris (A3 and A86) and Lille, and some cross-country stretches such as the A84 from Caen to

A sign at a gas pump points to *GPL* **(LPG) or** *gazole* **(gasoline)**

The scenic route around Mont Cenis Lake

SCENIC ROUTES

France's dense web of *Routes Nationales* and D–roads weave through some of the country's most gorgeous scenery. The most celebrated roads are in mountain regions, such as the Col du Galibier road over the Alps east of Grenoble (N91, then D902) but there are many others throughout the country. Some hug the coast, such as the roads along the Côte d'Azur or the rugged coasts of Brittany and Normandy. Information on these *routes touristiques* is available from tourist offices (*see p669*).

ROAD CONDITIONS

The French Highway Authorities' *Bison Futé* website (*see p687*) provides essential information for driving in France, with details of weather conditions, winter driving requirements, and road works. Check also www.autoroutes.fr for highway driving.

Motoring organizations like the **AA** and **RAC** sell tailor-made route-planning services, giving scenic options and road conditions (*see p687*).

Rennes, and the A75 south of Clermont-Ferrand.

Much of the autoroute network includes rest areas, gas stations every 25 miles (40 km) and emergency phones every mile (2 km).

OTHER ROADS

RN (*Route Nationale*) roads are the main alternative to highways for long-distance trips. They are often far more attractive, but can be more congested. To get really off the beaten track, travel by D (*départementale*) roads, which snake around the countryside.

Look out for *Bis/Bison Futée* signs, which indicate quieter, alternative routes.

Try to avoid traveling at the French vacation rush periods known as *grands départs*. The worst times are weekends in mid-July, and the beginning and end of August.

Certain signs are particularly useful to know when driving in and out of towns. Follow *Centre Ville* signs for the town center and *Toutes Directions* (all routes) to take you out of the center to where you can find ongoing routes. If your destination is not signposted, follow *Autres Directions*.

USING THE AUTOROUTE TOLL

Collect a ticket from the toll booth and keep it safe until you reach an exit toll where you will be charged according to the distance traveled and type of vehicle used. To pay at small tolls, just throw your coins into the large receptacle.

Gare de Péage de Fresnes

2000 m

Highway Sign
These signs (left) indicate the name and distance to the next toll booth. They are usually blue and white; some show the tariff rates for cars, motorbikes, trucks, and RVs.

Toll Booth with Attendant
When you hand in your ticket at a manned toll booth, the attendant will tell you the cost of your journey on the autoroute and the price will be displayed. You can pay with coins, bills, credit cards, or with a check in Euros. A receipt is issued on request.

Automatic Machine
On reaching the exit toll, insert your ticket into the machine and the price of your journey is displayed in Euros. You can pay either with coins or by credit card. The machine will give change and can issue a receipt.

USING AN HORODATEUR MACHINE

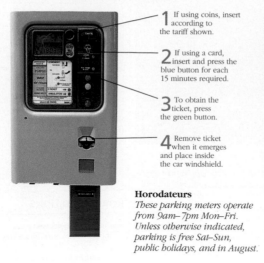

1 If using coins, insert according to the tariff shown.

2 If using a card, insert and press the blue button for each 15 minutes required.

3 To obtain the ticket, press the green button.

4 Remove ticket when it emerges and place inside the car windshield.

Horodateurs
These parking meters operate from 9am–7pm Mon–Fri. Unless otherwise indicated, parking is free Sat–Sun, public holidays, and in August.

PARKING

Parking regulations vary from town to town, but most cities have street pay-and-display machines *(horodateurs)*, with spaces marked out in blue. Some machines accept a parking payment card sold at *tabacs*. Parking is normally limited to 2 hours. Charges are relatively low, and in most provincial towns parking is free between noon and 1:30pm. In narrow streets, parking may be confined to one side of the street and this can alternate at different times of the month.

Finding a parking space in larger cities, especially in Paris, can be difficult and it is often easier to use a parking lot. These are well indicated by a large 'P' sign accompanied by the word *libre* to indicate that there are spaces available.

CAR RENTAL

All the main international car-rental companies operate in France, as well as local French-based companies like **ADA** and **Rentacar**, which often have very competitive prices. You will nearly always get the best rates by reserving a car in advance through an Internet car rental reservation service like **Auto Europe** or

Autos Abroad. Requirements for car rental vary, but in general you must be over 21 and have held a driver's license for at least a year. You will need to present your license, passport, and a credit card against a deposit.

The price quoted should include all taxes and unlimited mileage. All rental contracts include basic third-party insurance, and some companies also include comprehensive insurance. Extras such as car seats, snow chains, or an automatic car, should be indicated when reserving.

Before you drive away check the general condition of the car and also check it has a set of spare bulbs, a warning triangle, and a luminous jacket, which are all legal requirements in France *(see p684)*.

MAPS

Each chapter in this guide begins with a map of the region showing all the sights and information on getting around. As additional maps, the excellent **Michelin** Tourist and Motoring Atlas at a scale of 1:200,000 is the most comprehensive driving map available. The red-cover Michelin maps of the whole of France (scale 1:1,000,000) are useful for planning trips,

as are the regional maps with orange covers (scale 1:200,000). Larger scale Michelin maps with green covers are only for certain parts of France such as Paris and the French Riviera.

The **Institut Géographique National** (IGN), the equivalent of the British Ordnance Survey, produces high-quality maps in different scales. Particularly useful are their *Cartes de Randonnée* (scale 1:25,000), an excellent series of walking maps covering every part of the country. Also recommended, are the **Blay Foldex** town maps.

In France, all newsstands and gas stations stock maps and most tourist offices provide good free maps. In the UK, **Stanfords** is one of the best places to look for a full selection of French maps.

TRAVELING BY BUS

The French railroad is so fast and reliable that there is not much demand for long-distance buses and they tend to only operate in areas with poor train services.

Eurolines offers a wide range of low-priced international services, many of which make stops within France. These services are centered on the Porte de Bagnolet bus station in Paris (Métro Galliéni).

Veolia Transport runs an extensive network of buses that covers the Ile de France, and **Lignes d'Azur** provides a good service along the Côte d'Azur.

Local buses are definitely an important means of transportation, particularly in rural areas. These run in and out of villages from the *gare routière* (bus station), which is often located next to the SNCF train station of the main town of each *département* or area. Buses run mostly at peak times to take people to and from work and school.

TAXIS

There are taxi services in every part of France, although in rural areas you will normally have to reserve a car

Mountain cyclists in the Alps

by phone. Hotels, bars, and restaurants will have the numbers of local taxis. Otherwise, in towns look for a taxi stand *(station de taxi)* outside train stations, airports, or in the town center.

All taxis must use meters *(compteurs)*, but prices do vary from one region to another. In general, the pick-up charge should be about €2 plus €0.8 or more per mile. It is often possible to agree a fixed price for a long journey. For city taxis *see pp688–9.*

BICYCLING

Bicycling is extremely popular in France and facilities are steadily improving as part of the government-backed "Eco-mobility" scheme *(see p679).* Several long-distance **Voies Vertes** footpaths and bike tracks have been created, and more are being established. Every local tourist office has a leaflet on nearby *véloroutes*, and many have developed their own schemes, such as the network of bike routes around the main Loire Valley châteaux *(La Loire à Vélo).* Details are available from local tourist offices and *département* websites.

Bicycles can be taken on nearly all **SNCF** trains and on some routes you can reserve a rental bike at your destination station when buying a train ticket. There are also bike rental stores in nearly every town with standard and mountain bikes *(VTT)* for rent at reasonable prices. Tourist offices can advise on local companies.

More information on bicycling in France can be found on the Maisons de la France websites and through the **Fédération Française de Cyclisme** (in French only). Most cities offer rental bicycling schemes *(see p689).*

HITCHHIKING

It is not easy to get around France by hitchhiking, and it is not advisable to try either. There is, however, a safe car-sharing *(covoiturage)* program called Allostop (www.allostop.net), which has branches in many towns and through which you can set up rides at reasonable rates.

DIRECTORY

GENERAL DRIVING INFORMATION

AA
Tel 0800 085 7253.
www.theaa.com

RAC
Tel 0844 891 3111.
www.rac.co.uk

Société d'Autoroutes
www.autoroutes.fr

Zagaz
www.zagaz.com (for fuel price guide in French).

CAR RENTAL

ADA
Tel 0825 169 169.
www.ada.fr

Autos Abroad
Tel 0844 826 6536 (UK).
www.autosabroad.com

Auto Europe
Tel 1 888 223 5555
(USA & Canada).
www.autoeurope.com

Avis
Tel 0820 050 505
(France), 0844 581 8181
(UK). www.avis.com

Budget
Tel 0825 003 564
(France), 0844 544 3455
(UK). www.budget.com

Europecar
Tel 0825 358 358
(France), 0871 384 0235
(UK). www.europcar.com

Hertz
Tel 0825 861 861
(France), 0845 191 536
(UK). www.hertz.com

National/Citer
Tel 0800 131 211
(France),
0871 384 1140 (UK).
www.nationalcar.com

Rentacar
Tel 0891 700 200.
www.rentacar.fr

MAPS

Blay Foldex
www.blayfoldex.com

Institut Géographique National
www.ign.fr

Michelin
www.viamichelin.fr

Stanfords
12–14 Long Acre,
London WC2E 9LP, UK.
Tel 020 7836 1321.
www.stanfords.co.uk

BUS TRAVEL

Eurolines
Tel 0892 899 091.
www.eurolines.fr

Lignes d'Azur
www.lignesdazur.com

Veolia Transport
www.veolia-transport.com

BICYCLING

Fédération Française de Cyclisme
Tel 01 49 35 69 00.
www.ffc.fr

SNCF
www.velo.sncf.com
(for train and bicycle travel – in French only).

Voies Vertes
www.voiesvertes.com

Traveling within Cities

The charming centers of France's cities are best enjoyed on foot. If, however, you need to cover a fair amount of ground in a day, it is best to use the excellent range of public transportation available. Paris and many other cities have tram and underground rail networks, often integrated with local train and bus services, and efforts have been made to create user-friendly ticketing systems. France has led the world in encouraging urban bike use as an alternative to the car, with easy-access bike-rental programs. In each city, local tourist offices will provide full information on services, including free maps.

Marseille tram traveling along the Boulevard Longchamp

PARIS METRO, RER, AND TRAM

The **RATP** operates 14 Métro underground train lines. The Métro is the most convenient way to get around the city, and you are never far away from a station in central Paris. Each line can be identified by its color and number. The direction the train is traveling in is indicated by the name of the station on the front of the train – this is always the last station on the route, so it's worth checking the Métro map before boarding. Trains run frequently on each line from 5:20am–1:20am daily (to 2:20am Sat).

The newer RER lines complement the Métro and run across Paris and the suburbs. There are five lines (A–E), each with branches. The most useful for visitors are B3, from Charles-de-Gaulle airport; A4, to Disneyland Paris Resort; and C5, to Versailles.

Paris also has three tramway lines: from Gare de St-Denis to Noisy-le-Sec; La Défense to Porte de Versailles; and Pont du Garigliano to Porte d'Ivry.

OTHER METRO AND TRAM SYSTEMS

The cities of Lyon, Marseille, Toulouse, Lille, and Rennes all have Métro systems. The Lille Métro serves the whole conurbation known as Lille-Métropole, including towns such as Roubaix and Tourcoing. All Métros connect with SNCF railroads at main stations.

Rouen's two-line Métro is actually made up of overground trams (light rail lines) that connect the city to the outer suburbs. Some 22 other cities around France use trams as well as local buses, and Paris, too, has some suburban tram lines that connect with the Métro and RER.

BUSES

Every city has local buses. In Paris, RATP buses provide cheap opportunities for sightseeing. Throughout France, most routes operate from around 6am to midnight; routes and times are indicated at bus stops. Most French cities also have several night bus routes and in Paris and the Ile-de-France, 42 Noctilien bus routes operate throughout the night, passing the main train stations. A fast-growing number of buses in Paris and other cities have wheelchair ramps. On all French city buses, you must board at the front of the bus, and get off through the middle or rear doors. Tickets can be bought from the driver or in advance from a range of outlets, which saves time when boarding.

LOCAL TRAINS

Regional TER lines *(see p681)* are operated by SNCF and are well integrated with local transportation around cities. In some cases, tickets are interchangeable. Around Paris the SNCF Transilien lines form a third level of rail services with the Métro and RER.

TAXIS

In Paris and most other cities taxis have a light on top of the car which is white when the taxi is free, and orange, or just switched off, when it is taken. Paris taxi fares are more expensive between 5pm and 10am, Monday–Saturday, and all day Sunday and holidays, and cost more for any journey outside central Paris (limited by but including the Boulevard Périphérique). Many taxis take credit cards, but often only for fares over €15. At busy times the best places to find taxis in Paris are taxi stands *(station de taxis)* marked with a blue T sign. Ranks are found at major road junctions and train stations. Though operated by several companies, there is now a single number to phone for taxis in Paris. All taxis in France are required to carry wheelchair users for no extra charge, but in the Paris region **Taxis G7** provide a specialized service for passengers with mobility problems.

In other cities taxis are similarly operated by several companies. Taxi ranks are found at airports, most train stations, and around city centers. Otherwise tourist offices and hotels can provide you with local firm numbers.

Taking a bicycle from one of the Vélib' stands in Paris

BICYCLING

Great efforts are underway in French cities to encourage town bicycling. On Sundays, some major streets are closed to traffic to make way for bicyclists and rollerbladers. Paris city council has a world-leading pro-cycling program, and expects to have 373 miles (600 km) of cycle routes by 2013. The centerpiece of the program is the **Vélib'** scheme, where you can pick up a basic bike at any one of hundreds of Vélib' stations around Paris and leave it at another. To do this you must purchase a Vélib' card, which is available for a day (€1) or a week and can be bought from machines at the Vélib' bike racks, or by annual subscription. Other cities run similar bike-sharing schemes under different names (the **Vélo'V** in Lyon, **Le Vélo** in Marseille). Tourist offices will have full information on them.

TICKETS

In Paris, RATP T-tickets are valid for city buses, the Métro and the RER. Tickets are available singly or for lower prices in carnets of 10 and can be bought at Métro and RER stations, the airports, tourist offices, and *tabacs*. Single tickets can also be bought on board buses but are not valid for other forms of transportation. Don't forget to validate your ticket.

An alternative aimed at tourists is the ParisVisite card, which gives unlimited travel on all systems for 1, 2, 3, or 5 days, as well as discounted admission fees to sights. The card is sold at Métro, RER, and train stations, as well as at tourist offices or online.

Nearly all larger cities offer some kind of city pass for visitors, giving unlimited travel and other advantages for one or more days. Enquire at tourist offices for local plans.

SEINE CRUISES

A boat trip on the Seine is one of the classic ways to see Paris. The long-running **Bateaux-Mouches**, **Bateaux Parisiens**, and **Vedettes du Pont-Neuf** offer traditional cruises along the river with multilingual commentary. The **Batobus** is a more flexible alternative, allowing you to hop on and off as many times as you want during the day. Another option is to see a more intimate side of Paris with a cruise along the St-Martin canal. Full information is available from tourist offices.

Cruise boats plying the river Seine

DIRECTORY

TRANSPORTATION AUTHORITIES

Lille – Transpole
www.transpole.fr

Lyon – TCL
Tel 04 26 10 12 12.
www.tcl.fr

Marseille – Le Pilote/RTM
Tel 04 91 91 92 10.
www.lepilote.com

Paris – RATP
Tel 3246. www.ratp.fr

Rennes – STAR
Tel 0811 555 535.
www.star.fr

Rouen – TCAR
Tel 02 35 52 52 52.
www.tcar.fr

Toulouse – Tisséo
Tel 05 61 41 70 70.
www.tisseo.fr

TAXIS

Paris Taxis
www.taxis-paris.fr

Taxis G7
Tel 01 47 39 47 39;
specially adapted taxis:
01 47 39 00 91 or 3607.
www.taxisg7.fr

BICYCLING SCHEMES

Vélib' (Paris)
Tel 01 30 79 79 30.
www.velib.paris.fr

Le Vélo (Marseille)
Tel 0800 801 225.
www.levelo-mpm.fr

Velo'V (Lyon)
Tel 0800 083 568.
www.velov.grandlyon.com

SEINE CRUISES

Bateaux-Mouches
Tel 01 42 25 96 10.
www.bateaux-mouches.fr

Bateaux Parisiens
Tel 0825 010 101.
www.bateauxparisiens.com

Batobus
Tel 0825 050 101.
www.batobus.com

Vedettes du Pont-Neuf
Tel 01 46 33 98 38.
www.vedettesdupontneuf.com

General Index

Acknowledgments

Dorling Kindersley would like to thank the following people whose contributions and assistance have made the preparation of this book possible.

Main Contributors
John Ardagh, Rosemary Bailey, Judith Fayard, Lisa Gerard-Sharp, Robert Harneis, Alister Kershaw, Alec Lobrano, Anthony Roberts, Alan Tillier, Nigel Tisdall.

Contributors and Consultants
John Ardagh is a writer and broadcaster, and author of many books on France, among them *France Today* and *Writers' France*.

Rosemary Bailey has written and edited several guides to regional France, including *Burgundy, the Loire Valley*, and the *Côte d'Azur*.

Alexandra Boyle is a writer and editor who has worked in publishing in England and France for 20 years.

Elsie Burch Donald, editor and writer, is the author of *The French Farmhouse*.

David Burnie B.Sc. has written over 30 books on natural sciences, including *How Nature Works*.

Judith Fayard, an American based in Paris, was Paris bureau chief for *Life* magazine for 10 years, and is now European editor of *Town & Country*. She contributes to various publications, including the *Wall Street Journal*.

Lisa Gerard-Sharp is a broadcaster and author of several regional guides to France and Italy.

Robert Harneis is editorial correspondent for the English language newspaper *French News*.

Colin Jones is Professor of History at Exeter University. His books include *The Longman Companion to the French Revolution* and *The Cambridge Illustrated History of France*.

Alister Kershaw is an Australian writer and broadcaster who has lived in the Loire Valley for 30 years.

Alec Lobrano is an American writer, based in Paris. He is the European editor of *Departures* magazine and contributes to *International Herald Tribune, Los Angeles Times*, and *The Independent*.

Anthony Roberts is a writer and translator who has lived in Gascony for 15 years, contributing to various publications including *The Times, World of Interiors*, and *Architectural Digest*.

Anthony Rose is the wine correspondent of *The Independent* and co-author of *The Grapevine*.

Jane Sigal is the author of two books on French food, *Normandy Gastronomique* and *Backroom Bistros, Farmhouse Fare*.

Alan Tillier is the main contributor to the *Eyewitness Guide to Paris*. He has lived in Paris for more than 20 years as correspondent for various journals, including the *International Herald Tribune, Newsweek*, and *The Times*.

Nigel Tisdall is a travel writer and author of guides to Brittany and Normandy.

Patricia Wells is food critic of the *International Herald Tribune* and author of the *Food Lovers' Guide to Paris* and the *Food Lovers' Guide to France*.

Additional Contributors
Nathalie Boyer, Caroline Bugler, Ann Cremin, Jan Dodd, Bill Echikson, Robin Gauldie, Adrian Gilbert, Peter Graham, Marion Kaplan, Jim Keeble, Alexandra Kennedy, Rolli Lucarotti, Fred Mawer, Lyn Parry, Andrew Sanger, Katherine Spenley, Clive Unger-Hamilton, Roger Williams.

Additional Photography
Jo Craig, Andy Crawford, Michael Crockett, Mike Dunning, Philip Enticknap, Philippe Giraud, Steve Gorton, Alison Harris, John Heseltine, Roger Hilton, Andrew Holligan, Paul Kenwood, Oliver Knight, Eric Meacher, Neil Mersh, Roger Moss, Robert O'Dea, Ian O'Leary, Tony Souter, Alan Williams, Peter Wilson.

Additional Illustrations
Dinwiddie Maclaren, John Fox, Nick Gibbard, Paul Guest, Stephen Gyapay, Kevin Jones Associates, Chris Orr, Robbie Polley, Sue Sharples.

Additional Cartography
Colourmap Scanning Limited; Contour Publishing; Cosmographics; European Map Graphics; Meteo-France. Street Finder maps: ERAMaptec Ltd (Dublin), adapted with permission from original survey and mapping by Shobunsha (Japan).

Cartographic Research
Jennifer Skelley, Rachel Hawtin (Lovell Johns); James Mills-Hicks, Peter Winfield, Claudine Zarte (Dorling Kindersley Cartography).

Design and Editorial Assistance
Peter Adams, Azeem Alam, Elizabeth Ayre, Laetitia Benloulou, Steve Bere, Sonal Bhatt, Uma Bhattacharya, Hilary Bird, Anna Brooke, Arwen Burnett, Cate Craker, Maggie Crowley, Alison Culliford, Lisa Davidson, Simon Davis, Emer FitzGerald, Helen Foulkes, Fay Franklin, Tom Fraser, Anna Freiberger, Rhiannon Furbear, Catherine Gauthier, Camilla Gersh, Eric Gibory, Emily Green, Vinod Harish, Robert Harneis, Elaine Harries, Victoria Heyworth-Dunne, Paul Hines, Nicholas Inman, Rosa Jackson, Sarah Jackson-Lambert, Stuart James, Laura Jones, Nancy Jones, Kim Laidlaw Adrey, Cécile Landau, Maite Lantaron, Delphine Lawrance, Jude Ledger, Siri Lowe, Francesca Machiavelli, Carly Madden, Hayley Maher, Nicola Malone, Lesley McCave, Ella Milroy, Malcolm Parchment, Lyn Parry, Helen Partington, Shirin Patel, Alice Peebles, Alice Pennington-Mellor, Marianne Petrou, Pollyanna Poulter, Pete Quinlan, Salim Qurashi, Marisa Renzullo, Philippa Richmond, Nick Rider, Ellen Root, Baishakhee Sengupta, Shailesh Sharma, Kunal Singh, Shruti Singhi, Cathy Skipper, Andrew Szudek, Helen Townsend, Dora Whitaker, Fiona Wild, Nicholas Wood, Irina Zarb.

Special Assistance

Mme. Jassinger, French Embassy Press Department; Peter Mills, Christine Lagardère, French Railways Ltd.

Photographic Reference

Altitude, Paris; Sea and See, Paris; Editions Combier, Maçon; Thomas d'Hoste, Paris.

Photography Permissions

Dorling Kindersley would like to thank the following for their assistance and kind permission to photograph at their establishments: The Caisse Nationale des Monuments Historiques et des Sites; M. A. Leonetti, the Abbey of Mont St-Michel; Chartres Cathedral; M. Voisin, Château de Chenonceau; M. P. Mistral, Cité de Carcassonne, M. D. Vingtain, Palais des Papes, Avignon; Château de Fontainebleau; Amiens Cathedral; Conques Abbey; Fontenay Abbey; Moissac Abbey; Vézelay Abbey, Reims Cathedral, and all the other churches, museums, hotels, restaurants, stores, galleries, and sights too numerous to thank individually.

Picture Credits

a = above; b = below/bottom; c = center; f = far; l = left; r = right; t = top.

Works of art have been reproduced with the permission of the following copyright holders; ©ADAGP, Paris and DACS, London 2011: 29c, 29crb, 30bl, 63tl, 64–65, 65tl (d), 90t, 93cra, 93cb, 93bl, 93br, 99t, 213b, 351t, 335br, 482t, 508ca, 522b, 524bc, 524br, 529br; ©ARS, NY and DACS, London 2011: 92c; ©DACS, London 2011: 93t, 381br, 422t; © Succession H. Matisse/DACS, London 2011:29bl, 92bl, 526br; © Succession Picasso/DACS, London 2011: 88cl, 90b, 473t, 521t.

Photos achieved with the assistance of the EPPV and the CSI: 136–7; Photo of Euro Disneyland ⁻ Park and the Euro Disneyland Paris ® 178cr; The characters, architectural works, and trademarks are the property of The Walt Disney Company. All rights reserved; Courtesy of the Maison Victor Hugo, Ville de Paris: 91t; Musée National des Châteaux de Malmaison et Bois-Preau: 173b; Musée de Montmartre, Paris: 133t; Musée National de la Legion d'Honneur: 60t; © Sundancer: 142bl.

The publisher would like to thank the following individuals, companies, and picture libraries for permission to reproduce their photographs:

AIR FRANCE: D Toulorge 678tl; ALAMY IMAGES: Andy Arthur 420bc, Sébastien Baussais 674tr, Directphoto.org 669br, David R. Frazier Photolibrary, Inc 672cl, Glenn Harper 96tl, Philippe Hays 675cb, Hemis/Camille Moirenc 18, Neil Juggins 682tl, Michael Juno 239c, Justin Kase Zfivez 673tr, a la poste 676tr, 670b, Jack Sullivan 673cr, vario images GmbH & Co.KG/Rainer Unkel 676bl; ALPINE GARDEN SOCIETY/CHRISTOPHER GREY-WILSON: 460bl, 460br; AGENCE PHOTO AQUITAINE: D. Lelann 421tl; ANCIENT ART AND ARCHITECTURE COLLECTION: 47 crb, 50c, 50cb, 52br, 57bl, 252–3b, 335bl, 382t, 434t, 438b; PHOTO AKG, BERLIN: 45cra, 46bl, 58bc, 55crb, 402t, 403b; ARCHIVES PHOTOGRAPHIQUES, PARIS/DACS: 422t; by kind permission of WWW.ARTINSWFRANCE.COM: 660b; ATELIER BRANCUSI/CENTRE GEORGES POMPIDOU, PARIS: Bernard Prerost 93br; ATELIER DU REGARD/A ALLEMAND: 442cl, 442cr, 442b.

HOSTELLERIE BERARD: 660cl; BIBLIOTHÈQUE NATIONALE, DIJON: 49cb; F. BLACKBURN: 461bl; GERARD BOULLAY/ PHOTOLA: 87bl, 87cra; BRIDGEMAN ART LIBRARY: Albright Knox Art Gallery, Buffalo, New York 275br; Anthony Crane Collection 211br; Bibliothèque Nationale, Paris 50cr–51cl, 52t, 53cr, 69bl; British Library, London 52bl, 68br, 292c, 293br, 293tl; Bonhams, London 59tc, 62tl; Château de Versailles, France 69tr; Christies, London 29c, 513b; Giraudon 28tr, 28tl, 56cr–57cl, 57tl, 59tl, 69bc, 181b, 334c, 343c, 365t; Guildhall Library, Corporation of London 417b; Hermitage, St Petersburg 29bl; Index 472b; Kress Collection, Washington DC 293bl; Lauros-Giraudon 46t, 69br; Musée des Beaux Arts, Quimper 243c; Musée Condé, Chantilly 50tl, 57tr, 68bl, 69tc, 69tcl, 69cb, 204t, 293c; Musée d'Orsay, Paris 28cb; Musée du Quai Branly, Paris 112cb; Paul Bremen Collection 255t; Sotheby's New York 55tl; V&A Museum, London 338b; Walters Art Gallery, Baltimore, Maryland 356t; JOHN BRUNTON: 514b; MICHAEL BUSSELLE: 182–3; CAMPAGNE, CAMPAGNE: 350t; C. Guy 325t; Lara 191cr; B. Lichtstein 217b, 324cl; Pyszel 190bl; CNMHS, PARIS/DACS: Longchamps Delehaye 213tl; CASTELET/ GROTTE DE CLAMOUSE: 493b; CEPHAS: Stuart Boreham 260–1; Hervé Champollion 322tr, 334t, 350b; Mick Rock 38c, 398tl, 398cl, 471t, 518–9; JEAN LOUP CHARMET: 47b, 50br, 52clb, 58t, 62cl, 62clb, 63tl, 63tc, 64bl, 64br, 65crb, 214b, 243b, 265br, 269b, 274t, 281b, 300br, 343br, 358b, 359t, 361c, 401cr, 401br, 421b, 475t, 507t, CHATEAU DE LA LIQUIERE: 470ca; CHATEAU MARGAUX: 26cb, 26bc; CITÉ DES SCIENCES ET L'INDUSTRIE: Michel Lamoureux 136ca; NASA/ESA 136tr, 137br; Sylvain Sonnet 136clb; BRUCE COLEMAN: Udo Hirsch 371br; Flip de Nooyer 387br; Hans Reinhard 323tl, 323tr; COLLECTION CDT GARD: 325bl; CDT LOT: 439b; PHOTOS EDITIONS COMBIER, MÂCON: 203t; CORBIS: Gary Braasch 469c; Michael Busselle 13cl; Ray Juno 10cl, Patrice Latron 684br, Reuters 657tl, Robert Harding World Imagery/ Charles Bowman 685tl; JOE CORNISH: 116, 234–5, 370br, 448.

DANSMUSEET, STOCKHOLM/PETER STENWALL: 64cr–65cl; E. Donard; 35tr, 35c, 35cl, 35bc; EDITIONS D'ART DANIEL DERVEAUX: 400cr–401cl; PHOTO DASPET, AVIGNON: 504bl; DOHERTY: 245tc; DOMAINE DE LA COURTADE: 471cr; DOMAINE SARDA MALET: 470cb; DOMAINE TEMPIER: 471cl.

ET ARCHIVE: 300bl; Cathedral Treasury, Aachen 4t; 48cl; Musée Carnavalet, Paris 61tl; Museum of Fine Arts, Lausanne 55br; Musée d'Orsay, Paris 61cra; Musée de Versailles 56b; 299bl; National Gallery, Scotland 58br; Victoria and Albert Museum, London 53tl; 343bl; EUROPEAN COMMISSION: 675; MARY EVANS PICTURE LIBRARY: 9c, 46br, 50bl, 51c, 53b, 54tl, 56cla, 58c, 62b, 63cr, 63br, 65br, 113cl, 177b, 183c, 191t, 197b, 235c, 279t, 291b, 293tr, 301bl, 315c, 366b, 393c, 455t, 465c, 473b, 508tl, 545c, 667c; Explorer 31b, 54cb.

FESTIVAL D'AVIGNON: Marc Chaumeil 656cl; FESTIVAL INTERNATIONAL DU FILM DE LA ROCHELLE: 656br; PHOTO FLANDRE, AMIENS: 193b; FNOTSI: 668tc.

GETTY IMAGES: Axiom Photographic Agency/Ian Cumming 283tl, AFP/Jean Ayissi 689tl, De Agostini

Picture Library 484t, Manfred Mehlig 680bl, National Geographic/Ed George 683, Panoramic Images 151br, Sergio Pitamitz 689bl, Peter Scholey 669tl, WireImage/Tony Barson 67bc; Giraudon, Paris: 8–9, 15t, 29cra, 29br, 46ca, 48tl, 48clb, 49tl, 50cl, 52cr–53cl, 56tl, 56clb, 58cl, 60cl, 60cr–61cl, 333br, 347br, 369b, 491cb MS Nero EII pt.2 fol. 20V0; Lauros-Giraudon 44tl, 44bc, 45t, 45crb, 45cb, 45br, 47tc, 49tr, 51crb, 55cr, 60clb, 60br, 351b, 491cl; Musée d'Art Moderne, Paris 29tr; Musée de Beaux Arts, Quimper 28cl; Gîtes de France: 548cb; Ronald Grant Archive: 21b, 66clb. La Halle Saint Pierre: *Untitled* Stavroula Feleggakis 133br; Sonia Halliday Photographs: Laura Lushington 309tr; Robert Harding Picture Library: 30bl, 37tr, 39tr, 39cl, 43b, 112br, 240tl, 243tr, 322bl, 322br, 323br, 349t, 400cla, 437cr, 461tr, 489b, C. Bowman 452t; Explorer, Paris 39cr, 67br, 101br, 179b, 362t, 371tr, 460cb, 461tl, 484b, 497br, 660b, 671cl; R. Francis 86clb; D.Hughes 392–3; W.Rawlings 49br, 67tl, 237tl, 256b; A.Wolfitt 26tr, 170; Hemispheres Images: Hervé Hughes 259br; John Heeltuhei 139a, Honfleur, Musée Boudin: 262b; David Hughes: 367t, 367b; The Hulton Deutsch Collection: 191br, 301br, 473c, 516b; FJ Mortimer 190tl. The Image Bank: Peter Miller 372; Images: 323c, 460cl, 460tr; Jacana: F Gohier 460tl; JM Labat 461bc; Trevor Jones: 204b.

Magnum Photos ltd: Bruno Barbey 20b, 31tr, 36bl; R Capa 472tr; P Halsman 525b; The Mansell Collection: 31tl, 282t, 295b, 459b, 504tl; Mas Daumas Gassac: 470cr; John Miller: 224b, 336tr, 407b; Montpellier Danse Festival: 657br; Musée de l'Annonciade, St-Tropez: 524tr; Musée D'art Moderne et Contemporain de Strasbourg: Edith Rodeghiero 231t; Musée des Beaux Arts, Carcassonne: 489tl; Musée des Beaux Arts, Dijon: 343tl; Musée des Beaux Arts de Lyon: 381tr, 381bl, 381br; Musée de la Civilisation Gallo-Romaine, Lyon: 47cr, 378cl; Musée Departmental Breton, Quimper: 274bl; Musée Flaubert, Rouen: 265bl; Museum National d'Histoire Naturelle, Paris: 138c; Courtesy of the Musée Matisse, Nice: 526b; Musée National d'Art Moderne, Paris: 92clb, 93t, 93cr, 93cb, 335br; Succession Henri Matisse 92bl; Musée Réattu, Arles: M Lacanaud 508ca; Cliché Musée de Sens/J.P. Elie: 330tl; Musée Toulouse-Lautrec, Albi: 444b. Network Photographers: Barry Lewis 338t; Rapho/ Mark Buscail 661tl; Rapho/De Sazo 661tr Office de Tourisme de Vence: 668c; Orient-Express Hotels Trains & Cruises: 548tl; OTC Marseille: 688cla Photolibrary: Duncan Maxwell 2–3; Jean-Marc Romain 673crb, Widmann Widmann/F1 Online 674bl; Pictures Colour Library: 402b, 426, 544, 666–7; Michel le Poer Trench: 30br; Centre Georges

Pompidou: Bernard Prerost 93b; Popperfoto: 251c; La Poste: 677bl; Pyrenees Magazine/DR: 400bl. Redferns: William Gottlieb: 64clb; Restaurant de la Tour d'Argent: 598br; Retrograph Archive: M. Breese 474tl, 474tr; Réunion des Musées Nationaux: Musée des Antiquités Nationales 403c; Musée Guimet 111t; Musée du Louvre 57ca, 101bl, 102t, 102bl, 102br, 103tl, 103c, 103b; Musée Picasso 88cl, 90b, 473t; Musée de Versailles 179t; RF Reynolds: 245bc. M Reynard 674b; Rex Features: Sipa 22t; Rocamadour: 437t; Roger-Viollet: 113tc; Foundation Royaumont: J Johnson 172t; Réunion des Musées Nationaux: *Le Duo* (1937) by Georges Braque, Collections du Centre Pompidou, Musée Nationaux d'Art Moderne, 93ra.

Sipa Press: 132bl; Photo SNCM/Southern Ferries: 678br; SNCF – Societe National des Chemins de Fer: 680tl, 682bc, Fabro & Leveque 683tr; Spectrum Colour Library: P Thompson 249el; Frank Spooner Pictures: Bolcina 37b; Uzan 66br; Simon 67ca; Gamma Press 39b, 67crb; STA Travel Group: 670tl; Jean Marie Steinlen: 404; Tony Stone Images: 322c, 326; Sygma: 531t; C de Bare 36t; Walter Carone 150t; P Forestier 314–5; Frederic de la Fosse 520b; D Goldberg 21c; L'Illustration 108tl; T Prat 436c; L de Raemy 66br. Editions Tallandier: 42, 44cb, 47tl, 48br, 48br–49bl, 51t, 51b, 52cl, 53tr, 54br, 58clb, 58bl, 58cr–59cl, 59crb, 59bl, 61tr, 61crb, 61br, 63bl, 63bc, 64cla, 64crb, 65cl, 65tr; Telarci 49cr; Tourist Office Semur-en-Auxois: 335t; Collection L. Treillard: © Man Ray Trust/ADAGP, Paris and DACS, London 2011 65tl(d). Jean Vertut: 44br–45bl; Visual Arts Library: 28b; View Pictures: Paul Rafferty 135b. World Pictures: 323bl. Zefa: 178c, 351t; O. Zimmerman/Musée d'Unterlinden 6800 Colmar: 227t.

Front Endpaper: All special photography except The Image Bank rcb; Pictures Colour Library lcr; Jean Marie Steinlein lcl; Tony Stone Images rca. Back Endpaper: All special photography except Joe Cornish lbl.

Jacket
Front - DK Images: Max Alexander bl; Getty Images: Image Bank/Peter Adams main image. Back - Cephas Picture Library: Stuart Boreham tl; Corbis: Sygma/P. Forestier cla; DK Images: Max Alexander clb; Kim Sayer bl.Spine - DK Images: b; Getty Images: Image Bank/Peter Adams t.

All other images © Dorling Kindersley. For more information see www.dkimages.com

SPECIAL EDITIONS OF DK TRAVEL GUIDES

DK Travel Guides can be purchased in bulk quantities at discounted prices for use in promotions or as premiums. We are also able to offer special editions and personalized jackets, corporate imprints, and excerpts from all of our books, tailored specifically to meet your own needs.

To find out more, please contact:
(in the United States) **SpecialSales@dk.com**
(in the UK) **travelspecialsales@uk.dk.com**
(in Canada) DK Special Sales at
general@tourmaline.ca
(in Australia)
business.development@pearson.com.au